# POLITICAL PARTIES OF THE MIDDLE EAST AND NORTH AFRICA

Recent Titles of
The Greenwood Historical Encyclopedia of the World's Political Parties

A five-volume reference guide to the world's significant political parties from the beginnings of the party system in eighteenth-century England to the present. Each volume provides concise histories of the political parties of a region and attempts to detail the evolution of ideology, changes in organization, membership, and leadership, and each party's impact upon society.

Political Parties of the Americas: Canada, Latin America, and the West Indies
*Robert J. Alexander, editor*

Political Parties of Europe
*Vincent E. McHale, editor*

Political Parties of Asia and the Pacific
*Haruhiro Fukui, editor*

The Greenwood Historical Encyclopedia of the World's Political Parties

# POLITICAL PARTIES
# OF THE MIDDLE EAST
# AND NORTH AFRICA

*Edited by Frank Tachau*

GREENWOOD PRESS
Westport, Connecticut

JQ
1758
.A979
P65
1994

**Library of Congress Cataloging-in-Publication Data**

Political parties of the Middle East and North Africa / edited by
Frank Tachau.
    p.  cm.—(The Greenwood historical encyclopedia of the
world's political parties, ISSN 1062-9726)
    Includes indexes.
    ISBN 0-313-26649-2 (alk. paper)
    1. Political parties—Middle East.  2. Political parties—Africa,
North.  I. Tachau, Frank.  II. Series.
JQ1758.A979P65   1994
324.256—dc20        93-25067

British Library Cataloguing in Publication Data is available.

Library of Congress Catalog Card Number: 93-25067
ISBN: 0-313-26649-2
ISSN: 1062-9726

First published in 1994

Greenwood Press, 88 Post Road West, Westport, CT 06881
An imprint of Greenwood Publishing Group, Inc.

Printed in the United States of America

The paper used in this book complies with the
Permanent Paper Standard issued by the National
Information Standards Organization (Z39.48–1984).

10 9 8 7 6 5 4 3 2 1

5/04

# CONTENTS

| | |
|---|---|
| Tables | vii |
| Preface | ix |
| Introduction | xiii |
| Algeria | 1 |
| Arabian Peninsula States: Bahrain, Kuwait, Oman, Qatar, Saudi Arabia, and the United Arab Emirates | 69 |
| Egypt | 93 |
| Iran | 133 |
| Iraq | 174 |
| Israel | 198 |
| Jordan | 259 |
| Lebanon | 297 |
| Libya | 369 |
| Morocco | 380 |
| The Palestinians | 422 |
| Sudan | 476 |
| Syria | 500 |
| Tunisia | 530 |
| Turkey | 549 |
| Yemen | 611 |
| Appendix 1.  Chronology of Major Political Events | 641 |
| Appendix 2.  Genealogy of Parties | 653 |
| Index | 673 |
| About the Editor and Contributors | 709 |

# TABLES

**ALGERIA**

1. Elections, Plebiscites, and Referenda in Algeria, 1962–89     15
2. June 12, 1990, APC and APW Elections—Number of Lists Presented by Party     24
3. June 12, 1990, APC and APW Election Results     25
4. December 26, 1991, APN Election Results (First Round)     26

**ISRAEL**

5. Number of Parties or Lists Represented in the Israeli *Knesset* (1949–92)     200
6. Anticoalition Parties     201
7. Participation in Government Coalitions (1949–92)     202
8. *Knesset* Representation of the Largest and Second Largest Parties     203
9. Israeli Prime Ministers (1948–92)     204
10. Party Groupings in the Israeli Party System     205
11. Eight Phases in the Development of the Israeli Party System     210
Appendix A. *Knesset* Election Results: 1949–69     257
Appendix B. *Knesset* Election Results: 1973–92     258

**LEBANON**

12. Parliamentary Representation in Lebanon, by Political Party     301
13. Party Representation in Lebanon, in the 1992 Election     302
14. Sectarian Affiliation of Communist Party Martyrs in Lebanon     313

15. Lebanese Phalanges Performance in Parliamentary Elections, 1943–68                    331

16. Sectarian Composition of the Phalanges Party, 1969          333

## MOROCCO

17. Results of 1963 Moroccan Parliamentary Elections       387

18. Results of 1977 Moroccan Parliamentary Elections       390

19. Results of 1984 Moroccan Parliamentary Elections       393

20. Results of 1993 Moroccan Parliamentary Elections       396

## TURKEY

21. Grand National Assembly Election Results, 1950–57       560

22. Grand National Assembly Election Results, 1961–77       563

23. Grand National Assembly Election Results, 1983–91       576

## YEMEN

24. Results of the 1993 Yemeni Elections                   625

# PREFACE

*Political Parties in the Middle East and North Africa* is part of a series designed to provide a comprehensive guide to significant political parties in various parts of the world. The objective is to provide as much information as possible regarding the formation, evolution, and impact of these parties, including their interactions with each other as well as with the societies and governments within and under which they have functioned. The series is designed both for those in need of data on modern parties and related organizations as well as for those seeking historical background information.

The boundaries of the Middle East as a cultural and political region are somewhat ill-defined. Rather than discussing various definitions of the area, suffice it to say that this volume includes the countries lying between Morocco to the west and Iran to the east, north of the Sahara Desert, and south and east of the Mediterranean Sea, including Turkey. We do not include Afghanistan, Pakistan, or the countries of the Horn of Africa or central and west Africa. Although one may argue for the inclusion of some or even all of these countries on the grounds that their cultures have a great deal in common with Middle Eastern lands, they likewise share many characteristics with their other neighbors, that is, central and south Asia, and sub-Saharan Africa. This delimitation of the area is somewhat arbitrary. It does, however, coincide with the definition underlying most of the relevant scholarly and political literature.

The definition of political parties in the Middle East is also somewhat nebulous. We are unable, for example, to apply a simple criterion such as representation in parliament or nomination of candidates for election to public office. Neither parliaments nor competitive elections are common political institutions in the Middle East. The introduction provides elaboration of this point and seeks to establish the criteria that were utilized in the decision as to which organizations to include and which to exclude. In short, the reader will find sixteen chapters covering all of the states of the Middle East as we define it.[1] In general, each chapter is devoted to a specific state. The only exception is the chapter devoted to the royal states of the Arabian Peninsula. Because of their relatively small size, and particularly because these states have not yet established fully empowered parliamentary bodies or meaningful popular elections, it seems most appropriate to treat them in this rather summary fashion.

Within these parameters, we have tried to be comprehensive in our coverage. Generally, this means that even if a political organization does not appear to fit the definition of a pure political party, that organization has been included if it performs functions characteristic of a party, particularly given the nature of the regime or political system that forms the context of political action in the particular state.

The individual chapters utilize a standard format. Each begins with an introductory essay outlining the character and history of the party system under review. This is followed by descriptive material providing detailed information about the various parties. We have tried to incorporate all parties that can be identified. Those parties about which there is little or no information, or which have played virtually no role in politics, are listed with simple statements to this effect. Each chapter also includes a brief bibliography, placed at the end of the introductory essay.

Parties are listed alphabetically in the indigenous language as well as in English, with the descriptive text usually associated with the English listing. We make exceptions in the cases of Algeria and Morocco, where party names are given in French because of the almost universal use of French in discussions of the politics of these countries. There are also occasional exceptions in other cases in which a party is universally known by its name in its indigenous language (e.g., the Ba'th).

The appendices, country chronologies, and party genealogies may be found at the end of the volume. The genealogies are especially important for the more complex and highly developed political systems, particularly Algeria, Egypt, Israel, Lebanon, Morocco, and Turkey. They should enable the reader to trace the origins and evolution of individual parties, as well as party systems. Where appropriate, electoral alliances (especially in Israel), mergers, and splits are clearly indicated. The chronologies provide a profile of each political system as it developed over time. This helps place both individual parties and party systems in the context of the general political development of the various countries under review.

This volume is intended for both experts and nonexperts. A fine balance is therefore required. We need to be precise so that experts can find the information they need, and yet not so precise as to unnecessarily complicate matters for nonexperts. Those who are familiar with Middle Eastern languages are aware that transliteration presents a formidable problem in this connection. Ideally, transliteration should render words and expressions in a form that resembles their spelling and pronunciation in the original language as closely as possible. But this ideal is complicated in the case of a language that is divided into a profusion of widely divergent local dialects, as is the case with Arabic, the dominant language of all but three of the countries included here. The development of technologically sophisticated mass media, such as radio, television, and the popular press, has had a salutary effect in encouraging the use of classical Arabic forms as a standard accessible to speakers and readers throughout the Arab world. Nevertheless, a profusion of modes of transliteration remains.[2] In general in this volume we have opted to follow the transliteration system established by the Library of Congress and used by the *International Journal of Middle East Studies*, the leading scholarly journal in the field. However, in order not to overburden nonexpert readers while maintaining the greatest clarity and consistency possible, we have eliminated almost all of the diacritical marks in the transliteration of Arabic, Persian, and Hebrew names and expressions. We have also chosen to render certain well-known names and expressions in the form commonly used by Western journalists. Thus, we refer to Gamal Abdel Nasser, Nasserites, and Nasserism. We also use such common English versions as *Quran* (rather than the popular *Koran*) and *Hizbullah*. On the other hand, we prefer the usage of Saddam Husayn and King Husayn. We also accept the common transliteration of Aya-tollah Khomeini's name. In fact, the chapter on Iran renders many common Middle Eastern terms (such as Islam) in their Arabicized form rather than trans-literated according to the specifically Iranian standard. Turkish names and terms present few problems because of the radical linguistic changes initiated in 1928, specifically with the adoption of the Latin alphabet. The Israel chapter follows standard norms for transliteration of Hebrew names and expressions. As editor, I assume primary responsibility for these matters, with apologies to the contrib-utors, some of whom may disagree with the results.

A project of this magnitude requires the active participation of a large number of individuals. First, I want to express my appreciation to the contributors, all of whom put forth their best efforts. Their contributions speak for themselves. I can only add that, thanks to their dedication and diligence, the reader will find here an excellent reference work that is unique in its field.

Second, I owe a debt of gratitude to many others who were involved in one way or another in putting this project together. Foremost among these is the editorial staff of the Greenwood Press, including Mildred Vasan, Sally M. Scott, and Dina Rubin. Others who helped in various large and small ways along the road include: Marla Lane and Sheree Victorian of the staff of the Department of Political Science at the University of Illinois at Chicago, who cheerfully accepted often onerous requests for transmitting mountains of material by mail or by fax. Jacob Landau of the Hebrew University, Jeremy Salt of Bilkent University, Man-fred Wenner of Northern Illinois University, and Farouk Mustafa of the Uni-versity of Chicago provided valuable advice concerning a number of technical problems. In the latter stages, as the manuscript moved into production, a great deal of help was provided by the staff of the Department of Political Science at the Hebrew University, and its then Chairman, Professor Abraham Diskin; and the Department of Political Science and Public Administration of Bilkent Uni-versity and its Chairman, Professor Metin Heper. Ms. Efrat Yanco of the Hebrew University compiled the data for the chronology of events, and Ms. Simten Coşar of Bilkent University provided invaluable assistance in updating the chapter on Turkey and preparing the index.

Finally, my personal thanks go to Paula, my wife, whose continuing tolerance of the seemingly endless hours of academic chores and undimmed enthusiasm for the peripatetic academic life-style is truly awesome.

## NOTES

1. Generally, this volume covers political parties organized since the formation of the contemporary states in which they currently operate. For a review of early political associations and parties, see "Hizb" in *The Encyclopedia of Islam*, new ed., vol. 3, pt 1 (1965).

2. An especially prominent example is the rendition of the name of the Egyptian president who became the symbol of pan-Arab nationalism. In most of the Arab world, his name is rendered as Jamal 'Abd al-Nasir. In Egypt, however, his given name is Gamal. Hence, we are confronted with the dilemma of whether to represent his name in the form characteristic of his own country, or in conformity with the rigorous scholarly rules of transliteration. We indicate our own choice below. Also, the chapters on Algeria and Morocco render Arabic names somewhat differently to conform with local usage. Some other exceptions have also been retained.

Frank Tachau
December 1993

# INTRODUCTION

The political party is a singularly modern phenomenon. It arose in response to the need to mobilize masses of citizens for voting and related political activities. Its first appearance coincided with the introduction and development of such institutions as popularly elected legislatures and mass suffrage. In the early industrializing societies, these developments occurred in the nineteenth century. In societies that experienced socioeconomic and political development in later years, the political party emerged later. In every case, however, parties developed in tandem with the emergence of mass politics. As Joseph LaPalombara and Myron Weiner put it:

[T]he political party materialized when the tasks of recruiting political leadership and making public policy could no longer be handled by a small coterie of men unconcerned with public sentiments. The emergence of a political party clearly implies that the masses must be taken into account by the political elite, either out of a commitment to the ideological notion that the masses have a right to participate in the determination of public policy or the selection of leadership, or out of the realization that even a rigidly dictatorial elite must find the organizational means of assuring stable conformance and control.[1]

LaPalombara and Weiner further suggest that parties have four characteristics: (1) "continuity in organization," or longevity, so that the party "is not dependent on the life span of current leaders" or regimes; (2) "manifest and presumably permanent organization at the local level" and an institutionalized relationship between the local and national levels; (3) a conscious drive on the part of the leadership to seek governmental power, either alone or in coalition, and "not simply to influence the exercise of power"; and (4) "a concern on the part of the organization for seeking followers at the polls or in some manner striving for popular support."[2]

It is commonly assumed that parties are integrally associated with democratic political systems. Generally speaking, this may be true, but it is not an iron law of politics or of history. Since the beginning of the twentieth century, the world has seen numerous examples of political parties that, although they may proclaim democratic ideals and values, hardly qualify as genuinely democratic. Many of these parties have sought governmental power but not by means of the ballot box. Some have operated clandestinely and have not hesitated to employ violent means to gain their objectives. Mao Zedong's oft-quoted slogan that power grows out of the barrel of the gun epitomizes this point. Often parties are forced into such nondemocratic alternatives by the repressiveness of the regime under which they operate. This was certainly true of the communist parties of the former Soviet Union and China; the pattern has also manifested itself in the modern Middle East. Finally, some parties either become so enamored of the violent tactics they feel driven to adopt, or are so far removed from the possible attainment of governmental power by any means, that they are caught in an endless and unproductive maze in which they continue to proclaim their ideals and practice their techniques even though there is no hope of ever achieving power. Some of these parties actually go so far as to relinquish the goal of governmental power in favor of some "higher goal" that they continue to pursue like a will-o'-the-wisp. Generally speaking, however, parties of whatever type, in whatever kind of system, regardless of the specific tactics they employ, strive to—or at least claim to—represent the masses.

Giovanni Sartori has put this matter in more general terms:

[W]hen the society at large becomes politicized, the traffic rules that plug the society into the state, and vice versa, are established by the way in which a party system becomes structured. At this point, parties become channeling agencies, and the party system becomes the system of *political canalization* of the society.[3]

In other words, the manner in which parties function may differ from system to system. In fact, the differences may be so extreme that some might argue that there is no comparability between, say, dictatorial and democratic parties. However, if we recall the mobilizing function of parties, their common attributes should be evident. Styles of mobilization may differ from the voluntarism appropriate to competitive or democratic systems, to the coercive pattern commonly associated with authoritarian regimes. The mobilizing function, however, remains common to virtually all political parties.

In short,

The term "political parties" emerged in the nineteenth century with the development of representative institutions and the expansion of the suffrage in Europe and the United States. It designated organizations whose goal was the capture of public office in electoral competition with one or more other parties. Subsequently the term "party" was extended to include political organizations not engaged in electoral competition: minor parties which had no realistic expectations of gaining office through appeals to the electorate, revolutionary organizations seeking to abolish competitive elections, and the governing groups in totalitarian states.[4]

Scholarship on political parties has tended to focus on developed or industrialized countries. Apart from studies of individual parties or party systems, there have been only a few works that focus on political parties in less developed countries since LaPalombara and Weiner's volume in the series on political development in the 1960s—and even this work devoted nearly half its attention to the United States and Western Europe.[5] It is appropriate to attempt to fill this gap. The present volume hopefully will contribute to this effort.

Parties abound in the Middle East, but—partly for the reasons just alluded to—they do not necessarily manifest all of the attributes set forth above. Perhaps this is because the role of the masses in the politics of Middle Eastern states remains inadequately defined and poorly institutionalized. The populace has in fact played only a peripheral role in the politics of some of the political systems in the region. There are several cases in which mass organization has not offered a reliable means of gaining control of the government, or in which the regime has not so far felt a need for the services of a party to "assure . . . stable conformance and control." In other cases, the regime has responded to the first stirrings of mass political involvement by means of repression. Halim Barakat, for example, has suggested that political parties, labor unions, and voluntary organizations in the Arab countries generally have been "either not allowed, repressed, or at least dismissed as irrelevant."[6] Adeed Dawisha has delivered an even harsher judgment:

In every Arab state (apart from Lebanon), the centralisation of power in the hands of one man has been the dominant feature of Arab politics over the last four decades. Opposition parties and groups hardly exist except in clandestine form, and . . . where opposition officially exists, they are blatantly manipulated by the regime. Institutions, such as parliaments and assemblies are sometimes created by the regimes to act as rubber stamps for government policies. And when assemblies, parties and mass organisations outgrow their original purpose or begin to act independently, they are ruthlessly cast aside by the ruling group.[7]

And yet, mass political awareness and demands for greater and more effective political participation are evident throughout the region, even (perhaps especially) under repressive regimes. Hence, it is not surprising that political parties exist, though their precise form may not fully match the models observed elsewhere. Indeed, one observer has suggested that in the late 1980s and early 1990s there were signs of growing pluralism in such countries as Jordan, Egypt, Algeria, and Yemen, and that these signs have been ignored or overlooked by Western academics and journalists.[8] Similarly, it may be that, with the apparent end of the lengthy civil war and the first peaceful parliamentary election in twenty years in Lebanon, a modicum of democracy has reappeared in that strife-torn land. Even the fundamentalist Islamic regime in Iran employs the device of popular election of the president and the parliament, although competition is tightly restricted. Finally, functioning democracies obviously continue to prevail in Turkey and Israel, though in the former case there have been several military interregnums.

Only a handful of regimes in the Middle East has met the acid test of democracy: the peaceful change of the regime in power in the wake of a freely contested election.⁹ We cannot, of course, limit our elaboration of political parties to such a handful of cases. Political parties or quasi-party organizations, as we have suggested above, function in a variety of environments, not all of which are fully democratic. Furthermore, given the fact that some political systems are excessively repressive or at least nonconsensual, it should not surprise us that parties assume a variety of shapes and forms. In Lebanon, for example, the breakdown of the political system in the mid-1970s created an anarchic situation in which parties and factions were either forced to take up arms in their own defense and effectively become militias, or to seek the protection of other armed groups. Similarly, among the Palestinians, the exigencies of political survival have motivated factions to resort to arms.¹⁰

We come, then, to the question of the proper scope of the present volume. It seems fitting for a reference book of this sort to be inclusive rather than exclusive. Accordingly, we have included organizations that meet only some, rather than all, of the criteria of political parties. Thus, several of the mass political organizations established by post-1952 regimes in Egypt do not meet the test of longevity: They failed to survive the regime that established them. It would make no sense to omit them, however, because these organizations have performed many of the critical functions of political parties, and because neither the post-1952 politics of Egypt, nor the emergence of more genuine parties in recent years, would be understandable without reference to these mass organizations. Likewise, quasi-party organizations in traditional noncompetitive regimes (e.g., the Gulf states, Saudi Arabia) have also been included.

Political parties in the Middle East have played a variety of roles and have followed diverse lines of historical development. Among them may be found comprehensive nationalist parties that led the struggle for independence (such as the Republican People's Party [RPP] of Turkey, the National Liberation Front [FLN] of Algeria, the *Wafd* in Egypt, the *Dustur* and Neo-*Dustur* in Tunisia, and the *Istiqlal* in Morocco). There are secular socialist parties that have dominated hegemonic regimes (e.g., in Syria, Iraq, Libya, and Egypt); parties closely identified with religio-ethnic groups (e.g., in Lebanon); parties that espouse militant ethnic nationalist programs, such as pan-Arabism; parties created by regimes and serving as instruments of their creators (e.g., the various hegemonic parties created by Gamal Abdel Nasser in Egypt); and, most recently, parties carrying the banner of resurgent Islam (e.g., the Islamic Republican Party [IRP] of Iran; the Muslim Brotherhood and smaller Islamic groups in Egypt and Jordan; the Islamic Salvation Front [FIS] in Algeria; and the Islamic Tendency Movement [MTI] in Tunisia). Finally, there are proto-parties in political systems in which parties have been severely constrained or prohibited altogether (e.g., in Jordan and Kuwait).

Examination of political parties in the Middle East is particularly challenging because this area continues to undergo rapid socioeconomic change. Political parties play a key role in mobilizing masses of citizens for political action, as we have noted. Mass political participation is one of the hallmarks of modern political systems. The pressures of mass political demands that erupt during the process of change may give rise to serious instability and violence. Whatever form the transition from traditionalism to modernity takes, however, the phenomenon of combinations of the two emerges, including the grafting onto traditional social and political relations of such essentially modern structures as parties.[11] This is as true of one-party authoritarian regimes as it is of competitive or multiparty systems.

Parties and party systems are profoundly affected by their particular social, cultural, and historical environment. In a sense, the party may be envisaged as a generic construct whose specific manifestation is a product of its immediate context. Accordingly, a potential benefit of this volume may be to permit an analysis of the specific interactions among Middle Eastern parties, governments, and other social groups and institutions, to trace their historical evolution, and particularly the manner in which they have functioned as agents of political mobilization.

Political parties in the Middle East obviously have something in common with political parties elsewhere; otherwise, the concept and its definition would have no meaning. They are also part of the Middle East, however, which is to say that they reflect the culture of the Middle East and are shaped at least in part by it. Indeed, the Middle East presents a number of peculiarities that should be noted.

First, some of the contemporary states of the Middle East remain somewhat fragile. Their boundaries have not been universally accepted, either by their own citizens or by other governments and peoples.[12] Some political parties reflect this uncertainty. The Syrian Social National Party (SSNP), for example, has proclaimed as its goal the creation of a Greater Syria incorporating the territories of the present states of Lebanon, Jordan, and Israel (including the occupied territories). The reader will find discussions of this party and others like it in more than one country chapter in this volume.

Second, more generally, uncertainty regarding the identity and most appropriate form of the state remains a problem in the Middle East. Beginning with the rise of Arab political consciousness in the nineteenth century, nationalist thinkers, leaders, and activists have either disagreed among themselves or have manifested ambiguity or uncertainty as to what sort of state or states the Arab nation should maintain. Some have argued for a pan-Arab political entity that would encompass all of the Arab nation from the Atlantic coast in the west to the Persian Gulf in the east. Not surprisingly, political parties espousing pan-Arab ideas have emerged and have waxed and waned over time. These parties have organized and maintained chapters in several Arab countries as part of the effort to realize their goal. Accordingly, the reader will find discussions of such parties (most prominently, the Arab Socialist Resurrection [Ba'th] Party and the Movement of Arab Nationalists [MAN]) in more than one of the country chapters appearing in this volume.[13]

Third, given the Muslim resurgence in recent years, it is not surprising to note the presence in the Middle East of organizations, including political parties, dedicated to promoting the values and customs of traditional Islam. Many of these movements and their adherents deny the legitimacy of existing states or regimes because they are perceived as hostile to Islamic values and traditions. Indeed, Islamicists are rather indifferent to the precise form of the state, so long as they can be sure that the political community will be governed in conformance with the strictures of pure Islam (as they interpret them). Islamicist movements are present in many of the states considered in this volume. Some of them straddle existing state boundaries, as do some of the pan-Arab associations. The most prominent example is the Muslim Brotherhood, which appears or has appeared in Egypt, Jordan, and Syria, among the Palestinians, and elsewhere.

In this connection, one of the issues that has drawn some attention involves the question of whether modern democracy is compatible with Islam. This question has assumed particular significance in such countries as Jordan, Egypt, and Algeria. In each of these countries, militant Islamic groups have gained considerable popular support; indeed, in Algeria, the Islamic Salvation Front (FIS) appeared on the verge of a dramatic electoral victory over the regime party (the FLN) in 1992, when the military took overt control of the government and imposed harsh, repressive measures. In Egypt, Islamic militants quietly constructed a network of social support services that reportedly functioned more smoothly than the corrupt and inefficient government bureaucracy. These groups also insinuated themselves into the parliament by means of alliances with officially sanctioned parties. Some of the militants also took up arms, selecting foreign tourists as their targets with the aim of depriving the government of the considerable foreign currency income brought in by the tourist industry. In Jordan, the Muslim Brotherhood legitimately earned a position from which it could bid for a formal share of power by electing thirty-four candidates out of a total of eighty in the national parliament in 1989 to become the largest organized group in that body.

The issue of the compatibility of Islam and democracy remains, however. No Islamic party has yet gained governmental power by means of the ballot box. When it comes to prediction, observers sit on the fence, pointing to some elements in the Muslim tradition that might become the basis for acceptance of democratic principles and procedures, while acknowledging that traditional Islam's core principle of observance of the will of God hardly encourages or accepts the free and sometimes tumultuous competition of modern democracy.[14]

Fourth, another political group that has straddled existing political jurisdictions is the communist movement. In this regard, the Middle East is not unique and does not require further elaboration. Communist parties have existed or now exist in Algeria, Iran, Iraq, Israel, Jordan, Lebanon, Syria, Turkey, and Palestine under the British Mandate, as well as among contemporary Palestinians and possibly in Egypt.[15] Their significance has varied from state to state and over time. Although one might expect bitter relations between communists and such traditionalists as the Islamicists, in fact some communist parties have suffered the greatest hostility not from those who opposed their ideas, but from those whose own appeal overlapped with theirs. This has been particularly true of the secular, socialist *Ba'th* party, especially in Iraq, where the regime subjected members of the Iraq Communist Party to extremely brutal treatment. Clearly the Iraqi regime was not motivated by ideological principle, but rather by fear of undue competition. More recently, of course, communist parties in the Middle East, as elsewhere, have suffered from the collapse of the Soviet Union, once a major external source of support.

Fifth, the process of state formation is still in flux in the Middle East. Several political communities aspire to but have not yet achieved statehood. Foremost among these are the Palestinians and the Kurds. The status of both these communities is reflected in this volume in that political organizations claiming to represent these groups exist in a number of countries. Kurdish political organizations operate in Iran, Iraq, Lebanon, and Turkey. So far, however, none of these groups has declared the establishment of a sovereign Kurdish state as their goal. They have sought to defend and enhance Kurdish interests in the existing states in which they find themselves, or at best to demand autonomy within those states.[16]

The Palestinians, on the other hand, have consistently and insistently demanded their own state, and they have organized themselves within the states in which they reside to promote that ultimate goal.[17] Accordingly, this volume includes a chapter that deals explicitly and exclusively with the Palestinians, although a functioning Palestinian state has not existed heretofore. There is further justification for this treatment in that the Palestine Liberation Organization in many ways functions as a quasi-state, with the disparate factions within it playing the role of quasi-political parties.

The case of the Palestinians brings up another, sixth, facet of contemporary Middle East politics. At times, politics in the Middle East have been played out tragically with bullets rather than ballots. Under these conditions, armed militias rather than political parties necessarily may be the dominant political organizations. Thus, the reader will find that the chapters on the Palestinians and on Lebanon, for example, include groups whose status as political parties may be questionable. This is due to the fact that political conflict in these cases has taken the form of armed confrontation (in Lebanon, during the civil war between 1975 and 1990; and among the Palestinians, consistently from the beginnings in 1920 until the present). Some of these armed factions, in fact, transformed themselves into parties or quasi-parties when physical conflict ended (Algeria); or, conversely, parties or quasi-parties have become armed militias when civil conflict degenerated into civil war (Lebanon). Some observers suggest that the same will occur among the Palestinians some day.

Finally, Middle East politics is characterized by the survival of primordial ties and traditional loyalties that often permeate the existing structures of political parties.[18] In the current, highly charged atmosphere of rapid social and political change, this intertwining of the traditional and the modern often leads to ob-fuscation and confusion. Some political parties mask (with varying degrees of transparency) ethnic, tribal, clan, sectarian, and *zu'ama'* (leader) loyalties. In respect to the last of these, contemporary political parties reflect what many observers see as a long-standing feature of Middle Eastern society, namely, the authority structure of patrimonialism.[19] Although this may not be unique to the area, it is certainly characteristic of the traditional clan or tribal leader, or *shaykh*, as well as formal rulers such as shahs, sultans, and caliphs, and even such ven-erable figures as the Prophet Muhammad. Twentieth-century examples abound: Consider the cases of Reza Shah of Iran, Kemal Atatürk, and, for that matter, such leaders of competitive Turkish parties as Süleyman Demirel (leader of the Justice Party, 1964–80, and the True Path Party in the early 1990s); Necmettin Erbakan (National Salvation Party, 1973–80, Prosperity Party in the 1990s); Alpaslan Türkeş (Nationalist Action Party, 1965–80, Nationalist Work Party in the 1990s); and even Bülent Ecevit (Republican People's Party, 1972–80, Dem-ocratic Left Party in the 1990s).

Similarly, as parties have emerged, they have often incorporated within their structures and functions preexisting patron-client relationships. The party thus becomes a new political instrument of traditional local notables; or, alternatively, the party serves to rechannel a set of traditional relationships. This phenomenon is particularly evident in Lebanon and in the more traditional regions of Turkey, as well as throughout the Arab world and in Iran.[20]

Political parties in the Middle East have also reflected the impact of major events. In the Arab world, for example, pan-Arab movements became quite popular in the aftermath of the Arab defeat in the first Arab-Israeli war in the late 1940s, due to the disgrace of the more traditional leadership of most Arab states at the time. Subsequently, visions of Arab unification fell from favor in the wake of the devastating defeat of Arab arms in the 1967 war with Israel. In particular, President Gamal Abdel Nasser of Egypt, the chief spokesman and symbol of these visions, suffered a serious erosion in his power and influence. Paradoxically, the pan-Arab *Ba'th* party seized power in Syria and Iraq at this time. Far from carrying out its ideology by unifying these two neighboring states in the Fertile Crescent, however, relations between the two wings of the party and the respective regimes they controlled deteriorated to such an extent that they became bitter rivals and enemies. Symbolic of the depths of this animosity, Syria was the only Arab state that failed to support Iraq in the lengthy Iran-Iraq war during the 1980s; it actually supported Iran during the war. Moreover, Syria was among the Arab states that contributed troops to the United Nations coa-lition against the Iraqi regime during the crisis triggered by the invasion of Kuwait in 1990–91.

With pan-Arabism in decline, Arab parties and regimes opted for more con-servative—in a sense, parochial—programs. This phase was exemplified by the Sadat government in Egypt, which abandoned pan-Arab rhetoric in favor of a renewed emphasis on a specifically Egyptian identity. Similarly, the late 1960s saw the emergence of Yasir Arafat as leader of the Palestine Liberation Organization, heralding a new self-reliance of the Palestinian community, replacing the policy of dependence on Arab states and governments in the struggle for national liberation. Like Sadat, Arafat emphasized the more limited interests of the Palestinian community over and above the causes of the Arab world at large.

Finally, the 1980s witnessed the emergence on the political stage of the Middle East of parties advocating the resurgence of Islam. These parties seemed to enjoy their greatest political successes in countries plagued by what Alan Richards and John Waterbury have called "regime exhaustion": the failure of regimes to "develop any coherent mass base"; the failure of attempts at corporatism, resulting in increased prominence of the police in controlling the citizenry; and, finally, the failure to achieve economic prosperity for the masses.[21] Iran was the first country to fall to the Islamicists. The Sudan also succumbed; although it is a minor force in the Middle East and the Arab world, it is strategically situated as Egypt's neighbor to the south, and Egypt is a major player. By the early 1990s, a series of basically secular regimes seemed in some danger (including those in Algeria, Tunisia, and Egypt). Islamic militants had also made significant inroads in Lebanon, among the Palestinians, and in Syria, where in 1982 the Asad regime felt it necessary to put down an uprising of the Muslim Brotherhood with unrestrained brutality.[22] There were signs of Islamic revivalism even in the staunchly secular republic of Turkey. Overt advocacy of theocracy has been outlawed in Turkey; as a result, Islamicist parties have been somewhat more restrained in their public rhetoric than elsewhere. Although such parties have not so far gained more than roughly 10 to 15 percent in freely contested elections, their very presence on the spectrum of political parties has undoubtedly served to pull other formally secular parties somewhat in their direction.

The apparent popularity of Islamic revivalism may represent more than an upsurge of piety. Given the intense dissatisfaction with the perceived flaws and failures of existing regimes, it is possible that Islamic militancy is widely supported because it is viewed as an effective vehicle for the expression of frustration and despair. Suggestive of this interpretation is the widespread dismay reportedly caused by a pious official in the Ministry of Education in Jordan when he tried to impose far-reaching measures of segregation of the sexes in the schools, affecting even parents of children at public performances. These measures created a significant backlash.

In one sense, the success of the Islamicists may be explained without reference to the exhaustion of preceding regimes. Islam, after all, is clearly an indigenous expression of Middle Eastern culture. It is perhaps the only major political doctrine that cannot be labeled as "foreign." In this sense, it, more persuasively than any other ideology, can claim authenticity in the search for a distinct and congenial form of political identity. Islamicist regimes (so far only in Iran and Sudan) have not been in power long enough to indicate their ability to satisfy popular demands, nor to demonstrate their ability to maintain stable, long-term relations with other states, particularly non–Middle Eastern states. Above all, it remains to be seen if this particular political credo also fails in its turn, yielding to another round of regime exhaustion.

It is the task of the analyst to disentangle these phenomena in search of the social origins and true agendas of political parties. This task is made more difficult by the nature of political literature and party rhetoric, which mislead and disguise more than they inform and reveal. Many political parties are constrained to try to reconcile their narrowly based membership with their lofty slogans. Even the most narrowly based parties thus seek to broaden their appeal. For example, a modern Marxist-Leninist party might be better understood if the tribal balance in its leadership and membership were analyzed.[23] Other political parties in the Arab world serve no purpose other than to institutionalize support for the leader (whether he is a ruler or dictator or a local za'im); this tends to be true especially in Lebanon. In still other cases, parties have been suborned by the political organization of a dominant personal ruler or boss (za'im or rais), such as Nasser, Saddam Husayn, Hafez al-Asad, or Muammar Qadhafi.

In an earlier version of his contribution to this volume, Shahrough Akhavi put this matter in a neat nutshell. With reference to the question of what makes Iranian and Middle Eastern parties unique (or rather, why they may not be unique), he said:

To be sure, the region of the Middle East can be defined in ways that would distinguish it from other world regions, as for example by noting its topography, climatic conditions, social structures, cultural systems, and historical experiences. But it would be more apposite to compare Iranian political parties with third world parties rather than Middle Eastern ones per se. After all, those themes that we might adumbrate as uniquely Middle Eastern turn out not to be so after all. For instance, among these Iranian parties have been those with explicit commitments to Islamic perspectives. Yet, Islamic political parties may be found outside the Middle East region (in Africa and South and Southeast Asia).

Akhavi further argues that both Iranian and non-Iranian parties are based on "the urban petite bourgeoisie—shopkeepers, petty merchants, self-employed persons such as taxi drivers—and lumpenproletariat." They also manifest similarities in their organizational patterns that "appear to be based on the principle of centralized pyramidal hierarchy, with the local branches in the form of basic units, which are in turn subsumed by district units, regional units, and a national organization."[24]

While these organizational and social attributes may not be unique to Iran or the Middle East, without question they are characteristic of political parties in the region. In short, political parties are very much a part of the contemporary Middle East. Hopefully, the following detailed descriptions will prove useful in expanding our understanding and knowledge of these uniquely modern structures.

Finally, it is interesting to note that the concept of party was not unknown in the Middle East before the onset of modernizing change. The Arabic word hizb does not have the exact connotation that the word *party* has in English. Traditionally, it meant a community, sect, or a group of followers.[25] Although there are references in the *Quran* to *ahzab* (parties or groups), particularly the *Hizballah* (Party of God) and *Hizb al-Sheytan* (Party of the Devil), it is inaccurate to maintain, as present-day leaders of the Party of God in Lebanon do, that the *Quran* provides a recipe for the creation of modern political parties. In fact, according to the *Quran*, God warned Muslims against splitting into various sects and factions: "[B]e not of those . . . who have split up their religion, and have become sects, whose every party rejoices in what is their own."[26] And yet, as the historical record shows, the realm of Islam was split into sects or factions from a very early stage, as exemplified by rival caliphates in Spain and Baghdad and by the split between Shi'ites and Sunnis.

This history of factionalism and apparent fragility of the political community have spawned deep-rooted distrust of political parties. Nathan Brown and Timothy Pirot comment on this phenomenon in the chapter on Egypt, but it is observable in other countries of the Middle East as well. Even in Turkey, which has a fairly long history of vigorous party competition, there is inherent suspicion of any perceived challenge to national solidarity and integrity, and parties do not hesitate to accuse one another of undermining that solidarity and integrity.[27] In the last analysis, robust political parties exist in the Middle East, and, despite numerous setbacks and threats, the struggle to develop genuine democracy seemed to be making some headway in the early 1990s.

## NOTES

1. Joseph LaPalombara and Myron Weiner, eds., *Political Parties and Political Development*, (Princeton, N.J.: Princeton University Press, 1966), 4.

2. Ibid., 6.

3. Giovanni Sartori, *Parties and Party Systems* (New York: Cambridge University Press, 1976), 41.

4. Joseph A. Schlesinger, "Party Units," in D.L. Sills, ed., *International Encyclopedia of the Social Sciences*, (New York: The Free Press, 1968), Vol. 8, 428.

5. Ibid.

6. H. Barakat, "Ideological Determinants of Arab Development," in *Arab Resources*, ed. Ibrahim Ibrahim (London: Croom Helm), 173; quoted by Sharon Staunton Russell, "Migration and Political Integration in the Arab World," *The Arab State*, ed. Giacomo Luciani (Berkeley: University of California Press, 1990), 384.

7. "Arab Regimes: Legitimacy and Foreign Policy," in Giacomo Luciani, 288.

8. Michael Hudson, "After the Gulf War: Prospects for Democratization in the Arab World," *Middle East Journal*, 45:3 (Summer 1991), 407–26. Hudson is hardly so sanguine, however, as to suggest that the Arab world is about to achieve full-blown democracy.

9. Samuel P. Huntington suggests an even more stringent criterion for the consolidation of democratic regimes: *two* peaceful changes of government, which he dubs the "two turnover test." By his own admission, however, this test may be excessively severe. See his *The Third Wave*, (Norman: University of Oklahoma Press, 1991), 266f.

10. As the Palestinian chapter below indicates, a number of Palestinian factions emerged out of the conviction that armed struggle was the only means of achieving Palestinian goals. While they may have operated within the framework of the Palestine Liberation Organization (PLO) as parties or quasi-party factions, in the struggle against Israel they clearly functioned as armed militias. This pattern is not unknown in other parts of the world, including Europe, where fascist brown shirts and Nazi SA toughs played critical roles in intimidating more peacefully inclined rival parties. Similarly, in Turkey during the 1970s, armed factions of both right and left wreaked havoc in the larger cities to such an extent that they generated fears of outright civil war. The role of violence in politics is a complex subject. See H.L. Nieburg, *Political Violence: The Behavioral Process*, (New York: St. Martin's Press, 1969).

11. As Sartori makes clear, there is a distinct difference between party and faction, which stems from the essentially modern and generally more highly institutionalized nature of the former. This difference characterizes the historical background of parties almost irrespective of their specific cultural environment, which is to say that many parties began as factions in the traditional environment of pre-electoral, pre-mass politics, and assumed the form of true parties only as mass politics developed.

12. This does not imply that we disagree with Ilya Harik's observation that Middle Eastern states are far more stable and have stronger historical roots than has generally been thought. Egypt, Saudi Arabia, and Morocco are cases in point. On the other hand, the states of the Fertile Crescent, even those that have historical antecedents, such as Lebanon and Syria, not to speak of Israel, have suffered significantly from disagreements concerning their precise definition and/or borders. See Harik, "The Origins of the Arab State System," in Giacomo Luciani, 1–28.

13. The Ba'th Party is treated extensively in the country essays on Iraq, Lebanon, and Syria; the MAN in the essays on Jordan, Lebanon, and the Palestinians.

14. See, for example, John L. Esposito and James P. Piscatori, "Democratization and Islam," *Middle East Journal*, 45:3 (Summer 1991), 427–40.

15. To facilitate identification of these parties, they are generally listed under the heading of Communist Party in each country chapter.

16. Nevertheless, a de facto Kurdish government was created in northern Iraq in July 1992. Several months later, the Iraqi-Kurdish elected parliament announced its intention of creating a federal state, and its determination not to allow the Iraqi government to reassert control. Subsequently, Iran, Syria and Turkey jointly warned that they would not accept this implicit partition of their neighbor, Iraq. *New York Times*, November 15, 1992, 11. The joint statement is significant in that Iraq's three neighbors have not hesitated to support Kurdish dissidence in each others' territories in the past, nor have they ever before spoken on the Kurdish issue in such unambiguously unanimous terms. Political organizations specifically claiming to represent Kurdish interests in Turkey, Iraq, and Iran are treated in the respective country chapters. Because of the illegal and clandestine nature of these groups, especially in Turkey, it is difficult to acquire precise data concerning them.

17. The Israeli Arabs are an exception to this rule; they have operated within the Israeli political system, supporting a number of parties, including major Zionist parties such as Labor. This behavior is intended to promote their immediate interests. Should an autonomous Palestinian entity emerge in the occupied territories, its influence upon— and the management of its relations with—the Israeli Arab community will be complex and delicate.

18. James A. Bill and Robert Springborg, *Politics in the Middle East*, 3rd ed. (Glenview,

IL: Scott, Foresman/Little Brown Higher Education, 1990), 92–99.

19. "In the Islamic world, where religion and politics have always been inseparable, shahs, sultans, and shaykhs have tended to rule in a paternal, patriarchal, and patrimonial manner. Government has been personal, and both civil and military bureaucracies have been little more than extensions of the leader. . . . [T]he sovereign is located at the center of the political system. He is surrounded by advisers, ministers, military leaders, personal secretaries, and confidants. The one thing that all members of this inner circle share is unquestioned personal loyalty to the leader." Bill and Springborg, 153–54. Contemporary discussions of patrimonialism are generally based on Max Weber, *The Theory of Social and Economic Organization*, edited by Talcott Parsons (New York: The Free Press, 1964), 348ff.

20. Some years ago, Lloyd and Suzanne Rudolph called attention to this phenomenon in the case of India. See *The Modernity of Tradition: Political Development in India* (Chicago: University of Chicago Press, 1967); for excerpts, see F. Tachau, ed., *The Developing Nations: What Path to Modernization?* (New York: Dodd, Mead and Co., 1972), 41–51.

21. Alan Richards and John Waterbury, *A Political Economy of the Middle East: State, Class, and Economic Development* (Boulder: Westview Press, 1990), 432–33 and *passim*.

22. Most accounts refer to this incident in the city of Hama only in passing, but see Thomas L. Friedman, *From Beirut to Jerusalem* (New York: Farrar Straus Giroux, 1989), 76–87.

23. In this vein, the predominance of relatives and fellow townsmen among the Iraqi leadership, especially since the emergence of Saddam Husayn as strongman, has been widely noted. See, for example, Hanna Batatu, *The Old Social Classes and the Revolutionary Movements of Iraq: A Study of Iraq's Old Landed and Commercial Classes and of its Communists, Ba'thists, and Free Officers* (Princeton N.J.: Princeton University Press, 1978).

24. See the chapter on Iran, below.

25. See Butrus Al-Bustani, *Muhit Al-Muhit* (Beirut, 1866), Vol. 1, 384–85. The following passage is based partly on a draft originally prepared by As'ad Abukhalil. See also "Hizb" in *The Encylopedia of Islam*, new ed., vol. 3, pt. 1 (1965).

26. *The Koran*, translated from the Arabic by J.M. Rodwell (London: J.M. Dent and Sons, 1953), Sura XXX—"The Greeks," 213.

27. By the same token, overt threats to national solidarity and territorial integrity, such as the guerrilla campaign mounted by the PKK in eastern Turkey, tend to trigger a reaction of increased militant nationalism among Turks.

# POLITICAL PARTIES
# OF THE MIDDLE EAST
# AND NORTH AFRICA

# ALGERIA

The political history of Algeria is unique in the Arab world in both the duration and character of its colonial experience. In the early sixteenth century Algeria fell under Turkish domination and remained a distant outpost of the Ottoman Empire until the French conquest in 1830. The French remained in Algeria for 132 years, departing in 1962 following one of the bloodiest wars of independence of the twentieth century.

Algeria was never considered, strictly speaking, a colony, but was rather an integral part of France with (from 1900) a special legal status. This was so because of the heavy presence of European settlers (principally from France, Spain, Italy, and Malta) who migrated to Algeria following the 1830 conquest. The number of settlers had reached some 750,000 by 1900 (15 percent of the total population) and a little over 1 million in 1954.[1] In addition to occupying the best agricultural land, the settlers predominated in the major urban areas. In 1931, for example, the percentage of Europeans in the four largest cities was 69 percent in Algiers, 79 percent in Oran, 48 percent in Constantine, and 57 percent in Bône (Annaba).

The French conquest led to the severe repression of the Muslim population and the destruction of most precolonial institutions. Unlike in Tunisia and Morocco, which were protectorates of France, the entire Algerian social structure was upended and disarticulated during the colonial period. This had numerous consequences, two of which deserve note. First, Algerian society closed in on itself as a defensive response to the colonial occupier. For much of the colonial period Algerian Muslims remained at a relatively low level of cultural development, lagging behind trends and developments in the rest of the Arab world. Second, it resulted in the leveling of Algerian society and the marginalization of the precolonial urban bourgeoisie. This further solidified a cultural egalitarianism already deeply rooted in Algeria's essentially tribal society and greatly reduced the importance of class-based politics in the twentieth century.

Until 1946 the juridical status of the Muslim community was defined by the *Senatus Consulte* of 1865, which introduced the distinction between citizens and noncitizens. Under the *Senatus Consulte*, Algerian Muslims were regarded as subjects of France governed by Muslim personal status law—though the practice of Islam itself was tightly controlled, as was the teaching of classical Arabic. A qualified Muslim could request French citizenship but only by renouncing Muslim law, an act of apostasy very few were willing to take. The number of Muslims who became citizens thus remained insignificant throughout the colonial period. (This did not, however, exempt subject Muslims from conscription into the French army.)

The depersonalization experienced by the Muslim population was compounded by the repressive legal regime, known as the Code de l'Indigénat, to which they were subjected. This code involved a series of discriminatory laws and administrative measures enacted or decreed from the 1840s onward that closely controlled the movements of Muslims and imposed harsh penalties for a multitude of infractions. The final abrogation of all the provisions of the Code de l'Indigénat, which was a central demand of the Algerian nationalist movement, did not occur until the 1940s.

The second-class status of the Muslim population was reflected in the system of representation. Four levels of representation existed for residents of Algeria, most of which were established following the end of military rule in 1870. At the highest level was representation in the French parliament, which was fixed in 1881 at two deputies for each of Algeria's three departments (Algiers, Constantine, and Oran). Until 1944 only full French citizens were entitled to vote in elections to the National Assembly in Paris.

The second level, which covered the three departments of Algeria and was known as the Délégations Financières, was established in 1898 and remained in existence until 1945. Located in Algiers, the Délégations Financières was a tripartite corporatist body that enacted the colony's annual budget (Algeria having been granted budgetary autonomy in 1900). Representatives to the Délégations Financières were elected by three distinct economic groups: landowning Europeans or those connected in some way to agriculture, non-landowning Europeans registered on urban property tax rolls, and Muslim representatives. Until 1919 only some five thousand Muslims were eligible to vote, although it is to be noted that European suffrage for this body was restricted as well.

The third level included the three Conseils Généraux (departmental councils), which were created in 1875. Elected Europeans made up from four-fifths to five-sixths of the Conseils Généraux; the Muslim contingents were composed of landowners appointed by the Governor-General (the chief executive authority in the colony who answered to the minister of interior in Paris). A 1908 law provided for the election of the Muslim representatives, though it was based on the same restrictive suffrage as that for the Délégations Financières.

The fourth level of representation comprised the Conseils Municipaux (local councils). Until 1919 only about 5 percent of the adult male Muslim population was eligible to vote in municipal elections in the predominantly European *communes de plein exercice*. In addition, the percentage of Muslim representatives could not exceed one-fourth of the local council. And, until 1919, Muslim members of the municipal commissions of the predominantly Muslim *communes mixtes* were designated by an appointed European administrator.

Parallel to the Conseils Municipaux was the "djemaa" (*jama'a*), which was an elective council institutionalized in 1919 in the Muslim *douars* (villages) within the communes. The djemaas were made up of representatives elected from a special roll of several hundred thousand voters. Though the djemaas had several administrative attributes, they were essentially powerless and served primarily as an additional means of control over the rural population.

The discriminatory nature of these elective bodies was a major complaint of the Algerian national movement, whose first manifestation was the Jeunes Algériens. Emerging in the decade prior to World War I, the Jeune Algérien movement was not a political party but rather consisted of literate men from the small but growing middle class (a number of whom founded newspapers and intellectual clubs) who advanced demands for greater political equality and opposed the docility of the *vieux turbans* who occupied many Muslim seats on the representative bodies. The platform of the Jeunes Algériens was first spelled out in the 1912 "Manifeste Jeune Algérien," which was presented to the French government. Among the reforms demanded was the abrogation of the Code de l'Indigénat, equal taxation, enlarged suffrage for Muslims, and representation in the French parliament. The overall orientation of the Jeunes Algériens was assimilationist rather than nationalist, although the defense of Islam and the promotion of the teaching of classical Arabic were important themes for many.

The first move on the part of the colonial authorities to address the growing aspirations of Muslims came with the law of February 4, 1919. This law enlarged the categories of Muslims eligible to request French citizenship—still necessitating a renunciation of Muslim personal status law—to include, inter alia, all those who had served in the armed forces, farmed land or rented urban property, or could read and write French. Those fulfilling the new conditions but not wishing to take French citizenship were nonetheless registered on the Muslim electoral rolls for elections to the Conseils Généraux and Municipaux, thus creating an intermediate category between that of voteless subject and full citizen.[2] The law also raised the percentage of Muslim representatives to up to one-third of the Conseils Généraux and Municipaux, although, for the latter body, they were still not eligible to stand for mayor.

The 1919 law fell far short of the modest hopes of the Jeunes Algériens (though it was violently denounced in the European community). For, in addition to giving only the illusion of greater Muslim participation, the law formally organized the colonial administration's Muslim agents—the caïds, aghas, and bachaghas[3]—into a corps of state functionaries. The political role played by the caïds—which included the rigging of elections—enabled the colonial administration to improve its means of surveillance and control over the Muslim community.

The enactment of the 1919 law was followed by the emergence onto the political scene of Emir Khaled, who became the unofficial leader of the Jeune Algérien movement. Khaled, a graduate of the French military academy at Saint-Cyr and the grandson of Emir Abdelkader—who led the Algerian resistance to the French in the 1830s and 1840s—was regarded as a dangerous agitator by the

European community and shocked the colonial administration by getting elected to the Algiers municipal council in 1919. Over the subsequent four years he led a spirited campaign against the colonial system, furthering the demands of the Jeune Algérien movement. In addition to reiterating the 1912 Manifeste, Khaled called for equal rights for Muslims in all domains, an end to Algeria's special status and the juridical attachment of the three departments to the metropole, and the right of Muslims to acquire French citizenship without renouncing Muslim personal status law.

Khaled could be considered modern Algeria's first nationalist leader, though his solution to the condition of the Muslim population was total assimilation into France rather than independence. Khaled's militant rhetoric in favor of equal rights for Algeria's Muslims threatened the *colon* elite, however, who unleashed a merciless campaign against him. In 1923 he resigned his municipal council seat and left Algeria for voluntary exile in the metropole.

The departure of Khaled produced only a temporary void in Algerian Muslim politics. In the course of the 1920s four distinct forces in the Muslim community took form that would define the political debate in the colony for the coming two decades. The first were assimilationists of the Jeune Algérien movement, some of whom created the Fédération des Elus Indigènes Algériens in 1927. This was never a political party as such but rather a federation of independent elected officials not tied to the colonial administration. The men of the Fédération des Elus were principally members of the liberal professions and schoolteachers— many of whom were inculcated with the values of the French Revolution and *laïcité*[4]—and their rise came at the expense of the caïds, whose influence in the colony's elected bodies began to decline in the 1920s. This evolution was particularly pronounced in the Department of Constantine, where the Fédération des Elus was most influential.

The Fédération des Elus was personified by two politicians, Mohammed Bendjelloul, who was a medical doctor from Constantine, and Ferhat Abbas, a pharmacist from Sétif. Ferhat Abbas was a prominent publicist as well, and he became the leading intellectual and political advocate of assimilation in the late 1920s and 1930s. Ferhat Abbas's discourse centered on the lack of respect accorded to Algerian Muslims and the Islamic religion by the Europeans and the need to do away with the colonial system in order to assure entente between the two communities. For Ferhat Abbas there was no question of an independent Algerian nation—which, he maintained, in a celebrated 1936 newspaper article, had never existed in history—but rather of total assimilation into France and the right of Muslims to acquire French citizenship without having to abandon their personal status code. Ferhat Abbas declared that Algeria was French, that Algerian Muslims were Frenchmen, and that no interpretation of the *Quran* existed that could deny this fact.

A second force that emerged in the 1920s, Islamic reformism, gained organizational form in 1931 with the creation of the Association des Oulémas Musulmans Algériens, familiarly known by its shortened Arabic name, the *Jam'iyat* al-'Ulama. The Jam'iyat al-'Ulama was also not a political party but rather a religious and cultural association that played, however, an important political role until its dissolution by the colonial authorities in 1956. The Jam'iyat al-'Ulama was led by men from traditional middle-class backgrounds, the majority of whom were Arabophone schoolteachers. A number were graduates of the Islamic universities of Zaytuna in Tunis and al-Azhar in Cairo, where they were heavily influenced by thinkers of the Islamic salafiyya movement such as Jamal al-Din al-Afghani and Muhammad Abduh. Among the leading figures of the Jam'iyat al-'Ulama were Abdelhamid Ben Badis, a native of Constantine and founder of the association, and Bachir Ibrahimi, who succeeded Ben Badis as president following the latter's death in 1940.

The goals of the Jam'iyat al-'Ulama were expressed by Tawfik El Madani, one of the association's leading figures, in his famous 1931 formulation "Islam is my religion, Arabic is my language, Algeria is my homeland." As the vanguard of Islamic reformism, the Jam'iyat al-'Ulama struggled relentlessly against the folk Islam of the marabouts, the locally based holy men who, in addition to their supposed heretical practices, were seen (not always accurately) as agents of the colonial administration. The Jam'iyat al-'Ulama presented Islam as the national ideology of the Algerian people, which was the sole force capable of unifying all sectors of society. Though it opposed political nationalism, which it felt led to division and conflict (fitna) within the community (umma), the Jam'iyat al-'Ulama advocated a linguistic nationalism and promoted the Arabic language through its extensive press and publishing operations and, most important, in the parallel educational system it established in the 1930s and 1940s through which tens of thousands of Algerians passed, many of whom came from modest, small-town backgrounds.

The position of the Jam'iyat al-'Ulama on the national question was ambiguous. Though opposed to assimilation the association did not advocate independence and pledged loyalty to France, a stance it did not consider to be in contradiction with the return of the Algerian people to cultural and religious authenticity. In this respect it is to be emphasized that the Jam'iyat al-'Ulama was a socially conservative force and drew support from a traditional middle class that had enjoyed close ties to the colonial administration. (Ben Badis' father, for example, was a bachagha and representative to the Délégations Financières.) Nevertheless, the Islamic reformism and Arabism of the Jam'iyat al-'Ulama provoked the colonial administration into closely controlling the association's activities, leading the latter into overt alliances with the established parties of the nationalist movement.

The third force was the Parti Communiste Algérien (PCA),* which was officially created in 1936 out of the "Algerian Section" of the Parti Communiste Français (PCF), itself founded in 1920. The communist movement in Algeria was, until the late 1940s, principally concentrated among the petits blancs of the European community, though it did attract significant numbers of Muslim members and votes in the mid-1930s and immediately following World War II. The position of the PCF/PCA on the national question followed the vagaries of the Soviet line. This ranged from the demand for total independence for Algeria (late 1920s to mid-1930s) to the notion that Algeria was a "nation in formation" not yet ready for independence (late 1930s to mid-1940s) to a more pronounced nationalist stand but stopping short of advocating total separation from France (mid-1940s to 1955).

Despite the fluctuations of its line on the national question, the PCA was an unwavering defender of equal rights for Algeria's Muslims. It was, in addition, the sole party in colonial Algeria that attempted to bridge the chasm between the European and Muslim communities, articulating an ideology that denied the existence of immutable barriers between the different ethnic and confessional groups. In this regard, the PCA was able to recruit middle-class Muslim members who wished to overcome the ambient social segregation of the colonial system, and who were moreover attracted by the party's social program, introduction of new ideas, and sophisticated organizational structure involving the active participation of militants. These factors explained in good part the PCA's success in organizing important categories of the small but growing Muslim working class into the party-controlled Confédération Générale des Travailleurs (CGT).

The PCA failed in its endeavor to became a hegemonic force in the Muslim community, however, because of its own errors as well as factors beyond its control. The party's subservience to the PCF and the Soviet Union, its ambiguity on the national question, and political opportunism cost it much support in the Muslim community. On the other hand, the PCA came up against the reality of colonial Algeria's deeply divided society and the near impossibility of breaking down the barriers between Muslims and Europeans. Social contact was rare even between European and Muslim members of the same PCA cells, and it was no coincidence that the CGT was strongest in professions that were homogeneous rather than confessionally mixed. Attitudes toward Muslims on the part of European Communists were indeed hardly different from those in the rest of their community.

The failure of the PCA and its Communist ideology can also be attributed to its inability to compete with the Parti du Peuple Algérien (PPA),* which dominated Muslim politics from its creation in 1937 until 1954. The PPA was the incarnation of the Algerian nationalist movement, and its founder, Messali Hadj, was the first political leader to unequivocally call for Algerian independence. Through the charismatic personality of Messali—who ranks as the preeminent political figure in modern Algerian history—the PPA articulated an Islamo-populist ideology that resonated deeply in Algeria's egalitarian society. The Front de Libération Nationale (FLN),* which would later lead Algeria's war of independence, was a direct successor of the PPA, in terms of ideology, worldview, and political origins of its founders and early leaders.

The PPA was the immediate successor to the Etoile Nord-Africaine (ENA), which was founded in 1926 in Paris and led by Messali. The ENA was the first exclusively Algerian Muslim political party, although its activities were almost entirely limited to the French metropole until 1936. The rise of the ENA/PPA in the 1920s and 1930s coincided with the crisis in colonial agriculture and subsequent exodus of Muslims from the countryside, both to the urban areas of Algeria and into the metropole. The large-scale emigration of Algerian workers to France (most of whom were Kabyle Berbers)[5] began immediately following World War I, and it was from this group that the ENA drew its initial support, and where the PPA later became hegemonic. Unlike the emigrants in France, who were mainly concentrated in working-class occupations and petty commerce, the rural migrants in Algeria's cities were economically marginalized. Victims of colonial Algeria's low level of industrial development, large numbers were transformed into a sort of lumpenproletariat, who no longer fell under the control of the caïds or the sway of the marabouts.

It was from the "plebeians" of the towns and cities that the PPA drew its bedrock support; they remained unswervingly loyal to Messali during his long years in prison and internal exile (1937–59). Messali, a native of Tlemcen and an autodidact from a modest background, articulated the Islamo-populist ideology that appealed directly to this stratum of society, but also to the middle and secondary school graduates from small and medium-sized towns who made up the core of the PPA's base of militants. The PPA's discourse reflected the egalitarianism of Algerian society and the importance of honor (nif in the Algerian vernacular). This included the exaltation of "the people"—defined as all those involved in the struggle for independence—and the emphasis placed on dignity, which had been denied the people by the unjust and contemptuous attitude (hogra) of the colonial occupier.

Like the Jam'iyat al-'Ulama, the PPA accorded central importance to Islamic themes and a revival of the Arabic language, and Messali strongly supported the former's efforts in this regard. Despite their agreement on key cultural issues, however, the PPA and Jam'iyat al-'Ulama differed in several respects. The PPA's religious imagery was heavily drawn from the folk Islam of the zawaya (religious brotherhoods), and was both millenarian in tone and replete with references to jihad against the colonial occupier. All this was anathema to the Jam'iyat al-'Ulama, as was Messali's advocacy of mass mobilization, his uncompromising stand toward the French, and his call for land redistribution and nationalization of industry. The radical social program of the PPA was similar to that of the PCA, although the two parties were intensely distrustful of one another. Unlike the PCA, the PPA was unequivocally nationalist and had no presence whatsoever in the European community, and it was regarded for many years as a reactionary force by the communists.

The first coordinated effort by the Muslim political and social forces came in 1936, when the Fédération des Elus, Jam'iyat al-'Ulama, and PCA banded together to form the Congrès Musulman Algérien. This was not so much a separate structure as two conventions (held in August 1936 and July 1937), where the three forces put forth a common program of demands to the Popular Front government of Prime Minister Léon Blum. The demands were essentially a synthesis of those advanced over the years by Ferhat Abbas and Ben Badis, though they now had the possibility of being at least partially realized in the Blum-Violette bill proposed by the government in 1937.

Blum-Violette, which was supported by the Congrès Musulman, was the most far-reaching proposition advanced to that date to improve the status of Algeria's Muslims. Provided for in the bill was the right for several sizable categories of Muslims to acquire French citizenship without having to renounce their personal status code. Those who would be eligible under the bill included, inter alia, former officers and noncommissioned officers in the army, winners of military decorations and other official medals, and holders of diplomas down to the elementary school level. The ENA/PPA opposed Blum-Violette as totally inadequate and continued to demand the creation of a constituent assembly elected by universal suffrage, which would have been tantamount to granting independence. For this, the ENA/PPA was kept out of the Congrès Musulman, harassed by the authorities, banned once in 1937, and then banned again in 1939. Blum-Violette was also bitterly opposed by the European community, whose powerful lobby in Paris succeeded in scuttling the bill.

The failure to enact Blum-Violette threw the Congrès Musulman into disarray and ultimate breakup in 1938. It also furthered the radicalization of Muslim public opinion, now ever more susceptible to the PPA. In 1943, while Algeria was under Allied and Free French occupation, another effort was initiated to forge a united Muslim front. Spearheading the move was Ferhat Abbas, who, with the support of the PPA (many of whose leaders were in prison), the Jam'iyat al-'Ulama, and the Muslims in the Délégations Financières, presented the Manifeste du Peuple Algérien to the administration in February 1943. Among the demands of the Manifeste were the abolition of the colonial system, equality between Muslims and Europeans in all spheres, and, in the critical "addition" of May 1943, the recognition of political autonomy for Algeria as a sovereign nation (but still linked to France) and endowed with its own constitution adopted by a constituent assembly elected by universal suffrage.

The abandonment of the goal of assimilation by Ferhat Abbas, who had been its most ardent defender for over two decades, was a major event in Algerian colonial politics. Despite the united front behind the Manifeste, it was rejected by the Free French administration of General Charles de Gaulle, which countered with a series of ordonnances (executive edicts) enlarging the rights of the Muslim community. The most important one, decreed on March 7, 1944, accorded French citizenship to some 60,000 Muslims and gave all Muslim males over the age of twenty-one the right to vote, although French and non-French citizens still belonged to two separate electoral colleges. The ordonnance of August 17, 1945, accorded the noncitizen Muslim second college parliamentary representation in Paris on a par with the European-dominated first college (fifteen deputies each), and the ordonnance of September 15, 1945, abolished the Délégations Financières and replaced it with an Assemblée Financière elected by universal suffrage (though only male for noncitizen Muslims) and two-fifths of which was composed of representatives of the second college.

These reforms were dismissed as woefully inadequate by the PPA (which had operated clandestinely since its banning in 1939) and the Amis du Manifeste et de la Liberté (AML),* the party created by Ferhat Abbas in 1944 and banned the following year. The banning of the AML came on the heels of the events of May 1945, which was the turning point for the Algerian nationalist movement. On May 8, 1945, a number of PPA-led demonstrations, held principally in Sétif, degenerated into rampages that resulted in the deaths of over a hundred Europeans. In the three weeks that followed, the security forces undertook brutal reprisals in the areas around Sétif and Guelma, killing several thousand Muslims.

Differing lessons were drawn from the murderous campaign of the authorities. Moderates such as Ferhat Abbas concluded that it was futile, if not downright dangerous, to go too far in challenging the French and that the goals expressed in the 1943 Manifeste could only be realized by working within the existing representative structures. To this end Ferhat Abbas created the Union Démocratique du Manifeste Algérien (UDMA)* in 1946, which represented the declining numbers of politically engaged Muslims who were committed to evolutionary change.

An entirely different lesson from the events of May 1945 was drawn by the younger generation of militants in the PPA, who concluded that the only way for Algeria now to win its independence was through violence. A twin strategy was adopted to resolve the conflicting currents developing within the PPA. In October 1946 Messali created the Mouvement de la Triomphe des Libertés Démocratiques (MTLD), which would contest elections as the legal wing of the banned PPA. In the parliamentary elections held the following month, the MTLD won five seats, giving the nationalist movement representation in Paris for the first time. To complement its new electoral strategy, the PPA created in February 1947 a clandestine paramilitary wing, the Organisation Spéciale (OS), that would prepare the ground for armed struggle. Put in charge of the OS were Hocine Aït Ahmed and Ahmed Ben Bella, who would later emerge as founding members of the FLN.

With the Algerian question on the front burner in Paris, the French government moved to further increase the rights of the Muslim community and counteract the nationalist movement. The National Assembly had already enacted the law of May 17, 1946, the Lamine Gueye law, which accorded French citizenship to all Algerian Muslims, while maintaining intact the two separate electoral colleges. In 1947 the National Assembly debated a new status for Algeria, which was enacted in the law of September 20, 1947. The most important provision of the Statut d'Algérie, as the law was known, was the replacement of the Assemblée Financière by the Assemblée Algérienne, which was to enjoy greatly expanded powers of legislation. Each electoral college was to send sixty representatives to the Assemblée, where decisions were to be taken by a simple majority. A two-thirds vote would be required if the Governor-General, assembly finance committee, or one-fourth of the members so requested, however, thus ensuring effective European veto power.

The Statut d'Algérie was denounced by the PPA-MTLD as totally inadequate; it was bitterly opposed as well by a European community unprepared to countenance any significant concession to the Muslim majority. The extent of popular support for the PPA-MTLD was demonstrated in the municipal elections of October 1947. In the only free and fair election ever to be held in colonial Algeria, the MTLD won a huge victory. MTLD candidate lists swept all the major cities and did well even in the smaller towns and djemaas (where elections were held the following month). The nationalist score shocked the colonial authorities, who ensured that such a result would never be repeated. In the April 1948 elections for the Assemblée Algérienne, where the MTLD and UDMA were set to win a majority of second college seats, the second round was brazenly rigged in over two-thirds of the constituencies in order to ensure victory to officially sponsored "independents." Every election thereafter was rigged in similar fashion, further discrediting the electoral strategy in the eyes of the young OS activists. Furthermore, the MTLD and UDMA representatives in the Assemblée Algérienne found themselves isolated and rendered totally ineffective over the following three years in the face of the hostility of their European colleagues.

In the years from 1949 to 1954, the PPA-MTLD was rocked by three internal crises, which ultimately split the party and gave rise to the FLN. The first was the "Berber crisis" of 1949, which involved the purging from the PPA-MTLD of a group of militants who had countered the party's Islamo-Arabism with the exaltation of Algeria's Berber roots and its cultural specificity vis-à-vis the rest of the Arab world. The "Berber crisis," which brought to light an important ideological cleavage in the Algerian polity, was in part a cover for a larger power struggle that implicated non-Kabyles as well (and with many Kabyle militants supporting Messali against the "Berberists"). The net effect, however, was the loss to the PPA-MTLD of some of its most dedicated militants from the Kabyle and in France, two areas where the party had been particularly strong.

The second crisis was the discovery and dismantling of the OS by the colonial authorities in 1950, following which many militants were either arrested or went into hiding. The MTLD denied any link with the OS and did little to aid its militants who were in prison or on the run. The OS activists subsequently became even more isolated from the official structures of the MTLD and embittered toward its leadership. In the early 1950s Jacques Chevallier, a liberal European Assemblée member and (from 1953) mayor of Algiers, embarked on a strategy of engaging MTLD representatives in a dialogue and reorienting them toward a strategy of evolutionary change. Chevallier's effort at cooptation had its effects, and the MTLD—which now cast a wide social net and counted in its leadership numerous French-educated middle-class intellectuals—began to slip into the gradualist reformism so disdained by the activists of the OS.

This led to the third crisis, which unfolded in 1953 and 1954 and pitted the MTLD Central Committee against Messali, who had been banished to internal exile in the metropole in 1952. The conflict between the *centralistes* and *messalistes* took on the character of a pure power struggle for control of the party apparatus, but also of a more fundamental conflict between the reformism of the *centraliste* intellectuals and the populism of the *messaliste* "plebeians." The crisis reached a climax in the summer of 1954, when the *messalistes* and *centralistes* held rival congresses and expelled members of the other faction. Though the MTLD was now split, the unquestioned victor in the crisis was Messali, whose charismatic hold on the party faithful gave him a base of support that the *centralistes* could not hope to match.

In the spring of 1954, a third force emerged calling itself the Comité Révolutionnaire pour l'Unité et l'Action (CRUA), which was composed of ex-OS militants in hiding who hoped to reconcile the *centralistes* and *messalistes*. The efforts of the CRUA came to naught and it soon disbanded. With the MTLD headed toward an irrevocable split, the principal figures of the CRUA came together in the early summer in the Comité des 22, which was to plan for the armed struggle that the MTLD no longer seemed to envisage. The guiding light behind this effort was Mohamed Boudiaf, who was the primus inter pares among the nine founding members of the FLN who emerged from the Comité des 22.

The leaders of the FLN were ideologically and sociologically much closer to the *messalistes* than to the *centralistes*. Nevertheless, a number of them had developed a conflictual relationship with Messali, which was due mostly to Messali's failure to take seriously the young radicals of the OS and their desire to engage immediately in violent action against the French. This led the FLN to echo the greatly exaggerated *centraliste* criticism of Messali's "authoritarianism" and supposed building of a cult of personality around himself. Messali had, in fact, always accepted the principle of armed insurrection, though he maintained that this could not be undertaken without a high level of mass mobilization or before all avenues of nonviolent mass action had been exhausted. As for the "cult of personality" charge, it was undeniable that Messali conducted himself in a paternalistic manner. This was, however, a result of the fact that he was indeed a cult figure among PPA-MTLD supporters. In addition, Messali, unlike the *centralistes*, never deviated from the principles of the party.

The poorly manned, poorly equipped FLN launched its armed struggle on November 1, 1954, to the surprise of all the other political formations. The authorities were equally caught off guard and responded by banning the MTLD and arresting many of its leaders. The *messalistes* reacted to this by establishing the Mouvement National Algérien (MNA),* which also entered into armed action against the French. The first year of the insurrection was a period of both cooperation and intense competition between the FLN and MNA. In terms of support among partisans of the PPA-MTLD, the MNA dominated in the metropole, Algiers, and in central and western Algeria. The FLN was preeminent in the east, and the two forces were equally present in the Kabylie. There was much confusion in the popular mind—as well as among the fighters themselves—between the two, however, since the FLN and MNA shared the same political roots. The two attempted in early 1955 to reconcile their differences, but this came to naught.

The critical stumbling block was the FLN's insistence that, as the vanguard of the armed struggle, it was now the sole legitimate force in Algeria and there was henceforth no more role for the prewar parties whose strategies in dealing with the French had so abjectly failed. The conceptual brain behind this position was Abane Ramdane, who became the FLN's principal political strategist and most effective leader inside Algeria beginning in April 1955. The line as laid down by Abane Ramdane specified that the FLN was open to all leaders and militants of the other parties, provided that their parties disband and that they join the FLN as individuals. The parties initiated contacts with Abane Ramdane, and in September 1955 the MTLD *centralistes* rallied to the FLN, followed by the UDMA in January 1956 (with Ferhat Abbas personally joining the FLN that spring). The following month the leaders of the *Jam'iyat al-'Ulama* announced their support of the FLN and, during 1956 and 1957, the FLN recruited most members of the Algerian student association, the Union Générale des Etudiants Musulmans Algériens (UGEMA), founded in July 1955. Matters were more difficult with the PCA (which was banned in September 1955); it accepted FLN leadership in the summer of 1956, and integrated some of its militants into the FLN's Armée de Libération Nationale (ALN), but declined to disband its clandestine party structure.

The sole party that refused the FLN's diktat was its ideological soul mate, Messali's MNA. The two forces thus descended into a bloody internecine war— in the midst of the larger war against the French—that continued for over two years and cost the lives of some ten thousand on both sides, including many of the ex–PPA-MTLD's most dynamic cadres. With Messali in internal exile in France and the MNA lacking sophisticated leadership in Algeria, the FLN rapidly gained the upper hand and turned the MNA out of its strongholds in the Kabylie and Algiers. By 1958 the MNA was an all but defeated force, and the name of Messali Hadj, who lived out his life in isolation in France, henceforth became taboo in Algeria.

The launching of the armed insurrection and will to hegemony on the part of the FLN marked the end of multiparty politics in Algeria's Muslim community. A detailed analysis of the FLN's evolution during the war, which is essential in order to understand postindependence Algerian politics, is beyond the scope of this chapter. Three general points may be made, however.

1. As alluded to earlier, the FLN represented the continuation of the Islamo-populism of the PPA-MTLD, with its exaltation of "the people," references to Islam, intense nationalism and Arabism, and social conservatism. There were two important differences with the PPA-MTLD, however. In reaction to Messali's supposed cult of personality, the FLN officially minimized the role played by individual leaders (reflected in the wartime slogan, "one sole hero: the people"). The former OS activists also not only deemphasized popular mobilization but also displayed an intense distrust of the very idea. The FLN, both during the

war and after, and despite its populist rhetoric, was the antithesis of a mass-based party, and defense of the people never represented anything more than an abstract slogan justifying its monopolization of power. The FLN conceived of itself as a vanguard and its leaders as men of action, whose modus operandi was to impress the population through bold acts of violence against the colonial occupier rather than to engage in mass action or political education. The latter was, moreover, considered to be unnecessary given that the FLN's one goal—total independence—was regarded as nonnegotiable and judged a priori to be supported by the entire Algerian people, apart from collaborators and other "traitors." The latter were not insignificant in number, however, and it is to be emphasized that the extent of popular support for the FLN was far from evident throughout much of the war. Almost no popular manifestations of support for the FLN occurred before the spontaneous outpouring of December 11, 1960, and much of the population—which had been largely *messaliste* before the war—adopted a wait-and-see attitude. Among other things, this led to numerous acts of terror against Algerian civilians on the part of the FLN. These excesses paled in comparison to the terror of the French army, however, which, along with the injustice of the entire colonial system, ultimately pushed the population into open support of the FLN.

2. The second point, which cannot be overstated, is that *the FLN never existed as a political party or an independently functioning organism*. At its creation in 1954 the FLN and the ALN were intended to be complementary organs, with the former representing the political leadership and the latter the military wing. By the spring of 1955, however, all but two of the FLN's nine founding members (Larbi Ben M'hidi and Krim Belkacem) were either outside Algeria, captured, or dead. Abane Ramdane strived to endow the FLN with a political structure, and at its first congress, held in the Soummam valley in August 1956, the primacy of the political over the military was asserted. The decisions of the Soummam were vehemently opposed by many in the FLN-ALN, however, and on October 22, 1956, the leadership suffered a serious blow with the capture by the French of *chefs historiques* Boudiaf, Aït Ahmed, Ben Bella, and Mohammed Khider. Two governing bodies were created at Soummam, the Conseil National de la Révolution Algérienne (CNRA), which was to function as a sort of appointed parliament, and the Comité de Coordination et d'Exécution (CCE), which was to be the CNRA's executive body. The CNRA—whose thirty-four members were either in prison or scattered in and outside Algeria—did not hold its first meeting until August 1957, however, and the five-member CCE fled Algeria in March 1957 in the midst of the Battle of Algiers.

At the CNRA's 1957 meeting, which was held in Cairo, the decisions of the Soummam congress were overturned, and the primacy of military action was asserted. Abane Ramdane was marginalized at that moment, and on December 27, 1957, he was brutally murdered by his own associates. Abane Ramdane's efforts to turn the FLN into a veritable political party thus never got off the ground and ended altogether. The FLN continued to be what in fact it had been from its very beginning: an umbrella label for autonomous apparatuses headed by the functional equivalent of warlords who sometimes cooperated with one another and just as often engaged in nonideological power struggles, referred to in the Algerian vernacular as *luttes de clans*. The "clans" making up the FLN were composed of frequently shifting clientelistic networks of men in the same apparatus who owed their jobs or positions to the chief of the apparatus and who came together on the basis of some kind of affinity (family, tribe, region, school tie, common life experience, etc.) or sometimes just out of happenstance.[6] It was indeed the *luttes de clans* that were the driving force in the internal life of the FLN throughout its entire history.

By 1960 the FLN was effectively splintered into ten identifiable fractions, some of which were subdivided as well into autonomous power centers: the six *wilayate* (zones) of the ALN; the Etat-Major Général (general staff) of the ALN, head-quartered in Tunisia, which organized the external army of the frontiers; the Gouvernement Provisoire de la République Algérienne (GPRA), which succeeded the CCE in September 1958 and was also based in Tunisia; the clandestine Fédération de France du FLN; and the five FLN founding members who were imprisoned in France. Out of these apparatuses, two became dominant and prefigured the character of the postindependence Algerian state: the Etat-Major Général (EMG) of the ALN, which was commanded by ex-PPA militant Houari Boumediene, and the liaison and armaments ministry (MALG) of the GPRA, which was headed by Abdelhafid Boussouf. The MALG, the internal security apparatus of the FLN, was transformed into the Direction Centrale de la Sécurité Militaire—the secret police—after independence.

3. The third point in regard to the wartime FLN is that the leaders of the two prewar parties that disbanded at Abane Ramdane's behest, the MTLD *centralistes* and Ferhat Abbas' UDMA, assumed a nearly dominant position in the GPRA, which was the most important organ of the FLN along with the ALN-EMG. The two political forces that had been so criticized by OS activists for "reformism" and "electoralism" thus emerged onto center stage in the 1958–62 period, leading the FLN's highly successful diplomatic effort, negotiating the Evian Accords with France, and endowing the front with an ideological and programmatic content that it had heretofore lacked. Heavily recruited into the ministries of the GPRA, including the MALG, were young intellectuals of the UGEMA, many of whom were inculcated with Marxism but who were sociologically akin to the *centralistes*.

On July 5, 1962, Algeria gained its independence, after a seven-and-a-half year war that cost between 250,000 and 400,000 Muslim lives[7] and, contrary to the expectations or even the wishes of the FLN, culminated in the sudden mass exodus of the European community. In addition, the months immediately preceding and following independence witnessed the most serious internal crisis ever to shake the FLN, shattering the façade of unity the front had barely maintained during the war and defining Algerian politics for the subsequent three decades (see Table 1).

The summer 1962 crisis was a pure struggle over power, a pitiless *lutte de clans*

Table 1
Elections, Plebiscites, and Referenda in Algeria, 1962–89

| DATE | ELECTION PLEBISCITE REFERENDUM | OFFICIAL PERCENTAGE VOTING YES | OFFICIAL PARTICIPATION RATE |
|---|---|---|---|
| 20 Sep 1962 | Constituent Assembly | 99.9% | 83.8% |
| 8 Sep 1963 | Constitution | 98.0% | 82.7% |
| 15 Sep 1963 | Presidential | 99.6% | 88.6% |
| 20 Sep 1964 | National Assembly | n/a | n/a |
| 5 Feb 1967 | APC | | 71.0% |
| 25 May 1969 | APW | | 72.0% |
| 14 Feb 1971 | APC | | 76.7% |
| 2 Jun 1974 | APW | | 78.3% |
| 30 Mar 1975 | APC | | 79.1% |
| 27 Jun 1976 | Charte Nationale | 98.5% | 91.4% |
| 19 Nov 1976 | Constitution | 99.2% | 92.9% |
| 10 Dec 1976 | Presidential | 99.4% | 95.6% |
| 25 Feb 1977 | APN | | 78.5% |
| 7 Feb 1979 | Presidential | 99.5% | 94.7% |
| 7 Dec 1979 | APC | | 73.4% |
| 14 Dec 1979 | APW | | 71.4% |
| 5 Mar 1982 | APN | | 72.7% |
| 12 Jan 1984 | Presidential | 95.4% | 96.3% |
| 13 Dec 1984 | APC/APW | | 80.0% |
| 16 Jan 1986 | Charte Nationale | 98.4% | 95.9% |
| 26 Feb 1987 | APN | | 83.3% |
| 3 Nov 1988 | Constitutional amendments | 92.3% | 83.1% |
| 22 Dec 1988 | Presidential | 81.2% | 88.7% |
| 23 Feb 1989 | Constitution | 73.4% | 78.8% |

devoid of ideology and involving every faction of the FLN. On one side was the EMG of Colonel Boumediene, which was backed by the ALN's internal *wilayate* of the Aurès, Nord Constantinois, Oranie, and Sahara, and by Ferhat Abbas and his associates from the ex-UDMA. Leading this faction was Ben Bella, who was accompanied by FLN founders Khider and Rabah Bitat.

On the other side was the triumvirate of the GPRA (Boussouf, Lakhdar Ben Tobbal, and Krim Belkacem), who were backed by the GPRA's ex-*centralistes* (led by GRPA president Benyoucef Ben Khedda) and ex-UGEMA intellectuals, the ALN's *wilayate* of Kabylie and Algérois (as well as elements of Nord Constantinois), the Fédération de France du FLN, and FLN *chefs historiques* Aït Ahmed and Boudiaf. The complex unfolding of the summer 1962 crisis will not be detailed here, except to say that the crisis ended in victory for Ben Bella and the EMG, and defeat for the GPRA and those allied with it. The outcome confirmed the institutional domination of the army in newly independent Algeria.

Two observations may be made about the evolution of party politics during Ben Bella's years in power (1962–65). First, the FLN's theoretical monopoly on power was maintained, with the one-party system consecrated in the September 1963 constitution. In the elections to the constituent assembly, which were held on September 20, 1962, the FLN Political Bureau presented a single slate of 196 candidates drawn mainly from the victorious clans of the summer crisis. The only other party present on the terrain was the PCA, which declined to participate in the elections and was formally banned in November 1962. FLN *chefs historiques* Boudiaf and Aït Ahmed became dissidents in the wake of the summer 1962 crisis, founding, respectively, the Parti de la Révolution Socialiste (PRS)* and the Front des Forces Socialistes (FFS).* The underground opposition parties created over the subsequent twenty-five years were, however, little more than spin-offs of the *luttes de clans* within the FLN and hardly differed from their parent party in terms of internal organization or worldview (though this was less the case with the FFS). Their activities at the outset were, moreover, financed by FLN wartime funds embezzled by Khider, who had gone into dissidence in 1963. With Khider's murder in 1967 the funds dried up, and so did most of the activities of the exile-based opposition. Moreover, most of the exiled opposition leaders continued to receive salaries and pensions from the Algerian regime, thus ensuring a certain quiescence on their part.

Second, the FLN itself effectively ceased to exist in the wake of the summer 1962 crisis. As mentioned above, the wartime FLN served as nothing more than an umbrella label for the EMG-ALN, GPRA, and other apparatuses. With these organs now either dissolved or making up the armed forces of the Algerian state, the FLN-as-party was revealed as the empty shell it had always been. The task of building a party structure from scratch was assigned to Khider, who quickly fell out with Ben Bella over, inter alia, whether the FLN should define itself as a broad union of nationalists (Khider's position) or as a vanguard of socialism (Ben Bella's position). The FLN was to become neither, although the mass organizations under its theoretical tutelage—and especially the trade union federation, the Union Générale des Travailleurs Algériens (UGTA)—developed a certain dynamism.

In addition, Ben Bella's core of young Marxist advisors was charged with elaborating the FLN's doctrine. This yielded the Charte d'Alger, the ideological document issued at the FLN's April 1964 congress that consecrated the party's *marxisant* orientation. As with the 1962 Tripoli Program that preceded it, however, the Charte d'Alger was written by a handful of intellectuals, read in advance by practically none of the congress delegates (who primarily issued from the victorious clans of the summer 1962 crisis), and ultimately served as little more than an ideological veneer for an apparatus concerned above all with questions of power and pursuit of *luttes de clans*.

The FLN structures put in place at the 1964 party congress, as well as the National Assembly and constitution, were dissolved following the overthrow of Ben Bella in the June 19, 1965, coup d'état. Three points may be made about parties during Boumediene's years in power (1965–78).

1. The FLN was almost completely moribund. No congress was held, and no central committee was ever constituted. Informally substituting for the latter was the regime's Conseil de la Révolution, which from 1966 contained not a single member not issuing from the wartime ALN. Early on, Boumediene proclaimed the importance of building the FLN but successive efforts to do so came up against the cultural and intellectual indigence of the FLN's actually existing membership base, composed as it was mainly of illiterate ex-*mujahidin* (guerrilla fighters) and their kin, who were attached to the party primarily out of sentiment or prospects for personal enrichment. Furthermore, the priorities of the Boumediene regime were industrialization and building the state apparatus. Membership in the FLN was never a prerequisite for employment in the state administration (except at the very highest level) or in the public sector, a principle that was implicitly asserted in the 1966 civil service code and 1976 constitution. With party membership also difficult to obtain—necessitating sponsorship and a lengthy probationary period—there was little incentive for anyone with a minimal level of education to join the FLN.

2. The regime did nevertheless require a party to mobilize the population behind its policies, which became imperative with the launching of the agrarian revolution in 1971. Given the FLN's mediocrity and incompetence, Boumediene fell back on the semiclandestine Parti de l'Avant-Garde Socialiste (PAGS)*— the direct successor to the PCA—to assist in the task. The PAGS eagerly supported the regime's policies in the 1970s and used the back door provided it to infiltrate the mass organizations, state-controlled media, and sectors of the state apparatus.

The PCA/PAGS was not the only prewar formation to make its presence felt, however. Former members of the MTLD Central Committee and UGEMA—a number of whom were recruited back into the system by Boumediene—assumed a dominant position in the formulation of economic policy and elaboration of the regime's *marxisant, étatiste, tiers mondiste* ideology, the latter of which was expressed in the 1976 Charte Nationale. Leading figures in this regard included Minister of Industry and Energy Belaïd Abdesselam and Minister of Higher Education Mohamed Saddik Benyahia. In addition, graduates of the schools of the prewar *Jam'iyat al-'Ulama* gained an important presence in the cultural sphere and educational system. Key figures here were Minister of Culture Ahmed Taleb Ibrahimi, Minister of Religious Affairs Mouloud Kassim Nait Belkacem, and Secretary General of the Ministry of Education Abdelhamid Mehri.

3. Although men associated with the losing coalition of the summer 1962 crisis achieved important positions during the Boumediene period and drafted the Charte Nationale, they were still removed from the key levers of power, which continued to be held by those associated with the ALN-EMG during the war, namely, the army. This was borne out at the FLN congress held in January 1979, where the leadership of the party and succession to Boumediene (who had died the previous month) were contested by two men issuing from the ALN, Mohamed Salah Yahiaoui and Abdelaziz Bouteflika, and which was ultimately won by a compromise candidate, Colonel Chadli Bendjedid.

The FLN, which had heretofore played only a marginal role, became an important actor in the political system following the party's 1980 special congress, which put Mohamed Cherif Messaadia in charge of the apparatus and inserted the infamous "article 120" into party statutes. Article 120, which stipulated that officials of the mass organizations of UGTA, the Union Nationale de la Jeunesse Algérien (UNJA), and others henceforth had to be members of FLN, led to the purge of PAGS members from leadership posts in those mass organizations, thus emptying them—the only existing mobilizational organs—of their most dynamic cadres. The UNJA indeed became moribund as a result of article 120. As for the evolution of the FLN and the political opposition in the 1980s, the following comments can be made.

First, the FLN utterly failed to accomplish the objectives that had implicitly been laid out for it: to mobilize the population behind the regime and canalize popular discontent. Far from taking on the character of a political party, the FLN remained little more than a network of clans within the power structure whose sole objective was to colonize the state apparatus with their clients. Under Messaadia's direction, the FLN ballooned into a burgeoning bureaucratic apparatus with an annual budget exceeding the equivalent of $100 million, some 30,000 paid party workers, enormous real estate holdings, printing presses, thousands of automobiles and buses, and so on. The Political Bureau and Central Committee were entirely appointed by the summit of the party, and the base was totally excluded from any participation in decision making, to the point where even its proposed candidates for municipal councils were vetted by commissions appointed by the leadership (and which included representatives of the Sécurité Militaire). Conditions for joining the FLN remained arduous, moreover, and the party never made any effort to recruit educated, younger members who could eventually reproduce the existing political class. Younger, educated militants with reformist ideas did exist in the FLN, but its character as a multitude of autonomous clans and apparatuses vertically linked to the summit but having no interaction with one another created a system in which such individuals rarely had occasion to meet or even learn of the other's existence, let alone form cliques within the party to push for change. In this vein, the FLN never established clientelistic relationships with any corporate or regional groupings, and its local sections functioned in total isolation from their surrounding communities. Furthermore, the FLN played no role in the elaboration of policy or in overseeing the conduct of the state, despite what was mandated by the official texts (constitution, Charte Nationale). FLN Central Committee sessions indeed served as little more than sounding boards for decisions already taken by the presidency.

Second, the power struggle that shook the regime in the years from 1985 to 1988 had nothing to do with the decidedly modest economic liberalization scheme of the presidency. The so-called reform–hard line cleavage within the FLN in reality never existed. Talk of such a split only served as a cover for a bitter *lutte de clans* that unfolded over two key issues: the chafing of ministers and state managers over attempts by the FLN apparatus to encroach on their turf through the imposition of its clients and whether or not Chadli would serve a third term as president. The only significant policy disagreement within the power structure was over the language question, with the heavily *arabisant* FLN apparatus pushing for rapid Arabization and the more educated state functionaries wishing to maintain effective bilingualism. Even this debate, however, was never divorced from considerations related to the nonideological *luttes de clans*.

Third, worsening economic conditions and increasingly heavy-handed authoritarianism engendered popular discontent, which in turn gave rise to oppositional activity. Two such forces emerged in the 1980s, which the regime sought to repress. The first were the Berberists, who emerged onto the scene in April–May 1980 in a wave of nonviolent demonstrations in the Kabylie demanding *droit de cité* for the Tamazight language. The leaders of the Berber spring, as the spiritual successors of the PPA's Berberist dissidents of 1949, rejected the Arabist cultural totalitarianism of the FLN. The second force included the Islamists, whose growth was fueled by anger over the corruption of the regime and its supposed deviation from Islamic principles.

In the face of growing opposition, it is to be emphasized that the Islamo-populism of the FLN—with its accent on egalitarianism, social justice, nationalism, and traditional values—still largely reflected the values of Algerian society. The FLN had come to be hated by much of the population (which made no distinction between the party and regime), not on account of its ideology but rather because it was seen as deviating from it. In this respect Algerian society—atomized as it was and still suffering from the depersonalization of the colonial period—remained profoundly *messaliste* in its political sentiments.

The rising tide of anger against the FLN regime came to a head in October 1988, when Algeria was shaken by six days of street rioting that left some 500 people dead. The events of October 1988 represented the most serious political crisis since that of the summer of 1962 and led to the collapse of the one-party system. Multipartyism was consecrated in article 40 of the February 1989 constitution, which allowed for the existence of "associations of a political character," provided, however, that they "not be invoked to violate fundamental liberties, national unity, territorial integrity, the independence of the country, and the sovereignty of the people."

The interpretation given to article 40 was spelled out in the law on political associations (Law 89–11) that was passed by the Assemblée Populaire Nationale (APN)[8] in July 1989. Contained in Law 89–11 were three features giving the authorities wide powers to regulate—and restrict—the political terrain. The first was the necessity of a party to apply for and await official registration (*agrément préalable*) from the ministry of interior before it could legally operate. The ministry routinely registered the majority of parties in the 1989–91 period but refused in several cases. Though technical violations of Law 89–11 were cited, the real reasons were usually political. The second feature consisted of articles obliging parties to use classical Arabic in their official proceedings—in the face of the continued dominance of the French language in the affairs of state, the economy, the media, and intellectual life—and forbidding the existence of parties based on, *inter alia*, "behavior contrary to Islamic morals and to the Revolution of November 1, 1954" and on an "exclusively confessional, linguistic, regional . . . or professional basis." A politically motivated interpretation of the latter could have led to the dissolution of the principal parties opposing the regime. The third feature concerned severe restrictions on the financing of parties, thus rendering them either open to prosecution for violation of the law or heavily dependent on aid from the state.

Several comments may be made regarding the character of multiparty politics in the three years following the promulgation of the February 1989 constitution.

1. First and foremost, the Algerian presidency, which initiated the reforms, had no intention of ceding power and did not initiate any serious negotiations with the new parties. Pact making was never on the regime's agenda. The decision to permit multipartyism was in one sense forced upon the regime as a result of the events of October 1988, which both laid waste to the *unanimisme* of the FLN and rendered untenable its continued monopoly of power. More crucial, however, was the fact that the events of October 1988 and the subsequent decision to open up the political system occurred in the context of a bitter *lutte de clans* pitting President Chadli and his clan against the FLN party apparatus led by Messaadia. A multiparty system, the president hoped, would push his adversaries to quit the FLN and found their own parties, as opposed to remaining inside the FLN and pursuing *luttes de clans*; encourage the FLN, which kept its patrimony and state financing, to reform itself and recruit members of the educated postindependence generation, who had heretofore shown little interest in joining it; and, most important, spawn the creation of smaller parties and independents who would form part of a "presidential majority" and attract the support of those unwilling to back the FLN.

2. Some twenty-five parties had been registered by mid-1990 and close to sixty

by the end of 1991. However, the vast majority of these formations were little more than cliques with few members, with no base whatsoever in society, and led by personalities who were unknown not only to the public at large but also in their own localities. The handful of small parties that succeeded in recruiting members, had the semblance of an internal party life, or were led by known individuals encountered often insurmountable obstacles in attracting popular support and imposing themselves on the political terrain. In this respect, the domination of the state over the society and economy was partly to blame. In the absence of a real estate market, it was exceedingly difficult (or prohibitively expensive) to rent office space, for which the parties were thus constrained to turn to the state. And with the airwaves, printing presses, and distribution networks controlled by the state, spreading one's message also became highly problematic. The financial difficulties of the parties were most evident during electoral campaigns, during which they were heavily dependent on meager allocations from the authorities. Among other things, the dependence of the small parties on the state ensured that they would not adopt an oppositional position against the regime. Many of the parties did indeed criticize the FLN but almost never President Chadli.

3. The biggest obstacle confronting the smaller parties was that the political spectrum in Algerian society had in many respects not changed since the prewar period and was, moreover, already "occupied." As mentioned above, the Islamo-populist discourse of the FLN (and PPA-MTLD before it) still predominated, which was only to be expected in a society whose cultural values had barely evolved, where social conformity weighed heavily, and which lacked a dense network of associations and institutions mediating society's relationship with the state, giving rise to a political life based on the interplay of interests. It is to be noted in this regard that not only had the FLN proclaimed the "unity of the people" and the absence of legitimately diverging interests in society but so had much of the pre-1989 opposition. The discourse of the Islamists was as *unanimiste* as that of the FLN, as was that of the exile-based opposition parties issuing from *luttes de clans* within the FLN. The antidemocratic discourse of the FLN and Islamists was also echoed in a different form in Westernized intellectual circles, influenced as they were by the pro-Soviet PAGS and other strains of Marxism. Advocates of Western-style democracy and economic liberalism did not have *droit de cité* in almost any milieu in postindependence Algeria prior to the late 1980s.

4. The one exception to this were the Berberists, whose discourse was represented by the Mouvement Culturel Berbère (MCB) through most of the 1980s, then the FFS and Rassemblement pour la Culture et la Démocratie (RCD).* The FFS and RCD (both of which refused the label "Berberist") emerged in 1989 as the principal "democratic" forces on the political spectrum. Their commitment to democracy was for the most part genuine, mainly because the Kabyles rejected Arabism and were less influenced by the Islamic reformism than the rest of Algerian society, and also were less reticent about overtly appropriating Western

political models. Berberist demands also necessitated the recognition of cultural pluralism, which could logically only be assured with the existence of political pluralism. Two essential facts must be highlighted, however. First, Kabyle society remained highly traditional, and the FFS, in particular, attracted most of its support in playing on this cultural register—as well as on the charismatic authority of Aït Ahmed—and not on the content of its program as such. Second, Berberism had little appeal for non-Berbers, thus placing a ceiling on potential support for the FFS and RCD together at around 15 percent of the electorate.

5. The FLN utterly failed to institute internal reforms or transform itself into a genuine political party. The FLN's leadership and base were hostile to the introduction of multipartyism and clung to the party's populist and socialistic slogans. The FLN remained a bureaucratic apparatus totally financed by the state and riven by *luttes de clans*. Prime Ministers Mouloud Hamrouche and Sid Ahmed Ghozali tried to distance themselves from the party apparatus and seek alternatives, but they finally returned to the fold. Even those who formed their own parties, such as Ben Bella in the early 1980s or former Prime Minister Kasdi Merbah in 1990, talked of rejoining the FLN. To quit the richly endowed FLN, with all its privileges and points of access to the state, was to be consigned to political oblivion. As a bureaucratic apparatus it was thus inconceivable that the FLN be disconnected from the state. Were a hypothetical opposition party to come to power, end state financing of the FLN, and confiscate its holdings, the FLN would disintegrate and effectively cease to exist.

6. Filling the political and cultural void left by the FLN were the Islamists, whose incarnation was the Front Islamique du Salut (FIS).* Based in the thousands of mosques that had been built over the previous twenty years and that escaped the control of the state, FIS preachers unleashed incessant, incendiary sermons against the corruption and injustice of the FLN regime. Lacking a coherent economic program, the FIS centered its discourse on moralization of both the public and private spheres, implying that the multitude of ills plaguing Algerian society could be cured if only Shari'a law were implemented, the mixing of the sexes in the schools and public space were ended, and individuals followed the "path of God."

The FIS was indeed less a political party representing interests than a social protest movement against the power structure. It is to be emphasized, moreover, that the FIS's populist and millenarian rhetoric, with its accent on social justice and honor (*nif*), followed directly from that of the PPA. And just as the PPA drew the core of its support from the "plebeians," the FIS also found its strongest base among the urban popular classes, which were heavily made up of recent migrants from the rural areas and their offspring, for whom the conditions of daily life were most difficult and who suffered most directly from the economic crisis. It was also these recently urbanized popular strata who were most afflicted by the anomie resulting from the upending of Algerian society over the previous forty years and who were thus especially receptive to the FIS's call for a return to cultural authenticity. In this respect, the rhetoric of the FIS recalled that of the *Jam'iyat al-'Ulama*, or more precisely where the discourse of the latter intersected with that of the PPA. As with the PPA-MTLD the FIS did not, however, represent only plebeians but also included in its ranks many from the educated and more well-to-do strata, providing the FIS with the personnel to constitute a genuine counter-elite to that which had ruled Algeria since 1962.

If the FIS was, in a sense, a successor to the PPA, it could also equally claim direct descent from the wartime FLN. It was no coincidence that FIS leader Abassi Madani had been an operative in the OS and participated in the very first FLN operations on November 1, 1954. In the view of Abassi Madani, the war of independence had been fought in the name of Islam, and this is what the FLN represented until its "socialist deviation" took place in 1962. There was indeed little to differentiate the worldview of the FIS from that of the culturally conservative base of the FLN.

The emergence of the FIS as Algeria's dominant party was confirmed in the local elections of June 12, 1990, when it won 55 percent of the national popular vote (according to the official results of the ministry of interior) and 856 of the 1,541 Assemblées Populaires Communales (APC).[9] The FIS equally won an absolute majority of seats in thirty-one of the forty-eight Assemblées Populaires de Wilaya (APW)[10] and a plurality in three (see Tables 2 and 3). The FIS proved to be solidly implanted in most regions of the country, doing poorly only in the Kabylie and the sparsely populated south. The FIS won large majorities in almost all the large and medium-sized cities. In Algiers, Oran, and Constantine, the FIS won on the order of 70 percent of the popular vote. The FIS was far from a uniquely urban phenomenon, however, as it won a majority of the communes with populations of between 10,000 and 20,000. Even in communes of less than 10,000 inhabitants, the overall FIS score followed closely on the heels of the FLN.[11]

The elections constituted a crushing defeat for the FLN, which came in a distant second with an official 28 percent of the vote and 486 communes. In the same way as the MTLD landslide in the October 1947 municipal elections stunned the colonial administration, few in the Algerian regime expected a FIS victory, much less one of this magnitude. Determined not to permit the FIS a similar victory in the upcoming legislative elections, the government of Prime Minister Hamrouche changed the electoral system to one based on single-member constituencies elected in two rounds, which would thus polarize the contest between the FIS and the FLN and constrain the "democrats" (whose level of support was still thought to be significant, despite the 1990 results) to back the latter. More important, the constituency boundaries were egregiously gerrymandered to favor the FLN.

It is not at all clear that the FIS would have lost these elections, which were announced for June 27 and July 18, 1991. The government's manipulation of the electoral system to deny the FIS outright victory was so transparent, however, that Abassi Madani, seeking total power, called for a general strike to sabotage the process and force early presidential elections (not scheduled until December

Table 2

June 12, 1990, APC and APW Elections—Number of Lists Presented by Party*

| PARTY | NUMBER OF APC'S WITH CANDIDATE LIST | NUMBER OF APW ELECTION DISTRICTS WITH CANDIDATE LIST | NUMBER OF WILAYATE WITH CANDIDATE LISTS |
|---|---|---|---|
| FLN | 1520 (99%) | 269 (97%) | 48 (100%) |
| FIS | 1265 (82%) | 248 (90%) | 48 (100%) |
| PNSD | 378 (25%) | 119 (43%) | 38 (79%) |
| PSD ** | 217 (14%) | 105 (38%) | 39 (81%) |
| RCD | 212 (13%) | 68 (25%) | 24 (50%) |
| PRA | 155 (10%) | 88 (32%) | 40 (83%) |
| PAGS | 56 (3%) | 33 (12%) | 19 (40%) |
| Others *** | 10 | 9 | 6 |
| Independents **** | 1365 | 266 | 48 |

Notes: *As reported by the Ministry of Interior, April 14, 1990. A small number of lists were subsequently disqualified for technical violations of the electoral law.

**The PSD was split into two disputing factions at the time of the elections. No information is available on which lists were allied with which faction.

***Four parties. The FFS and MDA boycotted the elections. HAMAS, MNI, and MAJD had not yet been created.

****Multiple independent lists were presented in many communes and APW election districts.

Number of APC's: 1541

Number of APW election districts: 277

Number of wilayate: 48

1993). The strike, which took place May 25–June 7, 1991, created an insurrectionary atmosphere in Algiers, which led to the June 5 declaration of the state of siege, cancellation of elections, resignation of the Hamrouche government, and the arrest later that month and next of the principal FIS leaders.

President Chadli promised to reschedule the elections by the end of the year, giving the regime several months to pursue a new two-track strategy to counter the FIS. The first consisted of playing upon internal divisions within the FIS in order to bring about a split, in the hope that dissident FIS leaders would form a more "moderate" and "tamed" Islamist party willing to cooperate with the pres-

Table 3
June 12, 1990, APC and APW Election Results*

| PARTY | VOTES | APC'S WON | APC SEATS WON |
|---|---|---|---|
| FIS | 4,331,472 (54.2%) | 856 (55.5%) | 5,987 (45.7%) |
| FLN | 2,245,798 (28.1%) | 486 (31.6%) | 4,799 (36.6%) |
| Independents | 931,278 (11.7%) | 106 (6.9%) | 1,427 (10.9%) |
| RCD | 166,104 (2.1%) | 87 (5.7%) | 623 (4.7%) |
| PNSD | 131,100 (1.6%) | 2 (0.1%) | 134 (1.0%) |
| PSD | 84,029 (1.1%) | 2 (0.1%) | 65 (0.5%) |
| PRA | 65,450 (0.8%) | 2 (0.1%) | 61 (0.5%) |
| PAGS | 24,190 (0.3%) | 0 | 10 (0.1%) |
| Others | 5,367 | 0 | 7 |

Notes: *All figures relating to the popular vote as reported by the ministry of interior, June 20, 1990.
The breakdown of the popular vote by *wilaya* or commune was not made public.
Results of APW Elections According to Seats Won
Number of *wilayate*: 48
FLN majority        6
FLN plurality        4
FLN/FIS tie        1
FIS majority        31
FIS plurality        3
RCD majority        1
Independent majority        1
Independent plurality        1
Number of registered voters: 12,841,769
Number of votes cast: 7,984,788
Blank or spoiled ballots: 381,972
Rate of voter participation: 65.2 percent

idency. The second was the holding of a government-parties conference in July–August 1991, which gave the impression that the regime was now attempting to seriously engage the parties in a dialogue. Both these strategies were total failures. The dissident leaders of the FIS quickly discredited themselves in the eyes of their erstwhile followers as collaborators with a hated regime, and the government-parties conference turned into a charade staged principally for the media.

Table 4
December 26, 1991, APN Election Results (First Round)*

| PARTY | VOTES | CONSTITUENCIES WITH CANDIDATE | SEATS WON | RUNOFFS ** |
|---|---|---|---|---|
| FIS | 3,260,222 (47.3%) | 430 (100%) | 188 | 186 (144/42) |
| FLN | 1,612,947 (23.4%) | 429 (99%) | 16 | 171 (44/127) |
| FFS | 510,661 (7.4%) | 322 (75%) | 25 | 19 (4/15) |
| HAMAS | 368,697 (5.3%) | 380 (88%) | | 5 (1/4) |
| Independents | 309,264 (4.5%) | n/a *** | 3 | 6 (1/5) |
| RCD | 200,267 (2.9%) | 295 (69%) | | 5 (3/2) |
| MNI | 150,093 (2.2%) | 208 (48%) | | 2 (1/1) |
| MDA | 135,882 (2.0%) | 334 (78%) | | |
| PRA | 67,828 (1.0%) | 381 (89%) | | 1 (0/1) |
| PNSD | 48,208 (0.7%) | 243 (57%) | | |
| PSD | 28,638 (0.4%) | n/a | | 1 (0/1) |
| MAJD | 27,623 (0.4%) | 199 (46%) | | |
| Others **** | 177,389 (2.5%) | n/a | | |

Notes: *Popular vote figures as reported in the *Journal Officiel de la République Algérienne Démocratique et Populaire* (4 January 1992). The complete breakdown of the popular vote by constituency was not made public.

**Figures in parentheses refer to first place/second place finish. Candidates in first place were favorably positioned to win in the second round.

***There were 1,089 independent candidates throughout the country.

****Thirty-eight parties. The PAGS boycotted the election.

Number of registered voters: 13,258,554

Number of votes cast: 7,822,625

Blank or spoiled ballots: 924,906

Rate of voter participation: 59 percent

Number of constituencies: 430

With its legitimate leaders in prison, the FIS boycotted the conference, as did the FFS during the first series of deliberations, and the FLN—whose apparatus, now led by a tandem of Mehri and Hamrouche, was locked in a pitiless *lutte de clans* with the Ghozali government—walked out on one occasion.

In the autumn the government and the APN revised the electoral code and constituency boundaries, in large part to ensure a certain level of credibility for the elections, which were rescheduled for December 26, 1991, and January 16, 1992. The first round of the contest confirmed the trend set in the 1990 municipal elections, with the FIS obtaining 47 percent of the vote and the FLN 23 percent (see Table 4). Contrary to the hopes of the regime, the "democrats" and "moderate" Islamist parties, as well as independent candidates, obtained derisory scores. The single-member constituency system—which the regime believed would favor the FLN—inflated the score of the FIS, which won 188 of the 231 seats decided outright in the first round, as opposed to 25 for the FFS and only 16 for the FLN. There was indeed little doubt that the FIS would go on to win at least a two-thirds majority of the 430-seat APN in the second round.

Facing a certain FIS victory, President Chadli—who had become politically isolated and was at odds with the army general staff—entered into last-ditch secret negotiations with the provisional leadership of the FIS for a cohabitation arrangement between the two. The coming to power of the FIS counter-elite was unacceptable to the army, however, which had moreover entered into an extremely antagonistic relationship with the FIS over the previous three years. As the ultimate holder of power in Algeria, the army thus intervened on January 11, 1992, forced President Chadli to resign, replaced the presidency with the unconstitutional Haut Comité d'Etat led by a suddenly rehabilitated Mohamed Boudiaf, cancelled the second round of the elections, and, on March 4, 1992, officially dissolved the FIS.

With its largest political party outlawed, Algeria's three-year experience with multipartyism effectively came to an end. This experience revealed the ideological hegemony of Islamism, with its millenarian and antidemocratic discourse, the total disgrace of an undemocratic ruling party-apparatus determined to cling to power at seemingly any cost, and the inability of any democratically oriented party not playing on the register of Berberism to attract popular support. It was a balance sheet that rendered highly unlikely any transition to a genuine multiparty democracy in the years to come.

## Bibliography

Ageron, Charles-Robert. *Histoire de l'Algérie contemporaine*. Tome II, *De l'insurrection de 1871 au déclenchement de la guerre de libération (1954)*. Paris: Presses Universitaires de France, 1979.

Aït Ahmed, Hocine. *La guerre et l'après-guerre*. Paris: Les Editions de Minuit, 1964.

———. *Mémoires d'un combattant. L'esprit d'indépendance, 1942–1952*. Paris: Sylvie Messinger, 1983.

————. *L'affaire Mécili*. Paris: La Découverte, 1989.

Al-Ahnaf, Mustafa, Bernard Botiveau, and Franck Frégosi, comps. and eds. *L'Algérie par ses islamistes*. Paris: Karthala, 1991.

*Algérie, naissance d'une société nouvelle: Le texte intégral de la Charte nationale adoptée par le peuple algérien*. Introduction by Robert Lambotte. Paris: Editions Sociales, 1976.

Aron, Robert, François Lavagne, Janine Feller, and Yvette Garnier-Rizet. *Les origines de la guerre d'Algérie*. Paris: Fayard, 1962.

Belaïd, Abdesselam, Mahfoud Bennoune, and Ali El-Kenz. *Le hasard et l'histoire: Entretiens avec Belaïd Abdesselam*. 2 vols. Algiers: ENAG/Editions, 1990.

Bourges, Hervé. *L'Algérie à l'épreuve du pouvoir (1962–1967)*. Preface by Jacques Berque. Paris: Grasset, 1967.

Bromberger, Serge. *Les rebelles algériens*. Paris: Plon, 1958.

Burgat, François. *L'islamisme au Maghreb. La voix du Sud*. Paris: Karthala, 1988.

Chalabi, El-Hadi. *L'Algérie, l'Etat et le droit (1979–1988)*. Preface by Mohammed Harbi. Paris: Arcantère Editions, 1989.

Chikh, Slimane. *L'Algérie en armes ou le temps des certitudes*. Paris: Economica, 1981.

Collot, Claude. *Les institutions de l'Algérie durant la periode coloniale (1830–1962)*. Paris: Editions du CNRS, 1987.

Courrière, Yves. *La guerre d'Algérie*. 4 vols. Paris: Fayard, 1968–1971.

Duchemin, Jacques C. *Histoire du F.L.N*. Paris: La Table Ronde, 1962.

Etienne, Bruno. *L'Algérie, cultures et révolution*. Paris: Le Seuil, 1977.

Favrod, Charles-Henri. *Le FLN et l'Algérie*. Paris: Plon, 1962.

Gadant, Monique. *Islam et nationalisme en Algérie: D'après "El Moudjahid" organe central du FLN de 1956 à 1962*. Preface by Benjamin Stora. Paris: L'Harmattan, 1988.

Harbi, Mohammed. *Aux origines du Front de libération nationale: La scission du PPA-MTLD. Contribution à l'histoire du populisme révolutionnaire en Algérie*. Paris: Christian Bourgois, 1975.

————. *Le FLN: Mirage et réalité. Des origines à la prise du pouvoir (1945–1962)*. Paris: Editions Jeune Afrique, 1980.

————. *1954: La guerre commence en Algérie. La mémoire du siécle*. Brussels: Editions Complexe, 1984.

Jackson, Henry F. *The FLN in Algeria: Party Development in a Revolutionary Society*. Westport, Conn.: Greenwood Press, 1977.

Julien, Charles-André. *L'Afrique du nord en marche: Nationalismes musulmans et souveraineté française*. 3d ed., rev. Paris: René Julliard, 1972.

Kaddache, Mahfoud. *Histoire du nationalisme algérien: Question nationale et politique algérienne, 1919–1951*. 2 vols. Algiers: Société Nationale d'Edition et de Diffusion, 1980.

Leca, Jean. "Parti et Etat en Algérie." *Annuaire de l'Afrique du Nord* 7 (1968): 13–42. Paris: Editions du CNRS, 1970.

————. "Etat et société en Algérie." In *Maghreb: les années de transition*, edited by Bassama Kodmani-Darwish and May Chartouni-Dubarry, 17–58. Paris: Institut Français des Relations Internationales/Masson, 1990.

Leca, Jean, and Jean-Claude Vatin. *L'Algérie politique: Institutions et régime*. Paris: Presses de la Fondation Nationale des Sciences Politiques, 1975.

————. "Le système politique algérien (1976–1978): Idéologie, institutions et changement social." *Annuaire de l'Afrique du Nord* 16 (1977): 15–80. Paris: Editions du CNRS, 1979.

Le Tourneau, Roger. *Evolution politique de l'Afrique du nord musulmane, 1920–1961.* Paris: Armand Colin, 1962.

Merad, Ali. *Le réformisme musulman en Algérie de 1925 à 1940. Essai d'histoire religieuse et sociale.* Paris and The Hague: Mouton, 1967.

Nouschi, André. *La naissance du nationalisme algérien (1914–1954).* Paris: Les Editions de Minuit, 1962.

Ottaway, David B. "Algeria." In *Students and Politics in Developing Nations,* edited by Donald K. Emmerson, 3–36. New York: Frederick A. Praeger, 1968.

Ottaway, David, and Marina Ottaway. *Algeria: The Politics of a Socialist Revolution.* Berkeley: University of California Press, 1970.

Pervillé, Guy. "Les étudiants algériens en guerre (1955–1962)." In *Armées, guerre et politique en Afrique du Nord (XIXe–XXe siècles),* 53–80. Paris: Presses de l'Ecole Normale Supérieure, 1977.

Quandt, William. *Revolution and Political Leadership in Algeria, 1954–1968.* Cambridge, Mass.: MIT Press, 1969.

Redjala, Ramdane. *L'opposition en Algérie depuis 1962.* Tome 1, *Le PRS-CNDR et le FFS.* Paris: L'Harmattan, 1988.

Roberts, Hugh. "The Politics of Algerian Socialism." In *North Africa: Contemporary Politics and Economic Development,* edited by Richard Lawless and Allan Findlay, 5–49. New York: Saint Martin's Press, 1984.

Sadi, Saïd. *Le RCD à coeur ouvert: entretiens avec Saïd Sadi par Mohamed Habili.* Algiers: Editions Parenthèses, 1990.

Sivan, Emmanuel. *Communisme et nationalisme en Algérie, 1920–1962.* Paris: Presses de la Fondation Nationale des Sciences Politiques, 1976.

Stora, Benjamin. *Messali Hadj. 1898–1974.* Paris: Sycomore, 1982.

———. "La différenciation entre le FLN et le courant messaliste (été 1954–décembre 1955)." *Cahiers de la Méditerranée* 26 (June 1983): 15–82.

———. *Les sources du nationalisme algérien: Parcours idéologiques, origines des acteurs.* Paris: L'Harmattan, 1989.

Vatin, Jean-Claude. *L'Algérie politique: Histoire et société.* Rev. ed. Paris: Presses de la Fondation Nationale des Sciences Politiques, 1983.

Zartman, William. "L'élite algérienne sous la présidence de Chadli Bendjedid." *Maghreb-Machrek,* no. 106 (October–December 1984): 37–52.

## Political Parties

In the period between the enactment of Law 89–11 and the end of 1991, some sixty parties were registered by the ministry of interior. The majority of these were cliques with no base of popular support whose political activities consisted primarily of issuing communiqués to the media. Most of these parties, which do not merit detailed discussion, are listed at the end of this chapter.

The following entries include parties registered from 1989 through 1991 that demonstrated a certain level of popular support and/or showed signs of a relatively active internal party life, as well as those led by well-known personalities.[12] A dagger (†) denotes parties created prior to 1989 that no longer existed in 1992.

Preindependence parties with a primarily European base of support (except for the PCA) will not be treated here.

Each entry begins with the date on which the party submitted its request for registration to the ministry of interior. Only this date, and not the date of actual registration, is officially made public. According to Law 89–11 the ministry of interior must act on a request for registration within a forty-day period. The number in parentheses that follows the date refers to the order in which the party was registered by the ministry of interior.[13]

†AMIS DU MANIFESTE ET DE LA LIBERTE (AML) (*Friends of the Manifesto and Liberty*). The AML was founded by Ferhat Abbas (1899–1985) in March 1944. The goal of the AML was "to make known and to defend" the Manifeste du Peuple Algérien of February 1943. The program of the AML demanded that the Muslim population be treated as full equals and that all special privileges for the European community be ended. Both the clandestine Parti du Peuple Algérien (PPA)* and *Jam'iyat al-'Ulama* supported the AML, and Messali Hadj reluctantly endorsed Ferhat Abbas' proposal for an independent Algerian republic federated with France.

The AML was one of the most successful political movements that had existed in Algeria up to that time. Hundreds of thousands joined the party, which spread throughout the country. With the PPA outlawed, the AML became, by the end of 1944, the leading legal party in the Muslim community, though the colonial administration refused to enter into a dialogue with it. Using the PPA-led demonstrations on May 8, 1945, as a pretext, the colonial administration dissolved the AML and arrested its leaders, including Ferhat Abbas. The following year, Ferhat Abbas formed the Union Démocratique du Manifeste Algérien (UDMA).*

AML. *See* AMIS DU MANIFESTE ET DE LA LIBERTE.

COMMUNIST PARTY OF ALGERIA. *See* PARTI DE L'AVANT-GARDE SOCIALISTE.

ENA. *See* ETOILE NORD-AFRICAINE.

†ETOILE NORD-AFRICAINE (ENA) (*North African Star*). *See* PARTI DU PEUPLE ALGERIEN—MOUVEMENT POUR LA TRIOMPHE DES LIBER-TES DEMOCRATIQUES.

FFS. *See* FRONT DES FORCES SOCIALISTES.

FIS. *See* FRONT ISLAMIQUE DU SALUT.

FLN. *See* FRONT DE LIBERATION NATIONALE.

FRONT DE LIBERATION NATIONALE (FLN) (*National Liberation Front*). The FLN was founded in 1954 following the split in the MTLD (see PPA—MTLD). The founders of the FLN consisted almost exclusively of activists from the former Organisation Spéciale (OS), all of whom were living clandestinely or were wanted by the police. They came from all regions of the country and their backgrounds spanned the class spectrum. The FLN was preceded by the Comité Révolutionnaire pour l'Unité et l'Action (CRUA), which emerged during the spring of 1954 in an attempt to reconcile the *centralistes* and *messalistes*, and then the Comité des 22, which convened in Algiers in the early summer to plan the armed struggle. The meeting of the Comité des 22 selected a leadership of five men: Mohamed Boudiaf (1919–92), Didouche Mourad (1922–55), Mostefa Ben Boulaïd (1917–56), Larbi Ben M'hidi (1923–57), and Rabah Bitat (b. 1925). In August the leadership won the support of the pro-Messali armed bands in the Kabylie led by Krim Belkacem (1922–70), who became the sixth member of the leadership. These six were joined during the summer by the three leaders of the MTLD's external delegation in Cairo: Mohammed Khider (1912–67), Hocine Aït Ahmed (b. 1926), and Ahmed Ben Bella (b. 1918). Together these men made up the nine *chefs historiques* of the FLN.

The FLN-ALN divided Algeria into five *wilayate*, only two of which—*wilaya* I (Aurès), led by Ben Boulaïd, and *wilaya* III (Kabylie), led by Krim Belkacem—had a significant number of armed fighters at the outset. The insurrection, which was launched on November 1, 1954, remained at a fairly low level for the following nine months, during which time Didouche Mourad was killed, Ben Boulaïd and Bitat were captured, and Boudiaf—the real coordinator and operational brains behind the insurrection—quit Algerian territory. In March 1955 Krim Belkacem brought in fellow Kabyle and ex-OS activist, Abane Ramdane (1920–57), to assume control of the Algiers zone and help fill the void in the FLN's internal leadership. Abane Ramdane rapidly became the FLN's most effective leader inside Algeria and conceived the front's strategy of absorbing the leaders and militants of the other Muslim parties and formations. The notion of bringing into the FLN leaders of the "reformist" parties was anathema to many of the ex-OS activists (as well as to the *messaliste* Movement National Algérien, or MNA,* engaged at the time in delicate negotiations with Abane Ramdane), but they were in no position to oppose the policy.

The fighting intensified with the FLN's offensive on August 20, 1955, in *wilaya* II (Nord Constantinois). The following year saw the rallying to the FLN of almost all the Muslim parties and formations, the escalation of the dirty war between the FLN and the MNA, and the increased political and military vulnerability of the French following the independence of Morocco and Tunisia (in March 1956). On August 20, 1956, the FLN held its first congress in the Soummam valley in the Kabylie. The guiding hand at the congress was Abane Ramdane. Sixteen delegates were present, although there were none from *wilayate* I or V (Oranie) or from the exterior. The exclusion of the latter pushed the FLN toward an internal crisis, which was only averted when, on October 22, 1956, a plane carrying Boudiaf, Ben Bella, Aït Ahmed, and Khider was intercepted over the Mediterranean by the French and forced to land at Algiers. The arrest of these *chefs historiques* dramatically altered the internal dynamics of the FLN.

The Soummam congress platform centered on the necessity of pursuing the armed struggle until total independence was achieved. Of equal importance, the platform underscored the primacy of the internal wing of the party over the external and of the FLN's political leadership over the military commanders of the ALN. To ensure the latter, the congress endowed the FLN—whose leadership had heretofore functioned informally—with its first formal structures, including the thirty-four-member Conseil National de la Révolution Algérienne (CNRA) (the majority of whom were ex-OS activists) and a governing Comité de Coordination et d'Exécution (CCE). The CCE included ex-OS activists Abane Ramdane, Krim Belkacem, and Ben M'hidi, but also two ex-*centralistes*, Benyoucef Ben Khedda (b. 1920) and Saad Dahlab (b. 1919). The congress also reorganized and rationalized the ALN, whose *wilayate* had previously acted autonomously and with little coordination.

In the month following the Soummam congress, the CCE unleashed the year-long Battle of Algiers, which was designed both to bring the war to the door of the European community and to attract international attention. Though it succeeded in these respects, the FLN's terror campaign in Algiers was met by the ruthless counterterrorism of the French army, which ultimately succeeded in smashing the FLN in the city. Though the cruelty of the French army drove many Algerians into the arms of the FLN, the Battle of Algiers ended in disaster for the latter. Following the capture and murder of Ben M'hidi in February–March 1957, the CCE fled Algiers and relocated to Tunisia. The result of the debacle was the isolation of Abane Ramdane at the Cairo meeting of the CNRA on August 20–28, 1957, which overturned the decisions of the Soummam congress and elected a new nine-member CCE dominated by the emerging triumvirate of Krim Belkacem, Abdelhafid Boussouf (1926–80), and Lakhdar Ben Tobbal (b. 1923). Also mandated was the creation of a Comité d'Organisation Militarie (COM), which would run the operations of the ALN's *wilayate* from the Tunisian and Moroccan borders. Commanding COM-East in Ghardimaou, Tunisia, was the former German collaborator Mohammadi Saïd (b. 1912); commanding COM-West in Oujda, Morocco, was Houari Boumediene (1932?–78).

The Cairo meeting of the CNRA was a decisive moment in the history of the FLN. The second CCE established "departments" for each of its nine members, which were precursors to the ministries of the Gouvernement Provisoire de la République Algérienne (GPRA), which succeeded the CCE on September 19, 1958. These ministries emerged into outsized bureaucracies, each controlled by autonomous chiefs, which prefigured the postindependence Algerian state apparatus. Of equal significance, the completion in September 1957 of the heavily fortified Morice Line along the Tunisian border cut the FLN's governing organs and external ALN off from the internal *wilayate* and engendered the creation of a large standing army under the command of the two COMs, which were unified in January 1960 as the Etat-Major Général (EMG) under the single command of Boumediene in Ghardimaou. The 25,000-man "army of the frontiers"—recruited heavily from Algerian refugees in Tunisia and Morocco—would be transformed after 1962 into the Armée Nationale Populaire (ANP), which, in addition to being the ultimate holder of power, would be the dominant force at the summit of the postindependence FLN.

The establishment of the GPRA institutionalized the role of those emerging from formations other than the OS. Eleven members of the first GPRA—including its president, Ferhat Abbas—originated in the MTLD Central Committee, the Union Démocratique du Manifeste Algérien (UDMA)*, the Parti Communiste Algérien (PCA)*, Jam'iyat al-'Ulama, and the Union Générale des Etudiants Musulmans Algériéns (UGEMA). The only ex-OS activists represented were the triumvirate (plus the five chefs historiques imprisoned in France, who were accorded honorary titles). A parallel development of sorts occurred in the standing army of the ALN, which was joined by large numbers of defecting officers and noncommissioned officers from the French army. These men, with their relatively high level of training, would later play an important role in the ANP and in postindependence politics.

Tensions within the FLN—which was now more a mini-state apparatus than a political party—were aggravated following the month-long meeting of the CNRA in December 1959–January 1960, which saw the appointment of a second GPRA and CNRA, and the creation of the EMG and interministerial war committee (CIG) led by the triumvirate and charged with overseeing the war effort. The period from 1960 to 1962 was dominated by the rivalry between the GPRA and the EMG over control of the ALN and by how much emphasis was to be accorded to the military side of the war (that the French army had all but won but which the EMG, to preserve its own position within the FLN, wished to intensify), as opposed to negotiations (the responsibility of the GPRA). The lutte de clans was not alleviated with the appointment of the third GPRA at the CNRA meeting of August 9–27, 1961, which replaced Ferhat Abbas with Ben Khedda, abolished the CIG, and saw the relative weakening of the triumvirate.

The conflict came into the open at the FLN congress held in Tripoli on May 27–June 7, 1962, which followed the March 18 Evian Accords and cease-fire with France—the terms of which were opposed by the EMG—and the release of the chefs historiques. The key issues at the congress were the composition of the FLN Political Bureau and the insistence of the coalition led by Ben Bella and Boumediene that the GPRA disband now that its historical mission had been achieved. The GPRA refused, precipitating the summer 1962 crisis that nearly brought about a civil war between the rival groups in the FLN. All-out conflict was averted in August when the GPRA-led coalition accepted the Political Bureau decided upon at Tripoli (Ben Bella, Khider, Bitat, Mohammedi Saïd, and Ben Bella ally Hadj Ben Alla; Boudiaf and Aït Ahmed refused to take their seats).

Also decided at the Tripoli congress was the FLN's first program, which was drafted largely by the ex-UGEMA intellectuals. The Tripoli program criticized the lack of a coherent ideology during the war; endorsed socialism, nationalization of industry, and an Algerian culture that would be "national, revolutionary, and scientific"; and accorded a place to a modernistic Islam. As was to be the case with all future FLN documents, the Tripoli program mainly reflected the concerns of its intellectual authors and was not subjected to serious debate within the party.

The sole existing organ of the FLN in autumn 1962 was the Political Bureau, whose uncontested leader became Ben Bella after the resignation of party secretary-general Khider in April 1963. More significant than the party itself were the mass organizations, which Ben Bella sought to bring under the direct authority of the FLN. The Union Générale des Travailleurs Algériens (UGTA) was brought to heel in January 1963, though efforts made to subdue the Union Nationale des Etudiants Algériens (UNEA) were less successful. The leftward drift of Ben Bella's regime gained the support of the theoretically illegal PCA and the relatively large Marxist intelligentsia in Algiers (many of whom were foreigners), who aided in the effort at party building. As a result, the newly created youth group Jeunesse du FLN (JFLN) and the Algiers federation of the FLN recruited members and displayed a certain dynamism. Until the congress of April 16–21, 1964, the FLN leadership boiled down to Ben Bella and his Marxist intellectual advisors. This was reflected in the Charte d'Alger, written by several of these advisors, which spelled out with some sophistication the Algerian road to socialism. The Charte d'Alger was hardly of interest to most of the enlarged Political Bureau and Central Committee that emerged from the congress, however, which was made up mainly of members of the wartime ALN.

The coup d'état of June 19, 1965, put an abrupt end to the party building efforts. Most of the leaders and cadres of the UGTA, JFLN, UNEA, and FLN Algiers federation opposed the coup and joined the underground Organisation de la Résistance Populaire (ORP)*, which was quickly dismantled by the authorities. The FLN Political Bureau and Central Committee were dissolved, and the latter's functions were assumed by the new regime's Conseil de la Révolution headed by Colonel Boumediene. Following the coup, the regime set up a five-man Executive Secretariat of the FLN headed by Cherif Belkacem (b. 1933), who was a member of Boumediene's four-man wartime inner circle known as the Oujda clan. Since this yielded no positive results, Boumediene dismissed the entire Executive Secretariat in December 1967—on the eve of the failed putsch of former wilaya commanders led by Tahar Zbiri (b. 1930)—and replaced Cherif Belkacem with Oujda clan member Kaïd Ahmed (1921–78).

Kaïd Ahmed, who was a large landowner and former UDMA elected official in the early 1950s, proclaimed 1968 as the "year of the party," although his efforts were directed primarily toward subduing the recalcitrant mass organizations that considered Kaïd to be a "reactionary." The FLN once again seized control of the UGTA but failed with the UNEA, which Kaïd banned outright in 1971. In the meantime, the regime had instituted "elected" local government in the form of the Assemblées Populaires Communales (APC) and the Assemblées Populaires de Wilaya (APW). The APCs and APWs were partly intended to serve as recruiting agents for the FLN, which drew up the candidate lists; however, APC and APW councillors usually entered into clientelistic relationships with the state administration and escaped supervision by local FLN controlling organisms. Moreover, the conservative FLN base resisted the agrarian revolution launched in 1971 by Boumediene, leading the regime to "enlarge" rural APCs with members not chosen by the party. The agrarian revolution was also opposed by Kaïd Ahmed, and he was ousted as party head in 1972.

The FLN base up to this point had shown itself to be hopelessly incapable of performing any kind of mobilizing function. Boumediene thus assumed control of the party himself and indefinitely postponed the holding of a congress. In 1974 he appointed former ALN officer Mohamed Cherif Messaadia (b. 1924) as the official in charge of the party apparatus. The regime's institutionalization efforts accelerated in 1976–77, with the drawing up of the FLN's weighty ideological treatise, the Charte Nationale, the promulgation of the new constitution that reaffirmed the FLN's monopoly on power, the formal election of Boumediene to the presidency, and the election of the newly constituted APN. Moving toward the convening of an FLN congress, Boumediene demoted the conservative Messaadia in favor of the more dynamic Mohamed Salah Yahiaoui (b. 1932), who was the chief army ideologue and was regarded as a "leftist."

During Yahiaoui's tenure (1977–80), the number of full-time party workers increased from around 5,000 to 15,000. Of equal significance, he tacitly permitted the pro-regime Parti de l'Avant-Garde Socialiste (PAGS)* to consolidate its hold over the mass organizations—especially the UGTA—and succeeded in attracting idealistic nonparty youth into the recently founded Union Nationale de la Jeunesse Algérien (UNJA). At the 4th FLN congress held on January 27–31, 1979—one month after Boumediene's death—Yahiaoui was one of the two candidates for FLN secretary general and president of the republic (the two offices going together); the other candidate was longtime Minister of Foreign Affairs Abdelaziz Bouteflika (b. 1937), an Oujda clan member who was considered to be a pro-Western "liberal." When neither candidate received majority support, the congress, which was controlled by the army, opted for one of the senior members of the Conseil de la Révolution, the previously little-known Colonel Chadli Bendjedid (b. 1929).

The power brokers at the congress had intended that the dull and uneducated Chadli would last for only a short period of time, after which he would be replaced by somebody else. Chadli outwitted everyone, however, spending his first five-year term consolidating power and purging from the Central Committee those closely associated with Boumediene. An extraordinary congress was held on June 15–19, 1980, at which Yahiaoui was ousted in favor of Messaadia, who once again assumed control of the FLN apparatus. The congress also drew up new party statutes, which decreed that all officials in the mass organizations henceforth had to be members of the FLN. The coming period thus saw the purging from the UGTA and UNJA of all officials associated with the PAGS or Yahiaoui. In an effort to win popular support for President Chadli, the congress confirmed the regime's new consumption-oriented economic policy, symbolized in the slogan, "for a better life."

The drop in the world price of oil caused the regime to reorient its economic policy. This was indicated at the 5th FLN congress held on December 19–22, 1983, whose slogan was "work and austerity to guarantee the future." The congress also formally approved a second term for President Chadli. The unity displayed at the 5th congress was only a façade, however, and the leadership descended into renewed bitter factional conflict in 1985 over the proposal by the presidency to "enrich" the 1976 Charte Nationale. The "enrichment" involved modest changes to reflect the timid economic liberalization schemes of the regime. The "enriched" Charte Nationale was approved at an extraordinary congress held on December 24–26, 1985.

Given the rise in social tension and disturbances and the FLN's demonstrated inability to canalize the frustrations of the population, the presidency indeed sought a limited opening to "civil society" and a reduction in the prerogatives of the party apparatus. Fearing that he and his clan were about to be sacrificed, Messaadia and the apparatus fought a bitter three-year power struggle with the presidency with the aim of replacing Chadli at the end of his second term. The conflict climaxed with the events of October 1988, which were subjected to a high degree of manipulation by the opposing clans. The political outcome of the October events was a victory for President Chadli, who ousted Messaadia on October 30, 1988, and replaced him with former *centraliste* Abdelhamid Mehri (b. 1926). At the 6th FLN congress held on November 27–29, 1988, Chadli was supported for a third five-year term, and the presidency's new political reform program was ratified, ending the FLN's *formal* tie to the state. In February 1989 the presidency proposed a new constitution that allowed for multipartyism; this was approved in a referendum on the 23rd of that month.

In March 1989 the army withdrew all its actively serving officers from the Central Committee (10 percent of its members) and formally cut its ties to the party. On November 28–30, 1989, the FLN held an extraordinary congress to project its role in the new environment of political pluralism. The congress, which was both the first with no representatives from the army (who had usually made up 20 percent of previous congresses) and the first to have a majority of delegates selected by the base, reflected the disarray in the party over the loss of its monopoly of power. It also showed that the FLN, whose membership was overwhelmingly made up of those with a low educational level, had utterly failed to reform itself and recruit new militants from the younger generation. Furthermore, the FLN's continued dependence on the state was borne out in a large march it held in Algiers in May 1990, which was entirely organized by the ministry of interior; the incompetence of its militants was shown in their total incapacity to lead a campaign for the June 1990 local elections; and its divorce from the population was laid bare in the results of the June 1990 vote.

Far from sobering up the party, the June 1990 results plunged it into further disarray. The base, which still exercised no influence over the party leadership, received little guidance from the latter, which continued to pursue *luttes de clans*. At this particular time, the power struggle pitted the "reform" government of Prime Minister Mouloud Hamrouche (b. 1943) against secretary-general Mehri and the hard-liners on the Central Committee. The *lutte de clans* reached a climax of sorts when the Hamrouche group took control of the party's candidate selection commission for the aborted legislative elections of June–July 1991 and declined to select any of the FLN's hard-liners as candidates.

The shifting nature of the FLN's internal alliance system was demonstrated in the summer of 1991, when Hamrouche, Mehri, and the Central Committee hard-liners joined forces in a pitiless power struggle against newly appointed Prime Minister Sid Ahmed Ghozali (b. 1937), the director of the mammoth public sector oil and gas concern SONATRACH during the Boumediene period. Hamrouche succeeded in taking control of the candidacy commission for the legislative contests scheduled for December 1991–January 1992. The Ghozali government reacted by tacitly supporting independents and the smaller "democratic" parties. Both factions lost badly in the first round held on December 26.

The forced resignation of President Chadli and the cancellation of the second round on January 11, 1992, was in part the continuation of this *lutte de clan*, as it kept the Ghozali government in power and dealt a further blow to the FLN faction led by Mehri and Hamrouche, who even made overtures to the provisional leadership of the Front Islamique du Salut (FIS) and resisted attempts by the Ghozali clan to stage a takeover of the party apparatus. Seeing which way the wind was blowing, however, the majority of Central Committee members pledged fidelity to the new Haut Comité d'Etat and its president, FLN founding member Mohamed Boudiaf, despite Boudiaf's oft-stated desire to see the FLN disbanded and relegated to the history books.

Boudiaf was assassinated on June 29, 1992, by a presidential bodyguard. He was succeeded as president of the Haut Comité d'Etat by Ali Kafi (b. 1928), a prominent figure during the war against France who spent most of his postindependence career in the diplomatic service. Just prior to Boudiaf's assassination Ghozali was replaced as prime minister by Belaïd Abdesselam, a founder of the UGEMA in the 1950s and father of Algeria's industrialization effort during the Boumediene period. An unrepentant partisan of economic *dirigisme*, Abdesselam set out to reverse some of the reforms that had been undertaken during the previous three years. This only contributed to the worsening economic situation, however, and, in August 1993, Abdesselam was replaced by Rédha Malek, a former minister, ambassador to the United States and other important countries, and one of the FLN's leading intellectual figures since the 1950s. During this time the increasingly marginalized FLN party apparatus, still led by the Mehri-Hamrouche tandem, continued to oppose the government, call for a return to the electoral process, and advocate a dialogue with the outlawed FIS.

FRONT DES FORCES SOCIALISTES (FFS) (*Socialist Forces Front*). Request for registration: September 24, 1989 (no. 11). The FFS emerged in the course of 1990–91 as one of Algeria's principal political forces. The party was originally founded in September 1963 and has been an uncompromising voice of opposition to the Algerian power structure ever since. The FFS enjoys the unswerving support of a majority of Kabyle Berbers, who make up the overwhelming bulk of its base, and it is a leading proponent of Berber cultural rights. Since its inception, the FFS has been inextricably bound up with the personality of its founder and leader, Hocine Aït Ahmed, who is one of the historic figures of the Algerian nationalist movement. The FFS is, in fact, less a political party than the organized expression of Aït Ahmed's charismatic personality.

The creation of the FFS was the outcome of Aït Ahmed's final break with the regime of Ahmed Ben Bella. One month after it was founded, the FFS initiated an armed revolt against the regime, and was backed by the army commander in the Kabylie and numerous Front de Libération Nationale (FLN)* fighters from the war who had sided with the losing factions of the summer 1962 crisis. Though Aït Ahmed had hoped to rally the entire nation, the FFS rebellion never extended beyond the Kabylie and a few pockets in the Algiers region. The FFS maquis, which cost over a hundred lives, was crushed by the army in the summer of 1964. Aït Ahmed was captured and imprisoned soon after. Ben Bella and Aït Ahmed concluded a deal in June 1965, but this became moot after the coup d'état conducted that month. On April 30, 1966, Aït Ahmed escaped from prison and made his way to France and then to Switzerland, where he remained in exile for the next twenty-three years.

Three points can be made about the political and ideological orientation of the FFS during this period. First, in spite of the nearly total concentration of its base of support among Kabyles, the FFS was not, strictly speaking, a Berberist party and did not include Berberist issues in its list of political demands. It presented itself as a party for all Algerians and one that opposed the authoritarian Ben Bella and, subsequently, Boumediene regimes. Second, although the FFS referred to itself as "socialist," it was less insistent on this score than either the regime or other opposition parties. Despite the occasional employment of Marxist analysis and vocabulary, Aït Ahmed had a humanistic conception of socialism that was closer to European social democracy than to any model in the Eastern bloc or Third World. Aït Ahmed, in fact, exhibited a disdain for and disinterest in the Soviet Union and other communist regimes and was essentially pro-Western in his sentiments. Third, Aït Ahmed spoke out against a one-party system in the early months of Algeria's independence, differentiating himself from other opposition figures who either accepted the principle of an FLN monopoly of power or equivocated on the concept of multipartyism.

The FFS was essentially moribund during the late 1960s and 1970s, although a number of young intellectuals did join for a time and pressured Aït Ahmed to take a stronger stand on Berberist issues. In 1979 the FFS issued its first political program. It rejected the economic orientation of the Boumediene regime, in particular the agrarian revolution and the strategy of "industrializing industries," though it did not propose an alternative model. The Arabization policy of the regime was criticized, as was its "hostility" toward the French language. The program also criticized the regime's policy of repression of the Berber culture. It called for regional autonomy, presented as the most efficacious means to break the hold of regionally based clans over the state apparatus; for local autonomy, which would be realized through the resurrection of the "djemâa"; and for "personal autonomy," which involved, among other things, the right of the individual to protection from the arbitrary authority of the state.

During Aït Ahmed's years in exile, the FFS had only an embryonic clandestine structure within Algeria. Though a number of the leaders in the 1980 Berber spring in the Kabylie were FFS militants, the party tended to exaggerate its role in the movement. As a result of two decades of cultural repression on the part of the regime, Berberist sentiment swept through Algeria's Kabyle community. Berberist issues thus became an increasingly important component of the FFS's discourse.

With the legalization of political parties in 1989, the FFS was immediately faced with competition for Kabyle support from the newly created Rassemblement pour la Culture et la Démocratie (RCD),* led by former Aït Ahmed associate Saïd Sadi and veterans of the Mouvement Culturel Berbère (MCB).[14] There were almost no programmatic differences between the FFS and the RCD, but the bitter personal animosity that developed between Aït Ahmed and Sadi rendered impossible any cooperation between the two.

Aït Ahmed returned to Algeria on December 15, 1989. His political stance over the next two years was one of ardent opposition to the regime, although he was received by President Chadli on several occasions. The FFS boycotted the June 1990 local elections—which it denounced as a "masquerade"—and refused to engage in any alliance with other "democratic" parties. Aït Ahmed argued that most of them were creations of the presidency and the Sécurité Militaire designed to undermine support for the FFS. The FFS thus aimed much of its rhetoric against the "political police," whose abolition it demanded. It likewise developed a discourse supporting human rights and the expansion of democracy, equality of the sexes, the effective separation of religion and the state (though it did not overtly speak of laïcité), and the implementation of a market economy. Foremost, however, was the demand for the constitutional recognition of the Tamazight language and its equality with Arabic in all spheres, including in the schools. In arguing for multilingualism the FFS, without explicitly saying so, wished to safeguard the position of the French language in Algeria.

Aït Ahmed strove to build a nationwide base and was everywhere received with respect, but his efforts to attract significant non-Kabyle support came to naught. Aït Ahmed's impressive capacity to mobilize the Kabyles was borne out, however, in two mammoth FFS marches undertaken in Algiers in 1990, as well as in the 75 percent of abstention in the Kabylie in the June 1990 elections. The nature of the FFS base also became evident during this period. Though numerous educated Kabyles supported the FFS, its base was heavily concentrated in the *Kabylie profonde* and among Kabyles from the popular classes in Algiers. Berber cultural and linguistic rights were the overwhelming concerns of FFS supporters, who exhibited fervent devotion to the personality of Aït Ahmed. In this respect, Aït Ahmed's relationship with his supporters was not based on clientelism but rather on his historical legitimacy, both as a prominent nationalist figure in the 1940s and 1950s and as the leader of the 1963–64 FFS maquis. In addition to his opposition to every post-1962 regime, Aït Ahmed's maraboutic roots played no small part in the adoration of his followers.

The FFS held its first congress on March 13–16, 1991, which confirmed the party's social democratic orientation. In the first round of the aborted legislative elections held on December 26, 1991, the FFS came in third with 7.4 percent of the vote. The FFS vote was almost entirely concentrated in the Kabylie and the Algiers metropolitan area. The FFS made a nearly clean sweep of the seats in Tizi Ouzou and Bejaïa wilayate, where it took over 60 percent of the popular vote. In the face of the Front Islamique du Salut (FIS)* landslide, the FFS immediately became the nation's leading "democratic" force, and on January 2, 1992, it staged a mammoth demonstration in Algiers organized around the watchwords "neither a fundamentalist republic nor a police state." The FFS opposed the January 11, 1992, coup d'état and called for a return to the electoral process, even if it were to result in a victory for the FIS.

FRONT ISLAMIQUE DU SALUT (FIS) (*Islamic Salvation Front*). Request for registration: August 16, 1989 (no. 5). The FIS emerged in 1990–91 as Algeria's dominant political party. It was founded on February 18, 1989, at the al-Sunna mosque in Bab el Oued (Algiers). Present at the rally were several hundred preachers from across the country, many of whom had been active in clandestine fundamentalist groupings that had sprouted up over the years and had served prison sentences during the repression of the Islamist movement in the early and mid-1980s. A number of preachers had also been associated with the clandestine Mouvement Islamique d'Algérie (MIA)* of Mustapha Bouyali.

The political program of the FIS was unveiled on March 7, 1989. It was the only formal political document of its sort issued by the FIS over the next three years, inasmuch as the party never convened a congress. Though short on specific proposals, the program critiqued at length the economic *dirigisme* of the regime. The apparent liberalism of the FIS's economic orientation was indicated in the call for the valorization of the private sector and a strict demarcation of the role of the state in industry. The FIS only rarely addressed economic issues, however, and those few statements indicated that it had, in fact, few major disagreements with the *étatisme* of the Front de Libération Nationale (FLN),* at least in regard to the public sector.

Closer to the hearts of FIS militants, the program condemned *mixité* (the mixing of sexes) in all aspects of public life. In the section on women it called for the payment of "allowances" for work done in the home, although it did not address the issue of women working outside the home. On the language question, the program advocated the generalized use of Arabic, without, however, advocating monolingualism. Contrary to popular belief, the FIS engaged in less demagoguery over the role of the French language than did the FLN. Legislation in all areas was to be subjected to the "imperatives" of the Shariʿa. The existence of multipartyism was acknowledged, and no menacing references were made toward non-Islamic parties or movements.

Despite repeated references to the Shariʿa the overall tone of the program was relatively moderate, conflicting with the contradictory and often incendiary rhetoric of extremist FIS leaders. The best known example was that of the fiery FIS number two Ali Ben Hadj (b. 1956), a schoolteacher and itinerant preacher, who on numerous occasions condemned the concept of democracy, which he maintained was an un-Islamic concept. Ben Hadj and other FIS preachers often declared their intention to abrogate the constitution once in power and to outlaw any non-Islamic parties.

The directing organs of the FIS were its National Executive Bureau and the *Majlis al-Shura* (consultative council), including from thirty-five to forty members. The composition of these two bodies was never revealed, and until the summer of 1991 the identities of most of the principal figures in the FIS were unknown to the larger public. The secretiveness of the FIS in this regard exceeded even that of the FLN during the war. The FIS was, moreover, structured in a hierarchical, almost Leninist manner, with almost all actions of the base being decided by the leadership. Until the spring of 1991, the only FIS leader to give interviews to the media and issue formal public statements (apart from Ben Hadj on rare occasions) was Abassi Madani (b. 1931), a British-educated university professor and former Organisation Spéciale (OS) activist and FLN member, who was the official party spokesman and its effective president.

Until the spring of 1990, the authorities, state-controlled media, and Westernized Algerians in general underestimated the growing strength of the FIS. Panic was stirred at that time following a large FIS march held in Algiers and numerous acts of intolerance committed by hoodlum elements on the party's fringe. Complacency settled in once again, however, and few were prepared for the FIS's landslide victory in the June 1990 elections. The panic ensuing from this was short lived as well, as the FIS did little to implement its vision of society in the communes under its control: Beaches remained "mixed," restaurants continued to serve alcohol, and nightclubs were not forced to close. In other respects, there was little concrete evidence to back up the notion that the FIS mismanaged the affairs of local government; much evidence, in fact, pointed to concerted efforts made by the regime to undermine the Assemblées Populaires Communales (APCs) controlled by the FIS. A significant, and relatively unnoticed, feature of the FIS-controlled municipalities was the effective displacement of decision making from the APC to a local *Majlis al-Shura*, which, like all FIS bodies, did not reveal its membership and deliberated in secret.

Despite the FIS's 1990 landslide victory, the size and stability of its base were far from clear. The backlash vote certainly played a role in the election result; many voted for the FIS more out of anger with the FLN and the deteriorating conditions of everyday life than in support of the FIS's program and worldview. As with fundamentalist movements elsewhere, the FIS drew support from many in the educated classes. A number of FIS leaders were in fact engineers and technicians by training, and the largest concentration of Islamist support among university students was found in the science and technical faculties. The FIS also enjoyed support among the commercial strata and sections of the private sector, as well as among those engaged in "trabendo" (trafficking of goods on the parallel market). The case of the latter could be explained in part by the generally liberal (though not always consistent) rhetoric of the FIS on matters relating to commerce. The principal source of the FIS's considerable financial support did come from these groups.

The FIS's most important base, however, was among the mass of marginalized, frustrated, unemployed men under the age of thirty, who constituted a large and volatile segment of the population. It was this group that gave the FIS its character as a social protest movement against the regime, giving vent to the anger of those hit hardest by the worsening economic crisis and most outraged by the corruption of the political class.

Following the declaration of the state of siege on June 5, 1991, the FIS suffered considerable repression. Abassi Madani and Ali Ben Hadj were arrested later that month on a number of charges related to the FIS general strike held from May 25 to June 7, 1991, including incitement to violence. Numerous FIS leaders, elected officials, and militants were arrested as well, though most of these were released by the time the state of siege was lifted in September.

Internal divisions within the FIS leadership also came into the open following the declaration of the state of siege. Confirming widespread rumors, it was revealed that a number of figures in the *Majlis al-Shura* had been opposed to the general strike called by Abassi Madani and favored playing the electoral game as defined by the government, despite the gerrymandering of constituency boundaries. At a national FIS conference held in Batna on July 25–26, 1991, five prominent figures, including El Hachemi Sahnouni and Zebda Benazzouz (b. 1943), were suspended from the *Majlis al-Shura* for reasons that remain unclear. Another leading figure, Saïd Guechi (b. 1946), who was named minister of employment in February 1992, was marginalized and left the conference before its closing. Emerging as the spokesman of the FIS in the absence of Abassi and Ben Hadj was Abdelkader Hachani (b. 1957), a petroleum engineer previously unknown to the public.

Though the dispute within the FIS took on the character of a *lutte de clans*, important political issues were also at stake. The FIS was henceforth divided into two tendencies: the "Jazara," led by Hachani and in control of the party leadership since the July meeting, and the "Salafiyya," represented by those ousted from the *Majlis al-Shura*. The tendencies were not well understood, although the Jazara was nationalist in orientation and advocated an Algerianization of the

Islamist movement, and the Salafiyya was more orthodox and linked to the Hanbalite school of jurisprudence originating in the Arabian peninsula. It was not certain where Abassi Madani and Ben Hadj stood, although Abassi Madani was probably oriented toward the Jazara and Ben Hadj toward the Salafiyya.

The provisional party leadership was divided during the autumn of 1991 over the issue of FIS participation in the legislative elections while Abassi Madani and Ben Hadj remained in detention. Hachani, who had rapidly developed a popular following, led the fight within the party in favor of participation. Following the FIS landslide in the first round on December 26, 1991, there appeared little doubt that the party would form Algeria's next government. The rhetoric of the FIS over the subsequent two weeks was typically contradictory, sometimes reassuring as to its intentions, sometimes more menacing. It did take care, however, not to give the army a pretext for intervention.

Not prepared to allow the FIS counter-elite to take power, however, the army intervened anyway on January 11, 1992, and cancelled the electoral process. Hachani and all other FIS leaders at liberty were arrested soon after, state-appointed preachers took control of their mosques, FIS-controlled APCs were dissolved, and, on March 4, 1992, the party was formally outlawed. Among the pretexts for this act was the contention that the existence of the FIS was a violation of Law 89–11—which forbade parties based on religion—and that it should thus never have been registered in the first place.

HAMAS. *See* MOUVEMENT DE LA SOCIETE ISLAMIQUE.

MAJD. *See* MOUVEMENT ALGÉRIEN POUR LA JUSTICE ET LE DEVELOPPEMENT.

MDA. *See* MOUVEMENT POUR LA DEMOCRATIE EN ALGERIE.

MDRA. *See* MOUVEMENT DEMOCRATIQUE POUR LA RENOUVEAU ALGERIEN.

MIA. *See* MOUVEMENT ISLAMIQUE D'ALGERIE.

MNA. *See* MOUVEMENT NATIONAL ALGERIEN.

MNI. *See* MOUVEMENT DE LA NAHDA ISLAMIQUE.

MOUVEMENT ALGERIEN POUR LA JUSTICE ET LE DEVELOPPEMENT (MAJD) (*Algerian Movement for Justice and Development*). Request for registration: November 5, 1990 (no. 39). The MAJD (which signifies "glory" in Arabic) was exclusively identified with its founder and leader, Kasdi Merbah (1938–1993). A Kabyle, Merbah was head of the Sécurité Militaire from 1962 to 1979, after which he held several key ministerial portfolios and served as an alternate member of the FLN Political Bureau.

In November 1988, one month after the events of October, Merbah was appointed prime minister. His appointment at this sensitive moment had been based principally on his neutral stance in the *lutte de clans* that had ensued between the presidency and the Front de Libération Nationale (FLN) apparatus. Soon after his nomination, Merbah himself entered into a *lutte de clans* with the presidency, which reached a climax in September 1989 when he was removed from office. Over the following year he became a harsh critic of President Chadli. Feeling increasingly isolated in the FLN Central Committee, he quit the party in October 1990 to form the MAJD.

The program and worldview of the MAJD hardly differed from that of the FLN. Likewise, the party's membership was mainly made up of Merbah's friends and associates from the FLN and his Sécurité Militaire days. The MAJD indeed had no other purpose than to serve as a vehicle for Merbah's ambition to be president of Algeria. In the first round of the aborted legislative elections held on December 26, 1991, the MAJD won 0.4 percent of the national vote, indicating the insignificant level of its popular support.

Merbah was assassinated on August 21, 1993, in an ambush near Algiers. No group claimed responsibility and the assassins escaped without a trace. Few believed Merbah was murdered by Islamists, as he had been a leading advocate of a dialogue with the outlawed FIS.

MOUVEMENT DE LA NAHDA ISLAMIQUE (MNI) (*Islamic Revival Movement*). Request for registration: October 3, 1990 (no. 31). The MNI was an Islamist party (founded in 1990) exclusively identified with its founder and leader, Abdallah Djeballah (b. 1956). The MNI emerged out of a local association in Constantine called *Jam'iyat al-Nahda*, which Djeballah created in 1988.

Djeballah's decision to transform his association into a political party came in the early fall of 1990, following the rejection by the Front Islamique du Salut (FIS)* of Mahfoud Nahnah's call for an Islamic Alliance, which Djeballah had enthusiastically supported. Though close to the FIS, Djeballah claimed to have several differences with it. These included differing conceptions of *ijtihad*, of the utilization of mosques for partisan political activity—which Djeballah claimed to oppose—and over the manner in which Shari'a law should be implemented. Djeballah called for the holding of a national referendum on whether Algeria should be governed by the "Islamic model" or the "liberal model." This implied that he believed in at least the theoretical possibility that society could legitimately choose to be governed under a system other than the Shari'a. The most fundamental difference with the FIS, however, appeared to be the MNI's insistence that a multiplicity of parties could exist within the "*da'wa*" (call). The creation of the MNI was in fact partly a response to the FIS's claim to a monopoly of representation over the Islamist movement.

Djeballah's disagreements with the FIS made him a figure courted by the regime and sometimes earned him the reputation of a "moderate." Djeballah, who drew theological inspiration from the Muslim Brotherhood in Egypt, hardly differed from hard-line FIS preachers on several sensitive issues, however. For example, he advocated the imposition of Islamic dress on women and opposed the legal existence of laïc political parties. At one point in 1991 Djeballah referred to Sudan as his model of an Islamic state.

In the first round of the aborted legislative elections held on December 26, 1991, the MNI won 2.2 percent of the vote, scoring poorly even in its supposed strongholds in Constantine and other towns in the east.

MOUVEMENT DE LA SOCIETE ISLAMIQUE (HAMAS) (*Islamic Society Movement*). Request for registration: March 26, 1991 (no. 43). HAMAS (*Harakat al-Mujtama al-Islami*) is an Islamist party whose creation was announced in December 1990. It is the political expression of the national nonpolitical association *Jam'iyat al-Irshad wa al-Islah* (Association for Guidance and Reform), which was founded in 1989. HAMAS is exclusively identified with its founder and leader, Mahfoud Nahnah (b. 1942), who is one of the more significant figures in Algeria's postindependence Islamist movement. His association also emerged in 1989–90 as the principal Islamist competitor to the Front Islamique du Salut (FIS).*

The relationship between Nahnah and the FIS, which was marked by a certain level of animosity, was exacerbated by Nahnah's failure to endorse the FIS in the June 1990 elections. When Nahnah launched the idea of an Islamic Alliance in September 1990, it was rejected out of hand by the FIS. The FIS's contention that alliance (*tahaluf*) is proscribed by the Sunna pointed to several differences between it and the *Jam'iyat al-Irshad wa al-Islah*/HAMAS. Nahnah argued that numerous parties could coexist within the Islamist movement and called for a dialogue with non-Islamist parties, including those advocating *laïcité*. His apparent moderation extended to the debate over gender issues, with Nahnah dismissing the issue of *mixité* as a "false problem" and arguing that women are equal to men and have a right both to work and to lead a public life. The women's section of the *Jam'iyat al-Irshad wa al-Islah* indeed played an active role.

The principal issue separating Nahnah from the FIS was his emphasis on educating society in Islamic values as a necessary prelude to the establishment of an Islamic state, in contrast to the FIS's will to accede rapidly to power and impose Shari'a law. Regarding the institutional form of the future Islamic state, Nahnah advanced the concept of *shuraqratiya*, a system based on consultation and consensus and, according to Nahnah, more democratic than democracy itself. As for Nahnah's decision to enter the political arena, it came only after the FIS landslide in the 1990 municipal elections. The decision to create HAMAS was based primarily on the imperative of confronting the FIS on the political terrain and not allowing it to monopolize the Islamist movement in a future Assemblée Populaire Nationale (APN).

In this respect it is essential to underscore the cordial relationship between

Nahnah and the regime. The presidency had banked on the ability of the *Jam'iyat al-Irshad wa al-Islah*/HAMAS to draw support away from the FIS and to form a moderate Islamist component of the "presidential majority" so anxiously sought by the regime. Nahnah's soothing rhetoric earned him sympathetic coverage in the media, which chose to overlook his extensive ties to Islamist organizations abroad, affinity with the Muslim Brotherhood in Egypt, and sometimes less-than-moderate discourse when addressing audiences in Algeria's interior.

HAMAS held its constitutive congress on May 29, 1991. The extent of support for the *Jam'iyat al-Irshad wa al-Islah*/HAMAS was not clear at the outset, although it appeared to be principally drawn from the educated classes, particularly middle- and upper-level cadres in the state administration. In addition, Nahnah enjoyed significant support among private-sector entrepreneurs, who are an influential force in his hometown of Blida.

In the first round of the aborted legislative elections of December 26, 1991, HAMAS won 5.3 percent of the vote, scoring well mainly in Algiers and in the area around Tebessa. The result was considered disappointing by Nahnah and the presidency; HAMAS no doubt suffered due to its identification with the regime.

MOUVEMENT DEMOCRATIQUE POUR LE RENOUVEAU ALGERIEN (MDRA) (*Democratic Movement for Algerian Renewal*). Request for registration: November 14, 1989 (no. 17). The MDRA is principally distinguished by its association with the memory of Krim Belkacem, the wartime leader of the Front de Libération Nationale (FLN)* who founded the MDRA in Paris in October 1967. The MDRA had only an ephemeral existence as an opposition party, although it was linked to an assassination attempt made on Houari Boumediene in 1968. This led to the October 1970 murder of Krim Belkacem in West Germany by agents of the Sécurité Militaire. With Krim Belkacem's death, the MDRA vanished from the scene.

In 1989 one of Krim Belkacem's longtime subalterns, Slimane Amirat (1929–92), resurrected the MDRA. A small formation composed almost exclusively of Kabyles, the MDRA situated itself among Algeria's "democratic" and Berberist parties. The MDRA had few members and was hardly present on the political terrain. Its primary function indeed appeared to be the rehabilitation of Krim Belkacem's reputation and memory. In the first round of the aborted legislative elections held on December 26, 1991, the MDRA ran candidates in several dozen constituencies but received less than 0.2 percent of the vote.

MOUVEMENT EL-OUMMA (*al-Umma Movement*). Request for registration: May 21, 1990 (no. 24). The Mouvement El-Oumma is an Islamist formation created during the summer of 1989. Since it has declined to participate in elections, the extent of its popular support cannot be discerned. It is no doubt minimal, however, given that the party has engaged in few public activities and has given no evidence of a significant militant base. What makes the Mouvement

El-Oumma noteworthy is the identity of its founders and, in particular, its leader, Benyoucef Ben Khedda, who was a president of the Gouvernement Provisoire de la République Algérienne (GPRA) and a leading Mouvement pour la Triomphe des Libertés Démocratiques (MTLD) *centraliste*. Also associated with the Mouvement El-Oumma is another *centraliste*, Abderrahmane Kiouane.

The orientation of the Mouvement El-Oumma, which is strongly critical of socialism, centers on the notion that the Algerian people are searching for cultural authenticity and that this can be found only through a return to Islamic values. The vision is one of an Islam reconciled to modernity and of a polity structured around *shura* (consultation). The Mouvement El-Oumma explicitly sees itself as an heir of the PPA-MTLD and the pre-1962 Front de Libération Nationale (FLN),* which it maintains were based on Islamic principles. The Mouvement El-Oumma asserts that the FLN deviated from Islam after 1962 and that, in any case, its historical mission ended with independence.

The outlook of the Mouvement El-Oumma indeed reflects an important current that existed in the preindependence nationalist movement. The extremely weak popular support for the Mouvement El-Oumma is due only to the identity of its leaders, who are largely forgotten figures from the past, and not to its political vision, which is deeply rooted in contemporary Algerian history and has been appropriated by other parties.

†MOUVEMENT ISLAMIQUE D'ALGERIE (MIA) (*Islamic Movement of Algeria*). The MIA was an underground movement that led a violent campaign against the regime in the years from 1982 to 1987. It represented the first explicitly political Islamist movement since independence. The MIA was founded and led by Mustapha Bouyali (1940–87). From 1982 to 1985, the MIA set up sixteen armed cells across the country, which were made up of men from all social categories, many of whom were well educated and employed as state functionaries. The heart of the maquis was in the Mitidja, particularly around Bouyali's hometown of Larbaa. Though the maquis remained at a fairly low level, the MIA staged attacks on police stations and plotted, though it never carried out, the assassination of top officials of the Front de Libération Nationale (FLN).* Over 300 men associated with Bouyali were arrested in the early and mid-1980s. Two trials were held (in 1985 and 1987), in which the defendants were given relatively light prison sentences or acquitted. Among those implicated with Bouyali, who served time in prison, were a number of individuals who would later play prominent roles in the Front Islamique du Salut (FIS).*

The MIA maquis came to an end with Bouyali's death in a clash with police on January 3, 1987.

† MOUVEMENT NATIONAL ALGERIEN (MNA) (*Algerian National Movement*). The MNA was created by Messali Hadj in November 1954, following the launching of the Front de Libération Nationale's (FLN's)* insurrection and outlawing of the MTLD (*see* PPA-MTLD). The MNA, founded as a fighting force,

was a logical outcome of the *messaliste* Hornu congress of July 1954, which called for armed struggle against the French. The MNA was not founded as a reaction to the FLN; Messali did not initially take the FLN seriously and intended to absorb it into the MNA.

The MNA was initially much stronger than the FLN in terms of support, both among MTLD militants and on the popular level. With Messali in internal exile in France and the MTLD split and in disarray following its interdiction, however, the FLN was soon able to gain the upper hand owing to its greater fighting capacity and to the political sophistication of Abane Ramdane, who proved to be more adept than the MNA's leadership inside Algeria. The *messalistes*, with their emphasis on mass action, such as demonstrations and strikes, also gave less importance to clandestine activity, which put them at a disadvantage with the FLN in the context of the time.

During the first several months of the insurrection, the MNA saw little difference between itself and the FLN, and fighters of the two groups often cooperated. When efforts at reconciliation between the two broke down in 1955, however, they descended into a bloody internecine conflict. The tide turned in the autumn of 1955, when the FLN inflicted a devastating defeat on the MNA in the Kabylie. Progressively ejected from its strongholds and losing its most dynamic cadres to FLN assassins (particularly in France, where the Algerian community was overwhelmingly *messaliste*), the MNA fell into disarray, which was aggravated by the FLN massacre in the pro-MNA town of Melouza in May 1957. From that point on, a number of MNA commanders went over to the French (the best known being Bellounis) and descended into banditry. The French tried in 1961 to include the MNA in the negotiating process for Algerian independence, but this was refused by the FLN. In 1962 Messali changed the name of the MNA back to the PPA, but by then his party was effectively finished as a military and political force.

MOUVEMENT POUR LA DEMOCRATIE EN ALGERIE (MDA) (*Movement for Democracy in Algeria*). Request for registration: January 21, 1990 (no. 21). The MDA is exclusively identified with its founder and leader, Ahmed Ben Bella, who is one of the historic figures of the Algerian nationalist movement. In September 1962 he became Algeria's first head of government, and one year later he engineered a plebiscite which elected him to the newly created post of president.

Ben Bella's discourse during his years in power was characterized by a mélange of Arab nationalism, Islamism, and Fanonism, and punctuated by a *marxisant* rhetoric originating from his circle of youthful leftist advisors. Among other things, this ideological eclecticism was translated into improvisation and incoherence in all areas of policy, particularly economic policy. On this level, Ben Bella was most remembered for his bombast and swagger, symbolized by grandiose ceremonies to mark the nationalization of small commercial enterprises such as cinemas and cafés. His reign was also marked by increasingly authoritarian rule, as a result of which he managed to alienate or drive into opposition the majority of the political class. His moves to undercut the Oujda clan of Minister of Defense Houari Boumediene brought about the coup d'état of June 19, 1965.

Ben Bella never stood trial and spent the entire Boumediene period in prison. In July 1979 President Chadli had him transferred to house arrest, and he was freed entirely in October 1980. Feeling intense bitterness over his long period of incarceration, Ben Bella openly criticized the post-1965 power structure and became a potential pole of opposition in what was still an authoritarian, one-party state. Fearing rearrest he left Algeria for France in the summer of 1981, and then Switzerland two years later. On May 25–27, 1984, the constitutive congress of the MDA was held near Paris and was attended by Ben Bella's partisans in exile.

The MDA never served as anything more than a vehicle for Ben Bella's opposition to the regime and his ambitions to once again become president of Algeria. The political orientation of the MDA reflected Ben Bella's own ideological gyrations. He abandoned much of his erstwhile *marxisant*, pan-Arab nationalism, and he fully embraced Islam, becoming a fervent supporter of Ayatollah Khomeini's Iran for a time. Ben Bella's Islamism was typically eclectic, however, and did not, for example, induce him to alter his relatively progressive stance on the status of women. Despite contacts with Islamist opponents of the regime, no ongoing relationship was established between the MDA and the Islamist movement, partly due to the latter's long-standing distrust of Ben Bella.

Following the legalization of multipartyism in 1989, the MDA began to operate openly in Algeria. The regime hinted at possible prosecution of Ben Bella for a trumped up affair from the mid-1980s, however, leading him to delay his return from exile. Once the legal threat was withdrawn, Ben Bella returned to Algeria on September 27, 1990, and continued his harsh criticism of the regime.

It had been assumed by many that the MDA enjoyed a certain level of popular support, particularly in Ben Bella's native region of the Oranie. Ben Bella did indeed receive a relatively enthusiastic welcome on his first return visit to Oran. The MDA had almost no organizational structure, however, and was riven by internal conflicts that resulted in the departure of a number of militants. In addition, the Oranie voted massively for the Front Islamique du Salut (FIS)* in the June 1990 municipal elections, despite the MDA's call for a boycott of the contest.

In the course of 1990–91 Ben Bella's discourse moved away from emphasis on Islam and toward the traditional Arabism and populist-nationalism of the Front de Libération Nationale (FLN),* accented with his typically virulent anti-Western and anti-American diatribes. This served as confirmation that the MDA was not different from the FLN, either ideologically or in the sociological composition of its militant base, which was made up primarily of Ben Bella's *compagnons de route*. In the first round of the aborted legislative elections held on December 26, 1991, the MDA won but 2 percent of the national vote. No MDA candidates made it into a runoff even in the Oranie—where the FIS once again scored a landslide victory—indicating the extremely low level of popular support for Ben Bella's dream of reclaiming Algeria's presidency.

†MOUVEMENT POUR LA TRIOMPHE DES LIBERTES DEMOCRA-TIQUES (MTLD) (*Movement for the Triumph of Democratic Liberties*). See PARTI DU PEUPLE ALGERIEN—MOUVEMENT POUR LA TRIOMPHE DES LIB-ERTES DEMOCRATIQUES.

MTLD. *See* MOUVEMENT POUR LA TRIOMPHE DES LIBERTES DEMO-CRATIQUES.

OCRA. *See* ORGANISATION CLANDESTINE DE LA REVOLUTION AL-GERIENNE.

†ORGANISATION CLANDESTINE DE LA REVOLUTION ALGERIENNE (OCRA) (*Clandestine Organization of the Algerian Revolution*). The OCRA was created in April 1966 in Europe by a number of former figures in, or close to, the Ben Bella regime who either opposed the June 19, 1965, coup d'état or broke with Houari Boumediene soon after. The goal of the OCRA was to overthrow the "Boumediene clan" and restore "revolutionary legitimacy." The organization, which existed only in exile, splintered rapidly and disappeared in 1968.

†ORGANISATION DE LA RESISTANCE POPULAIRE (ORP) (*Popular Resistance Organization*). The ORP was created in July 1965 by leftist associates and supporters of the Ben Bella regime who opposed the coup d'état that had taken place the previous month. All of the ORP's leaders had been arrested by the end of the summer of 1965, as well as several dozen militants, so the ORP was never able to mount an effective opposition to the Boumediene regime. After the PCA-PAGS (*see* Parti de l'Avant-Garde Socialiste) withdrew its support from the ORP in April 1967, the organization vanished.

ORP. *See* ORGANISATION DE LA RESISTANCE POPULAIRE.

PAGS. *See* PARTI DE L'AVANT-GARDE SOCIALISTE.

†PARTI COMMUNISTE ALGERIEN. *See* PARTI DE L'AVANT-GARDE SOCIALISTE.

†PARTI DE LA REVOLUTION SOCIALISTE—COMITE NATIONAL POUR LA DEFENSE DE LA REVOLUTION (PRS-CNDR) (*Socialist Revolution Party—National Committee for the Defense of the Revolution*). The PRS was founded in a Paris suburb on September 20, 1962. Its founder and leader was Mohamed Boudiaf, who was the leading *chef historique* of the Front de Libération Nationale (FLN).* The decision to create the PRS was the result of Boudiaf's

conflict with Ahmed Ben Bella during the summer 1962 crisis and had little to do with ideology or principle. In July 1964 an effort to unify the opposition was made with the creation of the CNDR, which included the Front des Forces Socialistes (FFS).* An attempted putsch staged by the CNDR that month was nipped in the bud by the regime, however, and the CNDR disintegrated, though the PRS continued to use its name.

The putsch marked the end of Boudiaf's oppositional activity inside Algeria, and from then on the PRS-CNDR was almost exclusively limited to the emigré community in France. In the late 1960s Boudiaf settled permanently in Morocco, where he became a businessman, and the running of the PRS-CNDR in France was entrusted to his youthful leftist associates. The ideological orientation of the PRS-CNDR henceforth reflected the views of these men, and the party veered toward the extreme left, presenting itself as a Marxist-style vanguard of the proletariat.

The party's intellectual life enabled it to attract a number of Algerians studying at French universities. Boudiaf's support of Morocco in the Western Sahara dispute and his contacts with FLN dissidents provoked a series of crises within the PRS-CNDR, and many militants left the party in 1979 when Boudiaf sent a letter of reconciliation to President Chadli. The PRS-CNDR had effectively ceased to exist by 1982.

Having completely retired from politics, Boudiaf did not attempt to revive the PRS after multipartyism was legalized in 1989. He did not even show any interest in returning to Algeria, where he was largely an unknown figure among the postindependence generation. He suddenly reemerged in January 1992, however, when he was brought back from Morocco to head the newly created Haut Comité d'Etat following the forced resignation of President Chadli and the cancellation of the second round of the legislative elections. The army high command called upon Boudiaf for a number of reasons, including his historical stature and the fact that he had never sullied himself in power over the previous thirty years.

PARTI DE L'AVANT-GARDE SOCIALISTE (PAGS) (*Socialist Vanguard Party*). Request for registration: August 13, 1989 (no. 2). The PAGS has been one of the more significant forces in postindependence Algeria, and its political impact has far exceeded its actual size and base of support in society. It is the direct successor of the Parti Communiste Algérien (PCA),* which played an important role in colonial politics from the 1930s through the war of independence, as well as during the presidency of Ahmed Ben Bella.

The birth and development of communism in colonial Algeria closely followed that of the Parti Communiste Français (PCF), which was founded in 1920. From that date until 1936, the communist movement in Algeria functioned as the "Algerian section" of the PCF and drew the majority of its militants and supporters from the European community. Following the Comintern line of the period, the PCF advocated independence for Algeria. This placed the PCF in Algeria in an untenable position, based as it was among working class settlers—

the *petits blancs*—who were as attached to *Algérie Française* as the rest of the European community. The Algerian section of the PCF, which was not large to begin with, thus lost many members and was reduced to a tiny sect by the early 1930s.

Around this time the PCF began an effort to increase the number of Muslims in the party, whose presence had heretofore been almost nonexistent. Following the change in the Comintern line in 1934–35, the PCF supported the creation of a "popular front" with other parties in order to combat fascism and moved away from its advocacy of Algerian independence. Under pressure from the Comintern the Algerian section of the PCF was transformed in early 1936 to the PCA, which was in principle fully separate from its parent party in the metropole. In reality the PCA continued to function as an appendage of the PCF.

The popular front strategy led the PCA to play an active role in the Congrés Musulman in 1936, which included the Fédération des Elus and the *Jam'iyat al-'Ulama*. The popular front and Arabization policies paid dividends for the PCA, which claimed 1,100 Muslim members (out of a total of some 5,100) in early 1937. The failure of the Blum-Violette bill provoked an exodus of Muslim adherents later that year, however.

With the rise of the PPA in the late 1930s and early 1940s, the issue of Algerian independence would increasingly occupy center stage. The PCA's line on the national question was developed by PCF Secretary-General Maurice Thorez in 1939, who defined Algeria as a "nation in formation," which was thus, by implication, not ready for independence. This position, as well as its hostility to the Parti du Peuple Algérien (PPA),* limited considerably the PCA's impact in the Muslim community at this time. The PCA went so far as to place responsibility on the PPA for the events of May 1945, earning the communists the lasting enmity of the nationalist movement. In the nationwide French election held in October 1945, the PCA captured a quarter of the First College vote (European) and a fifth of the Second College (Muslim); over half the voters in the Second College abstained, however, following a boycott of the contest by the PPA and the Amis du Manifeste et de la Liberté (AML).*

The PCA reversed course in 1946 and took an increasingly nationalist position, going so far as to purge its leading Muslim figure, Amar Ouzegane (1910–81), for his previous attacks on the PPA. From this point, the PCA began to lose much of its support in the European community. Muslims became the majority on the Central Committee and joined the party in growing numbers, some of whom had left the PPA-MTLD after the Berber crisis or because of its lack of a social program. These new PCA cadres, many of whom were Kabyles and from the middle classes, included Sadek Hadjeres (b. 1928), Abdelhamid Benzine (b. 1926), and Bachir Hadj Ali (1920–91). The PCA also gained a foothold in urban Muslim quarters and enjoyed solid support among Muslim members of the party-controlled trade union, the Confédération Générale du Travail (CGT).

In the period from 1946 to 1954, the PCA cooperated with the Union Démocratique du Manifeste Algérien (UDMA)* of Ferhat Abbas and, in the early

1950s, with the increasingly *centraliste*-dominated MTLD. In 1951 the three parties formed a loose, short-lived alliance called the Front Algérien pour la Défense et le Respect de la Liberté. Although the PCA endorsed the principle of Algerian independence, it remained attached to the concept of a "nation in formation" and equivocated on when and how independence was to come about. The PCA's subservience to the PCF and the Soviet Union, as well as its attempt to straddle the widening gap between the European and Muslim communities, cost it much support during the war of independence. Since much of its Muslim clientele transferred its loyalty to the Front de Libération Nationale (FLN)* in 1954–55, the PCA's outspoken criticism of the colonial repression during this same period prompted the desertion of most of its remaining European support.

The PCA openly endorsed armed struggle in June 1955 and was banned by the colonial authorities in September of that year. The party, however, rejected both the FLN's demand that it disband and that its cadres join the front on an individual basis. The PCA instead created its own fighting force, the Combattants de la Libération, in March 1956, to channel pressures from the party's Muslim ranks and compel the FLN to treat it as an equal. Poorly conceived and lacking seasoned fighters, the Combattants de la Libération was a fiasco, and in July 1956 it negotiated its integration into the Armée de Libération Nationale (ALN). During the war, some 200 communists rallied to the ALN, but the PCA, led by Hadjeres and Hadj Ali, continued to function as a separate party. Though former PCA leader Amar Ouzegane was a key FLN figure in 1955–57, the FLN distrusted the communists who entered its ranks and kept them far from the centers of decision.

The PCA, which claimed 6,000 members in 1962, attempted to play a role at independence but came up against the FLN's unwillingness to countenance multipartyism. On November 29, 1962, the PCA was banned once again, this time by the government of Ahmed Ben Bella, though its militants circulated freely and the party maintained its important presence in the press. The PCA indeed became a strong supporter and principal prop of Ben Bella as his regime moved to the left.

The PCA was thrown into disarray by the June 19, 1965, coup d'état, which brought into power what it initially regarded as a reactionary regime. The party immediately allied itself with the Organisation de la Résistance Populaire (ORP),* which led to the arrest of a number of its militants, including secretary-general Hadj Ali. The PCA's hostility to Houari Boumediene began to mellow following his trip to the Soviet Union in December 1965. In 1966 the party changed its name to the PAGS and revised its analysis of the regime, which it still saw as being dominated by "reactionaries" but as also containing "progressive" elements. When Kaïd Ahmed acceded to the top FLN post in 1968, the PAGS stance toward the regime hardened, though it was thrown into a quandary over Boumediene's increasingly warm relations with the Soviet Union. As was always the case, the party's uncritical pro-Soviet tendency (led by Hadjeres and

Benzine) won out over those (led by Hadj Ali) who advocated a more independent line.

The turning point for the PAGS came in 1971, when the regime carried out the final wave of nationalization and promulgated the agrarian revolution. The party's stance toward the regime was now one of "critical support," which in actuality became total support following the ouster of Kaïd Ahmed in 1972 and the hardening of Boumediene's socialist and *tiers mondiste* rhetoric. The penultimate ideological document of the FLN, the 1976 Charte Nationale, was indeed enthusiastically supported by the PAGS. Though still an illegal party, the militants of the PAGS—familiarly referred to as *pagsistes*—began to operate increasingly in the open, though PCA-PAGS clandestinity had been somewhat of a fiction given that its leaders and cadres had always been under close surveillance by the security services and could have been arrested at any time.

Possessing a core of educated and motivated cadres, which is more than the FLN could claim at the time, the PAGS was tacitly permitted to create and run the *Volontariat*, set up in 1972, which were brigades of urban secondary school and university students who did weekend and summer volunteer work with farmers in the newly created "socialist villages." They also reported on foot-dragging or abuses on the part of local authorities charged with the implementation of the agrarian revolution. The enthusiastic response of students to the *Volontariat*, which lasted through the 1970s, provided the PAGS with fertile ground in which to spread its ideology and recruit members. In addition, the PAGS adopted the policy of *entrisme*, encouraging its militants to take posts of responsibility in the theoretically FLN-controlled mass organizations, particularly the Union Générale des Travailleurs Algériens (UGTA), and the Union Nationale de la Jeunesse Algérien (UNJA), the state-run media, the Ministry of Labor and Social Affairs, and other state organs.

The apogee of PAGS influence came at the 5th congress of the UGTA in 1978, when an ex-PCA militant, Abdallah Demene Debbih, was named secretary-general, and nearly total control of the union's leadership bodies was assumed by *pagsistes*. The PAGS infiltration of the mass organizations was now aided by the FLN's top official, Mohamed Salah Yahiaoui.

Boumediene's death in December 1978 had a devastating effect on the PAGS. The accession of Chadli Bendjedid to the presidency in February 1979 brought into power clans within the FLN who had been hostile to PAGS influence throughout the 1970s. At the FLN's congress held in June 1980, Yahiaoui was replaced by Mohamed Cherif Messaadia, a known rightist, and the infamous Article 120 was written into the party statutes, henceforth obliging all officials in the mass organizations to be members of the FLN. The coming period thus witnessed the witch hunt and purge of *pagsistes* from the UGTA and UNJA, though they were able to maintain their significant presence in the media and the universities.

The PAGS suffered considerable repression at the hands of the security services during the 1980s, and numerous *pagsistes* spent time in prison, where they were often subject to physical abuse. This did not prompt the PAGS to enter into open opposition, however. Though criticizing the "rightist drift" of the Chadli regime, the PAGS continued to see "progressive" elements inside the FLN and power structure and hoped for a return to the status quo of the 1970s. At no point did the PAGS enter into dialogue, let alone alliance, with the underground opposition parties; it had, in fact, gone so far as to initially denounce the 1980 Berberist demonstrations in the Kabylie. As an uncritical supporter of the Soviet Union, the PAGS was not about to break with the regime as long as the latter maintained warm relations with Moscow. In addition, the PAGS supported the economic *étatisme* of the regime and was ideologically comfortable with the one-party system, provided that it afforded the prospect of infiltration into the state apparatus.

With the 1989 legalization of multipartyism, the PAGS situated itself in the "democratic" camp, supporting the regime's economic program and cooperating with other parties in efforts to combat Islamist influence. The PAGS participated in the June 12, 1990, elections, presenting lists in 3 percent of the communes and receiving 0.3 percent of the vote. This was an unimpressive result for what had been the second most influential party during the first twenty-five years of Algeria's independence and which still had an impact out of proportion to its actual weight in society.

The 1990 vote came on the heels of the collapse of communism in Eastern Europe, which threw the PAGS into disarray. On December 13–16, 1990, the PAGS held its first congress, which saw the transfer of power from the party old guard, led by Hadjeres and Benzine, to a younger generation of party militants, led by the new secretary-general El Hachemi Cherif. As militants split from the party or drifted away, the PAGS once again bound itself to the regime, referred to the FLN as a "democratic" party, and engaged in strident calls for the outlawing of the Front Islamique du Salut (FIS).* The PAGS refused to participate in the aborted legislative election of December 26, 1991, and enthusiastically backed the coup d'état of January 11, 1992.

PARTI DES TRAVAILLEURS (PT) (*Workers Party*). Request for registration: December 26, 1989 (no. 20). Known as the Organisation Socialiste des Travailleurs (OST) until June 1990, the PT is a Trotskyist party affiliated with the Fourth International (International Reconstruction Center). The party was founded in 1974 as the Comité de Liaison des Travailleurs Algériens. A small formation with no popular base, the PT is noteworthy primarily for its colorful and outspoken leader, Louiza Hanoune (b. 1954), who is the only woman to head a political party in Algeria. The OST/PT boycotted the election contests held in 1990 and 1991.

†PARTI DU PEUPLE ALGERIEN—MOUVEMENT POUR LA TRIOMPHE DES LIBERTES DEMOCRATIQUES (PPA-MTLD) (*Algerian Peoples Party—Movement for the Triumph of Democratic Liberties*). The PPA-MTLD was Algeria's

leading nationalist force prior to the war of independence and, from the standpoint of ideology and lasting impact, can be considered the most significant political party in the country's history. The party's leader, Messali Hadj (1898–1974), likewise ranks as Algeria's preeminent political figure of the twentieth century.

The PPA was the direct continuation of the Etoile Nord-Africaine (ENA), which was founded in Paris in 1926. The creation of the ENA was in part inspired by Emir Khaled (1875–1936), who was living in voluntary exile in Paris, though he never played an important role in the organization. Also implicated in the ENA at its beginning was the Parti Communiste Française (PCF), which had set about organizing the large numbers of Algerian workers (over 100,000 in the mid-1920s) migrating to France. One of these Algerians was Messali, who had arrived in Paris in 1923 and was the real driving force in the ENA from its inception. Messali also succeeded in keeping the organization independent from the PCF and eradicated its influence in the early 1930s, engendering long-lasting distrust between himself and the Communists.

By the end of 1927, the ENA counted some 3,500 members and had drawn up its political program, which called for, inter alia, the immediate abolition of the "odious" Code de l'Indigénat; freedom of the press, association, and unionization; replacement of the Délégations Financières with a national assembly elected by universal suffrage; and the total independence of Algeria and withdrawal of all colonial troops. The program called for the restitution to the Algerian state of banks, railroads, and public services "monopolized by the conquerors," and the confiscation of large *colon* properties. The radical nature of the ENA's rhetoric led to its dissolution by the prefect of Paris in November 1929 (rescinded in 1935). The interdiction threw the movement into disarray, and it was mainly due to the efforts of Messali that the ENA was kept alive. Messali henceforth incarnated the continuity of the Algerian nationalist movement and achieved a mythic stature in the eyes of his followers. In these years, also, Messali established ties with Algerian students in France, marking the beginning of his long love-hate relationship with intellectuals. The ENA's message also began to develop a following in Algeria.

In 1934 Messali was arrested for his political activities and imprisoned for six months. In late 1935, fearing rearrest soon after his release, Messali fled to Geneva, where he came under the influence of the Lebanese pan-Arabist Shakib Arslan. Messali was granted amnesty by the newly elected Popular Front government in 1936, and in August of that year he made his triumphant return to Algeria after a thirteen-year absence. On the day of his arrival, he addressed the crowds at the first Congrés Musulman, where he eclipsed all the other politicians present. From that moment the ENA spread rapidly in Algeria, recruiting members throughout the country.

Messali's uncompromising opposition to the Blum-Violette bill led to the ENA's second dissolution in January 1937. Messali responded by creating the PPA in March of that year. The PPA did not differ from the ENA, though

Messali began to soften his rhetoric somewhat in speaking of an independent Algeria that would still be linked to France. The PPA's political and economic program remained excessively radical for the colonial administration, however, which arrested Messali in August 1937 and sentenced him to two years in prison. Continuing to direct the party from his cell, Messali supported the faction, led by Lamine Debaghine (b. 1917), that was hostile to any alliance with Germany against France. Despite his refusal to flirt with Germany (or later with Vichy), the colonial authorities maintained a hostile stance toward Messali—a stance that was aggravated by PPA local election victories in 1938 and big PPA marches in 1939. In July 1939 the PPA was banned, and Messali, who was released in August, was rearrested in September.

At his trial Messali was sentenced to sixteen years of forced labor for a series of supposedly treasonous offenses. Released in 1943, he spent the following three years in internal exile in different towns in Algeria's interior (1943–45) and the French Congo (1945–46). Though he consulted with Ferhat Abbas in 1943 over the Manifeste, which he ultimately supported, Messali began to lose touch with developments inside the clandestine PPA, which was led in his absence by the intellectual Debaghine. It was also during this period that a new generation of militants joined the party. These new members not only were more radical than their elders but also were more educated and, moreover, would be indelibly marked by the events of May 1945.

Messali was freed from internal exile in October 1946, although he was juridically forbidden to set foot in any of Algeria's major cities. It was at this moment that the debate heated up within the party over whether to participate in elections. Over the objections of the Debaghine-led antielectoralist group, Messali, who believed in an electoral strategy, created the MTLD which sent Debaghine, Mohammed Khider, and three others to the National Assembly in November 1946. The dispute over party strategy was partially resolved at the PPA-MTLD's first congress, which was held in secret in Algiers in February 1947 and attended by some fifty delegates. It was decided there that the party would have three structures: the legal MTLD, which would contest elections; the paramilitary Organisation Spéciale (OS), which would prepare the ground for armed struggle; and the clandestine PPA committees, which would oversee the MTLD in order to ensure that it not descend into reformism, as well as to assure a party structure in case the MTLD was dissolved by the authorities.

The PPA component of this triptych had only a fictitious existence, however, as most of those assigned to it were recuperated by the MTLD or OS. The electoralist strategy gained the upper hand with the municipal election landslide of October 1947, though it began to lose credibility following the rigged vote to the Assemblée Algérienne in April 1948. The actions of the OS were limited to a few minor acts of sabotage. Its most serious operation was the heist of the Oran post office in April 1949, which was planned by Aït Ahmed and Ben Bella but only netted a relatively small amount of money. More important for the OS activists was their experience in clandestinity and the esprit de corps it engendered, which would maintain the cohesion of the group after its breakup by the police in 1950.

That same year, Hocine Lahouel (b. 1917) was named party secretary-general, following the ouster of Debaghine during the Berber crisis (though Debaghine was not a Kabyle and, in fact, advocated pan-Arabism). The debate within the party over electoral versus clandestine action continued, with Messali supporting the double-track strategy as in the past. Messali's popularity remained as high as ever, prompting the authorities to banish him to internal exile in western France in 1952 following several enthusiastic rallies he held in Algeria's interior that spring. Messali, who would never again set foot in Algeria, continued to guide the party from a distance and proposed the candidates to the leadership posts at the MTLD's second congress in April 1953.

This congress was held legally, preventing OS militants in hiding from attending, and in July Benyoucef Ben Khedda was confirmed as secretary-general. In September, however, Messali denounced the Central Committee for reformism and demanded that it grant him full powers to run the party. The Central Committee refused, inaugurating a year-long crisis that would split the party. Numerous attempts were made in the intervening months to reconcile the *messalistes* and *centralistes* but without success. On July 13–15, 1954, the *messalistes* held an extraordinary congress in Hornu, Belgium, which rallied the powerful Fédération de France du MTLD and the leading sections of the PPA-MTLD in Algeria, reaffirmed the original program of the ENA, annointed Messali president for life of the party, and formally called for armed struggle to liberate Algeria. The *centralistes* held their rival congress on August 13–16 in Algiers, but it was a failure compared to the Hornu congress, and it equivocated on the question of insurrection. By then, and unbeknownst to either group, the ex-OS activists were preparing their own insurrection to begin on November 1.

The MTLD was dissolved by the authorities on November 5, 1954. Messali formed the Mouvement National Algérien (MNA)* that month. The *centralistes* rallied to the Front de Libération Nationale (FLN)* in September 1955.

In August 1989 Mohamed Memchaoui (b. 1917), a nephew of Messali and an important figure from the PPA-MTLD and MNA, resurrected the PPA and submitted a request for registration with the Ministry of Interior. After an internal debate, the request was refused by the regime, which maintained that the legalization of the PPA would constitute a violation of Law 89–11's provision against parties basing their creation on "behavior contrary to . . . the Revolution of November 1, 1954."

PARTI DU RENOUVEAU ALGERIEN (PRA) (*Algerian Renewal Party*). Request for registration: September 17, 1989 (no. 7). The PRA, whose creation was announced in August 1989, is exclusively identified with its founder and leader, Nourredine Boukrouh (b. 1950). An economist in the public sector, he became a private businessman in the mid-1980s. A publicist as well, he gained a certain notoriety for a series of biting critiques of the Front de Libération Nationale

(FLN)* and its brand of socialism that he published in the government weekly *Algérie-Actualité* in 1985.

Boukrouh claimed to draw his inspiration from the writings of the modernist Islamic thinker Malek Bennabi (1905–73), who was a prominent Algiers publicist and intellectual. The PRA thus gained the label of a moderate Islamist party, even though Islamic themes made up only a relatively minor part of its discourse. In addition, it developed a highly critical stance toward the Front Islamique du Salut (FIS).* The PRA, resolutely antisocialist, actively endorsed economic liberalism and foreign investment, though it spoke out against the importation of "foreign models" of development. On the political level, it presented itself as a party of the "opposition" and denounced the FLN but avoided criticism of President Chadli.

The PRA held its constitutive congress on May 3–4, 1990, which was attended by over 1,000 delegates. The delegates, over half of whom were reportedly middle and high-level cadres in the state administration, appeared to be more traditional in their views than Boukrouh and sabotaged an attempt to name a woman to the party's executive committee. The ability of the PRA to organize rapidly throughout the country gave rise to suspicions that it was being secretly aided by the presidency, although Boukrouh vehemently denied rumors to this effect. In the June 1990 municipal elections, the PRA took approximately 0.8 percent of the national vote and won control of two Assemblées Populaires Communales (APCs).

Although the PRA evidently had little popular support and held few public meetings, Boukrouh—who was in reality more of an intellectual than a politician—began to mount grandiose publicity campaigns around his persona. In the first round of the aborted legislative elections of December 26, 1991, the PRA won 1 percent of the national vote.

PARTI NATIONAL POUR LA SOLIDARITE ET LE DEVELOPPEMENT (PNSD) (*National Party for Solidarity and Development*). Request for registration: September 16, 1989 (no. 4). The Constantine-based PNSD emerged in 1990 as one of the more significant small parties. Founded in the summer of 1989, it issued few public declarations and little was known about it until the hugely successful appearance of its president, Rabah Bencharif, on a television interview program in March 1990. An agronomist in his early forties, Bencharif came across as an amiable and charismatic personality with potential appeal to less-educated members of the younger generation. His discourse revolved around a mixed economy with a strong private sector and a modernist interpretation of Islam, although he was remembered principally for his proposal to create an artificial sea in the Sahara as a means of raising agricultural output and creating employment. Bencharif was also noted for his characterization of the PNSD's ideology as being based on the previously unheard of concepts of "horizontal capitalism" and "vertical socialism."

In the weeks following Bencharif's television appearance, the press reported large numbers of recruits to the PNSD, including many younger, disenchanted Front de Libération Nationale (FLN)* militants. The latter indeed appeared to dominate the party. In the June 1990 elections, the PNSD won 1.6 percent of the vote and two Assemblées Populaires Communales (APCs). By this time, however, Bencharif had begun to fade from public view and had moreover become involved in an internal party feud over an alleged misuse of funds. In addition, suspicions increased over the PNSD's links to the regime. Bencharif admitted to having been an FLN militant in his youth but claimed to have left the party in 1979. It was later revealed, however, that he had been elected to the Constantine APC that same year and did not leave the FLN until 1989.

No direct evidence emerged that the PNSD was created and financed by the presidency, although it was noted that the party never criticized the regime. It held a congress on December 6–7, 1990, which only increased the turmoil within the party over Bencharif's conduct as leader. It was indeed reported that many PNSD members were rejoining the FLN. The PNSD almost never held public meetings, issued few public documents, and did not publish a party organ. In the first round of the aborted elections held on December 26, 1991, it won a mere 0.7 percent of the vote.

PARTI SOCIAL-DEMOCRATE (PSD) (*Social Democratic Party*). Request for registration: July 19, 1989 (no. 1). The PSD, whose creation was announced in March 1989, was the first party to be registered under Law 89–11. It was also the first of the newly created parties to hold a congress, which took place on October 12–13, 1989. Two distinct groups came together to form the PSD, one composed of intellectuals who advocated social democracy and the other made up of lawyers and private-sector operators, the latter of whom had formed an association of entrepreneurs in 1988 sponsored by the "reformist" faction of the regime. The links of some of these individuals to the regime led to the suspicion that the PSD had in fact been secretly sponsored by the presidency, although there was never any evidence to this effect.

The original PSD program was a synthesis of the views of the party's two groups. It called for liberalization of the economy, but with the preservation of a public sector, and the expansion of democracy and guarantees for individual liberties. It also spoke of the "profound inspiration" the PSD drew from Islam, which offered society "access to modernity," and of the "eminent place" the party accorded to the concept of *ijtihad*.

Tensions emerged within the PSD and came to a head in March 1990, when the party split into two rival factions, known as the PSD-I, led by Abderrahmane Adjerid (b. 1939), and the PSD-II, led by Ahmed Hamidi-Khodja (b. 1946). Both factions held "extraordinary" congresses that month, issued virulent attacks on the leaders of the other faction, and claimed exclusive legitimacy over the PSD. Basic incompatibility between the two groups was certainly a factor in the split. The PSD-II claimed to be inspired primarily by Northern European–style social democracy, whereas the PSD-I placed more emphasis on Islam. In reality, however, the split could best be explained as the result of a simple factional conflict within the party leadership.

The June 1990 municipal elections occurred in the midst of the party's crisis, with the two factions together obtaining 1.1 percent of the national vote and winning two Assemblées Populaires Communales (APCs). In January 1991, under pressure from the Ministry of Interior, the two factions met to resolve their internal crisis, resulting in a victory for the PSD-II. In the first round of the aborted legislative elections of December 26, 1991, the PSD won 0.4 percent of the vote.

PARTI SOCIALISTE DES TRAVAILLEURS (PST) (*Socialist Workers Party*). Request for registration: October 29, 1989 (no. 15). The PST is a Trotskyist party affiliated with the Fourth International. It was founded in the mid-1970s as the Groupe Communiste Révolutionnaire and became the PST in the early 1980s. Though possessing no base in society, the PST has a core of committed militants and enjoys close ties with fraternal Trotskyist parties in France and elsewhere. Its leader is Salhi Chawki (b. 1951). In the first round of the aborted legislative elections held on December 26, 1991, the PST won 0.1 percent of the vote.

PCA. *See* PARTI COMMUNISTE ALGERIEN.

PNSD. *See* PARTI NATIONAL POUR LA SOLIDARITE ET LE DEVELOP-PEMENT.

PPA-MTLD. *See* PARTI DU PEUPLE ALGERIEN—MOUVEMENT POUR LA TRIOMPHE DES LIBERTES DEMOCRATIQUES.

PRA. *See* PARTI DU RENOUVEAU ALGERIEN.

PRS-CNDR. *See* PARTI DE LA REVOLUTION SOCIALISTE—COMITE NATIONAL POUR LA DEFENSE DE LA REVOLUTION.

PSD. *See* PARTI SOCIAL-DEMOCRATE.

PST. *See* PARTI SOCIALISTE DES TRAVAILLEURS.

PT. *See* PARTI DES TRAVAILLEURS.

†RASSEMBLEMENT NATIONAL POUR LA DEMOCRATIE ET LA REV-OLUTION (RNDR) (*National Rally for Democracy and Revolution*). The RNDR was created in May 1977 by Kaïd Ahmed, a former member of Houari Boumediene's inner circle who went into exile in Morocco after being ousted as the head of the Front de Libération Nationale (FLN)* in 1972. Also associated with

the RNDR were dissident FLN personalities Ahmed Mahsas and Tahar Zbiri. The RNDR opposed the Boumediene regime but hardly differed ideologically from the FLN. The RNDR had no impact and vanished after Kaïd Ahmed's death in March 1978.

RASSEMBLEMENT POUR LA CULTURE ET LA DEMOCRATIE (RCD) (*Rally for Culture and Democracy*). Request for registration: August 16, 1989 (no. 3). The RCD is one of the most important of the new parties that emerged following the end of one-party rule in 1989. Composed almost exclusively of Kabyles, the RCD is a standard bearer of Berberism and a leading force among the smaller "democratic" parties. In addition to representing a portion of the Kabyle electorate, the RCD is supported by numerous non-Kabyle Westernized intellectuals.

The RCD has its roots in the unstructured Mouvement Culturel Berbère (MCB) which emerged in the wake of the Berber spring of 1980. The RCD's leader since its inception has been Saïd Sadi (b. 1947), a psychiatrist and occasional playwright. The core of the RCD's leadership and cadres were militants in the MCB, as well as founders of the 1985 Ligue Algérienne des Droits de l'Homme, and a number spent time in prison in the course of the 1980s for their activities. The decision to create the RCD came in the period following the events of October 1988, when the principal figures of the MCB decided that the time had come to give their movement both a formal structure and an explicitly political content. The creation of the RCD was formally announced at a meeting held in Tizi Ouzou on February 9–10, 1989.

Within six months of its creation, the RCD claimed to have enrolled some 32,000 militants. Its base took on a different character than that of its Kabyle *frère ennemi*, the Front des Forces Socialistes (FFS).* This different character, in large part, can be explained by generational and educational differences; the RCD leaders and militants were younger, more educated, and more Westernized than their FFS counterparts. Despite the conflict between Sadi and Aït Ahmed, relations between the militants of the two parties, who were often personal friends or even from the same families, were usually cordial.

On December 15–16, 1989, the RCD held its first congress, with approximately 950 delegates in attendance—one-tenth of whom were women, confirming the RCD's reputation as the most feminist of Algeria's parties. The program adopted at the congress ratified the party's political orientation. In economic policy, the RCD called for a market economy but with the continued existence of a public sector. Politically, it advocated the furthering of democracy and the rule of law, placed much emphasis on equal status for the Tamazight language, and demanded recognition of cultural pluralism. Despite its Berberist discourse, the RCD, like the FFS, insisted that it was open to all Algerians and vehemently rejected any accusations of regionalism.

On a programmatic level, the RCD and FFS hardly differed from one another. Several aspects of the RCD's discourse did stand out, however. The RCD was particularly insistent on the issue of equal rights for women and went farther than the FFS in including women in its executive organs. The RCD was somewhat more outspoken than the FFS on the language question. It called for the reinstitution of French in the educational system and other spheres of public life. The RCD rarely used Arabic in its official proceedings—a technical violation of Law 89–11—and Sadi distinguished himself as the sole leader of a political party to speak only in French whenever he appeared on television. Most significant among the RCD's positions was its outspoken advocacy of *laïcité*, or the explicit separation of religion and the state. The RCD's discourse on *laïcité* indeed made it the privileged target of verbal, and sometimes even physical, abuse from Algeria's Islamists.

The RCD diverged from the FFS in one important respect: its willingness to cooperate with the regime. Although the RCD was harshly critical of the Front de Libération Nationale (FLN),* it offered critical support to the reform program of the government of Prime Minister Mouloud Hamrouche. In the June 1990 municipal elections, the RCD benefitted from the FFS boycott, winning control of eighty-seven Assemblées Populaires Communales (APCs) and the Tizi Ouzou Assemblée Populaire de Wilaya (APW). Although it only took 2.1 percent of the national vote, the RCD did well in areas with a concentration of Kabyles and led an inspired, well-organized electoral campaign.

The trajectory of the RCD through 1990 and into 1991 confirmed that it was a small but dynamic party with potential appeal beyond its communitarian base. The RCD, more than any other party, articulated a vision of a democratic, secular, modern Algeria free from complexes about the former colonial master, France, and solidly oriented toward Europe. The RCD, like the FFS, had little interest in the Arab world beyond the Maghreb, an attitude shared by many Algerians, non-Berber as well as Berber. The seemingly democratic credentials of the RCD were enhanced, moreover, by the high intellectual level and collegial nature of its leadership, all of whose members came of age after independence and had never been associated with the FLN or implicated in any way with the regime.

The promise shown by the RCD diminished in the latter half of 1991, however, as Sadi began to lead the party in an authoritarian manner. Matters came to a head when Sadi called for an extraordinary congress to be held on November 29. This move, as well as the undemocratic manner in which the congress delegates were selected, was vehemently opposed by party number two Mokrane Aït Larbi (b. 1948), a longtime Sadi companion and one of the RCD's most valuable assets. The congress, which was little more than a claque for Sadi's leadership, ousted Aït Larbi and a number of other members of the executive bureau. The RCD thus descended into the same infernal logic of purges and *luttes de clans* as the other parties.

In the aborted legislative elections of December 26, 1991, the RCD won 2.9 percent of the national vote. It was bested by the FFS across the Kabylie, winning only from 20 to 25 percent of the vote there. Sadi was himself beaten in his supposed stronghold of Tizi Ouzou city by a minor FFS figure. In the face of this result, Sadi responded by calling for cancellation of the second round of the elections and assumption of power by the army, all in order to prevent a government led by the Front Islamique du Salut (FIS).* Sadi backed the coup d'état of January 11, 1992, further calling into question his already tattered democratic credentials.

†RASSEMBLEMENT UNITAIRE DES REVOLUTIONNAIRES (RUR) (*Unitary Rally of Revolutionaries*). The RUR, which also called itself the "FLN Clandestin," was created in France in April 1967 by several opponents of the Boumediene regime. The principal figure associated with the RUR was former minister and Ben Bella associate Bachir Boumaza (b. 1927), who had also been associated with the Organisation Clandestine de la Révolution Algérienne (OCRA).* Apart from the occasional publication of a newspaper, the RUR engaged in almost no activities. It disbanded in 1974.

RCD. *See* RASSEMBLEMENT POUR LA CULTURE ET LA DEMOCRATIE.

RNDR. *See* RASSEMBLEMENT NATIONAL POUR LA DEMOCRATIE ET LA REVOLUTION.

RUR. *See* RASSEMBLEMENT UNITAIRE DES REVOLUTIONNAIRES.

UDMA. *See* UNION DEMOCRATIQUE DU MANIFESTE ALGERIEN.

UFD. *See* UNION DES FORCES DEMOCRATIQUES.

AL-UMMA MOVEMENT. *See* MOUVEMENT EL-OUMMA.

†UNION DEMOCRATIQUE DU MANIFESTE ALGERIEN (UDMA) (*Democratic Union of the Algerian Manifesto*). The UDMA was founded in April 1946 by Ferhat Abbas. As with the Amis du Manifeste et de la Liberté (AML),* the UDMA based its program on the Manifeste du Peuple Algérien of 1943. The UDMA was not a direct continuation of the AML, however, as it represented the break in the alliance between Ferhat Abbas and the Parti du Peuple Algérien (PPA)* over the events of May 1945, the responsibility for which Ferhat Abbas placed on the PPA. Militants of the PPA had played an important role in the AML, and Ferhat Abbas vowed to keep them out of the UDMA.

The UDMA contested the June 1946 elections for the second Constituent Assembly and won a huge victory in the second college (though half the electorate abstained due to the PPA's call for a boycott). Its representatives were met with hostility by their counterparts in the assembly, however, who totally rejected the UDMA's project for an independent Algeria federated with France. At the same time, the UDMA pursued its quarrel with the PPA in calling for a boycott of the National Assembly elections that November (which was contested by the newly created MTLD), in order to demonstrate that support for the PPA and Messali Hadj was not as great as widely believed. Though the MTLD realized a certain success in the election, the abstention rate was significant nonetheless, mostly due to the confusion of Muslim voters bewildered by the Abbas-Messali feud.

Attempts were made over the next five years to reconcile with the PPA-MTLD, but they failed. On the other hand, the UDMA was tacitly supported by much of the leadership of the *Jam'iyat al-'Ulama*. In elections held during this period, the UDMA came in a solid second after the MTLD, although it too was a victim of the rigging practiced by the colonial administration. The gradualism and electoralism of the UDMA began to cost it support, however, and many of its members—who were mainly middle-class Francophones—defected to the PPA-MTLD. By 1951 the UDMA had fewer than 3,000 members. Although the party continued to be a significant force in elected bodies, it had completely lost out to the PPA-MTLD in the battle of ideas. The UDMA's reformism was overtaken by events in 1954, and in January 1956 it rallied to the Front de Libération Nationale (FLN),* which led to its dissolution by the authorities.

Though the UDMA no longer existed, many of its leaders and members, including Ferhat Abbas, played important roles in the wartime FLN (particularly the Gouvernement Provisoire de la République Algérienne, or the GPRA) and in Ben Bella's first government following independence.

UNION DES FORCES DEMOCRATIQUES (UFD) (*Democratic Forces Union*). Request for registration: September 27, 1989 (no. 10). The UFD is a clique noteworthy for the identity of its founder and leader, Ahmed Mahsas (b. 1923), who was an important operative in the Organisation Spéciale (OS) and the wartime Front de Libération Nationale (FLN).* Mahsas became minister of agriculture in 1963 and was identified with the policy of *autogestion* (self-management) in the agricultural sector. He sided with Houari Boumediene in the 1965 coup but went into exile the following year, where he joined the Organisation Clandestine de la Révolution Algérienne (OCRA)* and later the Rassemblement National pour la Démocratie et la Révolution (RNDR).*

The political orientation of the UFD, which draws its inspiration from the 1976 Charte Nationale, claims fidelity to socialism, "anti-imperialism," and "Arabo-Islamic values." In this respect it does not differ from the FLN. The UFD has few militants and little popular support. In the first round of the aborted legislative elections of December 26, 1991, the UFD won 0.1 percent of the vote.

†UNION POPULAIRE ALGERIENNE (UPA) (*Algerian Popular Union*). The UPA, which was founded in July 1938, was the first attempt made by Ferhat Abbas to create a political party. The UPA, which followed the collapse of the Congrès Musulman, advocated equality among all "races" in Algeria, as well as the transformation of Algeria into a "veritable French province." The UPA

specified that membership in the party was a "duty" for all Algerians who were French subjects and claimed French citizenship and French "freedoms."

The UPA succeeded in organizing chapters in a number of towns across the country, though many of those who joined did so due to the personality of Ferhat Abbas rather than the party's program. The UPA, which had little impact, was dissolved after the fall of France in 1940.

UPA. *See* UNION POPULAIRE ALGERIENNE.

### Other Parties Registered by the Ministry of Interior in 1989–91

Ahd 54 (*Pledge 54*)

Alliance Nationale des Démocrates Indépendants (ANDI) (*National Alliance of Independent Democrats*)

Alliance pour la Justice et la Liberté (AJL) (*Alliance for Justice and Liberty*)

Amane Islamique (AI) (*Islamic Protection*)

Association Populaire pour l'Unité et l'Action (APUA) (*Popular Association for Unity and Action*)

Ecologie et Liberté (EL) (*Ecology and Liberty*)

El-Jazaïr Musulmane Contemporaine (JMC) (*Contemporary Muslim al-Jaza'ir*)

Front des Forces Démocratiques (FFD) (*Democratic Forces Front*)

Front des Forces Populaires (FFP) (*Popular Forces Front*)

Front des Générations de l'Indépendance (FGI) (*Independence Generations Front*)

Front du Djihad pour l'Unité (FDU) (*Jihad Front for Unity*)

Front du Salut National/ex-Front National du Renouveau (FSN/ex-FNR) (*National Salvation Front/ex-National Renewal Front*)

Front pour l'Authenticité Algérienne Démocratique (FAAD) (*Front for Democratic Algerian Authenticity*)

Génération Démocratique (GD) (*Democratic Generation*)

Hizb El-Haq (HEH) (*Truth Party*)

Mouvement de la Jeunesse Démocratique (MJD) (*Democratic Youth Movement*)

Mouvement des Forces Arabo-Islamiques (MFAI) (*Arab Islamic Forces Movement*)

Mouvement Er-Rissala El-Islamiya (MRI) (*Islamic Message Movement*)

Mouvement Social pour l'Authenticité (MSA) (*Social Movement for Authenticity*)

Organisation des Forces de l'Algérie Révolutionnaire Islamique Libre (OFARIL) (*Revolutionary Free Islamic Algeria Forces Organization*)

Parti Algérien de l'Homme Capital (PAHC) (*Algerian Party of the Man of Capital*)

Parti Algérien pour la Justice et le Progrès (PAJP) (*Algerian Party for Justice and Progress*)

Parti de la Justice Sociale (PJS) (*Social Justice Party*)

Parti de l'Union Arabe Islamique Démocratique (PUAID) (*Arab Islamic Democratic Union Party*)

Parti de l'Unité Populaire (PUP) (*Popular Unity Party*)

Parti Libéral Algérien (PLA) (*Algerian Liberal Party*)

Parti National Algérien (PNA) (*Algerian National Party*)

Parti Progressiste Démocratique (PPD) (*Progressive Democratic Party*)

Parti Républicain/ex-Parti Algérien du Peuple (PR/ex-PAP) (*Republican Party/ex-Algerian Party of the People*)

Parti Républicain Progressiste (PRP) (*Republican Progressive Party*)

Parti Science, Justice et Travail (PSJT) (*Science, Justice, and Labor Party*)

Parti Social Libéral (PSL) (*Social Liberal Party*)

Rassemblement Algérien Boumedieniste et Islamique (RABI) (*Algerian Boumedienist and Islamic Rally*)

Rassemblement Arabo-Islamique (RAI) (*Arab Islamic Rally*)

Rassemblement des Jeunes de la Nation Algérienne (RJNA) (*Young Peoples' Rally of the Algerian Nation*)

Rassemblement National Algérien (RNA) (*Algerian National Rally*)

Rassemblement National pour le Progrès (RNP) (*National Rally for Progress*)

Rassemblement pour l'Unité Nationale (RUN) (*Rally for National Unity*)

Union des Forces pour le Progrès (UFP) (*Union of Forces for Progress*)

Union du Peuple Algérien (UPA) (*Algerian Peoples Union*)

Union pour la Démocratie et les Libertés (UDL) (*Union for Democracy and Liberties*)

## NOTES

1. From 10 to 15 percent of the European population was Jewish, most of whom were indigenous Algerians who acquired full French citizenship en bloc with the Crémieux Decree of 1870.

2. Differing figures have been advanced as to the percentage of Muslim males over the age of twenty-five who gained the right to vote in 1919. Mafoud Kaddache (1980), citing Ageron, put the figure at 43 percent; Collot placed it at only 9 percent.

3. An agha was a caïd (*qa'id*) with twelve years of seniority. Bachaghas were aghas with six years of seniority. Caids were recruited from a variety of backgrounds, including landed notables, families of cadis or imams, former officers or noncommissioned officers in the French army, and so on.

4. Often erroneously translated as "secularism," *laïcité* signifies the nonreligious character of the state and legal system, as well as the neutrality of the state vis-à-vis different confessional groups. This does not imply nonrecognition of religion, however, as a laic state may, for example, subsidize parochial schools with public funds.

5. Kabyle Berbers make up approximately 15 percent of the Algerian population and are concentrated in the Kabylie, the Algiers metropolitan area, and the emigré community in France. Unlike Algeria's two other principal Berber groups, the Shawia and the Mozabites, the Kabyles were never Arabized. They speak the Berber dialect Tamazight, and the vast majority of those who have gone to school are Francophone. Kabyles are over-

represented in the state administration and public sector, the liberal professions, and the intelligentsia, and they have a strong presence in the economic private sector.

6. The political clan in Algeria is akin to the *shilla* in Egypt. See Robert Springborg, "Patterns of Association in the Egyptian Political Elite," in *Political Elites in the Middle East*, ed. George Lenczowski (Washington, D.C.: American Enterprise Institute, 1975). See also the discussion of contingent interest groups in Clement Henry Moore, *Politics in North Africa: Algeria, Morocco, and Tunisia* (Boston: Little, Brown, 1970), 201–10.

7. Official Algerian mythology puts the number of dead at 1.5 million, though no evidence has ever been advanced to justify this figure. Cf. Xavier Yacono, "Les pertes algériennes de 1954 à 1962," *Revue de l'Occident Musulman et de la Méditerranée* 34 (1982): 119–34.

8. The APN was created following the promulgation of the 1976 constitution. Until the abolition of the one-party system, voters chose between two candidates (1977), and then three (1982 and 1987), in each district, all of whom were presented by the FLN. No veritable campaigning between the candidates occurred, and the elections were often rigged, with the victor decided upon in advance as a result of intraparty bargaining or *luttes de clans*.

9. Municipal councils, created in 1967. Local elections under the one-party system involved a single list presented by the FLN which had twice as many candidates as there were seats at stake. The 1990 elections were based on a proportional list system with a guaranteed 51 percent of the seats going to the party that obtained a plurality, and the rest divided up among lists obtaining a minimum of 7 percent of the vote.

10. *Wilaya* (department) councils, created in 1969.

11. For a detailed presentation and analysis of the election results, see Arun Kapil, "Portrait statistique des élections du 12 juin 1990: Chiffres clés pour une analyse," *Les Cahiers de l'Orient* 23 (Summer 1991): 41–63.

12. The entries on the FIS, HAMAS, and MNI are shorter and revised versions of the author's "Les partis islamistes en Algérie: éléments de présentation," *Maghreb-Machrek* 133 (July–September 1991): 103–11.

13. Parties in Algeria are known by their French names (and especially by their French acronyms), both in Algeria and in English-language writing. Even Algerian Arabophones often refer to parties by their French appellations. The parties are thus listed alphabetically by their names in French, which is how the reader will encounter them elsewhere.

14. The MCB was never a structured party as such but rather the self-designation of the informal grouping of activists issuing from the 1980 Berber spring. It engaged in nonviolent action against the regime throughout the 1980s.

Arun Kapil

# ARABIAN PENINSULA STATES: BAHRAIN, KUWAIT, OMAN, QATAR, SAUDI ARABIA, AND THE UNITED ARAB EMIRATES

Formal political parties have played a significant but tangential role in the internal affairs of the countries of the Arabian Peninsula. Liberal reform movements advocated the establishment of representative advisory councils in Bahrain, Kuwait, and Dubai (now one of the United Arab Emirates) during the 1920s and 1930s. The suppression of these movements led some prominent dissidents to form nascent parties-in-exile, while others became active members of regional political organizations, most notably the Movement of Arab Nationalists (MAN)* (see chapters on Jordan and The Palestinians). Such associations provided a potent alternative means of generating political legitimacy to the ties of kinship and tenets of Islamic law exercised by the ruling families and their allies. Consequently, local authorities openly colluded with one another throughout the 1940s and 1950s to limit the influence and spread of political parties in the Gulf area.

General opprobrium continued to lie at the heart of Gulf rulers' attitudes toward political parties in the postindependence era. Radical organizations, particularly the Arab Ba'th Socialist Party and the Popular Front for the Liberation of Oman and the Arab Gulf (PFLOAG),* posed a direct challenge to existing regimes during the 1960s and 1970s. This threat became more pronounced in the wake of the Ba'thi seizure of power in Baghdad in 1963 and the outbreak of the Dhofari rebellion in Oman two years later. Repeated Iraqi attempts to subvert neighboring governments in the mid-1960s and overt Soviet and Chinese support for the rebels fighting in Dhofar enabled Arab Gulf rulers to associate formal political parties with outside intervention in the region, which both facilitated their efforts to quash indigenous activists and diminished these organizations' popular appeal. Of the two Arab Gulf states that instituted elected parliamentary systems shortly after independence, Bahrain explicitly prohibited and Kuwait actively discouraged candidates and deputies to their respective assemblies from forming or joining any party. The rulers of Oman, Qatar, and the United Arab Emirates set up advisory councils during the 1970s, whose totally appointed memberships were likewise precluded from party membership. Saudi Arabia has proven the least hospitable of the Gulf states to organized parties, as the regime has consistently refused either to promulgate a constitution or to establish any form of representative council, while quashing the activities of all formal political associations.

## BAHRAIN

From the late eighteenth century to the present, the islands that make up the State of Bahrain have been ruled by the senior *shaykhs* of one powerful clan, the Al Khalifa, acting in partnership with a collection of influential rich merchant families. What distinguishes this country from the other smaller Gulf states, such as Kuwait and Qatar, is the presence of a large and indigenous Shi'ite population, whose forebears were already firmly established on the islands at the time of their conquest by the Al Khalifa. It was among this subjugated majority, made up of native farmers and fisherfolk (*al-Baharina*) and settlers from the Persian shore of the Gulf (the *Hawala*), that discontent erupted in 1923, leading British agents to depose the ruler and initiate a program of sweeping fiscal and administrative reforms. Sunni notables opposed to overt British interference in the country's internal affairs organized a Bahrain National Congress to demand the restoration of the old ruler and the creation of an advisory council to assist him. But the Shi'ites generally remained aloof from this movement, and British officials soon arrested its leadership and exiled activists to India.

With the beginning of oil production in 1932, the position of the Al Khalifa almost immediately strengthened relative to that of the commercial elite, and the number of state agencies increased. These trends alienated poorer Shi'ites—who gravitated into manual labor in the petroleum and construction industries—and second-tier merchants, on the one hand, from the ruling family and its corps of British advisers, on the other. Shi'ite notables unsuccessfully petitioned the ruler in 1934 to promulgate a basic law and institute proportional representation on the municipal and education councils. Sunni reformers demanded the creation of an assembly (*majlis*) and an end to administrative inefficiency four years later. When students and oil workers threatened a general strike in support of the *majlis* movement in November 1938, the regime arrested a number of prominent reformers and deported them to India. Several clandestine opposition groups—including the Representatives of the People,* the Secret Labor Union,* and the Society of Free Youth*—remained active on the islands following the suppression of the 1938 *majlis* movement, but none posed a significant challenge to the regime during the subsequent decade.

Widespread social unrest erupted again in 1953–54, culminating in a general strike on the islands in July 1954. Liberal reformers from both the Sunni and Shi'i communities organized a Higher Executive Committee (HEC) that October to call for a legislative assembly, trade unions, and an appellate court. Protracted negotiations between the ruler and the HEC led to the formal recognition of a Committee of National Unity in return for the HEC's ending its demands for the establishment of a popular assembly. Activists based in the industrial labor force responded by forming a National Liberation Front–Bahrain (NLFB)* to press for more radical changes in the country's political structure. Anti-British demonstrations at the time of the Suez war of 1956 precipitated a crackdown on all opposition forces and the declaration of a state of emergency that effectively terminated the reform movement of the 1950s.

March 1965 saw a series of demonstrations at the Bahrain Petroleum Company that escalated into a general strike, carried out under the auspices of a National Front consisting of members of the Movement of Arab Nationalists, the Ba'th, and other more leftist parties. Further strikes conducted in the spring of 1972 prompted the ruler, Shaykh 'Isa bin Sulman, who had taken the title of amir following Bahrain's independence the previous August, to propose the creation of a Constituent Assembly to draft a provisional constitution. Elections to this body that December were boycotted by the NLFB and local cadres of the PFLOAG. Nevertheless, the assembly approved a draft constitution in June 1973 which left the power to propose, enact, and execute laws in the hands of the amir; mandated an elected thirty-member National Assembly (*al-Majlis al-Watani*) authorized to advise the ruler, to approve the state budget, and to question, but not dismiss, cabinet ministers; prohibited all political parties; and sanctioned the formation of trade unions, so long as their activities did not subvert the national interest.

Elections for the first National Assembly were held on December 7, 1973. Again, the PFLOAG boycotted the proceedings, but NLFB activists joined Ba'this, trade unionists, and other leftists to campaign for delegates united into a People's Bloc,* eight of whose twelve candidates emerged victorious. Six representatives of rural and suburban Shi'i districts subsequently coalesced into a Religious Bloc,* while a heterogeneous group of Independents—including a number of liberals, veterans of the HEC era—rounded out the assembly's thirty seats. Over the next year and a half, assembly members engaged in lively debates concerning a wide range of issues, but no single bloc was capable of transforming its platform into law. A new wave of industrial actions in early 1974, coinciding with the formation of a Popular Front in Bahrain, led the amir to signal the government's intention to promulgate a revised security law. People's Bloc deputies insisted that any such law be submitted to the assembly for approval, but the cabinet balked at subjecting itself to such a procedure. By the end of the year, the People's Bloc had reached a tentative agreement with the Religious Bloc to oppose promulgation of the law in exchange for more restrictive social legislation. In response, the cabinet announced in May 1975 that it would no longer cooperate with the assembly, and three months later the police moved to break up the NLFB, the PFLOAG, and the Union of Bahraini Students. The prime minister then submitted his resignation, and in August the amir dissolved the assembly and suspended the article of the constitution mandating new elections.

Since 1975, organized opposition to the regime has come primarily from Bahrain's variegated Islamist movement. Advocates of moderate reforms can be found in the Sunni Society for Social Reform (Jam'iyya al-Islah al-Ijtima'iyya)* and Supporters of the Call (Ansar al-Da'wa),* as well as in the Shi'i Party of the Islamic Call (Hizb al-Da'wa al-Islamiyya). Proponents of more profound social transformation belong to the Islamic Action Organization (IAO) (Munadhdhama al-Amal al-Islami)* and the Islamic Front for the Liberation of Bahrain (IFLB) (Jabha al-Islamiyya lil-Tahrir al-Bahrain),* both predominantly Shi'ite. Popular demonstrations involving adherents to these associations broke out sporadically during late 1979 and early 1980, culminating in a series of large-scale marches in support of the Islamic Republic of Iran during April and May 1980. Security forces broke up these demonstrations by force, killing a number of marchers in the process.

In the wake of these events, underground groups such as the IAO changed their tactics, abandoning mass popular demonstrations and turning instead to isolated acts of sabotage carried out by small groups of committed cadres. This shift was reinforced by the formation of the IFLB in Tehran at the end of 1979; the clandestine operations envisaged by the leaders of this organization were epitomized by the December 1981 plot to overthrow the Al Khalifa and set up an Islamic Republic on the islands. Sizable caches of small arms belonging to underground groups of Shi'ites continued to be discovered on the islands as late as the fall and winter of 1983–84.

Concerted efforts on the part of the Bahraini authorities to expose and destroy cells of militant Shi'ites largely succeeded in disrupting the operations of the IAO and IFLB by mid-decade. A particularly large number of arrests and deportations of prominent Shi'ite activists took place in 1986. In December 1987 some 100 persons were charged with conspiring to assassinate the ruler and seize the country's main oil facilities, the radio and television stations, the international airport, and the American embassy; observers speculated that this group was affiliated with the IFLB, but Bahraini officials refused to implicate Iran in the plot. Instead, the government imposed strict curfews on Shi'ite residential districts and promulgated a regulation prohibiting Bahraini Shi'ites from taking jobs in the armed forces. Further arrests were made in the days following the death of the Ayatollah Khomeini in June 1989 and during the weeks around 'Ashura two months later. But with the exception of persistent but unconfirmed reports of isolated attacks on government installations, the Islamist opposition appeared by early 1992 to have been firmly suppressed by the state security forces.

## KUWAIT

From the amirate's founding in the early 1700s to the end of the nineteenth century, politics in Kuwait involved a series of delicate bargains between one powerful clan, the Al Sabah, whose leaders achieved preeminence by guaranteeing the security of local trade through their amicable relations with surrounding tribes, on the one hand, and a collection of merchant families residing in the port city who profited from the trade of the northern Gulf, on the other. A trio of rulers upset the rough parity that existed between the Al Sabah and the richer merchants prior to the 1890s by first entering into an exclusive treaty relationship with the British in 1899, whose terms included an annual subsidy to the ruling family of 15,000 rupees, then gradually extending Al Sabah control over indigenous pearl fishing and import-export commerce, and finally creating government health and educational institutions. When a range of new taxes was levied to support these activities, prominent rich merchants formed an informal council of notables and demanded a voice in selecting the new ruler and other administrative matters. This body soon collapsed as a result of internal squabbling, but it sparked the establishment of both an elected municipal council in 1930 and an elected education council six years later.

These councils laid the basis for a liberal reformist movement among Kuwait's Sunni commercial elite that in early 1938 demanded the creation of an elected assembly, substantial improvements in education and health facilities, and a crackdown on corruption within the Al Sabah. When the ruler and his British advisers ignored the dissidents' demands and arrested one of their leaders, several reformists emigrated to Iraq, where they organized a party called al-Shabiba* to cultivate Iraqi support for their program. Meanwhile, in Kuwait itself, members of the movement elected a fourteen-member assembly (*majlis*) that June; they then formed a party of their own, the National Bloc,* to buttress the *majlis* and engender a sense of Kuwaiti nationalism among the local citizenry. Faced with growing popular support for the assembly, the ruler, Shaykh Ahmad al-Jabir, gave it his endorsement, designating it the National Advisory Assembly (*Majlis al-Ummah al-Tashri'i*). The assembly formulated a basic law patterned on the 1923 Egyptian constitution and instituted a variety of economic and social reforms. But when it moved to circumscribe more narrowly the political and financial prerogatives of the ruling family, Shaykh Ahmad ordered its dissolution and deployed armed bedouin retainers to enforce his decree. The regime then super-vised the election of a new twenty-member *majlis* and submitted for its approval a revised constitution that granted the ruler the power to veto any measures it adopted. This document was rejected by the assembly, prompting Shaykh Ahmad again to dissolve the body and detain its most outspoken supporters. British acquiescence in these moves, along with developments in Palestine, transformed the liberal nationalist sentiment of the early 1930s into a broadly pro-Iraq and anti-British nationalism that spread throughout the Sunni community during the late 1930s and 1940s.

Organized opposition to the Al Sabah took a number of largely clandestine forms in subsequent years. Expatriate teachers founded a branch of the Muslim Brotherhood (*Ikhwan al-Muslimin*)* in the amirate in 1951; foreign and indige-nous oil workers organized the Kuwaiti Democratic League (KDL)* about the same time, while communists rooted in the local Iraqi and Iranian communities formed the Kuwait Democratic Youth*; and Syrians sympathetic to the Ba'th set up a social organization, the Union Club,* in the mid-1950s. With an eye to developments within the expatriate communities, prominent Kuwaiti merchants reiterated their calls for the establishment of an elected citizen's assembly and the implementation of fundamental administrative reforms in mid-1954. The ruler parried these demands by appointing a Higher Executive Committee to coordinate the activities of the existing advisory councils. Handbills distributed by KDL activists protested this move and demanded the committee's replacement with a national assembly. Similar demands were expressed the following year in the weekly *Sada al-Iman*, published under the auspices of the National Culture Club by a former MAN activist, Dr. Ahmad Muhammad al-Khatib. Subsequent petitions to the ruler, Shaykh Abdullah al-Salim, asking him to reinstitute an elected assembly, were routinely dismissed.

When Great Britain granted Kuwait independence in June 1961, Shaykh Ab-dullah, who now took the title of amir, announced the creation of an elected Constituent Assembly charged with drafting a new constitution for the amirate. This document, which was ratified by the amir in November 1962, mandated the establishment of a fifty-member National Assembly empowered to question members of the appointed cabinet, to veto legislation promulgated by the ruler, and to approve the national budget. Political parties were not explicitly prohib-ited by the constitution, but neither were they authorized. Consequently, existing pan-Arab organizations were allowed to continue their activities within the country, thereby providing the institutional foundations for Kuwait's virtually unregulated mass media.

Within the National Assembly, informal blocs of deputies united by per-sonal ties or, less commonly, ideological affinities took the place of formal par-ties. A sizable contingent of liberal nationalists, led by Ahmad al-Khatib, won seats in the first assembly, elected in January 1963. Only four members of this bloc won reelection four years later, although the grouping steadily regained strength as a result of the elections of 1971 and 1975. Supporters of the Al Sabah—loosely grouped into blocs representing the settled bedouin, the indigenous Shi'ites, and moderate Sunni Islamists—provided the primary counterweights to liberal forces in the assembly in the years after 1967. Rising tension between elected assembly members and the appointed cabinet, in conjunction with persistent attacks on the regime's foreign policy in the local press, convinced the heir apparent, Shaykh Jabir al-Ahmad, to resign his position as prime minister in August 1976, an act that precipitated the immediate suspension of the assembly.

Shaykh Jabir's accession to the rulership in January 1978 set in motion a series of deliberations both within and outside the Al Sabah that eventuated in new elections to the National Assembly in February 1981. Perhaps as a result of changes in the number and shape of the electoral districts, only three liberal nationalists and two Shi'ites emerged victorious from the balloting, while more than half of the assembly's membership consisted of bedouin tribespeople loyal to the ruling family. Virtually identical results were obtained in the February 1985 elections. The twenty-seven bedouin representatives who gained seats that year coalesced into a National Center Group,* pledged to improve conditions in the outlying tribal districts, but were riven by deep splits along kinship, ideological, and economic lines. Prominent liberals campaigned as a Democratic Bloc,* whose platform called for fundamental administrative reform to reduce governmental inefficiency; only three adherents to this bloc won seats in the assembly. Islamist groupings unfavorably disposed to the regime, notably the Shi'ite Social Cultural Society (al-Jam'iyya al-Thaqafiyyah al-Ijtima'iyya),* fared poorly in the voting as well, while the moderate Sunni Social Reform Society (Jam'iyya al-Islah al-Ijtima'iyya,* which grew out of the Muslim Brotherhood in the 1960s, and the quietist Sunni Heritage Revival Society (Jam'iyya Ihya al-Turath)* did little better.

Outside the assembly, underground parties gained strength as the 1980s began, most notably among the country's poorer Shi'ites. The most active of these organizations, the Iraqi opposition party al-Da'wa,* enjoyed close ties to the Islamic Republic of Iran, which enabled the Kuwaiti authorities to accuse it of serving as a front for foreign agitators. At the end of October 1983, for instance, the government announced that the armed forces had captured forty armed Shi'ite infiltrators attempting to enter the country by sea from Iran. Two months later, militant Shi'ites detonated explosive devices outside the U.S. and French embassies, as well as near a compound housing American missile experts installing a new antiaircraft defense system. Police arrested eighteen members of al-Da'wa in early December, all Shi'ite expatriates from Iraq and Lebanon, and charged them with planning and executing the attacks. The relative leniency of the court in dealing with these cases, combined with the deportation of large numbers of Iraqi and Iranian nationals at the turn of the year, undercut local support for the radical opposition, although members of the Lebanon-based Islamic Jihad (whom the authorities subsequently linked to al-Da'wa) attempted to assassinate the amir in May 1985, and a group calling itself the Organization of Revolutionary Brigades claimed responsibility for bombing a pair of cafés owned by the Al Sabah two months later.

Persistent economic difficulties associated with the drop in world petroleum prices and the collapse of the country's unofficial stock market (the *Suq al-Manakh*) sparked heated criticism of the cabinet on the part of liberals and Shi'ites in the National Assembly by mid-decade. In early 1986, members of other groupings gravitated to the critics' camp, raising the distinct possibility that a broad bloc opposed to the regime might arise. Partly to preclude such a possibility, the cabinet tendered its resignation on July 1, and Shaykh Jabir suspended the assembly two days later. In his address to the nation, the ruler observed: "Instead of pooling efforts and all parties cooperating in order to contain these crises, opinions were divided, and blocs and parties emerged which have led to the shattering of national unity and the interruption of work until the Council of Ministers has become unable to continue its task."

Agitation to reconvene the National Assembly intensified in early 1990. Professional associations, university students, and trade unionists petitioned the ruler to hold new elections, while a group of twenty-eight former assembly delegates met with the crown prince, Shaykh Sa'd al-Abdullah, at the beginning of March and convinced him to support a return to parliamentary government. The cabinet in late April approved the calling of a seventy-five-member National Council, one-third of whose members would be appointed by the amir, charged with assessing the past and future role of the assembly and monitoring the country's fiscal affairs. Former members of the Democratic Bloc*, who favored the immediate restoration of the National Assembly, announced that they would boycott the council elections; thirteen of their number were arrested in early May for attending what the authorities called illegal meetings to organize the boycott. Of the fifty members elected to the Council on June 10, twenty had held seats in the old National Assembly; following earlier practice, Shaykh Sa'd was named prime minister by the amir.

In the wake of the August 2 Iraqi invasion of Kuwait, Shaykh Sa'd hinted on several occasions that an elected assembly would be restored as soon as the Al Sabah regained control. The prime minister told a group of Kuwaiti notables in Jiddah in mid-October that "the people of Kuwait can only be rewarded for their trust and loyalty by further trust," and that women, who were ineligible to vote in earlier elections, could expect to "play a greater role in liberated Kuwait." (Quoted in *Middle East Economic Digest*, October 26, 1990.) Members of the former Democratic Bloc* welcomed Shaykh Sa'd's remarks, but expressed concern over intimations from other cabinet members that martial law would be imposed on the country during the initial period following an Iraqi withdrawal. When the Al Sabah returned to the country in March 1991, a state of emergency was indeed declared; the cabinet appointed in mid-April included no critics of the government. During the months of the Iraqi occupation, neighborhood committees and discussion groups (*diwaniyyat*) provided the primary locus for popular resistance on the part of Kuwaiti citizens unable to escape the country. The Social Reform Society* and the Heritage Revival Society* used their influence in the directorates of the state food cooperatives to coordinate the distribution of foodstuffs, medicine, and fuel throughout the amirate. Sympathizers of the Democratic Bloc* joined in these efforts as well, creating a de facto popular front opposed to the occupation. The hasty evacuation of Kuwait by the Iraqi armed forces provided members of the local committees with modern weapons, which they soon turned on suspected collaborators. Forces loyal to the Al Sabah undertook, as one of their first moves upon recapturing the country, to disarm these individuals with the assistance of U.S. military police.

Throughout the spring of 1991, liberal critics of the Al Sabah called for early elections to a resurrected National Assembly. The highest-ranking Kuwaiti army officer to remain in the country during the Iraqi occupation publicly observed that ignoring demands for popular participation in policy making might prove risky, given the number of weapons in private hands. When the ruler announced in June that an advisory National Council would be appointed to supervise parliamentary elections sixteen months later, opposition leaders organized a series of popular demonstrations demanding the reinstitution of the 1962 constitution in its entirety.

Campaigning for the new National Assembly began in earnest in September 1992. The ministry of the interior prohibited political parties from forming in order to contest the election, so candidates ran as individuals associated with loose coalitions advocating a wide range of platforms. In the balloting held on October 5, Islamist candidates won eighteen seats, giving recognized critics of the Al Sabah a total of thirty-six delegates in the fifty-member body. The Islamists quickly coalesced into two distinct blocs, an avowedly reformist Islamic Constitutional Movement and a comparatively conservative Islamic Popular Alliance. Both blocs advocated amending the constitution to make Islamic law (shari'a) the basis of the Kuwaiti legal system.

## OMAN

Eighty-five years of continual conflict between tribal forces loyal to the Ibadi imamate, centered in the valleys and plains of the Omani interior, and townspeople, subject to the Sultan in the port city of Muscat, came to an end with Sultan Sa'id bin Taimur's reconquest of the hinterlands around the capital and the resignation of the imam, Ghalib bin 'Ali al-Hinai, in December 1955. The former imam almost immediately joined his brother Talib in soliciting support from Omani laborers working in Saudi Arabia for an anti-sultanate organization, the Oman Revolutionary Movement (ORM).* Armed ORM units landed along the Batinah coast in June 1957 and after pushing the sultan's armed forces out of the area were themselves defeated by British troops and aircraft seconded to the ruler.

Five years later, discontented inhabitants of the southern province of Dhofar began raiding oil company and military installations around the town of Salalah. These guerrillas held a congress in June 1965 under the name Dhofar Liberation Front* and issued a platform calling for independence from the central government in Muscat. More radical activists, led by Muhammad bin Ahmad al-Ghassani, took control of the second congress in September 1968 and adopted both an anti-imperialist program and a new label: the Popular Front for the Liberation of the Occupied Arab Gulf (PFLOAG).* This new organization received assistance from the People's Republic of China, the Soviet Union, and Iraq and initiated a campaign of armed struggle against government officials and troops in the province. Early victories sparked the formation of a companion movement in the north, the National Democratic Front for the Liberation of Oman and the Arab Gulf (NDFLOAG),* which carried out unsuccessful attacks on two garrisons in the summer of 1970. The formation of this second organization prompted critics of the sultan within the regime to encourage his son, Qabus, to seize control of the country.

Immediately after taking power, Sultan Qabus initiated a dual policy of granting amnesty for any dissidents who would surrender to the central government and complementing military moves against the Popular Front with development projects in the districts from which it drew its support. This combination put Popular Front activists on the defensive, prompting them to reassess their primary objectives and merge with the NDFLOAG to form a Popular Front for the Liberation of Oman and the Arab Gulf (PFLOAG). A series of government victories on the battlefield during 1972–73 forced PFLOAG guerrillas to retreat to the most desolate areas of the province. Militants within the movement emerged from a divided May 1974 conference committed to continuing the armed struggle against the regime as the Popular Front for the Liberation of Oman.* But government forces overran the rebels' remaining strongholds during the following summer and fall, and by the end of 1976 the sultan was able to claim that order had been fully restored to the province.

In November 1980, Sultan Qabus ordered a ministerial committee to consider ways of broadening the process of formal consultation within policy-making circles. The deliberations of this committee resulted in the promulgation of a set of decrees creating a forty-five-member appointed State Consultative Council (al-Majlis al-Istishari lil-Dawlah) the following October; the sultan presided over the first session of the new council in early November. This body was given no legislative powers; its mandate was limited to advising the ruler on proposed laws, and its meetings were to be held in secret.

At the height of the Gulf crisis, in March 1991, Sultan Qabus announced that the council's powers would be expanded and that representatives would henceforth be determined by popular election. Notables in each of Oman's provinces nominated candidates for such an election that September, but in the end delegates were selected by the palace. The head of the old State Consultative Council was appointed to preside over the new body.

# QATAR

In 1868 the British political resident in the Gulf selected Shaykh Muhammad bin Thani as signatory of a mutual pact pledging Britain's protection in exchange for a renunciation of warfare on the part of the bedouin tribespeople residing on the Qatar peninsula. This treaty represented both the beginnings of Qatar as an autonomous entity and the origins of Al Thani predominance within local society. Pearl fishing and date cultivation provided only scant revenues for the regime, and conflicts among prominent Al Thani shaykhs and their more powerful allies remained endemic throughout the first half of the twentieth century.

Immediately after World War II, the onset of large-scale oil production coincided with the death of the ruler, Shaykh Hamad bin 'Abdullah, to precipitate a crisis within the Al Thani over the distribution of oil revenues and the succession to the rulership. British mediation in these conflicts secured a firm position for the newly appointed political agent in policy making, and a network of administrative agencies was soon put in place to supervise the country's internal affairs.

Sporadic strikes involving Qatar's petroleum workers erupted during the early 1950s, inspired perhaps by Dhofari activists. More threatening to the regime was a simultaneous series of clashes among different factions within the Al Thani. These two dynamics merged in early 1956, resulting in the formation of a national front espousing a broadly Arab nationalist platform. Supporters of the front staged a public demonstration in the capital city of Doha in mid-August, waving Egyptian flags and shouting anti-British slogans. The scale of the demonstration prompted the ruler to request the assistance of British marines in breaking up the march. Shaken by the episode, the ruler convened a meeting of the Al Thani and announced his intention to set up a regular police force to enforce order at all levels of society.

In April 1963 a handful of Qataris blocked a main thoroughfare in Doha while cheering the proposed federation of Egypt, Syria, and Iraq. One of the ruler's nephews, who found his car surrounded, fired on the revelers, an act whose temerity prompted a group of local notables to form a National Unity Front* consisting of oil workers and Al Thani dissidents. The front threatened a general strike to press demands for stricter limits on the ruler's prerogatives, greater Qatarization of the labor force, the right to set up trade unions, and the establishment of a municipal council for the capital. The authorities quickly broke up the movement by deporting its leaders and promising to implement a series of administrative reforms, including the appointment of a fifteen-member advisory council, which then failed to convene.

Upon taking power from his absent cousin in February 1972, Shaykh Khalifa bin Hamad declared Qatar an independent state, published a provisional constitution, and created a twenty-member appointed Advisory Council (*Majlis al-Shura*) empowered to debate proposed legislation and question cabinet ministers. The *majlis* was expanded to thirty members in 1975, and its term was repeatedly extended by the ruler's decree, obviating the need to hold popular elections. All proceedings of the Advisory Council are held in secret. With the exception of a handful of replacements occasioned by members' deaths, the original appointees continued to serve on the council for the ensuing decade and a half.

Persistent feuding within the Al Thani posed continual challenges to Shaykh Khalifa's authority throughout the 1970s. The ruler's younger brother Shaykh Suhaym, for example, was reported to have been conspiring with tribes in the north of the country to overthrow Shaykh Khalifa at the time of his death in August 1985. But generous budget expenditures for social services precluded the emergence of opposition to the regime from below, and even isolated acts of sabotage had become extinct by the end of the decade. No political parties had taken root in the country as of early 1992.

Nevertheless, popular discontent with the regime began to percolate more openly in the wake of the Gulf war of 1990–91. Representatives of fifty prominent Qatari families petitioned the ruler in January 1992 to set up an elected national council as a means of "guaranteeing an effective participation of the people" in public policy making. This council would be charged with drawing up a "permanent constitution capable of guaranteeing democracy and determining political, social and economic structures" for the country, thereby eliminating what its proponents perceived as widespread abuses of power by members of the Al Thani. Although couched in the form of a petition, and not as the program of an organized political party, the publication of this manifesto represented the most significant episode of political mobilization in the amirate since the days of the National Unity Front, some three decades earlier.

## SAUDI ARABIA

From its establishment in 1932, the Kingdom of Saudi Arabia has been governed by a coalition of leading shaykhs of the Al Sa'ud, prominent merchant families and influential leaders of the religious notability ('ulama), inspired by the teachings of the eighteenth-century reformer Muhammad bin 'Abd al-Wahhab (whose followers are known as Muwahhidun or, more pejoratively, Wahhabis). The campaign by members of this coalition to construct a unified political entity out of the autonomous provinces of the Arabian Peninsula during the 1910s and 1920s faced recurrent challenges not only from powerful bedouin tribes allied to the Al Sa'ud but also from the inhabitants of the comparatively urbanized western province of al-Hijaz, who continued to resist Al Sa'ud dominance and the puritanical values espoused by the Muwahhidun for several years after the Saudi conquest of the province in 1926. Opponents of the new regime coalesced as the Hijazi Liberation Party (Hizb al-Tahrir al-Hijazi)* in the early 1930s, and this party orchestrated a short-lived rebellion in the northernmost districts of the province in 1932. The rapid expansion of oil production in the years immediately after World War II provided the regime with sufficient resources both to ameliorate conflicts of interest among its constituents and to co-opt potential opponents in al-Hijaz, in the central province of al-Najd, and in the southern province of al-'Asir.

In the eastern province of al-Hasa, however, the consolidation of an indige-nous working class associated with the burgeoning petroleum sector generated a new kind of political challenge to the regime during the 1940s and early 1950s. Wartime shortages of food and labor provided the bases for a series of protests in the region in the spring of 1945, while discriminatory hiring and promotion practices at the Arabian-American Oil Company (ARAMCO), combined with widespread popular sympathy for the nationalization policies carried out by Dr. Mohamed Mosaddeq's Popular Front in Iran, sparked a general strike by petro-leum workers in October 1953. The regime responded to the strike by imple-menting a comprehensive economic and social development program aimed at improving the living conditions in the eastern province. This program effectively undercut the demands of more militant laborers, who continued to agitate for change by supporting an underground Workers' Committee. This group organ-ized a sizable anti-American demonstration on the occasion of King Sa'ud bin 'Abd al-'Aziz's visit to ARAMCO headquarters at Dhahran in May 1956. The governor of the eastern province ordered bedouin irregulars to break up the march, sparking a general strike in the oil fields a month later.

Several clandestine political associations arose out of the first Workers' Com-mittee. The Sons of the Arabian Peninsula*. and the communist National Lib-eration Front* issued periodic calls for the overthrow of the Al Sa'ud from bases across the border in North Yemen throughout the 1950s and early 1960s. These appeals were succeeded by a wave of attacks on government and ARAMCO installations launched in 1966 by members of the Society for the Liberation of the Holy Soil* and the Nasserist Union of the People of the Arabian Peninsula.* During the June war of 1967, demonstrators marched on the U.S. consulate in Dhahran and a nearby police barracks; state security forces broke up the dem-onstration by force and arrested a number of local labor activists in retaliation. Former MAN activists reemerged in 1970 to join a small group of Saudi Ba'this in forming a left-leaning Popular Democratic Party,* whose platform advocated armed struggle to overthrow the Al Sa'ud and the adoption of central planning as a way of promoting greater equity within the local economy.

The Iranian revolution of 1978–79 precipitated sporadic rioting among the Shi'a of al-Hasa, on the one hand, and the emergence of several clandestine Shi'i political parties, on the other. Among these were the Islamic Revolutionary Organization of the Arabian Peninsula* and the Liberation Party of the Penin-sula.* The coordinated efforts of the regime's National Guard and the eastern province's economic development office largely precluded such organizations from attracting a large following among the local population, although they were somewhat more influential in expatriate circles.

More threatening to the regime was the emergence of groups critical to the religious laxity and alleged immorality of the Al Sa'ud at the end of the 1970s. One such group, led by Juhaiman bin Muhammad Al 'Utayba, captured the

Grand Mosque in Mecca in November 1979 after issuing a series of pamphlets blasting the ruling family for its luxurious life-style and the state-sponsored 'ulama for their tolerance of Western culture in the kingdom. At the end of the year, militant Islamists in the eastern province set up a vigilante organization called al-Ikhwan* to purge the region of outside influence; this group forced the closure of a women's clerical school run by the Saudi national oil company, as well as a number of beauty parlors and a hotel in Dhahran that winter. In response to the actions of these groups, the regime ordered its own morals police to crack down on women who disobeyed regulations governing dress and behavior in public, and, at the same time, narrowed the range of activities open to female citizens.

Except for perennial disturbances associated with the pilgrimage, opposition to the regime was scarce during the 1980s. In December 1984, Saudi officials unearthed a plot to smuggle weapons and explosives into the country in trucks transporting agricultural products from Lebanon. New regulations requiring all trucks entering the kingdom to unload their cargos at border checkpoints were promulgated in the wake of this incident. Three years later, the government set up a National Committee for Combating Drugs to oversee efforts to stem the flow of narcotics into the kingdom.

March 1988 saw what appears to have been an attack on the petrochemical works at Jubail, followed by the discovery of a cache of explosives outside the Ras Tanura refinery. Four months later, a spokesperson for Hizbullah* in Beirut told reporters that the party's branch in the eastern province had assassinated a trio of Saudi police officers in al-Qatif. In response to these incidents, the regime asked the Council of Senior 'Ulama to approve the death penalty for saboteurs; this body authorized capital punishment "as a deterrent" against attacks on public installations at the end of August. Hizbullah threatened to escalate its operations in the kingdom following the subsequent execution of four Shi'ites charged with setting the March explosions.

Mass demonstrations broke out in al-Hasa at the beginning of 1989, and there were unconfirmed reports that the police had exposed a group plotting to overthrow the Al Sa'ud. Public mourning on the occasion of the Ayatollah Khomeini's death that June precipitated harsh countermeasures on the part of the state security services. And in July members of a shadowy Arab Fury Generation claimed responsibility for two bombings outside the Grand Mosque in Mecca; when sixteen Kuwaiti Shi'ites were publicly executed for their involvement in this incident in late September, a spokesperson for Hizbullah declared that the organization would "avenge the blood of these oppressed Muslims who were massacred in an act of terrorism" on the part of the Saudi regime. Attacks on Saudi facilities in Turkey and Lebanon followed, as did an attempt to bomb the ministry of interior's headquarters in Riyadh. In the wake of these attacks—and as discontent was reported to be spreading among the country's university students—the number of public executions tripled during 1989 from what it had been the year before.

The massive deployment of U.S. troops to the eastern province that took place during the fall of 1990 generated discontent among influential religious notables who felt that the regime was capitulating to American wishes. Speeches and sermons critical of the growing U.S. presence by such prominent *ulama* as the dean of Islamic studies at Umm al-Qura University in Mecca and the head of the kingdom's Sufi orders circulated widely on audio- and videotapes. Liberals responded favorably to these messages as well, and recordings of dissident poets soon joined those of religious notables in making the rounds. A small anti–Al Sa'ud demonstration took place in Jiddah in November 1990, accompanied by the well-publicized protest in Riyadh on the part of elite Saudi women against the custom of not allowing them to drive motor vehicles. King Fahd bin 'Abd al-'Aziz eventually commuted the sentences of those convicted of participating in the latter protest, but the regime stepped up its support for the state-affiliated morals police during the course of 1991.

At the beginning of 1992, leaflets and cassettes openly criticizing the regime for squandering public monies and neglecting its obligation to protect the Islamic character of the kingdom began spreading on university campuses and in mosques located in the towns and villages of central and eastern Saudi Arabia. State security forces responded by arresting some fifty younger *ulama*, described as being outside the country's official religious establishment, as well as a number of supporters of al-Da'wa, a clandestine Shi'ite political organization that had been active in the eastern province in the late 1970s.

As early as 1926, Emir Faysal bin 'Abd al-'Aziz, the governor of al-Hijaz, appointed a Constituent Assembly to formulate a constitution for the province. The basic law that emerged from this committee's deliberations in September that year included provisions authorizing a nine-member Consultative Council (*Majlis al-Shura*) and other representative bodies in the larger towns. The former was enlarged to twenty members in 1952 and expanded again to twenty-five, three years later. The provisional constitution published in 1960 for the kingdom as a whole mandated a 120-member National Council (*al-Majlis al-Watani*), two-thirds of whose members were to be nominated by provincial councils. In the wake of King Faysal's assassination in March 1975, King Khalid bin 'Abd al-'Aziz resurrected plans to set up a National Council, this time consisting of some seventy prominent appointees. A similar proposal was advanced in the aftermath of the 1980 occupation of the Great Mosque in Mecca. Four years later, King Fahd told reporters that the time was ripe for both a Consultative Council and a permanent constitution, but neither had appeared by the time the decade came to an end.

In the spring of 1991, a group of Islamist notables petitioned the ruler to create an appointed Majlis al-Shura to ensure that laws comply with the strictures of the *Quran* and the Shari'a. This manifesto coincided with growing criticism of the Al Sa'ud on university campuses, prompting the king to announce in November that the regime planned to promulgate a Basic Order of Government and set up a Consultative Council. The order, issued on March 1, 1992, guaranteed a wide range of political liberties but did not authorize the establishment of political parties, and the ruler told reporters that representatives to the council would be appointed rather than elected.

## UNITED ARAB EMIRATES

Of the seven principalities—Abu Dhabi, Dubai, Sharjah, Ras al-Khayma, Ajman, Umm al-Qaiwain, and Fujairah—that merged to form the United Arab Emirates (UAE) in 1971, only Dubai has a history of active political parties. As in Bahrain and Kuwait, domestic affairs in this port city were dominated throughout the nineteenth century by a condominium of the ruling Al Maktum and a class of rich merchants. When, in 1887, the commercial elite of Lingah on the Persian coast was displaced by the arrival of a customs administration subordinate to the government in Tehran, the city's ruler, Shaykh Maktum bin Hashar, invited its members to settle in Dubai. These merchants' activities gradually transformed the port into a major center of trade between the Indian subcontinent to the east and Persia and Iraq to the northwest.

In 1937 Shaykh Sa'id bin Maktum sold exclusive rights to prospect for oil around the city to a British enterprise for a small annual royalty. The income from this concession upset the delicate economic and political complementarity that existed between various leaders of the ruling family, on one hand, and the resident rich merchant community, on the other. In an effort to restore the balance, several senior shaykhs of the Al Maktum persuaded Shaykh Sa'id to set up an elected fifteen-member assembly (majlis) to supervise the disbursement of the oil revenues. The members of the majlis, which sat from October 1938 to March 1939, were chosen from among the city's elite families, with cousins of the ruler occupying the most influential posts. Shaykh Sa'id agreed to cooperate with this body only under duress. Finally he abolished the majlis with the assistance of his son, Shaykh Rashid, by catching the reformers off guard and expelling them from the city. It appears that the episode contributed to the old ruler's physical decline, and Shaykh Rashid bin Sa'id steadily consolidated his hold over Dubai's affairs over the next two decades, assuming the rulership upon his father's death in 1958.

Clandestine resistance to the Al Maktum during the 1950s centered around a National Front (al-Jabha al-Wataniyya),* composed of younger professionals sympathetic to the ideals of Arab nationalism. Support for this organization came from dissident members of the Al Maktum, and perhaps from Saudi Arabia as well.

Great Britain's announcement in 1968 that it intended to withdraw from the Gulf precipitated almost three years of intense negotiations among the smaller principalities concerning the shape of subsequent political arrangements in the region. When Bahrain and Qatar opted to declare their independence at the end of 1971, the remaining amirates merged to form a federation with the ruler of Abu Dhabi, Shaykh Zaid bin Sultan Al Nuhayyan, serving as president and Shaykh Rashid of Dubai as vice president. Disagreement between these two over the amount of control each member state would cede to the federal administration led to Shaykh Rashid's accepting the position of prime minister in 1979 in return for his acquiescing in a strengthened union.

According to the provisional constitution of 1971, a forty-member Federal National Council (al-Majlis al-Watani al-Ittihadi) is authorized to debate, approve, or amend draft laws for the federation, although the president may enact legislation despite objections from the council. Seats are distributed in accordance with the relative power of the various amirates: Abu Dhabi and Dubai each hold eight; Sharjah and Ras al-Khayma, six; and the rest, four. Members are appointed by the rulers of the respective constituencies. With the collapse of world oil prices after 1986 and the cloud of fiscal difficulty rising over the federation, debate in the council grew more heated. Deputies nevertheless express their opinions as individuals, and political parties continue to be prohibited by the draft constitution.

In the early 1980s, several isolated acts of sabotage were carried out against federal institutions by a clandestine group calling itself the Arab Revolutionary Brigades.* A spokesperson for this organization claimed responsibility for the crash of a Gulf Air airliner in September 1983, in retaliation for "fascist measures adopted by certain persons in power" against expatriates residing in the UAE, "especially Palestinians." Subsequent attacks were attributed by the authorities to underground groups allied to Syrian and Palestinian dissidents. As a way of combating such organizations, the UAE central administration set up a federal security agency in mid-1989. Plans to abolish all unlicensed community associations in the amirates were announced by the federal ministry of labor and social affairs in January 1991.

## Bibliography

Allen, Calvin H., Jr. Oman: The Modernization of the Sultanate. Boulder, Colo.: Westview Press, 1987.

Buchan, James. "Secular and Religious Opposition in Saudi Arabia." In State, Society and Economy in Saudi Arabia, edited by Tim Niblock. London: Croom Helm, 1982.

Crystal, Jill. Oil and Politics in the Gulf: Rulers and Merchants in Kuwait and Qatar. Cambridge, England: Cambridge University Press, 1990.

Dekmejian, R. Hrair. Islam in Revolution. Syracuse, N.Y.: Syracuse University Press, 1985.

Eickelman, Dale F. "Kings and People: Oman's State Consultative Council." Middle East Journal 38, 1 (Winter 1984) 51–72.

Gavrielides, Nicolas. "Tribal Democracy: The Anatomy of Parliamentary Elections in Kuwait." In Elections in the Middle East, edited by Linda Layne, 153–213. Boulder, Colo.: Westview Press, 1987.

Halliday, Fred. Arabia without Sultans. Harmondsworth, England: Penguin, 1974.

Kechichian, Joseph A. "Islamic Revivalism and Change in Saudi Arabia." The Muslim World 80, 1 (January 1990) 1–16.

Lackner, Helen. A House Built on Sand. London: Ithaca Press, 1978.

Lawson, Fred H. Bahrain: The Modernization of Autocracy. Boulder, Colo.: Westview Press, 1989.

Nakhleh, Emile A. *Bahrain*. Lexington, Mass.: D. C. Heath, 1976.
Peterson, J. E. *The Arab Gulf States: Steps toward Political Participation*. New York: Praeger, 1988.
Said Zahlan, Rosemarie. *The Making of the Modern Gulf States*. London: Unwin Hyman, 1989.

## Political Parties

ANSAR AL-DA'WA. *See* SUPPORTERS OF THE CALL.

ARAB REVOLUTIONARY BRIGADES. This clandestine political organization was active in the United Arab Emirates in the early 1980s. Members launched a series of attacks on government installations in response to alleged mistreatment of Palestinians and other Arab expatriates residing in the UAE.

BAHRAIN NATIONAL CONGRESS. This group of prominent Sunnis in Bahrain banded together in 1923 to demand an end to British interference in the country's internal affairs, the restoration of the ruler, and the creation of an advisory council to assist him.

BROTHERHOOD (*Ikhwan*). These militant disciples of the Wahhabi theologian, Muhammad bin 'Abd al-Wahhab, constituted the military formations used by 'Abd al-'Aziz bin Sa'ud Al Sa'ud to create the Kingdom of Saudi Arabia during the 1920s. Suppressed by the government of the new state in the mid-1930s, they provided the inspiration for contemporary proponents of strict social and cultural practices in the kingdom, who resurrected the movement under its old name in the early 1990s.

THE CALL (*Al-Da 'wa*). This underground Shi'ite political organization was active in Kuwait and the eastern province of Saudi Arabia during the late 1970s and early 1980s. Its program called for the overthrow of the existing regimes in these two states and their replacement with Islamic republics modeled on the Islamic Republic of Iran. Although founded by a revered leader of the Iraqi Shi'ites, the organization became more closely identified with Iran following the revolution of 1978–79. Its cells were largely broken up by the two countries' security services in the early 1980s, but signs that it continued to attract at least some degree of popular support appeared in Saudi Arabia at the beginning of 1992.

AL-DA'WA. *See* THE CALL.

DEMOCRATIC BLOC. This informal grouping of liberal representatives within the Kuwaiti National Assembly coalesced after the elections of February 1985 and continued to push for the restoration of parliament throughout the decade.

DHOFAR LIBERATION FRONT. This organization of opponents of the regime of Sultan Sa'id bin Taimur in Oman was formed in June 1965. The Front's platform called for independence for the southern province of Dhofar.

HERITAGE REVIVAL SOCIETY (Jam'iyya Ihya al-Turath). This Sunni Islamist organization, active in Kuwait during the mid-1980s, pursued a generally quietist political platform emphasizing social reforms.

HIJAZI LIBERATION PARTY (Hizb al-Tahrir al-Hijazi). This party was formed in the early 1930s to oppose the domination of the Al Sa'ud over the cities of al-Hijaz in western Arabia. Supported primarily by townspeople, it organized a revolt of bedouin tribes in the northern marches of the province in 1932 which was quickly suppressed by forces loyal to the Al Sa'ud.

HIZB AL-TAHRIR AL-HIJAZI. See HIJAZI LIBERATION PARTY.

HIZBULLAH. This Shi'ite political organization was founded in Lebanon in the late 1970s and began orchestrating demonstrations in the predominantly Shi'ite eastern province of Saudi Arabia at the end of the 1980s.

IAO. See ISLAMIC ACTION ORGANIZATION.

IFLB. See ISLAMIC FRONT FOR THE LIBERATION OF BAHRAIN.

AL-IKHWAN. See BROTHERHOOD.

IKHWAN AL-MUSLIMIN. See MUSLIM BROTHERHOOD.

ISLAMIC ACTION ORGANIZATION (IAO) (Munadhdhama al-Amal al-Islami). This Shi'ite political organization was active in Bahrain during the late 1970s and 1980s. Its platform called for the radical transformation of the local social and economic order.

ISLAMIC FRONT FOR THE LIBERATION OF BAHRAIN (IFLB) (Jabha al-Islamiyya lil-Tahrir al-Bahrain). This Shi'ite political organization was active in Bahrain during the late 1970s and 1980s. Their platform called for radical changes in the country's social and economic structure.

ISLAMIC REVOLUTIONARY ORGANIZATION OF THE ARABIAN PEN-INSULA. This clandestine Shi'ite political organization was active in the eastern province of Saudi Arabia in the months following the Iranian revolution of 1978–79.

JABHA AL-ISLAMIYYA LIL-TAHRIR AL-BAHRAIN. *See* ISLAMIC FRONT FOR THE LIBERATION OF BAHRAIN.

AL-JABHA AL-WATANIYYA. *See* NATIONAL FRONT.

JAM'IYYA IHYA AL-TURATH. *See* HERITAGE REVIVAL SOCIETY.

JAM'IYYA AL-ISLAH AL-IJTIMA'IYYAH. *See* SOCIAL REFORM SOCIETY.

AL-JAMI'A AL-THAQAFIYYA AL-IJTIMA'IYYA. *See* SOCIAL CULTURAL SOCIETY.

JAM'IYYA AL-ISLAH AL-IJTIMA'IYYA. *See* SOCIETY FOR SOCIAL REFORM.

KDL. *See* KUWAITI DEMOCRATIC LEAGUE.

KUWAIT DEMOCRATIC YOUTH. This communist organization, set up in Kuwait during the early 1950s, drew its support primarily from the expatriate Iraqi and Iranian communities.

KUWAITI DEMOCRATIC LEAGUE (KDL). This worker-based political organization was formed in Kuwait during the early 1950s.

LIBERATION PARTY OF THE PENINSULA. This clandestine Shi'ite political organization was active in the eastern province of Saudi Arabia in the months following the Iranian revolution of 1978–79.

MAN. *See* MOVEMENT OF ARAB NATIONALISTS.

MOVEMENT OF ARAB NATIONALISTS (MAN). This political organization was founded in Beirut in 1951–52 under the leadership of the Palestinian George Habash and the Kuwaiti Ahmad al-Khatib. The primary objective of the movement was to unite all Arab states in support of Palestinian rights, as a first step toward transforming existing political and economic orders throughout the Middle East. MAN activists were instrumental in setting up a wide range of radical political movements in virtually all the Arab Gulf states throughout the 1960s and 1970s. (*See also* chapters on Jordan and the Palestinians.)

MUHADHDHAMA AL-AMAL AL-ISLAMI. *See* ISLAMIC ACTION ORGANIZATION.

MUSLIM BROTHERHOOD (*Ikhwan al-Muslimin*). This Sunni Islamist organ-ization was founded in Egypt in 1928. Offshoots spread throughout the Gulf as Egyptian teachers and professionals took up residence in the region during the 1950s. It served as the inspiration for the reformist Islamist movements that emerged in the Arab Gulf states in the 1970s and 1980s, particularly those of Kuwait, but it is completely unrelated to the indigenous Ikhwan of Saudi Arabia. (*See also* chapter on Egypt.)

NATIONAL BLOC. This political organization was formed in Kuwait in 1938 to support the objectives of the liberal reform movement and to engender a sense of nationalism in the local population. The fourteen-member council elected by the Bloc was at first recognized as a National Advisory Assembly but was then forcibly dissolved by the ruler.

NATIONAL CENTER GROUP. This informal grouping of bedouin represen-tatives within the Kuwaiti National Assembly coalesced after the elections of February 1985.

NATIONAL DEMOCRATIC FRONT FOR THE LIBERATION OF OMAN AND THE ARAB GULF (NDFLOAG). This guerrilla organization was formed in northern Oman at the end of the 1960s, following the initial successes of the Popular Front for the Liberation of the Occupied Arab Gulf* in the southern province of Dhofar. The establishment of this front convinced critics of Sultan Sa'id bin Taimur within the Omani regime that he should be replaced by his son, Qabus. In the face of concerted counterattacks by government troops, the NDFLOAG merged with the Popular Front for the Liberation of the Occupied Arab Gulf to form the Popular Front for the Liberation of Oman and the Arab Gulf (PFLOAG)* in 1971.

NATIONAL FRONT (*al-Jabha al-Wataniyya*). The members of this clandestine grouping of younger professionals in Dubai (now the United Arab Emirates), in the 1950s, advocated a broadly Arab nationalist program in foreign and domestic affairs.

NATIONAL LIBERATION FRONT. The platform of this clandestine political organization in Saudi Arabia espouses a broadly Marxist-Leninist political pro-gram.

NATIONAL LIBERATION FRONT—BAHRAIN (NLFB). This political or-ganization was formed in Bahrain in the mid-1950s to push for radical changes in local politics, including the legalization of trade unions and limits on the prerogatives of the Al Khalifa.

NATIONAL UNITY FRONT. This informal grouping of Qatari notables, oil workers, and dissident members of the Al Thani formed in the spring of 1963 to demand stricter limits on the prerogatives of the ruler, the Qatarization of the labor force, and the right to form trade unions.

NDFLOAG. See NATIONAL DEMOCRATIC FRONT FOR THE LIBERATION OF OMAN AND THE ARAB GULF.

NLFB. See NATIONAL LIBERATION FRONT—BAHRAIN.

OMAN REVOLUTIONARY MOVEMENT (ORM). Formed during the mid-1950s, this organization was made up of Omani laborers working in Saudi Arabia. Units of the ORM attempted to overthrow the regime of Sultan Sa'id bin Taimur by force in 1957.

ORM. See OMAN REVOLUTIONARY MOVEMENT.

PEOPLE'S BLOC. This informal grouping of liberal representatives in the Bahraini National Assembly was active during the mid-1970s.

PFLOAG. See POPULAR FRONT FOR THE LIBERATION OF OMAN AND THE ARAB GULF.

POPULAR DEMOCRATIC PARTY. This clandestine organization of Saudi leftists was formed in 1970 by activists associated with the Movement of Arab Nationalists (MAN)* and the Arab Socialist Ba'th Party. The party's platform advocated armed struggle to overthrow the Al Sa'ud and the implementation of central planning to promote greater equity in the local economic order.

POPULAR FRONT FOR THE LIBERATION OF OMAN. This militant offshoot of the Popular Front for the Liberation of Oman and the Arab Gulf (PFLOAG)* was formed in May 1974 to continue armed struggle against the regime of Sultan Qabus bin Sa'id in the southern Omani province of Dhofar.

POPULAR FRONT FOR THE LIBERATION OF OMAN AND THE ARAB GULF (PFLOAG). This political organization was formed in Oman in 1970 as a result of the merger of the Popular Front for the Liberation of the Occupied Arab Gulf* and the National Democratic Front for the Liberation of Oman and the Arab Gulf (NDFLOAG).* Its cadres carried out a program of armed struggle to overthrow Sultan Qabus bin Sa'id until they were defeated by Omani, British, and Iranian forces in the mid-1970s.

POPULAR FRONT FOR THE LIBERATION OF THE OCCUPIED ARAB GULF. This radical offshoot of the Dhofar Liberation Front in Oman was organized in September 1968. The movement cultivated ties to the People's Republic of China, the Soviet Union, and Iraq, and it carried out a campaign of guerrilla warfare against government forces and petroleum installations during the next two years.

RELIGIOUS BLOC. An informal grouping of Shi'ite representatives in the Bahraini National Assembly, it was active during the mid-1970s.

REPRESENTATIVES OF THE PEOPLE. This clandestine political organization was active in Bahrain following the suppression of the reform movement of 1938.

SECRET LABOR UNION. This clandestine political organization was active in Bahrain following the suppression of the reform movement of 1938.

AL-SHABIBA. This organization of Kuwaiti expatriates was formed in Iraq in 1938 to support demands for a constitution, a popular assembly, and other restraints on the power of the ruling Al Sabah.

SOCIAL CULTURAL SOCIETY (al-Jam'iyya al-Thaqafiyya al-Ijtima'iyya). This Shi'ite Islamist organization was active in Kuwait during the mid-1980s. Its platform was broadly critical of the regime.

SOCIAL REFORM SOCIETY (Jam'iyya al-Islah al-Ijtima'iyya). This Sunni Islamist organization was active in Kuwait during the mid-1980s. Advocating a moderate reformist platform, it grew out of the Ikhwan al-Muslimin* sometime during the 1960s.

SOCIETY FOR SOCIAL REFORM (Jam'iyya al-Islah al-Ijtima'iyya). This Sunni Islamist organization was active in Bahrain during the mid-1970s and 1980s. It called for moderate social and economic reforms.

SOCIETY FOR THE LIBERATION OF THE HOLY SOIL. This clandestine political organization was active in Saudi Arabia during the mid-1960s. Its members carried out armed attacks on government installations and facilities of the Arabian-American Oil Company.

SOCIETY OF FREE YOUTH. This clandestine political organization was active in Bahrain following the suppression of the reform movement of 1938.

SONS OF THE ARABIAN PENINSULA. This clandestine political organization grew out of the Workers' Committee in Saudi Arabia in the late 1950s.

SUPPORTERS OF THE CALL (*Ansar al-Da'wa*). This Sunni Islamist organization was active in Bahrain during the mid-1970s and 1980s. Its platform advocated moderate social and economic reforms.

UNION CLUB. Set up in Kuwait in the mid-1950s, this social organization drew its support largely from the expatriate Syrian community.

UNION OF THE PEOPLE OF THE ARABIAN PENINSULA. This clandestine political organization was active in Saudi Arabia during the 1960s and 1970s. Its platform called for the overthrow of the Al Sa'ud and its replacement by a Nasserist regime committed to economic reform and a foreign policy congruent with the principles of Arab nationalism.

WORKERS' COMMITTEE. This clandestine political organization in the eastern province of Saudi Arabia was formed by militant oil workers in the mid-1950s to press demands for radical changes in the local social and economic order.

Fred H. Lawson

# EGYPT

Political parties in Egypt, in the sense of formal organizations dedicated to influencing the course of politics, have emerged over the last century. During that period, the Egyptian political system has undergone radical change several times. Before 1882, Egypt, though technically an Ottoman province, was autonomous in domestic affairs and led by a hereditary governor (*khedive*). In the late 1870s a nationalist movement arose challenging foreign influence and ultimately the khedive himself. Great Britain occupied the country in 1882, though Egypt remained an autonomous Ottoman province until 1914 when a protectorate was declared. A nationalist uprising after World War I led Britain to declare Egypt independent in 1922 (although the British role in politics remained fairly strong until the 1950s). A 1923 constitution provided for a strong monarchy but also a popularly elected parliament and remained in effect, with some interruptions, until 1952. In July of that year an army group, calling itself the Free Officers, seized power in a bloodless coup. One of the leading Free Officers, Gamal Abdel Nasser, had emerged by 1954 as the country's sole leader. Anwar al-Sadat, another Free Officer, became president upon Nasser's death in 1970. Under both Nasser and Sadat, Egypt was ruled from the presidency with little challenge from other organs of government. Sadat took uncertain steps in the direction of political liberalization. His successor, Husni Mubarak, who assumed the presidency after Sadat's assassination in 1981, has moved more boldly to liberalize political life, though he has stopped far short of allowing meaningful competition over his office.

Over this sometimes turbulent century, two generalizations can be made about the nature of party life in Egypt. First, political parties have usually been creatures of the political system under which they have operated. Few parties have survived longer than the system under which they were born. Some, such as the palace parties of the 1920s and 1930s—the Unionist Party* and the People's Party*— or the four parties formed by Nasser and Sadat—the Liberation Rally,* the National Union,* the Arab Socialist Union (ASU),* and the National Democratic Party (NDP)*—have been created by the regime itself. All of these parties (except the NDP, the most recent creation) disappeared after the regime lost its use for them. Other political parties emerged under circumstances created by the political system and existed only to influence politics under that system (for example, the Umma Party* under the British occupation or the Liberal Constitutionalist Party* under the 1923 constitution). Two notable exceptions to this rule are the Wafd* and the Muslim Brotherhood.* The Wafd emerged in the nationalist uprising of 1919 and thus predated the 1923 constitution. It disappeared shortly after the 1952 coup (though not without an admittedly ineffectual struggle) but reemerged in 1977. The Muslim Brotherhood arose in the late 1920s and 1930s. Following a formal ban on its activities in 1948, the Brotherhood has been either tolerated or suppressed by those in power. The Wafd and the Brotherhood aside, party organizations in Egypt have generally been weak and party loyalties malleable. As a result, Egypt's experience with parties has varied radically according to the prevailing political system.

The second generalization that has held throughout the history of political parties in modern Egypt is the aversion of the country's rulers (and many parties as well) to the idea of partisanship. The ideal of national unity has been powerful enough to politically active Egyptians, and loyalty to the regime sufficiently important to most rulers, that even the label of political party (hizb) has often been avoided in favor of more inclusive terms. While the Egyptian experience with political parties is fairly rich by Middle Eastern standards, party and government leaders have preferred terms with more universal, less divisive connotations. This has been notable from the beginning of Egypt's history of modern parties. The group of like-minded political leaders who called themselves the "Nationalist Party" (al-Hizb al-Watani)* in 1881, to oppose foreign influence and pressure the khedive, accepted the party label. The following year, when they found themselves involved in rebellion against the khedive and war against Britain, some internal documents suggest that rural leaders preferred the more inclusive term of the Party of God (Hizbullah). The Wafd eschewed the party label, viewing itself not as a political party but as the organized expression of Egyptian nationalism. Other parties found this perspective arrogant, but electoral results often supported the Wafd's self-image. Even today, Wafdist leaders who have accepted the title of political party (Hizb al-Wafd al-Jadid) and have obtained a small but significant share of the vote, will claim that Wafdists number 55 million (that is, the entire population of the country). The Muslim Brotherhood has similarly eschewed the party label even when it has attempted (in vain) to register as a political party, claiming that it represents all righteous Muslims rather than a political tendency. None of the organizations founded under Nasser (Liberation Rally, National Union, and Arab Socialist Union) deigned to accept the term "party." However, events over the past decade and a half have begun to make the term more respectable. The idea of a single mass organization seems discredited, and the political parties law of 1977 legitimates the party concept. Yet there remains a historically rooted discomfort with the concept of a political party, as it has sometimes seemed to many Egyptians to be a structure that divides the society. Without consensus on some basic questions—such as Egypt's identity and the proper political system for the country—many organizations have claimed that there are broader goals that should go beyond partisanship. While these organizations have effectively operated as parties, they have preferred to see themselves as expressing the will of the entire society.

Yet if parties have been weak organizations, and the very concept of partisanship questionable, Egypt has still passed through periods when very lively party systems have emerged, and it now seems on the verge of another such period. In general, viable parliamentary activity has been required for political parties to flourish. The phases of party life, then, correspond closely to the nature of the prevailing political system.

## ELITE PARTIES (UNTIL 1919)

The political parties that formed under the British occupation consisted of like-minded members of Egypt's political elite. Quasi-parliamentary bodies did operate during the period, but their powers were sufficiently restricted that the political parties showed little interest in transforming themselves into electoral organizations. Nor did they develop into mass movements, although the Nationalist Party did command enough support among students to be able to organize demonstrations. Indeed, without a viable parliamentary structure or widespread literacy, such parties rarely had much influence outside of official and professional circles. Instead they remained loose structures uniting prominent individuals who had similar positions on the issues of the day. The most salient issues during the period revolved around the British occupation, Egypt's relationship with the Ottoman Empire, and matters of internal government. Social issues, such as education and the position of women, could also become topics of lively debate.

Given this orientation, it is not surprising that the parties of the period expressed themselves primarily through newspapers. Indeed, the parties were largely born as newspapers. The Nationalist Party grew out of the daily al-Liwa, edited by Mustafa Kamil. It remained staunchly opposed to British rule and sympathetic to the Ottoman Empire. In 1907 Ahmad Lutfi al-Sayyid began publishing al-Jarida, which brought the Umma Party into being. Indeed it was the formation of the Umma Party that inspired the Nationalist Party to convert from an informal grouping to an official organization. The Umma Party was less favorably inclined toward the Ottoman Empire than the Nationalist Party, and it had the reputation of being more accommodationist with the British. Unlike the Umma Party (some of which was absorbed by the Wafd), the Nationalist Party did survive beyond the 1919 uprising. Yet the mantle of nationalist leadership had passed to the Wafd.

## EGYPT'S LIBERAL PERIOD (1919–52)

With the 1919 uprising, a dramatic new mass political organization appeared: the Wafd. The Wafd, though formed to demand representation at the Versailles Peace Conference, claimed to be deputized by the nation as a whole. Its founders, led by Sa'd Zaghlul, saw themselves as the legitimate political leaders of the nation. Other political organizations were treated by the Wafd with disdain and at first received little support. The Wafd commanded the support of student groups, incipient trade unions, and professional associations. Even after the enthusiasm of 1919 had subsided, the Wafd could still produce impressive demonstrations.

With the promulgation of the 1923 constitution, the focus of party activity shifted somewhat from the streets to the parliament. Accordingly, the Wafd made the transition to an electoral party effortlessly and dominated the next three decades of party life in Egypt. The first parliamentary elections, held in 1924, provided for a two-stage process by which voters would select electors who would in turn select the members of parliament. Such a system seemed stacked against the Wafd. Direct elections would clearly result in a tremendous Wafdist victory. With the two-stage system, however, the government in power and the palace could bring pressure to bear on the electors far more easily than they could sway the entire population. In spite of this system, the Wafd won a victory in the 1924 elections; it used its parliamentary majority to legislate a system of direct elections to parliament.

Despite the Wafd's dominance, three other sorts of parties did form. First, splinter groups from the Wafd formed over particularly contentious issues. The Liberal Constitutionalist Party, the Sa'dist Organization,* and the Wafdist Bloc* were all formed by dissident Wafdists.

Second, the palace, jealous of the influence of the Wafd, inspired other parties to form. The Unionist and People's parties fall into this category. Both came during periods when the palace was attempting to assert more direct control over the governing of the country. In order to bring these parties to power, however, it had to bend or suspend constitutional rule and rig elections. On two occasions, the two-stage election process was restored to make it easier to defeat the Wafd. The success of such efforts was generally real but short lived.

Third, other political parties formed, especially toward the end of the period. These parties cared much less for electoral competition and aimed instead at building popular movements. The Muslim Brotherhood and Young Egypt* were the two most prominent examples; Marxist movements also gained in significance toward the end of the period. While both the Muslim Brotherhood and Young Egypt did each enter the parliamentary election battle on one occasion, their true challenge to the domination of the Wafd lay in the streets and particularly with students and other youth. In the late 1940s, these movements grew increasingly radical in their politics and bold in their actions.

Thus only the Wafd had a sufficiently widespread popular following to compete effectively in national elections. Other parties could win seats, but splinter parties and palace parties could not rely on free elections to bring them to power. They could come to power by electoral manipulation or by palace intervention and were thus far from politically irrelevant. Yet even as the Wafd's share of the vote slowly but steadily declined, none emerged as an effective electoral alternative. The rejectionist parties, such as the Muslim Brotherhood, did not represent an electoral alternative either, but they could similarly influence politics through other methods. They tended to rely on rallies, demonstrations, and party publications. With the growing politicization of the urban population and with increased education and literacy, these methods were beginning to bring some successes by the late 1940s.

## NASSERIST EGYPT (1952–77)

The Free Officers mounted their coup in July 1952 without a clear consensus as to how to restructure the political system. Most pre-coup political parties remained fairly wary of the Free Officers but hoped to use the collapse of the monarchy to further their position. A few movements—most notably the Muslim Brotherhood and the Democratic Movement for National Liberation,* a Marxist group—even had established links with some of the Free Officers before the coup. Yet most parties, despite their hopes, soon demonstrated their impotence. The Wafd had been slowly losing legitimacy and voters before the coup; when the new regime put several leaders on trial for corruption, the party found that it could no longer depend on enthusiastic popular support. The extremist political movements, including the Muslim Brotherhood, demonstrated with their activities the extent to which the pre-coup political system had lost legitimacy, but none could marshall the support necessary to challenge the regime. In January 1953 the Free Officers banned political parties, after having pursued the idea of reform of the party system for six months. The parties put up little resistance until the following spring. At that time Muhammad Nagib, the titular leader of the Free Officers, and Nasser, the most influential member of the group, engaged in a protracted conflict. Nagib, who had come to favor an earlier return to constitutional life, attracted the support of many of the pre-coup parties. His decisive defeat by Nasser sealed the parties' fate.

The ease with which the Free Officers disbanded the parties can be taken as a sign of their weakness. In rural areas only notables had shown much interest in party politics. Such individuals often depended on access to government officials and were in no position to defend the endangered parties. In urban areas the Free Officers had easily co-opted and outmaneuvered the parties. Yet if the parties were weak, they did not disappear without a trace. The Wafd and Muslim Brotherhood reemerged later, and strong traces of Young Egypt can be seen in the Socialist Labor Party,* operating since 1978.

Having abolished the existing party system, Egypt's new rulers established a series of organizations that were granted the exclusive right of political organization. None of the three—the Liberation Rally, the National Union, or the Arab Socialist Union—was called a "party," but all three were assigned the task of organizing Egyptians politically. Election to parliament generally followed screening of candidates by these parties. All other political parties were banned throughout the period.

All three regime parties had several additional tasks beyond the electoral function. First, they were all designed to monopolize the political field and preempt other parties. Membership in other political organizations was treated as opposition to the regime if not to the state. Egyptians with aspirations for public office or access to government resources often had to work through the regime parties. All three organizations, especially the Arab Socialist Union, were also notable for their domination of professional associations and trade unions.

Second, the regime parties exercised control over those Egyptians who wished to participate in politics. Party ownership of newspapers, for instance, meant that journalists who deviated from official policy could be disciplined. Crude censorship, though sometimes practiced, was thus often superfluous. Similarly, party control of formal associations made it possible to be less obvious and heavy-handed in discouraging dissent.

Finally, all three regime parties were used to mobilize popular support for the regime. They did so through organization of demonstrations, turning out the vote at elections, and molding public opinion. These tasks were facilitated by the National Union's and the Arab Socialist Union's ownership of all of Egypt's daily newspapers. Created to support the policies of a regime that sometimes shifted course dramatically, all three organizations were deprived of a strong ideological focus. Supporting national unity and supporting the government were generally deemed synonymous, but the particular policies favored by the parties were dictated by those who held top positions in the government. Only the Arab Socialist Union managed to stake out some claims to a distinct ideology; its "Arab socialism" was often vague but not vacuous. The ideological nature of the ASU meant that the party went beyond merely supporting the regime to cementing its commitment to equity, public ownership, and Arab nationalism. When the regime scaled back its commitment to these goals under Sadat, the Arab Socialist Union was vitiated and eventually abandoned.

## CONTROLLED LIBERALISM (1977–PRESENT)

Upon coming to power after Nasser's death in 1970, Sadat began a slow process of revising and sometimes even abandoning many of Nasser's policies. In foreign policy, Sadat gradually reoriented the country away from the Soviet Union and toward the United States. In 1978 he negotiated a peace agreement with Israel at the U.S. presidential retreat, Camp David. In economic policy, Sadat moved uncertainly towards liberalization. He also presided over a gradual and uneven political liberalization. These policy shifts all dictated a reassessment and eventual abandonment of the Arab Socialist Union. In its place, Sadat allowed a strictly controlled multiparty system to emerge.

The first stage in this process came in the mid-1970s when a rather freewheeling debate emerged among leading figures in the regime, the ASU, and the press about the proper direction for the country's sole party. The chairman of the ASU's Executive Committee at that time was Rif'at Mahjub, a figure who loyally served Nasser, Sadat, and Mubarak in various capacities. With party unity breaking down under the force of the debate, Mahjub (with license from Sadat) allowed various platforms to form within the party in 1975. These platforms represented the left, center, right, and Nasserist wings of the party. The Nasserist wing never emerged beyond this stage, but the other three platforms ran competitive slates in the 1976 parliamentary elections. The center platform, which eventually evolved into the National Democratic Party, won the 1976 (and every subsequent) election handily. Egypt then had a competitive party system in everything but name.

In May 1977 a law on political parties was promulgated that formally ended Egypt's experience with one-party systems. Under the new law, the three platforms of the ASU were allowed to form into political parties. New parties could join them, so long as they met specific conditions. The most important of these conditions barred parties that formed on religious grounds, that duplicated the principles of existing parties, or that challenged the constitution or the basic policies of the regime. A Committee on Parties was established, with representation from the judiciary and the cabinet, to review the applications of would-be parties.

The new party system gave a significant opening to new parties; it also left the regime substantial weapons to use against parties that it wished to obstruct. The Muslim Brotherhood was banned on the grounds that it was a religious party. The New Wafd Party* succeeded in meeting the conditions of the law in 1977, but complained several months later that official harassment forced it to suspend activities. The left platform, transformed into the National Progressivist Unionist Forum (NPUF),* made similar complaints. Political parties were enjoined from opposition to the peace treaty with Israel. The continuation of the Emergency Law and other legislation gave the government the means to restrict the political liberties of its citizens whenever it desired.

Sadat's purpose seems to have been to construct a loyal opposition. This would bring dissent out into the open where it could be observed. The opposition would be robbed of a common focus for its complaints, and the latent divisions among Marxists, Islamicists, and nationalists would quickly manifest themselves. The ability of these groups to organize a mass following would be sharply restricted. They would be allowed a voice but no influence. Should they become either too strident or too popular, the repressive tools of the regime could be brought to bear once again.

Opposition political parties during this period, then, primarily served as forums both for expressing and containing dissent. Party leaders were aware of (and bitterly resented) this latter function. Some chose to operate under these conditions while protesting them (the Socialist Labor Party); others chose, or were forced, to suspend activities (the Wafd) or operate extralegally (the Muslim Brotherhood).

Since Sadat's assassination, the restrictions on parties have been considerably loosened. The courts have lifted some of the restrictions (most notably the ban on opposition to the Camp David accords) and have overruled the parties committee on numerous occasions. Parties have thus proliferated, although only a few have a notable presence on the political scene. The Muslim Brotherhood and the Nasserists are the only significant political actors that have failed to organize as parties.

The Mubarak government also worked to develop an electoral system that would guarantee the opposition parties a credible showing while preventing them from winning any election. In order to encourage the electoral role of opposition parties, the 1984 and 1987 parliamentary elections were based on the principle of proportional representation. Voters selected among party slates in multimem-ber districts; seats were allocated according to the share of the vote in that district. By attempting to restrict independents and by instituting the propor-tional representation system (by which a party did not need a majority in a district to win some seats), the government made every effort to ensure that those in-clined toward opposition would find the parties the most attractive avenue of political participation. Under the electoral law in effect in 1984, independents were barred from participating, but the Constitutional Court ruled this ban un-constitutional. In 1987, one seat was set aside in each district for which inde-pendents could compete. The Constitutional Court eventually struck down this system as well, forcing the government to abandon party slates in 1990. Subse-quently, the electoral law provided for two-member districts; voters cast ballots for two candidates and those receiving support from a majority of voters win seats in parliament. Runoff elections are held if no two candidates receive majority support.

Yet other electoral features made participation less attractive to the opposi-tion. Urban areas, where the opposition is stronger, are generally underrepre-sented in the parliament. Rural areas, where voters have generally been happy to vote for candidates favored by local officials, dominate the parliament. The government also guarantees National Democratic Party victories by having the administrative machinery to support the party in elections. Opposition parties are so distrustful of the government's administration of elections that they have demanded that the judiciary, rather than the Interior Ministry, take pri-mary responsibility for supervising polling (an idea many judges have en-dorsed). Many opposition parties boycotted the 1990 elections after the government refused these demands.

The opposition also complained that the electoral system retracted some of the benefits of proportional representation by requiring that parties obtain a specified share of the national vote nationally in order to obtain any seats. Similar provisions exist in Israel (with a 1.5 percent threshold), Germany (with a 5 percent threshold), and Turkey (10 percent). When the government proposed a 10 percent threshold in Egypt for the 1984 elections, an outcry from the opposition resulted in a lowering of the barrier to 8 percent. It re-mained at that level in 1987, despite opposition protests. In the 1990 elec-tions, when candidates ran as individuals, there was no longer any place for the threshold.

## EGYPT'S CURRENT PARTY SYSTEM

The Egyptian party system today is somewhat like that of Mexico. A dominant government party, built more on patronage than on principle or popular enthusiasm, possesses an electoral machine capable of winning any election. The dominant party and the state bureaucratic machinery are often intertwined. Opposition parties operate with some freedom, able to publish newspapers and obtain parliamentary representation (though never a majority). Yet, if the opposition parties can make a lot of noise, their influence over policy is at best indirect.

The party of the regime, the National Democratic Party, continues to carry out some of the functions of the single parties of the Nasser years. It turns out the vote for parliamentary elections and referenda. Rather than monopolizing the parliament, its share is restricted to approximately three-quarters of the vote. The NDP also attempts to mobilize public opinion in support of government policies, but its propagandistic arm is so much lighter and less ambitious than those of the Nasserist parties that its presence is hardly noticed.

The legal opposition parties have several functions. Perhaps most important, they serve to bring issues to public consciousness. For this reason, the most significant way in which opposition parties express their political presence is through their newspapers. Coverage of opposition parties and of parliamentary debates is spotty in the government-owned press and broadcast media. Yet opposition groups are given a wide degree of freedom in their own publications. The Wafd's newspaper, the only opposition daily, is particularly widely read. The leftist al-Ahali, published by the National Progressivist Unionist Forum, has readers among the intelligentsia. These and other opposition papers can give a very independent perspective on major issues that counterbalances those found in the government-controlled press. Yet the papers all incline to sensationalism (albeit to different degrees) and may thus undercut their credibility.

Second, opposition parties also serve as electoral parties. That this is, under existing conditions, a secondary function for them is demonstrated by their regular threats to boycott elections. The most significant opposition parties carried out this threat in the 1990 parliamentary elections. In deciding whether to participate in elections, opposition parties have a difficult choice. Entry into the parliament will give them a voice, but it might also imply acceptance of a system that gives them little hope of achieving political power.

Third, opposition parties have attempted to organize the Egyptian population at large. This is where they have realized the least success, however. The major opposition parties do have branches throughout the country. Some (most notably the Wafd) have links with some of the professional associations. The Socialist Labor Party and the National Progressivist Unionist Forum both have cultivated the leaders of Egypt's trade unions. Yet none of the legal parties seems to have attracted an enthusiastic constituency. None has had any sustained success in mounting large rallies (though the government would not look kindly on them if they did).

Yet Egypt's governing National Democratic Party and the various legal opposition parties do not exhaust the political field in Egypt. They are joined by a group of illegal organizations. Primary among them is the Muslim Brotherhood. The Brotherhood might be better regarded as extralegal rather than illegal since it has been officially tolerated under the Mubarak regime. It operates openly and probably commands the widest popular support of any opposition group (with the possible exception of the Wafd). Having failed to obtain court approval to form as a party, members of the Brotherhood have participated in parliamentary elections either on the slates of other parties or as independents. Except for its inability to run candidates on its own slate, the Brotherhood essentially operates like the legal opposition parties.

Less tolerated opposition groups include the radical Islamic opposition and Marxist groups. The small role that such groups have played under the Mubarak regime is testimony to the success of the legal party system. Those who reject the prevailing political system are given certain outlets where their activities are tolerated. Some refuse to take advantage of these legal opportunities, aware that they offer little likelihood of effecting meaningful political change. Yet the option of participating through one of the legal opposition parties is sufficiently attractive to draw off all but a minority of the potential opposition to the regime.

Yet despite the apparent flourishing of party life in Mubarak's Egypt, even those who pay attention to party politics get involved in them only at election time. Most Egyptians do not even do that much; only a fraction of those eligible actually vote. Egypt's party system is now freer than at any time since 1952, but it remains restricted and elicits little popular enthusiasm.

### Bibliography

Aly, Abdel Monem Said. "Democratization in Egypt." *American Arab Affairs* 22 (Fall 1987): 14–22.

Baker, Raymond William. *Sadat and After: Struggles for Egypt's Political Soul.* Cambridge, Mass.: Harvard University Press, 1990.

Beinen, Joel, and Zachary Lockman. *Workers on the Nile: Nationalism, Communism, Islam, and the Egyptian Working Class, 1882–1954.* Princeton, N.J.: Princeton University Press, 1987.

Berque, Jacques. *Egypt: Imperialism and Revolution,* translated by Jean Stewart. London: Faber and Faber, 1972.

Bianchi, Robert. *Unruly Corporatism. Associational Life in Twentieth-Century Egypt.* Oxford: Oxford University Press, 1989.

Binder, Leonard. *In a Moment of Enthusiasm: Political Power and the Second Stratum in Egypt.* Chicago: University of Chicago Press, 1978.

Botman, Selma. *The Rise of Egyptian Communism.* Syracuse, N.Y.: Syracuse University Press, 1988.

Brown, Nathan. *Peasant Politics in Modern Egypt.* New Haven, Conn.: Yale University Press, 1990.

Deeb, Marius. *Party Politics in Egypt: The Wafd and Its Rivals 1919–1939*. London: Ithaca Press, 1979.

Goldschmidt, Arthur, Jr. "The Egyptian Nationalist Party: 1892–1919." In *Political and Social Change in Modern Egypt*, edited by P. M. Holt. London: Oxford University Press, 1968.

Gordon, Joel. *Nasser's Blessed Movement: Egypt's Free Officers and the July Revolution*. Oxford: Oxford University Press, 1991.

Ismael, Tareq, and Rifa'at El-Sa'id. *The Communist Movement in Egypt, 1920–1988*. Syracuse, N.Y.: Syracuse University Press, 1990.

Jankowski, James P. *Egypt's Young Rebels, "Young Egypt": 1933–1952*. Stanford, Calif.: Hoover Institution Press, 1975.

Landau, Jacob. *Parliaments and Parties in Egypt*. Tel Aviv: Israel Oriental Society, 1953.

Mitchell, Richard P. *The Society of Muslim Brothers*. London: Oxford University Press, 1969.

Safran, Nadav. *Egypt in Search of Political Community*. Cambridge: Harvard University Press, 1961.

al-Sayyid Marsot, Afaf Lutfi. *Egypt's Liberal Experiment, 1922–1936*. Berkeley: University of California Press, 1977.

———. *A Short History of Modern Egypt*. Cambridge: Cambridge University Press, 1985.

Vatikiotis, P. J. *The History of Egypt*. Baltimore: Johns Hopkins University Press, 1980.

Waterbury, John. *The Egypt of Nasser and Sadat: The Political Economy of Two Regimes*. Princeton, N.J.: Princeton University Press, 1983.

Zayid, Mahmud. "The Origins of the Liberal Constitutionalist Party in Egypt." In *Political and Social Change in Modern Egypt*, edited by P. M. Holt. London: Oxford University Press, 1968.

## Political Parties

ARAB DEMOCRATIC NASSERIST PARTY (*al-Hizb al-'Arabi al-Dimuqrati al-Nasiri*). Sadat's economic liberalization and his peace initiative toward Israel led some Egyptians to conclude that he had betrayed Nasser's legacy. Beginning in the mid-1970s, several groups dedicated to restoring Egypt to the path of Arab nationalism and Arab socialism were formed. Several Nasserist groupings tried to form independent political parties; for many years, none had much success. Rivalries among the groups, organizational difficulties, and the hostility of the Parties Committee all obstructed formation of a party. Some who label themselves Nasserists joined the National Progressivist Unionist Forum (NPUF)*; others gravitated toward the Socialist Labor Party.* Even the tiny Socialist Liberal Party* tried to woo the Nasserists on occasion.

One Nasserist organization, *Thawrat Misr* (Egypt's Revolution), formed and carried out terrorist acts in the 1980s. When its members were apprehended, it became apparent that several of Nasser's relatives, including one of his sons, had been involved. This made the case politically embarrassing to the government, which seemed to dawdle deliberately in prosecuting the group. As the case dragged on, the group obtained support from Ahmad al-Khawaja, the head of the lawyer's syndicate.

In the mid-1980s, some Nasserists published a newspaper which was suppressed by the regime in 1988 amid charges that it had Libyan funding and had attacked some of Egypt's Gulf allies.

Finally, in 1992, a group led by Diya al-Din Dawud won a court case allowing them to establish a legal organization, to be known as the Arab Democratic Nasserist Party. While critics complained that the party's title was an oxymoron (because Nasserism was hardly democratic), party leaders claimed that the organization would accept Egypt's multiparty system.

ARAB SOCIALIST UNION (ASU) (*Ittihad al-'Arabi al-Ishtiraki*). Following the collapse of the union with Syria in 1961, Nasser's regime called for a National Conference of Popular Forces to discuss the proper political, social, and economic course for the country. The conference approved a Charter of National Action in June 1962 that called for the establishment of a single political organization, the Arab Socialist Union, to lead the country. Egypt's leaders once again showed their aversion to the idea of partisanship, claiming that the new organization was to represent all those who had the nation's true interests at heart.

Besides eschewing the term party, the ASU's title also ratified two broad and ambitious initiatives undertaken by the regime: pan-Arabism and socialism. The pursuit of Arab unity had been elevated to a high priority by the regime after the Suez crisis of 1956 and the formation of the United Arab Republic with Syria in 1958. The collapse of the union in 1961 diminished the regime's enthusiasm for pan-Arabism, but not its rhetorical commitment. The ASU itself was emulated in Iraq, Libya, and Sudan. Socialism gained prominence as the regime nationalized the holdings of foreigners and political enemies in the 1950s; in 1961, the nationalizations were extended to entire sectors of the economy, such as banking and international trade. The Arab Socialist Union was thus created to further policy directions on which the regime had already embarked; as with the Liberation Rally* and the National Union,* the policies created the party rather than the other way around. Yet since the regime had defined its course more precisely by the early 1960s, the ASU took on a much more ideological tone than its predecessors.

The ASU also surpassed its two predecessors in organizational capacity and influence. Like the National Union, it controlled the press. Membership in the ASU was supposed to be more restricted than the National Union, but since many influential positions were reserved for ASU members, the ranks soon swelled. The Arab Socialist Union also established a strong presence in the professional syndicates, and representation in both the ASU and the ASU-monopolized parliament was by occupation as well as residence. One half of all seats in elected organs were set aside for workers and peasants, although the definitions of these categories remained fairly broad. These features gave the ASU a strongly corporatist flavor. The ASU's domination of the political landscape in Egypt was nearly complete. In 1968 the judiciary, a holdout from the organization, voted to reject group membership in the ASU. The following year, those judges voting against membership were dismissed.

Leaders of the ASU worried that although such actions made the organization ubiquitous they also robbed it of cohesiveness. Membership seemed to some too universal; the party would be inert if it contained within it so many competing interests and groups. Accordingly a "vanguard" organization within the ASU was established. While many leftists had been calling for such a step to allow for radicalization of the organization, in fact leadership of the vanguard was entrusted to mainstream members of the regime. The vanguard organization proved to be a paper tiger as it was easily defeated in struggles within the party.

Husayn Shafi'i, one of the Free Officers, was selected to head the ASU at its inception. In 1965, however, 'Ali Sabri, a former prime minister, took over and proved to be a more dynamic leader. He furthered the leftist drift of the ASU and used his position to emerge as one of the leading figures of the regime. In 1969 he lost his position (though he remained a member of the party executive) after being charged with smuggling on returning from an official visit to the Soviet Union.

Sabri's fall and Nasser's death the following year greatly weakened the political position of the ASU. Sadat owed little to the ASU, and Sabri, still powerful within the party, stood as his chief rival. Sabri led the opposition to defeat against Sadat in a showdown in May 1971. Having watched the ASU turn into a haven for his opponents, Sadat allowed the organization to become increasingly irrelevant. Gradually turning from the pan-Arabism and socialism of the 1960s, Sadat robbed the ASU of its ideological underpinnings. By 1975 he was prepared to weaken the unity of the organization, and several platforms emerged within the ASU. These platforms competed against each other in parliamentary elections in 1976. In 1977 the new parties law allowed these platforms to transform themselves into independent political parties (National Progressivist Unionist Forum,* Socialist Liberal Party,* and eventually the governing National Democratic Party*). Most of the various organizations associated with the Arab Socialist Union were abolished. Little remained of the ASU, and it was abolished in 1980, with its remaining functions (such as ownership of the press) transferred to the Consultative Council, a newly created parliamentary body.

ASU. *See* ARAB SOCIALIST UNION.

BLESSED SOCIALIST PARTY (*al-Hizb al-Ishtiraki al-Mubarak*). The Blessed Socialist Party, established in 1909 by Dr. Hasan Fahmi Jamal al-Din, concerned itself with improving the lot of the poor and the peasants of Egypt. The party was short lived and left few traces.

COMMUNIST PARTY OF EGYPT. *See* EGYPTIAN COMMUNIST PARTY.

CONSTITUTIONAL PARTY (al-Hizb al-Dusturi). The Constitutional Party was established before World War I by Idris Raghib. The party supported a gradual rather than immediate institution of a constitutional regime.

CONSTITUTIONAL REFORM PARTY (Hizb al-Islah 'ala al-Mabadi al-Dusturiyya). Shaykh Ali Yusif established the Constitutional Reform Party on December 9, 1907, in order to defend the khedive against the activities of the Watani (see Nationalist Party*) and Umma Party.* The party supported the constitutional power of the khedive, and it promoted the administrative independence of Egypt. The party, however, never had any real grass-roots support, and in 1911 it became an association.

DEMOCRATIC MOVEMENT FOR NATIONAL LIBERATION. See EGYPTIAN COMMUNIST PARTY.

DEMOCRATIC UNION. See EGYPTIAN COMMUNIST PARTY.

DEMOCRATIC UNIONIST PARTY (Hizb al-Ittihad al-Dimuqrati). The Democratic Unionist Party, formed in 1990, is closely related to the Sudanese party of the same name (see chapter on Sudan). Its major purpose seems to be to organize Sudanese resident in Egypt while Sudan remains under military rule, although it has called for further economic liberalization. The party participated in the 1990 elections but won no seats. It is led by 'Abd al-Mun'im Turk, an Alexandria banker.

EGYPTIAN COMMUNIST PARTY (al-Hizb al-Shuyu'i al-Misri). In 1920 Mahmud Husni al-'Urabi took the lead in founding the Socialist Party of Alexandria Workers. The following year he joined with Jacob Rosenthal, an Italian Jewish labor organizer with Egyptian nationality, to form the Egyptian Socialist Party. Several Egyptian intellectuals with Fabian inclinations were also members, including Salama Musa, Mahmud 'Abd Allah 'Inan, and Mahmud Husni al-'Urabi. The platform of the party included pushing for the establishment of an eight-hour workday, fairer wages for Egyptian workers, a more equitable distribution of land to the peasants, agrarian reform, and the nationalization of many of the large estates in Egypt. They also adopted a nationalist posture against the British. In this regard, they supported the Wafd* in its attempt to remove the British presence from the country. Different ideological trends existed in the party from the beginning.

In 1922 the party associated itself with the Communist International and changed its name to the Egyptian Communist Party. The radicalization of the party led some of the Egyptian intellectuals, including Salama Musa, to leave. The party, then led by al-'Urabi, expelled Rosenthal (perhaps because of his foreign origin or because of tactical differences between him and al-'Urabi).

With its headquarters initially in Cairo, much of the party's activity centered around Alexandria. In July 1922, when the central government closed down the organ of the new party, *al-Shabiba*, it was decided to move the party's headquarters to Alexandria. The party's main concern was labor activity. The leaders of the party were arrested in March 1924 for labor agitation after a series of strikes in Alexandria. The foreign citizenship of many members and sympathizers, and the reluctance of their governments to protect them, made it easier for the Egyptian authorities to move against the party. Official harassment and arrests kept the communist movement dormant from the mid-1920s on.

Party leaders were generally middle class. Many were foreign, and this may have limited the party's appeal. Yet most of the membership was Egyptian, and the party did have some success in organizing labor unions and strikes.

After the suppression of the Egyptian Communist Party, a variety of organizations arose. These organizations, many clandestine, often split and merged, creating a welter that is disentangled only with difficulty. One of the first organizations to emerge was the Union of Peace Partisans (*Ittihad Ansar al-Salam*), formed in 1934 by Paul Jacquot-Descombes. The union recruited a number of middle-class Egyptian intellectuals, some foreigners, and even some disaffected Wafdists, although it never gained a wide following. By the outbreak of World War II, the organization disbanded.

Jacquot-Descombes established a new movement in September 1946, the Popular Vanguard for Liberation, known by its acronym, Tasht (*al-Tali'a al-Sha'biya lil-Taharur*). Other leaders involved in this association included Sadiq Sa'd, Ramon Duwayk, Yusif Darwish, and Ahmad Rushdi Salih. The movement survived the 1952 revolution, but it was swallowed up by other Communist movements in the late 1950s.

The Democratic Union (*al-Ittihad al-Dimuqrati*) was founded in early 1939 by Henri Curiel and Hillel Schwartz in Cairo and Alexandria. The aim of this group was to create a purely Egyptian Marxist movement. Toward this end, it wanted to Egyptianize its leadership, a process that set off conflict among Curiel, Schwartz, and a third leader, Marcel Israel. By 1943, the movement was dissolved, and its various leaders went on to establish other organizations. Marcel Israel went on to establish the People's Liberation Group (*Jama'at Tahrir al-Sha'b*) in 1939. Internal ideological disputes soon arose. In October 1941 the organization came under heavy government repression, and most of its cadres were arrested.

In 1942 a second organization, Iskra, was formed out of the breakup of the Democratic Union. Iskra principally recruited students and intellectuals, though it did attempt to integrate workers into its organization. It worked to instill class consciousness in Egyptian workers through the publication of magazines, the holding of lectures, and the recruitment of students. Its aim was the establishment of a workers' party.

Henri Curiel formed a third organization out of the disintegration of the Democratic Union after he was released from imprisonment in 1943. This organization, the Egyptian Movement for National Liberation (*al-Haraka al-Misriyya* lil-Taharur al-Watani), went by the acronym Hamtu. Curiel viewed the association as a prelude to the establishment of a real communist party. Toward this end, he wanted to create an awareness among Egyptian intellectuals regarding the writings of Marx. He believed that cells should be created among the various social groups within Egypt—peasants, workers, and rural groups. In 1947 the organization, then having between six and seven hundred members, merged with Iskra to form Hadetu (al-Haraka al-Dimuqratiyya lil-Taharrur al-Watani). Other groups, including the much weakened People's Liberation Group, also joined, to give Hadetu a membership numbering 1,600.

Hadetu's efforts concentrated on recruiting and mobilizing students and laborers. It was influential in organizing strikes at Cairo University in 1948. However, the movement soon began to fragment. One of the groups that split off was the Revolutionary Bloc (al-Takattul al-Thawri) led by Shuhdi 'Atiyya al-Shafi'i. Another splinter group, founded by Fu'ad Mursi and Isma'il Sabri 'Abd-Allah, called itself the Communist Party of Egypt (al-Hizb al-Shuyu'i al-Misri).

During the 1940s, as these groups worked to organize labor, students, and peasants, existing inequalities gave them some hope of success; however, personality and ideology caused many splits within the movement. Government repression also created fear within the movements themselves and sapped many of these Marxist groupings of their energy.

When the Free Officers came to power in 1952, Hadetu and other groups had some hope that the new regime would allow them to organize more freely. Cooperation between Marxist groups and the new regime was dealt a severe blow when the regime ordered the execution of the leaders of a strike held at Kafr al-Dawwar two months after the coup. In 1954 the officer with the strongest ties to the Marxist left, Khalid Muhi al-Din, lost out in a showdown among the Free Officers. After that point, Marxist groups operated semiclandestinely. Repression followed throughout much of Nasser's rule. Marxist groups attempted to unify in the face of this repression and succeeded in forming a unified Egyptian Communist Party in 1957, but this organization soon split.

In the 1960s, as the regime pursued a program of widespread nationalization and alignment with the Soviet Union, the divided Communist Party decided to dissolve itself. Members joined the Arab Socialist Union* as individuals. A few, such as Isma'il Sabri 'Abd-Allah and Fuad Mursi, eventually achieved positions of prominence. Suspicions between the regime and the Marxist left continued, even as Marxist intellectuals found that they could publish in official publications.

Under the Sadat regime, these intellectuals generally abandoned their Marxist beliefs or lost the privilege to write in legal publications. The 1970s saw several clandestine attempts to organize communists once again. With passage of the new parties law in 1977, the National Progressivist Unionist Forum (NPUF)* was able to form and garner the support of most of the veterans of the various Marxist organizations that had existed. The NPUF represents the closest that the communist movement has ever approached to constructing an electoral party; even the NPUF, however, is not exclusively communist. The government has continued to suppress all Marxist groups that lie outside of the NPUF.

Some leftist periodicals continue to be published. They attack the regime's foreign policy as excessively accommodationist with Israel and overly reliant on the United States. In domestic policy, they attack the economic liberalization policies of the regime and defend the Nasserist legacy.

EGYPTIAN DEMOCRATIC PARTY (al-Hizb al-Dimuqrati al-Misri). The Egyptian Democratic Party, established in June 1920, had a number of liberal adherents including Mustafa Abd al-Raziq, Mansur Fahmi, and Mahmud 'Azmi. The party supported the independence of Egypt and wanted it free of foreign domination. It supported the reform of the country's educational system. The party supported the activities of the Wafd* in its efforts to secure the independence of Egypt. It broke up in the early 1920s.

EGYPTIAN DEMOCRATIC PEOPLE'S PARTY (Hizb al-Sha'b al-Dimuqrati al-Misri). The Egyptian Democratic People's Party was formed in 1992 by Anwar 'Afifi, an engineer without previous political experience. The party had the support of one member of parliament, Abu al-Fadl al-Jizawi, elected before the party's formation. The party promised that it would operate on a democratic basis internally, but its platform remained very vague. Its founder avoided a clear position with regard to other parties. Its most concrete proposal was to reclaim 40 million acres of land for agriculture over the next forty years, which would increase Egypt's cultivated area approximately sevenfold.

EGYPTIAN MOVEMENT FOR NATIONAL LIBERATION. See EGYPTIAN COMMUNIST PARTY.

EGYPTIAN PARTY (al-Hizb al-Misri). This political party, established in 1908, arose because of differences between the Muslims and Coptic Christians in Egypt. Led by Akhnus Fanus, it called for the liberation of Egypt and the cancellation of the Capitulations (which gave those with foreign citizenship extraterritorial status), but it still supported friendship between Egypt and Britain. The party realized that the British had a strategic interest in maintaining safe passage to India, yet it felt that the independence of Egypt could still be preserved. The party supported the khedive in his policy toward the British. Despite some Christian support, the party soon disappeared from the political scene.

EGYPTIAN SOCIALIST PARTY. See EGYPTIAN COMMUNIST PARTY.

FREE NATIONALIST PARTY (al-Hizb al-Watani al-Hurr). The Free Nationalist Party was established on September 26, 1907, by Muhammad Wahid al-Ayubi. It changed its name to the Party of Free Egyptians in 1908. The party never had much influence in Egyptian party politics since it was dwarfed by the activities of the Umma Party* and Watani (Nationalist Party)*. When Lord Cromer finished his service in Egypt in 1907, the head of the party stirred controversy by sending a letter to an Egyptian newspaper calling for the liberation of Egypt. The party never developed into a strong social or political force.

GREEN PARTY (*Hizb al-Khudr*). The Green Party was formed in 1990 in order to bring environmental issues to the public's attention. The party participated in the 1990 parliamentary elections but won no seats. 'Abd al-Salam Dawud, who helped inspire the party, replaced Hasan Rajab as party leader in March 1992.

HADETU. *See* EGYPTIAN COMMUNIST PARTY.

HAMTU. *See* EGYPTIAN COMMUNIST PARTY.

AL-HAYA AL-SA'DIYYA. *See* SA'DIST ORGANIZATION.

HAYAT AL-TAHRIR. *See* LIBERATION RALLY.

HIZB AL-AHRAR AL-DUSTURIYYIN. *See* LIBERAL CONSTITUTION-ALIST PARTY.

HIZB AL-AHRAR AL-ISHTIRAKI. *See* SOCIALIST LIBERAL PARTY.

HIZB AL-'AMAL AL-ISHTIRAKI. *See* SOCIALIST LABOR PARTY.

AL-HIZB AL-'ARABI AL-DIMUQRATI AL-NASIRI. *See* ARAB DEMO-CRATIC NASSERIST PARTY.

AL-HIZB AL-DIMUQRATI AL-MISRI. *See* EGYPTIAN DEMOCRATIC PARTY.

AL-HIZB AL-DUSTURI. *See* CONSTITUTIONAL PARTY.

HIZB AL-FALLAH AL-IJTIMA'I. *See* SOCIALIST PEASANT PARTY.

HIZB AL-FALLAH AL-ISHTIRAKI. *See* SOCIALIST PEASANT PARTY.

AL-HIZB AL-ISHTIRAKI AL-MUBARAK. *See* BLESSED SOCIALIST PARTY.

HIZB AL-ISLAH 'ALA AL-MABADI AL-DUSTURIYYA. *See* CONSTITU-TIONAL REFORM PARTY.

HIZB AL-ITTIHAD. *See* UNIONIST PARTY.

HIZB AL-ITTIHAD AL-DIMUQRATI. *See* DEMOCRATIC UNIONIST PARTY.

AL-HIZB AL-JUMHURI. *See* REPUBLICAN PARTY.

HIZB AL-KHUDR. *See* GREEN PARTY.

AL-HIZB AL-MISRI. *See* EGYPTIAN PARTY.

HIZB AL-NUBALA. *See* NOBLES' PARTY.

HIZB AL-SHA'B. *See* PEOPLE'S PARTY.

HIZB AL-SHA'B AL-DIMUQRATI AL-MISRI. *See* EGYPTIAN DEMO-CRATIC PEOPLE'S PARTY.

AL-HIZB AL-SHUYU'I AL-MISRI. *See* EGYPTIAN COMMUNIST PARTY.

HIZB AL-TAJAMMU' AL-WATANI AL-TAQADUMMI AL-WIHDAWI. *See* NATIONAL PROGRESSIVIST UNIONIST FORUM.

HIZB AL-UMMA. *See* UMMA PARTY.

HIZB AL-WAFD AL-JADID. *See* WAFD.

AL-HIZB AL-WATANI. *See* NATIONALIST PARTY.

AL-HIZB AL-WATANI AL-DIMUQRATI. *See* NATIONAL DEMOCRATIC PARTY.

AL-HIZB AL-WATANI AL-HURR. *See* FREE NATIONALIST PARTY.

AL-IKHWAN AL-MUSLIMIN. *See* MUSLIM BROTHERHOOD.

ISKRA. *See* EGYPTIAN COMMUNIST PARTY.

ISLAMIC ASSOCIATIONS (*Jama'at Islamiyya*). The radical ideas developed by Sayyid Qutb have been influential among some Islamicists, pushing them beyond the sometimes loyal opposition of the Muslim Brotherhood* to advocacy of revolution. Since these groups have been illegal and frequently clash (often violently) with security forces, they remain somewhat shadowy. The Mubarak government's strategy seemed designed to channel Islamic opposition into the

Muslim Brotherhood, existing political parties, or nonpolitical activities. At times, however, repression of radical groups has not spared more mainstream figures. Many groups do indeed avoid the government rather than oppose it. There are, however, some very radical groups. Knowledge of these underground groups is necessarily limited. The writings of some intellectual figures associated with radical movements have gained some circulation; such writings claim that Egypt's government and even its society are non-Muslim and therefore a legitimate, even mandatory, target for political violence. The actions of radical groups have included attacks on the military academy (1974), often successful assassination attempts on leading government figures (e.g., the Minister of Pious Endowments in 1977, several ministers of the interior in the 1980s and 1990s, the speaker of parliament in 1990), bloody clashes with security forces in Cairo and towns of Upper Egypt, and attacks on videotape stores, police officials, Copts, and foreign tourists. Most of what is known, however, comes from official reports whose reliability is uncertain. Even the names of these groups are subject to dispute; groups termed by the government the Jihad Organization or Those Rescued from Hell have rejected these terms.

The major issues raised by these groups are domestic, related to the claim that the current Egyptian political system is inimical to Islam and must be changed. The nature of their support is difficult to gauge, but their intellectual influence is probably greater than their relatively small numbers would suggest. They have a reputation for militant and uncompromising insistence on adherence to Islamic principles. They seem to have the greatest appeal among students and the middle class, primarily in urban areas—though their presence in provincial towns, especially in Upper Egypt, south of Cairo, has grown.

These groups certainly are not allowed to publish openly, although some of their ideas seep into the legal press, where they are sometimes attacked by more mainstream Islamicist groups. Recent leading radical Islamic figures include Shaykh 'Umar 'Abd al-Rahman (whose alleged involvement with the group accused of the World Trade Center bombing in New York City captured global attention), Hafiz Salama, and Jalal Kishk. One would-be Islamic party, al-Sahwa, headed by Yusif al-Badri, has been unsuccessful in obtaining official sanction. In the 1990s, ties between the radical groups and the Socialist Labor Party grew.

ITTIHAD AL-'ARABI AL-ISHTIRAKI. *See* ARAB SOCIALIST UNION.

AL-ITTIHAD AL-DIMUQRATI. *See* EGYPTIAN COMMUNIST PARTY.

AL-ITTIHAD AL-QAWMI. *See* NATIONAL UNION.

JAMA'AT ISLAMIYYA. *See* ISLAMIC ASSOCIATIONS.

JIHAD ORGANIZATION. *See* ISLAMIC ASSOCIATIONS.

AL-KUTLA AL-WAFDIYYA. *See* WAFDIST BLOC.


LIBERAL CONSTITUTIONALIST PARTY (*Hizb al-Ahrar al-Dusturiyyin*). The Liberal Constitutionalist Party, formed on October 30, 1922, emerged out of a split in the Wafd* over the conduct of negotiations with Great Britain. 'Adli Yakan had formed a political organization called the Society of Independent Egypt to support his delegation to the talks he was holding with Lord Curzon; this organization formed the nucleus of the party. Other prominent members were Muhammad Mahmud, who served as prime minister four times, and Muhammad Husayn Haykal, a prominent writer. The split with the Wafd over how and what to negotiate with the British was bitter. For the Wafd, the Liberal Constitutionalists had usurped the right to represent the nation. For the Liberal Constitutionalists, the Wafd was incapable of respecting dissent.

Yet its enmity with the Wafd did not always lead the party to cooperate with the king. Like the old Umma Party,* the Liberal Constitutionalist Party pressed to restrict the king's authority, though not perhaps as much as did the Wafd. The program of the party, spelled out in 1922, demanded constitutional reform, the promotion of literacy among Egyptians, and improvement of the agricultural and industrial base of the country. The party also supported the independence of Egypt and took a leading role in writing the 1923 constitution. However, in 1923, the party adopted a much harder line in regard to independence. It espoused an Egyptian independence that would maintain the complete autonomy of the country with no foreign influence, Egyptian membership in the League of Nations, and the removal of all occupying military forces in Egypt and the Sudan.

The Liberal Constitutionalists found themselves between two powerful forces in Egyptian political life: the Wafd and the palace. Throughout their history, they usually had to decide which of the two was their greater adversary and which was worthy of cooperation. With the support of many large landowners, the party generally performed credibly at the polls. Because these landowners could induce their tenants to vote for the party, the Liberal Constitutionalists generally earned sufficient votes to finish an admittedly distant second to the Wafd in free elections.

A staunch proponent of the 1923 constitution, the party cooperated with its adversaries on occasion to defend it. When the king forcibly disbanded parliament in 1925, the Wafd, the Nationalists (see Nationalist Party), and the Liberal Constitutionalists denounced the action. Similarly, the Liberal Constitutionalists objected strenuously to the more authoritarian 1930 constitution and suspended their feud with the Wafd to cooperate in demanding that the 1923 constitution be reinstated. The two parties also joined in boycotting the 1931 elections. Yet due to the world depression of the 1930s, the large landowners who formed the basis of the party became more amenable to government pressure. While the 1930 constitution remained in effect, many of the members of the party joined the People's Party* and the Unionist Party.* With the return to the 1923 constitution in 1935, the party reemerged. In January 1938, the party's fortunes revived when its president, Muhammad Mahmud, became prime minister.

The revival of the party also meant the revival of the rivalry with the Wafd. For the 1938 elections, the party cooperated with the two former palace parties (the Unionist and People's) and the Nationalist Party. The elections were held under the supervision of a Liberal Constitutionalist government, and the anti-Wafdist coalition, backed by the palace, won a plurality. The Wafd, after returning to power with British help in 1942, organized new elections which the Liberal Constitutionalists boycotted. In 1944 the king dismissed the Wafd and, with the support of the Liberal Constitutionalists, new elections were organized in 1945. Mindful of its 1938 experience (in which the Wafdists felt they were victims of gerrymandering and fraud), the Wafd boycotted the 1945 elections, and the Liberal Constitutionalists became an influential parliamentary presence again. By this time, however, two younger splinter groups from the Wafd, the Sa'dists (see Sa'dist Organization) and the Wafdist Bloc,* had joined the Liberal Constitutionalists in decrying the Wafd's leaders as arrogant and corrupt.

Besides its presence in parliament, the party also took part in political debate through the newspaper al-Siyasa.

LIBERATION RALLY (Hayat al-Tahrir). After coming to power in 1952, the Free Officers faced a dilemma with regard to the existing political parties. On the one hand, most officers seemed strongly inclined to protect their independence and viewed most of the parties as corrupt. On the other hand, the officers had little national organization and no readily identifiable constituency outside of the army. On January 17, 1953, the regime finally banned all political parties. To fill the political vacuum, the Liberation Rally was founded six days later. Initially led by the two most influential officers, Nagib and Nasser, the Liberation Rally claimed to move beyond partisanship to organize the nation for progress.

Its program necessarily remained vague. Created to support a regime that was in the process of defining itself, the Liberation Rally was unable to develop a strong platform. Unlike the Arab Socialist Union,* the Liberation Rally did not even serve as an important power base for prominent individuals. It did forge links with professional syndicates and unions, but the purpose was tactical—to prevent other parties from obtaining support from such organizations. In the struggle between Nagib and Nasser, the Liberation Rally played no role except to facilitate Nasser's efforts to obtain trade union backing.

Nevertheless, the Liberation Rally served the regime in two ways. First, it prevented other political organizations from developing during a period in which political parties were illegal. The Liberation Rally attracted few senior political leaders from the old regime, but some lower ranking members of the banned parties did join. Second, the Liberation Rally did prove capable of mobilizing demonstrations on occasion. Such demonstrations displayed popular support for the regime. At the time of the Liberation Rally's existence, such support was probably fairly shallow, but that made public displays of support that much more welcome.

In 1957 the Liberation Rally, by that point quite moribund, was disbanded. Its place was taken by the National Union.*

MISR AL-FATAT. *See* YOUNG EGYPT.

MUSLIM BROTHERHOOD (*al-Ikhwan al-Muslimin*). The Muslim Brotherhood was established in 1928 by Hasan al-Banna. First concerned with narrowly religious issues, such as building mosques and furthering Islamic education, it later broadened its focus to political themes and Islamic revival. Inspired partly by the writings of Jamal al-Din al-Afghani and Muhammad 'Abduh, the Brotherhood decried the spiritual state of Egypt and the Muslim world. The Muslim Brotherhood called for Islamic education and revival, opposition to imperialism, and the fostering of Islamic principles in public life. While the organization took an active interest in rural areas, its support was almost entirely in the towns and cities, among teachers and the middle class.

The movement quickly attracted a large number of sympathizers, but it did not move directly into the political arena until the late 1930s and early 1940s. Having entered politics, the Brotherhood engaged in a prolonged search for appropriate allies and partners. Initially the Brotherhood seemed closer to the palace, but from 1942 to 1944 it worked with the Wafd.* Hasan al-Banna moved his support to the Sa'dist Organization in 1944. In the late 1940s, the Brotherhood struck out on an increasingly independent path, although it continued to work with other parties on occasion.

The organization's increasing political role and popularity (it claimed half a million members in the late 1940s), combined with a growing militancy, made many view it as a threat to the existing political system. The Brotherhood organized guerrilla units to fight in Palestine in 1947 and 1948. The formation of paramilitary units frightened the government into banning the movement. The organization did not go out of existence, however, and it was widely blamed for the assassination of the prime minister who presided over the banning of the Brotherhood, Mahmud Fahmi al-Nuqrashi, in December 1948. Al-Banna himself was assassinated on February 12, 1949, and succeeded by Hasan al-Hudaybi, a former judge. The death of al-Banna robbed the organization of its charismatic leader and its unity. Units trained by the Brotherhood undertook a campaign of guerrilla warfare against British troops in the Suez Canal area, leading to a prolonged diplomatic crisis between Britain and Egypt. The crisis helped contribute to the political instability that fostered the 1952 coup. Several of the Free Officers had been involved with the Muslim Brotherhood, and elements of the Brotherhood cooperated with the coup.

Yet the Brotherhood's hopes for a privileged relationship with the new regime were dashed. The organization was never legalized, and tension soon developed between the Brotherhood and the Free Officers. In 1954 the Brotherhood was blamed for an assassination attempt on Nasser, although members of the organ-ization claimed that the event was staged. In subsequent years, the Muslim Broth-erhood felt the brunt of official repression. Many Brotherhood leaders spent much of the 1950s and 1960s in jail or in exile. The organization continued to be a political presence in the country, however.

In the early 1960s, a Brotherhood resurgence led to a new round of official repression. The organization was charged with attempting to overthrow the gov-ernment, and the group's most prominent ideologue, Sayyid Qutb, was executed in 1966. Qutb had been pushing the Brotherhood in a more radical direction, and his ideas, which implicitly legitimized the use of violence in an effort to overthrow the existing political system, gained a considerable following after his death.

In the 1970s, Sadat allowed the Muslim Brotherhood to reemerge. Although the organization was never legalized, its members were released from jail or al-lowed to return from exile. For a brief period, they were even allowed to publish a magazine. The Brotherhood's response to Sadat was perhaps more ambivalent than he had hoped. On the one hand, Sadat's regime was far more gentle with the Brotherhood than Nasser's had been. On the other hand, Sadat balked at removing all restrictions on the Brotherhood and responded harshly to criticism of his policies. In the final years of Sadat's presidency, the gulf between him and the Brotherhood widened, and Brotherhood leaders were included in the wide-spread arrests of opposition elements that Sadat ordered shortly before his assas-sination.

Under Mubarak the Muslim Brotherhood has operated more freely than in any period since the late 1940s, although it remains illegal. Repeated efforts to gain permission to form a political party have failed in the courts; however, the Brotherhood did gain admission to parliament by running on the Wafd's slate in 1984. In the 1987 elections, Muslim Brotherhood candidates successfully ran as part of an alliance with the Socialist Labor Party* and the Socialist Liberal Party.*

The Muslim Brotherhood's platform is encapsulated in its slogan, "Islam is the solution." Critics charge that the Brotherhood's program is vague; certainly it advances few concrete proposals beyond the implementation of Islamic law. The organization also stresses cultural issues, calling for Islamicization of the media and educational system. In foreign policy, the Brotherhood views the conflict with Israel as an Islamic, not an Arab or Palestinian, cause. In that context, it strongly denounced Egypt's relations with Israel. The Brotherhood also remained suspicious of Egypt's strong ties with the United States. Many leading figures of the Brotherhood spent much of the 1950s and 1960s in the Gulf and retained ties there. This probably contributed to the sharp debate within the Brotherhood about Egypt's participation in the anti-Iraq coalition in the Gulf crisis of 1990–91. For most of the Brotherhood, siding with the United States against Iraq was anathema, even with the Iraqi regime's record of harsh treatment of Islamicist forces. A sizable minority, however, was more respectful of the government's stance because of the conviction that Saddam Husayn represented a threat to the Islamic world, and to the Gulf states in particular.

The Brotherhood organized semilegally for so long that it lost some of its organizational coherence. A loose organization suited the Brotherhood well, however, because it rendered official pressure and repression less effective. The Muslim Brotherhood managed to gain strong support in urban areas, especially in the professional syndicates. Many in the private business community also have been sympathetic with the Brotherhood. The organization's reputation for righteousness and Islamic authenticity gained it the respect of many Egyptians, even those who are not strongly religious. Election results in 1984 and 1987 suggest that the Brotherhood commanded the support of roughly a tenth of the voting population.

The strength of the Muslim Brotherhood led some Copts to advocate the formation of a Christian party, an effort criticized by the Coptic pope. The fear of prominent Christians has been that formation of such a party would establish a precedent for a religiously based party—a step that might lead to formal legalization of the Brotherhood.

Since the Muslim Brotherhood has not been a legal organization, it has had no official publications. Nevertheless, prominent figures associated with the Brotherhood have published several periodicals (including al-Da'wa, al-I'tisam, al-Mukhtar al-Islami, and Liwa al-Islam) that have served either as semiofficial Muslim Brotherhood publications or as forums for those sympathetic to the organization's themes.

Recent leadership of the Brotherhood has included Muhammad Hamid Abu al-Nasr, the general guide, and Mustafa Mashhur. Two descendants of former general guides, Mamun al-Hudaybi and Sayf al-Islam Hasan al- Banna, have also been prominent among the Brotherhood's leadership.

NATIONAL DEMOCRATIC PARTY (NDP) (al-Hizb al-Watani al-Dimuqrati). In 1976, when platforms were formed within the Arab Socialist Union,* President Sadat clearly favored the center platform, which soon attracted the support of the majority of the parliament. As the left and right platforms were transformed into political parties in 1977, the center platform became the Arab Socialist Party of Egypt. That party was absorbed by the National Democratic Party, created the following year with Sadat's encouragement. The NDP was thus born as the government party and has continued to win the vast majority of seats in every parliamentary election since then. It has also monopolized the Consultative Council, the relatively weak upper chamber of the parliament. After the assassination of Sadat, there was brief speculation that his successor would remain above party politics, but Mubarak quickly accepted the mantle of NDP leadership.

Since the NDP was created to support the policies of the regime, those policies have determined the party's platform rather than the reverse. Specifically, the party has supported the Camp David accords and the regime's limited economic liberalization.

Membership in the NDP is necessary to achieve high political position in Egypt. With uncontested control of the administrative machinery, it is not surprising that the NDP can regularly win overwhelming electoral victories. These victories, which are especially marked in rural areas, are perhaps better seen as an indication of the regime's ability to turn out voters rather than evidence of popular enthusiasm.

The party publishes a newspaper, al-Mayu, which is quite widely distributed but probably not as widely read. It also publishes a weekly religious newspaper, al-Liwa al-Islami, which seemed to achieve wide readership, especially in the early 1980s when the publications of Islamicist groups were sharply restricted.

Nominally headed by President Mubarak, the party is managed by Yusif Wali, a technocrat who also serves as minister of agriculture.

NATIONAL PROGRESSIVIST UNIONIST FORUM (NPUF) (Hizb al-Tajammu'al-Watani al-Taqaddumi al-Wihdawi). The NPUF emerged when leftist members of the Arab Socialist Union* formed a platform within the party in 1976. The left platform was transformed into a political party in its own right in 1977. Its leader, Khalid Muhi al-Din, was a member of the Free Officers movement with Marxist leanings. The NPUF claimed to be a coalition of the left, involving Marxists, Nasserists, and nationalists. Its increasingly strident criticism of the foreign and domestic policies of Sadat's government apparently led the regime to reconsider the wisdom of viewing the NPUF as the loyal leftist opposition. The regime encouraged the development of a new party, the Socialist Labor Party,* in order to appeal to a similar constituency. The NPUF charged that the government had singled it out as a target for harassment and repression and suspended its activities in 1978. Under the Mubarak government, the NPUF reemerged, and it has operated more freely, though some affiliated with the NPUF have been arrested for engaging in Communist political activity.

The NPUF failed to win any parliamentary representation in the elections of 1984 and 1987. In 1984 Mubarak used his authority to appoint ten members of the parliament to give a seat to a leading Coptic member of the NPUF, Milad Hinna. The NPUF denounced the appointment, however. In 1990, the NPUF was the only significant opposition party to take part in parliamentary elections. The party won six seats, enough to make Khalid Muhi al-Din leader of the opposition in parliament.

The NPUF opposes both the foreign and domestic policies of the government. In foreign policy, the NPUF viewed the Soviet Union far more sympathetically than it viewed the United States; even after the dissolution of the Soviet Union, the NPUF continued to view as noxious the regime's close ties with the United States. The NPUF opposed Egyptian participation in the Gulf war of 1991, but its tone was less strident than that of some other opposition groups. The NPUF continued to question the large American economic aid program to Egypt as well as military and security cooperation with the United States. The NPUF also strongly identified itself with the Arab world generally and with the Palestinians specifically, and it opposed normalization of relations with Israel and the Camp David accords (though legal restrictions on parties made open expression of this opposition difficult for many years). Palestinian participation in peace talks with Israel and the Palestinian-Israeli accord of September 13, 1993, softened but did not silence the NPUF's voice on this issue. It did not repudiate its previous opposition to Camp David, but it made clear (sometimes with reluctance) that it would accept the decisions of the leadership of the Palestine Liberation Organization (PLO). One leading member of the NPUF, Lufti al-Khawli, even accepted presidential appointment to the Madrid peace conference in October 1991.

On domestic issues, the NPUF has identified itself as a party of workers and peasants, and it has therefore stridently criticized what it viewed as the dismantling of Egypt's socialist experiment. It defended the public sector and attacked proposed changes in labor and landlord-tenant laws as well as IMF-inspired (International Monetary Fund) reforms.

Although it has been the chief party of the left, the NPUF failed to organize a significant mass following. It has won parliamentary representation only when the national threshold of 8 percent was not in effect. Generally its candidates have been successful only where they have had a notable personal, rather than party, following. The NPUF has attempted to establish its own peasant organization, but it does not seem to have struck deep roots. Certain party members from rural areas, most notably Khalid Muhi al-Din himself, seem to have local support. The NPUF has had more success in establishing links with the trade union movement. It is for this reason that some members were arrested after worker disturbances occurred in 1977 and 1984. Nevertheless, the NPUF probably has more credibility among leftist intellectuals than any other sector.

The NPUF's most visible presence on the Egyptian political scene has probably been its weekly newspaper, Al-Ahali. Some of Egypt's leading intellectuals contribute simultaneously to government-owned papers and the NPUF's weekly.

Khalid Muhi al-Din, who founded the NPUF, serves as the party's leader; his two deputies are Lutfi Wakid, also a former Free Officer, and Muhammad Ahmad Khalf-Allah. Rif'at al-Sa'id, a Marxist historian, serves as secretary-general.

NATIONAL UNION (al-Ittihad al-Qawmi). The National Union, the second of the three political parties created to support Nasser's regime, was formed in 1957 in the wake of the Suez crisis when popular support for the regime was probably at its height. The National Union, like its predecessor (the Liberation Rally*) and its successor (the Arab Socialist Union*) eschewed the label and, to a lesser extent, the concept of a political party. Its avowed purpose was to unite Egyptians in support of the revolutionary regime rather than to divide them by partisanship. Membership was open to all Egyptians, and strong official encouragement was given to join. It claimed 6 million members, meaning that perhaps a majority of adult male Egyptians had enlisted in the organization. This gave it a base far wider than any of the pre-1952 political parties (even the Wafd*), and its organizational structure reached down to the village level.

Since its purpose was more to support than to guide the regime, however, the National Union's strong organization did not translate into political influence. Still, it was given important tasks. Ownership of the newly nationalized press was assigned to the National Union, and it screened candidates for the country's first post-1952 parliamentary elections, held in July 1957. A broad new task was added in 1958 with the creation of the United Arab Republic. This union between Syria and Egypt was predicated on the establishment of the National Union in Syria and the abolition of political parties there. The National Union thus became the first international party operating in Egypt. Those parties in Syria supportive of the union (most notably the Ba'th) accepted dissolution, and their members flocked to the National Union. Many soon came to feel, however, that the union in general, and the National Union specifically, amounted to Egyptian subjugation of Syria rather than a union of equals. When the Egyptian-Syrian union collapsed in 1961, the Egyptian regime was compelled to consider fundamental restructuring. The National Union was a victim of this restructuring and was replaced by the Arab Socialist Union.

NATIONALIST ISLAMIC PARTY. *See* YOUNG EGYPT (1933–52).

NATIONALIST PARTY (*al-Hizb al-Watani*). The Nationalist Party was established in 1907 by Mustafa Kamil, viewed by many Egyptians as the founder of modern Egyptian nationalism. Kamil, the son of an engineer, did not receive a traditional Muslim education. He oriented his thinking more toward the concept of the nation-state, and he founded the daily *al-Liwa* in 1900. A group of like-minded nationalists came together under Kamil's leadership, with encouragement from the khedive.

Kamil glorified the sentiment of nationalism and promoted education as a way of achieving independence. He wanted to educate the population and mobilize it behind the slogans of independence, patriotism, constitutionalism, and Western education. Kamil's newspaper also exhibited Islamic loyalties which led it to support the Ottoman Empire even during the Taba affair, in which the Ottomans laid claim to territory that the British maintained lay within Egyptian borders.

In 1907 a group of notables, some of them former members of Kamil's group, formed the Umma Party.* The *al-Liwa* group replied immediately by forming the Nationalist Party. Prior to World War I, the leadership and mass of followers were predominantly urban. Leaders came from the middle class and especially from the legal profession. By 1908 there were 200 members in Cairo and in other towns and provinces.

Mustafa Kamil died in 1908, and Muhammad Farid became the president of the party. He carried on Kamil's program to win Egyptian independence, but he lacked Kamil's charisma. The relations between the khedive and the party oscillated, and the British increasingly looked upon the party with suspicion. Farid was charged and convicted for writing a foreword for a book deemed seditious; in 1912, he was tried in absentia for a speech critical of the government. Farid spent the rest of his life in Istanbul and Europe. With the campaign of official repression, the influence of the party began to wane.

The Nationalist Party therefore was in weakened form when the 1919 uprising erupted. Although it supported the anti-British cause, it rejected the claims of the Wafd* to exclusive national leadership. The Nationalists did support the demand for complete independence from Britain and opposed prior negotiations. The party was thus quite critical of Sa'd Zaghlul's abortive negotiations with the British. The Nationalists similarly opposed Britain's unilateral declaration of Egyptian independence in February 1922, regarding it, as did the Wafd, as incomplete. The party could not contest the Wafd's claim to the mantle of popular legitimacy, and it performed poorly in the 1924 parliamentary elections. In subsequent parliamentary elections, the Nationalists generally won only a handful of seats.

While the Nationalists had few differences with the Wafd on matters of principle, party leaders resented their loss of the leadership of the nationalist movement. They remained willing to criticize the Wafd but could not establish a credible alternative for Egyptian public opinion. The party had suffered under tremendous government pressure, and the Wafd co-opted several Nationalists (including Mustafa al-Nahhas, the successor to Sa'd Zaghlul, as head of the Wafd). Although the Nationalist Party had little popularity, it continued to attract the support of some prominent political leaders and intellectuals, and it survived until the abolition of political parties in 1953.

NDP. See NATIONAL DEMOCRATIC PARTY.

NEW WAFD PARTY. See WAFD.

NPUF. See NATIONAL PROGRESSIVIST UNIONIST FORUM.

NOBLES' PARTY (*Hizb al-Nubala*). The Nobles' Party was established in 1908 by Hasan Hilmi Zada. It supported the continuation of Turkish autocratic rule, defending the rights of the sultan and the khedive. With the coming of Egyptian nationalism the party quickly became an anachronism.

PARTY OF FREE EGYPTIANS. See FREE NATIONALIST PARTY.

PEOPLE'S LIBERATION GROUP (*Jama'at Tahir al-Sha'b*). See EGYPTIAN COMMUNIST PARTY.

PEOPLE'S PARTY (*Hizb al-Sha'b*). Isma'il Sidqi established the People's Party on November 17, 1930, in order to contest the parliamentary elections of 1931.

The king had suspended the 1923 constitution and, with Sidqi as premier, promulgated a new, more authoritarian constitution designed to break the hold of the Wafd* on the Egyptian public. Sidqi had attempted both to satisfy King Fuad and keep the support of the Liberal Constitutionalist Party.* The latter's withdrawal of support over the suspension of the 1923 constitution prompted Sidqi to form a new party. The People's Party had the trappings of a national political organization, but it was not a broadly based political movement like the Wafd or even the Liberal Constitutionalist Party. Its national political presence existed only because Sidqi was willing to use the state administrative apparatus to support it (and purge supporters of the Wafd).

Only from 1931 to 1936 did the party have a significant bloc in the parliament. In the 1931 elections, boycotted by the Wafd and the Liberal Constitutionalists, Sidqi's party captured 56 percent of the parliament's seats. In November 1938, the Unionist Party* and the People's Party* merged, but the new party played a marginal role in Egyptian political life. With its fall from power, the party lost confidence in Sidqi who had become a symbol of authoritarianism. Sidqi was replaced by 'Abd al-Fattah Yahya.

Isma'il Sidqi had close ties with Egyptian business groups, and he was strongly identified with calls for economic nationalism. The party emphasized Egyptian independence in the international arena, but it worked as well to maintain good relations with the British in order to safeguard the flow of British investment to Egypt.

POPULAR UNIONIST PARTY. See PEOPLE'S PARTY and UNIONIST PARTY.

POPULAR VANGUARD FOR LIBERATION (al-Tali'a al-Sha'biya lil-Taharur). See EGYPTIAN COMMUNIST PARTY.

REPUBLICAN PARTY (al-Hizb al-Jumhuri). The Republican Party was founded in 1907 by Muhammad Ghanam. Its political program was based on the writing of a new constitution for Egypt.

REVOLUTIONARY BLOC (al-Takattul al-Thawri). See EGYPTIAN COMMUNIST PARTY.

SA'DIST ORGANIZATION (al-Haya al-Sa'diyya). This party was formed from a split within the Wafd* in January 1938. Ahmad Mahir was expelled from the Wafd after voting against awarding the contract for the electrification of the old Aswan Dam to the English Electric Company. Together with Mahmud Fahmi al-Nuqrashi, he founded a new party, named for Sa'd Zaghlul and claiming to be true to the original principles of the Wafd. In the next round of parliamentary elections held in 1938, the Sa'dist Organization won eighty-four seats, denying the Wafd a majority. The party was involved in a number of coalition governments from 1938 to 1950. The two party leaders together served five terms as prime minister.

The Sa'dists' appeal was stronger in urban than rural areas; they attracted particular support from merchants and industrialists. Party organization was modeled on the Wafd, with a nationwide network of committees, but its presence in society was not as pervasive. The party's political program reflected many of the socioeconomic concerns of Egypt in the late 1930s. The party addressed the issue of cooperation among local and international business interests. Sa'dists promoted the protection of local industry and emphasized the political independence of the country and the protection of the constitution. The party also called vaguely for reform of the social and economic fabric of Egyptian society.

Sa'dist prime ministers participated in several controversial decisions. In 1945 a Sa'dist-led government, under Ahmad Mahir, secured Egypt's entry into World War II after a bitter parliamentary debate. Immediately after the vote, a nationalist lawyer assassinated him. In 1948 Nuqrashi led Egypt into war with the newly declared state of Israel; it was also under his premiership that the Muslim Brotherhood* was banned. In December 1948 Nuqrashi was assassinated, and the Brotherhood was widely held responsible.

AL-SAHWA. *See* ISLAMIC ASSOCIATIONS.

SLP. *See* SOCIALIST LABOR PARTY.

SOCIAL PEASANT PARTY. *See* SOCIALIST PEASANT PARTY.

SOCIALIST LABOR PARTY (SLP) (*Hizb al-'Amal al-Ishtiraki*). The SLP was formed in 1978 by Ibrahim Shukri. He had been a leader of the Young Egypt* movement before 1952; he had also served as minister of agriculture under Sadat. The party seemed at first to be a tamer leftist opposition party than the defiant National Progressivist Unionist Forum (NPUF).* Yet, especially under Mubarak, the SLP has become the most strident of the legal opposition parties, and it has increasingly directed criticism against Mubarak himself. The SLP ran in the 1984 elections but failed to pass the 8 percent threshold; however, Mubarak did appoint four party members to the parliament. In 1987 the party formed an alliance with the Muslim Brotherhood*; this alliance (also joined by the small Socialist Liberal Party*) won fifty-six seats (perhaps over sixty if sympathetic independents are included), allowing Ibrahim Shukri to replace Mumtaz Nassar of the Wafd* as leader of the parliamentary opposition. The alliance with the Muslim Brotherhood augmented an Islamicist tendency among some of the party's leadership. After a bitter struggle for control of the party (ending in a contest over the party's name and headquarters), Ibrahim Shukri and others succeeded in cementing the identification of the Socialist Labor Party with the Islamic opposition. The SLP joined the opposition boycott of the 1990 parliamentary elections.

While the party was founded as a socialist party, the true intellectual roots of the leadership lie with the Young Egypt movement of the pre-1952 period. That movement can best be described as nationalist and populist, eschewing Marxism and sympathetic to Islamic political currents. The SLP's populism led it to oppose some of the economic liberalization policies of the regime. Its nationalism led to bitter, even vitriolic, criticism of the regime's policies toward Israel, the United States, and, more recently, the Gulf war. While many members of the opposition objected to Egypt's participation in the Gulf war, the SLP leadership seemed to come closest to supporting Iraq. A high party official was briefly arrested for inciting public opinion during the war. And while much of the opposition objects to the Camp David accords, the SLP's newspaper goes to the greatest lengths to make its objections, even issuing claims that AIDS-infected Israeli women have been sent to Egypt to sap the military capabilities of the country's youth. Unlike the Wafd, which allied itself for electoral purposes with the Muslim Brotherhood in 1984, the SLP has made its alliance with the Brotherhood much more than a marriage of convenience and has increasingly introduced Islamic themes into its platform.

Standing alone, the party does not seem to have substantial support. Although it did not win enough votes in 1984 to pass the 8 percent threshold for parliamentary representation, it did outpoll the NPUF. Yet it does have a leadership known for its devotion to nationalist (and increasingly to Islamic) causes, probably earning it respect among the educated urban population.

The party's weekly newspaper, *Al-Sha'b*, has given it a public voice even in periods when it has not had parliamentary representation. The newspaper's sensationalist tone has attracted attention but also probably undermined its credibility, especially when compared with the comparatively understated (but still forceful) tone of the Wafd's newspaper. The newspaper is edited by 'Adil Husayn, who was a leading leftist intellectual in the 1970s but has become increasingly Islamicist in his orientation.

Ibrahim Shukri's deputy leaders have been Naji al-Shihabi and Majdi Ahmad Husayn, a son of the founder of the Young Egypt movement.

SOCIALIST LIBERAL PARTY (*Hizb al-Ahrar al-Ishtiraki*). The Socialist Liberal Party began as the rightist platform in the Arab Socialist Union* in 1976; it became an independent party with the promulgation of the parties law of 1977. It was founded and continued to be led by Mustafa Kamil Murad, a former Free Officer and head of the state-owned General Cotton Organization. The party's major theme is the need for economic liberalization. It has established some ties with Islamicist groups and has even allowed an Islamicist newspaper to be published in its name, in addition to the party's own newspaper. While calls for reform and even privatization of the public sector are frequently heard in Egypt, the government's economic reform program, though slow, robbed the party of its primary issue. Later, when the Wafd* came into being and picked up the banner of liberalization, the Socialist Liberal Party all but disappeared. It received few votes in the 1984 elections. In 1987 it joined the coalition of the Muslim Brotherhood* and the Socialist Labor Party.* In 1990 it joined the opposition boycott of parliamentary elections. The party, though small, experienced sharp divisions over the alliance with Islamicist forces and the proper response to the Iraqi invasion of Kuwait.

SOCIALIST PARTY OF EGYPT. *See* YOUNG EGYPT.

SOCIALIST PEASANT PARTY (*Hizb al-Fallah al-Ijtima'i* from 1938 to 1945; thereafter *Hizb al-Fallah al-Ishtiraki*). While rural issues such as land distribution and poverty gained increasing attention in Egypt after the 1930s, the Socialist Peasant Party was the only sustained party founded primarily to promote peasant interests. In the early 1930s, a variety of organizations arose among students and youth to promote social welfare and raise funds for poor Egyptians. The Socialist Peasant Party was one of two political movements to arise out of these organizations (the other was Young Egypt*). In 1938, the leaders of an organization called the Society for the Awakening of Villages, which had previously cooperated with the government to promote social welfare in rural Egypt, formed a political party in the name of the peasants. The party's platform reflected its philanthropic origins. It called for rural education and development but stopped far short of advocating any redistributive policies. The party aimed not at establishing a separate organization for peasants but only at drawing national attention to rural issues. It worked with other political forces, including the Wafd* and the palace, to accomplish this goal.

In the 1942 and 1945 parliamentary elections, the party unsuccessfully fielded candidates. The party's platform took a turn to the left in 1945 when it changed its name from the "Social" to the "Socialist" Peasant Party and began to stress nationalist and distributive issues. While it finally did begin organizational work in the countryside in the late 1940s, it attracted attention largely because of the actions of its leader, Ahmad Qutb. In 1948 Qutb confronted the prime minister in New York; he was also evicted from Sudan during a visit. The following year the party dropped the socialist label and deemphasized radical elements in its program, but it still failed to win a seat in the 1950 parliamentary elections. In 1951 the party attempted to hold a national conference on rural issues, but the government prevented the meeting and arrested the leadership. The party strongly endorsed the Free Officers' coup in 1952 but disappeared along with other political parties shortly afterward.

TASHT. *See* EGYPTIAN COMMUNIST PARTY.

THOSE RESCUED FROM HELL. *See* ISLAMIC ASSOCIATIONS.

UMMA PARTY I (*Hizb al-Umma*) (1907–World War I). The Umma Party was founded by Ahmad Lutfi al-Sayyid as a counterweight to Mustafa Kamil's Nationalist Party.* Because Kamil's group, although older, organized itself as a party after the Umma Party had done so, the Umma Party is Egypt's oldest formally organized political party. The intellectual core of the party included lawyers and urban figures, such as Fathi Zaghlul, his brother Sa'd Zaghlul, and 'Abd al-Khaliq Tharwat; several landowners were also prominent members. Many in the group also cooperated to found the Egyptian University in 1908. The party was most active in Egyptian politics from 1907 to 1914. Perhaps because of the aristocratic tinge of its leadership, the party never really developed into a full-fledged grass-roots political movement.

The political program of the party was promulgated in the newspaper *al-Jarida* under the editorship of al-Sayyid. The paper ceased publication in 1915. In many ways, the newspaper became more influential than the party itself.

The Umma Party's views were less pro-Ottoman than those of the Nationalist Party. Influenced by the ideas of Muhammad 'Abduh, the movement viewed Islamic reform sympathetically but had little interest in pan-Islamic themes. Al-Sayyid called on Egyptians to prepare themselves for self-rule. The program of the party also emphasized reforming and overhauling Egypt's educational system with special emphasis on higher education. These stands left the party open to the charge that it was excessively accommodationist with the British. Such criticisms seem ironic in retrospect, however, because many of the party's leaders became involved with the Wafd,* which replaced the Nationalist Party as the leading nationalist organization in 1919. The party gradually scaled back its operations and disappeared with the emergence of the Wafd, although many members of the party were tremendously influential in the interwar years.

UMMA PARTY II (*Hizb al-Umma*) (1984–present). The Umma Party was formed shortly before the 1984 parliamentary elections by Ahmad al-Sibahi. It was believed at the time that he wished to form a party that would allow Muslim Brotherhood* candidates to run under its banner. The Brotherhood's surprise alliance with the Wafd* made the Umma Party superfluous and led al-Sibahi to launch periodic attacks on the Brotherhood. While quiescent, the Umma Party remains in existence, calling for implementation of the Islamic Shari'a and political liberalization, including converting from a presidential to a parliamentary system. It has published a newspaper erratically.

UNION OF PEACE PARTISANS (*Ittihad Ansar al-Salam*). *See* EGYPTIAN COMMUNIST PARTY.

UNIONIST PARTY (*Hizb al-Ittihad*). On November 25, 1924, the king postponed the parliamentary session for a month and then dissolved the lower house. Fearful of a victory by the Wafd,* the palace encouraged the adoption of a two-stage election process in which voters selected electors who in turn chose members of parliament. In January 1925, the Unionist Party was formed to compete under these rules with a clear mandate from the king to limit the influence and power of the Wafd. The royalist nature of the party was clear from the beginning; Hassan Nash'at, its founder, was deputy and acting chief of the Royal Cabinet. Yet the party did attract some credible figures. It was headed by Yahya Ibrahim, who had led the provisional government overseeing the 1924 elections. 'Ali Mahir was the vice president, and Mahmud Abu al-Nasr was secretary general. Some former Wafdists did join the party.

The Unionist Party was more of a clique than a well-organized political party. The platform of the party borrowed heavily from the Liberal Constitutionalist Party,* but, as a palace party, it was more attuned to putting forth the agenda of the king in order to counterbalance the Wafd.

In spite of palace support and the manipulation of the electoral system, all that was accomplished was a diminution of the size of the Wafd's victory. The Unionist Party was able to organize an anti-Wafdist coalition government with the cooperation of Liberal Constitutionalists and independents. When new, direct elections were held for parliament in 1926, however, the party won only a single seat, making its lack of a popular base all too clear. The party continued to exist, however. In 1931 parliamentary elections were held under a new constitution that was clearly designed to undermine the Wafd. When the Wafd and the Liberal Constitutionalists boycotted the elections, the field was left to the Unionist Party and the People's Party,* a new palace party headed by Isma'il Sidqi. When the 1923 constitution was restored and new elections were held in 1936, the two palace parties combined to form the Popular Unionist Party. Yet without the benefit of electoral manipulation and palace pressure, the party gradually disappeared from the political map.

WAFD (al-Wafd; later Hizb al-Wafd al-Jadid). Egypt's oldest surviving party, the Wafd (delegation) operated between independence and 1952 as Egypt's largest political party. It reemerged in the 1970s as the New Wafd Party and continues to operate as one of the leading opposition parties in the country. The Wafd is therefore one of the few political parties in Egyptian history to outlive the political system under which it was born.

When Great Britain occupied Egypt in 1882, it did nothing formally to disrupt Egypt's legal status as an Ottoman province. When Britain and the Ottoman Empire became adversaries in World War I, this arrangement was no longer tenable, and Britain unilaterally declared a protectorate over Egypt. During the course of the war, the British requisitioned Egyptian crops and mobilized labor in support of their military effort. With Egypt's legal status ambiguous and with claims to have supported the victorious cause, a group of prominent Egyptian citizens, led by Sa'd Zaghlul, constituted themselves as a delegation and demanded the right to represent Egypt at the Paris peace conference. The Wafd claimed at its inception that it was not a political party but instead the legitimate representative of the entire Egyptian nation. When the British arrested and exiled Zaghlul and other Wafdist leaders in March 1919, a brief but violent national uprising ensued, lending credence to the Wafd's claims. Zaghlul quickly assumed the position of charismatic leader of the nationalist movement.

Negotiations between Britain and Egypt dragged on, as the British discovered that the Wafd's popular support undermined the position of alternative leaders and the Wafd itself proved a difficult negotiating partner. In 1922 Great Britain unilaterally declared the country independent, but it reserved claims over several areas (such as minorities and defense), ensuring that the nationalist issue would continue to dominate Egyptian politics. One year later, the king promulgated a constitution. Despite reservations, the Wafd entered the subsequent parliamentary elections, scoring a landslide victory. The Wafd had now made the transition from an elite movement to a mass movement and from a mass movement to an electoral party. The Wafd's often antagonistic relationships with the British and the king limited its ability to rule Egypt. It was also racked by internal splits. In spite of these problems, Zaghlul and his successor, Mustafa al-Nahhas, managed to win convincing victories in every free election up to 1952. The party's support penetrated every element of Egyptian society; it was particularly strong among the rural notability and the free professions.

The forces opposed to the Wafd had to rely on electoral manipulation or political repression to keep the party from power. Interwar elections often alternated between Wafdist landslides and rigged or restricted elections. This only increased the feeling of leading Wafdists that other parties were illegitimate. Over time, however, the Wafd proved more flexible in its relationships with the British and the palace. In 1936 a Wafdist government assumed power and negotiated a treaty with Britain. In 1942 the British, anxious to secure political stability in the country as Axis armies approached, surrounded the palace and forced the king to allow al-Nahhas to form a government. While al-Nahhas always denied advance knowledge of British actions, the incident severely tarnished the party's nationalist image. Indeed, a group of young nationalist activists, including Anwar al-Sadat, feeling the Wafd had betrayed them, almost succeeded in assassinating al-Nahhas a few years later.

In the heated political atmosphere of the 1940s and 1950s, the Wafdist coalition began to unravel. Other groups outflanked the Wafd on the nationalist issue, and charges of corruption increasingly embarrassed party leaders. The Wafd formed its last government in 1950, determined to resolve the country's relationship with Britain and confront the increasingly divisive social issues dominating the political agenda (such as poverty and land distribution). Relations with Britain rapidly deteriorated, and the Wafd denounced the 1936 treaty that it had itself negotiated. The Wafd was dismissed following violent anti-British rioting in Cairo in 1952.

When the Free Officers took power in July 1952, the Wafd agonized inconclusively over how to respond. Attempts to enlist the officers in their camp were unsuccessful, and the party leadership pressed for a return to constitutional rule. In March 1954, when rivalry among the officers led to a crisis in the regime, the Wafd joined with several other civilian political groups in rallying around the ruling faction. As the new regime solidified its grip, leading members of the Wafd (including al-Nahhas and Fu'ad Siraj al-Din) were stripped of political rights and tried for corruption. The officers portrayed the party as a corrupt remnant of the nationalist movement founded by Zaghlul. The Wafd was effectively silenced for over two decades.

It was therefore a surprise to many Egyptians when Fuad Siraj al-Din re-emerged in 1977. In a speech before the bar association, a traditional Wafd bastion, Siraj al-Din launched a stinging attack on the post-1952 regime. In early 1978 the New Wafd Party was legalized and quickly attracted support from those with liberal political inclinations and others who criticized the regime as excessively repressive. A few months later, however, the party suspended operations, protesting against what it viewed as the authoritarianism of the regime.

With Sadat's assassination and the reemergence of political pluralism under Mubarak, the party decided to resume operations. The Parties Committee refused it permission, arguing that the party itself had determined its dissolution, but the Wafd brought the matter to court and won. In 1984 the party ran in parliamentary elections for the first time in thirty-four years. Shortly before the election, the Wafd formed a surprising alliance with the Muslim Brotherhood.* Wafdist leaders were apparently anxious to ensure that they would pass the 8 percent threshold for parliamentary representation and therefore allowed Brotherhood candidates to run on the Wafd's slate. Although the alliance alienated many Coptic supporters of the party, the Wafd was the only opposition group to win any seats in the election.

The alliance with the Muslim Brotherhood collapsed, however, and in 1987 the Wafd participated in parliamentary elections on its own. The new Brotherhood alliance with the Socialist Labor Party* outpolled the Wafd, but both won parliamentary representation. In the 1990 elections, the Wafd joined much of the rest of the opposition in a boycott, claiming that the government's assurance that elections would be fair were unconvincing. Some Wafdists ran as independents against the wishes of the leadership; one party member (Muna Makram 'Ubayd) was suspended when she accepted President Mubarak's offer of one of ten seats he is allowed to fill by appointment.

The New Wafd Party's platform stresses the themes of economic and political liberalization. The party has viewed economic reform sympathetically and portrayed the regime as riddled with inefficiency and corruption. In public, party leaders have been respectful of President Mubarak, but they have sharply criticized what they view as the strong Nasserist elements still found in Egypt's political and economic systems. In foreign policy, the party launched stinging but rarely fundamental criticisms of the government. Wafdist leaders have criticized Israeli behavior, but stop far short of calling for abrogation of the 1979 peace treaty. While the Wafd criticized the regime before and after the Gulf war, claiming that it had abandoned Egyptian workers in Iraq, it issued a cautious endorsement of Egyptian participation in the anti-Iraq coalition. Since the Wafd was formed before Arab nationalism became prominent in Egypt, the party takes pride in Egypt's role in the Arab world, but it is also insistent on a distinctive Egyptian identity.

The Wafd's newspaper, Al-Wafd, the only opposition daily, is probably more widely read than the weekly papers of other opposition parties. The staff of the paper specializes in embarrassing accounts of official misdeeds and corruption. Its tone is more sarcastic than demagogic. Because of the paper's muckraking feats, it has become fairly influential.

As Egypt's only legal opposition party with a truly popular base, the Wafd has attracted diverse sources of support. Many of the families prominent in the pre-1952 Wafd have reemerged in the New Wafd Party. Some intellectuals are attracted by the party's attacks on restrictions of democratic freedom and official corruption. Egypt's professional associations have traditionally supported the Wafd, although some have recently taken on a more Islamicist orientation. The legal profession has traditionally provided much of the Wafd's leadership. The parliamentary leader of the Wafd after the 1984 elections was Mumtaz Nassar, a judge who had been dismissed in the 1969 "Massacre of the Judges" in which Nasser's government attempted to bring the judiciary under political control. The Wafd's appeal to national unity has won it much support from Copts, although many were alienated by the party's 1984 alliance with the Muslim Brotherhood.

Recent leadership of the party has consisted of Fuad Siraj al-Din and Ibrahim Faraj.

WAFDIST BLOC (*Al-Kutla al-Wafdiyya*). In May 1942, a serious rift developed between Mustafa al-Nahhas, the leader of the Wafd*, and Mustafa Makram 'Ubayd, the party's secretary-general. While Nahhas and 'Ubayd had occupied leading positions in the Wafd since the party's founding, the split assumed scandalous proportions when an anonymous *Black Book* was published, widely attributed to 'Ubayd and detailing charges of venality and political betrayal by al-Nahhas, his wife, and their associates. 'Ubayd was stripped of his cabinet position and expelled from the party. Several leading members left with him and established a new party, the Wafdist Bloc, which claimed to espouse the Wafd's original principles. The party won a handful of seats in the 1945 parliamentary election and supported several anti-Wafdist coalitions. In 1950, however, the Bloc received less than 1 percent of the vote and disappeared from parliament and the electoral map. Never having achieved a significant popular following, the Bloc's major accomplishment was to sully the reputation of the Wafd and its leadership.

YOUNG EGYPT I (*Misr al-Fatat*) (1933–52). Young Egypt was founded in October 1933 as a youth movement by Ahmad Husayn. Husayn was its only leader; his deputy was Fathi Radwan, a young journalist. The two sought to build a nationalist movement that appealed to Egyptian youth. At the time, several observers noted the similarity between Young Egypt and fascist movements in Europe, pointing to the group's paramilitary structure, its strident nationalism, and its organization of "Green Shirts" who were frequently involved in street violence. Ideological similarities did not extend to formal links; neither Fascist

Italy nor Nazi Germany exhibited any sympathy or support for the movement at its inception.

Young Egypt generally supported the monarchy and opposed the Wafd.* In 1936 and 1937 violent clashes erupted between the Green Shirts and Wafdist "Blue Shirts." One member of the group unsuccessfully tried to assassinate Mustafa al-Nahhas in November 1937. At the end of 1936, Ahmad Husayn announced that Young Egypt would be reorganized into a party. In 1938 the Green Shirts were disbanded under government pressure. In any event, its leaders were all under the minimum age for entry into parliament, which prevented the party from winning any seats.

Young Egypt's involvement in street violence continued in the late 1930s as its nationalist and antidemocratic ideology became more strident. The government began to move against the organization and its publications, levying fines and jailing Husayn for several months. The party was renamed the Nationalist Islamic Party in 1940, marking its increasingly religious tone. The group's agenda became more hostile to Britain, leading to suspicions that it would cooperate with the Germans and Italians. In the constricted political atmosphere of Egypt during World War II, however, the organization was largely inactive.

The party became more radical and leftist (though never Marxist) in the late 1940s, when it changed its name to the Socialist Party of Egypt. Under this banner, the group called for land reform and other programs to redistribute wealth and power in Egyptian society. The party scored its only electoral success at this time, sending its vice president, Ibrahim Shukri, to parliament in 1950. The movement's nationalism led it to endorse violent action against the British; its opponents charged that it was involved in organizing the "Burning of Cairo," a day of urban unrest and severe anti-British rioting in January 1952.

In its various incarnations, Young Egypt appealed especially to students, government employees, professionals, and shopkeepers. It had very little strength outside the cities and provincial towns, though it devoted increasing attention to agrarian issues in its final years. The organization did change its platform over time, dropping its royalism and adopting Islamic and then socialist themes. Its consistency lay in its hostility to the Wafd, the British, and the existing political system. Its spirit was motivated above all by a strong sense of Egyptian nationalism.

The leaders of Young Egypt welcomed the 1952 coup. Although some of the Free Officers had been involved with the organization, it was granted no special favors. The 1953 ban on political parties extended to the Socialist Party of Egypt, and the group ceased operations. Its influence did not disappear, however. Ibrahim Shukri served as agriculture minister under Sadat and established the Socialist Labor Party* in 1978. Fathi Radwan, who had left Young Egypt in the 1940s, joined the Socialist Labor Party, as did some relatives of Ahmad Husayn.

YOUNG EGYPT II (Misr al-Fatat) (1990–present). Young Egypt was formed in 1990 as a stridently nationalist party. It began publishing a newspaper that is perhaps the most sensationalist among all the opposition publications. It has attracted little attention or support. The party ran candidates in the 1990 parliamentary elections but won no seats. Sami Mubarak, the president's brother, was also a founding member, though he was defeated in an early battle for leadership of the party. In 1992 another battle for control was won by a faction that was far less strident in its criticism of the government. As a result of that battle, 'Abdallah Rushdi replaced 'Ala al-Din Salih as party leader. Muhammad al-'Isawi became editor of the party's newspaper.

Nathan J. Brown and Timothy J. Piro

# IRAN

## HISTORICAL EVOLUTION OF POLITICAL PARTIES

Iran (land of the Aryans), known prior to 1935 as Persia, is a large Middle Eastern country with a civilization and culture that goes back for several millennia. Although the frontiers of Iran have changed in various historical periods, the country has retained its cultural ethos and sense of identity. It is considered an "old new state" in the language of development theorists, who referred to newly independent non-Western countries after World War II as "new states." Although Iran has faced severe problems of modernization and development, its historical, linguistic, and literary-artistic continuity has served to attenuate certain development crises that have been difficult for most less developed countries. In this regard, Iran resembles such Middle Eastern neighbors as Egypt and Turkey.

The country, which covers approximately 636,000 square miles, is bounded on the West by Iraq, on the northwest by Turkey and the former Soviet republics of Armenia and Azerbaijan, on the north by the republic of Turkmenistan, on the east by Afghanistan and Pakistan, and on the south by the Persian Gulf. In the ancient period, major dynasties, such as the Achaemenid (550–330 B.C.) and the Sasanid (A.D. 226–651) ruled large areas of the Middle East under the Zoroastrian religion. After the Arab conquest of Iran in the 640s, the area became a region of the larger Arab and Islamic caliphates. The modern era of Iran can be said to have begun in 1501, when the leader of a millenarian revolt in eastern Turkey, inspired by Shi'ite messianic hopes, drove into Iran, reunified the country, and established the Safavid dynasty (1501–1722). From that time until today, Shi'ite Islam has been the dominant religion of the Iranian people. The Safavid dynasty eventually collapsed because of an invasion of Sunni Muslim Uzbeks from Afghanistan, but Shi'ism was not displaced, despite a serious effort to do so by Nadir Shah (ruled 1736–47). After a period of tribal chaos, power fell into the hands of another Turkic tribal group, the Qajars, who moved the capital to Tehran. It is in the Qajar period (1785–1925) that Iranian political parties first made their appearance.

Despite external challenges (especially Russian and British), severe economic hardships, and natural disasters, the political system never collapsed completely during this period. Toward the end of the Qajar dynasty, a social and political movement, known as the Constitutional Revolution (1905–09), broke out. This revolution had portentous consequences for the establishment of political societies, political parties, a legislature (majles), and the country's original fundamental law (1906/7–1979). Inspiring the emergence of political factions and parties were several political societies that emerged at this time. Among these were the Society of Culture (Anjoman-e Ma'aref); the Humanity Society (Anjoman-e Adamiyyat); a number of clandestine regional political organizations, including the two Azerbaijani-based organizations, the Secret Center (Markaz-e Ghaybi) and the Social Democrat Party* (Hezb-e Ejtema'iyyun-e 'Ammiyun); and two Tehran-based groups, the Revolutionary Committee (Komiteh-ye Enqelabi) and the Secret Society (Anjoman-e Makhfi). Most of these were more secular in their orientation, but the last was oriented to Shi'ite Islamic perspectives.

Political parties were represented in the early majles-es but mainly in the form of caucuses (fraksions or maslaks) clustering around particular individuals. In the first majles, which convened in October 1906, three major tendencies were visible: the proaristocratic Royalists (Mostabeddan), the traditional merchant-oriented Moderates (Mo'tadelan), and the faction representing the reform-minded intelligentsia, the Liberals (Azadikhvahan). The names given to factional groupings such as these suggest the power of particular ideas prevalent among reformers at the time. They invariably included such concepts as democracy, freedom, reform, equality, liberal, conservative, moderate, radical, socialist, and the like. These terms were also current among intellectuals and reformers in the neighboring Ottoman Empire at the turn of the century. Some of the Iranian groups were inspired by Russian organizations as well. The provenance of these terms, however, clearly was Europe. The concepts of the French revolution were particularly influential among Iranian reformers, many of whom were inspired by that event.

The second majles, which opened in November 1909, became sharply divided into the Moderate faction (Ferqeh-ye E'tedal) and the Democrat faction (Ferqeh-ye Demokrat). The Moderates were really conservatives intent on ensuring royal prerogatives against the Democrats, who continued the traditional reformist arguments of the Constitutional Revolution. These two factions also dominated the third majles, which convened shortly after the outbreak of World War I in August 1914. Toward the end of the decade, new political organizations were spawned, including the famous Jangali movement in the northern province of Gilan, as well as others in Azerbaijan, including those with communist or quasi-Communist leanings (e.g., the Justice Party* [Ferqeh-ye 'Adalat]).

The word party (hezb) was little used at this time. Thus, political parties got off to a very shaky start, as the shahs of the time fell under varying degrees of external and internal reactionary influence and hence moved to ban the parliament and political activity. Although the country's rulers were never able to eliminate the new institutions spawned by the Constitutional Revolution, the shahs did their best to ignore them.

World War I was particularly devastating to Iran's economy. In addition, the decline of the Qajar dynasty contributed to the general sense that the old order was unraveling. British efforts to impose a virtual protectorate over Iran in the form of a treaty of alliance (1919) were rebuffed by the parliament and cabinet. Out of this turmoil came a new dynasty, the Pahlavi, which was headed by Reza Khan, a former officer of the Russian-controlled Cossack Brigade. In a crafty series of moves, he led a coup in 1921 that overthrew the existing government and installed himself as minister of war; he then engineered another change in government in 1923, this time making himself prime minister; and finally, in 1925, he arranged for the departure of the last Qajar shah and the convening of a Constituent Assembly to install him as monarch under the sobriquet, Reza Shah Pahlavi.

The various political groups in the country oriented themselves to these developments in different ways. Some supported Reza Khan's ambitions, others feared that he would usher in a secular republic, while yet others hoped that the new monarch would adhere to the country's constitution (modeled after the 1830 constitution of Belgium) and leave matters of rule to the cabinet and the parliament. The four political parties that controlled the fourth and the fifth *majles*-es (1921–25)—the Reformers' Party* (*Hezb-e Eslah Talaban*), the Revival Party* (*Hezb-e Tajaddod*), the Socialist Party* (*Hezb-e Sosialist*), and the Communist Party* (*Hezb-e Komunist*)—enjoyed relative freedom in articulating and aggregating interests. Although by now the word *party* was in full use, most of these organizations continued to operate like the old caucuses. That is to say, they were loose coalitions of like-minded individuals who essentially extended their loyalties to particular individuals, rather than specific policies.

In the early 1920s, the shah and the *majles* cooperated with each other, but by 1926 he emasculated it, and it became a mere rubber stamp. It was to remain powerless until the early 1940s, when invading Soviet and British troops ousted Reza Shah in order to facilitate Allied wartime strategies. From 1941 to 1953, in the first period of the rule of Reza Shah's son, Mohammad Reza Pahlavi, the political system opened up; many political leaders were released from prison, exile, or house arrest, while many others began to try their hand at political organization and mobilization for the first time. A semblance of party discipline emerged during this period. A party system had seemingly been established, characterized by a proliferation of organizations for aggregating interests. These parties, groups, and movements enjoyed autonomy, but their ramification created problems, as the nation plunged into a period of great political flux.

Some of the most important Iranian political organizations were created during this time, including the Democrat Party,* the Iran Party,* and the Tudeh Party, as well as the nationalists' front organization or bloc, led by Mohammad Mosaddeq, known as the *Jebhe-ye Melli* (National Front).*[1] An intriguing fact about this period in terms of the creation of political parties is that the religious groups failed to establish their own political organization per se, even though two quasi-party institutions or movements were founded: the Devotees of Islam* (*Fada'iyan-e Islam*) and the Warriors of Islam* (*Mojahedin-e Islam*). But the leading cleric of the time, Ayatollah Mohammad Hosayn Borujerdi (d. 1961), admonished the clergy to stay out of the political arena. Even the activist clergyman par excellence, Ayatollah Abu al-Qasem Kashani (d. 1962), never created his own political organization, and although the Devotees of Islam tried to recruit him as their leader, he refused. It is true, however, that he had close ties to the leaders of the Warriors of Islam (for example, Shams al-Din Qanatabadi).

These halcyon days of party activity came to an abrupt halt in 1953 with the military coup d'état that overthrew Prime Minister Mosaddeq's nationalist government, with the assistance of Great Britain and the United States. In the wake of the coup, the shah tried to consolidate his power by imposing a two-party system on the country from above. These parties, known as the *Melliyun* (ironically called the Nationalists' Party*) and the *Mardom* (People's Party*), were headed by two of the shah's trusted cronies, Manuchehr Eqbal and Asadollah 'Alam. This experiment failed abysmally because the people refused to accept the two organizations as credible vehicles for their needs.

At the end of the 1950s, popular political protest against the government's policies crystalized and spilled over into the streets and university campuses. The Melliyun Party did not survive these protests against the shah's arbitrary rule, poor economic performance, and the deep-rooted animosity of the clergy against the monarch's reform program. After two notoriously rigged parliamentary election campaigns held in 1960 and 1961, the shah simply disbanded the parliament and ordered the prime minister to rule by decree. In late 1963, after narrowly averting a major crisis during which the shah arrested (and eventually exiled) his chief clerical critic, Ayatollah Ruhollah Khomeini, the regime created a new party—the New Iran Party* (*Hezb-e Iran Novin*)—in lieu of the Melliyun. Its leaders were relatively young technocrats and managers, newcomers who replaced the traditional aristocratic figures who had served at length as cabinet ministers, parliamentary deputies, and high-ranking civil servants.

The New Iran Party was the beneficiary of the state's largesse, as representatives of the professional bureaucratic intelligentsia—a new social class—who were highly trained in various fields, such as economics, finance, demography, agronomy, statistics, and management, were recruited into its ranks. The shah's practice of rewarding trained cadres with high-paying and prestigious jobs while denying them political autonomy seemed to be acceptable to this new social class as long as the economy continued to grow. Yet in the 1970s, the shah dissolved both the New Iran Party and the still existing Mardom Party and replaced them with a single new party, the Resurgence Party* (*Hezb-e Rastakhiz*).

The new party was supposed to be open to the broad masses of the population, who would demonstrate their active support of the shah's policies down the line. The shah made it plain that, if people did not join this party, they were either enemies of the state or else nattering critics of society who were welcome to emigrate. Although the fiction was maintained that two tendencies or wings, the "progressives" and the "liberals," existed in the party, in fact both groups were headed by the shah's trusted confidants.

The rhetoric used by the founders of the Resurgence Party suggested that Iran would emerge among the top five industrial powers of the world by the year 2000. Aryanization of the country's political culture was encouraged under the party's auspices, including a change from the Islamic to the "imperial" calendar, commencing with the onset of the rule of the Achaemenid ruler, Cyrus the Great.[2] It was asserted that the country's political, social, and economic development could best be secured under single party auspices. But those leading the new party exhibited a curious amalgam of views on the role of parties, some stressing discipline and "transmission belt" metaphors straight out of Marxist discourse, while others adopted more "bourgeois" language, such as that parties are indispensable vehicles for institutionalization, itself seen as the bedrock concept of political development.

Why the shah moved in the direction of a single party is not clear. To most observers, it hardly mattered, because he would never allow autonomous groups to compete for power. The most likely answer is that he had become so confident of his position at home and abroad that he felt he could orchestrate developments, much like a conductor leading musicians through a musical score. Various guerrilla organizations were challenging his rule. He also identified the clergy as a whole as his inevitable enemies. But those employed in the top positions in the civil service, the economy, and the state accepted his terms for employment, that is, get rich but stay out of politics. The shah apparently was convinced that he could now afford to do away with even the trappings of competitive party politics and assert his personal leadership to work toward the "Great Civilization."

Despite all the energy expended upon it, the experiment to make the Resurgence Party the key mobilizing force in Iranian politics proved to be an abysmal failure. While the shah was trying to launch the party, the country was forced to borrow on international financial markets because of a sudden glut of oil and the resultant decline in revenues. Meanwhile, tremendous inflation had distorted the economy as a consequence of heavy government spending. With increases in the cost of living, worker dissatisfaction rose, and job actions, strikes, and other forms of confrontation spread throughout the mid-1970s.

Political parties played some role in the revolution that finally broke out in 1978–79. Among the most important of these were the Tudeh Party, the Liberation Movement of Iran* (LMI), the People's Mojahedin Organization of Iran* (PMOI), and the Devotees of the Masses* (*Fada'iyan-e Khalq*). In addition, nonparty organizations, such as the Lawyers' Syndicate, the Writers' Society, and human rights watch organizations, became active. With the departure of the shah from Iran on January 16, 1979, the suddenly free atmosphere of political activity resembled the period in September 1941 when the authoritarian Reza Shah was forced from the throne into exile.

During the next two years, a proliferation of political parties and groupings took place, reflecting the entire gamut of the political spectrum. In addition to the Tudeh, LMI, PMOI, and the Devotees of the Masses, the following political organizations resumed or began their activities: the pro-Mosaddeq National Front; the National Democratic Front, a spinoff of the National Front, led by Mosaddeq's grandson; the Devotees of Islam; the Islamic Republican Party (IRP),* which was the vehicle of the staunchly pro-Khomeini clergy; and the Muslim People's Republican Party (MPRP),* an instrument of Ayatollah Khomeini's major clerical rival, Ayatollah Mohammad Kazem Shari'atmadari.

As these organizations sought to mobilize support for their views, the new regime authorized a series of referenda and elections to institutionalize its power. The first of these was the national plebiscite on the nature of the political system, which was held in March 1979, in which the population demanded the establishment of an Islamic Republic. Some political parties, like the IRP and the Tudeh, actively and without reservations supported the regime in this referendum. Other organizations, such as the MPRP and the PMOI, were unhappy with the formulation of the question on which the population was to vote, but they decided to participate nevertheless.

But significant differences were to appear at the next juncture, which was in August 1979 when elections were held for a Council of Experts whose task it would be to draw up a new constitution for the country. Again, the IRP and the Tudeh supported the elections, but objections were heard from Shari'atmadari's supporters and the National Front. They claimed that the regime had originally promised to hold elections for a more broadly based and more representative Constituent Assembly, but then reneged because it feared it could not control the debate in the assembly. Consequently, Khomeini ordered that the elections be held for a much more narrowly based council, chosen from among candidates vetted by the IRP itself. Such arrangements proved unacceptable to a number of organizations because they would merely guarantee the victory of one set of viewpoints over all other contending viewpoints on such matters as sovereignty, the relevance of the doctrine of velayat-e faqih (exercise of the imam's authority by the top-ranking clergyman), the powers vested in the branches of the government, and the like.

Disagreements also arose in late November and early December 1979 over participation in the referendum on the council's draft constitution. Some groups objected to the contradictions in the draft between provisions calling for national sovereignty and other provisions vesting sovereignty in the faqih (Khomeini), who supposedly derived it by deputation from God, the Prophet, and the Hidden Imam.[3] Nonetheless, the referendum was held and the draft was approved.

The next stage proved to be the elections for the presidency of the republic, in which most groups participated. Unexpectedly, the IRP candidate for the presidency was disqualified on a technicality. The winner, Abu al-Hasan Bani Sadr, was a devotee of Ayatollah Khomeini, to be sure, but he was not an IRP stalwart and indeed was independent of the clerical establishment. The margin of Bani Sadr's victory was so great (he won 80 percent of the vote) that it seemed he would be the most powerful individual in the country, next to Ayatollah

Khomeini himself. But Bani Sadr lacked any organizational support, and the roots of his popularity were actually quite shallow.

In the course of the next year and a half, Bani Sadr struggled with the Revolutionary Council, the de facto executive authority in Iran, over many key issues, including the conduct of the war with Iraq, civil rights issues, and educational policies. In the course of his disputes with the stalwart pro-Khomeini clergy on the Revolutionary Council, Bani Sadr became increasingly isolated. His patron, Ayatollah Khomeini, became more and more impatient with requests for his intervention to break deadlocks between Bani Sadr and the council. Meanwhile, the PMOI mounted an escalating series of assassinations of powerful pro-Khomeini clerics whom they accused of trying to monopolize political power. These attacks culiminated in two spectacular actions in June and August 1981, in which the headquarters of the Islamic Republican Party was destroyed and its leadership was killed. The parliament impeached President Bani Sadr in June 1981, but he managed to escape from Iran, incognito, with the assistance of the PMOI leader, Mas'ud Rajavi.

Thereafter, the IRP inexorably eliminated other political parties from the scene. It did not move against the Tudeh until March 1983, however, perhaps because the Tudeh had unhesitatingly supported the regime. The occasion for finally moving against the Tudeh Party was the Soviet Union's call for Iran to end the war with Iraq. Because Tehran had decided to seek to overthrow Saddam Husayn's regime in Iraq and replace it with an Islamic government friendly to Iran, the Iranian regime took umbrage at the Tudeh's position, rounded up its leaders, and dissolved the organization. The ease with which this was accomplished suggests how problematical the Tudeh's social base of support was.

Between 1983 and 1987, the IRP ruled as the country's unique political party, a situation not unlike the period between 1975 and 1978, when the shah's Resurgence Party monopolized the party system. But the similarity goes farther than this, since in neither case was the political party the repository of true and effective political power. Just as in the monarchical period political power lay in the court, the secret police, and the armed forces, so, too, in the Khomeini era, the IRP was a second-order political organization. More significant were the Friday Mosque prayer leader network, the Society of Militant Clergymen, the religious militia (Pasdaran), and the various revolutionary bodies (nahadha-ye enqelabi), such as the revolutionary committees, the revolutionary courts, the Reconstruction Crusade, the Disinherited Foundation, the Martyrs Foundation, and so on.

In early June 1987, Jomhuri-ye Islami, the organ of the IRP, dramatically announced the dissolution of the party upon the request of its leaders to Ayatollah Khomeini. The reasons for this action are complex, but they certainly are related to growing fears among the pro-Khomeini clergy that the IRP was becoming an autonomous force and, as such, was posing a threat to the continued monopoly of power in the hands of the clergy. The IRP's dissolution was met with seeming universal indifference. In any case, once again, the regime in Tehran showed its contempt for the idea of political parties or a party system. The corollary is that no political party or party system has ever truly struck deep enough roots into the soil of the Iranian political system to be able to avert these moves from above to eviscerate them.

Since 1987 the Islamic Republic of Iran has been led by a clergy-dominated regime without benefit of party structures. It is true that, after the death of Ayatollah Khomeini in June 1989, the ministry of interior announced that it would begin to entertain applications for the establishment of political parties. Predictably, however, no political parties, as such, have been licensed. The regime has made much of the fact that it has granted charters to two or three organizations, but they are not political parties. Rather, these are very small ethnic societies purporting to represent their clientele's interests. By contrast, when such organizations as the LMI have requested licensing by the state, the response has been either a studied neglect of such requests or an unambiguous rejection.

## ANALYTICAL OVERVIEW OF IRANIAN PARTIES

Thus, political parties have been rather ephemeral, fragile structures in twentieth-century Iranian politics. Whereas the single most important function of political parties historically has been the mobilization and aggregation of political interests, Iranian political parties have more often served as convenient milieus for the evolution of patron-client relations. That is to say, influential political leaders amalgamate support for themselves as dispensers of patronage to particular individuals. One thinks of Sayyid Zia al-Din Tabatabai's National Will Party,* Qavvam al-Saltaneh's Democrat Party, the various parties introduced by the shah—such as the Nationalists' Party, the People's Party, the New Iran Party, and the Resurgence Party—and the clergy's IRP. Institutionalization of political parties and of a party system has proven to be extremely elusive in the Iranian context. Perhaps the one exception to this is the Tudeh Party, which, as usual for Communist parties, surpassed other Iranian political parties in regard to discipline and those characteristics of institutionalization identified by Samuel Huntington as coherence, complexity, and adaptability.[4]

Since most of the post–World War II era in Iranian politics has been characterized by autocratic rule, it comes as no surprise that the transmission belt function, identified by some observers of party behavior, has featured top-down communications. However, one should not underestimate the ability of regional party organizations to reflect the interests of the populations of those regions. The Kurdish Democratic Party (KDP)* has stood out at various times since 1945, as has the Democrat Party in Azerbaijan. In fact, the northwestern part of the country generally speaking has been *the* nonpareil area of political consciousness since the Constitutional Revolution of 1905. Possibly, the short-lived MPRP was also representative of constituent interests, like the more lasting LMI, the PMOI, and perhaps in some respects even the IRP, despite its status as a regime party that sought to monopolize political power.

If these parties did represent the interests of various groups, then the Democrat Party reflected the opinion of ethnically Turkic Azerbaijanis seeking autonomy from Tehran, while the KDP represented mainstream Kurdish Iranians. And the MPRP, too, was an Azerbaijan-based organization, under the spiritual leadership of the Tabriz-born Ayatollah Shari'atmadari. Although Ayatollah Khomeini had many followers in Azerbaijan, affiliated with the IRP, their leaders perceived the MPRP as a major threat. Consequently, they closed its offices and eventually outlawed it.

The LMI has represented a different constitutency from the Democrat Party, the KDP, and the MPRP. These were ethnically based political parties, whereas the LMI has been rooted in the professional and intellectual strata—among one-time supporters of Mohammad Mosaddeq who felt that, as a populist democrat, he had not responded adequately to the religious aspirations of Iranian nationalists. The PMOI mainly represented religiously minded young Iranian students or graduates who objected to what they perceived to be the liberalism of the LMI. In its early years, the PMOI was essentially a guerrilla organization that engaged in terrorist attacks; since the early 1980s, its spokesmen have argued before Western media and politicians that it is the religiously minded and democratic pluralist organization par excellence in Iran.

The IRP's constituency varied over the nine years of its existence. It did garner the support of the *bazaaris,* that is, the urban merchant class. However, these merchants frequently clashed with the leftist economic policies of the governments of Prime Minister Mir Husayn Musavi, whose tenure began in 1981 and ended only in 1989, well after the IRP's dissolution. The ministers in these governments were overwhelmingly members of the IRP responsible for the regime's industrial, trade, and financial policies, policies that frequently had a redistributive thrust that threatened the property interests of the merchants. Other constituencies served by the IRP included the petite bourgeoisie and the urban poor, both of which backed Musavi's radical intentions and his favoritism toward them in regard to rationing, consumer prices, housing, and transportation. Ultimately, conflict between the IRP's conservative and radical wings proved too costly for Khomeini, and the party was dissolved without fanfare in 1987.

Various electoral laws over the decades have hampered political parties in their desire to seek political power through the ballot box. While these laws, implemented by the ministry of interior, have been very effective during periods of highly authoritarian rule, they have also been successful in denying parties the ability to campaign for victory even in times of more open politics. Thus, during the 1940s, a period of vitality in Iranian politics, complaints by various groups over the country's electoral law were rife. Indeed, one of the most famous organizations ever established in twentieth-century Iranian politics, the National Front, came into existence in fall 1949 precisely because, inter alia, its members found the electoral law to be intolerably restrictive.

In the 1906/7–1979 era, the country was technically governed under a constitutional monarchical system. The constitution of 1906/7, tailored after the

Belgian constitution of 1830, specified that the monarch be the nominal sovereign, with real power lodged in the parliament, which would devolve it at its discretion upon the cabinet headed by the prime minister. The constitution authorized the parliament to enact all legislation, including budgets, and to be responsible for ratification of treaties or any other agreements involving foreign loans, monopolies, and concessions. The parliament was empowered to appoint, investigate, and dismiss ministers, including the prime minister. The parliament's term was to be two years (later changed to four years), and its structure was bicameral, although the upper house was established only in 1949. The shah was given the right to nominate half of the sixty members of this upper house, a right that he finally exercised as part of a larger effort in the late 1940s to broaden his powers against powerful and active politicians with their own agendas.

The electoral laws changed noticeably over the years. The original electoral law of 1906, following a quasi-corporatist model, divided the country into six classes (tabaqat) as follows: royalty, clergy, aristocrats, established merchants (those with a fixed place of business), property owners whose property was worth at least 1,000 tumans (a very substantial sum in those times), and artisans and traders who belonged to established guilds. Tehran, the capital, was to have sixty seats, according to the following formula: royalty, four; clergy, four; aristocrats, ten; merchants, ten; and artisans, thirty-two. All the other areas, divided into electoral districts by province, were accorded ninety-six seats. Precisely how many candidates could be nominated in this way and how the balloting would take place to ensure these proportions, or how many candidates could run for each seat is unclear. In the provinces, elections would be two-staged, with each of the six classes in every district selecting a delegate; six delegates would then nominate candidates to run for office.

The electoral law was amended in 1909. It retained the distinction between Tehran and the rest of the country in terms of allocated seats but dropped Tehran's quota drastically from 60 to 15 (later, this number was reduced further to 12); raised the number of seats for other districts from 96 to 101; deleted the corporatist notion of representation by profession or social background; reduced the property qualification for voting from 1,000 to 250 tumans (a still not inconsiderable sum); and introduced the notion of guaranteed representation for religious minorities for the first time (1 seat for Jews, 1 for Zoroastrians, and 2 for Christians). A later amendment in the period of the third majles (1914–16) abolished the property qualification and opened the vote to all adult men. This measure, despite its liberal intention, had the effect of reinforcing the power of already powerful landed magnates who dispensed patronage to their peasants and expected the latter to vote for them in national elections for parliament.

This is how matters stood with the electoral system until after the abdication of Reza Shah and the emergence of a freer political climate in the 1940s. In 1944 Mosaddeq, then a member of parliament, urged amendments to the electoral law that would increase Tehran's quota to thirty deputies and require a literacy test for voting (thus undercutting the power of the conservative aristocracy, who, presumably, would no longer be able to shepherd their unlettered peasants to the ballot boxes to vote as their landlords ordered them to do). Indeed, in March 1946, Mosaddeq advocated a further amendment to the electoral law that would have enfranchised women. Neither effort came to fruition, however.

In 1952, then prime minister, Mosaddeq modified his proposal of eight years earlier to permit illiterates to vote, and he proposed to increase substantially the representation of the country's urban districts. However, this effort failed in the parliament. In fact, when it became clear that the National Front candidates were about to be overwhelmed by royalists and conservative landowners in the countryside, where the electoral process was historically a long and drawn out process, Prime Minister Mosaddeq ordered a halt to the elections there as soon as a quorum of seventy-nine deputies had been formally elected.

After Mosaddeq was overthrown, with the assistance of the United States and Britain, in the royalist coup of 1953, the electoral law once again became the tool of autocratic rule. This was the period of the shah's imposition of political parties from above. Heavy-handed rigging of the 1960 elections led to unusually strong protests and the shah's belated cancellation of the results, with new elections called the next year. But these elections, which proved to have been even more flagrantly rigged, generated greater popular anger. Thus, the shah ordered the cabinet to rule by decree in the absence of a sitting parliament, a violation of the constitution.

During the remaining years of the monarchy, the *majles* remained subservient to the crown, although its members showed some independent spirit briefly in 1964 when a large number refused to attend sessions debating a bill that extended diplomatic immunity to American military officials and their dependents. They felt that this proposal resurrected the infamous capitulations that had been granted to colonialists in earlier times.

In the late Pahlavi period, there was one innovation in the electoral law worth mentioning. This was the second principle of the shah's so-called White Revolution program, which enfranchised women. While critics derided this step as giving an essentially meaningless right to more than half the country's population, the symbolism of this move was significant. Indeed, after the shah's overthrow, the conservative clergy, which had been scandalized by this change and bitterly opposed it, did not abrogate women's suffrage, for all their constant rhetoric about the dangers of involving women in the public arenas of life.

Some major changes in the constitutional system occurred after the revolution of 1979 and the formation of the republic. The upper house was abolished; significant authority was vested by the constitution of 1979 in the office of the *faqih* (top clergyman, i.e., Khomeini); and the new office of president was created. The new constitution was patterned somewhat on the constitution of the fifth French Republic. The executive was headed by a president, but the office of prime minister was retained. This anomaly of two executives was eliminated by constitutional changes in 1989, when the prime ministry was abolished as part of a package of political changes following Ayatollah Khomeini's death.

Apart from the abolition of the senate, another change relative to the situation under the monarchy might be noted: the increase in the number of deputies to the parliament to 270. Tehran received an allocation of 30 seats while the rest of the country received 240 seats. Each major city acquired a fixed quota of seats; each rural area was given one seat only. In districts with multiple seats, candidates became subject to elections "at large"—that is, a candidate does not have to run from any particular quarter of a city to be elected; he or she must, however, be among the top thirty vote getters. In the event the candidate does not win a majority of the votes cast in the first round, he or she must win in a second round, but this time a majority is not required and a plurality suffices. One significant similarity in the electoral systems of the monarchy and the Islamic Republic is the principle of "winner take all."

Despite the fact that no political parties fielded any candidates in the 1988 elections, two rival lists were circulated in the Tehran municipality endorsing various candidates. One list was submitted by an economically conservative group, the Tehran Society of Militant Clergymen, and the other by a breakaway group that endorsed economically radical positions. These two lists agreed on eleven of the thirty candidates but disagreed on the remainder. Of the latter, sixteen who won were on the "radical" list, while three were on the "conservative" list.[5] But these results may be misleading, because some candidates on the "radical" list could not be regarded as true economic radicals. Moreover, the capital represents only 11 percent of all members of parliament, so it is difficult to generalize.

In fact, debate in the post-1979 parliament is more open than it was under the monarchy. There is some sense, too, that the electorate is at greater liberty, than it was under the shah, to register its dissatisfaction with the deputies by "throwing the rascals out" in the next election. It is true that in the Pahlavi period, there was sometimes large-scale turnover in the majles, for example in 1964, when the shah clearly responded to the electorate's anger at the blatant rigging that had taken place in 1960 and 1961, and a new generation of technocrats was voted into parliament. But the three elections for the majles since the overthrow of the monarchy (1980, 1984, 1988) have witnessed more changes in personnel than previously. (It should be added, however, that turnovers in the revolutionary period may be due as much to the regime's administrative methods to prevent the reelection of certain parliamentary deputies as to the electorate's voting behavior.)

For example, the 1988 majles saw a 55 percent turnover relative to the 1984 majles. The 1988 majles was younger than any of its predecessors, with the average age being forty-five. Probably most interesting of all, the proportion of the 1988 majles members who were clergymen declined markedly over the 1980 and 1984 parliaments. Whereas in the first two parliaments, the percentage of members who were clerics was about 45 percent, it declined to only 27 percent in the 1988 parliament.[6] What these data tell us about the role of the IRP (or, more accurately, the absence of any role, since it was abolished the year before) is unclear. The fourth *majles*, elected in spring 1992, had nine women members compared to only four in the previous *majles*; the average age was 38.5 years, as opposed to 42 years in the third *majles*; and the percentage of clergymen in the fourth *majles* fell again, to 24 percent of the total.

Although the IRP no longer exists, the LMI is in limbo (prevented from campaigning for political office but not technically proscribed), and the Tudeh, the PMOI, and the KDP have all been driven underground, these groups have all left their marks. These Iranian parties seem somewhat more disposed to redistributive policies in regard to property and education than parties elsewhere in the Middle East. Conservative groups within the IRP were very strong, however, and some even attribute its dissolution to alarm over the growing power of these groups.[7]

On the other hand, a principal similarity between Iranian and non-Iranian parties is that their social base appears to be the urban petite bourgeoisie— shopkeepers, petty merchants, and self-employed persons, such as taxi drivers— and lumpenproletariat. Organizationally, too, there appears to be a significant similarity between the Iranian and non-Iranian parties. Although the LMI is an exception, all the others appear to be based on the principle of centralized pyramidal hierarchy, with the local branches in the form of basic units, which are in turn subsumed by district units, regional units, and a national organization. In addition, the parties also are functionally organized in places of employment.

## Bibliography

Abrahamian, Ervand. *Iran between Two Revolutions*. Princeton, N.J.: Princeton University Press, 1982.

———. *The Iranian Mojahedin*. New Haven, Conn.: Yale University Press, 1988.

Amirahmadi, Hooshang, and Manoucher Parvin, eds. *Post-Revolutionary Iran*. Boulder, Colo.: Westview Press, 1988.

Arjomand, Said. *The Turban for the Crown*. New York: Oxford University Press, 1988.

Avery, Peter. *Modern Iran*. London: Benn, 1965.

Azimi, Fakhreddin. *Iran: The Crisis of Democracy*. New York: St. Martin's Press, 1989.

Bakhash, Shaul. *The Reign of the Ayatollahs*. New York: Basic Books, 1984.

Bashiriyeh, Hossein. *The State and Social Revolution in Iran*. London: Croom Helm, 1983.

Bill, James. *The Politics of Iran*. Columbus, Ohio: Merrill, 1982.

Bill, James A., and William Roger Stookey, eds. *Musaddiq, Iranian Nationalism, and Oil*. Austin: University of Texas Press, 1988.

Binder, Leonard. *Iran*. Berkeley: University of California Press, 1962.

Bruinessen, Martin van. *Agha, Shaikh and State*. Leiden: E. J. Brill, 1978.

Chehabi, Houchang. *Iranian Politics and Religious Modernism*. Ithaca, N.Y.: Cornell University Press, 1990.

Cottam, Richard W. "Political Party Development in Iran." *Iranian Studies* I, 3 (Summer 1968): 82–95.

———. *Nationalism in Iran*. Pittsburgh: University of Pittsburgh Press, 1979.

Eagleton, William, Jr. *The Kurdish Republic of 1946*. New York: Oxford University Press, 1963.

Elwell-Sutton, L. P. "Political Parties in Iran: 1941–1948." *Middle East Journal* III, 1 (January 1949): 45–62.

Ghods, A. R. *Iran in the Twentieth Century*. Boulder, Colo.: Lynne Rienner Publishers, 1989.

Halliday, Fred. *Iran: Revolution and Dictatorship*. Baltimore: Penguin Books, 1979.

Katouzian, Homa. *The Political Economy of Modern Iran*. London: Macmillan, 1981.

Keddie, Nikki. *Roots of Revolution*. New Haven, Conn.: Yale University Press, 1981.

Lenczowski, George. *Russia and the West in Iran*. Ithaca, N.Y.: Cornell University Press, 1948.

Parsa, Misagh. *The Social Origins of the Iranian Revolution*. New Brunswick, N.J.: Rutgers University Press, 1989.

Razi, Gholam Hossein. "Genesis of Party in Iran." *Iranian Studies* III, 2 (Spring 1970): 58–90.

Wilber, Donald. *Contemporary Iran*. New York: Praeger, 1963.

Zabih, Sepehr. *The Communist Movement of Iran*. Berkeley: University of California Press, 1966.

———. *Iran since the Revolution*. Baltimore: Johns Hopkins University Press, 1982.

Zonis, Marvin. *The Political Elite of Iran*. Princeton, N.J.: Princeton University Press, 1971.

**Political Parties**

ALLIANCE AND PROGRESS PARTY (*Ferqeh-ye E'telaf va Taraqqi*). This small, ephemeral party came into being in 1908, between the first and second *majles*-es. It appears to have left no trace.

COMMITTEE FOR THE RESURRECTION OF KURDISTAN. *See* KOMA-LEH-E ZHIAN-E KORDESTAN.

COMMUNIST PARTY I (*Hezb-e Komunist*). This short-lived organization splintered off from the Tudeh Party* in 1947 on the grounds that the latter was not radical enough on the issue of proletarian revolution. It was dissolved by its leaders several weeks later after vehement criticisms from Moscow.

COMMUNIST PARTY II (*Hezb-e Tudeh*). The Tudeh Party, in existence since 1941, has been suppressed several times, most recently in 1983, but it has survived and will likely be a factor in future Iranian politics. Undoubtedly the Tudeh has been the most disciplined and organized political party in Iranian history. Its origins date from 1937, when several individuals with ties to the older Communist Party of Iran* were arrested by Reza Shah's government. Although the Tudeh did not come into existence until 1941, its spiritual founding father was the erudite Dr. Taqi Arani, who died mysteriously in prison in 1940.

The social basis of the leadership of the Tudeh differed from that of the older Communist Party of Iran in that the latter consisted mainly of Azerbaijanis who had converted to Marxism as a consequence of interactions with Russian radicals; the Tudeh leadership, on the other hand, was primarily urban based (mainly in

Tehran) and consisted of ethnic Persian professionals. Unwilling to use the name "Communist," the Tudeh leaders preferred a title with a broader appeal—hence, *tudeh*, or masses.

In keeping with the general policy of the Comintern, the Tudeh pursued a policy of a united front against fascism. Domestically, it attacked the autocracy of the shah and called for the economic enfranchisement of the lower classes. However, it explicitly denied that it was a communist party in the sense of calling for a revolution from below, arguing that the country lacked the requisite level of institutions and awareness to rely on standard Marxist-Leninist techniques.

During a brief interregnum, the Tudeh aligned itself with the government of Qavam al-Saltaneh in 1946, but Qavam turned on it in short order, and it was harassed for the next several years. A clear manifestation of its influence was the large number of workers it was able to recruit into its ranks in the late 1940s, especially the oil workers in the southwest. The Tudeh revived in the early 1950s with the onset of the National Front* government of Mohammad Mosaddeq, 1951–53. The party supported Mosaddeq until the fatal days of the royalist coup d'état of August 1953. On August 16, the Tudeh brought out the crowds to destroy statues of the monarch and his father, and red flags were unfurled in various locations. Mosaddeq ordered the security forces to remove the Tudeh from the streets on the next day, and the party remained aloof when the pro-royalist mobs began mobilizing on August 18 and succeeded in driving Mosaddeq from office.

The Tudeh thereupon entered a long period of repression, beginning with a massive purge of its organization by the British, Americans, and loyalist officers in the period immediately after the reinstatement of the shah, who had fled in fright. Over the course of many years, the Tudeh was successful in recruiting a disproportionate number of Christians and Azeris, and the middle-class professional bureaucratic intelligentsia. Its appeals among the peasantry fell on deaf ears, but industrial workers did respond, even though they did not necessarily formally join the party in large numbers. The Tudeh underwent a number of splits in the 1960s and 1970s as a consequence of the Sino-Soviet dispute, but it managed to maintain its coherence, chiefly because its leaders kept its principles alive while in exile.

The Tudeh played an ambivalent role in the Islamic Revolution, adhering closely to the anti-Americanism and pro-masses positions adopted by the Khomeini clergy, while remaining skeptical of the latter's revolutionary credentials. The Tudeh's careful tactics in not offending the clergy was rewarded for a time by the government, which exempted it from its general policy of purges. But its turn came in March 1983, presumably because Moscow had begun to press Tehran to accept Iraq's offer to end the Iran-Iraq War, whereas Tehran was adamant in prosecuting that war to the finish. In this context, the Tudeh fell victim to its close association with the Soviet Union and was accused of treason. Although the Tudeh Party has on many occasions been prematurely written off, only to revive again at a later time, it is quite clear now that its organization was shattered and its membership was scattered into exile.

COMMUNIST PARTY OF IRAN (*Ferqeh-ye Komunist-e Iran*). This organization came into being in 1920 as the result of the change in name by the Justice Party* (*Ferqeh-ye 'Adalat*), which had been established in 1917. The Communist Party of Iran strongly supported the ideas of the separatist Jangali movement headed by Kuchik Khan in the northern province of Gilan (1915–19). Originally divided on the relative merits of emphasizing class versus ethnic solidarity, the party eventually oriented itself in favor of the latter. In their decision, party members were undoubtedly influenced by the triumph of Lenin's thesis on the national question at the Second Congress of the Third (Communist) International held in July 1920.

The party's fortunes declined after the national government suppressed Kuchik Khan's rebellion, and it adopted less militant methods of confronting the state— for example, organizing unions and calling for an end to British imperialism in Iran. Its major accomplishment was the creation of the Central Council of Federated Trade Unions in 1921. Not surprisingly, the party membership was mainly Azeri and Armenian, symptomatic of the important influence of Russian developments on the fortunes of the Iranian left. When the Comintern adopted a militant, sectarian, leftist line in the late 1920s, the party followed suit and called for the overthrow of Reza Shah and his regime. Accordingly, the government cracked down, banned labor unions, and arrested many of the party's leaders, some of whom died in prison while others served long jail sentences. Although the party formally survived until 1937, its vigor had been sapped many years before.

COMRADES' PARTY (*Hezb-e Hamrahan*). This party was formed in 1942 as a counter to the Tudeh Party,* with many of whose positions its members nonetheless sympathized. However, the Comrades' Party felt the Tudeh was too pro-Soviet. A small party, it consisted chiefly of educated intellectuals who urged the nationalization of foreign-held enterprises in Iran. The party split in mid-1944 over a tribal rebellion in the south and spawned the new Socialist Party (*see* Socialist Party II).

DASHNAK PARTY (*Hezb-e Dashnak*). Formed in Russian Armenia to fight for the independence of that land, this party also established a counterpart organization in Iran, where it influenced the course of the Constitutional Revolution. The date of the founding of the Iranian Dashnak Party is uncertain, but it probably did not antedate 1908, when the Armenian tradesman, Yeprem Khan, captured the Caspian town of Rasht on behalf of antimonarchical forces who were under the influence of Marxist ideas. The Dashnaks were persecuted under the regime of Reza Shah, and most of them joined the Tudeh Party* in the 1940s after Raga Shah was forcibly removed from the throne by the Allies in 1941.

DEMOCRAT PARTY I (*Ferqeh-ye Demokrat*). This party, formed in 1909, was led by some of the outstanding figures of the Constitutional Revolution, most of whom came from the north and northwest. Heavily influenced by the reformist currents of the times, the party also had links to the Baku-based Social Democrat Party.*

The organ of the party soon became the largest circulation newspaper and contained articles discussing European socialism and Marxism-Leninism. Among important concepts that figured in political discussions were feudalism, capitalism, imperialism, Oriental despotism, and secularism. During the Jangali movement (1915–19), led by Kuchick Khan, the Democrat Party flexed its muscles in Azerbaijan province, where it later spawned a new organization—the famous Democrat Party of Azerbaijan.* The Democrat Party itself quietly passed from the scene in 1921, at the time of the rise to power of Reza Khan.

DEMOCRAT PARTY II (*Hezb-e Demokrat*). Formed in June 1946 by the veteran political leader, Qavam al-Saltaneh, this important but short-lived organization was meant to be a counter to the second Democrat Party of Azerbaijan.* Qavam invoked the legacy of the old Democrat Party,* in attempting to institutionalize his power base against pro-British royalists and leftists who otherwise might have gravitated to the Tudeh Party.* The Democrat Party included in its ranks individuals who were to become important figures in the later Pahlavi period, including the extremely popular Hasan Arsanjani, who was the true father of the land reform program of the 1960s.

At the start, the Democrat Party stood for extensive reforms in the country's economy and social and administrative structures, including a reorganization of the army and police, distribution of state lands, enfranchisement of women, and invigorating provincial assemblies. It apparently had a deal with the Tudeh that it would stay out of workers' affairs if the Tudeh in turn left the peasant question in the Democrats' hands. The Democrat Party was widely suspected by the British and the royal court of being a communist front organization, particularly when its leader Qavam, as prime minister, formed a coalition government that granted three portfolios (health, education, and trade and industry) to the leaders of the Tudeh.

The Democrat Party's fortunes were severely tested after the outbreak of a tribal rebellion in the south in late 1946, probably fomented by the British and the crown, which additionally stimulated opposition to Qavam in the ranks of the officer corps of the Iranian army. The rebellion spread to many regions, including Isfahan, Fars, Kermanshah, and Khuzistan. After several months of intense pressure, Qavam (probably fearing a civil war) altered course by moving against the left and veering sharply rightward about a year after his initial leftward tilt.

The Democrat Party won a majority of the seats in the fifteenth *majles* (1947–49) as a consequence of Qavam's deft maneuvering, which prevented the British and the court from removing him from power. However, the party imploded as a consequence of the antagonistic positions for which its various members stood. Among its ranks were landowners, trade unionists, tribal khans, and secular-minded intellectuals. Eventually, Qavam resigned after losing the confidence of the parliament, as ongoing defections from the party revealed his deteriorating position. With Qavam gone, the party eventually fragmented, although some forty-five deputies continued to invoke its name in parliamentary debates throughout 1948. The attempted assassination of the shah in early 1949 and the declaration of martial law led to the Democrat Party's final demise.

DEMOCRAT PARTY OF AZERBAIJAN I (*Ferqeh-ye Demokrat-e Azerbaijan;* formerly the provincial branch of the national Democrat Party*). This party was created in 1917 by Shaykh Mohammad Khiabani, a cleric whose radical ideas were influenced by currents in southern Russia as well as his participation in the Constitutional Revolution and service as a member of parliament in Iran's second *majles*. Although there was some sentiment not to create a regional party out of what had been the provincial branch of the national Democrat Party, Khiabani and his associates prevailed. Among their demands were land reform, the convening of provincial councils (foreseen in the constitution of 1906–7 but never realized), and the reconvening of the prorogued *majles*. Angered by the Anglo-Iranian agreement of 1919, which would have converted the country into a virtual British protectorate, the party demanded the abolition of the monarchy, adopted a secessionist plank, and began referring to the region of Azerbaijan as *Mamlekat-e Azadestan* (the Land of Freedom). Khiabani was killed in September 1920 by Cossacks from the city of Tabriz, leading to his party's dissolution. During the three years of its existence, the party was subject to a tug of war involving various groups in southern Russia and in Iran that were affected by turbulent social movements then under way in those two countries.

DEMOCRAT PARTY OF AZERBAIJAN II (*Ferqeh-ye Demokrat-e Azarbaijan*). This party was created in 1945 by Ja'far Pishevari, an Azeri Iranian who had been elected from his province to the *majles* in 1944. When his credentials were rejected, Ja'far led the supporters of the old Democrat Party of Azerbaijan* (1917–20) and the Communist Party of Iran* (1920–37) into a rejuvenated Democrat Party of Azerbaijan. Among the positions of the party were the use of Azeri Turkish in the province's schools and government offices, the right of the provincial government to keep tax revenues generated within Azerbaijan for the benefit of the Azerbaijani population, and the convening of the provincial assemblies that had never met, despite provisions in the constitution for them to do so.

Although not originally secessionist, the party adopted a clear-cut stand for provincial autonomy, and its militance eventually led it to adopt sharply confrontational positions; with the support of the provincial branch of the Tudeh (Communist) Party,* it resorted to armed uprisings against the national government.

As these events were transpiring, Soviet troops were in northwestern Iran under the aegis of a 1941 wartime agreement with Great Britain and the United States, and these troops set up roadblocks to prevent the central Iranian government authorities from gaining access to Azerbaijan. The Iranian government appealed for international—especially American—assistance, alleging that the affairs of the province were under the direction of the Soviet government. But American and British consular officials wrote that, although Moscow was indeed directing the Red Army to prevent Tehran from reasserting its sway in Azerbaijan, the Azeris were acting on their own and were far from being mere puppets of Moscow.

The Democrat Party of Azerbaijan did not embrace the cause of class struggle, noting that its primary aim was to foster Azari national consciousness and unity. In November 1945, the party organized a National Congress of Azerbaijan—in effect, a constituent assembly that presented demands to Tehran and called for the convening of a provincial national assembly. This assembly met in December 1945 and was dominated by the party. The assembly created a government headed by Pishevari, which declared itself to be the Autonomous Government of Azerbaijan.

The central government reached a compromise agreement with this government but deferred the crucial issue of jurisdiction over military affairs in the province. Meanwhile, the Democrat Party of Azerbaijan undertook land redistribution by seizing land belonging to the government and hostile private landlords. On other issues, such as enfranchising women, creating oversight committees to review the work of local officials, and especially delivering services, the party's activities, according to some estimates, accomplished more for the local population than the central government had managed to do during the entire reign of Reza Shah. In the end, though, the Democrat Party of Azerbaijan was undermined by growing rapprochement between the Iranian prime minister, Ahmad Qavam al-Saltanah, and the Soviet government. Cooperation between Qavam's own Democrat Party (see Democrat Party II) and the pro-Moscow Tudeh Party on a number of domestic issues was part of the rapprochement; the other was Qavam's seeming willingness to grant an oil concession to Moscow in exchange for Red Army withdrawal from the north. When, in December 1946, the Iranian government sent its troops into the province, Pishevari's supporters abandoned their positions and fled, possibly encouraged to do so by the expectant Soviet government. Although the party was not officially disbanded at this time, it entered a period of quiescence until it merged with the national Tudeh Party in 1960.

DEVOTEES OF ISLAM (*Fada'iyan-e Islam*). This secretive and, for many years, clandestine mass movement emerged in the mid-1940s during a time of great flux in Iranian politics. Its major objectives were to work for the establishment of a theocratic regime that would implement the shari'a in all areas of life. Fundamentalist and dogmatic, it was founded by a young seminary student, and the movement's first act was the assassination of the famous nationalist thinker, Ahmad Kasravi, who attacked the Shi'ite establishment for several years. In fact, a polemical book, *Asrar-e Hezar Saleh-ye Iran* (Secrets of Iran's One Thousand Year History), written by one of Kasravi's disciples, provoked Sayyid Ruhollah Khomeini to write a rejoinder, *Kashf al-Asrar* (Revealing the Secrets [1941]).

The Devotees of Islam never created an organized, disciplined party, but they did exert influence in the streets. Other victims of the organization's assassins included three prime ministers: 'Abd al-Hosayn Hazhir (1948), 'Ali Razmara (1951), and Hasan 'Ali Mansur (1965); they also carried out an abortive attack on Mosaddeq's foreign minister, Hosayn Fatemi (1952). Although the Qomm clergy establishment distrusted the Devotees because of their predilection for violence, it never denounced them. In fact, the assassins of Kasravi were acquitted in large measure because of the clergy's defense of the Devotees. In the case of Razmara's death, again, pressure on the court from some clergymen led to the freeing of his murderer.

During the Mosaddeq period, the Devotees tried hard to win the support of Ayatollah Abu al-Qasem Kashani, the most politically active clergyman of the time. However, Kashani rebuffed them, and the relationship between him and the organization remained rather cool, even though Kashani's actions and positions in the parliament meshed closely with a number of their positions. After the restoration of the shah in 1953, the government arrested many of the group's leaders in a mass sweep. It thus drove a deeper wedge between the terrorist organization and the main body of the clergy.

After the 1978–79 revolution, the Fada'iyan resurfaced, but once again the high-ranking clergy kept their distance. It fell to Shaykh Sadeq Khalkhali, *majles* deputy from Qomm and known by the sobriquet of "the hanging judge," to become its leader. In the last analysis, the Devotees of Islam have acted as a quasi-veto group, preventing the adoption of certain policies or views because of the fear they have spread among the people. However, they have not been successful in carrying out their own prescriptions, except insofar as these mesh with initiatives taken by other groups.


DEVOTEES OF THE MASSES (*Fada'iyan-e Khalq*). This is one of the two major groups of urban guerrillas that emerged in the late Pahlavi period, in 1971, and established its reputation in armed clashes with the state's security forces. The founders of this organization were students of mathematics, engineering, political science, and literature in the 1960s at Tehran and Aryamehr universities. Some of the founders had belonged to the Tudeh Party*; others had been strong supporters of Mosaddeq's National Front.* Deciding that police penetration would make normal recruiting difficult, the Devotees of the Masses concentrated on "heroic deeds"—mounting armed attacks against regime targets. The party's actions were inspired by the People's War doctrine associated with Vo Nguyen Giap, Mao Zedong, and Che Guevara. True to organizations of this type, its leaders attacked the Tudeh for being too pro-Soviet and conservative on the issue of immediate proletarian revolution.

The party was crushed after an initial armed attack against a police post in Gilan province in February 1971. After a series of reversals, it split in 1975, with one faction joining the Tudeh, and the other, the "Majority Group" (*Goruh-e Aksariyat*) maintaining the distinctly un-Leninist line of spontaneous actions against the state. The Majority Group and the Tudeh both played an important role in distributing weapons to the people in the Zhaleh Square section of Tehran in February 1979, but otherwise they remained basically marginal players in the social drama that unfolded over the course of the revolutionary period from January 1978 until Khomeini's seizure of power. After the consolidation of clerical power, the Majority Group went underground and has not since been a significant actor in Iranian politics.

FATHERLAND PARTY. *See* NATIONAL WILL PARTY.

FADA'IYAN-E ISLAM. *See* DEVOTEES OF ISLAM.

FADA'IYAN-E KHALQ. *See* DEVOTEES OF THE MASSES.

FERQEH-YE 'ADALAT. *See* JUSTICE PARTY I.

FERQEH-YE DEMOKRAT. *See* DEMOCRAT PARTY I.

FERQEH-YE DEMOKRAT-E AZERBAIJAN. *See* DEMOCRAT PARTY OF AZERBAIJAN I.

FERQEH-YE DEMOKRAT-E AZERBAIJAN. *See* DEMOCRAT PARTY OF AZERBAIJAN II.

FERQEH-YE E'TEDAL. *See* MODERATE PARTY.

FERQEH-YE E'TELAF VA TARAQQI. *See* ALLIANCE AND PROGRESS PARTY.

FERQEH-YE KOMUNIST-E IRAN. *See* COMMUNIST PARTY OF IRAN.

FORQAN. The Arabic word *furqan* literally means proof, and when it is used with the definite article, *al-furqan*, it refers to the *Quran*. This political group, founded in 1978, suddenly made headlines in spring 1979 when it claimed responsibility for the assassination of Ayatollah Mortaza Motahhari, one of the Islamic Republic's leading intellectuals, as well as several other individuals. Forqan justified these actions by claiming that the revolution had been hijacked by reactionary clergymen, rich merchants, liberal political figures, and Marxists.

Forqan vanished from the scene as suddenly as it had appeared, and it is possible that its members affiliated with other, more permanent groups and simply came together for these brief actions that occurred in 1979.

FREEDOM PARTY (*Hezb-e Azadi*). This small, independent organization was established in 1944 by Dr. Hasan Arsanjani, who in the 1960s was to become famous as the major force behind the country's land reform program. It was merged with Qavam al-Saltaneh's Democrat Party (*see* Democrat Party II) in 1946.

HEZB-E 'ADALAT. *See* JUSTICE PARTY II.

HEZB-E AZADI. *See* FREEDOM PARTY.

HEZB-E DASHNAK. *See* DASHNAK PARTY.

HEZB-E DEMOKRAT. *See* DEMOCRAT PARTY II.

HEZB-E DEMOKRAT-E KORDESTAN. *See* KURDISH DEMOCRATIC PARTY.

HEZB-E EJTEMA'IYUN-E 'AMMIYUN. *See* SOCIAL DEMOCRAT PARTY.

HEZB-E ERADEH-YE MELLI. *See* NATIONAL WILL PARTY.

HEZB-E ESLAH TALABAN. *See* REFORMERS' PARTY.

HEZB-E ETTEHAD-E MELLI. *See* NATIONAL UNION PARTY.

HEZB-E HAMRAHAN. *See* COMRADES' PARTY.

HEZB-E IRAN. *See* IRAN PARTY.

HEZB-E IRAN-E NOW. *See* NEW IRAN PARTY I.

HEZB-E IRAN NOVIN. *See* NEW IRAN PARTY II.

HEZB-E JANGALI. *See* JUNGLE PARTY.

HEZB-E JOMHURI-YE ISLAMI. *See* ISLAMIC REPUBLICAN PARTY.

HEZB-E JOMHURI-YE KHALQ-E MUSALMAN-E IRAN. *See* MUSLIM PEOPLE'S REPUBLICAN PARTY.

HEZB-E KARGARAN-E SOSIALISTI. *See* SOCIALIST WORKERS' PARTY.

HEZB-E KOMUNIST. *See* COMMUNIST PARTY.

HEZB-E MARDOM. *See* PEOPLE'S PARTY I.

HEZB-E MARDOM. *See* PEOPLE'S PARTY II.

HEZB-E MELLIYUN. *See* NATIONALISTS' PARTY.

HEZB-E MELLIYUN-E IRAN. *See* IRANIAN NATIONALISTS' PARTY.

HEZB-E MIHAN. *See* NATIONAL PARTY.

HEZB-E MIHAN PARASTAN. *See* PATRIOTS' PARTY.

HEZB-E NEHZAT-E RADIKAL. *See* RADICAL MOVEMENT PARTY.

HEZB-E PAN-IRANIST-E IRAN. *See* PAN-IRANIST PARTY.

HEZB-E RANJBARAN. *See* TOILERS' PARTY.

HEZB-E RASTAKHIZ. *See* RESURGENCE PARTY.

HEZB-E SOSIAL DEMOKRAT. *See* SOCIAL DEMOCRAT PARTY.

HEZB-E SOSIALIST. *See* SOCIALIST PARTY I.

HEZB-E SOSIALIST. *See* SOCIALIST PARTY II.

HEZB-E SOSIALIST-E MELLI-YE KARGAR-E IRAN. *See* NATIONAL SO-CIALIST WORKERS' PARTY OF IRAN.

HEZB-E TAJADDOD. *See* REVIVAL PARTY.

HEZB-E TARAQQI. *See* PROGRESSIVE PARTY.

HEZB-E TUDEH. *See* COMMUNIST PARTY II.

HEZB-E VATAN. *See* FATHERLAND PARTY.

HEZB-E ZAHMATKESHAN-E MELLAT-E IRAN. *See* TOILERS' PARTY OF THE IRANIAN NATION.

HOJJATIYEH ORGANIZATION (*Sazman-e Hojjatiyeh*). This organization be-gan in the mid-1950s as an essentially anti-Bahai society and took part in the notorious anti-Bahai campaigns of that time. Not much is known of its activities in the later Pahlavi period, however. It emerged to challenge the Khomeini clergy's single party, the Islamic Republican Party (IRP),* after the revolution of 1978–79. For example, the Hojjatiyeh Society seemingly urged Iranian Shi'ites to emulate the teachings of apolitical top clergymen and not participate in the struggle for power but rather await the return of the messianic Hidden Imam. Some critics believe that the society, in the post–1978/79 period, has not been a genuine social force or group but simply a self-styled cluster of clergymen and their supporters who had no program beyond their anti-Bahai predilections. Oth-ers say that its followers joined the IRP and worked from within to undercut its ideology of *velayat-e faqih*, the doctrine that the clergy are entitled to rule until the return of the Hidden Imam.

IRAN PARTY (*Hezb-e Iran*, 1941–present). Created by engineering students returning from Europe, this party has progressed through many different stages. About as old as the Tudeh Party, it has been the preeminent political party of secular Iranian nationalism. Mehdi Bazargan was one of this party's founders. Although its leaders sought to recruit Mohammad Mosaddeq, he remained true to his desire to remain independent of all political groups and refrained from joining. In 1949 the Iran Party was one of the major founders of the National Front* coalition, which became Mosaddeq's most important base of support. Seeing itself as the natural heir of the radicals of the Constitutional Revolution at the turn of the century, the Iran Party called for an end to royal tyranny, the destruction of the power of the landlords, agrarian reform, rapid industrialization, state ownership of important industrial enterprises, and welfare programs of the type associated with Western social democracy.

During the prime ministry of Mosaddeq (1951–53), the Iran Party remained one of his most steadfast supporters by cleaving to the bedrock principles of secular nationalism, neutralism in foreign policy, and socialism at home. Its lead-ers were rounded up and either executed or imprisoned after the shah was restored to the throne by the coup d'état of August 1953. The Iran Party then vanished from the political scene. It made a brief reappearance in the 1960–63 period of civil unrest, but it failed to make common cause with other groups. The party hoped for American intervention to curb the autocracy of the shah and provide the secular nationalists with the opportunity to win seats in genuinely contested elections. However, it was not to be, and the shah had successfully suppressed demonstrations against his rule by mid-1963.

Thereafter, the Iran Party remained a minor element of the political scene until the revolution. Shortly before the outbreak of the revolution in 1977, it joined with a resuscitated National Party* and the Society of Socialists to form the third National Front (the second National Front had formed in 1965—*see* Liberation Movement of Iran). But it was perhaps too little too late, inasmuch as its leaders had aged so much that it had no credible spokesmen to argue its cause, namely, the establishment of a secular democratic republic. In this context, the party was easily shunted aside by the Khomeini clergy, whose own Islamic Republican Party* became the sole political party of Iran.

IRP. *See* ISLAMIC REPUBLICAN PARTY.

ISLAMIC REPUBLICAN PARTY (IRP) (*Hezb-e Jomhuri-ye Islami*). The IRP was the political party of the pro-Khomeini clergy, although probably not the most important mobilizing institution of the revolutionary regime. The IRP was established on February 18, 1979, about a week after the seizure of power by Ayatollah Khomeini supporters. Membership in the IRP was an important, although not mandatory, prerequisite for running for the parliament. Organizationally, the IRP was modeled after typical single mass parties, such as the League of Yugoslav Communists and the Algerian Front de Libération Nationale (FLN). But such organizations are meant to deny the opportunity to others to mobilize their interests through their own organizations rather than to act as effective independent vehicles of social and political mobilization. In fact, the speaker of the parliament, 'Ali Akbar Hashemi Rafsanjani, then one of the IRP's two top leaders, admitted as much at the party's only national conference (1984) when he said the original intent in creating the party was to coordinate diverse tendencies and prevent fissiparousness.

The IRP was dominated by the so-called Maktabi or Khatt-i Imam line, which insisted upon the ideology of *velayat-i faqih*. The IRP was particularly intent on ensuring cultural conformity to clerical positions—for example, in the area of ideology, education, relations among the nationalities and between the nationalities and the center, and women's issues. However, it was unable to maintain uniformity of beliefs on crucial social and economic issues, and even on certain political-legal ones.

The social base of the IRP consisted of the urban poor and the petite bourgeoisie. It was not well received among, and even bitterly opposed by, high-ranking clergy at the time of the revolution, although most of them were effectively silenced by threats or coercion. Rhetorically, redistribution was the catchword of the IRP, but significant differences existed in its ranks, differences that ultimately led to its dissolution in 1987. The question of property rights would haunt the IRP, as its parliamentary majority would repeatedly enact land reform legislation only to have it judged unconstitutional by the Guardian Council of the Revolution. Meanwhile, the substantial parliamentary minority opposed to major redistributive policies would activate its supporters outside of parliament, particularly in the key Friday Mosque Preacher network, the Society of Militant Clergymen, and the Society of Teachers of the Qomm Seminary.

Although the Maktabis would occasionally seek relief by asking Khomeini to intervene on behalf of redistribution, he demurred, although he supported it in his heart. Seemingly, he reasoned that it was preferable to have no meaningful land reform if the price for having it was the creation of deep rifts among his supporters, which would jeopardize the clergy's power.

However, conflicts between the conservatives and radicals within the IRP continued to mount. It is possible that, if Ayatollah Mohammad Hosayn Beheshti had not been assassinated by the People's Mojahedin Organization of Iran (PMOI)* in June 1981, the IRP would have become a disciplined and cohesive organization. Beheshti deliberately established programs to train the cadres of the IRP in various aspects of party ideology and organization. But after his death the IRP really had no central direction, even though Khomeini sought to ensure its vitality by appointing President 'Ali Khamanahi and Rafsanjani to take the helm.

As disputes became more heated, Khomeini and his close advisors became increasingly worried. Eventually, on June 1, 1987, the regime announced that Khomeini had agreed to the suggestion of Khamanahi and Rafsanjani that the IRP had served its purpose and should be dissolved. Some observers say that the IRP's dissolution was due to fear of continued outright conflict within the IRP. However, the regime could not stop conflict by simply eliminating the IRP. It is more likely that some party stalwarts seriously believed that the IRP should become a bona fide and viable political organization of professional revolutionaries in the Leninist sense.

In this regard, attention focused on the so-called Warriors of the Islamic Revolution group within the IRP, led by Behzad Nabavi, the nonclerical minister of heavy industries. Were such a transformation to occur, the mission of the party would be changed from trying to tame opposing viewpoints to that of articulating particular programs, especially those favoring workers. Ultimately, it is not unlikely that Khomeini and his close supporters feared that the Islamic nature of the revolution would become increasingly subject to secularization. Given that the war with Iraq was going badly at this stage, there was a real possibility that the people would blame the clergy's "Islamic politics" for their adversities and look toward the secular left for some answers.

However, until further information becomes available, it will not be possible to state with any finality why Khomeini dissolved the IRP when he did. Suffice it to say that when its dissolution was announced, neither of the IRP's "wings" was able to account publicly for this move.

JAMI'EH-YE SOSIALISTHA-YE IRAN. *See* SOCIETY OF IRANIAN SOCIALISTS.

JEBHE-YE MELLI. *See* NATIONAL FRONT.

JUNGLE PARTY (*Hezb-e Jangali*). This ephemeral party was founded in late 1945 in Gilan province. Its name was a throwback to the Jangali movement, which had briefly created the Soviet Socialist Republic in Gilan in 1921.

JUSTICE PARTY I (*Ferqeh-ye 'Adalat*). This organization was established in 1917 by social democrats who supported the Baku-based Bolsheviks in Russian Azerbaijan. Its leaders had spent time in revolutionary Russia and had participated in the Third International, which was established in 1919 in Moscow. In 1920 it changed its name to the Communist Party of Iran.*

JUSTICE PARTY II (*Hezb-e 'Adalat*). The Justice Party was formed in 1941 by the writer 'Ali Dashti and other intellectuals who had participated in the politics of the early 1920s before Reza Shah began to suppress political organizations. Deliberately established to counter the influence of the Tudeh Party,* its positions were more reformist than radical, calling for greater government commitment to education, lower military expenditures, and a preference for American advisers. The Justice Party ended its activities unceremoniously in 1947 when Prime Minister Qavam al-Saltaneh confiscated its assets as part of a general crackdown when he was trying to cultivate better relations with the left and the Soviet Union.

KDP. *See* KURDISH DEMOCRATIC PARTY.

KOMALEH-E ZHIAN-E KORDESTAN (*Committee for the Resurrection of Kurdistan*, or simply KOMALEH). This organization was established as a secret Kurdish nationalist organization in the Kurdish town of Mahabad in 1942. Two years later, the respected Sunni Kurdish judge Qazi Mohammad became its spokesman. Strangely, he never became a member of Komaleh's central committee. The organization stood for Kurdish autonomy within an independent Iran, but it apparently attracted the attention of non-Iranian Kurds, as well. Qazi Mohammad urged land reform and had the support of the Soviet occupation forces in northwestern Iran. Yet, the Komaleh at this time was anti-Tudeh and quite conservative. Despite the original position of seeking autonomy only, the Komaleh eventually moved to seek independence, but Qazi Mohammad was unenthusiastic about this. Other tribal leaders demurred from assisting the Komaleh when it called for armed support, but the Barzani Kurds of Iraq did ally themselves with Qazi Mohammad. In 1945 the Komaleh changed its name to the Kurdish Democratic Party (KDP).*

In the 1970s, the Komaleh was revived in the form of a radically leftist group that favored Maoist solutions to the social and economic problems of Iran. Disavowing Moscow's cautious policies on national liberation, the Komaleh insisted on a Kurdish worker-peasant alliance to bring about a Marxist revolution, a position that is at variance with the nationalist idea of either Kurdish secession or autonomy. Its main source of support was in southern Kurdistan. In the revolution, it aligned itself with the KDP, which retained a more moderate posture. The Komaleh was defeated by the Khomeini regime during the same campaign in which the KDP was vanquished, but neither organization has been totally suppressed.

KURDISH DEMOCRATIC PARTY (KDP) (*Hezb-e Demokrat-e Kordestan*). The KDP, whose roots were in the Komaleh,* began activity during the crisis between the Iranian government and separatists in the northwest in the mid-1940s. At that time, the KDP made common cause with the Democrat Party of Azerbaijan* in demanding independence for Azerbaijan and Kurdistan. However, the KDP and the Democrat Party of Azerbaijan clashed over territorial issues during this period, so their alignment against the center did not imply harmonious relations. The KDP in its early years was pro-Soviet, but on tactical grounds, for the presence of the Red Army in the northwest was what prevented Tehran from sending its security forces into the region to bring about the collapse of the Kurdish Republic of Mahabad that had been declared in late 1945. However, Tehran eventually prevailed in 1946.

For all intents and purposes, the KDP went into hibernation from 1946 until 1964, when it was revived by Kurds who decided to leave the Tudeh Party. The KDP stood for an end to autocracy and for Kurdish autonomy within an independent Iran. Interestingly, the KDP, in its call for armed struggle to achieve its objectives, held up the model of Yugoslavia, which it believed was an example of a successful amalgamation of different ethnic groups within one nation-state. After a few years of desultory efforts to begin a "people's war" against the regime, the KDP retrenched and emphasized slow but steady recruitment of young Kurds into political work.

During the 1960s and 1970s, Iraqi Kurds rebelled against the Baghdad government. Due to the porosity of the frontier between Iran and Iraq, armed Kurdish groups moved back and forth freely. U.S. government policy was to help the Iraqi Kurds with funds and arms, a policy apparently adopted at the behest of the shah of Iran in 1972. A fatal proviso for such assistance, however, was that the Kurds not be permitted to win against Baghdad. In 1975 the governments of Iran and Iraq reached a frontier settlement known as the Algiers Accord; part of the price for this agreement was abandonment of the Iraqi Kurds by Iran. No doubt, these events left their mark on Iranian Kurds, who participated actively in the revolution that overthrew the shah in 1978–79.

However, the KDP did not have it any easier with Khomeini. He personally vetoed an agreement that had been achieved by his own emissary, Ayatollah Mahmud Taleqani, with the KDP over its demands for autonomy. In a move that was met with bitterness in the Kurdish areas, Iranian religious militia, known as *Pasdaran*, were sent to Kurdistan to suppress Kurdish autonomy. In retaliation, the KDP aligned itself with the largest of the Iranian guerrilla organizations, the *Mojahedin-i Khalq*, in the early and mid-1980s. The two organizations, together with recently impeached Iranian president Abu al-Hasan Bani Sadr and other groups, formed a Council of National Resistance to prosecute their plans to overthrow the Khomeini regime. However, when the *Mojahedin* became too dependent upon Baghdad and seemed to be promoting their own cause at the expense of the KDP, the latter went its own way. The two organizations were not on good terms after that.

LIBERATION MOVEMENT OF IRAN (LMI) (*Nehzat-e Azadi-ye Iran*). The LMI, sometimes also called the Freedom Movement of Iran, was established in 1960 by two strong supporters of Mohammad Mosaddeq's National Front Coalition, Mehdi Bazargan and Sayyid (later Ayatollah) Mahmud Taleqani. After Mosaddeq's overthrow in the royalist coup d'état of 1953, those still faithful to the fallen Mosaddeq formed the National Resistance Movement. The regime's destruction of this movement by 1957 was not a final victory, however, as the years 1960–63 brought about a period of mounting internal conflicts between the opposition and the government. Taking advantage of this unrest, during a period in which the shah was on the defensive, the old Mosaddeq stalwarts, plus some younger individuals, resuscitated the National Front* (then known as the second National Front). This new organization embraced four different groups: the Iran Party* (the original core of the first National Front), the National Party,* the Society of Iranian Socialists,* and the LMI. In affiliating the LMI with the second National Front, Bazargan and Taleqani imparted a specifically religious thrust to it, which caused it to stand out. The LMI was willing to take clergymen under its wing who criticized the shah's autocracy yet opposed land reform and women's suffrage, whereas the other members of the National Front favored such reforms.

Because of internal conflicts after the regime's successful suppression of internal dissent, a split in the second National Front took place, in which the Iran Party went its own way and the LMI and the other two groups formed the third National Front. The leaders of the LMI were mostly under arrest or in exile during the period between 1965 and 1978. However, when the revolution broke out, the LMI was a major actor. Bazargan became Ayatollah Khomeini's emissary in the southwestern oil fields, where workers had taken a wait-and-see attitude on the mounting protests against the shah, and he was able to mobilize them in massive protests on behalf of the revolutionaries' goals. Later, in February 1979, Khomeini appointed Bazargan to be the first prime minister of the revolutionary regime.

During the time he was prime minister (February–November 1979), Bazargan often clashed with hard-line clergymen and their secular allies in the Revolutionary Council, which was the real power center. He frequently complained that his government had no effective power and was under constant threat of being undercut in its policies by the Revolutionary Council. Finally, while Bazargan was in Algiers meeting with U.S. national security advisor Zbigniew Brzezinski, early in November 1979, Iranian students overran the U.S. embassy in Tehran and took its diplomatic staff hostage. This caused Bazargan and his government to resign. Regarded as a "liberal" by his rivals in the Revolutionary Council, Bazargan believed that the excesses of the revolution had badly injured the country's international reputation. Further, he maintained that Khomeini had misled him in the beginning, when he had been given to understand that the clergy would not seek to rule but would retire to the mosques and leave governance to the politicians. Bazargan's critics have rejected this characterization, arguing that he must have been aware of Khomeini's writings, especially his book, *Islamic Government*, which contained a radically new argument that was intended to justify clerical rule in the absence of the Hidden Imam.

Taleqani had been a widely revered figure at the time of the revolution, having been imprisoned several times under the monarchy. He had always been an independent-minded clergyman, and, although he joined the Khomeini forces by serving on the powerful Revolutionary Council, he eventually boycotted its meetings because he disagreed with its policies and actions, despite the fact that he was its chairman. His sudden death in September 1979 removed the second most popular clergyman from the scene and opened the door for the influence of those who more forthrightly supported Ayatollah Khomeini. Taleqani's death was a major blow to Bazargan himself, not only because he had lost a colleague and cofounder of the LMI, but also because he had been a major intellectual force who had been important in shaping Bazargan's ideology.

After 1979, the LMI fought a losing battle against the government on several fronts. Although it was the one group that the Khomeini regime never completely suppressed, the LMI nevertheless became a shadow of its former self. It was largely reduced to the role of a helpless Cassandra warning against the excesses committed by the regime and its supporters in the name of the revolution. In its worst moments, the LMI has seen gangs of regime supporters calling themselves Hezbollah (those of the Party of God) attack its offices, physically beat its members (except for Bazargan), arrest and throw them into prison (again except for Bazargan), and destroy the LMI's property. It continued to issue statements critical of the regime, despite these untoward incidents, both inside the country and from abroad.

LMI. *See* LIBERATION MOVEMENT OF IRAN.

MARXIST-LENINIST STORM ORGANIZATION (*Sazman-e Marksist-Leninisti-ye Tufan*). The Tufan was a splinter from the Tudeh Party,* formed in 1965, which accused the parent organization of complacency and a servile attitude toward Moscow. It cleaved to the Chinese radical line on most major issues of the time, except that it believed that the revolution would begin in the cities. The Tufan's organization collapsed in 1977 in the wake of Mao Zedong's death.

MODERATE PARTY (*Ferqeh-ye E'tedal*, also known as the *E'tedaliyun-e 'Ammiyun*). This early group, originating in the second *majles*, in 1910, consisted of the two most active, conservative clergymen of the Constitutional Revolution— Sayyeds 'Abdollah Behbehani and Mohammad Taba'taba'i—and generally supported the interests of merchants, landlords, and civil servants. With strong roots in the bazaar, it was the main opposition group to the Democrat Party,* to which it referred as a group of atheists. The partisans of the Moderate and Democrat parties clashed over projected reforms in the parliament and the selection of the prime minister. Assassination and armed conflict were symptomatic of the collision course of these two organizations, and tribal uprisings made matters worse. The Moderate Party also had representatives in the third *majles*, and again the activist conservative clergy were well represented. The Moderate Party lapsed in the chaos of foreign occupation of Iran during World War I.

MPRP. *See* MUSLIM PEOPLE'S REPUBLICAN PARTY.

MUSLIM PEOPLE'S REPUBLICAN PARTY (MPRP) (*Hezb-e Jomhuri-ye Khalq-e Musalman-e Iran*). The MPRP was founded in 1979 by supporters of Ayatollah Mohammad Kazem Shari'atmadari, the main clerical rival of Ayatollah Khomeini in the Iranian revolution. Although the MPRP supported the notion of an Islamic Republic, it disagreed strongly with the doctrinal principle of *velayat-e faqih*, which sanctioned clerical rule. Arguing the importance of tolerating diverse points of view, Shari'atmadari was frequently interviewed by reporters seeking his opinions on public policy in the 1979–80 period. The MPRP's base was in Azerbaijan, and its membership was active in combating what it believed to be the abuses of the pro-Khomeini Islamic Republican Party.* After a number of attacks were made on MPRP offices and supporters, the party was closed in 1980, and Shari'atmadari was placed under virtual house arrest. He was later charged with misprision of a murder plot against Khomeini and "defrocked" by the Society of Teachers of the City of Qomm, where he died in 1986 while still in detention.

NATIONAL FRONT (*Jebheh-ye Melli*). The National Front was created in October 1949 when partisans of Mohammad Mosaddeq decided to create a coalition bloc of parties generally supportive of oil nationalization, Iranian nationalism, and domestic reforms. Included in the National Front were the Iran Party,* the National Party,* the Toilers' Party of the Iranian Nation,* and the Third Force.* Because of Mosaddeq's outstanding popularity, the National Front became virtually synonymous with Iranian nationalism. However, he himself was only its informal leader, inasmuch as he refused to join any political parties. Although the National Front was broken up after the royalist coup d'état in 1953, its partisans continued to nurture its goals, and it was resuscitated briefly during the collective protests of the 1960–63 era. A second National Front came into being in 1965, but it is not clear when it broke up. The third National Front came into being in 1977 but did not survive the 1979 revolution. Mosaddeq's grandson, Hedayatollah Matin Defteri, led an organization known as the National Democratic Front, established in the 1970s. It played a minor role in the revolution. Between 1979 and 1981, the third National Front and the National Democratic Front tried to cooperate in support of President Abu al-Hasan Bani Sadr, but with the latter's impeachment they were dissolved and their members went underground.

NATIONAL PARTY (Hezb-e Mihan). This was one of the constituent parties of the National Front* coalition that supported Mohammad Mosaddeq. Like most coalition members, the National Party attacked the court and foreign powers. It began as a fusion of several much smaller groupings in the mid-1940s, including the Paykar Organization,* Mihan Parastan, Istiqlal, and Azadi Khvakhan. Internal differences led to splits in the 1950s, leaving at the helm those who later were to affiliate with the National Front. Some of its members apparently held extremist positions against Jews, Bahais, and the Islamic clergy. It also harbored irredentist aspirations toward Afghanistan, Bahrain, and regions of the Caucasus and held out for a "greater Iran."

NATIONAL SOCIALIST WORKERS' PARTY OF IRAN (Hezb-e Sosialist-e Melli-ye Kargar-e Iran, or Somka). This neo-Nazi group was affiliated with the National Front* in the early 1950s but left little imprint on politics.

NATIONAL UNION PARTY (NUP) (Hezb-e Ettehad-e Melli). The NUP, a conservative anti-British, anti-Soviet organization, supported an active relationship with the United States briefly in the early 1940s. The NUP changed its name to the People's Party* in 1944.

NATIONAL WILL PARTY (Hezb-e Eradeh-ye Melli). This party was founded in 1944 by the activist pro-British politician, Sayyid Zia al-Din Tabatabai, upon returning from exile. Tabatabai had been an accomplice in Reza Khan's rise to power in 1921 but was almost immediately banished from Iran. This party had formerly been called the Fatherland Party (Hezb-e Vatan), but its name was quickly changed the next year and its structure was more centralized. The party appealed to the petite bourgeoisie in the bazaar and their allies in the religious establishment, as it called for an end to autocracy, preservation of traditional values, a halt to anti-religious publications, support for local handicrafts, and distribution of state lands to the peasants. Adopting a populist slant, the National Will Party attacked the diversion of large amounts of revenue into military expenditures and called for an end to aristocratic privileges. The National Will Party lost its coherence after the rise to the prime ministry of Qavam al-Saltaneh in 1946.

NATIONALISTS OF IRAN PARTY (Hezb-e Melliyun-e Iran). This organization, formed by pro-German Iranians during World War II, sought to mount a tribal rebellion among the Kurds and the Qashqais and disrupt Allied aid to the Soviet Union via Iran. One of its adherents was General Fazlollah Zahedi, whom the shah was later to appoint as prime minister to replace Mohammad Mosaddeq after the August 1953 coup that toppled his government. The party seemingly dissolved after the British arrested Zahedi.

NATIONALISTS' PARTY (*Hezb-e Melliyun*). This unabashedly pro-shah party was created by the monarch in 1957 in an effort to give legitimacy to his claim to be a constitutional ruler. It was never taken seriously, headed as it was by Manuchehr Eqbal, the Shah's self-admitted "servant." The fact that it took the name *Melliyun* was especially anathematized by the supporters of the fallen Mohammad Mosaddeq, who believed the term should be reserved for their leader and movement. The shah imperiously dissolved the party after mounting public protests took place against its rigging of the parliamentary elections of 1960 and 1961.

NEHZAT-E AZADI-YE IRAN. *See* LIBERATION MOVEMENT OF IRAN.

NEW IRAN PARTY I (*Hezb-e Iran-e Now*). The first New Iran Party was the successor and predecessor, respectively, of the Revival Party* and the Progressive Party.* It strongly endorsed the policies of Reza Shah.

NEW IRAN PARTY II (NIP) (*Hezb-e Iran Novin*). The NIP replaced the Nationalists' Party* after the shah realized that domestic opposition to his autocracy was creating serious credibility problems in the early 1960s. The party was closely identified with modernizing bureaucrats and civil servants, many of whom had at one time or another been associated with the Point IV technical assistance program of the United States or otherwise affiliated with state agencies, such as the Plan Organization, which drew upon managerial and technical expertise. Although the NIP was in power for more than a decade, it was hardly an autonomous political party and reflected its pro-shah orientations as faithfully as its predecessor. Oddly, it contained a group that was influenced by Lenin's concept of a vanguard party and democratic centralism. It was abolished when the shah suddenly decided in 1975 to create a single party, the Resurgence Party.*

NIP. *See* NEW IRAN PARTY II.

NIRU-YE SEVVOM. *See* THIRD FORCE.

NUP. *See* NATIONAL UNION PARTY.

PAN-IRANIST PARTY (*Hezb-e Pan Iranist-e Iran*). This party, formed in 1949, advocated the idea of "greater Iran," involving concepts of empire and nationalism bordering on chauvinism. It was eclipsed after the 1953 coup, but in summer 1978 the shah permitted its resuscitation as part of a general plan to defuse the explosive revolutionary situation in Iran. The party failed to rally support after the shah's overthrow and vanished from the scene in the general purge of parties implemented by the new clerical regime.

PATRIOTS' PARTY (*Hezb-e Mihan Parastan*). This conservative party was supported by those in favor of education reform in the period after Reza Shah's exile.
Consisting mainly of those who desired professionalization of standards in various
arenas of public life, the Patriots' Party included those who had been strong
supporters of Reza Shah's reforms of the 1920s and 1930s. The Patriots' Party
was a short-lived experiment in the fluid politics of the early 1940s and merged
into the National Party* in 1944.

PAYKAR ORGANIZATION (*Sazman-e Paykar dar Rah-e Azadi-ye Tabaqeh-ye
Kargar*). The Paykar Organization was formed during the Iranian revolution when
the Marxist-Leninist Branch of the People's Mojahedin, which had itself broken
away from the parent People's Mojahedin Organization of Iran (PMOI)* in 1975,
decided to unite with Maoists. The Paykar attacked the mainstream "Muslim"
People's Mojahedin for cooperating with the Khomeini regime in 1979–80.
When the regime turned on the People's Mojahedin in June 1981 when the
latter had called for a general mass uprising, the Paykar opposed the rebellion in
Leninist terms, calling it premature and "infantile." However, some of its representatives were caught up in the reign of terror that followed. The Paykar
criticized the People's Mojahedin after the June 1981 events and especially attacked its alliance with former president Abu al-Hasan Bani Sadr in the Council
of National Resistance.

PEOPLE'S MOJAHEDIN ORGANIZATION OF IRAN (PMOI) (*Sazman-e
Mojahedin-e Khalq-e Iran*). The PMOI began in 1965 after leftist university students of the Liberation Movement of Iran (LMI)* formed a more militant
organization but retained the religious-mindedness of the parent body. Some
members were trained in guerrilla activity by the Palestine Liberation Organization (PLO). The ideology of the PMOI was to interpret Shi'ism as a revolutionary belief system and to activate these beliefs through class struggle and
mobilization of the impoverished masses against internal "feudalism" and foreign
imperialism, especially the multinational corporations and governments of the
West. In short, the PMOI stood for Third World liberation through revolution.
In this regard, their views were similar to those of 'Ali Shari'ati. PMOI guerrilla
activity against the monarchy began in 1971, but its ranks were thinned by mass
arrests, incarcerations, torture, and executions.

In 1975 the PMOI split into two groups, one of which, retaining the PMOI
label, came to be known as the Muslim Mojahedin; the other openly advocated
communism and clung to the PMOI name until 1978, when it changed its name
to the Marxist-Leninist Branch of the PMOI, and finally merged with Maoist
groups in 1979 to form the Paykar Organization.

During the revolution, the PMOI (henceforth the reference is to the Muslim
Mojahedin) initially strongly supported the Khomeini clergy. This was manifested not only in the distribution of arms to the masses in the final days, but
also in its participation in the referendum on the nature of the political system

and the elections for the Council of Experts to draft the constitution in 1979. At a time when the revolutionary committees were ordering gangs to assault the offices of anticlerical newspapers and other establishments, the PMOI refused to criticize these actions by the regime.

However, the PMOI boycotted the plebiscite on the constitution on grounds that the draft made no provisions for equitable land redistribution, genuine local councils, rights for the nationalities, and nationalizing foreign assets. The leader of the PMOI, Mas'ud Rajavi, ran as a candidate for the presidency in 1980 and lost badly. Undeterred, the PMOI contested the parliamentary elections a few months later and were widely considered to have broad support in various localities. The regime resorted to coercion during the campaign and rigging during the two-stage elections to prevent any of the PMOI candidates from winning seats. Meanwhile, Khomeini delivered a speech on the occasion of the Iranian New Year in March 1980 in which he attacked those seeking to combine aspects of Marxism and Shi'ism, and he used the word *monafeq* (hypocrite[s]) to allude to the PMOI.

Accordingly, the Mojahedin moved into violent opposition. There followed a period of assassinations of leading figures of the regime, including much of the top leadership of the Islamic Republican Party (IRP)* who were killed in a massive bomb explosion at party headquarters in June 1981. Between May 1980 and June 1981, the Mojahedin assassinated many regime figures, both in the provinces and the capital. The impeachment of President Bani Sadr by pro-Khomeini clergymen in the parliament, under the urging of *Maktabi* IRP clergymen in the Revolutionary Council, led to the fateful alliance between Rajavi and the fallen president. Shortly after the IRP headquarters explosion, the two were smuggled out of Iran and went to France, where they formed the Council of National Resistance.

The regime's response to this wave of assassinations was to inaugurate a reign of terror that lasted until December 1982. In the course of this campaign, the membership of the PMOI was scattered, and many gave up the struggle, although others continued to adhere to the PMOI ideological line and remained in the movement underground. After his wife was killed in a shootout with the Khomeini security forces, Rajavi married the daughter of Bani Sadr and thus strengthened the alliance between the two men. However, when, during the course of the Iran-Iraq War, Rajavi reached a deal with Baghdad that authorized PMOI guerrillas to be stationed, trained, and provisioned along the border for the purpose of attacking Iran, Bani Sadr broke with the PMOI. Rajavi and his second wife divorced.

During the war, the PMOI was kept on a short leash by the Iraqi regime, although occasionally its members were involved in skirmishes with the Iranians. After the acceptance of the UN–arranged cease-fire in summer 1988, however, the usefulness of the PMOI to Baghdad lessened. This situation appears to have changed somewhat in the aftermath of the 1991 Gulf War as the Iranian government again adopted anti-Iraqi policies. However, it is not clear whether Iranian government conduct toward Baghdad will lead the latter to authorize the PMOI forces stationed on its soil to take the initiative and engage the Iranians in skirmishes once again.

The PMOI has, on the other hand, dramatically altered its political conduct and has, since the mid-1980s, striven to convince Western policymakers that the organization is an effective democratic opposition to the government of the Islamic Republic of Iran. In this connection, they have succeeded in winning the support of parliamentarians in a number of Western countries. In the United States, despite the State Department's admonitions that the PMOI had been responsible for the assassinations of Americans during the Pahlavi period, certain congressmen lent their support to the Mojahedin's new political line. This line essentially seems to be a parliamentary path to power, equal rights for all groups, political tolerance and pluralism, human rights, and even respect for private property (despite formal advocacy of nationalization of foreign trade).

However, the PMOI has been less successful with the Iranian groups that, at one time, were its allies in the Council of National Resistance. Because of the developing personality cult around Rajavi and certain gauche, if not outlandish, acts such as divorces and remarriages among the top leadership (Rajavi married yet again, this time to the recently divorced wife of one of his closest associates, who in turn took another spouse almost immediately), the PMOI became quite isolated among opposition groups. It therefore remains to be seen whether it will be an effective force in the future.

In November 1993, Maryam Ezadanlu, Rajavi's second wife, was elected President of the Government-in-Exile of the Republic of Iran. The Council of National Resistance was reorganized and restructured into eighteen "commissions," representing shadow cabinet ministries. Rajavi's name is missing from the list of the heads of these commissions, for reasons one can only speculate about. Ezadanlu and some two hundred of the top leadership of the Council of National Resistance are said to have gone to Paris in the fall of 1993, abandoning Iraq, where they had maintained their headquarters since 1986. It is possible that the Iraqis expelled them at the request of the Iranian government, foreshadowing a possible minimal rapproachement between the two countries as their governments poised themselves to pursue Gulf policies after the war in 1991. The presence of the PMOI in France once again was likely to raise eyebrows in Tehran, at the very least, and possibly might augur rough seas in the relationship between France and Iran.

PEOPLE'S PARTY I (*Hezb-e Mardom*). Formerly known as the National Union Party,* the People's Party came into being in 1944 as the organization of pro-U.S. royalists opposed to British and Soviet interests in Iran. Lasting only for three years, it appears to have left little mark on Iranian politics.

PEOPLE'S PARTY II (*Hezb-e Mardom*). This organization was created in 1957 by the shah to be the "loyal opposition" to the Nationalists' Party.* Unlike the latter, however, the shah permitted it to remain after the 1960–63 uprisings. Even under the terms set down by the government, the People's Party did badly in the parliamentary elections, and no one took it seriously because it was led by Asadollah Alam, one of the monarch's cronies. In 1975 it was abolished when the shah decided to create a single party, the Resurgence Party.*

PMOI. *See* PEOPLE'S MOJAHEDIN ORGANIZATION OF IRAN.

PROGRESSIVE PARTY (*Hezb-e Taraqqi*). The successor to the Revival Party,* this party was modeled upon an eclectic mixture of the Italian Fascist Party and the Republican People's Party of Turkey. Though a staunch supporter of Reza Shah, he dissolved it a year after it was founded, in 1932, for its putative republican ideology and intentions.

RADICAL MOVEMENT PARTY (*Hezb-e Nehzat-e Radikal*). This party, centered in Azerbaijan during the revolutionary period, presumably cooperated with the Muslim People's Republican Party* because it was led by one of Ayatollah Shari'atmadari's supporters, Rahmatollah Moqaddam Maraghehi.

REFORMERS' PARTY (*Hezb-e Eslah Talaban*). This party, which consisted of conservative heirs of the Moderate Party,* represented propertied interests in the 1920s. One of its partisans was Ahmad Qavam al-Saltaneh, who became prime minister in 1921 and was to play a key role again in the 1940s as prime minister.

RESURGENCE PARTY (*Hezb-e Rastakhiz*). This organization represented a short-lived effort by the shah in the mid 1970s to abolish even the semblance of pluralism by instituting a single-party quasi-corporatist system. Branches of the party spread into the workplace, and an attempt was made to orchestrate the representation of interests by occupation. The regime's rhetoric was that a single party was necessary for the difficult task of mobilizing all the resources necessary to bring the country into the front ranks of industrialized states by the end of the century—a long-held goal of the shah. The prime minister was made its secretary-general, and the shah himself, its leader. Although it was said that a large number of people enrolled, the shah's warning that those who did not were "free to leave" or face imprisonment probably served as the catalyst for many.

REVIVAL PARTY (*Hezb-e Tajaddod*). Forerunner to the first New Iran Party,* this organization strongly supported Reza Khan/Shah in the fourth through sixth *majles*-es. Its leaders included 'Ali Akbar Davar and 'Abd al-Hosayn Taymurtash, Reza Shah's chief civilian and military advisers, respectively. The Revival Party also became the home of many of the leading secularists of the Constitutional Revolution of 1905–09. Centralization of authority, nationalism, and Western-style modernization were the rallying points of the Revival Party, which led the effort in parliament to abolish the Qajar monarchy in 1925 and convene a Constituent Assembly to decide the form of state. The Revival Party dominated the assembly and resolved early in 1926 to make Reza Khan the new monarch of a new dynasty. The party disappeared in 1927 when Reza Shah made it clear that he would not tolerate political parties.

REVOLUTIONARY ORGANIZATION OF THE COMMUNIST PARTY ABROAD (Sazman-e Enqelabi-ye Hezb-e Tudeh dar Kharej). This organization was created as a consequence of a split in the Tudeh Party in 1966, when its youth section rebelled. Like the Tufan,* which also had split from the Tudeh, it adopted Maoist positions, although unlike the Tufan, it expected revolution to occur in the rural areas first and then spread to the cities. Because the Chinese supported the shah in an effort to isolate the Soviets, the party became disillusioned. Later, it changed its name to the Toilers' Party.*

SAZMAN-E HOJJATIYEH. See HOJJATIYEH ORGANIZATION.

SAZMAN-E ENQELABI-YE HEZB-E TUDEH DAR KHAREJ. See REVOLUTIONARY ORGANIZATION OF THE COMMUNIST PARTY ABROAD.

SAZMAN-E MARKSIST-LENINISTI-YE TUFAN. See MARXIST-LENINIST STORM ORGANIZATION.

SAZMAN-E MOJAHEDIN-E ISLAM. See WARRIORS OF ISLAM SOCIETY.

SAZMAN-E MOJAHEDIN-E KHALQ-E IRAN. See PEOPLE'S MOJAHEDIN ORGANIZATION OF IRAN.

SAZMAN-E PAYKAR. See PAYKAR ORGANIZATION.

SOCIAL DEMOCRAT PARTY (Hezb-e Ejtema'iyyun-e 'Ammiyun). This very early party was founded in 1904 in Baku, Russian Azerbaijan, by Iranian emigrés who played a significant role in the Constitutional Revolution. It recruited expatriate Iranian laborers in the Baku oil fields. The party's members were strongly influenced by the Russian Social Democratic Labor Party, in the activities of which they themselves had already played some part. Thus, it called for workers' rights, including the right to organize and to strike, insurance programs, better working conditions, an eight-hour working day, and the like. Additionally, it called for land redistribution to those actually farming the soil, free education, taxes on the rich, and civil liberties. It was dissolved in 1910, and its members joined the newly formed Democrat Party.*

SOCIALIST PARTY I (Hezb-e Sosialist). Despite the pejorative connotations associated with the concept of socialism among some Iranians in the early 1920s, the founders of the Socialist Party, several of whom had impeccable credentials as activists in the Constitutional Revolution, were optimistic that they could broaden their appeal beyond Tehran. Branches were indeed established in the provinces, and the centerpiece of its platform was nationalization of both industry and agriculture and broadening of civil liberties. The Socialist Party supported Reza Khan as prime minister in the parliament, presumably seeing in his commitment to centralization of authority the seeds of their own hopes. It also backed the transformation of Iran into a republic when Reza Khan appeared to be deliberating about the merits of this at the time of the fifth *majles*. When Reza Khan was crowned, he moved to dissolve the Socialist Party as part of his general action against virtually all autonomous political organizations.

SOCIALIST PARTY II (*Hezb-e Sosialist*). This small party was the outcome of a split in the Comrades' Party,* one faction of which was strongly opposed to cooperation with the Tudeh Party, and the other, the Socialist Party, disposed favorably toward that end. The party joined the United Front of Progressive Parties that had been formed in mid-1946 by the Iran Party* and Tudeh Party. It appears to have been dissolved that same year.

SOCIALIST WORKERS' PARTY (*Hezb-e Kargaran-e Sosialisti*). This party, which came into existence in the late Pahlavi period, was essentially a Trotskyite party that regarded itself as an affiliate of the Fourth International.

SOCIETY OF IRANIAN SOCIALISTS. See THIRD FORCE.

SOMKA. See NATIONAL SOCIALIST WORKERS' PARTY OF IRAN.

THIRD FORCE (*Niru-ye Sevvom*). The Third Force was created by Khalil Maleki, who had broken with the Tudeh Party in the 1940s and had helped found the Toilers' Party of the Iranian Nation* in 1951. However, he was expelled from the latter in 1953 when its leader, Dr. Mozaffar Baqai, broke with Mosaddeq. At this point, Maleki created the Third Force, which he said was an alternative to Western imperialism and Eastern communism. After the 1953 coup, Maleki, deeply devoted to the nationalist cause, changed the name of his organization to the Society of Iranian Socialists (SIS) and urged cooperation with the left wing of the shah's government to bring about gradual change, a move for which he was ostracized by some of the National Front* people. The SIS got a new lease on life during the upheavals of 1960–63, when it participated in the resuscitated National Front, but it seems to have disappeared from the scene after the unrest was put down.

TOILERS' PARTY (*Hezb-e Ranjbaran*). This Maoist-oriented, small guerrilla party was created when the Revolutionary Organization of the Communist Party

Abroad* changed its name. It competed with other Maoist groups, such as the Paykar,* for influence in the postrevolutionary period.

TOILERS' PARTY OF THE IRANIAN NATION (*Hezb-e Zahmatkeshan-e Mellat-e Iran*). The Toilers' Party, established by Dr. Mozaffar Baqai and Khalil Maleki in 1951, consisted of anti-Soviet Marxist and leftist intellectuals and workers. A major element of the National Front,* the party supported Mohammad Mosaddeq but then broke with the prime minister in early 1953. Some believe that Baqai himself was jealous of Mosaddeq; others maintain that his break with Mosaddeq was based on sincere differences in policy. A powerful personality, Baqai was able to bring a substantial group of the Toilers' Party with him through some rapid swings in political thinking. After the downfall of Mosaddeq, Baqai was treated with resentment by many Iranian nationalists, and his party sank into political oblivion.

TUDEH PARTY. *See* COMMUNIST PARTY II.

TUFAN. *See* MARXIST-LENINIST STORM ORGANIZATION.

WARRIORS OF ISLAM SOCIETY (*Sazman-e Mojahedin-e Islam*). This organization, created in the late 1940s, was led by Shams al-Din Qanatabadi, a clerical *majles* member of parliament allied to Ayatollah Kashani. The society was utilized by Kashani in his confrontations with Prime Minister Mosaddeq after the two leaders went their separate ways, a convenient demarcation date probably being the events of 30 Tir 1331, or July 20, 1952. The society sometimes aligned itself with the Devotees of Islam* in opposition to what they claimed was the drift toward secularism in Iranian public life. The society was so closely identified with Kashani that it did not survive his political eclipse after the coup d'état of August 1953.

## NOTES

I would like to thank Mark Batarseh and Mpwate Ndaume, both graduate students in the Department of Government and International Studies at the University of South Carolina, for their help in identifying sources for this chapter.

1. Homa Katouzian rather eccentrically argues that the term, National Front, is a misnomer and that the real translation of the term should be Democratic Front. His reason for this is that it was not nationalism that was the driving spirit behind the front's activities but democracy. In his opinion, the word nationalism is freighted with connotations of chauvinism, which Mosaddeq forces did not accept. See Homa Katouzian, *The Political Economy of Modern Iran* (London: Macmillan, 1990), 171.

2. Thus, the year 1354, or 1975, suddenly became the year 2535.

3. Twelver Shi'ites believe that the twelfth imam was commanded by God to enter into hiding lest he be murdered by the Sunni rulers of the time. His death would have extinguished the line of the imans, which would be a disaster because Shi'ites believe

that the imams are proof of God's existence. The Hidden Imam's occultation is said to have occurred in A.D. 873/74, and his return is devoutly anticipated by the faithful.

4. Samuel P. Huntington, *Political Order in Changing Societies* (New Haven, Conn.: Yale University Press, 1968). In regard to Huntington's fourth indicator, autonomy, however, one could argue that the Tudeh's ties to the Communist Party of the Soviet Union were such as to render problematical any claims it might make.

5. For details, see *Iran Times* (Washington), 6 Khurdad 1367 H. Sh., or May 27, 1988.

6. *Iran Times*, 20 Khurdad 1367 H. Sh., or June 10, 1988. These data are based on 260 of the 270 candidates surveyed by the ministry of interior. No explanation was provided for why ten deputies were not profiled in the ministry's report.

7. See Sa'id Ahmadi, "Dar Barah-ye Inhilal-e Hezb-e Jomhuri-ye Islami" (On the Dissolution of the Islamic Republican Party) *Aghaz-e Now* 5–6 (Summer–Fall 1987, or 1366 H. Sh.: 26–33. This journal is published by Iranian exiles in California.

Shahrough Akhavi

# IRAQ

Iraq became a modern state in 1920. Created by the League of Nations after the dissolution of the Ottoman Empire at the end of World War I, Iraq was composed of the former Ottoman provinces of Baghdad, Basra, and Mosul. Most of the population is Arab Muslim composed of approximately 40 percent Sunni and 60 percent Shi'ite. A large Kurdish minority lives in the north.

Historically, the territory of Iraq, called by the Greeks Mesopotamia (land between the two rivers—the Tigris and the Euphrates), bordered by Turkey on the north, Syria and Jordan on the west, Iran on the east, and Kuwait on the south, rarely constituted an independent political entity. The city-states of the ancient Sumerians were incorporated into the first empire in 2400 B.C.E. by the Semitic Akkadians, who controlled and maintained the irrigation works that made civilization possible in the Tigris-Euphrates river valley. Babylonians established imperial control of the Fertile Crescent until Persians, and later Macedonians under Alexander the Great, ruled the area.

With the Islamic conquest of the seventh century, Iraq, under the Abbasid Caliphate one hundred years later, became the center of a glorious Arab-Islamic civilization, but began to deteriorate in the ninth century as imported Turkish slaves serving in the army took power and the process of disunity and decline began. The culmination came with the sack of Baghdad in 1258 by the Mongols under Hulagu and the later coup de grace in 1401 under Timur the Lame, who conquered the area and destroyed the irrigation works. The decline of Middle Eastern land trade routes, the discovery of the sea route around the Cape of Good Hope by the Portuguese, and intermittent warfare between Ottoman Turks and Persian Safavids left Iraq depopulated and impoverished, a battleground between the two empires. With the Ottoman conquest of Iraq in 1634, local rule continued until the nineteenth century.

The Tanzimat, or era of reform in the Ottoman Empire, ushered in the modern period of Iraqi history when Midhat Pasha (1869–72) was sent by the Porte to centralize rule and begin the process of modernization of the three backwater provinces. Educational, military, and administrative reform resulted in the initiation of Iraqis into the Ottoman political process. Young Turk rule and the elections of 1908 resulted in seventeen delegates representing the three provinces in Istanbul. All from old, well-established families, these Iraqis received their first experience in government.

Currents of Arab opposition to Young Turk rule reached Iraqis both at home and in Istanbul. Although most Iraqis were loyal to the Ottoman Empire, there were local demonstrations of opposition to Turkish rule. In 1913 Talib Pasha, the son of the Naqib of Basra, presented a program advocating independence for Turkish Arabia and Iraq. By the end of Ottoman rule, two political parties, whose goal was to defend Arab rights against the Turks, the Covenant (al-'Ahd)* and Haras al-Istiqlal, were already in existence.

Army officers, who, beginning in the 1880s, used Ottoman military schools as a means for social mobility, were attracted to Arab nationalist secret societies that were organized in Baghdad and later played a crucial role in the Arab Revolt of 1916 led by Faysal, the third son of the Sherif of Mecca. After World War I, their loyalty to Faysal and the Arab nationalist cause meant leadership positions in the newly created country when the British placed Faysal on the throne of Iraq.

Local opposition to British plans to occupy and rule Iraq as they did India played a role in the British decision to opt for indirect rule of what would become their mandate authorized by the League of Nations. In June 1919, Arab officers in Faysal's Syrian government requested the establishment of a national government in Iraq, and an abortive revolt by one of the officers followed. In 1920 an alliance between Shi'ite religious leaders, Sunnis, and tribal leaders led to a nationalist rebellion against the British. British imposition of King Faysal, the installation of British advisors in government ministries, and a treaty of alliance, first signed in 1922 and brought up for renewal periodically, giving Britain military access to Iraqi territory, were the means by which the British controlled Iraq. Throughout the period of the monarchy (1921–58), the two major political issues that occupied the politicians were Iraq's relations with the British and the internal cohesion of the state.

At the Cairo conference held in 1921, the British sponsored Faysal as their candidate for king. After a controlled plebiscite, he was installed as ruler of a constitutional, representative government limited by law. This parliamentary government, modeled on that of the United Kingdom, lasted until 1958.

The king was the head of state and commander in chief of the armed forces. He had the power to select the prime minister, to issue orders to hold general elections, and to convene, adjourn, prorogue, and dissolve parliament. The bicameral legislature was composed of an appointed Senate whose members could not exceed one-fourth the total number of the elected Chamber of Deputies. There was one deputy for every 20,000 male voters if they were Iraqi subjects over the age of twenty and had not lost their civil rights, regardless of ethnic or religious affiliation. Deputies were elected directly through secret ballot and numbered eighty-eight until 1935, including eight Christians and Jews. In 1935 their number was increased to 108, and in 1943, to 118. The Electoral Law of 1946 raised the number of Christian and Jewish delegates to six for each community but, in 1952, the Jewish representatives were dropped, since most of the Jewish population had left the country. By 1958 the total number of deputies had risen to 135.

Political parties were established soon after Faysal took the throne and remained active from 1921 until 1958. Except for the Communist Party, which was established in the 1930s, parties were formed around personalities, mostly Sunni Arabs, who sought complete independence from British rule but who waxed and waned in their support of an Anglo-Iraqi treaty signed in 1922 and renewed in 1930. These politicians created short-lived parties, often as means for personal aggrandizement and the achievement of high office. They manipulated elections from which emerged parliaments that were unrepresentative of the people and obedient to the government of the moment with politicians resigning from parties and forming new ones as their personal allegiances shifted. Members of parliament were primarily Sunni landowners and former army officers, most of whom followed Faysal from Syria to Iraq. Often, political positions were influenced by personal and family relations. For example, Nuri al-Sa'id and Ja'far al-'Askeri, head of the nascent army, were brothers-in-law. Loyalty was to individuals, not political platforms, and party membership was based on potential patronage and spoils, enticements that became even more significant upon attainment of membership. From 1921 until 1958, there were fifty-eight Iraqi cabinets consisting of 780 positions. These posts were occupied by 166 different individuals, many of whom merely changed jobs with the changes in government. From King Ghazi's death in a car accident in 1939 until the end of the monarchy in 1958, power was shared by the preeminent politician of the old regime, Nuri al-Sa'id, and the regent for Faysal II, 'Abd al-Ilah.[1]

The three major parties active by 1926—the Nationalist Party (Hizb al-Watani),* founded in 1922 by Ja'far Abu al-Timan; the People's Party (Hizb al-Sha'b),* founded in 1925 by Yasin al-Hashimi; and the Progressive Party (Hizb al-Taqaddum),* founded in 1925 by 'Abd al-Muhsin al-Sa'dun—were concerned solely with the treaty issue. The Shi'ite opposition worked for a brief time in the 1920s through the Awakening Party (Hizb al-Nahda)* but, after 1926, submerged its interests within the Sunni-dominated parties.

With the signing of the renewed Anglo-Iraqi treaty in 1930, new political alliances were formed, and more parties were created. Nuri al-Sa'id, instrumental in the treaty negotiations, formed the Covenant, reviving the pre-war Covenant, with the aim of implementing the treaty and seeing Iraq to independence. Opposing Nuri and the treaty, leaders of the People's Party and the Nationalist Party merged to form the National Brotherhood Party (Hizb al-Ikha al-Watani).* Even though Yasin al-Hashimi and Ja'far Abu al-Timan distrusted each other, they worked together against the treaty, against oil concessions to Britain, and, even more, they opposed the acceptance by the Iraqi cabinet of the terms of the Anglo-Iraqi association, which was to give Britain access to military bases in Iraq. Allied with the nationalists was the Artisans' Society (Jam'iat Ashab al-San'a) which used a workers' strike in 1931 to try to topple Nuri from power and to achieve immediate independence.

With Iraqi independence in 1932, most of the existing parties became irrelevant because of their sole concern with the treaty. Faysal dismissed Nuri's government and called the political leadership together for discussion of the formation of new political parties to answer the needs of the newly independent state. He appointed a neutral cabinet headed by Naji Shawkat to oversee the elections that were called in February 1933. The electorate was indifferent as there were no important issues under discussion. The Nationalist Party boycotted the elections to protest political restrictions, but the National Brotherhood Party participated, anticipating the assumption of power. It won only fifteen seats, a majority of the deputies being personal followers of the prime minister, Naji Shawkat, or supporters of the new government. Despite his majority, Shawkat resigned in March because of vociferous opposition to him in parliament. A National Brotherhood cabinet under Rashid 'Ali al-Kaylani took power advocating government reform, exploitation of Iraq's economic potential, strengthening the army, and supporting treaty revision, despite the fact that it had consistently denounced the treaty. The National Brotherhood Party's handling of the Assyrian crisis in 1933 led to its downfall and the emergence of the army as a powerful factor in Iraqi politics. Nationalists hailed the Iraqi troops, who fired on unarmed British-backed Assyrian civilians—whose leader, Mar Sham'un, had demanded increased autonomy—as necessary for internal cohesion. The military commander, Bakr Sidqi, who was to lead the first military coup in Iraq three years later, was cheered by the public and supported by the heir to the throne. Faysal's death in September 1933 brought his young and inexperienced son, Ghazi, to power.

The fall of the government in 1933 led to political realignments. There were defections from the National Brotherhood Party by Hikmat Sulayman and Ja'far Abu al-Timan, who joined the *Ahali* Group,* a loose coalition of young, Western-educated Iraqis, who worked for economic reform along the lines of Fabian socialism. Politicians jockeyed for power, and four cabinets followed in the next year and a half, two headed by Jamil al-Midfa'i, a military man who ignored Shi'ite grievances over funds allocated to the army instead of the Gharraf project designed to irrigate Shi'ite areas. Two Shi'ite ministers resigned, and 'Ali Jawdat al-Ayyubi became prime minister in 1935.

New elections were called for August 1935, despite National Brotherhood unhappiness that their previous request for elections had been denied. The Chamber of Deputies was increased to 108 seats, and tribal shaykhs were more fairly represented. National Brotherhood politicians, who had dissolved the party just before the elections, were now alienated from the government and began to use tribal dissatisfaction and extralegal means in an effort to take power. When Yasin al-Hashimi was asked to form a government in March 1935, 'Ali Jawdat dissolved his own National Unity Party (*al-Wihda al-Wataniyya*).

Yasin al-Hashimi headed the new government but neglected to appoint Hikmat Sulayman minister of the interior, choosing pan-Arab nationalist Rashid 'Ali instead. Suppression of tribal revolts, al-Hashimi's attempts to concentrate power in his own hands, and an increase in the power of the army under the command of his brother, Taha al-Hashimi, led Bakr Sidqi and Hikmat Sulayman, in an alliance of politicized army officers and economic reformers, to overthrow the government in 1936.

The Bakr Sidqi coup initiated a period of five years of military coups by army officers increasingly influenced by pan-Arab ideas and the efficiency demonstrated by the dictatorships ruling Turkey, Germany, Italy, and Japan. While the Western-oriented reformers participated in the first coup and proposed economic and social reform, their views had less influence on the ruling military cliques after Bakr Sidqi was assassinated in August 1937 and Hikmat Sulayman was removed from the government a few days later.

A moderate, al-Midfa'i, was immediately asked to return to the government, signaling a continuation of the status quo, while, behind the scenes, the military exercised real control. When al-Midfa'i's minister of defense tried to retire or transfer Arab nationalist officers, these officers insisted that al-Midfa'i resign. Nuri al-Sa'id, out of power since 1932, sided with the officers and became prime minister in December 1938. Nuri held elections, filling parliament with his own supporters, and initiated proceedings to bring Hikmat Sulayman to trial for the coup of 1936, despite the amnesty law passed by Hikmat's government. Charges were brought, but Nuri was faced with a crisis when on April 4, 1939, King Ghazi died in a car crash, which some Iraqi nationalists were to blame on a British conspiracy, thus fueling anti-British sentiment and leading to the death of the British Consul in Mosul.

By 1939 pan-Arab roots had taken firm hold in the military among the younger officers educated in Iraq. Pan-Arab nationalist clubs were active in Baghdad, the ideology was taught in Iraqi schools, and paramilitary youth movements, such as the *Futuwwah*, were formed. With the failure of the revolt in Palestine (1936– 39), Hajj Amin al-Husayni, the Mufti of Jerusalem, came to Baghdad and initiated, with the support of the German ambassador, Fritz Grobba, an alliance with the pan-Arab military officers, who were led for a time by Taha al-Hashimi.

Nuri offered to resign in February 1940, his position becoming untenable because of dissension within his cabinet. The military officers were divided over loyalty to Nuri and his associate Taha al-Hashimi and reliance upon the regent, 'Abd al-Ilah, to charge a new cabinet. The younger colonels, Salah al-Din al-Sabbagh, Muhammad Fahmi Sa'id, Mahmud Salman, and Kamil Shabib (later dubbed the "Golden Square"), mobilized forces and, in another coup, forced the regent to ask Nuri to stay in power. On March 31, 1940, Nuri resigned as prime minister and handed the post over to Rashid 'Ali al-Kaylani, but he remained in the government with Taha al-Hashimi, supported by the four colonels. By now, the young officers were in complete control of the army.

International events began to impinge upon local Iraqi politics. When Italy declared war on the allies in June 1940, the British asked Iraq to break diplomatic relations with Rome. Nuri and his allies were pro-British, but Rashid 'Ali, allied with the colonels and the Mufti of Jerusalem, who was negotiating with the Italians and the Germans for support of his pan-Arab program, at first wished to keep Iraq out of the war and later became decidedly pro-German. The British pressured the regent and Nuri to force Rashid 'Ali from the government. He refused to step down, forcing Nuri to resign instead. Rashid 'Ali appointed pro-Arab nationalist ministers to the cabinet and asked the regent to call new elections. Rather than accede to the request, the regent left Baghdad for refuge in al-Diwaniyya (a British military base) with units loyal to the crown. Rashid 'Ali resigned on January 31, 1941, unwilling to face a constitutional crisis, and Taha al-Hashimi, deemed acceptable to both sides, took over the cabinet. By February, the colonels had become unhappy with Taha, who tried to transfer some of them out of the capital, and wished to restore Rashid 'Ali to power. On April 1, 1941, Taha announced his resignation, but the regent, joined by Nuri and other pro-British politicians, left Baghdad for asylum on a British ship without signing the resignation, forcing Rashid 'Ali and the colonels to take power illegally, committing what is known as the Rashid 'Ali coup.

In mid-April, the British asked the government for permission to land troops in Basra in accordance with the treaty. The colonels agreed to the presence of British troops on Iraqi soil for only a few days. On April 28 they decided to send Iraqi troops to al-Habbaniyyah air base, where the British were evacuating women and children. The Iraqis told the British that, if the planes took off, they would be fired upon. The British interpreted this as an act of war, and on May 2, 1941, the local commander fired on the Iraqi troops.

Iraqi defeat at the hands of the British resulted in a second British occupation. The regent and Nuri al-Sa'id returned to power with British support. Martial law was declared, and trials, internments, and executions of those involved in the pro-Axis movements followed. With the suppression of the nationalist movements, the parties of the left achieved more prominence. The Communist Party of Iraq (ICP)* became active, and underground newspapers were openly distributed. Communists were given positions, especially in education, and the party was supported by the intelligentsia and working class, despite persecutions during the late 1940s and 1950s.

Iraqi political life seemed stable, with the establishment politicians firmly in control, supported by landlord-shaykhs, a new urban wealthy class, and army officers. There was a relaxation of communal tensions. Jews, who were prominent in middle-class positions, left the country in 1950–51 and were replaced by the newly emerging middle-class Shi'ites. Oil income enabled the adoption of economic development programs. Nevertheless, despite an early attempt at liberalization by the regent, the regime failed to build strong political institutions to support its rule and overlooked opposition to its foreign policy. The regent would appoint Nuri to see his programs through parliament, opposition would erupt, and new faces would be brought in to attempt significant change. When the situation deteriorated again to riots and strikes, Nuri would be returned to power, and the cycle would be renewed. By and large, parliament represented the same establishment interests and was controlled either by Nuri or the regent.

Iraq's pro-British foreign policy during the postwar period sparked opposition especially with regard to the renegotiation of the treaty with Britain, the Arab defeat in Palestine and the establishment of Israel, and the emergence of new nationalist regimes and ideologies that galvanized the people. 'Abd al-Ilah's meddling in Syrian politics in his search for a throne, looking to the time when Faysal II would reach his majority, and Nuri al-Sa'id's attempts at regional organization under British or later American aegis, such as his Fertile Crescent scheme or even the Baghdad pact, were not looked upon favorably by Iraqi pan-Arabs.

In spite of acquiescence to the formation of new political parties by the regent and the Tawfiq al-Suwaydi government of 1946, the policy of liberalization failed. Five new parties manifested a reorganization of the old political thinking of the Ahali Group and the pan-Arab nationalists: the National Democratic Party (Hizb al-Watani al-Dimuqrati) (NDP)*; the Liberal Party (Hizb al-Ahrar)*; the Marxist People's Party (Sha'b);* the Marxist National Union Party (Hizb al-Ittihad al-Watani),* which stressed democracy and socialism; and the Independence Party (Istiqlal),* made up of former followers of Rashid 'Ali. The ICP, although not licensed, garnered significant support. None of the parties had much of an impact in rural areas.

In July 1946 the opposition attacked the government over an oil workers' strike in Kirkuk, which resulted in the death of eight workers when police fired into the crowd. When a similar strike in Abadan threatened to spread from Iran, the British called troops to Basra, and the Iraqi government fell. Asked by the regent to hold elections, Nuri agreed, but he stepped down after the conservatives won, bringing Salih Jabr, a Shi'ite, to head the new cabinet composed of Independence Party members included in the government in order to split the opposition. Jabr banned the two left-wing parties and brought NDP leader Kamil al-Jadirji and the Communist 'Abd al-Fattah Ibrahim to trial. Their death sentences were later commuted to long prison terms. Yusuf Salman (known as Comrade Fahd) and other leaders of the ICP were hanged in public in Baghdad in 1949.

Worse riots, the so-called Wathbah, were to follow in 1948, caused by the negotiation of the Portsmouth Treaty with Britain, ostensibly a revision of the old treaty, even before its expiration date. The Wathbah was also symptomatic of Iraqi opposition to British policy in Palestine, where Nuri had sent a token fighting force. Elections held in 1948, coincidental with the beginning of the war in Palestine, returned a conservative parliament with only seven representatives from the opposition in the 138-member body. Attempts by the governments of Muhammad al-Sadr and Muzahim al-Pachachi to restore order failed, and the regent asked Nuri to form a cabinet in January 1949. Between 1948 and 1958 there would be twenty cabinets in and out of office.

Declaration of martial law and a crackdown on the ICP followed. Three political parties remained: the Independence Party, which refused to cooperate with Nuri, goading him to form his Constitutional Union Party,* designed to include all shades of opinion, and Sami Shawkat's Reform Party.* Internal disorder was quelled temporarily; the regent asked 'Ali Jawdat, then Tawfiq al-Suwaydi, to head new governments that would be involved with 'Abd al-Ilah's political maneuvering in Syria, a policy that Nuri opposed. Nuri was brought back for another two years when popular disorder resumed. Martial law was declared again after a strike by Basra port workers escalated under the leadership of the Communists and riots were instigated by a coalition of members of the National Democratic Party and the Independence Party, which, petitioning the regent for free, direct elections and a policy of nonalignment, actually supported abrogation of the Anglo-Iraqi treaty. A new law providing for direct elections failed to remove Nuri and his supporters from power in 1953.

On May 24, 1953, Faysal II reached his majority and became the third king of Iraq. Western-educated with democratic ideas, Faysal was, however, shy and lacked political experience, leaving politics in the hands of 'Abd al-Ilah, now crown prince, who spent the next five years interfering in Syrian politics with the goal of realizing Hashimite unity (see chapter on Syria). Throughout this period, Nuri was in power, except for a brief lapse in 1954 when he was out of the country. He opposed 'Abd al-Ilah's meddling in Syria, and he pursued his own foreign policy, culminating with the Baghdad Pact signed in 1955 as a counterweight to Egyptian president Nasser's growing popularity and status in the Arab and nonaligned worlds.

The elections of June 1954 were the freest elections ever held in Iraq, with all licensed parties participating and 425 candidates standing for the 135 seats. Nuri's party did not control a majority; the NDP won 6 seats; the Independence Party, 2; and the United Popular Front,* 1. The balance of power lay with the Independents, who, presumably, were committed to Crown Prince 'Abd al-Ilah and his Syrian policy. Within two months, however, parliament was dismissed, and Nuri returned as prime minister for the twelfth time. He prorogued parliament, banned opposition parties, and suppressed political activity so that the elections of September 1954 were tightly controlled, with over one hundred delegates elected unopposed and only twenty-two seats contested. Nuri ignored internal dissatisfaction because of his preoccupation with the Egyptian leader Nasser, whose Arab socialist philosophy and defiant stand against Britain posed a threat to Iraqi leadership of the Arab world. Pro-Nasser demonstrations erupted during the Suez crisis in 1956, and Iraq was placed under martial law, its foreign policy diverging more and more from the rest of the Arab world. When Egypt and Syria announced the formation of the United Arab Republic on February 1, 1958, King Husayn of Jordan invited the Iraqis to form an Iraqi-Jordanian federation. Because the implementation of such a scheme required an amendment to the Iraqi constitution, elections were held in May. All but twenty-nine deputies were committed to the government, and on May 19, 1958, the last government of the monarchy was formed. It lasted twenty-five days and fell when King Husayn, fearing the spread of hostilities in Lebanon, invited Iraqi troops to Jordan in June. Instead of going to Jordan, the troops, led by Brigadier 'Abd al-Karim

Qasim, marched on Baghdad and overthrew the monarchy. The king, the regent, and Nuri al-Saʻid were all killed in the course of this revolution.

Opposition to the regime had come to the surface intermittently during the 1950s. Iraqi army officers, mostly lower-class Sunni Arabs who had studied in the Baghdad Military Academy, had been meeting secretly since 1952 and became increasingly impressed with Nasser's Egyptian political model. Their Free Officers movement perpetrated the coup in 1958 after attempts in 1956 and reports of possible coups in 1958 were thwarted or discounted by Nuri. In June 1956 the Independence Party and the NDP applied for and were denied permission to form a new party with a platform stressing neutrality, an Arab federation, the liberation of Palestine, and political freedom. In 1957 the Independence Party and the National Democratic Party formed the United National Front with the Communist Party (ICP) and the Arab Socialist Resurrection (Baʻth) Party* which had begun to attract followers in Iraq.

Dissatisfaction in the army and the opposition over the lack of a real pan-Arab nationalist policy by the same regime of former Ottoman army officers, relatives, and tribal shaykhs who had been in power since 1921 led to the beginning of a new political era in Iraq despite the old regime's accomplishments in bringing Shiʻites and Kurds into the government and middle-class positions and the implementation of an economic modernization policy.

With the end of the monarchy, political parties and political structures, except for the ICP and the Baʻth, disappeared. If Nuri's failure to allow the development of a healthy opposition and an effective system of succession led to the overthrow of the monarchy, then the revolutionary regimes that followed neglected to learn the political lesson. ʻAbd al-Karim Qasim and the pan-Arab ʻArif brothers who succeeded him, and indeed the Baʻth regime that followed, all degenerated into one-man rule with a coterie of cabinet advisors.

In 1958, soon after taking power, Qasim, who had undertaken the July 14 coup in coalition with ʻAbd al-Salam ʻArif and a group of Free Officers, abolished the monarchy and parliament. Qasim and ʻArif soon broke ranks over the issue of union with Egypt, which ʻArif and the pan-Arab nationalists, including elements from the old regime and the army, supported. Relying increasingly on support from the left—the ICP being the only party that had a developed political apparatus and could mobilize its supporters in the streets—Qasim was able to outmaneuver ʻArif and become "sole leader" after October 1958, freeing himself from subordination to Nasser, but opening himself up as a target for overt opposition.

In December 1958 pan-Arabs under the leadership of Rashid ʻAli, newly arrived from exile in Germany, attempted a coup, which was followed in March 1959 by a rebellion of pan-Arab pro-Nasser officers stationed in Mosul. In October 1959, the Baʻth, whose forces in the army had been removed or arrested in purges following the attempted coups, tried to assassinate Qasim. Failure by a group of young Baʻth party members, including Saddam Husayn, decimated the Baʻth and left the ICP as the most powerful political force in Iraq.

Its influence was quickly felt when Qasim withdrew Iraq from the Baghdad Pact and forged relations with the Soviet Union, initiating cultural and educational exchanges and the arms deals that made the Soviets Iraq's major military supplier. Purges of pan-Arabists in the army allowed Communists to rise to positions of power. Serious riots in Kirkuk, however, which began as a Communist rally on the anniversary of the revolution and degenerated into bloody Turcoman-Kurdish riots, led Qasim to remove the Communists from the government.

His announcement that a permanent constitution would be drawn up and political parties licensed triggered a brief flurry of political activity as parties applied for registration, despite restrictions forbidding army officers, government officials, and students to join political parties. Qasim did not license the official ICP, which was shut down in 1961, but he did approve of a dissident party, headed by Da'ud al-Sayigh, that he could control. Although Jadirji opposed Qasim, NDP member and Minister of Finance Muhammad Hadid supported the government. In October 1961, Jadirji closed the NDP and stopped publishing *al-Ahali*. The Kurdish Democratic Party (KDP),* organ of the Kurdish autonomy movement, licensed while it supported Qasim, ceased to function openly in 1961 when many of its members were in jail. An anti-Communist Islamic Party,* backed by Shi'ite *mujtahid* Muhsin al-Hakim, was similarly short lived and ceased to function in 1961. No Arab nationalist parties applied for license, and by the end of 1961, there were no real political parties functioning in Iraq.

Qasim had become increasingly demagogic in domestic and foreign affairs. A tribunal, the Mahdawi Court, was instituted to try members of the old regime and was used as a propaganda platform against the British, the Americans, and Nasser. Relations with the Kurds, who were originally invited to join his national unity government, soured when Kurdish leader Mustafa al-Barzani demanded more Kurdish autonomy than Qasim was prepared to allow. The Kurdish rebellion, which began in 1961–62, lasted intermittently until 1975, and resumed in the 1980s. Qasim put forward Iraqi claims to Iranian Khuzistan and questioned the validity of the 1937 Shatt al-'Arab agreement, which drew the border at the low-water mark on the Iranian side, leaving Iran in control of the area around Abadan. When, in 1961, Kuwait became independent, Qasim declared that it was an integral part of Iraq, claiming that Kuwait had once been part of the Ottoman province of Basra.

By the end of 1962, Qasim had alienated all potential allies in Iraq, except for a weakened ICP, a few army officers, and the Soviet Union. The war with the Kurds taxed the central government, and economic development, begun under the old regime and continued by Qasim, slowed. Meanwhile, 'Arif, planning to return to power, but under surveillance since 1958, allied with the Ba'th in order to overthrow Qasim. Coup attempts set for 1962 were called off after they were discovered by Qasim's intelligence services.

The successful overthrow of Qasim was an Arab nationalist coup, organized by the Ba'th which, because of its cell organization and clandestine nature, was best equipped for success. On 14 Ramadan (February 8, 1963), the Ba'th and its allies took over major institutions in Baghdad and the Rashid Military Camp; the army defeated Communist demonstrators; and, after requesting safe conduct out of the country in return for surrender, Qasim and three associates were shot to death on February 9 by the newly formed National Council of the Revolutionary Command (NCRC).

Thinking it could control him, the Ba'th decided to make 'Abd al-Salam 'Arif president and promoted him to field marshal because of his stature and his acceptability to Nasser. Ahmad Hasan al-Bakr was named prime minister, but real power was to be in the hands of the Ba'th. Persecution of former Qasim supporters and Communists began, and the regime's Kuwait policy was reversed. Ba'thist interest in federation with Syria and/or Egypt was renewed, even though the United Arab Republic no longer existed. Aggravated by Ba'th pan-Arab policy, the Kurds demanded more autonomy in Kurdistan, but the Ba'thists decided to crush the rebellion rather than pursue the defensive policy followed by the Qasim regime.

The major political issue at hand was a power struggle within the Ba'th, which soon enabled 'Arif to take power and left the party in disarray. To Iraqis, who had little sympathy for the Ba'th, internal party squabbles were viewed as Syrian intervention in Iraqi affairs. Thus, when on November 18 'Arif, allied with the Nasserites, announced that the armed forces were taking over the country, there was no opposition and the coup was bloodless.

The three-year rule of 'Abd al-Salam 'Arif was dominated by a National Revolutionary Council headed by 'Arif and former army officers. 'Arif was a staunch Muslim, a Sunni pan-Arab nationalist, who was attracted to Nasser's form of socialism but stressed Islam more than economics. Foreign relations were normalized, arms deliveries from the Soviet Union resumed, and there were short-lived attempts at a merger with Egypt, until the discovery of pro-Nasserite plots resulted in the removal of Nasserites from the government. By 1965 relations with Egypt had cooled, and 'Arif named a new cabinet headed by the civilian Arab nationalist 'Abd al-Rahman al-Bazzaz. Bazzaz, a former supporter of Rashid 'Ali in 1941 and dean of the Baghdad Law College, was prime minister in a civilian National Defense Council that ended when, on April 13, 1966, 'Arif died in a helicopter crash.

'Arif's brother, 'Abd al-Rahman 'Arif, was named president of Iraq four days later by the National Defense Council. Talks with the Kurds broke down after Barzani achieved rapprochement with the shah. The negotiated twelve-point Kurdish plan was not implemented; an attempted pro-Nasserite coup was aborted; and Bazzaz resigned, leaving the cabinet in the hands of Naji Talib, a moderate Arab nationalist, who also resigned shortly thereafter. On May 10, 1967, unable to find a suitable candidate, 'Arif himself became prime minister in a coalition cabinet of pan-Arab nationalists, Kurds, and Shi'ites. There were no political parties, but opposition to the regime was broad based. There was dissatisfaction with the lack of a pro-Western tilt and the regime's socialist tendencies, a desire for a more open political system, disagreement with Iraq's policy in the Arab-

Israel War of 1967, and a general feeling that 'Arif was weak. Opposition groups consisted of the ICP central committee and a splinter group founded in 1967 by 'Aziz al-Hajj; moderate nationalists of the NDP who rallied around Bazzaz; army officers, including pro-Nasserites; Ba'thists out of power since 1963; and the Kurds, who were displeased that the 1966 agreement had not been ratified.

On July 17, 1968, the 'Arif government was overthrown by a coalition of disaffected 'Arif supporters led by 'Abd al-Razzaq al-Nayif and Ibrahim Da'ud. They were allied with the Ba'th, which, being accustomed to clandestine activities, had been planning its own coup. Ahmad Hasan al-Bakr was proclaimed president, and a seven-man Revolutionary Command Council (RCC) was formed, including three men from the Sunni town of Tikrit. For the next two weeks, Bakr and the Ba'th first politically isolated and then removed Da'ud and al-Nayif, who was assassinated in London in 1978. By July 30, the Ba'th controlled the government.

Having learned well the lessons of their failure in 1963, the Ba'this' immediate goals were to suppress internal opposition, to consolidate the power of the party, and to ensure the predominance of the civilian wing of the party over the military, thus forestalling any possibility of further military coups. The elimination of opposition and the struggle within the party would result, by 1991, in personal autocratic rule by Saddam Husayn, who used the party less for ideological goals than as a mechanism for retaining power.

The July 1970 interim constitution, first promulgated in 1968, established a People's Democratic Republic in Iraq whose goal was to achieve a united Arab state under a socialist system. Islam was the state religion, despite the secular ideology of the party. The RCC of the Ba'th party was the supreme executive, legislative, and sometime judicial institution of the state and did not take orders from the pan-Arab or regional party leadership, ensuring that the Syrian branch of the Ba'th, which split with the Iraqi branch in 1966, could not interfere in Iraqi affairs. The chairman of the RCC was also the chairman of the regional (i.e., Iraqi) command, the president of the republic, and the commander in chief of the Iraqi armed forces.

Immediately upon taking power, the militia of the Ba'th party, the National Guard, set about intimidating, arresting, and executing suspected members of the opposition. The government also instituted show trials of alleged Communists and Syrian, CIA, and Israeli agents, resulting in hundreds of deaths, including the public hanging of a number of "Zionist" agents in January 1969.

The method for dealing with the major opposition groups—the Shi'ites, the Communists, and the Kurds—was either to neutralize or absorb them. The Shi'ites, a majority in the Arab population of Iraq, never managed to unite politically in order to gain control of the country. After World War II, with the migration of rural Shi'ites from the south to the slums of the major cities, especially Baghdad, they were attracted to the ICP, which dealt with economic issues rather than preaching Arab nationalism as did other parties. The leading 'ulama of al-Najaf formed a political organization, the Association of Najaf

'Ulama', whose goal was more to combat secularism, atheism, and communism than to act politically. This group became the nucleus for the Islamic Call (al-Da'wa al-Islamiyya),* the Shi'ite secret society that became active in 1968 and which, by the late 1970s, was advocating the overthrow of the Ba'th regime. A widespread purge of Shi'ites followed riots in al-Najaf and Karbala in 1977. The government alleged a Syrian-backed Shi'ite plot, and riots in 1979 were all the more threatening after the accession to power of the Ayatollah Khomeini in Iran and subsequent Iraqi fears of a spillover of the Islamic revolution from Iran to Iraq. Islamic Call leaders were arrested and executed, and tens of thousands of Shi'ites were exiled. At the same time, Saddam appointed Shi'ites to the RCC and poured money into Shi'ite areas in order to prevent Shi'ite support for the Khomeini regime in Iran. One of Iraq's stated reasons for war with Iran in 1980 was fear of an Islamic Iranian threat to the regime.

Both the Communists and the Kurds were asked to join the government in 1968 and both refused. For the next two decades, the Ba'th used a carrot and stick method—terror with concrete demonstrations of good faith—in order to control both groups. Initially, the Communists refused to cooperate with the Ba'th in a National Progressive Front until political parties were legalized and free elections were held. They saw their participation in a Ba'th government as a means for neutralizing or muzzling the opposition. With the backing of the Soviet Union and the signing of the Iraqi-Soviet Friendship Agreement in 1972, however, the party took collective action to participate in a national front with the Ba'th. By this time, most of the Communists had been released from jail and reinstated to jobs, and Communists were appointed to the cabinet. The Ba'th, however, used this period of cooperation to control mass organizations and unions in which Communist influence had been predominant, by filling posts in the hierarchies with Ba'th members. In 1975 the ICP withdrew its support in protest against the government's Kurdish policy. Mass arrests and executions of Communists took place in 1978 after the Soviet-supported coup in Afghanistan, as Saddam sought to destroy the party. By 1979 most of the leadership had fled the country, and the party went underground and ceased to be a political factor.

At the same time, the government was determined to crush the Kurdish opposition, despite the Ba'th's commitment to the implementation of the 1966 agreement. Ba'th support of such Kurdish opponents of Barzani as Jalal al-Talabani and Ibrahim Ahmad first led to clashes in 1968 and to full-scale war in 1969. In March 1970 Saddam Husayn negotiated an agreement with Mustafa al-Barzani and his Pesh Merga guerrillas, whereby the government agreed to Kurdish autonomy, proportional representation of Kurds within a national legislative body, a Kurdish vice president at the national level, and equitable allocation of oil revenues to Kurdish areas. In return, the Kurds agreed to turn over their heavy weapons to the government, to submit to a census, and to delay the implementation of the agreement for four years.

The Kurds remained Iraq's major internal problem. Relations between the Kurds and the government steadily deteriorated, even after the 1970 agreement was signed, to the point where war resumed in 1974–75. Fearing Soviet influence in Iraq, both the United States, through CIA subsidies, and Iran, with arms and men, intervened on the side of the Kurds. The ICP, traditional ally of the Kurds, did not fight because of pressure from the Soviet Union, whose influence in Iraq was based on the 1972 treaty. In 1975, through the mediation of Algeria, Saddam negotiated an agreement with Iran, by which, in exchange for withdrawal of support of the Kurds, Iran received recognition of its claims to the Shatt al-'Arab waterway. The Kurds, their weapons and materiel cut off, retreated as the government took over the north and confined them to their mountain strongholds. By 1976 the government began to implement provisions of the 1970 agreement, allocating some funds to Kurdish areas but, at the same time, initiated a policy of depopulation of Kurdish areas on the border with Iran through large-scale deportations of Kurds to the south. Guerrilla warfare continued throughout the Iran-Iraq War (1980–88), during which it was government policy systematically to raze Kurdish villages, deport Iranian Kurds, resettle Iraqi Kurds in the southwestern desert, and use chemical weapons against those who remained in the north.

As deputy to President Bakr, Saddam Husayn used the early years of Ba'th rule to consolidate his own position and build a political base that enabled him to emerge as head of the party and president of the republic in 1979. Named by Bakr as head of both the party apparatus and the president's national security force, the National Security Bureau of the RCC, Saddam, in turn, appointed his supporters to thousands of newly created civilian commissions throughout the country. This was accomplished by means of an elaborate party organization reaching far down to local levels. As the Ba'th consolidated its power in Iraq through the extension of party control from the national to the local level and by the institution of a number of overlapping intelligence services, all reporting independently to him and headed by family members or fellow Tikritis, Saddam took control of the party by ensuring loyalty on all levels of the party structure.

By 1970 Saddam Husayn became deputy head of the RCC, after successfully weeding out his chief political competitors, Hardan al-Tikriti and Salih Mahdi Ammash, both popular military men who had tried to create personal alternative power bases. Saddam continued to consolidate his hold on the party through changes in the RCC and the Regional (Iraqi) Command, ensuring that in 1974 and in 1977 the newly elected Iraqi leadership, including a number of Shi'ites, supported him. Because members of the Regional (Iraqi) Command joined the ruling RCC, the top echelons of the party consisted of a younger, better educated, regionally diverse group that owed its loyalty not only to the party but to Saddam himself. At the same time, Bakr's deputy was broadening his government duties to include foreign affairs, gradually changing Iraq's image from that of a radical subversive regime supporting South Yemen and armed struggle against Israel to that of a key player in inter-Arab affairs and a major power in the nonaligned camp, and even fostering diplomatic relations with the Gulf states. With its increased wealth after the nationalization of oil and the signing of the 1975

Algiers agreement, which pacified Iraq's eastern border and removed the Kurdish threat, Iraq hosted the Baghdad Arab summit of 1978 and emerged as the prospective host for the nonaligned summit meetings scheduled for 1982.

On July 16, 1979, on the eve of the eleventh anniversary of the Ba'th takeover, Bakr resigned for reasons of ill health and Saddam was sworn in as president. He also retained all key government posts: chairman of the RCC, secretary-general of the Ba'th Party, prime minister, commander in chief of the armed forces, and head of internal security, which had been his responsibility since the Ba'th took over in 1968.

If by 1974, the Ba'th had achieved one-party control in Iraq, by 1979 Saddam Husayn had made the party an instrument for one-man rule through a purge of all senior party cadres, leaving only his loyal supporters. In order to ensure control, he increased the popular militia to 250,000 and began to bypass the RCC, leaning more on his cabinet to carry out the increasing numbers of presidential directives. Iraq also held the first elections since 1958 for a newly created national assembly that was to have legislative duties along with the RCC. It could ratify budgets and treaties, and propose and enact legislation. The 1979 law provided for an assembly of 250 members to be elected by secret ballot every four years. All Iraqis over the age of eighteen were eligible to vote, and the country was divided into electoral districts. There was, however, only one list of government-approved Ba'th and sympathetic independent candidates. Even though subsequent elections in 1984 and 1989 would show more independent participation in the political process, it seems that nonparty members were carefully screened.

Under Saddam, Iraq became not a military dictatorship but a totalitarian state under the rule of a sole leader who instituted a cult of personality not unlike that of Josef Stalin. With his ubiquitous portrait representing the ruler as father of the country, benevolent provider, military savior against Iran, religious leader whose genealogy extends back to the Prophet Muhammad, and scion of newly Arabized ancient Mesopotamians, Saddam created a regime that dominated the lives of all Iraqis. Political power was based more on personal ties to Saddam, his family, and the extended family of Tikritis than on party membership or loyalty to Ba'th ideology.

Saddam's single-handed control of the party apparatus and government enabled him to embark on two disastrous military adventures: the Iraq-Iran War (1980–88) and the Persian Gulf War (1991). Legitimate fear of his hostile eastern neighbor, the Islamic regime in Iran, led Saddam to attack Iran in what he anticipated would be a quick victory. Instead, the war degenerated into an eight-year quagmire. Iranian tenaciousness and refusal to negotiate accelerated the war so that, by 1986, after the fall of Fao, Saddam had to accede to his generals' demand that he permit them to direct the war. The president retained control of the military through honors and gifts and sent the politicized popular militia to the front; at the same time, he isolated the Iraqi public from economic hardship and unpleasant war news. The cease-fire of 1988, achieved after Iraqi aerial bombardment of Iranian cities, loss of Iranian morale, and a superpower tilt toward Iraq, left the country more than $80 billion in debt.

With the cease-fire, Saddam turned his attention more toward threats from within than without because of Iraq's enormous economic problems. Concerned with retaining personal power, he used the party but disregarded the Ba'th platform in order to alleviate Iraq's economic distress, policies that led the West to perceive a shift toward moderation in the regime. During the war, Saddam allowed privatization of agriculture and business. In 1988 he pledged to establish a democratic multiparty system and to pardon political prisoners; however, although the elections of 1989 returned more independent candidates, it seemed that no one was allowed to run who was deemed dangerous to the regime. An emphasis on Mesopotamian roots and Iraqi nationalism, the resuscitation of the Hashimite monarchy for popular veneration, and Saddam's involvement in the Arab Cooperation Council in 1989 added to the new image of the regime. Western investment followed.

The lack of a peace treaty with Iran, however, meant that, at great cost to the government, the army could not demobilize. Requests to Kuwait to cancel the war debt and for contributions to Iraq's economy having failed, Saddam invaded Kuwait in August 1990. Miscalculating the American response to his actions, Saddam faced, by war's end in February 1991, virtual destruction of Iraq's infrastructure, United Nations sanctions against the regime, and opposition to a rule that has depended almost entirely on family ties.

## Bibliography

Baram, Amazia. "The Ruling Political Elite in Ba'thi Iraq, 1968–1986: The Changing Features of a Collective Profile." *International Journal of Middle East Studies* 21 (November 1989): 447–93.

Batatu, Hanna. *The Old Social Classes and the Revolutionary Movements of Iraq.* Princeton, N.J.: Princeton University Press, 1978.

Dann, Uriel. *Iraq under Qassem.* New York: Praeger, 1969.

Farouk-Sluglett, Marion, and Peter Sluglett. *Iraq since 1958: From Revolution to Dictatorship.* London: I. B. Tauris and Co., 1990.

Karsh, Efraim, and Inari Rautsi. *Saddam Hussein: A Political Biography.* New York: Free Press, 1991.

Khadduri, Majid. *Independent Iraq: A Study in Iraqi Politics from 1932 to 1958.* London: Oxford University Press, 1960.

———. *Republican Iraq.* London: Oxford University Press, 1969.

———. *Socialist Iraq.* Washington, D.C.: Middle East Institute, 1978.

Longrigg, Stephen H. *Iraq 1900 to 1950: A Political, Social, and Economic History.* London: Oxford University Press, 1953.

Marr, Phebe. *The Modern History of Iraq.* Boulder, Colo.: Westview Press, 1985.

———. "Iraq: Its Revolutionary Experience under the Ba'th." In *Ideology and Power in the Middle East: Studies in Honor of George Lenczowski,* edited by Peter J. Chelkowski and Robert J. Pranger. Durham, N.C.: Duke University Press, 1988.

Simon, Reeva S. *Iraq between the Two World Wars: The Creation and Implementation of a Nationalist Ideology*. New York: Columbia University Press, 1986.

Sluglett, Peter. *Britain in Iraq: 1914–1932*. Oxford: Oxford University Press, 1976.

## Political Parties

AHALI GROUP. This group of Western-educated reformers never became a real party. Inspired by Fabian socialism, they were known by the name of their newspaper. The group's leaders were Muhammad Hadid, from a wealthy Mosul family, who had studied at the London School of Economics; 'Abd al-Qadir Isma'il, who later became the leader of the Communist Party of Iraq (ICP)*; and Kamil al-Jadirji, who resigned from the National Brotherhood Party* in 1933 to join the Ahali Group. In 1934 Hikmat Sulayman and Ja'far Abu al-Timan also left the National Brotherhood Party to join the group.

AL-AHD. *See* THE COVENANT.

ARAB SOCIALIST RESURRECTION (BA'TH) PARTY (*Hizb al-Ba'th al-'Arabi al-Ishtiraki*). Established in Syria in the 1940s by Michel 'Aflaq and Salah al-Din Bitar, the party stood for pan-Arabism and socialism. Iraqi students studying in Syria introduced the Ba'th into Iraq under the leadership of Fu'ad al-Rikabi, a Shi'ite engineer. The Iraqi Ba'th was officially designated a regional branch of the party headquartered in Syria. In 1952 there were one hundred members in Iraq organized in cells drawn from schools and colleges and some military, although its leadership remained civilian. In 1957 the Ba'th joined the National Union Front.* With the declaration of the union of Syria and Egypt in the United Arab Republic in 1958, the Ba'th became anti-Nasser even though al-Rikabi, who supported Nasser, became minister of development in Qasim's government.

Convinced that there was too much support for Qasim, the party ordered his assassination. This was attempted in spring 1959 by Saddam Husayn and others, but the attempt failed. By this time, most of the leadership was in exile, and al-Rikabi fled to Syria and Egypt.

In 1962 the party came under new leadership, including Shi'ites, the most important of whom was 'Ali Salih al-Sa'di (Kurdish and Arab Sunni). In alliance with 'Abd al-Salam 'Arif, the Ba'th helped to overthrow Qasim in 1963. A split in Ba'th leadership between the militant, doctrinaire al-Sa'di; pragmatists Talib Shabib, Hardan al-Tikriti, and Tahir Yahya; and centrists Ahmad Hasan al-Bakr and Salih Mahdi Ammash led the latter to mediate between the other two groups. When, in November 1963, party members took to the streets in order to proclaim their views, the Iraqi leadership of the Ba'th appealed to the National Command of the party in Syria to settle the dispute. Michel 'Aflaq and Amin al-Hafiz arrived in Baghdad and removed most of the Ba'th leadership from power, leaving decision making in the hands of the National Command, based in Syria. The party was in disarray after it acquiesced in this Syrian intervention in Iraqi party matters. Shortly thereafter, 'Arif ousted the Ba'th from the government. Party membership in 1964 was about 2,500 full members, with approximately 15,000 candidate members.

In early 1966, the radical wing of the Syrian Ba'th overthrew the Syrian government of General Amin al-Hafiz, which had established a rival National Command in Damascus with the support of Salah al-Din Bitar. Ahmad Hasan al-Bakr and Saddam Husayn remained loyal to Bitar and 'Aflaq, inviting them to Baghdad. In 1968 the Iraqi Ba'th, now more practical and unified, overthrew 'Arif.

The party apparatus was designed to function hierarchically, beginning with the *halaqah* (cell) at its most basic level. The cell, consisting of from three to seven active party members, was intended to function at the neighborhood level. Next, the *firqah* (section), made up of from three to seven cells, was to operate in the area of a small urban quarter or village. It was to recruit new members, link lower and upper echelons of the party, and execute policy made at higher levels through party units located in bureaucratic structures such as offices, factories, and schools. Consisting of from two to five sections, the *shu'bah* (division), headed by an elected command, was designed to supervise a large, rural district or a major portion of a city. The *far* (branch), consisting of at least two divisions, with an elected command was to govern a major subdivision of the city of Baghdad or a rural area. Five *tanzims* (area commands), one each for Baghdad, the Euphrates, Central, Southern, and Northern areas, was to complete the Iraqi organization. Numerous professional unions, such as the Lawyers' Union or the General Federation of Farmers' Union, were to work parallel to the party structure. Some of these groups were founded under the monarchy, but were expanded by the Ba'th and controlled through election of Ba'thists to positions of influence within the organizations. Membership in the Ba'th party became a prerequisite for admission to higher education and jobs. Achievement of high status in the party took at least fifteen years of party service; very few members reached top leadership posts. (See also the chapters on Lebanon and Syria.)

AWAKENING PARTY (*Hizb al-Nahda*). The Awakening was revived after the Young Turk period under Shi'ite leadership in the 1920s. It was led by Amin al-Charchafchi. It lost support when Shi'ite and Sunnis united against the British.

BA'TH PARTY. *See* ARAB SOCIALIST RESURRECTION (BA'TH) PARTY.

COMMUNIST PARTY OF IRAQ (ICP) (*Hizb al-Shuyu'i al-'Iraqi*). With roots going back to the 1930s, the first central committee was created in 1935. In 1941 the party came under the leadership of Yusuf Salman (Comrade Fahd), a self-educated Chaldean Christian. The party appealed to journalists, teachers, lawyers, and other educated professionals. Almost half of its members were Jews,

Christians, and Shi'ites. On February 14–15, 1949, Fahd, the first secretary of the ICP, and two members of his politburo were publicly hanged in Baghdad.

Suppressed in the 1950s by Nuri al-Sa'id, the ICP had a hard-core membership of about 500. It was active during the Qasim era with approximately 20,000–25,000 officially registered members in 1959, mostly new recruits drawn from Shi'ites, Kurds, and the Iraqi intelligentsia. Qasim purged the army of nationalists and replaced them with Communists and sympathizers, but by September 1960, the party had been discredited, its leader, 'Abd al-Qadir Isma'il, jailed, and Communists in high positions removed.

ICP support for the Ba'th* ended in 1975, by which time the Ba'th had co-opted Communist organizations, leaving the ICP only with the official party organization. It opposed the government because of its Kurdish policy, its policy on Palestine, its failure to call for elections for a national assembly, its growing ties with the capitalist world after 1973, and Baghdad's deteriorating relations with the Soviet Union due to its increased oil revenues. The Ba'th, in turn, feared internal subversion from the ICP, especially after the Soviet-backed coup in Afghanistan in 1978. In May 1978, twenty-one Communists who had been in prison for forming cells in the army were executed, and the party apparatus was destroyed through harassment, attacks, and purges of Communist sympathizers in the government. By April 1979 most of the leadership had fled the country, and the party went underground.

CONSTITUTIONAL UNION PARTY (*Ittihad al-Dustouri*). This party was created by Nuri al-Sa'id in 1949.

THE COVENANT (*al-Ahd*). This Arab nationalist secret society/party was formed in 1913. A party of that name was revived by Nuri al-Sa'id in 1930 after the signing of the Anglo-Iraqi treaty. Its goal was to implement the treaty and achieve Iraqi independence. It was dissolved in 1932 after Iraq became independent.

AL-DA'WA AL-ISLAMIYYA. *See* ISLAMIC CALL.

FATAMID PARTY. This party, founded in 1969 to propagate Shi'ite rights, was short lived.

HARAKAT AL-QAWMIYYIN AL-'ARAB. *See* MOVEMENT OF ARAB NATIONALISTS.

HIZB AL-AHRAR. *See* LIBERAL PARTY.

HIZB AL-BA'TH AL-'ARABI AL-ISHTIRAKI. *See* ARAB SOCIALIST RESURRECTION (BA'TH) PARTY.

HIZB AL-IKHA AL-WATANI. *See* NATIONAL BROTHERHOOD PARTY.

HIZB AL-ITTIHAD AL-WATANI. *See* NATIONAL UNION PARTY.

HIZB AL-NAHDA. *See* AWAKENING PARTY.

HIZB AL-SHA'B. *See* PEOPLE'S PARTY.

HIZB AL-SHUYU'I AL-'IRAQI. *See* COMMUNIST PARTY OF IRAQ.

HIZB AL-TAHARRUR AL-WATANI. *See* NATIONAL LIBERATION PARTY.

HIZB AL-TAQADDUM. *See* PROGRESSIVE PARTY.

HIZB AL-WATANI. *See* NATIONALIST PARTY.

HIZB AL-WATANI AL-DIMUQRATI. *See* NATIONAL DEMOCRATIC PARTY.

ICP. *See* COMMUNIST PARTY OF IRAQ.

ICP CENTRAL COMMAND (*al-Qiyada al-Markaziyya*). The ICP Central Command broke off from the main body of the Communist Party of Iraq (ICP)* in September 1967. Led by 'Aziz al-Hajj, it opposed all alliances with 'Abd al-Rahman 'Arif or the Ba'th. The party advocated armed struggle and sabotage against the regime. Most of its members had been caught and imprisoned or executed by 1969.

INDEPENDENCE PARTY (*Istiqlal*). This pan-Arab nationalist party, composed of former supporters of Rashid 'Ali al-Kaylani, was licensed in 1946. The membership was primarily Sunni, although the leader, Muhammad Mahdi Kubbah, was a Shi'ite. Appealing to the literate middle class, it had no real social program, but it championed the Palestine cause.

ISLAH. *See* REFORM PARTY.

ISLAMIC CALL or MISSION (*al-Da'wa al-Islamiyya*). Formed in 1968, this party, led by Shi'ite religious leaders with close ties to Iran, was inspired by the Iraqi Ayat Allah Muhammad Baqir al-Sadr, who preached a return to Muslim precepts in government and social justice. In 1979, with riots in al-Najaf and Karbala, the government uncovered al-Da'wa, which was now dedicated to the overthrow of the regime with support from Iran. The party was suppressed by the government; al-Sadr was arrested and executed, and the party went underground.

ISLAMIC PARTY. An anti-Communist party, backed by Shi'ite mujtahid Muhsin al-Hakim, the Islamic Party opposed 'Abd al-Karim Qasim, who first refused to license it, but later agreed.

ISTIQLAL. *See* INDEPENDENCE PARTY.

ITTIHAD AL-DUSTOURI. *See* CONSTITUTIONAL UNION PARTY.

KDP. *See* KURDISH DEMOCRATIC PARTY.

KURDISH DEMOCRATIC PARTY (KDP). The KDP was founded in 1946 by Mustafa al-Barzani and Kurds who left Iraq for Mahabad, Iran, after an abortive revolt in Iraq. It drew its support from Kurdish groups active in the 1940s especially *Hiwa* (Hope). Mahabad had developed into the headquarters for the movement for Kurdish autonomy. In fall 1945, Qadhi Muhammad, a judge in Mahabad, formed the KDP at about the same time Barzani and his followers arrived from Iraq. The autonomous republic of Mahabad was proclaimed in January 1946 but was abandoned by March 1947 when the Iranian government mounted a successful offensive. Qadhi Muhammad was hanged. Barzani and his followers fled to the Soviet Union and remained in exile throughout the 1950s, during which time the Iraqi KDP developed independently from the Iranian party.

The ideology of the KDP was influenced by the Communist Party of Iraq (ICP),* but it was not Marxist. Many members had dual membership and supported Barzani when he was in exile in the Soviet Union. The leadership consisted of leftist intellectuals, such as the lawyer, Ibrahim Ahmad.

The party received a license in 1960, when 'Abd al-Karim Qasim authorized political parties, but military action in 1961 forced the party underground. The KDP ceased hostilities in order to cooperate with the Ba'th* in an attempt to overthrow Qasim.

Dealing with the 'Arif government in 1964, the KDP split between Barzani, who supported negotiations, and Jalal al-Talabani and Ibrahim Ahmad, who wanted more government concessions. Ahmad and Talabani were expelled from the party, taking many intellectuals with them, and leadership remained in the hands of Barzani and his tribal relatives who carried on the civil war with the government.

Concerned over the destabilizing effect of the war, Saddam Husayn began negotiations as soon as the Ba'th* came to power in 1968. An amnesty was declared, and the government promised to subsidize the KDP, but as Iranian Kurds were being expelled from Iraq, Barzani became disillusioned with the Ba'th. Barzani himself survived a number of assassination attempts, and, before he died in the United States in 1972, he turned to President Nixon for support, which was forthcoming. In 1974, as the government began to implement the 1970 autonomy plan, pro-Barzani Kurdish ministers resigned. With support from

Iran, the war resumed, leading to the 1975 Algiers Agreement, which severely damaged the Kurdish movement (see introductory essay).

Revived in 1975, the KDP was split between the supporters and opponents of Barzani. Barzani's sons, Mas'ud and Idris, took over active control of the party with Mas'ud elected chairman in October 1979. The struggle against the Ba'th continued in the form of guerrilla warfare inside Iraq. The KDP was sympathetic to the Khomeini revolution in Iran and enjoyed good relations with the new regime in Tehran. Talabani's group, on the other hand, was aligned with the Iranian KDP in opposition to the Iranian government. The two parties reunited in 1985, fighting continued throughout the rest of the Iran-Iraq War, and open rebellion broke out again during the Gulf War of 1990–91.

KURDISH DEMOCRATIC PARTY (NEW). Headed by 'Aziz Aqrawi, Hashim Aqrawi, and Isma'il 'Aziz, this party was founded in the 1970s as one of the progovernment Kurdish parties that joined the National Progressive Front.

KURDISH REVOLUTIONARY PARTY. Headed by 'Abd al-Sattar Tahir Sharif, this was one of the progovernment Kurdish parties in the 1970s. It joined the National Progressive front.

LIBERAL PARTY (*Hizb al-Ahrar*). Led by Tawfiq al-Suwaydi, this party was licensed in 1946 and dissolved in 1950. Moderate and centrist, it advocated mild reform.

MOVEMENT OF ARAB NATIONALISTS (*Harakat al-Qawmiyyin al-'Arab*). Organized in 1955, by 1963 the party had attracted army officers who became a political force under 'Abd al-Salam 'Arif. Their goal was Arab unity under the leadership of Egypt's Gamal Abdel Nasser.

NATIONAL BROTHERHOOD PARTY (*Hizb al-Ikha al-Watani*). Founded in 1930/31 (official opening in 1931) by leaders of the People's Party* and the Nationalist Party,* who merged their organizations, the party opposed the Anglo-Iraqi treaty and demanded immediate independence. Important leaders were Yasin al-Hashimi, Ja'far Abu al-Timan, Rashid 'Ali al-Kaylani, Hikmat Sulayman, 'Ali Jawdat al-Ayyubi, Naji al-Suwaydi, and Hamdi al-Pachachi. The party was dissolved in 1935.

NATIONAL DEMOCRATIC PARTY (NDP) (*Hizb al-Watani al-Dimuqrati*). Headed by Kamil al-Jadirji, this party was licensed in 1946 as an outgrowth of the old Ahali Group.* Its semi-socialist views attracted members from wealthy, well-established families, Shi'ites, and the left-leaning, educated middle class who did not believe in radical change.

The NDP split over 'Abd al-Karim Qasim; al-Jadirji opposed him, and Muhammad Hadid became Qasim's minister of finance. In October 1961 Jadirji closed the NDP and stopped publication of *al-Ahali*.

NATIONAL LIBERATION PARTY (*Hizb al-Taharrur al-Watani*). This party was an auxiliary of the Communist Party of Iraq (ICP)* in the 1940s. It was never legalized.

NATIONAL SOCIALIST PARTY (*al-Umma al-Ishtiraki*). Established in 1951 by Salih Jabr, who broke with Nuri al-Sa'id, this party challenged the perennial prime minister for political power. Its platform was similar to Nuri's Constitutional Union Party.* Jabr died of a heart attack in 1957.

NATIONAL UNION FRONT. Formed in 1957 as a secret organization of opposition parties, including Communists, the front was founded to coordinate opposition to the regime.

NATIONAL UNION PARTY (*Hizb al-Ittihad al-Watani*). A Marxist party, licensed in 1946, it was headed by 'Abd al-Fattah Ibrahim. The party advocated radical social reform within the limits of parliamentary democracy.

NATIONAL UNITY PARTY (*al-Wihda al-Wataniyya*). This party was founded by 'Ali Jawdat al-Ayyubi after he left the National Brotherhood Party* in 1934. It was in existence from 1934 to February 1935.

NATIONALIST PARTY (*Hizb al-Watani*). Founded in 1922 by Ja'far Abu al-Timan, the party was suppressed, then revived in 1926 and continued until 1933.

NDP. *See* NATIONAL DEMOCRATIC PARTY.

PATRIOTIC UNION OF KURDISTAN (PUK). Formed in June 1975, the PUK was headed by Jalal al-Talabani and other members of the Kurdish Democratic Party (KDP)* who repudiated the leadership of Mustafa al-Barzani. Leftist in orientation, it received support from Syria. In 1984 Talabani made peace with the government, but he realized no political gain. The PUK reunited with the KDP in 1985 in its war against the regime, and it was involved in the negotiations after the Gulf War of 1991.

PEOPLE'S PARTY I (*Hizb al-Sha'b*). The first People's Party was founded by Yasin al-Hashimi in 1925 and operated until 1928.

PEOPLE'S PARTY II (*Sha'b*). The second People's Party was licensed in 1946. Headed by judge 'Aziz Sharif, the party's membership was composed mostly of lawyers. Close in view to the Communist Party of Iraq (ICP),* it was suspected, at times, of being a Communist front organization.

PROGRESSIVE KURDISH MOVEMENT. Headed by 'Abd Allah Isma'il Ahmad, this was one of the progovernment Kurdish parties formed in the 1970s that joined the National Progressive Front.

PROGRESSIVE PARTY (*Hizb al-Taqaddum*). Founded in 1925 by 'Abd al-Muhsin al-Sa'dun, a wealthy Sunni landowner who supported the British and the Anglo-Iraqi treaty, the party dissolved when al-Sa'adun committed suicide in 1929.

PUK. *See* PATRIOTIC UNION OF KURDISTAN.

AL-QIYADA AL-MARKAZIYYA. *See* ICP CENTRAL COMMAND.

REFORM PARTY (*Islah*). Formed in 1949 by Sami Shawkat, former supporter of Nuri al-Sa'id, the party merged with the National Socialist Party* led by Salih Jabr.

SHA'B. *See* PEOPLE'S PARTY II.

AL-UMMAH AL-ISHTIRAKI. *See* NATIONALIST SOCIALIST PARTY.

UNITED POPULAR FRONT. This front was formed in 1950 by a group that included younger members of the establishment.

AL-WIHDA AL-WATANIYYA. *See* NATIONAL UNITY PARTY.

## NOTE

1. Ghazi succeeded to the throne when King Faysal, his father, died in 1933. Upon Ghazi's death, his son, then a minor, became King Faysal II.

Reeva Simon

# ISRAEL

## INTRODUCTION

Political parties have played a major role in Israel's democracy. They emerged well before the formation of the state within the World Zionist Federation and the Jewish community in Palestine as strong parties in terms of membership, organization, institutions, role expansion, and ideology. Initially, they had to struggle to gain dominance in the World Zionist Federation and establish a monopoly in their specialized domain representation. They grew steadily, however, as the main agents of public affairs, and they have survived the crisis of transition from community to state.

Political parties have successfully maintained their leading role in Israeli politics, but they have become weaker as institutions because of their change from strong programmatic mass parties toward more pragmatic electoral parties. The latter party model is more limited in its organizational resources, forced continuously to democratize, and is increasingly under pressure to adapt to a more volatile electorate.

The Israeli multiparty system is highly developed. It gives political expression to a wide, almost exhaustive, spectrum of organized constituencies, economic interests, historic political traditions, and ideological approaches.

Israeli parties have undergone a gradual process of change and consolidation through electoral alignments and realignments, party splits, and mergers. Since 1965 the Israeli party system has gradually changed its character and has moved slowly toward a more competitive system, with two major parties at its center, rather than one. The new condition led in 1977 to the first major turnover in government in Israel's history.

The Israeli political left—the Labor movement—enjoyed a clear advantage over the political right in political organization during the formative communal era, and maintained it well into the state era. Labor parties preceded the emergence of the non-Labor secular parties; they have constantly demonstrated their capacity to keep a framework of unity within the *Histadrut*, the General Federation of Labor, and have been able to cooperate throughout most of the pre-state and state eras in the general political arenas despite their strong ideological differences. The major Israeli Labor party, the social democratic Labor Party of

Israel, or *Mapai*,* managed to overcome its historic splits and reunite in 1968 with the two former factions: the Unity of Labor (*Ahdut Ha'avoda*),* which had split from *Mapai* in 1942, and the Israeli Workers List (*Rafi*),* which had split from the party in 1965. All three parties founded the Israeli Labor Party, which was joined in 1969 by the more radical United Workers Party (*Mapam*)* in an electoral alliance, the Labor Alignment* (*Mapam* quit the Alignment in 1984, when the Labor Party decided to form a Unity government with the rightist National Camp, or *Likud*).

The Israeli political right was relatively late to form a major political party, and it failed to unite the various factions of the political center and the radical wing of the non-Labor secular section of the Israeli party system. During the pre-state era, the initially nonpartisan General Zionists* did not produce an effective and united party, and the party of the radical nationalist wing, the Revisionist Party,* almost faded away prior to the formation of the state. Thus, the political right entered the state era divided, without a leading political party equal to Labor's *Mapai*, and hampered by the problem of legitimacy of its radical nationalist wing. The two parties of the political right—the General Zionists* (subsequently called the Liberal Party*) and the Freedom Party, or *Herut** (founded by the commanders of the *Irgun*, the Jewish anti-British secessionist underground in Palestine)—joined forces only in 1965, forming a joint electoral list and parliamentary bloc, *Gahal*.* This bloc served as the basis for the formation of the Likud bloc in 1977. The Likud proclaimed itself a united party in 1990.

The maintenance and development of a highly pluralistic multiparty system in Israel was possible because of the system of proportional representation, which lacks systemic barriers to fragmentation. Israel inherited this system from its democratic communal origins. This system was in effect in all the Jewish national institutions that preceded the State of Israel: in the Zionist Federation and in the political organization of the Jewish community in Palestine (*Knesset Yisrael*). It was even adopted by the Histadrut, the multiparty General Federation of Labor. The proportional system of representation was highly functional in the pre-state national institutions. It offered greater opportunities for participation and representation, which corresponded to the constant search for unity and authority in the absence of sovereignty (see Table 5).

The proportional system of election offered opportunities for party survival and strengthened party organization. The necessity to present a unified list of candidates (in decreasing order of importance, from top to bottom) to the entire electorate in a single national district increased the importance of the political party in nominations as well as in the election campaign. It encouraged the formation of a centralized party regime and strengthened the dominant role of the leadership of the party. Nevertheless, the system of party nominations underwent a process of democratization, beginning in the 1965 election, that gradually took away the power of nomination from secretive committees, but for a long time left the choice (with few exceptions) in the hands of the central party bodies, composed of regular party activists. The Labor Party adopted the system

Table 5
Number of Parties or Lists Represented in the Israeli *Knesset* (1949–92)

| Election Year | Number of Lists* | Number of Parties |
|---|---|---|
| 1949 | 12 | 15 |
| 1951 | 15 | 15 |
| 1955 | 12 | 14 |
| 1959 | 12 | 14 |
| 1961 | 11 | 12 |
| 1965 | 13 | 15 |
| 1969 | 13 | 15 |
| 1973 | 9 | 14 |
| 1977 | 11 | 15 |
| 1981 | 10 | 13 |
| 1984 | 15 | 21 |
| 1988 | 15 | 17 |
| 1992 | 10 | 13 |

Notes: *Several lists represented more than one party.

of nominating primaries in the selection of its candidate for prime minister and the candidates for the *Knesset* in the 1992 election. In 1993, the Likud chose its new leader, Benjamin Netanyahu, through a party primary.

The proportional system of elections[1] to Israel's unicameral parliament, the *Knesset*, made it virtually impossible for one party to gain a majority and form a government by itself. Government by a coalition of parties, thus, became a major feature of the Israeli political system. Coalition government in Israel has been fairly stable in terms of tenure in office of each government and each prime minister: an average of close to two years for each government, and five and a half years for each prime minister (not counting David Ben-Gurion's thirteen years in office). The average tenure in office of each *Knesset* has been close to three and a half years, out of the possible four years prescribed by law. The number of parties that were ruled out as coalition partners or considered themselves unavailable for participation in any coalition government has sharply declined over the years. The latter may be referred to as anticoalition parties in contrast to the noncoalition parties which refuse to join a particular coalition government (see Table 6).

Only one government lost a confidence vote in the *Knesset* (Shamir's government in 1990), although several governments agreed, under pressure, to early elections during the fourth year in the tenure of the *Knesset* (in 1977, 1984, and 1992). The system of coalition government weakened the position of the prime

**Table 6**
**Anticoalition Parties**

| Years | Parties |
|-------|---------|
| 1949-55 | Maki, Mapam, Herut, Agudat Yisrael (after 1952) |
| 1956-67 | Rakah, Herut, Agudat Yisrael* |
| 1967-77 | Rakah, Agudat Yisrael |
| 1977 | Hadash (Rakah), Progressive List for Peace, Arab Democratic Party |
| 1992 | Hadash |

Note: *Poalei Agudat Yisrael participated in the coalition government between 1961 and 1969.

minister and decentralized, to a large extent, the operation of the government, with the exception of the major areas of defense and foreign policy. It certainly provided the smaller coalition parties with the opportunity to gain concessions from the leading party in government on issues that were of particular interest to them, a condition that has increasingly frustrated the explicit will of the majority (see Table 7).

The Israeli coalition government was headed continuously by one party, the Labor Party (previously Mapai), until 1977. Its consistent coalition partners throughout most of this period were the National Religious Party (*Mafdal*) (NRP)* and the pro-labor Independent Liberal Party* (the former Progressive Party*). The parties of the radical left, the Unity of Labor (*Ahdut Ha'avoda*) and *Mapam*, joined Mapai's coalition in 1955. The General Zionists (subsequently, the Liberal Party) participated in Labor's coalition between 1951 and 1955. The political right (Gahal) entered the government as a unified bloc only in 1967. It served in the Labor-led unity government until 1970. The new bloc of the political right, the Likud, headed all governments but one between 1977 and 1992. Labor's prime minister Shimon Peres headed the new Unity government formed in 1984, for the first two years in office, with the Likud's prime minister Yitzhak Shamir serving until the dismantling of this government in 1990. He continued in office as the head of a Likud-led coalition government with smaller religious and rightist parties. Labor regained power in 1992.

The formation of coalition governments did not reach an impasse until 1984. Prior to that year, the leading party in the *Knesset* always succeeded in forming a coalition government. The transformation from a dominant party system with only one party contender to lead the coalition government to a more competitive party system with two major contending parties produced a crisis in coalition formation. The proportional representation system not only necessitates the formation of a coalition of parties in government, but also creates the possibility of elections without a winner in terms of government formation. The close competition between the Likud and the Labor Alignment,* and the growing pressure

Table 7
Participation in Government Coalitions (1949–92)

| Years | Parties |
|-------|---------|
| 1949-55 | Mapai, Hamizrahi, Hapoel Hamizrahi, Progressive Party, General Zionists (1952-55), Agudat Yisrael (1949-52) |
| 1955-61 | Mapai, Ahdut Ha'avoda, Mapam, Progressive Party, Mafdal (out of government Nov. 1958 - Dec. 1959) |
| 1961-66 | Mapai, Ahdut Ha'avoda, Poalei Agudat Yisrael, Mapam (from 1966), Independent Liberal Party (from 1966) |
| 1967-70 | Mapai, Ahdut Ha'avoda, Rafi, Mapam, Independent Liberal Party, Mafdal, Gahal (Herut and Liberal Party ) |
| 1970-74 | Labor Party (Mapai, Ahdut Ha'avoda, Rafi), Mapam, Independent Liberal Party, Mafdal |
| 1974-77 | Labor Party, Mapam, Independent Liberal Party, Mafdal (from 1975), Ratz (1974) |
| 1977-84 | Likud, Mafdal, Agudat Yisrael, DMC |
| 1984-90 | Likud, Labor Party, Mafdal, Shas, Agudat Yisrael, Yahad, Ometz |
| 1990-92 | Likud, Mafdal, Shas, Agudat Yisrael, Degel Hatorah, Hatehiya,* Moledet,* Tsomet* |
| 1992- | Labor Party, Meretz Bloc (Shinui, Mapam, Ratz), Shas |

Note: *These parties left the government prior to the 1992 election.

on the smaller parties to ally themselves with one of the two major parties, rather than to act as free agents, produced a stalemate in the efforts to form a coalition government following the 1984 elections. The Labor Alignment became the largest faction in the *Knesset* in that election but could not gain the support of a majority in the *Knesset* and was forced to form a grand coalition (Unity government) with the Likud. The outcome of the 1988 election was not much different.

The occurrence of two successive elections without a clear winner increased support for electoral reform in Israel. Already in 1984, the Likud and Labor signed an agreement to form a bipartisan committee to examine such a change. This committee recommended the adoption of a mixed system of election: half of the members of the *Knesset* to be elected in a regional election (twenty regions with three representatives each), the other half to be elected in a single national constituency under the present proportional system of election. The threshold for representation would be raised to 3.33 percent from the current 1.5 percent. The final outcome would still be proportional. Parties would be guaranteed representation according to their proportional share in the national election, which means that they would be compensated for a possible loss in the regional part of the election, and the total number of seats in the *Knesset* would, thus, remain open-ended to allow for this. This proposal did not reach the floor of the *Knesset* and did not gain the firm support of the two major parties prior to the 1992 election.

Another reform proposed by four members of the *Knesset* for the direct election of the prime minister initially gained greater support. It commanded the support of the Labor Party and some members of the Likud despite the decision of the party to oppose it. The *Knesset* finally passed this bill prior to the 1992 election, but did not apply it immediately (see Tables 8 and 9). The first test of the new system was thus postponed until the next election.

## TYPOLOGY OF ISRAELI PARTIES

The Israeli party system has comprised four groupings: (1) left (labor), (2) right (nationalist), (3) religious, and (4) Arab (radical and nationalist) (see Table 10).

Table 8
**Knesset Representation of the Largest and Second Largest Parties**

| Election Year | Largest Party | No. Seats | Second Largest Party | No. Seats | Total of both parties |
|---|---|---|---|---|---|
| 1949 | Mapai | 46 | Mapam | 19 | 65 |
| 1951 | Mapai | 45 | General Zionists | 20 | 65 |
| 1955 | Mapai | 40 | Herut | 15 | 55 |
| 1959 | Mapai | 47 | Herut | 17 | 64 |
| 1961 | Mapai | 42 | Herut | 17 | 59 |
| 1965 | Labor Alignment | 45 | Gahal | 26 | 71 |
| 1969 | Labor Alignment | 56 | Gahal | 26 | 82 |
| 1973 | Labor Alignment | 51 | Likud | 39 | 90 |
| 1977 | Likud | 43 | Labor Alignment | 32 | 75 |
| 1981 | Likud | 48 | Labor Alignment | 47 | 95 |
| 1984 | Labor Alignment | 44 | Likud | 41 | 85 |
| 1988 | Likud | 40 | Labor Party | 39 | 79 |
| 1992 | Labor Party | 44 | Likud | 32 | 76 |

**Table 9**
**Israeli Prime Ministers (1948–92)**

| Prime Minister | Party | Dates Served | Years in Office | Date of Birth | Age |
|---|---|---|---|---|---|
| David Ben-Gurion | Mapai | 5/48 - 12/53<br>11/55 - 6/63 | 13 yrs in 2 pds | 1886 | 62-76 |
| Moshe Sharett | Mapai | 12/53 - 11/55 | 2 yrs | 1894 | 59-61 |
| Levi Eshkol | Mapai | 6/63 - 2/69 | 5.5 yrs | 1895 | 68-74 |
| Golda Meir | Mapai | 3/69 - 6/74 | 5.5 yrs | 1898 | 71-76 |
| Yitzhak Rabin | Labor | 6/74 - 6/77 | 3 yrs | 1922 | 52-55 |
| Menachem Begin | Likud | 6/77 - 9/83 | 6 yrs | 1913 | 64-70 |
| Yitzhak Shamir | Likud | 9/83 - 9/84<br>10/86 - 7/92 | 1 yr<br>6 yrs | 1915 | 68-69<br>71-77 |
| Shimon Peres | Labor | 9/84 - 10/86 | 2 yrs | 1923 | 61-63 |
| Yitzhak Rabin | Labor | 7/92 - | | 1922 | 70- |

The political center disappeared as an independent partisan force following the formation of the Likud; the fading away of the independent Liberals (1981) and the Democratic Movement for Change (DMC)* (1981); and the decision of the remaining small centrist party (Shinui*) to join a radical dovish block on the left (Meretz,* 1992).

Each of the four party groupings was divided into two subsections, one of which consisted of a major and more moderate party, the other minor and radical. This description remained valid concerning the political right and the political left, but some elaboration is required concerning the religious party grouping. Until 1984, the NRP was the major religious moderate party on the central issue of its party grouping, religion. The move of the NRP to the political right, and its failure to manage internal cleavages, as well as the emergence of Sephardi religious parties, robbed it of its historically dominant position within the religious group of parties. It remained moderate on religious issues but became more extreme on national issues. The ultraorthodox parties, which were radical or extreme on issues of religion and more moderate on national issues, became the major subsection in the religious party grouping in the 1988 election.

The major ideological issues in Israeli politics—other than the legacy of the past which continues to sustain the traditional typology of Israeli parties—have been essentially national and religious. The confrontation of the social ideologies of the past gave way, as prime identifying issues, to the attitude toward the historic Labor institutions, primarily the Histadrut.

Table 10
Party Groupings in the Israeli Party System

| Left - The Labor Grouping |
|---|
| The Labor Party |
| The dovish radical parties:<br>Ratz*<br>Mapam*<br>Shinui* |
| **Right - The Nationalist Grouping** |
| The Likud |
| The radical nationalist parties:<br>Hatehiya#<br>Tsomet<br>Moledet |
| **The Religious Grouping** |
| The Mafdal (NRP) |
| The ultra-Orthodox parties (Haredim):<br>Agudat Yisrael,@<br>Shas,<br>Degel Hatorah@ |
| **The Arab Grouping** |
| Rakah - The Communist Party |
| The Democratic Arab Party<br>The Progressive List for Peace# |

Notes:  *Listed together as Meretz in the 1992 election.
@Listed together in the 1992 election.
#Failed to pass election threshold in 1992.


Party Attitudes toward the Occupied Territories

| *Political Left* | *Political Right* |
|---|---|
| For separation | For annexation |

Rakah–Meretz–Labor–Aguda–Shas–Likud–NRP–Tsomet–Hatehiya–Moledet

Issues relating to the occupied territories seized by Israel from Jordan and Syria in the 1967 war gradually became the prime national issue in Israeli politics. The overall differences among Israeli parties on this issue moved from a position favoring annexation on the extreme right to a position favoring withdrawal on the extreme left. In the 1992 election campaign, the question of the territories entailed four issues: the immediate future and the long-term future of the territories, the issue of Jewish settlements in the territories, and attitudes toward the *Intifada*—the Palestinian uprising—in the West Bank and the Gaza Strip.

The New Communist List, or *Rakah*,* and the other two Arab parties have been on the extreme left on these issues: They favored immediate withdrawal of

Israel from all the territories and were for the formation of a Palestinian state headed by the Palestine Liberation Organization (PLO). They were against Jewish settlement, and they supported the Palestinian *Intifada*.

The Jewish radical left (Meretz) was for the withdrawal of Israel from the territories on the basis of a negotiated, possibly gradual, settlement that would take into account Israel's security needs. Meretz was prepared to accept a Palestinian state under restrictive conditions and supported negotiation with the PLO to achieve such an overall settlement. Meretz was against Jewish settlement in the territories. It objected to the violent side of the *Intifada*, but refrained from castigating the *Intifada*'s political aims.

The Labor Party opted for partition of the territories between Israel and a Jordanian-Palestinian state. It accepted, however, the autonomy plan signed by Israel, Egypt, and the United States at Camp David (1978) as a necessary interim phase in the search for an overall solution. Labor supported the maintenance of Jewish settlements within a limited part of the territories and only for security purposes. It rejected "political settlements" designed to prevent separation of the territories from Israel. Labor was critical of the Palestinian *Intifada*, but it maintained that only a political solution would put an end to this conflict.

The ultra-religious parties—Sephardi Association of Observers of the Torah (*Shas*),* Association of Israel (*Agudat Yisrael*),* and Flag of the Torah (*Degel Hatora*)*—had a complex and not easily defined political position on this issue. From a religious point of view, which proclaims the sanctity of the promised land, these parties sided with the political right; politically, however, they were more moderate and pragmatic on this issue because of the need to save human lives and to avoid turning the world against Israel.

The Likud was opposed to separation of the territories from Israel, although it did not seek to impose Israeli law on them. It viewed Jewish settlements as the most potent weapon against future separation of the territories, regarding them as an interim phase in a lengthy process leading to the ultimate annexation of the territories by Israel. The Likud rejected Labor's contention that there can be only a political solution to the *Intifada*, but it pursued a bipartisan policy with Labor in the handling of the uprising under the pre-1990 Unity government.

The NRP moved to the political right on this issue after 1977. Its platform in the 1992 election called for the imposition of Israeli law in the territories, and rejected the autonomy plan. It supported Jewish settlements and espoused a very hawkish position concerning the Palestinian *Intifada*.

The radical parties of the political right were all for annexation and settlements. Among them, only *Tsomet** was prepared to negotiate the granting of municipal autonomy to the Palestinians. The Homeland Party (*Moledet*)* was for "transfer" of the Palestinian Arabs to Jordan by agreement.

The 1993 agreement negotiated between the government of Itzak Rabin and the PLO providing for mutual recognition and Palestinian autonomy in the West Bank (beginning with the town of Jericho) and the Gaza Strip transformed the Israeli political agenda concerning the territories. Labor, Meretz, and the Arab parties supported this agreement. Likud, Tsomet, the NRP, Moledet, and Agudat Yisrael rejected it and voted against it in the *Knesset*. Shas abstained, despite its participation in the coalition government up until just before the vote (the party's status vis-à-vis the coalition was thrown into doubt by a development that had nothing to do with the peace accord). The agreement generated a re-evaluation of former positions on this issue by the parties.

### Issue of State and Religion

| *Political Left* | *Political Right* |
|---|---|
| For separation of state and religion | Against separation of state and religion |
| For minimal aid to religious institutions | For maximal aid to religious institutions |

Meretz–Rakah–Labor–Tsomet–Likud–Hatehiya–Moledet–NRP–Shas–Aguda

The prime religious issues in Israeli politics relate to the relationship between state and religion. The historical Israeli formula limits separation of state and religion. Religious institutions, such as the Chief Rabbinate, are recognized and funded by the state; religious courts of the various religious communities have jurisdiction over matters concerning personal status (such as marriage and divorce); and the state system of elementary schools has a religious section.

On the radical left, Meretz is for the separation of state and religion. It supports the institutions of civil marriage and favors providing only minimal aid to religious institutions. *Rakah* is for separation of state and religion; however, it tends to shun this issue, as do other Arab parties, because of the role of tradition in the Arab communities and the growing influence of the fundamentalist Islamic groups among the Arab citizens of Israel.

The Labor Party bore primary responsibility for the original formulation of Israeli political arrangements concerning state and religion, which it negotiated with the NRP at the time of the formation of the state. While in opposition, Labor moved to the left on this issue, but in recent years it has tried to balance this position in its quest for renewal of the coalition partnership with the religious parties.

The Likud has adopted a proreligion stance and has tended to be responsive to religious demands. Competition with Labor for the support of the religious parties in the formation of a coalition government has reinforced this tendency.

Tsomet has been the only secular nationalist party. Its origins are in the Labor settlement movement. Initially it did not try to woo religious voters, but in 1993 Tsomet sought the support of the NRP for Rafael Eitan, its candidate for the prime ministership in the next election. The Revival Party (*Hatehiya*)* and the Homeland Party had a mixed group of leaders and constituencies and were pro-religion.

The religious parties have differed in their general attitude toward the state and its institutions. The Zionist NRP has had a generally positive attitude toward the state. Historically it has managed its own religious institutions, including the religious sector of the state elementary schools. The ultraorthodox parties, by contrast, originated in a political movement (Agudat Yisrael) that rejected Zionism. The Aguda accepted the State of Israel when it was established, but it remained distrustful of its secular government and separated itself from the official religious institutions and the state system of education. Degal Hatora was a faction of the historic Aguda, and Shas was born within the Sephardic constituency of the religious community.

The position of the ultraorthodox parties on the issues of state and religion has been complex and full of contradictions. These parties in principle opposed separation of state and religion, believing that the state must act according to the teachings of Jewish religious law. They have even tried to use the authority of the state to impose religious norms (e.g., the sanctity of the Sabbath) as well as to pass laws to support their interpretation of Jewish identity ("Who is a Jew"). On the other hand, these parties have tried to protect the independence of their religious and political institutions from the secular state, while objecting to the leftist demand that the status quo regarding state and religion be changed. A major rationale for their participation in the political process has been to gain state aid for their independent educational institutions.

### Prime Social Issue: Party Attitude toward the Histadrut

| *Political Left* | *Political Right* |
|---|---|
| Favorable | Unfavorable |

Labor–Meretz–NRP–Tsomet–Moledet–Shas–Aguda–Hatehiya–Likud

The prime social issue in recent Israeli politics has focused on institutions more than on partisan social ideology. The decline of socialist ideology and the movement of the rightist Likud toward a populist social stance made the attitude toward an institution like the Histadrut into a prime political issue. This issue highlights the partisan record of the past and has given expression to the institutional interests of the Israeli parties. Almost all Israeli parties have been represented in the multiparty Histadrut. There are, however, marked differences in their attitudes toward its structure, policies, and leadership.

In this regard, the Labor Party appears as the leading party of the left, since it has controlled the Histadrut and has been identified, more than any other party, with its institutional principles and interests. The more radical parties on the left, and the dovish Meretz, have been more critical of the Histadrut and identified to a lesser extent with its historical record and ideology. The NRP has been closest to the Histadrut among the religious parties; its federation of labor Hamizrahi Worker (*Hapoel Hamizrahi*)* participated in the trade union department of the Histadrut and in its medical insurance program. Shas, the new religious party, has been represented on Histadrut bodies by arrangement with the Labor Party.

Social issues have not been at the center of attention of the radical nationalist parties. Tsomet, however, originated in the Labor settlement movement and has had a generally pro-Histadrut position. The other two nationalist parties (the Revival Party and the Homeland Party) have had no identifiable position on this issue.

The factions of the Likud have been represented in the Histadrut since 1965, and the Likud gained close to 30 percent of the vote in the Histadrut election of 1985. Nevertheless, the two major parties of the Likud (Herut and the Liberal Party) were historically hostile to the Histadrut, especially in the pre-state era. The Likud has opposed Labor leadership of the Histadrut and opposed the ownership of economic enterprises by it. The debate over proposed legislation for national medical insurance in 1991 revealed the differences between the Likud and Labor in relation to the Histadrut. The Likud bill would separate the medical system from the Histadrut, while Labor's bill, at the time, would not. After coming to power in the 1992 election, Labor split on this issue. Labor's leaders in the Histadrut continued to demand protection of their institutional interests in the new plan for medical insurance, while Labor ministers in government were less prepared to go along with this.

## THE DEVELOPMENT OF THE PARTY SYSTEM

The origin of most Israeli parties can be traced to the pre-state era and, in some cases, even to the beginning of the century. The number of new parties that emerged outside the historic party system has been small, and most of them did not survive for very long. The strongest challenge to the historic party system was posed in the 1977 election by a reform centrist party, the DMC, which gained fifteen seats in the *Knesset*, but disintegrated within its first term and disappeared before the 1981 election. Its only surviving faction was the Shinui, which won three *Knesset* seats in the 1981 election. Other than the DMC, the challenge to the historic party system has come largely from ethnic and more extreme parties: Shas (ethnic-religious), Civil Rights Movement (*Ratz*)* (left), the Democratic Arab Party* (Arab, nationalist), the Progressive List for Peace* (Arab, nationalist), the Revival Party (Jewish, nationalist), Tsomet (Jewish, nationalist), and the Homeland Party (Jewish, nationalist).

The Israeli party system is thus still embedded in its historical framework. Longevity, however, does not indicate lack of change in Israeli parties but rather underscores the fact that most changes have taken place within the historic party system. Indeed, veteran parties have undergone frequent structural changes but have kept a residual link to the legacy of the past and, in most cases, have maintained their historic association with a network of supportive institutions (federations of labor, settlement movements, youth movements, and so on).

The attempt to identify phases or periods in the development of the Israeli party system is predicated on changes relating to the character and roles of the political parties and the structure and character of the party system as a whole (see Table 11).

Table 11
Eight Phases in the Development of the Israeli Party System

| Phase | Period | Years | Characteristics |
|-------|--------|-------|-----------------|
| I | Incipient | 1902-20 | Emergence of strong parties; search for legitimacy in their respective political settings. |
| II | Formative | 1920-48 | Completion of a party system; parties gain dominance. |
| III | Transitional | 1948-49 | Party realignment in the transition to the state. |
| IV | Dominant | 1949-65 | Dominance of Mapai; highly fragmented system. |
| V | Dev toward competitive system | 1965-77 | Realignment & consolidation on right & left. |
| VI | Competitive system | 1977-84 | First major turnover in govt.; completion of competitive party system. |
| VII | Competitive system in crisis | 1984-90 | Impasse between Likud & Labor; crisis in govt. formation. |
| VIII | Competitive system | 1990 | Resumption of limited majority govt. by Likud. |
| | | 1992 | Second major turnover in govt.; formation of Labor govt. |

## THE INCIPIENT PERIOD (1902–20)

The first parties, which eventually contributed to the emergence of the Israeli party system, appeared within the framework of the World Zionist Organization founded in 1897 in Basel, Switzerland, or in reaction to it. The formation of this worldwide Jewish National Federation prompted the organization of political parties that went beyond the commonly shared ideology and goals of the Zionist movement as a whole. These early parties represented well-defined communities with class or religious sectoral ideologies and a utopian view of the prospective Jewish State. As political minorities within the Zionist movement, they were determined to protect their interests through partisan representation rather than through the general nonpartisan Zionist federations organized in every state.

The Zionist religious party, *Hamizrahi*, was the first to organize in 1902. It was founded to protest the decision of the Fifth Zionist Congress to launch an education program. The religious delegates feared the decisions of the secular majority in the realm of education and culture. A further decision by the Tenth Zionist Congress (1911) to permanently engage in cultural activities caused a defection from Hamizrahi. The defectors joined forces in 1912 with an anti-Zionist group of rabbis to found the Association of Israel, or Agudat Yisrael.* The new party dedicated itself to the preservation and promotion of religious education, and it rejected the secular ideologies of national Zionism and social revolution. The Zionist Hamizrahi and the anti-Zionist Agudat Yisrael became the two major political religious movements in the Jewish diaspora, and following World War I, in the Jewish community in Palestine.

The first Jewish labor parties were founded in Palestine in 1905: Young Worker (*Hapoel Hatsair*)\* and Zionist Labor (*Poalei Tsiyon*).\* Young Worker, an entirely indigenous party, rejected Marxist socialism and class warfare, proclaimed the centrality of the Land of Israel in Jewish life, and believed in the revival of Hebrew culture and the "religion of labor" as a prescription for the redemption of the Jewish people in its ancestral land. By contrast, Zionist Labor in Palestine considered itself an integral part of the world Poalei Tsiyon party and the socialist movement and believed in the Marxist interpretation of Zionism, class warfare, and the advent of socialism in the world.

In the absence of fully elected Jewish national institutions in Palestine, political parties developed as communal parties and service organizations. The first labor parties engaged in political, educational, cultural, economic, social, and unionist functions. They failed, however, to prevent the emergence of independent regional labor federations (1911), which claimed the nonpolitical roles of the party for themselves. The institutional competition between the political party and the federation of labor became a major issue in the Jewish labor movement. It was finally resolved in 1920, but not before a short-lived attempt to expand the structure and the role of the federation of labor and do away altogether with the institution of the political party. This attempt was conceptualized and engineered by an independent group of leaders (the nonpartisans) who led the regional federations of labor in their quest for unity. This group questioned the legitimacy of the political party and developed a vision of an all-inclusive social organization that would fulfill the roles previously assumed by both the Federation of Labor and the political party. This innovative organizational scheme was adopted by a special convention of the labor community that founded the association for the Unity of Labor (*Ahdut Ha'avoda*) in 1919. The new scheme, however, was never fully tested, since one of the two labor parties, Young Worker, or Hapoel Hatsair, refused to abide by the decision of the labor convention, kept its independence, and developed along the lines designed for the single, unified Unity of Labor, or Ahdut Ha'avoda. The institutional conflict, between a party that was developing into a wider association of labor and an association of labor that was forced to become partisan, prompted the leaders of both organizations in 1920 to accept a new structural concept that finally recognized the legitimacy of both the institutions of the political party and the federation of labor, and structured the relationship between them. The agreement between the two competing organizations led to the formation of a united, General Federation of Labor (the Histadrut), in 1920, and accorded the parties a legitimate role in it.

In sum, in the incipient phase of the prospective Israeli party system, political parties emerged in the labor and religious wings of the Zionist movement and the Jewish community in Palestine (the *Yishuv*). They had to struggle for legitimacy within their own respective constituencies and in the general political arena. Only at the end of this period (1920) did the Labor Party gain full legitimacy, redefining its relationship with the General Federation of Labor. Political parties expanded their roles throughout most of this period but were not yet given a major role in the leadership of the political system, other than within the General Federation of Labor.

## THE FORMATIVE PERIOD (1920–48)

The year 1920 was a watershed in the development of the party system primarily because of the formation of two new political organizations that enabled the parties to exercise their specialized political role and put an end to the debilitating debate concerning their legitimacy: the Histadrut (General Federation of Labor) and the Knesset Yisrael, the general political organization of the Jewish community in Palestine.

The Histadrut institutionalized a unique multiparty regime by adopting a proportional representation system that accorded the founding parties of the Histadrut an opportunity to gain control. The Histadrut provided a powerful organizational base for the labor community and its political parties. The external labor parties became the internal political parties of the Histadrut, a unique feature of a democratic federation of labor. The latter, in turn, adopted the social and national ideology of the political parties and developed into a key institution within the Jewish community in Palestine. The major labor parties cooperated under the Histadrut umbrella in their quest to gain political hegemony in the Zionist movement. They achieved this goal in the critical election of 1933, which placed political parties for the first time at the helm of the Zionist movement.

The Histadrut has been exceptionally successful in organizing the workers and in providing social and medical services. It has provided strong institutional support to the labor parties and has served as a primary actor in the areas of Jewish settlement, economic development, defense (*Hagana* and *Palmah*), and in the mobilization of the labor community in the struggle for a Jewish state.

The Knesset Yisrael provided the *Yishuv* with a nonsovereign political system under the British mandate. Four times, the voters of the *Yishuv* chose the Elected Assembly which, in turn, elected the Executive National Committee and the Plenum of the National Committee, the permanent parliamentary body of Knesset Yisrael. Political parties had the upper hand in the election of the Elected Assembly. They did not, however, gain a monopoly in electoral politics. Ethnic Sephardi associations and economic groups competed, with diminishing success, with political parties for representation. The eventual penetration of the parties into the ethnic constituency and the gradual politicization of the civic and antilabor local groups finally gave the political parties almost an exclusive hold on electoral politics toward the beginning of the state era.

Most major parties emerged or took shape in the formative pre-state phase of the Israeli party system.

### The Political Left (Labor)

Mapai was formed in 1930 by a merger of the two major parties in the Histadrut (Ahdut Ha'avoda and Hapoel Hatsair). Mapai became the dominant party of the Histadrut and the leading party in the national institutions of the *Yishuv* and the Zionist movement. In 1942, however, it split on the issues of the future of Palestine, the socialist orientation of the party, and the role of the pioneer Kibbutz movement in the Histadrut and the party. A leftist faction headed by the leaders of the major Kibbutz movement of the time, *Hakibbutz Hameuhad*, defected and formed its own party, the Unity of Labor Movement (*Hatnuah Leahdut Ha'avoda*).* This radical opposition faction objected to the partition of Palestine—a policy promoted by David Ben-Gurion and most leaders of the party. It developed a Marxist socialist orientation, called for the democratization of the economic organization of the Histadrut, and aspired to a leadership role for the pioneer Kibbutz movement in the party and the Histadrut. Under Ben-Gurion's leadership, Mapai overcame this radical challenge from the left and regained a dominant position in the Histadrut, though with a curtailed majority. It emerged as the driving force in the political struggle for the partition of Palestine and the formation of the Jewish state.

On the left, the Unity of Labor Movement, or Hatnuah Leahdut Ha'avoda, moved toward cooperation with *Hashomer Hatsair*, another kibbutz-led party whose origin was in a pioneer youth movement, and in a Kibbutz movement, called *Hakibbutz Ha'artsi*. Unlike Hatnuah Leahdut Ha'avoda which was committed to the concept of Greater Israel, Hashomer Hatsair was antinationalist and tried in vain to promote the idea of a binational Jewish-Arab state. Nevertheless, the two kibbutz-centered parties that developed pro-Soviet Marxist orientations merged in 1948 to form the United Workers Party (*Mapam*).

### The Political Right

The Revisionist Party was the only effective attempt made by the political right to respond to the challenge of the Labor movement in Palestine. It was born in the diaspora (in Paris, in 1925) and embraced the political-diplomatic rather than the Labor-constructive brand of Zionism, planning the transfer of a million and a half European Jews to Palestine in 1935. Nevertheless, the Revisionists followed the example of Labor in forming a mass-based party. They established a federation of labor (instigated by the secession of the Revisionist faction from the Histadrut in 1934), a youth movement (*Betar*), and a settlement movement. The Revisionists led the anti-British military underground (the *Irgun*). The Revisionist Party sought to commit a decisive and redeeming political act in the form of a military revolt designed to acquire Jewish control over the entire territory of Palestine, and to save European Jewry from the onslaught of fascism. The Revisionist Party grew rapidly, especially in Poland. At its peak, in 1931, it gained 20 percent of the total vote both in the election of the Zionist Congress and in the national institutions of the *Yishuv*.

The 1933 election to the Zionist Congress had critical consequences in the development of the Zionist Federation and the Revisionist Party. The latter lost a heated race with the Labor movement, and it has been haunted ever since by a debilitating political affair that stemmed from the assassination of a Labor Zionist leader, H. Arlozoroff, who headed the political department of the Jewish Agency. Two members of an extreme nationalist organization within the Revisionist movement were charged with the assassination and then released for lack of evidence. A much belated judicial investigation of this historic affair, initiated by Prime Minister Menachem Begin, finally cleared them of this charge. For a very long time, however, the affair both reflected and intensified the political rift between the Labor movement and the Revisionist movement.

The demands for discipline and conformity within the Zionist bodies, against the background of ideological and political division and electoral loss, prompted Vladimir (Zeev) Jabotinsky, the leader of the Revisionist Party, to secede from the Zionist organization and to found the New Zionist Federation in 1935. The new federation failed to overtake the original one and later faded away, as did the party, following the death of its founder and mentor, Jabotinsky, in 1940. The secession of the *Irgun* and the death of Jabotinsky prevented the Revisionist Party from developing into the major party of the political right.

The General Zionists originated in the nonpartisan State Zionist Federations. The inroads made by the Zionist political parties (Hamizrahi, Labor, and the Revisionists) forced them to organize as an equal political organization (1931). The General Zionists were torn, however, between pressures for an opening to the left and an opening to the right. They split in 1935. One faction was pro-Histadrut (Labor) and moderate in its attitude toward Britain; the other faction, more critical of the Labor movement and the Histadrut, supported an anti-British Zionist foreign policy.

The split among the loosely organized and badly fragmented General Zionists, as well as the secession of the Revisionist Party from the Zionist Federation, forestalled the emergence of a major party of the political right in the pre-state era. Instead, a Civic Block (*Ihud Ezrahi*) was formed in 1941 in an effort to unite the anti-Labor groups against the emergence of labor's supremacy in the national institutions of the *Yishuv*. The Civic Block comprised the elected mayors of the political right, the private Farmers' Association, and other nonlabor economic groups. The leaders of this bloc eventually became the primary leadership group of the General Zionist Party at the outset of the state era.

### The Religious Parties

The religious parties emerged in Palestine after World War I (1918). Hamizrahi was instrumental in the formation of the Chief Rabbinate and the institution of a network of Zionist religious schools. In 1922 a Labor sector (*Hapoel Hamizrahi*) was founded within Hamizrahi and developed into an independent party. Hapoel Hamizrahi established a federation of labor, a settlement movement, and a youth movement. It developed a cooperative attitude toward the secular Labor movement despite its failure to integrate into the Histadrut and became a political ally of Mapai in the national institutions of the *Yishuv* and the government of Israel.

The strength of the religious sector within the national institutions of the *Yishuv* was curtailed by the secession of Agudat Yisrael. The latter boycotted both the Zionist Federation and Knesset Yisrael. It supported the Jewish demand for the partition of Palestine and the formation of an independent state only just prior to the UN General Assembly resolution endorsing this option (1947). The leaders of the Jewish Agency (the prospective leaders of the State of Israel) undertook in return to protect the main religious interests in the Jewish state. Reassured by these leaders, Agudat Yisrael joined the People's Assembly which proclaimed the State of Israel.

In the formative phase of the prospective Israeli party system, political parties emerged as strong organizations within weak political institutions. In the absence of national sovereignty, parties and their associated network of institutions fulfilled instrumental roles and developed political subcenters of the national institutions. The final structure of the Israeli party system was determined by a process of consolidation in the actual transition to the state.

## TRANSITION FROM COMMUNITY (*YISHUV*) TO STATE (1948–49)

The formation of the state did not produce a radical change in the existing party system. The parties of the *Yishuv* successfully adapted to the state after a process of realignment. Four new parties were formed in 1948 (three by mergers and one by a new group of leaders): (1) *Mapam*, the pro-Soviet Marxist party, formed in 1948 through a merger of two kibbutz-led parties—the Unity of Labor Movement and *Hashomer Hatsair*; (2) the Herut Party, founded by the former commanders of the *Irgun* under the leadership of Menachem Begin; (3) the Progressive Party,* founded by three centrist parties that aspired to become the major party of the former General Zionist movement—the pro-Histadrut moderate faction of the General Zionists, Zionist Worker (*Haoved Hatsiyoni*),* a labor faction founded by the leaders of a Zionist youth movement (*Hanoar Hatsioni*) within the General Zionist movement, and the New Immigration (*Aliyah Hadasha*)* party founded by leaders of the Zionist federation in Germany; and (4) the Communist Party of Israel,* founded in response to the pro-partition stance of the Soviet Union, brought together the Jewish and the Arab sections of the Communist movement in Palestine.

No new parties appeared in the religious section of the Israeli party system in the transition to the state. All the old parties—the Zionist Hamizrahi and Hapoel

Hamizrahi and the anti-Zionist and ultraorthodox Agudat Yisrael and Workers of the Association of Israel (*Poalei Agudat Yisrael*)*—aligned together, however, in a joint list of candidates for the first *Knesset.* The religious front disintegrated before the election of the second *Knesset,* and the religious parties appeared on separate lists in 1951. The structure of the electoral front or alignment, introduced by the religious parties in 1949, was subsequently adopted (beginning in 1965) by the major parties of the political left and the political right in a gradual process of realignment of the party system.

At first, the formation of the state strengthened the political parties as institutions. It accorded them an exclusive role in electoral politics and placed them at the head of sovereign governing institutions. They played a major role in the absorption of the mass immigration that doubled the size of the Jewish population in the first four years of the state. This successful effort was the responsibility of both the politicized Jewish Agency and the government ministries. It enabled party activists politically to socialize and organize the new immigrants in their respective parties and thus prevented the emergence of an organized challenge to the veteran parties despite the overwhelming change in the composition of the society. The process of change in Israeli society, the weakening of its ideological orientation, and the development of a more competitive economy and independent commercial press gradually undermined the political parties as organizations, but they maintained their pivotal role in electoral politics and government.

## THE DOMINANT PARTY SYSTEM (1949–65)

The fourth period in the development of the Israeli party system commenced with the election of the first *Knesset* (1949). Unlike the inclusive composition of the Provisional Government, which reflected the search for unity in the transition from community to state, the new coalition government, formed after the election, represented only a limited majority in the *Knesset* (73 out of 120 members) and had a dominant party (46 seats) at its center. Mapai assumed a primary role in the Jewish Agency beginning in 1933, and even earlier in the National Committee of the *Yishuv.* It did not, however, enjoy a majority position in these institutions nor did it dominate institutions endowed with the sanction of the law until the proclamation of the state. Mapai's newly acquired majority position in the executive of a sovereign state thus brought to a conclusion its ascendance to a position of dominance in the Israeli party system.

It is generally agreed that Mapai met Maurice Durverger's criteria for a dominant party. It outdistanced its rivals over a long period of time; it was "identified with the nation as a whole—its doctrines and ideas"; and it adopted a style "coinciding with those of the times."[2]

The dominant position of Mapai within a highly fragmented party system reached its peak between 1949 and 1965. The Israeli Labor Party clung to this position until 1977 as the party system gradually changed toward a more competitive structure. Until 1965 Mapai was the largest party by far, although it fell short of a majority. Its parliamentary faction numbered more than double that of the second largest party. The opposition lacked a unified center, and in each of the first three elections a different party emerged as the second largest party and the largest opposition party in the *Knesset* (see Table 8).

Under these circumstances, there was no alternative to Mapai's leading role in government; indeed, it headed all governments until 1977. Beyond its early permanent alignments in government, Mapai could still choose among possible coalition partners throughout most of this period (for example, in 1961, between the new Liberal Party* and Unity of Labor, or Ahdut Ha'avoda).

The dominant position of Mapai was at least passively supported by the majority position of the labor grouping of parties in the *Knesset*, even when they did not cooperate in government. This condition ruled out the emergence of a non-Labor government. Nevertheless, the initial ideological conflict between the social-democratic, pro-Western Mapai and the Marxist, pro-Soviet Mapam prevented their cooperation in government until after Mapam's split in 1954. The defection from Mapam of the more moderate Ahdut Ha'avoda accelerated a process of deradicalization on the Zionist left that eventually brought both former factions of Mapam once again into the mainstream of the Israeli labor movement.

Beyond its dominance in government, Mapai controlled three political subsystems. It maintained its majority position in the Histadrut, which became the largest social organization in Israel. It headed the executive of the Zionist Organization (the Jewish Agency), which was empowered by law to act in the areas of settlement and absorption of immigrants. Finally, it steadily gained a leading role in municipal government which, prior to the formation of the state, was dominated by the political right.

Under Ben-Gurion's leadership, Mapai was identified with the "nation as a whole" during the struggle for a Jewish National Home, the transition from community to state, and the formative period of the state. Ben-Gurion championed the principle of the partition of Palestine, which was eventually adopted by the UN General Assembly. In his capacity as the head of the provisional executive of the *Yishuv*, Ben-Gurion proclaimed the State of Israel in the historic meeting of the People's Assembly on May 14, 1948. Ben-Gurion's government led Israel in the war of 1948 (the War of Independence), gained international recognition for the newly born state, and mobilized Jewish support and foreign aid for the absorption of two groups of Jewish refugees that settled in Israel: survivors of the European Holocaust and Jews from Arab lands, who were uprooted by the war of 1948.

Mapai's leadership was not always united on issues of security and foreign affairs. Foreign Minister Moshe Sharett frequently challenged Ben-Gurion's hawkish policies until he was forced to resign from the government in 1956. Nevertheless, Mapai's overall authority in these areas was widely accepted by its coalition partners.

Ben-Gurion's government was responsible for the emergence of a national consensus, frail and limited in scope as it was on major issues of foreign and domestic policy beginning with the adoption of the partition plan and the proclamation of the state. Ben-Gurion's Mapai espoused an orientation toward the Free World and a pragmatic foreign policy toward postwar Germany. Ben-Gurion's acceptance of a "new Germany," however, encountered strong opposition from the radical right and radical left, as well as from many survivors of the Holocaust. Ben-Gurion maintained a moderate hawkish policy toward the Arab states and was largely supported by most parties in his effort to put an end to Palestinian guerrilla warfare against Israel through a policy of retaliation.

Ben-Gurion's leadership in security affairs culminated in the Sinai Campaign of October 1956. Israel's swift victory in this war shaped its offensive security strategy for years to come, signaling to its Arab neighbors and the world that it had the military capacity to survive despite its rejection by the Arab world. Israel was forced by American and Soviet pressure to withdraw from the Sinai Peninsula. However, it gained the stationing of UN forces along the Israeli-Egyptian border and freedom of passage through the Straits of Tiran.

In domestic politics, Mapai capitulated to the demands of the religious parties in maintaining the arrangements governing state and religion, which had begun under the Ottoman Empire and were carried over from the British mandatory regime. The most controversial aspect of this arrangement gave the religious court of each denomination exclusive jurisdiction in matters of personal status (such as marriage and divorce).

Ben-Gurion assented to basic religious demands as defined by the religious parties: kosher kitchens in the army, recognition of the sanctity of the Sabbath (without a special law), and religious elementary schools in the state system. He refused, however, to go along with all of their demands, and he frequently tested the strength and resolve of these parties while maintaining cooperation with them in government. Ben-Gurion's most critical reform in domestic politics forced his own Labor movement (the Histadrut) to make concessions and relinquish some of its pre-state responsibilities and functions. The formation of a State Labor Exchange (the Employment Service) robbed the Histadrut of its primary role under the previous system. The formation of a state system of elementary schools put an end to the politicized sectoral systems, including that of the Histadrut. Each one of these reforms touched off an intense debate within the Israeli labor movement and Mapai itself.

The most heated political debate, however, accompanied Ben-Gurion's decision to disband the *Palmah*, the Kibbutz-inspired pre-state military force of the Jewish Agency's *Hagana*, which became the backbone of the Israeli army in the War of 1948. The *Palmah* was virtually nurtured by *Hakibbutz Hameuhad*, which was led by members of the leftist Mapam. Ben-Gurion's decision to disband the *Palmah* came after a bitter clash with the *Irgun* over the distribution of weapons sent by the European command of this organization on the ship *Altalena* immediately after the official dismantling of the *Irgun* by mutual consent. The *Altalena* affair produced violent clashes between former members of the *Irgun*, who had just been integrated into the official army, and units loyal to the provisional government. The political conflict spread to the streets of Tel Aviv, involving civilian supporters of both camps.

The *Altalena* affair tested the authority of the provisional government, facing the residual claim of the *Irgun* to autonomy concerning the distribution of weapons. The resolution of this conflict by the use of force accelerated the dismantling of the *Irgun,* whose former commanders decided to form a political party, the Herut Party. It undermined, however, its overall legitimacy in Israeli politics for some time to come, perhaps until the formation of Gahal in 1965.

Ben-Gurion's campaign to put an end to the encroachment on the functions and authority of the government of the newly born state by pre-state sectoral organizations enhanced his overall national leadership, but it did not fully benefit him electorally. It certainly aroused the hostility of the affected political forces against him. His party's bid to gain a clear parliamentary majority was repeatedly rejected by the voters, and it constantly needed the collaboration of minor parties in order to sustain a majority coalition in the *Knesset.* Nevertheless, Mapai did establish a dominant position in government, due to its pivotal position in a fragmented party system, and its legitimacy as a pragmatic and effective ruling party that defined and articulated with considerable success a new consensus on major issues confronting the state.

Beyond its leading role in government, Mapai served as a model party. In particular, its organized appeal to the new immigrant constituencies and its pragmatic style of politics, which made it more like a catchall party, are notable. This contagious model contributed, in part, to the processes of deradicalization of the opposing extremes in Israeli politics. The two former parties of the pro-Soviet Mapam gradually moved toward the social-democratic center of the Labor movement, and resumed cooperation with Mapai. Their unbroken membership in the multiparty Histadrut made it possible to limit the damage done during their radical phase in terms of labor unity and legitimacy. On the political right, Herut belatedly developed its own search for party alliances and a more pragmatic style of politics, which culminated in the formation of Gahal in 1965 and the entry of Gahal into the Government of National Unity in 1967.

Mapai itself, however, was victimized after the late 1950s by internal strife caused by the challenge of the "Youngsters" to the veteran leaders of the party, and the ensuing conflict among the veteran leaders themselves. The Youngsters developed a claim to national leadership while serving outside the institution of the regular party, largely in the army, state bureaucracy, and the party-sponsored youth movement. They called for party reform and democratization and pressed for an abrupt change of generations in the leadership of the party. The Youngsters did, however, support Ben-Gurion, who appointed their national leaders (Moshe Dayan and Shimon Peres) to his 1959 government. Ben-Gurion's support for the Youngsters, as well as his personal style of leadership, gradually increased tensions and fomented a crisis among the veteran leaders of the party.

The friction between Ben-Gurion and the veteran leaders of the party came to a head during the Lavon affair, which lingered on for over a decade and triggered one of the most important political crises in the history of Israel.[3] The affair generated the most potent challenge to the dominance of Mapai in government and politics. It brought Ben-Gurion's leadership to an end and prevented his successor, Levi Eshkol, from uniting the party and solidifying his position as prime minister. The affair threatened to isolate Mapai and raised questions about the legitimacy of its divided leadership. Finally, it split the party and fomented a process of realignment of the Labor parties.

The General Zionists were the most volatile party in the historic Israeli party system. It was the only secular party that resembled a cadre rather than a mass party at the outset of the state era. The size of its constituency fluctuated sharply in the first four *Knesset* elections: seven seats (5.2 percent of the votes) in 1949, twenty seats (16.2 percent) in 1951, thirteen seats (10.2 percent) in 1955, and eight seats (6.2 percent) in 1959. In an effort to put a halt to this electoral decline, it first deposed its two senior leaders, and later in 1961 it merged with the Progressive Party to form the Liberal Party. The new party hoped to challenge the dominant position of Mapai from the center and to block the rise of Herut on the right. It failed to do either. Herut maintained its electoral position in 1961, gaining the same number of seats as the new Liberal Party (seventeen), and even a slightly higher number of votes. Mapai lost five seats in the "election of the affair" (declining from forty-seven to forty-two seats), but was still able to form a coalition government without the Liberal Party. The leaders of the General Zionists then turned to the political right in their search for a new party strategy. They reached an agreement with Herut to form a joint electoral list and parliamentary bloc (Gahal). The majority of the Liberal Party supported this move, and the leaders of the Progressive Party split and reinstituted their independent party in reaction to it (the Independent Liberal Party).

The process of unity did not bypass the religious parties. Hapoel Hamizrahi, initially a federation of labor, rose to a position of dominance within its parent movement (Hamizrahi) in Israel and then merged with the smaller party (Hamizrahi), actually integrating it into its own structure. The result of this merger was the NRP, formed in 1956.

## TOWARD A COMPETITIVE PARTY SYSTEM (1965-77)

The year 1965 marked the beginning of a meaningful change in the Israeli party system. Three developments inaugurated a process of change that gave the Israeli party system a more competitive structure (1965–69), eventually produced a more competitive electoral outcome (1973), and finally produced the first major turnover in government in the history of the state (1977).

In 1965, Mapai experienced two conflicting and balancing changes: It split and simultaneously entered into a new electoral alignment. The split separated Mapai from its historic leader, Ben-Gurion, who questioned the legitimacy of his successor, Eshkol. For a while, the split also separated Mapai from its two most important young leaders, Dayan and Peres. Their splinter party, the Israeli Workers List, or Rafi, defined itself as a labor party, but its young leaders developed new themes (modernization and economic reform) that moved it toward the political center.

Undeterred by Ben-Gurion's challenge, Mapai moved to form an alignment with the Unity of Labor, or Ahdut Ha'avoda. The new coalition of forces successfully maintained the leading position of Labor in the *Knesset* (forty-five seats) and reinstated its coalition government. Nevertheless, Rafi's electoral showing (ten seats) and its readiness to cooperate with the political right became an important factor in the resolution of the next political crisis (1967) which ended in a humiliating setback for Prime Minister Eshkol and the leadership of the Labor Alignment.

The move toward unity on the left, which was sufficient to offset the defection of Rafi, was matched by a move toward unity on the political right. The latter move was even more significant because it ended the seventeen-year isolation of the Herut Party. The formation of Gahal did not produce an immediate change in the electoral strength of the political right. In fact, Gahal failed to gain the number of *Knesset* seats that the Herut and Liberal parties together had gained in the 1961 elections—thirty-four seats in 1961, compared to twenty-six seats for Gahal in 1965.

The immediate impact of Gahal was lessened by its failure to expand beyond the former partisan boundaries of its member parties, and by the radical changes on the left. The competing labor lists gave new, vigorous expression to the old-time conflict between the conservative and anti–Ben-Gurionist and the reformist and pro–Ben-Gurionist forces within this movement. Paradoxically, the externalization of this conflict actually helped to increase the overall representation of the labor grouping of parties in the 1965 election: sixty-three in 1965 (including Rafi), as against fifty-nine in 1961. The 1965 developments were, however, only the beginning of a period in which state events—primarily the crises of war in 1967 and 1973—accelerated developments on both the political left and right.

The 1967 war, and especially the domestic political crisis that preceded it, produced short- and long-term impacts on Israeli parties and politics. Mapai had reached this political juncture under the leadership of Levi Eshkol, a relative newcomer in the area of national security, who lacked Ben-Gurion's charisma. Moshe Dayan and Shimon Peres, the Youngsters who acquired strong reputations in the area of defense, left the party in 1965, and the young leaders of the Unity of Labor, Ahdut Ha'avoda, especially Yigal Allon, who established a strong reputation in the 1948 war, were not yet fully integrated into the leadership of the party. Mapai's leadership was thus severely weakened in the area of national security just at the onset of the crisis of the Six Day War. Prime Minister Eshkol's decision to exhaust the search for a diplomatic solution in the face of the Egyptian blockade of the Straits of Tiran and the threatening move of the Egyptian army into the Sinai Peninsula, accompanied by warlike rhetoric, undermined support for the government and invited public pressure for the formation of a unity government. More particularly, there was a loud clamor for the appointment of Moshe Dayan as defense minister.

Eshkol and his veteran associates finally succumbed to growing pressure from the minor parties in the coalition government, as well as from within their own party. The appointment of Dayan to the defense post, which had been held until then by the prime minister himself, and the invitation to two leaders of the rightist Gahal (including Menachem Begin) to join the government considerably weakened the veteran leadership of Mapai. It turned Moshe Dayan into a national leader, and it further solved the initial problem of legitimacy for Menachem Begin and his party, Herut.

The veteran leaders of Mapai moved to rectify their new political vulnerability by initiating a party merger with Ahdut Ha'avoda. Under pressure from within the party, they were forced, however, to negotiate instead a tripartite merger of Mapai, Ahdut Ha'avoda, and Rafi. These negotiations finally led to the formation of the Israeli Labor Party (see Labor Party of Israel) in 1968. The new party was based initially on conflicting expectations. The veteran leaders wanted to join forces with Ahdut Ha'avoda in order to stifle the potential challenge of Rafi and Moshe Dayan. On the other side, Dayan and Peres were ready to reverse their 1965 course and merge with Mapai in order to sustain Dayan's position and rejoin their strong residual supporters in Mapai.[4] The Rafi faction did score several victories in the ensuing interfactional politics in the newly formed Labor Party, but it failed to gain control of party bodies. Instead, the Rafi leaders adopted a brinkmanship strategy, threatening to split the Labor Party in order to exploit Moshe Dayan's popularity among the voters. Rafi's leaders had already prepared for an independent run in the 1969 elections, but Dayan himself chose in the end to reach an agreement with Golda Meir, the new prime minister and leader of the party (following Eshkol's death in February 1969). The agreement related to representation in the party's list of candidates to the Knesset and the future government. It also incorporated into the party's platform some of Dayan's hawkish views, particularly on the subject of settlements in the occupied territories and their economic integration with Israel. The unity of the Labor Party was thus saved less than two years after its formation, but its leadership remained divided, and its structure remained factional until the elections of 1973. Other informal arrangements were devised to preserve the integration of the former factional leaders at all levels of the party.

The rise of Moshe Dayan and the formation of the Labor Party again turned the left into the prime arena and the center of attention in Israeli politics. Nevertheless, the Six Day War moved the political right a step farther toward a competitive position, which only the next war (the Yom Kippur War of 1973) finally helped to establish.

Upon entering legitimate Israeli politics, Begin and the former commanders of the Irgun first adopted a strategy of political confrontation which placed them at the radical end of the political right, isolated from their own potential allies.

The belated formation of Gahal extricated Herut from its prolonged isolation, and the subsequent 1967 war helped solve its initial legitimacy problem by virtue of the invitation to join the Unity government. Menachem Begin made the most of this opportunity by adopting a cooperative and relatively moderate course within the government, which enabled it to survive beyond the election. In 1970, after almost three years of service in the Unity government, Begin made his move. He led Gahal out of the government in reaction to the acceptance of Security Council Resolution 242 (calling for Israel's withdrawal from the occupied territories to secured and recognized borders) and the Rogers Plan, which produced a cease-fire agreement with Egypt in the war of attrition along the Suez Canal.

In 1973 Gahal became the center of a new political force, the Likud, which eventually enabled the political right to gain a primary role in government. The new political body was formed by a merger of Gahal (twenty-six members of the Knesset) with two splinter parties: Free Center (Merkaz Hofshi)* (two members), which defected from the Herut Party in 1966, and the State List* (four members), which defected from Rafi in 1968. A new group, the Labor Movement for Greater Israel,* was formed for the purpose of joining the Likud. A war hero, General Ariel Sharon—a native son of a cooperative farm (Moshav) and a former Mapai cardholder—played an important role in the formation of the Likud. The Likud proclaimed the issue of Greater Israel (or the future of the territories) above all other issues in Israeli politics. The participation of former Labor activists and intellectuals in its formation gave the Likud broader national appeal and helped somewhat to weaken the old historical cleavages between the political right and left.

The Likud was formed before the Yom Kippur War (October 1973); however, its first electoral run came after the war (December 31, 1973). The Yom Kippur War was perceived in Israel as a political and military earthquake. The Egyptian-Syrian surprise attack on the Jewish Day of Atonement shattered Israel's sense of security, which had emerged after the victory in the 1967 war, with control over the Sinai Peninsula, the West Bank, the Gaza Strip, and the Golan Heights. The 1973 war produced a crisis of confidence in government directed primarily against Defense Minister Dayan and Prime Minister Meir, who were blamed by the opposition and a large segment of the public for not reacting effectively to the signs of imminent attack. Menachem Begin, the leader of the Likud, articulated the claim that the government was guilty of gross negligence and should resign. In contrast, the dovish left raised the charge that the government could have prevented the war by attempting to negotiate peace and giving up the occupied territories.

The most potent challenge to the authority and legitimacy of Meir and Dayan emerged, however, outside the Knesset. The Labor government enjoyed a commanding majority—75 of 120 seats. The crisis preceding the 1967 war had produced only a mood of protest; the 1973 war produced actual protest movements that politicized many young citizens in uniform and turned part of Labor's historic constituency against it. Meir's government initially managed the threatening crisis by appointing a commission of inquiry, which was asked to investigate the availability of information concerning the surprise attack, the decisions made on the basis of this information, the preparation of the army, and its functioning in the early stages of the war.

After four months, the commission issued an interim report that actually placed the blame only on the military and failed to discuss the issue of ministerial responsibility. Moreover, the commission cleared Meir and Dayan of any personal negligence and recommended ending the tenure in office of the chief of staff and the removal from office of the commander of the southern front and the head of military intelligence. The interim report raised a political storm, although its recommendations were implemented by the government. The growing protest for not fixing at least ministerial responsibility on the defense minister and the prime minister set the stage for their eventual resignation.

The success of the Israeli army in overcoming its initial setbacks and launching a successful counteroffensive, forcing the Arabs to accept a cease-fire agreement, together with the appointment of the commission of inquiry, saved Meir's government from a repetition of the political humiliation of 1967. It also prevented a Labor defeat in the December elections. The Labor Alignment lost five *Knesset* seats in that election (declining from fifty-six to fifty-one), but succeeded in retaining its dominant role in the government. The Likud gained thirty-nine *Knesset* seats, the largest number ever gained by an opposition party. The numerical gap between the leading party and the major opposition party was thus considerably reduced. The competitive structure of the Israeli party system, inaugurated in 1965 by the formation of Gahal, finally resulted in a more competitive outcome which placed the Likud on the threshold of electoral victory and a turnover in government.

The interim report enabled Meir and Dayan to resign without assuming personal responsibility for the initial military setbacks. Encountering persistent criticism within her own party, Meir resigned and retired from politics in April 1974. Dayan did not join the new government but remained active in politics.

Yitzhak Rabin, Meir's successor, represented a new generation in office. He was twenty-four years younger than his predecessor, having entered office at the age of fifty-two, and he was younger than any of the former prime ministers. His selection marked the beginning of a new era in the nomination of the prime minister in the Israeli Labor Party. All previous prime ministers were initially selected by consensus among the leaders of the party and confirmed by a formal vote in a central party body. With the resignation of Prime Minister Meir—the last standard-bearer of the party from the veteran generation—the party accepted an open nominating contest not only as a legal possibility, but also as a fully legitimate feature of party life. Previously, veteran party activists viewed such a contest as divisive, self-seeking, and not in the best interests of the party. The democratization of the nominating process reflected the absence of a consensual leader and was a response to the crisis of succession at the end of the founder's era in the aftermath of the Yom Kippur War, which had raised questions about the legitimacy of the party in power.

Yitzhak Rabin won a close race against Shimon Peres. Rabin was supported by former members of Ahdut Ha'avoda and a majority of the former members of Mapai in the central committee of the Labor Party. Peres was supported by the former members of Rafi and a significant minority among the former members of Mapai in that body. The departure of Dayan from Labor's leadership enabled Peres to emerge as the leader of Rafi activists and to appear as a major contender for the office of prime minister. He succeeded Dayan as defense minister in Rabin's government.

The 1974 nominating contest opened an era of competition between Rabin and Peres for the leadership of the Labor Party, which continued until 1992. Unlike the American "winner take all" nominating convention, Israeli contests have been much more complex and could not be ended in the same conclusive fashion. At the end of the contest, the party must still present a unified list of candidates for the *Knesset,* and the nominee must therefore negotiate with the defeated candidate and appoint him to his government in order to unify the party (see Table 9).

In sum, the second period in the development of the Israeli party system during the state era, commencing in 1965, was marked by the interaction of structural change and political crisis. This process led to the emergence of a competitive party system and the first major turnover in the composition of Israeli coalition government.

## FIRST TURNOVER IN GOVERNMENT IN A COMPETITIVE PARTY SYSTEM (1977–84)

Electoral change in Israel was the product of a realigning electoral era commencing with the 1973 election and culminating in the 1981 election. The Likud received thirty-nine *Knesset* seats in 1973, forty-three in 1977, and forty-nine in 1981. The 1981 election was pivotal from this perspective because, had the Likud lost that election, Labor would have reinforced its claim to legitimacy as a ruling party. The 1977 electoral defeat would then have become merely a deviant episode in the long history of Labor dominance in Israeli politics. The Likud's victory in the 1981 elections, narrow as it was, thus turned the 1977 change in government into a more legitimate feature of Israeli politics.

The first major turnover in government, or the replacement of the leading party in the governing coalition, was possible primarily because of the crushing defeat of Labor, which declined from fifty-one to thirty-two *Knesset* seats, rather than the moderate electoral gain of the Likud from thirty-nine to forty-three *Knesset* seats (or forty-five seats together with Ariel Sharon's Independent List).

Labor could still have formed a government in 1977 had it held the loyalty of its former coalition partners, primarily the NRP, and had it won the support of the new reform party, the DMC. However, the lopsided electoral outcome undermined Labor's efforts to remain in power. The Likud managed first to form a narrow coalition with the religious parties. The DMC joined this government four months later, prior to the Camp David conference (which provided the framework for a peace agreement with Egypt). The DMC's decision to join the coalition government caused an irreparable rift in the new party, which eventually led to its disintegration.

The defeat of the Labor alignment in the 1977 election may be explained by the convergence of a gradual process of decline with an adverse set of circumstances prior to the election. Labor's decline had been apparent since the 1969 election, perhaps even since the 1961 election if we disregard the 1965 election (the election of the Affair).

In the 1969 elections, the Rafi splinter group, the State List, gained four seats in the Knesset. If we add these to the sum total of the Labor grouping (altogether sixty members), the decline does not appear significant. The State List, however, participated in the formation of the Likud in 1973. Its electoral showing may therefore serve as a partial indication of Moshe Dayan's potential electoral strength among those who were prepared to cross party lines, rather than as an indication of the strength of the Labor grouping in that election.

Five major reasons contributed to Labor's electoral defeat in the 1977 election, two of which relate to developments within the Labor camp. First was the loss of political efficacy and governing legitimacy. It began with the failure to maintain the unity of the party in the Lavon affair; it continued with Mapai's poor performance, or what was perceived as such, in the crisis preceding the 1967 war, and the initial setback of the 1973 war. The cumulative erosion of Labor's reputation as the governing party coincided with the growing ills of longevity in government, such as corruption, bureaucratic excesses, and partisanship. Second was the failure of the Labor Party to overcome the crisis of leadership succession following the change of generations in the leadership of the party (1974) and the democratization of the nominating process. Divisive competition for the leadership of the party has since become a major feature of the Labor Party.

Third, there was a change in the electoral behavior of a major group of Israeli voters: Sephardi Jews, who immigrated to Israel from Arab countries following the establishment of the State of Israel and the war of 1948. The almost destitute refugees came to a society that until 1948 was predominantly East European and Ashkenazi by origin and cultural orientation. The early economic and educational gaps placed the new immigrants at a disadvantage that tended to linger on for years. The historic parties, with Mapai leading the way, made an effort to politicize and integrate the immigrants into their ranks. Their success prevented the emergence of an ethnic immigrants' party. The new immigrants found themselves in centralized parties dominated by East European Jewish leaders who tended to maintain a patronizing attitude toward them. The Sephardi activists among the new immigrants rose fairly quickly to positions of local leadership in the party and the Histadrut, but until the late 1970s they gained only token representation in the Knesset and the national leadership of the party.

The early politicization of the new immigrants benefited Mapai. The new sense of political empowerment, however, together with growing alienation over the lingering gaps in education, occupation, and standard of living, produced disenchantment with Labor, which seemed to lose its capacity to govern effectively, and produced a greater affinity with the Likud. Mapai was perceived as the party of the veteran Ashkenazi elite; the Likud gave expression to the anti-Mapai sentiment, as well as to proreligious tradition and the trend toward political hawkishness that characterized the Sephardi voters. About two-thirds of the Likud voters in the 1977 and 1981 elections were of Sephardi descent, while about the same percentage of Labor's voters were of Ashkenazi descent.

Fourth, there was the ascendancy of the political right, which finally found in the Likud an effective political organization. The 1967 war made the political agenda and leadership of the Likud more acceptable to Israeli society. The occupation of the West Bank and the reunification of Jerusalem under Israel's rule raised again the issue of Greater Israel and the issue of the settlements in the occupied territories. The policy of settlement was first introduced by the Labor Party against the background of Arab refusal to negotiate with Israel, a position adopted at the Khartoum Arab Summit Conference in August 1967.

Fifth was the softening of historic party allegiances and the decline of the old Labor values and perceptions in a society that had become more pragmatic and individualistic. The Likud's prime minister, Menachem Begin, moved to enhance acceptance of his new government, both at home and abroad, by inviting Moshe Dayan to serve as foreign minister. (Dayan had been elected to the *Knesset* on Labor's list of candidates.) Begin also lured the new centrist party (the DMC) to join the government. This government was successful in achieving Israel's first peace treaty with an Arab country (Egypt) in 1979, after signing an initial accord and a framework for a comprehensive settlement in the Camp David Peace Conference held in 1978.

The 1981 election brought to its peak the process of political consolidation in the Israeli party system. A two-bloc dominance emerged at the center of the historically fragmented system and enhanced its competitive structure. The Likud gained an additional five *Knesset* seats (altogether forty-eight), and the Labor opposition regained its competitive position by gaining fifteen seats (altogether forty-seven). The two major blocs together controlled 95 seats in the 120-member *Knesset*, the highest total ever gained by the two largest parties in the *Knesset*.

The Likud edged out Labor by only one *Knesset* seat in the 1981 election. It was able to reinstate its government because of the alliance with the religious parties. The Likud thus scored primarily a coalition victory in the *Knesset* in that election.

Jewish ethnic tension appeared at the center of the 1981 election campaign. It was caused by the protest of voters of Sephardi descent against the veteran Ashkanazi social and political elites. Such protest was channeled in the main through the Likud. It expressed itself, however, in a more extreme fashion by the appearance of a new religious ethnic protest party, *Tami*.* Studies of the 1981 election found that the voters of Sephardi descent leaned toward the Likud because of its favorable attitudes toward religion, its hawkish position in foreign and security policy, and ethnic identity.

Tami gained three *Knesset* seats but failed to institutionalize as a permanent party. Another protest party, the Revival Party, or Hatehiya, appeared in the 1981 election as a reaction against the Camp David Accords and the agreement with Egypt. This party originated in a defection of activists from the Likud who, together with religious and labor activists, formed the most extreme nationalist party of the time.

Following a long period of electoral stability, the 1981 election produced a significant change among the religious parties. The NRP lost half its *Knesset* seats, while the Labor Association of Israel, or Poalei Aguda, lost its single seat. Overall representation of the religious parties was reduced from seventeen to thirteen seats. The change in the electoral position of the NRP was the direct outcome of the appearance of Tami and the Revival Party and, to a lesser extent, the centripetal electoral trend caused by the Likud-Labor confrontation.

In 1983 the Likud was hampered by the sudden resignation of its charismatic leader, Menachem Begin, who left public life in a state of physical and emotional exhaustion. His successor, Yitzhak Shamir, failed to unite the party and had to face successive challenges (1984, 1988, 1992).

Begin's exit from politics deprived the Likud of its founding leader, who had developed a special populist appeal to alienated groups. The Jewish Defense League (*Kach*)* was one of the beneficiaries of Begin's exit, gaining a single seat in the *Knesset* after failing in three previous attempts. Begin personalized the historic record of the Likud, having served as commander of the *Irgun* in the pre-state era, as well as leading the Likud to its primary achievement in government: the peace treaty with Egypt.

Following the 1981 election, Begin balanced his peacemaking record with the imposition of Israeli law on the Golan Heights (1981) and the military campaign against the PLO in Lebanon (1982). It is generally assumed that the failure to achieve the military and political objectives of that war was the primary reason for Begin's departure from public life. Beyond the continuing war in Lebanon and Begin's resignation, the Likud was hampered prior to the 1984 elections by rampant inflation, which further undermined the position of the government.

## THE CRISIS OF THE COMPETITIVE SYSTEM (1984–90)

The 1984 election realized the potential for impasse and crisis in government formation embedded in the system of proportional representation. This system makes it extremely difficult if not impossible for one party to gain a majority in parliament in a pluralistic society, and it does not necessarily produce a winner. Both major parties lost support in the 1984 election. Labor became the largest faction in the *Knesset*, but it still lost three *Knesset* seats (declining from forty-seven to forty-four seats) and could not form a coalition government. The Likud lost seven seats (declining from forty-eight to forty-one seats) and was unable to reinstate its previous coalition government. Each of these parties could only form an alliance of fifty-four *Knesset* members, seven short of the required majority. Thus, for the first time in the history of Israel, neither of the two major parties could form a coalition government under its own leadership.

Under these circumstances, the two major parties faced three options: (1) hold new elections, an unacceptable solution to both parties and to the entire *Knesset* because of the high cost of campaigning and the lack of encouraging polls indicating a possible change in the outcome; (2) continue the Likud in power as an interim government; and (3) form a grand coalition between the Likud and the Labor Party.

The leaders of the Labor Party and the Likud preferred the third option. The Likud was more resigned to this possibility. It even called for the formation of a government of national unity during the campaign. Labor was less inclined to join such a government because of its strong opposition to Likud policies and its reluctance to accord the Likud new legitimacy by sharing power with it. Indeed, the decision to form such a government caused a split in the Labor alignment. The radical Mapam left the Alignment upon the decision of the Labor Party to join the unity government. The structure of the Unity Government was based on parity in representation and rotation in the office of prime minister. Moreover, the Likud and Labor formed an inner cabinet, composed of five ministers from each party, which gave both parties an actual veto power over the decisions of the government.

The previous two unity governments in Israel had differed in structure and had come into being for different reasons. The Provisional Government, which served in 1948–49, may be considered a unity government because of its inclusive composition. This government served as an interim government for legitimate constitutional reasons (transition from a community to an independent state), and it acted as a mini-parliament due to the lack of a coalition agreement and discipline. The second unity government was formed in response to the political and security crisis preceding the 1967 war. It was formed to restore confidence in government in the face of an imminent war. This government, which had an irregular structure imposed on an existing government, was led by the dominant party (Labor). Following the 1969 elections, the unity government was restructured as a regular coalition government, under Labor leadership, and served until 1970.

The third unity government in 1984 was thus unique in its structure of parity. It was also unique in the reasons that brought it into being: a crisis in coalition formation rather than a critical national condition. The high rate of inflation, as well as growing difficulties in defining the goals and achieving the objectives of the continuing war in Lebanon, helped to gain acceptance for the formation of the unity government (a pivotal party, the NRP, refused to join any other government). However, it was the parliamentary deadlock in coalition formation that made it necessary to establish such a government.

The unity government initially avoided the potential paralysis embedded in its parity structure. It managed to adopt majority decisions on a new economic policy that put a halt to rampant inflation, and it withdrew the army from areas deep inside Lebanon to a security zone close to the Israeli border. Following rotation in the office of prime minister, the Unity government gradually evolved into a divided body comprising two partisan shadow governments. Labor finally broke away because of a disagreement with the Likud concerning the terms for negotiations with a Palestinian delegation about elections in the West Bank and Gaza.

Jewish ethnic tension was less apparent in the 1984 election campaign. Tami, the Sephardi protest party, lost two of its three *Knesset* seats. *Shas*, a new Sephardi party, offered a more moderate message and a wider base of legitimacy. Tami presented an ethnic protest message that was viewed by the media as contrary to the national ideology of integration. Shas subordinated the ethnic message to a religious one. It was founded by legitimate religious leaders, specifically the former Sephardi chief rabbi and heads of religious academies (*yeshivot*) who politicized a passive constituency within the ultraorthodox community. In doing so, Shas gained a wider appeal to religious Sephardi voters, some of whom had supported the Likud in previous elections. In sum, Tami presented a deviant pattern in traditional Israeli politics, while Shas conformed to it, because religion rather than ethnic ideology had been acceptable in Israeli society as a basis for forming political parties.

The 1988 election did not produce a clear winner either. It did, however, improve the chances of the Likud to form a government. The Likud once again became the largest faction in the *Knesset*, despite the loss of one more seat (from forty-one to forty). Labor lost five seats (from forty-four to thirty-nine seats), three to Mapam, which had left the Labor alignment. The Labor group of parties (including the centrist Shinui) remained the largest section in the *Knesset* (despite the decrease from fifty to forty-nine seats), but it did not have the votes to block the formation of a government by the Likud and the religious parties. This coalition of parties commanded a majority in the new *Knesset* due to a significant increase in the representation of the religious parties, which rose from twelve to eighteen seats. The overall strength of the potential Likud coalition alliance rose from sixty seats in 1984 to sixty-five seats in 1988. In 1984 the NRP refused to join any coalition but a unity government, but in 1988 it was prepared to join a Likud government. Prime Minister Shamir preferred, however, to reinstate the unity government (with Labor and the religious parties) rather than be constrained by the demands of the religious and nationalist parties.

The new unity government was based on the same policy platform and the same structure (equal representation) as the previous one. This time, however, there was no rotation in the office of prime minister. This was the initial net gain of the Likud in the 1988 election. The potential alternative government (with the religious and nationalist parties) was realized only in 1990 when Labor quit because of differences with the Likud concerning the terms for talks with the Palestinians. Shimon Peres, the leader of the Labor Party, believed at the time that he had struck a secret deal with two religious parties (Shas and the Aguda), but this was proven wrong when they finally decided to maintain their alliance with the Likud (Appendix B).

The increase in the representation of the religious party grouping in the Knesset was the most significant outcome of the 1988 election. The ultraorthodox parties emerged as the primary section in this grouping. Two major developments led to this change, besides the decline of the NRP: (1) the politicization of the Sephardi constituency of the ultraorthodox community by Shas, and (2) personal, religious, and political feuds within the ultraorthodox community, which contributed to the overall mobilization of this constituency in the 1988 election.

In sum, the 1981 election produced two-party dominance in a competitive multiparty system. The 1984 election realized the potential for crisis in a competitive system, which does not necessarily produce a winner in terms of a parliamentary majority and formation of a government. The 1988 election again enhanced the role of the small parties in the formation of a government.

The 1992 election brought about a second major turnover in the composition of the coalition government. Labor gained five seats and established a commanding lead over the Likud, which declined from forty to thirty-two Knesset seats. The united radical list on the left (Meretz) gained twelve seats, while the two nationalist lists won eleven seats (Tsomet, eight; the Homeland Party Moledet, three). The Revival Party, Hatehiya, did not pass the threshold for representation. The overall representation of the religious parties declined from eighteen to sixteen Knesset seats. Shas maintained its parliamentary strength (six seats); the NRP added a seat (from five to six); and the united Aguda list lost three seats (from seven to four seats). The Arab lists declined by one seat. The Democratic Front for Peace and Equality (Hadash)* (Rakah) lost one. The progressive list did not reach the threshold for representation, and the Democratic Arab Party gained one seat (from one to two).

Labor, together with Meretz and the Arab lists, gained a blocking majority against the formation of a Likud government in the 1992 election. The defection of Shas from the former Likud coalition enabled Labor to form a majority coalition, with the passive support of the Arab lists outside the government: Labor, forty-four; Meretz, twelve; Shas, six—a total of sixty-two Knesset seats.

### Bibliography

Akzin, B. "The Role of Parties in Israeli Democracy." In Integration and Development in Israel, edited by S. N. Einsenstadt et al., 4–46. Jerusalem: Israel University Press, 1970.

Arian, Asher, Politics in Israel: The Second Generation. Revised edition. Chatham N.J.: Chatham House, 1989.

Arian, Asher, ed. *The Elections in Israel 1969*. Jerusalem: Academic Press, 1972.

―――. *The Elections in Israel 1973*. Jerusalem: Academic Press, 1975.

―――. *The Elections in Israel 1977*. Jerusalem: Academic Press, 1980.

―――. *The Elections in Israel 1981*. Tel-Aviv: Ramot, 1983.

Arian, Asher, and Michal Shamir, eds. *The Elections in Israel 1984*. New Brunswick, N.J.: Transaction, 1986.

―――. *The Elections in Israel 1988*. Boulder: Westview Press, 1990.

Aronoff, Myron J. *Power and Ritual in the Israeli Labor Party*. Assen-Amsterdam: Van Gorcum, 1977.

Azmon, Y. "The 1981 Elections and the Changing Fortunes of the Israeli Labor Party." *Government and Opposition* 16, 4 (1981): 432–46.

Beilin, Y. *The Price of Unity: The Labor Party before the Yom Kippur War* (in Hebrew). Tel-Aviv: Revivim, 1985.

Ben Avram, Baruch. *Parties and Political Movements in the Yishuv Era: 1918–1948* (in Hebrew). Jerusalem: Shazar Center, 1978.

Brichta, A. *Democracy and Elections* (in Hebrew). Tel-Aviv: Am Oved, 1977.

Caspi, D., A. Diskin, and E. Gutmann, eds. *The Roots of Begin's Success: The 1981 Israeli Election*. London: Croom Helm, 1984.

Deshen, S. *Immigrant Voters in Israel*. Manchester, England: Manchester University Press, 1970.

Diskin, A. *Elections and Voters in Israel*. New York: Praeger, 1991.

Don-Yehiya, E. "The Politics of the Religious Parties in Israel." In *Public Life in Israel and the Diaspora*, edited by S. V. Lehman-Wilzig and B. Susser, 110–37. Ramat-Gan: Bar-Ilan University Press, 1981.

Elazar, D., and S. Sandler, eds. *Israel's Odd Couple: The 1984 Elections and the National Unity Government*. Detroit: Wayne State University Press, 1990.

Goldberg, Giora. *Political Parties in Israel: From Mass Parties to Electoral Parties* (in Hebrew). Tel-Aviv: Ramot, 1992.

Isaac, R. J. *Party and Politics in Israel: Three Visions of a Jewish State*. New York: Longman, 1981.

Kieval, Gershon R. *Party Politics in Israel and the Occupied Territories*. Westport, Conn.: Greenwood Press, 1983.

Medding, Peter Y. *Mapai in Israel: Political Organization and Government in a New Society*. London: Cambridge University Press, 1972.

Neuberger, B. *Political Parties in Israel* (in Hebrew). Tel-Aviv: The Open University, 1991.

Penniman, Howard R., and D. J. Elazar, eds. *Israel at the Polls: The Knesset Elections of 1981*. Washington, D.C.: American Enterprise Institute, 1986.

―――. *Israel at the Polls: The Knesset Elections of 1977*. Washington, D.C.: American Enterprise Institute, 1979.

Peri, Yoram. *Between Battles and Ballots: Israeli Military in Politics*. London: Cambridge University Press, 1983.

Rubenstein, Sondra M. *The Communist Movement in Palestine and Israel 1919–1984*. Boulder, Colo.: Westview Press, 1985.

Sandler, S. "The National Religious Party: Toward a New Role in Israel's Political System?" In *Public Life in Israel and the Diaspora*, edited by S. L. Lehman-Wilzig and B. Susser, 158–70. Ramat-Gan: Bar-Ilan University Press, 1981.

Schechtman, Joseph, and Y. Benari. *History of the Revisionist Movement*. Tel-Aviv: Hadar, 1970.

Schiff, Gary S. *Tradition and Politics: The Religious Parties of Israel.* Detroit, Mich.: Wayne University Press, 1977.

Shapiro, Y. *Chosen to Command—The Road to Power of the Herut Party* (in Hebrew). Tel-Aviv: Am Oved, 1989.

Shapiro, Yonathan. *The Formative Years of the Israeli Labor Party: The Organization of Power 1919–1930.* London: Sage, 1976.

Shavit, Ya'acov. *Jabotinsky and the Revisionist Movement 1925–1948.* London: Frank Cass, 1988.

Shimshoni, Daniel. *Israeli Democracy.* New York: Free Press, 1982.

Tzahar, Zeev. *On the Road to Yishuv Leadership—The Formative Years of the Histadrut* (in Hebrew). Jerusalem: Ben-Zvi, 1981.

Yanai, Nathan. *Split at the Top* (in Hebrew). Tel-Aviv: Levin-Epstein, 1969.

———. *Party Leadership in Israel: Maintenance and Change.* Ramat-Gan: Turtledove, 1981.

Yishai, Y. *Factionalism in the Labor Movement* (in Hebrew). Tel-Aviv: Am Oved, 1984.

## Political Parties

AGUDAT YISRAEL. *See* ASSOCIATION OF ISRAEL.

AHDUT HA'AVODA. *See* UNITY OF LABOR.

AHDUT HA'AVODA-POALEI TSIYON. *See* UNITY OF LABOR—ZIONIST LABOR.

ALIYA HADASHA. *See* NEW IMMIGRATION.

ALIYA HADASHA OVEDET. *See* LABOR NEW IMMIGRATION.

ASSOCIATION OF ISRAEL (*Agudat Yisrael*). This ultraorthodox party was founded in 1912 in Poland in opposition to the nationalist ideology and secular majority of the World Zionist Congress. The party (which commenced its activities in Palestine in 1919) also boycotted the national institutions of the organized Jewish community in Palestine (the *Yishuv*) until 1947. Agudat Yisrael participated in the governments of 1949–52 and 1977–92. The party does not recognize the Israeli Chief Rabbinate, maintains independent elementary schools, and is under the supreme authority of a body of rabbis, known as the Council of the Sages of the Torah.

BLACK PANTHERS (*Pantherim Shehorim*). This social protest movement was organized by young Sephardi activists in deprived urban neighborhoods. It ran in the 1973 *Knesset* election without gaining a single seat. However, it did gain representation in the Histadrut. The movement split, and one leader of the party was elected to the *Knesset* through the Democratic Front for Peace and Equality* (the electoral list dominated by the Communist Party). Another faction joined the Labor Party.*

BLOCK OF THE FAITHFUL (*Gush Emunim*). This politico-religious movement, for the settlement of the occupied territories that were seized by Israel in the Six Day War (1967), was founded in 1974. This movement attached religious messianic significance to the consequences of that war; initiated Jewish settlement projects in the territories, especially in Judea and Samaria; and protested official policies to curb Jewish settlement or any attempt to reach an agreement with the Palestinians and the Arab states involving the return of the territories. Gush Emunim did not develop into a political party, but its leaders were active in the National Religious Party* and the parties of the political right.

CIVIL RIGHTS MOVEMENT (*Ratz*). This radical, dovish, and anticlerical party was founded in 1973 by Shulamit Aloni, a noted civil rights activist, who failed to win renomination on the Labor Party* ticket. In 1975, the party participated in a futile attempt to form a wider party, the Togetherness Party (Yahad).* In 1992 it became the leading party in a new electoral list (Meretz) with two other small, radical, dovish parties: the leftist United Workers Party (Mapam)* and the centrist Shinui.

COMMUNIST PARTY OF ISRAEL (*Hamiflaga Hakomunistit Hayisraelit—Maki*). This party had its origin in the Hebrew Socialist Workers' Party, which participated in the founding convention of the Histadrut (six of sixty-seven delegates) in 1920. The Palestinian Communist Party (PCP)* was admitted to the International Association of Communist Parties (Comintern) in 1924, and it was expelled from the Histadrut because of its extreme anti-Zionist stand. Many Jewish members of the party emigrated to the Soviet Union during this period. The party objected to Jewish immigration and settlement in Palestine. During World War II, the party was less hostile to the Jewish cause in Palestine, and in 1944 it was again admitted to the Histadrut. In 1945 a Jewish faction (the Hebrew Communists) split the party and supported Jewish independence within a federated Arab-Jewish state in Palestine. The support of the Soviet Union for the UN Partition Plan and its immediate recognition of the State of Israel, upon its establishment, prompted the various factions of the PCP to reunite and form the Communist Party of Israel (*Maki*). In 1949 the Hebrew Communists left the party and joined the United Workers Party (Mapam).* The Communist Party split again in 1965. The largely Arab faction, which supported Nasser and pan-Arabism, found itself in a minority and founded the New Communist List (*Rakah*).* The Communist Party, which became a Jewish party, lost its primacy to the New Communist List because the majority of its voters were Israeli Arabs. Maki gained only one seat in the elections of 1965 and 1969; the New Communist List gained three seats in each of these elections. In 1973 Maki cooperated with another Jewish leftist group, the Moked Movement*; later it disappeared altogether. The New Communist List became the primary Arab nationalist party, despite its Jewish secretary-general (until 1990) and Jewish activists. This group lost its primacy as the 1992 election approached. (See also the chapter on the Palestinians).

COURAGE MOVEMENT (*Ometz*). This electoral list was formed in the 1984 election by the former State List* (after the dismantling of Telem*) under the leadership of Yigal Hurwitz, a former finance minister. The movement gained one *Knesset* seat and participated in the unity government (1984–1988) as an ally of the Labor Party.* Subsequently, it joined the Likud* (1988).

DEGEL HATORA. *See* FLAG OF THE TORAH.

DEMOCRATIC ARAB PARTY (*Hamiflaga Ha'arvit Hademocratit*). This party was founded in 1988 by 'Abd al-Wahhab Darawshe, who quit the Labor Party* in protest over its policies concerning the peace process and the Arab minority in Israel. Darawshe was reelected to the *Knesset* in 1988 on his new party's list. In the 1992 elections, the party gained two seats. (See also the chapter on the Palestinians.)

DEMOCRATIC FRONT FOR PEACE AND EQUALITY (*Hadash*). This political bloc and electoral list, centered around the New Communist List,* was formed in 1977 to enhance the List's electoral reach both among Arab and Jewish voters. In addition to the New Communist List, the front consisted of a group of elected Arab local officials, a Druze committee, and the Democratic Front for Nazareth. It also included several Jewish groups: a faction of the Black Panthers* (which left Hadash in 1991) and a group known as the Israeli Socialist Left. In 1977, Hadash gained five *Knesset* seats. In 1981, 1984, and 1988, it gained four seats, and in 1992 only three.

DEMOCRATIC MOVEMENT FOR CHANGE (DMC) (*Hatnua Hademocratit Leshinui*). A short-lived reform, centrist party, it was founded prior to the 1977 election under the leadership of Professor Yigael Yadin, a noted archeologist and a former chief of staff of the Israeli army. The new party was formed through a merger of Yadin's group and the Shinui* party. The DMC, which was subsequently joined by other groups, held the first nominating primary for the selection of its candidates to the *Knesset*. It gained fifteen seats in its only electoral run, and it joined the Likud* coalition government. It later split into various factions, primarily over the issue of participation in the Likud government; only one of these factions (Shinui) remained active.

DMC. *See* DEMOCRATIC MOVEMENT FOR CHANGE.

FIGHTERS' LIST (*Reshimat Halohamim*). This electoral list was founded by members of the Stern Group (*Lohamei Herut Israel*), the militant anti-British underground that split off from the *Irgun*. It appeared only in the election for the first *Knesset* in 1949, when it gained a single seat.

FLAG OF THE TORAH (*Degel Hatorah*). This party was founded in 1988 by a faction of the Association of Israel (Aguadat Yisrael)* under the leadership of Rabbi Eliezer Shach, the spiritual leader of one of the principal sections (the non-Hasidic *Litaim*) of the ultraorthodox *Yeshivot* (institutions of higher religious learning). In the 1992 election, Degel Hatorah formed a joint electoral list with Agudat Yisrael, the Labor Association of Israel (Poalei Aguadat Yisrael),* and the Heritage Movement (Morasha.)*

FOR THE PEOPLE (*La'am*). This party was founded within the Likud* bloc in 1976. It included the State List,* the Independent Center,* and the Labor Movement for Greater Israel.* The party ceased to exist prior to the 1981 election.

FREE CENTER (*Merkaz Hofshi*). Founded in 1966 by an opposition faction that split from the Freedom Party (Herut),* the faction comprised two groups: one headed by Shmuel Tamir, who challenged the leadership of Menachem Begin; the other, headed by Eliezer Shostak and leaders of the National Federation of Labor (*Histadrut Ovdim Leumit*), which was founded by the Revisionist Party* in 1935. The Revisionist Party was against Herut's decision to organize a faction in the Histadrut, the historical rival of the Revisionist movement. The Free Center party gained two *Knesset* seats in the 1969 election. It joined the Likud* in 1973 but left again in 1975. One faction, under the leadership of Tamir, joined the Democratic Movement for Change* in 1977; the other, under the leadership of Shostak, joined other groups in forming the For the People* party within the Likud.

FREEDOM PARTY (*Herut*). This nationalist party was formed in 1948 by the former commanders of the *Irgun*, the anti-British underground organization that espoused Revisionist ideology and refused to accept the authority of Jewish national institutions in Palestine. Under the leadership of Menachem Begin, the Freedom Party (Herut)* was effectively isolated in Israeli politics by its arch-rival, the Labor Party of Israel (Mapai),* and by its potential partners (the General Zionists*), until the formation of the Gahal* bloc in 1965. The violent confrontations between the former members of the *Irgun* and David Ben-Gurion's government over the *Altalena* affair (1948), and subsequently over the issue of reparations from Germany, as well as Begin's early radical and populist style of politics, contributed to Herut's prolonged isolation. The participation of Gahal in the 1967 unity government helped Herut and Begin to overcome their initial crisis of legitimacy. The primary ideological commitment of the Herut Party has been to the principle of Greater Israel. Herut fought the labor movement, but in 1965 it decided to organize a faction in the Histadrut, while challenging the Labor Federation's leadership and its ownership of economic enterprises. As principal party in the Gahal bloc, Herut became the center of a wider political bloc, the Likud,* in 1973. In 1977 the Likud won the election and became the ruling party. Its leader, Menachem Begin, became prime minister. He was succeeded in 1983 by Yitzhak Shamir. In 1990 the major parties of the Likud merged into a unified political party by this name. Herut gained fourteen *Knesset* seats in the 1949 elections, eight in 1951; fifteen in 1955; seventeen in 1959; and seventeen in 1961.

GAHAL—BLOC OF HERUT AND THE LIBERAL PARTY (*Gush Herut— Liberalim*). This joint electoral list and parliamentary block of the Freedom Party (Herut)* and the Liberal Party* was formed in 1965 and served as the basis for the formation of the Likud* in 1973.

GENERAL ZIONISTS (*Hatsiyonim Haklaliyim*). Initially, these nonpartisan groups were organized within the World Zionist Congress and the various state Zionist Federations. In 1921 the nonpartisan General Zionist delegates constituted 73 percent of the Zionist Congress; in 1931, only 36 percent. In 1929 a conference of General Zionists decided to form a political party which held its first world convention in 1931. The party proclaimed the supremacy of Zionist ideology over any other sectoral interest. It viewed itself, however, as the guardian of the interests of the middle class, and it called for the encouragement of free enterprise in Palestine. The new party was divided, almost since its foundation, into two factions: one (General Zionists A), which favored cooperation with the Labor movement and the Histadrut, and another (General Zionists B), which was inclined to cooperate with the upcoming Revisionist Party.* In 1935 the party split over this issue. The former established a faction in the Histadrut (Zionist Worker*), and the latter formed its own federation of labor which was dismantled in 1946. That year, the two General Zionist parties reunited, but then split again in 1948. General Zionists A merged with Zionist Worker and New Immigration* to form the Progressive Party.* General Zionists B remained an independent party, the backbone of which was the Civic Union (*Ihud Ezrahi*), an association of elected officials and civic and economic groups that were hostile to the institutions and the socialist ideology of the Labor movement in Palestine. Upon the foundation of the state, the General Zionists viewed their party as an alternative to the social-democratic Labor Party of Israel (*Mapai*.)* They tripled their representation in the election of the second *Knesset* in 1951 (from seven to twenty *Knesset* seats), but sharply declined in the next two successive elections (from twenty to thirteen seats in 1955, and from thirteen to eight in 1959). In the search for a new partisan and electoral orientation, the General Zionists merged in 1961 with the Progressive Party to form the Liberal Party.* Failing either to challenge Mapai from the new political center, or to force it to invite the new party to join its coalition government, the former General Zionists (the majority in the Liberal Party) decided in 1965 to form an electoral list with the Freedom Party (Herut)* (Gahal*). This cooperation led to the formation of the Likud bloc in 1973. The Liberal Party merged with Herut to form the Likud* party in 1990.

GREATER ISRAEL MOVEMENT (*Tnua Lema'an Eretz Yisrael Hashlema*). This party was founded in 1967, following the Six Day War, in order to promote the case for Greater Israel. In 1968 this movement initiated the renewal of Jewish settlement in Hebron. A faction of this movement (the Labor Movement for Greater Israel*) joined the Likud* in 1973. The Greater Israel movement ceased to exist with the formation of the Revival Party* in 1980.

GUARDIANS OF THE CITY (*Neturei Karta*). A small, extreme, and ultraorthodox organization, the Guardians of the City do not recognize the State of Israel and its institutions, believing that the existence of the Zionist secular state is in violation of the pure Jewish religious commitment. The party was founded in 1935 as a spin-off of the Association of Israel (Agudat Yisrael)* movement. It maintains independent religious and educational institutions, mostly in Jerusalem, and has remained largely stagnant and isolated even within the ultraorthodox community.

GUSH EMUNIM. *See* BLOCK OF THE FAITHFUL.

GUSH HERUT—LIBERALIM. *See* GAHAL.

HA'AVODA. *See* LABOR PARTY.

HADASH. *See* DEMOCRATIC FRONT FOR PEACE AND EQUALITY.

HAMIFLAGA HA'ARVIT HADEMOCRATIT. *See* DEMOCRATIC ARAB PARTY.

HAMAHANE HALEUMI. *See* LIKUD.

HAMIFLAGA HADATIT HALEUMIT—MAFDAL. *See* NATIONAL RELIGIOUS PARTY.

HAMIFLAGA HAKOMUNISTIT HAYISRAELIT. *See* COMMUNIST PARTY OF ISRAEL.

HAMIFLAGA HALIBERALIT. *See* LIBERAL PARTY.

HAMIFLAGA HAPROGRESIVIT. *See* PROGRESSIVE PARTY.

HAMIFLAGA HAREVZIONISTIT. *See* REVISIONIST PARTY.

HAMIFLAGA LIBERALIT ATSMAIT. *See* INDEPENDENT LIBERAL PARTY.

HAMIFLAGA LIBERALIT HADASHA. *See* NEW LIBERAL PARTY.

HAMIZRAHI. This Zionist religious party was the first to organize in the Zionist Congress (1902). It strove to make Zionism compatible with traditional Jewish religious beliefs, and to protect the interests of religious people and institutions in the *Yishuv*. It supported the Chief Rabbinate in the *Yishuv* and, subsequently, in the State of Israel. Hamizrahi cooperated politically with Hamizrahi Worker* (the religious Labor party) and in 1956 merged with it to form the National Religious Party.*

HAMIZRAHI WORKER (*Hapoel Hamizrahi*). This Zionist religious labor federation, associated with the National Religious Party (NRP),* was founded in Jerusalem in 1922, and for a brief period it established a faction in the General Federation of Labor (the Histadrut). This action caused a split in the party, which resumed its independence in 1927. Subsequently, Hamizrahi Worker developed as a political party which overshadowed its parent Hamizrahi* party in Israel. Eventually, in 1956, it merged with Hamizrahi to form the NRP. Following the merger, Hamizrahi Worker kept its independence as a federation of labor associated with party. Since 1953 *Hapoel Hamizrahi* Federation of Labor has participated in the trade union department of the Histadrut, and in its medical service (*Kupat Holim*). It has developed a settlement movement of both kibbutzim and moshavim.

HAOLAM HAZE. *See* THIS WORLD PARTY.

HAOVED HADATI. *See* RELIGIOUS WORKER.

HAOVED HATSIYONI. *See* ZIONIST WORKER.

HAPOEL HAMIZRAHI. *See* HAMIZRAHI WORKER.

HAPOEL HATSAIR. *See* YOUNG WORKER.

HARESHIMA HAMAMLAHTIT. *See* STATE LIST.

HARESHIMA HAMITKADEMET LESHALOM. *See* PROGRESSIVE LIST FOR PEACE.

HATEHIYA. *See* REVIVAL PARTY.

HATNUA HADEMOCRATIT LESHINUI. *See* DEMOCRATIC MOVE-MENT FOR CHANGE.

HATNUA LEADHUT HA'AVODA. *See* UNITY OF LABOR MOVEMENT.

HATSIYONIM HAKLALIYIM. *See* GENERAL ZIONISTS.

HAZIT DATIT MEUHEDET. *See* UNITED RELIGIOUS FRONT.

HERITAGE MOVEMENT (*Morasha*). The Heritage Movement was a religious national list in the 1984 elections, composed of a faction of the National Religious Party (NRP)* and the Labor Association of Israel (*Poalei Agudat Yisrael*)* and a Sephardi ultraorthodox faction, headed by Rabbi Yitzhak Peretz. The latter headed the Shas* list of candidates in the 1984 and 1988 elections, but left the party in 1990 in protest against its failed attempt to form a coalition government with the Labor Party.* Rabbi Peretz joined the joint ultraorthodox list of candidates in the 1992 election under the instructions of his mentor, Rabbi Eliezer Shach.

HERUT. *See* FREEDOM PARTY.

HITAHDUT HASEFARADIM. *See* SEPHARDI ASSOCIATION.

HITAHDUT HATEIMANIM. *See* YEMENITE ASSOCIATION.

HOMELAND PARTY (*Moledet*). A radical nationalist party founded by General Rehavam Zeevi in the 1988 election, the Homeland Party gained two *Knesset* seats and joined Yitzhak Shamir's government in 1990 following Labor's resignation. The Homeland Party quit that government following the beginning of the peace talks with the Arab states and the Palestinians in 1991. The most extreme nationalist party in the *Knesset*, it alone proposes a voluntary "transfer" of the Arabs out of the West Bank and the Gaza Strip.

INDEPENDENT CENTER (*Merkaz Atsmait*). This faction split off from the Free Center* within the Likud* in 1975. Headed by leaders of the National Federation of Labor, the party joined the For the People* party, within the Likud, in 1975.

INDEPENDENT LIBERAL PARTY (*Hamiflaga Liberalit Atsmait*). The Independent Liberal Party is the new name of the former Progressive Party* after it split from the Liberal Party* in 1965. The Independent Liberal Party gained five *Knesset* seats in the 1965 election, four in 1959, four in 1973, and only one in 1977. The party's electoral standing was hurt by the appearance of the Democratic Movement for Change* and Shinui* and the relatively advanced age of its veteran constituency. In the 1984 election, the party joined the Labor alignment. Later it entered into a brief alliance with Shinui. In the 1992 election, its representative appeared on Labor's list.

ISRAEL WORKERS LIST (*Reshimat Poalei Israel—Rafi*). The Israel Workers List (Rafi) was formed by David Ben-Gurion and his supporters (most notable among them: Shimon Peres, Moshe Dayan, and Yosef Almogy) who left the Labor Party of Israel (Mapai)* in 1965 after losing their fight in the party convention over the Lavon affair and against the formation of the Labor alignment. Rafi called for sweeping electoral reforms, including the adoption of the single-member district system in *Knesset* elections and the direct election of mayors. In the political crisis preceding the 1967 war, Rafi cooperated with other parties in forcing Prime Minister Levi Eshkol to appoint Dayan as defense minister and to form a government of national unity. Following this crisis, Dayan became Rafi's principal leader. Despite Ben-Gurion's objection, Rafi joined Mapai and the Unity of Labor Movement (*Hatnua LeAhdut Ha'avoda*)* in forming the Israeli Labor Party in 1968. The merger did not put an end, however, to the conflict between Rafi young leaders (the former Young Turks of Mapai) and the veteran leaders of Mapai. Dayan prevented the defection of Rafi from the Labor Party in 1969. He was isolated in the party, however, following the traumatic Yom Kippur War (1973). In 1977 he joined Menachem Begin's Likud* government, and Peres, his former associate in Rafi, became the leader of the Labor Party. Rafi gained ten *Knesset* seats in its single independent electoral run in 1965.

JEWISH DEFENSE LEAGUE (*Liga Lehagana Yehudit—Kach*). The most extreme nationalist party in Israel, it was founded by Meir Kahane, the leader of the American Jewish Defense League. Kahane gained a single *Knesset* seat in the 1984 election, after failing in two previous attempts. His list was prohibited from competing in the 1988 election by the Central Election Committee because of its anti-Arab racist platform. Kahane called for the expulsion of Arabs from Israel, arguing that Jews and Arabs cannot coexist. He was boycotted by all other factions in the *Knesset*. Following his assassination in 1990 in New York, his party split and its leaders presented two lists of candidates in the 1992 election campaign. Both were disqualified by the Election Committee.

KACH. *See* JEWISH DEFENSE LEAGUE.

LA'AM. *See* FOR THE PEOPLE.

LABOR ALIGNMENT (*Ma'arah*). The initial alignment of Labor parties, formed in 1965, consisted of the Labor Party of Israel (Mapai)* and the Unity of Labor (Ahdut Ha'avoda).* The larger Alignment, formed in 1969, included the Labor Party and the United Workers Party (*Mapam*),* which quit the alignment in 1984. The formation of the first Alignment was initiated by Prime Minister Levi Eshkol and the veteran leaders of Mapai in response to the challenge

of David Ben-Gurion (over the Lavon affair) and the long crisis in their relationship with a major group of young leaders of the party, the *Tsairim* (youngsters), under the leadership of Moshe Dayan and Shimon Peres. Mapai's decision
to form the Alignment was one of the contributing factors to the split in the
party, and to the formation of the Israel Workers List (*Rafi*).* The formation of
the larger Labor Alignment (1969) was a direct response to the three-party
merger that founded the Israeli Labor Party. Both the Labor Party and its Alignment with Mapam represented the greatest unity ever achieved by the Israeli
Labor movement. The Labor Alignment was the primary faction in the *Knesset*
and the government between 1969 and 1977. Upon its foundation, it held 63 of
120 *Knesset* seats. In the 1969 election, it gained only 56 seats, in 1973, 51 seats;
in 1977, 32 seats; in 1981, 47 seats; and in 1984, 44 seats.

LABOR ASSOCIATION OF ISRAEL (*Poalei Agudat Yisrael*). This labor federation and political party emerged within the Association of Israel (Agudat
Yisrael)* movement. Founded in 1922 in Poland, it began its activities in Palestine in 1925, where it formed a youth movement (*Ezra*) as well as a settlement
movement and *yeshivot*. Poalei Agudat Yisrael joined the trade union section
and medical service of the Histadrut. The party ran in most elections, together
with Agudat Yisrael in a joint list of candidates for the *Knesset*. In the 1984
election, it formed the Heritage Movement* list with the National Religious
Party.* In its independent runs, the party gained one or two *Knesset* seats. *Poalei
Agudat Yisrael* is under the spiritual guidance of the Aguda's Council of the Sages
of the Torah, although it has not always followed its instructions.

LABOR MOVEMENT FOR GREATER ISRAEL (*Tnuat Ha'avoda Lema'an Er-
etz Yisrael Hashlema*). The origins of this political group were in the Greater Israel
Movement. It was founded in the wake of the occupation of the West Bank and
Gaza Strip in the 1967 war. The group was among the founders of the Likud*
in 1973. In 1976, it joined two other groups: the State List* and the Independent
Center* in forming a new party, For the People,* within the Likud. In 1980
most of the leaders of this group left the Likud and joined the nationalist Revival
Party* in protest against the Camp David agreements signed by the Likud gov-
ernment.

LABOR NEW IMMIGRATION (*Aliyah Hadasha Ovedet*). This party has been
a labor faction of the New Immigration* in the Histadrut.

LABOR PARTY OF ISRAEL (*Mifleget Poalei Eretz Yisrael—Mapai*, 1930–68;
*Mifleget Ha'avoda Hayisraelit*, 1968–    ). The social-democratic Mapai was the
leading party in the *Yishuv* and the State of Israel from the time of its formation
in 1930. It was founded by the two major parties of the Histadrut, the Unity of
Labor (Ahdut Ha'avoda)* and Young Worker (Hapoel Hatsair)* which controlled over 80 percent of the Histadrut convention. Mapai became the major

party in the governing bodies (National Institutions) of the *Yishuv* and, after 1933, in the World Zionist Federation. Mapai (with its associated Sephardi list) gained 45.9 percent of the vote to the third Elected National Assembly in 1931, and 36.5 percent of the vote to the fourth Elected National Assembly in 1944. The Labor faction (with Mapai as the major party) gained 44 percent in the election to the Zionist Congress in 1933; 48.8 percent in 1935; 46.3 percent in 1937; 46.4 percent in 1939; and 39.9 percent in 1946.

Mapai's leader, David Ben-Gurion, headed the Histadrut between 1920 and 1935; served as the chairman of the Jewish Agency between 1935 and 1948; proclaimed the State of Israel on May 14, 1948; and served as its prime minister until 1963, with a brief retirement in Kibbutz Sde Boker in 1954–55.

Mapai failed to increase its representation in the elected parliament (*Knesset*) of the independent state. It did, however, establish a dominant position in Israeli politics because it was much bigger (more than double) than its closest competitor; it faced divided opposition that could not replace it in power; and it gained a majority position in government through coalition with other parties. Mapai continued to lead the powerful Histadrut and gradually established a major position in elected municipal governments.

Under Ben-Gurion's leadership, Mapai developed a constructive brand of democratic socialism and accepted the need for social and economic compromise; Ben-Gurion rallied the Zionist movement behind the concept of the partition of Palestine and developed the concept of statism (*Mamlahtiut*) that called for the assertion of the authority of the state, in the transition from a nonsovereign community, and to draw the lines between the army and the new institutions of the state and those of the political parties and communal bodies. Mapai gained forty-six *Knesset* seats in the 1949 election (plus two seats gained by its associated Arab lists); forty-five seats (plus five on the Arab lists) in 1951; forty (plus five on the Arab lists) in 1955; forty-seven (plus five on the Arab lists) in 1959; forty-two (plus four on the Arab lists) in 1961; and forty-five (plus four on the Arab lists) in 1965.

Mapai was split twice. In 1942 it was split by *Siah Beit* (Faction B), which gained the support of about a third of its national convention. Siah Beit was led by the leaders of the major kibbutz movement at the time—*Hakibbutz Hameuhad*. The latter objected to the partition of Palestine, adopted a Marxist ideology, and called for the democratization of the economic enterprises of the Histadrut. Mapai overcame the split and maintained its dominant position in the Histadrut and its major governing role in the institutions of the *Yishuv* and the Zionist movement.

Mapai was split again in 1965, this time by its longtime leader, Ben-Gurion, and his supporters who established the Israel Workers List (Rafi).* The split, which grew out of the Lavon affair, reflected the residual impact of the conflict between the veteran leadership of the party (Levi Eshkol, Golda Meir) and the party's Young Turks (under the leadership of Moshe Dayan and Shimon Peres).

Mapai reunited with its two former factions (Unity of Labor—Zionist Labor* and Rafi) in 1968 and formed the Labor Party of Israel. In 1969 the Labor Party formed an alignment with the more leftist United Workers Party (Mapam).* The Labor Alignment* nearly captured a majority of the seats in the Knesset (fifty-six seats in 1969; fifty-one in 1973). The party served as the ruling party until 1977, when it suffered a major electoral setback. In that election, it dropped from fifty-one to thirty-two seats. The party stayed in opposition until 1984, when it formed a unity government with the Likud* on the basis of equal representation and rotation in the office of the prime minister. The party quit the government in 1990, in dispute with the Likud over the peace process. The Labor Party continues the political traditions of the social-democratic Mapai. It leads the multiparty Histadrut and identifies with its historical structure and goals. It follows a moderate line concerning major issues in Israeli politics, in state, religious, social, defense, and economic policies, and it has supported the principle of territorial compromise concerning the future of the occupied territories and the resolution of the Arab-Israeli conflict. The renamed party's first leader was Prime Minister Levi Eshkol (1968–69); he was followed by Prime Minister Golda Meir (1969–74), Prime Minister Yitzhak Rabin (1974–77), and by Shimon Peres in opposition (1977–84) and as prime minister (1984–86). Rabin regained the leadership of the party in a nominating primary prior to the 1992 election, and he became prime minister again in the coalition government formed after that election. In 1993, this government reached an agreement with the PLO providing for mutual recognition and Palestinian autonomy in the West Bank and Gaza Strip. This government also tried to accelerate the pace of peace negotiations with Jordan, Syria, and Lebanon.

LIBERAL LABOR MOVEMENT (Tnuat Ha'avoda Haliberalit). This is the Histadrut faction of the Independent Liberal Party.*

LIBERAL PARTY (Hamiflaga Haliberalit). The Liberal Party was founded in 1961 by a merger of the General Zionists* and the Progressive Party.* The party gained seventeen Knesset seats in its single electoral run as a united party. In 1965 the leaders of the former Progressive Party split the Liberal Party because of their refusal to go along with the majority decision to form a joint bloc with the Freedom Party (Herut)* (Gahal*). The former Progressives reasserted the independence of their party as the Independent Liberal Party*; the Liberal Party became identified, after the split, with the General Zionists. The Liberal Party cooperated with Herut in Gahal and the Likud, and in 1990 merged with it to form the Likud Party.*

LIGA LEHAGANA YEHUDIT—KACH. See JEWISH DEFENSE LEAGUE.

LIKUD—THE NATIONAL CAMP (Likud—Hamahane Haleumi). The Likud is the major party of the political right in Israel. It was founded in 1973 as a joint list and parliamentary bloc comprising Gahal* (the bloc of the Freedom Party

(Herut)* and the Liberal Party*) and three minor parties (the Free Center,* the State List,* and the Labor Movement for Greater Israel*). It became the largest faction in the *Knesset* in the 1977 election with forty-three seats and formed the coalition government. It gained forty-eight seats in the 1981 election and remained the leading party in the government. It formed a national unity government with Labor after the 1984 election, from which it emerged with the second largest *Knesset* faction (forty-one seats).

In 1988 the Likud regained its position as the largest faction in the *Knesset* (forty seats). It reinstated the unity government with Labor, but without rotation in the office of prime minister. The Likud remained in power after Labor resigned from the government in 1990. Menachem Begin served as the leader of the Likud until 1983. Yitzhak Shamir succeeded him, but he had to face successive challenges to his leadership.

The Likud adheres to the idea of Greater Israel, though politically it has a more limited program: to intensify Jewish settlement in the West Bank (Judea and Samaria) and the Gaza Strip and to prevent the transfer of these territories to foreign sovereignty. In the Camp David conference (1978), Prime Minister Begin signed an agreement with Egypt offering autonomy to the Palestinians on the West Bank and the Gaza Strip.

MA'ARAH. *See* LABOR ALIGNMENT.

MAFDAL. *See* NATIONAL RELIGIOUS PARTY.

MAHANE SHELI. See SHELI PEACE CAMP.

MAKI. *See* COMMUNIST PARTY OF ISRAEL.

MAPAI. *See* LABOR PARTY OF ISRAEL.

MAPAM. *See* UNITED WORKERS PARTY.

MEIMAD. This liberal, dovish faction of the national religious movement ran independently in 1988 but won no seats. It was reorganized as an educational movement in 1993.

MERETZ BLOC (*Meretz*). Three radical, dovish parties formed this bloc in the 1992 election: the Civil Rights Movement (Ratz)* (five *Knesset* seats in the 1988 election), the United Workers Party (Mapam)* (three seats), and Shinui* (two seats). Meretz considers itself to be an ally of the Labor Party,* but it is prepared to negotiate with the Palestine Liberation Organization and accept a Palestinian state. It presses for the separation of state and religion. Meretz joined the Labor-led coalition government formed after the 1992 election.

MERKAZ ATSMAI. *See* INDEPENDENT CENTER.

MERKAZ HOFSHI. *See* FREE CENTER.

MIFLEGET HA'AVODA HAYISRAELIT. *See* LABOR PARTY OF ISRAEL.

MIFLEGET HAPOALIM HAMEUHEDET—MAPAM. *See* UNITED WORK-ERS PARTY.

MIFLEGET POALEI ERETZ YISRAEL—MAPAI. *See* LABOR PARTY OF ISRAEL.

MIFLEGET POALIM—HASHOMER HATSAIR. *See* WORKERS PARTY—HASHOMER HATSAIR.

MINORITIES LISTS (*Reshimot Miyutim*). These ad hoc minorities electoral lists, associated with the Labor Party of Israel (Mapai),* and subsequently the Labor Party,* organized for each parliamentary election, gained representation in the *Knesset* until the 1981 election. Altogether six lists fell into this category. They were based on regional, communal, and religious considerations. These lists gained two *Knesset* seats in 1945; five seats in the 1951, 1955, and 1959 elections; four seats in the 1961, 1965, and 1969 elections; three seats in 1973; and a single seat in the 1977 election. Following the 1977 elections, the Arab representatives were integrated into Labor's list of candidates.

MIZRAHI. *See* HAMIZRAHI.

MOKED MOVEMENT. This bloc comprised the Communist Party of Israel* and Techelet Adom (a splinter group from the United Workers Party, Mapam*). Moked gained one *Knesset* seat in the 1973 election and then merged with the This World Party* faction to form the Sheli Peace Camp* in the 1977 election.

MOLEDET. *See* HOMELAND PARTY.

MORASHA. *See* HERITAGE MOVEMENT.

NATIONAL CAMP. *See* LIKUD.

NATIONAL RELIGIOUS PARTY (NRP) (*Hamiflaga Hadatit Haleumit—Mafdal*). The party of the national religious movement originated in the World Zionist Hamizrahi* movement. It was founded in 1956 by a merger of Hamizrahi Worker* and Hamizrahi. It participated in all Labor coalition governments but one, and in all the Likud* coalition governments. For over twenty years, the NRP has been the primary religious party. It failed, however, to maintain its unity, and it suffered serious electoral setbacks in the 1981 election (declining from twelve to six *Knesset* seats), and in the 1984 elections (declining from six to four seats). It thus lost its historic primary position to the ultraorthodox parties. In the 1988 elections, the NRP gained only 5 of the 18 Knesset seats gained by the religious parties. The NRP was victimized by ethnic conflict, which caused a split of the Sephardi faction (Tami*) in the 1981 election, and a challenge from a nationalist faction (*Matzad*) which split the party in 1984. (It reunited with the party in 1988.)

Traditionally, the NRP has represented a moderate political position, but, following the ascendancy of the Likud, it has moved to the political right. It has continued, however, to maintain a moderate position on religious issues compared to the ultraorthodox parties. The NRP is associated with a Labor Federation (Hamizrahi Worker) which participates in the trade union section and medical services of the Histadrut.

NETUREI KARTA. *See* GUARDIANS OF THE CITY.

NEW COMMUNIST LIST (*Reshima Komunistit Hadasha—Rakah*). This party, formed before the 1965 election by a largely Arab faction of the Communist Party of Israel (Maki),* commanded the support of Arab voters, who constituted the majority of the voters of the former Communist Party. *Rakah* adopted an Arab nationalist position. It demanded Israeli withdrawal from the occupied territories, recognition of the Palestine Liberation Organization, and the formation of a Palestinian state. The party supported the *Intifada* (the Palestinian uprising in the territories) and criticized the Israeli occupation regime. *Rakah* accepts the existence of the State of Israel but objects to its definition as a Jewish state and demands recognition of the Arab minority as a national entity within it. Since the election of 1977, *Rakah* has led in a wider electoral bloc, the Democratic Front for Peace and Equality (Hadash).* (See also chapter on the Palestinians.)

NEW IMMIGRATION (*Aliya Hadasha*). Founded in 1942 in Palestine by leaders of the Association of Immigrants from Central Europe (Germany and Austria), this party had a moderate position concerning the British mandatory regime in Palestine, and a progressive social platform. It organized a labor faction in the Histadrut. It merged with the Zionist Worker* and a faction of the General Zionists* to found the Progressive Party* in 1948.

NEW LIBERAL PARTY (*Hamiflaga Liberalit Hadasha*). Founded in 1992 as a splinter group from the Liberal Party* and the Likud,* it was headed by Yitzhak Modai, who was serving as finance minister in Prime Minister Yitzhak Shamir's government. It failed to gain *Knesset* representation in the 1992 elections.

NRP. *See* NATIONAL RELIGIOUS PARTY.

OMETZ. *See* COURAGE MOVEMENT.

PALESTINE COMMUNIST PARTY (PCP). This was the Communist Party in Palestine prior to the foundation of the State of Israel. (See Communist Party of Israel, also chapter on the Palestinians.)

PANTHERIM SHEHORIM. *See* BLACK PANTHERS.

PCP. *See* PALESTINE COMMUNIST PARTY.

PEACE NOW (*Shalom Ahshav*). Peace Now was founded in the late 1970s as a political movement for the promotion of peace with the Palestinians and the Arab states. It developed as an antiwar movement during the Israeli invasion of Lebanon and the continued military involvement in that country (1982–85). Peace Now has been operating as a loosely organized protest movement and an umbrella organization to a host of groups and parties in mobilizing popular support for the cause of peace.

POALEI AGUDAT YISRAEL. *See* LABOR ASSOCIATION OF ISRAEL.

POALEI TSIYON. *See* ZIONIST LABOR.

POALEI TSIYON SMOL. *See* ZIONIST LABOR—LEFT.

PROGRESSIVE LIST FOR PEACE (*Hareshima Hamitkademet Leshalom*). This party was founded in 1984 by the Arab Democratic Front for Peace, under the leadership of Muhammad Miari, and a Jewish leftist group (the Alternative Movement), under the leadership of Uri Avnery and Matityahu Peled. The overwhelming majority of the voters for this list were Israeli Arabs, and it developed into an Arab nationalist party. The Progressive List gained two *Knesset* seats in the 1984 election (one of its two representatives in the *Knesset* was Jewish), and a single seat in the 1988 election. It did not gain representation in the 1992 elections.

PROGRESSIVE PARTY (*Hamiflaga Haprogresivit*). This centrist party was founded in 1948 by a merger of three groups: New Immigration,* Zionist Worker,* and a faction of the General Zionists* movement (General Zionists A). The party adopted a progressive social platform and very modern foreign and defense policy positions. It participated in government with the Labor Party of Israel (Mapai),* and its labor faction (Zionist Worker) cooperated with Mapai leadership in the Histadrut. The leader of the party, Pinhas Rosen, served for a long time as minister of justice. In 1961, the Progressive Party merged with the General Zionists and formed the Liberal Party.* The former leaders of the Progressive Party left the party following the decision to form an electoral bloc with the Freedom Party (Herut)* (*Gahal**). They reestablished their party under the name of the Independent Liberal Party* (1965). The Progressive Party gained between four and six seats in the first four elections to the *Knesset*.

RAFI. *See* ISRAEL WORKERS LIST.

RAKAH. *See* NEW COMMUNIST LIST.

RATZ. *See* CIVIL RIGHTS MOVEMENT.

RELIGIOUS WORKER (*Haoved Hadati*). This religious faction in the Histadrut was associated with the Labor Party of Israel (Mapai)* (subsequently, the Labor Party). Founded in 1943, the party gained between 1 and 4 percent of the vote in elections to the Histadrut convention. It supports the Labor Party list of candidates in *Knesset* elections.

RESHIMAT HALOHAMIM. *See* FIGHTERS' LIST.

RESHIMAT KOMUNISTIT HADASHA—(RAKAH). *See* NEW COMMUNIST LIST.

RESHIMAT POALEI ISRAEL—RAFI. *See* ISRAEL WORKERS LIST.

RESHIMAT MIYUTIM. *See* MINORITIES LISTS.

REVISIONIST PARTY (*Hamiflaga Harevzionistit*). This Zionist, nationalist party was founded in 1924 in Paris and led by Vladimir (Zeev) Jabotinsky, a leading writer and speaker within the Zionist Federation. Jabotinsky called for a more activist and militant Zionist policy toward Britain to pressure it to implement the commitment to establish a Jewish homeland in Palestine as articulated in the Balfour Declaration (1917) and in the Mandate over Palestine given to Britain by the League of Nations (1921).

The Revisionist Party challenged the leadership of the Zionist Federation and developed a confrontational policy toward the Histadrut and the Labor movement in Palestine. In 1934 it established its own federation of labor, the National Labor Federation. In 1935, it left the Zionist Federation and formed the New Zionist Federation. That year, the party prepared a plan for the transfer of a million and a half Jews from Europe, primarily from Poland, to Palestine; this plan failed to materialize.

The exit of the Revisionist Party from the Zionist Federation and the failure of its grand schemes focused attention on the activities of the *Irgun Tsvai Leumi* (the National Military Organization), which split in 1931 from the *Hagana* and gradually acquired a revisionist orientation and viewed Jabotinsky as its leader. Between 1928 and 1930, Jabotinsky lived in Palestine, and his movement became a major factor in the politics of the *Yishuv* (21 percent of the total vote in 1931). After 1930 he was not permitted by the British government to stay in Palestine, and his movement declined. Jabotinsky died in 1940, and his remains were transferred to Israel by the decision of the Eshkol government in 1964.

After World War II, the Revisionist Party returned to the Zionist Federation. The *Irgun*, under Menachim Begin's leadership, became the primary revisionist organization in Palestine, and subsequently it became a political party (the Freedom Party, Herut*) in the State of Israel. Most of the veteran revisionist leaders in Israel joined the Herut Party, after failing to gain representation in the 1949 *Knesset* election. The Revisionist Party continued to exist in the Jewish diaspora, in association with the Herut Party in Israel.

REVIVAL PARTY (*Hatehiya*). This nationalist party was founded in 1980 in protest against the Camp David Agreements and the evacuation of the Sinai Peninsula. It was formed by three groups, which responded to a call by Yuval Neeman (a former president of Tel Aviv University): a splinter group from the *Herut* Party,* headed by Geula Cohen; leaders of the Block of the Faithful (Gush Emunim)* (a religious settlement movement in the territories), and members of the Labor Movement for Greater Israel.*

The party favored the imposition of Israeli law in the occupied territories. It gained five *Knesset* seats in the 1984 election (together with Tsomet*), and three in 1988. It participated in Yitzhak Shamir's government, but it quit in protest against that government's decision to participate in the peace talks with a Palestinian delegation in Madrid in 1991. The party did not gain *Knesset* representation in the 1992 election.

SEPHARDI ASSOCIATION (*Hitahdut Hasefaradim*). An association of Sephardi Jews, this party was active in the politics of the *Yishuv*. It gained four *Knesset* seats in the 1949 election. Its parliamentary faction split. Two members joined the Labor Party of Israel (Mapai),* and two joined the General Zionists.*

SEPHARDI ASSOCIATION OF THE OBSERVERS OF THE TORAH. *See* SHAS.

SHALOM AHSHAV. *See* PEACE NOW.

SHAS—SEPHARDI ASSOCIATION OF THE OBSERVERS OF THE TORAH (*Shas—Hitahdut Hasefaradim Shomrei Tora*). *Shas* is an ultraorthodox religious party representing Jewish voters of Sephardi descent. It was founded in 1984 under the spiritual leadership of the former Sephardi Chief Rabbi of Israel, Ovadia Yosef. A revered Ashkenazi Yeshiva head, Rabbi Eliezer Shach also gave his blessing to the formation of Shas and remained spiritual mentor to some of its leaders. Shas gained four *Knesset* seats in the 1984 elections, and six seats in the 1988 and the 1992 elections, becoming the largest religious party. It has participated in the coalition government since the 1984 election. At first, it formed a political alliance with the Likud,* but following the 1992 elections, Shas joined the Labor coalition government.

SHELI PEACE CAMP (*Mahane Sheli*). This leftist, dovish party appeared in the 1977 election. It comprised the Moked Movement,* This World Party,* a Black Panther* faction, and Arie Eliav's group which had left the Labor Party.* Sheli gained two seats in that election.

SHINUI—CENTER PARTY (*Shinui—Mifleget Merkaz*). This dovish, centrist party was founded in 1974. It grew out of the antigovernment protest movement during the Yom Kippur War. Shinui was one of the two groups that founded the Democratic Movement for Change (DMC)* in the 1977 election. Its leaders objected to the decision of the DMC to join the Likud* coalition government. Shinui left the DMC and ran independently in the 1981 election. It gained two *Knesset* seats in 1981, three in 1984, and two in 1988. Shinui joined the Civil Rights Movement (Ratz)* and the United Workers Party (Mapam)* in forming a joint electoral list, Meretz,* in the 1992 election. Shinui, under the leadership of Professor Amnon Rubinstein, is centrist in economic and social policies, and dovish on foreign and security policy.

STATE LIST (*Hareshima Hamamlahtit*). The State List was founded in 1969 by members of the Israel Workers List (Rafi),* and supporters of Moshe Dayan (who remained in the Labor Party*). David Ben-Gurion headed the party's list of candidates for the *Knesset*. He was elected, but then he retired from politics. Running on the strength of Dayan's popularity, the State List gained four *Knesset* seats in the 1969 election. It joined the Likud* in 1973 and later merged with the Independent Center* and the Labor Movement for Greater Israel* to form the For the People* party within the Likud.

TAMI—MOVEMENT FOR THE TRADITION OF THE PEOPLE OF ISRAEL (*Tami—Tnuat Masoret Yisrael*). This Sephardi party is supported chiefly by Jewish voters of North African descent. It was founded by Aharon Abuhatzira, who left the National Religious Party (NRP)* in 1981. Three sources of protest led to the formation of Tami: (1) the charge that Abuhatzira was singled out for police investigation of alleged criminal activities; (2) the alienation of many Sephardi voters because of ethnic, social, and economic gaps in Israeli society; and (3) the rejection of Abuhatzira's demand for larger representation in the NRP's list of candidates for the *Knesset*. Tami gained three *Knesset* seats in the 1981 elections, and only a single seat in 1984. In 1988 Tami joined the Likud.*

TELEM—MOVEMENT FOR RENEWAL OF STATEHOOD (*Telem—Tnua Lehithadshut Mamlahtit*). This electoral list was formed by Moshe Dayan in the 1981 election. Dayan quit Menachem Begin's government in 1980 in protest against the government's reluctance to negotiate the full implementation of the Autonomy Plan as agreed to at the Camp David conference (1978) for the Palestinians in the West Bank and the Gaza Strip. Telem included the former State List* and supporters of Moshe Dayan. It gained two *Knesset* seats and was dismantled following Dayan's death later in 1981.

THIS WORLD PARTY (*Haolam Hazeh*). This party was formed in 1965 by the editors of an antiestablishment weekly magazine bearing this name. Led by Uri Avinery, the party moved to the radical, dovish left and was represented in the *Knesset* until 1973. Avinery and the majority of the party participated in two successive blocs of the radical, dovish left: Meretz* and Sheli Peace Camp.*

TNUA LEMA'AN ERETZ YISRAEL HASHLEMA. *See* MOVEMENT FOR GREATER ISRAEL.

TNUAT HA'AVODA HALIBERALIT. *See* LIBERAL LABOR MOVEMENT.

TNUAT HA'AVODA LEMA'AN ERETZ YISRAEL HASHLEMA. *See* LABOR MOVEMENT FOR GREATER ISRAEL.

TOGETHERNESS PARTY. *See* YAHAD.

TSOMET—MOVEMENT FOR ZIONIST RENEWAL (*Tsomet—Tnua Lehithadshut Tsiyonit*). This nationalist party has its origins in the Israeli Labor movement. It was founded and led by General (Res.) Raphael Eitan, a former chief of staff of the Israeli army and member of a cooperative settlement (*moshav*). Tsomet cooperated initially, in 1984, with an existing nationalist party, the Revival Party.* It gained five *Knesset* seats in the 1984 election. Tsomet ran independently in the 1988 election and gained two seats. Like the other two nationalist parties (the Revival Party and the Homeland Party)*, it favors the concept of Greater Israel. However, it supports the municipal Autonomy Plan for Palestinians in the West Bank and Gaza Strip, and it is less hostile to the Labor Party. Tsomet participated in Yitzhak Shamir's government (1990–91). It gained eight *Knesset* seats in the 1992 elections.

UNITED RELIGIOUS FRONT (*Hazit Datit Meuhedet*). This joint electoral list of the religious parties—Hamizrahi* and Hamizrahi Worker* (which subsequently merged to form the National Religious Party*), the Association of Israel* (Agudat Yisrael),* and the Workers of the Association of Israel (Poalei Agudat Yisrael)*—participated in the first *Knesset* elections in 1949. The front gained sixteen *Knesset* seats.

UNITED WORKERS PARTY (*Mifleget Hapoalim Hameuhedet—Mapam*). Initially, this was a leftist Zionist party, which was founded in 1948 by a merger of two kibbutz-centered parties: Workers Party—Hashomer Hatsair and Unity of Labor Movement—Zionist Labor.* The united party declared itself as Marxist-Leninist in 1951 without disavowing Zionism.

The united Mapam was subjected to conflicting pressures: the Unity of Labor Movement strove to arrest movement to the left, while a leftist faction, under the leadership of Moshe Sne (a former General Zionist* and head of the Haganah, who helped found Mapam), pressed for a more rapid transformation into a Communist party. Sne quit the party in 1953 and joined the Communist Party of Israel.* The Unity of Labor Movement split from the party in 1954.

Hashomer Hatsair, which became a majority faction in Mapam, maintained the name of the united party. It then followed the Unity of Labor Party back to the mainstream of the Labor movement, and in 1956 joined the Labor Party of Israel's (Mapai's)* coalition government. Mapam pressed for an Israeli peace initiative based on the return of most of the territories captured in 1967 and negotiations with the Palestinians. In 1969 Mapam entered into an alignment with the Labor Party, both in the Knesset and the Histadrut. It quit the alignment in 1984 upon the decision of the Labor Party to form a unity government with the Likud.* In the 1988 election, Mapam ran alone and gained only three Knesset seats (it had six seats within the Labor Alignment* in the previous election). In 1992 Mapam joined the radical, dovish bloc of parties to form Meretz.*

UNITY OF LABOR (Ahdut Ha'avoda). Founded in 1919 as an all-embracing labor association by the convention of Jewish workers in Palestine, Ahdut Ha'avoda was replaced as a federation of labor by the Histadrut in 1920. It continued as a political party until 1930, when it merged with Young Worker* to found the Labor Party of Israel (Mapai).*

UNITY OF LABOR MOVEMENT (Hatnua Leahdut Ha'avoda). This Labor kibbutz-led party was founded in 1944 by a faction of the Labor Party of Israel (Mapai)* (Faction B), which split the party in 1942. The leadership of the Unity of Labor (Ahdut Ha'avoda)* came largely from Hakibbutz Hameuhad, the major kibbutz movement at the time. The party espoused a radical program. It aspired to establish a position of ideological and moral leadership of the kibbutz in the Histadrut and in Israeli society. It supported the idea of Greater Israel in 1947, and it adopted a revolutionary Marxist ideology.

Ahdut Ha'avoda merged with a leftist splinter group, Zionist Labor—Left,* in 1946 and changed its name to the Unity of Labor—Zionist Labor (Ahdut Ha'avoda Poalei Tsiyon).* In 1948 the party merged with the Workers Party (Hashomer Hatsair)* and formed the United Workers Party (Mapam).* In 1954, it reasserted its independence as Leahdut Ha'avoda-Poalei Tsiyon (see Unity of Labor—Zionist Labor). The split accelerated the deradicalization of this leftist party, which in 1956 rejoined Mapai's* coalition government, and in 1965 formed the Labor Alignment* with it. In 1968 it merged with Mapai and the Israel Workers List (Rafi)* to form the Labor Party.*

In its independent electoral runs, the party won ten *Knesset* seats in the 1955 elections, seven seats in the 1959 elections, and eight seats in the 1961 elections.

UNITY OF LABOR—ZIONIST LABOR (*Ahdut Ha'avoda—Poalei Tsiyon*). This party was a merger of the Unity of Labor Movement* and Zionist Labor—Left* in 1946.

WORKERS' PARTY—HASHOMER HATSAIR (*Mifleget Poalim Hashomer Hatsair*). This party originated in a youth movement that was founded in 1912 in Galicia and later spread to Jewish communities in Poland and Russia. From a boy scout and sport organization, it evolved into an ideological and pioneer movement that later espoused Marxist socialism. This political movement developed under the leadership of its Kibbutz movement (Hakibbutz Ha'artsi—Hashomer Hatsair), which was founded in 1927. Hashomer Hatsair became involved in electoral politics in the Histadrut and the Yishuv. It refrained, however, from establishing a full-fledged political party until 1946, fearing that it might diminish the primacy of the Kibbutz and the educational appeal of its youth movement. Nevertheless, in 1936 it did form a political organization for its non-Kibbutz supporters in the Socialist League. Hashomer Hatsair accepted Marxist socialism and called for a compromise with the Arabs within a binational state. In 1948 it merged with the Unity of Labor Movement (Hatnua Leahdut Ha'avoda)* to form the United Workers Party (Mapam).*

YAHAD (*Togetherness Party*). This party was founded by General (Res.) Ezer Weizman in the 1984 election. The former leader in the Freedom Party (Herut)* and defense minister quit Menachem Begin's government in protest over its policies concerning the peace process. Weizman believed that Israel should take the initiative and move faster toward a wider agreement, following the peace treaty with Egypt. Yahad joined the 1984 unity government as part of the Labor faction. It joined the Labor Party* in 1988. In 1993, Weizman was elected president of Israel.

YEMENITE ASSOCIATION (*Hitahdut Hateimanim*). An association of Jews who emigrated from Yemen to Palestine, the party was active in the politics of the *Yishuv*. It gained a single *Knesset* seat in the elections of 1949 and 1951.

YOUNG WORKER (*Hapoel Hatsair*). This party was one of two Labor parties organized in Palestine in 1905. The Young Worker rejected Marxism and espoused a constructive, cooperative labor philosophy. The founders of the first kibbutz (Degania) and the first moshav (Nahalal) were members of this party. The party's refusal to dissolve and join the all-inclusive Unity of Labor (Ahdut Ha'avoda)* Association (1919) prompted the formation of the Histadrut (1920). The Histadrut did not preempt the role of Labor parties inside and outside the General Federation of Labor. The Young Worker merged with the Ahdut Ha-'avoda Party in 1930 and founded the Labor Party of Israel (Mapai)* after a long period of cooperation in the leadership of the Histadrut. Among the principal leaders of Mapai, Levi Eshkol was a former member of the Young Worker.

ZIONIST LABOR (*Poalei Tsiyon*). This Jewish Labor organization was founded in Palestine in 1905 as part of a Zionist, social-democratic party which held its first convention that year in Warsaw, Poland. Zionist Labor believed in socialism through class warfare and called for Jewish independence in *Eretz Yisrael* (Palestine) based on social-democratic principles. In Palestine the party developed into an independent party and adopted a constructive brand of socialism. In 1919 the party joined the Unity of Labor (Ahdut Ha'avoda)* association, which was formed to unify workers in a single organization. The leaders of Zionist Labor (David Ben-Gurion, Yitzhak Tabenkin, and Yitzhak Ben Tsvi) emerged among the leaders of Ahdut Ha'avoda, which subsequently developed into a political party and played a major role in the development of the Labor movement and the *Yishuv*.

ZIONIST LABOR—LEFT (*Poalei Tsiyon—Smol*). This Marxist socialist party, which originated in the Zionist Labor movement, was founded in Vienna in 1920 and formed in Palestine in 1923. In 1946 it merged with the Unity of Labor Movement.*

ZIONIST WORKER (*Haoved Hatsiyoni*). The Zionist Worker is a nonsocialist labor faction in the Histadrut. Founded in 1936, it was associated with a Zionist youth movement (*Hanoar HaTsiyoni*) and the pro-Labor faction of the General Zionists.* The party formed a settlement movement and played a major role in the Progressive Party, and, subsequently, the Independent Liberal Party.*

## NOTES

1. The only deviation from the proportional principle is the requirement of a minimal one-and-a-half percent of the total electoral vote cast as a threshold for representation in the 120-member *Knesset*.

2. See Maurice Duverger, *Party Politics and Pressure Groups* (London: Nelson, 1972), 36.

3. The Lavon affair originated in an investigation concerning responsibility for an order to activate a clandestine Israeli ring for subversive acts in Egypt (in 1954), designed to drive a wedge between Egypt and Britain and postpone the British evacuation of the Suez Canal Zone. The effort was a disastrous failure. The minister of defense, Pinhas Lavon, and the head of army intelligence, Benjamin Gibly, accused each other of giving this order. A secret investigating commission, appointed by Prime Minister Moshe Sharett, left a cloud of suspicion over both. Lavon was forced to resign, and Gibly was demoted. This personal feud took place against the background of suspicion and mistrust between the minister of defense and the prime minister and other members of the cabinet. Under pressure from party leaders, David Ben-Gurion was brought back from his kibbutz retreat to take over the ministry of defense, and following the 1955 election, again assumed the post of prime minister. Lavon was later restored to his old powerful post as secretary-general of the Histadrut, and it seemed as if the affair had ended. It reemerged, however, as a full-fledged political crisis that shook the Labor Party (Mapai) and Israeli politics in two cycles: 1960–61 and 1964–65.

4. The merger caused a split in the Israel Workers List (Rafi). A minority, with Ben-Gurion's support, objected and later ran independently in the 1969 elections under the name of the State List. The leaders of this list, without Ben-Gurion, subsequently moved farther to the political right and joined Gahal in founding the Likud. Ben-Gurion himself gave his blessing to the formation of the State List, and for a short while represented it in the *Knesset*, but he retired from active politics in 1970, at the age of eighty-four.

Nathan Yanai

## Notes to Appendix B (p. 258)

1. *Shinui* has been the only surviving faction of the DMC in Israeli politics.

2. The Independent Liberals subsequently gained representation (a single seat) in the Labor Party's list of candidates.

3. *Tami* joined the *Likud* and gained a single seat representation in its list of candidates in 1988.

4. *Kach* (Rabbi Kahane's list) was disqualified in the 1988 election.

5. *Degel Hatora* split from *Agudat Yisrael*.

6. *Poalei Agudat Yisrael* ran in 1984 together with a faction of the *Mafdal* (*Matsed*) under the name *Morasha*. In the 1988 and 1992 elections, *Poalei Aguda* ran in the *Aguda* list.

7. A faction of *Shas:* joined the *Aguda* list in the 1992 elections.

8. *Maki* appeared in a new list (*Moked*) with other leftist groups.

9. Two seats were gained by Ariel Sharon's list (*Shlomtsion*); two seats by a dovish leftist party (*Sheli*) and a single seat by a personal list (Flatto Sharon).

10. Two seats were gained by Moshe Dayan's list (*Telem*).

11. Three seats were gained by Ezer Weizman's list (*Yahad*); and one seat by *Ometz*.

# APPENDIX A.
Knesset Election Results: 1949–69

| Election Year | 1949 | | 1951 | | 1955 | | 1959 | | 1961 | | 1965 | | 1969 | |
|---|---|---|---|---|---|---|---|---|---|---|---|---|---|---|
| Eligible Voters (in thousands) | 507 | | 925 | | 1058 | | 1218 | | 1271 | | 1500 | | 1749 | |
| % Voting | 86.9 | | 75.1 | | 82.8 | | 81.6 | | 83.0 | | 81.7 | | | |
| List | No. Seats | % Vote | No. Seats | % Vote | No. Seats | % Vote | No. Seats | % Vote | No. Seats | % Vote | No. Seats | % Vote | No. Seats | % Vote |
| Mapai | 46 | 35.7 | 45 | 37.3 | 40 | 32.2 | 47 | 38.2 | 42 | 34.7 | 45 | 36.7 | 56 | 46.2 |
| Ahdut Ha'avoda | 19 | 14.7 | 15 | 12.5 | 10 | 8.1 | 7 | 6.0 | 8 | 6.6 | | | | |
| Mapam | | | | | 9 | 7.3 | 9 | 7.2 | 9 | 7.5 | 8 | 6.6 | | |
| Rafi | | | | | | | | | | | 10 | 7.9 | | |
| Ind. Liberals | 5 | 4.1 | 4 | 3.2 | 5 | 4.4 | 6 | 4.6 | 17 | 13.6 | 5 | 3.8 | 4 | 3.2 |
| Liberal Party | 7 | 5.2 | 20 | 16.2 | 13 | 10.2 | 8 | 6.2 | 17 | 13.8 | 26 | 21.3 | 26 | 21.7 |
| Herut | 14 | 11.5 | 8 | 6.6 | 15 | 12.6 | 17 | 13.5 | | | | | | |
| Free Center | | | | | | | | | | | | | 2 | 1.2 |
| State List | | | | | | | | | | | | | 4 | 3.1 |
| Mafdal | 16 | 12.2 | 10[a] | 8.3 | 11 | 9.1 | 12 | 9.9 | 12 | 9.8 | 11 | 8.9 | 12 | 9.7 |
| Agudat Yisrael | | | 3 | 2.0 | 6 | 4.7 | 6 | 4.7 | 4 | 3.3 | 4 | 3.2 | 4 | 3.2 |
| Poalei Agu. Yis | | | 2 | 1.6 | | | | | 2 | 1.9 | 2 | 1.8 | 2 | 1.8 |
| Maki | 4 | 3.5 | 5 | 4.0 | 6 | 4.5 | 3 | 2.8 | 5 | 4.2 | 1 | 1.1 | 1 | 1.1 |
| Rakah | | | | | | | | | | | 3 | 2.3 | 3 | 2.8 |
| Haolam Haze | | | | | | | | | | | 1 | 1.2 | 2 | 1.2 |
| Sephardi Assoc. | 4 | 3.5 | 2 | 1.7 | | | | | | | | | | |
| Yemenite Assoc. | 1 | 1 | 1 | 1.2 | | | | | | | | | | |
| Arab Lists[b] | 2 | 3.1 | 5 | 4.7 | 5 | 4.4 | 5 | 3.9 | 4 | 3.5 | 4 | 3.8 | 4 | 3.5 |
| Others | 2[c] | 2.4 | | | | | | | | | | | | |
| Total | 120 | | 120 | | 120 | | 120 | | 120 | | 120 | | 120 | |

[a] Including *Hamizrahi* which ran separately in that election.
[b] Arab lists associated with *Mapai*.
[c] One seat was gained by the *Wizo* list and one seat by the *Lohamim* list.

## APPENDIX B.

### Knesset Election Results: 1973–92

| Election Year | 1973 | | 1977 | | 1981 | | 1984 | | 1988 | | 1992 | |
|---|---|---|---|---|---|---|---|---|---|---|---|---|
| Eligible voters (in thousands) | 2037 | | 2236 | | 2490 | | 2655 | | 2894 | | 3409 | |
| % Voting | 78.6 | | 79.2 | | 78.5 | | 79.8 | | 79.7 | | 77.5 | |
| List | No. Seats | % Vote | No. Seats | % Vote | No. Seats | % Vote | No. Seats | % Vote | No. Seats | % Vote | No. Seats | % Vote |
| Labor Party | 51 | 39.6 | 32 | 24.6 | 47 | 36.6 | 44 | 34.9 | 39 | 30.0 | 44 | 34.6 |
| Mapam | 3 | 2.2 | 1 | 1.2 | | | | | 3 | 2.5 | | |
| Ratz | | | | | 1 | 1.4 | 3 | 2.4 | 5 | 4.3 | 12 | 9.5 |
| Shinuti | | | | | 2[1] | 1.5 | 3 | 2.6 | 2 | 1.7 | | |
| DMC | | | 15 | 11.6 | | | | | | | | |
| Ind. Liberals | 4 | 3.6 | 1 | 1.2[2] | | | | | | | | |
| Likud | 39 | 30.2 | 43 | 33.4 | 48 | 37.1 | 41 | 31.9 | 40 | 31.1 | 32 | 24.9 |
| Tami | | | | | 3 | 2.3 | 1 | 1.5[3] | | | | |
| Kach | | | | | | | 1 | 1.2[4] | | | | |
| Hatehiya | | | | | 3 | 2.3 | 5 | 4.0 | 3 | 3.1 | | |
| Tsomet | | | | | | | | | 2 | 2.0 | 8 | 6.3 |
| Moledet | | | | | | | | | 2 | 1.9 | 3 | 2.3 |
| Mafdal | 10 | 8.3 | 12 | 9.2 | 6 | 4.9 | 4 | 3.5 | 5 | 3.9 | 6 | 4.9 |
| Degel Hatora | | | | | | | | | 2[5] | 1.5 | | |
| Agudat Yisrael | 5 | 3.8 | 4 | 3.4 | 4 | 3.7 | 2 | 1.7 | 5 | 4.5 | 4 | 3.2 |
| Poalei Agudat Yis. | | | 1 | 1.3 | | 0.9 | 2[6] | 1.6 | | | | |
| Shas | | | | | | | 4 | 3.1 | 6 | 4.7 | 6[7] | 4.9 |
| Maki | 1[8] | 1.4 | | | | | | | | | | |
| Hadash (Rakah) | 4 | 3.4 | 5 | 4.6 | 4 | 3.4 | 4 | 3.4 | 4 | 3.7 | 3 | 2.3 |
| Progressive List | | | | | | | 2 | 1.8 | 1 | | | |
| Democratic Arab | | | | | | | | | 1 | 1.2 | 2 | 1.5 |
| Arab Lists | 3 | 3.3 | 1 | 1.4 | | | 4[11] | | | | | |
| Others | | | 5[9] | | 2[10] | | | | | | | |
| Total | 120 | | 120 | | 120 | | 120 | | 120 | | 120 | |

# JORDAN

Prior to 1921, the area of Jordan, or "Transjordan" as it was known from 1921 to 1946, did not constitute a unified, independent entity. The area, a major trade route, was occupied over the centuries by various conquerors, such as the Greeks and the Romans. In 1517 it came under Ottoman Turkish rule, although Ottoman rule eventually lapsed and was not reestablished until the 1850s, when several administrative districts were formed in the area.

During World War I, Britain entered into an agreement with Sharif Husayn bin 'Ali of Mecca by which Husayn promised to support Britain in its war against the Ottomans in return for British support for Arab independence from Turkey after the war. Following the Ottoman defeat, the area that became known as Transjordan came under the rule of Husayn's son, Amir Faysal, who attempted to establish an independent Arab kingdom throughout Greater Syria. Under the terms of the secret Sykes-Picot agreement of 1916 between Britain and France, however, the Allies decided to partition and rule the Arab Ottoman provinces themselves after the war. The San Remo Conference of 1920 ratified this agreement, and the area of Transjordan was assigned to British control and separated politically from the rest of Greater Syria. French forces occupied Damascus in 1920, defeating Faysal's troops and putting an end to his independent Arab kingdom. The newly created League of Nations later established British and French mandates in the Arab provinces of the Fertile Crescent. Transjordan was part of the British Mandate for Palestine.

In 1921, Faysal's brother, Amir 'Abdullah, arrived in Transjordan at the head of a body of troops with the proclaimed intention of liberating Syria from the French. Seeking to avoid problems with its ally, Britain came to an understanding with 'Abdullah on the basis of the Cairo and Jerusalem agreements of 1921 by which he forswore liberating Syria and agreed to become the ruler of the region east of the Jordan River, reigning as head of a titularly independent Arab government within the British Mandate. Transjordan was officially constituted as a united administrative unit in April 1921.

The first experiment in representative politics in Transjordan came in 1923, when Mandate authorities allowed elections for a twelve-member representative council. This council brought together two representatives from each district in the country, elected by the local municipal councils and the district administrative councils. In 1928 British authorities reached an agreement with 'Abdullah and defined the powers to be exercised by him, by the various Jordanian governmental branches, and by the officials of the British Mandate posted in Transjordan. Although this agreement and the constitution (Organic Law) agreed upon the same year placed great restrictions on the power of the amir—such as the condition that he seek British advice on most major issues, especially financial and foreign policy matters—it nevertheless vested legislative and executive powers in 'Abdullah's hands, to be exercised through a cabinet called the executive council. The representative council was replaced with a legislative body called the legislative council, although it had no power to propose legislation and could be dismissed at will by the amir.

True constitutional rule was hindered by 'Abdullah's reluctance to see the establishment of a democratic regime in Transjordan as well as by the fact that the political development of Transjordan was subordinated to British strategic interests and designs in the area. 'Abdullah played a key role in British designs by maintaining a stable regime in Transjordan, thereby enabling Britain to pursue its interests in the region without fear of undue unrest in the country. The establishment of truly democratic rule would have meant allowing nationalist opposition to British control or policies, a situation that was averted through the broad powers assigned to Amir 'Abdullah.

Elections for the legislative council were regulated in June 1928. The country was divided into three electoral zones, each of which sent representatives to the legislative council. Furthermore, the country's ethnic and religious communities were assigned a specific number of seats in the council. Elections were carried out by indirect balloting conducted on two levels—a primary and a final level—according to Ottoman law, still the basis of law in Transjordan. In the primary elections, all Transjordanian males over eighteen (except the bedouin) were eligible to vote. Those elected in turn elected the representatives to the council. Seats for the bedouins were filled by appointment and not by election. Appointment was made by a body of twenty tribal leaders selected personally by the amir.

Parties were registered on the basis of the Ottoman Associations Law of 1909. Political parties during the mandate era (1921 until 1946) can be characterized as follows. First, they represented two types of parties: ideological parties, such as the Istiqlal* party, and non-ideological, such as the Jordanian People's Party,* which was used as an instrument by the regime for its own purposes. This latter type of party did not enjoy a mass following but consisted of a clique centered around the party leaders. Bonds within such parties were formed on the basis of parochial loyalties, such as tribal divisions or personal relationships.

Second, politics during this period was preoccupied with issues related to mandatory rule, such as ending French rule in Syria, the character of British rule in Transjordan, and establishing the unity and independence of Greater Syria. Parties also concerned themselves with other issues of national independence, such as the fear of Zionist land purchases in Transjordan and the granting of concessions to foreign companies to exploit the country's natural resources. Domestically, these parties focused attention on the economic crisis of the 1930s, democratization of the government, and means to redress the socioeconomic hardships affecting the peasants and workers. Finally, the life span of these parties was very short, generally not lasting longer than a few years.

The period following the 1928 agreement witnessed heated debates both within and outside the legislative council, and constituted a promising beginning for parliamentary life in Transjordan, however short-lived it may have been. Whereas the Istiqlal labored for Greater Syrian unity, other opposition parties focused as well on national issues such as changing the electoral law and opposing the 1928 Transjordanian-British agreement. The opposition soon convened a National Congress in July 1928 and adopted a National Pact to articulate its views. The Congress boycotted the February 1929 elections for the first legislative council because of its objections to the Anglo-Transjordanian treaty of 1928 and the electoral law that allocated seats not on the basis of proportional represen- tation but on ethnic and religious lines. This provision served to guarantee the return of several pro-government legislators given that minorities such as the Circassians and Shishanis generally supported the regime. The opposition also argued that this system of representation was an obstacle to forming national unity since it only deepened existing ethnic and religious divisions, and it de- prived the bedouin of participation in the democratic experience (since the be- douin representatives in the legislature were not elected but appointed).

The opposition soon split, however. Several members of the Congress decided to run in the elections and won seats, their rhetoric notwithstanding. This de- velopment led to strife within the Congress and an eventual split, with those members in favor of a total boycott forming the Executive Committee of the National Congress Party (ECNC).* Members of the rump Congress who were elected to the legislative council, such as Shams al-Din Sami, continued their struggle in the legislature and formed an opposition bloc within it. They reiter- ated the demands of the National Pact for a separation of powers and objected to the granting of concessions to exploit Transjordan's natural resources to for- eigners.

The government hurriedly dismissed the legislative council in February 1931 after it had exercised its constitutional privileges by objecting to British inter- ference in the details of the budget, which the council was empowered to ratify. The dismissal of the legislative council was the first nail in the coffin of parlia- mentary democracy in Transjordan, and it clearly showed that the British and the regime wanted only the appearance of constitutional democracy in Trans- jordan.

New elections for the legislative council were held in June 1931. Only four members of the previous council were reelected. The split in the opposition worsened when certain prominent members of the ECNC decided to run and were elected, despite their earlier refusal to participate in the 1929 elections. The opposition's continued activity in the council forced the amir to change the government and include three members of the legislative council in his cabinet.

However, the split in oppositional ranks was deepened through the issue of tribal leaders' sale or lease of lands to Jews. The issue generated heated debates and accusations within the opposition, and it created a schism between the younger generation of nationalists and the tribal shaykhs and notables. This was evident in the convening of the Executive Committee of the General Congress of the Jordanian People in August 1933, led by Naji al-'Azzam and attended by 300 tribal shaykhs and notables. Its main aim was to question the authenticity of the Executive Council of the National Congress and refute the accusations of land sales to Jews.

This development weakened the opposition within the parliament, as evident in the amicable relationship that developed between the legislative and executive branches of government after the second council. Government harassment and repression led to the flight of ardent opposition leaders to Syria and elsewhere and to the dissolution of the ECNC. The opposition in exile aired its views through pamphlets, such as those issued by the Jordanian National Party* and the Jordanian Liberal Youth Association,* both based in Damascus around the influential opposition figure, Subhi Abu Ghanima. Abu Ghanima was the most persistent opposition figure, and thanks to him the opposition movement continued to function between 1934 and 1939.

Overall, the opposition succeeded in increasing popular awareness of foreign occupation and the need for a responsible, democratic government; calls that were reiterated in the 1950s and the 1990s. But the opposition was powerless to effect changes in the broader political and economic structure of the country. The British, in complete control, threatened to cut off the subsidy granted to Transjordan. Even the limited reform measures allowed by the British were motivated by specific concerns, such as a general colonial retrenchment policy throughout the Middle East.

Jordan acquired its independence on March 22, 1946, through the Treaty of London, followed by the establishment of a new constitution on February 1, 1947, which protected the authority and extensive powers of 'Abdullah (proclaimed King on May 25, 1946) and the executive under the façade of a constitutional monarchy. In March 1948, a new Anglo-Jordanian treaty was signed that relieved Jordan of direct British financial and administrative control while allowing Britain the use of bases and facilities. British officers continued to lead and serve in Jordan's army.

The most significant factor in the development of political parties in Jordan after independence was the 1948 Arab-Israeli war and the unification of that portion of Palestine known as the West Bank with Transjordan on April 25, 1950. Due to the tragic results of the war, many Palestinian intellectuals and professionals fled to Jordan or came under Jordanian rule in the West Bank. Due to their high level of education and their history of struggle against the Zionists and the British, these Palestinians participated with Jordanians in developing political organizations and parties with clear platforms and ideologies.

Three important characteristics distinguish these new parties from the pre-

1948 parties: first, they articulated more coherent ideologies and programs than pre-independence parties; second, they possessed larger mass followings; and finally, they rejected the monarchy and worked for its radical transformation. The emergence of mass-based ideological parties did not spell the end of status-quo political parties based on vague sloganeering and personal allegiance, however, and many parties of this type continued to exist after independence.

With the unification of the East and West Banks of Jordan in 1950, the legislative council was enlarged to reflect the new demographic and political developments. The lower house was increased from twenty to forty seats, allowing equal representation for both banks, and in April 1950 the first elections following unification were held. Five parties competed for the seats but on an unofficial level. Opposition parties such as the Jordanian Communist Party* and the National Front* won fourteen seats, while pro-regime parties, such as the Arab Constitutional Party and the Party of the Nation* won ten seats. Independents took the remainder of the seats.

These elections indicated the growing power of ideological parties, a power that they exercised effectively in the legislative council to pursue their objectives. These objectives centered on four main issues: revision of the 1947 constitution to make it more democratic; rejection of 'Abdullah's position on Palestine and his acceptance of the Rhodes armistice agreement; rejection of British financial and military aid and a request for its replacement by Arab aid; and rejection of the proposed governmental budget. The pressure of the opposition on the government was initially successful. King 'Abdullah formed a committee in May 1950 to study constitutional revision. Despite this, the government increased its harassment of the opposition and its censorship of the press and parliamentary debates, and finally dissolved the parliament in May 1951.

The emergence of the new ideological parties of the opposition initiated a tug of war between them and the palace (the king and his allies). With 'Abdullah's assassination on July 20, 1951, the struggle was transformed into one between the pro-regime old guard (exemplified in the persona of Tawfiq Abul-Huda and his followers) and the opposition, as 'Abdullah's assassination left the door open for palace protégés to increase their power independently of the monarchy and for the opposition to pursue its goal of democratizing the system from 1951 to 1952. The issue of succession between 'Abdullah's sons Talal and Nayif, Talal's coronation, and his eventual abdication and succession by his youthful son Husayn in 1952 allowed ample room for the old guard and the opposition to vie for power.

The opposition was initially victorious. It achieved its goal of a revision of the constitution in January 1952. Although this constitution still left significant power to the monarch, the revision was the most remarkable development of this period. Moreover, the opposition won a major victory by finally creating a government responsible to the people's representatives in parliament. Nevertheless, the tug of war continued. Between 1955 and 1957, Jordan underwent one of its most radical stages in terms of opposition demands and external influences.

This period was crucial in highlighting the vulnerabilities of the Jordanian state and regime, as well as indicating the limits of democracy under such constraints.

One such constraint was rooted in the Cold War, exemplified by the creation of the Baghdad Pact in 1955. The Baghdad Pact was a mutual cooperation pact designed by Great Britain to undertake political and military measures to face what it perceived as the Soviet threat in the Middle East. Britain made joining the pact a precondition for revision of the Anglo-Jordanian treaty. The inclination of King Husayn and his government to join the pact ushered in a stage of street politics in Jordan, for the newly politicized people joined the opposition's call, echoed by Egypt and Syria, for Jordan to refuse to join. Numerous demonstrations were held in the major cities and towns. There were indications that the opposition, which was backed financially by other Arab countries, used the popular resentment to gain popular support against the regime.

Similar nationalist fervor was exhibited against the U.S.-sponsored Eisenhower Doctrine. The doctrine, initiated in January 1957, promised American military and financial aid to ward off any "communist threat" in the Middle East. Nationalists noted the similarities in intent between the Baghdad Pact and the Eisenhower Doctrine, and rejected the doctrine as an extension of Western influence in the area and a plan to create schisms among the Arab states.

The liberalized atmosphere of the 1950s allowed opposition parties to push for greater democratization and greater resistance to the regime's pro-Western inclinations. New elections were held in October 1956. Eight political parties competed in the elections, many of which did not enjoy official recognition. One hundred forty-four candidates competed for forty seats, including seventy independents. The election results were the clearest indication yet of the success of the opposition in winning mass support and popularizing its programs. The National Socialist Party* won the most seats, with eleven representatives. Its general secretary, Sulayman al-Nabulsi, became prime minister and selected a cabinet that reflected the relative strength of opposition parties in the parliament, including his own party and the Arab Socialist Resurrection (Ba'th) Party.*

The opposition movement demonstrated a remarkable capacity for solidarity and consensus building, which enabled it to present a unified national stand, as indicated in the program of al-Nabulsi's government. The designation of al-Nabulsi as premier was a remarkable development in that period. Prior to this designation, prime ministers were hand-picked by the monarch. The prime minister, in turn, selected his cabinet with the monarch's approval. The cabinet did not necessarily include any members of the parliament, a practice still in force today.

An interesting development during this period was the resilience of the young King Husayn and his remarkable ability to juggle radical opposition forces on the one hand and his conservative allies—tribal shaykhs, parties, and palace men—on the other. The king was in favor of the Baghdad Pact and appointed the government of Hazza' al-Majali, a supporter of the pact, in December 1955 as a clear signal. However, under external and internal pressures, the king eventually decided against joining the pact and dismissed General John Glubb (the British commander of Jordan's army, known as the Arab Legion) and other British officers on March 2, 1956, as a concession to the nationalists.

The king knew how to play his cards well, however. Due to the geostrategic position of Jordan and the goal of Israel not to see a radical state in Jordan, the monarchy was ultimately saved. American military and economic aid, conservative Arab countries' aid, the loyalty of the Jordanian army to the king, and the ability of the state to utilize its coercive machinery combined to stave off what might have been a more democratic and radical system in Jordan. Backed by his conservative allies and knowing that the scales were tipped in his favor, the king dismissed Premier al-Nabulsi on April 10, 1957, after al-Nabulsi's government decided to exchange diplomatic representation with the Soviet Union and adopt a hostile stand toward the Eisenhower Doctrine. Although the dismissal of the democratically elected government was followed by mass demonstrations and, more significantly, by an attempted military coup on April 13, 1957, led by army Chief of Staff 'Ali Abu Nuwwar, Husayn was able to withstand such challenges and again prove his resiliency based on the bedouin elements within the army, his palace group, and American backing extended by the U.S. Sixth Fleet in the Mediterranean and Secretary of State John Foster Dulles's equation of the regime's security with American national interests.

The king's acceptance of the Eisenhower Doctrine and the dismissal of al-Nabulsi initiated a new period of retrenchment and signaled the end of the freewheeling political atmosphere of the 1950s. This repression was carried out through several measures, among them the declaration of martial law on April 17, 1957, the suspension of parliament, and the placing of many of its members under house arrest. Others fled into exile. The most important aspect of the crackdown, however, was the banning of all political parties that same year and clamping down on all avenues for political expression. Following these measures, parties went underground and did not operate openly again until 1989, with the exception of the Muslim Brotherhood,* which functioned legally as a charitable organization. Only independents and the Brotherhood stood in the elections of 1962 and 1967.

The November 1962 elections were the first in which parties were banned and candidates ran as independents. Balloting was relatively free and a high percentage of registered voters turned out (about 70 percent of the 450,000 registered voters). Palace protégés performed poorly; new, moderate politicians registered the largest gains. In March 1963, this parliament was the first to force the fall of a government when it refused to accept a new government proposed by the king and headed by the venerable Samir al-Rifa'i to replace the government of the nationalist prime minister Wasfi al-Tall, who had resigned over the king's refusal to support an Egyptian proposal to forge a union of Arab states.

Jordan's loss of the West Bank to Israel in the June 1967 war created a political crisis that still reverberates. This crisis centered around the question of who should speak for the Palestinians in the West Bank: Jordan or the Palestine

Liberation Organization (PLO) (see chapter on the Palestinians), which by 1969 was the most significant actor vying for the right to represent the Palestinians.

With half of its deputies trapped in the West Bank, the Jordanian parliament stopped holding sessions. In October 1974, the Arab League complicated the regime's problems by declaring the PLO to be the "sole, legitimate representative of the Palestinian people," in effect denying Jordan the right to speak for the West Bank Palestinians. That November, King Husayn dissolved the parliament and later postponed the proposed elections of 1975 and 1976 pending a constitutional amendment to deal with the question of what to do about the seats allocated to the West Bank. In 1972, the king formed the Jordan National Union* (later called the Arab National Union) as the country's only political party.

In January 1984, the National Assembly was finally reconvened, under the old constitutional arrangement, when Israel allowed West Bank deputies to travel to Amman. Those West Bank seats vacated since 1967 through death or resignation were replaced by parliamentary appointment, while elections were held in March to fill fourteen vacant seats, including eight from the East Bank. With parties still banned, 102 independents ran. A total of 558,581 voters registered, and women were allowed to vote for the first time (they had acquired the right to vote in 1974).

Two important observations apply to the results of the 1984 elections. The first is that participation in (underground) political parties and political representation in Jordan continue to be affected by tribal allegiance or tribalism. Allegiance to blood relatives takes precedence over personal merits. The issue of tribalism was debated at length during the 1984 elections, where votes were cast more on the basis of tribal linkages than on specific political affiliations. Although parties were still banned and therefore operated on an unofficial level, they did not fare as well as in earlier elections. A second important development was that the Muslim Brotherhood captured one-half of the vacant seats, signaling a shift in opposition politics away from leftist parties and toward the religious right.

In July 1988, Jordan formally relinquished its claim to the West Bank and deferred to the PLO's claim to represent the Palestinians living there. Subsequently, King Husayn dissolved the parliament since half of its members were drawn from the West Bank, which was now in effect no longer part of Jordan. New elections were promised upon a revision of the electoral laws. This process was given new urgency as a result of several days of serious rioting in central and southern Jordan in April 1989, triggered by International Monetary Fund austerity measures and price rises adopted by the government. The king dismissed Premier Zayd al-Rifaʻi, his longtime confidant, who was blamed for the economic problems, and agreed to allow the first general elections for parliament since 1967.

The November 1989 elections were the most significant since 1956. In all, 877,475 voters registered for the elections. Even though parties were still banned, 647 candidates presented themselves. In most respects, the election was free.

Parties were still illegal, but the Muslim Brotherhood was allowed to use its legal status as an "association" to present a list. As a result of the vote, the Brotherhood captured twenty-two of eighty seats, with independent Muslim candidates winning another twelve to fourteen seats, against eleven seats won by leftist and Arab or Palestinian nationalists and thirty-five by pro-government candidates. Political observers were stunned by the Islamic candidates' victory, which was conducted under the slogan "Islam is the Solution." Along with the radical leftists, they made their voice heard in parliament by opposing U.S. initiatives for solving the Arab-Israeli conflict.

Parliamentarians eventually organized themselves into six blocs: the Muslim Brotherhood (twenty-two seats), the National Bloc (sixteen seats), the Constitutional Bloc (twelve seats), the Independent Islamic Bloc (eight seats), the Liberal Bloc (seven seats), and finally, the leftist Democratic Bloc (six seats). The blocs serve an important function as power brokers in the confidence vote on a new government. The second government to be formed after the 1989 elections, headed by Tahir al-Masri, depended on the Constitutional Bloc for its approval in July 1991.

The 1989 elections signaled the formalization of sweeping new liberalizing reforms in Jordan. Anticommunist legislation was abolished in January 1990, political prisoners were freed, martial law was effectively repealed, and parties were allowed to function, albeit still unofficially. Because of the political openness, several political parties were created or regrouped after being banned in 1957. By September 1991, some ninety parties had registered for official approval. These parties can be categorized into three groups: parties formed in the early 1950s, such as the Jordanian Communist Party, the Muslim Brotherhood, and the Liberation Party*; parties formed underground in the early 1970s, such as the Democratic Front Organization in Jordan (MFJD)* and the Popular Front Organization in Jordan*; and, finally, parties formed in the 1980s or after the 1989 elections.

Overall, the parties that emerged after liberalization can be loosely grouped into four categories based on their ideological program or orientation: conservative-traditional, leftist, Islamic, and nationalist. The conservative trend, the least ideological, based its support on tribal or familial relations and social status. Parties of this type had no firm organizational structures like those of the ideological parties, and attempted to shift their programs to address current issues. The leftist trend enjoyed increased popularity after the 1989 riots due to the economic crisis and the organizational ability of the parties. However, the left's appeal was hampered by several factors, including the resurgence of Islamic groups and ideological rigidity among many on the left. The Islamic trend increased enormously, as can be seen in the 1989 parliamentary elections. This increase can be traced to the ability of religious groups to use mosques and Friday sermons to popularize their views as well as the basic religious orientation of the masses. These parties in many cases did not have a coherent, pragmatic program to address socioeconomic issues, but instead capitalized on deteriorating eco-

268 / Political Parties of the Middle East

nomic conditions and the political bankruptcy of other candidates. Finally, the nationalist trend, including Ba'thists, Nasserists, and members of the Movement of Arab Nationalists (MAN)* faced major challenges in terms of its orientation. This is especially true as the nationalists have dealt with the growth of Islamic groups, have encountered the belief that the Palestinian struggle should be led by uniquely Palestinian (not pan-Arab) leaders, and have faced the conception among many that these parties are residues of the past.

In April 1990, King Husayn formed a royal commission of sixty members to draft a national charter. The charter was meant to regulate political and social life, to allow for the return of political parties, and to function as the common denominator among the various political parties and ideologies. Those appointed to draw up the charter included leftists, liberals, Ba'thists, tribal leaders, and religious fundamentalists. After a year of deliberation, the charter was announced on June 9, 1991, at a national conference attended by 2,000 delegates. The eight-chapter charter was not legally binding and required regulations to formalize it. Wary of his experience in the 1950s, Husayn emphasized that only "national" parties—in terms of funding, methods, affiliation, and objectives—would be tolerated. Moreover, he cautioned against the abuse of democratization and warned against allowing partisan politics to paralyze the political process.

Jordan, in the early 1990s, was still plagued by three nagging issues: the struggle over the nature and bounds of democracy and the role of political parties in the country; the continued feeling that Jordan is an incomplete entity that needs to be reunited with some larger, organic whole (whether Arab or Islamic or both); and what political role Jordan should play in the Palestinian conflict, including the problem of whether Palestinians in Jordan should act politically as Jordanians or Palestinians (or both). These systemic questions have been reflected in party platforms from the 1920s until today, and they will no doubt continue to affect Jordanian politics for some time in the future. Although numerous parties emerged from the liberalization of 1989–90 advocating the familiar themes of Arab unity, Palestinian liberation, or social Islamicization, most also stressed their unique Jordanian identity and took pains to emphasize their commitment to working within the Jordanian political system.

The 1993 parliamentary election was an important milestone in the development of democracy in Jordan since it was the first multiparty parliamentary election since 1956. Some 1.2 million voters registered to select from among 536 candidates who ran for the eighty-seat parliament.

There was a 4.7 percent increase in the number of voters compared to that in 1989, despite the exclusion of members of the security forces. The higher number may be attributed to the large number of Jordanian citizens who returned from the Gulf countries following the Gulf War of 1991 (some 100,000 returnees registered to vote), increased trust in the regime and its attempts to democratize the system, and legalization of political parties. It was estimated that 20,000 Jordanians, 0.5 percent of the population, maintained a party affiliation.

The election reflected the preeminence of tribalism and regional identification over ideological or political affiliation. Twelve of twenty parties legalized prior to the election nominated candidates, while the remaining parties unofficially endorsed candidates. Sixty-seven party-affiliated candidates ran in the election. Only seven leftist/nationalist candidates won, although there were twenty officially registered parties of this type. This compared with thirteen winners in the 1989 election. The Islamic Action Front* (created by the Muslim Brotherhood) won sixteen seats, compared to twenty-two for the Muslim Brotherhood Association in 1989. Centrist parties like al-'Ahd, al-Mustaqbal,* and al-Yaqaza* won 3 seats. The remaining seats were captured by independent Islamists (five seats) and independents (forty-nine seats).

The predominance of tribal identity was indicated not only by the election results but also by the campaigns, which were conducted on tribal and personal bases. Voters cast ballots for their kinsmen or candidates endorsed by their tribe, as well as candidates hailing from their region. Jordanians of Palestinian origin tended to vote for Palestinian candidates, while those of Jordanian origin voted for East Bank Jordanian candidates. This pattern highlighted the schisms within Jordanian society over identity, a factor that was extensively debated during the election campaign, particularly after the Palestinian-Israeli accord of September 1993.

The biggest surprises in the election outcome were the victory of the first woman deputy and the decline in the number of Islamists. These surprises may be attributed, in the first case, to the minority quota system that prevailed (she was elected to represent a Circassian sect in Amman) and to the coordinated efforts of women activists. The second surprise was due to a change in the law to a one-person, one-vote system. Overall, the 1993 election was heralded as a dramatic step in consolidating democracy in Jordan, despite the fact that fifty activists protested that it was unfair and unfree.

## Bibliography

Abidi, Aqil Hyder Hasan. Jordan: A Political Study, 1948–1957. London: Asia Publishing House, 1965.

Abu-Jabir, Kamal S. "The Legislature of the Hashemite Kingdom of Jordan," Muslim World 59 (1969), 220–50.

Aruri, Naseer H. Jordan: A Study in Political Development (1921–1965). The Hague: Martinus Nijhoff, 1972.

Ayyad, Ranad al-Khatib. Al-Tayarat al-Siyasiyya fi'l-Urdunn (Political Trends in Jordan). Amman: 1991.

Chizik, I. "The Political Parties in Trans-Jordania," Journal of the Royal Central Asian Society 22 (January 1935).

Dann, Uriel. Studies in the History of Transjordan, 1920–1949. Boulder, Colo.: Westview Press, 1984.

Jordanian Political Parties, Civil Society and Political Life in Jordan. Amman: The New Jordan Research Center, 1993.

Madi, Munib and Musa, Sulayman. Ta'rikh al-Urdunn fi'l-Qarn al- 'Ishrin (History of

Jordan in the Twentieth Century), second edition. Amman: 1991. (First edition: M. Madi and S. Musa, 1959.)

"Malaf Al-Ahzab al-Siyasiyya fi'l-Urdunn" (File of Political Parties in Jordan). *al-Urdunn al-Jadid* (The New Jordan) 17/18 (Fall 1990).

Shwadran, Benjamin. *Jordan: A State of Tension*. New York: Council for Middle Eastern Affairs Press, 1959.

## Political Parties

ARAB COVENANT PARTY (*Hizb Al-'Ahd al-'Arabi*). This party was formed in December 1921 by ex-members of the Arab nationalist Covenant Society (*al-'Ahd*), a secret society of Ottoman Army officers of Arab origin established in 1913 by 'Aziz 'Ali al-Masri. The party was one of the most significant parties in the history of Arab nationalism. It sought the independence of all countries in the Arab east under the leadership of the *Sharif* Husayn bin 'Ali of Mecca and his heirs.

ARAB INDEPENDENCE PARTY. *See* ISTIQLAL.

ARAB NATIONALISTS MOVEMENT. *See* MOVEMENT OF ARAB NATIONALISTS.

ARAB NATIONAL UNION (*Hizb al-Ittihad al-Watani al-'Arabi*). *See* JORDAN NATIONAL UNION.

ARAB REVIVAL PARTY (*Hizb al-Nahda al-'Arabiyya*). Established in May 1947, this moderate party was founded by King 'Abdullah's protégés to support his plan for Greater Syrian unity under his rule. The party, led by Hashim Khayr, included a number of leading tribal shaykhs and influential merchants. Its goals were to rekindle the aims of the Arab revolt against the Ottomans during the First World War by achieving total independence from the British and unity of Greater Syria under 'Abdullah's rule. Unlike the opposition's stand, however, it echoed the palace's views in accepting the 1948 Anglo-Jordanian treaty.

The party's goals were popularized in a congress it held in September 1947, and in its two papers, *al-Jihad* (1948) and *al-Nahda* (1949–50). The party won four seats in the 1947 legislative council but was dissolved in 1950.

ARAB SOCIALIST RESURRECTION [BA'TH] PARTY—UNIFIED ORGANIZATION (*Hizb al-Ba'th al-'Arabi al-Ishtiraki—al-Tanzim al-Muwahhad*). Established after the April 1989 riots by Muhammad al-Zu'bi to distinguish itself from the Syrian and Iraqi wings of the Ba'th party (see Progressive Arab Resurrection [Ba'th] Party; Jordanian Socialist Resurrection [Ba'th] Party), this party aimed at representing specific Jordanian concerns within a Ba'thist context. The party's platform was based on the traditional Ba'thist slogans of "Unity, Freedom, and Socialism." It urged unity among all nationalist forces in Jordan as well as pan-Arab unity. Late in 1993, the party agreed to merge with the Jordanian Revolutionary People's Party* and two small factions to form a new organization, the National Action Front Party (Hizb Jabhat al-'Amal al-Qawmi). The new party applied for official registration in November 1993. (See also the chapters on Iraq, Lebanon, and Syria.)

ARAB UNION PARTY (*Hizb al-Ittihad al-'Arabi*). Established by Yusuf 'Izz al-Din, this party was a branch of the Egyptian-based Arab Union Association established by Fu'ad Abaza in 1942. The party's platform was embodied in the Pact of the Arab Nation (*Mithaq al-Umma al-'Arabi*), which advocated resistance to Zionism and foreign occupation and asserted economic and cultural Arab unity based on shared origins but also on the specificity of each Arab country.

BA'TH PARTY. *See* ARAB SOCIALIST RESURRECTION (BA'TH) PARTY—UNIFIED ORGANIZATION; JORDANIAN SOCIALIST ARAB RESURRECTION (BA'TH) PARTY; PROGRESSIVE ARAB RESURRECTION (BA'TH) PARTY.

THE CALL. *See* DEMOCRATIC ISLAMIC ARAB MOVEMENT.

COMMUNIST PARTY OF JORDAN. *See* JORDANIAN COMMUNIST PARTY.

COMMUNIST WORKERS PARTY IN JORDAN (*Hizb al-'Ummal al-Shuyu'i Fi'l-Urdunn*). This party was established in the late 1970s by Hisham al-Hijazi, Nizar al-Kayid, and Yusuf Hamid after it split from the Palestinian Communist Workers Party (see chapter on the Palestinians). The party, based on Marxist-Leninist ideology, made a point of stressing its political and ideological independence from the Soviet Union. Within Jordan, it urged greater democratization and respect for the constitution.

In 1992 the party joined with the Jordanian Democratic Party* to form the Jordanian Democratic Progressive Party.*

CONSTITUTIONAL ARAB FRONT (*Al-Jabha al-'Arabiyya al-Dusturiyya*). Established in 1975 by Milhim al-Tall with a program calling for adherence to the Jordanian constitution as the basis for political action, the party never enjoyed a mass following but gained some support among tribal leaders. In the 1989 elections, it won a few seats in Parliament and called for a national congress and cooperation among all political parties. However, it rejected the idea of a national charter because it felt that the constitution fulfilled that role. The party stressed the specificity of both the Palestinian and Jordanian national identities and called for the liberation of Palestine. It also urged the unity of Greater Syria as a prelude to an ultimate comprehensive Arab unity. The Front did not officially register prior to the November 1993 parliamentary elections, but it remained operative nonetheless.

CONSTITUTIONAL ARAB PARTY (Al-Hizb al-'Arabi al-Dusturi). This pro-government, conservative party was established in April 1956 by Riyad al-Muflih, Ahmad Tarawna, and supporters of Prime Minister Tawfiq Abu'l-Huda. Its platform called for liberation of Palestine, cooperation with Arab countries, and improvement of workers' and peasants' rights. Fourteen party members ran in the 1956 election as independents to avoid public animosity due to popular anger against pro-regime parties. They were able to win on the basis of tribal, familial, or class influences. The party was dissolved along with all other political parties in 1957.

DEMOCRATIC ARAB UNIONIST PARTY—PROMISE (Hizb al-Wahdawi al-'Arabi al-Dimuqrati—WA'D). Promise was formed out of a union of several parties, including the Unionist Democratic bloc,* and legalized in February 1993. Its leaders included Anis al-Mu'ashshir, Muhammad al-'Uran, and Talal al-'Umari. A centrist party, Promise stressed the unity of Jordan's soil and people and was committed to the Jordanian constitution. It supported the Palestinian struggle; it also supported the legal equality of all Jordanians, the strengthening of democratic freedoms, development of national education, and provision of equal opportunities in education and welfare. Economically, the party called for removal of impediments to economic activity and attraction of Arab and foreign capital.

DEMOCRATIC FRONT ORGANIZATION IN JORDAN (MAJD) (Muna-dhdhimat al-Jabha al-Dimuqratiyya fi'l-Urdunn). Known as MAJD, this underground organization was established in 1974 as a Jordanian branch of the Democratic Front for the Liberation of Palestine (DFLP), a Palestinian Marxist organization headed by a Jordanian, Nayif Hawatmeh (see chapter on the Palestinians). Even though it was a Palestinian organization, the DFLP has always remained interested in maintaining ties with leftists in Jordan. Certain activists felt, however, that a uniquely Jordanian organization should be formed to pursue a Jordanian agenda.

MAJD activists wrestled with the accusation that MAJD merely represented the DFLP in Jordan and was controlled by the parent organization. In 1989 MAJD activists created a political party to operate on the Jordanian political scene: the Jordanian Democratic People's Party (HASHD).*

DEMOCRATIC ISLAMIC ARAB MOVEMENT—THE CALL (Al-Haraka al-'Arabiyya al-Islamiyya al-Dimuqratiyya—Al-Du'a). Established in 1990 by Yusif Abu Bakir, this party rejected both Marxism and capitalism and adhered to the Quran and the Sunna (traditions of the Prophet Muhammad, a major source of Islamic theology) as its only comprehensive sources for belief, political life, and solutions to socioeconomic problems. But The Call sharply criticized other Islamic groups for their rigid interpretations of Islam and their focus on "trivial" issues of Islamicization of Jordan. It has also called for expanded political freedoms, the creation of an independent judicial system, and complete equality for women. In marked contrast to most Islamic parties, which called for the immediate application of Islamic law in Jordan, The Call urged delaying its application until the proper conditions have been met.

AL-DU'A. *See* DEMOCRATIC ISLAMIC ARAB MOVEMENT.

ECNC. *See* EXECUTIVE COMMITTEE OF THE NATIONAL CONGRESS PARTY.

EXECUTIVE COMMITTEE OF THE GENERAL CONGRESS OF THE JORDANIAN PEOPLE (ECGCJP) (*Hizb al-Lajna al-Tanfidhiyya Li-Mutamar al-Sha'b al-Urdunni*). The ECGCJP grew out of a congress held in August 1933 at the initiation of Naji al-'Azzam and attended by three hundred tribal shaykhs and notables who disagreed with the Executive Committee of the National Congress Party* and its followers. The party's agenda essentially restated that of the Executive Committee of the National Congress Party, although it affirmed its loyalty to the regime. The party participated successfully in the 1934 election, although al-'Azzam was not elected and therefore resigned from his leadership position. This led to the party's disintegration by October 1934.

EXECUTIVE COMMITTEE OF THE JORDANIAN CONGRESS PARTY (*Hizb al-Lajna al-Tanfidhiyya Lil-Mutamar al-Urdunni*). This party was established in September 1944 by Muhammad 'Ali al-'Ajluni and other ex-members of the Jordanian National Congress* party with the aim of reviving the ideals of their former party. Among the factors contributing to its demise three months later was government repression during World War II.

EXECUTIVE COMMITTEE OF THE NATIONAL CONGRESS PARTY (ECNC) (*Hizb al-Lajna al-Tanfidhiyya Lil-Mutamar al-Watani*). The ECNC was a pillar of the Transjordanian opposition established by Husayn al-Tarawna in April 1929 as the official body of the National Congress,* but it split from the parent body following a dispute over whether to boycott the 1929 legislative council election. While several Congress members ran and were elected, those who refused to participate broke with the Congress and formed the Executive Council of the National Congress Party. Other influential opposition figures of the time, such as 'Adil al-'Azma and Subhi Abu Ghanima, were also members. Its followers were Syrian nationals, Jordanian intellectuals, tribal leaders, and landowners.

The party believed strongly in the ideals of the former Istiqlal* party and was formed to implement the ideas embodied in the national pact (see National Congress). It generally adhered closely to the platform of its antecedent, the National Congress. Following the example of its parent body, it organized additional national congresses in December 1929, May 1930, March 1932, and

June 1933. The party's program was echoed in the pronouncements of these congresses, all of which were restatements of the national pact. The party urged a greater separation of powers in the government, sought to improve economic conditions in Transjordan, and expressed concern over the granting of foreign concessions in the country as well as of Zionist attempts to purchase land. The party, like all opposition groups, sought to amend the Anglo-Transjordanian Agreement of 1928 and called for the installation of a government responsible to the legislative council. It later focused increasing attention on the plight of the country's farmers.

A factional dispute led to the formation of the Moderate Liberal Party* in 1930, although the two groups later reconciled. The congress of March 1932 found the party facing internal turmoil once again over the question of whether to participate in elections for the legislative council. Certain prominent members withdrew their earlier objections, ran in the 1931 elections, and sat in the new legislative council, including Husayn al-Tarawna—an act of treason in the eyes of ECNC purists.

The ECNC party possessed the potential to become a mass movement and a strong party. It enjoyed the longest life span among parties of that period—over five years. However, its programs contradicted the interests of the British and the amir, and it was thus subjected to government attempts to weaken it. The first attempt was made by Amir 'Abdullah, who successfully co-opted party members such as Hashim Khayr (vice president of the party), who resigned and established the pro-government Moderate Liberal Party in 1930, and Tahir al-Juqqa (general secretary), who resigned to become the mayor of Amman in 1931. The government did not stop at co-optation: Party members and leaders were subjected to harassment under the defense laws of 1935 and the general repression in the aftermath of the 1936 Palestinian uprising. Several leading members went into exile, and the party disintegrated.

AL-FATAT. *See* ISTIQLAL.

FREEDOM PARTY (*Hizb al-Hurriyya*). This party was first established in January 1990 as the Jordanian Progressive Party by Fawwaz al-Zu'bi and other ex-members of the Jordanian Communist Party (JCP)* who left the JCP following the collapse of the Soviet Union and the onset of democratic reforms in Jordan. It later changed its name to Freedom Party and was legalized in February 1993. The party's platform called for strengthening the armed forces, realizing independence from foreign economic assistance, and combatting what it saw as an attempt by the so-called New World Order to reoccupy Jordan. It also supported the national struggle of the Palestinian people for self-determination. Internally, the party called for democratization of the political system through popular participation and freedom of the press. The party published a monthly newspaper, *al-Hurriyya*.

FUTURE PARTY (*Hizb al-Mustaqbal*). This centrist party was legalized in December 1992 with Sulayman 'Arar as its secretary-general. It advocated respect for private property, individual rights, and equality of women. It encouraged economic development through cooperation between the state and the private sector with the goal of national self-sufficiency. Politically, the party urged democratization of both the society and the political system. It published a weekly newspaper, *al-Mustaqbal*. The party won one seat in the 1993 parliamentary elections.

AL-HARAKA AL-'ARABIYYA AL-ISLAMIYYA AL-DIMUQRATIYYA. *See* DEMOCRATIC ISLAMIC ARAB MOVEMENT—THE CALL.

HARAKAT AL-QAWMIYYIN AL-'ARAB. *See* MOVEMENT OF ARAB NATIONALISTS.

HASHD. *See* JORDANIAN DEMOCRATIC PEOPLE'S PARTY.

HIZB AL-'AHD AL URDUNNI. *See* JORDANIAN PLEDGE PARTY.

HIZB AL-'AHD AL-'ARABI. *See* ARAB COVENANT PARTY.

HIZB AHRAR AL-URDUNN. *See* JORDAN'S LIBERALS PARTY.

AL-HIZB AL-'ARABI AL-DUSTURI. *See* CONSTITUTIONAL ARAB PARTY.

AL-HIZB AL-'ARABI AL-URDUNNI. *See* JORDANIAN ARAB PARTY.

HIZB AL-BA'TH AL-'ARABI AL-ISHTIRAKI AL URDUNNI. *See* JORDANIAN SOCIALIST ARAB RESURRECTION (BA'TH) PARTY.

HIZB AL-BA'TH AL-'ARABI AL-TAQADDUMI. *See* PROGRESSIVE ARAB RESURRECTION (BA'TH) PARTY.

HIZB AL-BA'TH AL-'ARABI AL-ISHTIRAKI—AL-TANDHIM AL-MUWAHHAD. *See* ARAB SOCIALIST RESURRECTION (BA'TH) PARTY—UNIFIED ORGANIZATION.

HIZB AL-DIMUQRATI AL-ISHTIRAKI AL-URDUNNI. *See* JORDANIAN SOCIALIST DEMOCRATIC PARTY.

AL-HIZB AL-DIMUQRATI AL-'ARABI AL-URDUNNI. *See* JORDANIAN ARAB DEMOCRATIC PARTY.

AL-HIZB AL-DIMUQRATI AL-URDUNNI. *See* JORDANIAN DEMO-CRATIC PARTY.

HIZB AL-HURR AL-MU'TADIL. *See* MODERATE LIBERAL PARTY.

HIZB AL-HURRIYYA. *See* FREEDOM PARTY.

HIZB AL-IKHA AL-URDUNNI. *See* JORDANIAN BROTHERHOOD PARTY.

HIZB AL-ISTIQLAL AL-'ARABI. *See* ISTIQLAL.

HIZB AL-ITTIHAD AL-'ARABI. *See* ARAB UNION PARTY.

HIZB AL-ITTIHAD AL-WATANI. *See* NATIONAL UNION PARTY.

HIZB AL-ITTIHAD AL-WATANI AL-'ARABI. *See* ARAB NATIONAL UNION/JORDAN NATIONAL UNION.

HIZB AL-JABHA AL-WATANIYYA. *See* NATIONAL FRONT PARTY.

HIZB JABHAT AL-'AMAL AL-ISLAMI. *See* ISLAMIC ACTION FRONT PARTY.

HIZB JABHAT AL-'AMAL AL-QAWMI. *See* ARAB SOCIALIST RESUR-RECTION (BA'TH) PARTY—UNIFIED ORGANIZATION; JORDANIAN REVOLUTIONARY PEOPLE'S PARTY.

HIZB AL-JAMAHIR AL-'ARABI AL-URDUNNI. *See* JORDANIAN ARAB MASSES PARTY.

HIZB AL-LAJNA AL-TANFIDHIYYA LI-MUTAMAR AL-SHA'B AL-URDUNNI. *See* EXECUTIVE COMMITTEE OF THE GENERAL CON-GRESS OF THE JORDANIAN PEOPLE.

HIZB AL-LAJNA AL-TANFIDHIYYA LIL-MUTAMAR AL-URDUNNI. *See* EXECUTIVE COMMITTEE OF THE JORDANIAN CONGRESS PARTY.

HIZB AL-LAJNA AL-TANFIDHIYYA LIL-MUTAMAR AL-WATANI. *See* EXECUTIVE COMMITTEE OF THE NATIONAL CONGRESS PARTY.

HIZB AL-MUSTAQBAL. *See* FUTURE PARTY.

HIZB AL-NAHDA AL-'ARABIYYA. *See* ARAB REVIVAL PARTY

AL-HIZB AL-SURI AL-QAWMI AL-IJTIMA'I. *See* SYRIAN SOCIAL NATIONALIST PARTY.

HIZB AL-SHA'B. *See* PEOPLE'S PARTY.

HIZB AL-SHA'B AL-DIMUQRATI AL-URDUNNI. *See* JORDANIAN DEMOCRATIC PEOPLE'S PARTY.

HIZB AL-SHA'B AL-THAWRI AL-URDUNNI. *See* JORDANIAN REVOLUTIONARY PEOPLE'S PARTY.

HIZB AL-SHA'B AL-URDUNNI. *See* JORDANIAN PEOPLE'S PARTY.

AL-HIZB AL-SHUYU'I AL-URDUNNI. *See* JORDANIAN COMMUNIST PARTY.

AL-HIZB AL-SHUYU'I AL-URDUNNI—AL-NAHJ AL-THAWRI. *See* JORDANIAN COMMUNIST PARTY—REVOLUTIONARY PATH.

HIZB AL-TADAMUN AL-URDUNNI. *See* JORDANIAN SOLIDARITY PARTY.

HIZB AL-TAHRIR. *See* LIBERATION PARTY.

HIZB AL-TAJAMMU' AL-WATANI AL-URDUNNI. *See* JORDANIAN NATIONAL ALLIANCE PARTY.

HIZB AL-TAQADDUM WAL-'ADALA. *See* JUSTICE AND PROGRESS PARTY.

AL-HIZB AL-TAQADDUMI AL-DIMUQRATI AL-URDUNNI. *See* JORDANIAN DEMOCRATIC PROGRESSIVE PARTY.

HIZB AL-TAQADDUMI AL-URDUNNI. *See* JORDANIAN PROGRESSIVE PARTY.

HIZB UMM AL-QURA. *See* UMM AL-QURA PARTY.

HIZB AL-UMMA. *See* PARTY OF THE NATION.

HIZB AL-'UMMAL AL-SHUYU'I FI'L-URDUNN. *See* COMMUNIST WORKERS PARTY IN JORDAN.

HIZB AL-'UMMAL AL-URDUNNI. *See* JORDANIAN WORKERS PARTY

HIZB AL-WAHDAWI AL-'ARABI AL-DIMUQRATI—WA'D. *See* DEMO-CRATIC ARAB UNIONIST PARTY—PROMISE.

HIZB AL-WATAN. *See* HOMELAND PARTY.

AL-HIZB AL-WATANI AL-ISHTIRAKI. *See* NATIONAL SOCIALIST PARTY.

AL-HIZB AL-WATANI AL-URDUNNI. *See* JORDANIAN NATIONAL PARTY.

HIZB AL-WIHDA AL-SHA'BIYYA—AL WAHDAWIYYUN. *See* POPULAR UNITY PARTY—THE UNIONISTS.

HIZB AL-WIHDA AL-SHA'BIYYA AL-DIMUQRATIYYA AL-URDUNNI. *See* JORDANIAN DEMOCRATIC POPULAR UNITY PARTY.

HIZB AL-YAQAZA. *See* REAWAKENING PARTY.

HOMELAND PARTY (*Hizb al-Watan*). This nationalist-centrist party, legalized in June 1993, was founded by 'Akif al-Fayiz and Hasan Kayid al-Sum. The party adhered to the principles of democracy and justice for the promotion of Arab-Islamic civilization and Arab unity. It called for ensuring national survival by safeguarding national unity, cultivating national pride, promoting women's role in society, and enhancing social justice and equal opportunity. It denounced corruption and encouraged investment.

INDEPENDENCE PARTY. *See* ISTIQLAL.

ISLAMIC ACTION FRONT PARTY (*Hizb Jabhat al-'Amal al-Islami*). This party was established in 1992 as the political wing of the Muslim Brotherhood Association,* which was technically not a party, and legalized in December of that year. Its first secretary-general was Ishaq Ahmad al-Farhan. Its platform resembled that of the Brotherhood, calling for the application of Islamic precepts; respect for democratic principles, pluralism, and human rights (as understood in Islam); and creation of a national economy based on Islamic principles of social justice. The party did not publish a newspaper, but its views were expressed in *al-Rabat*, the newspaper of the Muslim Brotherhood. The Islamic Action Front Party ran in the 1993 elections, winning sixteen seats.

ISTIQLAL (*Hizb al-Istiqlal al-'Arabi*, Arab Independence Party). This party emerged in February 1919 as a public expression of its antecedent, the secret Society of *al-Fatat* (the Young Arab Society), founded in 1911 by Arab students in France. The society was moved to Beirut in 1913 and then to Damascus where it enjoyed the membership of Amir Faysal bin Husayn and participated in drawing up the Damascus Protocol, which formed the basis for Arab support for Britain during World War I.

In the aftermath of the destruction of Faysal's independent Syrian kingdom by the French in 1920, many members of the party regrouped in Transjordan, Egypt, and the Hijaz. Upon the personal request of Amir 'Abdullah, party members officially established the Istiqlal as a political party in the summer of 1921. They called for an independent Arab state made up of Jordan, Palestine, Syria, Lebanon, and Iraq. They adopted an extremely hostile attitude toward the French and British mandates and vowed to free the Arabs from foreign rule once again. The party adopted military means to resist the mandates and infiltrated the Transjordanian army and the government thanks to the education and experience of its members. Party activists viewed Transjordan primarily as a base from which to launch attacks against the French in Syria. Because of their antimandate position and guerrilla attacks against the French, the Istiqlal incurred the wrath of the British and threatened to destabilize Anglo-French relations, not to mention stable British rule in Palestine and Transjordan.

Fearing French retaliation and seeking to stabilize the situation, the British increased their pressure on 'Abdullah to uphold the terms of his agreement with them in the Cairo and Jerusalem conferences and keep Transjordan pacified. 'Abdullah acquiesced in British designs to end the activities of the Istiqlal in Transjordan. Accordingly, he dismissed numerous party members from government and the military, including his chief minister, Rashid al-Tali' and the influential army officer, Fuad Salim. In August 1924, the British forced him to crack down even harder on the Istiqlal as the price for remaining in power.

The ideas of the Istiqlal found a receptive audience in Transjordan, especially among landowners and tribal leaders and in intellectual circles. However, it also incurred the wrath of many who viewed the party as merely using Transjordan for its own aims and depriving educated Transjordanian nationals of government employment. This resentment was vocalized in nativist slogans and in the platforms of many uniquely Transjordanian associations. The party ended in 1924 with the expulsion of eight of its leaders.

AL-ITTIHAD AL-WATANI AL-URDUNNI. See JORDAN NATIONAL UNION.

AL-JABHA AL-'ARABIYYA AL-DUSTURIYYA. See CONSTITUTIONAL ARAB FRONT.

JAMA'AT AL-IKHWAN AL-MUSLIMIN. See MUSLIM BROTHERHOOD ASSOCIATION.

JAMA'AT AL-SHABAB AL-AHRAR AL-URDUNNIYYIN. See JORDANIAN LIBERAL YOUTH ASSOCIATION.

JCP. *See* JORDANIAN COMMUNIST PARTY.

JDP. *See* JORDANIAN DEMOCRATIC PARTY.

JDPP. *See* JORDANIAN DEMOCRATIC PROGRESSIVE PARTY.

JDPUP. *See* JORDANIAN DEMOCRATIC POPULAR UNITY PARTY.

JORDANIAN ARAB DEMOCRATIC PARTY (*Al-Hizb al-Dimuqrati al-'Arabi al-Urdunni*). This party was established by ex-Ba'thists (see Ba'th Party) and legalized in July 1993 with Mu'nis Munif al-Razzaz as secretary-general. In keeping with Ba'thist tradition, the party supported the Palestinian cause, worked to strengthen inter-Arab relations to achieve Arab unity, and fought imperialism. It sought to protect the independence of the national economy and supported collective action and the work of unions and charitable societies. It won one seat in the 1993 parliamentary elections.

JORDANIAN ARAB MASSES PARTY (*Hizb al-Jamahir al-'Arabi al-Urdunni*). Under Secretary-General 'Abdal-Khaliq Hatat, this party was legalized in May 1993. Its program stressed national development; safeguarding Jordanians from economic, political, and cultural dependency; and giving priority to youth and women in the development process. It called for protection of the Jordanian experiment in democracy. Internationally, the party supported Palestinian rights and acknowledged the unique relationship between the Jordanian and Palestinian peoples. It also supported Arab unity, but only when all Arab countries achieve freedom and democracy.

JORDANIAN ARAB PARTY (*Al-Hizb al-'Arabi al-Urdunni*). Formed underground by followers of the influential opposition leader Subhi Abu Ghanima after it was denied official recognition in June 1946, the party elected Abu Ghanima as president and drew up a national pact resembling in tone the pact of 1928. It called for democratization of the system by enforcing the principle of separation of powers, a freely elected parliament, government by the people and responsible to the people's representatives in parliament, protection of civil liberties and cancellation of emergency laws, cooperation with the Arab League, and, finally, modification of the 1946 treaty to achieve true independence.

The regime was threatened by the party's success, and took steps to co-opt its leaders. Sulayman al-Nabulsi, for instance, was included in the 1947 government of Samir al-Rifa'i.

JORDANIAN BROTHERHOOD PARTY (*Hizb al-Ikha' al-Urdunni*). This party was established in September 1937 by ex-members of the Executive Committee of the National Congress Party* with Majid al-'Adwan as president. The party was formed to counter the attacks launched by the National Congress* party on the government and its policies, and it declared its loyalty to the government and to the amir. Its platform, calling for securing Transjordan's independence and unity with other Arab countries based on political and socioeconomic co-operation, as well as economic and educational improvement of the country, was similar to those of its rivals in the National Congress party and the Executive Committee of the National Congress Party. The party's ultimate demise can be attributed to internal disorganization and to the popularity of its rivals in the opposition movement.

JORDANIAN COMMUNIST PARTY (JCP) (*Al-Hizb al-Shuyu'i al-Urdunni*). The JCP rose out of the ashes of the Palestine Communist Party, which split along Jewish-Arab lines in the early 1940s over the party's stance toward Zionism (see chapter on the Palestinians). In the fall of 1943, Arab activists formed the National Liberation League (*'Usbat al-Tahrir al-Watani*). The 1949 cease-fire left Palestine divided, and communists within both the Arab and the Jewish sectors quickly established new party apparatuses. Within the Jordanian-occupied West Bank in 1950, communists from the National Liberation League split over the question of whether the organization should retain its largely intellectual char-acter or push for greater proletarianization. The faction of Fu'ad Nassar, who argued that the party's intellectual orientation fit the West Bank social fabric in which the party operated at that time (which contained virtually no working class), ultimately carried the day. The League organized against the Transjordan-ian annexation of the West Bank and changed its name to the Jordanian Com-munist Party in 1951 after the annexation took place, and the League's activists found themselves part of the Jordanian political scene.

The JCP has been one of the most significant Jordanian political parties in the post-1948 era. Highly-organized and committed to a pro-Soviet Marxist-Leninist line, the party has exerted an influence far beyond what its numbers would seem to warrant. The JCP has endured the special wrath of the Jordanian authorities, who passed several anticommunist laws during the 1940s and 1950s.

Activists took part in several elections surreptitiously during the 1950s, re-turning several "independents" to parliament and forming the National Front Party* along with the National Socialist Party* and the Ba'th Party.* During the 1960s, the JCP adopted the Soviet line of subordinating the proletarian struggle in the Arab world to the wider Arab nationalist struggle.

The party was rent once again in the late 1960s in the aftermath of the Israeli occupation of the West Bank. The JCP had always been a largely Palestinian party, and activists in the East Bank were split regarding the proper attitude toward the growing Palestinian guerrilla movement and the activities of Pales-tinian party members in it. In the West Bank, communist activists eventually broke away from the JCP to form their own uniquely Palestinian communist party (see chapter on the Palestinians). Schisms in the late 1980s led to the formation of several other Marxist parties in Jordan, such as the Jordanian Communist Party—Revolutionary Path* and the Jordanian Progressive Party.* Prior to the 1993 elections, a faction headed by 'Isa Mudaynat split off to form the Jordanian Socialist Democratic Party.*

The JCP remained active on the underground Jordanian political scene in the 1970s and 1980s. The government cracked down on the party periodically, such as after the 1986 student demonstrations at Yarmuk University, which led to the deaths of several students, and after the 1989 riots. But the party participated in the 1989 election and won a seat in Parliament. The political reforms that swept through Jordan beginning in that year were symbolized by the repeal of the decades-old anticommunist legislation in December 1989. The party was legalized in January 1993 under its secretary-general, Ya'qub Zayadin. It ran unsuccessfully in the 1993 elections.

JORDANIAN COMMUNIST PARTY—REVOLUTIONARY PATH (Al-Hizb al-Shuyu'i al-Urdunni—Al-Nahj al-Thawri). This revolutionary Marxist-Leninist party was formed in 1989 after it split from the Jordanian Communist Party.* The party called for a reassessment of the role of communism in the Middle East and of communists' relationship with Moscow in the wake of the collapse of communism in Europe. It has also urged greater democratization within the communist movement in Jordan.

In June 1991, six members of the party were arrested on charges of slandering Prime Minister Mudar Badran. The arrests sparked protests from numerous activists and parliamentarians who demanded that the regime live up to the democratic ideals it had enunciated in the liberalization program initiated in 1989. The party did not officially register prior to the 1993 elections, but it continued to function, largely among radical intellectuals.

JORDANIAN DEMOCRATIC PARTY (JDP) (Al-Hizb al-Dimuqrati al-Urdunni). The JDP is an expression of the traditional splits and internal turmoil faced by Jordanian activists associated with the Democratic Front for the Liberation of Palestine (DFLP), a Marxist Palestinian organization (see chapter on the Palestinians), over the "Jordanian-ness" of DFLP activists in Jordan (see Democratic Front Organization in Jordan [MAJD] and Jordanian Democratic People's Party [HASHD]).

The JDP broke with HASHD in August 1990 under the leadership of 'Ali 'Amir and Hani Hawrani. The JDP strove to serve as a forum within which to solve the internal factional crisis faced by HASHD over just how Jordanian the followers of the Palestinian DFLP should be. Even though HASHD was itself created in 1989 as a Jordanian party by DFLP-affiliated activists from MAJD, party members who later broke with HASHD and formed the JDP objected to the fact that, in their opinion, control of HASHD still lay in the hands of the Palestinian parent movement. The JDP aimed to serve the Jordanian national movement and continued to work in conjunction with, but not under the command of, the Palestinian national movement.

Another factor in the formation of the JDP was its criticism of what it termed the extreme centralization and authoritarianism within HASHD. It also criticized HASHD for its ties with "reactionary" parties.

In 1992 the party joined with the Communist Workers Party in Jordan* in forming the Jordanian Democratic Progressive Party.* That same year, Hawrani and other members of the central committee withdrew from the JDP and formed the Jordanian Democratic Platform along with members of various other leftist parties.

JORDANIAN DEMOCRATIC PEOPLE'S PARTY (HASHD) (*Hizb al-Sha'B al-Dimuqrati al-Urdunni*). Established in July 1989 by Taysir al-Zibri, HASHD was created by activists from the Democratic Front Organization in Jordan (MAJD).* MAJD was an underground group of Jordanians associated with a Palestinian Marxist organization, the Democratic Front for the Liberation of Palestine (DFLP) (see chapter on the Palestinians). HASHD broke from MAJD because it criticized the continued organizational links between MAJD and its Palestinian mentor, the DFLP. HASHD activists also felt that a uniquely Jordanian party was needed to reflect the increasing separateness of the respective struggles of the Palestinian and Jordanian peoples. This separation was forcefully demonstrated by the Palestinian uprising known as the *intifada*, the subsequent Jordanian decision to cut ties with the West Bank in July 1988, acknowledgement of the independence of the Palestinian state, and the 1989 antigovernment riots in Jordan.

HASHD began focusing on Jordanian priorities, such as the democratization movement, pluralism, freedom of political parties, and general guarantees for freedom and equality of Jordanian women. It still called for the total liberation of Palestine, however, and it supported the establishment of a Palestinian state under the leadership of the Palestine Liberation Organization (PLO).

Until 1991 both MAJD and HASHD were harassed by the authorities. However, HASHD has been able to publish its monthly paper *Tariq al-Sha'b* and intermittent leaflets, as well as to participate in the 1989 elections in which it won a seat. A youth organization, the Jordanian Democratic Youth Association (Rashad) was also created.

In 1990 dissatisfaction over how much control the Palestinian DFLP still maintained over HASHD led a group of activists to break away and form the Jordanian Democratic Party.* The party won one seat in the 1993 parliamentary elections.

JORDANIAN DEMOCRATIC POPULAR UNITY PARTY (JDPUP) (*Hizb al-Wihda al-Sha'biyya al-Dimuqrati al-Urdunni*). The JDPUP was established in November 1990 by 'Azmi al-Khawaja as a Jordanian party associated with the Popular Front for the Liberation of Palestine (PFLP), a Palestinian Marxist organization. Many of the party's members have also been ex-members of the Jordanian Revolutionary Peoples' Party* and the Popular Front Organization in Jordan, branches of the PFLP that operated underground in Jordan beginning in the early 1970s.

Like other leftist activists associated with Palestinian organizations, PFLP militants in Jordan created a specifically Jordanian party to address the new political reality in Jordan, which emerged after 1989, to deal with important developments in the Palestinian-Jordanian relationship in the late 1980s, and to rectify what it considered the mistakes committed by Jordanian and Palestinian leftists in Jordan. The party's platform asserts its Jordanian identity but still upholds its belief in the historic and geographic ties between Palestinians and Jordanians. It sees their struggles for liberation as a joint project.

Although party members and leaders have been harassed and jailed, the party has published Nida al-Watan and took part in the 1989 election, winning one seat.

JORDANIAN DEMOCRATIC PROGRESSIVE PARTY (JDPP) (Al-Hizb al-Taqaddumi al-Dimuqratiyya al-Urdunni). The JDPP was formed in 1992 by the Communist Workers Party in Jordan* and the Jordanian Democratic Party.* The party was legalized in January 1993 with 'Ali 'Amir as its secretary-general. It advertised itself as a party of national political realism, which depended upon scientific theories to realize social progress and freedom. It urged the building of a productive economy, support for the Palestinian struggle for statehood, and realization of democratic freedoms for the Arab people. On the international level, the JDPP denounced colonialism, Zionism, racism, and dictatorship. The JDPP published a paper, al-Masirah.

JORDANIAN LIBERAL YOUTH ASSOCIATION (Jama'at al-Shabab al-Ahrar al-Urdunniyyin). This association was established in 1946 by Transjordanian students in Damascus who were influenced by their contact with the opposition leader Subhi Abu Ghanima, then in exile in Syria. Its membership included Dayfullah al-Humud, Khalaf Haddadin, 'Abd al-Rahman Shuqayr, and 'Aqab Khasawna.

The group's agenda included Transjordan's complete independence from Britain, pan-Arab unity, support for the Palestinians' struggle, and political liberalization within Transjordan.

JORDANIAN NATIONAL ALLIANCE PARTY (Hizb al-Tajammu' al-Watani al-Urdunni). This party was legalized in December 1992 with Mijhim Haditha al-Khuraysha as its secretary-general. A nationalist party, it supported the objectives of the Jordanian constitution and defense of Jordanian territory and sovereignty. These broad nationalist goals were buttressed by equally broad calls for respect for individual rights, commitment to democratic principles, and adherence to the sense of belonging to the Arab nation. It won four seats in the 1993 parliamentary elections.

JORDANIAN NATIONAL PARTY (*Al-Hizb al-Watani al-Urdunni*) (I). Little is known about this party except that it was established prior to 1933. It was characterized by two features. The first was extreme Transjordanian nationalism, reiterating the call of "Jordan for Jordanians." It advocated loyalty to Amir 'Abdullah and replacement of non-Transjordanians occupying governmental and administrative positions. However, it welcomed all Arab businessmen to work and invest in Transjordan as long as they did not aspire to political posts. The second feature was its acceptance of the British mandate, although it argued for a reform of the Anglo-Jordanian relationship.

JORDANIAN NATIONAL PARTY (*Al-Hizb al-Watani al-Urdunni*) (II). This party was established as a secret political organization in Damascus by ex-leaders of the Executive Committee of the National Congress Party* who were in exile following government repression in 1936. It boasted the leadership of such influential opposition figures such as Subhi Abu Ghanima, 'Adil al-'Azma, Sulayman al-Sudi al-Rusan, and Muhammad 'Ali al-'Ajluni. The party popularized its views through a dedicated group of Jordanian students in Syria and through declarations in which it attacked traditional tribal leaders and the various governments of the 1940s. It also urged acceptance of the Peel Commission's recommendations for the partition of Palestine and the unification of its Arab portion with Transjordan.

Most significant, it was the first party that attacked the persona of Amir 'Abdullah through a 1938 book entitled *What Did the Amir Leave to Legend?*

JORDANIAN PEOPLE'S PARTY (*Hizb al-Sha'b al-Urdunni*) (I). Formed in March 1927 with Hashim Khayr as president, the Jordanian People's Party was composed of tribal shaykhs and a number of Palestinians and Syrians. The party called for the achievement of independence through peaceful means and had a broad program that included economic and social development and political liberalization. Moreover, it called for immediate Anglo-Jordanian negotiations toward the goal of ending the Mandate. The party helped organize the first national congress in 1928, and later, in 1930, it merged with the Executive Committee of the National Congress Party.*

JORDANIAN PEOPLE'S PARTY (*Hizb al-Sha'b al-Urdunni*) (II). The party was established in May 1947 by 'Abd al-Mahdi Shamayila and Syrian-educated individuals who formed a moderate opposition party calling for a general improvement in socioeconomic and political conditions, increased cooperation with Arab countries, support for Jordanian peasants, placement of nationals in government positions, and (later) modification of the 1946 and 1948 agreements.

The government dissolved the party in July 1947 on the ground that it deviated from legal norms. The true reason was that the party was slowly gaining mass support as a result of the attention it paid to the disadvantaged classes. It briefly resurfaced in October 1952 when it formed a new committee for the improvement of general economic and political conditions, but it soon died out.

JORDANIAN PLEDGE PARTY (Hizb al-'Ahd al-Urdunni). This pro-government, uniquely Jordanian, party was established in 1990 by 'Abd al-Hadi al-Majali to respond to economic and political conditions following the April 1989 riots. It affirmed its Jordanian identity and loyalty to the Hashemite regime. The party popularized itself as a Jordanian center, which aimed at realizing the democratization of the system through respect for the constitution, separation of powers, political pluralism, and respect for civil liberties. The party was legalized in December 1992 under its secretary-general, 'Abd al-Hadi al-Majali. It won two seats in the 1993 elections.

JORDANIAN PROGRESSIVE PARTY (Al-Hizb al-Taqaddumi al-Urdunni). *See* FREEDOM PARTY.

JORDANIAN REVOLUTIONARY PEOPLE'S PARTY (Hizb al-Sha'b al-Thawri al-Urdunni). Established in the 1970s by Burayq al-Hadid and Ahmad Mahmud Ibrahim as a Jordanian branch of the Arab Socialist Workers Party (Hizb al-'Ummal al-Ishtiraki al-'Arabi), the party affirmed its belief in the significance of the Arab cultural and intellectual heritage as a basis for intellectual advancement. It lamented the fall of the Soviet Union and the collapse of the socialist camp, which it felt allowed "imperialist forces," such as the United States, the UN Security Council, and the International Monetary Fund to increase their interference in developing countries. Late in 1993, the party agreed to merge with the Arab Socialist Resurrection (Ba'th) Party—Unified Organization* and two small factions to form a new organization, the National Action Front Party (Hizb Jabhat al-'Amal al-Qawmi). The new party applied for registration in November 1993.

JORDANIAN SOCIALIST ARAB RESURRECTION (BA'TH) PARTY (Hizb al-Ba'th al-'Arabi al-Ishtiraki al Urdunni). The Iraqi wing of the Ba'th Party was established in Jordan by Ahmad al-Najdawi to realize the Ba'thist slogan of "Unity, Freedom, and Socialism." While supporting unity, however, the party upheld the belief in the "specificity" of each Arab country and maintained that only by addressing basic Jordanian interests could it address wider Arab interests. Like the Syrian wing of the party, the Iraqi Ba'th pushed for greater democratization within Jordan. The party was legalized in January 1993 with Taysir Salama al-Humsi as its secretary-general. It ran successfully in the 1993 elections, winning one parliamentary seat.

JORDANIAN SOCIALIST DEMOCRATIC PARTY (JSDP) (Al-hizb al-Dimuqrati al-Ishtiraki al-Urdunni). This party was formed following the defection of a faction of the Jordanian Communist Party (JCP)* headed by 'Isa Mudaynat, and it was legalized in January 1993. Its platform calls for protecting national independence and unity, consolidating democracy through separation of powers, strengthening the powers of parliament, and other measures. The JSDP also urges strengthening and expanding the economy of Jordan, as well as protecting the rights of workers, peasants, women, and youth. The party publishes a newspaper, *al-Fajr al-Jadid*. The JSDP ran in the 1993 elections and won one seat.

JORDANIAN SOLIDARITY PARTY (*Hizb al-Tadamun al-Urdunni*). This short-lived party was established in March 1933 by tribal leaders, city notables, and landowners. A nativist party, the Solidarity Party restricted its membership to pre-1922 residents of Transjordan in order to exclude Syrians and Palestinians. Its broad program focused on protecting citizens' rights and working toward greater national solidarity.

JORDANIAN WORKERS' PARTY (*Hizb al-'Ummal al-Urdunni*). The party was established in September 1931, with the support of the opposition leaders Subhi Abu Ghanima and Shams al-Din Sami, to protect the rights of laborers and peasants. The party's importance stems from the fact that, through members and supporters in the legislative council, it made several proposals calling for the promulgation of a labor law, approval of labor unions, and regulation of employment procedures of foreign companies such as the Iraqi Petroleum Company. This call was repeated in November 1943 by 'Isa 'Awad, who urged compensation for work-related injuries. In both instances, the proposals were met by inaction on the part of the council and the government, both of which sought to protect the interests of large landowners and businessmen in need of labor at low wages. The party eventually ceased to function.

JORDAN NATIONAL UNION (*Al-Ittihad al-Watani al-Urdunni*). This was a short-lived nonideological party established by King Husayn in 1972 as a result of the United Arab Kingdom project that he initiated to unite Jordan and the West Bank. It lasted approximately two years. The party was dissolved because of the Palestinians' rejection of the idea of unity, and because of the death of Wasfi al-Tal, the originator of the project. The party was later renamed Arab National Union.

JORDAN'S LIBERALS PARTY (*Hizb Ahrar al-Urdunn*). This party was formed in about 1922 by ex-members of the Istiqlal* party. It represented Transjordanian intellectuals who felt that neither the Istiqlal nor the Umm al-Qura Party* fulfilled their needs. They accused the first of preoccupation with Syrian concerns and the second of being merely a front for its leader, 'Ali Rida al-Rikabi.

JUSTICE AND PROGRESS PARTY (*Hizb al-Taqaddum Wal-'Adala*). This was a centrist party under the leadership of 'Ali Farid al-Sa'd, which was legalized in January 1993. Its platform called for realization of individual and national goals through scientific planning and a realistic assessment of national, regional, and international factors. It supported a free economy based on private property, freedom of investment, and individual initiative. It also called for deepening democracy and political pluralism.

LIBERATION PARTY (Hizb al-Tahrir). The party was established by Shaykh Taqi al-Din al-Nabhani in November 1952 as a split from the Muslim Brotherhood Society in Jerusalem. The split stemmed from al-Nabhani's close links with Hajj Amin al-Husayni, a violently anti-Hashemite Palestinian nationalist figure (see chapter on the Palestinians), and al-Nabhani's criticism of the Brotherhood for its pro-Hashemite position. He also berated the Brotherhood for presenting what he felt was an "unauthentic" picture of Islam.

The party called for the "comprehensive" application of Islam in Jordan, including the establishment of a democratic, Islamic government, and advocated the revival of Arabo-Islamic civilization and rejection of foreign ideologies. Unlike the Muslim Brotherhood, the Liberation Party incurred the regime's wrath from its inception because it advocated replacing the Hashemite regime with a religiously based government as the first step toward pan-Islamic world unity and because it criticized the regime's pro-Western stance. The party was not allowed to register legally, and its publications, al-Raya and al-Sarih, were banned in 1954. Despite the harassment, it was able to operate underground and to popularize its views through Friday sermons, secret pamphlets, and underground cells. The party even returned an "independent" to the 1954 legislative and eight in 1956, mainly through the support of conservative West Bank towns such as Hebron, Janin, and Tulkarm. Led by 'Atta Abu Rashta, the party at last emerged in public during the liberalizations of 1989.

MAJD. See DEMOCRATIC FRONT ORGANIZATION IN JORDAN.

MODERATE LIBERAL PARTY (Hizb al-Hurr al-Mu'tadil). This short-lived party was established in June 1930 by Rufayfan al-Majali, Hashim Khayr, and other ex-members of the third national congress (May 1930) who split from the Executive Committee of the National Congress Party (ECNCP)* owing to personal differences. They called for a vague program stressing loyalty to the amir and the nation, modification of the Anglo-Transjordanian treaty, improvement of socioeconomic conditions and educational facilities, and protection of civil liberties and the legal rights of each individual. The party lacked cohesion among its members and was dissolved when it was reconciled with the ECNCP in November 1930.

MOVEMENT OF ARAB NATIONALISTS (MAN) (Harakat al-Qawmiyyin al-'Arab). Not strictly a Jordanian party, the MAN was rather a pan-Arab nationalist organization with branches throughout the Arab world. Along with the Ba'th Party,* it was the most significant pan-Arab party of the 1950s and 1960s, differing from the Ba'th largely in its uncompromising support of Egyptian President Gamal Abdel Nasser, the Ba'th's chief rival.

The MAN was established in Beirut after the 1947–49 Arab-Israeli war by several young Palestinian intellectuals, among them George Habash and Wadi' Haddad, both of whom later formed the Popular Front for the Liberation of Palestine, an MAN-inspired Palestinian guerrilla movement (see chapter on the Palestinians). A Jordanian branch of the MAN was established in late 1953 and drew strength from Palestinian intellectuals in the West Bank. The MAN urged the immediate union of Jordan with other Arab states, viewing Jordan's weakness as the result of its detachment from Greater Syria by the British and French in 1921. Extremely hostile to the pro-Western Hashemite monarchy, it was also accused of amassing arms to facilitate an anti-monarchical uprising.

The MAN's popularity lay in the angry slogans of its young leaders. It organized guerrillas to harass Israel and issued fiery statements urging revenge and the reconquest of Palestine. The MAN was avowedly pan-Arab and militantly anti-imperialist. It competed with the Ba'th and the Jordanian Communist Party* for followers, although it operated underground after 1954. It participated in the National Front in 1957 and was strongest in the late 1950s and early 1960s, when Nasser was at the peak of his popularity and the communists and Ba'thists were at their nadir.

The government cracked down on the MAN in the 1960s, and the party fell apart in the aftermath of the Arab defeat of 1967 when the myth of Nasser's invincibility was shattered. (See also chapters on the Arabian Peninsula and the Palestinians.)

MUNADHDHAMAT AL-JABHA AL-DIMUQRATIYYA FI'L-URDUNN. *See* DEMOCRATIC FRONT ORGANIZATION IN JORDAN.

MUNADHDHAMAT AL-JABHA AL-SHA'BIYYA F'IL URDUNN. *See* JORDANIAN DEMOCRATIC POPULAR UNITY PARTY.

MUSLIM BROTHERHOOD ASSOCIATION (*Jama'at al-Ikhwan al-Muslimin*). Established in 1946 by 'Abd al-Latif Abu Qura as an off-shoot of the Egyptian Muslim Brotherhood (founded in the late 1920s by Hasan al-Banna), the Brotherhood has been one of the most significant political movements in Jordan since the 1950s. Although the party was registered as a charitable society and not as a political organization, a major portion of its agenda is political. The Brotherhood believes that Islam is not only a religion and a set of personal ethical guidelines, but is also a complete and comprehensive system addressing spiritual, political, and socioeconomic issues. Its platform reflects this notion of "totality": Jordan must return to "true" Islamic principles and apply the shari'a (Islamic law) as the basis for Jordanian society. Only thereafter can the country move toward social justice and progress. Thus issues such as banning the sale of alcohol and separating men and women in the workplace hold more than just symbolic importance for the Brotherhood; they are steps toward the Islamicization of Jordan, which is itself a prerequisite for total social, political, and economic change.

The history of the organization is one of the most peculiar of any party in Jordan. Because of its vague program and its intent to represent itself as a non-threatening socioreligious organization, it has maintained an interesting courtship with the regime. Under the mandate, it won the support of Amir 'Abdullah as a spiritual organization. King Husayn also gave it his support and even, to an extent, his encouragement to counterbalance the challenge presented by leftist parties in the 1950s. This courtship became apparent after 1957, when all political parties were banned and only the Muslim Brotherhood remained operative. However, in the 1990s the party became a menace to the regime since it adopted the coloring of a political movement and provided a nonleftist alternative for opposition politics. The Brotherhood is one of the only truly mass-based movements in Jordan, deriving considerable strength from poorer, socially conservative areas. It is popular among both Palestinians and Jordanians.

The Brotherhood has enjoyed great success at the polls. Led by Muhammad 'Abd al-Rahman Khalifa in the 1950s and 1960s, it participated in every election successfully, including 1956, when it won four seats. But its most striking victory came in the 1989 election for the national assembly, when, as the only "party" permitted to compete, the Brotherhood staged a vigorous campaign under the slogan "Islam is the Solution." The establishment was stunned at the outcome: The Brotherhood captured twenty-two of eighty seats, the most of any party, and grouped together with ten independent Islamists to form an Islamic bloc. It was subsequently given five of twenty-four portfolios in the government of Mudar Badran, but it boycotted the government of Tahir al-Masri (formed in June 1991) because it opposed Masri's support for U.S.-led peace negotiations in the Middle East.

The Brotherhood's success has been based on addressing the grievances of the day in very general terms, such as abolition of martial law, protection of civil liberties, rejection of Western influence and "Western decadence," support of the Palestinian cause, and rejection of both Marxism and capitalism. The Brotherhood also joined with the left in supporting Iraq during the 1991 Gulf War, a popular stance at the time in Jordan. Several other factors account for its success. For years it operated as Jordan's only legal political "party," although it was formally considered as an "association." The Brotherhood was thus able to establish an effective organizational structure and reach the masses through use of the mosques, Friday sermons, and publications such as *al-Kifah al-Islami* in the 1950s, *al-Manar* in the 1960s, and *al-Rabat* in the 1990s. In 1992, the Brotherhood formed the Islamic Action Front Party* to function as its political wing.

AL-MUTAMAR AL-WATANI. *See* NATIONAL CONGRESS.

NATIONAL ACTION FRONT PARTY. *See* ARAB SOCIALIST RESURRECTION (BA'TH) PARTY—UNIFIED ORGANIZATION; JORDANIAN REVOLUTIONARY PEOPLE'S PARTY.

NATIONAL CONGRESS (NC) (Al-Mutamar al-Watani). The NC, chaired by
Husayn al-Tarawna, was convened on July 25, 1928, to group national opposition
forces together following the ouster of the Istiqlal.* It represented the beginning
of a uniquely Transjordanian political opposition. The Congress did not represent
a mass movement but consisted of some 150 influential landowners, tribal leaders,
and Syrian-educated intellectuals who were influenced by the anti–French liberation movement in Syria.

The Congress drew up a national pact (al-Mithaq al-Watani), a comprehensive
document detailing the views of the nationalist opposition on the political and
economic situation within the country. The demands contained in it focused on
two interconnected dimensions—those related to Transjordan's relations with
Britain and those related to the political process in the country. In terms of
relations with Britain, the nationalists demanded independence based on sovereign equality and the establishment of a constitutional Arab state headed by
'Abdullah, rejection of the Balfour Declaration to establish a national home for
the Jews in Palestine, and decreased British financial control over Transjordan.

Domestically, the Congress demanded separation of powers and the subordination of the executive to the legislature and not to the amir, a modification of
the electoral law, rejection of all exceptional laws, rejection of the legality of
loans and sales of state-land arranged prior to the council's formation, and rejection of any attempt to suppress freedoms. The Congress reiterated the demands
of the pact in letters sent to the British Resident in August 1928, to the High
Commissioner of Palestine in December 1928, and to the League of Nations. In
these letters, the Congress added such demands as replacement of British officials
with nationals, reduction in the military and civil list budget, and objections to
harassment of national leaders and to treaties and laws signed unilaterally by
Britain.

Following its boycott of the 1929 election, the Congress refused to acknowl-
edge the newly elected legislative council since it felt it did not represent the
will of the people. It issued The Black Book in the Jordanian-Arab Issue to spread
its views. However, the boycott of the election was not a unanimous decision
among the members of the Congress; three prominent members participated in
the election and won seats, and they sat in the council. Those who boycotted
the election broke with the Congress and formed a separate party, the Executive
Committee of the National Congress Party* in April 1929. The Congress died
out shortly thereafter.


NATIONAL FRONT PARTY (Hizb al-Jabha al-Wataniyya). The National Front
was an overarching Front composed of the Ba'th,* the Jordanian Communist
Party,* the National Socialist Party,* and the Movement of Arab Nationalists.*
The Front was able to win popular support through a comprehensive platform
calling for pro-Egyptian pan-Arab nationalism, liberation of Palestine, anti-
imperialism, abrogation of the Anglo-Jordanian treaty, and Arabization of the

army. It also pushed for internal democratization and improved standards of living.

Led by the National Socialist Party, the Front attempted to obtain official recognition in 1950 and in 1954, but it was refused on each occasion on the pretext that it advocated violence. However, it still presented ten candidates in the important 1956 election, including seven from the West Bank. The list included a number of communists, such as Rushdi Shahin and Ya'qub Zayadin, as well as prominent nationalists, such as 'Abd al-Rahman Shuqayr. The Front later expelled the Jordanian Communist Party from its ranks in 1958 due to the latter's support of the anti-Egyptian regime of 'Abd al-Karim Qasim in Iraq. The Front disintegrated after the Ba'th party came to power in Syria in 1963.

NATIONAL SOCIALIST PARTY (NSP) (Al-Hizb al-Watani al-Ishtiraki). This was one of the most significant parties during the important years of the 1950s. Established in July 1954, it was a vaguely leftist pan-Arab nationalist party formed by liberal landowners, businessmen, and professionals. It competed with the Ba'th Party* and the Jordanian Communist Party* for votes, but it was less revolutionary than either of these parties because it supported the constitution and did not seek to remove the monarchy.

The Arab nationalist philosophy of the NSP echoed the optimistic pan-Arab currents of the day. Its platform called for achieving independence from foreign domination and forging Arab unity. The party supported union between Jordan and Iraq, which was ruled by a cousin of King Husayn until 1958, as a step toward wider pan-Arab unity. It was also strongly anti-imperialist.

The party's program was greatly influenced by political developments in Jordan in the 1950s, such as the popularity of Gamal Abdel Nasser, the mass demonstrations against the pro-Western Baghdad Pact, and the strident calls for abrogation of the Anglo-Jordanian treaty. Socially, the party stood for a mild form of non-Marxist socialism, stressing vague notions of social justice through redistribution of land and state ownership of major economic sectors. However, it upheld private property and urged the integration of all sectors of society instead of encouraging class conflict.

During the important 1956 election, the party openly called for abrogation of the Anglo-Jordanian treaty, although it failed to clarify other positions and remained a generally disorganized party. Still, it won eleven seats, far more than any other party. Its strong showing in the election can be explained partially through the local prestige of the candidates it presented and partially through the strength of Arab nationalist, anti-Western feeling in Jordan at that time. King Husayn asked the party's new general secretary, Sulayman al-Nabulsi, to form a government. Relations between the new government and the pro-Western king soon began to deteriorate. Husayn issued several warnings in early 1957 expressing his fear of communist influence in Jordan. In contrast, the NSP-led government eventually decided to establish relations with the Soviet Union. The king also sought American aid, which the government bitterly opposed. The struggle between Nabulsi and Husayn reached its climax in April 1957, when the king dissolved the government, survived an unsuccessful coup, banned political parties, and declared martial law.

NATIONAL SYRIAN PARTY. *See* SYRIAN SOCIAL NATIONAL PARTY.

NATIONAL UNION PARTY (*Hizb al-Ittihad al-Watani*). This insignificant party was established in November 1952 with a platform calling for independence and prosperity in Jordan and support for Arab unity.

NC. *See* NATIONAL CONGRESS.

NSP. *See* NATIONAL SOCIALIST PARTY.

PARTI POPULAIRE SYRIENNE. *See* SYRIAN SOCIAL NATIONAL PARTY.

PARTY OF ARAB INDEPENDENCE. *See* ISTIQLAL.

PARTY OF THE NATION (*Hizb al-Umma*). This pro-regime party was formed in July 1954 by Samir al-Rifa'i with a broad platform calling for liberation of Palestine and the Arab world from foreign occupation and improvement of socioeconomic conditions in Jordan. The party ceased functioning in November 1954 in the wake of a crackdown on political expression throughout Jordan.

POPULAR FRONT ORGANIZATION IN JORDAN. See JORDANIAN DEMOCRATIC POPULAR UNITY PARTY.

POPULAR UNITY PARTY—THE UNIONISTS (*Hizb al-Wihda al-Sha'biyya—Al-Wahdawiyyun*). Legalized in December 1992 under the leadership of Talal Harun al-Ramahi, this party claimed to adhere to the goals of the Hashemite-led Arab Revolt of World War I and supported the rule of law and guaranteed freedoms. It also called for improvement in living conditions and employment opportunities.

PROGRESSIVE ARAB RESURRECTION (BA'TH) PARTY (*Hizb Al-Ba'th Al-'Arabi Al-Taqaddumi*). This party was unofficially formed in 1951 as a branch of the Syrian Ba'th party, which was established in 1940 by Michel 'Aflaq and Salah al-Din Bitar. Based on the party's slogan of "Unity, Freedom, and Socialism," the government rejected its petition to form a party in February 1952 on the pretext of radicalism and adoption of violent means. Although its request was also denied in 1953 and 1954, it managed to elect two representatives in the 1950 parliament and three in 1954. In 1955, the party was allowed to organize officially. Thereafter it ran in the 1956 election with sixteen candidates, won fifteen seats, and participated in the coalition government of Sulayman al-Nabulsi when its leader, 'Abdullah Rimawi, was appointed as foreign minister.

This enabled the party to present its nationalist views, which called for Arabization of the army, total independence from Britain, nonalignment, and Arab unity. The party was weakened in 1957 when political parties were banned; however, the party, now associated with the Syrian wing of the Ba'th party, staged a comeback in the 1980s, and it successfully competed in the 1989 election.

The party's support stemmed from intellectuals, students, and liberal professionals, as well as circles within the armed forces. In addition to the party's emphasis on Arab unity and defiance of "imperialist" powers, its supporters were attracted by the party's domestic agenda, which emphasized democratic freedoms, objected to the emergency laws, rejected class conflict, and called for improvement in the economic and social conditions of peasants and workers.

REAWAKENING PARTY (*Hizb Al-Yazaqa*). A nationalist-centrist group, this party was legalized in February 1993 with 'Abd al-Ra'uf al-Rawabda as secretary-general. It stressed consolidation of the national identity of the Jordanian people by deepening awareness of Jordan's history and heritage and developing the country through agricultural and educational development. It also supported democratic freedoms and the constitutional rights of individuals, women, and workers. The party won two seats in the 1993 parliamentary elections.

SSNP. *See* SYRIAN SOCIAL NATIONAL PARTY.

SYRIAN SOCIAL NATIONAL PARTY (SSNP) (*Al-Hizb al-Suri al-Qawmi al-Ijtima'i*) (also called the PARTI POPULAIRE SYRIENNE and the NATIONAL SYRIAN PARTY). The SSNP was established as a pan-Syrian party in the 1930s by a Lebanese, Antun Sa'ada, to promote the unification of Greater Syria, an area which includes today's Syria, Lebanon, Palestine/Israel, and Jordan (the party has included other areas as well over the years). The party played a much greater role in the politics of Syria and Lebanon than Transjordan, but cautiously welcomed Amir 'Abdullah's own advocacy of Greater Syrian unity under the Hashemite crown (see Arab Revival Party).

In July 1951, the Lebanese politician Riyad al-Sulh was assassinated by the SSNP while he was visiting Jordan. Although the killing was allegedly carried out by SSNP agents who had infiltrated from Lebanon, the Jordanian government cracked down on the party in Jordan in 1951–52. Another campaign was launched against the party in 1966. When the party resurfaced in 1990, it was led by Badi' 'Attiya and Hiyat 'Attiya al-Huwayk. However, it did not apply for registration in time for the 1993 elections.

AL-TAJAMMU' AL-DIMUQRATI AL-WIHDAWI. *See* UNIONIST DEMOCRATIC BLOC.

UMM AL-QURA PARTY (*Hizb Umm al-Qura*, Party of Mecca). This party was established in 1922 by 'Ali Rida al-Rikabi during his first term as prime minister of Transjordan. The party's aim was specifically to limit the power and influence of the Istiqlal* party in the administration and in the country. It declared its loyalty to Sharif Husayn (father of Amir 'Abdullah) and his call to liberate and unify the Arab world. Because it was composed mainly of personal followers of al-Rikabi, the party did not survive long after his dismissal.

UNIONIST DEMOCRATIC BLOC (*Al-Tajammu' Al-Dimuqrati al-Wihdawi*). The Bloc was established in 1983 as a semiunderground, center-left party by ex-members of the Ba'th Party* led by a prominent opposition figure, Jamal al-Sha'ir. The party's platform called for increased democratization through a return to parliamentary life, political pluralism, reform of the political party law, and a change in the system of appointments to the upper house of parliament. In its foreign policy, the party called for pan-Arab unity on a confederal basis, unity of the East and West Banks of Jordan, and adoption of a neutralist international policy. With this platform, it was able to attract a following of professors, civil servants, intellectuals, and lawyers. The party emerged in the open in 1989.

In June 1992, al-Sha'ir urged that the party dissolve itself, claiming that its main goals—a return to democratic life in Jordan and the legalization of political parties—had been achieved. He called for the formation of new parties to function on the new political scene in Jordan, and the Bloc tried to join with other like-minded parties, including various branches of the Ba'th Party. The Bloc later selected a new executive committee, headed by Muhammad al-'Uran, which did not include al-Sha'ir. The Bloc was finally dissolved when it united with other parties to form the Democratic Arab Unionist Party—Promise,* which was legalized in February 1993.

**Parties Formed after 1989 (but not registered in time for the 1993 elections) and Leading Figures:**

Arab Nationalist Movement (Ahmad al-'Is'is)

Arab People's Party ('Isa al-Raymuni)

Arab Popular Liberation Movement (Naji 'Allush)

Arab Popular Movement

Arab Revival Party (Taysir 'Amari)

Arab Unity Party

Arab Vanguard Movement (Minwir al-Rimawi)

Democratic Arab Party (Salim al-Zu'bi)

Democratic Justice and Unity Party ('Arif al-'Utayba)

Democratic Work Committees (Muwaffaq Mahadin)

Islamic Arab Rejuvenation Party (Usama 'Aknan)

Islamic Truth Party (Jamal al-Ma'lawani)

Jordanian Communist Party—Temporary Command

Jordanian Democrats Movement

Jordanian al-Khadir Party (Sultan al-Hattab)

Jordanian National Party—Urdunn (Nasib Abu Jabir)

Justice Bloc (Muhammad Khayr al-Kaylani)

Liberation Party, "al-Mu'tazala" Faction (*Shaykh* Amin Faris Dhiyab)

Nasserite Unionists in Jordan (Ahmad al-'Armuti)

National Bloc Party ('Abd al-Fatah Tuqan, Musa al-Sakit, Tha'ir al-'Ajluni)

National Reform Movement

National Union

One Arab Movement

Palestine Communist Party (Yusuf al-Tillawi)

Party of the Nation (Ahmad 'Uwaydi al-'Abbadi)

Popular Democratic Nationalists (Tariq Kayali)

Popular Movement

Progressive National Movement

Promise Movement

Revolutionary March Committees (Muhammad Isma'il al-Nahar al-'Abbadi)

Revolutionary Marxists in Jordan—New Leftist Formation

Salvation Movement (Mashhur al-Haditha)

Unionist Democratic Jordanian Party (Hamad al-Farhan)

Unionist Socialist Movement (Hisham Ghasib)

Unionist Socialist Movement in Jordan—New Leftist Formation

Workers' Party (Muhammad al-Qummayri)

Abla Amawi

# LEBANON

## THE STUDY OF POLITICAL PARTIES IN LEBANON: TOWARD A TYPOLOGY

Although pre-1975 Lebanon was an exception to the repressive regimes in the region, and although political parties were an observable phenomenon of Lebanese political life, studies of Lebanese political parties are nevertheless scarce. The classic study of Michael Suleiman was published in 1968.[1] The minor role that political parties played in Lebanese parliamentary life before the war shifted the attention of scholars away from the mysterious world of Lebanese party politics. In one chapter on political parties written in the mid-1960s, Labib Yamak maintained that "it is doubtful that there is a party system" in Lebanon because political groups are not rationally organized.[2] But it is possible to argue that two different party systems operated in pre-1975 Lebanon. The first, official, system was merely a vehicle for the institutionalization of the leadership of sectarian political bosses, better known as the *zu'ama'*. It is this form of political organization and mobilization that failed to express the aspirations and inclinations of Lebanese groups and, indeed, sectarian communities. Nevertheless, the traditional *zu'ama'*-led political parties, which should be referred to as *kutal* (blocs) rather than parties, were rational political actors that were intended to disguise the basis of the political leadership of the *zu'ama'*. The second system was comparable to party politics in Western democracies. It included parties with well-defined ideologies, sophisticated mechanisms for mobilization, and—at least in some cases—collective leaderships. Most of these parties were active outside the "official" political system due to the nature of the electoral system of the 1950s which favored sectarian *za'im*-like candidates. Moreover, the Lebanese state put its institutions and apparatus at the service of the traditional elite during elections. Most of those antiestablishment parties later transformed their organizations into militias and participated actively in combat in the course of the protracted civil war.

The study of political parties in Lebanon is made more difficult by fragmentation of the system into narrow, sectarian subcultures. Most Lebanese parties mobilize members of a particular sectarian group. This excessive fragmentation requires the introduction of a new typology based on two criteria. The first arises from the sectarian question. Many parties are "single sect-oriented parties." This group includes all the parties that reflect in their actions, policies, and the composition of their membership and leadership the advertised (real or imagined) interests of a single sect. This criterion is not limited to parties with a patently sectarian agenda. Some political parties adhere to an ostensibly secular ideology, although a clear sectarian preponderance characterizes the membership and leadership of the party. Such parties should be regarded as sectarian. (See the List of Lebanese Parties by Ethno-Religious Group and Ideology, which follows the profiles of individual parties, on page 364 ff.)

The second criterion is based on the type of "primary" national identity to which a party adheres. The word primary is used here because identity (in Lebanon and elsewhere in the Arab world) is often manifested in multiple loyalties in a group of concentric circles. The interconnection between group identity and the identity fashioned by the idea of the relatively new Lebanese entity will be examined.

## ORIGINS AND EVOLUTION OF PARTY POLITICS IN LEBANON

The rise of the *iqta'* (often translated, or mistranslated, as feudal) system in the Arab east in the ninth and tenth centuries and the decline of the Islamic center of government reinforced the particularistic feelings of people and strengthened the identification with the family and with the local leader or large landowner. The concentration of families and tribes of one sect into one geographical region in the area of Lebanon, in order to avoid persecution from a Sunni center, provided emotional security to individual members of sects which no alternative organized body could provide.

The beginning of modern political organization and activity in what is today Lebanon can be traced back to the first half of the nineteenth century. Various peasant revolts in the first half of the nineteenth century expressed sentiments influenced by the French Revolution. Crystallization of secular political consciousness, however, was impaired by virtue of the sectarian agitation and mobilization initiated by large landowners and the Maronite church. The first known organizations to appear in Lebanon were of a literary, scientific, and educational nature. The creation of the Mutassarifate of Mount Lebanon in 1861, in the wake of savage massacres between Druzes and Maronites, and the emerging role of Beirut, contributed to an enhanced political role for a rising middle class, which wanted to foster Muslim-Christian ties.

The promulgation of the Ottoman Constitution in 1876 raised the hopes of people in the area and increased political awareness. The demands of the populace were manifested in graffiti and leaflets circulated in the region. One of the leaflets distributed in Beirut and in other Syrian cities in 1880 contained a clear political program, with an emphasis on the necessity of Syrian independence in a state of unity with "our brothers the Lebanese," and an assertion of the Arab linguistic identity of the people.

The nascent revolutionary movement gained new momentum after 1909, with the ascension to power of the Ottoman Committee of Union and Progress in the imperial capital of Istanbul. The Turkification campaigns and the heavy-handed tyranny contributed to the emergence of a strong Arab nationalist movement that sought either full equality of Arabs with Turks, or—in some revolutionary circles—the complete independence of the Arab people.

After World War I, and with new signs of French interests in Lebanon, Lebanese popular organization entered a new era. Gone were the days of temporary Muslim-Christian solidarity. The idea of Lebanon was proposed by various Christian organizations and parties as a Christian nation representing Western culture. The birth of Lebanon's political parties, in a modern sense, stems from the lobbying of various Lebanese immigrant groups outside of Lebanon. Some groups wanted full independence for Lebanon, which meant in effect a French-sponsored, Christian-dominated polity isolated from Syria. Most Muslim groups opted instead for unification with Syria. However, there were no clear-cut sectarian lines of demarcation since many Christians led Arab or Syrian nationalist movements. Thus, in 1919, a group of Lebanese Christians residing in Argentina formed the Democratic National Party, which called for an American-style federalism encompassing Lebanon, Syria, and Palestine.

In this early period, many political movements centered around newspapers and magazines. Thus, supporters of a certain political line, reflected by the editorial policy of a particular newspaper, behaved like members of a political party. Opposition to the idea of a Lebanese entity expressed itself in political organizations that included Syria in their names; supporters of the idea of a Lebanese nation acted through organizations like the Board of Mount Lebanon, which wanted a French-protected Lebanon severed from Syria.

In 1920 France announced the creation of Greater Lebanon, which annexed the north, Beirut, the Biqa', and the south to Mount Lebanon. The 1926 constitution guaranteed French political supremacy. This lasted until 1943, when Lebanon gained its independence partly as the result of World War II. French troops did not evacuate Lebanese territory until three years later. The Lebanese constitution, aside from the provisions dealing with the authority assumed under the League of Nations mandate, remained virtually intact until reforms were introduced in 1990, according to what is now known as the Al-Ta'if Accords.

Under the constitution, the president was "the kingpin of the system."[3] He had the power to negotiate and ratify international treaties, to appoint ministers (including the prime minister), to dissolve the parliament, to veto bills, and to postpone parliamentary meetings. The constitutional reforms of 1990 shifted crucial powers from the hands of the president to the Council of Ministers as a whole. The nomination of the prime minister became the prerogative of the president and speaker of parliament, who both have to defer to the preferences of the deputies. Dissolution of the parliament became the prerogative of the Council of Ministers.

Sectarianism has been the most problematic dimension of Lebanese politics. The vague phraseology of the constitution that "the sects [al-tawa'if] shall be represented equitably in public posts and in the formation of the cabinet without impairing the interest of the state" actually favored the Christians over the Muslims. The sectarian formula, confirmed in 1943 when the so-called National Pact was agreed upon between the Maronite president and the Sunni prime minister, stipulated that the presidency would be reserved to the Maronites, the prime ministership to the Sunnis, and the speakership of parliament to the Shi'ites. Top posts in the government (primarily the military and intelligence posts) went to the Maronites, and Muslims were to accept the Lebanese entity and refrain from seeking unity with Syria (or any larger Arab entity), in return for a Christian promise to refrain from seeking "Western protection."

Although the National Pact was never written down, it survived the turmoil of contemporary Lebanese history, including the civil war. Amendments to the constitution left out the National Pact, which is still accepted as a formula for the distribution of the top government posts among the sects. Instead of the 6: 5 ratio (of Christians to Muslims) in parliamentary representation (which was part of the National Pact), equal representation between Christians and Muslims in parliament was agreed to in the 1990 reforms.

The constitution guarantees freedom of association and freedom to form societies. However, laws pertaining to the licensing of Lebanese political parties are still based on the Ottoman law established in 1909, due to a long-standing reluctance to recognize left-wing political parties. Most Lebanese left-wing political parties were licensed only in 1970 when Kamal Jumblat, the left-leaning, traditional Druze leader who, as minister of interior, insisted on legalizing these organizations.

Lebanese political organization has centered around the personalities of traditional leaders (zu'ama'). During the period of the French mandate, two individual Maronite leaders represented (both theoretically and organizationally) the two main political ideas in the country: Emile Iddi, who served as president before independence and stood for a French-sponsored, French-protected nation; and Bisharah al-Khuri, who became the first president of independent Lebanon and stood for an independent Lebanon with close ties to the Arab world. Both individuals formed parliamentary and extraparliamentary blocs (kutal), which were the major political players until the 1950s. The activities of parliamentary blocs associated with key zu'ama' have always been encouraged.

The domination of Lebanese politics by traditional blocs (kutal) led by zu'ama' has prevented organized or formal political parties from achieving significant development. Table 12 shows representation by political party in parliamentary elections from 1951 to 1972.

The last election prior to the civil war took place in 1972; the al-Ta'if accords called for the appointment of new deputies to fill the seats of the deceased depu-

**Table 12**
**Parliamentary Representation in Lebanon, by Political Party**

| Party | 1951 | 1953 | 1957 | 1960 | 1964 | 1968 | 1972 |
|---|---|---|---|---|---|---|---|
| SSNP | | | 1 | | | | |
| Ba`th | | | | | | | 1 |
| Nasserite Organization | | | | | | | 1 |
| Dashnak | 2 | 2 | 3 | 4 | 4 | 3 | 2 |
| Najjada | | | | 1 | | | |
| PSP | 3 | 2-4 | 3 | 6 | 6 | 5 | 4 |
| Phalanges | 3 | 1 | 1 | 6 | 4 | 9 | 7 |
| National Bloc | 2 | 3 | 4 | 6 | 2 | 5 | 3 |
| National Liberals | | | | 4-5 | 6 | 8 | 7 |
| Democratic Socialist Party | | | | | | | 3 |
| TOTALS | 10 | 8-10 | 12 | 27-28 | 22 | 31 | 28 |

Notes: The number of seats in the Lebanese Parliament was always a multiple of eleven, divided
    according to a ratio of six Christians to five Muslims; in the last several elections, the size of
    the chamber reached ninety-nine. Thus, members of organized parties were a minority in all
    sessions.
  Party names are as follows: PSP: Progressive Socialist Party; Nasserite Organization: Union of
    Forces of the Working People—Nasserite Organization; SSNP: Syrian Social National Party
Source: Adapted from Abdo Baaklini, *Legislative and Political Development: Lebanon, 1842–1972*,
    (Durham, NC: Duke University Press, 1976).

ties and to fill new seats to expand the parliament from 99 to 108 members. In
June 1991, the Council of Ministers appointed forty new deputies with various
party loyalties. New parliamentary elections were held after the civil war in 1992.
The distribution of parties in the new parliament is shown in Table 13. It is important to note that elections are not accurate measures of Lebanese public pref-

**Table 13**
**Party Representation in Lebanon, in the 1992 Election**

| Parties | No. of Deputies |
|---|---|
| Party of God | 8 |
| SSNP | 6 |
| PSP | 4 |
| Amal | 4 |
| Dashnak | 4 |
| Islamic Community | 3 |
| Ba'th Party (Syrian Wing) | 2 |
| Arab Socialist Union | 1 |
| Grouping of Popular Committees and Leagues | 1 |
| Popular Nasserite Organization | 1 |
| Al-Habashi Group | 1 |
| Toilers' League | 1 |
| Arab Democratic Party | 1 |
| Hanchak | 1 |
| Wa'd (Promise) Party | 1 |

Note: Figures are based on a preliminary study by the Beirut-based Institute for Research and Documentation, published in *Al-Hayat*, October 16, 1992.

erences. The representativeness of these deputies in particular is questionable because the Syrian government (and its Lebanese allies) rushed the elections, and the Christian Lebanese community organized a successful boycott of them. Furthermore, there were various irregularities reported in a number of electoral districts.

The 1991 appointments and 1992 elections reflect the growing weight of political parties, particularly those active on the Muslim/leftist side and those aligned with the Syrian regime. While the appointments can not be taken as a measure of Lebanese public opinion after more than fifteen years of civil strife and after the passage of twenty years since the last free election, it can be said that new political players have emerged in Lebanon. The new players, the militias and parties, reflect a segment of the Lebanese public whose membership, with the exception of the Israeli-sponsored South Lebanon Army, has been voluntary. But financial gains and "combat prestige" do help lure the unemployed, uneducated youths of the country into the militias. The longevity of militia rule in Lebanon suppressed the voices of civil society. Only a truly free election can determine the true sentiments and aspirations of the Lebanese people.

The sectarian element remains the strongest determining factor of party politics. Most parties and militias are associated with the interests of a single sect or ethnic group. The behavior and composition of a party are the critical features, whether it preaches nonsectarianism or secularism. The elitist nature of party politics has also not been altered by the civil war. In his classic study of political parties, Robert Michels maintains that "at the outset, leaders arise spontaneously; their functions are accessory and gratuitous. Soon however, they become professional leaders, and in this second stage of development they are stable and irremovable."[4] In Lebanon, however, parties, as well as traditional blocs, have been founded to perpetuate the influence of a leader within his own sectarian community and within his parliamentary clique. Clear-cut distinctions often cannot be drawn between the "party" and the "bloc."[5] Furthermore, elitism in party structure cuts across ideological lines; while the traditional leadership of the zu'ama' is rejected by Lebanese leftist groups, all types of parties suffer from an unusually high allegiance to the personality of the party leader, which hinders popular participation in policy-making. It is customary to treat the hero-idol of every party with special glorification.

The militia leadership, or war elite, has now eclipsed some sectarian zu'ama', but many zu'ama' of the Maronite and Christian community have remained powerful players. In some cases, new zu'ama' are sons and nephews of old or deceased leaders. Thus, for example, Walid Jumblat inherited his father's position as leader of the Druze community and head of the Progressive Socialist Party.* Dani Sham'un inherited his father's position as head of the National Liberal Party,* and when Dani was assassinated in 1990, he was succeeded by his brother Duri. The new war elite has its own style and its own preferences, but the pattern of traditional leadership, based upon primordial ties and sectarian allegiances, has not been broken. In the Shi'ite community, however, traditional leadership seems to have been a major loser from the war. New leadership has emerged with no ties to the traditional large landowning families of South Lebanon and the Biqa' valley where Shi'ites predominate.

The parties will be studied first in relation to a standard criterion to inform comparatively about the reality of each of the parties under study and second in terms of its own peculiarities.

## Bibliography

Abou-Jaber, Kamel. *The Arab Ba'ath Socialist Party: History, Ideology, and Organization.* Syracuse, N.Y.: Syracuse University Press, 1966.

Aboujaoude, Joseph. *Les partis politiques au Liban.* Kaslik: Bibliothèque de l'Université Saint-Esprit, 1985.

Abukhalil, As'ad. "Druze, Sunni, and Shi'ite Political Leadership in Present-Day Lebanon." *Arab Studies Quarterly* (Fall 1985).

———. "Ideology and Practice of Hizb-ul-Lah in Lebanon: The Islamization of Leninist Organizational Principles." *Middle Eastern Studies* 27, 3 (July 1991), pp. 390–404.

Abu Shaqra, Yusuf. *Al-Harakat fi Lubnan* (The Movements in Lebanon). Beirut: N.p., n.d..

Ajami, Fouad. *The Vanished Imam: Musa al-Sadr and the Shia of Lebanon.* Ithaca, N.Y.: Cornell University Press, 1986.

Al-Akhdar, Al-'Afif. *Al-Tandhim Al-Thawri Al-Hadith* (The Modern Revolutionary Organization). Beirut: Dar al-Tali'ah, 1976.

Bayhum, Muhammad Jamil. *Al-Ittijtihat al-Siyasiyya fi Lubnan min al-'intidab ila al-'Ihtilal* (Political Orientations in Lebanon from the Mandate to Occupation). Beirut: Jam'iat Bayrut al-'Arabiyyah, 1977.

Dakrub, Muhammad. *Judhur al-Sindiyanah al-Hamra'* (Roots of the Red Oak Tree). Beirut: Dar al-Farabi, 1974.

Deeb, Marius. *Militant Islamic Movement in Lebanon: Origins, Social Basis, and Ideology.* Washington, D.C.: Georgetown University's Center for Contemporary Arab Studies, Occasional Papers Series, 1986.

Dhibyan, Sami. *Al-Haraka Al-Wataniyya al-Lubnaniyya* (The Lebanese National Movement). Beirut: Dar al-Masirah, 1977.

Entelis, John. *Pluralism and Party Transformation in Lebanon: Al-Kata'ib, 1936–1970.* Leiden, Netherlands: E. J. Brill, 1975.

Hariq, Diyya. *Man Yahkum Lubnan?* (Who Rules Lebanon?). Beirut: Dar Al-Nahar, 1972.

Hudson, Michael C. *The Precarious Republic.* New York: Random House, 1968.

Ibrahim, Muhsin. *Limatha Munadhdhamat al-Ishtirakiyyin al-Lubnaniyyin?* (Why the Lebanese Socialist Organization?). Beirut: Dar al-Tali'ah, 1970.

Ishtay, Faris. *Al-Hizb al-Taqaddumi al-Ishtiraki wa Dawruhu fi-l-Siyasa-I-Lubnaniyya, 1949–1975* (The Progressive Socialist Party and its Role in Lebanese Politics, 1949–1975). 3 vols. Al-Mukhtarah: Al-Dar al-Taqaddumiyya, 1989.

Kubaysi, Basil. *Harakat al-Oawmiyyin al-'Arab* (The Movement of Arab Nationalists). Beirut: Dar al-Tali'ah, 1974.

Lebanese Ministry of Information. *Qadiyyat al-Hizb al-Qawmi* (The Case of the [Syrian Social] National Party). Beirut: Ministry of Information, 1949.

Mokdessi, Toufic, and Lucien George. *Les partis Libanais en 1959.* Beirut: L'Orient et al-Jarid, n.d.

Al-Nadi Al-Thaqafi al-'Arabi (Arab Cultural Club). *Al-Qiwa al-Siyasiyya fi Lubnan* (Political Forces in Lebanon). Beirut: Dar al-Tali'ah, 1970.

Norton, Augustus Richard. *Amal and the Shi'a: Struggle for the Soul of Lebanon*. Austin: University of Texas Press, 1987.

Rondot, Pierre. *Les institutions politiques du Liban*. Paris: L'Institut d'Etudes de L'Orient Contemporain, 1947.

Shruru, Fadl. *Al-Ahzab wa-l-Tandhimat wa-l-Qiwa-l-Siyasiyya fi Lubnan, 1930–1980* (Political Forces, Organizations, and Parties in Lebanon, 1930–1980). Beirut: Dar al-Masirah, 1981.

Suleiman, Michael. *Political Parties in Lebanon: The Challenge of a Fragmented Political Culture*. Ithaca, N.Y.: Cornell University Press, 1967.

Tabbarah, Bahige. *Les forces politiques actuelles au Liban*. Grenoble, France: These, 1954.

## Political Parties

ALWIYAT AL-SADR. *See* BRIGADES OF AL-SADR.

AMAL MOVEMENT *(Harakat al Amal)*. The original full name of this organization is *Harakat al-Mahrumin* (Movement of the Disinherited*). After 1978 the movement became known by the acronym of its militia *Afwaj al-Muqawama al-Lubnaniyya* (Detachments of Lebanese Resistance): AMAL. Amal also means "hope" in Arabic.

Any discussion of this movement should begin with its founder, Musa al-Sadr.[6] Al-Sadr was born in Iran, where he received his religious training. He relocated to Lebanon (his ancestral home) in 1959 and later received Lebanese citizenship.[7] His leadership of the Lebanese Shi'ites was the product of deep social problems within the community. In Norton's words, "Lebanon's Shi'as have been considered the most disadvantaged confessional group in the country. By most, if not all, of the conventional measures of socio-economic status, the Shi'as fare poorly in comparison to their non-Shi'a cohorts."[8] By the end of the 1960s, Musa al-Sadr became one of the most influential religio-political leaders in Lebanon. He constantly pressed the Shi'ite agenda, and he successfully challenged the political dominance of the traditional Shi'ite establishment.

In 1969 Musa al-Sadr's leadership was boosted when he was elected chairman of the Higher Islamic Shi'ite Council, which he himself had helped to create. This council intended to press for a separate Shi'ite agenda and, more important, to separate the Shi'ite agenda in Lebanon from the general Islamic agenda, which was championed by the traditional Sunni elite. By creating the council, Musa al-Sadr wanted to nourish the separate Shi'ite consciousness of the masses, which was helpful in political mobilization, given the masses' disillusionment with the traditional Muslim elite. Al-Sadr's chairmanship of the council also signaled the decline of the Shi'ite traditional elite, especially Kamil al-As'ad.

Al-Sadr's agenda was concerned primarily with the cause of South Lebanon. The residents of the south, who are overwhelmingly Shi'ite, suffered from the consequences of the Israeli-Palestinian war in their region. The Israelis, using the pretext of retaliation, did not distinguish in their bombing raids between civilian and military targets, or between Lebanese and Palestinians. The Israeli government took it upon itself to punish Lebanon and its people—not to mention Palestinian civilians in Lebanon—for Palestinian military and political activity in Lebanon. The destruction and the death toll in the south, in particular, became a national scandal as the Lebanese government refrained from taking any action against Israel, or in defense of the people of the south. There was a widespread perception in the south that the Lebanese government was unwilling, rather than unable, to protect the south. The Shi'ites resented the slogan raised by Lebanese president Charles Hilu (1964–70) who insisted that "Lebanon's strength lies in its weakness."

Al-Sadr stressed the plight of the southern Lebanese, and he also called attention to the general poverty of Shi'ites in Lebanon. He also criticized the government's neglect of the south, which alienated many Shi'ites. This alienation led to their attraction to radical Palestinian and Lebanese organizations. Leftist and ostensibly secular organizations appealed to the oppressed Shi'ites, who desperately sought to change their conditions. It was expedient for the Shi'ites to join the secular organizations, since sectarianism was basically to the advantage of the Maronite-Sunni elite, who had designed the National Pact. This political calculation can explain how and why thousands of Shi'ites later left their secular Palestinian and Lebanese organizations to join the various religiously oriented organizations that later took the helm of the Shi'ite political leadership. The radical ideologies addressed the growing Shi'ite resentment, which was ignored by the central government and the traditional Shi'ite leadership.

Al-Sadr articulated Shi'ite sentiments and began calling for immediate reforms in the Lebanese political system and for the defense of the southern Lebanese against Israeli military attacks. By 1972 al-Sadr had assumed a clearly political role. He made his political preferences clear in the election that year. More important, he realized how fascinated Shi'ites were with the notion of "armed struggle." Al-Sadr began to organize a militia of his own, although he claimed that he was merely helping the Shi'ites to defend themselves against Israeli aggression. The militia was originally supported and funded by the Fatah movement and by Syria, through its Palestinian organization, al-Sa'iqa, presumably to confront and limit the strong sweeping leftist tide in Lebanon, which al-Sadr and the two Palestinian organizations feared. (See also Islamic Amal Movement; Movement of the Disinherited.)

ARAB DEMOCRATIC PARTY (Al-Hizb al-'Arabi al-Dimuqrati). The origins of this 'Alawite-oriented party can be traced back to 1975, when 'Ali 'Id, a local 'Alawite leader from the Tripoli area who headed a small organization called Harakat al-Shabab al-'Alawi (the Movement of the 'Alawite Youths), founded the Confrontation Front along with Sunni deputy Talal al-Miri'bi and Shi'ite activist Suhayl Hamadah. The front, closely aligned with the Syrian army in Lebanon, benefited from the close ties between 'Id and key officials in Damascus.

The front's militia was nicknamed the Pink Panthers, and its fighters were notorious for their thuggery. The party, along with other pro-Syrian organizations in Lebanon, was subject to a crackdown in 1976 by the joint forces of the Palestine Liberation Organization (PLO) and the Lebanese National Movement.* The Syrian military intervention in the same year, however, brought out all those organizations from internal and external exile. The front's name was changed in the mid-1980s to the Arab Democratic Party. 'Ali 'Id was appointed a deputy in 1991.

ARAB LIBERATION PARTY. See PARTY OF ARAB LIBERATION.

ARAB SOCIALIST RESURRECTION (BA'TH) PARTY (Hizb al-Ba'th al-'Arabi al-Ishtiraki). The origins of the Ba'th party in Lebanon go back to the 1950s, when it emerged as an active player in radical Lebanese politics. The Ba'thists, a growing opposition force in the country, were included in the broad front of "progressive and nationalist" organizations headed by Kamal Jumblat. Lebanese Ba'thists held their founding congress in 1956 and elected a local leadership. The split between the pro-Iraqis and the pro-Syrians was finalized in 1964, when supporters of the "radical" faction of the Iraqi Ba'th party met in Beirut and elected a provisional national command. The new command drew the support of some leading Lebanese Ba'thists, although it was opposed by party founder Michel Aflaq. After the 1966 coup in Syria, the Ba'th party in Lebanon became almost entirely dominated by pro-Iraqi activists. Nevertheless, there was always a small, insignificant faction that pledged allegiance to Damascus.

In the 1972 parliamentary election, the pro-Iraqi Ba'thist leader, 'Abdul-Majid al-Rafi'i, was elected to a seat in Tripoli. Another pro-Iraqi Ba'thist sympathizer, 'Ali al-Khalil, was elected to parliament from Tyre. The Ba'th was very active in the south and utilized generous Iraqi aid for its own party activities and propaganda. Many newspapers and magazines espoused its line. The party, like the pro-Syrian party, which adds the word munadhdhamat (organization) to the full name of the Ba'th party to distinguish itself from the pro-Iraqi party using the same party name, participated in the civil war. The pro-Iraqi faction suffered a setback in 1976 in the wake of the Syrian miliary intervention in Lebanon, when the Syrian army forced all pro-Iraqi Ba'thists either to flee abroad or go underground. Some were assassinated. Al-Rafi'i, who still heads the pro-Iraqi faction, still resides abroad. The small pro-Syrian faction benefits from Syrian influence in the country. In 1991 'Abdallah al-Amin, the current leader of the pro-Syrian faction, was appointed to the parliament along with two other leading members from the north. Al-Amin also served in the cabinet.

ARAB SOCIALIST UNION (Al-Ittihad al-Ishtiraki al-'Arabi). There are literally dozens of small, Sunni-oriented organizations that use this name. They all agree on allegiance to Gamal Abdel Nasser's legacy but disagree on everything else. The main organization, formally established in 1975, was headed by 'Umar Harb,

308 / Political Parties of the Middle East

Hasan Shalhah, and Abdur-Rahim Murad, who was appointed to parliament in 1991. The efforts of Libya, the main patron of Nasserite groups in Lebanon, to unite all Nasserites in Lebanon failed over the years. This organization benefited from Libyan aid to engage in social programs in the Biqa'. It participated in the civil war on the side of the Lebanese National Movement.*

The union held a general congress in 1979, which developed sophisticated organs and tried to institute democratic procedures. It continued to have special ties with Libya, and formed good ties with revolutionary Iran. One leader of the movement, Hasan Sabra, left it in the early 1980s, and founded the weekly magazine Al-Shira', which broke the Iran-Contra scandal. The movement, however, was never able to attain a mass appeal.

ARAB SOCIALIST UNION (THE NASSERITE ORGANIZATION) (Al-Ittihad al-Ishtiraki al-'Arabi [al-Tandhim al-Nasiri]). This is a splinter group of the main Arab Socialist Union. It split off from the latter in 1976, was led by Munir al-Sayyad, and was confined to the Sunni quarter of 'Ayn al-Muraysah.

ARMENIAN SECRET ARMY FOR THE LIBERATION OF ARMENIA (ASALA). This small, secretive organization, founded in January 1975, has attracted ultraleftist Armenian activists. This organization has engaged in violent attacks against Turkish interests around the world in pursuit of its strategy of "armed struggle." The party has been active in Lebanon in attacking Turkish interests and individuals. In 1980 the party began to publish its own newspaper. The party has aligned itself with Lebanese and Palestinian leftist organizations and has reportedly received financial and military aid from them.

ASALA. See ARMENIAN SECRET ARMY FOR THE LIBERATION OF ARMENIA.

BA'TH PARTY. See ARAB SOCIALIST RESURRECTION (BA'TH) PARTY.

BRIGADES OF AL-SADR ('Alwiyat al-Sadr). This organization announced itself after 1978, when Musa al-Sadr disappeared while on a visit to Libya. It claimed responsibility for various violent attacks aimed at Libyan interests.

COMMUNIST ACTION ORGANIZATION (Munadhdhamat al-'Amal al-Shuyu'i). This is the second most influential Communist party in Lebanon. It started as a radical alternative to the Communist Party of Lebanon (LCP)* but later changed its stance to become indistinguishable from the LCP. The organization was born as a result of the merger in 1969 of the Organization of Lebanese Socialists (which split off from the Movement of Arab Nationalists) and the Organization of Socialist Lebanon (a splinter group of the Ba'th Party*). It was led by Muhsin Ibrahim, whose leftist criticism of George Habash led to the collapse of the Movement of Arab Nationalists. Muhsin Ibrahim, one of the most skilled pamphleteers and polemicists in the entire Arab world, came to dominate the organization. The organization was officially set on foot in a founding congress in May 1971. The Organization of Socialist Lebanon provided the new organization with effective and experienced cadres who had a long experience in the recruitment of students and teachers. As soon as the organization was founded it suffered from defections and factionalism, which limited its size and effectiveness.

The organization purged its ranks and introduced more centralization. It benefited from Ibrahim's ties to Kamal Jumblat, which ensured a prominent political role for Ibrahim in leftist Lebanese politics. The organization soon abandoned its past radical leftist stance. It dismissed the LCP as a reformist party and adopted an orthodox communist line. By 1975 the organization forged an alliance with the LCP and participated in combat. Ibrahim's close ties to Yasir Arafat provided the organization with resources beyond its limited means. After 1982 the organization was one of the few to remain supportive of Arafat's Fatah. It has never expanded in size, and it has never had a mass appeal. In recent years, its relations with the LCP have worsened.

COMMUNIST PARTY OF LEBANON (LCP) (*Al-Hizb al-Shuyu'i al-Lubnani*). The LCP is one of the oldest parties in Lebanon. The embryonic formation of the party can be traced back to the early 1920s when socialist, romantic writers used a local literary newspaper in Zahlah to express ideas of "class brotherhood, respect for the poor and the humble, and opposition to monopoly companies."[9] The newspaper, *al-Sahafi al-Ta'ih*, became the voice of dedicated socialist writers who were at pains to avoid offending religious authorities and to assert that the messages of Jesus and Muhammad were consistent with socialism. The death of V. I. Lenin provided an opportunity for a middle-level employee at the Beirut port, Yusuf Ibrahim Yazbak, to inform readers about the contributions of Lenin and to glorify his work and actions. But the creation of the Communist party in Lebanon (and Syria) was the result of the efforts of three individuals: Fu'ad al-Shimali (a Lebanese activist worker who was expelled from Egypt for his revolutionary activities), Yusuf Ibrahim Yazbak, and a Bolshevik envoy. So the creation of the party was partly spontaneous and partly the direct result of Comintern activity.

The party, officially founded in October 1924, comprised both workers and intellectuals. It deliberately decided to camouflage its ideology by adopting the name Lebanese People's Party, and Fu'ad al-Shimali was chosen as its first secretary-general. The party made itself known to the public in a May 1 celebration in 1925 in Beirut, where reformist proposals dealing with the workers' welfare were presented. The successful celebration prompted Yazbak to publish a new newspaper devoted to the communist cause, but it was soon banned. The outbreak of the Syrian revolt against the French in 1925 was enthusiastically received by the Lebanese communists who began circulating leaflets and agitating against the French army. The French authorities cracked down against party cells and arrested Shimali and other leaders. Yazbak fled to France where he made contacts with French communists.

The party continued its campaigns of secret agitation and mobilization but faced serious problems in recruitment. A Party report in 1928 indicated that 60 percent of its members were Armenians, and complained of the difficulty of glorifying the proletariat in a society that had the largest section of its workers in the agricultural—not the industrial—sector of the economy. The party decided to focus more on agricultural workers and started attacking the authority of large landowners and the clerical authorities.

The party was transformed in 1930, when Khalid Bakdash became a leading member and began a movement to Arabize the party. This led to a conflict between Arab members of the party and Jewish envoys of the Comintern, who were active in the communist movement in Palestine. In 1932 Khalid Bakdash succeeded in replacing Shimali as the leader. While the party continued to suffer from persecution and oppression, its leaders focused on the translation into Arabic of the major works of Marxism-Leninism.

The party's credibility declined when it softened its stance toward France as a result of the ascension of Leon Blum's socialist government in France in the 1930s. The party gained official recognition, and its leaders were allowed to operate openly for the first time. Their credibility was further undermined when they supported the cession of Alexandretta to Turkey. Nevertheless, the party continued to champion workers' rights and to call attention to the plight of the Palestinians who were struggling against the Zionist movement. The party also was interested in developing a solution to the problems of minorities in the Arab world, and party leaders advocated a democratic arrangement to absorb the various ethnic and confessional minorities in the region.

The beginning of World War II ushered in a new round of arrests and persecution against the communists, which did not end until 1943. In the first national party congress, the Syrian Communist Party leadership decided to split into a Lebanese and a Syrian party, and each began to develop its own independent institutions. The split was imperative for the Lebanese communists to end the tyrannical rule of Khalid Bakdash, who was notorious for promoting his personality cult in the party, and for ignoring opinions other than his own.

The most fateful crisis of the Arab communist movement was posed by the Palestinian problem. The subservience of the Arab communist movement to the Stalinist leadership in the Soviet Union led Arab communist parties to support the 1947 partition plan of Palestine, which discredited communism in Arab eyes. The party also argued against Arab nationalism, which was a position that the party later regretted. The party started to focus on working within the Lebanese political system by fielding candidates for parliamentary elections. It was not, however, able to win a parliamentary seat although some of its candidates in Beirut, in the north, and the south polled large numbers of votes. The party was compromised by virtue of Khalid Bakdash's continued interference in internal party affairs, and the leadership was regarded as dependent on Bakdash and the Soviet Union, which looked upon the unpopular Bakdash as the ideal Arab communist leader.

The party engaged in various political and social struggles in the 1950s, and it was at the forefront of anticorruption campaigns and the struggle against Western policies in the Middle East. Another crisis occurred in 1958, when it was decided to oppose the popular leadership of Gamal Abdel Nasser and to label his creation, the United Arab Republic, a mistake. This position cost the party members, and it cost the party its own leader, who was arrested by the internal security services of the United Arab Republic, for murdering party leader Farajallah al-Hilu by immersion in acid.

In the 1960s, the party began witnessing a new phenomenon: Factions began forming and eventually splitting from the organization. In 1964 a group of party militants expressed their identification with the Chinese line of communism and later formed the pro-Chinese Socialist Revolution Party. Another faction, which comprised veteran party leaders, split in 1964–65 and formed what was known as the Ila al-'Amam (Forward) group, which condemned the personality cult in the party and other bureaucratic ills. This group later merged with the Union of Lebanese Communists (headed by Nasib Nimr), which never succeeded in gaining a mass following. Although it continued to exist up until the civil war, it was confined to a handful of intellectuals. Another split occurred in 1966, when two leading members, Hasan Quraytim and Sawaya Sawaya, split off in disagreement with the party's analysis of the Intra Bank crisis. In the midst of these organizational crises, the party began to focus on broadening its circle of alliances and valued the struggle within a broad front that would comprise the "progressive and national" parties in Lebanon.

The party held its second national congress in 1968. The new congress elevated a new, youthful leadership (which would take over at the outset of the civil war in 1975), and tried to adjust the party's ideology to the public mood. The party began grudgingly to support the Palestinian revolution as a way to solve the Palestinian problem after years of opposing "armed struggle." This change was more the result of the public climate in the wake of the defeat in the 1967 war. The party never advocated a radical solution to Lebanese problems; instead, it adopted what its leftist critics rightly called the reformist approach. The party called for a series of reforms in the Lebanese political system that were consistent with the platforms of other parties in the Lebanese National Movement.* Furthermore, the party believed in the efficacy of change within the Lebanese system. Thus, elections were considered to be an appropriate vehicle for progressive change in Lebanon. The party, however, continued to adhere to Marxism-Leninism in its literature. The subservience of the party to the Soviet Union was, by the late 1960s, less the disadvantage that it had been in the 1940s and 1950s, and became a political asset given the popularity of the Soviet Union as "a friend of the Arabs."

The party participated in the civil war and created its own militia, which participated on various fronts. The LCP, unlike other parties in Lebanon, was successful in creating cells in all areas of Lebanon including East Beirut, although the Phalangists banned communist activity from areas under their control after 1975. Also, the war heralded the emergence of a new leadership in 1975 with the rise of George Hawi as the most powerful man in the party. Hawi was no less dogmatic or Stalinist than the old leadership, but he was far more supportive of the Palestinian revolution and the Arab nationalist cause.

While the party was started by a multisectarian group of intellectuals and workers, it had become a strong vehicle for Shi'ite radicalization as early as the 1950s. The Shi'ite composition of the membership was visible not only in the composition of the membership, but also in the very discourse of the party. The term *mahrumin* (deprived) was, for example, used by party leaders to depict the lot of the people and villages in South Lebanon. The sectarian affiliation of those who voted for party leader Niqula al-Shawi in the 1972 election for a seat in Tripoli reveals a differential in the various polling places. For example, he obtained heavy support from the 'Alawites of Tripoli (around 45 percent of their votes), while the support in Maronite polling places declined to 4.4 percent and 3.2 percent.

It is not possible to conduct an empirical study of the exact sectarian composition of the membership of the LCP because the party does not release information on the subject. The question is made more difficult by the multisectarian composition of its ruling body, the Central Committee. But leadership of political parties in Lebanon has never been reflective of the parties' real composition. Members of ruling bodies are often chosen for propaganda purposes. The only record of the sectarian characteristics of the LCP was found in a study conducted by a party organization. The study presented figures on the social and economic characteristics of a random sample of party martyrs, defined as card-carrying members who died—not necessarily in combat situations—between 1975 and December 31, 1980. The findings of the survey are summarized in Table 14.

Interestingly, when the party conducted a similar survey of party martyrs who died between 1980 and 1987, no mention was made of sectarian affiliation. However, although Shi'ites constitute the overwhelming majority of members, Christians still constitute a disproportionate percentage. Of the Central Committee members elected in the Fifth Party Congress in February 1987, Christian members constituted 43.59 percent.[10] The percentage of Christians in the leadership was resented by some party members, who were pushing for Islamicization of the party. Secretary-general George Hawi was accused of stacking leading bodies with his Greek Orthodox coreligionists.

In the course of the preparation of the Fifth Party Congress, the party witnessed a strong sectarian schism. There was a strong movement within the party, initiated by Shi'ite members, to replace George Hawi with the Shi'ite leader Karim Muruwwah. A recent Central Committee was still split along sectarian lines; George Hawi headed a faction that comprised most of the Christians; Karim

Table 14
Sectarian Affiliation of Communist Party Martyrs in Lebanon

| Sect | Percentage |
|---|---|
| Druzes | 6 |
| Shi`ites | 58 |
| Sunnis | 7.5 |
| Armenians | 4.5 |
| Greek Orthodox | 9 |
| Greek Catholics | 3 |
| Maronites | 7.5 |
| Others | 4.5 |

Source: *Al-Nida*, September 21, 1986, pp. 34–36.

Muruwwah, assistant secretary-general (who called for a marriage between Marxism and Shi'ism), headed a Shi'ite faction. But many leftist parties appear to enjoy a Shi'ite presence in their membership due to the appeal of radical ideologies among Shi'ites in Lebanon.

While the party prepared for its Sixth Party Congress, events in Eastern Europe and the Soviet Union affected the policies of the party. The party was now embarrassed by its Marxist legacy, and LCP leader George Hawi insisted that the party was not atheistic but that it stood for faith. It was possible that the party might change its name back to the 1924 name of the People's Party to rid itself of the stigma of communism. It was also engaged in a political initiative that aimed at reconciliation with the enemies of the past, including the right-wing parties. It was further possible that the new congress might replace Hawi, who was criticized for his lavish life-style and corruption.

CONSTITUTIONAL BLOC (*Al-Kutla al-Dusturiyya*). This organization was founded in 1936 by Bisharah al-Khuri and his supporters, who demanded Lebanese independence from France. Bisharah al-Khuri became the first president after independence, and the bloc became one of the most influential political parties (or, more accurately, a *za'im* bloc). The bloc continued to play a political role until the 1960s. It does not play any political role today, although Bisharah's son, Khalil, who has lived in France since the beginning of the civil war, still considers himself leader of the party.

THE COURSE, OR PATH (Al-Nahj). This parliamentary (and extraparliamentary) bloc supported Fu'ad Shihab in the 1960s and 1970s. It has no political role in present-day Lebanon.

DASHNAK PARTY. The Dashnak Party was founded in 1890 in Tiflis in Russia to call attention to the conditions of Armenians living under Ottoman rule. Although the party began as a revolutionary organization, it "is no longer revolutionary nor a federation."[11] The Lebanese Dashnak Party also parted ways with the original ideology of socialism. It stands for the free enterprise system, and it is considered to be part of the right-wing, Maronite-oriented establishment. The party opposes Marxism and rejects ideologies that seek to transcend nationalism.

The membership of this party is exclusively Armenian, and it has become the major voice for Lebanese Armenians. It operates in all areas of Lebanon where Armenians reside (mostly in and around Beirut and in the Biqa'). This party has been able to recruit from various social classes, although its leadership is indistinguishable from the Armenian political and economic elite. On the Lebanese ideological spectrum, the party is considered rightist because of its historical alliance with the Maronite establishment. Most Armenian deputies and ministers have been either members of or sympathizers with this party.

The party came under pressure in the late 1970s and early 1980s from the leadership of the Lebanese Forces,* which wanted it to contribute more to "the war effort." The Armenian leadership chose to take a moderate stance in the course of the war to avoid antagonizing any of the Lebanese groups. The party refused to create its own militia, although individual members of the party participated in the war, mostly on the side of the Maronite-oriented organizations.

DEMOCRATIC SOCIALIST PARTY (Al-Hizb al-Dimuqrati al-Ishtiraki). This is not really a party; it is more a body for the followers of traditional Shi'ite za'im Kamil al-As'ad, who held the speakership of parliament from 1970 to 1984. Al-As'ad was fearful of the growing popularity of leftist organizations among Shi'ites in the late 1960s and early 1970s, so he decided to organize his own following. He developed a party from one that his father (another traditional za'im in his time) had developed in the 1940s, and he gave it a socialist name, although he himself is known to be a conservative, right-wing, large landowner who has become a symbol of insensitivity to the plight of the poor. Al-As'ad wanted to compete with the rhetoric of the left and that of Musa al-Sadr. With Syrian help, al-As'ad also formed a militia for the party.

The only significance of the party is that it belonged to a traditional leader who dominated Shi'ite politics for decades. Those who needed al-As'ad's help for the attainment of jobs and services were forced to join the party. Al-As'ad continued to play an important political role until 1982, when he reversed his earlier decision and agreed to hold a presidential election with Israeli forces occupying large parts of Lebanon. It was widely reported at the time that Bashir Jamayyil's camp paid several millions to al-As'ad as a bribe to facilitate the election of Bashir as president. Syria never forgave him for his role in that election, and supported his rival Husayn al-Husayni in the 1984 election for speakership of parliament. The party was no longer significant in the politics of Lebanon in the 1990s, although it held its first meeting in years in 1990 at its Beirut headquarters.

EAGLES OF AL-BIQA' (Nusur al-Biqa'). This small, obscure organization was formed by 'Ali Hamadah, the son of the late Shi'ite za'im Sabri Hamadah, who held the speakership of parliament for years. Hamadah basically attempted to compete with the militias of the PLO and the LNM in the Biqa'. The party failed to attract any substantial following, and the family went into political eclipse.

FITYAN 'ALI. See THE YOUTHS OF 'ALI.

FORCES OF MARADA (Quwwat al-Marada). This is more a militia of the powerful Franjiyyah family in Zgharta-'Ihdin than a party. It had its origins in the Zgharta Liberation Army, which was founded in 1968. This militia benefited in 1970 from the election of Sulayman Franjiyya (the head of the Franjiyya family confederation) as president of the republic. Sulayman supplied his own militia from the warehouses of the Lebanese army. In 1975 all the important families of Zgharta decided to support the militarization of the populace, and the Zgharta Liberation Army was renamed Liwa' al-Marada (the Brigade of al-Marada), while other "brigades" were formed with names given to them by the various large families in the north Lebanon region. Al-Marada is the name of the historical (and partly mythical), tough Maronite fighters who inhabited the northern area of Mount Lebanon. This organization participated actively in the civil war, particularly in the front against Tripoli, which was dominated by a coalition of Muslim, leftist, and Palestinian forces.

With the rise of the Lebanese Forces* and Bashir Jamayyil, the brigade did not have a significant role beyond the political role of Sulayman Franjiyya within the Lebanese Front.* After the conflict between the Lebanese Forces and the Franjiyya family in 1978, Toni Franjiyya (Sulayman's eldest son and head of the brigade) was assassinated by forces loyal to Bashir Jamayyil. The death of Toni hardened the resolve of the Franjiyya family, who relied on their Syrian friends to revive the brigade under the leadership of Toni's brother, Robert. Robert ensured that the region under his control would be free of the influence of the Lebanese Phalanges Party* or the Lebanese Forces. The brigade also developed its own radio and television stations and pursued a line that was compatible with

Syrian policy in Lebanon. In the mid-1980s the teenage son of Toni (Sulayman Toni Franjiyya) began to assert himself. He expressed his independence of his uncle Robert. In August 1990, Sulayman Toni Franjiyya launched "a white revolution"[25] against the forces of his uncle, and took complete control of the organization, which was renamed the Forces of al-Marada. Sulayman served as minister in 1990, and he was appointed as a deputy in 1991 to replace his father.

GROUPING OF POPULAR COMMITTEES AND LEAGUES (*Tajammu' al-Lijan Wa-l-Rawabit al-Sha'biyya*). This group split off from the Ba'th party in the wake of the Arab defeat in the 1967 war. It believed in the primacy of grass-roots organization in contrast to the theorizing of a few intellectuals. The grouping had an insignificant role in the Lebanese civil war.

GUARDIANS OF THE CEDARS PARTY (*Hizb Hurras al-Arz*). One of the most extreme right-wing parties in Lebanon, the Guardians was established in September 1975, when Communiqué No. 1 was issued to denounce advocates of the partition of Lebanon. The second communiqué contained a bitter attack on the Palestinians. The third articulated the party's attitude on the issue of Lebanese identity: Lebanon should dissociate itself from Arabism. The party spread its messages by means of graffiti in East Beirut, including such slogans as: "No to Syria, no to the [Palestinian] Resistance, no to Arabism; Lebanon will be the graveyard of the Palestinians; kill a Palestinian and enter heaven." Some of the slogans bore the signature of the Front of the Guardians of the Cedar (sometimes known by its Arabic acronym, JIHA), which was a small organization that held similar views to those of this party, but had not been heard from since the 1975–76 phase of the Civil War.

The party formulated fourteen "truths." It was committed to the territorial integrity of Lebanon, and to the "eternal" existence of the Lebanese "nation." The party believed that the Lebanese people form a nation that is superior to what it considers the "fictitious Arab nation." The party took an extremely negative view of Arabism; party literature often ridiculed Arab culture and Arab nationalism. It associated Arabism with backwardness and desert life, while it associated Lebanese nationalism with Westernization and progress. The founder and leader of the party, Abu Arz (a code name for Ityan Saqr), announced in early 1976 that Lebanon should not be associated with anything but itself, and particularly not with Arabism "which is [a] backward movement."

The party took a principled stand against sectarianism and believed that all Lebanese should be treated equitably by the state. It has been one of the staunchest advocates of full secularization in Lebanon, although it remained sectarian in the composition of its membership and its leadership. Moreover, it subordinated itself to the leadership of the Maronite establishment, whether it was Bashir Jamayyil before 1982, or General 'Awn after 1988.

The party has also distinguished itself with its attitude on the Palestinian question. It has consistently called for the expulsion of all Palestinians from

Lebanon and for their distribution among the Arab countries. The party has openly allied itself with Israel, and has called for defense and diplomatic treaties between Lebanon and Israel. It lists its eight major enemies: the press, Arabism, traditional politicians, leftism, "acute capitalism," sectarianism, Al-Gharib (literally the alien, a reference to the non-Lebanese Arab residents of Lebanon), and the Palestinians.[12] The party was associated in its early days with the great poet Sa'id 'Aql. He later dissociated himself from the party not so much because of disagreement with its policies but primarily because of personal differences with its leadership.

The party played a limited military role in the civil war because of its small membership. Its fighters gained a reputation for savagery and ruthlessness, particularly against the Palestinians. As was said earlier, the party went along with the leadership of the Lebanese Forces* until the rise of General 'Awn, who was championed as a hero by the party. The party continues to operate; lately, it has added the term Harakat al-Qawmiyya al-Lubnaniyya (the Movement of Lebanese Nationalism) to its name. In a statement in 1990, it greeted the occupation of Kuwait by Saddam Husayn by asserting that "Arabism is the undisputed lie of the 20th century." It called upon the people to rally around the leadership of General 'Awn, and it demanded the withdrawal of Lebanon from the Arab League.

The party suffered a setback in October 1990 when the Syrian army and Lebanese government troops forced 'Awn out of power. Abu Arz suffered an unspecified injury and was forced to seek refuge in Israeli-occupied South Lebanon. The party's effectiveness and influence was diminished markedly after the defeat of 'Awn.

AL-HABASHI GROUP. A small, Sunni fundamentalist group, centered around the Burj Abi Haydar mosque in West Beirut, it is headed by a former mufti from Ethiopia (hence his nickname, The Abyssinian). It is strict and anti-Shi'ite. It is also very secretive, and very little is known about it.

HARAKAT AL AMAL. See AMAL MOVEMENT.

HARAKAT AL AMAL AL-ISLAMIYYA. See ISLAMIC AMAL MOVEMENT.

AL-HARAKAT AL-ISLAMIYYA FI LUBNAN. See ISLAMIC MOVEMENT IN LEBANON.

HARAKAT AL-NASIRIYYIN AL-MUSTAQILLIN—"AL-MURABITUN." See MOVEMENT OF INDEPENDENT NASSERITES—"AL-MURABITUN."

HARAKAT RUWWAD AL-ISLAH. See MOVEMENT OF THE PIONEERS OF REFORM.

HARAKAT AL-TAWHID AL-ISLAMI. *See* ISLAMIC UNIFICATION FRONT.

HARAKAT 24 TISHRIN. *See* OCTOBER 24 MOVEMENT.

AL-HARAKAT AL-WATANIYYA AL-LUBNANIYYA. *See* LEBANESE NATIONAL MOVEMENT.

HARAKAT AL-WIHDAWIYYIN AL-NASIRIYYIN. *See* MOVEMENT OF UNIONIST NASSERITES.

HELPERS PARTY *(Hizb al-Najjada)*. This Sunni-oriented party, founded in 1936, was a major political vehicle for Sunni Muslims in Lebanon. The party participated in the 1958 revolt, and adopted Nasserism after that. Some of its members have held parliamentary and ministerial positions over the years. In 1974 the military cadres of the party split off to form their own "Corrective Movement" led by Jamil Da'bul. The party lost its political significance as early as the 1970s. Its veteran leader 'Adnan al-Hakim passed away in 1989 or 1990.

HIZB AL-'AMAL AL-'ISHTIRAKI AL-'ARABI—LUBNAN. *See* SOCIALIST ARAB ACTION PARTY—LEBANON.

AL-HIZB AL-'ARABI AL-DIMUQRATI. *See* ARAB DEMOCRATIC PARTY.

HIZB AL-BA'TH AL-'ARABI AL-ISHTIRAKI. *See* ARAB SOCIALIST RESURRECTION (BA'TH) PARTY.

AL-HIZB AL-DIMUQRATI AL-ISHTIRAKI. *See* DEMOCRATIC SOCIALIST PARTY.

AL-HIZB AL-DIMUQRATI AL-MASIHI AL-ISHTIRAKI—HIZB AL-'AMAL. *See* SOCIALIST CHRISTIAN DEMOCRATIC PARTY—THE ACTION PARTY.

HIZB HURRAS AL-ARZ. *See* GUARDIANS OF THE CEDARS PARTY.

HIZB AL-KATA'IB AL-LUBNANIYYA. *See* LEBANESE PHALANGES PARTY.

HIZB AL-NAJJADA. *See* THE HELPERS PARTY.

AL-HIZB AL-SHUYU'I AL-LUBNANI. *See* COMMUNIST PARTY OF LEBANON.

AL-HIZB AL-SURI AL-QAWMI AL-IJTIMA'I. *See* SYRIAN SOCIAL NA-TIONAL PARTY.

HIZB AL-TAHARRUR AL-'ARABI. *See* PARTY OF ARAB LIBERATION.

AL-HIZB AL-TAQADDUMI AL-ISHTIRAKI. *See* PROGRESSIVE SOCIAL-IST PARTY.

HIZB AL-WA'D. *See* PROMISE PARTY.

HIZB AL-WATANIYYIN AL-AHRAR. *See* NATIONAL LIBERAL PARTY.

HIZBULLAH. *See* PARTY OF GOD.

HUNCHAK PARTY. This originally Marxist-oriented party, which was founded in 1887 in Geneva, moderated its doctrine to fit the environment in Lebanon. The party has no ties to Marxist organizations in Lebanon.[13] Like the Dashnak Party, this party has avoided taking controversial positions, and it has maintained good relations in recent years with the major Armenian party in Lebanon, the Dashnak, although the two parties have engaged in bloody clashes, particularly in the 1950s. Considered the second strongest Armenian party in Lebanon after the Dashnak, it has been successful in recruiting in working-class Armenian districts, although it has intellectuals in its leadership and membership.

ISLAMIC AMAL MOVEMENT (*Harakat al Amal al-Islamiyya*). The Islamic Amal Movement, headed by Husayn al-Musawi, split from the Amal Movement* in June 1982 when Nabih Birri agreed to participate in the Salvation Committee, which former president Ilyas Sarkis (1976–82) formed after the Israeli invasion, and which included, among other members, Bashir Jamayyil. Al-Musawi consid-ered Birri's participation tantamount to treason, given Bashir's relations with the Israelis and his anti-Muslim attitudes. Islamic Amal rejects the "secular" orien-tations of Amal.

Al-Musawi came from a middle-class background, from a prestigious family that claims descent from the Prophet (a *sayyid* family). He is a former school-teacher whom Musa al-Sadr had expelled from Amal in the mid-1970s (according to sources in Amal's leadership) because of his insistence on establishing an Islamic republic in Lebanon. Al-Musawi denied to this writer that he was ex-pelled by al-Sadr, although he acknowledged some differences with him at the time.

Islamic Amal has been strongly backed by the Islamic Republic in Iran, but the movement is still confined to areas near Ba'albak, the area from which al-

Musawi hailed. His relations with the Party of God* have been obscure. Iran pressured him to unify Shi'ite militia movements in Lebanon, while al-Musawi insisted upon maintaining his separate organizational existence, although he became one of the leaders of the Party of God. He is reported to have become a member of the highest ruling body of the Party of God.

ISLAMIC COMMUNITY (Al-Jama'a al-Islamiyya). This Sunni militant movement was founded in 1964 in Tripoli. It was led by influential Sunni fundamentalist thinker Fathi Yakan and Sunni writer Muhammad 'Ali al-Dinnawi. It advocated the establishment of an Islamic society in Lebanon that would be based solely on Islamic laws. The organization believed in the efficacy of political violence and established its own militia, Al-Mujahidun (the Religious Strugglers) in 1976. The militia participated in the civil war on the side of the leftist-Islamic coalition in Tripoli. The organization, which bitterly opposed secularism and communism, considered the best solution to the Lebanese morass to be based on Islam.

ISLAMIC MEETING (Al-Liqa' al-Islami). This grouping had its origins in the meetings held by the Sunni mufti (jurisconsult), Hasan Khalid, in his house in 'Aramun in 1975 to discuss Muslim affairs with key Muslim officials. It was later formalized and called Al-Tajammu' al-'Islami (the Islamic Grouping). It embraced the "club" of traditional Sunni politicians, mostly the prime ministerial aspirants. It includes former prime ministers, former ministers, current and former deputies, and individual traditional Sunni politicians. The Islamic Meeting takes a moderate stance, usually supporting the incumbent prime minister.

ISLAMIC MOVEMENT IN LEBANON (Al-Harakat al-Islamiyya fi Lubnan). This highly secretive organization first announced its existence in a leaflet in 1983, but its leader, Shaykh Sadiq al-Musawi, had been active in militant Shi'ite politics since the 1970s. This obscure organization preceded the Party of God* in its call for the immediate establishment of an Islamic republic in Lebanon. It considered the Party of God too moderate and not sufficiently dedicated to the objective of an Islamic order in Lebanon. The party is very active in distributing leaflets calling for the "election" of a Muslim cleric as president of Lebanon. Al-Musawi had close ties to the Iranian government, and he was frequently featured in the Iranian press, where he sometimes wrote commentaries on Lebanese affairs.

ISLAMIC UNIFICATION FRONT (Harakat al-Tawhid al-Islami). This is the most important movement in Tripoli. Its leader, or prince, according to the movement's terminology, Shaykh Sa'id Sha'ban, was able to assert his authority over the whole city in 1983 in defiance of Syria's wishes. Sha'ban, who comes from a lower-middle-class background, had been successful in attracting the numerous and highly active lumpenproletariat of Tripoli. Sha'ban was originally a member of the conservative, pro-Saudi movement of the Muslim Brotherhood in Tripoli before founding his Unification Movement in 1982. The movement was born of a merger of three Tripoli-based Islamic fundamentalist groups: Jundullah,* al-Muqawama al-Sha'biyya, and the Movement of Arab Lebanon. The first two groups had split from the Unification Movement by the summer of 1984, denying Sha'ban important power bases in the neighborhoods of Tibbanah and Abu Samra. Sha'ban saw no way out of the civil war except through an application of the Shari'a in Lebanon under an Islamic authority. Strongly hostile to the communist movement in Muslim countries, in 1983 the movement engaged in bloody massacres of communists and their families in Tripoli. Their bodies were thrown into the sea, to rid the soil of their evil. The movement dominated the city for a few years, and imposed strict Islamic laws on the people, until Syrian forces entered the city and savagely brought about the defeat of Sha'ban. In recent years, Sha'ban had become a close ally of Iran, and he has improved his ties with Syria.

AL-ITTIHAD AL-ISHTIRAKI AL-'ARABI. See ARAB SOCIALIST UNION.

AL-ITTIHAD AL-ISHTIRAKI AL-'ARABI (AL-TANDHIM AL-NASIRI). See ARAB SOCIALIST UNION (THE NASSERITE ORGANIZATION).

ITTIHAD QUWWAT-SHA'B AL-'AMIL (AL-TANDHIM AL-NASIRI). See UNION OF THE FORCES OF THE WORKING PEOPLE (THE NASSERITE ORGANIZATION).

AL-JABHA AL-LUBNANIYYA. See LEBANESE FRONT.

JABHAT AL-TAHRIR AL-YAZBAKIYYA. See YAZBAKI LIBERATION FRONT.

AL-JAMA'A AL-ISLAMIYYA. See ISLAMIC COMMUNITY.

JUNDULLAH. See SOLDIERS OF GOD.

KURDISH DEMOCRATIC PARTY (Al-Parti). This party was founded by Jamil Mihhu in 1960. It operated without a license until 1970, when it obtained legal status. First and foremost, it espouses the cause of Kurdish nationalism, and views as one of its primary activities instilling Kurdish consciousness among the masses. Its official platform, on the basis of which the Lebanese state licensed the party, is "the upgrading of the general level of Kurds in Lebanon." The party rose in Lebanon at a time when some Kurds obtained Lebanese citizenship, which had been denied them because of Maronite suspicions of their Muslim identity. According to one estimate, only 10,000 Kurds were naturalized out of over 75,000 living in Lebanon.

The founder of the party, Jamil Mihhu, ran for parliament in 1968 but lost.

The party and its leader suffered because of their support of the Iraqi regime, and Mihhu was put under house arrest between 1971 and 1974 by Mustafa al-Barzani in northern Iraq. The party's support for the Iraqi regime also put it at odds with the powerful Syrian army in Lebanon. The party was a member of the Lebanese National Movement* (the left-wing coalition of parties and organizations), but was later replaced by a left-wing offshoot. Both factions participated in combat during the civil war.

KURDISH DEMOCRATIC PARTY (Al-Parti)—PROVISIONAL LEADER-SHIP. In 1977 Muhammad Mihhu, Jamil Mihhu's son, split off from his father's party and formed his own. He wanted closer relations with the Lebanese National Movement,* and he was a firm believer in the Kurdish national cause. Muhammad Mihhu controlled his father's party while Jamil was in prison, and he was able to build a following.

AL-KUTLA AL-DUSTURIYYA. See CONSTITUTIONAL BLOC.

AL-KUTLA AL-WATANIYYA. See NATIONAL BLOC.

LCP. See COMMUNIST PARTY OF LEBANON.

LEBANESE FORCES (LF) (Al-Quwwat al-Lubnaniyya). The protracted civil war led to the bizarre transformation of militias into political parties, and political parties into militias. On the one hand, political parties that wanted to survive the new military phase of Lebanese politics felt pressured to militarize their ranks to hold onto members and to attract new ones. On the other hand, aware of a possible future, nonmilitary phase of Lebanese politics, militias tried to institutionalize support and to adapt to the changing aspects of Lebanese politics. The relatively successful disarming of the militias in 1991 by the Lebanese army, according to the Al-Ta'if Accords, did not end the role of the Lebanese Forces. Press reports in June 1991 pointed to the possible transformation of the LF into a political party headed by their commander, Samir Jaja.

The origin of the LF goes back to the battle of Tal al-Za'tar and to the 1975–76 military campaigns conducted by the rightist (predominantly Christian) militias and their allies in the Lebanese army against the Palestinian and Lebanese Shi'ite presence in the suburbs of East Beirut. The suspicious death of William Hawi, head of the war council, the main military apparatus of the Lebanese Phalanges Party,* paved the way for Bashir Gemayyel to assume control of the party's military arm and eventually of the entire military force in East Beirut.

The LF was officially established in August 1976 on the creation of its Joint Command Council with its first chairman, Bashir Gemayyel, who was clearly dissatisfied with the policies of his father and comrades in the leadership of the Phalanges Party. By forming a powerful, unified military force, Bashir increased his political power and eventually controlled the Phalanges

Party also. He achieved his goals, through the ruthless, often brutal, elimination of his foes.

The Command Council initially comprised "the command" of the Phalanges, the National Liberal Party,* Al-Tandhim,* Guardians of the Cedars,* and other nonaffiliated armed groups in East Beirut. Soon Bashir and his fighters represented an important group within the Phalanges Party who were disillusioned with "moderates" like his father, Pierre Jamayyil. Bashir fought alongside his fighters on several fronts, and he became a symbol of their growing militancy in East Beirut. The displacement of Christian people from their villages and towns by fighters of the leftist/Muslim-PLO coalition created a powerful group in East Beirut who wanted to take revenge. Bashir offered a simple formula for ending the war: Lebanon would regain its sovereignty, and peace would prevail only if the *aghrab* (the aliens, i.e., the Palestinians, and, after 1978, the Syrians) were expelled. Bashir's first major attempt to eliminate Maronite rivals began in June 1978 when Toni Franjiyya, the leader of the Marada Forces,* and his family were killed and his military force was defeated in the Ihdin massacre. Franjiyya had resisted Bashir's extension of the rule of the LF to areas in north Lebanon, a stronghold of the powerful Maronite Franjiyya family. By 1979 it became clear that Bashir would not allow any rival military force to exist in East Beirut, and he formed a new military force, which theoretically was not affiliated with any political party in East Beirut. In July 1980, in one of the bloodiest episodes against his Maronite enemies, he ruthlessly exterminated the militia of the National Liberal Party, the Tigers (*Al-Numur*), and forced surviving commanders to flee to West Beirut. Thus the LF integrated all the armed men of East Beirut into one militia.

Bashir's rise to political supremacy was enhanced by his control of all military units in East Beirut and by financial and military aid from the Likud government of Israel. Theoretically, the LF and Bashir were subordinate to the leadership of the Lebanese Front,* the coalition of major Christian-oriented organizations and personalities. However, he clearly became the uncontested neo-*za'im* of the East Beirut region. His tough anti-Syrian message and clashes between the Syrian army in Lebanon and the LF from 1978 to 1982 helped to determine its main ideological line—the full restoration of Lebanon's independence and sovereignty. Enemies of the LF were considered "guilty" of violating the sovereignty of Lebanon, and the militia invited outside forces to intervene in Lebanon to bolster their cause, including the Israelis, and after 1984 the Iraqi regime and forces loyal to Yasir Arafat.

The Israeli invasion of 1982 was instrumental in Bashir's election as president, which had been utterly unthinkable only weeks earlier. Bashir cleverly exploited the invasion, first by attempting to distance himself from Israeli war activities in Lebanon, and second by summarizing his political objectives, using the area of Lebanon as his slogan. The "catchy" slogan of Lebanon's area appealed to many Lebanese who thought that Bashir was serious in wanting to rid Lebanon of all foreign forces, and it also promoted the myth that Lebanon's problems were all the product of foreign intervention in Lebanon. By 1982 most Lebanese were too exhausted by the violent clashes to question his leadership. In September of that year he was assassinated by a Christian member of the Syrian Social National Party.*

The ascension of Fadi Frem to command the LF ushered in a new era. First, the party dealt with a new image shaped by its involvement in the Sabra and Shatila massacre. Second, the newly elected president, Bashir's brother Amin, had never been on good terms with the forces loyal to his brother. Furthermore, the LF had become more than a fighting force, consisting also of a large bureaucracy that had forcibly replaced governmental structures in East Beirut. The size of its military arm and its intelligence apparatus expanded with a new system of conscription in July 1982, and an illegal system of tax levying and collection financed the bureaucracy. Despite efforts to appeal to the Lebanese population as a whole, the Lebanese Forces remained predominantly Maronite, although "their ranks include unspecified numbers of Greek Catholics, Greek Orthodox, Armenian Catholics, Assyrians, and other Christians."[14]

Elie Hubayqah became commander of the LF in 1985 after the brief tenure of Fu'ad AbuNadir, relative and protégé of Amin Gemayyel. Hubayqah, the longtime head of the intelligence apparatus of the Lebanese Forces, was associated with Israeli intelligence and was prominent in the investigation of the Sabra and Shatila massacre. However, he chose to improve ties with the Syrian government, and in December 1985 he signed what is now called the Tripartite Agreement between the LF, Nabih Birri (on behalf of the Amal Movement*), and Walid Jumblat (on behalf of the Progressive Socialist Party*). The agreement made major concessions to Lebanese Muslims and to Syria that were later incorporated into the Al-Ta'if Accords. His signature cost him his position and led to his ouster in January 1986 when he became a member of the pro-Syrian coalition in Lebanon.

His successor, Samir Jaja, took over the command in January 1986 and remained there until July 1991. Jaja also comes from a notoriously violent background and was involved in the Ihdin massacre in 1978. His eccentric personality and his Christian fundamentalist outlook solidified his sectarian power base. His legitimacy was based upon his objection to the Tripartite Agreement. But his tenure was marred by Israel's diminishing interest in the LF, the tendency of the Christian community to fragment, and the rise of General Michel 'Awn, who was appointed by Amin Gemayyel as a caretaker president in 1988. Initially, 'Awn struck a precarious alliance with Jaja in his war against the Syrian presence in Lebanon in March 1989, but in December 1989 'Awn turned against the LF in order to emulate Bashir's "unification of the Christian gun."

Although 'Awn's forces were defeated and he sought asylum at the French embassy in October 1990, due to Syria's military intervention, the crisis of the Lebanese Forces did not end. 'Awn's campaign against the LF was based on widespread resentment against the militias in East Beirut and corruption, extortion, and embezzlement, both on official and individual member levels.

In theory, the Lebanese Forces are run collectively by the command council;

in reality, with two exceptions, one man has tended to dominate the organization. Although the LF is divided into various departments, which cover financial, social relief, military, foreign relations, public services, counterintelligence, and security affairs, each commander rules through his own trusted clique, which penetrates all facets of the militia/party. However, in contrast to the militia rule in West Beirut, the LF imposed a rigid security system that achieved some degree of prosperity for East Beirut under Bashir.

The disarming of the Lebanese Forces in spring 1991 marked the beginning of a new era in the life of the movement. The post-'Awn era used the political arena to resolve Lebanese conflicts. Although new relationships between the Lebanese Forces, the Phalanges, and the Syrian regime were costly from the Christian perspective, Samir Jaja was the LF leader for some time. He shrewdly designated his deputy, Roger Dib, to assume most of the visible political duties, including negotiations with Damascus and membership in the cabinet. Ja'ja' seemed to be getting ready to create his own political party to dissociate himself from Syria. The imposition of Syrian power in Lebanon eclipsed his role, however, and his failure to win the leadership of the Phalanges Party weakened him as well. He did form a political party for the Lebanese Forces but failed to transform the old militia into an effective political force. He maintained good ties with various Lebanese factions (including former enemies such as the PSP and Amal), and he was critical of the parliamentary elections of 1992.

Although the LF experienced important changes, forced by the rise of General 'Awn, the movement still stood for its original ideological agenda: the physical protection of Christians in Lebanon (and indeed in the Arab east), and protection of Lebanon's sovereignty and independence against outside forces. The LF called for a measure of political decentralization in Lebanon that enemies consider a thinly disguised call for the partition of the country. The political discourse of the Lebanese Forces is now full of references to "al-mujtama' al-masihi al-hurr" (the free Christian society), which has narrowed the party's appeal.

LEBANESE FRONT (Al-Jabha al-Lubnaniyya). The Lebanese Front, as the name indicates, is not a political party. It is rather a body that brings together all the important Maronite-oriented parties and organizations in East Beirut. It defines itself as a general leadership council for all Christians in Lebanon. The front has its root in Jabhat al-Hurriyya wa-l-'Insan fi Lubnan (the Front of Freedom and Man in Lebanon), which declared its existence in January 1976 in a brief statement that affirmed the priority of "restoring sovereignty" to Lebanon. The statement was signed by Father Sharbil al-Qassis (head of the Maronite Order of Monks), Kamil Sham'un (head of the National Liberal Party*), Pierre Gemayyel (head of the Lebanese Phalanges Party*), Fu'ad al-Shimali (head of Al-Tandhim* militia), Shakir AbuSulayman (secretary-general of the Maronite League), Charles Malik (a well-known right-wing thinker), and Sa'id 'Aql (a famous poet and guide of the Guardians of the Cedars*). Charles Malik was instrumental in drafting the vow of the front in February of 1976, which included—among other things—affirmation of the unity of Lebanon, a demand for the expulsion of the non-Lebanese "aggressors" from Lebanon (a reference to the Palestinians), a call for respect of the International Declaration of Human Rights (which Charles Malik helped draft), and praise for the free enterprise system. This original draft was later diluted before it was published owing to the reservations of Pierre Gemayyel.

This front was initially formed to unify political action in the Christian camp. Later it evolved into an ideological movement that gradually broke with Lebanon's Arab identity and sanctioned Bashir Gemayyel's alliance with Israel. By 1977 the front's name became the Lebanese Front and it included Kamil Sham'un, as president; Sulayman Franjiyya; Pierre Jamayyil; Edward Hunayn (a gifted writer and a deputy who deserted the National Bloc,* on which list he won the election in 1972), who served as its secretary and writer of its eloquent statements; Abbot Sharbil al-Qassis, head of the Permanent Congress of the Lebanese Monastic Order* (who was succeeded by Abbot Bulus Na'man); Charles Malik; and Fu'ad Afram al-Bustani (a former president of the Lebanese University and a distinguished scholar). The new front declared its "charter" at a special meeting at the monastery of Sayyidat al-Bir in January 1977. This document emphasized "the eternal existence of the Lebanese entity" and affirmed the members' commitment to the preservation of Lebanon's "distinctive characteristics," which—in Muslim eyes—had become a code word for Maronite political supremacy.[15] Also included was a call for modification of the national pact, but only in order to "accommodate some sort of decentralization or federation within a comprehensive framework of a single unified Lebanon." Although partition was rejected, many opponents of the front flatly considered its declaration at Sayyidat al-Bir as the first separatist move on the part of the leadership of the Maronite establishment.

While the front was initially established to serve as the political directorate for the Christian community (or what front leaders call Al-Mujtama' al-Masihi [the Christian society]), the influence of Bashir Jamayyil began to rise as soon as it was established. By 1980, when Bashir eliminated the military presence of all rival Christian groups, including the Tigers militia of Sham'un, and in the wake of the withdrawal of Sulayman Franjiyya, the Lebanese Forces* became the dominant element in the leadership of the front, and Bashir was a regular participant in its meetings, although military commanders were ostensibly excluded from leadership positions.

The death of Bashir in 1982 and the death of Pierre Jamayyil in August 1984 weakened the front. The uprising of Elie Hubayqah in 1985 against Amin Gemayyel's influence in the Lebanese Force marginalized the front, and its headquarters was bombed in November. The victory of Samir Jaja against Hubayqa in 1986 revived the front in a new form. Its leadership body was expanded to include non-Maronite figures and organizations, like deputy Rashid al-Khuri; deputy Michel Sasin and Habib al-Mutran from the National Liberal Party; Karim Baqraduni of the Lebanese Forces; Albert Milki representing the League of Christian Minorities; Dimitri Bitar of the Lebanese League of the Greek Orthodox; and publisher Jubran Tuwayni. The credit for the expansion of the front's leadership beyond the traditional confines should go to Samir Jaja, who consistently made efforts to expand the appeal of his movement to encompass all Christian sects and organizations.

The status of the front's leadership changed in the summer of 1987, when its president, Kamil Sham'un died, and his place in the party leadership was taken by his son Dani Sham'un. The leadership of the front went to George Sa'adah, the head of the Phalanges Party. The signing of the Al-Ta'if Accords and the rise of General 'Awn split East Beirut, and the front had its last meeting in the fall of 1989, during the Al-Ta'if meetings. The front itself was split asunder: George Sa'adah still insisted that he remain the legitimate president of the front, while Dani Sham'un, who opposed the Al-Ta'if Accords and who became a staunch ally of General 'Awn, claimed that the front had now been transferred to new hands. The revived front (which began to meet in April 1990) became known as the "new" Lebanese Front, and was led by Dani Sham'un, who had a hard time expanding the leadership body. Most of the historical and traditional leaders refused to join, and the new front comprised young and mainly obscure political activists who agreed only on their staunch support for General 'Awn. The new front also included defectors from the Lebanese Forces and the Phalanges Party who wanted to voice their support for General 'Awn. Until the defeat of General 'Awn in October 1990, the front included Dani Sham'un; Jubran Tuwayni; a representative of the Guardians of the Cedars; Walid Faris of the Socialist Christian Democratic Party*; the head of the Lebanese League of Greek Orthodox; the head of the Northern Liberation Grouping (a pro-'Awn instrument); a representative of the General Greek Orthodox Organization; a representative of the Christian minorities; a representative of the Greek Catholic League; and other activists.

The new front served to rationalize and articulate General 'Awn's policies. In the summer of 1990 it even tried to open channels of communication with Muslim factions to help end 'Awn's isolation. With his defeat, the front suffered a major setback, particularly with the assassination of Dani Sham'un soon after. Many members of the front chose to leave Lebanon: Its secretary, Jubran Tuwayni, continued to make statements on its behalf in Europe and in Lebanon.

LEBANESE KURDISH PARTY (*Riz Kari*) (I). This party was founded in 1975 by Faysal Fakhru, who preferred to align his party with the Syrian regime in Lebanon. It criticized the Mihhu family's party for failing to appeal to a broad section of the Kurdish population. It also charged that the Kurdish Democratic Party* (Al-Parti) has been transformed into a Mihhu family apparatus. It supported Barzani's revolt in northern Iraq. In December 1976, the Kurdish Democratic Party and the Lebanese Kurdish Party decided to put aside their differences and form the Broad Kurdish National Front to unify Kurdish political action in Lebanon. The party criticized its own past pro-Syrian policies, leading a dissident faction to announce the expulsion of Faysal Fakhru and to continue the previous political line. Faysal Fakhru continued to claim that he represented party legitimacy. The party's militia participated in the civil war.

LEBANESE KURDISH PARTY (Riz Kari) (II). Following the creation of the joint front between the Kurdish Democratic Party and the Lebanese Kurdish Party, a faction within the latter party split off and accused Faysal Fakhru of catering to the wishes of Jamil Mihhu and of returning to Kurdish clannishness. They also protested against the "domination" by Mihhu of the front. This faction has consistently supported Syrian policy in Lebanon.

LEBANESE MONASTIC ORDER (Al-Ruhbaniyyat al-Lubnaniyya). This organization operates under the name of the Permanent Congress of the Lebanese Maronite Monastic Order. Originally nonpolitical, this changed in 1966 when the Order issued a statement protesting foreign ownership of lands in Lebanon. The Permanent Congress was then formed to follow up on this issue and to "defend Lebanese territory." The Order is hierarchically structured and is independent of the local Maronite patriarchate. It has representatives wherever Lebanese reside, inside and outside of Lebanon. The Order was originally concerned with social and educational services. It enjoys rich financial resources, owning—according to one credible account—27 percent of the land in the Mount Lebanon region.[16] It also receives aid from the Vatican and from Catholics around the world. Of all the monastic orders in Lebanon, the Maronite Order constitutes the largest, with almost 500 monks in 1976 at the beginning of the civil war. All monastic orders in Lebanon suffer from small memberships.

The role of the Maronite Monastic Order was expanded in 1966 when the Holy Spirit University was founded in Junyah. For the first time, Lebanese monks became responsible for the education of Lebanese clerical students. The campus became active in organizing conferences and lectures dealing with "Lebanese nationalism" and various aspects of "Maronitism." The "Lebanese Research Committee" at the university played a major role in theorizing for the Lebanese Front* and the Lebanese Forces.* It promoted the vision of "the Lebanese nation" as one which is unique, indivisible, and not linked with the Arab/Muslim environment. The Order did not confine itself to the political and intellectual realm, however, but threw its support behind the ultrarightist Al-Tandhim* militia.

The Order assumed a prominent political role in the 1975–76 phase of the civil war, and its president, Sharbil al-Qassis, became a major figure of the Maronite establishment participating in crucial meetings that decided the policies of the Lebanese Front and later the Lebanese Forces. Al-Qassis was a detested figure among Muslims for what was perceived to be his blatantly anti-Muslim bias. In a memorandum submitted to the Lebanese parliamentary deputies in 1975, the Order did not choose to blame all of Lebanon's problems on the outsiders, but rather accused the Muslims of violating the terms of the National Pact and, consequently, of causing the collapse of the Lebanese political system. The Order refuses to commit Lebanon to any of the Arab issues because it understands the Pact to require Lebanese neutrality, because Arab identity (which in its mind is akin to Muslim identity) threatens the "civilizational uniqueness" of the Lebanese Christians. Similarly, the Order rejects the state of war between Lebanon and Israel and calls upon the Lebanese state to abdicate the responsibility that emanates from the Joint Arab Defense Pact. On the specific issues of internal reforms, the Order emphasizes the importance of the Maronite identity of the president in Lebanon. It rejects any diminution of the powers of the president because "the Maronitism of the president without his powers becomes meaningless."

The most controversial stand of the Order was its pessimistic assessment of the prospects for Muslim-Christian coexistence in Lebanon. For example, it stated that Islamic civilization cannot coexist with Christian civilization. Moreover, Maronites cannot accept Arabism or Islam, because Maronites constitute a distinctive "civilization" and anti-Muslim movement. The Order was accused by its enemies of favoring partition because it called for a confederal arrangement in Lebanon.

Sharbil Qassis was succeeded by Abbot Bulus Na'man, who was a very close advisor to Bashir Gemayyel. Na'man has continued the policies of Qassis, who seems to have retired from political life. Na'man also has encouraged the alliance with Israel that was vigorously pursued by Qassis. In recent years, the Order has taken a lower profile. It has been frustrated by the conflict between General 'Awn and the Lebanese Forces, trying to mediate between the two Maronite parties. The new president of the Order (Abbott Hashim) has not taken the same overtly political stands of his predecessors.

LEBANESE NATIONAL MOVEMENT (Al-Harakat al-Wataniyya al-Lubnaniyya). This is not a party, but a broad front that first operated in 1964 under the name of the Front of National and Progressive Parties, Bodies, and Personalities. It was reorganized in 1969, and was named the Grouping of the National and Progressive Parties. Kamal Jumblat was the leader and founder of both fronts, which were intended to support the Palestinian revolution and the program of internal reforms in Lebanon. The Front focused on the right of the PLO to carry arms in Lebanon and to perpetrate military operations against Israel from Lebanese territories.

In 1975 the Front was renamed the Lebanese National Movement, which was formally reorganized in July 1976, when the Central Political Council was formed to centrally guide the organizations operating within the movement. The council comprised representatives of the Progressive Socialist Party,* the Communist Party of Lebanon,* the Communist Action Organization,* the Syrian Social National Party,* the Movement of Independent Nasserites (Al-Murabitun),* the Ba'th Party,* the Lebanese Movement in Support of the Revolution, the Organization of the Socialist Arab Ba'th Party, the Popular Nasserite Organization,* the Arab Socialist Union (the Nasserite Organization),* Al-Afwaj al-'Arabiyyah, the Forces of Nasser, the Leftist Kurdish Party,* the Socialist Arab Action Party—Lebanon,* the Democratic Christians, and pro-Jumblat personalities, such as Albert Mansur, 'Usamah Fakhuri, Muhammad Qabbani, 'Isam Ni'man, 'Izzat Harb, and Fu'ad Shbaqlu. The movement ceased to exist after the Israeli invasion of 1982, and all efforts to revive it failed given the dramatic changes in the political map of Lebanon after 1982.

LEBANESE PHALANGES PARTY (*Hizb al-Kata'ib al-Lubnaniyya*). Although the Lebanese Forces* emerged from the womb, so to speak, of the Phalanges Party, the history of the party is distinctive and precedes the independence of Lebanon.

The Phalanges Party was founded in November 1936 by Pierre Jamayyil and four other Christians in the wake of his visit to Germany where he was a member of the Lebanese delegation to the infamous 1936 Olympic Games in Berlin. Jamayyil never denied his desire to replicate the youth organizations of Nazi Germany. In his own words: "In Germany, I witnessed the perfect conduct of a whole, unified nation."[17] The movement was unquestionably political, and was founded as a response to the rise of "unionist" calls among Muslim and some Christian groups in Lebanon, who sought the unity of Lebanon with either Syria, or any Arab country as part of a larger would-be Arab nation. The name al-Kata'ib means battalions, and was intended to underline the military purpose of the organization.

Although the party was to be led by the five-man founding committee, Pierre Jamayyil soon assumed the leading role. Loyalty to the leader became one of the duties of the membership as early as April 1937, when it was decided to transfer the prerogatives of the founding committee to Pierre Jamayyil. The first crisis in the party's life occurred in November 1937 when French mandate authorities decreed the dissolution of all paramilitary organizations in Lebanon, a ban directed primarily against the Phalanges and the al-Najjadah (Helpers)* organization, the Muslim sectarian counterpart to al-Kata'ib. And, as al-Najjadah declared its commitment to the incorporation of Lebanon into Syria, the Phalanges asserted its commitment to Lebanese independence. When clashes between these two groups spread to different parts of Lebanon, Jamayyil took an anti-French stand and led demonstrations against the government ban against all paramilitary groups. The mandate authorities continued to tolerate Phalanges activities; theoretically, the party pledged to confine its activities to the athletic realm. In 1938 the Phalanges officially advocated an independent Lebanon bound by ties of friendship and alliance to France. The party's real agenda regarding French rule in Lebanon remained vague, however, due to the split in the Christian camp between those who wanted complete independence and those who believed that the French presence was a protection against Muslim/Arab ambitions. The latter view was represented by France's major ally in Lebanon, Emile Iddi, head of the National Bloc.*

**Table 15**
**Lebanese Phalanges Performance in Parliamentary Elections, 1943–68**

| Year | Candidates (no.) | Elected (no.) | Elected (%) |
|---|---|---|---|
| 1943 | 0 | 0 | 0 |
| 1945 | 1 | 0 | 0 |
| 1947 | 4 | 0 | 0 |
| 1951 | 5 | 3 | 60 |
| 1953 | 2 | 1 | 50 |
| 1957 | 4 | 1 | 25 |
| 1959 | 1 | 1 | 100 |
| 1960 | 7 | 6 | 86 |
| 1964 | 9 | 4 | 44 |
| 1968 | 9 | 9 | 100 |
| TOTAL | 42 | 25 | 60 |

Source: John Entelis, *Pluralism and Party Transformation in Lebanon: Al-Kata'ib, 1936–1970* (Leiden, Netherlands: E.J. Brill, 1975), p. 151.

In 1943 the Phalanges leaders broke with Iddi and supported the rising tide of popular opinion that called for immediate independence. This gave the party national legitimacy without costing it any significant loss of Christian support. The party's ideology also stressed that "Lebanon has an Arab tongue and it is Arab in neighborhood and interest, but the Lebanese are not of the Arab race. We believe in the existence of a Lebanese nationalism that equals Arab nationalism. . . . We are like the Italian and English races."[18] Jamayyil viewed Lebanese nationalism as equivalent to Arab nationalism. Yet the concept of Lebanese nationalism is fundamentally opposed to the very idea of Arab nationalism and the dissolution of boundaries between Arab countries that it implies. This is why the concept of Lebanese nationalism is politically charged. It does not have the same connotation that Italian nationalism has, for example. In the Lebanese political lexicon the term is understood to mean ultranationalism. Thus, the affirmation of Lebanese nationalism is meant—according to many Arab nationalists (Christian as well as Muslim)—to negate the Arab dimension of Lebanese identity. This conflict over identity lies at the heart of Lebanon's communal strife. The precarious National Pact of 1943 left the identity question unsettled; the Muslim and Christian political elites merely agreed that Lebanon is not entirely Arab, but it is not non-Arab either.

The party adjusted quickly to postindependence politics by deciding to field candidates for the Lebanese parliament in the by-election of 1945 and by officially changing its name from Phalanges Libanaises to Hizb al-Kata'ib al-Lubnaniyyah. In reorganizing, the party created a politburo and instituted an annual congress to democratize its structure and to dilute its image as a neofascist party. The party continued to field "social democratic" candidates for parliament with little success until the 1958 civil war, which boosted the popularity of the party in Christian eyes. As sectarian polarization tore the country apart, the Phalanges emerged as a well-organized party with a militia. The party's increased success in parliamentary elections can be seen in Table 15.

As the party grew in popularity, it became more sophisticated in its recruitment and propaganda techniques. Phalanges leadership was so keen on building its power in Lebanon that it sought financial help from Israel and received a modest sum to support an electoral campaign as early as 1951.[19] But the sectarian agitation and mobilization in the country during and after the 1958 civil war helped the party more, and the party began to articulate its message in clearer terms. Amin Naji, a pen name for the party's main ideologue, Antoine Najm, published a manual in 1966, pledging strict dedication to traditional values; hence, the party's motto: God, Homeland, Family. The party professed its dedication to democracy, private property, and the free enterprise system, and it stated its opposition to individualism, leftism, and communism. The party also claimed, before the 1975 war, that it stood for secularism as long as respect for all religions in Lebanon was maintained.

The party grew dramatically in the 1960s for two reasons: It was the best organized Lebanese organization and the one with the largest militia, and it appealed to Christian youths who feared that the Lebanese state was too weak to defend itself against "the Palestinian threat." The issue of al-'amal al-fida'i (guerrilla action or Palestine Liberation Organization [PLO] activities in Lebanon) split the Lebanese in 1975 when the civil war began. Jamayyil was concerned that Palestinian revolutionism might threaten the 1943 National Pact and that the PLO militia in Lebanon might threaten the existence of Lebanon.

The more Muslims in Lebanon raised the issue of internal political reforms and the more they emphasized the changing demographic balance in the country (which accrued to their advantage), the more Pierre Jamayyil fixated on the Palestinian presence. Jamayyil may have sincerely believed that Muslim resentment of Christian status would not have arisen but for Palestinian revolutionary

**Table 16**
**Sectarian Composition of the Phalanges Party, 1969**

| Sect | Membership (%) |
|---|---|
| Maronites | 80 |
| Non-Maronite Christians | 10 |
| Jews | 2 |
| Shi`ites | 6 |
| Sunnis | 1 |
| Druzes | 1 |

Source: John Entelis, *Pluralism and Party Transformation in Lebanon: Al-Kata'ib, 1936–1970* (Leiden, Netherlands: E.J. Brill, 1975), p. 110.

influence on the Lebanese masses. It is also entirely possible that Jamayyil did not want to deal with the issue of reform because he did not wish to make any concessions to the Muslim side. He believed that Maronite privileges in Lebanon were merely *damanat* (guarantees) against Christians being swallowed up by Arabism. His political position was stated in quasi-religious terms as he emphasized that any change in the "unique formula" of Lebanon would lead the Christians to "give up their features and characteristics."

The major thrust of the Phalanges Party has been its sectarian appeal and power base, which have clearly reflected Christian Maronite preponderance. In 1969 its sectarian composition was as shown in Table 16.

John Entelis, who wrote a rather sympathetic study of the Phalanges, states that "Christian percentages are somewhat deflated, non-Christian ones, inflated."[20] A study conducted by party officials in 1974 claimed that the proportion of Muslims in the party had been increasing steadily, from 4 percent in 1960 (when Christians constituted 96 percent of the party members according to the same study) to 10 percent in 1970.[21] But those figures may not be reliable, and they differ from Entelis's figures for 1969. A Politburo member and a major ideologue of the party also admitted in 1982 that the party had failed to recruit Muslims. He blamed this failure on intimidation by "zealous Muslims."[22] Finally, there are no Muslims whatsoever among the party's leaders.

Maronites predominate among Phalanges members; an internal party document states that this preponderance is "natural" because "the nationalist doctrine of the Phalanges" expresses "the political will" of the Maronites.[23] One of the most serious organizational crises occurred when a non-Maronite Christian, Elie Karama, assumed the leadership of the party upon Pierre Jamayyil's death in 1984. Threatened by the dramatic ascendancy of the Lebanese Forces, the leadership chose to replace Karamah in 1986 with the Maronite deputy George Sa'adah.

The sectarian appeal of the Phalanges Party can also be documented through a study of the sectarian composition of votes for Pierre Jamayyil in the 1972 parliamentary election. Jamayyil ran for the Maronite seat of the First District of Beirut and won about 90 percent of the votes in this overwhelmingly Christian district. He also received 100 percent of the votes in a Jewish polling place in Al-Marfa. The results were different in Muslim polling places where he received from 16.2 to 24.4 percent of the votes.

The Phalanges became a voice of militarism in the 1960s when it formed the Tripartite Alliance (Al-Tahaluf al-Thulathi) along with two other Maronite-oriented parties, the National Liberal Party* and the National Bloc.* The Tripartite Alliance won in almost all Christian areas in the 1968 election. As the party focused on "the Palestinian threat" in Lebanon, it engaged in militia building and training. The party's line was that the state was too weak and indecisive "to save Lebanon" from its external enemies.

The Phalanges was involved in clashes with PLO forces in various parts of Beirut and its eastern suburbs in the 1970s. The party received aid from President Sulayman Franjiyyah, who helped the militia and other right-wing organizations. In April 1975, party militiamen ambushed a busload of Palestinian civilians in the suburb of 'Ayn al-Rummana. The incident became known as the incident of 'Ayn al-Rummana, or the Sarajevo of the civil war. The party's military then became heavily involved in the fighting throughout Lebanon. William Hawi headed its council of war. After Hawi's mysterious death in 1976, Bashir Jamayyil became the overall head of the military apparatus of the party.

However, the rise of the Lebanese Forces, with Jamayyil at the helm, marginalized all other political and military forces in East Beirut, including the Phalanges Party. There was, however, some overlap between the Lebanese Forces and the Phalanges. Some members of the Phalanges politburo were also members of the Command Council of the Lebanese Forces. Indeed, Bashir Jamayyil became the single most important decision maker in East Beirut. Although the party was marginalized by virtue of Bashir's monopoly over the decision-making process in East Beirut, the Phalanges Party also benefited from his popularity. Although he always gave credit to the party, nevertheless it lost its independent voice and became subordinate to its fighters' wing which was incorporated into the Lebanese Forces.

The year 1982 was a watershed in the history of the party. First, Bashir was elected president of Lebanon. After his assassination, Amin Jamayyil, his brother, became the first Phalangist to assume the presidency of the republic. This was provocative to many critics, Muslims and Christians alike, who attributed the party's success to Israel's desire to redraw Lebanon's political map according to its own wishes in the aftermath of its 1982 invasion. Amin's election signaled an Israeli-Phalangist alliance, after years of denials by Phalangist leaders. However, Amin Jamayyil's tenure in office was not beneficial to the party, which needed to make clear that his election did not mean that his party had assumed power. For one thing, the Lebanese constitution refers to the election of a person, not a party. But Amin made appointments mostly on the basis of old Phalangist connections, and the distribution of seats among his party clique was a factor that led to the February 1984 uprising in West Beirut, which ejected Amin's forces from Muslim areas, and led to the withdrawal of the Multinational Forces (MNF) from Lebanon because of American support for Amin's regime.

Amin wanted to control the party through a trusted circle of sycophants. After the death of Pierre Jamayyil in 1984, Amin insisted that his deputy become the permanent leader of the party, although he was not popular and—probably more important—non-Maronite. The ascension of Elie Karamah, a Greek Catholic, further weakened the party by driving many members to the Lebanese Forces, which was perceived to be more independent and more militant in its relations with Syria and in terms of internal reforms. Elie Karamah's tenure marked the ultimate marginalization of the party in Lebanese politics. The Lebanese Forces made Jamayyil's task in controlling East Beirut more difficult. In a bitter—but fairly honest—party election, the Lebanese Forces' choice, George Sa'ada, was elected to the presidency of the party in 1986.

Sa'ada, part of the faction that called for improved ties with the Arab world, participated in meetings with Syrian officials as early as 1973 to bring the party out of its regional isolation. His reputation as a moderate Arabist helped the party in the late 1980s, when Syrian influence in Lebanon culminated in the signing of the Treaty of Cooperation, Friendship, and Coordination between the Syrian and Lebanese governments. Sa'ada resumed ties with Syrian officials and facilitated contacts between leaders of the Lebanese Forces and the Syrian government. The party, as well as the Lebanese Forces, was forced to improve ties with Damascus as they both faced General 'Awn, whose populist appeal threatened to undermine the power base of both movements.

Sa'ada also promised to end the dominance of the Jamayyil family and to transform the party from "the party of the founder to the party of institutions." But the new leadership was paralyzed by the presence in the leadership of such powerful men as the leader of the Lebanese Forces, Samir Jaja. According to one analysis, the party "has begun to change from a 'powerful party' into a party of 'powerful men,' each of whom wants the party to fill his measure and ambitions."[24] There is still no consensus within the party over the necessary procedures and regulations for the election of the president given the last problematic election. A special committee is now assigned to design new procedures to democratize the electoral procedures within the party. Sa'adah now seems intent on sharing the decision-making process with the largest number of leaders, and he now presides over regular meetings that bring together the highest leading organs of the party: the Politburo, the Central Council, and the Consultative Council.

LEBANESE YOUTHS (Al-Shabiba al-Lubnaniyya). The Lebanese Youths, an organization founded within the structure of the National Bloc* party, was headed by Marun Khuri, known as Bash Marun. Marun opposed Raymond Iddi's rejection of a separate militia for the party. Marun was reportedly supported by the Lebanese Phalange Party* in restructuring his organization in 1975 as a separate militia to embarrass Iddi. After the end of the first phase of the civil war (1975–76), the organization seems to have ceased to exist, and its members were incorporated into other existing militias in East Beirut.

LF. See LEBANESE FORCES.

AL-LIQA' AL-ISLAMI. See ISLAMIC MEETING.

LNM. See LEBANESE NATIONAL MOVEMENT.

MOVEMENT OF THE DISINHERITED (Harakat al-Mahrumin). This organization was founded in 1974, and it was successful in recruiting some of the Shi'ite masses by advocating armed struggle. But Imam al-Sadr was playing with fire, toying with too revolutionary a notion. He preached the idea of political violence but only to shake up the traditional Shi'ite political families, especially al-As'ad. Al-Sadr's famous slogan, "Weapons are the ornaments of men" (Al-Silah Zinat al-Rijal) is a clear illustration of the new, fashionable approach to political change in Lebanon. Nevertheless, the Shi'ites of Lebanon remained by and large supportive of the leftist Palestinian and Lebanese parties, whose expression of Shi'ite class resentment and sufferings was more eloquent and sophisticated than that of al-Sadr, who was eagerly trying to enter the Lebanese political game by unconventional means.

The existence of a well-organized military arm of the Movement of the Disinherited was revealed in July 1975, when an explosion in a training camp (supervised by Palestinian military experts) near Ba'albak, which killed thirty-six people, forced al-Sadr to announce the existence of Amal. The movement was based on general principles that were written by al-Sadr to constitute the mithaq (pact) of the organization. It included passionate calls for an end to injustice and oppression, and for the end of the inequities of the sectarian political system in Lebanon. It also called for the abolition of economic exploitation and for the creation of equal opportunity and social justice for all Lebanese. As far as national loyalty is concerned, the pact emphasized that the movement is patriotic and committed to national sovereignty and the territorial integrity of the country. The pact also referred to the Arab nation, asserting the necessity of defending the Palestinian people and underlining its opposition to Zionism and its commitment to the liberation of Palestine.

The war of 1975–76 went beyond Amal's intentions. It proved how costly the slogan of armed struggle was for a leadership with reformist orientations. Suddenly, al-Sadr assumed a new, moderating role after years of preaching political violence. He tried to pressure the warring factions to cease fighting through a hunger strike and a sit-in. Al-Sadr secluded himself in a mosque and called for an immediate halt to "all armed actions in all Lebanese territories." After years of demonizing the social and economic conditions in Lebanon, al-Sadr began calling for the return to the previous "normal situations." His appeals for pacification and reconciliation were not enthusiastically received in the Shi'ite community. Although the movement had a minimal military role in combat in the first phase of the war, several hundred of its fighters participated—very often on their own without the movement's authorization—in armed combat.

The movement was soon discredited in Shi'ite, as well as Muslim and leftist, eyes due to the fall of Al-Nab'a. This Shi'ite district in East Beirut was subject to vicious attacks by right-wing forces in the summer of 1976, and the Amal leadership decided to remain neutral, which facilitated the fall of the area and the subsequent massacre of civilians by right-wing forces. That a predominantly Shi'ite quarter would be left undefended was confusing to many Shi'ites, many of whom believed that the Amal leadership had gone too far in its collaboration with the Syrians and, indeed, with the Phalangists. In July 1976 the Palestinian-Lebanese alliance defeated Amal's negligible military force as part of a general crackdown against all pro-Syrian organizations. That the offices and bases of Amal were eliminated in two days reflected the weak popular support it mustered at the time. Although Musa al-Sadr emerged as a prominent Shi'ite leader in the late 1960s and early 1970s, his total allegiance to the Syrian regime had marginalized his role and the role of his movement by the end of the first phase of the civil war (1975–76).

Ironically, al-Sadr was not as popular and influential among Lebanese Shi'ites as he became after his "disappearance" in 1978, when the Imam was presumed kidnapped during an official trip to Libya. He was popular as long as he articulated Shi'ite grievances and resentment; he failed when he tried to lead the community according to the dictates of his own regional alliances.

The second phase of Amal's history developed in the late 1970s, when several parallel factors were at play. First, the Shi'ites of Lebanon were increasingly alienated by the politics and misconduct of fighters belonging to the PLO and the Lebanese National Movement.* The slogans of these organizations did not particularly address Shi'ite demands for more political and economic power. Indeed, the policies of the two movements were dictated more by regional calculations than by purely Lebanese conditions. The showmanship and corruption of commanders and fighters of the PLO and the Lebanese National Movement dealt a heavy blow to those who had hoped that the two movements would lead the way to radical change in Lebanon. Particularly severe was the situation in the south, where local Lebanese and Palestinian commanders engaged in acts of theft, rape, and general oppression. While all areas of Lebanon suffered under the detested militia rule, the situation in the south was more chaotic and subject to Israeli attack and intervention. Hostile attitudes toward the Palestinian presence emerged in the south. The Shi'ites began using the Palestinians as scapegoats. This climate of anti-Palestinian feelings was exploited by Amal to mobilize the disenchanted Shi'ites along narrow chauvinist Lebanese and Shi'ite sectarian lines. Furthermore, hostile attitudes against the Palestinians were exacerbated by the PLO's bloody battles with Amal prior to the Israeli invasion in 1982. Once the PLO and the Lebanese National Movement recognized the growth of the Amal movement in the late 1970s and early 1980s, they tried to crack down on its bases through sheer military force. Fierce battles were fought between the Lebanese National Movement and the PLO, on the one hand, and the Amal movement, on the other, between 1980 and 1982. In the course of the fighting, some villages were indiscriminately bombarded by Lebanese-Palestinian forces. For this reason, the war of the camps (1985–87), between Palestinians and armed Shi'ite groups, was a continuation of old disputes and an extension of an old conflict.

This mood among the Shi'ites coincided with the disappearance of their Imam, Musa al-Sadr in 1978 in Libya. His disappearance reminded Lebanese Shi'ites of the *ghaybah* (absence) of their twelfth Imam. According to Shi'ite religio-political tradition, the twelfth Imam, who disappeared in the ninth century A.D., will return one day to dispense justice and to end oppression. The disappearance of al-Sadr revived this messianic belief, and raised the hopes of the desperate Shi'ite masses. Like the twelfth Imam, *Al-Mahdi al-Muntadhar* (the Awaited Guide), al-Sadr is believed to be on his way back to rescue his people.

Finally, the victorious Iranian model of revolution provided the Lebanese Shi'ites with an applicable alternative to "alien" ideologies: a Shi'ite Islamic republic. The Iranian revolution restored the Shi'ite faith in communal power. It was the Amal movement that combined all three elements in a purely Shi'ite framework in order to achieve a solid basis for mobilization and recruitment. The movement was reorganized after the disappearance of al-Sadr, and deputy Husayn al-Husayni (who later became the speaker of the Lebanese parliament) took over the leadership. But Husayni's moderate line was opposed by his deputy Nabih Birri, who wanted to develop the military capabilities of the movement. In 1980 the movement held a general congress in which Birri took over as the head. He introduced some organizational centralization. He also established a command council (later named the Politburo) as the highest body of the organization. Birri, who had marked the movement with his influence, has remained at its helm since 1980.

The Amal movement is the major political organization claiming to represent the Shi'ites of Lebanon. The secret of its relative longevity lies in the movement's extension to all regions inhabited by Shi'ites: the Biqa', the south, and Beirut and its suburbs. However, to underline the broad geographical base of the movement is not to attribute cohesiveness to its organizational structure, or to dismiss the schismatic implications of its strong particularistic tendencies. The Amal movement resembles the past organizational structure of Fatah in Lebanon. It advocated an ill-defined and vague ideology, which was often expressed in general and ambiguous terms. This feature is far from being a weakness within the rapidly changing nature of the Lebanese political and social context; it enabled Amal to adjust to the growing radical mood of the Shi'ites. Amal also managed to support a leader who enjoyed the endorsement of conflicting cliques within the ruling elite. As in Fatah, Amal regional leaders care very little about policy consistency because recruitment in a particular area draws heavily upon a certain regional context. Muhammad Ghaddar, for example, who was a Politburo member and a leader of Amal in Al-Ghaziyya, openly supported the Israeli invasion of 1982. Later, when Ghaddar's activities began to embarrass Birri, his membership in the movement was suspended. In contrast to Ghaddar, another Amal regional leader in Sidon, Mahmud al-Faqih, actively opposed the Israelis. These two examples illustrate that Amal's various geographical branches were not tied to a central ideological and political position, but rather were subject to the particularistic tendencies of each region and to the idiosyncrasies of each regional leader.

Regarding the internal organization of Amal, its two leading bodies, the Politburo and the Executive Committee, appeared to balance between two conflicting socioeconomic groups. The first group was educated, upper middle class, and relatively secular in orientation. Its members came from prominent Shi'ite families. The second group was composed of members who had been with the movement since its inception, and who generally are of peasant origin; it was religiously oriented in its political outlook. It appears that the first group, the Birri clique, was still in control in the early 1990s. One member from the first group, Muhammad Baydun, joined the movement in 1980 after years of activism with the Communist Action Organization.* He represented the movement at the Geneva and Lausanne peace talks in 1983. In 1985 he was appointed head of the crucial Council of the South, the body that administered monies for reconstruction and development in South Lebanon; and he was appointed a deputy in 1991.

The Amal movement faced numerous crises in the 1980s. After the uprising of February 1984, when Amal and the Progressive Socialist Party (PSP)* joined hands (with the support of Syria) to expel Amin Jamayyil's forces from West Beirut, Amal became the unofficial ruling power in West Beirut, the suburbs, some parts of the Biqa', and in parts of South Lebanon where Israel was not an occupying power. The rule of the Amal militia, just like the rule of the leftist Lebanese and PLO organizations before it, was detested by large numbers of Lebanese. Its fighters became involved in thuggery and internecine fighting, which exhausted the movement and discredited it in public eyes. Furthermore, Amal was in a difficult position due to its representation (through Nabih Birri) in cabinets since 1984. On the one hand, the leading Amal elite profited from participation in government; on the other hand, the participation in the highly detested Jamayyil government provided Amal's enemies, such as the Party of God* (Hizbullah) with political ammunition.

But the most serious crisis was the protracted war of the camps (1985–87), which the Amal movement started (possibly at Syria's instigation) against the Palestinian camps in Beirut and the south. The Amal movement wanted to disarm Palestinian fighters who were returning to Lebanon. The war was fought under the slogan of "fighting Arafat's forces," which was consistent with the Palestinian policy of the Syrian regime at the time. But Amal fighters fought indiscriminately against all residents of the refugee camps, and they imposed a siege that deprived refugees of water and food for months. On the military level, the Amal movement was not able to bring about a surrender of the Palestinians in a few weeks, as it had hoped. The Palestinians fought tenaciously, and Amal was bogged down in an exhausting conflict for three long years. As if "the war of the camps" was not enough, the Amal movement also fought battles against Sunni and Druze militias in West Beirut. The poor military performance of Amal was caused by disorganization and factionalism within the movement and the series of defections that rendered its fighting force obsolete at times.

Savage fighting between Amal and the Party of God (Hizbullah) began sporadically in 1987 and exploded with full force in 1988. As A. R. Norton states, "[F]rom 1988 to 1990, Amal and Hizballah were locked in a savage turf war which began in the south with the February 1988 kidnapping of US Marine Corps officer Lieutenant Colonel William R. Higgins . . . and spread subsequently to the Beirut suburbs."[26] Amal barely kept control of a few positions in West Beirut and lost most of the southern suburbs to Hizbullah. While the south remained mostly in Amal's hands, the fighting in Iqlim al-Tuffah benefited the Party of God. The diminishing power of Amal, as well as the series of defections from its ranks, led Birri to lose faith in his militia. With Syria's help, he started to develop the Sixth Brigade of the Lebanese Army (which is mostly Shi'ite) as an alternative military tool. Hence, the militia of Amal became a burden for Birri, rather than an asset.

To add to Birri's problems, top leaders of Amal either resigned to protest Birri's autocratic tendencies, or were assassinated by a variety of parties. Those active in anti-Israeli activity in the south were most probably killed by Israeli agents; those active in the war against the Hizbullah were probably killed by members of the latter militia. Furthermore, Birri's own deputy, Hasan Hashim, a charismatic and popular leader of Amal who was close to Musa al-Sadr, resigned in 1986 to protest Birri's "undemocratic" behavior. Other leaders who resigned included 'Ali al-Husayni, Mustafa al-Dirani, 'Aql Hamiyyah, and Zakariyya Hamza. The last three were the top military commanders of the movement. All four were more oriented toward Islam and Iran than Birri, who was perceived to be more pro-Syrian.

The disarming of the militias in 1991 was beneficial to Birri. He appeared to be most enthusiastic about the end of militia rule because he was losing turf to Hizbullah. The appointment of Birri to the Lebanese parliament in 1991, along with Muhammad Baydun and Mahmud AbuHamdan (two pro-Birri Amal leaders), could make Amal a strong parliamentary voice, significant inasmuch as Shi'ite problems remained unresolved.

MOVEMENT OF INDEPENDENT NASSERITES—"AL-MURABITUN" (*Harakat al-Nasiriyyin al-Mustaqillin*—"*Al-Murabitun*"). This movement is closely associated with the name of its founder and leader, Ibrahim Qulaylat. The movement started informally in 1958 when the young Ibrahim participated actively in the 1958 disturbances, championing the cause of Gamal Abdel Nasser in Lebanon. His movement at the time was confined to the Sunni quarter of Abu Shakir, where his father had been a local leader before him. Ibrahim was regarded as a militant Nasserite who would do anything to support Nasserite principles in Lebanon and punish Nasser's enemies. In 1961 he was accused of bombing the house of the minister of finance, who was regarded as anti-Nasser. Qulaylat spent a month and a half in jail.

Qulaylat became a prominent figure only in 1966, when the Lebanese government alleged that he was the instigator of the assassination of Kamil Muruwwah, the publisher and editor in chief of the Beirut daily, *Al-Hayat*. Muruwwah was virulently anti-Nasser and supported pro-Western Arab regimes in his paper. Qulaylat, who professed his innocence, was jailed for a year and a half and was then released without trial. The case made him a hero in some circles, particularly among Nasser's many Muslim supporters. After 1967 Qulaylat informally used the name of Independent Nasserites to underline his independence from the numerous Nasserite organizations in Sunni Muslim areas in Lebanon. His armed men clashed with the authorities as early as 1969, and his quarter of Abu Shakir was immune from the state police. The movement came to public prominence when government troops tried to crack down on the movement's headquarters, which led to popular sympathy with Qulaylat on the part of the Muslim and leftist masses.

Qulaylat often asserted that his organization was not a political party, but rather a broad-based movement that aimed at the mobilization of Nasserites in Lebanon. The movement adhered to the writings and speeches of Nasser as its source of ideological formulation. It also was on record, before the outbreak of the civil war, as favoring the use of violence for political ends. It also staunchly supported the right of the PLO to engage in armed conflict with Israel from Lebanese territory, and it was rewarded by Yasir Arafat's Fatah with generous financial and military aid. But the Libyan regime was believed to be the main benefactor of the movement. The movement emerged as a major militia in the 1975–76 phase of the civil war, not so much because its fighters made up the backbone of the Lebanese anti-Phalangist fighting force, but because Qulaylat knew how to promote his movement in the press, sometimes pressuring local newspapers and magazines to run favorable stories. The promotion of the militia led to the association of the movement with the name of its militia, *al-Murabitun*, which is the common name for the movement.

Qulaylat ran the movement autocratically, although he created the façade of a collective leadership. Many Sunni professionals flocked to the movement after 1977 because they thought it provided opportunities for employment and upward mobility. The leadership was predominantly Sunni, although a token presence of one Shi'ite in the leadership was often advertised. The militia also had a significant Shi'ite component, but the sectarian orientations of the movement were expressive of Sunni urban professionals. Between 1977 and 1982, Qulaylat was one of the masters of the street in West Beirut, and often received foreign dignitaries and ambassadors. He was perceived as the Muslim voice in the city, and the PLO supported his representative claims. His militia lost its popularity when it engaged, like other militias, in plunder, blackmail, and thuggery. The Israeli invasion of 1982 dealt a setback to all the elements of the Lebanese National Movement,* including al-Murabitun, which was a founding member of the movement. But Qulaylat continued to operate in the city until 1984, when Amal* and the Progressive Socialist Party* imposed their dominance over the city and gradually eliminated all rival Sunni militias in West Beirut. In 1985 fighters of the movement were defeated in bloody battles, and Qulaylat was forced to flee. In recent years he has resided in Europe, dividing his time between Switzerland and France. He has continued to issue political statements from exile criticizing his enemies and asserting his Muslim credentials.

MOVEMENT OF THE PIONEERS OF REFORM (Harakat Ruwwad al-Islah). This movement, founded in 1973 by Tammam Salam, the son of traditional Sunni leader Sa'ib Salam, was intended to compete with the sophisticated and armed leftist groups that were popular in Muslim areas. In 1975 the militia of the movement did not participate in armed combat, although it had rich military resources thanks to Saudi support for Salam.

MOVEMENT OF UNIONIST NASSERITES (Harakat al-Wihdawiyyin al-Nasiriyyin). This small organization was founded by Ibrahim Qulaylat's former deputy in the movement of Independent Nasserites—"al-Murabitun."* After 1982 Qulaylat's deputy, French-educated Samir Sabbagh, decided to rebel against the autocratic tendencies of the head of al-Murabitun. He initially formed a small organization that he called the National Grouping, which he later renamed the Movement of Unionist Nasserites. It is a small, Beirut, Sunni-based organization that claims to speak on behalf of Sunnis in West Beirut. It aligned itself with Syria and the Progressive Socialist Party.*

MUNADHDHAMAT AL-'AMAL AL-'ISHTIRAKI AL-THAWRI. See ORGANIZATION OF REVOLUTIONARY SOCIALIST ACTION.

MUNADHDHAMAT AL-'AMAL AL-SHUYU'I. See COMMUNIST ACTION ORGANIZATION.

"AL-MURABITUN." *See* MOVEMENT OF INDEPENDENT NASSERITES.

AL-NAHJ. *See* THE COURSE, OR PATH.

AL-NAJJADA. *See* HELPERS.

NASSERITE FORCES (*Quwwat Nasir*). This is a splinter and self-declared corrective movement of the Union of the Forces of the Working People.* 'Isam al-'Arab split off from the union in 1974 to protest Kamal Shatila's support of Anwar al-Sadat's policy at the time. Al-'Arab was supportive of Libya, which supported the movement financially and militarily. The movement was active in the civil war on the side of the anti-Phalangist coalition, but it always had a small membership and limited effectiveness. Al-'Arab was assassinated in the mid-1980s.

NASSERITE ORGANIZATION. *See* UNION OF THE FORCES OF THE WORKING PEOPLE.

NATIONAL BLOC (*Al-Kutla al-Wataniyya*). This party was also a vehicle for a political leader. It began as a "club" of supporters of Emile Iddi, president of Lebanon in the 1930s. It emerged officially in 1936 when the Lebanese parliament split into two blocs: one (the Constitutional Bloc* of Bisharah al-Khuri), which wanted complete independence for Lebanon and called for close ties between Lebanon and the Arab world; the other (the National Bloc), which supported Iddi's line of Lebanese ultranationalism, and rejected identification with the Arab world while calling for a continued French presence in Lebanon. It defined Lebanon's cultural identity as Phoenician. Iddi was blatantly sectarian and was accused by Muslims of calling for their expulsion to Mecca. Iddi emphasized the Christian character of Lebanon and lobbied Lebanese emigrants to return so as to increase the Christian component of the population.

Lebanese independence in 1943 dealt a severe blow to Iddi's agenda. He suffered political isolation and was expelled from parliament, and his supporters were purged from the civil service. In May 1946, Iddi revived his political movement by forming the National Bloc party. Its platform stated that "the Lebanese people form one nation and that Lebanon is a sovereign, independent state." This latter affirmation was necessary, given Iddi's past support for French "protection." The president of the party (who was called 'amid [dean] according to the party terminology) is elected by the party council and the Executive Committee, which is the highest body. Iddi served as the first dean of the party, and he attracted supporters in Mount Lebanon.

Following the death of Emile Iddi in 1949, his son Raymond became dean, and the party has since been inextricably linked to him. His brother Pierre also played an important role in the party; both brothers assumed several ministerial posts. Raymond's strong and charismatic personality was an asset to the party.

This *za'im*, who always harbored presidential ambitions, transformed the party from a pro-French movement that resisted Lebanese independence into a modern organization that had a significant impact on public debate.

The party supports the free enterprise system and the democratic system of Lebanon. It does not have a distinctive ideology; rather, it stands for general principles that many parties in Lebanon share. But the idiosyncrasies of Raymond Iddi were incorporated into the party's agenda. In the 1960s he often stressed that three dangers faced Lebanon: communism, Zionism, and Shihabism. Iddi's stiff opposition to the policies of President Fu'ad Shihab (and to the policies of his successor, Charles Hilu), and to the intervention of the military in politics, earned him the wrath of the state apparatus, which fought candidates of the party in state and local elections.

Raymond Iddi was an active, respected parliamentarian who took his duties seriously. He was responsible for the banking secrecy laws of Lebanon, the creation of the special security forces (Troop 16), and for a sizable body of legislation. Iddi was also a constant critic of government policy toward southern Lebanon. He proposed the deployment of United Nations forces in South Lebanon in the 1960s to protect Lebanese territory from Israeli bombing and Palestinian infiltration. The PLO and its Lebanese allies rejected the proposal. Iddi was also a firm believer in secularism, and he constantly called for the legalization of civil marriage in Lebanon, which is opposed by clerics of all sects.

Although Iddi's party was regarded in the 1960s as part of the traditional Maronite establishment because it was a member of the Tripartite Alliance (which included the Lebanese Phalanges Party* and the National Liberal Party*), Raymond Iddi took a distinctly political stand throughout the civil war. He objected to the militarization of Maronite ranks, and he refused to create a militia for the party. The outbreak of the civil war in 1975 led to the marginalization of the party on the popular level where combat became fashionable. Iddi took a consistent position against the Maronite establishment (represented by the Lebanese Front*) and considered intra-Maronite conflicts as threatening to the stability of Lebanon. Iddi's position was not popular among some of his supporters, and one of his deputies, Edward Hunayn, resigned from the party and became the secretary-general of the Lebanese Front. Iddi also expelled deputy Ahmad Isbir from the party for insubordination.

But the political position that almost cost Iddi his life was his adamant opposition to Syrian intervention in Lebanon. Iddi considered the Syrian army an occupation force, and he consistently called for its withdrawal. Iddi also maintained a principled position against Israeli occupation of parts of Lebanon and called for an end to Israeli intervention in Lebanese affairs. In 1976, in the aftermath of an assassination attempt for which Iddi held Syria responsible, the dean of the National Bloc party chose to leave Lebanon and settle in Paris, where he has remained ever since. He still maintains a deep interest in Lebanon and still calls for the evacuation of Syrian and Israeli forces. There are indications that Iddi's ties to Iraq might have influenced his views over the past few years. While the party organization in Lebanon still exists, it has lost all significance.


NATIONAL LIBERAL PARTY (*Hizb al-Wataniyyin al-Ahrar*). This party was founded in 1958 by former Lebanese president Kamil Sham'un. It was the political instrument of a charismatic *za'im* who saw the influence of party mobilization in the 1958 civil war. Sham'un did not want to be outflanked by the Lebanese Phalanges Party*; he wanted to organize his supporters as soon as he left the office of president. The party was such an informal group of Sham'un supporters that it did not even bother to publish a program until the mid-1960s. Sham'un, who previously was active in the Constitutional Bloc* of Bisharah al-Khuri, was identified with a pro-Western policy that alienated many of his former Muslim and Christian supporters. Nevertheless, his sectarian appeal won him new supporters.

The party, which included even some non-Maronite and some non-Christian members in its leadership, is classified here as Maronite-oriented because it was closely associated with the person of Kamil Sham'un. According to party by-laws, Sham'un appointed delegates, who then regularly elected him as president of the party. The late Shi'ite deputy Kadhim al-Khalil served for a long time as Sham'un's deputy, but power and decision making always remained firmly in the hands of the autocratic Sham'un, who had little patience with consultation and deliberation. Thus, in the lexicon of Lebanese politics, this party should be understood more as a *kutla* (parliamentary bloc) than as a regular political party. The charisma of Sham'un, however, guaranteed that the party would muster enough supporters and members for public rallies and party festivals.

The party resolved the dilemma regarding the identity of Lebanon by calling for respect for Lebanon's commitment to the League of Arab States. In other words, the party saw no harm in Lebanon's ties with the Arab world as long as its "distinctive character" was retained. Economically, the party firmly believed in the free enterprise system and called for close relations with Western nations. It shared the view of the Phalanges Party in regarding communism as one of the dangers facing Lebanon, and it claimed that "international leftism" aimed at destroying the foundations of the Lebanese political system and its economy. Like the Phalanges Party, the National Liberal Party opposed legalization of leftist parties because they allegedly were disloyal to Lebanon.

In the 1960s, the party's alliance with the Phalanges helped both of them score electoral victories. Their collaboration in the Tripartite Alliance (along with the National Bloc*) presented them to the masses as crusaders for a great Maronite cause. Like the Phalanges, the National Liberal Party began organizing a militia known as the Tigers long before the outbreak of the civil war in 1975. Benefiting from financial and military aid from his friend King Husayn of Jordan, Sham'un believed that the Palestinian presence in Lebanon posed a threat that the Lebanese state was unwilling or unable to cope with. King Husayn was obviously interested in funding a cause that aimed at defeating his Palestinian enemies at the time.

The party's militia was active in the early part of the civil war, but it was overshadowed by the Phalanges Party and the Lebanese Forces.* The party did not—unlike the Phalanges Party—develop into a sophisticated apparatus. It remained a mere instrument for Sham'un, who treated it as his own personal property. Thus, his son Duri was "elected" secretary-general, and his other son, Dani, was "elected" secretary of defense. Duri, who was not skilled politically, appeared to have been forced into politics against his will (he regularly left Lebanon for months at a time and focused more on his business deals), whereas Dani was interested in the military aspect of his party involvement.

As mentioned earlier, when Bashir Jamayyil decided in 1980 that the Tigers militia should cease to exist, his fighters perpetrated a massacre of the Tigers in July 1980 in Safra. This was the party's most fateful crisis. Nevertheless, Sham'un did not boycott the Lebanese Front,* and he continued his political alliance with Bashir Jamayyil until Jamayyil was assassinated in 1982.

After the Israeli invasion of 1982, Dani Sham'un tried to revive the party and its militia, but he was not able to compete with the Phalanges and the Lebanese Forces. The death of Kamil Sham'un in 1987 resulted in an organizational crisis in the party. Young, educated activists apparently took advantage of Sham'un's death to press for democratization of the party and to end the Sham'un family's dominance over party affairs. The conflict over this issue was not satisfactorily resolved. Instead, the rebellious group decided to defect. This small faction, however, was not able to play a significant political role. The party as a whole remained marginal until 1989 when Dani Sham'un headed the "new" Lebanese Front in 1989 to promote the agenda of General 'Awn. His outspoken support for 'Awn and his staunch opposition to the Syrian government and the Al-Ta'if Accords gave him much visibility and indeed popularity in East Beirut.

The defection of the small faction made Sham'un sensitive to the accusation of family dominance over the party. Thus, in August 1990, he called the General Congress of the party to elect a new president and vice president. Not surprisingly, he won the presidency, receiving 243 votes while his opponent (who boycotted the session) received only 3 votes. Opponents of Sham'un within the party, including longtime party leader Musa Prince, challenged the results; nevertheless, the movement against Sham'un remained insignificant because the party was founded primarily to organize those who were susceptible to Kamil Sham'un's charisma. The dominance of the Sham'un family did not offend most members, who saw a benefit in terms of legitimacy and the electoral appeal of the party. The small faction, however, continued to operate using the name of the Political Council of the National Liberal Party Convening in Saudico (a quarter in East Beirut), and it included such party veterans as Musa Prince, Marun Hilu, Nabil Karam, and Nuhad Shalhat.[27]

The assassination of Dani Sham'un in 1990 dealt a serious blow to the party. Duri Sham'un, who had given up his political career, came back to Lebanon and was elected president of the party in 1991. For obvious reasons, Duri chose to take a less anti-Syrian stand than his brother. The party, which was founded to exploit the leadership of Kamil Sham'un, is unlikely to regain the prominence that it enjoyed under his leadership.

NUSUR AL-BIQA'. *See* EAGLES OF AL-BIQA'.

OCTOBER 24 MOVEMENT *(Harakat 24 Tishrin)*. This small, Tripoli-based organization takes its name from the revolt led by its leader, Faruq al-Muqaddam, on October 24, 1969, when (with Fatah's help) he occupied the city's fortress to protest government policies against the Palestinians. This charismatic leader was a student in France in the 1960s, and he came back to Lebanon to try to create a pro-PLO movement in Tripoli to further the Palestinian cause and to champion the cause of the poor Lebanese. The confrontation in Tripoli in 1969 brought national fame to Muqaddam and his movement. He presented his movement as a radical alternative that stood outside the parameters of the Lebanese National Movement.* In other words, he considered the Movement to be too reformist and too moderate. However, the election of 1972 was too tempting for Muqaddam, who set aside his talk of the futility of reformism and "struggle within"; he ran for the parliamentary seat of Tripoli and lost.

This organization, like many similar ones in Lebanon, lacks a coherent ideology. The literature of the movement combines Nasserite rhetoric with romantic socialist ideas. The movement idolized "armed struggle" and participated in combat in the 1975–76 war proportionate to its small size. It confined its activities to the Tripoli region.

The movement underwent some mysterious changes in the late 1970s when Muqaddam began to improve ties with the Lebanese state and was often accused of ties to the Lebanese intelligence services. In the early 1980s, he aligned himself with the Lebanese Phalanges Party,* and later with the regime of Amin Jamayyil. He relocated to East Beirut, and was said to have resided for a while in France, where he spent most of the 1980s.

THE ORGANIZATION *(Al-Tandhim)*. This small party was founded in 1969 in the wake of major clashes between the Palestinian forces in Lebanon and the Lebanese army (which was aided by right-wing militias). Its founders split off from the Lebanese Phalanges Party* in protest against its leadership's reluctance to engage in nationwide military training and arming of the Lebanese population to engage in full-scale war against the Palestinians in Lebanon. Since its inception, this party has exhibited a fixation with the militarization of the Lebanese in order to "defend Lebanon." This ostensibly secretive program was made public in 1973 when the Organization participated in clashes between Palestinian forces, on the one hand, and the coalition of Lebanese army troops and right-wing militias, on the other. The Organization developed into a political party in

1975 and became an active (albeit largely insignificant) member of the Lebanese Forces.*

ORGANIZATION OF LEFTIST KURDISH PARTY. A faction of the *Parti* opposed the formation of a joint front by the Kurdish Democratic Party* and the Lebanese Kurdish Party* in 1976, and cautioned against the insulation of Kurdish forces from the Lebanese conflict. The new faction asserted that Jamil Mihhu was fundamentally anti-leftist. The Lebanese National Movement* welcomed the creation of this party and accepted it within the leading bodies of the movement.

ORGANIZATION OF REVOLUTIONARY SOCIALIST ACTION (*Munadhdhamat al-'Amal al-Ishtiraki al-Thawri*). This is the Lebanese sister party of the Popular Front for the Liberation of Palestine (PFLP)–General Command (GC) that participated briefly in the Lebanese civil war. It claimed responsibility for the kidnapping of U.S. Colonel Morgan, who was released in 1975 after the U.S. embassy delivered food to refugee camps.

AL-PARTI. *See* KURDISH DEMOCRATIC PARTY.

PARTY OF ARAB LIBERATION (*Hizb al-Taharrur al-'Arabi*). This small organization was formed by the late Sunni prime minister, Rashid Karami. It was a renamed version of a parliamentary bloc formed by his father, 'Abdul-Hamid Karami, in the 1940s.

PARTY OF GOD (*Hizbullah*). *Hizbullah* was officially established in the wake of the Israeli invasion in 1982; however, its formation can be traced to the 1960s, to some Shi'ite militants who were displeased with the agenda of Imam Musa al-Sadr. Shaykh (or Ayatollah) Muhammad Husayn Fadllalah, who is regarded as the spiritual guide of the party, said that he never liked or trusted al-Sadr because he was promoted as "a star by the Christians."[28] Fadllalah himself, after youthful Islamic activity in southern Iraq, was active in his quarter in Al-Nab'ah, promoting his Islamic vision through his own organization called the Family of Brotherhood ('*Usrat al-Ta'akhi*). Nevertheless, Fadllalah's theological views were consistent with the mainstream Shi'ite notion of *al-Shura*, which suggests that Muslims should rule according to the Quranic principle of consultation. This theory holds that the ideal Islamic order is impossible as long as the Twelfth Imam remains concealed. But Fadllalah's religio-political outlook went through a dramatic change over the years. By his own admission, it was the Iranian revolution that led him to believe in the efficacy of the notion of *velayat-e faqih* (the Guardianship of the Jurisconsult) as a model for political order and consequently in the necessity of establishing an Islamic republic.[29] The call for an Islamic order in the absence of the Twelfth Imam is the main feature of Ayatollah Khomeini's political outlook; it is a revolutionary idea as it constitutes a recipe for action after centuries of Shi'ite tolerance of Sunni rule. In Lebanon, advocates of *velayat-e faqih* staunchly opposed what they perceived to be Christian domination of the government.

The single most important event in the history of Shi'ite militant groups in Lebanon was the creation of the Salvation Committee by president Ilyas Sarkis in June 1982. Sarkis formed the committee, which included, among others, Nabih Birri and Bashir Jamayyil, to deal with the repercussions of the Israeli invasion. Birri's membership on the committee reinforced the rift in the Shi'ite political movement between Birri and those who were pushing for a more hardline Islamic path in accordance with Iranian designs in Lebanon. Husayn al-Musawi, a leading figure in the Amal Movement* at the time, objected to Birri's acceptance of membership in the committee and called for Iranian arbitration of the matter. The dispute was referred to the Iranian ambassador in Damascus at the time, 'Ali Akbar Mohtashemi (formerly minister of interior and later member of the *majles* [parliament], who ruled against Birri's participation in the committee. Birri did not abide by the ruling, and Musawi decided to resign from Amal and form his own Islamic Amal Movement.*

On the day of Birri's participation in the meeting of the Salvation Committee, the official Amal representative in Iran, Shaykh Ibrahim al-Amin, held a press conference in the offices of the Iranian newspaper *Keyhan* in which he attacked the committee and its members. It was then that the organization of Hizbullah was formed under the sponsorship of the Iranian Revolutionary Guards stationed in the Biqa' at the time, although the organization declared its existence officially in 1984 when a statement commemorating the massacre of Sabra and Shatila was issued over the party's signature.

The role of Fadllalah in the establishment of the Party of God is unclear. One account maintained that Fadllalah preferred to have Muslim Shi'ite fundamentalists working within the body of the Amal Movement in order to reach the broadest possible audience in the Shi'ite community. But the tide of pro-Iranian sentiments within the Shi'ite community was growing at a pace that could not be restrained within the confines of Amal's alliance with the Syrian regime. Furthermore, Iran wanted to have a loyal and obedient organization in Lebanon to further its influence among the Shi'ites and to strike at its enemies. The presence of Israeli troops and U.S. Marines in Lebanon added another incentive for direct Iranian involvement in Lebanon.

Hizbullah's ideology emphasizes the Quranic origins of its terminology. Almost all the political terms that the party uses in its political literature are derived from the *Quran*. One party leader states that most of the activities and "movements" of Muslims should be based on Quranic verses (*Ayats*). However, the claim that all the policies and actions of the Party of God are derived from the *Quran* is unpersuasive, although the party does legitimize all its actions through Islamic rationalization. The word *Hizbullah* itself is from the *Quran*, but it was not used to advocate party formation in the modern sense; the term *Hizbullah* in the *Quran* simply denotes the body of Muslim believers.

Organizationally, the party paradoxically follows Leninist organizational centralization. While the Leninist party is based on the doctrine of "democratic centralism," the Party of God is based upon a similar doctrine that one Islamic ideologue calls "the centralism of the method of *Hizbullah*, or the centralism of the *'ulama*." Hizbullah's power flows from the ruling clerics down to the entire membership, although there is an unspecified, nonclerical minority in the leadership. The party, however, allows for the taking of initiatives by local party leaders as the situation requires. The leadership is aware that rigid centralism can render the organization ineffective.

In Hizbullah's ideology, justice and equality can be achieved through human efforts, through a revolutionary process. The party's ideology represents a radical, revolutionary strand of Shi'ite theology. The conservative and orthodox Shi'ite theological school believes that justice and equality can be achieved only with the return of the Twelfth Imam. The concept of *velayat-e faqih* calls for a political revolution to establish an Islamic order headed by the deputy of the Imam on earth, a title that only Khomeini held in recent times. The ideology also introduces a new distinction between the revolutionary *'ulama* and what Khomeini called *Fuqaha' al-Salatin* (the Sultan's theologians, in reference to those *'ulama* who support the secular, ruling government).

It is not possible to determine the exact nature of the relationship between the party and Iran. It is not clear whether its subservience is similar to that which bound Arab communist parties to the Soviet Union. It is clear, however, that Iranian influence among members and leaders of the party stems primarily from the moral and political standing of Khomeini in the Shi'ite world. He was the link between the Shi'ite community and the blood lineage of the Prophet. His death is destined to lead to more political independence of the party vis-à-vis the Iranian government, which is perceived by some party leaders and members as being too moderate.

The party emulates the Leninist pattern of organization, which ensures party discipline and strict allegiance to the leadership. The leadership body (which comprises from ten to twelve members) was initially called the *Shura* Council, but is now known as the Politburo. Decisions within the Politburo are reached by consensus, or by a majority vote when a consensus is not reached. The leadership may also decide to refer matters to the Iranian government. Responsibilities are divided according to typical party functions: there are seven committees for thought, finance, political affairs, information, military affairs, judicial affairs, and social affairs. The party organization in Lebanon is also divided geographically into three regions: Beirut and its suburbs, the Biqa', and the south.

The swift and dramatic rise of the party occurred after 1984. The party benefited from its stiff confrontational stance vis-à-vis the U.S. Marine presence in Lebanon and the Israeli occupation in the south. The association of the Hizbullah with the bombing of the U.S. Marine barracks in Lebanon and the series of hostage takings boosted the radical credentials of the party. It originally maintained a low profile and focused on the slow formation of cells, but the TWA airliner hijacking in 1985 focused more attention on the party (although the party has never admitted responsibility for hostage taking or hijacking acts), and the party became visibly active in the Lebanese political and military arena. The party declared its manifesto in 1985, three years after its birth. It is primarily known for its strategic objective: the creation of an Islamic republic in Lebanon. The party is committed in its literature to bringing an end to "Maronite domination" of Lebanon. It refuses to associate itself with the conventional Lebanese political game and emphasizes its ideological uniqueness within the context of Islamic thinking.

During the war between Amal and Hizbullah in 1988–90, the party scored some successes on both political and military fronts. While Amal was discredited, the party intensified its attacks against Israeli forces and their allies in South Lebanon. Amal was viewed as one of the many traditional political players in Lebanon that was lured by the political benefits of membership in the government, while the Hizbullah asserted the need for a radical overthrow of the Lebanese system and stressed the urgency of an Islamic order in Lebanon. More important, the party proved to be far more sophisticated in its recruitment procedures and its propaganda campaigns than Amal. The party takes seriously the indoctrination of members and holds lectures and seminars for members and sympathizers alike. It also publishes a large number of periodicals that are aimed at children, women, and militant youths. To be sure, Hizbullah reportedly has benefited for years from generous financial aid from Iran, but there is no solid information on this subject.

The party also created a variety of social services for desperately impoverished Shi'ites in various parts of Lebanon. It tried to fill a gap that the Lebanese government had created in predominantly Shi'ite areas before the outbreak of civil strife. Party speakers utilize the crucial platform of the Friday prayer sermon to propagate the party message to large sectors of the population. It has effectively used its radio and television stations to expand its following in Lebanon. More important, the party has profited from the discipline and dedication that its members display, unlike Amal. It is this discipline that characterized the military success of the numerically inferior Party of God against Amal.

The end of the intra-Shi'ite war in 1991, as well as the disarming of the militias, provided the party with a challenge. Could it maintain the credibility of its uncompromising revolutionism and adapt to a purely political struggle? The party also had to adjust to the change of government in Iran and the rise of the Rafsanjani line, which believed less in the efficacy of the immediate creation of an Islamic republic in Lebanon. Furthermore, the Rafsanjani government seemed more interested in maintaining good relations with Damascus than in furthering Islamic revolutionary goals in Lebanon.

While the party has not abandoned armed struggle, and has indeed moved most of its weapons to safe areas in the Biqa', the leadership appears prepared to engage in conventional political battles. Leaders now hold meetings with various Lebanese political factions, including bitter enemies of yesterday, like the Phalangists (see Lebanese Phalanges Party) and the communists (see Communist Party of Lebanon). They have even met with representatives of the Lebanese government and its army. This would have been inconceivable until recently.

After years of postponement, the Party of God held its Second National Congress in May 1991. The congress, which was attended by members and cadres from all parts of the party, elected a secret new leadership. The secretary-general of the party, Subhi At-Tufayli, was replaced by ʻAbbas al-Musawi, who was killed in an Israeli raid in 1992. Ibrahim al-Amin, who was absent from party activity in the last three years, was elected deputy secretary-general. The new leadership could very well prepare the party for the new, difficult stage of post-militia politics. Whether the party will succeed in its new political role remains to be seen.

PHALANGES PARTY. See LEBANESE PHALANGES PARTY.

POPULAR NASSERITE ORGANIZATION (Al-Tandhim al-Shaʻbi al-Nasiri). This organization, based in Sidon, is closely associated with the name of a local activist, Maʻruf Saʻd, whose assassination in 1975 marked the beginning of the Lebanese civil war for some. He was succeeded in the leadership of the movement by his son Mustafa Saʻd, formerly an engineering student in Moscow. Mustafa Saʻd became interested in modernizing the organization's militia, which was later named the Popular Liberation Army. Saʻd survived the detonation of a car bomb near his house in 1985, which killed his daughter and cost him his eyesight. Israel was widely believed responsible for the explosion, which was presumably meant to punish him for support of anti-Israeli actions in the south. After 1982 the PLO began to support Saʻd and his militia because Sidon was the last remaining stronghold in the PLO's hands, free of Syrian domination. The entry of the Lebanese army into Sidon in the summer of 1991 appeared likely to undermine the power of Saʻd, whose militia was detested by the local population. The movement lacks an ideology, and it should be considered, rather, a local gang.

PROGRESSIVE SOCIALIST PARTY (PSP) (Al-Hizb al-Taqaddumi al-Ishtiraki). This party is closely associated with the name of its founder, Kamal Jumblat, who hails from one of the leading Druze families of Lebanon. Jumblat came from a family that transfers political leadership from father to son. Although Kamal was not politically inclined in his youth, he was elected to parliament in 1943, and political leadership became inescapable for him when his mother died.

Ironically, Kamal's first involvement in politics was in the ranks of a right-wing, Maronite-oriented party; he won the election in 1943 as a member of the National Bloc* party, and he served in the party until 1946. Jumblat formed the PSP in 1949. The founding committee included an impressive group of intellectuals from various sects. In his first public statement as party head, Jumblat announced that the party intended to organize the masses of "men of thought, workers, and peasants." The party opened branches in most of Lebanon and presented several proposals that dealt with improving the conditions of workers and peasants. It also called for free education and health care. When it intensified its opposition to the administration of Bisharah al-Khuri, security forces clamped down.

Jumblat became a key parliamentary leader (what is known in the Lebanese lexicon as *Qutb*, literally, a pole), and he was instrumental in the formation of a broad front in 1952 that led to the end of the administration of al-Khuri, who was forced to resign from the presidency. Jumblat protested British and American policy in the Middle East and gradually became a supporter of Nasser of Egypt.

The radicalization of the party put it at odds with the administration of President Kamil Sham'un, who dissolved the party. But a civil war broke out in 1958, and Jumblat was one of the leaders of the so-called popular resistance. The party militia took part in the fighting in various parts of Lebanon. The party soon changed from one that was established by a group of secularly oriented intellectuals into an organizational tool through which the Jumblati family leadership successfully mobilized and recruited Druze followers. The secular and progressive rhetoric of the PSP helped Kamal Jumblat extend his leadership and appeal well beyond his community, but it failed to make the party a nonsectarian organization, at least as far as membership composition was concerned. Furthermore, Jumblat always maintained a traditional "feudal" image among his constituency, which referred to him as the "lord of the Mukhtarah [his hometown]," a title he himself accepted. According to a former leading member, the PSP was one of the traditional confessional groups working "within the framework of conservative politics of Lebanon" as early as the mid-1950s.

The sectarian nature of Kamal Jumblat's leadership is also revealed by the composition of the voters who supported the PSP in the election of 1972. In the Shuf region, for example, where Jumblat was a candidate, he received more than 90 percent of the votes in the Druze polling places. By contrast, in non-Druze polling places, Jumblat received less than 10 percent of the votes.

Jumblat's influence grew in the aftermath of the 1958 civil war, and he played an important role in the 1960s, especially since President Fu'ad Shihab (1958–1964) admired him. But the party's sectarianism also increased as the party became identified with particularistic Druze concerns. In addition, Jumblat had decided to expel eighteen prominent members after 1958 due to their disagreement with his position during the civil war. Almost all of those expelled were Christians. Jumblat was a frequent cabinet member. He formed the National Struggle Front as a parliamentary bloc comprising all PSP members in parliament, as well as deputies who sympathized with him.

Jumblat's undoubtedly unique charisma appealed to Muslims who were increasingly disenchanted with their traditional leaders (*zu'ama*). Moreover, Jumblat was the only one among the *zu'ama* who challenged the very foundations of Lebanese legitimacy and questioned the ability of the political system to survive without reform. Of course, Jumblat never went so far as to call for revolutionary change. He was mainly concerned with internal reforms. His disillusionment with the traditional political elite and his pan-Arab stance led

354 / Political Parties of the Middle East

him to begin organizing a front that would include all leftist and Muslim anti-establishment organizations and parties. In 1964, he formed the Front of National and Progressive Parties, Personalities, and Bodies in Lebanon, which was modified in 1969 to operate under the name of The Grouping of National and Progressive Parties.

The PSP (as a member of the Grouping) played a major role in the demonstrations and strikes that were launched in defense of the Palestinian Resistance Movement and internal Lebanese reforms throughout the late 1960s and 1970s. Jumblat, however, angered some of his leftist allies when he decided to support Sulayman Franjiyyah in the 1970 presidential election. By 1975 Jumblat had become a major Arab figure who was admired for his staunch support of the PLO. He also became closely aligned with the communist movement in Lebanon.

The PSP never articulated a coherent ideology. Instead, the party espoused general and vague ideas of socialism and Arab nationalism. It believed in the betterment of social and economic conditions of the workers and peasants. It also called for an end to "feudal" relations of production in Lebanon, although Jumblat himself (as well as his large extended family) belonged to the large landowning class. The party also favored closer relations with the Arab world and a specific definition of the Arab identity of Lebanon, in contrast to the vague formulation of the National Pact, which designated only "Lebanon's face" as Arab. Jumblat also wanted a dilution of the pro-Western orientation of Lebanon, and closer cooperation with the Soviet bloc, which won him the Lenin Order.

The PSP had its own militia, which was inferior to the militias of the right-wing parties, but it benefited from the military expertise of the PLO. Furthermore, the party benefited from the ancient social values among the Druzes, who "measured a man by his ability to use a rifle." Of course, the weapons available to Druze men could not match the sophisticated weaponry of the Maronite-oriented militias. For that, Jumblat had to rely on the help of the Syrian regime and the PLO.

When war broke out in 1975, Kamal Jumblat become the main spokesperson for the Leftist/Muslim coalition. But although he became one of the two main protagonists in the civil war, his own party did very little fighting. Jumblat preferred to insulate the Druze heartland from the ferocity of the civil strife. Jumblat even prohibited his PLO allies from operating in Druze areas. Nevertheless, he was the most prominent member of the leftist coalition. He was instrumental in organizing what became known as the Lebanese National Movement (LNM),* which comprised leftist and Nasserite organizations. Jumblat headed the committee that announced the program of the National [or patriotic] and Progressive Forces and Organizations in August 1975. The program, known as *Al-Barnamaj al-Marhali* (the Phased Program) was not the radical program that its Phalangist (see Lebanese Phalanges Party) critics claimed. It included certain provisions for the reform (not the abolition) of the Lebanese political system, and it called for the diminution of sectarian representation but not for full secularization.

Although the PSP did not play a role in major combat operations (people in

West Beirut remarked that Jumblat was going to fight his enemies to the last Shi'ite), Jumblat devoted party resources to the construction of an effective and modern militia. Early on, he formed the Popular Liberation Army, as the major military arm of the PSP, and indeed of the Druze community, given his popularity within it. Due to the militarization of the Druze youths, and the prominent pan-Arab and Lebanese role that was played by Kamal Jumblat, the influence of the traditional Druze rivals of the Jumblati family confederation, the Arsalans, declined dramatically. The Arsalans, who have headed the Yazbaki family confederation, erred—in Druze eyes—by remaining allies of the Maronite establishment, specifically of Kamil Sham'un.

While Jumblat was officially the president of the Central Political Council (the highest ruling body) of the Lebanese National Movement, which was thoroughly organized and structured in July 1976, decision making in areas under the control of the PLO and the Lebanese National Movement was in reality in Yasir Arafat's hands. The leadership of the Palestine Liberation Organization (PLO) made sure that all important decisions of the LNM accorded with Palestinian political wishes, which created resentment among many Lebanese Muslims, and also led to frequent complaints by Jumblat. Jumblat, for example, wanted the Lebanese civil war to be fought to the fullest in order to bring about the demise of the Maronite establishment, while the PLO wanted a limited and manageable conflict.

Yet, the major crisis in the political life of Kamal Jumblat and the PSP was his conflict with Syria. While Jumblat was planning an all-out war to achieve for the LNM full control of Lebanese territory, the Syrian regime began to shift in 1976 to the side of the Maronite coalition. The intervention of Syrian troops in the spring of 1976 against the PLO–LNM forces led to the defeat of Jumblat's camp.

The conflict with Syria dashed Jumblat's hopes and denied his coalition crucial military aid. So angered was Jumblat about the changing Syrian role that he refused various Arab appeals to mend fences with Damascus. With Syrian political ascendancy in Lebanon, Jumblat kept a low profile until he was assassinated in March 1977. As with all assassinations in Lebanon, the perpetrators are still unknown. His conflict with Syria, and the artificially deliberate attempt by the assassins to leave evidence linking Syria's archenemy Iraq to the deed, led many to blame the Syrian regime for the assassination.

The real confessional and traditional nature of the PSP was clearly revealed when Walid Jumblat, Kamal's only son, inherited the leadership of the party upon the death of his father in 1977, along with large estates, the Siblin factory, and the Mukhtarah palace. Party leadership, then, is one of the family holdings transmitted from father to son to secure Jumblati leadership of the Druze community. The "secular" and progressive rhetoric of the PSP helped Kamal and Walid to extend their leadership and appeal well beyond the community. Like his father, Walid saw no difficulty in reconciling the progressive rhetoric of the PSP with his sectarian and traditional leadership. In his own words, "[J]e suis féodal à ma façon et progressiste à ma façon." (I am feudal in my own way and progressive in my own way.)[30]

Walid Jumblat introduced changes by ending the feud with the Syrian regime and expanding the militarization of the party. He reorganized the Popular Liberation Army and established army-style barracks for the fighters. However, he continued to insulate the Druze areas from combat and fighting. The Lebanese National Movement chose him to succeed his father as its head, but he was not able to play the same regional or international role as his father. He did not break with his father's main policies, except in his relations with Syria. He was also different from his father in temperament; Walid was known to indulge in worldly pleasures.

As the 1982 Israeli invasion changed the political map of Lebanon and helped install a Phalangist as President of the Republic, Walid kept a low profile and even agreed to meet with Israeli military and political leaders. While the Lebanese National Movement ceased to exist by virtue of the dramatic political changes in the country and the rise of religiously oriented parties, the PSP benefitted from the presence of Druzes in the Israeli army. Many Israeli Druze soldiers extended clandestine help to the members of the PSP, in the form of weapons and freedom of movement in Israeli-occupied areas. The Israeli occupation of Lebanon also facilitated interaction between Lebanese Druzes and their coreligionists in Israel, who formed a domestic lobby to help the Druze in Lebanon.

The consequences of the Israeli invasion inadvertently led to the enhancement of Walid's leadership. The introduction of Lebanese Forces troops into the Druze heartland antagonized the Druze community and led in 1983–84 to one of the bloodiest chapters in the history of the civil war. The "war of the mountain," as it is known in Lebanon, led to savage confrontations between the Lebanese Forces* and the PSP militia. It resulted in an eventual victory for the Druze fighters, but at a tremendous cost in human life on both sides. The war also intensified sectarian agitation on both sides and transformed a seemingly political conflict into sectarian warfare reminiscent of the bloody nineteenth-century feuds between Maronites and Druzes. As a result of the war, those Christians who survived were forcibly evicted from Druze areas. The war boosted the popularity of Walid in his community, which regarded him as its ultimate defender. Walid became even more popular as a Druze leader than his father, since he has spent less time and effort on non-Druze concerns.

Like his father, however, Walid propagates two different messages. The first is a purely Druze message that sees in the war with the Phalangists a continuation of the nineteenth-century sectarian feuds between Druzes and Maronites. It appeals to Druze emotions. The second is the propaganda that keeps an eye on the larger Muslim Arab community and the Socialist International, in which the PSP is represented; it tries to appeal to the Muslims by stressing the anti-Israeli policies of the PSP, and by exaggerating the party's progressive objectives. In reality, Walid appears to be primarily concerned with the interests of his community, which he calls "my tribe." Those interests include survival as an independent confessional group free from persecution and humiliation. They also entail the preservation of a peculiar identity that has maintained Druze separateness. Of course, whenever possible, a Druze leader who is able to achieve more power for his community will be rewarded with more support and loyalty.

The victory of the PSP facilitated Jumblat's task of ensuring Druze separateness. He was accused—even by some of his former allies—of creating a Druze canton, which was not an entirely unfair accusation. In 1983–84 Walid formed what he called *Al-'Idarah al-Madaniyyah* (the civil administration), which put the PSP in charge of the areas under its control and permitted the party to replace the Lebanese state in all of its functions. He even ordered a separate flag and a separate anthem to replace the Lebanese flag and national anthem. While this narrow sectarian endeavor displeased many Lebanese, it increased Jumblat's popularity within his community.

The separate Druze entity was threatened in 1990–91 when the Lebanese state began to expand its authority and when the PSP was forced to surrender its weapons to the Syrian army under the terms of the Al-Ta'if Accords. But the disarming of the PSP will not threaten the leadership of Walid Jumblat, who is the most secure political leader among all militia leaders in Lebanon. Some militia leaders in Lebanon will lose their leadership positions once their militias are disarmed. Walid, by contrast, is a leader in peacetime as he was in wartime. Furthermore, Walid's political influence was increased when four of his supporters (along with himself) were appointed to the parliament in 1991.

Finally, Walid ensured uncontested political supremacy within the party by banning factionalism within its ranks and by expelling those who did not display full allegiance.

PROGRESSIVE VANGUARDS (*Al-Tala'i' Al-Taqaddumiyya*). This very small, Beirut-based organization was founded in 1973 by Muhammad Zakariyyah 'Itani. It consistently supported Syrian policy in Lebanon.

PROMISE PARTY (*Hizb al-Wa'd*). It is inaccurate to call this group a political party. In reality, it is a clique, or gang, of the former head of the Lebanese Forces, Elie Hubayqa. Hubayqa was the commander of the Lebanese Forces until January 1986, when Samir Ja'ja' staged a coup within the leadership and ousted Hubayqah for his acceptance of the Tripartite Agreement of December 1985, which was signed in Damascus by Hubayqah (representing the Lebanese Forces), Nabih Birri (representing Amal), and Walid Jumblat (representing the Progressive Socialist Party). The agreement was opposed by some Christian factions because it gave more power to Muslims, and because it guaranteed Syrian political supremacy in Lebanon.

After his defeat, Hubayqah moved to Zahlah in the Biqa' and claimed to represent the "authentic" Lebanese Forces. He subsequently became a close ally of the Syrian regime and set up an office in Damascus. With millions of dollars from the Lebanese Forces' budget, Hubayqah was able to maintain a militia of his own, although he always wanted to return to East Beirut. The Hubayqah militia incorporated all those fighters and cadres who were expelled from East Beirut on account of their subservience to him. In September 1986, Hubayqah launched a military operation (with Syrian help) to take control of East Beirut. The Lebanese Army loyal to General 'Awn repulsed the attackers and Hubayqah went back to his headquarters in Zahlah.

Hubayqah entered East Beirut victoriously in October 1990 in the wake of the defeat of General 'Awn. He opened offices for his organization, which he said would operate as a political party (the Promise Party) in the postmilitia phase. Several of his men tried to settle old scores with enemies from the past, engaging in sporadic clashes with supporters of Jaja. The Syrian forces later restrained the Hubayqah forces after loud protests from Christian leaders. In his appointment to the expanded parliament in 1991, Hubayqah gained the Beirut seat which was vacated by Pierre Jamayyil. To many Phalangists his appointment to that very seat was a provocative act. His Syrian patrons continue to demonstrate their strong willingness to reward him for his support of the Tripartite Agreement.

PSP. See PROGRESSIVE SOCIALIST PARTY.

QUWWAT HUSAYN AL-INTIHARIYYA. See SUICIDAL FORCES OF HUSAYN.

AL-QUWWAT AL-LUBNANIYYA. See LEBANESE FORCES.

QUWWAT AL-MARADA. See FORCES OF MARADA.

QUWWAT NASIR. See NASSERITE FORCES.

RABITAT AL-SHAGHILA. See TOILERS' LEAGUE.

RAMGAVAR PARTY. This party, founded in 1921 when two liberal and democratic Armenian parties merged together, is considered the party of Armenian intellectuals. It has benefited from the conflict between the Dashnak Party* and the Hunchak Party.* The party has emphasized the necessity of preserving Armenian culture and heritage in the diaspora. The party participated in the 1960s in creating an opposition front against the political dominance of the Dashnak.

REVOLUTIONARY COMMUNIST BLOC (Al-Tajammu' al-Shuyu'i al-Thawri). This is one of the smallest of the numerous, clandestine communist organizations in Lebanon. It adheres to Trotskyism, and calls for violent revolutionary change in Lebanon. It is one of the few organizations of the left that has taken a consistently anti-Syrian line. Its membership is small and multisectarian.

REVOLUTIONARY NASSERITE ORGANIZATION (Al-Tandhim al-Thawri al-Nasiri). This is an offshoot of the Forces of Nasser. In 1977, 'Isam al-'Arab's deputy, Hasan Qubaysi, split off from the Forces to form his own small Nasserite organization. The movement had some Shi'ite members.

RIZ KARI. See LEBANESE KURDISH PARTY.

AL-RUHBANIYYAT AL-LUBNANIYYA. See LEBANESE MONASTIC ORDER.

AL-SHABIBA AL-LUBNANIYYA. See LEBANESE YOUTHS.

SOCIALIST ARAB ACTION PARTY—LEBANON (Hizb al-'Amal al-Ishtiraki al-'Arabi—Lubnan). When the Movement of Arab Nationalists was dissolved, George Habash's supporters in the Lebanese branch decided to form an organization of their own. The party, founded in 1969, presented itself as an alternative version of Marxism-Leninism that considered the Communist Action Organization* and the Communist Party of Lebanon* to be too moderate and reformist. The party declared itself a revolutionary communist party that admired the Bulgarian version of Marxism-Leninism. It was known as the Lebanese sister party of the Popular Front for the Liberation of Palestine (PFLP). The party held its first national congress in 1975 and elected an Iraqi-born union leader, Hashim 'Ali Muhsin, as its leader. The party held its second national congress in 1980.

The party, which has advocated armed struggle throughout its history, participated in the civil war. It was linked by Abu Iyad to the assassination of the American ambassador in Lebanon in 1976. It has consistently advocated intensification of hostilities to achieve revolutionary change. Its links with the PFLP gained it representation in the Lebanese National Movement.* In 1981 the PFLP decided to sever its ties with the party. The party remained insignificant.

SOCIALIST CHRISTIAN DEMOCRATIC PARTY—THE ACTION PARTY (Al-Hizb al-Dimuqrati al-Masihi al-Ishtiraki—Hizb al-'Amal). This party is associated with Walid Faris, who was until 1989 the head of the "immigrants' apparatus" in the Lebanese Forces* command. He took the side of General 'Awn in his conflict with the Lebanese Forces and joined the ranks of the new Lebanese Front* where he was put in charge of immigrants' affairs. This party combines the anti-Syrian stand of 'Awn with vague formulations about the necessity of Christian socialism in Lebanon.

SOLDIERS OF GOD (Jundullah). This is not really a party; it is rather a small armed group in the quarter of Abu Samra in Tripoli. This militia stood for the establishment of an Islamic order in Lebanon, and its fighters have acted on their own, refusing to cooperate with the Lebanese National Movement.*

SUICIDAL FORCES OF HUSAYN *(Quwwat Husayn al-Intihariyya)*. This little-known Shi'ite organization has participated in the fighting in the heavily Shi'ite populated area of Al-Shiyyah. The organization has not been heard from in several years.

SSNP. *See* SYRIAN SOCIAL NATIONAL PARTY.

SYRIAN SOCIAL NATIONAL PARTY (SSNP) *(Al-Hizb al-Suri al-Qawmi al-Ijtima'i)*. This is one of the oldest political parties in the Arab East. It was founded by Antun Sa'adah in 1932. The party was founded according to a rigid, hierarchical system, and it preferred clandestine operations to visible political activity. In 1937 party members had their first serious clash with Lebanese authorities. By 1939 it had become one of the most influential parties in the entire Arab East. It was particularly popular among intellectuals. Some of the most prominent names in contemporary Arabic literature and political thought were at one point or another members of the party.

The party advocated the unity of Greater Syria, which includes the Fertile Crescent and Cyprus. Sa'adah spelled out his ideas by chanting the slogan: "Syria is for the Syrians and the Syrians form one nation." He also opposed sectarianism and called for Christian-Muslim brotherhood within the context of Syrian nationalism. Sa'adah also attacked the clerical authorities and called for secularization in Lebanon to solve the acute sectarian problem. He often stated that his experience in South America (where he lived for some time) convinced him that a new ideology should be formulated to unify the Syrians who were split by sectarian and particularistic sentiments. Ideas of unity and discipline were paramount in Sa'adah's thinking.

In the first constitution of the party in 1934, Sa'adah was declared "the leader (*za'im*) of the party for life; . . . members absolutely support the leader in all his constitutional legislation and administration." The fascist inclinations of the party led some to charge that "Sa'adah was recruited to set up the party as an agent for Il Duce of Fascist Italy."[31] There is also a connection between pan-Germanism and Sa'adah's version of Syrian nationalism. Sa'adah's ideological formulations were articulated in a book that was first published in 1937 under the title *Nushu' al-Umum* (The Genesis of Nations). He asserted that the "natural environment" is the most important element in defining the national composite, yet he himself was confused in defining what he meant by "natural Syria." Initially, Syria was to comprise Palestine, Jordan, Lebanon, and Syria. Later, he added Iraq and Cyprus. While Sa'adah called for the unification of Syria into one nation, he was adamant about the exclusion of Jews. In fact, the party's ideology is virulently anti-semitic. Even the non-Jewish enemies of Sa'adah were called *Yahud al-Dakhil* (the Jews of the Interior).

The most controversial aspect of the party was its obvious emulation of Nazi organization. Michael Suleiman best analyzes this aspect:

While glorifying the folk, i.e., the Syrian nation, considering it as an organic whole endowed with life, Sa'adah, borrowing from Italian Fascism, elevated the state to the same position and recognized it as an integral realization of the Syrian nation. Like Hitler and Mussolini, Sa'adah had no regard for the masses and argued that in essence a self-constituted, self-proclaimed elite should lead the nation to glory behind the leader. Giving himself the title of al-Za'im (Der Fuhrer), Sa'adah imitated Hitler and the Nazis in almost every possible manner. Thus, the Syrian national anthem . . . sang "Syria, Syria, uber alles." . . . The hand gestures in saluting and the "long live the leader" bore striking resemblances to the Nazi practice. The swastika was replaced with a hurricane as a [party] symbol.[32]

The party's ideology is also based on the belief that there are "in humanity excellent, advanced races and inferior races."

Sa'adah believed in the superiority of the Syrian nation and was very critical of the Arab nation because—unlike the Syrian nation—the Arabs—in Sa'adah's mind—intermarried with the "black race" of North Africa.[33] Economically, Sa'adah did not formulate specific theories, but he rejected Marxism and called for state intervention in the economy. He was also bitterly opposed to the notion of class struggle owing to its divisiveness. The ideas of racial categorization and prejudice and the fascist organizational structure did not prevent the party from expanding in Lebanon, Syria, Palestine, and Jordan. Many Arabs, and in particular intellectuals, suffering from the despair and frustration of the 1948 loss of Palestine, felt that its ideology provided them with a sense of power and superiority. What was very attractive in party ideology was the emphasis on the centrality of the Palestinian question.

Sa'adah declared armed revolt against the Lebanese state in 1949, which gave the government the pretext to crack down on the party and eventually to arrest and execute him in July 1949. The execution of Sa'adah expanded the party's appeal and gave it a principled, uncompromising image. But it suffered in the 1950s from schismatic tendencies after the death of the leader, and also from ideological isolation caused by the rise of Arab nationalist ideas, as exemplified by Gamal Abdel Nasser and the Ba'th. The party became known as a right-wing party that supported Kamil Sham'un's administration in Lebanon and was close to the Jordanian regime and its Western patrons. Ironically, the party fought in 1958 in support of Sham'un against the very same organizations that were to become allies in 1975.

The most serious crisis in the party's history was the coup attempt launched by the party in 1961; it was the only coup d'état in Lebanon's history, if one is to exclude the comical, Fatah-supported coup of Aziz al-Ahdab in 1976. The failed coup led the Shihabi regime to persecute suspected party members and sympathizers ruthlessly. This almost destroyed the party, but the prison experience of party leaders led to a revolutionary change in its ideology. Party leaders like In'am Ra'd and Munir Khuri read Marxist works and introduced new in-

terpretations of Sa'adah's writings that—while continuing to stick to the idoli-
zation of the *za'im*—were intended to end the party's political isolation.

The party began talking about social justice and the necessity of achieving an
equitable distribution of income. It also ended its ideological opposition to Arab
nationalism and began preaching reconciliation between Arab nationalism and
Syrian nationalism. The party also championed the Palestinian revolution and
identified with the Lebanese leftist coalition headed by Kamal Jumblat. The
release of the party leadership in 1969 and the convocation of the Melkart party
congress led to the institutional legitimization of Arabization and the introduction of Marxist influences into the party's ideology. This led to a split that came
out in the open in 1974. The main party was led by In'am Ra'd; the small splinter
group was led by Ilyas Qunayzih. The Ra'd faction participated in the civil war
on the side of the Lebanese-Palestinian coalition. The two branches fought
bloody battles in 1976 when Ra'd's branch opposed Syria's policies in Lebanon
while Qunayzih's branch supported Syrian objectives.

While the SSNP is ostensibly a secular party, its membership does not reflect
a universalistic trend. It has been very popular, for example, among the Greek
Orthodox. Al-Kurah, a Greek Orthodox area, has always been a stronghold of
the party. In the election of 1972, a candidate of the SSNP there, 'Abdallah
Sa'adah, polled 6,639 votes, although he lost the election. The SSNP has also
attracted Druze members, but mostly from the Yazbaki family confederation.
Thus, in many Druze regions, the party became a traditional and sectarian rival,
albeit a weak one, to the Jumblati family leadership of the Druze community. It
could be said that the SSNP is now at the helm of the Yazbaki family confederation. The party has a modest Shi'ite following. However, members of the
same sect within the party (and indeed in other ostensibly secular parties) tend
to cling together. Hence, Shi'ite members within the party are less influenced
by the teachings of Sa'adah than by their prevailing sectarian consciousness. In
1987 an entire Shi'ite faction, within the party, defected under the leadership
of a certain commander Jamal, and joined the Party of God (Hizbullah).*

The party was reunited in 1978 when veteran party leader 'Abdallah Sa'adah
headed the new united party and improved ties with Syria, while continuing
special relations with the Libyan regime. But the unity was artificial and did not
affect the separate cells of each of the two factions. The crisis was intensified in
the wake of the Israeli invasion when all members of the Lebanese National
Movement* suffered from demoralization and ideological confusion. The party
then elected 'Isam al-Mahayri, a close ally of the Syrian regime, as head of the
party. But the schismatic tendencies were still at play, and the two factions split
apart in 1987, when Mahayri's branch (the one that attracted the support of the
majority of members) added the title of *Majlis al-Tawari* (the Emergency Council); the other, pro-Libyan, pro-Arafat branch operated under the name SSNP—
*Al-Majlis al-A'la* (the Higher Council). Efforts at reunification succeeded in a
unity conference in 1991. Nevertheless, the two factions clashed again in the
summer of 1991.

The Syrian regime helped Mahayri's branch to benefit from the new political reforms in Lebanon. Mahayri's aide, As'ad Hardan, was appointed minister in 1990, and a leading member of the party was appointed a deputy in 1991.

TAJAMMU' AL-LIJAN WA-L-RAWABIT AL-SHA'BIYYA. *See* GROUPING OF POPULAR COMMITTEES AND LEAGUES.

AL-TAJAMMU' AL-SHUYU'I AL-THAWRI. *See* REVOLUTIONARY COMMUNIST BLOC.

AL-TALA'I' AL-TAQADDUMIYYA. *See* PROGRESSIVE VANGUARDS.

AL-TANDHIM. *See* THE ORGANIZATION.

AL-TANDHIM AL-SHA'BI AL-NASIRI. *See* POPULAR NASSERITE ORGANIZATION.

AL-TANDHIM AL-THAWRI AL-NASIRI. *See* REVOLUTIONARY NASSERITE ORGANIZATION.

TOILERS' LEAGUE *(Rabitat al-Shaghila)*. This very small, Marxist-Leninist organization is headed by deputy Zahir al-Khatib, who replaced his brother Dhafir who died in combat early in the war. Founded in 1974, it was established as a self-styled revolutionary organization that called for violent overthrow of the government. The league is an insignificant player which has benefited from Zahir's close ties to Syria.

UNION OF THE FORCES OF THE WORKING PEOPLE (THE NASSERITE ORGANIZATION) *(Ittihad Quwwat-Sha'b al-'Amil [al-Tandhim al-Nasiri])*. This organization was born in the midst of the revolutionary upheavals of April 1969, when the Lebanese army clashed with PLO forces in Lebanon and with their Lebanese supporters. It was founded by a Sunni student leader, Kamal Shatila, who remains the head of the organization. The organization successfully utilized the legacy of Gamal Abdel Nasser to recruit students from public schools and the publicly run Lebanese University. The movement achieved national fame in 1972, when its Greek Orthodox candidate, Najah Wakim, won the Greek Orthodox seat of West Beirut. His landslide victory, made possible by Muslim votes, displeased the Greek Orthodox establishment. The movement was known (and in some eyes stigmatized) for its total allegiance to the Syrian regime.

In the spring of 1976, the movement suffered a tremendous setback when its offices and bases in Beirut were occupied by the PLO–LNM* alliance in retaliation for its blind support of Syria, which was sympathetic to the Phalangist-led coalition (see Lebanese Phalanges Party) at the time. Leaders of the movement were arrested and forced to criticize Syria. They were later allowed to seek haven in Damascus. When Syria gained the upper hand in Lebanon, the movement was allowed back, and Syria ensured that it played a prominent political role. In 1976 Kamal Shatila (by this time deputy Najah Wakim had left the movement permanently) announced the formation of *Al-Jabha al-Qawmiyya* (The [Pan-Arab] National Front) to counter the LNM. The front comprised all pro-Syrian organizations in Lebanon, but it failed to attract a mass following. The LNM continued to outflank the Front, which witnessed a slump in popular support.

The Union suffered a crisis in the early 1980s, when Syria forced Shatila and his organization out of Lebanon. Still unclear is what ruined the special relations between Shatila and Syria, but it was rumored that he leaked a copy of a top secret Syrian Ba'th document to an anti-Syrian magazine in Lebanon (*Al-Hawadith*), which proved to be embarrassing to the Syrian government. The editor in chief of the magazine was later found dead in West Beirut. Shatila was later based in Paris, where he issued statements critical of pro-Syrian militias. He then took a pro-Saudi line.

YAZBAKI LIBERATION FRONT *(Jabhat al-Tahrir al-Yazbakiyya)*. This small organization was formed by Farid Hamada, who hails from a prominent Druze family. He intended to oppose the leadership of the Jumblat family by reviving the historical Yazbaki-Jumblati feud within the Druze community. His alliance with the Lebanese Forces* and his residence in East Beirut, however, discredited him in Druze eyes. This organization has an insignificant role in Lebanese politics; it was merely a tool in the hands of the Lebanese Forces to undermine Walid Jumblat's leadership.

YOUTHS OF 'ALI *(Fityan 'Ali)*. This organization was a splinter of the Amal movement.* It was led by a militant local street leader, 'Ali Safwan, who participated in the 1975–76 war on the Al-Shiyah front.

**Lebanese Parties by Ethno-Religious Group and Ideology**

*I. The Single-Sect (or Single-Ethnic Group) Parties*

## A. THE MARONITE-ORIENTED PARTIES
Al-Hizb al-Dimuqrati al-Masihi al-'Ishtiraki-Hizb Al-'Amal (Socialist Christian Democratic Party—The Action Party)
Hizb Hurras al-Arz (Guardians of the Cedars Party)
Hizb al-Kata'ib al-Lubnaniyya (Lebanese Phalanges Party)
Hizb al-Wa'd (Promise Party)
Hizb al-Wataniyyin al-Ahrar (National Liberal Party)
Al-Jabha al-Lubnaniyya (Lebanese Front)
Al-Kutla al-Dusturiyya (Constitutional Bloc)
Al-Kutla al-Wataniyya (National Bloc)

*Al-Nahj* (The Course, or Path)
*Al-Quwwat al-Lubnaniyya* (Lebanese Forces)
*Quwwat al-Marada* (Forces of Marada)
*Al-Ruhbaniyyat al-Lubnaniyya* (Lebanese Monastic Order)
*Al-Shabiba al-Lubnaniyya* (Lebanese Youths)
*Al-Tandhim* (The Organization)

## B. ARMENIAN PARTIES

Armenian Secret Army for the Liberation of Armenia (ASALA)
Dashnak Party
Hunchak Party
Ramgavar Party

## C. KURDISH PARTIES

Kurdish Democratic Party *(Al-Parti)*
Kurdish Democratic Party *(Al-Parti)*—Provisional Leadership
Lebanese Kurdish Party *(Riz Kari I)*
Lebanese Kurdish Party *(Riz Kari II)*
Organization of Leftist Kurdish Parti

## D. 'ALAWITE-ORIENTED PARTIES

*Al-Hizb al-'Arabi al-Dimuqrati* (Arab Democratic Party)

## E. DRUZE-ORIENTED PARTIES

*Al-Hizb al-Taqaddumi al-'Ishtiraki* (Progressive Socialist Party)
*Jabhat al-Tahrir al-Yazbakiyya* (Yazbaki Liberation Front)

## F. SHI'ITE-ORIENTED PARTIES

*Alwiyat al-Sadr* (Brigades of Al-Sadr)
*Fityan 'Ali* (Youths of 'Ali)
*Harakat al-Amal* (Amal Movement)
*Harakat al-Amal al-'Islamiyya* (Islamic Amal Movement)
*Al-Harakat al-Islamiyya fi Lubnan* (Islamic Movement in Lebanon)
*Al-Hizb al-Dimuqrati al-Ishtiraki* (Democratic Socialist Party)
*Hizbullah* (Party of God)
*Nusur al-Biqa'* (Eagles of Al-Biqa')
*Quwwat Husayn al-Intihariyya* (Suicidal Forces of Husayn)

## G. SUNNI-ORIENTED PARTIES

*Harakat al-Nasiriyyin al-Mustaqillin*—"*Al-Murabitun*" (Movement of Independent Nasserites—"Al-Murabitun")

*Harakat Ruwwad al-Islah* (Movement of the Pioneers of Reform)
*Harakat al-Tawhid al-Islami* (Islamic Unification Front)
*Harakat 24 Tishrin* (October 24 Movement)
*Harakat al-Wihdawiyyin al-Nasiriyyin* (Movement of Unionist Nasserites)
*Hizb al-Najjada* (Helpers Party)
*Hizb al-Taharrur al-'Arabi* (Party of Arab Liberation)
*Al-Ittihad al-Ishtiraki al-'Arabi* (Arab Socialist Union)
*Al-Ittihad al-Ishtiraki al-'Arabi (al-Tandhim al-Nasiri)* (Arab Socialist Union [The Nasserite Organization])
*Ittihad Quwwat-Sha'b al-'Amil (al-Tandhim al-Nasiri)* (Union of the Forces of the Working People [The Nasserite Organization])
*Al-Jama'a al-'Islamiyya* (Islamic Community)
*Jundullah* (Soldiers of God)
*Al-Liqa' al-Islami* (Islamic Meeting)
*Quwwat Nasir* (Nasserite Forces)
*Al-Tala'i' al-Taqaddumiyya* (Progressive Vanguard)
*Al-Tandhim al-Sha'bi al-Nasiri* (Popular Nasserite Organization)
*Al-Tandhim al-Thawri al-Nasri* (Revolutionary Nasserite Organization)

## II. Parties with Secular Ideologies

### A. PAN-SYRIAN PARTIES
*Al-Hizb al-Suri al-Qawmi al-'Ijtima'i* (Syrian Social National Party)

### B. PAN-ARAB PARTIES
*Al-Haraka al-Wataniyya al-Lubnaniyya* (Lebanese National Movement)
*Hizb al-Ba'th al-'Arabi al-Ishtiraki* (Arab Socialist Resurrection Ba'th Party)
*Tajammu' al-Lijan Wa-l-Rawabit al-Sha'biyya* (Grouping of Popular Committees and Leagues)

### C. COMMUNIST PARTIES
*Hizb al-'Amal al-'Ishtiraki al-'Arabi-Lubnan* (Socialist Arab Action Party—Lebanon)
*Al-Hizb al-Shuyu'i al-Lubnani* (Communist Party of Lebanon)
*Munadhdhamat al-'Amal al-Ishtiraki al-Thawri* (Organization of Revolutionary Socialist Action)
*Munadhdhamat al-'Amal al-Shuyu'i* (Communist Action Organization)
*Rabibat Al-Shaghila* (Toilers' League)
*Al-Tajammu' al-Shuyu'i al-Thawri* (Revolutionary Communist Bloc)

## NOTES

1. Michael W. Suleiman, *Political Parties in Lebanon: The Challenge of a Fragmented Political Culture* (Ithaca, N.Y.: Cornell University Press, 1967). The first serious study was made by Lucien George and Toufic Mokdessi, *Les Partis Libanais en 1959* (Beirut: L'Orient [1960]). One recent study was a descriptive volume written by a Politburo member of the Popular Front of the Liberation of Palestine—General Command: Fadl Shruru, *Al-Ahzab wa-l-Tandhimat wa-l-Qiwa al-Siyasiyya fi Lubnan, 1930–1980* (Political Forces, Organizations, and Parties in Lebanon, 1930–1980) (Beirut: Dar al-Masirah, 1981). More recent is Joseph Aboujaoude, *Les partis politiques au Liban*, vol. 12 (Kaslik: Bibliothèque de l'université Saint-Esprit, 1985).

2. See Labib Zuwiyya Yamak, "Party Politics in the Lebanese Political System," in *Politics in Lebanon*, ed. Leonard Binder (New York: John Wiley, 1966), 155–56.

3. David C. Gordon, *The Republic of Lebanon: Nation in Jeopardy* (Boulder, Colo.: Westview Press, 1983), 78.

4. Robert Michels, *Political Parties: A Sociological Study of the Oligarchical Tendencies of Modern Democracy* (Gloucester, Mass.: Peter Smith, 1978), 400–401.

5. Kenneth Janda rightly distinguishes between "traditionalist blocs" and "doctrinal" parties. The blocs are defined as ones that are "oriented toward controlling seats in parliament and winning governmental positions for personal and sectarian gains within the framework of the traditional sectarian-feudal system." The "doctrinal" party is defined as one that "is more ideological in character and less committed to maintaining the traditional political system." Janda lists the PSP and the Phalanges Party as examples of doctrinal parties. See Kenneth Janda, *Political Parties: A Cross-National Survey* (New York: The Free Press, 1980), 841–42. But one can talk of parties in Lebanon that have features of both the traditionalist bloc and the doctrinal party. The PSP and the Phalanges Party have both served as vehicles for controlling seats in parliament and winning benefits and posts for their leaders, as well as for the dissemination of ideologies that have benefited the leaderships of both parties. Also, these two parties may not be as opposed to the traditional system as Janda suggests.

6. Students of the Amal Movement are indebted to the original and informative work of Augustus Richard Norton. His *Amal and the Shi'a: Struggle for the Soul of Lebanon* (Austin: University of Texas Press, 1987) is the best available source in any language. Even in Lebanon, its Arabic translation is used as the classic study of the movement. For a brief and succinct study of the movement, see also Augustus Richard Norton, "Harakat Amal," in *The Emergence of a New Lebanon: Fantasy or Reality?* ed. Edward Azar et al. (New York: Praeger, 1984), 162–204.

7. For Musa al-Sadr, see Fouad Ajami, *The Vanished Imam: Musa Al-Sadr and the Shia of Lebanon* (Ithaca, N.Y.: Cornell University Press, 1986); and Peter Therou, *The Strange Disappearance of Imam Moussa Sadr* (London: Weidenfeld and Nicholson, 1987).

8. Norton, "Harakat Amal," 163.

9. 'Ali Shu'ayb, *Tarikh Lubnan: Mina-l-Ihtilal Ila-l-Jala, 1918–1946* (The History of Lebanon: From Occupation to Withdrawal, 1918–1946) (Beirut: Dar al-Farabi, 1990), 102–114; and Samir Ayyub, *Al-Hizb al-Shuyu'i fi Surya wa Lubnan, 1922–1958* (The Communist Party in Syria and Lebanon, 1922–1958) (Beirut: Dar al-Huriyya, 1959).

10. This figure is a rough estimate based on this writer's identification of the sectarian affiliation of the members from the list in Lebanese Communist Party, *Documents of the Fifth Congress* (in Arabic), 1988, 140.

11. Suleiman, *Political Parties in Lebanon*, 191.

12. See *Al-Diyar*, December 14, 1975.

13. Suleiman, *Political Parties in Lebanon*, 194; Aboujaoude, *Les partis politiques au Liban*.

14. Lewis Snider, "The Lebanese Forces: Wartime Origins and Political Significance," in *Emergence of a New Lebanon*, 13.

15. A sympathetic analysis of "the charter" is found in Snider, "Lebanese Forces," 135–37.

16. See Antoine Butrus, *Wathiqat Harb Lubnan* (The Document of Lebanon's War) (Beirut: Dar al-Sayyad, 1977), 502.

17. See Gemayyel's interview with *Magazine*, February 1, 1968; cited in John Entelis, *Pluralism and Party Transformation in Lebanon: Al-Kata'ib, 1936–1970* (Leiden, Netherlands: E. J. Brill, 1975), 46.

18. See the interview with Gemayyel in *Daily Star*, March 2, 1969. The best sources on the Phalanges Party are Entelis, *Pluralism and Party Transformation in Lebanon*; and the official Lebanese Phalanges Party, *Tarikh Hizb-i-l-Kata'ib-i-l-Lubnaniyya* (The History of the Lebanese Phalanges Party) (Beirut: Dar al-'Amal, 1979). See also Hazim Saghiyyah, *Ta'rib al-Kata'ib al-Lubnaniyya: al-Hizb, al-Sultan, al-Khauf* (The Arabization of the Lebanese Phalanges: The Party, the Government, and Fear) (Beirut: Dar al-Jadid, 1991).

19. See Benny Morris, "Israel and the Lebanese Phalange: The Birth of a Relationship, 1948–1951," *Studies in Zionism* 5, 1 (1984): 142.

20. Entelis, *Pluralism and Party Transformation in Lebanon*, 110.

21. The figures are from an unpublished mimeographed report by the Phalanges Party, 1974, given to this writer by an official of the party.

22. An interview by this writer with Antoine Najm, November 1982.

23. An unpublished and untitled internal report of the Phalanges Party, p. 14.

24. *Al-Shirà*, November 26, 1990.

25. See *Al-Nahar*, August 21, 1990.

26. Augustus Richard Norton, "Lebanon after Ta'if: Is the Civil War Over?" *Middle East Journal* 45, 3 (Summer 1991): 13.

27. See *Al-Nahar*, August 15, 1990.

28. An interview by this writer with Muhammad Husayn Fadllalah, conducted in August 1985.

29. This information is based upon a revealing taped speech concerning *velayat-e Faqih*, February 1983, taped and distributed by Fadllalah's followers in Bir al-'Abd.

30. See the interview with Walid Jumblat in *Magazine*, April 27, 1987.

31. Suleiman, *Political Parties in Lebanon*, 92–93.

32. Ibid, 111–12.

33. Antun Sa'adah, *Al-Muhadarat al-'Ashr* (The Ten Lectures) (Beirut, 1956), 51–52.

As'ad AbuKhalil

# LIBYA

Libya witnessed the very beginnings of political participation when it was still an integral part of the Ottoman Empire. The Municipalities Law of 1871 led to the election of some members of the municipal councils of Tripoli, Khums, Benghazi, and Darnah (while others were appointed). By 1894 thirteen more towns had municipal councils. All administrative units (*Sanjak* and *Qada*) in Libya had councils with elected and appointed members.[1] With the triumph of the Young Turks and the elections that followed in which Libyans participated, both Cyrenaica and Tripolitania elected representatives during the period from 1908 to 1911 from leading Libyan notable families, including Sulayman al-Baruni, Mukhtar Ku'bar, and 'Umar Mansur al-Kikhya.[2] Thus the Ottoman reforms and, in particular, the Ottoman parliament after 1908 provided Libyan notables and their followers the first taste of political participation, which was a precursor of future party politics.

The Italian invasion of Libya in September 1911 and the Treaty of Lausanne of November 1912, between the Ottoman Empire and Italy, was a watershed in further developing the political awareness of the Libyan notables. The status of Libya, which was given autonomy by the Ottomans but was virtually annexed by Italy, forced the notables either to accept cooperation with Italians or to continue to fight them. There were three potential loci of struggle against the Italians. The first and most important was the Sanusiya movement, an Islamic Sufi order, whose mainstay of power was Cyrenaica. The second was the coast of Tripolitania with Misrata as the center of the opposition led by Ramadan al-Suwayhli who had support from the Ottomans. The third was the Ibadi and Berber Jabal al-Gharb led by Sulayman al-Baruni, who, before and after the Young Turk revolution, had entertained the idea of an autonomous Ibadi province.

The Sanusiya was a religious movement that united the tribes of Cyrenaica in particular and played a vanguard role in resisting the Italians. Through the mediation of the British, the Italians recognized the autonomy of the Sanusiya in Cyrenaica in the Agreement of 'Ikrima in April 1917.

The second mainstay of opposition was the coast of Tripolitania with Misrata as its headquarters, which had become the second most important urban center after Tripoli by the end of the first decade of the twentieth century.[3] Unlike

Cyrenaica, the opposition to the Italians, which was centered in Misrata, was not completely indigenous as the Ottomans had virtual control over Misrata, which had become an important supply port for the Ottomans and the Germans during World War I. The Ottoman troop commander, Nuri Bey, backed Ramadan al-Suwayhli, a local notable who was a rival of the Muntasir clan which supported the Italians. With Ottoman backing, Ramadan al-Suwayhli was able to defeat Sanusi troops in 1916 when they tried to extend the influence of the Sanusiya beyond Sirt into Tripolitania proper. In 1917 Ramadan al-Suwayhli was appointed local governor by the Ottomans, and he presided over quite an extensive administration encompassing eastern Tripolitania.[4]

The third mainstay of resistance against the Italians was the Ibadi Jabal al-Gharb under the leadership of Sulayman al-Baruni who was, not unlike Ramadan al-Suwayhli, supported, but to a lesser extent, by the Ottomans. Nevertheless al-Baruni's political objectives were separatist in nature, and his relations with the Ottomans were not always cordial.

In emulation of the Sanusiya movement—whose leader Sayyid Idris was able to wrest local autonomy in Cyrenaica from the Italians in 1917, and with President Woodrow Wilson's support of national self-determination in January 1918, in addition to the defeat of the Ottomans in October 1918—the Tripolitanians, who had hitherto cooperated with the Ottomans, were forced to seek local autonomy of their own. In November 1918 a meeting, held in Misallatah, was attended by notables from various regions of Tripolitania who declared the formation of the Tripoli Republic (al-Jumhuriya al-Tarabulusiya), a short-lived experiment that lasted less than one year and was run by a Republican Council of four members: Ramadan al-Suwayhli, Sulayman al-Baruni, Ahmad Murayyid, and 'Abd al-Nabi Bilkhayr. A Consultative Council of twenty-four was established, as well as a four-member Shar'ia Council of clergymen.[5] The Tripoli Republic contained the seeds of its own destruction because the four leaders were at loggerheads with each other. After they signed an agreement with the Italians in April 1919, the Tripoli Republic was transformed into a protopolitical party or faction called the Association for National Reform.

The demise of the Tripoli Republic was accompanied by the elimination of Ramadan al-Suwayhli by the Muntasir family in cooperation with Bilkhayr, a sectarian conflict between the Ibadis and the Sunnis which devastated Jabal al-Gharb and forced al-Baruni into exile. Only the Sanusiya movement was strong enough to survive, even though its leader, Sayyid Idris, moved to Egypt. It remained the only mainstay of struggle against the Italians until the capture of the commander of the Sanusi forces, 'Umar al-Mukhtar, in 1931.

The liberation of Libya by the British in 1942 paved the ground for the rise of political parties. The first political party was formed in 1942 by a group of Sanusi followers who resided in Egypt. They called the party the 'Umar al-Mukhtar Society, which was not a sporting society as it claimed, but a political society with Sayyid Idris, the Sanusi leader, as its patron. On the whole, Cyrenaica was united in its adherence to the Sanusiya; therefore, the political consciousness as embodied in the al-Mukhtar group was more cohesive than in Tripolitania, which had been bedeviled by fragmentation. Except for a division between the Darna and the Benghazi branches of the al-Mukhtar Group, when the latter changed its official name to the National Association* in 1950, there was a basic underlying unity which was furnished by the dominance of the Sanusiya in Cyrenaica. This was clearly demonstrated by the formation in 1948 of the National Congress* under the leadership of Sayyid Idris's brother al-Rida al-Sanusi.

The emergence of political parties in Tripolitania in the aftermath of the British liberation of Libya was not unexpected as Tripolitanians had to contend with the rising leadership of Sayyid Idris. The first party to be formed was the Nationalist Party* in 1944. Later the leaders of the Nationalist Party joined a wider political organization called the United National Front.* Six new political parties emerged during the period 1944–49 either as splinter parties or as attempts to reunite parties in the form of broader political organizations.

The rise of these political parties reflected an attempt to voice aspirations for independence, or to take a stand on whether Libya should be a federal or unitary state, or to determine whether to support or oppose the leadership of Sayyid Idris. The heyday of political parties lasted for a decade from 1943 to 1952 when all political parties were banned, and the leader of the Tripolitanian National Congress, Bashir al-Sa'dawi, the main opposition to the Sanusi ruling establishment, was exiled. Although political parties ceased to exist in the open during the period 1952–69, some continued to work underground and, in their different shades, represented the major political ideologies of the Arab east (Mashriq).

The September 1, 1969, revolution, which brought a group of army officers to power, was characterized by strong opposition to the activities of all political parties, whatever their form. Only one political party, the ruling party, the Arab Socialist Union,* modeled on its Egyptian counterpart, was permitted. Later even this party was abolished when the Mass Republic (Al-Jamahiriya) was declared. All parties that emerged from the mid-1970s to the 1990s were opposition parties active either underground or abroad with the main common objective of overthrowing the Qadhafi regime.

### Bibliography

Allen, J. A. Libya since Independence: Economic and Political Development. London: Croom Helm, 1982.

Anderson, Lisa. "Nineteenth Century Reform in Ottoman Libya." International Journal of Middle East Studies 16,3 (August 1984).

———. The State and Social Transformation in Tunisia and Libya, 1830–1980. Princeton, N.J.: Princeton University Press, 1986.

Deeb, Marius K., and Mary-Jane Deeb. Libya since the Revolution: Aspects of Social and Political Development. New York: Praeger, 1982.

———. "Libya: Internal Developments and Regional Politics." In The Middle East: Annual Issues and Events, edited by D. V. Partington, vol. 4. Boston: G. K. Hall, 1985.

Joffe, E.G.H., and K. S. Mclachlan, eds. *Social and Economic Development of Libya*. Wisbech, Cambridgeshire: Middle East and North Africa Studies Press, 1982.
Khadduri, Majid. *Modern Libya: A Study in Political Development*. Baltimore: Johns Hopkins University Press, 1968.

## Political Parties

ARAB SOCIALIST RESURRECTION (BA'TH) PARTY (*Hizb al-Ba'th al-'Arabi al-Ishtiraki*). This branch of the Ba'th party of the Arab East was active underground during the 1950s and 1960s, recruiting members primarily among students and youth. The party had a large following among the intelligentsia which prompted the Libyan authorities to arrest 159 Ba'thists in December 1961. It was led by 'Abdallah Sharaf al-Din and Ibrahim al-Hanqari.

ARAB SOCIALIST UNION (*al-Ittihad al-Ishtiraki al-'Arabi*). This party was formed by Muammar al-Qadhafi on June 11, 1971, as the only political party, modeled in structure and function on the Egyptian Arab Socialist Union of the 1960s and the early 1970s. Qadhafi was strongly influenced then by the Nasserite ideology and the Libyan union reflected that influence.

BA'TH PARTY. *See* ARAB SOCIALIST RESURRECTION (BA'TH) PARTY.

EGYPTIAN-TRIPOLITANIAN UNION PARTY (*Hizb al-Ittihad al-Misri al-Tarabulusi*). This party was formed on December 16, 1946, by two members of the Free Nationalist Bloc,* 'Ali Rajab and Yusuf al-Mushayriqi. Rajab, the leader of this new party, called for a union between Egypt and Tripolitania with Tripolitania retaining its autonomous status under the Egyptian monarchy.

FREE NATIONALIST BLOC (*al-Kutla al-Wataniya al-Hurra*). This was a splinter party from the United National Front* of Tripolitania. It was formed on May 30, 1946, by 'Ali al-Faqih Hasan and his brother Ahmad al-Faqih Hasan. It had a small following of some 800 members, but it actively opposed the Sanusi leadership and the spread of its influence to Tripolitania. It had republican leanings and was therefore opposed to the establishment of a Sanusi monarchy.

FREE UNIONIST OFFICERS MOVEMENT (*Harakat al-Dubbat al-Wahdawiyyin al-Ahrar*). According to Muammar al-Qadhafi, this party originated by forming its first cell in Sebha in 1959 prior to al-Qadhafi's enrollment in the military academy in 1963. Later it referred to the group of army officers, led by al-Qadhafi, who managed to take power in 1969. It was basically an organization with military officers as its backbone with a civilian wing of supporters and followers.

AL-HARAKA AL-WATANIYYA AL-DIMUQRATIYYA AL-LIBIYA. *See* LIBYAN NATIONAL DEMOCRATIC MOVEMENT.

AL-HARAKA AL-WATANIYYA AL-LIBIYA. *See* LIBYAN NATIONAL MOVEMENT.

HARAKAT AL-DUBBAT AL-WAHDAWIYYIN AL-AHRAR. *See* FREE UNIONIST OFFICERS MOVEMENT.

HARAKAT AL-QAWMIYYUN AL-'ARAB. *See* MOVEMENT OF ARAB NATIONALISTS.

HIZB AL-AHRAR. *See* LIBERAL PARTY.

HIZB AL-BA'TH AL-'ARABI AL-ISHTIRAKI. *See* ARAB SOCIALIST RESURRECTION (BA'TH) PARTY.

HIZB AL-ISTIQLAL. *See* INDEPENDENCE PARTY.

HIZB AL-ITTIHAD AL-MISRI AL-TARABULUSI. *See* EGYPTIAN-TRIPOLITANIAN UNION PARTY.

HIZB AL-MUTAMAR AL-WATANI. *See* NATIONAL CONGRESS PARTY.

AL-HIZB AL-SHUYU'I AL-LIBI. *See* LIBYAN COMMUNIST PARTY.

HIZB AL-TAHRIR AL-ISLAMI. *See* ISLAMIC LIBERATION PARTY.

HIZB AL-'UMMAL. *See* LABOR PARTY.

AL-HIZB AL-WATANI. *See* NATIONALIST PARTY.

AL-IKHWAN AL-MUSLIMIN. *See* MUSLIM BROTHERHOOD.

INDEPENDENCE PARTY (*Hizb al-Istiqlal*). This party was formed in 1948 by Salim al-Muntasir, who had a disagreement with Bashir al-Sa'dawi, and consequently resigned from the presidency of the United National Front* to establish a separate political party. The followers of the new party were opposed to Sa'dawi and the role of the Arab League.

ISLAMIC JIHAD (*al-Jihad al-Islami*). This party was formed in the early 1970s with an ideology similar to that of the Islamic Jihad in Egypt. Al-Qadhafi tried, with some success, in 1973 and 1986–87, to undermine its underground organization after it had engaged in a campaign of terrorism against the Libyan authorities.

ISLAMIC LIBERATION PARTY (*Hizb al-Tahrir al-Islami*). This is a branch of the Jordanian party with a similar ideology. It is probably the most powerful, covert Islamic fundamentalist political organization in Libya. In 1984 al-Qadhafi publicly hanged student leaders who belonged to the Islamic Liberation Party on the campus of al-Fatih University.[6]

AL-ITTIHAD AL-DUSTURI AL-LIBI. *See* LIBYAN CONSTITUTIONAL UNION.

AL-ITTIHAD AL-ISHTIRAKI AL-'ARABI. *See* ARAB SOCIALIST UNION.

AL-JABHA AL-WATANIYYA. *See* NATIONAL FRONT.

AL-JABHA AL-WATANIYYA LI INQADH LIBYA. *See* NATIONAL FRONT FOR THE SALVATION OF LIBYA.

AL-JABHA AL-WATANIYYA AL-MUTTAHIDA. *See* UNITED NATIONAL FRONT.

JAMA'AT 'UMAR AL-MUKHTAR. *See* 'UMAR AL-MUKHTAR GROUP.

AL-JIHAD AL-ISLAMI. *See* ISLAMIC JIHAD.

AL-KUTLA AL-WATANIYYA AL-HURRA. *See* FREE NATIONALIST BLOC.

LABOR PARTY (*Hizb al-'Ummal*). This party was formed in September 1947 by Bashir bin Hamza after he was forced to leave the Free Nationalist Bloc.*

LAJNAT AL-TAHRIR AL-LIBIYA. *See* LIBYAN LIBERATION COMMITTEE.

LIBERAL PARTY (*Hizb al-Ahrar*). This party was formed on March 11, 1948, by a former vice president of the Nationalist Party.*

LIBYAN COMMUNIST PARTY (*al-Hizb al-Shuyu'i al-Libi*). The communists were active in the 1950s without much success. By the 1960s, their influence was confined to the writings of few leftist intellectuals like Kamil al-Maghur and 'Abdallah al-'Uwari.

LIBYAN CONSTITUTIONAL UNION (*al-Ittihad al-Dusturi al-Libi*). This organization was formed in Manchester, England, by Muhammad Abdu bin Ghalbun in October 1981. He pledged his allegiance to the Sanusi monarchy.

LIBYAN LIBERATION COMMITTEE (*Lajnat al-Tahrir al-Libiya*). This group was formed in March 1947 in Cairo, Egypt, and was led by Bashir al-Sa'dawi with the backing of the secretary-general of the League of Arab States, 'Abd al-Rahman 'Azzam. Al-Sa'dawi organized the Libyan Liberation Committee, which was composed of Tripolitanians, to reconcile their differences and to convince them to support Sayyid Idris as the head of a united Libya. Al-Sa'dawi moved the headquarters of the party to Tripoli in 1948.

LIBYAN LIBERATION ORGANIZATION (*Munadhdhamat al-Tahrir al-Libiya*). This party was formed in Cairo in 1982 by a former prime minister under the monarchy, 'Abd al-Hamid Bakkush.

LIBYAN NATIONAL DEMOCRATIC MOVEMENT (*al-Haraka al-Wataniyya al-Dimuqratiyya al-Libiya*). This party is an offshoot of the Libyan National Grouping formed in 1978 by 'Umar al-Muhayshi and Fadil Mas'udi. (See also Libyan National Democratic Rally.)

LIBYAN NATIONAL DEMOCRATIC RALLY (*al-Tajammu' al-Watani al-Dimuqrati al-Libi*). This rally represented the healing of the rift between Mahmud Sulayman al-Maghribi and Fadil Mas'udi and the coalescing, in 1982, of their respective organizations, the Libyan National Grouping and the Libyan National Democratic Movement.*

LIBYAN NATIONAL MOVEMENT (*al-Haraka al-Wataniyya al-Libiya*). This party was formed in 1980 by pro-Iraqi Ba'thists led by 'Umran Burways. It is active mainly among Libyan exiles in Europe.

LIBYAN NATIONAL RALLY (*al-Tajammu' al-Watani al-Libi*). In August 1975 'Umar al-Muhayshi, a colleague of al-Qadhafi, in cooperation with two other members of the Revolutionary Command Council, tried to overthrow al-Qadhafi. The coup failed, and al-Muhayshi fled to Egypt. In 1976 al-Muhayshi formed the Libyan National Rally, headquartered in Cairo, with another exiled member of the Revolutionary Command Council, 'Abd al-Mun'im al-Huni, and a prominent journalist, Fadil Mas'udi. Later they were joined by a former prime minister, Mahmud Sulayman al-Maghribi.

LIJAN THAWRIYA. *See* REVOLUTIONARY COMMITTEES.

MOVEMENT OF ARAB NATIONALISTS (MAN) (*Harakat al-Qawmiyyun al-'Arab*). This was a branch of the movement that had been established in Beirut,

Lebanon, in the early 1950s (see chapters on Jordan and the Palestinians). It began its activities in the early 1960s assisted by its support for Egyptian President Gamal Abdel Nasser and by the decline of the influence of the Ba'thists. Its ideological radicalization in the mid-1960s and the military training given to its members prompted the Libyan government to arrest and put on trial its leading members in June 1967 thus curbing its ability to operate.

MUNADHDHAMAT AL-TAHRIR AL-LIBIYA. *See* LIBYAN LIBERATION ORGANIZATION.

MUSLIM BROTHERHOOD (*al-Ikhwan al-Muslimin*). The influence of the Muslim Brotherhood in Libya goes back to the early 1950s owing to the impact of the powerful Egyptian Muslim Brotherhood. In Libya the Muslim Brothers appealed to students and graduates of both religious and modern schools. The organization broke into three factions, one of which became Nasserite; a second faction distanced itself from any political activity and confined itself to the practice of religion.[7] The third faction continued in the same tradition as the Muslim Brothers. With al-Qadhafi's anticlerical and Islamic reformist policies, the Muslim Brotherhood has become one of the major political opposition forces against the revolutionary regime whether as such or under the rubric of the National Front for the Salvation of Libya.*

AL-MUTAMAR AL-WATANI. *See* NATIONAL CONGRESS.

AL-MUTAMAR AL-WATANI AL-TARABULUSI. *See* TRIPOLITANIAN NATIONAL CONGRESS.

NATIONAL ASSOCIATION (*al-Rabita al-Wataniyya*). This association was the 'Umar Mukhtar Group* or club which filed for permission to organize on January 14, 1950. It had to change its name because the Mukhtar family objected to the continued use of the name of their heroic ancestor.

NATIONAL CONGRESS (*al-Mutamar al-Watani*). This congress was formed in January 1948 after Sayyid Idris ordered the dissolution of all political parties in Cyrenaica. Consequently, a meeting of tribal leaders and politicians led to the establishment of the National Congress. It was at a meeting of the National Congress on June 1, 1949, that Sayyid Idris declared the independence of Cyrenaica.

NATIONAL CONGRESS PARTY (*Hizb al-Mutamar al-Watani*). This party was the successor organization to the Tripolitanian National Congress,* which was headed by Bashir al-Sa'dawi. It contested the first general parliamentary elections held under the monarch in February 1952. The party, which ran against the federal system hoping to revise the constitution, won in the city of Tripoli but was defeated by the government candidates in the Tripolitanian countryside. Because of its defeat in the tribal regions, the National Congress Party encouraged "the tribes to seize power by force."[8] Consequently, al-Sa'dawi was promptly deported, which led to the demise of the party.

NATIONAL FRONT (*al-Jabha al-Wataniyya*). The National Front was formed in August 1946 by the tribal chiefs of Cyrenaica to unite all the leading politicians of Cyrenaica. Its main purpose was to present the case of Cyrenaica to the international commission of inquiry, which was sent to find out the wishes of the people with respect to the future political status of Cyrenaica. By November 1946, it had seventy-five members and a steering committee of nineteen.

NATIONAL FRONT FOR THE SALVATION OF LIBYA (NFSL) (*al-Jabha al-Wataniyya Li Inqadh Libya*). The NFSL was formed on October 7, 1981, on the thirtieth anniversary of the promulgation of the constitution of the Sanusi monarchy. The NFSL is led by a former diplomat, Muhammad Yusuf Maqarif. It is the largest, most powerful opposition organization challenging the Qadhafi regime. In June 1988, it established a military wing called the Libya National Army (LNA). More than 1,200 volunteers joined the LNA, many of them former prisoners of war taken by Chad in its 1987 defeat of al-Qadhafi's forces. The NFSL comprises members of diverse political views. There are those with Islamic leanings, including supporters of the Muslim Brotherhood.* Others are Sanusi in their outlook. Still others are leftists and pan-Arab nationalists. The NFSL aspires to establish, in the wake of al-Qadhafi's overthrow, a democratic, pluralistic polity. It "believes in the freedom of thought, and the importance and necessity of political parties."[9] The NFSL has published a bimonthly periodical called *al-Inqadh* since 1982 and a monthly leaflet called *Akhbar Libya* dealing with the Libyan domestic situation.[10]

NATIONALIST PARTY (*al-Hizb al-Watani*). This party was originally formed in 1944 as a secret political party, led by Ahmad Faqih Hasan. It gained official recognition on April 8, 1946. It served the interests of the Tripolitanians and advocated the complete independence of Libya either under the sponsorship of the Arab League or as an Egyptian protectorate. Due to differences within its ranks, Mustafa Mizran became its leader, replacing Ahmad Faqih Hasan. It claimed that it had fifteen branches with a total membership of 15,000.[11]

NFSL. *See* NATIONAL FRONT FOR THE SALVATION OF LIBYA.

AL-RABITA AL-WATANIYYA. *See* NATIONAL ASSOCIATION.

RABITAT AL-SHABAB. *See* YOUTH LEAGUE.

REVOLUTIONARY COMMITTEES (*Lijan Thawriyya*). These committees were formed by al-Qadhafi in 1977 to facilitate the process of transforming Libya into a Republic of the Masses (*al-Jamahiriya*). They acted as a mobilizing undeclared political party to motivate the apathetic Libyan public to participate in the popular committees and popular congresses. They select the candidates for the popular committees, bring to trial antiregime elements, and exercise the power of censorship. They publish a weekly called *al-Zahf al-Akhdar* (the Green March).

AL-TAJAMMU' AL-WATANI AL-DIMUQRATI AL-LIBI. *See* LIBYAN NATIONAL DEMOCRATIC RALLY.

AL-TAJAMMU' AL-WATANI AL-LIBI. *See* LIBYAN NATIONAL RALLY.

TRIPOLITANIAN NATIONAL CONGRESS (*al-Mutamar al-Watani al-Tarabulusi*). This organization, a result of the merger of the Nationalist Party* and the United National Front,* was formed on May 14, 1949, because of apprehensions that Italy would be given a trusteeship over Tripolitania in accordance with the British-Italian Bevin-Sforza plan. On June 1, 1949, Cyrenaica declared its independence; consequently, the Tripolitanian National Congress, led by al-Sa'dawi, invited Amir Idris to visit Tripoli so that the Tripolitanians could demonstrate their allegiance to the Sanusi leadership. The congress was able to sway the opinion of the Tripolitanian notables to a large extent toward favoring a united independent Libya under Amir Idris.

'UMAR AL-MUKHTAR GROUP (*Jama'at 'Umar al-Mukhtar*). This group began in 1942 among Libyan exiles in Egypt as the 'Umar al-Mukhtar Sporting Society, which was in reality a political association or group. The leading organizer was As'ad bin 'Umran. Later, when the members moved to Cyrenaica, they formally declared its establishment on April 4, 1943. They elected as its head Shaykh Khalil al-Kawwafi. Although it was political from the outset, the 'Umar al-Mukhtar Society became openly political in 1944–45, and Mustafa bin 'Amir became its president and Bashir al-Mughayribi its secretary. Its ideological stand was pro-Sanusi, but as it was dominated by younger notables of Cyrenaica, it was also anti-British. The 'Umar al-Mukhtar Society was officially dissolved on December 7, 1947, when Sayyid Idris called for the dissolution of all political parties. Nevertheless, the members changed the society to a sports organization and continued to be involved in politics. In fact, when the parliamentary elections were held in independent Cyrenaica in June 1950, the 'Umar Mukhtar Group managed to win ten seats out of a total of sixty.[12]

UNITED NATIONAL FRONT (*al-Jabha al-Wataniyya al-Muttahida*). This organization, formed on May 10, 1946, was headed by Salim al-Muntasir. It included as members prominent notables of Tripolitania. The front was to seek an independent Libya and not to accept any Italian trusteeship. It sought the support of Sayyid Idris to be the head of an independent Libya, and the vast majority of the members were in favor of the Sanusi leadership. Those not in favor of a Sanusi monarchy left the front and formed their own political parties.

YOUTH LEAGUE (*Rabitat al-Shabab*). To counter the influence of the 'Umar al-Mukhtar Group* among the younger generation, elder politicians sponsored in 1945 the formation of a dissident political association called the Youth League. The leading figure of this organization was Salih Buwaysir. The Youth League represented the parochial interests of older conservative politicians who were unhappy about the challenge to their power represented by the 'Umar al-Mukhtar Group.

## NOTES

1. Lisa Anderson, "Nineteenth-Century Reform in Ottoman Libya," *International Journal of Middle East Studies* 16, 3 (August 1984): 330–31; Mahmud Muhammad al-Naku', *Budhur al-Dimuqratiyya fi Libya* (Seeds of Democracy in Libya) (Dar al-Afaq: n.p., 1989), 33.

2. Majid Khadduri, *Modern Libya: A Study in Political Development* (Baltimore: Johns Hopkins University Press, 1968), 9.

3. Marius K. Deeb and Mary-Jane Deeb, *Libya since the Revolution: Aspects of Social and Political Development* (New York: Praeger, 1982), 110.

4. Lisa Anderson, "The Tripoli Republic 1918–1922," in *Social and Economic Development of Libya*, edited by E. G. H. Joffe and K. S. Mclachlan (Wisbech, Cambridgeshire: Middle East and North Africa Studies Press, 1982), 48–49.

5. Tahir Ahmad al-Zawi, *Jihad al-Abtal fi Tarabulus al-Gharb* (The Jihad of Heroes in Tripoli), 2nd. ed. (Tripoli, Libya: Al-Nur Publications, 1970), 326.

6. Mary-Jane Deeb, "Libya," in *Religion in Politics: A World Guide*, edited by Stuart Mews (Essex, England: Longman, Harlow, 1989), 170–71.

7. Salaheddin Hasan, "The Genesis of the Political Leadership of Libya 1952–1969: Historical Origins and Development of Its Component Elements" (Ph.D. diss., George Washington University, 1973), 384–85.

8. Khadduri, *Modern Libya*, 219–20.

9. National Front for the Salvation of Libya, *Libya under Gaddafi and the NFSL Challenge: An Anthology of the NFSL Newsreport 1989–1992* (Chicago, Ill., 1992), 277–78.

10. Marius Deeb and Mary-Jane Deeb, "Libya: Internal Developments and Regional Politics," in *The Middle East: Annual Issues and Events*, vol. 4, *1984*, edited by D. V. Partington (Boston: G. K. Hall 1985), 139.

11. Khadduri, *Modern Libya*, 85.

12. Ibid., 62–65, 78.

Marius K. Deeb

# MOROCCO

Morocco, the western terminus of the Arab world, more closely approximates the West than do its fellow Arab states in its multiplicity of political parties. In the activity, relative freedom, and number of its parties, Morocco has generally stood alone in the Arab world, its dizzying array of fissiparous factions confusing even for the Moroccan political pundit. Dozens of Moroccan party groupings are discussed in this chapter, however, numerous other organizations connected to the parties or otherwise involved in national politics could be added.

The meaning of this extraordinary party activity for Moroccan and Arab politics more generally is harder to ascertain. The overall trend has been for Morocco's party system to evolve toward increasing diversity and decreasing political importance for individual parties. But what is the primary lesson of this developmental course? Is it, as various observers have argued, the divisive and defensive nature of Moroccan political culture, the continued relevance or manipulative acumen of the Moroccan monarchy, the difficulty modern political organizations face transplanted in Arab soil, or the importance of a built-in choke valve providing democratic window dressing in a personalistic authoritarian system? Is the steady existence of parties on the Moroccan political landscape evidence of the emergence of a civil society many would see as essential for democratization? Or is the limited role and mobilizational capacity of parties a sign of the failure of partial pluralism in a political system dominated by one of the world's oldest royal dynasties?

In general, it can be said that the close, symbiotic relationship between the country's monarch and its parties has deterred the development of the latter into Western-style institutions with strong ideologies or client bases. The ultimate test of the adaptive capacity of Moroccan parties will come if and when the king's traditional and continuing central political role diminishes.

## BACKGROUND

With its nearly 26 million citizens, Morocco is the world's most populous nation with a monarch who both reigns and rules. The nation, which gained independence from French colonial rule in 1956, consists almost entirely of Muslims of the majority Sunni denomination. Morocco's 30,000 Christians are virtually all French people who have remained since decolonialization. Morocco prides itself on a tradition of tolerating a vibrant Jewish community. However, since the creation of the State of Israel and the Arab world's hostility to it, almost all of Morocco's Jews have emigrated to the Jewish state or other nations, leaving about 10,000 Jews in the kingdom.

Not including the former Spanish colonial territories in the Western Sahara, which Morocco has virtually integrated, the kingdom occupies 173,000 square miles with long coastlines both on the Mediterranean Sea and Atlantic Ocean. Rabat, the capital, is located on the Atlantic coast fifty-seven miles east from Casablanca, the country's industrial and trading center. Morocco has a higher proportion of arable land (18 percent) and a correspondingly lower proportion of desert than most other Arab countries. However, independent Morocco inherited and furthered a legacy of agricultural mismanagement from the French, and it has faced stiff competition from southern European Community members for its traditional northern European citrus fruit and other agricultural export markets.

Morocco has little natural oil or gas, importing most of its needs from other Arab states. Morocco's major natural resource is phosphates, of which it is the world's largest exporter and third largest producer. Including the Western Saharan territories, Morocco may possess as much as two-thirds of the world's phosphate resources. Morocco also has a growing fishing industry, like phosphates an economic sphere that would expand with the additional resources available should Morocco's sovereignty over the Western Sahara be legally recognized.

To try to establish this sovereignty, the kingdom has waged war on forces fighting for Western Saharan independence for over fifteen years, forcing it to allocate as much as 40 percent of its yearly budget to defense spending, or almost $700 million each year. Combined with the rise in oil prices of the early 1980s, this tapped Morocco's economic resources to the point that the country had become one of the world's largest debtors by the middle of the decade. With pressure from the International Monetary Fund, increases in phosphate production, and several exceptionally good harvests, Morocco was managing economic expansion and debt reduction as the 1990s began. But insecurity about future economic growth led the government to seek greater macroeconomic coordination with its North African neighbors and to hope that final resolution of the Western Saharan problem on its terms was imminent.

## MOROCCAN INDEPENDENCE AND THE ISTIQLAL PARTY

Morocco's geography includes three large bands of mountains, as well as another range of mountains in the northeast. The separation of different regions that this has produced has contributed to a view of Moroccan history that emphasizes fragmentation and tribalism over common development. The early inhabitants of the country, now known as Berbers, were overwhelmed by Arab conquest in 710 A.D. with the invaders settling and gradually spreading their dominance from the coastal plains. Yet, from the start, Arab-Berber intermarriage and Berber conversion to Islam intermingled the two groups. In 792 the first Moroccan proto-state and the first successful breakaway Arab dynasty were founded by Idris II, who established the city of Fez as a center of political and religious importance. Thus began Moroccans' self-image as an independent people, as well as the preeminence of Fez and its inhabitants in Moroccan cultural, religious, and economic life.

As the balance of military power increasingly shifted from the Islamic world to Europe, Morocco had to struggle to maintain its independence. For the most part, a series of indigenous dynasties was able to provide the country with some autonomy, although this came largely by trying to play off different European powers and linking the Moroccan economy to these powers. The latest of these dynasties, the 'Alawites (no relation to the Syrian Shi'ite minority), emerged in 1666 with the dynasty's founder Moulay Rachid's seizure of the throne. But the 'Alawites really established themselves during the reign of Moulay Ismail, from 1672 to 1727, who succeeded in increasing Moroccan centralization and driving out a Spanish presence. The 'Alawis have continued to this day as Morocco's ruling dynasty; the current King Hassan II is the fifteenth of his line ruling by general recognition.

Even with continuing dynastic succession, Europe's might and Morocco's proximity virtually ensured colonial conquest. The Treaty of Fez of 1912 codified arrangements that had been worked out among the European powers, establishing most of Morocco as a French protectorate and a much smaller zone in the north as a Spanish enclave. Morocco lacked any power to contest this arrangement, although it was the last North African state to lose its autonomy. Under the Protectorate, the 'Alawi ruler retained formal sovereignty; however, his laws, known as *zahirs*, were promulgated on the basis of "suggestions" from a resident general of the colonial government.

A rebellion in the northwest Rif mountains of the Spanish zone, led by the charismatic leader 'Abd al-Krim, was put down only through combined French and Spanish military intervention. The French strategy to control its new colony was based on exaggerating the differences between the country's regions and between the Arabs and Berbers. In 1930 the French made their most famous Moroccan miscalculation, adopting a decree taking mountainous Berber regions out of the administration of traditional central Islamic courts, hoping to polarize coastal Arabs and rural Berbers. The strategy completely backfired and, instead, encouraged the growth of Moroccan nationalism and popular identification with the 'Alawi ruler Moulay Muhammad.

The Berber *zahir* also stimulated the development of Morocco's first political party. By this time, two circles of well-educated intellectuals had formed in Fez and Rabat. Although 'Allal al-Fassi's Fez group arose from efforts to modernize Islam and Ahmed Belafrej's Rabat circle was stimulated by Arab nationalism, the two were easily able to link up in general hostility to further French control after the Berber *zahir*. More important, popular perceptions that the French and

Spanish wished to substitute not only their governments for Morocco's kings but also Western ideas for Islam provided the newborn nationalist movement with millions of potential adherents.

In 1933, several years after the *ʒahir*, the proto-nationalist intellectuals began publishing a journal in French, criticizing various aspects of the protectorate without yet openly calling for independence. After this journal was suppressed, in December 1934, the ten leading activists petitioned the authorities with a plan of reforms, referring to themselves as the Moroccan Action Committee (CAM).* The nationalists' act was not meant to create a political party, and the CAM was not one, but it was the skeleton which, when given flesh, would become Morocco's Istiqlal (meaning either "independence" or "liberation") party.

The small group of nationalists that started as the CAM went through several cycles of activity, expansion, repression, and reorganization before it emerged as the Istiqlal Party* in January 1944. Despite the CAM's unified political purpose, it remained at first a very narrow collection of intellectuals without strong organization or local cells. When the broad terms of the plan of reforms were rejected by the French, the CAM tapped into popular hostility to the Berber *ʒahir* and staged more vocal demonstrations.

The French governor general outlawed the CAM in 1937; several of its members fled to Paris and formed a successor party in 1938, the National Party for the Realization of the Reform Plan* or, more simply, the National Party. This organization created the basic structures from which the Istiqlal would eventually assimilate much of Morocco's male population as members. Even before the National Party period, the CAM had begun collecting dues from and submitting prospective members to loyalty oaths.

The Allies' rhetoric in World War II made Moroccan nationalists hopeful about the prospects for independence following the fighting. In this general climate, the Istiqlal Party was born in December 1943, consisting of the same activist leaders, although many of these were living in exile. The new party, like its predecessor the CAM, commenced its activities by publishing a petition of political demands. However, the January 1944 manifesto differed from the earlier one in two critical respects. First, it clearly called for Moroccan independence from French rule. Second, the 1944 manifesto had been approved by Sultan Muhammad before its submission to the French resident general.

For the first few years after its formation, the Istiqlal remained a small party. Its initial membership was about 3,000; its early structure consisted of small, secret cells, designed to educate nationalist activists, which imposed stringent commitments on prospective members. Illiteracy and hostility to the French pervaded the country; the new party did not want to be crippled or suppressed on account of members' unauthorized violence or general lack of discipline.

By 1947 two developments had helped change the party's strategy. First, the increasingly evident popular appeal of the sultan threatened to deprive the nationalist intellectuals of any control of the nationalist crusade and, consequently, postindependent politics. Second, the disappointing postwar intransigence of the French heated up the struggle and made less relevant the mostly journalistic and persuasive tactics of the party. The Istiqlal opened its doors to all kinds of new members, swelling its ranks, but decreasing its coherence. The party became the conduit of mass nationalist activism, synonymous in fact as well as word with the nationalist movement. Its diverse members were motivated by the leadership and inspiration of 'Allal al-Fassi and the idea of independence, but not any other political ideology. In so expanding its activity and sponsoring all sorts of nationalist agitation, it also became the Sorcerer's Apprentice of Moroccan nationalism—it unleashed forces that it could not control.

Nonetheless, other Moroccan political parties had developed by 1956, when Morocco achieved its independence. The Spanish protectorate zone had its own political parties, most notably, the Islah ("reform") Party.* However, the power of the Istiqlal and the lack of urbanization and importance of the Spanish zone relative to the much larger and more central area controlled by the French meant that, in practical terms, the Spanish zone parties coordinated their activities and eventually merged with the Istiqlal.

Several parties developed as alternatives to the Istiqlal. One of the original CAM members, Muhammad al-Ouazzani, split from the movement in 1937, starting his own journal and, later, a party called the Popular Movement.* Imprisoned until 1946, he reformed his group with a new name, the Democratic Party of Independence (PDI).* Although the PDI put more emphasis on intellectuals and less on Islam than the Istiqlal, Ouazzani probably formed the party as much out of a desire not to be subordinated to other nationalist leaders as for ideological reasons. This was the most important of the splits from and alternatives to the Istiqlal emerging before independence, and a general template of the series of party divisions that would occur thereafter. The Moroccan Communist Party* also established itself before independence, in 1943, at first as a derivative of the French Communist Party.

Despite these other parties, between 1947 and independence, the Istiqlal's pervasiveness led it to be known as "the party." And, in 1951, all of the Moroccan parties agreed to cooperate for independence as the Moroccan National Front.* The political counterweight to the Istiqlal came not from other parties, but from the sultan. By 1953 Muhammad V's popularity, as a symbol of independence and legitimacy, had grown so much that the French staged a coup, exiled Muhammad, and put a more pliable 'Alawi relation on the throne. This proved to be another miscalculation—turning the person of the traditional, sacred ruler into a martyr and further galvanizing the Moroccan people. The Istiqlal was the organizational channel for this popular outrage, but the sultan was at least as much its beneficiary. In putting its independence campaign in terms of the restoration of Morocco's traditional monarchy, Istiqlalis may have been pursuing the only viable strategy, and one in which many believed. But the result was to amplify enormously the stature of Muhammad V and to set up a confrontation for control between the two dominant Moroccan political forces once the French (and Spanish) caved in to the pressure for independence in 1956.

## FROM 1956 TO 1961: MUHAMMAD V AND THE ISTIQLAL

Having regained its independence in 1956, Morocco was left with two strong political axes, King Muhammad V and the Istiqlal Party, both of which agreed that the new government should be a constitutional monarchy. Their divergence, a major one, concerned how much actual political power the monarch would wield. The Istiqlal leadership did not mind the king's initial central political role, but assumed that the party's numbers and status would erode that role over time.

Yet the Istiqlal underestimated the king's strength, overestimated its own importance, and mistakenly emphasized large membership over party coherence. Morocco's first post-1956 government included nine ministerial portfolios for Istiqlalis, but it also incorporated six ministers from the rival PDI and six with no party affiliation. With these appointments, Muhammad acknowledged the Istiqlal's importance, but he also provided checks on its influence. The prime minister himself was independent of any political party.

With the king unwilling to step aside and let the Istiqlal rule, and the Istiqlal as large as it was in part on account of its prenationalist loyalty to the monarchy, the party faced a difficult strategic decision. If the king would not let it run the country, should it articulate a specific program and become the party of opposition to the government? This decision was encumbered by the fact that the cooperation between Muhammad and the party had been genuine before 1956, even as their divergent visions of Moroccan politics were based on more than lust for power.

Initially, the Istiqlal chose to remain part of the government, perhaps due to a combination of Muhammad's popularity and the party's ideological incoherence. But the very diversity of the party that led to this incoherence created dissension about this decision. In 1959 an Istiqlali named Mehdi ben Barka, a generation younger than the party's founders, formed a new party from the more radical intellectual elements of the Istiqlal. The National Union of Popular Forces (UNFP),* the second major breakaway group from the Istiqlal, became the opposition party that the Istiqlal was at first unwilling to be.

The UNFP was not the only new political party formed in the few years after 1956. As widespread as the membership of the Istiqlal had become during the struggle for independence, it remained primarily an urban organization. In 1957 Abdelkrim Khatib, a rural intellectual and former anti-French resistance leader, allied with Mahjoubi Aherdane, governor of the province containing the Moroccan capital Rabat, to form a clandestine party called the Popular Movement (MP).* After two years of direct and indirect involvement with rural uprisings, the MP's party status was legalized. The king decided to give his tacit support to parties that could counter the dominance of the Istiqlal.

By the time Muhammad V died suddenly in 1961 of complications during surgery, the Moroccan monarchy had established its political primacy over the Istiqlal. In retrospect, the king's traditional legitimacy and the unprecedented popularity he enjoyed after his symbolic equation with Moroccan nationalism had put him in a much better position to subdue diverse political factions than the loose, lumbering coalition that was the Istiqlal.

## FROM 1961 TO 1974: THE ROYAL PATTERN OF PARTY FISSION AND REPRESSION

King Muhammad's death left the country ruled by his son, Crown Prince Hassan, who lacked both the experience and popularity of his father. Moreover, the new king and the Istiqlal had not developed the same habits of cooperation and mutual respect necessitated by Muhammad V's exile and the Istiqlal's might during the struggle for independence. The new king and the old party could each easily imagine a political system in which the other played no important role.

One resource that King Hassan did have was his knowledge of his father's experience with political parties. Muhammad had been able to erode the Istiqlal's influence. The transplantation of Western-style political parties to Moroccan soil did not engender popular interest in parties on the basis of ideological platforms. Politics in Morocco were traditionally based on patron-client relations. A party was valuable to its potential members largely in terms of whether it was linked to established patronage networks or established new ones. But the king was the central patron in the entire system, as well as being the acknowledged central national and cultural symbol. This gave him the ability to play diverse groups off against each other, in particular, by nurturing the conflicts within political parties enough to help the formation of breakaway groups.

Much of the postindependence history of Moroccan parties can be understood in terms of this dynamic. As is true in most countries marked by illiteracy and apathy to imported ideologies, parties were unable to attract a wide following through coherent doctrines. Those parties, such as the Istiqlal, the MP, and the UNFP—with an established history, a client base, and a long-standing group of intellectuals committed to the organization—have been the most successful at developing relevance to Moroccan politics. But these parties have had to work closely with the king in order to do this, with the result that party activity has, on the whole, actually strengthened the king's legitimacy and political capacity.

Knowing some of these things, King Hassan II moved quickly to prevent the Istiqlal from increasing its strength. Following up on a promise made by his father, Hassan drafted a constitution that established a unicameral parliamentary political system with contested elections but with tremendous power vested in the monarchy. This constitution, prepared without input from the Istiqlal and the UNFP, guaranteed that the king would remain at the center of the political system. In December 1962, Hassan held a national referendum on his draft constitution, which the UNFP boycotted. Faced with a choice between the king's constitution and no constitution, and aware of the monarchy's popular legitimacy, the Istiqlal reluctantly supported the referendum. The referendum overwhelmingly approved the draft constitution, arming King Hassan with new mechanisms for continuing the Istiqlal's political marginalization.

Fearing that his lack of established competence or reputation would undermine his rule and destabilize the country, King Hassan adopted a general strategy through the 1960s of eroding alternative organizational sources of power. He moved both to disempower potential opposition parties, as seen above with the Istiqlal, and midwifed the birth of counterweights, just as his father had done with the MP.

In 1963 the minister of interior, close political ally of the king, Ahmed Reda Guédira, grouped the MP, some of the PDI—now known as the Democratic Constitutional Party (DCP)*—and many nonparty politicians under the umbrella of the Front for the Defense of Constitutional Institutions (FDIC)* to foster greater coordination among the promonarchy candidates for the first election of representatives to the parliament. Guédira had tried unsuccessfully to organize promonarchy independents before; this time he had the backing of the king, who hoped that the FDIC would marshall the resources to capture enough seats to eliminate real opposition to government programs in the new parliament.

The king had grounds for concern. Rightly sensing Hassan's determination to enervate their party, the Istiqlali ministers in Hassan's first government resigned in January 1963, shifting the party into the opposition. Although far less than a majority, the seats in parliament won by the Istiqlal and UNFP were enough to allow the two parties, provided they cooperated, to paralyze government legislation (see Table 17). Meanwhile, the UNFP channeled its energy into a series of protests against the regime. The government claimed that the UNFP was involved in a plot to unseat the king, and, as a result, prominent party members were arrested or sent into hiding.

Table 17
**Results of 1963 Moroccan Parliamentary Elections**

| Party Grouping | No. of Seats Won |
|---|---|
| FDIC | 69 |
| Istiqlal | 41 |
| UNFP | 28 |
| TOTAL | 138 |

Notes: 1. On November 30, 1963, the Supreme Court annulled the election of several delegates. Following replacement elections on January 2, 1964, the FDIC attained a majority of seats. Delegate counts of the contested seats changed from the original result of three, FDIC; three, Istiqlal; and one, UNFP, to five, FDIC; two, Istiqlal; and zero, UNFP, thus giving the FDIC a total of seventy-one seats.
2. King Hassan declared a state of exception and suspended parliament on June 7, 1965.

The next two years exacerbated the growing political polarization between the government and party opposition. The Istiqlal and the UNFP enhanced their cooperation and stalemated government legislative initiatives in the parliament. Violent border disputes between Morocco and neighboring Algeria, coupled with price and unemployment rises within the kingdom, created an incendiary climate which blew up with widespread rioting in Casablanca, the country's largest city, in March 1965. About 400 people died in the riots. King Hassan, genuinely alarmed at the event, attempted to put together a new government drawn from all of the parties to implement a comprehensive reform package. But this government was stillborn. The king instead declared a constitutional "state of exception," suspended parliament and elections, appointed a government of loyal technocrats with himself as prime minister, and banned all party activity.

The state of exception lasted for five years, until 1970. During this period, due to the direct and absolute nature of the king's rule, the parties withered. The opposition parties retained their activists, but what grass-roots support they had eroded greatly. The loyal FDIC had collapsed, along with the Social Democratic Party,* which had emerged from under the FDIC umbrella in 1964; both failed to emerge as real political forces. Though the MP still existed, proroyalist parties had little to do at a time when the king controlled politics without using mobilizational organizations. Although party activities were restored before Hassan II ended the state of exception in 1970, the UNFP's sense of incapacity in the face of Hassan's power led it to boycott the first municipal and rural communal elections in 1969.

The end of the state of exception was a reenactment of the situation in 1962, but all of the political actors were weaker. Hassan II promulgated a new constitution, giving himself more power and the parliament less power than in the earlier document. He submitted the constitution to popular referendum, which the Istiqlal and the UNFP, now united as a National Front,* urged Moroccans to boycott. Not surprisingly, the constitution was resoundingly approved, and the first parliamentary elections of the summer of 1970, also boycotted by the National Front, put promonarchy delegates in all but 20 of the 240 seats. The two opposition parties, the only political parties left with any real organizational structure, were very weak.

But the king's strength also was limited. Having chipped away at autonomous political groups before and especially during the state of exception, Hassan now found himself vulnerable to other forces. In 1971 and 1972, dramatic military plots came very close to killing the king and establishing a right-wing army junta. The king's survival, which seemed almost miraculous, increased his popularity among Moroccans in general but illustrated his political fragility to antimonarchy activists. The National Front parties had grounds both for working with Hassan and for believing he could be nudged from power.

In 1972 the king drafted a third constitution in which, although he retained royal control, more concessions were made to political pluralism. The constitution provided for parliamentary elections every six years. Although two-thirds of the seats would be filled by direct elections, another third were chosen through an electoral college of local officials generally dependent on the king. The National Front took a neutral stance on the new constitution, which was passed by another referendum. When the king and the opposition parties began negotiating power sharing, the parties overestimated their strength and the king's willingness to compromise. The king established yet another government of loyal technocrats which clamped down hard on opposition party activities, especially after the discovery of an antigovernment plot in March 1973. The Istiqlal and UNFP ended their National Front cooperation, and the UNFP itself polarized into two distinct factions.

Hoping to find an enduring basis of popular support, Hassan II turned to symbolic politics and nationalism, perhaps making use of his father's example. The king improved his grass-roots image by sending troops to the 1973 Arab-Israeli war. But this was a minor rehearsal for what was to come the following year when Hassan made the status of the Western Saharan territories into the central issue of Moroccan politics for years to come. By identifying himself firmly with popular sentiment for "reclaiming" the Western Sahara, to the point of calling on Moroccans to march *en masse* to these territories, the king succeeded in identifying himself with the essence of Moroccan nationalism, as the Istiqlal had helped his father do. Hassan II now had the political strength he needed to bypass the political elite entirely.

## FROM 1974 TO 1990: MORE PARTIES, MORE PARTY WEAKNESS?

With the increased popularity the king gained by his stand on the Western Sahara, the political climate warmed somewhat. Restrictions on opposition party activity were lifted. As virtually all Moroccans fervently supported the country's dominion over the Western Sahara, many of the opposition leaders were willing to work on behalf of Hassan's irredentist policy, including traveling abroad to represent this policy to other governments. In 1974 Hassan let it be known that parliamentary elections would be held, although he gave no firm date.

The net result of these developments was a proliferation of new parties the same year. Morocco's generally outlawed communist party was able to reestablish itself overtly as the Party of Progress and Socialism (PPS).* One of the two UNFP factions, based on the Rabat section, officially split off to form the new Socialist Union of Popular Forces (USFP).* A rural intellectual, Abdullah Senhaji, created the Party of Action (PA)* to represent less established rural interests than those connected with the MP.

During the next few years, Morocco devoted more and more of its resources to annexing the Western Sahara. Although the United Nations and most governments did not recognize Morocco's claim, the kingdom began a costly war against pro-Saharan independence guerrilla groups backed by neighboring Algeria. The first years of the war continued to strengthen the king's popular position. The king was happy to allow the activity of political parties so long as he did not see any one, or a combination of several, as a challenge to his authority, and to the extent that party leaders agreed with his policies. Both these conditions were satisfied during the first years of the Saharan conflict. Therefore, provincial elections were scheduled for 1976, and parliamentary elections for 1977 (see Table 18). Furthermore, Hassan's 1976 government included ministers from almost every political party.

But the king's tolerance for political pluralism remained limited. The UNFP, now overshadowed by the breakaway USFP, boycotted the elections entirely. In both elections, the largest bloc of successful candidates were progovernment independents, leading many party members and outside observers to believe the results were rigged. Nonetheless, the elections represented a significant political liberalization and allowed a greater degree of free expression than had occurred for years. In this climate, the Istiqlal, which won the most parliamentary seats after the independents, agreed to join the 1977 government. The following year, the king urged Prime Minister Ahmed Osman to make a new attempt at bringing the loyalist representatives under a party rubric, and the National Rally of Independents (RNI)* was born. It appeared that the king could foster limited political reform, allow party activity, and retain control.

Yet the Saharan war dragged on, at tremendous cost to Moroccan economic reform. Within four years of political liberalization, less wealthy Moroccans had exhausted their patience with the sacrifices they had had to endure because of the government's continued prime emphasis on the Sahara. Spurred on by a new

**Table 18**
**Results of 1977 Moroccan Parliamentary Elections**

| Party | Seats by Direct Election | Seats by Indirect Election | Total |
|---|---|---|---|
| Non-party Independents | 81 | 61 | 142 |
| Istiqlal | 45 | 4 | 49 |
| MP | 29 | 15 | 44 |
| USFP | 16 | 0 | 16 |
| Moroccan Labor Union | 0 | 6 | 6 |
| DCPM | 2 | 1 | 3 |
| PA | 2 | 0 | 2 |
| PPS | 1 | 0 | 1 |
| Genl Union of Moroccan Workers | 0 | 1 | 1 |
| TOTAL | 176 | 88 | 264 |

Note: The Moroccan Labor Union is the country's oldest labor movement, not specifically affiliated to a political party, but subsidized by the government. The General Union of Moroccan Workers is a labor union affiliated with the Istiqlal.

labor union affiliated with the USFP, workers in Casablanca staged a series of protests, which culminated in riots in June 1981 that rivaled the riots of 1965 in scope and significance. The government immediately clamped down on USFP activity, without first establishing the party's complicity in the events. As a result, the USFP withdrew its delegates from the parliament, and the party's relations with the king soured considerably.

The 1981 riots roughly coincided with another of Morocco's frequent party fissions, this time within the RNI. A group of wealthy rural landholders, led by Abdelamid Kassimi, objecting both to the RNI's deemphasis on agricultural policy and Ahmed Osman's lackluster leadership, formed a breakaway party called the National Democratic Party (PND).* The king, apparently also disappointed with Osman, asked the considerably weakened RNI to become the opposition party in parliament, after the USFP withdrawal had destroyed the façade of majority and minority factions in the representative body. Hassan hoped that the RNI could do better in helping to establish his ideal mix of royal control and apparent political pluralism than it did in trying to make the various progovernment parliamentarians march to the same political beat.

The next year brought renewed political calm. Not only had the violence of 1981 gone beyond what Moroccans wanted, international organizations, most notably the Organization of African Unity, showed increasing sympathy for the independence forces in the Western Sahara. This reminded all Moroccan political factions of the need for unity on the Saharan issue. King Hassan released many USFP leaders who had been imprisoned for their imputed role in the riots; and communal elections, which had been postponed, were scheduled for 1983, with parliamentary elections to come soon thereafter.

The approach of new elections stimulated a new round of political party formation. Since the RNI had proved little better than the FDIC in reining in progovernment parliamentarians, Hassan II midwifed a third attempt at this task. Prime Minister Maati Bouabid started the Constitutional Union party (UC),* which attempted to develop a more modernist, youth-oriented message than previous loyalist parties. A new leftist party, formed from previous clandestine movements of radicalized UNFP and USFP members, the Organization of Democratic and Popular Action (OADP),* also emerged in 1983.

The communal elections had the usual result; the bulk of successful candidates were progovernment with no party affiliation. However, the UC fared best among the parties. As in prior elections, both the Istiqlal and the USFP charged the government with undercounting their voting strength. These charges were widely believed by outside observers. Nonetheless, the government considered the communal election returns a vindication of its strength; certainly, popular support for King Hassan was high.

Yet 1984 heralded a renewal of the tensions that had boiled over in 1981. Although the king had put in place a government drawn from all the major parties, including the USFP, economic austerity measures pushed onto Morocco by the International Monetary Fund triggered an outbreak of urban dissatisfaction, as it had done three years earlier. The 1984 riots were less severe, and the government was less inclined to blame them on the USFP. Parliamentary elections, postponed until September 1984, saw major successes for the UC, the worst showing ever for the Istiqlal, and a correspondingly larger share of representatives for the USFP, once again amidst widespread charges of election fraud and government interference (see Table 19).

It was true that the government had many mechanisms to achieve favorable election results. Local governors, appointed by the Ministry of the Interior, supervised elections both for communal leaders and for parliament. The two-tiered electoral system for parliamentary seats ensured extra manipulative latitude for pro-government forces in the one-third of the seats that were indirectly elected. Slightly more than half of this indirect one-third is chosen by local provincial organizations usually dependent on the king; the rest is selected by a special body representing professional and labor groups. Thus, Morocco's electoral system favored parties loyal to the king even without the vote fraud alleged by opposition parties. Nonetheless, that the political system had included contested elections and uninterrupted parliamentary activity since 1977 gave political parties an incentive to be involved in the system, particularly those that hoped parliament might develop into a vigorous and salient political forum.

## CONCLUSION

The pattern of the early 1980s remained largely in place in the early 1990s. Though occasionally a locus of spirited political dispute, parliament did not emerge as a real center of legislative or other power. When domestic affairs, particularly those relating to the economy, stood out, the Istiqlal, USFP, and smaller leftist parties tended to speak out against the government and make use of their labor union affiliates to threaten or carry out strikes. On the other hand, when international crises, particularly those concerning the Western Sahara, were prominent, the parties tended to support the government.

The first tendency emerged prominently in mid-1990. The mid-1980s saw several years of exceptional agricultural production, which contributed to good economic performance at the same time that the Saharan territories seemed increasingly Moroccanized. The king's standing was high, and articulated opposition was minimal. But 1989 and 1990 were years of economic decline. In May 1990, the Istiqlal and USFP once again united in an opposition National Front,* introducing a motion of no confidence in the government for the first time since 1964. The motion was defeated by the UC, MP, PND, and RNI representatives who made up two-thirds of the parliament. But the Istiqlal and USFP media carried the debates for weeks, leveling severe criticism at the government for its management of domestic economic and social policy. The king responded with a ministerial shuffle.

The atmosphere of confrontation over domestic issues continued through the year, culminating in a general strike in December that was organized by the labor

**Table 19**
**Results of 1984 Moroccan Parliamentary Elections**

| Party | Seats by Direct Election | Seats by Indirect Election | Total |
|---|---|---|---|
| UC | 56 | 27 | 83 |
| RNI | 39 | 22 | 61 |
| MP | 31 | 16 | 47 |
| Istiqlal | 24 | 17 | 41 |
| USFP | 35 | 1 | 36 |
| PND | 15 | 9 | 24 |
| Moroccan Labor | 0 | 5 | 5 |
| CDT | 0 | 3 | 3 |
| General Union | 0 | 2 | 2 |
| PPS | 2 | 0 | 2 |
| OADP | 1 | 0 | 1 |
| Unaffiliated | 1 | 0 | 1 |
| TOTAL | 204 | 102 | 306 |

Note: CDT is the Democratic Confederation of Workers, the labor affiliate of the USFP.

organizations affiliated with the Istiqlal and USFP. The strike got out of control in Fez, resulting in violent clashes between the military and strikers and scores of deaths.

Yet the second tendency has counteracted the confrontation to a large extent. New flare-ups in the Western Sahara and the publication of a book in France widely critical of Hassan II's human rights practices catalyzed a uniform party response behind the king and his Saharan absorption policies. Even regarding the king's widely unpopular decision to send Moroccan troops against Iraq in the 1991 Persian Gulf War, the opposition parties refrained from stoking the fires of the king's vulnerability.

King Hassan, like his father before him, has used his political assets and skill to assist the transformation of a large, powerful party into a group of weaker, less autonomous parties. While the king has allowed parties increased freedom, he has used carrots and sticks to ensure that they work within the basic monarchical rules of the Moroccan regime rather than articulating an alternative to the political status quo.

But increasing talk of democratization in Eastern Europe, in the Third World, and in the Arab countries, as well as Hassan's increasing age, have invited speculation as to whether any of the political parties could articulate a broad enough agenda to survive in a political system in which they could play a more central role. So far, all of the parties have kept their ideas firmly under the umbrella of the monarchy. In contrast, other organizations, such as the new human rights groups and the clandestine radical Islamic movements, have enjoyed no history of cooperative engagement with the monarchy but stood to benefit from their youthful membership and their lack of association with traditional politics.

Because Kings Muhammad and Hassan have been able to keep political parties bound up with the monarchy as an institution, the parties' survival could depend on the king. So long as Morocco continues to have a king as its actual head of state, he will undoubtedly continue the long-standing strategy of using parties as legitimizing mechanisms with limited autonomy and mobilizational capacity. The parties, for their part, to the extent they have developed solid bases of support, will hope for more success in their attempts to nudge politics toward a Western-style constitutional monarchy than they have enjoyed heretofore.

Late 1992 promised to be an interesting test of these competing strategies and represented a potentially wide window of political opportunity for the parties. In April, the king announced that new communal elections and the first legislative elections since 1984 would be held toward the end of the year. In response, the Istiqlal, USFP, UNFP, OADP, and PPS strengthened their cooperation under the aegis of the Democratic Bloc,* hoping thereby to muster a strong showing in the elections.

There were signs that this hope had some substance. In part because of pressure from the Democratic Bloc, King Hassan lowered the minimum legal age for voting and for running for office, and he also promised a commission independent of the government to oversee the election. The pro-government parties showed few signs of a popular clientele or populist message. Moreover, the king proposed reforms to the constitution to subject the prime minister to popular election, guarantee a specific timetable and process for parliamentary approval of legislation, and authorize parliament to conduct political investigations independent of the government.

However, the prospects for increased party relevance suggested by these reforms were counterbalanced somewhat by the results of a national referendum held on the new constitution on September 4. Even though both pro-government and opposition parties supported the constitution, the officially reported 99.98 percent approval vote and 97.4 percent participation rate were reminiscent of previous manipulated elections. These results tended to underscore the malleability of the political system, in contrast with the centrality of the monarchy.

The year of political jockeying and elections that followed approval of the new constitution amplified this combination of system manipulability and monarchical guidance. A lackluster and confused electoral campaign for local officials in October 1992 led to the apparent emergence of the RNI as the leading party, with 21.7 percent of the seats. Yet the RNI was perhaps the least partisan, with virtually no defined ideology. Furthermore, amid widespread charges of fraud and vote buying, candidates unaffiliated with any party garnered the second largest share of offices—with 13.9 percent of the seats. Two major parties that had hoped to do well, the Constitutional Union and Istiqlal, were embarrassed with third- and fourth-place rankings, garnering 13.45 percent and 12.5 percent of the seats, respectively. The ability of independents to outmaneuver both pro-government and well-organized opposition parties produced tacit agreement across the political spectrum that the blatantly corrupt behavior of these independents had to be stopped.

Both government and opposition parties wished to avoid a repetition of these election results in the far more visible parliamentary contests; consequently the king announced postponement of these elections. The opposition hoped that its organization and independence would translate into significant popularity in the atmosphere of free and fair elections promised by the king. Opposition leaders also believed that the king would want them to join the next government, if only to mute their intensified criticism of the government's economic development policies. Therefore, between December 1992, the intended date for elections, and June 1993, when they actually occurred, the opposition sharpened its strategy of testing its bargaining leverage with the regime. Istiqlal and USFP members argued loudly with the government over details of voter registration and election monitoring procedures, and they disputed many of the local election results. Allegations of vote buying and intimidation continued, as official tribunals annulled 191 local election results on grounds of fraud.

As the parliamentary election campaign began in earnest in late spring 1993, officials clearly hoped that the process would highlight Moroccan moves toward democratization in the eyes of western nations, whose economic investments assumed a high priority. King Hassan himself gave speeches in April and June, calling on all Moroccans to exercise their national duty by voting and helping to build true democracy. Yet many citizens had been alienated by the cynical local election process and by the belief that, even under the new constitution, parliament had little real political significance. For the first time, the government allowed all parties equal access to state-controlled media so they could present their programs and platforms to the voters.

Although the campaign was greeted by widespread voter apathy, the opposition hoped that its superior organization and discipline would gain more seats and improve its political bargaining power. Consequently, the two major opposition parties, the Istiqlal and the USFP, jettisoned the smaller Democratic Bloc parties and tightened bipartisan coordination. They arranged to support only one candidate in each constituency, though that candidate would still be identified by party. In response to this move, and in the face of the RNI's success in the local election, four pro-government parties—the UC, MP, National Popular Movement, and PND—formed their own electoral alliance, the National Accord.* This alliance was not as well coordinated as the Democratic Bloc, however.

The opposition strategy paid off. The June 25 election, generally regarded by international observers as the fairest in Morocco's history, produced a victory for the Istiqlal-USFP coalition. The USFP won 48 and the Istiqlal 43 of the 222 seats determined by direct popular vote (see Table 20). Had there been fair counting in the relatively few districts where fraud was thought to have occurred, even more USFP candidates might have won.

Subsequent events, however, once again called into question the ability of the two best organized parties to turn their political strength into real power in a system in which the ultimate arbiter of all power remains clear. The communal and professional representatives, elected in October 1992, who chose the remaining one-third of parliament on September 17, 1993, compensated for the

Table 20
Results of 1993 Moroccan Parliamentary Elections

| Party | Seats by Direct Election | Seats by Indirect Election | Total |
|---|---|---|---|
| Constitutional Union | 27 | 27 | 54 |
| USFP | 48 | 4 | 52 |
| MP | 33 | 18 | 51 |
| Istiqlal | 43 | 7 | 50 |
| RNI | 28 | 13 | 41 |
| MPN | 14 | 11 | 25 |
| PND | 14 | 10 | 24 |
| PPS | 7 | 5 | 12 |
| PDI | 3 | 6 | 9 |
| CDT | 0 | 4 | 4 |
| Moroccan Labor | 0 | 3 | 3 |
| General Union | 0 | 2 | 2 |
| ODPA | 2 | 0 | 2 |
| Action Party | 2 | 0 | 2 |
| Unaffiliated | 1 | 1 | 2 |
| TOTAL | 222 | 111 | 333 |
| RESULTS BY BLOC | | | |
| National Accord | 88 | 66 | 154 |
| Democratic Bloc | 100 | 22 | 122 |
| Others | 34 | 23 | 57 |

Notes: These figures are accurate as of late 1993 when the outcome of several races remained in doubt. Although the government reported the results by Bloc, they were essentially loose alliances that experienced major difficulties in cooperation and coordination throughout the campaign.

popular strength of the Istiqlal and the USFP when they cast their ballots. At the end of the second, indirect election process, the parties of the Democratic Bloc held 37 percent of the seats, as compared to 27 percent in the previous session (see Tables 19 and 20). Thus, although they had gained strength, they were still likely to remain in opposition.

With their bargaining power reduced by these developments, the king invited these parties to assume a numerically dominant position in the new government, although he stipulated that he would not offer them such major positions as that of prime minister, minister of the interior, or minister of foreign affairs. This insult, added to the disappointment the Istiqlal and the USFP had with the election results, led them to reject the offer. The government, which was organized in November 1993, consisted of technocrats with no party affiliation, with the prime minister and minister of the interior remaining unchanged from the previous, pre-election government.

The combination of a nonpartisan government and a badly divided parliament suggested that the relation between political efficacy and party activism would become even more complex than in the past. The loosely organized pro-government parties in the National Accord feared marginalization by a government oriented more to the king than to them. The Democratic Bloc's decision not to join the government meant it would continue to be sidelined because of its demand for a share of power appropriate to what it perceived to be its popularity. In any event, the Bloc disintegrated as a result of interparty disputes.

Thus, as the 1993 election faded into history, the essential dilemma of Morocco's many political parties remained what it had been since the kingdom gained independence: Can political organizations dependent on subservience to an unelected, unquestioned ruler become agents of independence and innovation? This question was particularly vexing with regard to the popular image of the parties. Despite the genuine popularity of some of the 1993 candidates, particularly from the USFP and Istiqlal, could parties accustomed to being played off against one another by the ruler retain popular accountability or capacity for action? If Morocco's political history of royal dominance is clear, the future of the complex symbiosis between the king, the parties, and the people is not.

## Bibliography

*Annuaire de l'Afrique du Nord* (North Africa Yearbook). Vols. 1–28. Aix-en-Provence, France: Centre National de la Recherche Scientifique, 1962–89.

Ashford, Douglas E. *Political Change in Morocco*. Princeton, N.J.: Princeton University Press, 1961.

Entelis, John. *Culture and Counterculture in Moroccan Politics*. Boulder, Colo.: Westview Press, 1989.

Nelson, Harold D., ed. *Morocco: A Country Study*. 5th ed. Washington, D.C.: Government Printing Office for Foreign Area Studies, American University, 1985.

Parker, Richard B. *North Africa: Regional Tensions and Strategic Concerns*. New York: Praeger, 1984.

Rezette, Robert. *Les Partis Politiques Marocains* (Moroccan Political Parties). Paris: Armand Colin, 1955.

Waterbury, John. *The Commander of the Faithful: The Moroccan Political Elite—A Study in Segmented Politics*. New York: Columbia University Press, 1970.

Zartman, I. William. *The Political Economy of Morocco*. New York: Praeger, 1987.

———. "Opposition as Support of the State," in *The Arab State*, edited by Giacomo Luciani. Berkeley: University of California Press, 1990.

**Political Parties**

EL-'ADL W'AL IHSAN. *See* JUSTICE AND CHARITY MOVEMENT.

BLOC DEMOCRATIQUE. *See* DEMOCRATIC BLOC.

COMITE D'ACTION MAROCAINE. *See* MOROCCAN ACTION COMMITTEE.

COMMUNIST PARTY. *See* MOROCCAN COMMUNIST PARTY.

CONSTITUTIONAL UNION (UC) (*Union Constitutionnelle*). The Constitutional Union party, Morocco's youngest major party, was created to represent a more progressive, progovernment perspective than the National Rally of Independents (RNI),* from which it broke off. Maati Bouabid, who served as Morocco's prime minister in 1983, formed the party that year to be modernist, responsive to popular needs, representative of both cities and the countryside, and imbued with a social conscience. Bouabid's move was a response to the growing sense that the government did not adequately represent the aspirations of the younger generation who had not personally experienced the independence struggle.

The UC held itself out as nonideological, nonaligned on foreign affairs, and supportive of the interests of small and medium-size private sector enterprises. Whether because of this approach or, more likely, because of the king's strong support, the UC emerged within a year of its formation as the country's big winner in communal and parliamentary elections. It gained fifty-six seats directly and twenty-seven seats indirectly in the 1984 Chamber of Deputies, making it the largest party in parliament (see Table 19).

However, like earlier royalist party groupings of independents, the UC did not manage to establish a stable clientele or a set of political positions. In 1986 clashes between Bouabid and the group of financial advisors to the king precipitated decreased royal support for the UC. Without the strong backing of the king, the UC, like the Front for the Defense of Constitutional Institutions* and the RNI, the two previous efforts at umbrella party groupings of independent candidates, it may fade in importance in the next elections. If prior history is a guide, another party of the king's supporters, perhaps the RNI, is likely to emerge that is more in tune with current issues than the UC.

DCP. *See* DEMOCRATIC CONSTITUTIONAL PARTY.

DCPM. *See* DEMOCRATIC AND CONSTITUTIONAL POPULAR MOVEMENT.

DEMOCRATIC AND CONSTITUTIONAL POPULAR MOVEMENT (DCPM) (*Mouvement Populaire, Démocratique et Constitutionnel*). Abdelkrim Khatib led a group of members away from the Popular Movement* to form their own group under his leadership in 1967. Khatib's organization represented and favored a more urban orientation than that traditionally favored by the main party. However, the DCPM never developed into anything larger than a small group of Khatib loyalists. The party went from three parliamentary seats in 1977 to none in 1984.

DEMOCRATIC BLOC (*Bloc Démocratique*). On several occasions, Morocco's leading opposition parties have worked together to contest government policies, calling themselves the National Front.* In May 1992, the two major opposition parties, the Istiqlal* and the Socialist Union of Popular Forces,* along with the smaller National Union of Popular Forces,* the Party of Progress and Socialism,* and the Organization of Democratic and Popular Action,* came together under this new name to coordinate their strategy and tactics for the communal and legislative elections announced for later that year. The heads of the five parties specifically called for electoral reforms to strengthen the rule of law, to guarantee fair elections, to reduce the minimum age for voting and for political candidacy, and to strengthen parliament. King Hassan then proposed amendments to the constitution that encompassed some of the bloc's demands. The bloc hoped that cooperation would aid the constituent parties' efforts at making a strong showing in the elections.

DEMOCRATIC CONSTITUTIONAL PARTY (DCP) (*Parti Démocratique Constitutionnel*). Former nationalist leader, Muhammad al-Ouazzani, built the DCP in 1959 on the remnants of his former party, the Democratic Party of Independence (DPI).* However, the DCP never managed to achieve even the modest political role of its predecessor. Many of the members of the DPI, who had joined in the hopes that the DCP could provide an alternative political forum to the dominant Istiqlal,* changed their allegiance to the more radical and better-organized National Union of Popular Forces (UNFP).* The small DCP that remained was unable to find a niche in Moroccan politics. In the first years of its existence, Ouazzani failed at efforts to make the party independent of the royal government, the Istiqlal, and the opposition politics of the UNFP. Then, in 1963, he attempted to build a new clientele for the party under the rubric of the umbrella organization for political forces loyal to the king known as the Front for the Defense of Constitutional Institutions.* But other parties and factions within this grouping received greater royal patronage and, hence, greater success. The DCP faded into insignificance after the mid-1960s. Nonetheless, the party changed its name back to the DPI in the 1993 election campaign, and managed to win nine seats.

DEMOCRATIC PARTY OF INDEPENDENCE (DPI) (*Parti Démocratique de l'Indépendence*). Muhammad al-Ouazzani, an early Moroccan nationalist, formed this party in 1946 as the result of personal differences with the Istiqlal* leader, 'Allal al-Fassi, that dated back to 1937. The DPI was distinct from the dominant Istiqlal primarily in the animosity between the two party leaders, but Ouazzani's party was at first more willing than the Istiqlal to compromise with the French on the timing of Moroccan independence. The party had limited success in developing its own policies and members, but it saw many of its adherents join the National Union of Popular Forces* in 1959. Following this diminution of forces, Ouazzani reestablished the party as the Democratic Constitutional Party.* In 1993, the party reemerged under a modified version of its original name and captured nine seats, six by the indirect election process geared toward individual personalities. Because of its lack of representation in the 1984 parliament, the party was the only one not to receive government subsidies during the election campaign.

DPI. See DEMOCRATIC PARTY OF INDEPENDENCE.

FDIC. See FRONT FOR THE DEFENSE OF CONSTITUTIONAL INSTITUTIONS.

FORWARD (*Ilal Amam*). Ilal Amam, meaning "forward" or "toward the future" in Arabic, was a leftist fringe group that broke away from the Party of Liberation and Socialism,* the predecessor of Ali Yata's Party of Progress and Socialism (PPS),* in 1970. Because Ilal Amam supported self-determination in the Western Saharan territories, it was outlawed, and its leader, Abraham Serfaty, was imprisoned. The members of this small group have mostly reaffiliated themselves with the major socialist party, the Socialist Union of Popular Forces,* or the PPS.

FRONT FOR THE DEFENSE OF CONSTITUTIONAL INSTITUTIONS (FDIC) (*Front pour la Défense des Institutions Constitutionnelles*). Founded in March 1963 by the king's friend and minister of the interior, Ahmed Reda Guédira, this was the first of several organizations Hassan II encouraged to provide diverse candidates for elected office loyal to the monarchy with the potential electoral advantages of party discipline. Progovernment, French-educated "independents," informally organizing under the rubric of Liberal Independents, had been a factor in Moroccan politics since the independence struggle; both Muhammad V and Hassan II appointed such loyalists to important ministerial portfolios in the country's first governments to counter the influence of the Istiqlal.* In January 1963, the prominence of Guédira in the government prompted three ministers from the Istiqlal to resign from the government and move the party into opposition with the more leftist National Union of Popular Forces (UNFP). In response, the king encouraged the independents to group together more formally; he promoted Guédira's efforts to form the FDIC. Guédira had previously tried without success to provide institutional structure for the king's nonparty supporters.

As its name implies, the new organization was more a loose coalition than a unitary party. In fact, the FDIC included in its ambit the core of two extant parties—the Popular Movement (MP)* and the Democratic Constitutional Party (DCP)*—as well as Guédira's liberal independents. The FDIC's goal was to win the parliamentary and communal elections scheduled for May and the summer, respectively. But Guédira's organization failed to provide the diverse parliamentary candidates running under its aegis with a common ground; and the FDIC did not attain a majority in the new legislative body.

Although the FDIC won 85 percent of the seats in the subsequent communal elections in July, this was due in no small part to the opposition parties' decision not to field candidates in light of mounting disagreements with the government. From the moment the FDIC failed to realize its primary purpose of attracting votes, its demise was foreseeable. When the MP members of the front attempted increasingly to dominate the organization, Guédira changed tactics and formed a new party in 1964, the Social Democratic Party.* This effort to build a more cohesive party also failed.

The collapse of the FDIC eventually led to Guédira's loss of political influence. The next effort to group monarchy loyalists, the National Rally of Independents (RNI),* was pursued by Ahmed Osman in 1978.

FRONT NATIONAL. See NATIONAL FRONT.

FRONT NATIONAL MAROCAIN. See MOROCCAN NATIONAL FRONT.

FRONT POUR LA DEFENSE DES INSTITUTIONS CONSTITUTION-NELLES. See FRONT FOR THE DEFENSE OF CONSTITUTIONAL INSTITUTIONS.

ILAL AMAM. See FORWARD.

ISLAH PARTY (Party of National Reform). Founded in 1936 by Abdel Khalek Torres, this was the largest party agitating for independence in the northeast area of Morocco occupied by the Spanish before 1956. The party, which operated independently of the nationalist movement in French-occupied Morocco, was largely an expression of the personal views of its founder. Islah was most active in publishing newspapers and organizing demonstrations between 1936 and 1939, while attempting to cooperate somewhat with the Spanish during this period. After World War II, the Islah was in a difficult position trying to reorient and reestablish itself after Torres's open pro-German posture during the war and a personal financial scandal. Nonetheless, Torres was able to revive his party, operating out of the city of Tetouan. For a few years, the Islah worked with the Spanish, stopping short of a call for full Moroccan independence from Spain. By 1947 the Islah was in full cooperation with the Istiqlal Party,* joining the latter in favoring unified Moroccan efforts toward independence of both the French and Spanish zones under the leadership of Sultan Muhammad V. After Torres returned from a trip to Egypt in late 1947, the Spanish refused to allow him entry into Morocco and cracked down on the party. Permitted to operate openly again in 1952, the Islah was eclipsed in importance by the unification of the vast majority of Moroccan nationalists under the aegis of the Istiqlal. With Morocco's independence and reunification in 1956, the Islah disappeared.

ISLAMIC YOUTH (Al-Shabiba al-Islamiyya). This has been the best-known clandestine Islamic political movement seeking the overthrow of the monarchy and the establishment of a new Islamist political system along lines similar to those advocated by Islamic opposition groups in other Arab countries. 'Abd el-Karim Muti, once active in the Moroccan leftist secular opposition, founded Islamic Youth in 1969. In 1975, probably without basis, the government accused Muti's movement of assassinating 'Omar ben Jelloun, the editor of al-Muaharrir, the former newspaper of the Socialist Union of Popular Forces.* Since that time, the government has cracked down on the movement. Following riots in 1984, seventy-one people connected to the movement were arrested for subversive activities; twenty-six received heavy sentences. In the late 1970s and early 1980s, increasing infighting among Islamic Youth members led the movement to split into four factions, despite Muti's efforts to exercise firm control.

A secret organization forbidden by the government, the strength of Islamic Youth's different factions has been hard to estimate. The Mujahidin Movement* of Abdeslam Namani has become the most active of these factions. These groups have appealed primarily to educated technical workers and students. Throughout the 1980s and early 1990s, violent clashes between students affiliated with non-Islamist leftist parties and Islamic Youth took place on many of Morocco's campuses. Yet King Hassan's status as a descendant of the prophet Muhammad, the traditional religious legitimacy accorded the Moroccan monarch, and the king's public acts of religious piety have led some observers to downplay the political threat posed by radical Islamist movements, even though the regime's crackdown on the movements has demonstrated that it has taken this threat seriously.

ISTIQLAL PARTY (Parti Istiqlal). The Istiqlal is historically Morocco's most important party, and it remains, with the Socialist Union of Popular Forces (USFP),* a vital political unit for the legal articulation of opposition views. The Istiqlal, the Arabic term for independence, led Morocco's struggle for independence from French colonialism and aspired to be the institutional center of Morocco's postindependence political system. However, King Hassan's father, Muhammad V, took advantage of the tendency for the Istiqlal to factionalize. He outmaneuvered the party and revitalized the Moroccan monarchy, weakening the Istiqlal's political clout in the process.

The history of the party overlays the history of Morocco's campaign for independence. The Istiqlal's formal organization dates back to World War II; its founding members had created the Moroccan Action Committee (CAM)* and the National Party for the Realization of the Reform Plan* before the Istiqlal. These early nationalists represented two sociopolitical tendencies. 'Allal al-Fassi came from a prominent family of traditional urban merchants, close to the religious establishment of Fez. Ahmed Belafrej received a French education and spoke for a newer, Western-style middle class.

Belafrej, Muhammad Lyazidi, and the other leading members of the nationalist movement of the 1930s gathered in December 1943 to form the Istiqlal, although al-Fassi, who would become the head of the new party, was in exile at the time. Of critical importance is that the nationalists first consulted the future king, Sultan Muhammad, and obtained his approval before establishing the party. The party was created on the principle that nationalist cooperation with the French could occur only after explicit recognition of the principle of Moroccan independence. The new organization's first act was to draft a manifesto for independence, which it sent to Sultan Muhammad, the French resident general (the real governing authority under colonialism), and the World War II Allied powers. The sultan had agreed to this move as well, pledging to do nothing to help the French undermine the nationalists' efforts. The manifesto specifically left to Sultan Muhammad the task of creating Morocco's postindependence political regime along democratic lines.

Thus, from its very beginnings, the Istiqlal tied its fortunes to Morocco's traditional monarchy. This made sense for two reasons. First, the sultanate was an appealing symbol to the many Moroccans who might not be moved by the Western educational background and orientation of many of the nationalists. Second, the political reputation of the sultanate during colonialism had decayed to the point that the nationalists could easily imagine paying homage to the symbol without later having to lose power to the man.

The Istiqlal grew rapidly to become the spearhead and rallying point for Moroccan independence. The party's membership increased tenfold from 1947 to 1951, from ten to one hundred thousand. This expansion was fueled in large part by a third socioeconomic group, the urban poor and new migrants. Though these generally younger party members did not always agree with the traditional merchant and Westernized intellectual party chiefs, all Istiqlalis could unite under the broad banner of independence, nationalism, and Sultan Muhammad.

Yet, the Istiqlal's rapid expansion and direction of the independence struggle triggered French repression. From 1953 until independence, the party's prominent leaders were exiled. The party had been able to channel independence sentiment through its own essentially nonviolent mobilizational strategies before the French cracked down on it. Once headless, this became much more difficult. Particularly in the cities, independence agitation after 1953 became increasingly confrontational with the French. Sultan Muhammad, too, had been exiled. Much more than the Istiqlal's decapitation, Muhammad's ouster galvanized the Moroccan grass-roots population to act against the French.

The erosion of the Istiqlal's influence and the martyrdom of Sultan Muhammad put the latter in a strong political position when Morocco achieved its independence in 1956. The Istiqlal's potency was also undercut by internal problems. The party's coalition of Islamic reformers, traditional merchants, the modern middle class, intellectuals, and the urban lower middle class only worked to the extent that all could band together on the immediate goal of independence. Even then, the exile of the party's leaders undermined the fragile cohesion that existed. While the Istiqlal was known to many Moroccans as "the party," in fact small rival parties, such as the rural Popular Movement* and Muhammad al-Ouazzani's National Democratic Party,* had formed before independence.

Independence heightened the challenges to the Istiqlal. Al-Fassi returned to Morocco in 1956 to find his party in no shape to dictate the terms of the new regime. Muhammad V, now the king of Morocco, was the undisputed political hero of the nation. Under the guise of establishing a government representative of the country's diversity, the king appointed a cabinet of ministers from all of the parties, thereby limiting the Istiqlal's influence.

The king's strategy accentuated frictions within the party. The Istiqlal was founded on the principle of accepting the monarch's legitimacy, but continuing to serve within Muhammad's government threatened to undermine the party's status as Morocco's preeminent political organization. Generally, the Istiqlal's younger members responded to this dilemma differently from al-Fassi, Belafrej, and their followers. Led by Mehdi ben Barka, Istiqlalis who opposed further cooperation with the king formed a breakaway party in 1959, the National Union of Popular Forces (UNFP).*

The Istiqlal's fission was a pivotal event in Moroccan politics, establishing a pattern of monarchical encouragement and exploitation of factionalism that would work to the king's advantage. Muhammad took direct control of the government in 1960, on the ground that the diverse political interests of his ministers had fostered political instability. When Muhammad died suddenly in 1961, his son Hassan became king. The new king continued to rule personally, and he promulgated a constitution which he submitted to a popular referendum in 1962.

The Istiqlal was once again presented with a dilemma. On the one hand, the party's leaders served in the government as ministers. On the other, the new constitution would formalize the monarch's political preeminence, without providing for any particular status for the party. The Istiqlal supported the new constitution lukewarmly. The document was approved overwhelmingly. However, upon learning that King Hassan intended to force the Istiqlalis from his government to further work against the party's power, the party's ministers resigned in January 1963. The Istiqlal thereby completed its transition from the mass organization that paved the way for the monarch's return to a party of opposition.

Parliamentary and communal elections under the new constitution were set for 1963. The king encouraged his supporters to field candidates under the newly created Front for the Defense of Constitutional Institutions (FDIC).* The FDIC managed to win sixty-nine seats in parliament to the Istiqlal's forty-one (see Table 19); working with the UNFP, the Istiqlal refused to field candidates for the communal elections, fearing the government would prevent fair campaigning and voting. Thus, the party found itself less politically influential than ever, particularly in the rural areas where it had always been weakest.

Nonetheless, if the Istiqlal and UNFP pooled their delegates to parliament, they could block legislation. In fact, the two deposed a motion censoring the government in 1964, and they succeeded in pressuring Hassan to hold an extraordinary session of parliament later that year. It was only a symbolic victory, however; the session produced no legislation opposed by or constraining the monarch. In 1965, large-scale urban rioting triggered by restrictive government educational reform led the king to declare a state of exception. He again assumed direct political control, recalling parliament, serving as the prime minister, and curtailing party activity. These measures included the Istiqlal, which had been only marginally involved in the riots.

The restrictions of the following years further undermined the Istiqlal's political base. The king authorized renewed party activity and stepped down as prime minister in 1967, but his government continued to keep the opposition tightly leashed. The Istiqlal boycotted municipal and rural communal elections in 1969, again dissatisfied with government restrictions on campaign activities. When Hassan ended the state of exception and proposed a referendum on a new constitution in 1970, the Istiqlal coordinated its activities with the UNFP as the National Front.* The front opposed the new constitution, which granted the king greater authority than the earlier system. But the referendum reportedly passed with a nearly 99 percent approval rate.

But in 1971 and 1972 the king was distracted from his ongoing efforts to marginalize the opposition parties by two coup attempts from within the army, which came close to killing him. While Hassan concluded from these events that he could not trust any political forces not beholden to him, Istiqlali leaders believed the time was finally ripe for them to realize their goal of one-party government. The National Front had collapsed; the Istiqlal refused to be part of any new governments without the king's conceding some of his authority.

This strategy proved to be a miscalculation. 'Allal al-Fassi died in 1973 and, with him, an important symbol of the Istiqlal's historical role. More significant, King Hassan managed to increase his power and popular standing tremendously through the Green March, his 1975 mobilization of about 350,000 Moroccans to walk to the Western Saharan territories over which Morocco claimed sovereignty. Ironically, recuperation of all formerly Moroccan territories had always been one of the Istiqlal's founding principles. Both as a matter of principle and pragmatism, the party, now led by Muhammad Boucetta, had no choice but to follow mass sentiment and support the king's clear dedication to the territorial issue. With one broad gesture, Hassan both boosted his own legitimacy and removed the Istiqlal from its own place of historical leadership of Moroccan nationalism.

The popularity of the king's Western Sahara policies encouraged him to initiate a new phase of political openness starting in 1977, when communal and parliamentary elections again took place. In these new elections, the success of the independent promonarchy candidates reflected the genuine mass sentiment about the Green March more than campaign or procedural irregularities, which were slight. But the Istiqlal fared far better than any other party, winning 49 of the 264 parliamentary seats at stake (see Table 18). As a result, the Istiqlal felt strong enough to agree to join the government for the first time since 1963. Boucetta was made minister of foreign affairs; the party controlled the politically sensitive ministry of education as well.

The party remained in the government until major urban rioting occurred in 1981, a result of Morocco's growing economic problems. The Istiqlal saw its already limited status watered down by its minority representation in the government. Moreover, the issue of the Western Sahara became less pressing than economic issues. Consequently, the party broke with the regime and once again went into opposition. The Istiqlal campaigned for economic reform and Islamic socialism in the 1984 elections, but it ended up with a disappointing 14 percent of the seats in an enlarged parliament (see Table 19).

Because the king postponed parliamentary elections several times, the Istiqlal did not have an opportunity to increase its share of delegates after 1984. But it tried to revitalize its oppositional image. As economic hardship and, to a lesser extent, democratization have eclipsed the Western Saharan question in recent years, Morocco's original nationalist party has found itself working with the UNFP's progeny, the Socialist Union of Popular Forces (USFP),* to challenge the regime on domestic policy. The two parties reestablished the National Front* for the purpose of coordinating a parliamentary motion of censure in May 1990. The motion was symbolic in that the small size of the opposition parties' representation ensured its defeat. But debate on the motion was carried by the media, allowing the delegates on the Istiqlal side, most notably Abdelhaq Tazi, to voice the party's grievances before the Moroccan public.

By December 1990, many Moroccans not only were uncomfortable with economic issues, they also opposed King Hassan's decision to commit Moroccan troops to the allied force against Iraq. The labor union associated with the Istiqlal, the General Union of Moroccan Workers (UGTM), worked with the Democratic Confederation of Workers (CDT) to carry out a general strike and urban demonstrations. These turned violent, resulting in forty-nine deaths, according to USFP estimates. This violence raised the political temperature. In 1991 the Istiqlal continued to work with the USFP to put pressure on the king's government in parliament and, through the UGTM, to mobilize protests in the cities. The party openly called for reform of the monarchy.

The Istiqlal has remained predominantly an urban party, drawing its strength from loosely organized chapters in cities. The party's main themes continue to be territorial nationalism, Islam, education, and broad slogans of socioeconomic justice, but it has tried in recent years to be more aggressive in taking on social democratic themes such as democratization, the minimum wage, and unemployment to widen its appeal to students and workers. It publishes two independent, respected daily newspapers, *l'Opinion* in French and *el-'Alam* (the flag) in Arabic.

The Istiqlal has gone through many changes. After independence, it gradually lost its status as "the party" and became one of many political organizations beholden to the prime mover in Moroccan politics, the king. The party became more associated with traditional urban merchants and pragmatic reformist intellectuals, but its basic policy orientations toward gradual democratization, a nonaligned foreign policy stance, Islam, and socioeconomic reform have largely remained stable. The question for this venerable party is whether its long history and established structure would help or hinder its efforts to adapt itself to an important role in Morocco's political future.

JUSTICE AND CHARITY MOVEMENT *(El-'Adl W'al Ishan)*. Since the mid-1970s, former Ministry of Education inspector 'Abdessalem Yassin has attracted followers in his crusade to establish a new Moroccan government based on a stricter adherence to Islamic principles. In 1974 Yassin wrote a long, open letter to the king calling for total restructuring of the government. This resulted in Yassin's incarceration in a psychiatric facility for three years. In 1979 he started a sporadic magazine, known as *al-Jama'a* ("the community"), which the regime frequently censored and then banned outright in 1983. By this time, Yassin had won several thousand adherents to his cause. Imprisoned for several years in the mid-1980s and subjected to constant police surveillance at other times and under house arrest since 1989, Yassin became a popular symbol of antiestablishment Islam.

Yassin and his supporters, known as the Justice and Charity Movement, have distinguished themselves somewhat from the Islamic Youth* movement in advocating less violent tactics. Nonetheless, some of Yassin's followers were implicated and arrested in rioting and fighting on Moroccan university campuses in the early 1990s. Part of the government's effort to crack down on illegal Islamist groups, the trial of six members of the movement in Rabat in 1990 generated large protests and subsequent sporadic university violence. Observers have differed in their sense of the ability of movements such as Yassin's to attract widespread support given the plethora of legal Moroccan parties and the real Islamic legitimacy King Hassan has enjoyed among important segments of the Moroccan population.

AL-KUTLA AL-DIMUQRATIYYA. *See* DEMOCRATIC BLOC.

AL-KUTLA AL-WATANIYYA. *See* NATIONAL FRONT.

LIBERAL INDEPENDENTS. *See* FRONT FOR THE DEFENSE OF CONSTI-TUTIONAL INSTITUTIONS.

MARCH 23 MOVEMENT (*Mouvement de 23 Mars*). Muhammad ben Said established this Marxist-Leninist group in 1970 from within the ranks of the former main socialist party, the National Union of Popular Forces (UNFP). The movement took its name from the day in 1965 when massive discontent with the government erupted in major riots in Casablanca and other urban centers. This clandestine movement was divided over whether to support King Hassan's policies of Western Saharan integration. Its adherents either joined the current dominant leftist party, the Socialist Union of Popular Forces (USFP),* in the late 1970s or formed part of the newer Organization of Democratic and Popular Action,* created in 1983.

MOROCCAN ACTION COMMITTEE (CAM) (*Comité d'Action Marocaine*). The Moroccan Action Committee, formed in 1934 by ten leading agitators for Moroccan independence, was the proto-party from which emerged the National Party for the Realization of the Reform Plan* and its successor, the Istiqlal Party.* This small group of activists consisted of men with a traditional Islamic education, and others with French university training. The CAM grouped together after the French suppressed the nationalist journal, *l'Action du Peuple* (People's Action), published during 1933 and 1934. The journal's suppression led its organizers to group together as the CAM in order to present a list of desired reforms to the French. The expansion of membership and activities of the CAM between 1934 and 1937 led the colonial authorities to outlaw it in 1937; it reemerged as a slightly more structured party later that year.

MOROCCAN COMMUNIST PARTY (*Parti Communiste Marocain*). The first communist party in Morocco grew out of a few cells of the French Communist Party organized in Casablanca. The Frenchman Léon Sultan created the party in 1943 along the lines of a Marxist-Leninist, European, communist party. When Sultan died in 1945, Ali Yata took over as party secretary, and the party's membership became dominated by Moroccans, rather than French expatriates. Moroccanization of the party also meant a growing similarity of purpose between the party and other preindependence Moroccan parties. Yata's party, never strong to begin with, had to cooperate with the dominant Istiqlal Party* in the drive for Moroccan independence. After independence, the Moroccan government outlawed the small party in 1960, but allowed it to function from time to time. In 1968 political liberalization allowed the party to reemerge legally under a new name, the Party of Liberation and Socialism.*

MOROCCAN NATIONAL FRONT (*Front National Marocain*). Stimulated by the suggestion of Egyptian political activists, the political parties of preindependence Morocco formed the National Front in 1951 as a limited effort at cooperation and coordination. The Moroccan parties drafted a statement of general agreement on the goal of independence and engaged in several unified publicity campaigns abroad. Nonetheless, the front did not result in the unification of the preindependence parties; the Istiqlal Party* remained by far the dominant party organization.

MOUVEMENT DE 23 MARS. *See* MARCH 23 MOVEMENT.

MOUVEMENT POPULAIRE. *See* POPULAR MOVEMENT.

MOUVEMENT POPULAIRE, DEMOCRATIQUE ET CONSTITUTION-NEL. *See* DEMOCRATIC AND CONSTITUTIONAL POPULAR MOVEMENT.

MOUVEMENT POPULAIRE NATIONALE. *See* NATIONAL POPULAR MOVEMENT.

MUJAHIDIN MOVEMENT. 'Abdelaziz Na'mani headed this breakaway faction of the Islamic Youth* society. A clandestine movement seeking the overthrow of the Moroccan monarchy and the establishment of a more leftist regime based on Islam, the group has been involved in violent disputes with other radical movements on Moroccan university campuses. Because it has been repressed by the government, its strength and influence are difficult to estimate. As the name suggests, the Mujahidin has been thought to have closer ties to Iran than Morocco's other Islamist groups.

NATIONAL ACCORD (ENTENTE NATIONALE) (*Al-Wifaq al-Watani*). During the parliamentary election campaign of spring 1993, four of the pro-government parties—the Constitutional Union,* the National Democratic Party,* the National Popular Movement,* and the Popular Movement*—formed a bloc known as the National Accord. The move was a reaction to the 1992 communal election victory of those parties' rival, the National Rally of Independents (RNI),* which was thought to be tacitly supported by the king. The Accord was also an attempt to counter the effectiveness of the Democratic Bloc,* which united the opposition parties during the election. Since each Accord party fielded its own candidates and offered its own program, it is unclear whether the bloc involved significant coordination. Nonetheless, it was still in place when the 1993 Moroccan government was formed from among technocrats outside its ranks.

NATIONAL DEMOCRATIC PARTY (PND) (*Parti National Démocrate*). Abdelamid Kassimi led a group of rural, landholding notables from the National Rally of Independents (RNI)* to form this breakaway party in 1981. The group was frustrated with the leadership of RNI chief Ahmed Osman, whom they did not consider to be supportive of agricultural interests. Specifically, the PND advocates government aid for large-scale commercial agriculture, central food subsidies, and protectionist agricultural law to keep out cheaper foreign competition.

Immediately after its formation, the PND held sixty-one seats in the Chamber of Representatives and five ministerial portfolios. The minister of labor at the time, Arsalane al-Jadidi, emerged as the party's leader. In 1983 the PND founded a student group, the National Union of Democratic Students (UNED), as part of an effort to broaden its organizational base. But, that same year, Maati Bouabid organized the Constitutional Union (UC)* party in an attempt to fill the same political niche aspired to by the PND—that of the major promonarchist party replacing the RNI. Because the PND's limited support came from rural elites, it fared much less well than the UC in the 1984 parliamentary elections, winning only twenty-four seats. As a result, it held onto only two ministerial portfolios in the 1985 cabinet. In late 1992, the party was still part of the coalition of royalist parties in parliament, but less important than either the RNI or the UC.

NATIONAL FRONT (*Front National*). Not actually a political party, the front has emerged twice in recent Moroccan political history as the opposition parties' effort at coordinating their strategy against the government. The Istiqlal Party* and the National Union of Popular Forces (UNFP)* combined to form the National Front in 1970 to combat King Hassan's new, highly centralized proposed constitution. The National Front dissolved with the clampdown on antiregime political activity precipitated by two nearly successful coup attempts made against the king in 1971 and 1972. The Istiqlal and the Socialist Union of Popular Forces (USFP),* along with the much smaller UNFP, the Party of Progress and Socialism,* and the Organization of Democratic and Popular Action,* reestablished the front in 1990 to press opposition demands for social and economic change. This more recent version of the front was revitalized and invigorated in May 1992 under the name of the Democratic Bloc,* when the component parties articulated a platform and pledged increased cooperation in preparation for national communal and legislative elections announced for the end of the year.

NATIONAL PARTY FOR THE REALIZATION OF THE REFORM PLAN (*Parti National*). Formed in 1937, this was the name for the grouping of Moroccan nationalists that began as the small Moroccan Action Committee* in 1934 and eventually grew into the dominant party grouping of the Istiqlal Party.* Between 1937 and 1943, the National Party generally operated clandestinely, organizing protests on the themes of independence and the restoration of authority to the Moroccan sultan.

NATIONAL PARTY OF UNION AND SOLIDARITY (*Parti de l'Union et de la Solidarité Nationale*). This small, obscure party emerged in 1983 to field candidates for the 1984 parliamentary elections. It failed to gain a single seat or build a constituency and faded thereafter.

NATIONAL POPULAR MOVEMENT (*Mouvement Populaire Nationale*). In response to his removal from leadership of the Popular Movement,* a post he had held since 1958, Mahjoubi Aherdane started this party in July 1991. Expected to retain the Berberist, agrarian, monarchist orientation of the old party, the party failed to attract the twelve parliament members necessary to form a caucus. Later in 1991, Mohand Laenser, who represented a group of party members who believed Aherdane incapable of modernizing the organization's image and structure, ousted Aherdane as leader of the party. Aherdane formed a breakaway party, the National Popular Movement.* Laenser worked to project a more pragmatic, contemporary, disciplined orientation for the old party and was rewarded with fifty seats in the 1993 parliament, once again the third best showing.

NATIONAL RALLY OF INDEPENDENTS (RNI) (*Rassemblement National des Indépendents*). Ahmed Osman, a former prime minister and brother-in-law of King Hassan, founded the National Assembly of Independents in 1978 as a way of organizing and centralizing the coalition of independent candidates who supported the king and formed the majority of members of parliament. Thus, the party was created not to represent a particular ideological perspective or constituency, but to facilitate communication and coordination among Moroccans who already enjoyed social status and political power.

Independents had already begun publishing newspapers in French and Arabic before forming the RNI. Once the party was established, its platform conformed to the general orientation of the king and the governments he formed. The RNI favored rapid socioeconomic modernization through large industry, liberal provisions for foreign investment, and a pro-Western stance in foreign policy. Like all other political parties, the RNI was a staunch supporter of Moroccan sovereignty over the former Spanish territories in the Western Sahara.

Dissatisfied with Osman's leadership, Abdelamid Kassimi and a group of wealthy rural landowners formed their own breakaway faction of independents, the National Democratic Party (PND)* in 1981. Osman, by this time, was no longer prime minister, and the RNI's delegate share in the 1981 parliament was reduced from 141 seats to 84. King Hassan himself delivered a further blow to the RNI's status by encouraging the formation of a new promonarchy party in 1983, the Constitutional Union (UC).* This new party relegated the RNI to the status of second largest parliamentary group in the 1984 elections, with sixty-one seats.

After its loss to the UC, the RNI's continued existence depended on Osman's prestige. In the early 1990s, the former prime minister served as the president of the Chamber of Deputies. Because the UC was not much more successful than the RNI in developing an appealing national message or base, elections scheduled for late 1992 held out the possibility of renewed royal patronage and, therefore, the renewed support of progovernment voters.

NATIONAL UNION OF POPULAR FORCES (UNFP) (*L'Union Nationale des Forces Populaires*). In September 1959, a radical breakaway faction of the

Istiqlal Party* founded the UNFP. Led by Mehdi ben Barka, this group of predominantly French-trained intellectuals was dissatisfied with the deferential, nationalistic, Islam-based reform and royalist program of the Istiqlal. In practice, the new group's approach was distinguished by its active confrontation with the king. First known as the National Confederation of the Istiqlal, it had the support of the only organized labor syndicate, the Moroccan Labor Union (UMT) and the only student union, the National Union of Moroccan Students (UNEM). Initially, King Muhammad V encouraged this development of a separate leftist organization, no doubt in order to water down the Istiqlal's strength. But the new party objected to Muhammad V's intention to rule as well as reign, resulting in the arrest of some of its leaders and the seizure of its journal late in 1959.

The death of Muhammad V and the succession of Hassan II in 1961 led the UNFP to mount a new challenge to royal rule. It joined with the Istiqlal in calling for a constitution as a means to undermine royal authority. When Hassan drafted a constitution in 1962 without opposition input, the UNFP called for a boycott of the public referendum on the new document scheduled for November. The Istiqlal, on the other hand, supported the constitution; the UMT refused to agree to the boycott and broke with the UNFP in February 1963. The constitution was overwhelmingly approved in December 1962.

Ben Barka's criticisms of the Moroccan political system during this period were quite sharp, and included public pronouncements on Tunisian state radio. But his role was hampered somewhat by his exile from Morocco between 1960 and 1962, and again later that year.

In March 1963, Morocco held its first parliamentary elections under the new constitution. The UNFP fielded candidates, but the government interfered with the results, giving the party a smaller number of seats than was consistent with its share of the popular vote. In July, the government announced the discovery of a subversive plot, laying the primary blame on the UNFP. More than 130 UNFP members were arrested for participation in the alleged plot, including twenty-one of the twenty-eight parliamentary deputies from the party (see Table 19). Nine members, including the exiled Ben Barka, were sentenced to death.

The UNFP's internal problems and continued royal efforts at undermining the influence of the Istiqlal party paved the way for increasing Istiqlal–UNFP cooperation. Late in 1964, the two parties' delegates to the Chamber of Deputies joined in voting to censure the government for its economic mismanagement. Somewhat influenced by this, but more worried by student and urban workers' riots in the major cities in March 1965, King Hassan granted general amnesty to all political prisoners the following month, including UNFP members. The king explicitly invited Ben Barka to return from exile. This muted UNFP criticism for a few months, but not sufficiently to prevent a successful no-confidence vote in parliament against the government. As a result of the opposition activity, King Hassan declared a state of exception, suspending the constitution in June 1965 and ruling directly for the next five years.

During this time, the king neutralized the capacity of the major opposition parties. Most of the UNFP's leaders remained in exile; the party languished without them. Ben Barka himself disappeared in Paris in October 1965; French courts convicted General Muhammad Oufkir, a close associate of the king then serving as minister of the interior, of assassinating the UNFP leader. Abdallah Ibrahim succeeded Ben Barka as leader of the party and reorganized it in 1967. Overt political party activity did not start again until 1969, when communal and provincial elections were held. The UNFP boycotted local elections and denounced the government for campaign irregularities. In these elections, the UNFP won only 32 of more than 10,500 council seats, amid widespread charges of election rigging.

Emboldened by this result, King Hassan promulgated a new constitution in 1970, increasing the monarch's powers. This prompted the UNFP to form a National Front* with the Istiqlal in an effort to defeat the new constitution. The document was overwhelmingly approved. Furthermore, the Front's boycott of parliamentary elections later that year allowed 219 of the 240 seats to be captured by progovernment candidates. Although the king's power was shaky enough during the early 1970s for two military-based coup efforts to come close to succeeding, the UNFP was not able to take advantage of the turmoil to improve its own standing.

This pattern of attempting to prove its political relevance by opting out of the king's efforts at political manipulation through quasi-democratic methods was a consistent UNFP strategy. It was partly a result of the UNFP's organization—a group of French-educated intelligentsia directing a party based on a labor union, the UMT, which it could not control, trying to broaden its appeal to urban merchants, civil servants, and farmers. Oftentimes, the rank and file was unsympathetic to the intelligentsia's propensity to avoid complicity with the king's centralizing policies, especially when this propensity seemed to result in more power for the monarchy and weakness for the party. This problem was illustrated by the constant tensions between the UMT and the UNFP. The party's organizers put no small weight on working-class political agitation. Yet the union found itself wishing to preserve its autonomy because of its leaders' calculus as to when cooperation with the government best served worker interests. Between 1965 and 1967, the UMT went so far as to break with the UNFP and ally itself once more with the Istiqlal. Similar tensions existed between the UNFP and its student affiliate, the UNEM. Even more significant was the UNFP's split into two rival factions. The head of the UNFP's Rabat section, Abderrahim Bouabid, increasingly advocated different policies and strategies from Abdullah Ibrahim. The government had in fact suspended the Rabat section in early 1973 while leaving the party's status as a whole unchanged. Bouabid was willing to act as a spokesman on behalf of the government's policy of considering the territories of the Western Sahara, about to be decolonized by Spain, as an integral part of Morocco. This led to an official break between his group and the UNFP. The breakaway group, the Socialist Union of Popular Forces (USFP),* held its first congress in 1975. Its combination of a progovernment nationalist position on the increasingly central Western Sahara issue and willingness to advocate other antigovernmental policies from within the political structures approved by the king led the USFP to quickly outstrip the UNFP in importance. As it had in the past, the UNFP boycotted parliamentary elections in both 1977 and 1983. This strategy proved ineffective in light of the popular support for the king inspired by his Western Saharan irredentism. By 1984 the UNFP was practically nonexistent. The bulk of its supporters were willing to participate within the royalist framework through the USFP; others moved to more radical, clandestine organizations such as the March 23 Group.*

OADP. *See* ORGANIZATION OF DEMOCRATIC AND POPULAR ACTION.

ORGANISATION DE L'ACTION DEMOCRATIQUE ET POPULAIRE. *See* ORGANIZATION OF DEMOCRATIC AND POPULAR ACTION.

ORGANIZATION OF DEMOCRATIC AND POPULAR ACTION (OADP) (*Organisation de L'Action Démocratique et Populaire*). In January 1983, Muhammad ben Said reformed a clandestine leftist organization into a party known as the March 23 Movement,* named for the date in 1965 on which the infamous Casablanca riots occurred. The new party, the OADP, also attracted a handful of adherents of the Forward* movement and the old National Union of Popular Forces (UNFP).* The OADP was able to establish itself as a legal party because its members staunchly supported the king's Western Saharan reintegration policies. It adopted a slightly more populist socialist agenda than the other opposition parties. But it has failed to garner any substantial support. It won only one seat in the 1984 parliamentary elections (see Table 19). It is part of the general grouping of opposition parties known as the National Front.*

PA. PARTY OF ACTION.

PARTI D'ACTION DU PEUPLE. *See* PEOPLE'S ACTION PARTY.

PARTI DE L'ACTION. *See* PARTY OF ACTION.

PARTI DE L'AVANT GARDE DEMOCRATIQUE SOCIALISTE. *See* PARTY OF THE DEMOCRATIC SOCIALIST AVANT-GARDE.

PARTI DU CENTRE SOCIAL. *See* SOCIAL CENTER PARTY.

PARTI COMMUNISTE MAROCAIN. *See* MOROCCAN COMMUNIST PARTY.

PARTI DEMOCRATIQUE CONSTITUTIONNEL. *See* DEMOCRATIC CONSTITUTIONAL PARTY.

PARTI DEMOCRATIQUE DE L'INDEPENDANCE. *See* DEMOCRATIC PARTY OF INDEPENDENCE.

PARTI ISTIQLAL. *See* ISTIQLAL PARTY.

PARTI LIBERAL ET DU PROGRES. *See* PROGRESSIVE LIBERAL PARTY.

PARTI DE LIBERATION ET SOCIALISME. *See* PARTY OF LIBERATION AND SOCIALISM.

PARTI NATIONAL. *See* NATIONAL PARTY FOR THE REALIZATION OF THE REFORM PLAN.

PARTI NATIONAL DEMOCRATE. *See* NATIONAL DEMOCRATIC PARTY.

PARTI DU PROGRES ET DU SOCIALISME. *See* PARTY OF PROGRESS AND SOCIALISM.

PARTI SOCIALISTE DEMOCRATIQUE. *See* SOCIAL DEMOCRATIC PARTY.

PARTI DE L'UNION ET DE LA SOLIDARITE NATIONALE. *See* NATIONAL PARTY OF UNION AND SOLIDARITY.

PARTI DE UNITE MOROCAIN. *See* PARTY OF MOROCCAN UNITY.

PARTY OF ACTION (*Parti de l'Action*). Abdullah Senhaji, a resistance network organizer for the Istiqlal Party* before independence and a founder of both the Popular Movement (MP)* and the National Union of Popular Forces (UNFP),* formed the Action Party in September 1974. Its purpose was to provide a more leftist and innovative rural elite than the MP. The party comprised primarily Berber intellectuals, but opposed divisive political platforms based on race, tribe, or region. Most of its support was rural, and its leadership came from the Sous Plain and Middle Atlas, although a few administrators and businessmen were attracted to it as well. It won only two parliamentary seats in 1977 and faded from the Moroccan political scene after that, gaining no seats in the 1984 elections.

PARTY OF THE DEMOCRATIC SOCIALIST AVANT-GARDE (*Parti de l'Avant Garde Démocratique Socialiste*). Two respected lawyers from Rabat, Abderrahim ben Amor and Ahmed ben Jalloun, created this party late in 1991 as a breakaway group from the Socialist Union of Popular Forces.* The party faced an uphill battle trying to establish itself as a secular, democratic, socialist alternative to the well-known larger party from which it emerged and the older leftist parties, the pro-communist Party of Progress and Socialism* and the Organization of Democratic and Popular Action.* It had no significant impact on Moroccan politics in its first year of existence.

PARTY OF LIBERATION AND SOCIALISM (PLS) (*Parti de Libération et Socialisme*). In 1968, Ali Yata, head of the outlawed Moroccan Communist Party,* formed this new organization in an effort to gain legal status. The PLS consisted of the same small group of Moroccan students and intellectuals who had been in the Communist Party. Attempting to limit antigovernment political organizations, King Hassan II outlawed the PLS two years later. After two military-based coups were attempted in the early 1970s, the king began a policy of more open encouragement of diverse political parties, with the result that PLS adherents were permitted to reconstitute themselves legally in 1974 as the Party of Progress and Socialism.*

PARTY OF MOROCCAN UNITY (PMU) (*Parti de Unité Morocain*). The second preindependence party in the portion of Morocco occupied by Spain before 1956, the Party of Moroccan Unity was formed in 1937 by Mohammed Naciri. Naciri had been a protégé of Abdel Khalek Torres, the founder of the Islah Party,* the Spanish zone's other major preindependence party. Naciri broke away from the Islah in order to build a political organization with a better defined program. But this organization dwindled within a few years. Moreover, the Spanish were able to play off the two parties against each other effectively before World War II. Before and during the war, the PMU assumed a cooperative stance toward the Spanish, who generally adopted more conciliatory policies toward Moroccan nationalists than did the French. After the Allies' 1942 landing in North Africa, Naciri's party worked with the Islah in a call for full independence of both the French and Spanish zones under Sultan Muhammad. After the war, the PMU compromised less with Spain, and coordinated more with the Istiqlal Party.* The PMU, based in Tangier, gradually dwindled in importance, especially as its confluence of goals with the much larger Istiqlal increased. The reunification of the French and Spanish zones into independent Morocco in 1956 resulted in the end of the parties rooted in the Spanish zone.

PARTY OF NATIONAL REFORM. *See* ISLAH PARTY.

PARTY OF PROGRESS AND SOCIALISM (PPS) (*Parti du Progrès et du Socialisme*). Created in 1974, this is essentially a new organizational name for the Moroccan Communist Party,* which was banned in 1960. The PPS maintained the same leadership as the old organization, continuing under the stewardship of secretary-general Ali Yata, the grand old man of contemporary Moroccan politics.

The PPS held its first national congress in February 1975; this was the first time Moroccan communists had been allowed to conduct an open conclave. Although Yata's party espoused communist doctrine generally in line with that of official communist parties in Eastern Europe and the Soviet Union, its tactics were nonrevolutionary, showing a willingness to work within the monarchical political system. Ali Yata was elected to the parliament in 1977. The PPS gained a second parliamentary seat in 1984, obtaining about 1 percent of the vote (see Tables 19, 20).

The PPS claims a following of around 50,000, largely urban students and teachers. American government estimates put PPS members at a considerably lower number. It publishes a daily newspaper, *al-Bayane*, in French and Arabic versions. On many issues, it has taken stances consistent with Soviet communism, including support of nationalization, price controls, and an anti-Western foreign policy. However, the party has generally taken care not to criticize the monarchy directly or to oppose Moroccan integration of the Western Saharan territories. Yata's party has worked with the Socialist Union of Popular Forces* and the Istiqlal Party* on numerous occasions, including on the defeated motion to censure the government because of its economic policies in May 1990.

The PPS provides a narrow focus of fairly sharp criticism of Moroccan politics, which is tolerated for its moderate tactics, the stature of its leader, and its relatively insignificant power. With its small following, it remains to be seen how independent of the two main opposition groups the party will remain in light of the breakdown of the communist regimes in Eastern Europe and the former Soviet Union.

PEOPLE'S ACTION PARTY (*Parti d'Action du Peuple*). The intellectual and nationalist leader Muhammad al-Ouazzani started this small organization in 1937 in an effort to exercise more influence over the Moroccan nationalist movement than he could as one of the members of the Moroccan Action Committee.* Also known as the Popular Movement,* this group was of little significance in the short time before the French put al-Ouazzani under house arrest late in 1937. He established a new party, known as the Democratic Party of Independence,* when he was freed in 1946.

PLS. *See* PARTY OF LIBERATION AND SOCIALISM.

PMU. *See* PARTY OF MOROCCAN UNITY.

PND. *See* NATIONAL DEMOCRATIC PARTY.

POPULAR MOVEMENT (MP) (*Mouvement Populaire*). This term refers to two distinct Moroccan parties. The first of these was a second name for the relatively unimportant preindependence grouping of nationalists around Hassan al-Ouazzani founded in 1937 and also known as the People's Action Party.* This party emphasized more secular themes than its larger rival, the National Party for the Realization of the Reform Plan,* but it was basically dominated by al-Ouazzani. The latter's house arrest from 1937 until 1946 led to the disappearance of the Popular Movement. Al-Ouazzani founded a new party, the Democratic Party of Independence,* in 1946.

The second, and more important party, with the name Moroccan Popular Movement (MP), founded clandestinely in 1957, was an expression of rural re-

418 / Political Parties of the Middle East

sentment at the urban orientation of Istiqlali-dominated party politics. Muhammad V encouraged its emergence as a method of undercutting the Istiqlal Party.* The Popular Movement, legalized in 1959, was organized around a group of rural leaders who had marshaled resistance to French colonialism in the central and northern mountainous regions. Mahjoubi Aherdane served as the party's secretary-general until a group of party members removed him in 1986. The party's new collective leadership disagreed with Ahardane's political strategy and heavy-handed leadership style.

The MP is best known for its strong ties to important rural Berber families and its unswerving loyalty to the king. During the early years of independence, the party more specifically advocated economic austerity, nonalignment, selective nationalization, and "Islamic socialism," meaning the minimization of gross economic inequalities between cities and the countryside. It joined the coalition of monarchist forces known as the Front for the Defense of Constitutional Institutions (FDIC)* in 1963. This exposed personality differences between Ahardane and his more urbanized rival Abdelkrim Khatib, who was pushed out of the MP in 1966. Khatib formed a new party called the Democratic and Constitutional Popular Movement* in 1967 which failed to develop any real support.

Because the MP has an established political base and a tradition of supporting the king, its leaders have found themselves cabinet members in many governments. The party won forty-one seats in the 1977 elections (see Table 20) to the Chamber of Deputies and increased that number to forty-seven in 1984 (See Table 21). The 1984 election thus enabled the MP to retain its position as the third largest party in parliament. Aherdane's ouster as party chief resulted when he pulled the party out of the government following the 1984 elections. The party remained staunchly pro-king and rural, but independent of the progovernment coalition in parliament. However, the large migration of rural Moroccans to the cities in the past few decades has weakened the MP.

PPS. *See* PARTY OF PROGRESS AND SOCIALISM.

PROGRESSIVE LIBERAL PARTY (*Parti Libéral et du Progrès*). Aknoush Ahmadou Belhaj headed this party, which was founded in 1974 by a small group of wealthy landowners and merchants from the western mountainous Sous region. The party's agenda stressed free markets and civil liberties. It failed to win any seats in the 1977 elections for parliament, and it faded from the scene thereafter.

RASSEMBLEMENT NATIONAL DES INDEPENDENTS. *See* NATIONAL RALLY OF INDEPENDENTS.

RNI. *See* NATIONAL RALLY OF INDEPENDENTS.

AL-SHABIBA AL-ISLAMIYYA. *See* ISLAMIC YOUTH.

SOCIAL CENTER PARTY (*Parti du Centre Social*). This very small party has a slightly left-of-center political orientation. It won one parliamentary seat in the 1984 national elections.

SOCIAL DEMOCRATIC PARTY (*Parti Socialiste Démocratique*). In 1963 Ahmed Reda Guédira, one of King Hassan's closest supporters, tried to bring together all political forces supporting the monarchy or against the influence of the Istiqlal Party* under the banner of the Front for the Defense of Constitutional Institutions.* Following legislative elections in which Guédira's forces won only a few more seats than the Istiqlal and its antigovernment ally, the National Union of Popular Forces* (see Table 19), Guédira realized that an even stronger effort was needed to organize the many independent progovernment members of parliament. Thus, he and his supporters formed the Social Democratic Party in 1964.

The party produced a platform, hard to distinguish from the platforms of the other established parties, calling for support of business and the king. It failed to develop a popular clientele. Further, widespread rioting in March 1965 eventually led the king to dissolve parliament and crack down on party activity. For these two reasons, the party had fallen apart by 1966. Subsequent efforts to organize progovernment politicians into a party have included the National Rally of Independents* and the Constitutional Union,* which together made up a parliamentary majority in the late 1970s and 1980s.

SOCIALIST UNION OF POPULAR FORCES (USFP) (*L'Union Socialiste des Forces Populaires*). The USFP, created by a breakaway faction of the National Union of Popular Forces (UNFP),* itself a breakaway faction of the Istiqlal Party,* has inherited the UNFP's mantle of Morocco's leading left-of-center party. Along with the Istiqlal, the USFP became the major legal voice of political criticism in contemporary Morocco. The party emerged from the Rabat branch of the UNFP; its head, Abderrahim Bouabid, disagreed with the direction taken by the national party organization. In part, this disagreement stemmed from the personal animosity between Bouabid and UNFP chief Abdullah Ibrahim. Bouabid's faction objected to the UNFP's strategy of boycotting Morocco's infrequent local and parliamentary elections. Nonetheless, the Rabat faction was outlawed by the government from the time it broke away from the UNFP in 1972 until it emerged as the USFP in 1972.

At the USFP's first national congress in 1975, the party established its essential parameters. It advocated policies along the lines of what might be expected from a Western European social democratic party. These included nationalization, pressure for increased civil liberties, and land reform. On the other hand, the party aligned itself firmly behind King Hassan's assertion of Morocco's complete right to all former and remaining Spanish colonial enclaves in North Africa. The USFP won 6.5 percent of the seats in the communal elections of November 1976 and sixteen seats (based on 14.6 percent of the votes) in the parliamentary elections the following year (see Table 20). Contravening the UNFP's policy, the USFP fielded candidates in national elections. Bouabid stood for parliament in

1977; he was the only major party leader to be defeated. Nonetheless, by this time, the USFP had surpassed the UNFP in importance and began attracting the core of the earlier party's following.

The party is linked to the Democratic Labor Confederation (CDT), whose formation the party oversaw. The CDT has a strong urban membership including several key state economic sectors. In June 1981, widespread antigovernment violence, during a general strike called by the CDT, led to many deaths and the government's suppression of much USFP activity. Bouabid himself was arrested and imprisoned. The riots led the government to postpone scheduled parliamentary elections, as a result of which the USFP delegates resigned. However, the king granted Bouabid and several other party leaders a royal pardon in February 1982. The USFP gradually showed itself willing to work within the system once again. It fielded candidates in local elections in 1983, but it complained that it won only 3 percent of the votes because of government interference. Still wary of the widespread political and economic disorder of the early 1980s, the USFP participated in a national unity government in 1983 and 1984. The USFP withdrew from the national unity government in preparation for parliamentary elections in late 1984. The party won thirty-six seats; its CDT affiliate won three seats (see Table 21). After 1984, the USFP was the leading opposition party. Like its UNFP parent, the party has attracted a mixture of young people, low-level state employees, workers, and intellectuals. It is primarily a party of the urban intelligentsia. It advocates increased attention to human rights, democracy, economic planning, and egalitarian social policy within a secular, nationalistic framework that accepts the monarchy. The party publishes a weekly French magazine and a daily Arabic newspaper, al-Ittihad al-Ishtiraki, which has been banned by the government on frequent occasions. Bouabid died early in 1992; Abderrahman Youssoufi then headed the party as first secretary.

The USFP walked a fine line between working within the political rules of the monarchy and providing a credible challenge to the government. Generally, the party supported the king's foreign policy, particularly with respect to the Western Saharan territories. However, the USFP opposed Hassan's 1990 decision to send Moroccan troops to aid the multinational force against Iraq, putting pressure on the government to allow pro-Iraqi demonstrations early in 1991. The party has been more inclined toward antigovernment agitation on social and economic issues, on which it attempts to portray itself as the champion of the common person. The USFP and CDT were behind the riots against the reduction of food subsidies in 1984, and a general strike over economic policy issues that led to widespread rioting and casualties in Fez in 1990. In parliament, the USFP worked with the Istiqlal to call attention to government policies. In May 1990, the two parties introduced a motion to censure the government for its mismanagement of the economy. This motion, though defeated by the progovernment majority in the Chamber of Deputies, received extensive national media coverage, giving USFP parliamentarian and economics professor Fathallah Oualalou a chance to level a wide variety of charges against the government.

At the same time, the USFP's autonomy to criticize the government has largely been a function of its willingness not to call the monarchy itself into question. The party has tried to prove its relevance not only by providing an outlet for the expression of popular frustration but also by offering constituents the hope of gaining the king's ear. Hassan has used consultation with the USFP alternatively as a means of placating it and of playing it off against other political factions. An important component of the USFP's 1981, 1984, and 1990 antigovernment agitation consisted of complaints that the king had suspended dialogue with the party or its CDT affiliate.

More than any other political group, the USFP has been able to maintain a balance between its own agenda and sufficient cooperation with the government to be allowed to function. Whether this balance has made it difficult for the party to develop a strong program of its own, which could make it part of a future government, is less clear. After 1990, the party tried to mitigate this problem through greater public exposure as part of a more coordinated coalition with the Istiqlal and the smaller secular leftist factions. Additionally, its CDT affiliate stepped up a program of labor unrest, in cooperation with the Istiqlal's labor affiliate.

In April 1992, the king announced new communal and legislative elections for later that year. Also, the government attempted to undermine workers' strikes by arresting the head of the CDT, Nabir Amaoui, a member of the USFP's political committee. These two events put the party in the tricky position of having incentives to step up its confrontation with the government, on the one hand, and, on the other hand, to augment its activity with the Istiqlal within the system in an attempt to gain more influence in the next parliament. In fact, in mid-1992, it was thought that the king favored a greater USFP presence in the government to reinforce the impression that the political system is made up of diverse ideological bases.

The future of the USFP depends on its ability to remain a salient, independent voice in Moroccan politics and to offer an appealing message to the increasing number of young Moroccans inclined to involve themselves with mostly clandestine radical Islamic political movements.

UC. *See* CONSTITUTIONAL UNION.

UNFP. *See* NATIONAL UNION OF POPULAR FORCES.

UNION CONSTITUTIONNELLE. *See* CONSTITUTIONAL UNION.

L'UNION NATIONALE DES FORCES POPULAIRES. *See* NATIONAL UNION OF POPULAR FORCES.

L'UNION SOCIALISTE DES FORCES POPULAIRES. *See* SOCIALIST UNION OF POPULAR FORCES.

USFP. *See* SOCIALIST UNION OF POPULAR FORCES.

David M. Mednicoff

# THE PALESTINIANS

## HISTORICAL BACKGROUND

The Palestinians include some five million Arabs who live or lived in Palestine, the region comprising today's Israel, the West Bank, and the Gaza Strip. Palestine was ruled by the Ottoman Turks from 1517 until Turkey's defeat in World War I, although it did not constitute a single political or administrative unit within the Ottoman Empire. Britain administered Palestine through a Mandate granted by the League of Nations after the war without establishing local legislative bodies or elections until 1948, after which it abandoned its rule in the country.

A central element of British policy was the Balfour Declaration, which pledged Britain to foster the establishment of a national home for the Jewish people in Palestine, a policy bitterly attacked by the majority Arab inhabitants of the country. Under British rule, hundreds of thousands of Jews immigrated to Palestine as Arab anger over the policy festered and erupted into resistance and violence, including a general strike and campaign of guerrilla warfare conducted from 1936 to 1939. A 1939 British White Paper, signaling an end to British support for the Jewish national home, was in turn bitterly attacked by the Zionists, some of whom launched a guerrilla campaign against British targets.

By 1947 the population of Palestine stood at approximately two-thirds Palestinian Arab and one-third Jewish. Increasing strife between the two communities, combined with Jewish attacks against the British, prompted frustrated British authorities to declare their intent to evacuate Palestine and turn over the future settlement of Zionist and Arab claims to the country to the newly created United Nations. On November 29, 1947, the UN General Assembly voted to partition Palestine into two states, one for each of the two peoples. Fighting broke out immediately after the announcement because the Palestinians rejected any proposal that would give away part of Palestine.

Localized Jewish-Palestinian fighting escalated in May 1948 when the British finally withdrew and the Zionists declared the establishment of their own state, which they called Israel. Troops from five Arab states entered Palestine to fight Jewish forces, which had captured portions of that area of Palestine assigned to the proposed Arab state by the UN. By the time cease-fire agreements were signed in 1949, much of Palestine was under the control of Jewish forces and subsequently was incorporated into Israel. The remainder of Palestine, controlled by Arab forces, constituted the area that became known as the West Bank (occupied by Jordanian forces and annexed to Jordan in 1950) and Gaza (occupied and administered by Egypt). Some 725,000 Palestinians fled or were driven from their homes, settling as refugees in the West Bank, Gaza, and surrounding Arab countries. Some 120,000 Palestinians remained in what became Israel.

## THE NATURE OF PALESTINIAN PARTIES AND POLITICS

By 1949, the Palestinians who remained in Palestine lived under the jurisdiction of three different states; many others were spread out throughout the Arab world and farther as refugees. Palestinian politics in each major sphere of operations—Israel, the West Bank and Gaza (hereafter called the occupied territories), and in exile from Mandate-era Palestine—took on a different face, dealing with different problems and facing different constraints.

Any discussion of Palestinian political movements and parties, both before and after 1949, must therefore deal with a unique set of circumstances. The most obvious is that until 1993 the Palestinians did not enjoy political sovereignty in an independent state. As a result, the question of achieving national independence dominated all facets of Palestinian political life, both as exercised in Mandate-era Palestine and in exile.

Second, the quest for national independence meant walking a tightrope between two divergent tendencies. The first viewed Palestinian liberation as part and parcel of some form of wider liberation for the Arab peoples from colonial and neo-imperialist domination, whether within a pan-Arab nationalist, Marxist, or Islamic framework. The second tendency conceives of Palestinian nationalism as a unique phenomenon, integrally linked to wider Arab and Third World concerns but possessing its own agenda and goals that are often, if not usually, quite divergent from the goals and strategies of other Arab actors.

Third, the interconnectedness between Palestinian politics and the politics of surrounding Arab states, which has resulted from ideological and logistical factors (such as the large numbers of Palestinians living in Arab countries), has greatly affected Palestinian political expression and more than once drawn the Palestinians into destructive conflicts bearing little relationship to the nationalist goal of liberation and self-determination.

Finally, the national movement has been severely hampered by factional discord since the 1920s. Personal and ideological rivalries have been exacerbated by external actors as well as by the lack of an independent state and a single set of institutions within which politics can be pursued.

Because of their significantly different nature, this introduction will discuss

Palestinian political organizations within four different geographical and historical arenas: parties and organizations in Mandate-era Palestine before the creation of the state of Israel in 1948, political groups in exile outside of Palestine after 1948, politics in the West Bank and Gaza after 1948, and parties and movements among Palestinian citizens of Israel after 1948 (the "Israeli Arabs").

## ARENA ONE: PARTIES IN PALESTINE UP TO 1948

Some of the political associations that emerged during the period of British rule in Palestine (1917–48) traced their roots to various underground Arab nationalist groups that had pushed for Arab independence from Ottoman rule, such as the al-Fatat (Youth). Others coalesced around influential politicians in Jerusalem or took the form of religious and cultural clubs opposed to Zionism.

But whatever their origin, Arab political activists at the dawn of British rule struggled with two main issues: the prospect that Zionism could turn Palestine into a Jewish state, thereby depriving the Arabs of potential sovereignty over their own country, and the question of how to deal with the breakup of the region of historic Syria into several different states controlled by either Britain or France. While most politically minded Palestinians agreed on the need to combat Zionism, they differed on what to do about the breakup of Syria. Pan-Arabists (or, more appropriately, pan-Syrianists) agitated for the return of Palestine to Syria, while others argued for accepting the partition of Syria but pushing Britain to allow the creation of independent national institutions to be created in Palestine instead.

The localist approach carried the day, particularly after the destruction of the Syrian kingdom in 1920. Nationalist leaders were convinced that the British could be pressured into granting the Palestinians some form of home rule. In August 1921, a delegation left for London to present demands to the British government: abolish the Balfour Declaration, establish a national government responsible to a parliament elected by the existing population of Palestine, halt Jewish immigration pending a national formula decided upon by the new parliament, and include Palestine within a federation with surrounding Arab states. Their demands were rejected.

The British then offered the Palestinians a legislative council in 1922, but the Palestinians rejected the offer because it was contingent upon Palestinian recognition of the Balfour Declaration and would have created a parliament in which British and Zionist representatives together would have constituted a majority (at a time when the Palestinians constituted some 89 percent of the population). Elections for a legislature were eventually canceled after Arab boycotts. As a result, Palestinian politics failed to acquire a parliamentary forum in which to operate.

The battle over the legislature in the 1920s revealed several factors within Palestinian politics that led to greater fragmentation of the nationalist movement and to the proliferation of parties. The first was the lack of a historical sense of national unity. Palestine had never constituted a unified administrative unit. Urban notables (particularly those from Jerusalem) dominated politics, but their authority was not accepted in all parts of the country nor by all sectors of society. The second trend was the emergence of ideological and personal conflicts that rent the movement as well, spawning numerous contending parties. The most significant rivalry centered around two Jerusalem families locked in a bitter arch-rivalry, the al-Husayni and al-Nashashibi families. Their rivalry was partly ide-ological as well, centering on the degree to which Palestinians should cooperate with the British mandate in trying to secure their rights. The final factor was lack of British recognition. Unlike the official Jewish Agency, no single Arab body was recognized by the British as the official representative of the Pales-tinians.

The Husayni-Nashashibi rivalry was particularly pronounced, and spread across the Palestinian political scene, from the 1920s to the 1940s. The Husaynis, led by Hajj Amin al-Husayni, consolidated their power base in several important institutions during this time: the Arab Executive,* which was the most significant Palestinian political association from 1924 to 1934; the Supreme Muslim Coun-cil,* a religious-cum-political body; and the Arab Higher Committee.* All three advocated confronting British authorities, and all three were shrill in their refusal to recognize the legitimacy of British rule in Palestine. The Husaynis also formed a party, the Palestine Arab Party,* in the 1930s following the breakup of the Arab Executive. The Nashashibis, led by Amin al-Husayni's bitter foe, Raghib al-Nashashibi, who were more willing to work within the framework of mandate rule, formed two parties, the National Party* and, later, the National Defense Party.*

Both the nationalist struggle and the Husayni-Nashashibi rivalry reached a new stage in April 1936 when the Arab Higher Committee was formed to co-ordinate a nationwide strike staged by Palestinians to protest Zionism and British rule. The strike, which lasted six months, developed into a three-year rural guer-rilla war against both British and Jewish targets. The guerrillas were eventually overwhelmed by British military force, but not before turning to vicious inter-necine political violence.

The British victory in the 1936–39 uprising disarmed the Palestinians and decapitated their leadership. Over 3,000 leaders were deported or fled, including Hajj Amin. The result was a demoralized and leaderless population, unprepared for the exigencies of 1947–49. By comparison, the various Zionist factions were able to cooperate successfully within a quasi-government, legislative body, and military.

Parties during this period were not able to mobilize the vast majority of Pal-estinians. Those Palestinians who did respond to their calls for action did so on general nationalist or religious grounds during times of turmoil, not because of ideological conviction or even allegiance to the Husaynis or Nashashibis. The most striking example of this was the 1936–39 revolt, which was overwhelmingly a rural explosion beyond the control of the urban parties.

## ARENA TWO: PALESTINIAN POLITICS IN EXILE AFTER 1948

Following the Arab defeat in the 1947–49 fighting and the flight of the Palestinian refugees, the Palestinian national question was transformed into a crusade to regain the lost homeland. Much as they had during the war, Palestinians sought outside Arab help in regaining their country. Because of conditions in the Arab world during the first two decades after the creation of Israel, Palestinian political expression was generally subordinated to wider Arab struggles for independence and unity which treated the liberation of Palestine as but one of several goals.

For the thousands of Palestinians living outside Mandate-era Palestine—in Jordan, Lebanon, Syria, the Gulf states, and elsewhere—political expression was channeled in the direction of several Arab nationalist groups, including the pan-Arab Ba'th Party, the pan-Syrian Syrian Social National Party, and various movements that supported the pan-Arab stance of Egyptian president Gamal Abdel Nasser, such as the Movement of Arab Nationalists. For these movements, the solutions to the Palestinians' problems lay in some form of higher unity; embryonic "regionalist" Palestinian-focused movements were condemned.

These movements were able to channel the frustrated nationalism and sense of loss of the Palestinian people into support for a return to a more organic unity, whether pan-Syrian or pan-Arab. Nasser's popularity and the perception of his success on the global level led many Palestinians to believe that the Arab states and parties would realize their liberation for them.

The Palestinians' faith in the ability of the Arab regimes and parties to realize their national goals suffered a rude shock as a result of the disastrous Arab defeat in the June 1967 war with Israel. Despite decades of posturing and rhetoric, the armies of Egypt, Syria, and Jordan quickly crumbled under the Israeli onslaught. Even worse for the Palestinians, Israeli forces occupied the West Bank and Gaza, bringing all of Mandate-era Palestine under Israeli control.

The impact on Palestinian politics was profound. The Arab states appeared no more than "paper tigers," and the often harsh restrictions placed on Palestinians living in their midst suggested that the regimes' talk of assisting their brothers and sisters was empty. New voices began to emerge calling for a uniquely Palestinian struggle for Palestinian national aims, waged alongside the Arab regimes and parties but separate from them and ultimately concerned with their own goals and needs.

This reappraisal coincided with, and was strengthened by, the growth of Palestinian politico-military commando organizations that staged attacks on Israeli positions from neighboring Arab countries. One group stands out in terms of its early decision to shift toward "Palestinianism": Fatah* (the Conquest), headed by Yasir Arafat. Formed in exile in the 1950s, Fatah waited until 1964 to launch attacks against Israeli targets. In the aftermath of the 1967 war, Palestinian commando groups multiplied quickly as the Palestinians' spirits were lifted by the sight of young men taking up arms to liberate their country, instead of waiting for the Arab states to do it for them.

While advocating different approaches to liberation, these groups shifted the focus of the national question to Palestinians working for Palestinian goals. The takeover of the Arab League–sponsored Palestine Liberation Organization (PLO)* by the commandos in 1969 signaled the beginning of a new phase of Palestinian politics, dominated by the PLO, which began by emphasizing Palestinian military confrontation with Israel and, by September 1993, produced an agreement with Israel for achieving Palestinian self-rule in the occupied territories, a move that triggered considerable turmoil within the Palestinian national movement.

The rise of the commandos, while galvanizing the Palestinian people, brought numerous tensions to the surface. Several contentious issues from past decades reemerged. The first was the age-old question of the relationship between the Palestinians and the Arab world or, more precisely, the relation between the Palestinian struggle for national liberation and other struggles urged by various Arab actors. Fatah argued for cooperation with the Arab states but maintained the priority of Palestinianism. Leftist groups, such as the Popular Front for the Liberation of Palestine (PFLP)* and the Democratic Front for the Liberation of Palestine (DFLP),* argued that Palestinian liberation would come only as part of a wider socioeconomic and political revolution within the Arab world and a wider Arab anti-imperialist struggle internationally.

Second, militants have argued over the tactics of cooperation with the enemy, much as the Husaynis and Nashashibis had during the 1920s and 1930s. Some Palestinians, such as those in the PFLP, pushed the demand for total liberation of Palestine by armed struggle and accepted the 1974 PLO move toward a two-state solution only reluctantly and late in the day. Bitter disputes continue to erupt over the wisdom of pursuing diplomatic initiatives toward this end at the expense of military action. Fatah has supported such moves, while the PFLP, DFLP, and some Islamic militants have been more reticent.

The emergence of the PLO marked the beginning of a new era in Palestinian politics. Although commando tactics failed to liberate Palestine and instead instigated numerous bloody confrontations with the Arab states, the PLO and its constituent organizations were able to mobilize political action in a number of areas and to retain the Palestinians' loyalty in the face of numerous adversities. The PLO's success lies in its ability to channel popular hopes for liberation with a sense that, at last, Palestinians themselves are doing something for their own future. The PLO's control over all aspects of life in exile, from health care to pensions for the families of slain guerrillas, also increases its importance as an agent of mobilization on the Palestinian scene. Not a single exilic organization has laid a significant rival claim to the allegiance of the Palestinian people since 1970.

However, the PLO's decision to enter into negotiations with Israel with the formal opening of Arab-Israeli peace talks in 1991 in Madrid drew harsh criticism from many Palestinian quarters. Factions within and outside the PLO opposed to negotiations coalesced into a grouping known as the "Damascus Ten," which was transformed in October 1993 into the National Democratic and Islamic Front,* following the signing of the PLO-Israel agreement for Palestinian self-rule in the occupied territories. Formation of the Front represented growing difficulties for the PLO in maintaining its dominant position within the Palestinian nationalist movement.

## ARENA THREE: POLITICAL ACTIVITY IN THE WEST BANK AND GAZA AFTER 1948

Much like the situation in exile, Palestinian political expression in the West Bank and Gaza centered around the Arab states' and parties' ability to liberate Palestine. The West Bank was controlled by Jordanian forces during the 1948–49 fighting and was annexed to Transjordan in 1950. Palestinians there became Jordanian citizens. Gaza was administered by Egypt but not annexed.

One short-lived attempt made by Palestinians to manage their own affairs in the occupied territories took place in September 1948. In that month, the exiled nationalist leader Hajj Amin al-Husayni formed an "independent" Palestinian government in Gaza, claiming authority over all of Mandate-era Palestine. Al-Husayni and the reconstituted Arab Higher Committee had been pressuring the Arab League since 1946 to establish a Palestinian government that could assume control of the country after British withdrawal in 1948. The Arab League assented, partially to appease public opinion and partially as a way to frustrate the plans of al-Husayni's bitter foe, Abdullah of Jordan, to annex the Arab-controlled portions of Palestine.

Despite recognition by several key Arab states, the "All Palestine Government" never evolved into a full-fledged Palestinian state due to lukewarm Arab support. The government, which had neither income nor a regular army, was unable to claim the undisputed allegiance of most Palestinians. In October 1948, Jordanian forces disarmed al-Husayni's followers in the West Bank, and a renewed Israeli offensive against Egyptian troops further reduced the government's status. The government collapsed after the Jordanian annexation of the West Bank and Egypt's decision to stop supporting al-Husayni.

During the 1950s and 1960s, uniquely Palestinian parties and movements were subordinated to wider Arab parties and personalities as they were in exile. In the West Bank, Palestinians were attracted to the pan-Arab Ba'th Party and its pro-Nasser rival, the Movement of Arab Nationalists. Islamic parties were also strong, particularly the Muslim Brotherhood and the Liberation Party. Also, intellectuals were drawn to the highly organized Jordanian Communist Party, which rose from the ashes of the Palestine Communist Party (PCP).* Jordan banned political parties in 1957 with the exception of the Muslim Brotherhood. Only it and the communists survived Jordanian repression and the onset of Israeli occupation in 1967 with any strength. Palestinians in Gaza had less political room in which to maneuver. Nasser was locked in a bitter rivalry with the communists and the Muslim Brotherhood, and he clamped down on their activities in Gaza. Egypt instead used the PLO and its army, the Palestine Liberation Army (PLA), to channel and contain Palestinian political energies in Gaza.

Although anti-Israeli protest movements among traditional leaders developed shortly after the Israeli occupation in 1967, it was the rise of the commando groups in exile and their takeover of the PLO that spurred widespread resistance politics in the occupied territories. Serious guerrilla fighting broke out in Gaza, but it was ruthlessly suppressed by the Israeli army in 1971. In the West Bank, which had been disarmed by the Jordanians, nonmilitary resistance was on the rise in the mid-1970s as the PLO and the PCP (which was re-formed out of the Jordanian Communist Party) began making inroads into the area at the expense of pro-Jordanian politicians. Local town council elections in April 1976 returned several strongly pro-PLO candidates in a move that signaled a shift in Palestinian sentiments in the occupied territories in favor of the PLO.

Thanks to pressure from the communist-led Palestine National Front,* the PLO established a Committee for the Occupied Homeland in March 1977 to increase its links with the territories, especially since the PLO had by then shifted strategies in favor of establishing a Palestinian state in the occupied territories. During the late 1970s and early 1980s, nationalist activity centered around the National Guidance Committee,* a coalition of local interests and groups affiliated with various PLO groups and factions. Islamic movements, such as the Muslim Brotherhood and Islamic Jihad,* were also on the rise, particularly in Gaza. Increased land expropriations and the introduction of Israeli settlers into the occupied territories, which accelerated after the 1977 electoral victory of the Likud bloc, led to greater frustration among the population, despite the growing international focus on the territories as the logical place for the establishment of a Palestinian homeland as part of a peaceful settlement of the Arab-Israeli dispute.

In December 1987, a massive anti-Israeli uprising known as the Intifada broke out in Gaza and spread to the West Bank. Eventually coordinated by the Unified National Command of the Uprising (UNCU)* in conjunction with the PLO, the uprising captured headlines worldwide and garnered considerable sympathy for the Palestinians in the face of harsh Israeli attempts to put down the unrest. Despite PLO involvement, the uprising also led to a marked increase in popular support for militant Islamic organizations operating outside the PLO, such as Hamas* and Islamic Jihad.* Popular participation in the Intifada dwindled after the 1991 Gulf War and stringent Israeli repression. Increasingly, the Intifada assumed the form of isolated armed attacks carried out by youthful militants. Israel continued to exert forceful efforts to combat this new development, including a mass deportation of 415 Palestinians to southern Lebanon in December 1992 on the grounds that they were linked to Islamic groups like Hamas.

The PLO has enjoyed amazing success in the occupied territories since 1967, rivaled only by the increasingly powerful Islamic groups. This can be linked to the belief among Palestinians in the occupied territories that their ultimate lib-eration, and the creation of an independent state, depends upon linking their own resistance activities within the occupied territories with the political and diplomatic position of the PLO internationally.

Yet Israeli-Palestinian negotiations over self-rule in the territories, which opened with the October 1991 Madrid peace conference, tarnished PLO prestige in the territories. The negotiations highlighted differences of priorities between activists in the territories (some of whom sat at the negotiating table) and the PLO leadership in exile, which directed the negotiations. Furthermore, Hamas and Islamic Jihad successfully combined their continued attacks on Israeli targets with vocal opposition to the negotiations to attract a significant level of support at the expense of the PLO.

Secret negotiations between the PLO and Israel, carried out without the knowledge of the Palestinian negotiating team, culminated in September 1993 with an agreement for Palestinian self-rule in the territories. This produced fur-ther divisions within the Palestinian national movement. Nevertheless, the PLO pressed on with implementation of the agreement, and the Palestine Central Council approved the formation of a "Palestinian National Authority" in Oc-tober 1993.

## ARENA FOUR: PALESTINIAN POLITICAL ACTIVITY IN ISRAEL AFTER 1948

Palestinians' political behavior in Israel has always been tempered by the re-ality of their status as an Arab minority within a Jewish state that is at war with their kinfolk beyond the borders. With the partial exception of Druze Arabs, who agreed to participate as loyal citizens and serve in the military, Palestinians in Israel have faced both suspicion and legal barriers in their quest for full equality with their Jewish fellow citizens.

Arab politics within Israel have been dominated by three trends: the search for equality with Jewish citizens, the search to maintain both an Arab identity and spiritual links with Palestinians beyond the borders, and the search to es-tablish Arab political parties free from government harassment or co-optation by Zionist parties. Arab politics in Israel have also been hampered by voter apathy, government hostility, and social rivalries that many maintain have been delib-erately fanned by the authorities.

For the first three decades of Israeli independence, the Arab vote was largely captured either by Zionist parties, by small Arab electoral lists affiliated with a particular Zionist party, or by the Communist Party of Israel and its Arab-dominated offshoot, Rakah.* Formal membership in Zionist parties has not al-ways been possible (the Labor Party began admitting Arab members only in 1973), and while some parties campaigned directly for Arab votes, the usual pattern for Zionist parties has been to sponsor separate Arab electoral lists affiliated with the party. One example was the United Arab List, a group of candidates affiliated with the Labor Party, which appeared in the 1977 Knesset elections. The Labor Party has also supported several lists simultaneously throughout the country, exploiting local rivalries. In 1988 a prominent Palestinian parliamentarian broke with Labor to form the Democratic Arab Party* because of his disagreement with the party's stance on the *Intifada*. The move signaled an overall decline in Arab support for Zionist parties, although 40 percent of the Arab vote still went to such parties in the 1980s. One factor in this phenomenon has been the pattern of village leaders delivering votes to several different lists during the same election, hoping to secure favors from several victorious parties at once.

The main Arab-oriented party has remained the Communist Party of Israel and Rakah, its Arab-dominated offshoot. Because it followed the Soviet line of accepting Israel's right to exist, Rakah has always been willing to work within the Israeli system and has consistently returned Arab deputies to the Knesset since its inception in 1965. As a communist internationalist party dominated by Arabs, Rakah has tried to balance its struggle to achieve equal rights for Arabs with an overall pro-PLO, Palestinian nationalist stance. In 1977 Rakah formed the Democratic Front for Peace and Equality* to include non-communist village mayors and other influential leaders who could deliver votes traditionally beyond Rakah's grasp.

While Rakah/Democratic Front for Peace and Equality was traditionally the most significant Arab political force in Israel, it never completely dominated Arab political behavior in Israel. Electorally, the majority of Palestinians voted for Zionist parties in the 1960s. In its first electoral apearance in 1965, for instance, Rakah captured only 23 percent of the Arab vote, while in 1977 it garnered some 49 percent. In addition to the votes taken by Zionist parties, the communists have faced significant challenges from non-communist Arab nationalist groups. The first nationalist challenge came from the *al-Ard* (The Land)* movement in the late 1950s, when Nasser's influence was at its peak and his rivalry with the communists in Egypt and Iraq affected Arab support for the communists in Israel. Similar tensions led to the growth of the Palestinian nationalist Abna' al-Balad (Sons of the Country)* movement in the 1970s, which urged greater confrontation with the authorities, and the Progressive List for Peace* in the 1980s.

Finally, both communists and nationalists have faced the challenge posed by Islamic movements among the Arabs of Israel. The Islamists' power lies at the local level, where they have been active in establishing much-needed social services. In February 1989, Islamic candidates won several local village council elections at the expense of the Democratic Front for Peace and Equality. The most significant occurred in the large village of Umm al-Fahm, where Islamists had gained popular approval in the community through the establishment of the social services group, the Islamic Association, in 1985. The Islamists' ability to deliver on such promises had played a key role in their success.

In the 1988 Knesset elections, Rakah and the Democratic Front for Peace and Equality returned four parliamentarians, and the Progressive List for Peace and the Democratic Arab Party one each. In 1992, the Democratic Front for Peace and Equality won three seats and the Democratic Arab Party two, while the Progressive List for Peace gained none. Although Arab voter turnout has grown, some 40 percent of the Arab vote continued to be directed toward Zionist parties, while 30 percent of Arab voters did not vote at all.

## Bibliography

Cobban, Helena. *The Palestinian Liberation Organisation: People, Power and Politics.* Cambridge, England: Cambridge University Press, 1984.

Cohen, Amnon. *Political Parties in the West Bank under the Jordanian Regime, 1949–1967.* Ithaca, N.Y.: Cornell University Press, 1982.

"The Islamist Movements in the Occupied Territories. An Interview with Iyad Barghouti." *Middle East Report* 183 (July/August 1993), 9–12.

Jiryis, Sabri. *The Arabs in Israel.* Translated by Inea Bushnaq. New York: Monthly Review Press, 1976.

Lesch, Ann Mosely. *Arab Politics in Palestine, 1917–1939: The Frustration of a Nationalist Movement.* Ithaca, N.Y.: Cornell University Press, 1979.

Lustick, Ian. *Arabs in the Jewish State: Israel's Control of a National Minority.* Austin: University of Texas Press, 1980.

———. "The Changing Political Role of Israeli Arabs." In *The Elections in Israel—1988,* edited by A. Arian and M. Shamir, 115–34. Boulder, Colo.: Westview Press, 1990.

Ma'oz, Moshe. *Palestinian Leadership on the West Bank: The Changing Role of the Arab Mayors under Jordan and Israel.* London: Frank Cass, 1984.

Mattar, Philip. *The Mufti of Jerusalem: Al-Hajj Amin al-Husayni and the Palestinian National Movement.* New York: Columbia University Press, 1988.

Muslih, Muhammad Y. *The Origins of Palestinian Nationalism.* New York: Columbia University Press, 1988.

Peretz, Don. *Intifada: The Palestinian Uprising.* Boulder, Colo.: Westview Press, 1990.

Porath, Yehoshua. *The Emergence of the Palestinian Arab National Movement 1918–1929.* London: Frank Cass, 1974.

———. *The Palestinian Arab National Movement.* Vol. 2, *From Riots to Rebellions.* London: Frank Cass, 1977.

Quandt, William B., Fuad Jabber, and Ann Mosely Lesch. *The Politics of Palestinian Nationalism.* Berkeley: University of California Press, 1973.

Sahliyeh, Emile. *The PLO after the Lebanon War.* Boulder, Colo.: Westview Press, 1985.

———. *In Search of Leadership: West Bank Politics since 1967.* Washington, D.C.: Brookings Institution, 1988.

Steinberg, Matti. "The Worldview of Habash's 'Popular Front.'" *Jerusalem Quarterly* 47 (Summer 1988): 3–26.

———. "The Worldview of Hawatmeh's 'Democratic Front.'" *Jerusalem Quarterly* 50 (Spring 1989): 22–40.

Zureik, Elia T. *The Palestinians in Israel: A Study in Internal Colonialism.* London: Routledge and Kegan Paul, 1979.

## Political Parties

The following list of parties and political associations requires some explanation. First, by necessity brief, it includes only the most important groups and trends within the four historical arenas of Palestinian political expression. Second, because the extremely varied nature of Palestinian political expression over the past eighty years renders defining a "party" or other political group somewhat difficult, the list includes a wide variety of political actors, from parties to clubs, associations to politico-military commando groups, all of which express a form of Palestinian consciousness and serve to mobilize Palestinian political consciousness. This policy leads to the inclusion of militant groups seemingly devoid of any ideology or following but which exist as an expression of a wider political agenda pursued by some Palestinians, such as the continuation of armed struggle and the rejection of "surrenderist" solutions to the Arab-Israeli conflict.

Some organizations are generally known by their Arabic names, in which case they have been listed accordingly. In other cases, the recognized English form of a group's name has been used even when it is not the grammatically correct translation.

ABNA AL-BALAD (*Sons of the Country*). Abna al-Balad is a movement of Palestinian nationalists in Israel. The movement traces its roots to the Palestinian village of Umm al-Fahm, where the group was established by Muhammad Kiwan as an electoral list for local village council elections in the early 1970s. Abna al-Balad is a movement of local groups of intellectuals seeking to reform local Arab community councils rather than a structured organization.

As nationalists, the movement's activists sought self-determination for the Palestinians within Israel, embraced the Palestine Liberation Organization (PLO),* and supported its original ideological commitment to establishing a secular, democratic state in Palestine/Israel. They advocated active confrontation of the Israeli authorities, rejected working with Zionist parties and movements, and opposed traditional political networks based on kinship as divisive social forces that weaken a united stand in favor of Palestinian identity.

While many activists supported the Popular Front for the Liberation of Palestine* during the factional struggle within the PLO during the early and mid-1980s, followers of Fatah* broke from Abna al-Balad and formed their own group, al-Ansar (see al-Ansar II).

ABU MUSA GROUP. *See* FATAH-UPRISING.

ABU NIDAL GROUP. *See* FATAH–REVOLUTIONARY COUNCIL.

ACTION ORGANIZATION FOR THE LIBERATION OF PALESTINE (AOLP) (*Al-Hay'a al-'Amila Li-Tahrir Filastin*). A short-lived commando group established in February 1969 by 'Isam al-Sartawi, the AOLP was later absorbed by Fatah.*

ALF. *See* ARAB LIBERATION FRONT.

AL-ANSAR I (*The Partisans*). This short-lived communist guerrilla group was established in March 1970 by activists from several pro-Soviet Arab communist parties. In 1974–75, the group changed its name to the Palestine Communist Organization and eventually formed the Palestine Communist Party in 1982.*

AL-ANSAR II (*The Partisans*). This movement of Palestinians in Israel broke away from the Abna al-Balad* movement during the factional struggle that took place within the Palestine Liberation Organization (PLO)* during the early and mid-1980s. While most Abna' al-Balad activists supported the position of the Popular Front for the Liberation of Palestine* during the intra-PLO crisis of the 1980s, those who supported Fatah* left to form al-Ansar. Its influence, however, has never extended beyond the village of Umm al-Fahm.

AOLP. *See* ACTION ORGANIZATION FOR THE LIBERATION OF PALESTINE.

ARAB CLUB (*Al-Nadi al-'Arabi*). Formed in Damascus in late 1919 as an offshoot of the Arab nationalist al-Fatat movement the Arab Club was a group of approximately 500 anti-Zionist members of the young, urban Palestinian elite who supported inclusion of Palestine within a larger Arab kingdom of Syria headed by King Faysal I in Damascus. The Arab Club also urged Faysal to oppose Zionism, despite the fact that he eventually signed an agreement with Chaim Weizmann, leader of the Zionist movement. The leadership of its Jerusalem branch was dominated by members of the Husayni family.

ARAB EXECUTIVE (*Al-Lajna al-Tanfidhiyya Lil-Mutamar al-'Arabi al-Filastini, The Executive Committee of the Palestinian Arab Conference*). The Arab Executive, formed to coordinate the various Palestinian national congresses held during the 1920s, was the main Palestinian nationalist body from 1924 to 1934.

The Arab Executive was presided over by Musa Kazim al-Husayni, a venerable politician from one of Jerusalem's most distinguished families. Faced with both the lack of a representative national legislature within the framework of the British mandate in Palestine and the increasing threat posed by Zionist immigration, the Arab Executive adopted old-school diplomatic tactics such as sending delegations and submitting petitions in its attempts to gain self-determination for the Palestinian people.

Members and opponents of the Arab Executive within the Palestinian community faced off along personal and family factional lines. Foremost in this arena were the "councilists" (*majlisiyyun*), coalesced around the Husayni family, and the "opposition" (*mu'aridun*), led by their rivals in the Nashashibi family. Intra-Palestinian rivalries and factionalism eventually led to the disintegration of the Arab Executive upon Musa Kazim al-Husayni's death in 1934.

ARAB FRONT. *See* AL-ARD.

ARAB HIGHER COMMITTEE (*Al-Lajna al-'Arabiyya al-'Uliya Li-Filastin*). The "Higher Arab Committee for Palestine," a nationalist coordinating body, was formed in April 1936 to supervise a general strike observed by Arabs throughout Palestine from April to October 1936. The strike came in reaction to the killing of two Palestinians by Zionists bent on avenging the deaths of three Jews shortly before, but it was also the culmination of years of frustration over the failure to stop Jewish immigration and land purchases and to realize Palestinian self-determination.

The Arab Higher Committee included representatives from six parties in the Palestinian community and was headed by Hajj Amin al-Husayni, the major Palestinian nationalist figure in the 1930s and 1940s. The committee continued its work as the leading nationalist voice among Palestinians even after the strike ended and guerrilla bands began attacking British and Zionist targets from late 1936 until 1939. The committee began to fall apart in July 1937, however, when the pro-Nashashibi National Defense Party* withdrew from it. British authorities banned the committee that October and exiled many of its leaders when Palestinian guerrilla attacks intensified.

The Arab Higher Committee was reestablished by the Arab League in 1946, and it lobbied the Arab states to establish a Palestinian government that could operate after the British withdrawal from the country was announced in 1947. A short-lived "All Palestine Government" was established in Gaza in 1948, but it soon died out (see Introduction). A group calling itself the Arab Higher Committee continued to function long afterward, although as a marginalized relic from a former era.

ARAB LIBERATION FRONT (ALF) (*Jabhat al-Tahrir al-'Arabiyya*). The ALF, a Palestine Liberation Organization (PLO)* commando group, was established in early 1969 by the Iraqi wing of the pan-Arab Ba'th Party.* The Syrian wing of the Ba'th formed its own armed group as well (see al-Sa'iqa). Early leaders included Zayd Haydar and a Jordanian of Syrian origin, Munif al-Razzaz.

As an Iraqi-sponsored organization, the ALF has consistently pushed for a pro-Iraqi policy within the PLO and exerts limited influence among Palestinians. In the early 1980s, it was led by 'Abd al-Wahhab Kayyali, until 'Abd al-Rahim Ahmad assumed the leadership post in 1982. In 1993 the ALF was led by Mahmud Isma'il. The ALF opposed the peace process initiated by the 1991 Madrid conference.

ARAB SOCIALIST LIST. *See* AL-ARD.

AL-ARD (*The Land*). Al-Ard, a pan-Arab nationalist movement, was formed as a non-communist alternative for Palestinian nationalist expression in Israel from 1958–64. While accepting the 1947 partition of Palestine into Jewish and Arab states, the al-Ard movement supported the reigning pan-Arab nationalist stance championed by Egyptian president Nasser and pushed for Arab rights within Israel.

From 1949 to 1958, the Communist Party of Israel* (see also chapter on Israel) had exercised a monopoly over anti-Zionist Arab activism in Israel. In 1958 the Arab Front (later called the Popular Front) was formed to provide an avenue for joint struggle among communists and non-communist Arab nationalists. By 1959 the Front had broken up along communist-nationalist lines in response to the bitter rivalry between Nasser and 'Abd al-Karim Qasim, the Iraqi leader who ruled with the support of the Iraqi Communist Party. The pro-Nasser nationalists formed the al-Ard movement that year, which was led by Sabri Jiryis, Habib Qahwaji, Muhammad Mi'ari, Salih Baransi, and Mansur Qardush, among others.

The al-Ard movement quickly became a significant voice for Arab dissent within Israel, to the extent that the Israeli authorities formally banned it in 1964. The following year, al-Ard activists attempted to run in the Knesset elections as the Arab Socialist List, but they were banned once again. Several prominent leaders of al-Ard fled into exile.

ASSOCIATION OF BROTHERHOOD AND PURITY (*Jam'iyyat al-Ikha Wa al-'Afaf*). Formed in 1918, the Association of Brotherhood and Purity is thought to have been an armed wing of the Arab Club* and the Literary Society.* By 1919 the association claimed some 200 members, but British authorities soon disbanded it.

ASSOCIATION OF THE MUSLIM BROTHERHOOD. *See* MUSLIM BROTHERHOOD.

BA'TH PARTY. *See* ARAB LIBERATION FRONT and AL-SA'IQA.

BLACK JUNE ORGANIZATION. *See* FATAH–REVOLUTIONARY COUNCIL.

COMMITTEE FOR THE DEFENSE OF ARAB LANDS (*Al-Lajna Lil-Difa' 'An al-Aradi al-'Arabiyya*). Increasing confiscation of Palestinian land by Israeli authorities in the Galilee region of Israel during the 1970s led to the formation of the Committee for the Defense of Arab Lands in the fall of 1975. Its importance lay in its call for Palestinian observance of Land Day on March 30, 1976, to protest the confiscations. The resulting general strike among Palestinian communities in Israel came as a shock to the authorities, who until then had considered the Arabs of Israel politically passive. Six Palestinian citizens were killed by security forces during protests. Land Day is now regularly commemorated by Palestinians worldwide.

COMMUNIST PARTY OF ISRAEL (*Hamiflaga Hakomunistit Hayisraelit—Maki*). Maki, an acronym for the party's name, was formed in 1948 by communists in what had become Israel, although Maki's roots extend back to 1919 and the establishment of the Palestine Communist Party (PCP).* The joint Arab-Jewish membership of the PCP had been divided over the national struggle of the two peoples throughout its history, and the party eventually collapsed. In the fall of 1943, Arab militants formed the National Liberation League ('Usbat al-Tahrir al-Watani).

After the war, the Soviet Union urged Palestinian and Jewish members in what became Israel to unite, and Maki was formed in 1948. National Liberation League militants in what became the Jordanian-annexed West Bank formed the Jordanian Communist Party (see Jordanian Communist Party and Palestine Communist Party). But the national question continued to plague Maki throughout the 1950s. Arab nationalist sentiment, preached by Gamal Abdel Nasser and carried over the airwaves, was strong among Palestinians in Israel. Tension mounted further as the Soviet Union developed a marked pro-Nasser, pro-Arab policy that was resented by Jewish members of Maki. Jewish members, while anti-imperialist and supportive of Arab liberation from neo-colonialism, rejected the unqualified support extended by Arab members of the party to Arab regimes such as that of Egypt. The Jewish members perceived these regimes as reactionary and considered support for them in the name of anti-imperialism to be hypocritical. They also criticized Soviet support for leaders like Nasser, who ruthlessly crushed communism in Egypt. The Jewish criticism became an overall reassessment of the party's view of the Soviet Union as the bastion of a new socialist order.

In August 1965, Maki split along generally Jewish-Arab lines. Under Moshe Sneh, Jewish members continued to function as Maki, while Arab militants formed the New Communist List, or Rakah,* under the leadership of the Jewish communist, Meir Vilner. Maki ceased to be a factor within Palestinian politics after that and, ironically, was also effectively dismissed by the mainstream Israeli body politic as well for its anti-Zionist Marxism, by then out of vogue among Israeli Jews (see chapter on Israel).

COMMUNIST PARTY OF JORDAN. *See* JORDANIAN COMMUNIST PARTY.

COMMUNIST PARTY OF PALESTINE. *See* PALESTINE COMMUNIST PARTY.

DAMASCUS TEN. *See* NATIONAL DEMOCRATIC AND ISLAMIC FRONT.

DEMOCRATIC ALLIANCE (*Al-Tahaluf al-Dimuqrati*). The Democratic Alliance was formed in March 1984 in the midst of serious internal conflicts within the Palestine Liberation Organization (PLO)* prompted by the Fatah-Uprising's challenge of Yasir Arafat's leadership (see Fatah and Fatah-Uprising). The alliance comprised four constituent organizations of the PLO—the Democratic Front for the Liberation of Palestine (DFLP),* the Popular Front for the Liberation of Palestine (PFLP),* the Palestine Liberation Front,* and the Palestine Communist Party (PCP)*—which, while supporting PLO unity, voiced significant criticism of Arafat's leadership of the organization and called for reforms.

The alliance was based in Syria, which had poor relations with Arafat and which served as a base for anti-Arafat Palestinians. As a loyal opposition, the Democratic Alliance did not go as far as the National Alliance* in its calls for reform, but it did urge the reformation of the Palestine National Front* to press for reforms within the PLO.

In 1985 the DFLP withdrew from the Democratic Alliance, signaling its demise. The PFLP later joined with the National Alliance to create the Syrian-backed Palestinian National Salvation Front.*

DEMOCRATIC ARAB PARTY (Al-Hizb al-'Arabi al-Dimuqrati). The Democratic Arab Party was formed in time for the November 1988 Knesset elections in Israel. The party was spearheaded by 'Abd al-Wahhab Darawsheh, a Palestinian Knesset member representing the Labor Party, who split with the party over the harsh measures applied by Israeli security forces in combatting the *Intifada* in the occupied territories under the direction of then Defense Minister Yitzhak Rabin (see chapter on Israel, Labor Party).

The party is one of the three main Arab parties in Israel, the other two being the communist-dominated Democratic Front for Peace and Equality* and the Progressive List for Peace.* While openly Arabic in orientation, the party places greater emphasis upon achieving equal rights for Palestinian citizens of Israel than upon general Palestinian issues.

In the 1988 elections, the party won one seat, capturing 10.8 percent of the Arab votes cast; in 1992, it won two seats. (See also chapter on Israel.)

DEMOCRATIC FRONT FOR THE LIBERATION OF PALESTINE (DFLP) (Al-Jabha al-Dimuqratiyya Li-Tahrir Filastin). The DFLP is the third most significant organization within the Palestine Liberation Organization (PLO)* after Fatah* and the Popular Front for the Liberation of Palestine (PFLP).* The Marxist DFLP has exerted a more significant intellectual influence than its numerical strength alone would imply. Its main leaders have been the Jordanian Nayif Hawatmeh, Yasir 'Abd Rabbuh, 'Abd al-Karim Hammad, and Qays Samarra'i.

The DFLP, which broke from the PFLP in February 1969 as the result of ideological disputes, was originally called the Popular Democratic Front for the Liberation of Palestine (al-Jabha al-Sha'biyya al-Dimuqratiyya li-Tahrir Filastin). Younger PFLP cadres such as Nayif Hawatmeh argued that the PFLP needed to overcome the petty bourgeois nature of its urban, educated leadership headed by George Habash. The dispute also centered on the harsh criticism focused by the Hawatmeh group on Gamal Abdel Nasser, once the idol of PFLP cadres while they were members of the Movement of Arab Nationalists,* after the 1967 Arab defeat. The DFLP exerted great efforts to maintain the unity of the PLO, particularly during the 1980s. It has often been critical of Yasir Arafat, such as during the period of serious dissent within the PLO from 1984 to 1987. In March 1984, the DFLP helped form the dissident Democratic Alliance,* and, although it withdrew in 1985, it did not resume activity within the PLO Executive Council until 1987. But overall, the DFLP has stood by Arafat in order to preserve PLO unity.

The DFLP has advocated a solution to the Palestinian problem along with a wider sociopolitical revolution within the Arab world. It is also credited by some with first introducing the concept of a secular, democratic state in Palestine/ Israel to serve as a home for Jews and Arabs alike as the long-term strategic goal of the Palestinian national movement, to replace the original PLO goal of liberating the homeland and establishing an Arab state. The PLO eventually adopted the secular, democratic state goal in 1974. Later, the DFLP supported the concept of an independent, Palestinian state in the occupied territories and emphasized realizing national liberation first and deferring social revolution until later. The DFLP has never advocated extending the process of liberation outside the Middle East, and it has eschewed such activities as airplane hijackings. Consistent with its ideology, the DFLP has maintained fraternal cooperation with revolutionary groups in other Arab states, particularly Jordan. Its Jordanian wing incorporated itself as a Jordanian political party called the Jordanian Democratic People's Party in 1989 (see chapter on Jordan). The DFLP has been unabashedly pro-Soviet over the years. While the DFLP is not disproportionately made up of Christian activists, Christians have often been attracted to it and other organizations that advocate secular (and often Marxist) positions within an overwhelmingly Muslim body politic. It focuses a great deal of energy on organizing labor groups as well.

Throughout its history, the DFLP has been much more flexible in its ideological positions and more willing to deal with right-wing Palestinian elements than the other main Marxist Palestinian organization, the PFLP, consistent with its policy of "revolutionary realism."

Friction between factions loyal to Hawatmeh and 'Abd Rabbuh began developing in the spring of 1990 over issues such as how to react to U.S.–led diplomatic initiatives as well as the question of how involved the DFLP should become in non-Palestinian politics, particularly in Jordan. Hawatmeh and DFLP military commanders in Syria and Lebanon were extremely skeptical of Arafat's interest in a U.S.–brokered peace. 'Abd Rabbuh and DFLP political leaders have stood by Arafat's diplomatic efforts, although they too remained skeptical of U.S. moves to convene a Middle East peace conference in the fall of 1991. The strife led to armed clashes between the two sides in Syria in August 1990, and in April 1991, the organization split. 'Abd Rabbuh claimed his faction was abandoning Marxism-Leninism. Mediation efforts failed, and 'Abd Rabbuh changed the name of his faction to the Palestinian Democratic Union.* Both groups retained representation on the PLO Executive Comittee.

The DFLP was critical of the Arab-Israeli peace process that began in the fall of 1991, not so much because of ideological opposition to a negotiated settlement, but because it opposed the conditions that it felt were imposed on the Palestinians. The DFLP became associated with the oppositional "Damascus Ten" groups in 1992. Hawatmeh played an important role in the eventual transformation of the Ten into the Democratic Nationalist and Islamic Front* in October 1993, following the signing of the PLO-Israeli agreement the previous month. The DFLP also played a role in creating a new leadership to guide the *Intifada* (See Unified National Command of the Uprising).

The intra-Palestinian crisis precipitated by the agreement and PLO Chairman Yasir Arafat's style of leadership (see Palestine Liberation Organization) also led to a reconciliation between the PFLP and DFLP. The two groups agreed to merge their leadership bodies twenty-five years after the DFLP broke off from the PFLP.

DEMOCRATIC FRONT FOR PEACE AND EQUALITY (*Hazit Demokratit L'Shalom ve Shivyon* [Hebrew]; *Al-Jabha al-Dimuqratiyya Lil Salam Wal-Musawa* [Arabic]). This front, known by its Hebrew acronym, HADASH, was established by the Arab-dominated communist RAKAH* in 1977 as a nation-wide alliance among Arab political figures in Israel to align Rakah with traditional leaders who could deliver non-communist votes on the local level. The front won many village council elections despite its growing rivalry with the Progressive List for Peace,* the Democratic Arab Party,* and Islamic movements in the mid-1980s. The latter in particular began making serious inroads at the front's expense. During the 1989 village council elections, the front lost to Islamist candidates in several large communities.

During the 1988 Knesset elections, the front garnered four seats and captured 33 percent of the Arab vote. While it outran the Progressive List and the Democratic Arab Party, these results, along with the Islamic movements' successes at the local level, indicated that the front and the communists faced stiff competition for political support among Israel's Arab citizens. In the 1992 Knesset elections, the front won only three seats (see also the chapter on Israel).

DFLP. *See* DEMOCRATIC FRONT FOR THE LIBERATION OF PALESTINE.

FARMERS' PARTY (*Hizb al-Zurra'*). In 1924 several Farmers' Party organizations were established in Nazareth, the Nablus-Janin region, and the area around Hebron, which were composed of village leaders opposed to the policies of the Arab Executive* and who championed rural issues. The party was accused of receiving funds from Zionist organizations; it disappeared after 1927.

FATAH (*Harakat al-Tahrir al-Watani al-Filastini, Palestinian National Liberation Movement*). "Fatah," a backwards acronym, is derived from the group's name, which means "the conquest." Fatah is the largest, wealthiest, and most significant organization within the Palestine Liberation Organization (PLO)* and has wielded great influence over the Palestinian national movement since the 1960s.

Fatah coalesced around several activists in Cairo and Kuwait during the 1950s. Some of its early leaders continued to occupy positions of power within the movement throughout its history, including Yasir Arafat (known as Abu 'Ammar), Faruq al-Qaddumi (Abu Lutuf), Salah Khalaf (Abu Iyyad), Khalil al-Wazir (Abu Jihad), Muhammad Yusuf al-Najjar (Abu Yusuf), and Khalid al-Hasan (Abu Sa'id).

Fatah's success has lain in the primacy it has given to Palestinian national liberation without heavy emphasis upon ideological abstractions, particularly those derived from Marxism. Palestinian society is by and large socially conservative and Islamic, and Fatah's mainstream Arab nationalist stance and overwhelmingly Muslim leadership have appealed to a broad spectrum of Palestinians. Fatah has always stood for Palestinians spearheading their own liberation rather than depending upon events or forces in the Arab world to do it for them. By emphasizing such general interests, it has attracted Palestinians holding widely divergent ideological and tactical viewpoints over the years.

Another of Fatah's bedrock principles has been noninterference in the affairs of Arab states. Unlike the leftists, Fatah has generally not preached revolution throughout the Arab world as a prerequisite for the liberation of Palestine. It stressed just the opposite: cooperation with all types of Arab governments, from monarchies to military regimes. This nonthreatening approach has made for good relations between Fatah and most Arab regimes and has helped it garner by far the most financial and diplomatic support of all the groups. However, Fatah forces were drawn into conflict in Jordan in 1970–71 and Lebanon in 1976 despite this policy (see PLO). Arafat's public embrace of Iraqi president Saddam Husayn during the 1990–91 Gulf crisis also damaged Fatah's relations with Egypt, Saudi Arabia, and the Gulf states.

Fatah took the political struggle to the battlefield in late 1964, when fighters began launching raids against Israel, using the name *al-'Asifa* (the storm) to separate themselves from Fatah should the raids fail. Fatah grew into the largest Palestinian guerrilla group, especially after its fighters joined Jordanian army units in inflicting relatively heavy casualties when the Israeli army crossed the border to attack Palestinian commando bases in March 1968 at al-Karama, Jordan. Although they lost the battle, Fatah fighters were seen in the Arab world as the only force still actively confronting the Israelis in the aftermath of the 1967 defeat. Within days, thousands flocked to join the organization.

Unlike the groups favoring internationalization of the struggle, such as the Popular Front for the Liberation of Palestine (PFLP),* Fatah initially wavered between support for and condemnation of exploits such as hijacking airplanes and hostage taking outside of the Middle East. Fatah generally opposed such activities; however, elements within Fatah are believed to have been responsible for carrying out several such actions in the early 1970s through a shadowy group calling itself Black September. Following a 1974 decision to freeze international operations, Fatah usually restricted its armed activities to the Middle East.

In 1968 Fatah and the other commando groups forced the PLO to include them in the organization's structure. In February 1969, Fatah's chairman, Yasir Arafat, was elected chairman of the PLO. From that point on, Fatah has remained the most powerful and influential movement within the PLO, and it has played a strong role in guiding overall PLO policy. In 1983 internal tensions within Fatah led to full-scale combat in Lebanon between pro-Arafat loyalists and Syrian-backed dissidents (see Fatah-Uprising), which led to the loyalists' evacuation from northern Lebanon under UN supervision.

Fatah, once a fairly solid base of Arafat's leadership within the PLO, experienced serious internal discord concerning the September 1993 agreement with Israel, as well as Arafat's overbearing style of leadership. The Fatah Revolutionary Committee approved the agreement, but rejectionists within the movement soon emerged. Although Fatah officially withdrew from the Unified National Command of the Uprising* following the agreement, some factions opposed the decision and continued to work with new *Intifada* leadership. Another serious indication of the level of discord within the organization surfaced when approximately one-half of the 105 members of the Fatah Revolutionary Committee boycotted its meeting in November 1993 as a protest against the peace accord and Arafat's leadership. Among the major Fatah figures in this new opposition was Faruq al-Qaddumi, one of its founding members and the PLO's "foreign minister."

Fatah remains the most important PLO group, with strong support among Palestinians within the occupied territories and in exile.

FATAH—INTIFADA. *See* FATAH-UPRISING.

FATAH—AL-MAJLIS AL-THAWRI. *See* FATAH–REVOLUTIONARY COUNCIL.

FATAH–REVOLUTIONARY COUNCIL (*Fatah–Al-Majlis al-Thawri*). Known in the West as Black June and the Abu Nidal group, the organization's leader, Sabri Khalid al-Banna, or Abu Nidal, is believed to have split from the mainstream Fatah* movement in the early 1970s. Violently hostile to the mainstream Palestine Liberation Organization (PLO),* Fatah–Revolutionary Council has been blamed for several assassinations of PLO figures and moderate Palestinians, as well as attacks against Jordanian, Israeli, Jewish, and Western targets.

The Fatah–Revolutionary Council has operated with support from several Arab regimes, reportedly operating first with Iraqi and later Syrian and Libyan assistance. Al-Banna has been sentenced to death in absentia by the PLO.

FATAH–UPRISING (*Fatah–Intifada*). This dissident group split from Fatah* in the wake of the 1982 Israeli invasion of Lebanon. Activists associated with this organization consider themselves the true heirs of Fatah and continue to use the name Fatah. Other Palestinians refer to the group as Fatah-Uprising.

The dissident movement gained force in the wake of the withdrawal of Palestine Liberation Organization (PLO)* forces from Beirut in August 1982. Some Fatah activists were particularly incensed that certain military officers who had been criticized by rank-and-file fighters for their poor performance or outright cowardice in the face of the Israeli onslaught were promoted by Yasir Arafat, head of both Fatah and the PLO. The dissidents took their case to the battlefield under Colonel Sa'id Musa Muragha (known as Abu Musa), a Fatah military officer who had seen service in the Jordanian army. Abu Musa and his followers did not originally seek to break from Fatah. As military men, they felt that Fatah needed to be cleansed of what they perceived as cronyism and corruption among the movement's politicians and politicians-cum-officers.

Efforts to avoid an armed clash failed, and fighting between the two Fatah factions broke out in 1983. Fatah-Uprising forces drove loyalist Fatah troops out of their bases in northern Lebanon and laid siege to them near the city of Tripoli. The internecine fighting ended with a UN–sponsored evacuation of loyalist Fatah forces in December 1983. The Popular Front for the Liberation of Palestine–General Command (PFLP–GC)* joined Fatah-Uprising forces, although other anti-Arafat groups within the PLO remained neutral.

The insurrection spawned a wide-reaching crisis within the PLO, amidst many calls for reforms within both Fatah and the PLO as a whole. Eventually, Fatah-Uprising broke with Arafat and the PLO and helped form the Syrian-backed dissident Palestinian National Salvation Front (PNSF)* (see National Alliance* and Palestinian National Salvation Front).

In the wake of warmer relations between the PNSF and the PLO in 1991, Fatah-Uprising reportedly indicated its willingness to abide by the resolutions of the PLO-controlled Palestine National Council while not actually participating in it.

As one of the "Damascus Ten" groups opposed to the Israeli-Palestinian negotiations that began with the 1991 Madrid peace conference, Fatah-Uprising denounced the September 1993 agreement between Israel and the PLO and joined the National Democratic and Islamic Front.*

FIDA. *See* PALESTINIAN DEMOCRATIC UNION.

AL-FIDAIYYA (*Those Who Sacrifice Themselves*). Al-Fidaiyya, a nationalist organization, was established in Jaffa in early 1919, with branches in other towns. It died out in 1923.

FOLLOW UP COMMITTEE ON THE GENERAL CONCERNS OF THE ARABS OF ISRAEL (*Lajnat al-Mutabi'a lil-Shuun al-'Amma Li-'Arab Israil*). The committee, an organization dealing with the concerns of Palestinian citizens of Israel, comprises prominent Arab citizens of Israel, including Knesset members, mayors, officials of the Histadrut (Israel Labor Federation), and representatives of other Arab organizations in Israel. Among its activities, the committee has organized demonstrations in solidarity with the *Intifada* and has donated food, clothing, and medicine to Palestinians in the occupied territories.

FRONT OF PALESTINIAN FORCES REJECTING SURRENDERIST SO-LUTIONS. *See* REJECTION FRONT.

HADASH. *See* DEMOCRATIC FRONT FOR PEACE AND EQUALITY.

HAMAS (*Harakat-al-Muqawima al-Islamiyya, Islamic Resistance Movement*). Hamas (zeal) is an acronym derived from the organization's full name. The creation of Hamas as an armed wing of the Islamic revivalist Muslim Brotherhood* movement in Gaza in August 1988 represented a strategic and tactical change in the Brotherhood's philosophy. Before the *Intifada* broke out in December 1987, the Muslim Brotherhood concentrated on religious proselytizing and social purification, and it was overtly hostile to the activities of secular Palestinian nationalists. But the popularity of the nationalist message prompted the Brotherhood to change tactics. In 1984 Israeli authorities arrested thirteen members of the Brotherhood and captured an arms cache. Mass participation in the *Intifada* furthered the Brotherhood's conviction that a shift in tactics was justified, and Hamas was created.

The August 1988 Hamas charter declared that all of Palestine is Islamic trust land and an integral part of the wider Islamic world, and it can never be surrendered to non-Muslims. While Hamas joined with the secular nationalists in calling for the establishment of a Palestinian state, it broke with the official Palestine Liberation Organization (PLO)* policy of creating a Palestinian state in the occupied territories alongside Israel by calling for total liberation of all of Mandate-era Palestine and the establishment of an Islamic Palestinian state. It rejected Western-led moves toward a Middle East peace conference as a policy designed to force Palestinian acquiescence in the partition of Palestine.

Hamas agreed to work with the Unified National Command of the Uprising (UNCU)* during the *Intifada* beginning in October 1988, although it never joined the UNCU. Instead, Hamas operated parallel to it, declaring its own hours and days of general strike, which differed from those called by the UNCU, and issuing its own proclamations. In 1989 it also agreed to abide by the decisions of the Palestine National Council, the PLO's "parliament in exile," until the creation of a Palestinian state. By 1991 it was calling for elections for membership in the council, which would be held both in exile and within the occupied territories, where the strength of Hamas lies.

As popular participation in the *Intifada* waned after the 1991 Gulf War, the uprising increasingly took the form of isolated armed attacks against Israeli targets. Hamas activists, such as those in the "Martyr 'Izz al-Din al-Qassam Brigades," were among those who carried out such attacks, especially in Gaza. Their militancy struck a responsive chord, particularly among young people, as frustration at the lack of tangible moves toward Israeli withdrawal from the territories mounted. Hamas also benefitted from Saudi financial assistance, which flowed from Saudi bitterness over the pro-Saddam stance adopted by PLO Chairman Yasir Arafat during the 1991 Gulf War (see PLO).

The ideological and even personal differences between youthful Islamic militants and secular nationalists led to tension and even confrontations in the occupied territories in early 1990. In early June 1991, a week of mounting tension led to a gun battle in the streets of Nablus, long one of the centers of secular nationalism in the West Bank, between Hamas and Fatah militants. The two groups issued a joint call for unity after conciliation meetings. Violence between the two groups also broke out in Gaza in July 1992.

Hamas's main support comes from the Gaza Strip. Its leadership has included Shaykh Ahmad Yasin (sentenced to life imprisonment by the Israelis in 1991), Shaykh Khalil Qawqa, and 'Abd al-'Aziz Rantisi (deported by Israel in December 1992). Hamas rejected the principle of a negotiated Middle East peace settlement.

Hamas used its increased prestige and presence to mount a significant challenge to the PLO's former monopoly over the anti-Israel struggle in the territories, although it was not averse to working with secular nationalists on some matters. As one of the "Damascus Ten" groups opposed to the Israeli-Palestinian negotiations that began at the 1991 Madrid peace conference, Hamas denounced the September 1993 agreement between Israel and the PLO and joined the National Democratic and Islamic Front.* Hamas's true position on the agreement and the proposed elections for the new Palestinian authority was harder to ascertain, however, as statements by certain Hamas figures suggested that some factions within the movement questioned whether militant noncooperation might lead to a loss of Hamas influence in the territories.

HARAKAT AL-MUQAWIMA AL-ISLAMIYYA. *See* HAMAS.

HARAKAT AL-QAWMIYYIN AL-'ARAB. *See* MOVEMENT OF ARAB NATIONALISTS.

HARAKAT AL-TAHRIR AL-WATANI AL-FILASTINI. *See* FATAH.

AL-HAYA AL-'AMILA LI-TAHRIR FILASTIN. *See* ACTION ORGANIZATION FOR THE LIBERATION OF PALESTINE.

HAZIT DEMOKRATIT LSHALOM VE SHIVYON. *See* DEMOCRATIC FRONT FOR PEACE AND EQUALITY.

HIGHER COMMITTEE FOR NATIONAL GUIDANCE (*Al-Majlis al-A'la lil-Tawjih al-Watani*). This committee was organized soon after the Israeli occupation of the West Bank in 1967 to coordinate anti-Israeli protests. Its leaders were established members of the pro-Jordanian West Bank establishment. The committee soon disappeared.

HIZB AL-AHRAR. *See* LIBERAL PARTY.

AL-HIZB AL-'ARABI AL-DIMUQRATI. *See* DEMOCRATIC ARAB PARTY.

AL-HIZB AL-'ARABI AL-FILASTINI. *See* PALESTINE ARAB PARTY.

HIZB AL-DIFA' AL-WATANI. *See* NATIONAL DEFENSE PARTY.

HIZB AL-ISLAH. *See* REFORM PARTY.

HIZB AL-ISTIQLAL AL-'ARABI. *See* PARTY OF ARAB INDEPENDENCE.

HIZB AL-SHA'B AL-FILASTINI. *See* PALESTINE COMMUNIST PARTY.

AL-HIZB AL-SHUYU'I AL-FILASTINI. *See* PALESTINE COMMUNIST PARTY.

AL-HIZB AL-SHUYU'I AL-THAWRI AL-FILASTINI. *See* PALESTINIAN REVOLUTIONARY COMMUNIST PARTY.

AL-HIZB AL-SHUYU'I AL-URDUNNI. *See* JORDANIAN COMMUNIST PARTY.

HIZB AL-TAHRIR. *See* PARTY OF LIBERATION.

HIZB AL-'UMMAL AL-SHUYU'I AL-FILASTINI. *See* PALESTINIAN COMMUNIST WORKERS PARTY.

AL-HIZB AL-WATANI AL'ARABI AL-FILASTINI. *See* PALESTINIAN ARAB NATIONAL PARTY.

HIZB AL-ZURRA. *See* FARMERS' PARTY.

ISLAMIC JIHAD (*Al-Jihad al-Islami, Islamic Holy Struggle*). It is suspected that Islamic Jihad was established as a splinter movement from the Muslim Brotherhood* by activists frustrated with the Brotherhood's strongly antinationalist ideology. Unlike the social Islamicization program of the Brotherhood, militants of Islamic Jihad felt that Palestinian liberation could not wait until Palestinians became observant Muslims, but required immediate Islamic struggle against Israeli occupation.

The group first came to light in October 1986 after an attack was made on Israeli soldiers in Jerusalem. It staged several daring attacks on Israeli troops in Gaza in 1987 but afterward saw many of its rank and file arrested. Shaykh 'Abd al-'Aziz 'Awda was an early leader of Islamic Jihad until he was deported by Israeli authorities in April 1988. His successor, Fathi 'Abd al-'Aziz Shiqaqi, was deported and subsequently operated from Lebanon.

Islamic Jihad has participated in the *Intifada* alongside, but separate from, the Unified National Command of the Uprising (UNCU).* It seeks the liberation of the occupied territories but as a stepping stone to the total liberation of Palestine. Islamic Jihad has operated as a dedicated group of highly motivated armed militants rather than as a broadly based movement, in contrast to the strategy of the other main Islamic movement, Hamas.* As one of the "Damascus Ten" groups opposed to the Israeli-Palestinian negotiations that began at the 1991 Madrid peace conference, Jihad denounced the September 1993 agreement between Israel and the PLO and joined the National Democratic and Islamic Front.*

ISLAMIC HOLY STRUGGLE. *See* ISLAMIC JIHAD.

ISLAMIC RESISTANCE MOVEMENT. *See* HAMAS.

ISTIQLAL. *See* PARTY OF ARAB INDEPENDENCE.

AL-ITTIHAD AL-DIMUQRATI AL-FILASTINI. *See* PALESTINIAN DEMOCRATIC UNION.

AL-JABHA AL-DIMUQRATIYYA LIL-SALAM WAL-MUSAWA. *See* DEMOCRATIC FRONT FOR PEACE AND EQUALITY.

AL-JABHA AL-DIMUQRATIYYA LI-TAHRIR FILASTIN. *See* DEMOCRATIC FRONT FOR THE LIBERATION OF PALESTINE.

AL-JABHA AL-SHA'BIYYA LI-TAHRIR FILASTIN. *See* POPULAR FRONT FOR THE LIBERATION OF PALESTINE.

AL-JABHA AL-SHA'BIYYA LI-TAHRIR FILASTIN-'AMALIYYAT KHARAJIYYA. *See* POPULAR FRONT FOR THE LIBERATION OF PALESTINE–EXTERNAL OPERATIONS.

AL-JABHA AL-SHA'BIYYA LI-TAHRIR FILASTIN–AL-QIYADA AL-'AMMA. *See* POPULAR FRONT FOR THE LIBERATION OF PALESTINE–GENERAL COMMAND.

AL-JABHA AL-SHA'BIYYA AL-THAWRIYYA LI-TAHRIR FILASTIN. *See* POPULAR FRONT FOR THE LIBERATION OF PALESTINE.

AL-JABHA AL-WATANIYYA AL-DIMUQRATIYYA WAL-ISLAMIYYA. *See* NATIONAL DEMOCRATIC AND ISLAMIC FRONT.

AL-JABHA AL-WATANIYYA AL-FILASTINIYYA. *See* PALESTINE NATIONAL FRONT.

JABHAT AL-INQADH AL-WATANI AL-FILASTINIYYA. *See* PALESTINIAN NATIONAL SALVATION FRONT.

JABHAT AL-NIDAL AL-SHA'BI AL-FILASTINI. *See* PALESTINIAN POPULAR STRUGGLE FRONT.

JABHAT AL-QUWA AL-FILASTINIYYA AL-RAFIDA LI'L-HULUL AL-ISTISLAMIYYA. *See* REJECTION FRONT.

JABHAT AL-TAHRIR AL-'ARABIYYA. *See* ARAB LIBERATION FRONT.

JABHAT AL-TAHRIR AL-FILASTINIYYA. *See* PALESTINE LIBERATION FRONT.

JAMA'AT AL-IKHWAN AL-MUSLIMIN. *See* MUSLIM BROTHERHOOD.

AL-JAM'IYYA AL-FILASTINIYYA. *See* PALESTINIAN SOCIETY.

AL-JAM'IYYA AL-ISLAMIYYA AL-MASIHIYYA. *See* MUSLIM-CHRISTIAN ASSOCIATION.

JAM'IYYAT AL-IKHA WA AL-'AFAF. *See* ASSOCIATION OF BROTHERHOOD AND PURITY.

JAM'IYYAT SHABAB FILASTIN. *See* SOCIETY OF PALESTINIAN YOUTH.

JAM'IYYAT AL-SHUBAN AL-MUSLIMIN. *See* YOUNG MEN'S MUSLIM ASSOCIATION.

JAYSH AL-TAHRIR AL-FILASTINI. *See* PALESTINE LIBERATION ARMY.

JCP. *See* JORDANIAN COMMUNIST PARTY.

AL-JIHAD AL-ISLAMI. *See* ISLAMIC JIHAD.

JORDANIAN COMMUNIST PARTY (JCP) (*Al-Hizb al-Shuyu'i al-Urdunni*). The JCP traces its roots to the Palestine Communist Party (PCP)* (see also Communist Party of Israel). The Jewish-Arab PCP membership split in the early 1940s over the question of Zionism. In the fall of 1943, Arab communists split from the party and formed the National Liberation League ('Usbat al-Tahrir al-Watani). After the partition of Palestine in the wake of the 1947–49 war, League members who found themselves in the West Bank began organizing to oppose Jordanian annexation of the territory. Annexation took place in 1950, and the militants now found themselves operating within the Jordanian political arena (those who remained in what became Israel formed the Communist Party of Israel).

In 1950 a split occurred within the movement when activist Radwan al-Hilu pushed for greater proletarianization of the largely intellectual party. He was opposed by Fu'ad Nassar, who argued that the party's intellectual orientation fit the West Bank social fabric, which contained virtually no working class. The Nassar faction was victorious, and in June 1951, the League changed its name to the Jordanian Communist Party (see also chapter on Jordan).

The JCP grew in influence throughout the West Bank and the East Bank of Jordan itself during the 1950s despite government crackdowns in 1953 and 1958. It was associated with Sulayman al-Nabulsi and the National Front in the October 1956 elections, sending three members to the parliament—more than any other party.

Over the years, Palestinian communists both inside the occupied territories and in exile began focusing on their unique Palestinian identity and problems rather than on political events within Jordan as a whole. Over the JCP's objections, militants in the West Bank eventually formed their own party, the Palestine Communist Party. The rump JCP continued to function in Jordan as an important opposition force.

AL-KUTLA AL-WATANIYYA. *See* NATIONAL BLOC.

AL-LAJNA AL-'ARABIYYA AL-'ULIYA LI-FILASTIN. *See* ARAB HIGHER COMMITTEE.

AL-LAJNA LIL-DIFA' 'AN AL-ARADI AL-'ARABIYYA. *See* COMMITTEE FOR THE DEFENSE OF ARAB LANDS.

AL-LAJNA AL-QUTRIYYA LI-RUASA AL-MAJALIS AL-MAHALIYYA

AL-'ARABIYYA. *See* NATIONAL COMMITTEE OF HEADS OF ARAB LOCAL COUNCILS.

AL-LAJNA AL-TANFIDHIYYA LIL-MUTAMAR AL-'ARABI AL-FILASTINI. *See* ARAB EXECUTIVE.

LAJNAT AL-MUTABI'A LIL-SHU'UN AL-'AMMA LI-'ARAB ISRA'IL. *See* FOLLOW UP COMMITTEE ON THE GENERAL CONCERNS OF THE ARABS OF ISRAEL.

LAJNAT AL-TAWJIH AL-WATANI. *See* NATIONAL GUIDANCE COMMITTEE.

THE LAND. *See* AL-ARD.

LIBERAL PARTY (*Hizb al-Ahrar, Party of the Liberals*). Established in late 1927 by prominent residents of Jaffa and Gaza, the Liberal Party emerged as a new voice on the increasingly polarized Palestinian political scene. The party criticized the rivalry between the Husayni and Nashashibi families of Jerusalem. It advocated a program of Palestinian independence and social reforms but felt that Zionism was a reality with which the Palestinians had to deal. Never an active party, it died out after 1931.

LITERARY SOCIETY (*Al-Muntada al-Adabi*). The Literary Society, an anti-Zionist association of younger members of the Palestinian urban elite, was established in November 1918. It had originally surfaced in Istanbul in 1909 as a club for Arabs in the Ottoman capital. Chapters were established in several Palestinian towns after 1918. The Jerusalem branch was the most significant, where its leadership was dominated by members of the influential al-Nashashibi family.

AL-MAJLIS AL-A'LA LIL-TAWJIH AL-WATANI. *See* HIGHER COMMITTEE FOR NATIONAL GUIDANCE.

AL-MAJLIS AL-ISLAMI AL-A'LA. *See* SUPREME MUSLIM COUNCIL I, II.

MAKI. *See* COMMUNIST PARTY OF ISRAEL.

MIFLAGA KOMUNISTIT YISRAELIT. *See* COMMUNIST PARTY OF ISRAEL.

MOVEMENT OF ARAB NATIONALISTS (MAN) (*Harakat al-Qawmiyyin al-'Arab*). The MAN was an important political movement established in Beirut in 1948 to further armed resistance against Israeli rule in Palestine. Its initially vague ideology soon shifted toward the pan-Arab nationalism espoused by Gamal Abdel Nasser, whom the movement idolized.

The MAN was not a specifically Palestinian movement, despite the fact that many young, educated Palestinians flocked to it, both in the occupied territories and in exile. Following the pan-Arab climate of the time, the MAN viewed the solution to the Palestinian problem as part and parcel of wider Arab liberation from colonial and neo-imperialist rule. Palestinian "regionalist" thought was condemned.

The MAN competed with the Ba'th Party* and the communists for followers, and its fortunes were often dependent upon Nasser's popularity and success. Nasser and the pan-Arab movement shifted positions in the mid-1960s by allowing Palestinians to maintain organizations that focused on their own regionalist concerns. In 1964, for instance, Nasser and the Arab League decided to sponsor the Palestine Liberation Organization* to allow Palestinians a forum in which to voice their own specific agenda. Palestinians in the MAN, such as George Habash, also formed their own mini-movements within the MAN to deal with uniquely Palestinian issues. These eventually merged with several other organizations to form the Popular Front for the Liberation of Palestine* in 1967–68, through which the pan-Arab legacy of the MAN continues to affect the Palestinian national liberation movement in many ways.

MUNAZZIMAT FILASTIN AL-'ARABIYYA. *See* ORGANIZATION OF ARAB PALESTINE.

MUNAZZIMAT AL-TAHRIR AL-FILASTINIYYA. *See* PALESTINE LIBERATION ORGANIZATION.

AL-MUNTADA AL-ADABI. *See* LITERARY SOCIETY.

MUSLIM BROTHERHOOD (*Jama'at al-Ikhwan al-Muslimin, Association of the Muslim Brotherhood*). The Muslim Brotherhood organization that emerged in Palestine was closely connected with the mother organization founded in Egypt in 1928 by Hasan al-Banna (see chapter on Egypt). The Brotherhood, one of the first mass-based Islamic sociopolitical reform movements in the Arab world in this century, has exerted tremendous influence wherever it has been organized, including among Palestinians.

The Muslim Brotherhood was first established in Palestine in Jerusalem in May 1946. That same year, branches were set up in Jaffa, Lydda, Haifa, Nablus, and Tulkarm. Members of the Egyptian organization serving with the Egyptian expeditionary forces in southern Palestine in 1948 were instrumental in setting up a branch in Hebron in 1948. When the creation of Israel in 1948 left a divided Palestine, the Brotherhood flourished in the West Bank where Jordanian authorities allowed it to exist openly despite the 1957 ban on all other political organizations (see chapter on Jordan). It operated underground in Egyptian-occupied Gaza, which emerged as the center of Muslim Brotherhood activity following the Israeli occupation of the West Bank and Gaza in 1967. By the early 1980s, it had developed its base at the Islamic University of Gaza and increasingly clashed with secular nationalists from the Palestine Liberation Organization (PLO)* over ideological questions. Its most influential leader has been Shaykh Ahmad Yasin of Gaza, who was imprisoned for life by Israeli authorities in 1991.

While the parent organization was active in the anti-British guerrilla movement in Egypt in the 1940s, the Brotherhood's program in the Israeli-occupied territories since 1967 centered around social and economic reform through a return to "authentic" Islamic values and living rather than overt military struggle. The Brotherhood preached that human liberation flows from pious Islamic living. Its policy on national liberation for the Palestinians derives from this viewpoint; the Palestinians will achieve liberation through Islamic action, which can occur only after the Islamicization of Palestinian society.

The Brotherhood's ideology has long collided with that of secular nationalists and communists in the occupied territories. In January 1980, Islamic militants attacked the office of the Palestine Red Crescent Society, a PLO-affiliated organization. The Brotherhood did not initially take part in the anti-Israeli uprising known as the *Intifada,* which broke out in December 1987, although other Islamic militants did. The popular support won by the uprising in the occupied territories prompted a revision of the Brotherhood's traditional reluctance to engage in overt resistance activities and work alongside the secular nationalists. In August 1988, the Brotherhood established a resistance wing, Hamas,* to coordinate with other groups in more forcefully combating Israeli occupation.

MUSLIM-CHRISTIAN ASSOCIATION (*Al-Jam'iyya al-Islamiyya al-Masihiyya*). The Muslim-Christian Association, a forerunner of Palestinian political organizations, was first formed in Jaffa in November 1918. It appeared in Jerusalem and other Palestinian cities shortly thereafter. By late 1919, it claimed some two hundred adherents, mostly members of the older generation of the Ottomanized urban elite. While not overtly a political organization, the Muslim-Christian Association stressed biconfessional unity in the face of Zionism and Palestinian self-determination. Reticent to criticize British rule directly, it even received encouragement from some British sources in Palestine.

MUTAMAR AL-SHABAB. *See* YOUTH CONGRESS.

AL-NADI AL-'ARABI. *See* ARAB CLUB.

NATIONAL ALLIANCE (*Al-Tahaluf al-Qawmi*). The National Alliance was a grouping of Palestinian resistance movements based in Syria that opposed Yasir Arafat's leadership of the Palestine Liberation Organization (PLO).* The alliance was established in 1984 in the wake of the intra-PLO crisis prompted by the military defeat of Fatah* forces in northern Lebanon by the Syrian-backed dissidents of the Fatah-Uprising,* a process that led to criticism of Arafat's leadership and calls for reform from other groups as well.

Groups such as the Popular Front for the Liberation of Palestine (PFLP)* and the Democratic Front for the Liberation of Palestine (DFLP),* which sought reform but stressed the unity of the PLO, formed the Democratic Alliance,* a type of "loyal opposition." The National Alliance, however, comprising Fatah-Uprising, the PFLP–GC,* al-Sa'iqa,* and the Palestinian Popular Struggle Front (PPSF),* rejected the Democratic Alliance's 1984 call for a re-formation of the Palestine National Front* to press for reforms within the PLO, seeking support instead for a tougher, anti-Arafat program. The National Alliance found support in Syria, then strongly opposed to Arafat. The National Alliance was transformed into the Palestinian National Salvation Front (PNSF)* in March 1985.

NATIONAL BLOC (Al-Kutla al-Wataniyya). The National Bloc was one of the minor parties established in Palestine during the 1930s. Founded in 1935 by 'Abd al-Latif Salah, a notable from Nablus, the party shifted back and forth between support for the Nashashibi and Husayni families and their respective political parties (see National Defense Party and Palestine Arab Party). The party had only a limited following, even within Nablus.

NATIONAL COMMITTEE OF HEADS OF ARAB LOCAL COUNCILS (Al-Lajna al-Qutriyya Li-Ruasa al-Majalis al-Mahaliyya al-'Arabiyya). The National Committee was formed in 1975 by Palestinian mayors in Israel to push for equal government funding of Arab town and village councils, which received lower budgets from the central government than comparably sized Jewish communities.

In the late 1980s, the National Committee began to emerge as one of the most important Palestinian political voices in Israel. The committee has successfully articulated Arab concerns over discrimination against them as non-Jewish citizens of Israel and as such has linked nationalist questions with local economic issues. In May 1987, the National Committee called for a one-day strike in the Arab sector to protest the underfunding of the councils. The strike was widely supported among Arab villages. A similar strike was carried out in September 1987 to push for improved conditions in Arab schools. In 1991 it was headed by Zaydan Muhammad of the village of Kufr Manda.

NATIONAL DEFENSE PARTY (Hizb al-Difa' al-Watani). The National Defense Party was formed in 1934 by the powerful al-Nashashibi family of Jerusalem as the most important element in the "opposition" movement challenging the Husayni family's leadership of the Palestinian national movement after the collapse of the Arab Executive* in 1934.

Friction between the two families and their supporters, which had been mounting since the 1920s, extended beyond family rivalry to embrace conflicting views on the best strategy for combating British-supported Zionism in Palestine. The National Defense Party and its antecedents, such as the Palestinian Arab National Party,* were anti-Zionist but advocated dealing with the British. The Husaynis pushed for a more militant, noncooperative approach. The National Defense Party was also on friendly terms with Amir 'Abdullah, the ruler of Transjordan, who openly courted Palestinian opinion and proposed that Palestine be annexed by Transjordan and ruled by himself. The leading figure in the National Defense Party was Raghib al-Nashashibi.

As the 1936–39 Palestinian uprising petered out, a wave of assassinations erupted in which some supporters of the Nashashibis were murdered by agents of their rivals. Several prominent members of the family fled into exile.

NATIONAL DEMOCRATIC AND ISLAMIC FRONT (Al-Jabha al-Wataniyya al-Dimuqratiyya Wal-Islamiyya). In September 1992, ten Palestinian groups opposed to the Palestinian-Israeli negotiations, which began with the 1991 Madrid peace conference, formed an alliance based in Damascus. The groups—the Popular Front for the Liberation of Palestine (PFLP),* Democratic Front for the Liberation of Palestine (DFLP),* PFLP–General Command,* Palestinian Popular Struggle Front,* Palestine Liberation Front,* Fatah-Uprising,* Palestinian Revolutionary Communist Party,* al-Sa'iqa,* Hamas,* and Islamic Jihad*—were known as the "Damascus Ten" and included groups from both within and outside the PLO.

The "Damascus Ten" thus inherited the role of Syrian-backed opposition to the policies pursued by Palestine Liberation Organization (PLO) Chairman Yasir Arafat, which had formerly been expressed by groups such as the PFLP, DFLP, and the Palestinian National Salvation Front.* The emergence of this group indicated the growing scope and intensity of anti-Arafat and anti-negotiation sentiment. Not only had a large number of groups come together, but they also included groups that had not been linked traditionally to Syria, such as Hamas and Islamic Jihad. The Ten also represented a significant degree of cooperation between committed secularists and Islamists.

The influence of the Ten extended to the occupied territories as well. Protest strikes against the peace process, called by the group, were reportedly observed in refugee camps in the territories. Representatives of the Ten also met with Iranian officials in Iran and discussed their mutual opposition to the negotiations.

In the wake of the agreement signed by Israel and the PLO in 1993, the DFLP was instrumental in prompting the group of ten to rename itself the National Democratic and Islamic Front. Formation of the Front, combined with significant divisions within Arafat's own Fatah* movement arising from the agreement, reflected the serious crisis that gripped the Palestinian nationalist movement as it wrestled with the impact of the agreement, the secret manner in which it was negotiated, and Arafat's heavy-handedness in trying to implement it.

NATIONAL GUIDANCE COMMITTEE (NGC) (Lajnat al-Tawjih al-Watani). The NGC was a group of nationalists active in the West Bank coordinating the anti-Israeli nationalist struggle. Unlike the earlier Palestine National Front,* the

NGC was composed of representatives of local corporate and geographical interests, not merely representatives of political groups in exile; therefore, although it bore allegiance to the Palestine Liberation Organization (PLO),* it was also attuned to local concerns.

The NGC was established in November 1978 in the wake of the Camp David Accords, which were bitterly opposed by most Palestinians for failing to address their nationalist demands. It was also established at a time when the nationalist movement within the occupied territories was assuming a more important place within overall Palestinian politics.

The NGC suffered from friction among competing groups beginning in 1980, but it was an Israeli crackdown that finally led to its dissolution in March 1982.

NATIONAL LIBERATION LEAGUE. *See* COMMUNIST PARTY OF ISRAEL, JORDANIAN COMMUNIST PARTY, and PALESTINE COMMUNIST PARTY.

NATIONAL PARTY. *See* PALESTINIAN ARAB NATIONAL PARTY.

NEW COMMUNIST LIST (*Reshima Komunistit Hadasha, Rakah*). Rakah, an acronym for the New Communist List, is an overwhelmingly Arab communist party in Israel that traditionally has garnered the largest number of Arab votes of any non-Zionist party in Israeli elections since 1965.

By 1965 the Communist Party of Israel,* or Maki, was rent with ideological disputes centering around the Arab-Israeli dispute. Arab members wholeheartedly supported the Arab regimes and Gamal Abdel Nasser in particular, whom they viewed as a leader in the anti-imperialist struggle in the Arab world. Jewish communists were more critical of the support extended by Arab communists to anti-communist leaders such as Nasser. The pro-Arab orientation of the Soviet Union also affected the debate.

In August 1965, the party split, with Arab members (and some Jews) leaving Maki to form the New Communist List, or Rakah. The Soviet Union threw its support behind Rakah rather than Maki. While Rakah's chairman, Meir Vilner, is Jewish, the rest of the party's leadership and its rank and file are Arab. Other important leaders have included Tawfiq Tubi, Emile Habibi, and Emile Tuma. The level of overall support for Rakah's positions among the Palestinian citizens of Israel was reflected in the November 1965 elections, when Rakah won three seats in the Knesset to Maki's one. In December 1975, Rakah candidate Tawfiq Zayyad was elected mayor of Nazareth, Israel's largest Arab city, as part of a front called the Nazareth Democratic Front. Since 1977, Rakah has functioned as part of a nationwide alliance called the Democratic Front for Peace and Equality.*

NGC. *See* NATIONAL GUIDANCE COMMITTEE.

OAP. *See* ORGANIZATION OF ARAB PALESTINE.

ORGANIZATION OF ARAB PALESTINE (OAP) (*Munazzimat Filastin al-'Arabiyya*). The OAP, a small commando organization, was established in the fall of 1968 by Ahmad Za'rur. Za'rur, who had been a member of the Popular Front for the Liberation of Palestine (PFLP),* left the group along with Ahmad Jibril when ideological quarrels tore it apart in 1968. Together they established PFLP–General Command,* although Za'rur soon broke with Jibril and established his own group, called the PFLP–General Command (B). He later changed the name to the OAP. Many OAP members were absorbed by Fatah,* and the OAP eventually ceased to exist.

PALESTINE ARAB PARTY (*Al-Hizb al-'Arabi al-Filastini*). The Palestine Arab Party was established in 1934 by the powerful al-Husayni family of Jerusalem in the wake of the collapse of the Arab Executive* that same year.

The Palestine Arab Party advocated a policy of noncooperation with British authorities in pursuit of the twin goals of curbing the Zionist movement and pushing for Palestinian independence. Although the leader of the party was Jamal al-Husayni, its spiritual leader was his cousin, Hajj Amin al-Husayni. Amin al-Husayni was the mufti of Jerusalem (a title of respect, referring to his status as chief Islamic jurist), the leader of the Supreme Muslim Council I,* and the most powerful figure in Palestinian politics, a man who did not suffer rivals lightly. He fled into exile after the British broke up the leadership of the Arab Higher Committee* in 1937.

PALESTINE COMMUNIST PARTY (PCP) (*Al-Hizb al-Shuyu'i al-Filastini*). The PCP has seen a long and turbulent history. It was formed approximately in 1919 by Marxist Jews who had immigrated to Palestine from Eastern Europe. Arab members were brought into the party, and the PCP soon came to support Palestinian nationalism, even in its violent, anti-Zionist aspects. This policy led to the party's estrangement from Jewish leftists who were influenced by Zionist socialist parties committed to the establishment of a Jewish state.

By the early 1940s, the party had disintegrated over Jewish-Arab disagreements about Zionism and the future of the country. Arab activists broke from the party and formed the National Liberation League ('Usbat al-Tahrir al-Watani) in the fall of 1943. Following the 1947–49 war, league activists who found themselves in the West Bank formed the Jordanian Communist Party (JCP)* in 1950 while those in Israel joined forces once again with Jewish members and created the Communist Party of Israel* in 1948. Thus the PCP ceased to exist and was replaced by two different communist organizations.

After the Israeli occupation of the West Bank and Gaza in 1967, Palestinian members of the Jordanian Communist Party in the West Bank shifted their focus away from Jordanian politics toward their own pressing problems as Palestinians living under Israeli occupation. They eventually formed their own branch of the JCP in 1975 called the Palestinian Communist Organization (PCO), over objections from the JCP. In February 1982, the PCO made a complete break with the JCP and formed the Palestine Communist Party, adopting the name of the pre-1948 party. Eventually, the PCO in Lebanon joined the new party as well.

The (new) Palestine Communist Party remains active in the occupied territories. It was a driving force behind the formation of the Palestine National Front* in 1973 and has been a member of the Unified National Command of the Uprising,* which coordinated nationalist activities during the *Intifada*. Its rivalry with Islamic militants in Gaza grew heated in 1991.

Party militants in Lebanon were divided over whether the party should take up arms. The debate concerned not only the party's role in the Palestinian national movement but also its position in Lebanon, which was locked in a bitter civil war beginning in 1975.

The PCP supports the Palestine Liberation Organization (PLO)* and its goal of establishing a Palestinian state in the occupied territories. It became an important member of the "loyal opposition" to PLO chairman Yasir Arafat, however, and joined the reformist Democratic Alliance,* which was established in 1984. In April 1987, it joined the PLO Executive Committee for the first time when its leader, Sulayman al-Najjab, was given a seat on that body. In the wake of communism's collapse in the Soviet Union and the Eastern Bloc, the PCP changed its name to the Palestinian People's Party (Hizb al-Sha'b al-Filastini). The Palestinian People's Party supported the 1993 agreement between Israel and the PLO, but it also called for reforms within the PLO and urged the PLO to enter into serious discussion with factions opposed to the agreement.

PALESTINE LIBERATION ARMY (PLA) (*Jaysh al-Tahrir al-Filastini*). The PLA is not a political group but the regular armed forces of the Palestine Liberation Organization (PLO).* However, it has at times played a political role within the Palestinian community.

Created in 1964 to serve as a Palestinian army in exile, it comprised Palestinians trained by host Arab armies and serving in regular military formations. While the PLA has been theoretically under PLO command, it has in fact been under the control of the Arab countries in which its units have been posted. The 'Ayn Jalut brigade has operated under Egyptian authority; the Hittin brigade and, after the early 1970s, the Qadasiya brigade, have come under Syrian control (the Qadasiya brigade was originally controlled by Iraq). The Badr Forces have been stationed in Jordan since 1982 when they were evacuated from Lebanon.

While theoretically nonpolitical, the PLA was initially hostile to the commandos. It established its own commando forces, the Popular Liberation Forces (Quwwat al-Tahrir al-Sha'biyya), to compete with them and later rebelled against PLO authority when the guerrillas took over the PLO in 1969.

But the most serious PLA–PLO friction has resulted from the Arab states' control over PLA units on their soil. Syria ordered elements of the PLA stationed there to attack PLO fighters in Lebanon in 1976 during the Syrian intervention in the Lebanese civil war, although many fighters defected to the PLO. In October 1983, the PLA commander, Tariq Khudra, cast his lot with the growing anti-Arafat movement within the Palestinian resistance movement by issuing a statement from Damascus urging Arafat's ouster as chairman of the PLO.

According to the 1993 agreement between Israel and the PLO, a Palestinian police force was to be deployed in the territories after the withdrawal of Israeli troops. Certain PLA troops stationed in Egypt and Jordan received training in police work in the fall of 1993 to prepare them for service as the nucleus of a Palestinian police force in the territories.

PALESTINE LIBERATION FRONT (PLF) (*Jabhat al-Tahrir al-Filastiniyya*). The Palestine Liberation Front, a Palestine Liberation Organization (PLO)* commando group, split from the Popular Front for the Liberation of Palestine–General Command (PFLP–GC).* Its first leader, Muhammad Abu-l-'Abbas, tried to take over the PFLP–GC in 1976 because he disagreed with the PFLP–GC's support for Syrian intervention against PLO forces in Lebanon in 1976. He failed and left to form his own group in 1977 (which is not to be confused with a group by the same name that helped to form the PFLP).*

In 1983 Abu-l-'Abbas signaled his shift away from Syria and toward Yasir Arafat and the mainstream PLO by moving the PLF's headquarters from Damascus to Tunis, site of the PLO's headquarters, leaving another faction behind in Syria. This faction itself split the following year, with 'Abd al-Fattah Ghanim throwing his support to Iraq, while the Tal'at Ya'qub faction remained in Damascus. Ya'qub and Abu-l-'Abbas were reconciled in July 1987.

Abu-l-'Abbas was the subject of intense international scorn for the PLF's 1985 hijacking of the Italian cruise ship *Achille Lauro* during which an American Jewish passenger was murdered. Abu-l-'Abbas was again in the public eye when Israeli authorities foiled an attempted seaborne PFL raid near Tel Aviv in May 1990. The attack led to a suspension of the U.S.–PLO dialogue begun in December 1988 (see PLO) after the United States charged that, by failing to discipline Abu-l-'Abbas, the PLO was wavering in its prior pledge to renounce terrorism.

Abu-l-'-Abbas resigned from the PLO Executive Committee during the September 1991 meeting of the Palestine National Council in Algiers, although the PLF as an organization retained its seat on the committee.

As one of the "Damascus Ten" groups opposed to the Israeli-Palestinian negotiations that began at the 1991 Madrid peace conference, the PLF denounced the 1993 agreement between Israel and the PLO and joined the National Democratic and Islamic Front.*

PALESTINE LIBERATION ORGANIZATION (PLO) (*Munazzimat al-Tahrir al-Filastiniyya*). The PLO, an umbrella organization that encompasses a number of commando groups, social welfare organizations, unions, and independents, has guided most aspects of Palestinian social and political life and has served essentially as a government in exile. It undoubtedly represents the most significant manifestation of Palestinian political mobilization since the end of Ottoman rule.

The PLO was established by the first summit of Arab leaders held in Cairo in

1964 to serve as a specific Palestinian voice within the broader Egyptian-led pan-Arab nationalist movement. Ahmad Shuqayri was selected as its first chairman, and its headquarters were set up in Cairo. Its first national conference, held in East Jerusalem in May 1964, formulated the organization's constitution, the Palestinian National Charter. A military force, the Palestine Liberation Army (PLA),* and a parliament, the Palestine National Council (PNC), were also established.

Rising independent political-commando groups, such as Yasir Arafat's Fatah* movement, were critical of the PLO during the mid to late 1960s, dismissing its leaders as bombastic "armchair revolutionaries" dominated by Gamal Abdel Nasser. The defeat of 1967, coming in contrast to the fierce rhetoric uttered by Shuqayri over the Voice of Palestine radio before the war, symbolized to the commandos the bankruptcy of the PLO's policy of waiting for pan-Arab military support to liberate Palestine. As commando raids against Israel increased after 1967, Palestinians (and the entire Arab world) came to see the commandos as dashing young heroes who were continuing the armed struggle against Israel in the face of hopeless odds while the Arab states sat by helplessly.

Riding the crest of popular Arab opinion, the commando groups successfully pressured the PLO to dismiss Shuqayri and assign them positions in the PLO leadership in 1968. In February 1969, Arafat was elected chairman of the PLO, replacing Yahya Hammuda. The PLO was then transformed into an activist coordinating committee for all aspects of the Palestinians' national liberation struggle and consolidated its influence over all aspects of Palestinian life. The PLO established unions, professional organizations, medical services, orphans' and widows' charities, and rehabilitation clinics, in addition to persevering in its strategy of armed struggle. All this was made possible through subsidies from Arab states, assistance from the communist bloc, a tax collected by Arab Gulf states from the wages of expatriate Palestinian workers there, and the PLO's own business activities.

The Arab states were far from happy about this turn of events, however. Recovering from the disastrous 1967 defeat and suffering from coups and political instability, the Arab regimes did not relish the prospect of PLO raids against Israel, which might prompt a new round of fighting. Even more threatening to Lebanon and especially Jordan was the growing armed PLO presence in the refugee camps. PLO raids drew Israeli counterstrikes which created havoc, and the thousands of armed Palestinians began creating what were, in effect, states-within-states within those two countries.

The tension led to armed conflict. Fighting broke out between the PLO and the Lebanese army in 1969, leading to the signing of the Cairo Accords, which allowed the PLO to operate in Palestinian areas, especially around Beirut and in the south of the country. But the situation was different in Jordan. The growing numbers of PLO fighters, combined with arrogant behavior and the Marxist commando groups' talk of overthrowing the regime of Jordan's King Husayn, drew the Palestinians into increased strife with the Jordanian army. On September 6, 1970, commandos of the Popular Front for the Liberation of Palestine (PFLP)* hijacked three international commercial airliners and flew two of them to Jordan. After evacuating the passengers six days later under the glare of international media attention, they destroyed the aircraft as the Jordanian authorities watched helplessly. The embarrassment of this infringement on Jordanian sovereignty drove King Husayn to order his army to attack the PLO. On September 17, full-scale fighting erupted. The fighting was halted ten days later by a truce brokered in Cairo by the other Arab states, but not until many civilians had died. Palestinians remembered the bloodshed as "Black September." Subsequent Jordanian attacks in July 1971 drove the PLO completely out of Jordan. New headquarters were set up in Beirut.

The defeat in Jordan led to numerous changes within the PLO. Most important, it sobered the organization. The PLO changed its strategy from one of simple liberation and the creation of an Arab Palestinian state to espousing the establishment of a secular, democratic state in Palestine/Israel after liberation. In 1974 the PLO decided to shift away from the secular state strategy and announced that a Palestinian political entity would be established in any portion of the homeland that could be liberated—meaning that it now favored creation of a Palestinian state in the occupied territories, the only areas ever likely to be evacuated by Israel. This decision to support a two-state solution (Israel and Palestine) created much dissension within the movement. The PFLP, the traditional leader of dissent, joined the Democratic Front for the Liberation of Palestine (DFLP),* the PFLP–GC,* and the Arab Liberation Front (ALF)* in forming the Iraqi-backed Rejection Front* in 1974, which opposed conceding the goal of total liberation.

The same year also witnessed two momentous diplomatic victories for the PLO. In October 1974, the Arab League voted to recognize the PLO as the "sole, legitimate representative of the Palestinian people," a major diplomatic triumph for the PLO within the Arab world just three years after its defeat in Jordan. In November, Arafat was invited to address the UN General Assembly, which voted to grant the PLO observer status. The PLO had now garnered international support for its espousal of Palestinian rights as well.

The PLO changed in other ways during the mid-1970s. Spectacular acts of terrorism subsided amidst Palestinian criticism of their detrimental effect on world opinion. The PLO also struggled to learn from the experience of 1970 and avoid interference with Arab regimes. But one area proved too difficult for the PLO: Lebanon. The political and communal strife that shook Lebanon in the mid-1970s soon sucked the PLO into the civil war, which broke out in April 1975. Leftist Palestinian groups joined the fray immediately. In January 1976, Fatah forces (the majority of PLO forces in Lebanon) also joined a coalition of "leftist" (often Muslim and Druze) militias battling "right-wing" Christian forces. The PLO–leftist forces were on the verge of victory in the spring of 1976 when Syria intervened to stop the war, battling the PLO and forcibly lifting its siege of Christian positions. For the second time in six years, the PLO had suffered a serious military setback at the hands of an Arab state, and Syrian–PLO relations entered a cold war that would endure for years.

The PLO suffered a serious diplomatic setback in 1977 when Egyptian president Anwar al-Sadat flew to Israel and initiated a peace process that culminated in the 1979 Egyptian-Israeli peace treaty. The PLO joined with such Arab states as Syria and Iraq in opposing the Egyptian move, which removed the Arab world's most powerful army from confrontation without winning any significant Israeli concessions to the Palestinians.

With military pressure greatly reduced after the peace treaty with Egypt, Israel invaded Lebanon in June 1982 and attacked PLO forces and the organization's headquarters there. Forced to evacuate from Beirut after nearly three months of siege, intense bombardment, and high Palestinian and Lebanese civilian casualties, the PLO moved its headquarters to Tunisia and dispersed its forces throughout the Arab world. In 1983 a dispute within Arafat's own Fatah movement over the group's role in the fighting (see Fatah-Uprising) led to a full-scale Fatah civil war in which the Syrian-backed dissidents forced the withdrawal of pro-Arafat loyalists in Tripoli, northern Lebanon, that December. The mutiny prompted other groups, such as the influential PFLP and the DFLP, to escalate their own perennial complaints about Arafat's leadership and to press for serious reform measures within the movement. The PLO-wide rebellion was contained and unity prevailed, although a coalition of anti-Arafat groups, the Palestinian National Salvation Front (PNSF),* was established in March 1985 with Syrian support, and groups such as Fatah–Revolutionary Council* stepped up their attacks on PLO targets.

As the prospects of armed liberation faded, the PLO intensified its diplomatic campaign on behalf of the establishment of an independent Palestinian state in the West Bank and Gaza. With Iraq tied down in a bloody war with Iran and with Syrian–PLO relations at their nadir, Arafat turned to Egypt in 1983, by then an important U.S. ally. The PLO also recognized the important role Jordan would play in any diplomatic solution, and entered a period of dialogue with Jordan on joint diplomatic moves that culminated in a February 1985 agreement to create a Palestinian-Jordanian confederation in the occupied territories in the event of an Israeli withdrawal. In July 1988, Jordan's King Husayn declared that Jordan was renouncing its claims to sovereignty over the West Bank, thereby challenging the PLO to take the diplomatic initiative on behalf of its people living under Israeli occupation. On November 15, 1988, the Palestine National Council issued a "declaration of independence" for the "State of Palestine." It declared that an independent Palestinian state existed in the West Bank and Gaza, and furthermore it accepted UN Security Council Resolution 242. The resolution, issued in 1967, called for the return of territories seized in 1967, but it had long been rejected by Palestinians because it implicitly recognized Israel and failed to discuss Palestinian national rights. Arafat was eventually given the title of president of Palestine, and PLO offices were converted into full-fledged embassies in several countries. But while the new "state" was recognized by many nations, the overall political climate in the Middle East did not change.

Despite overwhelming international support and UN backing for its cause, the PLO's diplomatic efforts failed in one major respect: The United States, the major actor capable of bringing the Arab-Israeli conflict to a negotiated settlement, refused to include the PLO in any proposed peace talks. Deferring to its Israeli ally, the United States dismissed the PLO as a "terrorist" organization and established a list of criteria to which the PLO must adhere before the United States would consider formally dealing with the organization, including a renunciation of terrorism and the recognition of Israel. Following an address delivered by Arafat to the UN General Assembly in Geneva in December 1988, the United States declared that the PLO had met these criteria and opened a limited dialogue through the American ambassador to Tunisia. Following months of fruitless talks and accusations that the PLO continued to sanction terrorist activities, U.S. president George Bush suspended the dialogue in the wake of an aborted May 1990 raid against Israel by the Palestine Liberation Front (PLF).*

Even more than the PLO's diplomatic moves, the uprising in the occupied territories known as the *Intifada*, which broke out on December 9, 1987, shifted international attention to Israel's continued occupation of the West Bank and Gaza and the Palestinians' demands for an independent state. The casualties resulting from Israeli security forces' stringent attempts to halt the protests (nearly 1,000 dead by early 1992) generated considerable sympathy for the Palestinians. The PLO worked with *Intifada* militants in the occupied territories in guiding the uprising through the Unified National Command of the Uprising (UNCU).* But international support declined precipitously following PLO and popular Palestinian support for Iraq in the 1991 Gulf War, as did the financial support formerly received by the PLO from the Arab Gulf states, which bitterly resented Arafat's embrace of Iraqi president Saddam Husayn. Israeli repression—including shootings, arrests, and the mass deportation of 415 Palestinians in December 1992 on grounds that they were linked to such Islamic resistance groups as Hamas*—also had a significant impact on the *Intifada*. The uprising increasingly took the form of sporadic armed attacks by youthful militants. The *Intifada* also allowed Islamic groups like Hamas and Islamic Jihad* to gain considerable support among Palestinians, sometimes at the expense of the PLO.

The PLO suffered another serious political blow in July 1991 when the Syrian-backed central government of Lebanon deployed its army in Sidon and Tyre in southern Lebanon and routed PLO troops stationed there. Furthermore, the collapse of communism in Eastern Europe and the Soviet Union led to a drying up of the traditional diplomatic and military support extended by those countries.

With practically no significant diplomatic support, the PLO debated whether to authorize Palestinian participation in the peace negotiations set up by the United States and the Soviet Union in 1991. Israel, Egypt, Jordan, Saudi Arabia, Lebanon, and, after decades of confrontation, even Syria, decided to attend. But Israel, backed by the United States, refused to participate if any Palestinians affiliated with the PLO attended the conference. The September 1991 PNC meeting in Algiers voted to recommend sending Palestinian independents to the conference as part of a joint Jordanian-Palestinian delegation, although the PFLP, the Hawatmeh wing of the DFLP, and Islamic groups such as Hamas* sharply criticized the move, and many Palestinians were skeptical of the entire process. They saw the negotiations as an attempt to marginalize the PLO and force significant concessions from the Palestinians with no guarantee of any tangible gains. The PLO subsequently approved a team of delegates who participated in the 1991 Madrid conference and subsequent negotiations and who remained in constant contact with the PLO during the talks despite the fact that Israel officially refused to deal with the PLO. (The delegates sat as part of a joint Jordanian-Palestinian negotiating team.)

The negotiations marked a major turning point in the PLO's history. They symbolized the organization's commitment to a negotiated settlement with Israel as well as the fruition of its long campaign to become a legitimate player in diplomatic solutions to the Arab-Israeli conflict (although it remained a behind-the-scenes player during the negotiations). The PLO was particularly anxious for a diplomatic breakthrough given that it was suffering from an unprecedented financial crisis as well as from serious internal criticism. The decision to participate in the negotiations had generated serious opposition from Palestinians who felt that the PLO was compromising on fundamental principles. Arafat's heavy-handed approach to his critics only exacerbated the mounting tensions. Ten factions opposed to the talks came together in Damascus in September 1992 to form the "Damascus Ten." The Ten—which included significant groups like the PFLP, DFLP, and Hamas—commanded a significant level of support both in exile and among Palestinians in the occupied territories.

In the late summer of 1993, details emerged of secret, direct talks between Israel and the PLO in Norway that were conducted outside the official negotiations. The revelations caught many by surprise given that the public peace process was still underway and that the PLO had informed neither the Palestinian negotiating team nor the other Arab participants. The secret talks produced an agreement that was publicly signed by the two sides in Washington in September 1993 that called for Palestinian self-rule and an eventual Israeli withdrawal from at least part of the occupied territories, with details on most major points to be worked out by the two sides. Arafat signed a statement recognizing Israel's right to exist and accepting UN Security Council Resolutions 242 and 338. And in a dramatic departure from precedent, the Israeli government formally recognized the PLO as the representative of the Palestinian people. Even the United States was obliged to change its hostile attitude toward the PLO, as evidenced by its decision to allow Arafat to attend the signing ceremony.

These dramatic events rocked the Palestinian national movement even further. The Unified National Command of the Uprising* in the territories was split over the question of whether or not the *Intifada* should now be halted. The Palestine Central Council approved the September agreement on October 11, 1993, but the influential PFLP and DFLP boycotted the meeting. The same meeting approved formation of a "Palestinian National Authority" in the territories with Arafat at its head. Units of the Palestine Liberation Army* also began training to serve as the nucleus of a new Palestinian police force in the territories. Opposition mounted, however, despite some initial popular support shown for the agreement in the territories. In October, the "Damascus Ten" renamed themselves the National Democratic and Islamic Front* and continued to push for serious restructuring of the PLO. Formation of the Front and serious divisions within Arafat's own Fatah movement, reflected the mounting crisis gripping the PLO in the fall of 1993 as it continued to discuss implementation of the September agreement with Israel.

The PNC, which consisted of 484 members as of its September 1991 meeting, serves as a type of parliament-in-exile for the Palestinian people and includes representatives from PLO factions as well as independents. Since the PNC meets infrequently, the Palestine Central Council undertakes policy decisions when the PNC is not in session. The Palestine Central Council was composed of 107 members at its October 1993 meeting. Implementation of policy is carried out by the PLO Executive Committee, which functions as a type of cabinet. Its members are elected by the PNC; in early 1992, eighteen members sat on the Executive Committee. The PNC also elects the PLO chairman, who, since 1969, has been Yasir Arafat of Fatah.

PALESTINE NATIONAL FRONT (PNF) (Al-Jabha al-Wataniyya al-Filastiniyya). The Palestine National Front was established in August 1973 to resist the Israeli occupation of the West Bank and Gaza. Communist militants were instrumental in its creation, although the PNF garnered broad backing, including support from Fatah,* Democratic Front for the Liberation of Palestine (DFLP),* and Ba'th Party* activists. The influential Popular Front for the Liberation of Palestine (PFLP)* refused to participate because the PNF urged the Palestine Liberation Organization (PLO)* to create a Palestinian state in the occupied territories, should they be liberated. The PFLP contended that this contradicted the strategy of total liberation. Although the PLO did change its policy in 1974 to espouse the creation of a Palestinian state in the territories, it still felt challenged by the PNF's leadership of the national struggle in the occupied territories because of the prominence of the communists, who were not part of the PLO at that time.

Israeli repression and the political prominence assumed by pro–PLO mayors elected in 1976 led to the PNF's demise. It was briefly revived in 1979 by the PFLP (which dropped its earlier opposition to the PNF), the DFLP, communists, and Ba'thists, all of whom were dissatisfied with the leadership role then being played by the successor to the PNF, the National Guidance Committee.*

In 1983 the Palestine National Council adopted a resolution calling for the re-activation of the PNF, a call strongly supported by the PFLP and the DFLP but dismissed by Fatah, which had grown suspicious of the PNF. In the mid-1980s, the Democratic Alliance* once again called for the re-formation of the PNF.

PALESTINIAN ARAB NATIONAL PARTY (*Al-Hizb al-Watani al-'Arabi al-Filastini*). The Palestinian Arab National Party, or National Party, was established in November 1923 as one of the first expressions of opposition to the Arab Executive.* The party was formed by nationalists who broke with the Arab Executive and its leaders in the Husayni family, such as 'Arif al-Dajani and several members of the Nashashibi family.

The Palestinian Arab National Party was anti-Zionist and, like the Arab Executive, supported Palestinian independence, but it did not explicitly reject British rule as the Husaynis and their allies did. It and its successors, such as the Nashashibi-dominated National Defense Party,* continued the tradition of moderate opposition to the British and the Zionists, preferring a degree of cooperation with the authorities to the rejectionist strategy of more militant nationalist parties.

PALESTINIAN COMMUNIST ORGANIZATION. *See* PALESTINE COMMUNIST PARTY.

PALESTINIAN COMMUNIST WORKERS PARTY (*Hizb al-'Ummal al-Shuyu'i al-Filastini*). This group is composed of Palestinian leftists who left other organizations in the early 1970s. Its ideologically sophisticated activists succeeded in forging numerous alliances with other leftist groups in the Arab world. However, the party's activists have never achieved a mass following.

PALESTINIAN DEMOCRATIC UNION (*Al-Ittihad al-Dimuqrati al-Filastini*). This organization was born out of a major split in the Democratic Front for the Liberation of Palestine (DFLP)* in the early 1990s. Factionalism emerged over a variety of issues, including how involved the DFLP should become in non-Palestinian politics (particularly in Jordan) and to what degree the movement should support diplomatic means to solve the Arab-Israeli dispute. Yasir 'Abd Rabbuh's faction broke from the DFLP in April 1991, and by 1993 had established a new organization, the Palestinian Democratic Union. The Union is sometimes referred to by an Anglicized Arabic acronym, FIDA.

'Abd Rabbuh was more supportive of Palestine Liberation Organization (PLO)* diplomatic efforts, which intensified after the opening of the 1991 Madrid peace conference. While supportive of the September 1993 PLO-Israel agreement, the Union maintained certain reservations about the accord. It soon initiated a reformist movement within the PLO to deal with such issues.

PALESTINIAN NATIONAL LIBERATION MOVEMENT. *See* FATAH.

PALESTINIAN NATIONAL SALVATION FRONT (PNSF) (*Jabhat al-Inqadh al-Watani al-Filastiniyya*). The PNSF, a dissident alliance based in Damascus, challenges Yasir Arafat's leadership of the Palestine Liberation Organization (PLO).* The internal PLO crisis prompted by an uprising within Fatah (see

Fatah-Uprising, PLO) eased in 1985, and the groups constituting the Democratic Alliance* improved their relations with the mainstream PLO, with the exception of the Popular Front for the Liberation of Palestine (PFLP),* which joined with the more militantly anti-Arafat National Alliance* to form the PNSF in March 1985. Syria backed this dissident movement.

The PNSF continued to voice its opposition to Arafat's leadership of the PLO, although the PFLP was reconciled with the PLO in 1987 and left the PNSF. Syrian backing of the PNSF began to fade, and in the aftermath of the 1991 Gulf War, PLO–Syrian relations began to improve. In the spring and summer of 1991, top-level PLO delegations traveled to Damascus and met with Syrian officials as well as PNSF leaders to discuss improvements in PLO–Syrian and PLO–PNSF relations. Although the PNSF called for PLO–PNSF dialogue on several issues, including configuring the Palestine National Council (PNC) to determine the possibility of PNSF participation in that body, no talks were held before the PNC was convened in September 1991, and the PNSF boycotted the meeting.

Opposition to PLO support for Israeli-Palestinian negotiations after the 1991 Madrid peace conference prompted the formation of a new and wider grouping of factions opposed to Arafat, leading to the formation of the "Damascus Ten" in September 1992. This grouping later formed the National Democratic and Islamic Front* in the wake of the September 1993 framework signed by Israel and the PLO. The Palestinian National Salvation Front continued to issue statements thereafter, although the new National Democratic and Islamic Front represented a far more significant source of Syrian-based opposition to Arafat. The chairman of the PNSF at the time was Khalid al-Fahum.

PALESTINIAN PEOPLE'S PARTY. See PALESTINE COMMUNIST PARTY.

PALESTINIAN POPULAR STRUGGLE FRONT (PPSF) (Jabhat al-Nidal al-Sha'bi al-Filastini). The PPSF, a Palestine Liberation Organization (PLO)* commando group, was formed in early 1968 around Bahjat Abu Gharbiyya and a former Palestine Liberation Army (PLA)* officer, Major Fayiz Hamdan. The group was dormant in the early 1970s but was later revived with Syrian and Libyan support.

Recently led by Samir Ghawsha, the PPSF has often taken an oppositional line within the PLO. In 1974 it helped form the Rejection Front* to oppose the PLO's shift in its strategic goal from total liberation to the establishment of an independent Palestinian state in the occupied territories. Internal strife led to the appointment of Khalid 'Abd al-Majid as secretary general over Ghawsha's objections in April 1992. Despite this move, Ghawsha remained the effective leader of the group.

As one of the "Damascus Ten" groups opposed to the Israeli-Palestinian negotiations that began with the 1991 Madrid peace conference, the PPSF denounced the 1993 agreement between Israel and the PLO and joined the National Democratic and Islamic Front.*

PALESTINIAN REVOLUTIONARY COMMUNIST PARTY (PRCP) (Al-Hizb al-Shuyu'i al-Thawri al-Filastini). This party was born out of an ideological debate among Palestinian communists in Lebanon over whether they should wage armed struggle against Israel. A faction headed by 'Arabi 'Awwad decided in favor of armed action and formed the PRCP. It eventually joined with other Syrian-oriented movements in opposing Yasir Arafat and the mainstream Palestine Liberation Organization (PLO).* As one of the "Damascus Ten" groups opposed to the Israeli-Palestinian negotiations that began with the 1991 Madrid peace conference, the PRCP denounced the 1993 agreement between Israel and the PLO and joined the National Democratic and Islamic Front.*

PALESTINIAN SOCIETY (Al-Jam'iyya al-Filastiniyya). Established in 1919 in Damascus by many of the leaders of the Society of Palestinian Youth,* the purpose of this party was to support the Palestinians' struggle against Zionism among Arabs in Syria.

THE PARTISANS. See AL-ANSAR I and AL-ANSAR II.

PARTY OF ARAB INDEPENDENCE (Hizb al-Istiqlal al'Arabi). Known as the Istiqlal, this influential pan-Arab nationalist party was established in December 1918 by the secretive al-Fatat (Youth) movement to support the establishment of a unified, independent Arab nation after the fall of the Ottoman Empire. In 1932 a Palestinian branch of the party, formed under the leadership of 'Awni 'Abd al-Hadi of Nablus, was one of the first Palestinian parties not dominated by members of the major Jerusalem families of al-Husayni, al-Nashashibi, al-Khalidi, and al-Dajani. It was critical of the Husayni-Nashashibi rivalry.

The Palestinian Istiqlal vehemently opposed British colonial policy and Zionism in Palestine, and its formation signaled a move away from more genteel methods of trying to persuade Britain to stop its support for Zionism and the beginning of a more militant Palestinian response.

PARTY OF LIBERATION (Hizb al-Tahrir). Hizb al-Tahrir, an Islamic revolutionary party, operated underground in the West Bank during the period of Jordanian annexation (1950–67). It was founded in Jerusalem in November 1952 as a split from the Muslim Brotherhood.* Its early leaders were Shaykh Taqi al-Din al-Nabhani, Da'ud Hamdan, 'Adil Nabulsi, Ghanim 'Abduh, and Munir Shuqayr, and it drew most of its support from conservative Islamic districts such as Hebron, Tulkarm, and Janin.

The party differed from the program of Islamic social reform offered by the Muslim Brotherhood, which operated legally in Jordan and the West Bank. Hizb al-Tahrir advocated the Islamic liberation of occupied Palestine through clandestine action, and it viewed its struggle as part of a larger Islamic revolution. As a pan-Islamist organization, Hizb al-Tahrir was strongly opposed to secular

Arab movements. It was also strongly anti-Western because it perceived the West as antithetical to Islam, and it opposed the Jordanian authorities because of Jordan's pro-Western stance.

Hizb al-Tahrir operated study groups in the West Bank and was particularly active in trying to convert Jordanian army officers to its cause. Unity talks between the Muslim Brotherhood and Hizb al-Tahrir failed, and the rivalry between the two Islamic movements never lessened.

Hizb al-Tahrir's influence waned, and it has been overshadowed by more significant Islamic groups in the occupied territories, such as Hamas* and Islamic Jihad.*

PCP. See PALESTINE COMMUNIST PARTY.

PFLP. See POPULAR FRONT FOR THE LIBERATION OF PALESTINE.

PFLP–GC. See POPULAR FRONT FOR THE LIBERATION OF PALESTINE–GENERAL COMMAND.

PLA. See PALESTINE LIBERATION ARMY.

PLF. See PALESTINE LIBERATION FRONT.

PLO. See PALESTINE LIBERATION ORGANIZATION.

PNF. See PALESTINE NATIONAL FRONT.

PNSF. See PALESTINIAN NATIONAL SALVATION FRONT.

POPULAR DEMOCRATIC FRONT FOR THE LIBERATION OF PALESTINE. See DEMOCRATIC FRONT FOR THE LIBERATION OF PALESTINE.

POPULAR FRONT FOR THE LIBERATION OF PALESTINE (PFLP) (Al-Jabha al-Sha'biyya li-Tahrir Filastin). After Fatah,* the Marxist PFLP and its offshoots have exerted the greatest influence on Palestine Liberation Organization (PLO)* politics since the late 1960s, and it remains the second most significant group within the PLO. Important leaders have included George Habash, Ahmad al-Yamani, and Abu 'Ali Mustafa.

The PFLP was formed in late 1967 and early 1968 by a merger of four groups. The first was a grouping of Palestinian militants associated with the pan-Arabic Movement of Arab Nationalists (MAN),* such as George Habash and Wadi' Haddad and a Syrian, Hani al-Hindi. During the mid-1960s, these activists began pushing for a unique Palestinian voice within the MAN, which in general criticized "Palestinianism" as a regionalist deviation from the pan-Arab cause. They merged with three other organizations: the Palestine Liberation Front, headed by Ahmad Jibril (not to be confused with a group bearing the same name, discussed earlier, which emerged in 1977); the Heroes of the Return, led by Wajih al-Madani and Shafiq al-Hawt; and the Vengeance Youth, led by Nayif Hawatmeh, a Jordanian who came up through MAN ranks as well.

In 1968 factionalism split the PFLP. Younger, ultra-left members, led by Hawatmeh, criticized Habash and the PFLP leadership and eventually left to form the Democratic Front for the Liberation of Palestine (DFLP)* but not before Jibril and other less ideological military men had left in disgust to form the PFLP–GC.* In 1972 friction over internal organizational matters led to the establishment of yet another offshoot, the Popular Revolutionary Front for the Liberation of Palestine (al-Jabha al-Sha'biyya al-Thawriyya li-Tahrir Filastin), although it soon disappeared.

The PFLP, which has long contended with Fatah over the future of the Palestinian resistance movement, has been the pillar of the PLO opposition. Unlike Fatah, the PFLP sees Palestinian liberation as part of a wider process of sociopolitical revolution within the Arab world. The PFLP has voiced shrill criticism of "reactionary" Arab regimes and has urged their overthrow. It has also been quicker than Fatah to become involved in the affairs of Arab states, joining the leftist coalition in the 1975–76 Lebanese civil war much sooner than Fatah and calling for the overthrow of the Jordanian government in 1970, a call that eventually led to the disastrous PLO–Jordanian confrontation of 1970–71 and the expulsion of the PLO from Jordan.

PFLP militants have consistently supported maximalist solutions to the Arab-Israeli conflict. The PFLP has long favored armed struggle over diplomacy and has advocated the liberation of all of Palestine. In 1974 the PFLP broke with the PLO and formed the Rejection Front* after the PLO abandoned the goal of total liberation in favor of a two-state solution. Unlike the DFLP, the PFLP only grudgingly accepted this concept in 1981, but it insisted that the establishment of an independent state represented only a tactical pause in the revolution.

The PFLP also attempted to internationalize the Palestinian problem through airplane hijackings, hostage taking, and other violent activities inside and outside the Middle East. In September 1970, it hijacked three aircraft, flew two of them to Jordan, and blew them up after evacuating the passengers—an act that directly triggered the PLO–Jordanian confrontation of 1970–71. The PFLP halted hijackings in 1971.

Fundamental differences of philosophy, strategy, and tactics between the PFLP on the one hand and Fatah and the PLO mainstream on the other have long placed the PFLP in an oppositional role within the PLO. At various times, the PFLP has even operated outside the PLO, both voluntarily and as a result of expulsion. It helped found the Rejection Front from 1974 to 1978, and it was later estranged from the PLO between 1985 and 1987 when it was associated with the Palestinian National Salvation Front.* It has always drawn support from Arab states opposed to PLO positions, such as Syria.

While the PFLP is not disproportionately composed of Christian activists, Christians have often been attracted to it and to other organizations that advocate secular (and often Marxist) positions within an overwhelmingly Muslim body politic. The PFLP's consistency and determination contrasts with the ideological and tactical flexibility shown by the DFLP, for instance.

The PFLP has remained skeptical of diplomatic solutions to the Palestinian problem, only reluctantly agreeing to the diplomatic moves carried out by the PLO during the late 1980s. Its long-standing criticism of the Soviet Union stemmed in part from the latter's support of a two-state, diplomatic solution. In 1991 the PFLP sharply criticized the Arab-Israeli peace negotiations backed by the United States and the Soviet Union and froze its membership in the PLO Executive Council after the PLO authorized Palestinian delegates to participate in the negotiations.

In September 1992 in Damascus, the PFLP joined with nine other factions opposed to the negotiations to form the "Damascus Ten." The PFLP denounced the 1993 agreement between Israel and the PLO and established the National Democratic and Islamic Front* along with the other nine groups. It also helped create a new leadership group for the Intifada (see Unified National Command of the Uprising).

The intra-Palestinian crisis posed by the 1993 agreement and PLO Chairman Yasir Arafat's style of leadership (see Palestine Liberation Organization) also led to a reconciliation between the PFLP and the DFLP. The two groups agreed to merge their leadership bodies twenty-five years after the DFLP had broken off from the PFLP.

POPULAR FRONT FOR THE LIBERATION OF PALESTINE–EXTERNAL OPERATIONS (Al-Jabha al-Sha'biyya li-Tahrir Filastin–'Amaliyyat Kharajiyya). The PFLP–External Operations was formed in the early 1970s as an offshoot of the Popular Front for the Liberation of Palestine (PFLP)* by Wadi' Haddad and Fayiz Jabir, whose earlier disagreements with certain aspects of PFLP policy had led them to form the short-lived Popular Revolutionary Front for the Liberation of Palestine. External Operations was formed after the two again broke with the PFLP in disagreement over the PFLP's 1971 decision to halt certain activities, such as international hijackings.

POPULAR FRONT FOR THE LIBERATION OF PALESTINE–GENERAL COMMAND (PFLP–GC) (Al-Jabha al-Sha'biyya li-Tahrir Filastin–Al-Qiyada al-'Amma). The PFLP–GC, a Palestinian commando group, was established by Ahmad Jibril and Ahmad Za'rur in 1968 as a result of factional strife within the Popular Front for the Liberation of Palestine (PFLP).* The PFLP–GC itself soon split, and Za'rur formed the Organization of Arab Palestine.* Jibril was left in control of the PFLP–GC by the fall of 1968.

Jibril, a Palestinian who served in the Syrian army, has long advocated a pro-Syrian line within the Palestine Liberation Organization (PLO),* even supporting the Syrian decision to intervene against the PLO in Lebanon in 1976. That decision sparked dissent within the Front, and a splinter group, the Palestine Liberation Front,* was eventually formed in 1977. In 1983 Jibril's forces joined with those of Fatah-Uprising* to fight Fatah troops loyal to Yasir Arafat in northern Lebanon. Since that time, the PFLP–GC has ceased to operate under the PLO umbrella, and Jibril's membership in the Palestine National Council was suspended in 1984. In 1985 the PFLP–GC joined the anti-Arafat Palestinian National Salvation Front.*

The PFLP–GC, which advocates maximalist positions within Palestinian politics, has earned a reputation for sophisticated methods of pursuing the armed struggle against Israeli and Western targets. Because it has been so closely linked with Syrian policy, it has not made major inroads into the Palestinian community outside of the refugee camps that it controls. Nevertheless, its innovative armed operations against Israel, such as a November 1987 attack on an Israeli army base by a guerrilla who flew into Israel on a hang glider, and a major exchange of prisoners it effected with Israel in May 1985 (which freed detainees from other groups as well) have earned it a degree of admiration among Palestinians in the occupied territories.

As one of the "Damascus Ten" groups opposed to the Israeli-Palestinian negotiations that began with the 1991 Madrid peace conference, the PFLP–GC denounced the 1993 agreement between Israel and the PLO and joined the National Democratic and Islamic Front.*

POPULAR LIBERATION FORCES. See PALESTINE LIBERATION ARMY.

POPULAR REVOLUTIONARY FRONT FOR THE LIBERATION OF PALESTINE. See POPULAR FRONT FOR THE LIBERATION OF PALESTINE AND POPULAR FRONT FOR THE LIBERATION OF PALESTINE–EXTERNAL OPERATIONS.

POPULAR STRUGGLE FRONT. See PALESTINIAN POPULAR STRUGGLE FRONT.

PPSF. See PALESTINIAN POPULAR STRUGGLE FRONT.

PRCP. See PALESTINIAN REVOLUTIONARY COMMUNIST PARTY.

PROGRESSIVE LIST FOR PEACE (Qa'imat al-Taqaddumiyyin lil-Salam). The Progressive List emerged in the early 1980s in Israel to reach Palestinians who did not feel comfortable voting for Zionist parties or for Rakah.* Like the al-Ard* movement of the early 1960s, the Progressive List was made up of noncommunist Palestinian nationalists. It was led by a former member of al-Ard, Muhammad Mi'ari, and a Jewish leftist and former general, Mattityahu Peled. The Progressive List places great emphasis upon Palestinian concerns and pays less concern to issues of equality for Arab citizens of Israel, as espoused by the Democratic Arab Party* and Rakah, the two other main Arab parties in Israel.

The Progressive List put forth its first electoral list in the 1984 Knesset elections, and its candidates were bitterly attacked by Rakah as opportunists who split the Arab vote. The fact that the Progressive List received a degree of support from the Palestine Liberation Organization (PLO)* also infuriated Rakah, which until then had dominated the Arab electoral scene. In the 1988 Knesset elections, the Progressive list won one seat, capturing 14 percent of Arab votes cast. The Progressive list gained no representation in the 1992 Knesset election.

QA'IMAT AL-TAQADDUMIYYIN LI'L-SALAM. *See* PROGRESSIVE LIST FOR PEACE.

AL-QIYADA AL-WATANIYYA AL-MUWAHHADA LI'L-INTIFADA. *See* UNIFIED NATIONAL COMMAND OF THE UPRISING.

QUWWAT AL-TAHRIR AL-SHA'BIYYA. *See* PALESTINE LIBERATION ARMY.

RAKAH. *See* NEW COMMUNIST LIST.

REFORM PARTY (*Hizb al-Islah*). The Reform Party was established in June 1935 by Husayn Fakhri al-Khalidi and drew supporters mainly out of respect for the prominent al-Khalidi family. Al-Khalidi strove to maintain a balance between the two major parties, the National Defense Party* and the Palestine Arab Party,* although its positions resembled those of the former much more than the latter. It accepted the concept of a legislative council within the framework of British rule and urged Palestinian unity along with certain social reforms.

REJECTION FRONT (*Jabhat al-Quwa al-Filastiniyya al-Rafida Lil-Hulul al-Istislamiyya, Front of Palestinian Forces Rejecting Surrenderist Solutions*). The Rejection Front, an Iraqi-backed alliance including the Democratic Front for the Liberation of Palestine (DFLP),* the Popular Front for the Liberation of Palestine (PFLP),* the Popular Front for the Liberation of Palestine–General Command (PFLP-GC),* and the Arab Liberation Front,* existed from 1974 to 1978 to protest the Palestine Liberation Organization's (PLO)* change in strategy from total liberation to the establishment of a Palestinian state in the occupied territories.

RESHIMA KOMUNISTIT HADASHA—RAKAH. *See* NEW COMMUNIST LIST.

AL-SA'IQA (*Talai' Harb al-Tahrir al-Sha'biyya–Quwwat al-Sa'iqa, Vanguards of the Popular Liberation War–Forces of the Lightning Bolt*). Al-Sa'iqa is a commando group formed by the Syrian wing of the pan-Arab Ba'th Party in 1966 as its contribution to the growing Palestinian liberation movement. (The Iraqi Ba'th party formed its own movement; see Arab Liberation Front.) Its pan-Arab base was seen in its three main leaders, none of whom were Palestinians: Zuhayr Muhsin (Syrian), Yusuf Zu'ayyin (Syrian), and Mahmud al-Mu'ayita (Jordanian).

Al-Sa'iqa's consistently pro-Syrian line has alienated it from the Palestinian mainstream. It has never made extensive inroads into the Palestinian community outside of the refugee camps it controls in Syria. Many of its substantial number of troops are in fact Syrians. Al-Sa'iqa has even supported Syria during times of serious Palestine Liberation Organization (PLO)*–Syrian conflict, such as during the fighting in Lebanon in 1976, when al-Sa'iqa forces fought alongside the Syrians against the PLO.

Once one of the largest groups within the PLO, it ceased functioning within the PLO rubric in 1983 and saw its membership in the Palestine National Council suspended in 1984 for its oppositional line. In 1985 it joined the anti-Arafat Palestinian National Salvation Front.* In the wake of warmer relations with the PLO, al-Sa'iqa indicated a desire to work with the PLO in trying to determine a formula for its participation in the Palestine National Council. It has recently been led by 'Isam al-Qadi and Sami al-'Attari.

As one of the "Damascus Ten" groups opposed to the Israeli-Palestinian peace negotiations that began at the 1991 Madrid peace conference, al-Sa'iqa denounced the September 1993 agreement signed by Israel and the PLO and joined the National Democratic and Islamic Front.*

SOCIETY OF PALESTINIAN YOUTH (*Jam'iyyat Shabab Filastin*). The society was established in Damascus ca. 1919 by young members of several prominent Palestinian families to carry out attacks in Palestine and to signal to British military authorities that the Palestinians intended to fight Zionist colonization and Britain's support for it.

SONS OF THE COUNTRY. *See* ABNA AL-BALAD.

SUPREME MUSLIM COUNCIL (I) (*Al-Majlis al-Islami al-A'la*). The Supreme Muslim Council was not a political body per se but a religious authority established by the British mandatory government in 1922 to supervise Islamic affairs in Palestine. However, the council afforded its president, Hajj Amin al-Husayni, a base from which he could consolidate his political power and influence the Arab Executive* and, later, the Palestine Arab Party.*

Al-Husayni used his position in the Supreme Muslim Council to promote his followers and dismiss his enemies within Islamic bodies in Palestine. Al-Husayni and the council were bitterly opposed by the "opposition" led by the Nashashibi family. The British allowed the council to continue functioning after al-Husayni went into exile in 1936, although it lost the political significance he had imparted to it.

SUPREME MUSLIM COUNCIL (II) (Al-Majlis al-Islami al-A'la). This council was one of several short-lived movements to coordinate civil disobedience in the West Bank immediately after the 1967 Israeli occupation. Consisting of members of the Muslim establishment in the West Bank, it was particularly concerned with preserving the Arab-Islamic character of East Jerusalem after it was formally annexed by Israel in 1967.

AL-TAHALUF AL-DIMUQRATI. See DEMOCRATIC ALLIANCE.

AL-TAHALUF AL-QAWMI. See NATIONAL ALLIANCE.

TALAI' HARB AL-TAHRIR AL-SHA'BIYYA–QUWWAT AL-SA'IQA. See AL-SA'IQA.

THOSE WHO SACRIFICE THEMSELVES. See AL-FIDAIYYA.

UNCU. See UNIFIED NATIONAL COMMAND OF THE UPRISING.

UNIFIED NATIONAL COMMAND OF THE UPRISING (UNCU) (Al-Qiyada al-Wataniyya al-Muwahhada li'l-Intifada). The UNCU (often translated as the Unified National Leadership of the Uprising) was an underground committee that supervised the activities of the Palestinian Intifada (see Palestine Liberation Organization) in the occupied territories in coordination with the PLO leadership in exile. The UNCU, a secretive, four-member body, was composed of representatives of Fatah,* the Popular Front for the Liberation of Palestine (PFLP),* the Democratic Front for the Liberation of Palestine (DFLP),* and the Palestinian People's Party.* Its shadowy leadership, drawn from younger, lesser-known activists, initially functioned well despite numerous arrests by Israeli authorities as new leaders quickly replaced those detained.

UNCU tactics were articulated through periodic pronouncements that were circulated within the occupied territories calling for specific actions to take place in specific locations. The UNCU also specified days and times for general strikes among Palestinian merchants. The UNCU coordinated its activities with the external PLO leadership. Early friction with Islamic revivalists gave way to a degree of cooperation as the Intifada progressed. The UNCU struck an agreement with the Islamic revivalist group Hamas* in October 1988 under which the two pledged to coordinate activities during the Intifada. Islamic Jihad* also worked independently but alongside the UNCU.

Several important factors affected the UNCU beginning in 1991, including mounting arrests, the general slowdown in the pace of the Intifada after the Gulf War, and the controversial PLO decision to enter negotiations with Israel. The

DFLP and PFLP opposed the talks, as did groups outside the UNCU, such as Hamas* and Islamic Jihad.* After the Israeli-PLO announcement of a "Palestinian National Authority" in the territories to coordinate the transition to self-rule, Fatah and the Palestinian People's Party, which supported the agreement, withdrew from the UNCU to work toward peaceful implementation of the accord. The DFLP and PFLP then decided to work with Hamas to create a new *Intifada* leadership, joined by certain Fatah members who opposed the agreement.

'USBAT AL-TAHRIR AL-WATANI. *See* COMMUNIST PARTY OF ISRAEL, JORDANIAN COMMUNIST PARTY, AND PALESTINE COMMUNIST PARTY.

VANGUARDS OF THE POPULAR LIBERATION WAR–FORCES OF THE LIGHTNING BOLT. *See* AL-SA'IQA.

YMMA. *See* YOUNG MEN'S MUSLIM ASSOCIATION.

YOUNG MEN'S MUSLIM ASSOCIATION (YMMA) (*Jam'iyyat al-Shuban al-Muslimin*). The YMMA was established in 1927 on the model of the Young Men's Christian Association. The YMMA's founding principle was protest over what it perceived as Christian domination of civil service jobs in Palestine, which it blamed on deliberate British policy. The YMMA became more vocally militant in the early 1930s, but it never became a significant political actor in Palestine.

YOUTH CONGRESS (*Mutamar al-Shabab*). The Youth Congress was established in December 1932 to criticize the lack of job opportunities for educated Muslim youths in Palestine, echoing the concerns of the Young Men's Muslim Association.* As with many other Palestinian associations, the congress became a voice for political concerns as well, although it never played a major role in Palestinian politics.

Michael R. Fischbach

# SUDAN

Sudan, known officially as the Democratic Republic of the Sudan, is the largest country in Africa, comprising some 1 million square miles. Stretching from the Nubian desert in the north to the tropical rain forests of the south, and from the Red Sea coast in the east to the hill country of Darfur in the west, it borders eight states (Egypt, Libya, Chad, Central African Republic, Zaire, Uganda, Kenya, and Ethiopia) and contains a vast array of ethno-linguistic and cultural groups. Of Sudan's approximately 25 million people, perhaps 40 percent consider themselves Arabs (i.e., of Arab descent). These are almost all Muslims, practicers of agriculture, trade, and pastoralism in the northern half of the country. Another 30 percent of the population are northerners of non-Arab descent, including Nubians near the Egyptian border; Beja nomads in the Red Sea hills; the Ingessana of the upper Blue Nile; the various Nuba peoples of the southern Kordofan mountains; the Fur, Masalit, and other peoples of western Darfur province; and a large resident West African population (mainly of Fulani background) known locally as Fellata. These are likewise mainly Muslim, though the Nuba and Ingessana are also known to practice Christianity and traditional religions. The final 30 percent of the population consists of southern Sudanese. These are divided into the Nilotes (Dinka, Shilluk, and Nuer), who practice a mix of pastoralism, agriculture, and hunting and fishing along the upper Nile and in the grasslands region of the southeast and southwest, and the various agriculturalists of the extreme south (such as the Bari, Turkana, Moru, and Azande). Traditional religions and Christianity mainly prevail among the southerners, though Islam has made some inroads here as well. While the structure of Sudanese society as a whole may be conceived in a number of ways—according to socioeconomic, ethno-linguistic, regional, religious, and sectarian differences—the history of this vast territory bespeaks a sharp distinction between the largely Muslim north and the traditionalist and Christian south; and it is this distinction that animates the country's struggle in the twentieth century for political coherence and, indeed, for survival.

The development of the Sudan as a nation began with the rise of the sultanates of Sinnar and Darfur in the sixteenth century, when strong centralized administrations were established and processes of socioeconomic change ("modernization") got under way. It is to the Turco-Egyptian conquest of 1820–22, however, that the Sudan owes its territorial integrity.[1] Governing from Khartoum at the confluence of the Blue and White Niles, the Turco-Egyptian regime (or "Turkiyya" as it was known to the Sudanese) gradually extended an infrastructure of improved transportation and communication to the outlying territories, until with the conquest of Darfur in 1874 most of the present-day Sudan had been brought under at least nominal governmental control. The apparent advantages of modern administration, however, went unappreciated by most Sudanese. Government monopolies on various export goods, an ongoing attempt to eradicate the slave trade, and the burden of heavy taxation caused untold suffering and drove many northern riverain Sudanese off their land into a diaspora in the west and southwest. Meanwhile Turco-Egyptian attempts to impose a more orthodox version of Islam, complete with government-sponsored Shari'a courts and Egyptian-trained 'ulama', posed a direct challenge to the authority of the local holymen (fakis) and Sufi brotherhoods. The presence of Christian foreigners in government, including a number of Europeans in the service of the Egyptian khedive, was an added indignity during times of great hardship and served to sharpen the distinction between the local population and the increasingly unpopular "Turks." Massive discontent combined with rising millenarian sentiments eventually found expression in the uprising of Muhammad Ahmad b. 'Abdullah, a Sufi holyman from the Nubian region of Dongola, who in 1881 declared himself to be the expected Mahdi (divinely guided one) and called for jihad against the Turkish regime.

Both circumstance and personality played roles in the astonishing success of the Mahdi's revolt.[2] Initially, the government was slow to respond to the menace, and then it found itself short on leadership and low in morale. Every Mahdist victory in battle—and they came quickly and dramatically—served to bolster the Mahdi's reputation and diminish the stature of the government. Families, communities, and entire tribes of northern Sudanese flocked to the Mahdi's standard, attracted in some cases by the lure of booty and the desire to avoid taxes but also, undeniably, by the charismatic leadership of the Mahdi himself. Like the Prophet Muhammad's community at Medina upon which they deliberately modeled themselves, the Mahdi's followers saw themselves playing out a sacred drama between the forces of Islam and unbelief: Their mission was ultimately the universal acceptance of the Mahdi's rule. As the Prophet had done, the Mahdi assumed the role of lawgiver and leader to his people who, in imitation of the early Muslims, styled themselves as ansar (helpers). By early 1883 the western provinces of Kordofan and Darfur had gone over to the Mahdi, as well as much of the north and east; by 1884 the government capital at Khartoum was under siege, and despite a spirited defense, it eventually fell on January 26, 1885, costing the life of its British commander, General Charles G. Gordon. A mere six months later, after a sudden and brief illness, the Mahdi himself died, and with him went much of the inspiration as well as the dream of universal conquest. It was left to his successor, a westerner known as Khalifa 'Abdullahi al-Ta'ayshi, to rule Sudan as a territorial state.

The challenges facing the *khalifa* during his thirteen-year reign were enormous: The tribal basis of Sudanese society militate against the Mahdist ideal of a unified *ansar*, and tensions between pastoralist westerners (*awlad al-'Arab*) and the settled riverain population (*awlad al-balad*) were especially pronounced; resistance to the Mahdist regime from some segments of the population, particularly the Mirghani family and its Sufi order the Khatmiyya, continued unabated; and environmental disasters with resulting social dislocations combined to make the Sudan almost ungovernable. Ultimately, however, it was European imperial interests in the region that undermined the *khalifa*'s rule. After a two-year Anglo-Egyptian invasion, the final blow came at the battle of Omdurman, outside the Mahdist capital, on September 2, 1898. The victors soon proclaimed a condominium or joint-rule agreement over Sudan, with Britain the effective master of the country, and Mahdism was pronounced dead. In fact the legacy of the Mahdiyya, as the period of the Mahdi and *khalifa* came to be known, was to have far-reaching effects on the political development of the country, lending focus to the identity of northern Sudanese.

While sporadic acts of resistance to the condominium marked its first twenty years, these were without effect and had almost no bearing on the later nationalist movement. Of greater import was the establishment in 1918 of the Sudan Schools' Graduate Club in Omdurman, which served as a site both for social gathering and for antigovernment literary activity.[3] In 1920 a group of graduates formed the Sudanese Union Society (SUS)* with the aim of fostering nationalist sentiment and encouraging political unity with Egypt. In 1923 SUS members favoring direct confrontation with the government formed the White Flag League (WFL),* choosing as their insignia a map of the Nile Valley with the Egyptian flag in one corner. Though relatively small in number, the WFL was well organized with contacts among government employees, army officers, students, merchants, and others in both the capital area and the provinces. A series of demonstrations in northern towns in 1924 led to the arrest of the WFL leadership and government repression of the movement, but this in turn sparked mutinies in a number of Sudanese battalions of the Egyptian army. After the assassination of the British governor-general of Sudan, Sir Lee Stack, in Cairo and a serious mutiny in November 1924, Britain demanded the withdrawal of Egyptian troops from the country and harshly put down the rebellion. By the end of 1924, the WFL ceased to exist, but its idea of nationalist struggle based on a strategic alliance with Egypt had been broached and its non-elite challenge to the country's establishment had been registered.

The emergence of political parties in Sudan initially was linked to the influence of the country's two preeminent religious leaders: Sayyid 'Abd al-Rahman al-Mahdi, the posthumous son of the Mahdi and leader of the Ansar sect, and Sayyid 'Ali al-Mirghani, leader of the Khatmiyya sect. The "two Sayyids," as they were known, wielded enormous religious influence and economic power and enjoyed the respect and services of a large number of clients. The coteries of graduates, merchants, and government officials that formed around them operated, in the words of Tim Niblock, as "quasi-political groupings" to further the Sayyids' political and commercial interests. The condominium government meanwhile encouraged and cultivated the support of these traditional elites, both to facilitate the government policy of indirect rule and to minimize the radical threat of the WFL disturbances. Divided by the history of Mahdist-Khatmiyya enmity, the Sayyids competed for prestige and influence in government; by the 1930s they had also exploited differences within the Graduates Club and the Omdurman literary groups that were then in vogue.

The period of World War II witnessed an increase in nationalist activity among Sudanese graduates. In 1937 the Sayyid 'Ali–affiliated Abu Ruf faction formed a Graduates Congress as a first step toward a national political institution, and in this it had the support of the Sayyid 'Abd al-Rahman–affiliated al-Fajr faction and the neutral Ashiqqa* faction. While not a legislative body, but rather an instrument to further graduate interests, the Graduates Congress was intended eventually to serve a national political movement. From its founding conference in 1938 until 1940, the congress pursued moderate policies, unable or unwilling to challenge the government during a time of war and dominated by the influence of senior graduates, including the Graduates Congress president Isma'il al-Azhari. At least in principle, the factions were avowedly antisectarian, agreeing to subordinate their differences in favor of nationalist objectives. By the end of 1941, however, open competition had broken out among them, as they vied to form alliances with the coteries of the two Sayyids and control the congress. In 1942 the congress's governing Committee of Fifteen came under the control of a younger, more radical group of graduates determined to play a direct role in political affairs. A committee letter to the Sudan's governor-general, expressing hopes for eventual Sudanese self-determination, met with a public rebuke though private assurances of sympathy; this presented the committee with a difficult decision of political strategy, and it split the congress into opposing "moderate" and "confrontationist" camps. Elections to the committee later that year deepened the split within the congress, and with the victory of the confrontationist camp, Sayyid 'Abd al-Rahman threw his support behind the moderates. This shift in political alliance left the governing Ashiqqa faction without a source of establishment support, and, concerned to secure short-term political influence, it aligned itself with Sayyid 'Ali. Thus was established a central feature of Sudanese politics: the use of the religious establishment by the parties to obtain the immediate, practical support of the Sayyids' large followings, as opposed to direct mobilization of the masses; and the use of the parties by the two Sayyids to counter each other's influence and ambitions.

As competition between the moderate and confrontationist camps sharpened, each side advocated cooperation with a rival power of the condominium: Sayyid 'Abd al-Rahman's moderates sought to work closely with the British-dominated government through existing representative channels, while Sayyid 'Ali's confrontationists called for a vaguely defined "union" with Egypt. While each camp's policy was tactical, linked to the perceived shortest route to independence, the resonance of nineteenth-century history (namely, the Mahdist revolt and Egyptian support of the Khatmiyya) undoubtedly also played a role in these alliances. Finally, in 1945 the Ashiqqa-controlled Graduates Congress rejected cooperation with the government's Advisory Council of Northern Sudan, precipitating an irreparable split in the graduates' ranks: The moderates resigned from the congress to form the Umma Party,* which called for a transitional period during which power would be transferred to the Sudanese; while the congress essentially became the base for the Ashiqqa Party, which advocated Sudanese independence under the Egyptian crown. Three other unionist parties also appeared during this period: the Unionist Party* (*Ittihadiyyin*), which called for a democratic Sudanese government with dominion status under the Egyptian crown; the Liberal Party* (*Ahrar*), which advocated a confederal relationship with Egypt; and the Unity of the Nile Valley Party,* which supported integration of Sudan into a single Egyptian state. These were eventually merged into the National Unionist Party (NUP)* in 1952.

Meanwhile a party concerned with transforming the socioeconomic structure as well as achieving independence appeared in 1946: Developed among Sudanese communists and influenced by both British and Egyptian leftists, the Sudanese Movement for National Liberation (SMNL)* waged campaigns to mobilize workers, peasants, and students directly in an anticolonial struggle. Critical of the "bourgeois" tendencies of the two dominant parties with their establishment support, the SMNL was influential in boycott movements and university students' activities in the immediate pre-independence period. A final political group to emerge at this time, though it did not operate as a party until years later, was the Muslim Brotherhood (MB),* established among students at Khartoum University as an extension of the original Egyptian movement. True to the ideals of its sister organization, the MB sought the revival of Islamic society and the creation of an Islamic state in Sudan.[4]

After the Egyptian revolution of 1952, Sudan was given the choice of union or independence, and a framework for self-determination was agreed upon in 1953. In that year's election for an internally autonomous government, the NUP won forty-six of ninety-two seats in the representative assembly, and in January 1954 Isma'il al-Azhari assumed power as prime minister with an all-NUP cabinet. Almost immediately al-Azhari began to distance himself from his patron Sayyid 'Ali, dismissing three of the Sayyid's associates from his cabinet (they, in turn, formed the Republican Independence Party) and working toward the complete independence of Sudan. Withdrawal of British troops and the transfer of power to the Sudanese was completed in 1955, and on December 23 al-Azhari succeeded in passing through parliament a declaration of independence. On January 1, 1956, Sudan officially became an independent sovereign state.

The first two years of Sudan's independence affirmed the Sayyids' political dominance. In February 1956 al-Azhari was forced to accept a "national government," forming a coalition with the rival Umma Party. In June of that year, members of parliament with ties to Sayyid 'Ali's Khatmiyya sect defected from the NUP to form a rival party with the Independent Republicans, the People's Democratic Party (PDP).* By July, the Umma and PDP were able to force al-Azhari's resignation, and a coalition government headed by Umma secretary-general 'Abdallah Khalil took power. Now in opposition, the NUP adopted a more radical posture and began to espouse a policy of "secular nationalism." As the 1958 elections approached, the Umma–PDP government carefully restructured the electoral framework to give greater representation to those rural areas where their support was based, a process that included actual gerrymandering of districts to ensure Umma or PDP control. Anxious to uphold the status quo, the two parties agreed not to oppose each other in the constituencies. Election returns yielded sixty-three assembly seats for the Umma, twenty-six for the PDP, and forty-four for the NUP. The Umma–PDP coalition thus remained in power with 'Abdallah Khalil as prime minister.

Unaddressed during the country's first parliamentary period was the problem of the south. Southern Sudanese had been largely victimized by the policies of the Turkish and Mahdist regimes and kept isolated and underdeveloped during the condominium. The so-called Southern Party,* established in 1953 and renamed the Liberal Party in 1954, lacked coherent organization and programs and was able to win only nine of twenty-two southern province assembly seats in the 1953 elections. The disunity among southern members of parliament enabled the northern government to overlook their concerns, and the "sudanization" of administration prior to independence benefited southerners little. While northern parties sought to integrate the south into the country—a process that included the abolition of the southern command of the Sudan Defense Forces and the Arabization of southern education—southerners favored constitutional protection for their regional interests. In 1956 the northern-dominated national assembly defeated a southern bid for federal government. By then, however, a southern garrison had already mutinied and fled into the bush, later to form the nucleus of the Anya Nya* guerrilla movement.

Political maneuvering after the 1958 election, aimed at the formation of an Umma–NUP coalition government, threatened the position of 'Abdallah Khalil as prime minister, and in an attempt to preserve his authority the embattled politician invited the military to seize power, which it did on November 17. Doubtless the Umma leader imagined himself returning to power after a brief coup, but the military regime of Major General Ibrahim 'Abboud had other ideas. After declaring a state of emergency, suspending the transitional constitution, and dissolving the political parties, 'Abboud announced the formation of the Supreme Council of the Armed Forces (SCAF), reserving for himself full legislative, judicial, and executive powers and assuming the positions of prime minister and minister of defense. Sudan's first military dictatorship was dedicated to restoring political order by suppressing the electoral system and most civil rights, but significantly it maintained close ties to the country's religious establishment. Ansar and Khatmiyya support for the regime varied in accordance with their mutual competition, such that when Sayyid 'Abd al-Rahman's son and successor

Sayyid Siddiq agitated against the SCAF in 1960, Sayyid 'Ali's Khatmiyya provided a crucial pledge of allegiance to the regime. Only in 1963 did the regime offer a limited form of electoral representation, but in the absence of party politics this never gained credibility.

With regard to the southern Sudan, the 'Abboud regime opposed the idea of a federalist structure. More significantly, it attempted to eliminate all traces of southern particularism with a program of Arabization and Islamicization that included establishing Koranic schools, making Arabic (instead of English) the language of instruction, replacing Sunday with Friday as the day of rest, and limiting the activities of Christian missionaries in the region. The result of these policies was an affirmation of southern political consciousness and armed resistance: In 1962 the Sudan African Closed Districts National Union* (SACDNU) was founded in Uganda as a leadership in exile; renamed the Sudan African National Union (SANU)* in 1963, it advocated independence for the southern Sudan. Meanwhile the army mutineers of 1955 joined with exiles to form Anya Nya in 1963, and by 1964 a full-fledged civil war had erupted in the south.

It was in part the regime's inability to resolve the southern problem that brought it down. On October 22, 1964, the army used force to break up a Khartoum University meeting discussing the situation in the south, and two students were killed; antigovernment protests in the capital area followed, and a Professionals Front of university staff, teachers, doctors, judges, lawyers, and civil servants formed to demand a return to civilian rule. After a short but effective general strike, elements of the armed forces convinced the SCAF to dissolve itself. On October 30, a transitional government was formed with 'Abboud as president (he was forced to resign on November 14), an unaffiliated civil servant named Sirr al-Khatim al-Khalifa as prime minister, and a cabinet containing seven members of the Professionals Front, two southerners, and one member each from the Umma, NUP, PDP, Islamic Charter Front (ICF) (i.e., MB), and Communist Party of Sudan (CP).* Political parties were again legalized, censorship was lifted, and the provisional constitution was reinstated.

Unlike parties of the dominant political tradition, the Professionals Front did not owe its influence to religious and tribal leadership, but rather to mobilized urban workers and rural tenants; not surprisingly, its executive council was dominated by members of the CP. Once in power in the transitional government, it sought to make radical changes in the country's domestic and foreign policy, including nationalization of foreign banks, imposition of a state monopoly on foreign trade, reformation of the agricultural system, and extension of the suffrage to women. In the political realm, the Professionals Front proposed that half of all assembly seats be reserved for worker and peasant representatives. Such a threat to establishment interests could not go unchallenged, and a United Front of the Umma, PDP, NUP, and ICF began to press for early elections. In the ensuing contest between the traditionalist following (e.g., Ansar) and the government's backers, the former prevailed, largely through protest actions; and in February 1965 Sirr al-Khatim was forced to form a new cabinet with ministers from the Umma, NUP, ICF, and Southern Front.* Sudan thus returned to its pre-1958 style of politics, in the wake of which the Professionals Front ultimately dissolved.

Meanwhile an attempt was made to resolve the southern problem with the convening of a round table conference in Khartoum in March 1965. Present were representatives of northern and southern parties, including SANU and the Southern Front, as well as a number of foreign African observers. Southerners pressed for a plebiscite to choose among the options of federation, national union, and southern independence; however, no consensus was reached and the conference essentially failed. A month later national elections were held, though fighting in the south precluded meaningful voting there. The results confirmed the status quo: Umma won seventy-six seats and NUP won fifty-four; the ICF won five; the CP won eight (including the first woman member of parliament), all from a special graduates' constituency that contained fifteen seats; PDP boycotted the elections but still managed to win three seats; and in the absence of organized southern political activity, twenty mainly northern merchants were elected to southern assembly seats. In a new development, some twenty independents won seats, including the regionalist parties of the Beja Congress* (ten seats) and Nuba Mountains Federation* (seven seats). In May 1965 Muhammad Ahmad Mahjoub took office at the head of an Umma–NUP coalition government with a cabinet of six Umma ministers, six NUP ministers, and two southern ministers. Rivalry between Mahjoub and the NUP's al-Azhari, however, undermined the stability of the coalition and dissipated the political will necessary to confront the raging violence in the south. The Umma Party meanwhile experienced its own problems, as rival factions emerged led by the Ansar leader Imam al-Hadi and the grandson of Sayyid 'Abd al-Rahman, Sadiq al-Mahdi.

The remainder of Sudan's second parliamentary period saw a continuation of divisive politics, as the dominant parties formed coalitions, split apart, and failed to rise above their sectarian and personality differences. In July 1966 Sadiq al-Mahdi was elected to parliament and immediately challenged Mahjoub for the premiership; with the support of the NUP's al-Azhari (and against the wishes of Imam al-Hadi), Sadiq became prime minister with a new Umma–NUP cabinet. In May 1967 al-Azhari took advantage of a divided Umma Party to bring down the government, which next was led by Mahjoub in an Umma (Imam faction)–NUP coalition. In December, the NUP and PDP merged to oppose a divided Umma in the 1968 elections, forming the Democratic Unionist Party (DUP).* The results of these elections were predictable: The DUP won 101 seats in the assembly, the Umma-Sadiq faction won 36 (Sadiq himself failed to win reelection), Umma-Imam won 30 and independent Umma candidates won 6 seats; in addition, SANU won 15 seats, the Southern Front won 10, and a variety of smaller parties (representing regional interests) and independents won 20 seats. In the DUP–Umma (Imam faction) government that followed, Mahjoub was retained as prime minister with a cabinet composed of ten DUP ministers, five Umma-Imam ministers, and two ministers from the Southern Front. Senior statesman al-Azhari was made president of the Supreme Council of State, from which position he could continue to influence events (and vex Mahjoub).

Such an unsettled political climate naturally precluded any resolution of the southern conflict. Elections in the south in 1967 had been boycotted by the Southern Front and generated very little enthusiasm: Of the thirty-six contested constituencies, fifteen went to the Umma and five to the NUP, ten went to SANU, and the remainder (six) were split between smaller parties and independents. A constitutional drafting committee formed later that year included only seven southerners among its forty-two members. Meanwhile, in an attempt to eliminate the radical political threat, the Umma and NUP-dominated parliament had voted (at the behest of the MB) to outlaw the CP in 1965, which measure was carried out over the objections of the Supreme Court. The string of Umma-unionist governments were thus preoccupied with their internal rifts and matters of foreign policy. As the fighting in the south continued and the economy began to collapse from neglect, the Sudanese public grew increasingly disenchanted with the parties, politicians, and the political process. In April 1969 the Umma healed its rift and planned for the 1970 elections against the DUP; one month later, a group of Free Officers led by Colonel Ja'far Nimeiri took power in a military coup with no overt opposition.

The May Revolution, as it came to be known, followed the example of the earlier 'Abboud coup in dissolving the provisional constitution, the Supreme Council of State, and parliament, and banning the political parties. Nimeiri promoted himself to the rank of major general and president of the ruling Revolutionary Command Council (RCC), taking firm control of the state. At least initially, the regime seemed to have a leftist orientation. Perhaps a third of the members of Nimeiri's cabinet were communists or leftists, including some members of the 1964–65 transitional government, and during its first year in power the regime adopted a number of the CP's policies. The CP was not, however, exempt from the ban on political parties. Clearly the most pressing concern for the new government was with the dominant parties. In August 1969 al-Azhari died, and the DUP thereafter appeared to be conciliated with the regime. Sadiq al-Mahdi was placed under house arrest shortly after the coup and eventually went into exile. Imam al-Hadi, however, chose to retreat to the Ansar base of Aba Island on the White Nile and defy Nimeiri. In March 1970 the government launched an attack on Aba that resulted in high Ansar casualties and government confiscation of the Mahdi family's property; Imam al-Hadi was later killed fleeing into Ethiopia. Nimeiri next turned his attention to the communists, instituting purges of the RCC and officer corps in November and arresting leading communist civilians. In 1971 Nimeiri accused the communists of subversion, and he was proven correct in July when several deposed RCC officers led a countercoup that briefly succeeded in creating a new, pro-communist RCC. This regime, however, misjudged the strong anti-communist sentiment among the Sudanese and the popular support for Nimeiri, who quickly returned to power and executed both coup leaders and communist officials, including the leader of the CP, 'Abd al-Khaliq Mahjoub. Having purged the government and the army of the leftist threat, Nimeiri held a referendum in September which affirmed his hold on power with a six-year presidency, and a new cabinet was sworn in with Nimeiri as prime minister.

In 1973 Nimeiri gave Sudan its first permanent constitution, which established a presidential system of government with authority vested in the head of state. The president was given sweeping powers, including the right to suspend the constitution, and authority over the judiciary. All political parties were officially abolished, being replaced by the Sudan Socialist Union (SSU), an ideologically vague organization that strengthened Nimeiri's political control. The People's Assembly was shorn of real authority and served mainly as a rubber stamp for the president.

Meanwhile among the southern Sudanese a measure of political and military unity had been achieved, and Nimeiri came to appreciate the futility of a military policy toward the south. In February 1972 meetings were held in Addis Ababa, Ethiopia, between representatives of the government and Joseph Lagu's Southern Sudanese Liberation Movement (SSLM),* leading to an accord known as the Regional Self-Government Act for the Southern Provinces. This provided for a cessation of hostilities and the grouping of the three southern provinces into a self-governing region with its own regional assembly and High Executive Council. The authority of the southern government extended to matters of local administration, education, public health, mineral resources, and so on, ensuring (ideally) steady progress toward social and economic development and the maintenance of national unity. Ethnic and personal rivalries within the southern leadership, however, undermined its effectiveness, and southern disunity invited the Nimeiri government's intervention in 1980 and 1981 to "restore order." It is worth noting that neither Nimeiri nor Joseph Lagu had the support of their respective constituencies to negotiate the Addis Ababa agreement. As one scholar has noted, "[B]y operating through a process which excluded the majority of organized Sudanese political opinion (both north and south), the negotiations failed to create a respect for and loyalty to the constitutional guarantees which alone could have ensured the agreement's survival."[5] In 1983 Nimeiri decided that the experiment had failed, and he redivided the south into three regions. By this time, however, southern distrust of the central government and frustration with the slow pace of development had encouraged the renewal of armed resistance.

A failed but bloody coup attempt in 1976, planned by Sadiq al-Mahdi from exile, convinced Nimeiri of the need to conciliate his opponents among the traditional leadership. A secret meeting with the Umma leader in Port Sudan in 1977 led to a number of agreements and a declaration of amnesty, and in September al-Mahdi returned from exile in a visible display of "national reconciliation." A pretense to assembly elections was held in 1978, involving not parties but individuals associated with the old parties, and this yielded eighty seats combined to the Umma, DUP, and MB. Actual political power still resided in the

SSU, to whose Political Bureau Nimeiri appointed his former opponents al-Mahdi and Hasan al-Turabi, leader of the MB.

Political reconciliation between Nimeiri and al-Mahdi did not last long. In 1982 al-Mahdi rejected his affiliation with the government, and a year later he was arrested and imprisoned. As the Sudanese economy began to collapse under the weight of civil war, inflation, foreign debt, drought, and corruption, Nimeiri sought to deflect criticism of his regime—much of it coming from sectarian quarters—with a strident religious posture. Hasan al-Turabi was named attorney general as Nimeiri imposed Shari'a law on the country. Rather than ameliorating Sudan's political and economic problems, the September Laws (as they came to be known) exaggerated them. In particular, southerners resumed their armed resistance to northern domination: Anya Nya II,* a tribally based separatist group, was created and then quickly superseded by the Sudan People's Liberation Army (SPLA),* a leftist, antiseparatist group established in 1983 by Colonel Dr. John Garang. With a source of arms and safe haven in Ethiopia, the SPLA scored successive victories against government forces, until by 1986 it controlled most of the south.

The baleful effects of Shari'a on Sudan's economy and polity marked the last years of the Nimeiri regime and contributed to a persistent crisis. In 1984 Nimeiri declared a state of emergency and authorized the application of Koranic punishments (hudud), including flogging and the amputation of hands. In 1985, Mahmud Muhammad Taha, the elderly leader of the Republican Brothers, who had been a critic of Nimeiri, was publicly hanged for "heresy." Eventually even Hasan al-Turabi, one of the last supporters of the regime, was arrested and imprisoned on suspicion of plotting a coup. A visit to the United States in April 1985 was the occasion for Nimeiri's overthrow; the military seized power in response to antigovernment riots and a general strike. Nimeiri entered exile in Egypt as a Transitional Military Council (TMC), led by General 'Abd al-Rahman Siwar al-Dhahab, was established to rule the country.

During the year that it was in power, the TMC acted more as a caretaker regime than as a source of political leadership. Almost immediately it suspended Nimeiri's constitution and dissolved the SSU, but all laws—including the September Laws—remained in effect, awaiting review by an elected government. As in the post-'Abboud period of 1964–65, a struggle for power ensued between progressive and traditional political forces; in this case, between the Alliance of National Forces for National Salvation (a coalition of mass organizations and trade unions) and the old parties. While the former advocated a long transitional period in which to create new political structures, the parties demanded immediate elections; as had been the case years earlier, the superior organization of the parties with their sectarian-based mass following prevailed.

The elections of April 1986 returned Sadiq al-Mahdi to power as premier of an Umma–DUP coalition government. Forty-seven political parties had contested the 264 assembly seats in the elections, though most represented narrow sectarian, regional, or tribal bases and garnered little support. By contrast, Umma won ninety-nine seats while the DUP won sixty-three seats. Fighting in the south and an SPLA boycott of the elections prevented polling there. Perhaps the biggest beneficiary of the elections was the National Islamic Front (NIF)* (formerly the ICF), which won the majority of the twenty-eight seats allotted to the special Graduate College constituency for a total of fifty-one seats and went into opposition with parliamentary influence in excess of its actual electoral support. The headship of state in this parliamentary government was once again embodied in a five-member Supreme Council of State, which was chaired by the son of Sayyid 'Ali, Ahmad al-Mirghani.

The government of Sadiq al-Mahdi was confronted with a number of vital issues, including the war in the south, the nature of a permanent constitution, Shari'a law, and the ravaging effects of famine and assorted natural disasters. Needing the support of the NIF for his economic reforms, al-Mahdi was unable to take action on the matter of Shari'a and consequently the war in the south raged on. To some extent a challenge from within the Umma, from Wali al-Din, the son of Imam al-Hadi, further hamstrung him politically. From 1987 to 1989, al-Mahdi pursued a harsh military policy toward the southern conflict while his coalition partners in the DUP favored a negotiated settlement with the SPLA. An Umma–NIF coalition government, with the DUP in opposition, was a short-lived (and unsuccessful) attempt to achieve political stability. Finally, in February 1989, the army delivered an ultimatum to al-Mahdi to make progress toward peace in the south. A cease-fire was arranged, the Umma and DUP–dominated parliament agreed to a freeze on Shari'a, and a date was set—September 1989—for the convening of a constitutional conference to decide the permanent character of the Sudanese nation. Three months short of the conference, on June 30, 1989, the military again seized power in a bloodless coup.

In the first three years of its rule, the government of Lt. General 'Umar Hasan al-Bashir resembled earlier Sudanese military regimes. A Revolutionary Command Council served as the supreme state authority; trade unions and political parties were abolished and all forms of dissent prohibited; and the constitution was suspended by a government that ruled by decree. Unique to this regime, however, was its strident support of Islamic fundamentalism, as outlined in the programs of the NIF. The military policy toward the south was continued with renewed vigor, accompanied by a declaration of jihad against the southern rebels, and an Iranian-style Popular Defense Force (with Iranian advisors and Chinese weapons) was created as a popular militia to offset a politically unreliable national army. Meanwhile, the range of Shari'a law was broadened, and human rights abuses by the regime appeared unprecedented.[6] While the political program of the regime continued to evolve, the government made clear its intention to establish local congresses and committees throughout the country on behalf of an "Islamic" decentralized system. Some type of autonomy for the south was apparently also envisioned. While Hasan al-Turabi had no official role in the government (he was in fact briefly arrested after the coup, along with Sadiq al-

Mahdi), it is obvious that he was the intellectual force and spiritual mentor of the Bashir regime.

In conclusion, it may be useful to consider comparatively the operation of Sudan's political parties.[7] Identity in Sudan has historically been a function of various factors (regional, ethnic, tribal, and sectarian affiliation) which are expressed in the composition and programs of political parties. There is hence some question as to whether "national politics" truly exist or whether all Sudanese politics are essentially local; clearly, the Sudanese nation is a work in progress. Among the dominant northern parties there are few ideological differences, and membership can be ascribed to one's relationship to the Ansar and Khatmiyya traditions. Both the Umma and PDP/DUP have been able to draw upon the mass following and hierarchy of their associated sects; the NUP, in the absence of a rural organizational structure, has had to rely upon Khatmiyya support during periods of alliance, and otherwise promote itself as a modern and secular alternative to the more traditional parties. All three dominant parties have tended to recruit support from their fixed clienteles with little attempt to attract one another's followers; virtually the only areas of electoral contest have been parts of Blue Nile Province and the capital cities. Meanwhile, the two so-called radical parties, the MB (ICF/NIF) and CP, have successfully appealed to the educated young who are disillusioned with the inability of the traditional parties to address the nation's problems. Ideologically these two parties are diametrical opposites: The CP's program has been defined by the struggle against imperialism, while the MB has advocated a return to orthodox Islamic policies and practices. Finally, the regional parties have developed among various non-Arab peoples (e.g., Fur, Nuba, Beja, and southerners) who have felt oppressed, exploited, or neglected by the "Arab-Nubian" governments. These parties have taken the form of political blocs with vague and limited objectives, distinct parties with clear objectives, and exile movements with both military and nonmilitary objectives. Almost by definition the regional parties have been less concerned with ideology than the structure of the state that governs and distributes resources.

In all of Sudan's elections, the Umma, NUP, and PDP/DUP have accounted for most of the votes and have obtained the majority of the assembly seats. These parties have not always operated effectively, however. Peter K. Bechtold identifies three weaknesses of the dominant parties: their haphazard means of fund-raising with an emphasis on voluntary contributions, their failure to maintain active organizations in the provinces except during elections, and the absence of primary elections or other processes to nominate party candidates, resulting in multiple candidates contesting an election. This last shortcoming has frequently cost parties a constituency, as their candidates split the vote and enabled a rival to win with a small plurality. The CP and MB have exhibited a greater degree of effectiveness, drawing on the commitment and internal cohesiveness of their members and avoiding entirely the problem of multiple candidates. The harsh opposition these parties have faced from centrist governments (both civilian and military) has often forced them to operate in a clandestine manner, though the present regime is obviously sympathetic to the ideals of the MB. Finally, the regional parties have lacked national influence due to a paucity of assembly seats, which renders almost meaningless their local appeal and potential for coalition. At the same time, organizational problems have cost these parties assembly seats in their own regions. The southern parties in particular have been plagued by problems of disunity, often emanating from tribal and personal animosities, although the poverty and underdevelopment of the region, to say nothing of the devastating effects of civil war, naturally mitigate against an effective political process. As the war and its accompanying effects continue to exact a huge toll on the southern population, there is a serious question as to whether certain southern cultures will survive intact, while the Bashir government's apparent intention to impose a military solution on the south seems reminiscent of Nimeiri's attempt at Addis Ababa—ultimately a failure—to bypass the political process and dictate a Sudanese national arrangement.

## Bibliography

Afaf Abdel Majid Abu Hasabu. *Factional Conflict in the Sudanese Nationalist Movement, 1918–1948*. Khartoum, Sudan: Graduate College, 1985.

Bechtold, Peter. *Politics in the Sudan: Parliamentary and Military Rule in an Emerging African Nation*. New York: Praeger, 1986.

Daly, M. W. *Empire on the Nile: The Anglo-Egyptian Sudan, 1898–1934*. Cambridge, England: Cambridge University Press, 1986.

———. *Imperial Sudan: The Anglo-Egyptian Condominium, 1934–1956*. Cambridge, England: Cambridge University Press, 1991.

Holt, P. M., and M. W. Daly. *A History of the Sudan*. 4th ed. London: Longman, 1988.

Johnson, Douglas. *The Southern Sudan*. London: Minority Rights Group Report no. 78, 1988.

Mohamed, Omer Beshir. *The Southern Sudan: Background to Conflict*. London: Hurst, 1968.

———. *Revolution and Nationalism in the Sudan*. London: Rex Collings, 1974.

Muddathir, Abd al-Rahim. *Imperialism and Nationalism in the Sudan*. London: Oxford University Press, 1969.

Niblock, Tim. *Class and Power in the Sudan: The Dynamics of Sudanese Politics, 1898–1985*. Albany, N.Y.: State University of New York, 1987.

Wai, Dunstan M. *The African-Arab Conflict in the Sudan*. N.Y.: Africana Publishing Company, 1981.

Warburg, Gabriel. *Islam, Nationalism and Communism in a Traditional Society*. London: Frank Cass, 1978.

Woodward, Peter. *Condominium and Sudanese Nationalism*. London: Rex Collings, 1979.

———. *Sudan, 1898–1989: The Unstable State*. Boulder, Colo.: Lynne Rienner, 1990.

## Political Parties

ANTI-IMPERIALIST FRONT (*Al-Jabha al-Mu'adiyya lil-Isti'mar*). Established in 1953 by the Communist Party* to compete in assembly elections, it won one seat. It ceased operation after the 1958 military coup.

ANYA NYA. This militant southern secessionist movement was named for a type of snake venom. Created in 1963 by exiles and veterans of the 1955 mutiny of the Equatorial Corps of the Sudan Defense Forces, it served as the military branch of the Sudan African National Union.* Originally composed mainly of Equatorians, it attracted Nilotes (Dinka, Nuer, and Shilluk) in the 1960s. After the Addis Ababa agreement ending the civil war (1972), it was absorbed into the national army and police.

ANYA NYA II. This militant southern movement was formed by veterans of the original group in the late 1970s in resistance against Ja'far Nimeiri's policies which kept the southern region underdeveloped and divided and allowed for state (i.e., northern/Muslim) intervention in southern affairs. Composed primarily of Nuer and Equatorians, it merged into the Sudan People's Liberation Army (SPLA)* after July 1983, forming a dissident secessionist wing of that body. It continues as an opposition group to the Garang-led SPLA/SPLM which, since 1984, has accused it of cooperating with the national army.

ASHIQQA. Initially one of three literary study groups in post-1924 Omdurman, it was named for the three brothers who formed it. Originally not aligned with either of the two Sayyids, Ashiqqa was an effective manipulator of Graduate politics. It formed an alliance with Sayyid 'Abd al-Rahman and Isma'il al-Azhari in 1941 and served as part of the confrontationist camp of the Graduate Congress, allied with Sayyid 'Ali, in 1942. It raised the slogan of "Unity of the Nile Valley" in 1944, in effect becoming a political party calling for Sudanese self-determination under the Egyptian crown. It controlled the Graduate Congress in 1945, after which date the congress essentially merged with the Ashiqqa Party. The party recruited support from the congress organization and Khatmiyya network. Supported financially by Khatmi merchants, Ashiqqa merged into the National Unionist Party (NUP)* in 1952.

AZANIA LIBERATION FRONT. See SUDAN AFRICAN NATIONAL UNION.

BEJA CONGRESS (Mu'tamar al-Bija). Founded in 1954 to represent the interests of eastern, non-Arab Sudanese, the Beja Congress was led by Muhammad Ahmad 'Awad. After a failed bloc with the Nuba Mountains Federation,* it contested the 1965 elections and won ten seats, but it was reduced to three seats in the 1968 elections.

COMMUNIST PARTY OF SUDAN (CP) (Al-Hizb al-Shuyu'i al-Sudani). The Communist Party established the Sudanese Movement for National Liberation (SMNL) in 1945, being influenced by the Egyptian Movement for National Liberation (MNL) (see Egyptian Communist Party) and the British communists serving in Sudan. The CP attempted initially to radicalize the Ashiqqa;* then it concentrated on mobilizing the population. Organized into a network of cells, it was influential among students, workers on the Sudan Railways and Gezira Agricultural Scheme, the intelligentsia, and women's organizations, and it was active in boycott movements and University College Student Union politics in the 1940s and 1950s. From 1949 until his execution by Ja'far Nimeiri in 1971, the CP was led by 'Abd al-Khaliq Mahjoub. In 1953, the party established the Anti-Imperialist Front.\* Active in the National Front and Transitional Government of 1964–65, it was outlawed in November 1965 by the Umma–National Unionist Party\* government. In January 1967, former members of the CP formed a short-lived Socialist Party. The CP was suppressed and dismantled by Nimeiri in 1971 after a communist-inspired coup attempt. Advocating a form of communism supposedly compatible with Islam, it was otherwise staunchly anti-imperialist and in favor of socioeconomic reforms threatening to the politico-religious elite. Of limited appeal nationally, it won eleven of fifteen Graduate constituency seats in 1965 and garnered perhaps a quarter of the capital-area total vote. At the height of its popularity (1970), the CP could claim from 6,000 to 8,000 members.

The party suffered a severe blow when its leader, Mahjoub, and other party officials were executed in 1971. After the fall of Nimeiri in 1985, the CP surfaced again, but it was banned and its leaders jailed by the Islamic junta in 1989.

CP. *See* COMMUNIST PARTY.

DEMOCRATIC UNIONIST PARTY (DUP) (*Al-Hizb al-Ittihad al-Dimuqrati*). Formed in 1967 by a merger of the People's Democratic Party (PDP)\* and National Unionist Party (NUP),\* the DUP won a plurality of assembly seats in the 1968 elections and formed a coalition government with the Umma Party.\* The DUP served as a coalition partner with Umma from 1986 until the 1989 coup and negotiated the November Accords—rejected by Umma—with the Sudan People's Liberation Army (SPLA)\* to bring a halt to the civil war. Like other previous unionist parties, the DUP represents the political and economic interests of the conservative Khatmiyya religious sect and its associates (see also chapter on Egypt).

DUP. *See* DEMOCRATIC UNIONIST PARTY.

AL-HARAKA AL-SUDANIYYA LIL-TAHARRUR AL-WATANI. *See* SUDANESE MOVEMENT FOR NATIONAL LIBERATION.

AL-HIZB AL-AHRAR. *See* LIBERAL PARTY.

AL-HIZB AL-AHRAR AL-JANUBI. *See* SOUTHERN LIBERAL PARTY.

AL-HIZB AL-ITTIHAD AL-DIMUQRATI. *See* DEMOCRATIC UNIONIST PARTY.

HIZB AL-ITTIHADIYYIN. *See* UNIONIST PARTY.

AL-HIZB AL-JANUBI. *See* SOUTHERN PARTY.

AL-HIZB AL-JUMHURI AL-ISHTIRAKI. *See* SOCIALIST REPUBLICAN PARTY.

AL-HIZB AL-JUMHURI AL-MUSTAQILL. *See* INDEPENDENT REPUBLI-CAN PARTY.

AL-HIZB AL-SHA'BI AL-DIMUQRATI. *See* PEOPLE'S DEMOCRATIC PARTY.

AL-HIZB AL-SHUYU'I AL-SUDANI. *See* COMMUNIST PARTY OF SU-DAN.

HIZB AL-WAHDA AL-SUDANI. *See* SUDAN UNITY PARTY.

HIZB WAHDAT WADI AL-NIL. *See* UNITY OF THE NILE VALLEY PARTY.

AL-HIZB AL-WATANI AL-ITTIHADI. *See* NATIONAL UNIONIST PARTY.

HIZB AL-WATANIYYIN. *See* NATIONALIST PARTY.

AL-IKHWAN AL-MUSLIMIN. *See* MUSLIM BROTHERHOOD.

INDEPENDENT REPUBLICAN PARTY (*Al-Hizb al-Jumhuri al-Mustaqill*). This party was formed by followers of Sayyid 'Ali in the assembly, led by Mirghani Hamza, Khalafallah Khalid, and Ahmad Jayli, who defected from the National Unionist Party (NUP)* in 1955 to vote with the Umma Party* against Isma'il al-Azhari. The party joined with other Khatmi members of parliament in May 1956 to form the People's Democratic Party (PDP),* helping to bring down the Azhari government.

ISLAMIC CHARTER FRONT. *See* MUSLIM BROTHERHOOD.

ITTIHAD JIBAL AL-NUBA. *See* NUBA MOUNTAINS FEDERATION.

AL-JABHA AL-ISLAMIYYA AL-QAWMIYYA. *See* NATIONAL ISLAMIC FRONT.

AL-JABHA AL-MU'ADIYYA LIL-ISTI'MAR. *See* ANTI-IMPERIALIST FRONT.

JABHAT AL-JANUB. *See* SOUTHERN FRONT.

JABHAT AL-MITHAQ AL-ISLAMI. *See* ISLAMIC CHARTER FRONT.

JAM'IYYAT AL-ITTIHAD AL-SUDANI. *See* SUDANESE UNION SOCIETY.

LIBERAL PARTY (*Al-Hizb al-Ahrar*). This short-lived unionist group advocated a confederal relationship with Egypt. Formed in 1945, it split in 1946 into the Liberal Secessionists, which merged with the Umma Party,* and the Liberal Unionists, most of whom later joined the Communist Party.*

AL-LIWA' AL-ABYAD. *See* WHITE FLAG LEAGUE.

MB. *See* MUSLIM BROTHERHOOD.

AL-MUNADHDHAMA AL-SUDANI AL-DIMUQRATI. *See* SUDANESE DEMOCRATIC ORGANIZATION.

MUSLIM BROTHERHOOD (MB) (*Al-Ikhwan al-Muslimin*). This group was established in about 1954 at Khartoum University by professors and students, although some type of MB presence had possibly been introduced into the Sudan as early as 1946. The MB formed the Islamic Charter Front (ICF) after the October Revolution of 1964 to recruit followers into the political program and to contest elections, party ideology being determined by the MB. The party was active in the Transitional Government of 1964–65. It is a steadfast opponent of the "alien ideology" of the Communist Party (CP).* Drawing on a social base of students and graduates, the MB/ICF presented itself as an alternative to the Umma Party* and the People's Democratic Party (PDP)* and advocated the revival of Muslim society, the creation of an Islamic state, and worldwide Muslim unity. The MB's emphasis on self-improvement and nonsectarianism has proven extremely popular among university students, and its support comes mainly from the northern and eastern provinces and the capital area. Its support increased greatly in the 1986 elections, which it contested as the National Islamic Front, and it effectively thwarted the Umma governments of 1986–89. Led by Hasan al-Turabi, it became the guiding ideological movement of the military regime of Lt. General 'Umar Hasan al-Bashir.

MU'TAMAR AL-BIJA. *See* BEJA CONGRESS.

NATIONAL ISLAMIC FRONT. *See* MUSLIM BROTHERHOOD.

NATIONAL UNIONIST PARTY (NUP) (*Al-Hizb al-Watani al-Ittihadi*). Formed from a merger of smaller unionist parties in 1952, the NUP was aligned initially with Egypt; after its 1953 election victory under Isma'il al-Azhari it moved toward complete independence for Sudan. Success of the party came from the personal charisma of al-Azhari and the organizational skill of his ex-Ashiqqa* associates. The NUP lost support of Khatmi members of parliament in 1955 and 1956, and it was forced into a coalition with the Umma Party* in 1956 and lost the government in July of that year. Assuming a more radical posture after 1956, it advocated "secular nationalism" in the 1958 elections in a National Front with the Communist Party (CP),* trade unions, and professional associations. Involved in the Transitional Government of 1964–65, it dominated the 1965 elections, which led to a coalition with Umma. The NUP merged with the People's Democratic Party (PDP)* in 1967 to form the Democratic Unionist Party (DUP).* Membership was drawn from the young, educated, and nonsectarian portions of the population, mainly in the urban north; some support came from the northern Blue Nile Province and from the Kababish tribe of Kordofan, who are non-Khatmi Arabs with a historic enmity against the Ansar. The party has been dominated by Isma'il al-Azhari, a master of political maneuvering whose positions have varied over time, but who has attempted to maintain a central position between Umma and PDP policies.

NATIONALIST PARTY (*Hizb al-Wataniyyin*). This short-lived party merged with the Umma Party* in 1946.

NUBA MOUNTAINS FEDERATION (*Ittihad Jibal al-Nuba*). Founded in 1954, it developed out of the Black Bloc (al-Kutla al-Suda), established in 1938 by Adam Adham with a membership of Nuba, Fur, and Fellata living in the Khartoum area. The party advocated Nuba unity, the revival of Nuba Mountains Province as a separate administrative unit, abolition of the poll tax, a school construction program, and the "Africanization" of Sudan. Under the leadership of Philip Abbas, the party won seven seats in the 1965 election, and in 1968 it formed a bloc with the Sudan African National Union (SANU)* and the Southern Front* calling for a federal structure of government and the removal of allusions to Arabism and Islam in the constitution.

NUP. *See* NATIONAL UNIONIST PARTY.

PDP. *See* PEOPLE'S DEMOCRATIC PARTY.

PEOPLE'S DEMOCRATIC PARTY (PDP) (*Al-Hizb al-Sha'bi al-Dimuqrati*). The PDP was formed in May 1956 by ex–National Unionist Party (NUP)* Khatmi members of parliament, led by 'Ali 'Abd al-Rahman, who were disaffected from the al-Azhari government. The PDP helped force al-Azhari's resignation in June 1956 and joined a coalition government with the Umma Party.* Involved in the Transitional Government of 1964–65, the PDP merged with the NUP to form the Democratic Unionist Party (DUP)* in 1967. The PDP was advised by and drew on the traditional following of Sayyid 'Ali. Party support came from the Khatmiyya sect, particularly the tribes of the rural north and east, most of whom had opposed the Mahdists in the nineteenth century. The PDP advocated close relations with Egypt; otherwise, its positions were similar to those of Umma regarding an Islamic constitution and the maintenance of a free-enterprise system.

PEOPLE'S PROGRESSIVE PARTY. This southern party, post 1983, originally supported the existence of three separate southern provinces. It represents the interests of the Bari community of eastern Equatoria.

SANU. *See* SUDAN AFRICAN NATIONAL UNION.

SOCIALIST REPUBLICAN PARTY (*Al-Hizb al-Jumhuri al-Ishtiraki*). This short-lived party emphasized cooperation with the British administration. Its support came from a segment of the rural tribal leadership. The party was dissolved in 1953.

SOUTHERN FRONT (*Jabhat al-Janub*). Created after the October Revolution of 1964 of southern civil servants and students in the capital area, the party was led by Clement Amboro. It was associated with the Professionals Front of 1964 and given three ministerial positions in the Transitional Government of 1964–65 and one seat on the Supreme Council of State. The party was involved in the round table conference of 1965. It contested the 1968 elections and won ten seats, earning it two cabinet positions in the 1968 Democratic Unionist Party*–Umma Party* government.

SOUTHERN LIBERAL PARTY (*Al-Hizb al-Ahrar al-Janubi*). Originally known as the Southern Party,* it was renamed the Liberal Party* in 1964. This was the sole southern party until 1958. It won forty seats in the 1958 election and advocated a federal structure of government. This party is not related to the earlier (northern Sudanese) Liberal Party of 1945–46. It split in 1958 and died out after the 1964 overthrow of the 'Abboud regime.

SOUTHERN PARTY (*Al-Hizb al-Janubi*). This party was founded in 1953 and won nine of twenty-two Southern Province seats in that year's elections. It advocated a federal government. It was renamed the Southern Liberal Party* and later was known as the Liberal Party.*

SOUTHERN SUDAN POLITICAL ASSOCIATION. This Khartoum-based party, advocating the return of a unified southern regional government, is associated with many ministers of that former government. The party elected representatives from the three southern provinces to the national assembly in the 1986 elections.

SOUTHERN SUDANESE LIBERATION MOVEMENT (SSLM). Formed in 1969 by former army lieutenant Joseph Lagu from a number of exiled southern political movements and guerrilla groups, it negotiated the Addis Ababa accord with Ja'far Nimeiri in 1972. Lagu went on to serve as the second president of the southern High Executive Council (1978–80), leading the Equatorial bloc within the regional government.

SPLA. See SUDAN PEOPLE'S LIBERATION ARMY.

SSLM. See SOUTHERN SUDANESE LIBERATION MOVEMENT.

SUDAN AFRICAN CLOSED DISTRICTS NATIONAL UNION. See SUDAN AFRICAN NATIONAL UNION.

SUDAN AFRICAN CONGRESS. This Khartoum-based southern party has advocated the return of a unified southern regional government. It was created in opposition to the Southern Sudan Political Association* by southern intellectuals.

SUDAN AFRICAN LIBERATION FRONT. See SUDAN AFRICAN NATIONAL UNION.

SUDAN AFRICAN NATIONAL UNION (SANU). Formed in 1962 as the Sudan African Closed Districts National Union by Fr. Saturnino Lahure, Joseph Oduho, and William Deng, it was renamed SANU in 1963 with headquarters in Kampala, Uganda. Composed of southern political leaders in exile, including administrators and teachers, it advocated independence for the southern Sudan. It was involved in the round table conference of 1965. The party split in 1965 into two factions: one led by William Deng, committed to working within Sudan as a legal party, and the other led by Aggrey Jaden in exile. The former faction (SANU) won fifteen seats in the 1968 elections and was a rival of the Southern Front.* The latter faction further split into the Azania Liberation Front and the Sudan African Liberation Front; these factions reunited later that year as the Azania Liberation Front, pursuing a militant policy toward the government. In 1969 the factions united into the Southern Sudanese Liberation Movement.*

SUDAN AFRICAN PEOPLE'S CONGRESS. This southern party, post 1983, originally supported the existence of three separate southern provinces. It represents the interests of the people of western Equatoria.

SUDANESE DEMOCRATIC ORGANIZATION (*Al-Munazzama al-Sudani al-Dimuqrati*). This faction of the Communist Party* split from the Sudanese Movement for National Liberation* in 1952, and eventually dissolved in 1953.

SUDANESE MOVEMENT FOR NATIONAL LIBERATION. *See* COMMUNIST PARTY OF SUDAN.

SUDANESE UNION SOCIETY (SUS) (*Jam'iyyat al-Ittihad al-Sudani*). Formed by graduates in 1920 to raise national consciousness and to oppose the condominium regime, it stressed political unity and common struggle with Egypt against Britain. It attempted to facilitate Sudanese student travel to Egypt. SUS activists formed the White Flag League* in 1923, which led the direct action campaigns of 1924. The party did not survive the suppression of the White Flag League campaigns in 1924.

SUDAN PEOPLE'S FEDERAL PARTY. This southern party, post 1983, originally supported the existence of three separate southern provinces. It is associated with Anya Nya II* with a Nuer political leadership.

SUDAN PEOPLE'S LIBERATION ARMY (SPLA). This main southern military resistance force has operated with a political wing, the Sudan People's Liberation Movement (SPLM). Formed initially of Anya Nya II* and various mutinous army units, it was created in Ethiopia in July 1983 after Ja'far Nimeiri's attempt to replace southern soldiers with northern garrisons to quell an insurrection, and after his division of the unified southern administrative region into three provinces. Support for SPLA/SPLM grew after the September 1983 declaration of Shari'a law throughout the country. It has been led since its inception by Colonel John Garang, an American-educated Dinka from the region of Bor, who has served as commander of the SPLA and chairman of the SPLM. Advocating a complete restructuring of the country with strengthened regional authorities, clearly defined limits to central government authority, socialist economic development, and a secular law code, the SPLA/SPLM has faced opposition from both northern political leaders and southern secessionists. The party refused to recognize the Transitional Military Council (TMC) in 1985, calling it a continuation of northern military rule, and it boycotted national elections in 1986. Resisting any discussion of a "southern problem," instead it linked the south to larger issues of uneven regional development and national character. By 1986 the SPLA controlled most of the southern countryside and was extending operations into southern Kordofan province. The downfall of Ethiopia's Marxist regime in 1991, however, cost the SPLA its main haven and source of supplies. Split into two factions, apparently along tribal (Dinka-Nuer) lines, and weakened by the successive assaults of national government troops, the SPLA quickly lost control of most southern towns. In May 1992 both SPLA factions agreed to attend peace negotiations with representatives of the Bashir regime in Abuja, Nigeria.

SUDAN PEOPLE'S LIBERATION MOVEMENT. *See* SUDAN PEOPLE'S LIBERATION ARMY.

SUDAN UNITY PARTY (*Hizb al-Wahda al-Sudani*). A short-lived southern party founded by Santino Deng in 1964, it opposed the Sudan African National Union* and the Southern Front* and advocated a unitary system of government for the country.

SUS. *See* SUDANESE UNION SOCIETY.

UMMA. Formed of the moderate camp of the Graduate Congress under the patronage of Sayyid 'Abd al-Rahman in 1945, Umma's membership base came from the Ansar sect. Originally the party advocated a transitional period for self-determination and the transfer of power to the Sudanese; hostile to Egypt, it insisted upon absolute independence. It formed a coalition government with the People's Democratic Party (PDP)* in 1956, won the 1958 election, and was involved in the Transitional Government of 1964–65. The party split in 1965 into factions led by Imam al-Hadi (traditionalist) and Sadiq al-Mahdi (modernist). It dominated the 1965 elections and formed coalition governments with the National Unionist Party (NUP)* from 1966 to 1967. Umma ruled in coalition with the Democratic Unionist Party (DUP)* from 1986 until the coup of 1989. Leadership of the party has been in the Mahdi family, and the party has drawn upon the hierarchical organization and geographic and tribal representation of the Ansar movement. Support for the Umma has come from the Ansar communities of Dar Fur, Kordofan, the White Nile region (especially Aba Island and Kosti and vicinity), and the Dongola region; the Hadendowa tribe of the east have also been Umma supporters; they were staunch Mahdists in the nineteenth century. The Umma, like the PDP/DUP, has favored an Islamic constitution and a free-enterprise system.

UNIONIST PARTY (*Hizb al-Ittihadiyyin*). A small unionist party led by Hamad Tawfiq, 'Abdallah Mirghani, and Khidr Hamad, and including members of the Abu Ruf faction of the Graduate Congress, it was formed in about 1945. The party advocated a free and democratic Sudan with dominion status under the Egyptian crown. Officially antisectarian, the party had many links to the Khatmiyya. It merged with other unionist parties into the National Unionist Party (NUP)* in 1952.

UNITY OF THE NILE VALLEY PARTY (*Hizb Wahdat Wadi al-Nil*). This small unionist party, led by Dirdiri Ahmad Isma'il and formed ca. 1945, sought the complete integration of Sudan into a single Egyptian state. It merged with other unionist parties into the National Unionist Party (NUP)* in 1952.

WHITE FLAG LEAGUE (WFL) (*Al-Liwa' al-Abyad*). Formed by members of the Sudanese Union Society (SUS)* in 1923, it led a campaign of demonstrations against the condominium government in 1924. The party's leaders included 'Ali 'Abd al-Latif, a Sudanese of Dinka-Nuba heritage and former army lieutenant with a nationalist reputation. The WFL had important links to the "black" communities (southern and Nuba) in the capital, the military, students, merchants, artisans, and petty officials. It espoused independence with some form of union with Egypt. Composed of a small core group of followers, it was well organized. The WFL was a short-lived but influential nationalist movement.

## NOTES

1. For the political and social structures of the Keira and Funj sultanates, see R. S. O'Fahey and J. L. Spaulding, *Kingdoms of the Sudan* (London: Methuen, 1974). The history of the Turco-Egyptian period is treated by Richard Hill in *Egypt in the Sudan, 1820–1881* (London: Oxford University Press, 1959).

2. For the history of the Mahdist period, see P. M. Holt, *The Mahdist State in the Sudan, 1881–1898*, 2d ed. (Oxford: Oxford University Press, 1970).

3. A bibliography of works on the nationalist and independence periods is provided. The content of much of the social and political analysis is taken from Tim Niblock, *Class and Power in Sudan: The Dynamics of Sudanese Politics, 1898–1985* (Albany: State University of New York Press, 1987).

4. Mohamed Omer Beshir gives 1952 as the date for the founding of the MB in Sudan: *Revolution and Nationalism in the Sudan* (London: Rex Collings, 1974), 186. For a different account, see Peter K. Bechtold, *Politics in the Sudan: Parliamentary and Military Rule in an Emerging African Nation* (New York: Praeger, 1976), 89, 98 n. 17.

5. Douglas Johnson, *The Southern Sudan* (London: Minority Rights Group Report no. 78, 1988), 5.

6. See, for example, the Africa Watch Report, "Denying the Honor of Living: Sudan, a Human Rights Disaster" (New York: 1990).

7. What follows is a paraphrasing of Peter K. Bechtold, *Politics in the Sudan*, 78–95.

Robert S. Kramer

# SYRIA

Political parties have played a central role in Syrian politics since at least the early 1900s. In the beginning, the associations that called themselves parties consisted of loose groupings of like-minded individuals, led by one or two prominent patrons. The elite nature of Syria's political parties continued to be in evidence throughout the intermittent periods in which an elected parliament operated during the 1920s and 1930s. It was only in the mid-1940s, with the formation of the Ba'th Party* and the radical peasants' movement, which later became the Arab Socialist Party,* that mass-based political organizations entered the domestic political arena. When these two parties merged in the months preceding the parliamentary election campaign of 1954, the new Arab Socialist Ba'th Party's mass base provided firm support for the principled socialism espoused by Ba'thi ideologues. Nevertheless, elite politicians continued to dominate the electoral system, and the Ba'th proved unable to win a working majority in any of the successive National Assemblies of the 1950s and early 1960s.

In the wake of the March 1963 coup d'état, which put military commanders sympathetic to the party in charge of the state apparatus, the Ba'th Party's primary offices began to intermingle with those of the regular armed forces and central administration. This state of affairs buttressed the Ba'th's revised conception of itself as a Leninist-style vanguard party; in the years after 1966 the party captured virtually every major institution in Syrian society, molding them to conform to the vision and interests of the Ba'thi leadership in Damascus.

## ARAB NATIONALIST AGITATION

Political parties began to coalesce in Syria in the aftermath of the July 1908 revolution in Istanbul organized by the Committee of Union and Progress (CUP). Members of an underground CUP branch in Damascus, in collaboration with clandestine cells of local intellectuals who advocated a greater degree of Syrian autonomy within the overarching Ottoman imperial administration, led popular demonstrations in the city in support of the 1908 uprising. Prominent religious notables ('ulama) in Damascus reacted by forming an organization of their own, the Muslim Union,* which protested the changes introduced by the CUP, most notably concerning women's dress and their participation in affairs outside the home. Candidates sympathetic to the Muslim Union emerged victorious from the parliamentary elections held in early 1909. More important, influential advocates of Syrian autonomy, associated with the Arab Renaissance Society,* joined the opposition to the CUP in Damascus, accusing it of undermining the cosmopolitan nature of the Ottoman Empire by emphasizing the empire's Turkish component. Liberal opponents of the CUP, such as Shafiq Mu-'ayyad al-'Azm, Rushdi al-Sham'a, and Shukri al-'Asali, denounced the authorities in Istanbul from within the chambers of parliament, prompting the CUP to call for new elections in April 1912. These elections were rigged to ensure that only CUP supporters would win seats in the new assembly.

In the wake of the 1912 elections, prominent Syrian liberals emigrated to Cairo, where they formed the Ottoman Party of Administrative Decentralization.* This party, which maintained branches in a number of Syrian cities and towns, advocated greater administrative autonomy for the Arab-speaking provinces of the empire. Its program was complemented by anti-CUP agitation on the part of several secret societies, including the Istanbul-based Qahtan Society,* the Paris-based Young Arab Society,* and the Iraq- and Syria-based Society of the Covenant.* It was among these societies that the seeds of Arab nationalist sentiment germinated throughout Syria in the years just prior to World War I.

Wartime security measures resulted in the forced exile or imprisonment of virtually all of the leaders of both the Ottoman Party of Administrative Decentralization and the secret societies. With the outbreak of the Arab revolt in mid-1916, a handful of prominent Syrians—particularly members of Young Arab Society (al-Fatat)—opted to join the Sharif Husayn of Mecca in fighting for independence from the Ottoman Empire. The majority of Syria's notables, distrustful of Husayn's political ambitions, remained on the sidelines to await the outcome of the contest. A handful of exiled members of the Ottoman Party of Administrative Decentralization in Cairo set up a Party of Syrian Unity* in late 1918. This association gained strength among the notables of Damascus when Husayn's son, Amir Faysal, was appointed ruler over the city by the British in October 1918.

Popular resentment against the Hashimis flared into overt opposition when Faysal agreed to accept increased Jewish immigration into Palestine beginning in January 1919. The Arab Club* in Damascus publicly criticized this arrangement; al-Fatat, on the other hand, kept its support for the Palestinian national movement under wraps, partly to prevent the banning of its front organization, the Party of Arab Independence* which had been formed in December 1918. At the other extreme, the Society of the Covenant, some of whose Iraqi members were at the time serving as cabinet ministers in the Hashimi administration, openly supported Faysal's decision on this issue.

When Faysal attempted to regain popular support for his regime by calling parliamentary elections in mid-1919, CUP sympathizers and other conservatives won most of the seats representing Damascus. Nevertheless, members of al-Fatat and its adjunct Party of Arab Independence dominated the remainder of the assembly. In cooperation with independents from the north-central cities of Aleppo, Hama, and Homs, these representatives succeeded in transforming the parliament into a forum for Arab nationalist propaganda. The fall of 1919 saw Damascene members of al-Fatat forming a Committee of National Defense to resist Faysal's alleged willingness to capitulate to the French. Faysal retaliated by organizing his remaining supporters into a National Party* whose platform called for the establishment, with French assistance, of a constitutional monarchy. But the National Assembly, led by Hashim al-Atasi of Homs, parried this proposal by acclaiming Faysal as king of an independent Greater Syria. Faysal's apparent acquiescence in this action prompted the French army to move against Damascus in July 1920, scattering the leaders of Syria's first organized political parties.

## POLITICS UNDER THE MANDATE

Following the expulsion of Faysal and the arrest and execution of a number of prominent nationalists who remained in the country, the French mandatory authorities outlawed Syria's prewar political parties and proscribed the formation of new ones. In 1922, returned nationalist leaders formed the clandestine Iron Hand Society* under the leadership of 'Abd al-Rahman Shahbandar in Damascus. The society orchestrated a series of massive anti-French demonstrations in the capital that April. Agitation against the French authorities in the north was organized by the Red Hand Society* based in Aleppo.

It was not until a reform-minded French High Commissioner, General Maurice Sarrail, lifted the ban on political associations in 1925, however, that a new generation of formal parties emerged, starting with the People's Party.* This party, led by 'Abd al-Rahman Shahbandar and a corps of Damascene notables, advocated independence for Greater Syria, including the neighboring territories of Lebanon and Alexandretta; explicit constitutional guarantees of individual liberties, including freedom of the press and of association; government protection for Syria's nascent industrial enterprises; and the establishment of universal elementary education. It also openly supported the Druze rebellion of July 1925, which led to the party's suppression in the wake of the revolt. The rump of the membership coalesced in the fall of 1927 into the National Bloc,* whose fifteen founding leaders carried on the old organization's liberal reformist program.

Several other political parties took an active part in National Assembly debates following the 1928 elections. The Syrian Union Party* was formed with the assistance of the French authorities as a counterweight to the People's Party. Disaffected members of the National Bloc set up a Party of National Unity* in 1935 to push for a firmer line on negotiations for independence from the French. A less well-known faction, al-Mu'tadilin,* on the other hand, attempted to achieve Syrian independence by means of active cooperation with the French authorities. Moderates sharing broadly similar views led by Haqqi al-'Azm made up the Reform Party.* The Liberal Constitutional Party,* led by Subhi Barakat, the governor of Aleppo, at first stood in opposition to the National Bloc, but during the course of negotiations over the 1936 treaty on Syrian independence shifted to a decidedly pro-Bloc position. The resurrected Party of Arab Independence demanded the immediate creation of a pan-Arab federation uniting Syria, Lebanon and Iraq. Finally, two royalist groupings, Hizb al-Umma* and Hizb al-Maliki,* favored the establishment of a monarchy in Damascus, perhaps with the Hashimi regent of Iraq, Amir 'Abd al-Illah, as king.

At the grass roots level, social and economic disruptions in the cities and towns precipitated the formation of a network of Islamist societies (jam'iyyat) throughout Syria beginning in the mid-1920s. These associations, led by local religious notables, drew financial and moral support from urban artisans and tradespeople, whose enterprises suffered most from the influx of western manufactured goods into provincial markets. The jam'iyyat pushed the National Bloc to provide material assistance to the 1936 rebellion in Palestine, but these societies became major political actors only during World War II, when they organized a series of public demonstrations in Damascus to protest the growing participation of women in public life and the secularization of Syria's schools.

Meanwhile, in Beirut, the clandestine Party of the Lebanese People was founded in 1924. A year later, a branch of this organization merged with a Lebanese Armenian communist association called Spartacus to form the Communist Party of Syria and Lebanon. Syrians took the leading role in the party with the election of Khalid Bakdash to the first secretaryship in 1932. Under orders from the French Communist Party, the communists supported the abortive 1936 Syrian independence treaty, severely compromising their nationalist credentials. In July 1944, the Syrian and Lebanese wings of the party split into separate organizations, with Bakdash remaining first secretary of the reconfigured Syrian Communist Party.*

Also of Lebanese origin was the Syrian Social National Party (SSNP),* founded as a secret society in November 1932 by Antun Sa'adah. This organization's constitution, circulated two years later, called for the creation of an independent Greater Syria, based on the shared national consciousness of its Arab inhabitants.

## INDEPENDENT SYRIA

At independence in May 1946, four powerful domestic forces struggled for control over Syrian politics. Large landholders and the merchant elite, whose members had profited from wartime shortages in grain and manufactured goods, dominated the revived parliament by means of the National Bloc; independent small farmers concentrated in the 'Alawi and Druze districts, and poor and landless peasants in the central plains, agitated for reform and criticized the evident corruption and nepotism of the old regime. Poorer peasants, led by Akram Hawrani of Hama, initiated a campaign early in 1947 to force the government to change the electoral laws to allow direct elections to the National Assembly. But the president, Shukri al-Quwwatli, responded by ordering a state of emergency designed to limit the activities of radical populist parties, particularly the communists, Hawrani's peasant movement, and the Ba'th Party, which had been founded in 1943–44 and had convened its first congress in Damascus in April 1947. The state of emergency ensured victory for the National Bloc's successor, the revived National Party, in the parliamentary elections of July 1947, but set the stage for serious splits between liberals and conservatives within the regime over the best way to respond to future challenges to the established order.

Following the 1947 elections, party politics began to fragment along regional lines, reflecting deep conflicts of interest between the rich merchants of Damascus and those of Aleppo. Deputies representing the latter, notably Nazim al-Qudsi and Rushdi al-Kikhiyya, mobilized discontented parliamentarians into informal groupings such as the Constitutional Parliamentary Group and the People's Parliamentary Group. The commercial elite of Damascus, represented in the National Assembly by such figures as Faris al-Khuri, Jamil Mardam, and Sabri al-'Asali, remained loyal to the National Party. Both factions courted Syria's large landholders, who were able to mobilize electoral support in the rural areas by manipulating their ties with the poor and landless peasants.

Domestic political infighting, focused on efforts by the government to amend the constitution to allow President al-Quwwatli to run for a second term, precluded an effective response to the escalating Palestinian conflict in the spring of 1948. And although the Syrian brigade that moved into northern Galilee was the only Arab contingent to capture new territory during the first Arab-Israeli war, accusations of incompetence and misappropriation of funds rose in the National Assembly immediately following the cease fire. Members of parliament dissatisfied with the leadership of the National Party re-formed the People's Party in August. This party consisted of both representatives of Aleppo's rich merchant community, who hoped to reestablish connections with the trading centers of northern Iraq, and landed interests around Homs, including Hashim al-Atasi. As one of its first actions, the People's Party petitioned President al-Quwwatli to merge with Iraq as a way of meeting the strategic threat posed by the new State of Israel. National Party deputies rejected this proposal, but failed to maintain parliamentary support for their prime minister, Jamil Mardam. In late November, a strike by students sparked a widespread rebellion that forced the government to resign and led the army chief of staff, Colonel Husni Za'im, to order troops into the streets to restore order.

Continued popular and parliamentary discontent over both the defeat in Palestine and the state of Syrian domestic affairs prompted Za'im to overthrow the elected government in March 1949, with the blessing if not the active support of the United States embassy in Damascus. This move may have been precipitated by the vitriolic criticisms levied against Za'im in the National Assembly by Faysal al'Asali, the leader of the Cooperative Socialist Party.* Unable to convince the leadership in parliament to cooperate with his regime, Za'im abrogated the 1930 constitution, suppressed all political parties, and began ruling by decree. Hawrani's peasant movement joined the Ba'th Party in expressing guarded approval for the steps taken by the new regime to prepare Syria for internal revolution. In June, after the Ba'th began criticizing increased restrictions on free speech, its leaders and those of the resurrected People's Party were arrested. Za'im then proclaimed himself president and orchestrated popular approval of this move by means of a referendum. Two months later, his growing ostentation and the extradition of Antun Sa'adah to Lebanon precipitated Za'im's assassination by a military clique closely tied to the SSNP, which staged a comparatively peaceful coup d'état against his remaining supporters in mid-August.

Colonel Sami Hinnawi, who eventually emerged as the leader of the post-Za'im regime, promised to restore civilian government and called for general elections to select a constituent assembly to frame a new constitution. These elections, in which women voted for the first time, gave a clear majority to the Aleppo-based People's Party, which renewed its demand for immediate union with Iraq. Representatives of the SSNP, which had moved its headquarters to Damascus in the wake of the August 1949 coup, also supported moves toward Arab unity on the part of the new government. But influential opponents of union—in particular Hawrani; the Muslim Brotherhood,* which had been formed out of the *jam'iyyat* during 1945–46 under the leadership of Mustafa al-Siba'i; and senior officers in the armed forces—blocked virtually all parliamentary business during the last two months of the year; and on December 19 a group of junior officers, led by Colonel Adib Shishakli, ousted Hinnawi.

Shishakli reconvened the constituent assembly and ordered it to resume work on the draft constitution. This document, promulgated on September 5, 1950, provided for the restoration of a parliamentary system of government, guaranteed a lengthy list of civil rights, and promised a number of social and economic reforms. But Shishakli and his fellow army officers, who manipulated the various cabinets that succeeded one another at regular intervals, adopted increasingly severe tactics in an attempt to control the labor unions, which enjoyed close ties to the Ba'th, and the peasant movement, which had organized as the Arab Socialist Party* the previous January. In November 1951, the regime once again dissolved the parliament and suspended the constitution. For six months the army ruled Syria directly, without even a cabinet, and in April 1952 it abolished all political parties, replacing them with a regime-sponsored Arab Liberation Movement.* A year later, Shishakli issued a new constitution that mandated a presidential form of government. Under the terms of this document, Shishakli was elected president by plebiscite in July 1953, but his authoritarian methods aroused deep-seated opposition among both establishment politicians and younger army officers, who joined forces to end the military dictatorship in February 1954.

## CRISIS PARLIAMENTARIANISM

The military-civilian coalition that seized power in early 1954 named as president the elderly and highly respected former president Hashim al-Atasi, of the

People's Party. Al-Atasi restored the constitution of 1950 and permitted political parties to operate freely. When general elections were finally held in September 1954, the People's Party and the National Party secured control of the National Assembly by a slim margin, but the new Arab Socialist Ba'th Party,* which had been formed in February 1953 as the amalgamation of the Arab Socialist Party and the Ba'th, emerged as the strongest contender against the old guard. Despite an impressive showing at the polls, the Syrian Communist Party succeeded in electing only one member to the parliament; one SSNP delegate was also seated; and even though the Muslim Brotherhood abjured campaigning, several members of the organization ran as independent candidates. The resurrected Cooperative Socialist Party* also contested the elections, but without success.

The three largest parliamentary blocs compromised to permit the formation of a loose coalition government early in October, with Faris al-Khuri of the People's Party serving as premier. Five months later, when al-Khuri's efforts to maintain a neutral stance in inter-Arab affairs collapsed, Sabri al-Asali of the National Party took over as premier and, with the encouragement and assistance of the Ba'th, implemented a wide-ranging program of industrial and agricultural reforms. Startled by this move, as well as by the resurgent trade union movement in the larger cities, conservative members of parliament blocked a proposed law designed to protect the rights of farm workers and began mobilizing support for the National Party's Shukri al-Quwwatli in the presidential elections of August 1955. At the same time, conflicts between pro-Western and neutralist officers in the armed forces intensified, especially in the wake of the April 1955 assassination of Colonel Adnan al-Malki, the neutralist deputy chief of staff, by a member of the SSNP. The subsequent suppression of the SSNP and the attendant purge of pro-Western officers laid a basis not only for later collaboration between Ba'thi and other leftist military commanders but also for the rise of the army's chief of intelligence, 'Abd al-Hamid Sarraj.

Closer ties with Egypt greatly enhanced the power of Sarraj, who was a firm supporter of Egypt's President Gamal Abdel Nasser, while at the same time persistent United States and Iraqi attempts to provoke internal instability in Syria undermined popular support for the People's Party, many of whose leaders enjoyed close ties to the pro-Western regime of Nuri al-Sa'id in Baghdad. During the summer and fall of 1956, Syrian military intelligence uncovered an extensive plot to topple al-Quwwatli's government, ostensibly sponsored by Iraqi agents. The urgency of the situation was highlighted in August, when Iraqi weapons were smuggled into Jabal al-Druze in anticipation of the Israeli-British-French strike against Egypt. In December, forty-seven high-ranking pro-Iraqi members of the People's Party were brought before a military court chaired by Colonel Afif al-Bizri and summarily convicted of treason. Prime Minister al-Asali immediately removed People's Party ministers from the cabinet, replacing them with prominent Ba'this and overtly anti-American independents.

Subsequent U.S. attempts to destabilize the new government by dumping American wheat into Syria's traditional markets in Greece and Italy generated widespread popular sympathy for leftist parties. The disclosure of an alleged American plot to overthrow al-Quwwatli and replace him with a military junta sent Sarraj and al-Bizri to Cairo to discuss possible Egyptian assistance in the event of a coup. By the end of 1957, fear of the rising influence of the communists prompted the Ba'th Party to join the People's Party in refusing to take part in municipal elections, a move that resulted in the indefinite postponement of the elections, and prevented the communists from gauging the level of their electoral support. In early January 1958, the Ba'thi leadership persuaded newly appointed Chief of Staff al-Bizri to travel to Egypt in secret to ask Nasser for an immediate union between the two countries. A month later, al-Quwwatli flew to Cairo to announce the creation of the United Arab Republic (UAR).

## UNITED ARAB REPUBLIC AS INTERLUDE

Egyptian officials dictated two primary conditions in return for agreeing to the union: The Syrian army must stop interfering in politics and all political parties must be abolished in Syria, as they had been in Egypt five years earlier. The Syrian people acceded to these demands by enthusiastically approving the merger in a referendum on February 21, 1958; the union took effect the following day. A provisional constitution provided for a single president and cabinet for the union as a whole, as well as for separate executive councils for the Northern and Southern Regions of the UAR, as Syria and Egypt were now called. In the summer of 1959, the government in Cairo authorized the Egypt-based National Union* to be the country's sole legal political organization. More significantly, the combined executive appointed 'Abd al-Hamid Sarraj as minister of the interior with sole authority over the Syrian security services. Under Sarraj's direction, the rising communist influence in the country was curtailed, but at the cost of the gradual elimination from public office of the Syrian politicians who had originally sponsored the union.

Egyptian efforts to create a unified political entity out of these two disparate countries evidenced more vigor than imagination. Officials based in Cairo sought to apply development programs designed for the Nile valley to the wholly different social and economic conditions prevailing in Syria. When the UAR's central administration introduced a comprehensive socialist program in the summer of 1961, largely in reaction to developments within the Southern Region, merchants and tradespeople in Syria's cities started agitating against the union; and with the reassignment of Sarraj to Cairo, the Egyptian hold over the Northern Region weakened, opening the door to more effective Syrian resistance. Even the generally pro-Nasser Ba'th Party joined the rising opposition to the Egyptian-sponsored socialist program on the grounds that it was designed merely to deflect popular criticism and to impose a greater degree of state control over the Northern Region's internal affairs. These circumstances made it relatively easy for a heterogeneous civilian-military coalition to orchestrate Syria's secession from the UAR in September 1961.

## RETURN TO SOVEREIGNTY

Syria's preunion political parties found themselves decimated by the actions of the Egyptian secret police during the three and a half years of the UAR. Within the Ba'th, a radical wing associated with Akram Hawrani early on favored secession, while the more moderate wing of the party led by Michel Aflaq refused to endorse any retreat from Arab unity. The communists were prohibited from playing any role in the revived nation, and most of their leaders remained imprisoned until early 1962. The old National and People's Parties no longer elicited popular support, while Nasserists continued to occupy many of the top posts in the trade unions and central bureaucracy.

Under these circumstances, the leaders of the secessionist movement could at first find no one to head a new Syrian government. They finally convinced Ma'mun al-Kuzbari, the former secretary of the National Union in Damascus, to form a cabinet made up of oldtime National and People's Party notables. But this government required continued intervention by the military and state security agencies to forestall widespread opposition, particularly on the part of the trade unions and the peasant movement. Backed by the army high command, al-Kuzbari's ministers began dismantling the country's public sector and encouraging private enterprise. This program was bolstered by the results of the non-party December 1961 parliamentary elections, which gave former People's Party and National Party candidates a working majority. Former Ba'this, most notably allies of Akram Hawrani, formed the largest opposition bloc. Nevertheless, the People's Party–dominated cabinet that took office in the wake of the elections denationalized most of Syria's commercial and industrial firms, rescinded UAR–era legislation expropriating British, French, and Belgian properties, and modified the 1961 land reform law in favor of the country's larger agriculturalists.

Throughout the winter of 1961–62, demands for democratization were increasingly voiced by leftist delegates to the National Assembly such as Hawrani and the independent radical Khalid al-'Azm. These demands finally forced the resignation of the cabinet on March 25, 1962. Three days later, an army faction headed by the original secessionists arrested most of the members of parliament and attempted to coerce them into reinstating the economic and social policies of the UAR period; three days after that, Nasserist officers based in Homs carried out an unsuccessful countercoup; finally, on April 1, the army commander in chief ordered a meeting of senior commanders in Homs to formulate a unified program of action. The agreement reached at this meeting removed doctrinaire socialists from the armed forces and restored civilian government, but it also dissolved the parliament and named the commander in chief, Major General 'Abd al-Karim Zahr al-Din, as minister of defense, bringing the army's role in politics out into the open.

In September, after six months of unrest among workers and peasants throughout the country, the military high command reinstated the parliament and appointed Khalid al-'Azm as prime minister; al-'Azm rescinded the UAR ban on political parties and formed a cabinet that included representatives of all parties and factions except those advocating outright reunification with Egypt. But the prime minister's outspoken opposition to continued military involvement in politics, along with the eruption of public protests organized by Nasserists and the Muslim Brotherhood in Damascus and the Hawran in January 1963 and the Ba'thi coup d'état in Iraq the following month, precipitated yet another coup d'état in Syria that March.

## THE BA'THI ERA

Although not a part of the official party organization, the Military Committee of the Ba'th that came to power in Damascus following the March 1963 coup shared the objectives of promoting socialism and securing Syrian independence within the framework of a pan-Arab regional order held by the established Ba'thi leadership. Salah al-Din Bitar was asked to serve as the country's first Ba'thi prime minister, while Colonel Amin al-Hafiz was recalled from exile in Argentina to act as minister of the interior and military governor. A National Council for Command of the Revolution was formed to direct the country's affairs. Initially, it was made up of Ba'thists, Nasserists, and self-proclaimed independent progressives. The predominance of the Ba'th became more evident within a few months, however; in early August, a cabinet was formed consisting exclusively of Ba'this and closely allied socialist unionists.

During its first months in power, the new government carried out a two-pronged program to reduce the level of exploitation in Syrian society. It nationalized all indigenous and foreign banks and insurance companies, and it enacted a new agrarian reform law that set strict limits on the size of private landholdings. At the same time, however, it undertook to reassure private entrepreneurs that wholesale nationalization was not being considered; Prime Minister Bitar announced that private ownership would be maintained "in productive industrial sectors, which sincerely serve the interests of the people." Fluctuations between these two poles characterized the regime's economic policies from 1963 to 1965.

Politically, the Military Committee took charge of the Regional (Syrian) Command of the Ba'th Party. The officers made common cause with younger, more doctrinaire party members who felt little sympathy for elder statesmen like Aflaq and Bitar, who tended to patronize the newer cadres streaming into the party in the wake of the March 1963 coup. Collaboration with such ambitious newcomers enabled the Military Committee to capture the key institutions of the Syrian state during the summer and fall of 1963. The committee thus achieved a position from which it could dictate dramatic revisions of Ba'th ideology at the Sixth National (Pan-Arab) Congress that convened in Damascus in October of that year.

The doctrinal statements adopted during this Congress declared the Ba'th's primary objective to be the establishment of socialism through the mechanism of a type of Leninist "revolutionary vanguard." Arab unity, once a coequal goal of the party, was now treated as little more than a means for the more effective advancement of socialism. In the words of Itamar Rabinovich, "For the majority at the Sixth National Congress the immediate goal appeared to be the establishment of a socialist society, while Arab unity became a sacred slogan still deserving of proper respect."[1] Furthermore, the very notion of socialism articulated by the congress differed sharply from that implicit in the pronouncements of the party's founders: It was now couched almost in Marxist-Leninist terms, with references to class struggle and the dialectical development of social relations. Such shifts in Ba'thi ideology presaged significant changes in the composition of the Syrian government, as Colonel al-Hafiz replaced Bitar as prime minister at the conclusion of the congress and brought new and younger ministers into his cabinet, such as the radical technocrat Yusuf Zu'ayyin.

In spring 1964, opposition to the restructured Ba'th erupted in several cities in the north-central part of the country. Students in Hama vandalized government and party buildings in April, and prominent 'ulama castigated the government's socialist policies in their Friday sermons. Radicals based in the Ba'th's provincial branches responded to the unrest by nationalizing a number of larger industrial firms in the cities of Aleppo and Homs and setting up a form of self-management within them. By the summer, these same cadres had succeeded in pressuring the government to acquiesce in the formation of countrywide trade union federations and to adopt a new labor law that greatly increased the state's role in guaranteeing workers' rights. In the fall, a party-affiliated General Peasants' Union was formed, and in mid-December the state reserved for itself all future revenues from oil production in the country.

These steps set the stage for a radical restructuring of Syria's politico-economic system that began in January 1965. A series of measures, known as the Ramadan Socialist Decrees, extended state control over Syria's most important economic enterprises; additional nationalizations occurred over the subsequent six months. This program finally cut the remaining ties between the Ba'th and artisans and tradespeople of the cities and towns who had supported the party's broadly nationalist objectives. Tensions between these two coalitions erupted in a series of riots and demonstrations in Syria's cities during the spring and summer of 1965, precipitating a power struggle between General al-Hafiz and General Salah Jadid over the future course of the Ba'thi revolution. The former, who had served as president since 1964, turned to the National (Pan-Arab) Command of the party for support, while the latter consolidated his hold over the Regional (Syrian) apparatus with the help of strategically placed Syrian military commanders. Supporters of Salah Jadid, including the influential commander of the air force, General Hafiz al-Asad, finally ousted al-Hafiz and his allies in late February 1966.

Jadid's regime represented the triumph of the socialist state administration over private enterprise in Syrian society and therefore marked a dramatic shift in the country's politics. The new government played down even further the pan-Arab tenets of the Ba'th Party, concentrating its attention instead on purely Syrian issues. It set up extensive state agricultural projects and organized the land that had been sequestered in earlier land reforms into state-supervised cooperatives, and it introduced a central economic planning organization in 1968, after having adopted measures that concentrated all wholesale trade in the public sector. More important, the new regime revived the Ba'th's earlier alliance with the Syrian Communist Party, appointing prominent communists to positions in the cabinet.

These policies alienated the urban petite bourgeoisie in the provincial cities and towns, who were coerced into complying with party directives by the party-affiliated workers' militia, led by Khalid al-Jundi. Anti-Ba'th protests once again broke out in the north-central cities in the spring of 1967, precipitated by an editorial in the army's weekly magazine that was widely held to be atheistic. The regime retaliated by mobilizing both the workers' and peasants' militias and various Palestinian guerrilla formations stationed on Syrian soil. The spiral of militarization that accompanied this effort helped push the country into the disastrous June war with Israel.

Syria's economy was severely damaged by the 1967 war, as was the reputation of the Jadid regime, whose leadership was held responsible not only for the poor showing of the army and air force but also for the loss of the strategically important Golan Heights. Persistent domestic economic difficulties generated another round of anti-regime violence in urban districts throughout 1968 and 1969. These uprisings were spearheaded by the comparatively militant northern branches of the Syrian Muslim Brotherhood, known as the Fighting Vanguard,* led by Marwan Hadid and supported by comparatively militant branches of the organization based in the north-central cities. Challenges from below accompanied a growing split within the regime itself that pitted radicals associated with Jadid, who favored greater state control over the economy and the subordination of the military with the civilian wing of the party, against pragmatists allied with al-Asad, who wanted to encourage private enterprise and maintain the autonomy of the military with civilian authority. By January 1970, the pragmatists had pushed through a set of regulations that subsidized private factories and workshops and relaxed restrictions on a variety of imports. The popularity and success of these measures provided the foundations for the coup d'état that brought Hafiz al-Asad to power in November 1970.

Shortly after taking power, the al-Asad regime announced the creation of a reconfigured parliament, the People's Assembly, charged with drafting a permanent constitution to supersede the provisional ones promulgated by the Ba'th in 1964 and 1969. Members of the assembly were to be selected by the president and his closest advisers so as to represent the Ba'th and its four officially sanctioned competitors—the Syrian Communist Party; the Arab Socialist Union,* which had broken from the Ba'th in 1961; the Socialist Unionists' Movement,* an offshoot of the Arab Socialist Union; and the Arab Socialist Movement, the successor to Akram Hawrani's Arab Socialist Party—although a few independents and representatives of opposition organizations were also included. In March

1972, Syria's five main political parties coalesced into a National Progressive Front.*

A year later, the revised constitution was ratified by plebiscite. It provided for a popularly elected president, who was to be nominated by the Ba'thi leadership for a seven-year term of office, approved by the People's Assembly, and confirmed by an absolute majority in a national referendum. The president was empowered to appoint and remove the vice president(s), the prime minister and other members of the cabinet, or Council of Ministers; to dissolve the People's Assembly and assume its legislative functions until it reconvened; to call for national referenda to approve measures not adopted by the assembly; to select judges for the high courts; and to appoint provincial governors. He was also made commander in chief of the armed forces, while the Ba'th Party was designated "the leading party of the society and state." On the other hand, the 1973 constitution gave the People's Assembly the authority to veto or amend presidential decrees by a two-thirds vote, although this provision remained dormant throughout the 1970s and 1980s.

Festering discontent among artisans and tradespeople of the north-central cities convinced leaders of the northern branches of the Muslim Brotherhood to launch a campaign to overthrow the al-Asad regime by force in the first months of 1976. The Islamist opposition gained strength and momentum as Syria's intervention in the Lebanese civil war bogged down, and between 1978 and 1980 intermittent strikes and demonstrations paralyzed the north-central cities of Aleppo, Hama, Homs, and Idlib. These protests culminated in the formation of an Islamic Front in Syria* at the end of 1980. The Front's published manifesto called for the overthrow of the al-Asad regime and the establishment of an elective parliamentary order firmly grounded in the principles of Islam. Running battles between Islamist militants on one hand and the armed forces and state security services on the other escalated throughout 1980 and 1981, leading to a citywide revolt in Hama during the first week of February 1982. The ferocity with which the government suppressed this rebellion crushed both the militant northern and the more quietist Damascene branches of the Muslim Brotherhood, although the exiled leadership of the Islamic Front announced the creation of a successor National Alliance for the Liberation of Syria in May 1982.

Following three months of intense jockeying for position among potential successors while he was recuperating from a serious illness, President al-Asad named three of his most powerful lieutenants to be vice presidents of the republic on March 11, 1984. The strongest of these, his brother Rif'at, at the time commanded the well-armed Defense Brigades responsible for guarding official buildings in the capital, although he was relieved of this command two months later and many of his former battalions were subsequently incorporated into units of the regular army. These steps put him more or less on a par with the other two vice presidents—'Abd al-Halim Khaddam and Zuhair Masharqah—who had previously served as the country's foreign minister and as deputy secretary of the Regional Command of the Ba'th Party, respectively. Less than a year after his appointment as vice president, Rif'at al-Asad was expelled from Syria on charges of corruption. He remained in exile for the rest of the decade, reportedly attempting to gauge public support for a new party tentatively named Young Syria.

General elections to the People's Assembly have taken place approximately every four years since 1973. The Ba'th has dominated each session of the assembly, nominally in collaboration with its partners in the National Progressive Front. The 1986 elections gave Ba'thi representatives 129 of the assembly's 195 seats; the remaining parties in the National Progressive Front captured 57 seats, while the Syrian Communist Party took 8 seats. Four years later, the Ba'th won 137 of the assembly's expanded total of 250 seats; other National Progressive Front parties won 31; the remainder went to independent candidates. In the wake of the 1990 elections, a new Islamic party was added to the National Progressive Front in an effort to bolster the front's appeal in future campaigns.

More important than the regularly scheduled sessions of the People's Assembly are the occasional congresses of the Regional (Syrian) Command of the Ba'th. The January 1985 congress, the first since 1980, highlighted the effective demotion of Rif'at al-Asad. Although the president's brother retained fifth place in the senior party hierarchy, three of his closest associates were relieved of their posts entirely. These congresses displayed considerable debate concerning the government's economic and social programs on the part of rank-and-file delegates, but domestic political and foreign policy issues remained definitively off-limits. Uncertainties arising from the dramatic changes in Eastern Europe led to the indefinite postponement of the ninth Regional Congress, which had been scheduled to convene in March 1989.

## Bibliography

Abd-Allah, Umar F. *The Islamic Struggle in Syria*. Berkeley, Calif.: Mizan Press, 1983.

Chizik, I. "Political Parties in Syria." *Journal of the Royal Central Asian Society*, 22,1 (October 1935), pp. 556–65.

Devlin, John F. *The Ba'th Party*. Stanford, Calif.: Hoover Institution Press, 1976.

Khoury, Philip S. *Urban Notables and Arab Nationalism*. Cambridge: Cambridge University Press, 1983.

———. *Syria and the French Mandate*. Princeton, N.J.: Princeton University Press, 1987.

Perthes, Volker. "Syria's Parliamentary Elections: Remodeling Asad's Political Base." *Middle East Report*, 174 (January–February 1992), pp. 15–18.

Petran, Tabitha. *Syria*. New York: Praeger, 1972.

Rabinovich, Itamar. *Syria under the Ba'th, 1963–66: The Army-Party Symbiosis*. New York: Halsted Press, 1972.

Roberts, David. *The Ba'th and the Creation of Modern Syria*. New York: St. Martin's Press, 1987.

Van Dam, Nikolaos. *The Struggle for Power in Syria*. New York: St. Martin's Press, 1979.

Yamak, Labib Zuwiyya. *The Syrian Social Nationalist Party: An Ideological Analysis*. Cambridge, Mass.: Harvard Middle East Monographs, 1966.

**Political Parties**

AL-'AHD. *See* SOCIETY OF THE COVENANT.

ARAB CLUB (*al-Nadi al-'Arabi*). This secret society, founded in Damascus, was critical of the regime of Amir Faysal following World War I. Its members were outspoken in their criticism of the regime of the Hashimi Amir Faysal, who had been appointed ruler of Syria by the British. The club particularly opposed Faysal's willingness to cooperate with the British in facilitating Jewish immigration into Palestine in 1919–20.

ARAB LIBERATION MOVEMENT (*Haraka al-Tahrir al-'Arabi*). This mass organization was set up in April 1952 by the regime of Adib Shishakli to take the place of the existing political parties in Syria. Its candidates, running virtually unopposed, captured a great majority of seats in the October 1953 parliamentary elections. Acts of retribution against Shishakli's supporters led to the revival of the party in the months leading up to the elections of September 1954. One of those who played a major role in reviving the movement at this time, Ma'mun al-Kuzbari, later played a key role in the National Union,* a similar organization set up during the United Arab Republic period. The movement won two seats in the National Assembly in 1954, but it carried little weight in subsequent debates and quietly disappeared later in the decade.

ARAB RENAISSANCE SOCIETY (*Jam'iyya al-Nahda al-'Arabiyya*). This secret society was formed just after 1908 by a group of Syrian notables who advocated greater Syrian autonomy in response to what they saw as the "Turkification" of the hitherto multiethnic Ottoman Empire by the reformist Committee of Union and Progress.

ARAB SOCIALIST PARTY (*Hizb al-'Arabi al-Ishtiraki*). This radical party was founded by Akram Hawrani of Hama in January 1950 with widespread support from the poorer peasants of Syria's north-central plains. The party grew out of the peasant movement that emerged in the mid-1940s under Hawrani's leadership; this movement proposed measures that would have imposed strict limitations on the size of private agricultural landholdings in successive sessions of the National Assembly throughout the late 1940s. Hawrani initially supported the military regime of Husni Za'im because he felt that its policies prepared the ground for a revolutionary transformation of Syrian society. But he parted company with Za'im as restrictions on freedom of expression and assembly were promulgated during the summer of 1949.

In February 1953, while the Shishakli regime maintained a ban on all political parties, Hawrani held meetings in Beirut with the leaders of the Ba'th Party,* which resulted in the merger of the two organizations to form the Arab Socialist Resurrection (Ba'th) Party (see Ba'th Party). The popular base that had been cultivated by Hawrani in the Syrian countryside during the 1940s enabled the new Ba'th to raise its representation in the National Assembly from one delegate in 1949 to twenty-two in the elections of September 1954. At the insistence of Hawrani and his followers, the greatly strengthened Ba'th encouraged successive Syrian governments to carry out fundamental reforms in the agricultural and industrial sectors of the local economy during the 1950s. By 1957, however, Hawrani's left wing of the Ba'th found itself eclipsed by independent socialists like Khalid al-'Azm, who frightened the party's mainstream into pursuing a political union with Egypt in the form of the UAR (formed in February 1958).

Former Arab Socialist Party cadres welcomed the collapse of the UAR three years later but were unable to regain positions of influence within the Ba'th Party after the dissolution of the union with Egypt. Hawranists won a convincing victory in the December 1961 nonpartisan parliamentary elections, but their repeated calls for greater democratization were ignored by various governments of the day. When Ba'thi officers seized control in the aftermath of the March 1963 coup d'état, Hawrani's supporters were gradually marginalized within the Ba'th. Although the Arab Socialist Party's later successor, the Arab Socialist Movement, was one of the founding members of the Ba'th-dominated National Progressive Front,* the party completely lost influence over policy making after the al-Asad regime took power in November 1970. In May 1982, the leaders of the old Arab Socialist Party joined exiled Islamists, Nasserists, and dissident Ba'this in forming a National Alliance for the Liberation of Syria.

ARAB SOCIALIST RESURRECTION (BA'TH) PARTY. *See* BA'TH PARTY.

ARAB SOCIALIST UNION (*Ittihad al-'Arabi al-Ishtiraki*). A formal party organization set up by members of the Ba'th Party* sympathetic to the principles and programs of the United Arab Republic. With the collapse of the UAR in September 1961, these unionists formally split with the Ba'th, whose leadership had grown increasingly disenchanted with the UAR as an experiment in Arab unification. The party that emerged as a result of the split continued to cooperate closely with its parent organization, particularly in the wake of the March 1963 coup d'état that brought Ba'thi officers to power in Damascus. The Arab Socialist Union, one of the founding members of the Ba'thi-dominated National Progressive Front,* continues to put forward candidates for election to the People's Assembly under the auspices of the front.

BA'TH PARTY (*Hizb al-Ba'th al-'Arabi*). This pan-Arab nationalist organization was founded in Damascus in the early 1940s by a trio of committed Arab nationalists: the Greek orthodox Michel Aflaq, the Sunni Muslim Salah al-Din Bitar, and the 'Alawi Zaki Arsuzi. The party grew out of an earlier grouping called the Arab Resurrection (*al-Ba'th al-'Arabi*), organized by Arsuzi in Damascus in 1940. Angered by Aflaq and Bitar's appropriation of the name, Arsuzi disbanded his group in 1944.

Meanwhile, the group led by Aflaq and Bitar began to pick up steam, attracting the attention of Sami al-Jundi and 'Abd al-Halim Qaddur, disciples of Arsuzi, as well as the young reformers Akram Hawrani and Jamal al-Atasi. Aflaq and Bitar were candidates in the parliamentary elections of 1943, but neither was elected. After the election, they referred to themselves as leaders of the Ba'th Party, and in July 1945, they attempted to register the party with the French authorities. The application was denied; nevertheless the party convened a general membership meeting in Damascus in December of that year. As John Devlin has noted, "During this period, [the Ba'th] acted pretty much as would any conventional political party in an Arab state. The party was not a secret organization in any sense."[2]

By the time Syria gained its independence in May 1946, the Ba'th had established local branches throughout the country. Aflaq and Bitar traveled to Latakia early in 1947 to persuade Arsuzi to join them. Their discussions led directly to the first official congress of the party, convened in Damascus in April 1947. The congress elected Aflaq as head of the organization, and it selected Bitar, Jalal al-Sayyid, and Wahib al-Ghanim, a representative of Arsuzi, to serve as the governing council. This council supervised the publication of the party's newspaper, al-Ba'th, and authorized the establishment of district branches (firr) in Syrian cities and towns. Branches were also set up in Jordan, Lebanon, and Iraq during the late 1940s. (See the chapters on Jordan, Lebanon, and Iraq.)

Efforts by the National Bloc* to restrict the activities of radical parties prevented the Ba'th from winning seats in the National Assembly elections of July 1947. But as the mainstream parties fragmented along regional lines over the next two years, Ba'th Party spokespersons stepped up their criticism of the "feudalists, reactionaries and exploiters" who dominated the government. These attacks prompted President Shukri al-Quwwatli to close several of its offices and to order Aflaq's arrest in the fall of 1948. Nevertheless, the Ba'th's consistent demands for political reform attracted adherents from all classes. This theme even played a role in motivating Colonel Husni Za'im to overthrow the elected government in March 1949.

The Ba'th joined Akram Hawrani's peasant movement in expressing guarded approval for the policies adopted during the first weeks of the Za'im regime on the assumption that they would help prepare Syrian society for a long-awaited revolution. It was not long, however, before the demands for greater freedom of expression began to grate on the new president; in mid-June 1949, the leaders of the Ba'th were arrested. After the overthrow of Za'im in August 1949, the party opened talks with the People's Party* to form a joint list of candidates for the resuscitated parliament. These discussions soon collapsed, and the Ba'th made overtures instead to Hawrani's newly established Arab Socialist Party.* These negotiations bore valuable fruit: In February 1953, the Ba'th formally merged with the Arab Socialist Party to form the Arab Socialist Resurrection (Ba'th) Party.

Invigorated by the supporters of the Arab Socialist Party, and gaining sympathy for its commitment to a foreign policy of nonalignment and its opposition to persistent U.S. efforts to undermine the government of Shukri al-Quwwatli in the mid-1950s, the Ba'th became increasingly influential in Syrian politics. Ba'thi candidates won approximately sixteen seats in the parliamentary elections of September 1954, thanks largely to a clean sweep of the districts around Hama by Hawrani's allies. These deputies provided a crucial margin of support for the reform program carried out by Prime Minister Sabri al-'Asali beginning in March 1955. Paradoxically, the party exerted considerably less influence over the radical-dominated cabinets of 1956–57, which drew their strength from the Ba'th's major rivals, the Syrian Communist Party* and the independent Khalid al-'Azm. Confronted by the rising power of these competitors, Ba'thi leaders took the initiative in persuading Syrian and Egyptian officials to form the United Arab Republic in February 1958.

Egypt's president Gamal Abdel Nasser proved no more palatable as a partner than had Syria's indigenous radicals, provoking the Ba'th to join the coalition that orchestrated the dissolution of the United Arab Republic in September 1961. Officers sympathetic to the party took control of Syria's central administration in the wake of the March 1963 coup d'état; the following year, militant party cadres in the north-central cities began sequestering private enterprises and turning them over to the workers. These actions set the stage for a series of nationalizations in 1965 and 1966, culminating in the February 1966 coup that brought a radical Ba'thi leadership to power in Damascus. This leadership steadily increased state control over the economy and forged closer ties to the Syrian Communist Party and the Soviet Union. The 1966–70 period also saw the consolidation of Ba'thi control over trade unions, youth organizations, the peasant union, and the women's federation, each of which became a virtual subsidiary of the Ba'th. Intraparty rivalry pitting the more radical Salah Jadid against the more pragmatic Hafiz al-Asad ended with the latter's seizing power in November 1970. Over the subsequent two decades, the Ba'th has functioned as Syria's predominant political institution, dictating the program of the umbrella National Progressive Front.*

In structural terms, the civilian apparatus of the Ba'th Party consists at bottom of a layer of distinct cells made up of from three to five members. Such cells may be based in a particular district or neighborhood or may be associated with a specific economic enterprise or government agency. The membership of the cells is supposed to be a closely guarded secret for security reasons; communication across different cells is thus actively discouraged. Half a dozen or so cells constitute a section (firqa), headed by an elected executive committee. Sections are grouped into thirteen branches, broadly congruent with Syria's thirteen administrative provinces, each of which also elects its own executive committee. It is likely that the military wing of the party is constructed in a severely hierarchical fashion as well. In any case, policy has always been set at the pinnacle of the Ba'thi apparatus, with directives from the top passed down through successive layers of the party hierarchy for implementation.

Ba'thi doctrine was most authoritatively codified in the party's theoretical statement *Some Theoretical Starting Points* (*Ba'd al-Muntalaqat al-Nadriyya*), drafted by Michel Aflaq for the Sixth National (Pan-Arab) Congress held in Damascus in October 1963. This statement introduced the slogan: "Unity, Freedom and Socialism" (*Wahda, Hurriyya wa Ishtirakiyya*). Steps to promote effective unity among the existing Arab states were thus given highest priority. The party's concept of freedom appears largely derivative of the political philosophy of Jean-Jacques Rousseau: It bears little resemblance to liberal democratic thought, tolerating neither unbridled individual liberties nor representative government. The third Ba'thi goal, socialism, has proven the most elastic of all. From 1963 to 1966, it largely signified a mixed economic program that included both measures designed to redistribute income and state support for "non-exploitative" private enterprise; from 1966 to 1970, a more radical notion of socialism that entailed widespread collective ownership and comprehensive state planning predominated; with the advent of the al-Asad regime in November 1970, government economic policy shifted once again to encourage the reintroduction of private ownership throughout the local economy. The very flexibility of Ba'thi doctrine, while engendering profound frustration on the part of ideologues in other parties, has provided a touchstone for the disparate leaderships that have governed Syria beginning with the March 1963 coup d'état. (See also chapters on Iraq, Jordan, and Lebanon.)

COMMUNIST PARTY OF SYRIA. *See* SYRIAN COMMUNIST PARTY.

COOPERATIVE SOCIALIST PARTY (*Hizb al-Ishtiraki al-Ta'awwuni*). This party first appeared in the immediate aftermath of the 1948 Palestinian war, when its leader, Faysal al-'Asali, strongly criticized the armed forces for failing to defeat the infant Israeli army. Al-'Asali's invective against Chief of Staff Husni al-Za'im provoked the latter's wrath against the National Assembly in general, thereby contributing to Za'im's decision to wrest control of the government from the civilian leadership in the March 1949 coup d'état. The party reemerged in the parliamentary election of September 1954, but it failed to win any seats and evaporated soon thereafter. Its platform has been described by Patrick Seale as a broadly right-wing, pan-Islamist one.

AL-FATAT. *See* YOUNG ARAB SOCIETY.

FIGHTING VANGUARD (*al-Tali'a al-Muqatila*). These secret cells of militant members of the Syrian Muslim Brotherhood* emerged under the leadership of Marwan Hadid of Hama province in the late 1960s. Hadid, who had studied in Cairo under the chief ideologue of the Egyptian Muslim Brotherhood, Sayyid Qutb, argued that the association faced ultimate extinction at the hands of the state unless it defended itself through armed struggle (*jihad*). Although this message did not appeal to the mainstream leaders of the Syrian Muslim Brotherhood in Damascus, who favored nonviolent means to undermine the power and legitimacy of the Ba'thi regime, younger members in the north-central cities, particularly Hama and Aleppo, rallied to his side.

Hadid's followers organized into clandestine cells (*usrahs*) of a dozen or so members, supported by artisans and tradespeople who made up the majority of the membership of the northern branches of the Syrian Muslim Brotherhood. These cells organized a series of anti-Ba'thi uprisings in Aleppo, Hama, Homs, and Idlib in 1968 and 1969. In the early 1970s, they coalesced under the rubric of the Fighting Vanguard, attracting the support of one of Syria's most prominent Islamist ideologues, Sa'id Hawwa.

Throughout the 1970s, the Fighting Vanguard carried on a campaign of assassination and intimidation against Ba'th Party officials. Marwan Hadid was captured in the course of one of these operations in Damascus in 1976, and he died in prison shortly thereafter. Leadership was then disputed among several rivals, including Hawwa and Adnan 'Uqlah. But the organization continued its campaign to destabilize the regime, striking at more and more targets. These attacks culminated in a brief but bloody civil war in the north-central cities in the spring of 1980. During this struggle, state security services decimated the Fighting Vanguard, capturing or killing most of its leaders. Remnants of the organization, led by 'Uqlah, cooperated with the Islamic Front in Syria* during the February 1982 rebellion in Hama but refused to join the front in setting up the National Alliance for the Liberation of Syria in May. In January 1985, 'Uqlah ended three years of fruitless clandestine agitation against the regime by surrendering to the authorities under the terms of a general amnesty.

HARAKA AL-TAHRIR AL-'ARABI. See ARAB LIBERATION MOVEMENT.

HIZB AL-'ARABI AL-ISHTIRAKI. See ARAB SOCIALIST PARTY.

HIZB AL-BA'TH AL-'ARABI. See BA'TH PARTY.

HIZB AL-HURR AL-DUSTURI. See LIBERAL CONSTITUTIONAL PARTY.

HIZB AL-ISLAH. See REFORM PARTY.

HIZB AL-ISTIQLAL AL-'ARABI. See PARTY OF ARAB INDEPENDENCE.

HIZB AL-ITTIHAD AL-SURI. See PARTY OF SYRIAN UNITY.

HIZB AL-LAMARKAZIYYA AL-IDARIYYA AL-'UTHMANI. See OTTOMAN PARTY OF ADMINISTRATIVE DECENTRALIZATION.

HIZB AL-MALIKI. This monarchist party played an active role in Syrian parliamentary debates in the late 1920s. Its platform called for the establishment of a constitutional monarchy in Damascus, perhaps with the regent of Iraq, Amir 'Abd al-Illah, as king.

HIZB AL-SHA'B. *See* PEOPLE'S PARTY.

HIZB AL-SHUYU'I AL-SURI. *See* SYRIAN COMMUNIST PARTY.

HIZB AL-SURI AL-QAWMI AL-IJTIMA'I. *See* SYRIAN SOCIAL NA-TIONAL PARTY.

HIZB AL-TADAMAN AL-WATANI. *See* PARTY OF NATIONAL UNITY.

HIZB AL-UMMA. This monarchist party played an active part in Syrian parliamentary debates in the late 1920s. The party's platform called for the establishment of a constitutional monarchy in Damascus, perhaps with the regent of Iraq, the Amir 'Abd al-Illah, as king.

HIZB AL-WAHDA AL-SURIYYA. *See* SYRIAN UNION PARTY.

AL-HIZB AL-WATANI. *See* NATIONAL PARTY.

IKHWAN AL-MUSLIMIN. *See* MUSLIM BROTHERHOOD.

IRON HAND SOCIETY (*Jam'iyya al-Qabda al-Hadidiyya*). This secret society was founded in Damascus in 1922 under the leadership of 'Abd al-Rahman Shahbandar. Its members were mostly drawn from the corps of Syrian nationalists who had been forced to flee the country during World War I. The society orchestrated a number of antimandate demonstrations in Damascus in April 1922. When the reform-minded French High Commissioner for Syria, General Maurice Sarrail, rescinded the ban on political parties, Shahbandar and his allies formed the People's Party* to continue the struggle against the French mandatory regime.

ISLAMIC FRONT IN SYRIA (*al-Jabha al-Islamiyya fi Suriyya*). This umbrella organization was formed by the leaders of the Syrian Muslim Brotherhood* in the aftermath of the 1980 civil war against the Ba'thi regime. The front represented an attempt by a coalition of prominent Islamists to reunify the disparate factions of the organization in Syria. It published a manifesto in October 1980 calling for all wings of the Muslim Brotherhood to unite to overthrow the al-Asad regime and replace it with a liberal democratic political system firmly rooted in the tenets of Islam.

ISTIQLAL. *See* PARTY OF ARAB INDEPENDENCE.

AL-JABHA AL-ISLAMIYYA FI SURIYYA. *See* ISLAMIC FRONT IN SYRIA.

AL-JABHA AL-WATANIYYA AL-TAQADDAMIYYA. *See* NATIONAL PROGRESSIVE FRONT.

JAM'IYYA AL-'AHD. *See* SOCIETY OF THE COVENANT.

JAM'IYYA AL-NAHDA AL-'ARABIYYA. *See* ARAB RENAISSANCE SOCIETY.

JAM'IYYA AL-QABDA AL-AMARIYYA. *See* RED HAND SOCIETY.

JAM'IYYA AL-QABDA AL-HADIDIYYA. *See* IRON HAND SOCIETY.

AL-JAM'IYYA AL-QAHTANIYYA. *See* QAHTAN SOCIETY.

JAM'IYYA AL-UMMAD AL-'ARABIYYA AL-FATAT. *See* YOUNG ARAB SOCIETY.

AL-KUTLA AL-WATANIYYA. *See* NATIONAL BLOC.

LIBERAL CONSTITUTIONAL PARTY (*Hizb al-Hurr al-Dusturi*). This party, which was active in parliament during the late 1920s, was founded by the mandatory governor of Aleppo, Subhi Barakat. Its platform originally called for collaboration with the French as a means of achieving Syrian independence. During the course of the negotiations over the 1936 treaty, however, it appears to have shifted to a less moderate position on this issue and effectively allied itself with the National Bloc.*

MUSLIM BROTHERHOOD (*Ikhwan al-Muslimin*). This umbrella Islamist organization was formed in 1945–46 under the leadership of Mustafa al-Siba'i of Homs. Students and religious notables (*'ulama*) who had been influenced by the Egyptian Muslim Brotherhood returned to Syria during the late 1930s and 1940s and set up local Islamist benevolent societies (*jam'iyyat*) to carry out the movement's program of social and moral improvement. The *jam'iyyat* also put pressure on the National Bloc* to provide assistance to the Palestinian Arabs during the 1936 rebellion and organized mass demonstrations against French-sponsored reforms in the educational system during World War II. As the war drew to a close, these societies formed a national organization, and in the summer of 1946 they elected al-Siba'i to be general director of one of the Syrian branches of the Muslim Brotherhood. The association set up its headquarters in Damascus and established close ties with the Egyptian Muslim Brotherhood, led by Hasan al-Banna.

The Syrian Muslim Brotherhood played an active role in local politics in the late 1940s and early 1950s, when it competed with the Syrian Communist Party* and the Ba'th Party.* al-Siba'i refused to characterize the organization as a formal party, referring to it instead as a "spirit that permeates the very being of the community." In line with this conception, the national leadership declined to sponsor candidates in the parliamentary elections of September 1954. Nevertheless, the organization did form a short-lived Islamic Socialist Front at the end of 1949 to block moves by the People's Party* to unite Syria with Iraq. Eight years later, the Brotherhood vehemently but unsuccessfully opposed Syria's political union with Egypt, whose leader, Gamal Abdel Nasser, had ruthlessly crushed the Egyptian Muslim Brotherhood in 1953–54. The ineffectiveness of the opposition to the formation of the United Arab Republic (UAR) persuaded the leaders to take a more active part in politics, and the organization sponsored popular demonstrations against the post-UAR regime in 1963–64. As a result of these activities, al-Siba'i's successor as general director of the Brotherhood, 'Isam al-'Attar, was deported to Germany in 1964.

During the 1960s, the Brotherhood in Syria gradually split into a relatively quietist branch centered in Damascus and a comparatively militant northern branch. Northerners, organized into the Fighting Vanguard,* led by Marwan Hadid, launched a campaign to overthrow the Ba'thi regime by force. This campaign precipitated a crisis in the organization's leadership, which eventuated in its division into two distinct entities. The northern branch escalated its campaign of assassination and sabotage in the early 1970s, culminating in a virtual civil war in the north-central cities in the spring of 1980. After the forcible suppression of the rebellion, leaders of various factions of the Muslim Brotherhood created an Islamic Front in Syria.* In October 1980, the front elected as its secretary general Shaykh Muhammad Abu al-Nasr al-Bayanuni of Aleppo. A month later, it published a comprehensive manifesto calling for the overthrow of the Ba'thi regime and its replacement by a liberal democratic political system firmly rooted in the principles of Islam.

Continuing action against the Islamic Front by the state security forces in 1981 and 1982 heightened antiregime sentiment in the cities and towns of north-central Syria. The front advised the inhabitants of these areas not to resist the operations of the security services, lest overt resistance provide the government with a pretext for obliterating the Muslim Brotherhood. When a large-scale rebellion broke out in Hama in February 1982, Islamic Front militants joined the fighting. They resisted the Syrian army's efforts to dislodge them for three weeks but eventually they were crushed by furious artillery and air strikes that reduced whole districts of the city to rubble. Meanwhile, calls by al-Bayanuni and Sa'id Hawwa for a nationwide uprising against the al-Asad regime went unheeded.

After the suppression of the Hama uprising, the leadership in exile of the Islamic front joined liberal and socialist opponents of the Ba'th to form a National Alliance for the Liberation of Syria (al-Tahaluf al-Watani li-Tahrir Suriyya). This step was criticized by militants led by 'Adnan 'Uqlah of the Fighting Vanguard, who vowed to continue the struggle against the Ba'th from within Syria. In response, the Islamic Front leaders expelled 'Uqlah and appointed Hawwa as commander of the organization's military formations. In January 1985,

'Uqlah's surrender to the authorities under a general amnesty ended significant political activity by members of the Syrian Muslim Brotherhood. (See also chapter on Egypt.)

MUSLIM UNION (*Ittihad al-Muslimin*). This clandestine organization was formed in 1908 and 1909 by religious notables in Damascus to protest the secularizing reforms carried out by the Committee of Union and Progress in Istanbul. Members of the Muslim Union made a strong showing in parliamentary elections at the beginning of 1909, but the party evaporated with the coming of World War I.

AL-MU'TADILIN (*The Upright*). This party, which was active in Syrian parliamentary debates in the late 1920s, advocated a program of active collaboration with the French mandatory authorities as the most effective means of achieving Syrian independence.

AL-NADI AL-'ARABI. *See* ARAB CLUB.

NATIONAL BLOC (*al-Kutla al-Wataniyya*). This umbrella organization was formed by the leadership of the People's Party* in the fall of 1927 to perpetuate its liberal reformist agenda after its suppression by the French mandatory authorities. The bloc assumed a dominant role in the National Assembly following the 1928 elections. With Syrian independence in 1946, the bloc's leading figure, Shukri al-Quwwatli, became president of the republic. The first months of 1947 saw a dramatic intensification of conflict between the National Bloc and such radical movements as the precursor of the Arab Socialist Party.* When President al-Quwwatli declared a state of emergency in the spring of 1947, the bloc was superseded by the resurrected National Party.

NATIONAL PARTY (*al-Hizb al-Watani*). In its first incarnation, this party was set up in Damascus by the Hashimi King Faysal in the fall of 1919 to prepare the way for the creation of a constitutional monarchy in Syria. The party was revived following the dissolution of the National Bloc* in 1947, and it served as the basis of parliamentary support for President Shukri al-Quwwatli. It was repeatedly banned by the series of military governments during the late 1940s and early 1950s, but it resumed a leading role in parliamentary politics following the 1954 parliamentary elections when its leaders shared power with those of the People's Party* in a number of cabinets and al-Quwwatli returned as president of the republic.

NATIONAL PROGRESSIVE FRONT (*al-Jabha al-Wataniyya al-Taqaddamiyya*). This umbrella organization was formed in March 1972 by the new Ba'thi regime of Hafiz al-Asad. The five founding components of the front were the Ba'th Party,* the Syrian Communist Party,* the Arab Socialist Union,* the Socialist

Unionists' Movement,* and the Arab Socialist Movement (see Arab Socialist Party*). According to the constitution promulgated in January 1973, front policy was to be determined by the Ba'th. Other parties were prohibited from operating within the armed forces or among students, although each of the parties that made up the front was permitted to draw up its own electoral lists for quadrennial elections to the People's Assembly. It was reported that a regime-sponsored Islamic party was added to the front in the wake of the 1990 parliamentary election campaign.

NATIONAL UNION (*Ittihad al-Qawmi*). This mass organization was imported into Syria from Egypt during the years of the United Arab Republic (1958–61) to take the place of the country's existing political parties.

OTTOMAN PARTY OF ADMINISTRATIVE DECENTRALIZATION (*Hizb al-Lamarkaziyya al-Idariyya al-'Uthmani*). This party was formed by Syrian exiles in Cairo sometime after 1912. Its platform called for greater administrative autonomy for the Arab-speaking provinces of the Ottoman Empire, effectively opposing the reforms introduced by the Committee of Union and Progress in Istanbul.

PARTY OF ARAB INDEPENDENCE (*Hizb al-Istiqlal al-'Arabi*). This front organization was set up by the Young Arab Society* in December 1918. Representatives of this party dominated the Syrian parliament elected in mid-1919, transforming the institution into a forum for Arab nationalist debate.

PARTY OF NATIONAL UNITY (*Hizb al-Tadaman al-Watani*). This party was formed by disaffected members of the National Bloc* in 1935 to push for a harder line in negotiations with the French concerning Syrian independence.

PARTY OF SYRIAN UNITY (*Hizb al-Ittihad al-Suri*). This offshoot of the Ottoman Party of Administrative Decentralization* was organized in Cairo at the end of 1918.

PEOPLE'S PARTY (*Hizb al-Sha'b*). This party was formed by the leader of the Iron Hand Society,* 'Abd al-Rahman Shahbandar, and other Damascene notables in 1925. Its platform advocated a range of liberal nationalist objectives, including the independence of Greater Syria, freedom of the press and of association, government protection for indigenous industry and the institution of universal education. It supported the Druze rebellion of July 1925, and it was subsequently suppressed by the French authorities. The party was resurrected in August 1948 by a collection of Aleppine notables, and it won a plurality in the National Assembly elections in November 1949. Its close connections with Iraq caused the party to lose popular support during the mid-1950s, and forty-seven of its members were convicted in December 1956 of conspiring with the regime of Nuri al-Sa'id in Baghdad to overthrow the government of Syrian president Shukri al-Quwwatli. This incident precipitated the demise of the party as a potent force in Syrian politics.

QAHTAN SOCIETY (al-Jam'iyya al-Qahtaniyya). This clandestine association was founded in Istanbul by Syrian intellectuals around 1912 to oppose the policies adopted by the reformist Committee of Union and Progress.

RED HAND SOCIETY (Jam'iyya al-Qabha al-Ahmariyya). This clandestine nationalist organization was active in the north-central city of Aleppo during the early 1920s. Virtually nothing is known about its leadership, ideology, or structure; these features presumably mirrored those of the Iron Hand Society* based in Damascus.

REFORM PARTY (Hizb al-Islah). The members of this parliamentary party, led by Haqqi al-'Azm, favored active cooperation with the French authorities as a means of achieving Syrian independence.

SOCIALIST UNIONISTS' MOVEMENT (al-Wahdawiyyin al-Ishtirakiyyin). This offshoot of the Ba'th Party* was formed late in 1961 under the leadership of Sami al-Jundi and Sami Sufan. Its members openly championed the founding principles of the United Arab Republic in the face of criticism of the union on the part of middle-level Ba'thi cadres. It was a founding member of the Ba'th-dominated National Progressive Front,* and it continues to put forward candidates for the National Assembly under the front's auspices.

SOCIETY OF THE COVENANT (Jam'iyya al-'Ahd). This clandestine association of Syrian nationalists opposed the Committee of Union and Progress. It was founded around 1912 and included branches in both Syria and Iraq.

SSNP. See SYRIAN SOCIAL NATIONAL PARTY.

SYRIAN COMMUNIST PARTY (Hizb al-Shuyu'i al-Suri). This clandestine Marxist organization was founded in Beirut in 1924. A year later, two of its founders, Yusuf Yazbek and Fu'ad al-Shamali, joined Artin Madoyan, the leader of an Armenian communist group, to form the Communist Party of Syria and Lebanon. After a two-year hiatus, during which the leaders languished in prison, a cell of the party was organized in Damascus in 1928. The party came under Syrian control with the election of Khalid Bakdash to the post of first secretary in 1932, and it was legalized by the French when the Popular Front gained power in Paris four years later. Its leaders were imprisoned again at the outbreak of World War II, but they were freed when British forces occupied Syria in 1941.

Syrians on the party's central committee split away from their Lebanese colleagues in July 1944 and set up a separate Syrian Communist Party. The party planned to participate in the parliamentary elections of July 1947, but it was prevented from doing so when all radical organizations were outlawed by the al-Quwwatli regime. Popular support was further undermined by Bakdash's continuing ties with the French Communist Party and then by the decision of the Soviet Union to support the creation of a Jewish state in Palestine in November 1947. These developments persuaded the central committee to disband the party in January 1928.

Communist party members reemerged as part of the underground opposition to Adib Shishakli in 1953–54. After Shishakli's ouster, Bakdash tried to build an alliance with the Ba'th Party* and the prominent independent socialist Khalid al-'Azm, but Bakdash failed to overcome their deep-seated anticommunist sentiments. Party members participated in the parliamentary election of September 1954 but were forced to run as independents because the new civilian government maintained the ban on the party imposed during the period of military rule. The party won a single seat in the National Assembly, occupied by Bakdash.

During early 1955, the influence of the Syrian Communist Party began to increase once again. Minister of Defense al-'Azm signed an economic cooperation agreement with Moscow in February of that year, and Prime Minister Sabri al-'Asali met with the Soviet foreign minister a month later to discuss joint responses to Turkish threats along Syria's northern border. The party collaborated with the Ba'th to crush the Syrian Social National Party (SSNP)* after the assassination of Deputy Chief of Staff 'Adnan al-Malki in April. Subsequent attempts by the United States to interfere in Syrian internal affairs generated widespread sympathy for the party, which formed a de facto alliance with al-'Azm and Colonel 'Afif al-Bizri, a key member of the military high command, to shape foreign and domestic policy. The rising influence of the Syrian Communist Party contributed significantly to the Ba'th's decision to pursue political union with Egypt early in 1958.

Bakdash left Syria for Eastern Europe as soon as the United Arab Republic (UAR) was formed. In mid-1959, the Cairo-based government of the UAR outlawed all political parties except the regime-sponsored National Union.* The leaders of the Syrian Communist Party who remained in Syria soon found themselves imprisoned by UAR authorities, and they remained in custody until well after the dissolution of the union in September 1961. The party reemerged when Prime Minister al-'Azm revoked the prohibition against political parties in the fall of 1962, but almost immediately fell out with the military leadership that seized control of the government in March 1963.

Party spokespersons applauded the nationalization policies implemented by the Ba'thi regime beginning in January 1965. Candidates sympathetic to the communists emerged victorious from comparatively free trade union elections later that year. As a result, prominent members and allies of the Syrian Communist Party were offered key government positions in the wake of the February 1966 coup d'état that put a more radical wing of the Ba'th Party in control of Syria's central administration. The central committee of the party launched a campaign to increase both its size and influence throughout the country early in 1968. But at the Regional (Syrian) Congress of the Ba'th in Damascus in October, simmering discontent over the rising communist involvement at all levels of government came to a boil in a lengthy diatribe against Prime Minister Yusuf Zu'ayyin by the powerful minister of defense, General Hafiz al-Asad. In the cabinet reshuffle that followed, compliant communist apparatchiks were substituted for the outspoken ministers who had played such an important role in earlier governments.

When the radical wing of the Ba'th was overthrown in November 1970, the new al-Asad regime allowed the Syrian Communist Party to join the Ba'th-dominated National Progressive Front.* Participation in the front was enthusiastically encouraged by officials in Moscow, who saw active collaboration with the regime as a step toward the establishment of socialism in Syria. Under the auspices of the front, the party fielded a succession of candidates for election to the 195-seat People's Assembly, winning 6 seats in 1977 and 8 in 1986. Party leaders firmly supported the Ba'th in the struggle against the Muslim Brotherhood* in the late 1970s and early 1980s, and joined in condemning Egypt for signing the Camp David Accords with Israel in 1979.

Several factions opposed to Bakdash's leadership were reported to have broken away from the Syrian Communist Party in the mid-1970s. Bakdash's longtime rival Riyad al-Turk led one of these breakaway groups; Yusuf Murad founded another, called the Base organization, in 1980; a Communist Party Political Bureau published a series of calls to arms during the mid-1980s. As the decade came to an end, international human rights organizations formally protested the drastic measures taken by the Syrian security services against such clandestine splinter groups as the Party for Communist Action and the Union for Communist Struggle.

SYRIAN SOCIAL NATIONAL PARTY (SSNP) (*Hizb al-Suri al-Qawmi al-Ijtima'i*). Founded as a secret society in Beirut in 1932 by Antun Sa'adah, this party's platform called for the creation of an independent Greater Syria based on the shared national consciousness of the Arab population of the territory. Its original incarnation, the Syrian National Party (Hizb al-Suri al-Qawmi), formed clandestine cells in Syria beginning in 1934; and the party's first general congress convened a year later. In November 1935, Sa'adah and the rest of the leadership were arrested by the French on charges of conspiring against the mandatory state. While in prison, Sa'adah wrote a comprehensive manifesto for the party and rechristened it the Syrian Social National Party (SSNP).

Despite its evocative appellation, the SSNP played only a minor role in the politics of Syria proper. During the late 1940s, its ideals generated considerable enthusiasm within the Syrian officer corps. Sa'adah enjoyed cordial personal relations with Colonel Husni Za'im, who led the March 1949 coup d'état in Damascus. When fighting erupted in June 1949 between the party militia and the paramilitary Lebanese Phalanges, Sa'adah sought refuge in Damascus. But when Za'im's plans to use the SSNP to undermine the government of Riyad al-Sulh in Beirut began to unravel a month later, the Syrian leader did not hesitate to turn Sa'adah over to the Lebanese authorities, who executed him at dawn on July 8.

Za'im's evident complicity in Sa'adah's extradition, combined with his pronounced tendency toward autocratic rule, convinced SSNP members in the Syrian armed forces to begin planning his overthrow. In August a military clique headed by Colonel Sami Hinnawi arrested and executed Za'im and his prime minister, Muhsin al-Barazi. The SSNP's headquarters were moved to Damascus in the wake of the coup. When parliamentary elections were held the following November, nine SSNP members won seats in the National Assembly; these deputies expressed strong support for the majority People's Party,* whose leadership had begun calling for immediate union with Iraq. Opposition to such a move on the part of Akram Hawrani's peasant movement and the Muslim Brotherhood* precipitated yet another coup in mid-December. After a brief period of parliamentary rule, the leader of the new regime, Adib Shishakli, dissolved the National Assembly and suspended the constitution, sending the Syrian branch of the SSNP underground once again.

The military-civilian coalition that ousted Shishakli in February 1954 had little sympathy for the SSNP. Only one member of the party won a seat in the parliamentary election of September 1954. When the army's deputy chief of staff, Adnan al-Malki, was assassinated by a member of the party the following April, leftist officers with close ties to the Ba'th Party* purged all SSNP members and sympathizers from the armed forces, destroyed the party's headquarters, and confiscated its literature. Laibib Yamak has rightly observed that these actions resulted in "the virtual liquidation of the party in Syria."[3] (See also the chapter on Lebanon.)

SYRIAN UNION PARTY (Hizb al-Wahda al-Suriyya). This organization was formed in the late 1920s with the assistance of the French mandatory regime to counteract the influence of the People's Party.*

AL-TALI'A AL-MUQATILA. See FIGHTING VANGUARD.

AL-WAHDAWIYYIN AL-ISHTIRAKIYYIN. See SOCIALIST UNIONISTS' MOVEMENT.

YOUNG ARAB SOCIETY (Jam'iyya al-Ummad al-'Arabiyya al-Fatat). This secret association of Syrian nationalists was founded in Paris around 1912. Its members opposed the Committee of Union and Progress in Istanbul and openly supported the Arab revolt led by the Hashimi Sharif Husayn of Mecca in 1916. The society created a front organization, the Party of Arab Independence,* in

December 1918, which played an active role in parliamentary politics throughout the 1920s.

## NOTES

1. Itamar Rabinovich, *Syria under the Ba'th, 1963–66: The Army-Party Symbiosis* (New York: Halsted Press, 1972), p. 88.

2. John F. Devlin, *The Ba'th Party* (Stanford, Calif: Hoover Institution Press, 1976), p. 13.

3. Labib Zuwiyya Yamak, *The Syrian Social Nationalist Party: An Ideological Analysis* (Cambridge, Mass.: Harvard Middle East Monographs, 1966), p. 70.

Fred H. Lawson

# TUNISIA

Tunisia, derived from the term "Tunis," a Phoenician settlement, was known to the Romans and later to the Arabs as Africa or Ifriqiya. Despite being subjected over the centuries to the foreign rule of the Phoenicians, Romans, Byzantines, Arabs, Ottomans, and eventually the French, Tunisia retained its own political and cultural identity over a period of nearly 3,000 years.

## POLITICAL PARTIES IN PRE-INDEPENDENCE TUNISIA

The origins of modern political organizations and parties, however, can be said to have begun under the French protectorate of Tunisia (1881–1956). In 1908 the first nationalist political organization known as the Evolutionist Party of Young Tunisians* was formed. It was made up of two earlier groups who had reacted to the French protectorate by demanding that its influence be restricted and that Tunisia's traditional Arab-Islamic culture be restored.

'Ali Bash Hambak, an intellectual figure and graduate of the Sadiki College, a bilingual and bicultural lycée located in Tunis, wanted selectively to adopt Western social and scientific culture to modernize Tunisia's political system and society. He was one of the founders of the Association des anciens du Sadiki in 1905. In 1907 the Association of the Zaytuna Mosque Students* was set up by graduates of that traditional Islamic institution; it called for the revival of Arab and Islamic culture in Tunisia. The Khalduniya Institute, founded in 1896 and headed by Bashi Sfar, a follower of 'Ali Bash Hambak, served as the meeting place for these two elites: the bilingual reformist Sadiki College elite and the monolingual, more traditional Zaytuna graduates. Together they formed the Evolutionist Party of Young Tunisians, better known as the Young Tunisians, which aimed at articulating nationalist demands for greater Tunisian participation in the political life of their country.[1] They also published a newspaper, Le Tunisien, to convince the French administration and the French public that Tunisians were fully capable of sharing in the government of their own country.

The Young Tunisians were an elite group of intellectuals whose education and family background placed them above the rest of the Tunisian population. They became directly involved in the affairs of the nation, however, when they took the side of Tunisian workers demanding jobs in fields (such as transportation) that had become the exclusive preserve of foreigners. The workers demonstrated and led a boycott of the tramways, which the Young Tunisians publicly supported. They also backed the Zaytuna graduates who, because of their inability to communicate in French, were being excluded from their traditional positions in government, education, and law. In 1910 demonstrations by Zaytuna students turned into public riots which took a distinctly nationalist turn, appearing as a protest against French rule. Exacerbating the situation was the French decision to register *habus* land under Islamic jurisdiction and to put it under protectorate administration. The riots that followed resulted in a number of casualties, both French and Tunisian, and the imposition of harsh sentences on the Tunisians for their demonstrations. Some of the leaders of the Young Tunisians were exiled; others were imprisoned; and in 1912, the organization was banned. *Le Tunisien* was closed down, and a state of emergency was declared that lasted until 1921.

In the aftermath of World War I, three major political organizations emerged. The first was the Liberal Tunisian Constitutional Party,* better known as the Dustur Party. It called for independence and a complete break from France. The second party was the Socialist Federation of Tunisia, whose primarily French members professed socialist and later communist views. Third was the Reformist Party, which chose to compromise with the French rather than demand complete independence and a constitution. Both the Reformist and the Dustur parties were heirs of the Young Tunisians.

The Dustur Party was founded in 1920 by Sheikh 'Abd al-'Aziz al-Tha'labi, a Young Tunisian and a graduate of the Zaytuna Mosque, who had been exiled in 1912. The Dustur's leadership did not differ significantly from that of the parent party, as it represented landowning, professional, and merchant families of Tunisia, rather than the poorer strata of the society. In 1919 al-Tha'labi wrote a manifesto, *La Tunisie Martyre*, in which he argued that the French protectorate had, in fact, frozen the progress Tunisia had been making in "education, economic development, constitutional government and administraton of justice",[2] and he demanded an end to the protectorate, a constitution, the election of a deliberative assembly, and universal suffrage for Tunisians. As the Young Tunisians had done earlier, the Dusturians argued for an independent Tunisian state that would maintain a formal association with France. They also recognized the Bey of Tunis as the legitimate head of state and tried to protect his powers from erosion by the French administration.

This time the French were more flexible. They began instituting reforms, opening up the Ministry of Justice to Tunisians wishing to gain employment there and permitting the creation of a Grand Council giving Tunisians a greater say in the government of their country. The Grand Council, however, was a far cry from the parliament the Dusturians had demanded, although it did have the structure of a legislature. It was divided into two sections: one Tunisian and one European. Tunisian delegates were elected indirectly through regional councils; European delegates were directly elected or joined as representatives of the Chamber of Commerce. This system ensured the dominance of European delegates, while permitting some Tunisian representation. The final part of the reform package included the granting of French citizenship to qualified Tunisians by virtue of their services or their education.

These reforms were not sufficient to satisfy the demands of the Dusturians who continued agitating throughout the 1920s and the early 1930s. The Grand Council was seen as a travesty of a legislature that maintained the power of the French almost unchanged. The naturalization issue led to a major confrontation with religious 'ulama in Tunisia who maintained that those who gave up their Tunisian citizenship to become French would not be buried in a Muslim cemetery. The dissatisfaction among Tunisians was compounded in the early 1930s by a dismal economic situation brought about by the depression in Europe and inclement weather conditions that ruined agriculture. Finally, Tunisians spontaneously took to the streets in April 1933 in mass demonstrations against the French administration. The Dustur Party supported the demonstrators and pursued their demands for independence, including both internal and external sovereignty.

The French responded by passing decrees limiting Tunisians' rights to free expression and assembly, and they followed this by closing down the Dustur's newspaper, L'Action Tunisienne. Finally, on May 31, 1933, the French resident general in Tunis ordered the disbanding of the Dustur Party. Despite the French decision to dissolve the party, it continued to exist and to grow in membership as it established between 70 and 130 new cells throughout Tunisia in 1934.[3]

## THE NEO-DUSTUR PARTY

The Dustur, however, was being weakened and undermined not so much by French repression as by divisions within the party itself. In 1934 some of its youngest and brightest members split from the mother party and established a new party that called itself the Neo-Dustur Party.* Those included Mahmoud Materi, 'Ali Bouhajeb, Bahri Guiga, and Habib Bourguiba and his brother Muhammad Bourguiba, the editorial team of L'Action Tunisienne. Others, such as Tahir Sfar, were also among those who broke away from the Dustur Party and joined them.

The young generation of nationalist leaders believed in mobilizing mass support in both rural and urban areas, while the old, primarily urban-based Dusturians belonged to a wealthy and educated stratum of the population. The Neo-Dusturians, like the members of the older party, advocated the creation of a transitional legislature in which Tunisians would share power equally with Europeans until they could take power and rule themselves in an independent state. Neo-Dusturians also supported the traditional institution of the beylicate, but they planned eventually to establish a Tunisian republic.

Habib Bourguiba was elected secretary of the Neo-Dustur Party, and Mahmoud Materi became the president in 1934. But it was Bourguiba who began traveling all over Tunisia mobilizing people to join the new party, helping to create new party cells, and taking over existing cells of the old Dustur. It is in those early days that Bourguiba discovered that he was a great orator and that he could move crowds. His oratory and his skill for organization and for planning enabled him to achieve the leadership of the Neo-Dustur very rapidly. He became known as the supreme combatant (*al-mujahid al-akbar*).

The French cracked down on the Neo-Dustur in late 1934 and in early 1935, arresting all its main leaders including Bourguiba. This led to mass protests that were put down, and the members of the Neo-Dustur began working clandestinely. In April 1935, on the eve of the coming to power of the new government of Léon Blum in France, Bourguiba was set free. He hoped that the new government would be more liberal and would undertake some of the reforms Tunisians were demanding. When this did not happen, the Neo-Dustur organized simultaneous mass demonstrations in Tunis, Bizerte, Sfax, Moknine, and Bourgel in February 1936, resulting in the ouster of the resident general and the appointment of a new one, Armand Guillon. In 1938, after more protests and general strikes, the French administration once again arrested the leaders of the Neo-Dustur and dissolved the party. Bourguiba spent the next five years in prison in Tunisia, France, and Italy.[4] The Neo-Dustur weathered the crisis by electing a new round of leaders each time the previous ones were arrested. Among those who continued the struggle for independence were Bahi Ladgham, Hadi Sa'idi, and Salah al-Din Bouchoucha.

In 1943 Bourguiba was set free, and he returned to Tunisia as a national hero. During the next two years, he concentrated on rebuilding the grass-roots infrastructure that had been decimated by the French during his incarceration. He toured the country making speeches and recreating the party cells that had all but disappeared in his absence. When the French administration realized he was reviving the Tunisian nationalist movement, they made it difficult for him to move out of Tunis for any reason.

By that time, however, other organizations and movements had joined the Neo-Dustur in their demands for independence. In 1945 a national front made up of the Neo-Dustur, the old Dustur Party (which was still alive), the Reformists, representatives of the Zaytuna institution and of the Tunisian Jewish community, as well as other organizations, formed the Comité des Soixantes, which issued a manifesto calling for the complete independence of Tunisia from France.[5] Although this strengthened the legitimacy of the Neo-Dustur domestically, it was dismissed by the French and produced no tangible results.

The Neo-Dustur then decided to put international pressure on France to permit self-government for Tunisia as a first step to complete independence. Bourguiba, fleeing from the French police who were about to arrest him in March 1945, took up residence in Cairo for the next four years. From there he took it upon himself to rally Arab support for the Tunisian cause, and he toured the Arab world in search of allies and political supporters. He found little interest on the part of the Arab nations of the east for Tunisia's plight, and that in turn affected his attitude and that of the postindependence Neo-Dustur toward the Arab world.

In January 1947, Bourguiba flew to the United States to seek U.S. support for Tunisian independence. At a party hosted by Prince Faysal of Saudi Arabia in New York, he met with Dean Acheson, then U.S. under secretary of state, and emerged from the meeting with a statement that the United States was ready to back Tunisia's demand for independence when presented at the United Nations.

In 1949 Bourguiba was back in Tunisia, having kept links with the Neo-Dusturians in Paris who were led by Muhammad Masmudi, and with the neo-Dusturians in Tunisia who were led by Salah ben Youssef, who would become his major rival for the control of the party. At the time of his return, a guerrilla movement known as the *fallaqah* began attacking French installations, particularly communication and transportation systems. At least some in the Neo-Dustur Party supported those activities that brought considerable pressure on the French administration to introduce reforms. These reforms were so limited, however, that they produced only more anger and protests. Bourguiba also resumed the task of rebuilding the Neo-Dustur by touring the countryside and the small towns and by campaigning for independence. In 1952 he was arrested for the third time, and he spent the next two years in prison. His arrest produced nationwide demonstrations which were put down forcefully and resulted in hundreds of casualties.

In 1954 the French government began negotiating with the Neo-Dustur for self-rule as a step toward recognizing the complete independence of Tunisia, and in June 1955 it granted internal autonomy. However, the Bardo Treaty of 1881, signed by the Bey of Tunis and the representative of France, giving the French the right to control Tunisia's defense and foreign affairs, remained in force.

It was over the Bardo Treaty that the Neo-Dustur split. One faction, headed by Salah ben Youssef, demanded complete and unconditional independence, while Bourguiba's faction moved more gradually, accepting what concessions it could wring from the French authorities, then negotiating to get more. Bourguiba's faction was able to mobilize support for its position at a party congress in Sfax in 1955, after which ben Youssef went on the attack. He resorted to guerrilla warfare and urban terrorism, and he brought the country to the brink of civil war, claiming that his faction represented the authentic Neo-Dustur. It was only after a large-scale French military intervention in Matmata in June 1956, and the granting of independence to Tunisia, that the matter was put to rest, and Bourguiba became the uncontested leader of the Neo-Dustur.

In March 1956, after the declaration of independence, elections were held for a Constituent Assembly. Bourguiba became the president of the assembly, and the Neo-Dustur swept the elections with the only opposition coming from Communists and Independents who together garnered a mere 1.3 percent of the vote. The election thus consolidated the power of the Neo-Dustur as the single most important political force in the country at independence.[6]

The next step to complete independence took place when Prime Minister Ben Ammar signed a series of six agreements with his French counterpart Edgar Faure. These agreements dealt with French-Tunisian economic and financial relations, administrative and cultural cooperation, and judicial and internal administrative reforms. The Bardo Treaty, which allowed France to maintain control of Tunisia's defense and foreign relations, remained in force, however. Bourguiba supported this agreement, but his longtime ally Salah ben Youssef turned against him over the Bardo Treaty and organized an opposition movement from exile in Cairo against the French as well as against Bourguiba's supporters.

Bourguiba continued to work for independence by pushing for internal reforms. The Bey of Tunis, al-Amin Bey, was pressured to agree to accepting a Constitutional Assembly and to ratifying an electoral law that had been prepared by Bourguiba. This law ensured that the Neo-Dustur Party would select the candidates and would win the elections. The hope was that the elected assembly could put pressure on France to give Tunisia its independence. Finally, the Bardo Treaty of 1881 was abrogated, and a protocol recognizing Tunisia's independence was signed. Bourguiba then took over the portfolios of foreign affairs and defense.

Five days later, the Constituent Assembly was elected and Bourguiba became its president by acclamation. Most of the elected members of the new assembly were also members of the Neo-Dustur Party. The assembly then formed a number of committees to draft a new constitution, the first article of which declared Tunisia an independent and sovereign state, with Arabic as its official language and Islam as its religion. In 1957 the assembly voted unanimously to depose al-Amin Bey and declare Tunisia a republic. Its members then proclaimed Habib Bourguiba president of the new republic.

It can, therefore, be said that the Neo-Dustur Party, led by Habib Bourguiba, not only enabled Tunisia to obtain its independence but also was the main political force that shaped Tunisia's postindependence political system and institutions.

After independence, the Neo-Dustur was transformed from an independence movement into a mass political party. All other political organizations and opposition groups, except for the Tunisian Communist Party (TCP),* were delegitimized, and the Tunisian political system became a de facto single-party system.

The Neo-Dustur became a highly structured organization with party cells in villages and urban neighborhoods and in educational, business, and administrative organizations. The structure was centralized by means of regional coordination committees headed by a central committee elected at the national level, above which stood a political bureau the members of which were directly appointed by Bourguiba himself.

In 1964 the party's name was changed to the Dusturian Socialist Party (PSD)* to reflect the new economic policies of the Tunisian state. Since 1955 the trade union movement, the Union Générale Tunisienne du Travail (UGTT), headed by Ahmad ben Salah, had been advocating centralized state planning. Bourguiba did not favor such planning and eventually forced Ben Salah from the leadership of the trade union movement by supporting a split in the UGTT that undermined his power. By 1960, however, Bourguiba had shifted his position to support the concept, which he called Dusturian socialism, combining state and private own-ership and limited state control of the economy. Over the next few years, cen-tralized state planning increased very significantly, and Ben Salah, once more in favor with Bourguiba, became the head of a new government planning agency. Ben Salah introduced many economic changes in Tunisia, some of which have remained in place, as can be seen in the very large and vigorous public sector still functioning today. Others, such as the socialization of agriculture, failed abysmally and led to disastrous consequences and to his dismissal and impris-onment in 1969. Ben Salah escaped to Algeria in 1972, and in 1973 he moved to Europe and created his own socialist party, the Movement for Popular Unity (MUP).* The socialist experiment lasted eight years.

Attempts to open up the political system to other parties and views failed during the 1970s. In 1973 Bourguiba forced out of the legislature two eminent ex-members of the PSD, Ahmad al-Mestiri and Bahi Ladgham, who had been advocating greater political liberalization. Mestiri, who had been expelled from the party the previous year, eventually created his own political party, the Move-ment of Socialist Democrats (MDS)*; and Ladgham had resigned from the party earlier in 1973. There were further purges of prominent party figures at the 1974 party congress, including Habib Boulares, Hasib ben ʿAmmar, Sadiq ben Jumʿa, and Benji Qaʿid al-Sebsi. Their offense was signing a declaration objecting to some of the arbitrary decisions taken by the leadership of the PSD. The party congress also elected Bourguiba party president for life and gave him the right to appoint the twenty-one members of the Political Bureau of the party, as well as the prime minister and other cabinet ministers.

By the mid-1970s, student and labor strikes and demonstrations were becoming frequent. In 1976, for instance, tobacco, textile, and metal workers joined work-ers in public sector fields, such as those in transportation, health care, and util-ities, and staged a major walkout. They were attempting to improve their conditions and pressure the government to give in to their demands. By 1977 the government of Habib Bourguiba was using the military as well as the police force to put down the strikes. In January 1978 the confrontation between the major trade union, the UGTT, and the government reached an unprecedented state of violence. A general strike was met with military action, which resulted in a number of deaths and injuries, and the day came to be known as Black Thursday. Labor leaders were arrested and tried, and new ones supporting the party and the government were installed in their place.

In the 1980s, Bourguiba began introducing political reforms to liberalize the system to some degree. The TCP of Muhammad Harmal was legalized in 1981, and in 1983 both the MDS of Ahmad al-Mestiri and the Party of Popular Unity (PUP)* of Muhammad Belhaj ʿUmar were legally recognized. Strikes and dem-onstrations continued, however, and in the last week of 1983 there was an out-break of serious street violence that was met once again with military force.

The PSD in the 1980s was faced by a new challenge: Militant Islamic move-ments took over where students and labor left off. As early as 1979, an Islamic group calling itself the Islamic Tendency Movement (MTI)* organized strikes on campuses and in the streets of major cities against government policies, and the state again resorted to force to crack down on its members. The MTI tried unsuccessfully to gain acceptance as a political party within the constitutional framework of Tunisia throughout the 1980s and resorted to violence to pressure the government to introduce Islamic policies.

The confrontation between the Tunisian state and the MTI culminated in 1987 when four tourist hotels were bombed and MTI members were accused of the crime. The State Security Court sentenced seven of the arrested MTI members to death, its leader Rached Ghannouchi to life imprisonment, and sixty-seven members to from two years to life imprisonment. In October 1987, the first death sentences were carried out when two MTI members were hanged. By the end of that month, it became apparent that Bourguiba was planning to reopen the trials and extend the death penalty to other MTI members. Fearing the repercussions of such an action on the political stability of the country, the prime minister, Zine al-'Abdin ben 'Ali, with the support of both party and state leaders, ousted Habib Bourguiba from power on November 7, 1987.

As the new Tunisian leader, Ben 'Ali began immediately to introduce major political reforms. He renamed the PSD the Democratic Constitutional Rally (RCD)* to break away from the old party associated with Bourguiba, and he made some changes in the leadership but retained its structure and organization. He then opened up the system to pluralist competitive organizations and announced the democratization of the political system. A national pact was drafted in the fall of 1988 with the participation of a number of political parties that were legalized that year, including the Socialist Rally of Progressive Unity (RSP),* the Social Progress Party (PSP),* and the Union for Democratic Unity (UDU).*

In April 1989, free and fair presidential and parliamentary multiparty elections took place. The RCD won all the seats based on the single-member constituency system, which had been inherited from the previous regime. The MTI was not allowed to participate in the elections as a party, but its leaders ran as independents under the banner of the Nahda or Renaissance Party.* Although it did not win any seats in parliament, the MTI fared extremely well and established itself as the second most important political organization.

Municipal elections were held in June 1990. In response to objections by the opposition, the Tunisian government amended the electoral system to allow for proportional representation in some districts, and the taking of half the seats by the leading party in other districts. Opposition parties, feeling too weak to compete with the RCD, boycotted the elections, and the Renaissance Party, still unrecognized, ran lists of independents in only a few municipalities. As a result, 99 percent of the municipal council seats were won by the RCD. Thus the RCD remains the single most powerful political party in Tunisia today, and unless the Renaissauce Party is legalized it will remain unchallenged in the coming few years.

## Bibliography

Anderson, Lisa. *The State and Social Transformation in Tunisia and Libya, 1830–1980.* Princeton, N.J.: Princeton University Press, 1986.

Camau, Michel, ed. *Tunisie au present.* Paris: Editions du CNRS, 1987.

Deeb, Mary-Jane. "Militant Islam and the Politics of Redemption." *Annals of the American Academy of Political and Social Science* 521 (November 1992): pp. 52–65.

Hermassi, El-Baki. *Leadership and National Development in North Africa.* Berkeley: University of California Press, 1972.

Leveau, Remy. "Tunisie: Equilibre interne et environment arabe." *Maghreb-Machrek* 124 (April 1989): 4–17.

Moore, Clement Henry. *Tunisia since Independence.* Berkeley: University of California Press, 1965.

———. "Political Parties," in I. William Zartman and William Mark Habeeb, eds., *Polity and Society in Contemporary North Africa,* Boulder, Colo.: Westview Press, 1993, pp. 42–67.

Nabli, Mustafa K., and Jefrey B. Nuggent, eds. *The New Institutional Economics and Development Theory: Theory and Tunisian Case Studies.* Amsterdam: North Holland Press, 1989.

Nelson, Harold D., ed. *Tunisia: A Country Study.* Washington, D.C.: U.S. Government Printing Office, 1987.

Perkins, Kenneth. *Tunisia: Crossroads of the Islamic and European Worlds.* Boulder, Colo.: Westview Press, 1986.

Salem, Norma. *Habib Bourguiba, Islam, and the Creation of Tunisia.* London: Croom Helm, 1984.

Stone, Russell. *Change in Tunisia.* Albany: State University of New York Press, 1976.

Vanderwalle, Dirk. "From the New State to the New Era: Toward a Second Republic in Tunisia." *Middle East Journal* 42, 4 (Autumn 1988): pp 602–20.

Ware, Louis. "The Role of the Tunisian Military in the Post-Bourguiba Era." *Middle East Journal* 39 (1984): 27–47.

Zartman, I. William, ed. *Tunisia: The Political Economy of Reform.* Boulder, Colo.: Lynne Rienner, 1991.

## Political Parties

AFAQ TUNISIYA. *See* TUNISIAN PERSPECTIVES.

AL-'AMIL AL-TUNISI. *See* TUNISIAN WORKER.

ASSOCIATION OF THE ALUMNI OF SADIKI (*Jam'iyat Khariji al-Sadiqiyya*). 'Ali Bash Hambak, an intellectual figure and graduate of the Sadiki College, a bilingual and bicultural lycée in Tunis, wanted selectively to adopt Western social and scientific culture to modernize Tunisia's political system and society. He was one of the founders of the *Association des anciens du Sadiki* in 1905. See also the Association of the Zaytuna Mosque Students.

ASSOCIATION OF THE ZAYTUNA MOSQUE STUDENTS (Jam'iyyat Tulab Jami' al-Zaytuna). This association was set up by graduates of the traditional Zaytuna Mosque institution in 1907. It called for the revival of Arab and Islamic culture in Tunisia. The Khalduniya Institute, founded in 1896 and headed by Bashi Sfar, a follower of 'Ali Bash Hambak, served as the meeting place for these two elites: the bilingual reformist Sadiki College elite and the monolingual, more traditional Zaytuna graduates. Together they formed The Evolutionist Party of Young Tunisians, also known as the Young Tunisians, which aimed at articulating nationalist demands for greater Tunisian participation in the political life of their country.

BA'TH MOVEMENT (Harakat al-Ba'th). The origin of the Ba'th Movement in Tunisia can be traced to the cultural league, al-Qalam al-Jadid, or the New Pen, founded in 1962 in Tunis to study Arab nationalist thought. Its members sought to infiltrate major trade unions and the Union Générale Tunisienne du Travail (UGTT) in particular. In 1967 they organized a number of student demonstrations in support of Arab causes, and later some Ba'thists were arrested on charges of threatening national security. The Tunisian government attempted to suppress the movement throughout the 1970s and 1980s, but Ba'thists continued to have support in labor and educational institutions.

In December 1987, the Ba'thists applied for permission to legalize the movement so that it could become an official party and its members could participate in the national elections. To qualify, its leader Fawzi Snoussi, described it as a purely Tunisian movement, the activities of which were limited to the geographical boundaries of Tunisia, and which had no connection whatsoever with any party of the same name in the Arab world. Permission was not granted.[7]

COMMUNIST PARTY OF TUNISIA. See TUNISIAN COMMUNIST PARTY.

DEMOCRATIC CONSTITUTIONAL RALLY (RCD) (Al-Tajamu' al-Dusturi al-Dimuqrati). This was the name of the PSD* adopted by President Ben 'Ali in 1987.

DUSTUR PARTY. See TUNISIAN LIBERAL CONSTITUTIONAL PARTY.

DUSTURIAN SOCIALIST PARTY (PSD) (Hizb al-Dusturi al-Ishtiraki). This was the name adopted by the Neo-Dustur Party* in 1964.

EVOLUTIONIST PARTY OF YOUNG TUNISIANS (Hizb al-Tatawwuri li Tunis al-Fatat). See Association of the Zaytuna Mosque Students.

HARAKAT AL-BA'TH. See BA'TH MOVEMENT.

HARAKAT AL-DIMUQRATIYYIN AL-ISHTIRAKIYYIN. *See* MOVEMENT OF SOCIAL DEMOCRATS.

HARAKAT AL-ITTIJA AL-ISLAMI. *See* ISLAMIC TENDENCY MOVEMENT.

HARAKAT AL-TAJADUD AL-ISLAMI. *See* MOVEMENT OF ISLAMIC RENEWAL.

HARAKAT AL-TUNISIYYA AL-WATANIYYA. *See* TUNISIAN NATIONALIST MOVEMENT.

HARAKAT AL-WAHDA AL-SHA'BIYA. *See* MOVEMENT FOR POPULAR UNITY.

HIZB AL-'ADALA. *See* JUSTICE PARTY.

AL-HIZB AL-DUSTURI AL-HURR AL-TUNISI. *See* TUNISIAN LIBERAL CONSTITUTIONAL PARTY.

HIZB AL-DUSTURI AL-ISHTIRAKI. *See* DUSTURIAN SOCIALIST PARTY.

HIZB AL-DUSTURI AL-JADID. *See* NEO-DUSTUR PARTY.

HIZB AL-ISHTIRAKI AL-DIMUQRATI. *See* SOCIALIST DEMOCRATIC PARTY.

HIZB AL-NAHDA. *See* RENAISSANCE PARTY.

AL-HIZB AL-SHUYU'I AL-TUNISI. *See* TUNISIAN COMMUNIST PARTY.

HIZB AL-TAHRIR AL-ISLAMI. *See* ISLAMIC LIBERATION PARTY.

HIZB AL-TAQADDUMI AL-IJTIMA'I. *See* SOCIAL PROGRESS PARTY.

HIZB AL-TATAWWURI LI TUNIS AL-FATAT. *See* EVOLUTIONIST PARTY OF YOUNG TUNISIANS.

AL-HIZB AL-'UMMAH AL-SHUYU'I. *See* TUNISIAN COMMUNIST WORKERS' PARTY.

HIZB AL-WAHDA AL-SHA'BIYYA. *See* PARTY OF POPULAR UNITY.

ISLAMIC LIBERATION PARTY (*Hizb al-Tahrir al-Islami*). This secret Islamic organization traces its origins to a Palestinian shaykh, Taqi al-Din al-Nabahani, whose objectives include the reestablishment of the Islamic caliphate. Some of its members were arrested and tried in 1983 and again in 1985 for belonging to illegal organizations. A number of those members were military officers.

ISLAMIC TENDENCY MOVEMENT (MTI) (*Harakat al-Ittijah al-Islami*). In 1979 a group broke away from the Movement of Islamic Renewal* and formed the MTI. Its members, unlike those of the other Islamic organizations, sought to reconstruct their movement into a political party based on the guidelines set by the Tunisian government. They set up organized committees all over the country but primarily in cities, and they developed very rapidly into a significant force in Tunisian politics. Rached Ghannouchi, one of the principal leaders and ideologues of the MTI, argued that Westernization was destroying Islamic civilization, and that it was imperative to establish an Islamic state, by means of a jihad if necessary, to liberate the land of Islam and save all Muslims from domination by the West. He also called for a more equitable redistribution of the wealth of Islamic countries to resolve their economic problems.

After having encouraged the development of the Quranic Preservation Society,* the Tunisian government refused the MTI's request to be recognized as a political party. From 1979 it began cracking down on MTI leaders and members, a confrontation that culminated in massive arrests in 1987 and the dismantling of much of the organizational structures of the MTI. In November 1987, Habib Bourguiba's decision to sentence some of the leaders of the MTI to death led to his eviction from power by Zine al-'Abdin ben 'Ali, with the support of many in government who feared that this action would lead to social polarization and civil strife in Tunisia.

In December 1987, the new Tunisian leader, Ben 'Ali, granted amnesty to 2,487 prisoners including 608 members of the MTI and dropped charges against another 60 MTI members. Rached Ghannouchi was pardoned and set free in July 1988 with a number of MTI members who had been imprisoned on charges of having committed crimes "against public rights." The secretary general of the MTI, 'Abd al-Fattah Mourou, was also allowed to return from exile in September of that year.

AL-ITTIHAD AL-DIMUQRATI AL-WAHDAWI. *See* UNION FOR DEMOCRATIC UNITY.

ITTIHAD QIWA AL-SHA'B AL-TUNISI. *See* UNION OF TUNISIAN PEOPLE'S FORCES.

AL-JABHA AL-WATANIYYA AL-DIMUQRATIYYA. *See* NATIONAL TU-NISIAN DEMOCRATIC FRONT.

AL-JABHA AL-WATANIYYA AL-TAQADDUMIYYA LI TAHRIR TUNIS. *See* NATIONAL PROGRESSIVE FRONT FOR THE LIBERATION OF TU-NISIA.

AL-JABHAT AL-WATANIYA AL-TAQADDUMIYYA. *See* TUNISIAN NATIONAL PROGRESSIVE FRONT.

JAM'IYYAT AL-HIFADH 'ALA AL-QURAN. *See* QURANIC PRESERVA-TION SOCIETY.

JAM'IYYAT KHARIJI AL-SADIQIYYA. *See* ASSOCIATION OF THE ALUMNI OF SADIKI.

JAM'IYYAT TULAB JAMI' AL-ZAYTUNA. *See* ASSOCIATION OF THE ZAYTUNA MOSQUE STUDENTS.

JUSTICE PARTY (*Hizb al-'Adala*). This is a party whose leadership comes from the traditional trade unions such as the UGTT. Its leader is Khalifa 'Ubaid, an old trade union leader who applied for party recognition in 1988 but did not receive it.

KUMUNAT 26 YANAYIR. *See* 26 JANUARY MOVEMENT.

MOVEMENT FOR POPULAR UNITY (MUP) (*Harakat al-Wahda al-Sha'bi-yya*). The 1970s saw the emergence of new political forces in Tunisia. In 1973 the Movement for Popular Unity emerged, first in Paris, then in 1978 in Tunisia, headed by Ahmad ben Salah, the former secretary of state for planning and finance (see Dusturian Socialist Party). Some of his close associates included Sulayman Duggi, Hisham Mussa, and 'Abd al-Qadir Zuwawi. In 1975 the group published a manifesto entitled *Towards a New Tunisia*, in which they advocated socialism. The members of the MUP were very critical of Habib Bourguiba's economic policies, which they described as capitalistic and colonialist in nature, aimed at benefiting the elite in Tunisia. They called for free parliamentary elec-tions in 1977, organized by a transitional government. Ben Salah was pardoned in 1988 by President Ben 'Ali and was able to return to Tunis after sixteen years in exile.

MOVEMENT OF ISLAMIC RENEWAL (*Harakat al-Tajadud al-Islami*). An off-shoot of the Quranic Preservation Society,* this movement was created in 1978 by a loose coalition of Islamists who began voicing the economic and political grievances of many Tunisians, defining the framework of their opposition to government policies in religious terms.

MOVEMENT OF SOCIALIST DEMOCRATS. *See* SOCIALIST DEMO-CRATIC PARTY.

MTI. *See* ISLAMIC TENDENCY MOVEMENT.

MUP. *See* MOVEMENT FOR POPULAR UNITY.

AL-MUQAWAMA AL-TUNISIYYA AL-WATANIYYA. *See* TUNISIAN NATIONAL RESISTANCE.

NATIONAL PROGRESSIVE FRONT FOR THE LIBERATION OF TUNISIA (*Al-Jabha al-Wataniyya al-Taqadumiyya li Tahrir Tunis*). No information is available about this party.

NATIONAL TUNISIAN DEMOCRATIC FRONT (*Al-Jabha al-Wataniyya al-Dimuqratiyya*). This front was established in 1962 in Morocco. Its members were loyal to Salah ben Youssef, who was assassinated in Frankfurt in 1961 on orders from Habib Bourguiba.

NEO-DUSTUR PARTY (*Al-Hizb al-Dusturi al-Jadid*). In 1934 some of the youngest and brightest members of the Tunisian Liberal Constitutional Party (Dustur Party)* split from the mother party and established a new party that called itself the Neo-Dustur. Those included Mahmoud Materi, 'Ali Bouhajeb, Bahri Guiga, and Habib Bourguiba and his brother Muhammad Bourguiba, the editorial team of *l'Action Tunisienne*. Others such as Tahir Sfar were also among those who broke away from the Dustur Party and joined them. With Bourguiba's emergence as national leader, this party became the dominant Tunisian political party. See the introductory essay for further details.

PARTY OF POPULAR UNITY (PUP) (*Hizb al-Wahda al-Sha'biyya*). In 1980 an offshoot of the Movement for Popular Unity (MUP) was created in Tunisia and was authorized to function by the state in an attempt to undermine Ahmad Ben Salah's own organization. It changed its name to the Party of Popular Unity and was officially legalized in 1983. It remains a very small organization and is headed by Muhammad Belhaj 'Umar. The PUP, an organization of the left, advocates socialist solutions for Tunisia's economic problems. In the elections of April 1989, it received a negligible number of votes at the national level.

PCT. *See* TUNISIAN COMMUNIST PARTY.

PDS. *See* SOCIALIST DEMOCRATIC PARTY.

PSD. *See* DUSTURIAN SOCIALIST PARTY.

PSP. *See* SOCIAL PROGRESS PARTY.

PUP. *See* PARTY OF POPULAR UNITY.

QURANIC PRESERVATION SOCIETY (*Jam'iyat al-Hifadh 'ala al-Quran*). This Islamic cultural association, founded in 1970 in the Zaytuna Mosque, was to constitute the springboard for the Islamic movement and party that became part of Tunisia's political life in the 1980s and 1990s. Its development was encouraged by the Tunisian government in the 1970s to counterbalance the leftist groups on the various campuses of the Tunisian university.[8]

RALLY OF THE UNITED MAGHRIB (RMU) (*Tajamu' al-Maghrib al-Muwahhad*). This movement was formed in 1988 when it asked for legalization but was refused. Its leader is Al-Shadhli Zuwaytin whose vision extends beyond Tunisia to incorporate the whole of the Maghrib where he sees the need for economic and political liberalization.

RCD. *See* DEMOCRATIC CONSTITUTIONAL RALLY.

RENAISSANCE PARTY. *See* ISLAMIC TENDENCY MOVEMENT.

RMU. *See* RALLY OF THE UNITED MAGHRIB.

RSP. *See* SOCIALIST RALLY OF PROGRESSIVE UNITY.

AL-SHU'LA. *See* THE TORCH.

SOCIALIST DEMOCRATIC PARTY (PDS) (*Hizb al-Ishtiraki al-Dimuqrati*). Political dialogue on the evolution of the Tunisian political system continued within the Neo-Dustur Party* and the Dusturian Socialist Party* long after independence. Two leading members of the party, Ahmad al-Mestiri and Hasib ben 'Ammar, were longtime proponents of liberalization of the Tunisian political system. They favored the development of a multiparty system. By 1971 they felt they had enough support within the party to push for major policy changes. Habib Bourguiba won the showdown that ensued, and al-Mestiri was banished from the party. In 1974, after the party congress, eight more liberals were dismissed from the Dusturian Socialist Party.

The liberals headed by al-Mestiri continued to protest government policies and in 1977 attempted to organize a conference on human rights in Tunis but were prevented from doing so at the last minute. In 1978 they began publishing two newspapers: a weekly in Arabic, *Al-Ra'iy*, and a monthly in French, both of which had a checkered history of being closed down each time the government did not like their editorials.[9] Finally, in June 1978, they formed the Movement of Socialist Democrats (MDS) but were denied official recognition until 1983 when the party was finally legalized. *Al-Mostaqbal* (*The Future*) became the party's organ. Although it suffered from the same problems as did its predecessors, it has continued to publish. The party has been accused of being bourgeois and liberal and of appealing to the upper middle class of professionals and businessmen.

In April 1989, in the first multiparty elections held in Tunisia since 1956, five opposition parties, a coalition of leftists, and twenty-one independent candidates ran for 141 seats in parliament. In Tunis, the MDS's stronghold, it obtained only 5.3 percent of the votes, while at the national level its gains totaled less than 4 percent of the votes. As a consequence of the rather dismal election results, Ahmad al-Mestiri, who had been the longtime leader of the party, resigned and turned over the leadership to a three-man council composed of Muhammad Muwa'da, Isma'il Boulahya, and Mustafa ben Ja'far. Mawa'da eventually took over the leadership of the party.

SOCIALIST RALLY OF PROGRESSIVE UNITY (RSP) (*Al-Tajamu' al-Ishtiraki al-Taqaddumi*). This is yet another socialist party formed in 1980 and headed by Ahmad Najib al-Shabbi. In 1983 it began publishing a weekly entitled *Al-Mawqif* (*The Position*). After the takeover of the presidency by Zine al-'Abdin ben 'Ali, the RSP along with a number of other parties was legalized in 1988. In the April 1989 elections, it received only a tiny proportion of the votes at the national level.

SOCIAL PROGRESS PARTY (PSP) (*Hizb-al Taqaddumi al-Ijtima'i*). This party was founded in 1988 a few months before the national elections were held, and it was legalized the same year. It claims to be a liberal democratic party and is headed by a lawyer, Munir Beji. In the elections of April 1989, it obtained an insignificant number of votes at the national level.

TAJAMU' AL-DUASAT WAL AL-'AMAL AL-ISHTIRAKI. *See* TUNISIAN SOCIALIST STUDY AND ACTION GROUP.

AL-TAJAMU' AL-DUSTURI AL-DIMUQRATI. *See* DEMOCRATIC CONSTITUTIONAL RALLY.

AL-TAJAMU' AL-ISHTIRAKI AL-TAQADDUMI. *See* SOCIALIST RALLY OF PROGRESSIVE UNITY.

TAJAMU' AL-MAGHRIB AL-MUWAHHAD. *See* RALLY OF THE UNITED MAGHRIB.

AL-TAJAMU' AL-MARKISI AL-LININI AL-TUNISI. *See* TUNISIAN MARXIST-LENINIST GROUP.

AL-TAJAMU' AL-WAHDAWI LIL DIMUQRATIYYA. *See* UNIONIST RALLY FOR DEMOCRACY.

THE TORCH (*Al-Shu'la*). This Marxist-Leninist group was active among Tunisian workers in France in the 1960s.

TUNIS AL-FATAT. *See* YOUNG TUNISIANS.

TUNISIAN COMMUNIST PARTY (PCT) (*Al-Hizb al-Shuyu'i al-Tunisi*). The Tunisian Communist Party, founded in 1921 as part of the French Communist Party, became an independent Tunisian party only in 1934. It was the second major party that emerged in the pre-independence period. Muhammad Harmal was the founding father of the party that included, among its better known members, Muhammad al-Nafa'a and 'Abd al-Hamid ben Mustafa. Despite its claims to be the party of the workers and the *fallahin*, or peasants, it was primarily a party of intellectuals who took a pro-Soviet stand in foreign affairs and were never very effective on the domestic scene.

In 1963 the party was banned by Habib Bourguiba after a plot to assassinate him was discovered in December 1962. Some of the PCT members were implicated along with Ben Youssef's supporters, army elements, and members of the old Dusturian party. This action left the Neo-Dustur Party* as the only legal political organization in Tunisia for the next fifteen years.

In 1981 the party was legalized, and it reemerged on the political scene weak but ready to work with other leftist groups. It ran in local elections in 1989 as part of a leftist coalition. The coalition did very poorly, receiving only 4.2 percent of the votes in Monastir, 5 percent of the votes in Gafsa, and only 0.36 percent of the total vote at the national level.[10]

TUNISIAN COMMUNIST WORKERS' PARTY (*Al-Hizb al-'Ummah al-Shuyu'i*). Formed in 1988 and headed by Hamma al Hammami, this party has not been legalized.

TUNISIAN LIBERAL CONSTITUTIONAL PARTY (DUSTUR) (*Al-Hizb al-Dusturi al-Hurr al-Tunisi*). This party, also known as the Dustur Party, was founded in 1920 by Sheikh 'Abd al-'Aziz al-Tha'labi, a Young Tunisian and graduate of the Zaytuna Mosque, who had been exiled in 1912. The Dustur's leadership did not differ significantly from that of the parent party, as it represented landowning, professional, and merchant families of Tunisia, rather than the poorer strata of the society. In 1919, Al-Tha'labi wrote a manifesto, *La Tunisie Martyre*, in which he argued that the French Protectorate had in fact frozen the progress Tunisia had been making in "education, economic development, constitutional government and administration of justice," and he demanded an end to the protectorate, a constitution, the election of a deliberative assembly, and universal suffrage for Tunisians. As the Young Tunisians had done earlier, the Dusturians argued for an independent Tunisian state that would maintain a formal association with France. They also recognized the Bey of Tunis as the legitimate head of state and tried to protect his powers from erosion by the French administration. The Dustur Party was superceded by the Neo-Dustur Party* and later renamed Dusturian Socialist Party.*

TUNISIAN MARXIST-LENINIST GROUP (Al-Tajamu' al-Markisi al-Linini al-Tunisi). This group was formed in 1970.

TUNISIAN NATIONAL PROGRESSIVE FRONT (Al-Jabhat al-Wataniyya al-Taqaddumiyya). This front represents three groups: the Nasserite Arab Socialist Union of Tunisia, the Ba'thist Arab Socialist Movement of Tunisia, and the Youssefists or followers of Salah ben Youssef.

TUNISIAN NATIONAL RESISTANCE (Al-Muqawama al-Tunisiyya al-Wataniyya). No information is available about this party.

TUNISIAN NATIONALIST MOVEMENT (Harakat al-Tunisiyya al-Wataniyya). No information is available about this party.

TUNISIAN PERSPECTIVES (Afaq Tunisiyya). This party was created in the early 1960s in Paris. A branch was founded in Tunis in 1970.

TUNISIAN SOCIALIST STUDY AND ACTION GROUP (Tajamu' al-Duasat wal al-'Amal al-Ishtiraki). This group was formed in Paris in 1964. It held Trotskyite views, and some of its members were arrested in the early 1970s.

TUNISIAN WORKER ('Al-'Amil al-Tunisi). This party was active among workers in the 1970s, and some members were arrested in 1975.

26 JANUARY COLLECTIVE (Kumunat 26 Yanayir). No information is available about this party.

UDU. See UNION FOR DEMOCRATIC UNITY.

UNION FOR DEMOCRATIC UNITY (UDU) (Al-Ittihad al-Dimuqrati al-Wahdawi). This party was founded in 1988 by 'Abd al-Rahman Tlili and legalized by the Tunisian government that same year. An Arab nationalist party, it claims organizational independence from other similar groups in the Arab world, and it advocates Arab unity, democracy, and pluralism. It did better than a number of other parties in the elections of 1989, but it received only 0.61 percent of the total vote at the national level.

UNION OF TUNISIAN PEOPLE'S FORCES *(Ittihad Qiwa al-Sha'b al-Tunisi)*. No information is available about this party.

UNIONIST RALLY FOR DEMOCRACY *(Al-Tajamu' al-Wahdawi lil Dimuqratiyya)*. This pro-Qadhafi group, formed in 1988, is headed by Bashir al-Sid.

YOUNG TUNISIANS. See EVOLUTIONIST PARTY OF YOUNG TUNISIANS.

## NOTES

1. See Harold Nelson, ed., *Tunisia: A Country Study*, Foreign Area Studies, American University (Washington D.C.: U.S. Government Printing Office, 1979), 39–40. See also Norma Salem, *Habib Bourguiba, Islam and the Creation of Tunisia* (London: Croom Helm, 1984), 42–51.

2. Salem, *Habib Bourguiba*, 54.

3. Ibid., 92.

4. See L. B. Ware, "Habib Bourguiba," in *Political Leaders of the Contemporary Middle East and North Africa: A Biographical Dictionary*, ed. Bernard Reich (New York: Greenwood Press, 1990), 119–26.

5. Salem, *Habib Bourguiba*, 115.

6. Clement Henry Moore, *Tunisia since Independence: The Dynamics of One Party Government* (Berkeley: University of California Press, 1965), 74.

7. Ridha al-Maluli, "Al-'Amal al-Qawmi bi-Tunis: Al-Waqi wal-Afaq," *Al-Sabah* (Tunis), 25 June 1988.

8. Susan Waltz, "Islamist Appeal in Tunisia," *Middle East Journal* 40, 4 (Autumn 1986): 651–70.

9. Russell A. Stone, "Tunisia: A Single-Party System Holds Change in Abeyance," in *Political Elites in Arab North Africa: Morocco, Algeria, Tunisia, Libya and Egypt*, ed. I. William Zartman et al. (New York: Longman, 1982).

10. Habib Slim, "Reflexions autour des resultats des elections legislatives de 1989 en Tunisie: Implications et perspectives" (Paper prepared for the Middle East Studies Association of North America Conference, Toronto, Ontario, November 1989).

Mary-Jane Deeb

# TURKEY

The Republic of Turkey was established on October 29, 1923, following a long and bloody war with Greece. Although much smaller than the Ottoman Empire, which was defeated in World War I and subsequently partitioned, Turkey still comprises some 310,709 square miles (776,773 square kilometers), mostly in Anatolia, with its European segment in Eastern Thrace, up to and including Edirne (Adrianople). Thus, Turkey straddles the Bosphorus, which enhances its strategic importance. Its loss of territory was offset by the advantage of a more homogeneous population, especially after the Turkish-Greek population exchange. Turkey's overall population reached 57 million in 1990; the only significant minority is the Kurds, in the southeast, while the Greek, Jewish, and Armenian populations have dwindled to numerical insignificance, although they still account for a number of urban professionals and businessmen. About 99 percent of all inhabitants are Muslims, principally Sunnis.

Mustafa Kemal (Atatürk), the Republic's first president (1923–38) and leader of Turkey's only political party at the time, the Republican People's Party (RPP),* was largely responsible for harnessing the national effort to start Turkey on the road toward becoming a Westernized state. Together with a few trusted assistants, he strove to give the Turks pride in a new, Turkey-oriented nationalism, as well as a new sense of national purpose. The ideology expressed in his multifaceted reforms is often referred to as "Kemalism." Mustafa Kemal disestablished institutionalized Islam, closed down the religious schools, introduced secular civil law, changed the alphabet from Arabic to Latin characters, banned polygamy and granted women equal rights, introduced European clothes, founded a new modern capital in Ankara, supervised most of the economy via state institutions, and strengthened the military forces—although he was as careful in keeping them out of politics as he was in preventing any Turkish involvement in war.

His successor as president, İsmet İnönü (1938–50), followed in his footsteps and succeeded in carrying Turkey through a difficult period. It was he who decided, in 1945, to allow the formation of opposition parties, thus inaugurating the multiparty era in the republic (political parties had existed during the late Ottoman period in the parliaments convened by the Young Turks just before and during World War I). Upon the establishment of the republic in 1923, the

People's Party (later renamed the Republican People's Party) assumed power and ruled single-handedly in the unicameral parliament and in the country as a whole, disregarding a few short-lived political groups. The 1945 decision to switch from a hegemonic to a pluralistic party system began an era of lively competition for the popular vote. The change was a breakthrough in the institutionalization of free and competitive elections, the legitimization of opposition, and more generally the extension of political participation. The expanding scope of party politics drew new forces into national politics at the levels of both the ruling elite and the mass public.

At the beginning of the era of competitive politics, both major parties were middle-of-the-road pluralist groupings, directing their populistic appeal toward mobilizing the entire population and frowning on those smaller parties that appealed to class or other narrower, special-interest groups. To a striking extent, all parties have frequently been dominated by prominent personalities. In brief, numerous political groups mushroomed since the late 1940s, testing the new atmosphere of freedom. Many merely registered legally, showing no signs of further activity; others were much more solidly based. Either way, politics increasingly became everybody's business. A growing political organization, the Democrat Party (DP),* won the general elections of 1950 and ruled Turkey for the entire decade. Political leadership became more diversified, rural landowners and others being recruited into the political elite. The new leadership inclined toward encouraging more private enterprise in the economy, requesting and accepting massive U.S. financial aid, and granting Islam a more favored standing (although not retreating from secularism in any drastic manner).

Competition between the Republican People's Party and the Democrat Party dominated Turkish politics—and the entire public scene—from 1946 to 1960, not only on the national level, but also on the local level. Most remarkably, this also applied to rural Turkey, until then only modestly involved in politics. In practically all general elections, based on the electoral system during the multiparty era, voter participation was proportionately greater in the less-developed, rural areas. This cannot be attributed solely to the massive mobilization of the peasant vote by landowners and other local leaders. Indeed, feelings ran so high in some villages that separate coffeehouses had to be maintained for supporters of the respective parties; in some cases, fathers who supported one party refused to let their daughters marry men affiliated with the other.

The multiparty era can be subdivided into shorter periods marked by military interventions in 1960, 1971, and 1980. The first, on May 27, 1960, was a protest against the increasing authoritarianism of the Democrat Party as much as it was an attempt to reassert Kemalist ideology. However, with the voluntary transfer of government from military to civilian rule in 1961, another epoch commenced in Turkish politics. Competition between the two mass parties—now the Republican People's Party and the Justice Party (JP)* (successor to the banned Democrat Party)—was accompanied by no less severe a rivalry among smaller groups. This resulted largely from the change in the electoral system: Prior to

1960, there was a majority list system, whereas the subsequent, mixed system was based predominantly upon proportional representation. Many of the groups that mushroomed during the 1960s and 1970s were ideologically based, some of extreme nature adopting Marxist, ultranationalist, or Islamic philosophies; several of these wore the mantle of radical protest. There was greater issue orientation, too. In particular, there was a preoccupation with developmental problems; the growing of social interests contributed to ideological polarization in the party spectrum. At the same time, political mobilization of workers and farmers by the parties assisted their integration into politics; parties became an indispensable channel for political and social mobility to elective positions. As a result, the urban-rural dichotomy slightly but perceptibly declined.

Increasing violence brought about a second military intervention via a memorandum issued by the armed forces on March 12, 1971. The government resigned and was succeeded by coalition cabinets, serving rather to increase fragmentation in political organization, which generally favored accelerated radical tendencies. Stronger ideological commitment in politics was prompted by the continuing failure of the authorities to cope with Turkey's special problems (such as mass migration to urban centers) and economic difficulties (such as unemployment and inflation). Similarly, liberalization of the regime, following the 1960 military intervention, encouraged the further fragmentation of the party system through the formation of additional parties (both new ones and splinter groups), either ideological or pragmatic, but everyone vying for a share of the seats in the two houses of parliament set up under the 1961 constitution. Frequent elections made party rivalry a common feature of Turkish politics. Significantly, some of this activity, particularly violence, took place outside parliament.

Party structure and certain features of party activity were regulated by the 1965 Party Law, which drew upon earlier laws concerning political behavior, as well as upon the constitution, regarding prevention of abuse and misuse of political freedom. Briefly stated, the Party Law set down the structural models to which parties were required to conform regarding organization and registration. Following Western European patterns, parties were expected to establish branches linked to a central bureau, which was in turn responsible to an annual or biennial party convention that elected the various party officials and bodies. Disciplinary boards were designed to control the party members and institutions. Obligatory party registration and state control (including, for example, the membership dues parties may collect) ensured legality. Parties were barred from exploiting ethnic divisions or religious sentiments for propaganda and could not advocate a violent change of regime. Marxism and advocacy of a *sharia* state were outlawed and still are. However, in order to prevent the majority party from simply disbanding its rivals, the Party Law stipulated that only the Constitutional Court, a nonpolitical institution established in 1961, would be qualified to determine the legality of party activity.

The military memorandum of 1971 changed nothing in either the political structures or party activity, but the third military intervention of September 12,

1980, did. Lasting for three years, it focused much of its activity on attempting to change the political structure in a way that would reduce tension and violence, which had been the catalyst for the intervention. On October 16, 1981, all political parties were closed down by the military, and active politicians were barred from politics for up to ten years. For the first time in the history of the Turkish Republic, all political parties were banned (in 1960, only the Democrat Party had been banned.) Nonetheless, public debate about political parties continued and, in 1983, A. Yaşar Oğuz even published a 156-page book, entitled *An Ideal Party Program (İdeal Bir Parti Programı)*, in which he envisioned a party committed to achieving the best for everybody in Turkey.

The return to civilian rule found expression in the 1982 constitution and the November 6, 1983, general elections, to a five-year, one-house parliament of 400 seats (later, since 1987, 450 seats). Three parties ran, all other competitors having been vetoed by the military. Of these, two had been sponsored by the military regime; it was symptomatic of public attitudes that the third one, the Motherland Party,* won an absolute majority in parliament. In the 1987 parliamentary elections, several parties ran, but only three succeeded in winning seats, due to the laws laid down by the military regime, which established a barrier of 5 percent in each constituency and 10 percent nationally.

With rare exceptions, Turkey's political parties obeyed the law; they skillfully skirted controversial issues, alluding to them rather than adopting clear positions. In addition, they supplied the authorities (and the public) with only the minimum information required concerning their organizational aspects; thus, they studiously avoided revealing details concerning the extent of membership or sources of party financing. Turkish parties were generally kept under tight control by their respective leaders, who were responsible for most of the policy making, consulting at most only their own parliamentary groups. These groups showed considerable discipline and actually handled most of the activity connected with their parties.

### Bibliography

### TURKISH SOURCES

Abadan, Nermin. *Anayasa hukuku ve siyasî bilimler açısından 1965 seçimlerinin tahlili* (An Analysis of the 1965 Elections from the Perspective of Constitutional Law and Political Science). Ankara: Siyasal Bilgiler Fakültesi, 1966.

Ahmad, Feroz, and Bedia Turgay. *Türkiye'de çok partili politikanın açıklamalı, kronolojisi (1945–1971)* (A Chronology of Multiparty Politics in Turkey, 1945–1971). Ankara: Bilgi Yay ınevi, 1976.

Arar, İsmail. *Hükumet programları, 1920–1965* (Government Programs, 1920–1965). Istanbul: Tipo Neşriyat, 1968.

Bilâ, Hikmet. *C.H.P. tarihi, 1919–1979* (A History of the Republican People's Party, 1919–1979). Ankara: DMS Doruk Sanayii, 1979.

Boran, Behice. *Türkiye ve sosyalizm sorunları* (Turkey and the Problems of Socialism), 2d ed. Istanbul: Tekin Yayınevi, 1970.

Coşkun, Süleyman. *SHP: Bir oluşumun arkası* (The Social Populist Party: Behind the Scenes of Its Formation). Ankara: Esen Yayınları, n.d. [1986].

Demirel, Süleyman. *Büyük Türkiye* (Great Turkey). Istanbul: Dergâh Yayınları, 1975.

Doğru Yol Partisi, *Doğru Yol Partisi neyin mücadelesini yapıyor?* (Why Does the True Path Party Pursue Its Struggle?) Ankara: Doğru Yol Partisi Yayınları, n.d. [1984].

Erbakan, N. *Millî görüş ve anayasa değişikliği* (The National Outlook and the Revision of the Constitution). Istanbul: Dergâh Yayınları, 1975.

İpekçi, Abdi. *Liderler diyor ki (röportajlar)* (The Leaders Are Saying: Reports). Istanbul: ANT Yayınları, 1969.

Tezic, E. *100 soruda siyasî partiler* (Political Parties in a Hundred Questions). Istanbul: Gerçek Yayınevi, 1976.

Toker, Metin. *Tek partiden çok partiye* (From Single-Party to Multi-Party). N.p.: Milliyet Yayınları, 1970.

Tunaya, T. Z. *Türkiyede siyasal partiler* (Political Parties in Turkey), vols. I, II, III. Istanbul: Hürriyet Vakfı Yayınları, 1984–89.

## SOURCES IN OTHER LANGUAGES

Ahmad, Feroz. *The Turkish Experiment in Democracy, 1950–1975*. London: C. Hurst, 1977.

Akarlı, E. D., and G. Ben-Dor, eds. *Political Participation in Turkey*. Istanbul: Boğaziçi University Publications, 1975.

Akyüz, Yahya. *Le parti politique unique de la Turquie (1923–1946) et l'éducation politique du peuple*. Nancy, France: Université de Nancy, 1966.

Dodd, C. H. *Politics and Government in Turkey*. Manchester, England: Manchester University Press, 1969.

———. *Democracy and Development in Turkey*. Walkington, England: Eothen Press, 1983.

———. *The Crisis of Turkish Democracy*. 2d ed. Walkington, England: Eothen Press, 1990.

Frey, F. W. *The Turkish Political Elite*. Cambridge, Mass.: MIT Press, 1965.

Hale, W. M., ed. *Aspects of Modern Turkey*. London: Bowker, 1976.

Harris, G. S. *The Origins of Communism in Turkey*. Stanford, Calif.: Hoover Institution Press, 1967.

Heper, Metin, and J. M. Landau, eds. *Political Parties and Democracy in Turkey*. London: I. B. Tauris, 1991.

Karpat, K. H. *Turkey's Politics: The Transition to a Multi-Party System*. Princeton, N.J.: Princeton University Press, 1959.

Karpat, K. H., et al. *Social Change and Politics in Turkey: A Structural-Historical Analysis*. Leiden, Netherlands: Brill, 1973.

Kışlalı, A. T. *Forces politiques dans la Turquie moderne*. Ankara: 1968.

Kündig-Steiner, Werner. *Die Türkei*. Tübingen, Germany: Horst-Erdmann Verlag, 1974.

Landau, J. M. *Radical Politics in Modern Turkey*. Leiden, Netherlands: Brill, 1974.

———. "The National Salvation Party in Turkey." *Asian and African Studies* 11(1976): 1–57.

———. *Politics and Islam: The National Salvation Party in Turkey*. Research Monograph no. 5. Salt Lake City: Middle East Center, University of Utah, 1976.

———. *Pan-Turkism in Turkey: A Study in Irredentism*. London: C. Hurst, 1981.

———. "The Nationalist Action Party." *Journal of Contemporary History* 17(1982): 587–606.

———. *The Politics of Pan-Islam: Ideology and Organization.* Oxford, England: Oxford University Press, 1990.

Landau, J. M., ed. *Atatürk and the Modernization of Turkey.* Boulder, Colo.: Westview Press; Leiden, Netherlands: Brill, 1984.

Landau, J. M., Ergun Özbudun, and Frank Tachau, eds. *Electoral Politics in the Middle East: Issues, Voters and Elites.* London: Croom Helm, 1980.

Lewis, Bernard. *The Emergence of Modern Turkey.* London: Oxford University Press, 1966.

Lewis, Geoffrey. *Modern Turkey.* New York: Praeger, 1974.

Mango, Andrew. *Turkey.* London: Thames and Hudson, 1968.

Ortaylı, İlber, ed. *Liberal Elements in the Programmes of Turkish Political Parties.* Ankara: TES-AR, 1992.

Özbudun, Ergun. *Social Change and Political Participation in Turkey.* Princeton, N.J.: Princeton University Press, 1976.

Özbudun, Ergun, and Frank Tachau. "Social Change and Electoral Behavior in Turkey: Toward a 'Critical Realignment'?" *International Journal of Middle East Studies* 4 (1975): 460–80.

Party of Social Democracy. *For Democracy, Equality, Peace and Progress.* N.p., n.d. [1985].

Rustow, D. A. "The Development of Political Parties in Turkey," in *Political Culture and Political Development,* edited by J. LaPalombara and M. Weiner. Princeton, N.J.: Princeton University Press, 1966.

Sherwood, W. B. "The Rise of the Justice Party in Turkey." *World Politics* 20 (1967–8): 54–65.

Social Democratic Populist Party. *Historical Background, Platform, Program, Bylaws, List of Executive Members.* Ankara: SHP, 1986.

Tachau, Frank. *Turkey: The Politics of Authority, Democracy and Development.* New York: Praeger, 1984.

Tachau, Frank, and M.J.D. Good. "The Anatomy of Political and Social Change: Turkish Parties, Parliaments and Elections." *Comparative Politics* 4 (1973): 551–73.

Tachau, Frank, and Metin Heper. "The State, Politics and the Military in Turkey." *Comparative Politics* 16 (1983): 17–33.

Tachau, Frank, and A. H. Ülman. "Dilemmas of Turkish Politics," in *Turkish Yearbook of International Relations, 1962* (1964): 1–34.

Toprak, Binnaz. *Islam and Political Development in Turkey.* Leiden, Netherlands: Brill, 1981.

Turan, İlter. "Political Parties and the Party System in Post-1983 Turkey," in *State, Democracy and the Military: Turkey in the 1980s,* edited by M. Heper and A. Evin. Berlin: Walter de Gruyter, 1988.

Weiker, W. F. *Political Tutelage and Democracy in Turkey: The Free Party and Its Aftermath.* Leiden, Netherlands: Brill, 1973.

———. *The Modernization of Turkey from Ataturk to the Present Day.* New York: Holmes and Meier, 1981.

## Political Parties

ADALET PARTİSİ. *See* JUSTICE PARTY.

AHALİ CUMHURİYET FIRKASI. *See* PEOPLE'S REPUBLICAN PARTY.

ANADOLU PARTİSİ. *See* ANATOLIAN PARTY.

ANATOLIAN PARTY (*Anadolu Partisi*). Founded on January 25, 1991, this party was led by Zeki Çeliker, an independent member of the Grand National Assembly from Siirt province at the time; Hüseyin Özalp, an independent deputy from Sırnak, was vice-chairman. Initially named the Great Anatolian Party,* the name was changed in order to distinguish it from pre-1980 parties with this name. Its program emphasized national sovereignty, national unity, and the supremacy of the national will. It emphasized national security and it favored free enterprise, privatization of state economic enterprises, and decentralization of the state. The party also advocated compulsory religious education in public primary and secondary schools.

ANAVATAN PARTİSİ. *See* MOTHERLAND PARTY.

ARITMA KORUMA PARTİSİ. *See* Purification and Preservation Party.

BANNER PARTY (*Bayrak Partisi*). This party was founded on July 29, 1983, by Yaşar Yürtoven, an industrialist. Its program aimed at fostering the liberty and prosperity of society, within a democratic secular framework, and at encouraging both technology and the national and moral values of the Turkish nation. Little is known of its activity; some of its members later participated in setting up the Reformist Democracy Party.*

BAYRAK PARTİSİ. *See* BANNER PARTY.

BİRLİK PARTİSİ. *See* UNITY PARTY.

BİZİM PARTİ. *See* OUR PARTY.

BROTHERHOOD PARTY OF TURKEY (*Türkiye Kardeşlik Partisi*). Established in Ankara on November 24, 1973, this party has displayed little to no activity.

BÜYÜK ANADOLU PARTİSİ. *See* GREAT ANATOLIA PARTY.

BÜYÜK BİRLİK PARTİSİ. *See* GREAT UNITY PARTY.

BÜYÜK DEĞİŞİM PARTİSİ. *See* GREAT CHANGE PARTY.

BÜYÜK KUVVET PARTİSİ. *See* GREAT POWER PARTY.

BÜYÜK TÜRKİYE PARTİSİ. *See* GREAT TURKEY PARTY.

BÜYÜK VATAN PARTİSİ. *See* GREAT HOMELAND PARTY.

COMMUNIST PARTY OF TURKEY (CPT) (*Türkiye Komünist Partisi*). This party is the only party to have survived from the 1920s into the 1990s. Illegal until 1990, it consistently operated clandestinely as a small organization of several hundred members that never succeeded in gaining grass-roots support, despite its numerous calls for popular antifascist associations. In addition, it has suffered repeatedly from rifts among the leadership. However, its greatest drawback may well have been the special circumstances under which it operated in a newly established state, conditioned by its leaders for revolutionary reform; communism had a difficult task in competing with powerful and dynamic nationalism. The republic's leadership watched communist activity closely, since it began in Turkey right after the end of World War I under the leadership of Mustafa Suphi (the party held its first general convention on September 10, 1920). A paragraph in the 1924 constitution, forbidding changes in the regime, was probably directed against the CPT. Mustafa Kemal even briefly established a rival Communist party, headed by some of his closest associates, to push the CPT aside.

As a rule, however, the activities of the party were officially discouraged, particularly after 1927. The CPT's leaders and activists were either jailed or exiled from Turkey, and its publications were seized. Although there was a letup on the part of the authorities during World War II, when Turkey was striving for neutrality, the CPT remained illegal. Even after the 1960–61 military intervention and the subsequent liberalization of political activity, the CPT's hopes to obtain legal status were not realized. It became legal only in 1990, in the renamed United Communist Party of Turkey.*

The small, tightly knit party leadership was dominated by Marxists, such as the CPT's secretary general, Şefik Hüsnü Değmer, a physician; then Zeki Baştımar, alias Yakup Demir; later I. Bilen; and finally Nihat Sargın, a physician. The authority of the party's central bodies, organized like communist parties elsewhere, spread to the local cells. Membership consisted of intellectuals (including some students) and workers; the intellectuals apparently predominated, at least in decision-making positions. Party pamphlets, leaflets, and journals were clandestinely prepared and distributed. Although the journals were short lived, they apparently had a stronger impact than was realized at the time. Indeed, while the CPT had only a marginal impact throughout its career, it did not remain without effect on the numerous small leftist groups that were legally established in Turkey after the end of World War II, many of which echo the teachings of the CPT to varying degrees.

The party ideology, toeing Moscow's line, bore a marked similarity to that of other communist parties in the Third World. Consistently fighting other leftist groups in Turkey, the CPT always argued that it was the only true Leninist group in the country and, as such, was the only party equipped to cure Turkey's ills on all levels. The CPT accordingly stressed the relevance of its solutions in the Turkish context. Consequently, there has been a marked change in points of emphasis. In 1945 Değmer proclaimed the new goal of the CPT to be the unfettered establishment of political parties, free activity of trade unions, the right to strike, free speech, distribution of land through agrarian reforms, equality for ethnic minorities, tax reform, and a rapprochement with the Soviet Union.

When several of these demands were implemented during the postwar period, the CPT's 1978 program followed another tack. It defined the party's role as the fight against Turkey's "capitalist progress," in the context of a national-social struggle for the democratic transformation of Turkey. The CPT wanted Turkey to get out of NATO, close down all U.S. military installations, abolish all foreign monopolies, protect local industries, and promote democracy by establishing stronger trade unions and cooperatives, fighting unemployment, setting up a system of social security, and distributing land to the needy through nationalization.

The party enjoyed the support of Turkish broadcasts from *Bizim Radyo* (Our radio) in Leipzig and of various Turkish periodicals, published irregularly, such as *Tan* (published during the 1940s), *Yurt ve Dünya, Komünist, Kızıl Yıldız, Adımlar, Yeni Edebiyat,* and others.

CONSERVATIVE PARTY (*Muhafazakâr Parti*). Established in Ankara, on July 7, 1983, the party's first chairman was Mehmet Pomak, an official and financier. When he was vetoed by the military regime's National Security Council, Ahmet Özsay, a pharmacist, became chairman in his stead, soon followed by İsmail Hakkı Yılanlıoğlu, a veterinarian who had been a close associate of Alparslan Türkeş, in the Nationalist Action Party (NAP).* In early 1985, Ali Koç, a lawyer and businessman, became chairman. A sizable number of members and sympathizers had been in the NAP previously, and the party's strongly nationalist ideology also resembled the NAP's, with its emphasis on a powerful Turkey. At the general convention held on November 30, 1985, the party's name was changed to the Nationalist Work Party.*

CONSTITUTION PARTY (*Düstur Partisi*). Established in February 1961, this party displayed little to no activity.

CPT. *See* COMMUNIST PARTY OF TURKEY.

CUMHURİYET HALK FIRKASI. *See* REPUBLICAN PEOPLE'S PARTY.

CUMHURİYET HALK PARTİSİ. *See* REPUBLICAN PEOPLE'S PARTY.

CUMHURİYETÇİ DEMOKRATİK GENÇLIK PARTİSİ. *See* REPUBLICAN DEMOCRATIC YOUTH PARTY.

CUMHURİYETÇİ GÜVEN PARTİSİ. *See* REPUBLICAN RELIANCE PARTY.

CUMHURİYETÇİ KÖYLÜ MİLLET PARTİSİ. *See* REPUBLICAN PEAS-ANTS' NATION PARTY.

CUMHURİYETÇİ MESLEKÎ ISLAHAT PARTİSİ. *See* REPUBLICAN PRO-FESSIONAL REFORM PARTY.

CUMHURİYETÇİ MİLLET PARTİSİ. *See* REPUBLICAN NATION PARTY.

CUMHURİYETÇİ PARTİ. *See* REPUBLICAN PARTY.

ÇALIŞMA PARTİSİ. *See* LABOR PARTY.

ÇIFTÇİ VE KÖYLÜ PARTİSİ. *See* FARMERS' AND VILLAGERS' PARTY.

DEMOCRACY PARTY *(Demokrasi Partisi [DEP])*. Led by Yaşar Kaya, this party was established on May 7, 1993. It includes a number of members of parliament identified as Kurdish, some of whom were subject to procedures for lifting their parliamentary immunity late in 1993 in order to allow their prosecution for alleged links with the Kurdish Workers Party (PKK)* and the guerrilla-style insurrection in the southeast. The party's program devoted special attention to the Kurdish question, citing a series of international documents, including the Universal Declaration of Human Rights. The party declared its opposition to "political, economic, and cultural coercion." It favored replacement of the 1982 constitution with a charter based on the principles of international law. In its first year of operation, this party controlled seventeen seats in the parliament. It was generally considered as the successor to the outlawed People's Labor Party (HEP).* Hatip Dicle was elected party chairman late in 1993, at a convention marked by positive rhetoric regarding the PKK and reported remarks by Greek guests favoring the Kurdish struggle.

DEMOCRAT PARTY I (DP) *(Demokrat Parti)*. Established in Ankara on January 7, 1946, by an opposition group within the Republican People's Party (RPP),* the DP stood for democracy (hence its name), political liberalization, and greater leeway for private enterprise in the economy. Personal rivalry between İsmet İnönü, an ex-general and the RPP's chairman, and a rival leader, Celal Bayar, an economist (who had been prime minister at the time of Mustafa Kemal's death), was a contributing factor in the DP's foundation. Bayar, together with Adnan Menderes, a landowner, Fuat Köprülü, a professor of history, and Refik Koraltan, a lawyer, established the DP and set about making it the focus of opposition to the RPP. The new party succeeded in benefiting from private and public dissatisfaction with the strong-handed, long-lasting, single-party rule of the RPP and its apparent responsibility for shortages during World War II.

Noting the DP's rising strength, the RPP cabinet advanced the elections by about a year to July 21, 1946. The DP obtained sixty-two seats in the Grand

National Assembly. This was a remarkable feat for Turkey in that period, as was the phenomenal increase in DP membership: By the end of 1946, less than a year after its foundation, it had—so Bayar claimed—over 1 million members. The DP held its first general convention on January 7, 1947 (its first anniversary) and adopted its first detailed program.

In the May 14, 1950, general elections, the DP achieved a major victory with 53.3 percent of the vote, which further improved to 56.6 percent in 1954. Even when its proportion of the vote decreased to 47.3 percent in 1957, the DP maintained a majority of seats in the Grand National Assembly (thanks to the majority list electoral system) (see Table 21). The DP governed Turkey for an entire decade; between 1950 and 1960, Bayar served as state president and Menderes as chairman of the DP and prime minister. During the late 1940s and throughout the 1950s, Turkey's political history revolved around the power struggle between the two mass parties of the time: the RPP and the DP.

The DP's program, largely pragmatic and directed against the RPP, focused on liberalization of controls, both political (greater freedom for the press, changes in the election laws, better security for the secret ballot) and economic (a retreat from etatism toward more private enterprise). In government, the DP favored the development of rural areas, investing in the mechanization of agriculture and providing farmers with better seeds and fertilizers—all of which brought handsome returns from peasant voters, appreciative of agricultural progress and industrial development in rural areas. Other groups supporting the DP were rural notables and rich landowners, who continued to enjoy their position as intermediaries between the peasants and the government; urban business, commercial, and industrial circles, which benefited from the government's support for free enterprise; members of ethnic minorities; tradesmen-artisans; and the nonsalaried middle class.

Although not retreating from secularism as a guiding principle, the DP was less rigid in enforcing it. For example, it allowed the call to prayer to be sounded in Arabic once again, reopened the tombs of holy men for worship (as historical monuments), and invested in the repair of mosques and the construction of new ones. To finance their vast economic projects, the DP governments attracted foreign capital investments and grants from the United States—one aspect of its rapprochement with the United States and the West, in addition to Turkish military participation in the Korean War and Turkey's joining NATO (1952) and the Baghdad Pact (1955). On a parallel level, the authorities curtailed leftist activities and arrested some of the more extreme leftists, particularly in 1951.

As in other mass parties with heterogeneous membership, there were several rifts in the DP; some of its leaders, too, subsequently left the party. As early as 1948, a religious conservative group split to form the Nation Party* (see NP 1). More of the DP's followers became disenchanted, especially after 1955; in that year, another breakaway group formed the Freedom Party.*

During the later 1950s, the economic leap forward slowed down visibly. Poor harvests and rising inflation reduced the DP's popularity among certain peasant

**Table 21**
**Grand National Assembly Election Results, 1950–57**

| ELECTIONS | | DP | RPP | Inds and other parties |
|---|---|---|---|---|
| 1950 | % of vote | 53.3 | 39.9 | 7.9 |
| | Seats won | 396 | 69 | 10 |
| | % of seats | 83.8 | 14.2 | 2.0 |
| 1954 | % of vote | 56.6 | 34.8 | 6.3 |
| | Seats won | 490 | 30 | 15 |
| | % of seats | 91.6 | 5.6 | 2.8 |
| 1957 | % of vote | 47.3 | 40.6 | 10.9 |
| | Seats won | 419 | 173 | 10 |
| | % of seats | 69.6 | 28.7 | 1.7 |

Note: The total number of seats varied from 487 (with twelve vacancies) in 1950, to 610 (with eight vacancies) in 1957.

and salaried circles. The DP's popularity declined still further due to the government's harsh policies toward other parties, the press, and so on. The DP's leadership displayed considerable impatience with criticism and increasingly called upon the armed forces to maintain order—and keep them in power. On May 27, 1960, the military intervened; DP leaders, including the state president, the cabinet, and all DP members of the Grand National Assembly were arrested and subsequently tried. Menderes and two other ministers were executed; others (including Bayar) were jailed. The DP was disbanded on September 29, 1960. Most of the party's members ultimately supported the Justice Party,* which was established in the following year. (Another party, also called the Democrat Party, was founded in Ankara on January 22, 1975, by an old member of the DP, Necati Turgut; this party bears no relation, however, to the banned DP.)

The DP's grass-roots support was wide, and its popular support was heterogeneous. As it originally broke away from the ranks of the RPP, it included most of the elements making up the RPP. One major RPP component not much in evidence within the DP, however, was the military; Bayar was Turkey's first president who had not been a high-ranking officer. However, the very creation of the DP markedly enlarged the Turkish political elite and institutionalized interparty and intraparty strife. The growth of the political elite and increasing differentiation within Turkish society compounded the difficulties of the DP in appealing to various groups and classes. This is probably the main reason why the DP's ideology was so pragmatic and moderate.

The Turkish press played a major role in the DP's rise and fall—more so than in the case of most other Turkish parties. During the party's early years (1946–50), when it was in opposition, the DP was the darling of the Turkish press. Toward the end of its rule, in the late 1950s, however, it lost much of its popularity. *Vatan* was the most important daily supporting the DP consistently. Later, however, with the exception of *Zafer*, the party's national daily, and several local papers, such as Izmir's *Ege Ekspres* and *Yeni Asır*, the Turkish press turned against the party on various grounds, particularly because of the DP's attempts to control the press and impose political censorship.

DEMOCRAT PARTY II (*Demokrat Parti*). This party was founded November 29, 1992; its chairman was Hayrettin Erkmen, and its leaders included several former members of parliament (including the pre-1980 Senate) as well as Nilüfer Gürsoy, daughter of the late president of Turkey and founder of the first Democrat Party, Celal Bayar. The party claimed to be the true heir of the first Democrat Party, a claim disputed by Democrat Party III.* Its program was virtually identical with its putative ancestor, including nationalism and secularism; it also declared firm opposition to any attempts to disrupt national unity and territorial integrity (i.e., Kurdish separatism). Like its namesake, the party favored private enterprise and supported the privatization of state economic enterprises.

DEMOCRAT PARTY III (*Demokrat Parti*). Founded on December 12, 1992, this party immediately ran into a legal problem because its name is identical to that of another party formed scarcely two weeks earlier (see Democrat Party II). Its program rejected communist ideology and supported a mixed economic system.

DEMOCRATIC CENTER PARTY (*Demokratik Merkez Partisi*). This party was founded, on May 17, 1990, by Bedrettin Dalan, an erstwhile mayor of Istanbul. He and another former member of the Motherland Party* represented this party in parliament until 1991. It spoke up for a liberal ideology. It shut down on September 14, 1991.

DEMOCRATIC LEFT PARTY (*Demokratik Sol Parti*). Established on November 14, 1983, a week after the parliamentary elections, this party was first led by Rahşan Ecevit, the wife of Bülent Ecevit, former chairman of the Republican People's Party (RPP),* then, after 1987, when the ban on political activists was lifted, by her husband himself. Many members and supporters came from the RPP, as did the new party's ideology (social-democratic and Kemalist). Indeed, the party claimed to be the RPP's successor. In the 1987 parliamentary elections, the party obtained 8.53 percent of the total vote, but it did not get any seats (due to the 10 percent barrier). In the 1990 local elections, it improved its percentage of the vote. In the 1991 parliamentary elections, it obtained seven parliamentary seats.

DEMOCRATIC PARTY (*Demokratik Parti*). The Democratic Party, to be distinguished from the Democrat Party (DP)* of the 1940s and 1950s, was established on December 18, 1970, by sixty-nine former members of the Justice Party
(JP).* Of these, forty-one were members of the Grand National Assembly, some
of whom had been expelled from the JP after having voted against the budget
bill presented by the JP cabinet; others had resigned of their own free will. The
founders of the Democratic Party were led by Ferruh Bozbeyli (an erstwhile
speaker of the National Assembly), who became the new party's chairman, S.
Bilgiç, a physician, and Y. Menderes, a political scientist, who became deputy
chairmen. Other prominent members were T. Asal, a lawyer, F. Sükan, a physician, and M. Turgut, a lawyer. There were personal rivalries between the founders and their supporters, as well as between the founders and the chairman of
the JP, Süleyman Demirel. Beyond these, moreover, there was a clash of interests
between the urban entrepreneurs, who had a decisive say in the JP's affairs, and
those leaders and members within the Democratic Party who represented those
with large rural holdings. Other supporters of the new party came from the ranks
of the banned Democrat Party, including the ex-president, Celal Bayar (until
1974). Not unexpectedly, one of the most important goals of the Democratic
Party was its out-and-out opposition to any reform in land tenure. The party
succeeded in convincing the Constitutional Court to nullify a law reforming land
tenure, contending that it was unconstitutional on procedural grounds.

Otherwise, much of the party's activity was parliamentary. During the 1973
presidential election crisis (the president of Turkey was elected jointly by the
two houses of the Grand National Assembly), the en bloc vote of the Democratic
Party forced the election of a compromise candidate. Later on, in the elections
held on October 14, 1973, the Democratic Party obtained 11.9 percent of the
vote to the National Assembly, giving them forty-five seats (out of 450) (see
Table 22); Senate election results (one-third of the Senate stood for reelection)
were only slightly less impressive for a first attempt—10.4 percent (although no
seats were won, owing to different methods of vote distribution). Support came
chiefly from poorly or moderately developed areas; much of it was at the JP's
expense.

Thus, the Democratic Party became the fourth largest group in the 1973 National Assembly, negotiating separately with both the Republican People's Party
(RPP)* and the JP for a governing coalition. With the former, there was obvious
ideological incompatibility; the latter was agreeable, but the Democratic Party
wanted a partnership without Demirel, which was rejected by the JP's leadership.
As a result, the parliamentary group of the Democratic Party dwindled, thanks
to desertions back to the JP, of which the most serious was that of a group led
by Bilgiç; the loss of the prestigious Bayar was another grievous blow.

In the June 5, 1977, general elections, the National Assembly vote for the
Democratic Party declined sharply to 1.9 percent (even Bozbeyli, the party's
chairman, failed to obtain a seat), and the Senate vote (one-third stood for
reelection) declined to 2.2 percent (thus it obtained no seat). It seems that many

Table 22
Grand National Assembly Election Results, 1961–77

| ELECTIONS | | NTP | JP | RPP | Inds and other parties |
|---|---|---|---|---|---|
| 1961 | % of votes | 13.7 | 34.8 | 36.7 | 14.8 |
| | Seats won | 65 | 158 | 173 | 54 |
| | % of seats | 14.4 | 35.1 | 38.4 | 12.0 |
| 1965 | % of votes | 3.7 | 52.9 | 28.7 | 14.7 |
| | Seats won | 19 | 240 | 134 | 57 |
| | % of seats | 4.2 | 53.3 | 29.8 | 12.6 |
| 1969 | % of votes | 2.2 | 46.5 | 27.4 | 23.9 |
| | Seats won | 6 | 256 | 143 | 45 |
| | % of seats | 1.3 | 56.9 | 31.8 | 9.9 |
| 1973 | % of votes | ------ | 30.6 | 33.5 | 37.0 |
| | Seats won | ------ | 149 | 185 | 116 |
| | % of seats | ------ | 33.1 | 41.1 | 25.5 |
| 1977 | % of votes | ------ | 36.9 | 41.6 | 21.7 |
| | Seats won | ------ | 189 | 213 | 48 |
| | % of seats | ------ | 42.0 | 47.3 | 10.4 |

Note: There were 450 seats in the National Assembly between 1961 and 1980. The Senate is not considered here.

of the former supporters of the Democratic Party returned to the JP in the 1977 election. The only Democratic Party candidate who obtained a seat in the National Assembly was Faruk Sükan, who joined with the RPP and several others in a coalition cabinet early in 1978. Party pressure, exerted through Sükan, is believed to have prevented the government from abolishing articles 141–142 of the penal code (which outlaw the formation of Marxist parties).

The party's program, approved by the Ministry of the Interior in December 1970, was somewhat modified at its first general convention held on December 16–17, 1972. As amended, the ideology of the party stood for freedom of thought, conscience, and religion; social justice; equitable taxation; the encouragement of investment (both private and foreign); closer cooperation with the EEC; industrialization based on research; improvements in transportation, housing, tourism, and public health; and raising the level of agriculture. In a later handbill, the party especially emphasized "right-of-center policies, nationalism and democracy" (which they saw as interacting), as well as a free and national economy, which, for them, meant private enterprise, encouraging savings, and a progressive technology (all within the context of the Islamic faith).

**DEMOCRATIC UNION PARTY** (*Demokrat Birlik Partisi*). Established in Sivas on April 23, 1968, as a local group, it displayed little to no activity.

**DEMOCRATIC WORKERS' PARTY** (*Demokrat İşçi Partisi*). This party was established in Istanbul in 1950 by Orhan Arsal, a lawyer (chairman); Üzeyir Kuran, a labor unionist (secretary general); Nizamettin Yalçinyuva, a leftist activist; and Ferruh Apaydin, a lawyer. The party claimed a membership of about 600. It ran unsuccessfully in the by-elections of 1951, obtaining a mere 221 votes. Several branches were organized in the various quarters of Istanbul, although without any visible popular support. It appears to have disbanded in 1953 or 1954. The party stood for public and individual freedoms, emphasizing the right to universal employment, although its main goal was to bring the working class to political power.

DEMOKRASİ PARTİSİ (DEP). *See* DEMOCRACY PARTY.

DEMOKRAT BİRLİK PARTİSİ. *See* DEMOCRATIC UNION PARTY.

DEMOKRAT İŞÇİ PARTİSİ. *See* DEMOCRATIC WORKERS' PARTY.

DEMOKRAT MERKEZ PARTİSİ. *See* DEMOCRATIC CENTER PARTY.

DEMOKRAT PARTİ. *See* DEMOCRAT PARTY (I) (II) (III).

DEMOKRATİK PARTİ. *See* DEMOCRATIC PARTY.

DEMOKRATİK SOL PARTİ. *See* DEMOCRATIC LEFT PARTY.

DEMOKRATLAR PARTİSİ. *See* PARTY OF DEMOCRATS.

**DEVELOPMENT OF TURKEY PARTY** (*Türkiye Yükselme Partisi*). Established in Istanbul on July 3, 1947, the party did not organize to any significant extent, although several of its founders ran unsuccessfully in the general elections of 1950 and 1951, mostly as independents. Party activity subsequently ceased. The party called for rapid development, chiefly in economics and education.

DEVRİM PARTİSİ. *See* REFORM PARTY.

DİRİLİŞ PARTİSİ. *See* REVIVAL PARTY.

DOĞRU YOL PARTİSİ. *See* TRUE PATH PARTY.

DUTY FOR THE FATHERLAND PARTY (*Yurt Görev Partisi*). Established in Iskenderun (Hatay) on August 15, 1946, the party was inactive and disbanded during the same year.

DÜSTUR PARTİSİ. *See* CONSTITUTION PARTY.

EMINENT DUTY PARTY (*Yüce Görev Partisi*). Headed by Baha Vefa Karatay, an ex-ambassador, the party was founded in 1983 and closed down in the same year.

EQUALITY PARTY (*Müsavat Partisi*). Established on February 13, 1961, the party displayed little to no activity.

ERGENEKON KÖYLÜ VE İŞÇİ PARTİSİ. *See* ERGENEKON PEASANTS' AND WORKERS' PARTY.

ERGENEKON PEASANTS' AND WORKERS' PARTY (*Ergenekon Köylü ve Işçi Partisi*). Established in Istanbul on June 21, 1946, it had branches in Izmir and Balıkesir and claimed a membership of 200. Its Kemalist platform emphasized nationalism. Activity was minimal, and the party eventually disappeared completely.

FARMERS' AND VILLAGERS' PARTY (*Çiftçi ve Köylü Partisi*). Established in Bursa on April 24, 1946, its founders were landowners: Sıddık Sümer, İbrahim Öztürk, and Şükrü Tokay. The party was ordered to disband on June 2 of the same year for anticonstitutional activity which, in this case, appears to have meant the use of religion in politics. The party was conservative and called for the maintenance of traditions and the strengthening of Islam.

FATHERLAND PARTY (*Vatan Partisi*). This party was established in Istanbul on October 29, 1954, by Hikmet Kıvılcımlı and fourteen others, eight of whom were workers. Kıvılcımlı, a known Marxist, became the party's chairman. The party established branches in Istanbul and Izmir, running unsuccessfully in the 1957 general elections. It was banned in the same year. Its main activity was the publication of books and articles by its leaders, designed to familiarize Turkish intellectuals with Marxism. The party called for cooperation between workers and peasants, eradication of unemployment, lowering the cost of living, and increased national productivity.

Disbanded in 1957, the Fatherland Party was reconstituted in Istanbul on January 21, 1975, by Emine Kıvılcımlı, the widow of Hikmet Kıvılcımlı (who had died in 1971). Its chairman was Mehmet Özler, a Marxist. Several other surviving members of the defunct Fatherland Party, such as Ahmet Cansızoğlu and Arif Şimşek, were among those who revived it in 1975: The 1954 and 1975 party platforms resemble each other closely. Undaunted by the lack of popular support, the reconstituted party, based in Istanbul, repeatedly called for a socialist front in Turkey. The party would provide leadership for all those believing in scientific socialism. Its new organs were the weekly *Sosyalist* and the monthly *Çağri*.

FAZİLET PARTİSİ. *See* VIRTUE PARTY.

FOR THE FATHERLAND ONLY PARTY (*Yalnız Vatan İçin Partisi*). Established in Istanbul on June 21, 1946, this party ran but won no seats in the 1946 general elections. It showed little other activity and disbanded voluntarily early in 1952. It claimed to be republican, Kemalist, and etatist, strongly emphasizing nationalism (as its name implied). Its ideology resembled certain aspects of Italian fascism.

FP. *See* FREE PARTY.

FREE DEMOCRATIC PARTY I (*Hür Demokrat Partisi*). Established in 1983, the party soon closed down.

FREE DEMOCRATIC PARTY II (*Serbest Demokrat Partisi*). Established in Izmir in August 1948, it showed no activity and merged with the Nation Party* in July 1949. The party's goals were to strive for true democracy and a liberal economic system in Turkey.

FREE PARTY (FP) (*Serbest Fırka*). This party was established on August 12, 1930, by several prominent personalities who resigned from the Republican People's Party (RPP),* encouraged by Mustafa Kemal himself, who was apparently sincere in moving toward a multiparty system. One of Mustafa Kemal's close associates, Fethi Okyar, was asked by him to lead the FP, while his own sister, M. Atadan, joined the party, which soon branched out throughout Turkey. Although it was supposed to be a loyal opposition, the FP soon clashed with the RPP, inside and outside the Grand National Assembly. The FP, while officially adopting and supporting Kemalist ideology, drew considerable popular support from anti-Kemalist circles, religious groups, proponents of greater private enterprise and of foreign capital investments in Turkey, and those eager for more clear-cut individual freedoms. FP supporters loudly demonstrated in Western Anatolia, particularly in Izmir; a violent incident, resulting in one death, occurred in the village of Menemen. There was an evident danger that the FP would not be as tame an opposition party as envisaged and that the RPP's power might be jeopardized. There was also a clash of personalities between Okyar and the RPP prime minister, İsmet İnönü. FP participation in the local elections of October 1930 heated up the political atmosphere still further. When Mustafa Kemal himself came out against the party, it decided, on its own volition, to disband, on November 17, 1930, after an existence of only ninety-nine days.

During its brief career, the FP aroused considerable interest and public sentiment. Although the party did not publish a periodical of its own, it was supported
by several newspapers in Istanbul and Izmir, especially *Son Posta* and *Yarın*.

FREEDOM PARTY (*Hürriyet Partisi*). The Freedom Party was established on
December 20, 1955, by nineteen members of the Grand National Assembly, some
of whom had left the Democrat Party (DP)* voluntarily, while others had been
expelled from it. Within the DP, the nineteen had opposed some of the policies
of its leader, Adnan Menderes. The issue that led them to leave and join in the
founding of a new party concerned their demand that the press be allowed to
publish all antigovernment statements that could be proven, a stand rejected by
a majority of the DP. Most prominent among the Freedom Party's founders were
E. H. Üstündağ, a lawyer (the new party's chairman); F. L. Karaosmanoğlu, an
agronomist; and F. Çelikbaş, E. Alican, and Aydın Yalçın, all economists. They
were joined by other former members of the DP who were disappointed in their
former party. The Freedom Party began to organize its following in the Aegean
coast region, a DP stronghold. Its formation was a serious blow to the DP, since
it demonstrated that opposition to the DP was not limited to the Republican
People's Party (RPP).*

In the 1957 general elections, the party obtained only 3.8 percent of the vote
and a mere four seats in the Grand National Assembly—all from Burdur, whose
voters remained loyal to Çelikbaş. As a consequence of their disappointment
over these meager results, the Freedom Party, in an extraordinary general convention on November 24, 1958, decided to disband after a life span of less than
three years. Most members joined the RPP; a minority returned to the DP; others
joined leftist groups. The failure of the Freedom Party to make further headway
was at least partly due to its composition and ideology. Party leadership was made
up primarily of intellectuals (including several professors from Ankara University), thus limiting grass-roots support. Its ideology was liberal, emphasizing individual liberties and aiming at constitutional changes to guarantee a more
balanced parliamentary system, an independent judiciary, a free press, autonomous universities, and unrestricted trade union activity. In brief, the leaders of
the Freedom Party claimed to stand for true democracy which (as they saw it)
the DP had betrayed. Several periodicals supported the party, particularly the
weekly *Forum*, edited by A. Yalçın, published in Ankara since 1953.

GREAT ANATOLIA PARTY I (*Büyük Anadolu Partisi*). Established in Ankara
on December 19, 1972, it displayed little to no activity.

GREAT ANATOLIA PARTY II. This party was founded on March 14, 1986,
with no known activity.

GREAT CHANGE PARTY (*Büyük Değişim Partisi*). Led by Aydın Menderes, a
son of the late founder of the Democrat Party (I) (DP)* and longtime prime

minister, Adnan Menderes, this party was founded on May 21, 1993. It favored free enterprise, including privatization of social security systems and the educational system.

GREAT HOMELAND PARTY (*Büyük Vatan Partisi*). Established in 1983, it closed down in the same year.

GREAT POWER PARTY (*Büyük Kuvvet Partisi*). Established in Istanbul on March 30, 1973, it displayed little to no activity.

GREAT TURKEY PARTY (*Büyük Türkiye Partisi*). Founded on May 20, 1983, by Ali Fethi Esener, a retired general, it was joined by members of the banned Justice Party (JP)* and propounded the JP's ideology. It was closed down, by an order of the military regime's National Security Council, on May 31, 1983, and its leaders were arrested. This act led to the establishment of a kindred organization, the True Path Party.*

GREAT UNITY PARTY (*Büyük Birlik Partisi*). Founded January 29, 1993, and chaired by Muhsin Yazıcıoglu, this party began as a breakaway from Alparslan Türkeş's Nationalist Action Party.* It emphasized nationalism and religion, declaring that Turkey should become the leader of the Muslim world and the protector of Muslims living in non-Muslim states. The party opposed the principle of secularism as practiced in Turkey, and emphasized that Islam lies at the foundation of Turkish society. It opposed education in foreign languages. It favored an economy based on private enterprise, and supported privatization of state economic enterprises. The party also supported unemployment compensation. During its first year of existence, it accounted for seven seats in the parliament.

GREENS' PARTY (*Yeşiller Partisi*). This party was founded on June 6, 1988.

GÜDEN PARTİSİ. *See* GUIDING PARTY.

GUIDING PARTY (*Güden Partisi*). A local group, established in Istanbul on July 14, 1951, it displayed little to no activity.

GÜVEN PARTİSİ. *See* RELIANCE PARTY.

HALK FIRKASI. *See* REPUBLICAN PEOPLE'S PARTY.

HALK PARTİSİ. *See* REPUBLICAN PEOPLE'S PARTY.

HALKÇI PARTİ. *See* POPULIST PARTY.

HALKIN EMEK PARTİSİ. *See* PEOPLE'S LABOR PARTY.

HÜR DEMOKRAT PARTİSİ. *See* FREE DEMOCRAT PARTY.

HÜR TÜRKİYE ADALET PARTİSİ. *See* JUSTICE PARTY OF FREE TUR-
KEY.

HÜRRİYET PARTİSİ. *See* FREEDOM PARTY.

HÜRRİYETÇİ MİLLET PARTİSİ. *See* LIBERAL NATION PARTY.

İDEALİST PARTİSİ. *See* PARTY OF IDEALISTS.

İLERLEME VE KORUMA PARTİSİ. *See* PARTY OF ADVANCE AND PRES-
ERVATION.

INDEPENDENT TURKISH SOCIALIST PARTY (*Müstakil Türk Sosyalist Partisi*). This party was established in Istanbul on September 19, 1948, by Arif Oruç,
a worker. In the following year, it distributed manifestos in several provincial
towns and participated in the 1950 general elections, but won no seats. Otherwise, it displayed little activity; the party ceased operation following the death
of its founder and leader, Oruç. The party's platform was socialist and egalitarian.
It aimed at reforming the regime, without disturbing the national structure, by
establishing a socially just and economically fair system. It demanded distribution
of land to landless peasants, curbing exploitation, utilizing Turkey's natural resources for the public good, increasing productivity, guaranteeing employment
and decent pay to one and all, and safeguarding individual liberties.

ISLAHATÇI DEMOKRASİ PARTİSİ. *See* REFORMIST DEMOCRACY
PARTY.

İSLÂM DEMOKRAT PARTİSİ. *See* ISLAMIC DEMOCRATIC PARTY.

İSLÂM KORUMA PARTİSİ. *See* PARTY FOR THE DEFENSE OF ISLAM.

ISLAMIC DEMOCRATIC PARTY (*İslâm Demokrat Partisi*). This party was established in Istanbul, during August 1951, by Cevat Rıfat Atılhan, an anti-
Semitic writer (chairman), who had already established the Turkish
Conservative Party* in 1947. The party was joined by Zühtü Bilimer (deputy
chairman), a doctor who had been one of the founders of the Party for Land,
Real Estate and Free Enterprise* in 1949, and several others. The party claimed
to have 2,000 members, organized in 150 branches in ten provinces. The party
was frankly traditional, voicing a high regard for Turkey's past and Islam and
equally strong disapproval of such clandestine groups as the Communists and

Freemasons. Although it claimed to speak for freedom of conscience and for the progress of Turkey, it was brought to court, in 1952, for stirring up intercommunal trouble; activity seems to have ceased after that time.

İŞÇİ PARTİSİ. *See* WORKERS' PARTY.

JP. *See* JUSTICE PARTY.

JUSTICE PARTY (JP) (*Adalet Partisi*). The JP was established in Ankara on February 11, 1961, during the military interregnum following the outlawing of the Democrat Party (DP).* Its initial platform demanded justice for the banned DP, whose leaders had been jailed in the wake of the 1960 military intervention (hence the name). Its founders were connected with DP circles, although not of the greatest prominence (the DP's more outstanding personalities were on trial). The JP's first chairman was a retired chief of staff, Ragıp Gümüşpala; after his death, in 1964, he was succeeded by Süleyman Demirel, a hydraulic engineer, who continued to head the party until the third military intervention closed down all parties on October 16, 1981. In the 1961 general elections, the JP competed with other right-of-center parties for the popular support that the defunct DP had enjoyed, indeed obtaining most of it: 34.8 percent of the vote and 158 seats (out of 450) in the National Assembly and 34.5 percent of the vote and 71 (out of 150 standing for election) in the Senate. Its vote was inferior only to that of Republican People's Party (RPP),* trailing by less than 2 percent of the vote (see Table 22).

Having adopted much of the DP's program, the JP was identified by many as the DP's successor and soon became a grass-roots party. Thus the 1950s' government/opposition seesaw of DP/RPP was recreated as a JP/RPP rivalry in the 1960s. However, the JP prudently kept a lower profile in times of tension, with the aim of supplying no pretext for a new military intervention (which might have proved perilous for it). This was probably the main reason behind the JP's joining a coalition cabinet led by İsmet İnönü of the RPP soon after the 1961 general elections; half a year later, however, the JP left the cabinet. As the DP's successor, the JP's apprehensions about military sentiment were not unfounded; there were, in fact, two unsuccessful military coups, directed largely against this party, in the following years. The JP grew more confident, however, after succeeding in both the 1963 local elections and the 1964 partial Senate elections. Demirel, the new chairman, organized the other parliamentary groups to bring down the İnönü cabinet and to form a new government, without the RPP. Although this cabinet was headed by a neutral prime minister, a member of neither mass party, the JP was clearly the main force behind it.

The JP's impressive victory in the 1965 general elections to the National Assembly gave it 52.9 percent of the vote and an absolute majority of 240 (out of 450) seats. Obviously, by that time, the JP had captured most of the DP's inheritance and formed an all–JP Cabinet. In 1969 the JP further increased the number of its National Assembly seats to 256, although its countrywide electoral support had declined to 46.5 percent (see Table 22). Indeed, although voter support had increased slightly in less-developed areas, it had declined perceptibly in the more developed ones. More trouble was brewing. The JP governments had indeed stimulated economic growth, and there was a 7 percent increase in the GNP. However, this was accompanied by inflation and currency devaluation; little had been done to resolve such pressing socioeconomic issues as unemployment. In addition, the party's public relations suffered from a financial scandal involving Demirel's own family (although not himself). An issue no less portentous was the 1970 resignation of several prominent JP members after an unsuccessful struggle with Demirel for the party leadership. These joined forces with several politicians, formerly active in the banned DP, who were unhappy about the JP's ostensibly meager efforts to restore their political rights. Together they established the new Democratic Party,* and the JP cabinet consequently lost its majority in the National Assembly. The government had to resign; Demirel formed another cabinet thanks only to the tenuous support of three members of the assembly who had left the Unity Party* to join the JP.

When the government failed to cope effectively with the 1968 student unrest and subsequent violence and terrorism in 1969–71, the military moved in a second time, staging a "coup by memorandum" (March 12, 1971). Their memorandum demanded and obtained Demirel's resignation. Mindful of the modest results of the 1960 military intervention, the chiefs of the armed forces in 1971 contented themselves with imposing mainly technocratic cabinets. These cabinets generally received the JP's nominal support in the National Assembly, without which democratic forms of government would have been impossible to maintain. In the meantime, the JP fought for a return to a fully civilian regime, collaborating with the RPP, which, under its new chairman, Bülent Ecevit, desired this as much as the JP. The civilian regime was fully restored, however, only after the 1973 elections.

The 1973 general elections repeated the pattern of 1961. Although the RPP obtained a plurality in the National Assembly, the JP ran a close second with 29.8 percent of the vote and 149 seats, probably reflecting the decline in its popularity. In the Senate, it came second as well, with 31.0 percent of the vote and 22 seats (out of the 52 standing for reelection). In 1974, when a coalition cabinet headed by the RPP collapsed after nine months, the JP returned to form and lead coalition cabinets from early 1975 to late 1977. In the 1977 general elections, the pattern was repeated with minor variations; the JP gained ground but was still second to the RPP. In the National Assembly, the JP obtained 36.9 percent of the vote and 189 seats (see Table 22).

The JP's ideological stance was conditioned by its establishment and development, despite the RPP opposition, as well as by military intervention in politics. The JP looked with disfavor upon these two forces and had some reservations about laws passed during the first military intervention and even about the 1961 constitution itself. The JP stood for increasing the powers of parliament (in which it had a majority until 1970) and safeguarding individual liberties. In the context of the latter, the party fought for years over the major issue of granting amnesty to the leaders of the banned DP and restoring their political rights. This was a popular issue and one likely to appeal to the supporters of the JP. As a mass party, the JP emphasized elements that could appeal to as many moderate center and right-of-center Turks as feasible, such as its unwill-ingness to impose property taxes. However, since the party opted for a centrist position, it displayed interest in the less well-to-do also, as in their introduction of certain social benefits for the working classes. There is no doubt, however, about the JP's intention to encourage private enterprise (assisted by government incentives); indeed, the party considered private enterprise the essence of a dem-ocratic, liberal regime. The party was equally committed to attracting foreign capital, as part of its commitment to the rapprochement with the West; it wanted to encourage, for example, the activity of foreign firms in Turkey (such as oil prospecting), provided Turkey received a fair share. These attitudes were anath-ema to the RPP, particularly to its left-wingers, and to other groups even farther left.

Demirel, technocrat and politician, showed himself to be the JP's chief deci-sion maker, with remarkable staying power. The party's supporters, however, although numerous and distributed throughout Turkey, changed somewhat in character over the years. In the early 1960s, the JP had support from among middle-class circles and from officers who had been cashiered during and after the 1960 military intervention; a large segment of the military establishment and the intelligentsia, however, opposed it. During the 1970s, minority ethnic groups displayed some signs of disappointment with the JP, while the officers it had promoted continued to support it. During the 1960s, much and possibly most of the JP's electoral support came from the more developed areas in Turkey. In the 1970s, however, its urban support showed signs of declining, although business and commercial circles in the cities and towns continued to vote for the JP. Rural JP supporters apparently remained loyal. In any case, the growth of the Turkish political elite and increasing differentiation within Turkish society compounded the JP's difficulties in appealing to various groups and classes with equal persua-siveness.

Several newspapers supported the JP at various times, such as the national dailies *Adalet, Zafer, Son Havadis,* and *Yeni İstanbul,* as well as a few local papers. However, in the late 1970s, the JP was supported principally by *Son Havadis,* with a small circulation of only a few thousand.

JUSTICE PARTY OF FREE TURKEY (*Hür Türkiye Adalet Partisi*). A local group, established in Bolu on June 24, 1959, it displayed little to no activity.

KEMALİST GENÇLİK PARTİSİ. *See* PARTY OF KEMALIST YOUTH.

KURDISH WORKERS' PARTY (PKK). This party, known by its Kurdish acronym, was established in the early 1970s as an illegal Marxist group. Its most prominent leader and ideologue, Abdullah Öcalan, has consistently advocated verbal—then physical—violence against rival Kurdish groups and the Turkish authorities. The tough countermeasures undertaken by the Turkish police and the military may have increased the PKK's popularity among the Kurds; during the 1980s and early 1990s, it increased its armed attacks on Turkish civilian and military officials in the Kurdish areas of the southeast as well as Turkish diplomatic posts and commercial businesses in Europe. While the PKK has not clearly indicated that its objective is separation of these Kurdish-speaking areas from Turkey, many Turks, especially government officials, suspect that this is the party's ultimate goal.

LABOR PARTY (Çalışma Partisi). The Labor Party was established in Ankara on September 12, 1950, by Cevat Mimaroğlu, Ömer Fahri Ünsal, Bedrettin Örtensoy, and Mehmet Emin Özdemir. The party's name notwithstanding, only Özdemir was actually a worker: the first three were, respectively, lawyers and an automobile repair shop owner. The party opened branches in Ankara and Istanbul, showing little activity; it disbanded the same year. The party called for social justice, economic prosperity, secularism (without neglecting religion), the preservation of private property, universal employment, and international cooperation, particularly with the United Nations.

Another party of the same name was established in Ankara on February 11, 1961; it displayed little to no activity.

LABOR PARTY OF TURKEY. See WORKERS' PARTY OF TURKEY.

LIBERAL DEMOCRATIC PARTY (Liberal Demokrat Partisi). Established in Istanbul on March 11, 1946, the party, with branches in Istanbul and Bursa, ran unsuccessfully in the general elections of 1946 and disbanded soon afterward. The party intended to work for increased economic prosperity and the encouragement of culture, morals, and arts in Turkey.

LİBERAL DEMOKRAT PARTİSİ. See LIBERAL DEMOCRATIC PARTY.

LİBERAL KÖYLÜ PARTİSİ. See LIBERAL PEASANTS' PARTY.

LIBERAL NATION PARTY (Hürriyetçi Millet Partisi). Established on November 20, 1979, it was banned, in 1981, along with all other parties, by the military regime. Its main objectives were to improve and watch over individual rights and freedom of the press; to reexamine the constitution by selected experts every twenty years; to improve the work of the executive and judiciary, banking and health services, social security, education, and industry; and to protect the family and foster patriotism and morals.

LIBERAL PEASANTS' PARTY (*Liberal Köylü Partisi*). This party, formed in Istanbul in 1950, included the Party for Land, Real Estate, and Free Enterprise* and several others. Noteworthy among the seventeen founders of the Liberal Peasants' Party was Lütfü Aksu, a lawyer. It displayed little activity; in mid-1952, it merged into the Peasants' Party of Turkey.* The party claimed to be republican, neither left nor right; secularist, without being antireligious; and nationalist, without being chauvinist. The reforms sought by the party were chiefly in the constitution (more emphasis on individual liberties), the electoral system, and the judiciary (introduction of trial by jury).

MEDENİYET HAYVANSEVER EKONOMİ VE TARIM PARTİSİ. *See* PARTY FOR CIVILIZATION, CHERISHING ANIMALS, ECONOMY, AND AGRICULTURE.

MEMLEKETÇİ SERBEST PARTİ. *See* PATRIOTIC FREE PARTY.

MİLLET PARTİSİ. *See* NATION PARTY.

MİLLETE HİZMET PARTİSİ. *See* SERVICE TO THE NATION PARTY.

MİLLİ GÜVEN PARTİSİ. *See* RELIANCE PARTY.

MİLLİ KALKINMA PARTİSİ. *See* NATIONAL DEVELOPMENT PARTY.

MİLLİ NİZAM PARTİSİ. *See* PARTY FOR NATIONAL ORDER.

MİLLİ SELAMET PARTİSİ. *See* NATIONAL SALVATION PARTY.

MİLLİYETÇİ ÇALIŞMA PARTİSİ. *See* NATIONALIST WORK PARTY.

MİLLİYETÇİ DEMOKRASİ PARTİSİ. *See* NATIONALIST DEMOCRACY PARTY.

MİLLİYETÇİ HAREKET PARTİSİ. *See* NATIONALIST ACTION PARTY.

MODERATE LIBERAL PARTY (*Mütedil Liberal Parti*). Established in Ankara on February 6, 1961, it did not display any particular activity and disbanded the same year.

MOTHERLAND PARTY (MP) (*Anavatan Partisi*). This party was founded in Ankara, on May 20, 1983, by Turgut Özal, a distinguished economist, who had served in 1969 as the director of the State Planning Organization, in 1979 and 1980 as economic adviser to Prime Minister Süleyman Demirel, and as deputy prime minister in the military regime until 1982. The party's first secretary-general was Veysel Atasoy, an official. The party won the parliamentary elections of November 6, 1983, with 45.1 percent of the total vote and an absolute majority of 211 seats (out of a total of 400). It did very well in the local elections of March 25, 1984, coming in first with 41.6 percent of the total vote. In the general election of November 29, 1987, however, it obtained only 36.3 percent of the total vote, even though this was enough to net 292 seats (out of a total of 450). By March 26, 1989, its popular appeal had declined even farther, and it came in third in the local elections on that occasion, with a mere 21.8 percent of the total vote. This was at least partly a result of resentment of the high rate of inflation (about 80 percent in 1989). On October 20, 1991, the Motherland Party lost its parliamentary majority, obtaining only 24 percent of the total vote and 115 seats (out of a total of 450). It thus became the main opposition party (see Table 23).

Özal defined his party, in 1983, as "nationalist, conservative, social policy-minded, promoting a controlled market economy." The party succeeded in providing a broadly acceptable, pro-establishment program for a large segment of the public that had had enough of the pre-1980 disruptive forces and the parties that had not coped successfully with them. The party assumed the image of a new center-right party, representing traditional values and market rationality, favored by many Turks eager for stability and prosperity. This pragmatic image, carefully avoiding ideological issues, constantly emphasized an entrepreneurial approach of service to the citizens, stressing the relationship between taxes paid and benefits supplied. The argument was enhanced by the energetic, dedicated mayors sponsored by the party and their reputation for getting things done in their respective municipalities.

When, in 1989, Özal was elected by the Grand National Assembly to become the president of Turkey, one of his close associates, Yildirim Akbulut, a member of parliament, became prime minister. Özal continued to be considerably involved in both his party's and parliamentary affairs, much more so than the immediately preceding Turkish heads of state. However, Özal's influence was weakened by the election of the energetic Mesut Yılmaz to the party leadership and his assumption of the office of prime minister. The party was severely weakened by its loss to the True Path Party* in the 1991 election. After Özal's death in spring 1993, and the election of the True Path Party leader Süleyman Demirel to the presidency, this internal party struggle ceased to be a factor. It remained to be seen whether the Motherland Party could take advantage of problems emerging in the TPP, with whom it was electorally most competitive, and recoup its own political fortunes in the process.


MUHAFAZAKÂR PARTİ. *See* CONSERVATIVE PARTY.


MÜSAVAT PARTİSİ. *See* EQUALITY PARTY.

Table 23
Grand National Assembly Election Results, 1983–91

| ELECTION | | MP | PP/SDPP | NDP | TPP | Other Parties |
|---|---|---|---|---|---|---|
| 1983 | % of votes | 45.1 | 30.5 | 24.0 | --- | ---- |
| | Seats won | 211 | 117 | 71 | --- | ---- |
| | % of seats | 52.8 | 29.3 | 17.8 | --- | ---- |
| 1987 | % of votes | 36.3 | 24.8 | ---- | 19.1 | 19.8 |
| | Seats won | 292 | 99 | ---- | 59 | ---- |
| | % of seats | 64.9 | 22.0 | ---- | 13.1 | ---- |
| 1991 | % of votes | 24.0 | 20.8 | ---- | 27.0 | 27.8* |
| | Seats won | 115 | 88** | ---- | 178 | 69* |
| | % of seats | 25.5 | 19.5 | ---- | 39.5 | 15.4 |

Notes: The total number of seats was 400 in 1983 and 450 thereafter. Many members in the 1991 session changed parties after the election, and a number of new parties were established in 1992 and 1993. As of late 1993, the breakdown of seats was as follows: TPP: 180; SDPP: 53; MP: 98; Welfare Party: 40; RPP(II): 20; DEP: 17; Nationalist Action Party (formerly Nationalist Work Party): 13; Great Unity Party: 7; Democratic Left: 3; Nation Party (III): 2; New Party: 3; Independent: 6.

*These votes were distributed as follows: 10.8 percent of the vote and 7 of the seats went to the Democratic Left Party; 16.9 percent of the vote and 62 of the seats went to the combined ticket of the Prosperity (approximately 40 seats) and Nationalist Work (approximately 19 seats) parties, which thus were able to surmount the 10 percent threshold.

**Approximately 20 of these seats were held by members of the People's Labor Party (HEP), which had formed an electoral alliance with the SDPP. HEP was closed down by court order in 1993; its place was taken by DEP.

MÜSTAKİL TÜRK SOSYALİST PARTİSİ. See INDEPENDENT TURKISH SOCIALIST PARTY.

MÜTEDİL LİBERAL PARTİ. See MODERATE LIBERAL PARTY.

NAP. See NATIONALIST ACTION PARTY.

NATION PARTY I (Millet Partisi). This was the first of three (not directly related) parties bearing this name (see Nation Party II and III). It was established on July 20, 1948, by several members of the Grand National Assembly, part of the Democrat Party (DP)* contingent which had left the DP for widely varying reasons, some personal and some ideological. Among the latter, several considered the DP to be insufficiently militant, not supporting liberal ideals, or indifferent toward Islam. Most prominent among the founders were Fevzi Çakmak, retired chief of staff and the party's honorary chairman; Hikmet Bayur, a well-known historian and the party's chairman; Osman Bölükbaşı, a scientist; and S. Aldoğan, a retired general. They were joined by A. Tahtakılıç, a lawyer; H. Dincer, a judge; and A. Oğuz, a teacher. The party aimed to fight the two mass parties, the Republican People's Party (RPP)* and the DP, but it achieved only limited results, partly because of the bitter fight of the RPP and the DP against it. Indeed, in the 1950 general elections, it obtained 240,209 votes out of nearly eight million and only one seat in the Grand National Assembly. This was partly due to the death of two leading figures, Çakmak and Öner, before the elections, and partly to the disparate character of the party's supporters and the difference in outlook between the party leadership, which was chiefly liberal, individualist, and secularist, and a large segment (perhaps a majority) of their followers, who were more religious and traditional, and had initially been impressed by the party's leaders. General conventions, held annually, witnessed much heated argument, but no agreement. On January 27, 1954, the Nation Party was disbanded by a court order. Two weeks after the first Nation Party had been outlawed, several of its leaders revived it under the name Republican Nation Party.*

The party platform demanded honest elections; ending etatism; placing the state at the disposal of the individual, rather than vice-versa; affording the individual greater opportunities for work and enterprise; raising the standard of living; and affording youth an education that would be both nationalist and religious. The party was supported by the daily *Kudret* (Istanbul), and the periodical *Millet*, among others.

NATION PARTY II (*Millet Partisi*). The second of three (not directly related) parties bearing this name (see Nation Party I and III), this party was established on June 15, 1962, by Osman Bölükbaşı together with twenty-eight members of the Grand National Assembly and their supporters who had left the Republican Peasants' Nation Party (RPNP)* in opposition to the RPNP's decision to participate in a coalition cabinet. The new party assumed the name of Nation Party, which had been the title of the party disbanded by the court in January 1954. This Nation Party, led by Bölükbaşı, obtained 6.3 percent of the vote and 21 (out of 450) seats in the Grand National Assembly in the general elections of 1965 (see Table 22). In 1966 and 1968 it received, respectively, 5.5 percent and 6.3 percent of the vote for the Senate, obtaining one seat each time out of those standing for reelection. In the 1969 general elections, its votes dropped to 3.2 percent and to only 6 (out of 450) seats in the Grand National Assembly. With the retirement of Bölükbaşı from politics in 1972, the party sank into insignificance. Led by a retired chief of staff, Cemal Tural, in the 1973 general elections, it obtained a mere 0.6 percent of the vote and not a single seat in the Grand National Assembly. The party fared no better in the 1977 general elections, when it was led by a wealthy businessman, M. Erkovan. The military intervention, which banned all parties, sealed its fate on October 16, 1981.

The ideology of the second Nation Party, as defined and expressed by Bölükbaşı, was conservative (without emphasizing religion) and right of center. Although it claimed to be both anticommunist and antifascist, it was mainly concerned with opposing leftism in all its forms. It was not anti-Kemalist, but it did support private enterprise strongly, thereby appealing to small merchants.

NATION PARTY (III). *See* REFORMIST DEMOCRACY PARTY.

NATIONAL DEVELOPMENT PARTY (*Millî Kalkınma Partisi*). Founded in Istanbul on July 18, 1945, this was the first opposition party to be set up in the multiparty era. The founders were Nuri Demirağ, a businessman (party chairman), and Cevat Rıfat Atılhan, a known anti-Semitic writer. The party began to establish branches and increased its propaganda campaigns, but through inefficiency, it failed to elicit any significant support in the 1946 local elections or in the 1950 general elections. In 1954 Demirağ was elected to the Grand National Assembly in Istanbul as an independent on the Democrat Party (DP)* ticket. After his death in 1957, the party seemed to disintegrate, and it was disbanded on May 22, 1958.

The party's propaganda lacked a coherent, detailed program; it was primarily directed against the Republican People's Party (RPP).* It rejected etatism and called for free competition; it frowned on secularism, at least by implication, striving to strengthen Islam (e.g., by calling for the foundation of a Muslim Technical University for Turks and Muslims from other lands, as one step toward the creation of a Pan-Muslim Union). Furthermore, the party was articulate in its opposition to communism and to the Soviets.

NATIONAL RELIANCE PARTY. *See* RELIANCE PARTY.

NATIONAL SALVATION PARTY (NSP) (*Millî Selamet Partisi*). This Islamic party was virtually a reconstitution of the Party for National Order (PNO),* which had been outlawed in May 1971. The NSP was established on October 11, 1972, by nineteen persons, most of whom had been connected with the PNO. The founders, however, were careful to disclaim any connection with the banned PNO; the NSP's founder and promoter, Necmettin Erbakan (who had been the PNO's chairman) prudently kept a low profile for a while, allowing Süleyman Arif Emre (the PNO's secretary-general) to lead the NSP during its first year. By the summer of 1973, the NSP had branches in all of Turkey's sixty-seven provinces, and it moved into high gear after the party's extraordinary general convention of July 22, 1973. All NSP resources were mobilized in the campaign for the general elections of October 14, 1973. The party's leaders traveled and spoke indefatigably: muezzins, imams, and others canvassed on a person-to-person basis or addressed small groups in private homes. The results were most gratifying from the party's point of view: The NSP obtained 11.8 percent of the vote for the Grand National Assembly, 48 of its 450 seats (see Table 22), and 12.3 percent of the vote for the Senate for 3 of the 52 contested seats. Thus, in its first trial, the NSP became the third largest group in the Grand National Assembly, after the Republican People's Party (RPP)* and the Justice Party (JP).* The NSP used its own position, neither definitely left of center nor decidedly right of center, to enter a cabinet coalition, first with the RPP (from February to September 1974) then with the JP and smaller parties (from April 1975 to June 1977). In the cabinet, the NSP stressed mostly educational and economic policies, all in the name of Islamic morals and virtue. For example, it strove to promote religious education; to disburse funds for religious purposes; to ban alcohol, immoral dress, and pornography; and to oppose Turkey's joining the European Economic Community, to which it preferred a Common Market of the Islamic States. The NSP's rather modest success in all the above may have cost it votes in the June 5, 1977, elections and halved its Grand National Assembly seats to twenty-four. This decline came about, in part, when several religious groups transferred their support to the JP and the Nationalist Action Party (NAP).* The NSP briefly entered a cabinet coalition with the JP once again after the 1977 elections, although this was subsequently brought down by a no-confidence vote sponsored by the RPP, which then headed the cabinet without the NSP. The party, along with all others, was shut down by the military regime on October 16, 1981.

The NSP's ideology was essentially identical with that of the PNO. Basically anti-Kemalist, it aimed at eliminating secularism and establishing a theocracy in Turkey. Its religiosity was mixed with a strongly nationalist ingredient, identifying Turkish patriotism with Islam. Furthermore, it was based on a fairly sophisticated economic program. The NSP openly represented a protest against change in the traditional structures and values of Turkish society as well as a reaction against unbalanced, too rapid economic and social change. The party's programs aimed at bringing the nation happiness and security via moral and material progress. Moral progress postulated the need for a virtuous society: one based on the ideals of Islam and enforced by Turkey's glorious heritage. Material progress required general development, speedy industrialization, and balanced socioeconomic progress. For example, the party argued that Turkey's much needed industrialization should not be at the expense of the little man, such as the artisan (its opposition to Turkey's joining the EEC was meant to protect this sector). It was this combination of morals and religion with the advocacy of industrialization that made up the party's ideological image and probably differentiated it from other religiously based parties. This was at least partially due to the personal character of the party leadership.

The NSP's leadership—Erbakan, a few of his former students at the Technical University of Istanbul, and several very orthodox Muslims—was a dedicated group which ably utilized modern methods of political organization and propaganda. The NSP—judging by voting patterns—included numerous religiously minded persons who, for the first time in fifty years, were given an opportunity to come out of the political wilderness, as well as many small artisans, who made and sold their own products and were economically threatened by major manufacturers. The NSP emerged as a protector of this large group in its opposition to Turkish membership in the European Economic Community (among other things). It is no coincidence that the NSP's main electoral support came from Turkey's less-developed areas and smaller towns. In addition to Islamic-oriented newspapers, which supported the NSP, the party had its own daily, *Millî Gazete*, published in Istanbul, as well as several periodicals in other cities.

NATIONAL WOMEN'S PARTY OF TURKEY (*Türkiye Ulusal Kadınlar Partisi*). This party was established in Istanbul, on November 17, 1972, by a woman, Mübeccel Toruner, who became the party's chairperson. Most of the party members were women, although it did include some men who supported its feminist views. It displayed little activity.

NATIONALIST ACTION PARTY (NAP) (*Milliyetçi Hareket Partisi*). Sometimes called the Nationalist Movement Party, the Nationalist Action Party is the name assumed by the Republican Peasants' Nation Party (RPNP)* in 1969. This change of name was the logical outcome of the increasingly militant character imposed on the RPNP after it had been taken over, in August 1965, by Alparslan Türkeş, an ex-colonel (the new chairman) and his supporters. Türkeş, then in uniform, had been a prominent member of the National Unity Committee set up by the military regime in 1960. In 1969, before the general elections, Türkeş gave his party a more appealing name and enacted new regulations to tighten the chairman's hold over the party. The NAP hardly increased its vote in the 1969 elections (from 2.2 percent [in 1965] to 3 percent). However, an amendment in the electoral law, adversely affecting smaller parties, reduced the number of its seats in the Grand National Assembly from eleven to only one (Türkeş himself). In the 1973 general elections, the NAP's vote remained virtually unchanged, but it gained three seats. Owing to the fragmented character of the 1973 Grand National Assembly, these three seats were essential to the Justice Party (JP)* when it formed a coalition cabinet, including a total of four parties, that remained in power from April 1975 to the June 1977 general elections. Türkeş became a deputy prime minister, and another NAP member of the Grand National Assembly became minister of state. This sharing of power was put to good use by the NAP; in the 1977 general elections, its votes doubled and it obtained sixteen seats, thus becoming the fourth largest group there. Consequently, it again entered a coalition cabinet, which remained in power for several months, until the end of 1977, after which a cabinet led by the Republican People's Party (RPP)* took office. Along with all other parties, the NAP was closed down by the military regime on October 16, 1981.

The ideology of the NAP—already laid down within the RPNP after Türkeş's takeover in 1965—was militantly nationalist, as formulated in the party's official publications and in Türkeş's writings, especially in his brochure, *Nine Lights*, first issued in 1965 and reprinted several times, which served as a constant inspiration to party stalwarts. The "nine lights" were the following: nationalism, idealism, moralism, social mindedness, a scientific attitude, support for freedom, peasant progress, development and populism, and industrialization and technology. Of these, nationalism was given greatest emphasis by Türkeş and other NAP spokesmen. Tinged with chauvinism and pan-Turkist ambitions, the party sought inspiration from Turkey's glorious past for the creation of a Great Turkey, populous and extending over all territories inhabited by people of Turkic origins. The party was uncompromisingly anticommunist, both because of its nationalist ideology and because many people of Turkish origin lived under Communist rule. The NAP's ideology was also authoritarian, although without attacking Turkey's democratic regime, which it claimed to cherish. After the 1969 elections, the NAP strove to present the electorate with the image of a party favoring religion; Türkeş even demonstratively performed the pilgrimage to Mecca. This most probably had an impact on some voters, particularly in the 1977 general elections to the Grand National Assembly when certain religious groups, formerly supporting the National Salvation Party,* switched their support to the NAP and the JP.

The NAP apparently had only limited support among intellectuals; many of its supporters were middle-class people, particularly those circles for whom nationalism has been a long-term credo. The party expended considerable effort, probably more than most other political parties, in recruiting for its youth organization, the Gray Wolves (bozkurtlar). These youths were trained in party ideology and sports and, according to the NAP's opponents, in the use of firearms, at summer camps. They became a familiar sight in the 1970s with their marches, demonstrations, and fights with leftist groups, thereby supplying ammunition to those political rivals who accused the NAP of fascist tendencies.

The party's main organ, Devlet (state) at first a semimonthly, then a weekly, was first published in Ankara, then in Konya. In 1978 it became a monthly, published in Ankara. A monthly directed at youth, Bozkurt (gray wolf) ceased publication in 1977, probably because of lack of funds. Another monthly, dealing principally with ideology, Töre (tradition), was published in Ankara.

NATIONALIST ACTION PARTY (II). See NATIONALIST WORK PARTY.

NATIONALIST DEMOCRACY PARTY (NDP) (Milliyetçi Demokrasi Partisi). Set up in Ankara in July 1983, with the encouragement of the military regime of the time, this was the first party to be established after all parties had been banned on October 16, 1981. Its first chairman was Turgut Sunalp, an ex-general, then Bülent Ulusu, an ex-admiral and a member of the group that had engineered the military intervention of September 12, 1980. The secretary-general was Doğan Kasaroğlu, a journalist and member of parliament. The party obtained 24 percent of the vote in the November 6, 1983, parliamentary elections and became the third largest parliamentary group with seventy-one seats (see Table 23). However, in the local elections of March 25, 1984, it was only fifth, and subsequently it disbanded of its own volition. Its program offered the best for everybody, on the basis of Kemalist ideology, emphasizing constitutional government, secularism and freedom of conscience, individual liberties, national culture, and technology. Its moderately right-of-center attitude was expressed chiefly in its advocacy of a market economy, limiting the role of the governmental sector in economy.

NATIONALIST MOVEMENT PARTY. *See* NATIONALIST ACTION PARTY.

NATIONALIST WORK PARTY (NWP) (*Milliyetçi Çalışma Partisi*). At its general convention held on November 30, 1985, the Conservative Party* changed its name to the Nationalist Work Party. Like the Conservative Party, the NWP was largely led and staffed by former members and sympathizers of the Nationalist Action Party (NAP).* In 1987 its leadership was assumed by the NAP's erstwhile leader, Alparslan Türkeş, following the referendum that permitted party leaders to return to politics. Ideologically, also, the NWP largely resembled its predecessors (with the addition of environmental issues). In the 1987 parliamentary elections, it obtained only 2.93 percent of the vote and no seats, but it improved this record in the local elections of 1990. In 1991 it entered the electoral contest in a joint slate with the Prosperity Party* and obtained 19 seats for itself (out of a total of 450). In 1993, the party changed its name to Nationalist Action Party.

NEW DEMOCRATIC PARTY (*Yeni Demokrat Parti*). Established in Ankara on December 18, 1961, with the aim of replacing the banned Democrat Party,* the party displayed little to no activity.

NEW ORDER PARTY (*Yeni Düzen Partisi*). Chaired by Vehap Esendağ, an ex-officer, the party was established in 1983 but soon closed down.

NEW PARTY (*Yeni Parti*). This party was founded on October 7, 1993, by Yusuf Bozkurt Özal, a member of parliament from Malatya, and brother of the late president of Turkey, Turgut Özal. The party declared its belief in the principles of the late president. It favored maximum freedom for free enterprise, privatization, avoidance of monopoly, and reliance by the state on macroeconomic policy for regulatory purposes. It favored attracting foreign investment, save for the field of national security. It endorsed the principle of privatization in education and health insurance as well. The party initially won over three members of parliament who had been with the Motherland Party.*

NEW PEASANTS' PARTY (*Yeni Köylü Partisi*). Set up in Izmir on June 22, 1964, this party displayed little activity.

NEW TURKEY PARTY (NTP) (*Yeni Türkiye Partisi*). One of the new parties established in the wake of the 1960 military intervention, the NTP was set up on February 12, 1961, with the virtually open support of General Cemal Gürsel, head of the National Unity Committee (the officers responsible for the 1960 military intervention). Gürsel and others would have preferred that the NTP, rather than some other, unpredictable group, inherit the political support of the banned Democrat Party (DP).* Among the NTP's founders were Ekrem Alican, a former Republican People's Party (RPP)* finance minister (chairman), and professors Aydın Yalçın and Cahit Talas. Some of the NTP's leaders had been active in the Freedom Party* during the years from 1955 to 1958; others had served in governments sponsored by the National Unity Committee. This internal contradiction—the NTP's campaign for DP-supporter votes, although they were protégés of the officers who had brought about the DP's downfall—hindered the party from achieving more than ephemeral success and eventually brought about its decline.

The New Turkey Party strove for support from the rural areas of eastern and southeastern Turkey, which remained the main basis of its electoral strength. In 1961, following a preelection agreement with the Justice Party (JP),* the NTP obtained 13.7 percent of the vote in the general elections and 65 (out of 450) seats in the Grand National Assembly, where it was the third largest group (see Table 22). The NTP participated in coalition cabinets with the RPP and supported it even when it was not a partner in the government. In 1964–65, it was a partner with the JP in a non-RPP cabinet. Its very moderate attitude seems to have cost it votes in the general election of 1965, when it obtained 3.7 percent of the vote and nineteen seats in the Grand National Assembly and in 1969, when it declined to 2.2 percent of the vote (six seats). The NTP did not run in the 1973 and 1977 general elections and has virtually disappeared from the political scene. After 1961 part of its support apparently passed to the Justice Party, and another part, later on, to the National Salvation Party.*

The liberal stance of the party and its moderate attitude in the RPP–JP rivalry was not calculated to recruit extensive popular support. The middle-of-the-road views of the NTP's leaders had only limited appeal. These factors probably outweighed Alican's resignation from the party before the 1969 elections and his replacement by Y. Azizoğlu, who was quite popular in Turkey's southeast.

NSP. See NATIONAL SALVATION PARTY.

NTP. See NEW TURKEY PARTY.

NWP. See NATIONALIST WORK PARTY.

OUR PARTY (Bizim Parti). This party, set up in 1983 by Mithat Ceylan, an ex-general, was closed down by its leaders in the same year.

ÖZ DEMOKRATLAR PARTİSİ. See PARTY OF GENUINE DEMOCRATS.

PARTY FOR CIVILIZATION, CHERISHING ANIMALS, ECONOMY, AND AGRICULTURE (*Medeniyet Hayvansever Ekonomi ve Tarım Partisi*). Established on October 4, 1989, this party has shown little activity.

PARTY FOR LAND, REAL ESTATE, AND FREE ENTERPRISE (*Toprak, Emlâk ve Serbest Teşebbüs Partisi*). This party was established in Istanbul on September 30, 1949, by Süreyya Paşa (İlmen), an ex-officer and real estate owner; Asaf İlbay, a businessman; and Zühtü Bilimer, a physician. The founders had formerly belonged to the Association of Owners of Real Estate. In 1950 the party merged with the recently established Liberal Peasants' Party.* The party claimed to be humane, moral, and traditional; moderately liberal to conservative; with a positive attitude toward enlightened religion. Presumably, its most important goal was to work for the preservation of private property.

PARTY FOR NATIONAL ORDER (PNO) (*Millî Nizam Partisi*). The PNO was the first *legal* party in Republican Turkey officially committed to the promotion of Islam. Established on January 26, 1970, it was created and headed by Necmettin Erbakan, independent member of the Grand National Assembly from Konya, formerly a professor of automotive engineering at Istanbul Technical University. The party's first general convention, held in Ankara on February 8, 1970, proved a starting point for establishing branches in other population centers, a role in which the PNO's chairman, Erbakan, and its secretary-general, Süleyman Arif Emre, were particularly active. The party's strong advocacy of Islam caused the attorney general's office to prosecute it before the Constitutional Court, on the grounds of exploiting religion for political purposes. The court disbanded the PNO on May 20, 1971. Some of its leaders subsequently established the National Salvation Party,* with the same ideological orientation. An attempt to revive the party in Ankara, on January 14, 1976, under Hüsamettin Akmumcu's chairmanship, did not lead to tangible results.

The party's ideology represented a retreat from the secularism that had been one of the guiding principles of the Turkish Republic and as such had been inscribed in its constitution. While the PNO could not officially oppose secularism, it opposed any interpretation that was hostile to religion. Furthermore, while it could not include Islam proper within its program, its call for "morals and virtue" was loud and clear. The party identified moral recovery with social justice, happiness, and peace; it attempted to assume a forward-looking image by arguing that Islam was not only progressive, but fully consonant with whatever was best for Turkey. An oft-repeated demand was the reinstitution and encouragement of religious education in all Turkish schools. The fact that the party founder and chairman had distinguished himself as an automotive engineer added credibility to the PNO's stand in favor of technological progress. Other leaders were orthodox Muslims; these circles, previously frowned upon by the ruling strata, provided most and perhaps all supporters of the PNO during its brief life span. Although the party did not possess its own newspaper, periodicals that had worked assiduously to foster Islam during the 1960s supported the PNO enthusiastically.

PARTY FOR THE DEFENSE OF ISLAM (İslâm Koruma Partisi). Established in Istanbul on July 19, 1946, its main goal was to support and work for Islam. Since it mixed religion with politics (thus breaking the law), the authorities disbanded it on September 12, 1946, less than two months after it was founded.

PARTY OF ADVANCE AND PRESERVATION (İlerleme ve Koruma Partisi). A local party, established in Gaziantep on July 11, 1950, this party displayed no activity whatsoever.

PARTY OF DEMOCRATS (Demokratlar Partisi). Established in Ankara on June 22, 1971, this party displayed little to no activity.

PARTY OF GENUINE DEMOCRATS (Öz Demokratlar Partisi). Established in Afyonkarahisar on August 8, 1948, this local party for the province of Afyon showed little activity and merged with the Nation Party I* on July 5, 1949. The party claimed to strive for greater democracy in Turkey, a better electoral system, social justice, and a liberal economy. In foreign policy, it favored support for and cooperation with the United Nations. Its organ was Demokrat Afyon.

PARTY OF IDEALISTS (İdealist Partisi). Established in Istanbul on January 10, 1947, this party did not show any activity and disbanded during the same year. Its main goal was to struggle for reforms on all levels in order to render Turkey a more advanced state.

PARTY OF KEMALIST YOUTH (Kemalist Gençlik Partisi). Established in February 1961, this party showed little activity and disbanded in 1966.

PATRIOTIC FREE PARTY (Memleketçi Serbest Parti). Established in Ankara on February 11, 1961, it displayed little to no activity and disbanded (in 1964?).

PEASANTS' PARTY OF TURKEY (Türkiye Köylü Partisi). This small group was established in Ankara on May 19, 1952, mainly as a result of a rift in the Adana District branch of the Democrat Party (DP).* Among the founders were Ethem Menemencioğlu (honorary chairman), Remzi Oğuz Arık (chairman), Tahsin Demiray, Hakkı Kâmil Beşe, Süreyya Endik, and Yusuf Ziya Eker. The first two founders were university teachers; the third, a writer and publisher. The leaders were members of the Grand National Assembly who had left the DP, apparently for personal reasons. They and probably many of their supporters were intellectuals who, while disclaiming class struggle, urged more interest in raising the standard of living among Turkey's peasants, whom they considered the most important component of Turkish society. Other points in their program included: greater liberalization, the need for a constitutional court, decentralization, and keeping the armed forces out of politics. In 1952 the party was joined by members of the Liberal Peasants' Party,* which merged with it. Nevertheless, in the 1954 general elections, it received only 0.56 percent of the vote and no seats in the Grand National Assembly. It fared somewhat better in the 1955 local elections. The party did not contest the 1957 general elections and merged with the Republican Nation Party* on October 16, 1958, which then assumed the name of the Republican Peasants' Nation Party.* Some members of the Peasants' Party of Turkey continued to work as a separate group within the new party and had a minor role in the 1961 establishment of the Justice Party.*

PEOPLE'S LABOR PARTY (Halkın Emek Partisi—HEP). On June 7, 1990, eleven members of parliament left the Social Democratic Populist Party (SDPP),* which was not radical enough for them, and established the People's Labor Party. It was headed by Fehmi Işıklar, a trade unionist. It entered an electoral coalition with the SDPP in the 1991 election, electing approximately twenty candidates. The party was closed by court order on July 14, 1993, on charges of violation of the law protecting the solidarity of the state (i.e., against Kurdish separatist activity). Its place in the political arena was assumed by the Democracy Party.*

PEOPLE'S PARTY I. See REPUBLICAN PEOPLE'S PARTY.

PEOPLE'S PARTY II (Halk Partisi). Founded on December 20, 1989, this party soon closed down.

PEOPLE'S REPUBLICAN PARTY (Ahali Cumhuriyet Fırkası). This party was established in Adana on September 29, 1930, by Abdülkadir Kemalî, a lawyer and a former member of the Grand National Assembly. The declared aims of the party were to increase the prosperity of the whole nation by decreasing state expenditures and by repayment of state loans to the people through disposition of state property. The authorities ordered the disbanding of the party on January 21, 1931, less than four months after its establishment. The party organ was Tok Söz, published in Adana.

PKK. See KURDISH WORKERS' PARTY.

PNO. See PARTY FOR NATIONAL ORDER.

POPULIST PARTY (PP) (Halkçı Parti). The Populist Party was established in Ankara, on May 20, 1983, with the approval of the military regime of the time. Its first chairman was Necdet Calp, a lawyer and ex-government official, then (after June 1985) Aydın Güven Gürkan, a professor and member of parliament.

The secretary-general was Niyazi Araz, a retired judge, then Özer Gürbüz, an offical. In the November 6, 1983, parliamentary elections, the party obtained 30.5 percent of the vote and became the main opposition party with 117 seats (see Table 23). However, in the local elections of March 25, 1984, it came in fourth, with just 8.3 percent of the vote. Considering this decline in the vote, the party's first general convention, held in Ankara, on June 29, 1985, decided to unite with the Social Democratic Party, renamed the Social Democratic Populist Party.* Both parties had claimed to be the successor of the Republican People's Party,* so they found much common ground, ideologically.

PROGRESSIVE IDEALS PARTY OF TURKEY (*Türkiye İleri Ülkü Partisi*). Established in Istanbul on June 24, 1971, it displayed little to no activity.

PROGRESSIVE REPUBLICAN PARTY (*Terakkiperver Cumhuriyet Fırkası*). This party was established on November 17, 1924, by a group of members of Turkey's Grand National Assembly and others who opposed the government on both ideological and personal grounds. Foremost among these were several heroes of the war of independence: Ali Fuat (Cebesoy), the new party's secretary-general, and Kâzim Karabekir, Rauf (Orbay), Adnan (Adıvar), Refet (Bele), and Cafer Tayyar (Eğilmez). Not daring to criticize Mustafa Kemal (Atatürk) himself, they directed their criticism instead at his trusted lieutenant, İsmet İnönü, who was prime minister at the time. The party argued, however, that its opposition to the government and the policies of the Republican People's Party (RPP)* was purely ideological and that it stood for the rights of the individual against the tyranny of the few. It described itself as republican, but it claimed to be liberal and democratic as well (implying that the RPP was not). Furthermore, it stood for limiting state intervention in the economy and increasing freedom of religion (thus expressing some reservations concerning both the etatism and the secularism advocated by the RPP). As a consequence of the strong criticism voiced by the Progressive Republican Party, the İnönü government resigned in late November 1924, and a new one, headed by Fethi (Okyar), was formed. Soon afterward, however, on February 11, 1925, a large-scale Kurdish revolt broke out in the southeast, with demands for the establishment of a Kurdish independent state and the restoration of the caliphate. The government of Fethi Okyar failed to suppress the revolt and İnönü became prime minister once again. Strong criticism of the Progressive Republican Party and accusations of "reactionism" brought about its disbanding on June 5, 1925, just over six months after its establishment, under a new Emergency Law. Party leaders refrained from active political participation during the rest of Mustafa Kemal's lifetime; only after his death in 1938 did several of them return to activity within the ranks of the RPP. During its brief life span, the Progressive Republican Party succeeded in setting up branches in only a few urban centers such as Istanbul, Izmir, Urfa, and Sivas; one general convention was held in Istanbul, during mid-May 1925. The party had no periodicals of its own, although several Istanbul newspapers supported it.

PROSPERITY PARTY (*Refah Partisi*). Established on July 19, 1983, the first chairman of this party was Ali Türkmen, a lawyer. When he was vetoed by the National Security Council, he was succeeded by Ahmet Tekdal, a businessman, formerly a religious official. In 1987, after the ban on pre-1980 political leaders had been lifted, Necmettin Erbakan, former head of the National Salvation Party (NSP),* became chairman. The party came in sixth in the local elections of March 25, 1984, with 4.8 percent of the vote, but it improved on this result in the 1987 parliamentary elections, when it received 7.16 percent, but no seats (due to the 10 percent barrier). It entered the 1991 parliamentary elections in a joint list with the Nationalist Work Party,* obtaining forty-three seats for itself (see Table 23). Its ideology is close to the NSP's, but it is more cautiously expressed, in a coating of Kemalist slogans (except in the domain of secularism). There is strong emphasis on development in an atmosphere of freedom of thought (i.e., for religious Turks) and an increase in prosperity.

PURIFICATION AND PRESERVATION PARTY (*Arıtma Koruma Partisi*). This party was established in Ankara, on June 26, 1946, as a political party with religious views. Displaying little activity, it disbanded on March 12, 1947.

RADICAL FREEDOM PARTY (*Radikal Hürriyet Partisi*). This local party, established on April 11, 1953, in Kırklareli (Thrace), displayed little activity.

RADICAL PARTY (*Radikal Parti*). Established in Istanbul on May 28, 1962, it displayed little to no activity.

RADIKAL HÜRRIYET PARTISI. *See* RADICAL FREEDOM PARTY.

RADİKAL PARTİ. *See* RADICAL PARTY.

REBIRTH PARTY I (*Yeni Doğuş Partisi*). Chaired by Zeyyat Kocamemi, a landowner, this party was established on August 9, 1989, then closed down by its own founders.

REBIRTH PARTY II (*Yeniden Doğuş Partisi*). Founded on November 26, 1992, this party is opposed to any economic activity by the state and even favors the privatization of education and the health care system. It advocates Turkey's identification with Islamic civilization and upholds the sanctity of the family and moral values.

REFAH PARTISI. *See* PROSPERITY PARTY.

REFORM PARTY (*Devrim Partisi*). Established in Izmir on November 3, 1961, this party displayed little to no activity.

REFORMIST DEMOCRACY PARTY (*Islahatçı Demokrasi Partisi*). This party was set up in Ankara on March 23, 1984. Among its founders was a group from the Banner Party.* Its chairman was Aykut Edibâli, a lawyer and journalist, and its secretary-general was H. Ali Özdemir, an engineer. It held its first general convention on October 20, 1985, but it was not otherwise very active. Its 1984 program emphasized liberalism, secularism, peace, and Turkish culture through legally sanctioned reforms in the social, political, and moral structures of Turkish society. In 1992, this party changed its name to Nation Party, the third party with this name.

RELIANCE PARTY (RP) (*Güven Partisi*). The first party with this name, established in February 1961, was an ephemeral one. A longer-lived one was established in Ankara in May 1967, by forty-eight Grand National Assembly members and senators who had left the Republican People's Party (RPP)* after the RPP had announced its opening to the left. The new party was led by professor Turhan Feyzioğlu, member for Kayseri in the Grand National Assembly. Under the banner of "a right-of-center party," the RP held its first general convention on March 1–2, 1968, and elected Feyzioğlu as its chairman. Initially, the party did fairly well in the 1968 elections for a third of the Senate, obtaining 9.2 percent of the vote; in the general elections of 1969, it obtained 6.6 percent of the vote and 15 seats (out of 450) in the Grand National Assembly. On January 17, 1971, an extraordinary general convention changed the party's name to the National Reliance Party (*Millî Güven Partisi*). After the second military intervention (the "intervention by memorandum") of March 12, 1971, the RP supported the various governments that assumed office, and a member of the party, Ferit Melen, even formed and headed one of them. On March 2, 1973, the RP merged with the Republican Party* to form a new group, the Republican Reliance Party.*

The ideology of the Reliance Party was only partly expressed in its slogan, "Internal security, external security, rely on the Reliance Party!" The party claimed to be Kemalist and secularist, as well as antisocialist. Furthermore, it called for a mixed economy in Turkey: a compromise between statism and private enterprise. Many of its supporters came from Turkey's wealthier urban circles. Gradually, however, its support, at least as indicated in elections, dwindled and became concentrated in the provinces of Kayseri (stronghold of Feyzioğlu) and Van (stronghold of Melen).

REPUBLICAN DEMOCRATIC YOUTH PARTY (*Cumhuriyetçi Demokratik Gençlik Partisi*). This party, set up on June 9, 1989, has shown little activity, if any.

REPUBLICAN NATION PARTY (*Cumhuriyetçi Millet Partisi*). This party was established on February 9–10, 1954, by several leaders of the Nation Party I,* two weeks after a court had ordered the latter to disband. The chairman of the new party was Osman Bölükbaşı, a scientist. Other prominent figures were A.

Tahtakılıç, a lawyer, and S. Batur, an architect. In the 1954 general elections, the party received 480,000 votes and obtained five seats in the Grand National Assembly. In the assembly, the party consistently fought against the government formed by the Democrat Party.* Its main power base was the province of Kırşehir (loyal to Bölükbaşı), from which it gained four seats in the Grand National Assembly in the general elections of 1957. Soon afterward, in October 1958, it merged with the Peasants' Party of Turkey,* jointly assuming the name Republican Peasants' Nation Party.*

The party appears to have been one of the most conservative Turkish parties of the 1950s, although perhaps less so than the Nation Party from which it had split. While not coming out against secularism, it took a positive stand toward Islam and called for favorable mention of both trends in Turkey's constitution.

REPUBLICAN PARTY (*Cumhuriyetçi Parti*). The Republican Party was formed in September 1972 by former members of the Republican People's Party (RPP)* who had left it in July 1972, following Bülent Ecevit's takeover. Led by Kemal Satır, they established the new Republican Party. Early in March 1973, the Republican Party merged with the National Reliance Party, also a split from the RPP, formerly called simply the Reliance Party,* and formed the Republican Reliance Party.*

REPUBLICAN PEASANTS' NATION PARTY (RPNP) (*Cumhuriyetçi Köylü Millet Partisi*). The RPNP was established on October 16, 1958, through the merger of the Republican Nation Party* and the Peasants' Party of Turkey,* with the former predominating. The leader of the former, Osman Bölükbaşı, became the chairman of the RPNP. The party continued the oppositionist tradition of its components, fighting against the Democrat Party (DP)* in the Grand National Assembly. With the advent of the military intervention in 1960, the DP was outlawed, and the RPNP became one of the contenders for its legacy. In fact, it obtained 14 percent of the National Assembly vote (54 out of 450 seats) and 12.5 percent of the Senate (16 out of the 150 elected seats) in the 1961 general elections. The RPNP participated in governing coalitions in 1962–63 and again in 1965. However, it split in June 1962, with Bölükbaşı and his supporters leaving and reconstituting the Nation Party II.* The weakened RPNP, led by A. Tahtakılıç, a lawyer; H. Dincer, a judge; and A. Oğuz, a teacher, co-opted several of those military officers who had engineered the 1960 intervention and were subsequently ousted, hoping to increase its popularity by including nationally known personalities. Of these officers, the best known was Alparslan Türkeş, who exploited his role as the party's inspector general to assume leadership of the RPNP at its general convention in August 1965. Tahtakılıç, Dincer, and Oğuz left the party, whereupon Türkeş and his supporters assumed full control. In the general elections to the Grand National Assembly which soon followed, the RPNP obtained 2.2 percent of the vote and eleven seats. On a formal basis, the party did not change any of its regulations until it changed its name to the Nationalist Action Party* in 1969. However, its ideology did change soon after Türkeş's takeover, going from mildly conservative to militantly nationalist. This became even more apparent in the late 1960s and the 1970s. The mass circulation *Tercüman* (Istanbul) and the extreme right-wing *Yeni İstanbul* (Istanbul) supported the party intermittently.

REPUBLICAN PEOPLE'S PARTY (RPP) (*Cumhuriyet Halk Partisi*). Turkey's longest-lived legal party was established in Ankara on September 11, 1923, by members of the Society for the Defense of the Rights of Anatolia and Rumelia, as the nationalist organization of Mustafa Kemal was called. At first, it was called Halk Fırkası (People's Party); then Cumhuriyet Halk Fırkası (Republican People's Party) on November 10, 1924. It was renamed Cumhuriyet Halk Partisi (Republican People's Party) in 1935. Its first chairman was Mustafa Kemal (Atatürk) himself; the vice chairman, İsmet (İnönü); and the secretary-general, Recep (Peker). The RPP was truly a comprehensive nationalist party. For an entire generation, it governed alone (short-lived attempts at allowing the formation of other parties notwithstanding). The party was an instrument of government; its leadership was largely identical with that of the state, from Mustafa Kemal (and then from İnönü) on down; and it identified with nation building (a frequently displayed slogan was "One Party, One Nation, One Leader"). As expected, it continued to aspire toward this role even after 1950, when it became the leading opposition party.

During its first generation, the RPP's program was Turkey's as well. Indeed, the Six Arrows (i.e., principles) of the RPP, adopted between 1927 and 1931, were inserted into the constitution, in a 1937 amendment. These "arrows" were republicanism, populism, nationalism, etatism, secularism, and reformism. Although variously interpreted, they served as guidelines for the modernization of Turkey as carried out largely by the party. Both within and outside the Grand National Assembly, the RPP was a major factor in instilling respect for the newly established republic and for the popular will. A new type of nationalism, focusing on Turkey itself, gave the embattled Turks a new sense of purpose. Political independence, considered sacrosanct, was ensured by strict neutrality ("Peace at home and peace in the world"). Economic independence and stability were furthered by an etatist policy, in which the state controlled all larger economic enterprises; this was expressed also in the construction of an economic infrastructure and the beginnings of industrialization. Islam was disestablished, and religious courts and schools were closed down and replaced by secular institutions; women were emancipated and enfranchised, and the veil was discouraged. A spirit of reformism prevailed, aiming at modernization and Westernization, carried out by the party. The RPP helped strengthen the central government at the expense of feudalist and particularistic trends; it trained cadres for a modern bureaucracy and prepared Turkey for contemporary statehood.

One of the most significant contributions of the RPP was its 1945 decision to switch to a multiparty regime. Somewhat surprised at the extent of popular support for the newly established parties, the RPP advanced the general elections by one year to 1946, and received a comfortable majority in the Grand National Assembly (although the Democrats claimed there was fraud). The RPP was defeated, however, in the 1950 elections, when it received only 39.9 percent of the vote and a mere 69 (out of 487) seats (because of the electoral system). Support for the Democrat Party (DP),* founded in 1946, surpassed that for the RPP, which remained in opposition for an entire decade. In 1954 the RPP received 34.8 percent of the vote and a mere 30 seats (out of 535); in 1957, it received 40.6 percent of the vote and 173 seats (out of 602) (see Table 21). The RPP, led by İnönü, showed itself to be a militant opposition, fighting the DP governments tooth and nail. Furthermore, it strove to change its formerly authoritarian character and assume a more liberal image, as the defender of democracy. The RPP accused the DP of authoritarianism, proposing a system of checks and balances to limit assembly powers. Thus, the RPP proposed the establishment of a senate and of independent bodies more representative of Turkey's elites.

Following the 1960 military intervention, the RPP witnessed the implementation of several of the above recommendations (the establishment of a senate and a constitutional court). The party was instrumental in ensuring a return to civilian government in 1961 and ruled Turkey, at the head of several coalition cabinets, between 1961 and 1964. Party support consistently amounted to approximately one-third of the vote. In 1961 it obtained a plurality in the Grand National Assembly, with 36.7 percent of the vote and 173 seats (out of 450) (see Table 22). In the Senate, it was the second largest group with 36.1 percent of the vote and 36 seats (out of 150 standing for election). The RPP's delicate balance with the Democrat Party, which had characterized the years 1946–1960, now continued with the Justice Party (JP)* which, in that year, was the second largest group in the National Assembly and the first in the Senate.

In 1965, before the general elections, İnönü proclaimed a moderate left-of-center stance for the RPP which may have contributed to the RPP's serious decline in popular support when it obtained only 28.7 percent of the vote (its poorest results up to that time) and 134 seats (out of 450) (see Table 22). The JP won with an absolute majority and formed its own cabinet, with the RPP returning to the opposition benches. In subsequent elections for a third of the Senate (1966, 1968), the same pattern was repeated. The RPP also suffered from a split in which several of its National Assembly members and senators broke away to establish the Reliance Party* in 1967 because of the RPP's leftward swing. In the 1969 general elections to the National Assembly, the RPP fared even worse than in 1965, with just 27.4 percent of the vote, although it increased its representation to 143 (thanks to a 1968 change in the electoral law, favoring the larger parties) (see Table 22). The JP, with an absolute majority in the National Assembly once again, formed a cabinet that was compelled to resign as a result of the military "coup-by-memorandum" (March 12, 1971). The RPP, however, had its own troubles, particularly after the party's secretary-general, the young and dynamic Bülent Ecevit, had taken over the chairmanship in 1972.

Supporters of the ousted İnönü, led by Kemal Satir, a banker, left to establish the Republican Party.* The RPP was as eager as the JP for a return to civilian government, and the military eventually reinstituted it.

In the 1973 general elections to the National Assembly and to a third of the Senate, the RPP, led by Ecevit, was the only left-of-center party to run, since the Workers' Party of Turkey* had been disbanded in 1971. Consequently, it strove to present a united left-of-center image against a divided right. The RPP was first in the National Assembly, with 33.3 percent of the vote and 185 seats (out of 450), as well as in the Senate, with 43.4 percent of the vote and 25 seats (out of 54 standing for reelection) (see Table 22). Early in 1974, the RPP formed a coalition cabinet with the theocratically minded National Salvation Party (NSP),* a retreat from its secularist views. The most notable event of this RPP–NSP government was the Cyprus Operation in July 1974. The partners claimed, separately, credit for the success of the Cyprus Operation and could not agree on most other issues. The cabinet resigned nine months after its formation, and the RPP returned to the opposition.

In the 1977 general elections, the RPP was first again in the National Assembly vote, improving its share to 41.4 percent of the vote and 213 seats (see Table 22); in the partial elections to the Senate, it obtained 42.4 percent of the vote and 28 seats (out of 50 standing for reelection). Thus, it still fell short of an absolute majority (i.e., 226 seats out of 450) in the National Assembly. It was only early in 1978 that Ecevit succeeded in forming a coalition cabinet supported by the RPP, as well as several line-crossers and independents. The most notable event during the RPP's 1978 rule appears to have been Ecevit's rapprochement with Moscow, which did not visibly impair Turkey's ties with the West. Along with all other parties, the RPP was closed down by the military regime on October 16, 1981.

There is an evident disproportion between the RPP's achievements before and after 1950. During the first period, it constituted the entire government or at least its major component. Afterward, however, it was either in the opposition, where, in the Kemalist tradition, it became the watchdog of democracy, or in the government for brief periods (between 1961 and 1964, in 1974, and again in 1978–79), always in coalition cabinets which obviously limited its freedom of action. Nevertheless, it proved to be one of the most important forces—in some years, the major force—in Turkish politics.

The party's ideology underwent perceptible change. During the single-party period, the Six Arrows constituted its very credo. Later, while not renouncing the Six Arrows, the party gave some of them a new interpretation. This resulted both from its new position in opposition and in response to criticism from within party ranks. Such criticism, coming from various directions, did not make the life of party leaders any easier. During the years from 1950 to 1965, the RPP's response was to demand individual freedoms and a curb on government authoritarianism; much of this was embodied in the 1961 constitution. In 1965 an

opening to the left became increasingly evident. However, İnönü's leftward leanings were less obvious than Ecevit's.

Ecevit's left-of-center stance brought about some much-needed support for the
RPP from leftist circles, which became increasingly articulate in the 1960s. Ecevit
maintained that the RPP, under his leadership, became a social democratic party,
a term that was interpreted differently by various groups within the party. Some,
though not all, of his positions displayed affinity with those of West European
social democrats. The party consensus seemed to be that, while the RPP continued to be committed to integration, mobilization, and development, emphasis
should be placed on an egalitarian approach to social welfare and on more elaborate economic planning. In other words, greater social justice and less economic
inequality should be stressed. In a mass party such as the RPP, programmatic
differences of opinion must evidently arise. The leadership appeared to have
agreed on the need for greater socioeconomic equality, without which political
equality is hardly meaningful. However, leftist groups within the RPP spoke up
(with varying degrees of insistence) for changes in land ownership, the development of Turkey's natural resources—in the common interest of all Turks—
and the nationalization of banks.

As a mass party with a long history, the RPP was sometimes unable to prevent
rifts, which altered the character of its leadership and membership. During the
single-party era, the leadership was composed largely of retired military officers
and bureaucrats. This carried over into the multiparty era as well. In the 1970s,
however, intellectuals, professionals, and career politicians also assumed a place
within the party. The new leadership also had a more youthful look, particularly
after the takeover of Ecevit and his appointees. Party support varied in nature
over the years. In 1946 many wealthy landowners were still close to the RPP;
quite a few passed to the opposition, in that year, in reaction to the RPP's plans
for land reform. Most of the ethnic minorities were opposed to the RPP, since it
had downgraded private enterprise; however, many Shiites, apprehensive of a
religious (i.e., Sunnite) revival under DP rule, favored the RPP. In general, the
broad popular support enjoyed by the RPP appears to have been mostly evident
among urban intellectuals, professionals, workers, the military, and the bureaucracy, and less so among business circles and landowners. After 1969 the party's
electoral support largely came from the more developed parts of Turkey. After
having lost ground in the urban centers during the 1950s and the 1960s, it began
to gain votes there during the 1970s, probably at the expense of the JP. Perhaps
its greatest strength was in its support from many different areas in Turkey. This,
of course, was also a source of potential weakness, as the growth of the political
elite in Turkey and the increasing differentiation within Turkish society have
compounded the RPP's difficulties in appealing effectively to various groups and
classes.

Various publications have supported the RPP over the years. In the single-
party era, most of the press was partial to it in varying degrees. In the multiparty
era, many newspapers turned against the RPP but returned to support the party

after their disappointment with the DP. In recent years, the daily *Ulus* and the monthly *Özgür İnsan* (both published in Ankara) were considered party organs, although several national dailies, such as *Milliyet*, *Cumhuriyet*, and *Günaydın* (all published in Istanbul) had also supported the RPP.

REPUBLICAN PEOPLE'S PARTY II (RPP) (*Cumhuriyet Halk Partisi*—CHP). This party, founded on September 9, 1991, broke away from the SDPP.* Its leader was former Professor Deniz Baykal, a one-time close associate of Bülent Ecevit early in his tenure as leader of the original RPP in 1972. Later in September 1992, fifteen members of parliament formed an interim party (lasting two days) for the purpose of joining the new RPP. The party claims to be a reincarnation of the original RPP. It characterized itself as a democratic left party, and it rejuvenated the six principles (six arrows) of the old RPP. Its program favored a state-led economy, particularly concerning the public service, traditional state monopolies, strategic industries, and those industries that might otherwise be monopolized by private concerns; it also opposed partnership between public and private firms. It specifically rejected privatization of state economic enterprises. It also favored autonomy for mass communications media and public pension systems, and it called on the state to encourage artistic and cultural activities. Late in 1993, the party included twenty members of parliament; its organizational leadership included a number of members of pre-1980 parliaments, such as Haluk Ülman.

REPUBLICAN PROFESSIONAL REFORM PARTY (*Cumhuriyetçi Meslekî Islahat Partisi*). Established in Ankara on February 11, 1961, this party displayed little activity.

REPUBLICAN RELIANCE PARTY (RRP) (*Cumhuriyetçi Güven Partisi*). This party was established through the March 3, 1973, merger of the Republican Party* with the Reliance Party,* which had already changed its name to the National Reliance Party. The RRP's chairman was Turhan Feyzioğlu, a professor of law; the deputy chairman, Ferit Melen, former minister of finance and defense; and the secretary-general, Orhan Öztrak, a lawyer. In the general elections held the same year, the RRP obtained 5.3 percent of the vote and 13 (out of 450) seats in the National Assembly. From early 1975 to mid-1977, the party was a component of the right-of-center cabinet coalition, together with the Justice Party,* the National Salvation Party,* and the Nationalist Action Party.* Feyzioğlu was accordingly one of the deputy prime ministers. In the general elections of June 5, 1977, the RRP's support declined sharply, perhaps as a result of increased support for the Republican People's Party*; it obtained only three seats, one of them for Feyzioğlu himself. The RRP did succeed in using the situation in the National Assembly to its advantage; early in 1978, it joined the Republican People's Party and several other members of the National Assembly in a government headed by Bülent Ecevit, the chairman of the Republican People's Party.

The merger ended the independent existence of the RRP. In this coalition, Feyzioğlu again became a deputy prime minister.

During its brief career, the RRP emphasized that it considered itself "a national party, not a class party." Its platform for the 1977 general elections expanded upon this theme. Claiming that it was a Kemalist, middle-of-the-road party, it belonged neither to the radical left nor to the extreme right. Its platform supported nationwide social security, respect for private property, freedom of religion and conscience, clean air, pure water, and an honest administration. Furthermore, the RRP desired national prosperity, a minimum wage, just taxation (which it prudently did not specify), agricultural insurance, provision of housing for families, employment for the young, and the serious pursuit of industrialization.

REVIVAL PARTY (*Diriliş Partisi*). Founded on March 26, 1990, the program of this party favored a strong state and presidential system, an economic policy of Income Substitution Industrialization (ISI), family values, "establishment of state controlled moral institutions" to bolster the moral character of youth, and empowerment of the Interior Ministry to monitor intellectual expression. It showed little activity.

REVOLUTIONARY WORKERS'-PEASANTS' PARTY OF TURKEY (*Türkiye İhtilalcı İşçi Köylü Partisi*). This illegal party worked mainly underground. Established on May 21, 1969, it became active chiefly in 1971, when its first central committee took office. The party kept a low profile during the martial law era from 1971 to 1973; even afterward, it appears to have operated clandestinely, mostly outside Turkey (little is known of its activity within Turkey). Its first general convention was also held abroad, in Milan, on September 9–10, 1977. The minutes of this convention, particularly the political report of the party's central committee, give an idea of the party's ideology. The entire address was delivered in a rigid spirit of Marxism-Leninism, with frequent and admiring references to Mao Zedong's interpretations. In this respect, two items relating specifically to Turkey are most interestingly emphasized: the demand for an agricultural revolution, to be carried out by peasant communes (most likely following the Chinese pattern), and insistence on solving what the party considered to be the national problems of the Kurds living in Turkey, Iran, Iraq, and Syria by allowing them a separate state of their own. The Marxist outlook of this party bears close resemblance to those of the Workers'-Peasants' Party of Turkey*; both parties attack virtually every other Turkish leftist group but refrain from attacking each other. Thus, there appears to be a possible link between the two parties. The party's organ, *Şafak*, was published irregularly.

RP. *See* RELIANCE PARTY.

RPNP. *See* REPUBLICAN PEASANTS' NATION PARTY.

RPP. *See* REPUBLICAN PEOPLE'S PARTY.

RRP. *See* REPUBLICAN RELIANCE PARTY.

SALVATION PARTY (*Selamet Partisi*). Established in Izmir on July 14, 1962, this party displayed little activity.

SDPP. *See* SOCIAL DEMOCRATIC POPULIST PARTY.

SELAMET PARTİSİ. *See* SALVATION PARTY.

SERBEST DEMOKRAT PARTİSİ. *See* FREE DEMOCRATIC PARTY.

SERBEST FIRKA. *See* FREE PARTY.

SERENITY PARTY OF TURKEY (*Türkiye Huzur Partisi*). Chaired by Ahmet Çelebi, a former religious official, it was founded in 1983 and was closed down in the same year by a decision of the Constitutional Court.

SERVICE TO THE NATION PARTY (*Millete Hizmet Partisi*). Established on February 13, 1961, it showed little to no activity and disbanded in the same year.

SOCIAL DEMOCRATIC PARTY I (*Sosyal Demokrat Parti*). This party was established in Ankara on September 22, 1964, by Sıtkı Ulay, an ex-officer, and A. Tiritoğlu, one of the founders of the Socialist Party I.* The party apparently did not organize to any significant extent, and its activity was negligible. It disbanded in 1965. The party's platform attacked both mass parties, the Republican People's Party* and the Justice Party,* as obsolete. It considered social democracy to be the only way to ensure Turkey's progress; this concept was not developed further, however.

SOCIAL DEMOCRATIC PARTY II. *See* SOCIAL DEMOCRATIC POPU-LIST PARTY.

SOCIAL DEMOCRATIC POPULIST PARTY (SDPP) (*Sosyal Demokrat Halkçı Partisi*). Established with the same name as the party founded in 1964, the Social Democratic Party I,* it had no other connection with it. The Social Democratic Party II was set up on June 6, 1983, by Erdal İnönü, a professor of physics and the son of Turkey's second president, İsmet İnönü. Its first secretary-general was Ahmet Durakoğlu, a retired official and former member of parliament, then Deniz Baykal, a political scientist, then Hikmet Çetin, an economist. It was prohibited from participating in the parliamentary elections of November 6, 1983, by the military regime, but it did run in the local elections of March 25, 1984, coming in second nationally with 23.4 percent of the total vote. Claiming 200,000 reg-

istered members, it united, on September 26, 1985, with the Populist Party,*
which was ideologically close to it. The union was approved by the two former
parties on November 2 and 3, respectively. Renamed the Social Democratic
Populist Party, this regrouping came in second in the November 29, 1987, parliamentary elections, obtaining 24.7 percent of the vote and ninety-nine seats
(see Table 23); it did even better in the March 26, 1989, local elections, when
it achieved first place nationally with 28 percent of the total vote. It did rather
less well in the October 23, 1991, parliamentary elections, when it obtained only
20.8 percent of the total vote and eighty-eight seats. It then entered a coalition
cabinet with the True Path Party.*

The SDPP posits two principal claims, not necessarily mutually compatible. It
claims to be a direct continuation of the Republican People's Party,* simultaneously calling itself a new social democratic grouping. Consequently, its ideology is partly Kemalist, partly West European social democratic. Thus, it is
committed to "a social state," in the European social democratic tradition, based
on both a market economy and social justice with economic problems resolved
in a manner suitable for the twenty-first century: more productive employment
of labor, a fairer distribution of profits, a freer and more democratic society, and
better social legislation. These ideals appeal to Turkey's growing urban intelligentsia and to many moderate left-of-center groups, which consider the SDPP
Turkey's main leftist party.

SOCIAL JUSTICE PARTY (Sosyal Adalet Partisi). This party, established in
Istanbul on February 28, 1946, remained in existence until 1952, when its general
convention decided to dissolve the party. Its activity appears to have been minimal; it never participated in an election. Its principal merit apparently lay in
having been the first legitimate post–World War II party to espouse socialism,
albeit in a moderate form associated with democracy and etatism. The party's
publications (it had no regular organ) indicate that it interpreted socialism as
the defense of workers and landless peasants.

SOCIALIST PARTY I (Sosyalist Parti). This party, the first of three unrelated
parties bearing this name, was established on January 19, 1960, by Âtıf Akgüç
(chairman), Alâadin Tiritoğlu (secretary-general), and several others. Most of
the founders and members were lawyers; several had experience in leftist political
activity or had contributed to leftist publications. Several of the founders had in
fact been active in the Socialist Party of Turkey.* The party began to organize
meetings for lectures on socialism and to publish a pamphlet on the same subject.
Additional activities were planned, but the party weakened considerably with
the resignation of both Akgüç and Tiritoğlu in 1961. The remnants of this party,
led by A. Haydaroğlu, merged with the Workers' Party of Turkey I* on May 12,
1962.

SOCIALIST PARTY II (*Sosyalist Parti*). This party, the second of three unrelated parties bearing this name, was established in Istanbul, on May 30, 1975, by Mehmet Ali Aybar and several associates. Aybar, a lawyer and journalist, had been chairman of the Workers' Party of Turkey I (WPT I)* from 1962 until his forced resignation in 1969, in the rift caused by the 1968 Soviet intervention in Czechoslovakia and the following failure of the party in the 1969 parliamentary elections. Several members of the WPT I joined Aybar in the Socialist Party, although the latter party enjoyed little of the popular support gained by the former in the 1960s. The party's secretary-general was Cenan Bıçakçı, a writer. Along with all other parties, it was closed down by the military regime on October 16, 1981.

Although a Marxist, Aybar consistently advocated an independent type of sui generis Turkish socialism. He always praised the virtues of the Turkish parliamentary system. The Socialist Party's claim that it stood for revolutionary socialism notwithstanding, the party's platform was more pragmatic than those of other far-left parties in Turkey. It considered itself as the party of the working class and of those peasants, revolutionary youths, and socialist intellectuals who wished to join in their struggle. The party had a far-reaching goal: to strive for the socioeconomic regime to be established by the workers upon assuming power—a democratic socialist order within a truly independent Turkey. Their more immediate goal was to imbue the workers and peasants with political awareness in order to achieve worker power, thus paving the way for democratic socialism. Among its other aims were the following: nationalization, necessary for economic independence; reform in land tenure, favoring the landless; improving education and the judicial system; establishing social security; and pursuing an independent foreign policy with no binding pacts. The party had two organs, *Sosyalist Yol* and the weekly *Sosyalist Yarın*.

SOCIALIST PARTY III (*Sosyalist Parti*). This party, the third of three unrelated parties bearing this name, was established on February 1, 1988. Its chairman was Ferit İlsever, an engineer, and its main ideologue was Doğu Perinçek, a Marxist journalist and activist, who had headed the Workers'-Peasants' Party of Turkey.* Its ideology was characteristically Marxist, so it was not surprising that it sent a delegation, headed by Perinçek (a convinced Maoist), to the general convention of the French Communist Party, in December 1990.

SOCIALIST PARTY OF TURKEY I (*Türkiye Sosyalist Partisi*). This party was established on May 14, 1946, by Esat Âdil Müstecaplıoğlu, Aziz Uçtay, and others already involved in leftist activities (a party of the same name had existed briefly in 1919). Suspicions by the military authorities concerning the political leanings of the party's founders and the Marxist tenor of its platform led to the invocation of martial law and the disbandment of the party on December 16, 1946. The founders were tried for communist activities but acquitted. The party was subsequently revived in 1950. By 1952 it was again ordered to disband, on charges of disseminating communist propaganda. The party's leaders were brought to court and were acquitted eight years later, following lengthy proceedings. The party was reestablished once again, as the Socialist Party I* in Ankara, on January 19, 1960. The party was allegedly infiltrated by communists, vying for power with the founders who claimed to be noncommunist socialists. On May 12, 1962, it merged with the Workers' Party of Turkey.* It has not existed independently since that time.

The party had no success in the general elections of 1946 nor in the by-elections of 1951 (in Istanbul, it polled a mere 220 of approximately 175,000 valid votes cast). Nevertheless, its incessant propaganda, chiefly in its periodical *Gerçek*, appears to have had a greater impact on leftist intellectuals than the mere vote count implied. The party platform was avowedly Marxist. It claimed to be democratic, nationalist, socialist, internationalist, and secularist. Its socialist credo found expression in its demands for improving the people's prosperity, culture, and health; doing away with economic and social injustice; and raising the dignity of labor. Other demands were made for Turkey's development and independence; guaranteed employment for all Turks; increased production; state responsibility for social security, education, and health care; safeguarding individual liberties; and the formation of cooperatives. The party respected private property but aimed at nationalizing the means of production and the larger landholdings. The reconstituted party of the early 1960s also laid emphasis on preventing exploitation of the people by interest groups.

SOCIALIST PARTY OF TURKEY (II) (*Türkiye Sosyalist Partisi*). Founded on November 6, 1992, this party supports an extreme version of socialism, including nationalization of all means of production and a planned economy. The party characterized the Kurdish problem as a problem of "national identity," and it supported the right of "the nations" (i.e., the Kurds) to secede from the country.

SOCIALIST POWER PARTY (*Sosyalist İktidar Partisi*). Relations between this party and the Socialist Party of Turkey (II)* and Socialist Party* are unclear; there may have been mergers of one sort or another. Its program consists of a single sentence declaring faith in scientific socialism. It was established on August 16, 1993.

SOCIALIST REVOLUTION PARTY (*Sosyalist Devrim Partisi*). This party was founded on December 27, 1992, and claimed to be the heir of a party of the same name allegedly established in 1975. The party proclaimed its belief in science (presumably scientific socialism) and advocated "revolution" led by the proletariat. Its chairman was Cenan Bıçakçı.

SOCIALIST UNITY PARTY (*Sosyalist Birlik Partisi*). Founded on January 15, 1991, this party was headed by Sadun Aren, a former university professor and activist in earlier socialist parties. The party claimed to represent industrial workers and laborers in general, and it expressed its opposition both to capitalism and to state socialism. It advocated ideological and political pluralism and emphasized human rights. It proposed state planning in education and, at a time when private fee-supported institutions were developing in Turkey, insisted on free education and equality of opportunity. The party also advocated official recognition of the separate national identity of the Kurds.

SOCIALIST WORKERS' AND PEASANTS' PARTY OF TURKEY (*Türkiye Sosyalist Emekçi ve Köylü Partisi*). This party was established in Istanbul on June 19–20, 1946, by leftist activists, including Şefik Hüsnü Değmer (party chairman and a known Marxist), Ragıb Vardar, Fuat Bilege, and several others, including a Greek and a Jew (both rather rare in Turkish party politics). The party hardly had time to establish an organization before it was accused of disseminating communist propaganda and dissolved by the military authorities on December 16, 1946, following less than half a year of existence. Despite its brief activity, the party did have some impact, chiefly on leftist intellectuals, via its periodical, *Sendika*, and another, *Yığın*, which supported its views. The party's ideology was outspokenly Marxist. It called for granting the workers a greater say in internal and external policies; helping workers and peasants join ever-growing economic and political organizations; forming trade unions, socioeconomic associations, and clubs; organizing the workers and peasants against exploitation and pressures; guaranteeing the rights of collective bargaining and social security; and, as a more distinct goal, placing all means of production under the control of the entire nation.

SOCIALIST WORKERS' PARTY OF TURKEY I (*Türkiye Sosyalist İşçi Partisi*). This party, the first of three unrelated parties of the same name, was established in Istanbul on May 24, 1946, by Sabit Şevki Şeren, a civil servant. The party had no noteworthy activity, and it was ordered to disband on September 10, 1948. Its name notwithstanding, the party was not fully socialist in its aims. It advocated the establishment of cooperatives and the betterment of conditions for workers and their families, but it respected the rights of private ownership.

SOCIALIST WORKERS' PARTY OF TURKEY II (*Türkiye Sosyalist İşçi Partisi*). This party, the second of three unrelated parties of the same name, was established on June 21–22, 1974. Among the party's most prominent leaders were Ahmet Kaçmaz, a lawyer (chairman); Yalçın Yusufoğlu, a lawyer (secretary-general); and Ms. Oya Baydar (Sencer), a sociologist, who was perhaps its leading theoretician. Some of the members came from the Workers' Party of Turkey* after the latter had been disbanded. In 1975 the party claimed to have branches in twenty-one (out of sixty-seven) provinces, with a membership of 2,500. The party reportedly sponsored unauthorized rallies for "Work, Bread, and Freedom" in six major provincial centers; several of its officials were arrested in Ankara in 1975 and charged with illegal dissemination of communist propaganda. The party

602 / Political Parties of the Middle East

took Moscow's side in intercommunist conflicts and advocated socialism and the leadership of the working class as the road to Turkey's salvation, principally through organization of the entire population for political action. The party's platform considered unemployment and the high cost of living in capitalist Turkey to be a social catastrophe. Interpreting everything in terms of class struggle, it aimed to lead Turkey's working class in its anti-imperialist struggle. The party favored nationalization, central planning, industrialization, development, redistribution of land, democracy, freedom of belief and thought, secularism, an anti-imperialist foreign policy, and social rights for the workers. The monthly *Ilke* and the weekly *Kitle* closely reflected the party's views; a bimonthly associated with the party, *Yeni Genç İşçi*, was intended for the youth.

SOCIALIST WORKERS' PARTY OF TURKEY (III) (*Türkiye Sosyalist İşçi Partisi*). Established January 3, 1993, nothing is known about this party other than that it advocated the establishment of a socialist regime, and that its chairman was named Turgut Koçak.

SOCIETY FOR THE DEFENSE OF THE RIGHTS OF ANATOLIA AND RUMELIA. *See* REPUBLICAN PEOPLE'S PARTY (I).

SOSYAL ADALET PARTİSİ. *See* SOCIAL JUSTICE PARTY.

SOSYAL DEMOKRAT HALKÇI PARTİSİ. *See* SOCIAL DEMOCRATIC POPULIST PARTY.

SOSYAL DEMOKRAT PARTİ. *See* SOCIAL DEMOCRATIC PARTY.

SOSYALİST BİRLİK PARTİSİ. *See* SOCIALIST UNITY PARTY.

SOSYALİST DEVRIM PARTİSİ. *See* SOCIALIST REVOLUTION PARTY.

SOSYALİST İKTİDAR PARTİSİ. *See* SOCIALIST POWER PARTY.

SOSYALİST PARTİ. *See* SOCIALIST PARTY.

TERAKKİ PERVER CUMHURİYET FIRKASI. *See* PROGRESSIVE REPUBLICAN PARTY.

TIP. *See* WORKERS' PARTY OF TURKEY I.

TOPRAK, EMLÂK VE SERBEST TEŞEBBÜS PARTİSİ. *See* PARTY FOR LAND, REAL ESTATE, AND FREE ENTERPRISE.

TRUE PATH PARTY (TPP) (*Doğru Yol Partisi*). This party was established in Ankara on June 23, 1983, following the order closing down the Great Turkey Party.* Its first chairman was Nusret Tuna, a former Justice Party* minister of agriculture, then E. Yıldırım Avcı, later Hüsamettin Cindoruk, a lawyer (one of the founders of the Great Turkey Party), and finally, since 1987, Süleyman Demirel, chairman of the banned Justice Party, after he regained the right to enter politics (through a constitutional referendum). Not allowed by the military regime to run in the November 6, 1983, parliamentary elections, it did compete in the November 29, 1987, election and came in third, winning 19.1 percent of the vote and 59 seats (out of a total of 450). In the local elections of March 25, 1984, it came in third again, with 13.3 percent of the vote, but in those of March 26, 1989, it succeeded in coming in second. The party did very well in the October 23, 1991, parliamentary elections, obtaining 27 percent of the total vote and 178 seats (out of a total of 450), making it the strongest party (see Table 23). Thereupon, Demirel formed a coalition cabinet, together with Social Democratic Populist Party,* with himself as prime minister.

In May 1993, after the death of Turgut Özal, Demirel was elected president of the republic, necessitating his resignation from the party. The subsequent contest for party leadership was won by Mrs. Tansu Çiller, a U.S.-trained Ph.D. in Economics; she thus became the first female prime minister in the history of the Republic of Turkey. Her position as party leader was overwhelmingly confirmed by a regular party congress in the fall of 1993, but her longterm prospects were somewhat doubtful in view of a general expectation that the True Path Party would not do well in the municipal elections scheduled for March 1994.

Although the party's name, Doğru Yol, may have referred to the Koranic sirât al-müstakîm (straight path) to attract the vote of the traditionally minded, its avowed objectives were to guard individual rights in the framework of social justice, to foster a democratic secular state, and to promote advanced development and prosperity. The party's founders and leaders repeatedly have defined it as committed to the nation's liberal democracy, based on the free will of the people. Ideologically, the True Path Party has emphasized its identification with the Justice Party—a primarily right-of-center, liberal set of doctrines—just as its chairman and many officials had been leading members of the Justice Party. In this, it has had to compete with the main right-of-center rival, the Motherland Party.* Both the True Path Party and the Motherland Party have resorted to a clientelistic approach (expressed in party patronage, machine politics, and distributive governmental policies).

TURKISH CONSERVATIVE PARTY (Türk Muhafazakâr Partisi). This party was established in Istanbul on July 8, 1947, by Cevat Rıfat Atılhan. Although its two periodicals Mücadele and Millî İnkılâp supported it, the party displayed very little activity and disbanded in 1952. The party program called for family values, democracy, justice, prosperity, and morals; judging by its publications, it was strongly pro-Islamic, anticommunistic, and anti-Semitic.

TURKISH PEOPLE'S LIBERATION PARTY (Türk Halk Kurtuluş Partisi). An illegal organization, this party was formed in the late 1960s along with the Turkish People's Liberation Front with which it was linked. Led by Mahir Çayan, a known Marxist, members maintained a compact Marxist ideology, which found expression in their monthly *Kurtuluş: İşçilerin-Köylülerin Gazetesi* (Independence: The Newspaper of Workers and Peasants), published in Ankara in 1970. The militancy of party members manifested itself in terrorist acts that provoked military intervention. Many were arrested, and several were executed; others were killed in fighting the security forces. One may gauge the extent of violence to which this group was committed by the fact that the 1974 amnesty freed 465 party members from prison.

TURKISH SOCIAL DEMOCRATIC PARTY (*Türk Sosyal Demokrat Partisi*). This party was established in Istanbul on April 26, 1946. Although the party does not seem to have had any effective organization, nor a regular publication, it participated (unsuccessfully) in several elections. The party disbanded in 1951, following the death of Cemil Alpay, its founder and leader. A characteristic social democratic group, the party expressed considerable interest in individual rights, social security, and other social matters, including a reform in land tenure. As a result, it was considered to be moderately socialist in outlook.

TÜRK CUMHURİYET AMELE VE ÇİFTÇİ PARTİSİ. *See* WORKERS' AND FARMERS' PARTY OF THE TURKISH REPUBLIC.

TÜRK HALK KURTULUŞ PARTİSİ. *See* TURKISH PEOPLE'S LIBERATION PARTY.

TÜRK MUHAFAZAKÂR PARTİSİ. *See* TURKISH CONSERVATIVE PARTY.

TÜRK SOSYAL DEMOKRAT PARTİSİ. *See* TURKISH SOCIAL DEMOCRATIC PARTY.

TÜRKİYE BİRLEŞİK KOMÜNIST PARTİSİ. *See* UNITED COMMUNIST PARTY OF TURKEY.

TÜRKİYE BİRLİK PARTİSİ. *See* UNITY PARTY.

TÜRKİYE EMEKÇİ PARTİSİ. *See* WORKERS' PARTY OF TURKEY II.

TÜRKİYE HUZUR PARTİSİ. *See* SERENITY PARTY OF TURKEY.

TÜRKİYE İHTİLALCI İŞÇİ KÖYLÜ PARTİSİ. *See* REVOLUTIONARY WORKERS'-PEASANTS' PARTY OF TURKEY.

TÜRKİYE İLERİ ÜLKÜ PARTİSİ. *See* PROGRESSIVE IDEALS PARTY OF TURKEY.

TÜRKİYE İŞÇİ KÖYLÜ PARTİSİ. *See* WORKERS'-PEASANTS' PARTY OF TURKEY.

TÜRKİYE İŞÇİ PARTİSİ. *See* WORKERS' PARTY OF TURKEY I.

TÜRKİYE İŞÇİ VE ÇİFTÇİ PARTİSİ. *See* WORKERS' AND FARMERS' PARTY OF TURKEY.

TÜRKİYE KARDEŞLİK PARTİSİ. *See* BROTHERHOOD PARTY OF TURKEY.

TÜRKİYE KOMÜNİST PARTİSİ. *See* COMMUNIST PARTY OF TURKEY.

TÜRKİYE KÖYLÜ PARTİSİ. *See* PEASANTS' PARTY OF TURKEY.

TÜRKİYE SOSYALİST EMEKÇİ VE KÖYLÜ PARTİSİ. *See* SOCIALIST WORKERS' AND PEASANTS' PARTY OF TURKEY.

TÜRKİYE SOSYALİST İŞÇİ PARTİSİ. *See* SOCIALIST WORKERS' PARTY OF TURKEY (I) (II) (III).

TÜRKİYE SOSYALİST PARTİSİ. *See* SOCIALIST PARTY OF TURKEY.

TÜRKİYE ULUSAL KADINLAR PARTİSİ. *See* NATIONAL WOMEN'S PARTY OF TURKEY.

TÜRKİYE YÜKSELME PARTİSİ. *See* DEVELOPMENT OF TURKEY PARTY.

UNITED COMMUNIST PARTY OF TURKEY (*Türkiye Birleşik Komünist Partisi*). This party, set up on June 4, 1990, was basically the old Communist Party of Turkey,* which was allowed to register and act legally. It assumed this new name in the hope of attracting all Marxist groups in Turkey. Its leader was Nihat Sargın, a physician, who had been secretary-general of the reconstituted Workers' Party of Turkey.* It shut down on July 16, 1991.

UNITY PARTY (UP) (*Birlik Partisi*). This had been the name of an ephemeral party established in Istanbul in 1957. A more substantial party was set up in October 1966 by a group led by Hasan Tahsin Berkman, a retired general who became the party's first chairman, and Cemal Özbey, a lawyer, the party's secretary-general. The chairmanship later passed to Hüseyin Balan, member of the National Assembly for Ankara, who left the Nation Party* to join the UP; it was then assumed by Mustafa Timisi, member of the National Assembly for Sivas. After November 28, 1971, the party called itself the Unity Party of Turkey (Türkiye Birlik Partisi). When the party's opponents accused it of being financed and supported by the Alevis (Shiites) of Anatolia, the UP's spokesman denied it, arguing that it was a centrist Kemalist party, which in the 1970s had assumed a left-of-center platform of socioeconomic reform. The UP was beset by rifts, which hampered its political activities, particularly at election time. It succeeded reasonably well in the 1969 general elections, obtaining 2.8 percent of the vote and 8 seats in the National Assembly (out of 450). It lost five seats, however, when former members joined the Justice Party* in 1970. This was a factor in the party's sharp decline in the 1973 general elections, when it obtained a mere 1.1 percent of the vote to the National Assembly and only a single seat. Subsequently, the UP had no real significance; it lost even its single seat in the 1977 general election.

UP. *See* UNITY PARTY.

VATAN PARTİSİ. *See* FATHERLAND PARTY.

VIRTUE PARTY (*Fazilet Partisi*). This party, founded in 1983 by Alparslan Demirel, an ex-general, was disbanded in the same year.

WORKERS' AND FARMERS' PARTY OF TURKEY (*Türkiye İşçi ve Çiftçi Partisi*). This party was established in Istanbul on June 17, 1946, by Ethem Ruhi Balkan (party chairman), Salâhattin Yorulmazoğlu, Mehmet Şükrü, and others. Several of the founders were workers and farmers; others were members of the free professions. Later, upon the death of Balkan in 1949, Suavi Raşidoğlu, a lawyer, became the party's chairman. The party began with great hopes, reportedly opening seventeen branches throughout Turkey, but it was unsuccessful in the 1946 general elections, obtaining only about 16,000 votes. In 1948 younger people joined the party, which then held its first general convention. The party ran again in the 1950 general elections in Istanbul and was unsuccessful once again (with a mere 465 votes this time). Two years later, it still claimed a membership of 500 in Istanbul, Eskişehir, and Amasya. The party maintained that it was a class party, aiming to protect the classes it represented—workers and farmers. However, it also claimed that it stood for democracy, parliamentarism, nationalism, and secularism, as well as etatism and a controlled economy.

Another party of the same name was established in February 1961; it disbanded, after a brief life span, in 1968.

WORKERS' AND FARMERS' PARTY OF THE TURKISH REPUBLIC (*Türk Cumhuriyet Amele ve Çiftçi Partisi*). This party was established in Edirne (Adrianople) on September 29, 1930, by Kâzim-bey, a local engineer-architect. Although the party's proposed platform opposed communism and bolshevism (as well as religious fanaticism), the authorities refused to grant it permission to operate, probably because its other tenets included protection of workers and farmers from capitalists, making it illegal under the penal code, because of suspicion of Marxism.

WORKERS' PARTY (İşçi Partisi). This party was founded on March 2, 1992; Dogu Perinçek became its chairman on July 26, 1992. The party's ideology was clearly socialist and opposed to capitalism, imperialism, and the "collaborator" bourgeoisie. The party also declared its intention to end the divide between the "vanguard" and the masses. The party supported a mixed economy and the nationalization of foreign trade, industry, banks, insurance firms, and foreign investments, and it supported the right of the labor unions to strike.

WORKERS' PARTY OF TURKEY I (WPT) (Türkiye İşçi Partisi—TIP). This party, the first of two unrelated parties bearing this name, is sometimes also referred to as the Labor Party of Turkey. It was established in Istanbul on February 13, 1961, and became Turkey's first avowed Marxist party to participate in parliamentary elections legally and continuously. Established by twelve trade union leaders, it was intended at first solely to further the interests of unionized workers. Only after one year, when the founders selected Mehmet Ali Aybar, a Marxist intellectual, as the WPT's chairman, did the party adopt an active leftist stance. Aybar was also largely responsible for organizing WPT branches throughout Turkey and for convening the party's first general convention in 1964. Strengthened by the support of several leftist intellectuals, mostly journalists and writers, such as Çetin Altan, the party received 3 percent of the vote in the 1965 general elections, seating 15 of its candidates in the 450-member National Assembly. The WPT's contribution to the debates of the assembly was chiefly of nuisance value. Its support dwindled, particularly after bitter quarrels within the WPT leadership concerning the 1968 Soviet invasion of Czechoslovakia. Aybar sharply criticized the invasion, while a more doctrinaire group, led by Ms. Behice Boran, a sociologist who was a committed Marxist, defended it just as strongly. Partly because of this very controversy, voter support in the 1969 general elections dropped to 2.7 percent, and only two seats were gained in the National Assembly. Aybar, who was blamed for this setback, resigned from the chairmanship on November 15, 1969. The WPT's leadership was taken over by the more doctrinaire group, headed by Boran. Since one of the decisions of the party's general convention of 1970 was to encourage Kurdish separatism (thus contravening the law), the WPT was brought before the Constitutional Court, which ordered it to disband in June 1971; several of its leaders, including Boran, were sentenced to jail. The WPT was reconstituted following an amnesty on April 30, 1975, with Boran as chairman and Nihat Sargın, a physician, as secretary-general. The party ran without success in the 1977 general elections. The third military regime banned it, along with all other parties, on October 16, 1981.

From 1962 on, the WPT averred that it was socialist, not communist (had it been communist, it would doubtlessly have been disbanded sooner). It argued insistently that its ideology was the only one that could both improve the lot of the Turkish workers and save Turkey from its backward socioeconomic situation. Consistently careful to praise Turkey's democracy and parliamentary regime, the WPT's propaganda nonetheless became more radical. At first, the WPT's platform supported full employment, a more equitable distribution of income, the nationalization of natural resources, and respect for private property. In 1964, however, the WPT's propaganda emphasized wider nationalization through overall planning and state supervision, along with a redistribution of land among the peasants. Its anti-American theme also became more pronounced. Such "Turkish socialism" had not been to the liking of the WPT's more doctrinaire group, led by Boran, which persisted in its view that there is only one socialism, "scientific socialism" (presumably, Marxism-Leninism). In 1975 the reconstituted WPT argued, indeed, that as Turkey was a capitalist state, it did not require a national democratic revolution but a socialist one. The party's program for 1977 maintained that the WPT, a party of and for the working class, would pave the way for socialism.

The WPT's following was never large, probably about 12,000 in its heyday (1965–67). Most of its support appears to have come from intellectual circles in Istanbul and Turkey's more developed Western areas. Although the leadership maintained a delicate balance of intellectuals and workers, the former were offered the key positions in the decision-making process. During its early years, the party did not enjoy the full support of any periodical (with the exception of a bulletin for its own members), although several leftist dailies like *Akşam*, or weeklies, like *Yön*, did offer it qualified support. After reconstitution in 1975, several periodicals, such as *Yürüyüş*, *Ürün*, and *Yurt ve Dünya*, were generally believed to reflect its views; the bimonthly *Çark Başak* served as its official publication.

WORKERS' PARTY OF TURKEY II (*Türkiye Emekçi Partisi*). This party was established on February 12, 1975, by Mihri Belli, an economist and leftist who had already been arrested and sentenced for communist activity. Belli was the party's chairman, and Şadan Ormanlar, an engineer, was its secretary-general. While little is known of the party's activities, one may obtain a good idea of its ideology from the party's platform and the report of the proceedings of its first general convention, which was held in Istanbul in February 1978. Although leaning toward Moscow, the party did not commit itself irrevocably in the Sino-Soviet controversy. Concerning other issues, it saw Turkey as a backward agricultural country whose means of production were privately owned and whose capitalist class cooperated with world imperialism. In order to halt this process, a national democratic revolution was necessary. For complete independence, Turkey's exclusive command of its own military forces was required, as well as nationalization of banks and major industries, securing basic rights, planning economic development, land tenure reform, just taxation, and a foreign policy supporting nations struggling for national liberation. The monthly *Emekçi* and the bimonthly *Bağımsız Türkiye* reflected the party's views.

WORKERS'-PEASANTS' PARTY OF TURKEY (*Türkiye İşçi Köylü Partisi*). This party was organized in the mid-1970s and was officially formed, in Ankara, on January 28, 1978, under the chairmanship of Doğu Perinçek, an erstwhile assistant at Ankara University's law faculty and a confirmed Marxist who had already edited or managed such leftist journals as *Aydınlık* and *İşçi-Köylü*. The thirty-nine founders of the party had some experience with leftist activity, some of it illegal; several had been tried and found guilty of sedition. They came from all over Turkey, the oldest of them was sixty-four years of age and the two youngest were twenty-three. The following Marxists formed the party's Central Committee: Doğu Perinçek, Gün Zileli, Durmuş Uyanık, Hasan Yalçın, and M. Kemal Çamırkan. The party displayed little activity, although its main views and goals were known. Its platform defined it as the political revolutionary party of Turkey's working class. Its final goal was to create a classless society through a national-democratic revolution, which would eradicate imperialism and feudalism. The party opposed both American and Russian imperialism, striving for liberation of the proletariat of all countries and persecuted peoples everywhere. The party's Marxist views closely resembled those of the Revolutionary Workers'-Peasants' Party of Turkey*; Perinçek was involved in both parties. Both attacked virtually every other leftist group in Turkey but refrained from attacking one another. Consequently, there appears to be a link between the two. The party's views were reflected in the daily *Aydınlık* and the biweekly *Halkın Sesi*.

WPT. *See* WORKERS' PARTY OF TURKEY I.

YALNIZ VATAN İÇİN PARTİSİ. *See* FOR THE FATHERLAND ONLY PARTY.

YENİ DEMOKRAT PARTİ. *See* NEW DEMOCRATIC PARTY.

YENİ DOĞUŞ PARTİSİ. *See* REBIRTH PARTY.

YENİ DÜZEN PARTİSİ. *See* NEW ORDER PARTY.

YENİ KÖYLÜ PARTİSİ. *See* NEW PEASANTS' PARTY.

YENİ PARTİ. *See* NEW PARTY.

YENİ TÜRKİYE PARTİSİ. *See* NEW TURKEY PARTY.

YENİDEN DOĞUS PARTİSİ. *See* PARTY OF REBIRTH.

YEŞİLLER PARTİSİ. *See* GREENS' PARTY.

YÜCE GÖREV PARTİSİ. *See* EMINENT DUTY PARTY.

YURT GÖREV PARTİSİ. *See* DUTY FOR THE FATHERLAND PARTY.

Jacob M. Landau

# YEMEN

The Yemen Republic came into existence in May 1990 as a result of the merger between the two previous Yemens: the Yemen Arab Republic (North Yemen) and the People's Democratic Republic of Yemen (South Yemen). Neither of the two predecessor states had fully functioning party systems (in the Western sense); on the other hand, both of them had organizational structures that had many of the characteristics and performed some of the functions of political parties in Western states. It is, therefore, both necessary and desirable to pay some attention to the predecessor states and to the political systems that obtained in them.

## NORTH YEMEN (YEMEN ARAB REPUBLIC)

Upon the conclusion of World War I, and the departure of the Ottoman forces that had been stationed in the country, Yemen became an independent state, although it took some years before most of the world's countries were willing to recognize its independence officially. The reins of government were in the hands of imams—the religio-political leaders of the Zaydi community, the largest Islamic sect in the new country. The reigning imam was Imam Yahya, who had led the two-decade-long revolt against Ottoman rule prior to the outbreak of World War I. The imam's domestic priorities, as well as his orientation to the world, were severely limited by his very parochial upbringing in the mountain fastnesses of the interior. And, in fact, the political system created by the imam was authoritarian (though in keeping with the political traditions of the Zaydi highlands), highly centralized, and not oriented to participation by others in decision-making processes.

It was, of course, precisely this authoritarianism that led those excluded from participation to demand reforms. While much of the support for reform came from elite elements who had been influential in the past and who had been excluded from power under the system established by the then current elite (the Hamid al-Dins), there were others whose exposure to the outside world and its ideologies and intellectual currents led them to support such contemporary ideas as democracy, popular sovereignty, and mass participation in the making of public policy.

No doubt the major opposition came from those families and clans that had wielded great political influence in the past, including providing imams (e.g., the Wazirs). These members of the traditional elite opposed the monopolization of power by the Hamid al-Din family, especially since it appeared that the family was planning to retain the imamate within its ranks for three generations, a very clear violation of Yemeni politico-religious traditions.

However, despite the deliberate effort made by Imam Yahya to permit as few interventions and influences from the outside world as possible, a policy of complete autarky was clearly not feasible. Even if he could have kept contemporary political ideals (including Arab nationalism) from penetrating Yemen, it was not possible to keep out some of the newer ideas and ideals that were circulating in Islamic circles, particularly those associated with the Muslim Brotherhood.

Even more subversive and alien to the traditionalist orientation of the Hamid al-Dins were those ideas coming from the West: popular sovereignty, democracy, and mass participation in the making of public policy. These ideas had also made their way into the thinking of at least some Yemeni exiles, usually as a result of their exposure to such ideas during a stay abroad. The most important of such "exiles" from Yemen were those young men sent abroad by Imam Yahya in the 1930s to learn more sophisticated military technology and techniques at the hands of the Iraqis—the beginning of a long association with Iraq that extends into the 1990s.

Other elements of the population, however, began to express dissatisfaction with the imam's policies. Foremost among these was probably the younger generation of urban intellectuals who had both the education and the inclination to become involved in the country's domestic (as well as foreign) affairs. In Yemeni parlance, these are known as *shabab* (youth). By the late 1930s, the *shabab* had created a number of organizations whose membership soon included the returning members of the missions sent to Baghdad. The locus of the activities (primarily discussions) of these intellectuals was, however, limited to Sana'a.

In the meantime, the situation in the southern portion of the country was also changing. The southern area of Yemen, located around Ta'izz, is known as the Hujjariyya district: Predominantly agricultural and Shafi'i, its location on the border with British-held Aden (protectorates) exposed its population to rather different economic as well as intellectual influences. If nothing else, the population had access to the newspapers and journals being printed in Aden (and elsewhere in the Arab world), and it was therefore exposed to different ideas than those supported or propagated by the imam.

Other loci of opposition began to develop outside of Yemen itself; the two most important of these were Aden Colony (i.e., the port and major commercial, industrial, and political center of the British presence on the Arabian Peninsula) and Cairo. In Cairo, a number of prominent Yemeni intellectuals discovered a joint interest in bringing political and economic reform to Yemen and were, at the same time, exposed to some other important strains in contemporary Arab and Islamic thought, the most notable of these being those advocated by the Muslim Brotherhood.

Collectively, these opposition elements were involved in the publication of a number of journals, newspapers, and other literary endeavors, as well as in a great variety of clubs and similar organizational frameworks. Eventually, most of these coalesced into the first of the "parties" that modern scholars identify as the major impetus for the political reform of Yemen: the Free Yemeni Movement (FYM).* Organizationally, the FYM may be traced to these scattered groups in Sana'a, Hujjariyya, Aden, and Cairo. Most important, however, from a contemporary political science perspective, is the fact that the FYM deliberately sought to represent and include Zaydis and Shafi'is—the two major religious sects in the country. The desire to include many factions and categories of Yemenis led them similarly to recruit from all regions of the country, as well as from among the rather substantial number of Yemeni exiles, both in the region (in such places as Djibouti and Aden) and outside of it (in such places as Cardiff, Wales, and other cities in Great Britain that had small communities of Yemenis).

In fact, at the outset there was some disagreement concerning the grouping's name; one of its major founders argued for Al-Amr bil Ma'ruf wal Nahi an al-Munkar (from the *Quran*, meaning "those who enjoin Good and forbid Evil"); eventually, the majority were persuaded that Hizb al-Ahrar al-Yamaniyyun (which actually means "Party of Yemeni Liberals," but which has been commonly given as the "Free Yemeni Party" or "Free Yemeni Movement" in English-language literature) was a better choice.

Due to a combination of factors involving both the Yemenis and the British, the Free Yemeni Party (FYP) was by war's end reduced to ineffectiveness. It was replaced by the Grand Yemeni Association (GYA),* which was founded and operated by essentially the same individuals. This time, however, the movement had a constitution as well as a newspaper (*Sawt al-Yaman*), which allowed it to operate on a much larger scale than before.

In terms of their program and goals, the members of the GYA (as well as the FYP) were definitely not radical: In their communications with the Yemeni government, they asked for such things as a cabinet, a consultative assembly, a limitation upon the powers of the sons of the imam, and similar reforms. Occasionally obtaining declarations of support or membership from some members of the Hamid al-Din clan, the GYA eventually succeeded in getting the imam to start a counter-publication, *al-Iman* (The Faith) in order to counter the declarations, announcements, proposals, accusations, and other material appearing in *Sawt al-Yaman*.

Of some importance to the later development of political movements and organizations in Yemen is the rise of Village Associations in southern Yemen (i.e., in the Hujjariyya region). Originally founded as a mechanism by which villagers could exchange information and the news that affected their area (including the availability of jobs in Aden), these associations also raised funds from among their members in order to fund local development projects (since the central government was neither interested nor able to undertake such projects).

Usually a small school was the first priority, although later clinics, roads, and water projects joined the list of priorities.

The GYA, in its efforts to recruit members and expand its influence, tied itself to the development of these village associations and helped to found numerous ones in the Hujjariyya area. It also expanded its influence and support among Yemeni exiles in the Red Sea region (primarily Djibouti and Ethiopia), East Africa, and Sudan, as well as in the cities of Europe and North America. It was estimated in the early 1950s that approximately one million Yemenis were living abroad, which amounted to roughly 20–25 percent of the population. If indeed these exiles could be persuaded to support the GYA, both financially and politically, the GYA could become a potent force for change within Yemen (though presumably not until after the death of Imam Yahya, which many believed was imminent in any event, particularly after a team of American doctors reported on his poor health in 1947).

Meanwhile, within Yemen itself, others were secretly organizing to accomplish some of the same goals as the GYA, and in fact appear to have had a working relationship with that organization: the Reform Association* (or Group) and the Literary Post (al-Barid al-Adabi). Somewhat surprisingly, however, these were joined in their demands for various kinds of reform by the 'ulama (religious scholars) of Sana'a (in 1946), which developed into important allies of the Free Yemenis. Perhaps even more surprising was the support that developed among some prominent tribal leaders from both of the major confederations—the Bakil and the Hashid. The motives involved were often quite varied, involving both the desire to support some progressive reforms and the desire to resist the encroachments on tribal prerogatives, which the imam's policies threatened to restrict. In fact, the support of such prominent tribal leaders as the al-Ahmar of the Hashid was to prove of immense importance to the ability of the republic to survive the efforts of the royalists to overthrow it.

By 1948 a highly varied but extensive network of different political orientations and elements decided to eliminate Imam Yahya and introduce some major reforms into the Yemeni political system. On February 17, he was assassinated and replaced as imam by Abdullah al-Wazir. The circumstances and events, as well as the aftermath, of the assassination are by now well documented; within a few weeks, Yahya's son Ahmad had succeeded in undoing the work of the conspirators, and he established himself as the new imam. Although he had either intimated or directly indicated to the reformers that he sympathized with (at least some of) their aims, once he became imam the relationship between the remaining reformers and Imam Ahmad changed dramatically. Furthermore, the remaining members of the Free Yemeni movement did not wish to risk the lives of their colleagues who had been captured by the imam and placed in Hajja Prison. The result was that, for some years after the attempted coup, there was little activity on the part of the reformers.

Imam Ahmad, though not as narrow, uninformed, and reactionary as his father, was not prepared to relinquish the powers and prerogatives of his office; nor was he prepared to abandon many of his father's policies with respect to the powers of the tribes. His reign, therefore, eventually led to a resurgence of opposition. New organizations surfaced, primarily in Aden: the League of the Sons of the South, which, however, seemed too sympathetic to Imam Ahmad to many Yemenis, and, of greater importance, the Yemeni Union. Imam Ahmad, no doubt to forestall any extensive opposition efforts to dislodge him, announced many measures designed to accommodate the major demands of the reformers—for roads, schools, hospitals, clinics, and so on. The reality, however, was that little changed. The inevitable result of this was that the groups and individuals who favored reforms that went beyond the symbolic statements Ahmad offered to his critics reestablished old links, created new organizations (especially in Aden and Cairo), and once again agitated for significant change. The essential mechanisms remained the same: statements, leaflets, literary endeavors of various sorts (poetry, essays, etc.), manifestos, and so forth. In the early 1950s, however, a new technique was introduced: the radio. The construction of much more modern and powerful radio broadcasting facilities by the Egyptians and others, as well as the widespread availability of low-cost, small (easily concealed) Japanese transistor radios, made it possible to reach a far larger portion of the population, and radio was used to spread the various critiques, analyses, accusations, reform proposals, and the like to a much wider audience. Some indication of the effectiveness of these efforts, of the extent of the disillusionment with Imam Ahmad, and of the perceived need to take direct action to accomplish any change is provided by the fact that it took only about seven years for the next major effort to rid Yemen of the imam and his system (1955). This particular assassination effort failed, however, and the imam was able to reassert his authority. More important, however, it persuaded him that compromise or negotiation with the critics of his rule was useless and dangerous. The gulf between the regime and its critics grew larger, more extensive, and more bitter. Indeed, the past had seen many individuals willing to reach some sort of agreement with the imam; those who adopted this position after 1955 were very few and lacking in influence. On the other hand, there were still many who believed that the imam's son, Muhammad al-Badr, was capable of providing effective leadership, and that he would wholeheartedly support the program of reforms sought by various critics in the political, economic, and social systems.

By the late 1950s, however, the majority of those who sympathized with reform programs were no longer much interested in retaining the imamate; rather, a significant element believed that a revolution was necessary: The imamate itself had to be replaced with an entirely new political system (a republic). The numerous officers, expatriates, disillusioned Zaydi and Shafi'i elements, Muslim Brotherhood reformers, and many others were prepared to support a new effort to change the system. When the imam died (in September 1962) and Muhammad al-Badr took over as imam and king, it was only one week before a revolution broke out. The new imam, however, escaped into the northern areas from which both his grandfather and father had waged their campaigns to regain the imamate for the Hamid al-Din clan. Like his predecessors, he mounted a campaign to restore himself to power, in which goal he was supported by many of the same tribal elements that had assisted both Imams Yahya and Ahmad.

The result was a civil war. On the one side there was the republic, supported by most of the Shafi'i south as well as some important tribal elements in the north (most important of all, the al-Ahmars of the Hashid confederation), collectively known as the "republicans." On the other side there were most of the Zaydi tribal elements of the north, northwest, and east (including the Jawf region), collectively known as the "royalists." Between 1962 and 1967, this conflict drew into it a number of other elements: the Egyptians and the Soviet Union on the side of the republicans; the Saudis and the British on the side of the royalists. The list of those who at one point or another sought to influence the outcome, or whose presence was a factor in the fray, eventually included the United States, Iran, and Jordan, not to mention the ineffective effort made by the United Nations to play a "neutral" role as arbiter and "peace keeper"—the United Nations Yemen Observation Mission (UNYOM)—between the contending parties.

Eventually, the Yemenis themselves settled their differences and reached the now famous "Compromise" that ended the war: A new government that included both republicans and royalists was created, and the country started on the long process of reconstruction, reconciliation, and modernization (of both the economic and political systems). It is important to note that many of the individuals who today play important roles in the Yemeni political system were active participants in these events, and that many of their ideals and programmatic concerns stem from the events and political developments of the post–World War II era. A brief listing of the major political organizations and movements to which these individuals belonged is found below, listed alphabetically; it is in them that one can find the origins of most of today's political parties and organizations:

1. al-Barid al-Adabi (1945) (The Literary Post)

2. Fatat al-Fulayhi (c. 1935) (The Youth of Fulayhi)

3. Hayat al-Nidal (1935–36) (Life Devoted to Struggle)

4. Hizb al-Ahrar al-Yamaniyyin (1944–45) (Free Yemeni Party)

5. al-Ittihad al-Yamani (1952–62) (Yemeni Unity)

6. Jam'iyyat al-Islah (1944) (Reform Association)

7. al-Jam'iyya al-Yamaniyya al-Kubra (1946–48) (Grand Yemeni Association)

8. al-Katiba al-Ula (1938–40) (The First Brigade)

9. Nadi al-Islah (1935) (Reform Club)

10. Shabab al-Amr bil-Ma'ruf wal-Nahi an al-Munkar (1941) (The Youth who Enjoin Good and Forbid Evil).

## SOUTH YEMEN (PEOPLE'S DEMOCRATIC REPUBLIC OF YEMEN)

In the 1940s, when what was to become the People's Democratic Republic of Yemen (PDRY) still consisted of the Crown Colony of Aden and the Aden Protectorates (its hinterland), the differences between the two were inconceivably vast—in terms of income levels, social stratification, ethnic differentiation, and economic development, not to mention political sophistication and development. The rather well-developed economy of the port of Aden, precisely because of its harbor facilities and the trade, manufacturing, and industrial enterprises associated therewith, meant that many different trades and occupations were practiced there. It was probably inevitable that the first associations of a political nature would be founded there as well. Since those who carried out these functions were overwhelmingly Arabs, whether from the protectorates or the southern areas of what was then the Kingdom of Yemen, the first politico-economic organizations encountered, and then founded or joined, by the Yemenis were the rather conservative or moderate ones permitted by the British authorities.

The first semipolitical organizations among the Adenis were the variety of social clubs founded in the years just before World War II; the first of these appears to have been the Arab Reform Club (Nadi al-Islah), founded in 1930. During this period, there were also the Arab Literary Club (Nadi al-Arabi), the Adeni Club (Nadi al-Adani), the Islamic Association* (al-Jam'iyya al-Islamiyya), and the Yemeni Union (al-Ittihad al-Yamani)—all based in Aden. These organizations were founded by and operated for the benefit of old Adeni merchant families, many of whose members played prominent roles in various political organizations between the 1930s and independence (1967), and even thereafter in other Yemeni political institutions, both North and South. Some of the recurring names include Luqman, who published the first newspaper in Aden, *Fatat al-Jazirah* (Youth of the Peninsula), in 1940; al-Makkawi, a prominent businessman who once served as chief minister in Aden; al-Asnaj, who played an important role in South Yemen, and later in North Yemen; Bayoomi, a leader of the South Arabian Federation; and al-Jifri, who founded the South Arabian League.* Somewhat surprisingly, in view of the low opinion held by the Adeni families and the population of the level of sophistication of the residents of the protectorates, even these had some quasi-political groupings. The People's Club (Nadi al-Sha'b) in Lahij, the Nationalist Party (al-Hizb al-Watani) in the Qu'ayti Sultanate, and the Committee for the Unification of the Hadhramaut (Lajnat al-Amal li-Wahdat Hadhramawt) and the Reform Association (Jam'iyyat al-Islah) in the Kathiri Sultanate give some indication of the extent of widespread if fragmented discontent with British policy in the area.

Another among the early political organizations in South Yemen was the Islamic Association, an association of local businessmen and notables who were sympathetic to the policies and programs of the British in Aden. It should be remembered that the Crown Colony of Aden was heavily influenced by and oriented toward India at the time, since for many decades it had been governed by the Bombay Presidency. The ethnic composition of Aden reflected this past: There was a large Indian element, and many Adenis sent their children to India for an education. Furthermore, the economy of the city was also oriented toward India. Its currency for many decades had been the Indian rupee (it was shifted to the East African shilling only in 1951, reflecting changes in the pattern of trade, ethnic composition, and political priorities of Aden). Most of these early organizations were pronouncedly sympathetic to the British, in part because of the much greater political (and economic) freedom that the British authorities permitted in Aden, at least compared to Yemen and the rest of the Red Sea states.

The postwar era brought considerable change to the economy of Aden. Its importance in the Indian Ocean basin increased considerably at the same time as its importance was established as an entrepôt in the Europe–Southeast Asia trade and communications explosion. By the 1950s, Aden became the third busiest port in the world (after New York and Liverpool). There was a massive building and development boom, which drew tens of thousands of Yemenis into the Colony, thereby considerably altering the older ethnic mix.

In the 1950s, the first "modern" political organization was founded: the Aden Association.* Its leaders were members of the established families already enumerated—Luqman, Bayoomi, and Makkawi—whose wealth, education, and control of the media made them Aden's "influentials." The association in fact came into being precisely because many influentials felt that the clubs were too close to the British and insufficiently concerned with the status and prerogatives of the Arab population of the Colony. The association's slogan was "Aden for the Adenis," and it advocated a measure of self-government, leading eventually to independence within the Commonwealth.

Founded at roughly the same time, the South Arabian League (SAL)* had as its primary goal the uniting of the British-dominated principalities of the Protectorates into an independent state.

Both of these organizations, however, despite the fact that they became more militant and determined in pursuit of their goals as a result of the political competition that developed in the Colony, eventually proved to be too conservative and establishment oriented for the next generation of nationalists. In part this was an almost inevitable result of the revolution in (North) Yemen in 1962 and the establishment of a republic more attuned to the various currents of Arab nationalism that were then influential throughout the Arab World (in no small part due to the career of Gamal Abdel Nasser in Egypt).

Other organizations that were part of the political milieu that brought about this political shift among the elites of the Colony (and the rather much smaller equivalent in the Protectorates) included:
• A coalition of SAL members, trade union activists, and other nationalists who,

in 1955, created the United National Front (UNF),* which called for independence from Great Britain and, eventually, for union with (North) Yemen. Those from the SAL, as well as others associated with the People's Socialist Party (PSP),* were upset over the close ties which the SAL had with the sultans and other rulers in the principalities, over the nepotism that developed within it, and over the SAL's decision to participate in the elections for the Adeni Legislative Council. Among its prominent members were Abdullah al-Asnaj and Abdullah Ba-Dhib, the first public Yemeni communist; its secretary-general was Muhammad Nu'man, one of the most famous Free Yemenis. When al-Asnaj formed the Aden Trades Union Congress (ATUC) and the British deported Nu'man, the UNF ceased to function.

• The ATUC was formed in 1956 as a result of the various Adeni trade unions coalescing into a new and rather more nationalist grouping. Under the leadership of Abdullah al-Asnaj, the ATUC developed into a major social and political force in the Colony because of the increasingly nationalist orientation of the (overwhelmingly Yemeni Arab) Adeni labor force.

• The PSP was created in 1962 by the ATUC because of its perceived need to broaden its scope of influence (previously restricted solely to Aden Colony) as a result of the threat of Aden's being included in the Federation of Arab Emirates of the South, a British proposal that would significantly decrease the political power of the labor movement and the influentials of Aden.

• The Organization for the Liberation of the Occupied South (OLOS)* was founded in 1965 by elements of the PSP, the ATUC, the SAL, the small Committee for the Liberation of the Occupied South, and some pro-Nasserite sultans who had defected from the Federation in June 1964—all of whom had concluded that the accommodating and conciliatory policies of the older organizations were no longer an appropriate mechanism for dealing with the British and their unwillingness to accord the population any degree of self-government.

• Last, but eventually the most important of the newer and more nationalist groupings, was the National Front for the Liberation of Occupied South Yemen, usually known as the National Liberation Front (NLF),* founded in 1963. The NLF was unusual in that it, like the SAL, at first drew the majority of its support from the Adeni hinterland (as opposed to OLOS and other organizations which essentially based their appeal only upon Aden). Its intellectual as well as political origins may be found in two sources: (1) an early dispute between two groups in the Hadhramaut that was actually fought out in Indonesia in the 1920s; this dispute was essentially one between the upper classes of traditional Hadhrami society (which included the *Sada*, i.e., the sayyid class that traces its ancestry to the family of Muhammad) and the commoners and (2) to the Movement of Arab Nationalists (MAN),* created in the aftermath of the 1948–49 Arab-Israeli war by a group of Palestinian intellectuals (e.g., George Habash). A branch of the MAN was formed in Aden in 1959; among its members were a number of individuals who later became important in the politics of the PDRY:

Sayf al-Dali', Faysal Abd al-Latif, Qahtan al-Sha'bi, Salim Ruba'i, and Abd al-Fatah Isma'il.

In fact, the NLF was an amalgam of some seven groupings, all of which had met in Sana'a in 1963 to discuss strategy against the British position in southern Arabia (among which was the MAN branch in South Yemen); later the front was joined by three additional organizations. All of the organizations agreed on the necessity of military action in order to accomplish their goals, something many elements of the other groups, including the PSP, would not accept.

The ideology and objectives of the NLF were first spelled out in a document called the National Charter, which was adopted by the NLF at its first congress, held in Ta'izz, North Yemen, in June 1965. At this congress, many of the divisions that were to become important in the evolution of the party after independence first became evident. The major division was between those whose views were heavily influenced by Nasserist and Arab nationalist thought, and who had their origins and experience largely outside South Yemen, and those whose outlook had been radicalized by the experience of the armed struggle against the British, whose origins were in the protectorates, and whose views were increasingly influenced by the Marxist wing of the MAN (and the views and actions of Frantz Fanon, Che Guevara, Mao Zedong, and Vo Nguyen Giap).

These divisions eventually surfaced publicly when, in January 1966, some members of the NLF left to create the Front for the Liberation of Occupied South Yemen (FLOSY),* which was supposed to represent a merger between the OLOS and the NLF, but excluded elements of the SAL. In fact, the "merger" represented an effort by the Egyptians to retain some kind of influence over the course of the campaign against the British presence in southern Arabia. Most of the leadership, meeting at the second congress in June 1966, rejected the merger.

By December 1966 the two wings were reconciled, though only as a temporary measure in order to increase the NLF's influence in the ongoing battle over the future of South Arabia and the inevitable negotiations with the British over who would control the successor government. In fact, the ideological split would continue to plague the party's entire tenure as the dominant political grouping in what eventually became the People's Democratic Republic of Yemen. It is of some interest that the more radical faction (Abd al-Fatah Isma'il and his supporters) were overwhelmingly from North Yemen or the Hadhramawt, whereas the more moderate faction tended to draw its support from the South, especially Lahij and Dathina.

In any event, by the end of 1967, it was clear that the NLF had won the battle for dominance in both Aden and the Protectorates, and so it was that the British turned over the reins of government to the leaders of the NLF in November. At the next congress of the NLF (March 1968), which after independence changed its name to the National Front (NF), the more radical faction succeeded in essentially taking over control of the machinery of the party. It is not until June 1969, however, that it succeeded in taking over the state, in what became known as the "Corrective Movement." In the following years, the more radical faction proceeded to erect the political infrastructure of a communist state; since at the outset it clearly did not have either the cadres or the resources to accomplish its goals, the process was necessarily slow and often resisted (sometimes with a degree of success). This resistance came primarily from elements of the more moderate wing of the NLF, as well as elements of the older groupings which were now necessarily based outside the PDRY, but which continued to receive support from North Yemen or Saudi Arabia. Both of these sought to maintain some leverage over the rather more aggressive and combative PDRY leadership through the provision of a safe haven as well as financial assistance to these forces.

Nevertheless, the NF continued its programs of nationalization; radical social reforms; aggressive foreign intervention in North Yemen, Oman, and the Gulf states; and the complete subordination of political life to party control. In 1975 it merged with two small parties that had been allowed to continue to exist: (1) the People's Democratic Union,* a pro–Soviet Union party that had been founded in 1961 by Abdullah Ba-Dhib, and (2) the Popular Vanguard Party,* led by Anis Hasan Yahya, a Ba'thist party that was independent of and rather more leftist than its namesakes in Syria and Iraq. The new coalition was named the Unified Political Organization of the National Front (UPONF).* Organizationally and ideologically, no significant change occurred when the two parties were integrated into the NF's governing system. In October 1978, the NF's leadership decided that the party was now mature enough, and had the necessary cadres and resources, to rename itself the Yemeni Socialist Party (YSP),* that is, a "vanguard party" carrying out the various responsibilities associated with a party attempting to carry out a political, social, and economic revolution.

Despite the continuing conflicts within its ranks, most clearly evident to the outside world as a result of the brief civil war that broke out in January 1986 when Ali Nasir Muhammad and his allies decided to try to eliminate the more radical elements associated with Abd al-Fatah Isma'il, the party continued in power—under rather more moderate leadership. It was this group, under the leadership of Haydar Abu Bakr al-Attas, that unified the PDRY with North Yemen in 1989–90. And it is this group that has continued to guide the YSP within the unified state.

## CONSTITUTIONAL AND LEGAL FRAMEWORK FOR POLITICAL PARTIES

The legal basis for the operations of political parties in the contemporary Yemen Republic rests on two documents: the Constitution and the Political Parties Law.

The constitution, which is the result of negotiations and discussions between North and South Yemen during the period from 1971 through 1989, but has as its base the constitution of (North) Yemen that was promulgated in 1970, was enacted into its final version by the parliaments of the two predecessor states in 1990 and approved by a popular referendum in the north and south in 1991.

Essentially, the right to participate in political life is found in Part Two, the Basic Rights and Duties of Citizens, Article 26, which guarantees "Every citizen the right to participate in the political, economic, social, and cultural life of the country." This is amplified by Article 39, which says that "citizens may organize themselves along political, professional, or union lines. They have the right to form associations in scientific, cultural, social and national unions in a way that serves the goals of the constitution. . . . The state shall guarantee all freedoms to the political, union, cultural, scientific, and social organizations."

The Political Parties Law (Law Number 66, of 16 October 1991) is divided into seven chapters: (1) Names and Definitions; (2) Foundations, Objectives and General Principles; (3) Procedures for Establishing a Party; (4) Resources and Financial Provisions; (5) Rights and Duties; (6) Penal Provisions; and (7) General and Transitional Provisions (which requires that all political parties adjust their status to the provisions of the Parties Law no later than December 30, 1991, especially with respect to Articles 3 and 10.

Article 3, which refers to Article 39 of the constitution, after reaffirming political pluralism and a party system based on the constitution (which may not be canceled, limited, or restrained), goes on to say that "no party or political organization may misuse this right in contradiction with the national interests and in preserving sovereignty, security, stability, and national cohesion."

Articles 5 through 7 outline the functions of political parties.

Article 8 is an extensive listing of provisions that must be observed by political parties; specifically, that their principles, objectives, programs, and means may not contradict Islamic precepts and values, may not threaten the sovereignty and unity of the country, the republican system of government, or Yemen's "affiliation" with other Arab and Muslim states; that they have a system of regulations and by-laws, that they not be "based upon regional, tribal, sectarian, class, professional, or any other form of discrimination among citizens on the basis of their sex, racial origin, or color"; and that they not be based upon concepts contrary to Islamic law, or claim to represent Islam exclusively, the revolution, or nationalism. Interestingly, the article specifically prohibits parties from establishing military or paramilitary forces (not to mention a prohibition on advocacy or instigation of violence). In view of Yemen's past, it is also interesting that later in the same article (part nine), the law once again specifically prohibits the formation of political parties which "limit membership to any geographic region."

Article 9 details the internal regulations and by-laws of the parties.

Article 10 sets out the specific conditions for membership in any Yemeni political party: (1) one must be a Yemeni national; (2) one must be at least eighteen years old; (3) one must enjoy full political rights; one cannot be under a court order that limits these (presumably as a result of a felony conviction); and (4) one must not belong to the judiciary, police, or military forces, or be assigned to the diplomatic corps outside Yemen.

Chapter 3 creates a Committee for the Affairs of Parties and Political Organizations and outlines the procedures that must be followed in order to found any political party or organization; the committee screens and ensures that applications to found parties and political organizations meet the requirements of the law. Most interesting here is that subsection (b) requires that any party or political organization must have at least 2,500 members from "most of the governorates including Sana'a city."

Chapter 4, Article 17 lists government subsidies, as well as subscriptions, contributions, and investments as sources of party funds. The committee is given the authority to propose to the Council of Ministers the annual total amount of support or subsidy that the state will allocate to the parties and political organizations; this amount is considered a part of the government's budget. Article 19 indicates how this subsidy is allocated and divided.

Last, but also of importance, is Article 31, which says that the "government media has [sic] a duty to enable all parties and political organizations to equally use them to carry their viewpoints to the citizens." This would appear to be the equivalent of the "equal access" regulation that characterizes access to the media of most of the world's democracies. Exactly how and at what times the various parties would obtain access to the media is to be regulated by later legislation.

In general, the new political system and the new regulations on political organizations have produced an extremely active and varied set of new political parties and organizations; indeed, their total number is greater than that found in any other Arab country. Furthermore, the newly open system has resulted in the founding of eighty-eight newspapers, magazines, and other periodicals to express the variety of political ideologies and orientations that have surfaced.

In the period immediately after unity, the new government authorized the existence of forty political parties—parties that would be entitled to receive the electoral subsidy (assuming they qualified) and other benefits under the Political Parties Law. In mid-1992, however, due to the nature of some of the disputes that developed, as well as the threat that Saudi Arabia presented to the fragile new system, the number of authorized parties was halved (to twenty). A number of mergers and amalgamations had already taken place; it was reported that more than thirty mergers and affiliations were agreed to in the last week of March 1992 alone. In order to guarantee that democratic procedures would be adhered to, and that the results of the elections would be accepted by all, the two major governing parties—the People's General Congress (PGC)* and the YSP—proposed a National Pact, which all the parties would sign, guaranteeing their adherence to these general principles, including especially the constitution and a republican, pluralist political system. The first draft was produced by a joint committee of the PGC and the YSP in mid-March 1992; the parties not represented in the government, however, asked for the right to amend various parts of the pact, though evidently not with the purpose of negating its basic purpose. A revised version was submitted to the parties somewhat later, and the parties were asked to approve this version in May.

The three most important parties in terms of influence, numbers, and resources are the PGC, the YSP, and the Yemeni Congregation for Reform.* They, and the Republican Party,* the Nasserite Organization of Yemen,* and the League of the Sons of Yemen* are members of another group, known as The Signatory Parties of the Declaration, which signed a declaration to set the limits of civil debate on the future of the new republic, and committed themselves to refrain from taking extremist positions in an attempt to curry favor or gain votes from disaffected elements and to concentrate their efforts on the establishment of a democratic system.

During 1992 a number of conferences were held to discuss various aspects of the elections, including the National Cohesion Conference, the Solidarity Conference, and the National Conference. In August the government created a Supreme Elections Committee (SEC) to handle the responsibilities of establishing the electoral districts, voter registration, and so on; this body had members from a number of parties as well as two independents. Although the SEC completed the work of creating the districts and had prepared a budget by the fall of 1992, it appeared in November that the elections would be postponed until April 1993, due to some major differences among the parties and their notables, as well as the fact that the months prior to the anticipated date saw a significant increase in the incidence of political violence (some assassinations as well as bomb explosions against officials and residences of party members). Responsibility for these incidents was never clearly determined.

Despite the numerous obstacles that the process of preparation threw in the path of the elections, they were in fact held on April 27, 1993. Although accusations of electoral fraud were made by various individuals and groups, most observers (including foreigners) agreed that the elections were as free of fraud and manipulation as elections in West Europe and North America.

The results, as reported in the Yemeni media, are shown in Table 24. As expected, the YSP received its greatest support in the districts of the former South Yemen, while the PGC did best in the urbanized areas of the former North Yemen. One of the most interesting new features of the Yemeni political landscape was the strong showing of the Yemeni Congregation for Reform, which ran second in ten of the eighteen governates, indicating substantial support for a stronger role for Islam in the political system; on the other hand, its performance should not be overestimated; it did not receive more than 25 percent of the vote in any district, and in many governates it garnered only 10 percent. Another interesting new feature was the strong support for independents, probably reflecting traditional tribal and local ties with candidates rather than widespread opposition to major parties. Of the nearly fifty parties that announced their existence, only twenty-one actually fielded candidates in at least one constituency (these are marked with the symbol [#] in the list of parties).

Following the creation of a government by the three major parties (PGC, YSP, and Yemeni Congregation for Reform [al-Islah]), which produced a seemingly interminable dispute over ministries and personalities, a coalition of opposition parties formed another bloc in the new parliament. This new opposition bloc consisted of members from the following parties: League of the Sons of Yemen,

Table 24
Results of the 1993 Yemeni Elections

| Party | % of vote | Seats | % of seats |
|---|---|---|---|
| People's General Congress | 32 | 122 | 40 |
| Yemeni Socialist Party | 25 | 57 | 18 |
| Reform Party (al-Islah) | 21 | 62 | 21 |
| Independents | 15 | 47 | 15 |
| Ba`th Party<br>Truth Party<br>Corrective Nasserite Organization<br>United Nasserite People's Orgn.<br>Nasserite Democratic Party<br>Disputed or unknown | 6 | 7<br>2<br>1<br>1<br>1<br>1 | 6 |
| TOTALS: | 99 | 301 | 100 |

Notes: Total Number of Candidates: 3,621
Total Candidates after Withdrawals: 2,731
Total Eligible Voters: 5,848,253
Total Registered Voters: 2,687,221
Votes Cast: 2,250,414
Turnout: 84 percent of registered voters.

Gathering of United Yemenis,* Union of Popular Forces,* Truth Party,* and United Nasserist People's Organization.* Moreover, a Bakil Tribal Group also made its appearance, evidently displeased with the inordinate political power that the new arrangements gave to the Hashid Confederation; the former was lead by Sinan Abu Luhum, while the latter was headed by Abdullah al-Ahmar, paramount shaykh of the Hashid.

## Bibliography

Burrowes, Robert. The Yemen Arab Republic. Boulder, Colo.: Westview Press, 1987.
Douglas, J. Leigh. The Free Yemeni Movement 1935–1962. Beirut: American University of Beirut, 1987.
Gavin, R. J. Aden under British Rule 1839–1967. London: C. Hurst, 1975.
Halliday, Fred. Arabia without Sultans. Hammondsworth, England: Penguin Books, 1974.
———. Revolution and Foreign Policy. Cambridge, England: Cambridge University Press, 1990.
Ismael, Tareq Y., and Jacqueline S. Ismael. PDR Yemen. London: Frances Pinter, 1986.
Kazziha, Walid. Revolutionary Transformation in the Arab World. London: Charles Knight, 1975.
Kostiner, Joseph. The Struggle for South Yemen. London: Croom Helm, 1984.
Lackner, Helen. P.D.R. Yemen. London: Ithaca Press, 1985.
Ledger, David. Shifting Sands: The British in South Arabia. N.p.: Peninsula Publishing, 1983.
Little, Tom. South Arabia: Arena of Conflict. London: Pall Mall, 1968.

Page, Steven. *The Soviet Union and the Yemens*. New York: Praeger, 1985.

Pridham, Brian, ed. *Contemporary Yemen: Politics and Historical Background*. London: Croom Helm, 1984.

Stookey, Robert W. *Yemen: The Politics of the Yemen Arab Republic*. Boulder, Colo.: Westview Press, 1978.

———. *South Yemen: A Marxist Republic in Arabia*. Boulder, Colo.: Westview Press, 1982.

Trevaskis, Kennedy. *Shades of Amber*. London: Hutchinson, 1968.

Wenner, Manfred. *Modern Yemen 1918–1966*. Baltimore: Johns Hopkins Press, 1968.

———. "The People's Republic of South Yemen." In *Government and Politics of the Contemporary Middle East*, edited by Tareq Y. Ismael. Homewood, Ill.: Dorsey Press, 1970.

*Yemen Times* (Sana'a). Issues of April and May 1993.

## Political Parties

ADEN ASSOCIATION (*Al-Jam'iyya al-Adaniyya*). This party was established in the 1950s in Aden. Its leaders were members of the established families of Aden influentials. The association came into being precisely because many influentials felt that the clubs were insufficiently concerned with the status and prerogatives of the Arab population of the Colony. The association's slogan was "Aden for the Adenis," and it advocated a measure of self-government for the population, leading eventually to independence within the Commonwealth.

ARAB SOCIALIST BA'TH PARTY (*Hizb al-Ba'th al-'Arabi al-Ishtiraki*). This organization was founded in Aden in the 1950s. In Yemen, as elsewhere, it split into Syrian and Iraqi factions. Its leader has been Mujahid Abu Shawarib; its organ is *Al-Jamahir*. Like its counterparts in other countries, it opposed foreign influences and called for the establishment of a new economic order and an end to exploitation. See also chapters on Iraq, Jordan, Lebanon, and Syria.

CHARITY ASSOCIATION. *See* REFORM ASSOCIATION.

COMMUNIST PARTY. *See* PEOPLE'S DEMOCRATIC UNION.

CONSTITUTIONAL LIBERAL PARTY (*Hizb al-Ahrar al-Dusturi*). This modern descendant of the Free Yemeni Party of the 1940s has had a membership of about 10,000. Its organ is *Sawt al-Yaman*. It reportedly was making an effort to represent Yemen's various minorities (e.g., the Akhdam) in the elections.

CORRECTIVE POPULAR NASSERITE ORGANIZATION (*Al-Tandhim al-Nasiri li-Tashih al-Sha'bi*). This organization was created in 1991 as a result of the merger of (1) the Democratic United Corrective Front (Jabha al-Tashih al-Dimuqrati al-Mutahhida), and (2) the Nasserite Organization of Yemen (Al-Tandhim al-Nasiri fi al-Yaman). Its membership has been estimated at over 100,000, primarily in Sana'a, the Jawf region, Dhamar, Ibb, Aden, and Hadhramawt. It has drawn heavily on the ideas and traditions associated with Gamal Abdel Nasser, as well as the programs and policies of Ibrahim al-Hamdi.

DEMOCRATIC UNITED CORRECTIVE FRONT. *See* CORRECTIVE POP-ULAR NASSERITE ORGANIZATION.

FLOSY. *See* FRONT FOR THE LIBERATION OF SOUTH YEMEN.

FREE YEMENI MOVEMENT. *See* FREE YEMENI PARTY.

FREE YEMENI PARTY (FYP) (*Hizb al-Ahrar al-Yamaniyyun*). Founded by Yemeni exiles during Imam Yahya's reign, this party, also called the Free Yemeni Movement (FYM), has operated primarily in Aden. Organizationally, it may be traced to scattered groups in Sana'a, Hujjariyya, Aden, and Cairo. The FYP sought to represent and include Zaydis and Shafi'is. The desire to include as many factions as possible led to recruitment from all regions of the country, as well as among the other Yemeni exiles, both in the region (in such places as Djibouti, Aden, etc.) and outside of it (in such places as Cardiff, Wales, and other cities of Great Britain that had small communities of Yemenis).

Due to a combination of factors involving both the Yemenis and the British, by war's end the FYP was reduced to ineffectiveness. It was replaced by the Grand Yemeni Association (GYA) (*al-Jama'iyya al-Yamaniyya al-Kubra*),* founded and operated by essentially the same individuals.

FRONT FOR THE LIBERATION OF SOUTH YEMEN (FLOSY) (*Jabhat Tahrir Janub al-Yaman al-Muhtal*). This organization was founded in Aden in the 1960s by some members of the National Liberation Front. Supposedly it represented a merger between the Organization for the Liberation of the Occupied South (OLOS)* and the National Liberation Front (NLF),* but excluding elements of the South Arabian League (SAL).* In fact, the "merger" represented an effort by the Egyptians to retain influence over the campaign against the British in southern Arabia. Most of the leadership rejected the "merger." By December 1966 the two wings were reconciled, although only temporarily. The ideological split plagued the party's entire tenure as the dominant political grouping in what eventually became the People's Democratic Republic of Yemen.

FYM. *See* FREE YEMENI PARTY.

FYP. *See* FREE YEMENI PARTY.

GATHERING OF UNITED YEMENIS (*Al-Tajammu' al-Wahdawi al-Yamani*). Sometimes referred to as the Unitarian Yemeni Congregation (Tajammu' al-Yamaniyyin al-Mutahhidin), this organization appears to draw its support primarily from intellectuals. Established in 1990 in Sana'a, its organ is *al-Tajammu'*, with a circulation of about 12,000 copies per week. Its support is primarily in the south, as well as in Ibb, Amran, and Zabid, and it is headed by 'Umar al-Jawi. The party opposes tribalism and favors popular election of cabinet ministers, the Presidential Council, and judges. It also rejects a recently concluded border treaty with Oman and opposes border negotiations with Saudi Arabia.

GRAND YEMENI ASSOCIATION (GYA) (*Al-Jam'iyya al-Yamaniyya al-Kubra*). This is one of the many anti-Imamic organizations created in Aden in the 1950s. It replaced (and retained the same leadership as) the Free Yemeni Party,* which had been reduced to ineffectiveness. The new organization adopted a constitution and published a newspaper (*Sawt al-Yaman*), which allowed it to operate on a much larger scale than the old organization.

In terms of program and goals, the GYA (as well as the FYP) was definitely not radical: in its communications with the government it asked for such things as a cabinet, a consultative assembly, limits upon the powers of the sons of the imam, and similar reforms. Occasionally obtaining declarations of support or membership from some members of the Hamid al-Din clan, the GYA eventually succeeded in getting the imam to start a counterpublication, *al-Iman* (the Faith) in order to counter the declarations, announcements, proposals, accusations, and other material appearing in *Sawt al-Yaman*.

GYA. *See* GRAND YEMENI ASSOCIATION.

HARAKAT AL-QAWMIYYIN AL-'ARAB. *See* MOVEMENT OF ARAB NATIONALISTS.

HIZB AL-AHRAR AL-DUSTURI. *See* CONSTITUTIONAL LIBERALS PARTY.

HIZB AL-AHRAR AL-YAMANIYYUN. *See* FREE YEMENI PARTY.

HIZB AL-'AMAL AL-YAMANI. *See* NATIONAL DEMOCRATIC FRONT.

HIZB AL-BA'TH AL-'ARABI AL-ISHTIRAKI. *See* ARAB SOCIALIST BA'TH PARTY.

AL-HIZB AL-DIMUQRATI AL-THAWRI AL-YAMANI. *See* NATIONAL DEMOCRATIC FRONT.

HIZB AL-HAQQ. *See* TRUTH PARTY.

AL-HIZB AL-ISHTIRAKI AL-YAMANI. *See* YEMENI SOCIALIST PARTY.

HIZB IBNA' AL-YAMAN. *See* LEAGUE OF THE SONS OF YEMEN.

HIZB AL-JABHA AL-TAHRIR. *See* LIBERATION FRONT PARTY.

AL-HIZB AL-JUMHURI. *See* REPUBLICAN PARTY.

HIZB AL-MINBAR AL-YAMANI AL-HURR. *See* UNION OF POPULAR FORCES.

AL-HIZB AL-NASIRI AL-DIMUQRATI. *See* NASSERITE DEMOCRATIC PARTY.

HIZB AL-RABITA AL-SHA'BIYYA AL-YAMANIYYA. *See* YEMENI PEOPLE'S LEAGUE PARTY.

HIZB AL-SHA'B AL-ISHTIRAKI. *See* PEOPLE'S SOCIALIST PARTY.

HIZB AL-TAJAMMU' AL-WAHDAWI AL-YAMANI. *See* GATHERING OF UNITED YEMENIS.

HIZB AL-TAJAMMU' AL-WATANI AL-YAMANI. *See* PEOPLE'S GENERAL CONGRESS.

HIZB AL-TALI'AH AL-SHA'BIYYA. *See* POPULAR VANGUARD PARTY.

THE ISLAMIC ASSOCIATION (*Al-Jam'iyya al-Islamiyya*). Among the early political organizations in South Yemen, this was an association of local businessmen and notables who were sympathetic to the policies and programs of the British in Aden.

ITTIHAD AL-QUWA AL-SHA'BIYYA AL-YAMANIYYA. *See* UNION OF POPULAR YEMENI FORCES.

ITTIHAD AL-SHA'BI AL-DIMUQRATI. *See* PEOPLE'S DEMOCRATIC UNION.

ITTIHAD QUWWAT AL-SHA'B. *See* UNION OF POPULAR FORCES.

JABHA AL-ISLAH AL-YAFA'IYYA. *See* NATIONAL FRONT.

AL-JABHA AL-NASIRIYYA. *See* NATIONAL FRONT FOR THE LIBERATION OF SOUTH YEMEN.

AL-JABHA AL-QAWMIYYA LI-TAHRIR AL-JANUB AL-YAMAN AL-MUHTAL. *See* NATIONAL FRONT FOR THE LIBERATION OF SOUTH YEMEN.

JABHAT TAHRIR JANUB AL-YAMAN AL-MUHTAL. *See* FRONT FOR THE LIBERATION OF OCCUPIED SOUTH YEMEN.

JABHA AL-TASHIH AL-DIMUQRATI AL-MUTAHHIDA. *See* CORRECTIVE POPULAR NASSERITE ORGANIZATION.

AL-JABHA AL-WATANIYYA. *See* NATIONAL FRONT FOR THE LIBERATION OF SOUTH YEMEN.

AL-JABHA AL-WATANIYYA AL-DIMUQRATIYYA. *See* NATIONAL DEMOCRATIC FRONT.

AL-JABHA AL-WATANIYYA AL-MUTAHHIDA. *See* UNITED NATIONAL FRONT.

AL-JAM'IYYA AL-ADANIYYA. *See* THE ADEN ASSOCIATION.

AL-JAM'IYYA AL-YAMANIYYA AL-KUBRA. *See* GRAND YEMENI ASSOCIATION.

JAM'IYYAT AL-ISLAH. *See* THE REFORM ASSOCIATION.

AL-JAM'IYYA AL-ISLAMIYYA. *See* THE ISLAMIC ASSOCIATION.

LABOR PARTY. *See* NATIONAL DEMOCRATIC FRONT.

LEAGUE OF THE SONS OF YEMEN (*Rabitat Ibna' al-Yaman*). Perhaps better known as the League of Yemenis, this party was formally founded in 1948 as the South Arabian League.* It was led most recently by Abd al-Rahman Ali al-Jifri. Its main concern appears to focus on rural affairs: It favored the establishment of a ministry of rural affairs and village reconstruction. It also supported independent oversight of oil revenues and reduction of the period of military service.

LEAGUE OF YEMENIS. *See* LEAGUE OF THE SONS OF YEMEN.

LIBERATION FRONT PARTY (*Hizb al-Jabha al-Tahrir*). The major themes of this party's program included demands for greater public participation in all aspects of government, an end to governmental corruption, greater emphasis on the Shari'a and consultation in public decision making, and reform of the judicial system. The party also proposed amnesty for all Islamic and other political detainees, including exiles; elimination of police posts in the countryside; limits on government expenditures, including the military; independent supervision of radio and television and greater access thereto; and reparations from Great Britain for alleged damages inflicted on South Yemen during the colonial period.

AL-MINBAR. *See* UNION OF POPULAR FORCES.

MOVEMENT OF ARAB NATIONALISTS (*Harakat al-Qawmiyyin al-'Arab*). This organization was created in the aftermath of the 1948–49 Arab-Israeli war by a group of Palestinian intellectuals, including George Habash. A branch was formed in Aden in 1959; among its members were a number of individuals who later became important in the politics of South Yemen, such as Sayf al-Dali', Faysal Abd al-Latif, Qahtan al-Sha'bi, Salim Ruba'i, and Abd al-Fatah Isma'il. (See also the chapters on Jordan, Lebanon, and the Palestinians.)

MUNAZZAMAT AL-AHRAR AL-SIRRIYA LIL-JANUB AL-YAMANI AL-MUHTAL. *See* NATIONAL FRONT FOR THE LIBERATION OF SOUTH YEMEN.

MUNAZZAMAT HIZB AL-BA'TH AL-'ARABI AL-ISHTIRAKI. *See* ARAB SOCIALIST BA'TH PARTY.

MUNAZZAMAT AL-MUQAWMIYYIN AL-YAMANIYYIN. *See* NATIONAL DEMOCRATIC FRONT.

MUNAZZAMAT SHABAB MINTAQAT AL-MAHRA. *See* NATIONAL FRONT FOR THE LIBERATION OF SOUTH YEMEN.

MUNAZZAMAT TAHRIR AL-JANUB AL-MUHTAL. *See* ORGANIZATION FOR THE LIBERATION OF THE OCCUPIED SOUTH.

AL-MUNAZZAMAT AL-THAWRIYYA FI JANUB AL-YAMAN AL-MUHTAL. *See* NATIONAL FRONT FOR THE LIBERATION OF SOUTH YEMEN.

MU'TAMR AL-SHA'B AL-'AM. *See* PEOPLE'S GENERAL CONGRESS.

NASSERITE DEMOCRATIC PARTY (*Al-Hizb al-Nasiri al-Dimuqrati*). This party won a parliamentary seat in the 1993 election. It generally supports the ideas identified with the late Egyptian president, Gamal Abdel Nasser, as elucidated in the 1950s and 1960s. Thus, it considers Yemen to be an integral part of the Arab nation, and it favors the unification of the two Yemens as part of the process of Arab unification. On the other hand, unlike Nasser, the party considers the Shari'a to be one of the sources of legislation, considers Nasserite socialism to be compatible with Islam, and describes Yemen as a part of the Islamic nation.

NASSERITE FRONT. *See* NATIONAL FRONT FOR THE LIBERATION OF SOUTH YEMEN.

NASSERITE ORGANIZATION OF YEMEN. *See* CORRECTIVE POPULAR NASSERITE ORGANIZATION.

NATIONAL DEMOCRATIC FRONT (NDF) *(Al-Jabha al-Wataniyya al-Dimuqratiyya)*. The NDF was organized in North Yemen in 1976 by the leaders of six of the progressive parties: the Organization of Yemeni Resisters, the People's Democratic Union, the Revolutionary Democratic Party of Yemen, the Yemeni Labor Party, the Ba'th (Syrian Wing), and the Ba'th (Iraqi Wing) (see Arab Socialist Ba'th Party).

It was led by Sultan Ahmad Umar and Yahya al-Shami. Many of the participants were members of leftist groupings that had been effectively eliminated from influence and power in 1968; others clearly had ties to the South Yemeni government. The latter came to dominate the organization and undertake activities that promoted the interests of the People's Democratic Republic of Yemen in the 1970s (against the government of Ali Abdullah Salih). The NDF was eliminated as a major threat to the government in 1982 after it suffered major military and diplomatic defeats in its campaign to alter the government of North Yemen. Its leaders were later integrated into the political system as a result of the process of accommodation and integration between the two Yemens that took place in the 1980s.

NATIONAL FRONT. *See* NATIONAL FRONT FOR THE LIBERATION OF SOUTH YEMEN.

NATIONAL FRONT FOR THE LIBERATION OF SOUTH YEMEN *(Al-Jabha al-Qawmiyya li-Tahrir al-Janub al-Yaman al-Muhtal)*. This organization, originally known as the National Liberation Front, was founded in 1963. After independence, its name changed to National Front (NF). It was formed through the agreement of several groupings, two of which adhered later (1975): the Nasserite Front, the Patriotic Front, the Revolutionary Pioneers, the Revolutionary Organization in Occupied South Yemen, the Secret Organization of Freemen of Occupied South Yemen, the Secret Organization of Free Officers and Soldiers, the Tribal Organization, the Yafa'i Reform Movement, and the Youth Organization of the Mahra District.

In 1969, the NF took control of the state in South Yemen in what came to be known as the "Corrective Movement."

NATIONAL YEMENI CONGREGATION *(Al-Tajammu' al-Watani al-Yamani)*. This organization merged with the People's General Congress (PGC)* in August 1991.

NDF. *See* NATIONAL DEMOCRATIC FRONT

NF. *See* NATIONAL FRONT FOR THE LIBERATION OF SOUTH YEMEN.

NLF. *See* NATIONAL FRONT FOR THE LIBERATION OF SOUTH YEMEN.

OLOS. *See* ORGANIZATION FOR THE LIBERATION OF THE OCCUPIED SOUTH.

ORGANIZATION FOR THE LIBERATION OF THE OCCUPIED SOUTH (OLOS) *(Munazzamat Tahrir al-Janub al-Muhtal)*. This organization was founded in 1965 by elements of the People's Socialist Party (PSP),* the Trades Union Congress (TUC), the South Arabian League (SAL),* the small "Committee for the Liberation of the Occupied South," as well as some pro-Nasserite sultans who had defected from the Federation in June 1964—all of whom concluded that the accommodating and conciliatory policies of the older organizations were no longer appropriate mechanisms for dealing with the British.

ORGANIZATION OF YEMENI RESISTERS. *See* NATIONAL DEMOCRATIC FRONT.

PATRIOTIC FRONT. *See* NATIONAL FRONT FOR THE LIBERATION OF SOUTH YEMEN.

PEOPLE'S DEMOCRATIC UNION *(Ittihad al-Sha'bi al-Dimuqrati)*. The Communist Party was founded in 1961 in Aden by Abdullah Ba-Dhib. It was a member of the National Democratic Front.*

PEOPLE'S GENERAL CONGRESS (PGC) *(Mu'tamr al-Sha'b al-'Am)*. The main political organization of North Yemen, the PGC was founded by Ali Abdullah Salih in 1982 as an umbrella political organization to include all existing political interests. Headquartered in Sana'a, its newspaper is *al-Mithaq*. Its membership is estimated at between 300,000 and 500,000, although most of its members are in the former North Yemen. Its primary programmatic emphasis is on economic development.

PEOPLE'S SOCIALIST PARTY (PSP) *(Hizb al-Sha'b al-Ishtiraki)*. The Aden Trades Union Congress created the PSP in 1962 because of its perceived need to broaden its scope of influence (previously restricted solely to Aden Colony) as a result of the threat of Aden being included in the Federation of Arab Emirates of the South. The Federation was a British proposal that would significantly decrease the political power of the labor movement and the influence of Aden.

PGC. *See* PEOPLE'S GENERAL CONGRESS.

POPULAR VANGUARD PARTY *(Hizb al-Tali'ah al-Sha'biyya)*. Led by Anis Hasan Yahya, this Ba'thist party was independent of and more leftist than its namesakes in Syria and Iraq. In 1975, the Popular Vanguard merged with the small People's Democratic Union* (the Communist Party) and the National Front* to form the Unified Political Organization of the National Front (UPONF).*

PSP. *See* PEOPLE'S SOCIALIST PARTY.

THE PULPIT. *See* UNION OF POPULAR FORCES.

RABITAT IBNA' AL-YAMAN. *See* LEAGUE OF THE SONS OF YEMEN.

RABITAT AL-JANUB AL-'ARABI. *See* SOUTH ARABIAN LEAGUE.

REFORM ASSOCIATION (*Jam'iyyat al-Islah*). Sometimes incorrectly translated as the Charity Association, this organization was founded by and operated for the benefit of old Adeni merchant families, many of whose members played prominent roles in various political organizations between the 1930s and independence in 1967, and even thereafter in other Yemeni political institutions, both North and South. Some of the recurring names include Luqman, al-Makkawi, al-Asnaj, Bayoomi, and al-Jifri. Somewhat surprisingly, in view of the low opinion that the Adeni families and population had of the residents of the Protectorates, even these had some quasi-political groupings: The *Nadi al-Sha'b* (People's Club) in Lahij, *al-Hizb al-Watani* (Nationalist Party) in the Qu'ayti Sultanate, as well as the *Lajnat al-Amal li-Wahdat Hadhramawt* (Committee for the Unification of the Hadhramaut) and the *Jam'iyyat al-Ihsan* (Reform Association) in the Kathiri Sultanate give some indication of the extent of widespread if fragmented discontent with British policy in the area.

REPUBLICAN PARTY (*Al-Hizb al-Jumhuri*). Led by Shaykh Sadiq al-Ahmar (son of Shaykh Abdullah al-Ahmar), this party was a member of another group known as *al-Ahzab al-Muwaqi'a 'ala al-'Ilan*, which was made up of parties who signed a declaration created to try to set the limits of civil debate on the future of the new republic. That is, they committed themselves to refraining from taking extremist positions in an attempt to curry favor or to gain votes from disaffected elements, and to concentrating their efforts on the establishment of a democratic system.

REVOLUTIONARY DEMOCRATIC PARTY OF YEMEN. *See* NATIONAL DEMOCRATIC FRONT.

REVOLUTIONARY ORGANIZATION IN THE OCCUPIED SOUTH YEMEN. *See* NATIONAL FRONT FOR THE LIBERATION OF SOUTH YEMEN.

REVOLUTIONARY PIONEERS. *See* NATIONAL FRONT FOR THE LIBERATION OF SOUTH YEMEN.

SAL. *See* SOUTH ARABIAN LEAGUE.

SECRET ORGANIZATION OF FREE OFFICERS AND SOLDIERS. *See* NATIONAL FRONT FOR THE LIBERATION OF SOUTH YEMEN.

SECRET ORGANIZATION OF FREEMEN OF OCCUPIED SOUTH YEMEN. *See* NATIONAL FRONT FOR THE LIBERATION OF SOUTH YEMEN.

SEPTEMBER DEMOCRATIC ORGANIZATION (*al-Tandhim al-Sabtambiri al-Dimuqrati*). The name of this party indicates its full support for the principles of the 1962 revolution against the Imam. Its platform included several unusual provisions, such as support for environmental protection (unique among Yemeni parties) and support for restrictions on migration to urban areas.

SOUTH ARABIAN LEAGUE (SAL) (*Rabitat al-Janub al-'Arabi*). One of the early south Arabian political groupings seeking independence for the Protectorates. (See essay for details. See also League of the Sons of Yemen.)

AL-TAJAMMU' AL-WAHDAWI AL-YAMANI. *See* GATHERING OF UNITED YEMENIS.

AL-TAJAMMU' AL-WATANI AL-YAMANI. *See* YEMENI NATIONALIST GATHERING PARTY.

AL-TAJAMMU' AL-YAMANI LIL-ISLAH. *See* YEMENI CONGREGATION FOR REFORM.

TAJAMMU' AL-YAMANIYYIN AL-MUTAHHIDIN. *See* GATHERING OF UNITED YEMENIS.

AL-TALA'I AL-THAWRIYYA. *See* REVOLUTIONARY PIONEERS.

AL-TANDHIM AL-NASIRI LI-TASHIH AL-SHA'BI. *See* CORRECTIVE POPULAR NASSERITE ORGANIZATION.

AL-TANDHIM AL-NASIRI FI AL-YAMAN. *See* CORRECTIVE POPULAR NASSERITE ORGANIZATION.

AL-TANDHIM AL-SABTAMBIRI AL-DIMUQRATI. *See* SEPTEMBER DEMOCRATIC ORGANIZATION.

AL-TANDHIM AL-SHA'BI AL-WAHDAWI AL-NASIRI. *See* UNITED NASSERITE PEOPLE'S ORGANIZATION.

AL-TANDHIM AL-SIYASI AL-MUWAHHAD: AL-JABHA AL-QAWMIYYA. *See* UNITED POLITICAL ORGANIZATION OF THE NATIONAL FRONT.

TASHKIL AL-QABA'IL. *See* NATIONAL FRONT FOR THE LIBERATION OF SOUTH YEMEN.

AL-TASHKIL AL-SIRRI LIL-DUBAT WA AL-JUNUD AL-AHRAR. *See* NATIONAL FRONT FOR THE LIBERATION OF SOUTH YEMEN.

THE TRIBAL ORGANIZATION. *See* NATIONAL FRONT FOR THE LIBERATION OF SOUTH YEMEN.

THE TRUTH PARTY (*Hizb al-Haqq*). This party was established in 1990, and it merged with The Pulpit* in January 1992 to create the Union of Popular Forces.* Membership was estimated at more than 300,000, concentrated overwhelmingly in such Zaydi strongholds as Sa'ada, the Jawf, and Shibam. This party represents the more conservative elements among the *'ulama*, the muftis, and so on. Its secretary-general is Ahmad Muhammad ibn Ali Shami, who founded the party, and the assistant secretary-general is Ahmad Sharaf al-Din. Programmatically, the party expressed concern regarding the judicial system, including election of judges to a Justice Council, and it favored the adoption of a system of proportional representation in elections and the creation of a bicameral parliament.

UNIFIED POLITICAL ORGANIZATION OF THE NATIONAL FRONT (UPONF) (*Al-Tandhim al-Siyasi al-Muwahhad: al-Jabha al-Qawmiyya*). This organization resulted from the 1975 merger of the People's Democratic Union* (the Communist Party) and the Popular Vanguard Party* with the National Front.* The latter was the dominant element in the new organization, both organizationally and ideologically. Ultimately, the organization was renamed the Yemeni Socialist Party.*

UNION OF PEOPLE'S FORCES. *See* UNION OF POPULAR FORCES.

UNION OF POPULAR FORCES (*Ittihad Quwa al-Sha'b*). This organization (sometimes called the Union of People's Forces), was created in January 1992 as a result of the merger between The Pulpit* and The Truth.* Its secretary-general has been Ibrahim ibn Ali al-Wazir. It is essentially an Islamic-oriented party, but it favors separation of religion and state and a secular state of Yemen in which religious freedom and a modernized version of Islam coexist; that is, it appeals to more progressive Islamic elements as well as some traditionalist elements that supported the al-Wazirs in the past.

UNION OF POPULAR YEMENI FORCES (*Ittihad al-Quwa al-Sha'biyya al-Yamaniyya*). This party was primarily concerned with the judicial system. It emphasized the Shari'a and the principle of consultation and it favored life tenure for judges, abolition of the ministry of Awqaf (endowments or trusts) and the ministry of information, and popular election of provincial governors and local security officials.

UNITARIAN YEMENI CONGREGATION. *See* GATHERING OF UNITED YEMENIS.

UNITED DEMOCRATIC CORRECTIVE FRONT. *See* CORRECTIVE POPULAR NASSERITE ORGANIZATION.

UNITED NASSERIST PEOPLE'S ORGANIZATION (*Al-Tandhim al-Sha'bi al-Wahdawi al-Nasiri*). This organization apparently draws its support from elements of the business community and educated laymen. Its major figures are Ali Sayf Hasan, and Abd al-Ghani Thabit. Its program favors government by a broad national coalition representing all classes, term limits for members of parliament, and government subsidies for basic commodities.

UNITED NATIONAL FRONT (*Al-Jabha al-Wataniyya al-Mutahhida*). This party is a coalition of members of the South Arabian League,* trade union activists, and other nationalists, created in 1955. It called for independence from Great Britain, and eventually, for union with (North) Yemen.

UNITED POLITICAL ORGANIZATION: NATIONAL FRONT. *See* UNIFIED POLITICAL ORGANIZATION OF THE NATIONAL FRONT.

UPONF. *See* UNITED POLITICAL ORGANIZATION OF THE NATIONAL FRONT.

YAFA'I REFORM FRONT. *See* NATIONAL FRONT FOR THE LIBERATION OF SOUTH YEMEN.

YAFA'I REFORM MOVEMENT. *See* NATIONAL FRONT FOR THE LIBERATION OF SOUTH YEMEN.

YCR. *See* YEMENI CONGREGATION FOR REFORM.

YEMENI CONGREGATION FOR REFORM (YCR) (*Al-Tajammu' al-Yamani lil-Islah*). This group represents a "marriage of convenience" of many of the tribal elements of the north, including especially Shaykh Abdullah al-Ahmar, the paramount shaykh of the Hashid Confederation, as well as the more conservative ("fundamentalist") elements of the Zaydi clergy (e.g., Abd al-Majid Zindani). However, the tribal element of the party appeared to be divided into at least two factions (the second one led by Shaykh Naji Abd al-Aziz Shayif). It was clearly one of the three most important parties in the run-up to the elections originally scheduled for late 1992. Its newspaper, Al-Nahdha, is edited by Faris al-Saqqaf, who is the deputy director of the Information Committee of the YCR. Its overwhelming emphasis programmatically is on Islamic issues, with constitutional reform as the first priority.

YEMENI FREE FORUM PARTY. See UNION OF POPULAR FORCES.

YEMENI LABOR PARTY. See NATIONAL DEMOCRATIC FRONT.

YEMENI NATIONALIST GATHERING PARTY (Al-Tajammu' al-Watani al-Yamani). This party was established in 1981 in the PDRY; its membership is estimated at about 10,000, mainly detribalized tribesmen, laborers, and students, including many people exiled from the south in the 1970s.

YEMENI PEOPLE'S LEAGUE PARTY (Hizb al-Rabita al-Sha'biyya al-Yamaniyya). This party claims it was founded in the 1940s. It went public in 1951. Its headquarters are in Sana'a, where it publishes al-Haqq. It has an estimated membership of 10,000, primarily in the south.

YEMENI SOCIALIST PARTY (YSP) (Al-Hizb al-Ishtiraki al-Yamani). This party was established officially in 1978 as the successor organization to the National Front* by Abd al-Fattah Isma'il in the PDRY. It has been one of the members of the National Democratic Front.* It probably represents a majority of the most politicized elements of society, although mostly in the south, and it is clearly the second most important party in the republic. Its secretary-general is Ali Salim al-Bidh, who is the vice president of the Republic. It favors the establishment of an Islamic university as well as new universities in Ta'izz and Hadhramawt, and it supports court reform. (See also the Unified Political Organization of the National Front.)

YOUTH ORGANIZATION OF THE MAHRA DISTRICT (Munadhamat Shabab Mintaqat al-Mahra). This organization was a member of the National Liberation Front.*

YSP. See YEMENI SOCIALIST PARTY.

**Parties About Which No Detailed Information is Available**

Hadhramawt Islamic Cooperative Party (*Al-Hizb al-Islami al-Ta'awuni al-Hadhrami*)

Hadhramawt Reform Association (*Jam'iyyat al-Ihsan al-Hadrami*)

Islamic Labor Party (*Hizb al-'Amal al-Islami*)

National Union Party (*Hizb al-Ittihad al-Watani*)

Organization of the People's Constitutional Conference (*Ha'yat al-Mu'tamr al-Dusturi al-Sha'bi*)

People's Association Party (*Hizb al-Rabitah al Sha'biyyah*)

People's Organization for the Liberation Front (*Al-Tandhim al-Sha'bi li-Jabha al-Tahrir*)

September Party (*Hizb al-Sabtambir*)

Unitarian Congregation for Political Participation (*Al-Tajammu' al-Ittihadi lil-Musharika al-Siyasiyya*)

Yemeni Renaissance Movement (*Harakat al-Nahda al-Yamaniyyah*)

Manfred W. Wenner

# CHRONOLOGY OF MAJOR POLITICAL EVENTS

## ALGERIA

| | |
|---|---|
| 1830 | Conquest of Algeria by France from the Ottoman Empire. |
| May 8, 1945 | End of World War II; violent demonstrations by Algerian nationalists and repression by French authorities presage war of national liberation. |
| November 1, 1954 | National Liberation Front (FLN) launches armed struggle against French rule. |
| October 22, 1956 | Five leaders of the Algerian nationalist movement are arrested after their plane, bound from Rabat to Tunis, was brought down in Algiers by order of the French government. |
| September 19, 1958 | Formation of a provisional government headed by Ferhat Abbas was announced in Cairo. |
| July 3, 1962 | France formally recognizes the independence of Algeria. |
| September 20–29, 1962 | General elections held; new government formed with Ahmed Ben Bella as Prime Minister. |
| September 1963 | Ben Bella elected president. |
| June 19, 1965 | Defense Minister Colonel Houari Boumediene as leader of Revolutionary Council deposes Ben Bella in a bloodless coup. |
| June 27, 1976 | Nationwide referendum on a National Charter preparatory to adopting a new constitution. |
| December 11, 1976 | Boumediene elected president. |
| December 27, 1978 | Boumediene dies. |
| December 26, 1985 | FLN adopts revisions in the charter to promote the private sector and to stress the importance of small business. |
| June 12, 1990 | Islamic Salvation Front (FIS) wins 55 percent of the votes in local elections. |
| June–July 1991 | General strike, declaration of state of siege, cancellation of elections, resignation of the government, and arrest of FIS leaders. |

| December 26, 1991 | First round of rescheduled parliamentary elections; FIS wins 47 percent of the votes; FLN, 23 percent. |
| January 11, 1992 | President Chadli Bendjedid resigns; presidency replaced by High Council of State under military influence; second round of parliamentary elections cancelled. |
| March 4, 1992 | FIS dissolved by government decree. |

**ARABIAN PENINSULA: *See* Kuwait; Oman; Saudi Arabia**

**EGYPT**

| September 9, 1881 | Coup against Khedive perpetrated by military forces under Ahmad 'Urabi. |
| 1882 | British protectorate begins. |
| 1919 | Wafd Party organized; first mass party. |
| 1923 | Constitution promulgated; monarchy inaugurated; Fuad became king. |
| December 1923 | First parliamentary elections, won by Wafd. |
| April 1936 | King Fuad died; Farouk became king. |
| August 26, 1936 | Conclusion of Anglo-Egyptian Treaty, ending British occupation of all Egyptian territory except for the Suez Canal Zone. |
| February 2, 1942 | British intervene to force resignation of anti-British government during World War II. |
| May 14, 1948 | Declaration of martial law; Egyptian government announces its decision to intervene in Palestine against "Zionist terrorist bands." |
| January 26, 1952 | Anti-foreign (especially anti-British) riot in Cairo with loss of sixty lives and extensive property damage, following escalating armed clashes between British troops and Egyptian police in the Canal Zone. |
| July 23–26, 1952 | Military coup by Free Officers; General Muhammad Nagib declares himself commander in chief of the army. King Farouk goes into permanent exile and abdicates in favor of his seven-month-old son. |
| May 18, 1953 | Lieutenant Colonel Gamal Abdel Nasser appointed vice president of the governing Revolutionary Council. |
| October 26, 1954 | Assassination attempt on Nasser during public speech; assailant identified as a member of the Muslim Brotherhood. |
| June 24, 1956 | Nasser elected president, and a new constitution approved in a national plebiscite. |
| July 26, 1956 | Nasser proclaims the nationalization of the Suez Canal. |
| October–November 1956 | War between Egypt and Israel, Great Britain, and France, as Israel invades the Sinai Peninsula and Britain and France invade the Suez Canal Zone. U.S. and Soviet pressure and UN resolution bring war to an end and initiate deployment of UN emergency force to patrol Israeli-Egyptian border. |
| February 1, 1958 | Egypt and Syria unite to form the United Arab Republic. |
| September 28, 1961 | Military coup in Syria dissolves United Arab Republic. |

| | |
|---|---|
| September 26, 1962 | Egyptian involvement in the Yemeni civil war begins. |
| June 6, 1967 | Six Day War with Israel; severe defeat for Egypt. |
| September 28, 1970 | Death of Nasser. |
| October 7, 1970 | Election of Anwar al-Sadat as president. |
| October 6, 1973 | Surprise joint Egyptian-Syrian attack launches war against Israel. |
| November 19, 1977 | Sadat visits Israel; addresses formal session of Knesset, representing major political and psychological breakthrough. |
| March 26, 1979 | Formal conclusion of peace treaty between Israel and Egypt. |
| October 6, 1981 | Assassination of Sadat by Muslim militants. |
| October 7, 1981 | Election of Husni Mubarak as president. |

## IRAN

| | |
|---|---|
| 1905–09 | Constitutional revolution, leading to formation of first political parties, a *majles* (parliament), and a fundamental law. |
| 1921–25 | Emergence of Reza Khan as dominant political figure; assumption of title of shah, inaugurating the Pahlavi dynasty. |
| 1941 | Reza Shah ousted by joint British-Soviet action; his son, Mohammad Reza Shah, becomes Shah. |
| April 28, 1951 | Mohammad Mosaddeq elected prime minister by *Majles*, which also votes to nationalize the Anglo-Iranian Oil Company; law comes into effect May 1. |
| August 11, 1952 | Mosaddeq voted full dictatorial powers for six months. |
| August 16, 1953 | Shah and queen flee to Rome amid political disorder. |
| August 19, 1953 | Mosaddeq overthrown in bloody attacks by royalist forces. |
| August 21, 1953 | Shah returned to throne. |
| November 15, 1961 | Shah launches "White Revolution," including land reform and literacy campaign. |
| November 4, 1964 | Khomeini exiled because of oppositional activities. |
| January 1978 | President Carter in Tehran lauds shah as "an island of stability" in the Middle East. Government attacks Khomeini in the press, triggering riots by religious dissidents. |
| September 1978 | Khomeini calls for overthrow of the shah; martial law imposed in Tehran; hundreds of demonstrators killed by police on Black Friday. |
| October 1978 | Khomeini expelled from Iraqi exile; moves to Paris; oil workers begin strike. |
| November 1978 | Strikes spread to television and central bank; shah forms a military government that arrests eight former high officials of the regime; Khomeini declares that an Islamic Republic will be formed after the Shah's overthrow. |
| December 1978 | Antigovernment demonstrations involve millions; Shahpour Bahtiyar of National Front agrees to form a new cabinet. |
| January 1979 | Shah departs; Carter commits U.S. to support Bahtiyar. |
| February 1, 1979 | Khomeini returns from fifteen-year exile. |

| February 1979 | Khomeini appoints Mehdi Bazargan to lead a provisional government; Bahtiyar goes into hiding; Imperial Guard defeated by revolutionaries; Evin prison stormed and inmates freed; armed forces declare neutrality; Islamic Republican Party formed; U.S. Embassy attacked. |
| April 1979 | Referendum approves establishment of the Islamic Republic. |
| October 1979 | Shah admitted to United States for treatment of cancer. |
| November 4, 1979 | U.S. Embassy seized by radical "students"; more than fifty hostages taken; Bazargan resigns. |
| December 1979 | Islamic Constitution ratified over opposition by Ayatollah Shariatmadari and the National Front; uprising by Shariatmadari supporters in Tabriz. |
| January 1980 | Abol Hassan Bani Sadr elected president. |
| April 1980 | United States severs diplomatic relations and imposes economic sanctions; abortive military effort to rescue embassy hostages. |
| September 1980 | War breaks out between Iraq and Iran. |
| August 20, 1988 | Cease-fire ends Iran-Iraq War. |
| June 4, 1989 | Death of Ayatollah Khomeini. |
| July 3, 1990 | Hashemi Rafsanjani elected president of the Islamic Republic. |

## IRAQ

| 1920 | League of Nations awards Mandate to Great Britain. |
| 1930 | Anglo-Iraqi treaty concluded. |
| 1932 | Independence of Iraq, with Faysal as king. |
| 1933 | Faysal dies; succeeded by his son Ghazi. |
| 1939 | Death of King Ghazi. |
| April 1, 1941 | Rashid 'Ali coup against British influence. |
| July 14, 1958 | Military units, commanded by Colonel 'Abd al-Karim Qasim, overthrow the government, killing the king, the regent, and longtime prime minister Nuri al-Sa'id. |
| February 8, 1963 | Assassination of Qasim in a bloody coup staged by the Ba'th Party. |
| November 18, 1963 | Overthrow of the Ba'th regime by President 'Abd al-Salam 'Arif, with the support of the armed forces. |
| July, 1968 | Successful coup against Arif, bringing Ba'th back to power. |
| July 16, 1979 | Saddam Husayn sworn in as president. |
| September 2, 1980 | Denunciation of Iran-Iraq border agreement by President Saddam Husayn marks beginning of full-scale war between Iran and Iraq. |
| August 20, 1988 | Cease-fire ends the war. |
| August 2, 1990 | Iraq invades Kuwait, initiating a far-reaching crisis in the region. |
| January 17, 1991 | Anti-Iraq coalition of nations led by the United States launches war to eject Iraqi forces from Kuwait, implementing a number of UN Security Council resolutions. |

## ISRAEL

| | |
|---|---|
| November 2, 1917 | Balfour Declaration issued by Great Britain, favoring the establishment of a Jewish National Home in Palestine. |
| April 20, 1920 | League of Nations awards Mandate to Great Britain. |
| November 29, 1947 | UN General Assembly passes Partition Plan for Palestine by a vote of thirty-three to thirteen, with ten abstentions. |
| May 15, 1948 | Formal end of British Mandate. The State of Israel proclaimed, with David Ben-Gurion as prime minister of a provisional government. |
| February 16, 1949 | Chaim Weizmann elected first president of Israel. |
| October 1953 | Ben-Gurion resigns; Moshe Sharett becomes prime minister. |
| July 1955 | Ben-Gurion returned as prime minister. |
| October 29, 1956 | Suez War against Egypt; Israeli troops overrun Sinai Peninsula; British and French troops invade Suez Canal Zone. |
| June 1963 | Ben-Gurion resigns as prime minister for the last time; Levi Eshkol becomes prime minister. |
| June 5, 1967 | Outbreak of six-day war resulting in Israeli conquest of Sinai and the West Bank, including East Jerusalem. |
| March 1969 | Eshkol dies; Golda Meir becomes prime minister. |
| October 6, 1973 | Outbreak of war with Syria and Egypt. |
| June 1974 | Yitzhak Rabin becomes prime minister. |
| May 17, 1977 | The Likud wins the elections, ending domination of Israel's politics by Labor. Menachem Begin becomes prime minister. |
| November 19, 1977 | Egyptian President Anwar al-Sadat visits Israel and delivers address to formal session of Knesset. |
| September 17, 1978 | Camp David agreements reached between Israel and Egypt providing for recession of Sinai to Egypt and establishing procedure for negotiation of self-rule in West Bank and Gaza. |
| March 26, 1979 | Formal conclusion of Israeli-Egyptian peace treaty, including opening of formal diplomatic relations. |
| June 6, 1982 | Israeli invasion of Lebanon. |
| September 1983 | Resignation of Prime Minister Begin in wake of his wife's death and massacre of Palestinians in Lebanon. |
| November 1984 | National Unity government of Likud and Labor formed in wake of elections with rotating prime ministership. Shimon Peres serves as prime minister first, followed by Yitzak Shamir starting in 1986. |
| March–June 1985 | Withdrawal of Israeli forces from Lebanon except for "security zone" in the south. |
| December 9, 1987 | Outbreak of the *Intifada* (uprising) against Israeli rule in Gaza and the West Bank. |
| November 1, 1988 | Parliamentary elections lead to continuation of National Unity government, but with Labor in a subordinate position. |
| Spring 1990 | Labor resigns from the coalition government. |

| October 30, 1991 | Peace talks with Arab governments and Palestinians begin in Madrid, Spain, by joint invitation of American and Soviet governments. |
| June 23, 1992 | Parliamentary elections won by Labor; Yitzhak Rabin becomes prime minister and assumes a more conciliatory position in the peace talks than had the Shamir government. |
| September 13, 1993 | Agreement on principles signed between Israel and the Palestine Liberation Organization (PLO), providing for Israeli withdrawal from Gaza and Jericho, and for Palestinian self-rule. |

## JORDAN

| April 1921 | Separation of territory of Transjordan from Palestine Mandate. |
| March 22; May 25, 1946 | Emirate of Transjordan becomes independent as Kingdom of Transjordan with Abdullah on the throne. |
| April 25, 1950 | Annexation of West Bank to form Kingdom of Jordan. |
| July 20, 1951 | King Abdullah assassinated; Talal becomes king. |
| August 11, 1952 | Parliament removes King Talal on grounds of ill health and proclaims his son, Crown Prince Husayn, as the new king. |
| May 2, 1953 | King Husayn sworn in on his eighteenth birthday. |
| April 17, 1957 | Declaration of martial law; political parties banned. |
| September 1970 | All-out conflict between Jordanian army and Palestine Liberation Organization (PLO) forces in Amman with many casualties and ultimate expulsion of the PLO from Jordan; Syria threatens to intervene, but withdraws its forces at the last minute. |
| July 1988 | Jordan relinquishes claim to sovereignty over the West Bank. |
| November 1989 | Parliamentary election signals political liberalization; parties legalized; Muslim Brotherhood gains the largest number of seats. |
| June 9, 1991 | Formal announcement of new "national charter." |
| September 1993 | Agreement with Israel on principles for negotiation of peace, in wake of Israel-PLO agreement. |
| November 1993 | Parliamentary elections weaken Islamists somewhat and bolster the monarchy. |

## KUWAIT

| June 19, 1961 | 1899 agreement for British protection canceled; Kuwait assumes full independence. |
| June 25, 1961 | Iraqi claims of sovereignty over Kuwait trigger return of British troop contingent. |
| October 1963 | Iraq formally recognizes Kuwaiti independence. |
| August 1976 | Dissolution of elected National Assembly. |
| November 1984 | Full agreement on frontiers between Iraq and Kuwait. |
| July 1986 | Dissolution of elected National Assembly. |
| August 2, 1990 | Invasion and occupation by Iraqi troops. |

| | |
|---|---|
| January–March 1991 | Air and land attack by U.S.-led coalition ejects Iraqi forces and restores Kuwaiti government. |
| 1992 | Election of new National Assembly. |

# LEBANON

| | |
|---|---|
| August 31, 1920 | League of Nations awards Mandate to France. |
| 1943 | Conclusion of "National Pact" providing for sectarian division of political offices. |
| December 1945 | Lebanon becomes independent. |
| 1952 | Kamil Sham'un elected President. |
| May, 1958 | Civil war develops as Sham'un tries to amend constitution to allow for reelection of president; Tripoli is reported in a state of siege, opposition forces barricade Beirut streets, the road to Damascus is barred, and armed men are intercepted as they enter Lebanon from Syria. |
| July 1958 | U.S. marines land in Lebanon to prevent feared takeover by Nasserist forces in the wake of the Iraqi revolution. Fuad Shihab, Lebanese army commander, elected president. |
| 1970 | Sulayman Franjiyya elected president. |
| April 13, 1975 | Violent clash between the Phalanges and Palestinian Fatah, marking the beginning of civil war. |
| April 1976 | Syrian troops enter Lebanon |
| May 1976 | Elias Sarkis elected president. |
| October 21, 1976 | Deployment of an "all-Arab force" dominated by the Syrian army; declaration of a cease-fire. |
| March 16, 1977 | Assassination of Druze leader Kamal Jumblat and renewed outbreak of civil war. |
| March–June 1978 | Israeli incursion into southern Lebanon; formation of Israeli-controlled "security zone" in southern Lebanon. |
| June 6, 1982 | Massive Israeli invasion. |
| August 21, 1982 | Yasir Arafat and Fatah forced to evacuate their forces from Beirut and give up their base of operations. |
| August 23, 1982 | Bashir Jamayyil elected president of Lebanon. |
| September 14, 1982 | Bashir Jamayyil assassinated. |
| September 24, 1982 | Amin Jamayyil elected president. |
| June 1985 | Withdrawal of Israeli troops except for "security zone" in southern Lebanon. |
| February 1986 | Large Syrian force takes full control of West Beirut. |
| June 1, 1987 | Assassination of prime minister and prominent Sunni leader Rashid Karami. |
| March 20, 1988 | Election of pro-Syrian Elias Hrawi as president. |
| September 22, 1989 | President appoints six-man military government. |
| June 9, 1990 | End of civil war with Beirut under control of the Syrian army. |
| August 1992 | National Assembly elections held; Christians boycott. |

## LIBYA

| | |
|---|---|
| March 8, 1951 | Newly appointed government of Tripolitania takes over authority from the British administration. |
| October 7, 1951 | Constituent Assembly formally approves the constitution for an independent, federal kingdom under Amir Idris al-Sanusi. |
| December 24, 1951 | Declaration of independence under King Idris. |
| September 1, 1969 | Military coup and declaration of a republic. |
| December 1969 | U.S. and British withdrawal from military bases. |
| January 1970 | Qadhafi becomes prime minister. |
| March 3, 1977 | Mass Republic (*Jamahariya*) declared by People's Congress. |

## MOROCCO

| | |
|---|---|
| November 1955 | Muhammad V declared Sultan and returned to Morocco; French government reaffirms its commitment to Moroccan independence. |
| April 4, 1956 | Spanish protectorate canceled. |
| August 1957 | Muhammad becomes king. |
| February 1961 | Death of King Muhammad; Hassan II proclaimed king. |
| July 1971 | Unsuccessful military coup. |
| August 1972 | Unsuccessful military coup. |

## OMAN

| | |
|---|---|
| July 1970 | Son of Sultan Saud Ibn Taymur takes control of the country after coup against his father. |
| 1971 | Oman becomes independent. |
| October 1981 | A consultative assembly is established. |

## PALESTINIANS

| | |
|---|---|
| May 28, 1964 | Creation of Palestine Liberation Organization (PLO) announced at meeting of Palestine National Congress (PNC) in Jerusalem. |
| July 10, 1968 | PNC dismisses Chairman Ahmad Shuqayri. |
| February 1969 | Yasir Arafat becomes chairman of the PLO. |
| September 1970 | Heavy fighting between PLO forces and Jordanian Army results in expulsion of PLO from Jordan. |
| 1974 | Acceptance of "two-state" formula; Arab states recognize the PLO as "sole, legitimate representative" of the Palestinians; PLO granted observer status in UN; Arafat addresses General Assembly. |
| July 1982 | Expulsion of PLO forces from Beirut; Syrian President Hafiz al-Asad refuses to allow PLO to relocate to Damascus. |
| December 1983 | PLO forces ejected from Tripoli, Lebanon, by dissident anti-Arafat group backed by Syria. |

| December 9, 1987 | Beginning of *Intifada* (uprising) against Israeli authority in Gaza and the West Bank. |
| November 15, 1988 | Arafat renounces terrorism and implicitly recognizes right of Israel to exist as a state. PNC declares the "State of Palestine" in West Bank and Gaza, and accepts UN Security Council Resolution 242. |
| October 30, 1991 | Opening of peace negotiations between Arabs and Israelis under U.S.-Soviet auspices, with Palestinians included in a joint delegation with Jordanian representatives. |
| September 13, 1993 | Agreement on principles signed between Israel and the Palestine Liberation Organization, providing for Israeli withdrawal from Gaza and Jericho, and Palestinian self-rule. |

## SAUDI ARABIA

| 1924 | Ibn Sa'ud conquers the western (Hijaz) region, expelling Sherif Husayn from the holy places in Mecca. |
| January 1926 | Ibn Sa'ud becomes king. |
| September 18, 1932 | Unification of the Kingdom of Saudi Arabia. |
| November 11, 1953 | Death of King Ibn Sa'ud. Sa'ud becomes king. |
| November 2, 1964 | Faysal becomes king. |
| October 1973 | In wake of Arab-Israel war, Saudi government announces embargo of oil exports to United States and Netherlands and sharp price increase, a move known as the price revolution. |
| March 1975 | Faysal assassinated; Khalid becomes king. |
| 1979 | Nationalization of the oil company. |
| November 20, 1979 | Seizure of the Grand Mosque in Mecca by militant religious group. |
| June 1982 | Death of Khalid; Fahd becomes king. |
| July 31, 1987 | Saudi security forces kill over 400 demonstrators during religious pilgrimage when Iranian pilgrims stage political demonstration in front of Grand Mosque in Mecca. |
| August 1990–March 1991 | Saudi Arabia hosts massive armed force led by U.S. to free Kuwait from Iraqi control; withdrawal of Saudi financial support from PLO because of PLO support of Iraq. |

## SUDAN

| January 1, 1956 | Sudan becomes formally independent. |
| June 1956 | General elections. |
| November 17, 1958 | Military coup under General Ibrahim 'Abboud; political parties banned. |
| May 25, 1969 | Military coup under Ja'far al-Nimeiri. |
| September 1971 | Nimeiri elected president. |
| April 1972 | New constitution adopted. |
| April 6, 1985 | Military coup. |
| April 1986 | First free elections held since 1968. |
| June 30, 1989 | Coup led by Brigadier Umar Hassan Ahmad Bashir overthrows al-Mahdi government and installs an Islamist regime. |

## SYRIA

| | |
|---|---|
| July 25, 1920 | League of Nations awards Mandate to France. |
| April 17, 1946 | Syria becomes independent. |
| December 18, 1947 | Communist Party outlawed in protest against Soviet UN vote in favor of Partition Resolution on Palestine. |
| March 30, 1949 | Bloodless coup led by Brigadier General Husni Zaim. |
| August 14, 1949 | Military coup brings Colonel Sami Hinnawi to power; Zaim executed. |
| November 29, 1951 | Coup led by Colonel Adib Shishakli. |
| February 1, 1958 | Syria and Egypt unite to form the United Arab Republic (UAR). |
| February 4, 1958 | Nasser announces the decision to dissolve all political parties in the Syrian region of the UAR. |
| September 28, 1961 | Military coup dissolves union with Egypt. |
| March 28, 1962 | Military coup ousts the government of President al-Qudsi and Prime Minister al-Dawalibi. |
| March 8, 1963 | Military coup leads to emergence of Ba'th Party as dominant force. |
| April 25, 1964 | New constitution proclaims Syria as a socialist democratic people's republic. |
| February 23–25, 1966 | Military coup; Atassi named head of state. |
| November 13, 1970 | Coup led by Defense Minister Hafiz al-Asad removes Atasi and General Salah al-Jadid from power. |
| March 1, 1971 | Asad elected president. |
| February 1982 | Suppression of uprising of Muslim Brotherhood in city of Hama with heavy loss of life. |

## TUNISIA

| | |
|---|---|
| 1881 | Beginning of French Protectorate. |
| March 20, 1956 | Agreement to make Tunisia independent. |
| July 25, 1957 | Tunisia declared a republic; Bourguiba elected president. |
| July 1, 1968 | Adoption of a new constitution. |
| November 7, 1987 | Eighty-four-year-old Bourguiba removed from presidency. Prime Minister Ben-Ali assumes the position of chairman of Dusturian Socialist Party. |

## TURKEY

| | |
|---|---|
| October 29, 1923 | Formal declaration of the Republic and election of Mustafa Kemal (Atatürk) as president. |
| June 3, 1925 | Law for the Restoration of Order, outlawing opposition parties. |
| August 12–December 1930 | Formation and dissolution of the Free Party, intended as opposition to Republican People's Party. |
| November 10, 1938 | Death of President Mustafa Kemal Atatürk; election of Ismet Inönü as president. |

| | |
|---|---|
| May 19, 1945 | President Inönü announces policy of allowing opposition parties to form. |
| May 26, 1947 | The governing council and the Parliamentary group of the Republican People's Party adopt a resolution favoring permission for religious instruction in schools, banned since 1923. |
| May 14, 1950 | Democrat Party wins election, ending the twenty-seven-year reign of the Republican People's Party. |
| May 2, 1954 | Democrat Party wins its second election. |
| October 27, 1957 | Democrat Party wins its third election, but with a reduced plurality and with sharply increased representation for the opposition Republican People's Party. |
| September 11, 1959 | Members of the European Economic Community (EEC) were reported to have approved unanimously Turkey's application for associate status. |
| May 27, 1960 | The Democrat Party government of Prime Minister Adnan Menderes is ousted by a military coup after a crescendo of protest in the streets of the major cities. The Committee of National Unity, a body consisting of thirty-eight mostly senior military commanders headed by General Cemal Gürsel, assumes control of the government. |
| July 1961 | New, more liberal constitution passed by thin margin in popular referendum. |
| October 26, 1961 | General Gürsel, head of the military junta, elected president of the republic by newly elected Parliament. |
| March 12, 1971 | Military commanders force resignation of government led by Süleyman Demirel; government of non-partisan technocrats formed; Constitution amended to provide more power to executive branch of government. |
| October 14, 1973 | Parliamentary election won by Republican People's Party; Bülent Ecevit becomes prime minister. |
| 1974–1979 | Alternation in power of personal rivals Ecevit and Justice Party leader Demirel amid rising tide of political violence of right- and left-wing extremists. |
| January 24, 1980 | Adoption of far-reaching economic reform plan conceived by Deputy Prime Minister Turgut Özal. |
| September 12, 1980 | Military coup led by Chief of General Staff Kenan Evren; closure of all political parties, including Republican People's Party. |
| November 8, 1982 | Election of Evren as president and adoption of new constitution in popular referendum. |
| November 6, 1983 | Parliamentary elections held under carefully controlled conditions; surprise victory of Motherland Party, led by former Deputy Prime Minister Turgut Özal. |
| November 29, 1987 | Second electoral victory of Motherland Party. |
| October 31, 1989 | Özal elected president of the Republic. |
| October 20, 1991 | Parliamentary election reduces Motherland Party to third rank; coalition government formed, headed by center-right True Path Party leader Süleyman Demirel and supported by center-left Social Democratic Populist Party led by Erdal Inönü. |

| April 17, 1993 | Death of President Özal. |
| May 16, 1993 | Election of Süleyman Demirel as president. |
| June 1993 | Appointment of Mrs. Tansu Çiller as prime minister. |

## YEMEN

| September 30, 1947 | Yemen formally admitted to the UN. |
| February 1, 1948 | Imam Yahya Hamid al-Din killed; his son, Abdullah ibn Ahmad al-Wazir, succeeds him as imam. |
| March 8, 1958 | Federation agreement signed with United Arab Republic. |
| September 19, 1962 | Imam Ahmad dies; Crown Prince Muhammad al-Badr succeeds him. |
| September 26, 1962 | Military coup led by Brigadier General Abdallah al-Salal leads to establishment of republic and outbreak of civil war between royalists loyal to the imam and republicans. Ultimately, Egypt becomes involved in support of the republicans, while Saudi Arabia supports the loyalists. |
| November 1967 | Former British Aden Colony becomes independent as Republic of South Yemen. |
| June 1969 | National Front takes over the state of South Yemen in "corrective movement"; South Yemen becomes the People's Democratic Republic of Yemen (PDRY). |
| 1989/1990 | Unification of the Yemen Arab Republic and PDRY (South Yemen). |
| April 1993 | Free competitive parliamentary elections held. |

# GENEALOGY OF PARTIES*

## ALGERIA

ETOILE NORD-AFRICAINE (ENA), 1926–37
  founded and led by Messali Hadj
  renamed in 1933 the GLORIEUSE ETOILE NORD-AFRICAINE
  renamed in 1935 the UNION NATIONAL DES MUSULMANS NORD-AFRICAINES
  readopted original name ENA in 1935
  other leading figures: Amar Imache, Belkacem Redjeff, Ahmed Yahiaoui, Amar Khider
  succeeded in 1937 by the PARTI DU PEUPLE ALGERIEN

PARTI COMMUNISTE ALGERIEN (PCA), 1936–66
  originally known as the "Algerian Section" of the PARTI COMMUNISTE FRANCAIS (PCF), 1920–36
  principal Muslim figures: Amar Ouzegane, Bachir Hadj Ali, Abdelhamid Benzine, Sadek Hadjeres
  renamed in 1966 the PARTI DE L'AVANT-GARDE SOCIALISTE (PAGS)

PARTI DU PEUPLE ALGERIEN–MOUVEMENT POUR LA TRIOMPHE DES LIBERTES DEMOCRATIQUES (PPA–MTLD), 1937–54
  founded and led by Messali Hadj
  succeeded the ENA in 1937
  known exclusively as the PPA until 1946
  MTLD created in 1946 as the legal wing of the PPA
  clandestine Organisation Spéciale (OS) created in 1947
  other leading figures include Lamine Debaghine, Asselah Hocine, Ahmed Bouda, Tayeb Boulahrouf, Chawki Mostefaï, Mohammed Belouizdad, Hocine Aït Ahmed (OS), Ahmed Ben Bella (OS), Hocine Lahouel, Benyoucef Ben Khedda
  PPA–MTLD split in 1954: some members formed or joined the FRONT DE LIBERATION NATIONALE (FLN); others the MOUVEMENT NATIONAL ALGERIEN (MNA)

UNION POPULAIRE ALGERIEN (UPA), 1938–40

---

*All entries in this genealogy are listed chronologically rather than alphabetically.

founded and led by Ferhat Abbas
predecessor of AMIS DU MANIFESTE ALGERIEN (AML)

AMIS DU MANIFESTE ALGERIEN ET DE LA LIBERTE (AML), 1943–45
founded and led by Ferhat Abbas
joined by many members of the PPA
succeeded by the UNION DEMOCRATIQUE DU MANIFESTE ALGERIEN (UDMA)

UNION DEMOCRATIQUE DU MANIFESTE ALGERIEN (UDMA), 1946–54
founded and led by Ferhat Abbas
other leading figures: Ahmed Francis, Ahmed Boumendjel
members rallied to the FLN in 1955–56

FRONT DE LIBERATION NATIONALE (FLN), 1954–present
formed by activists from the PPA–MTLD's clandestine wing OS
joined in 1955–56 by members of the MTLD Central Committee, UDMA, and some from the PCA
notable figures during war of independence include Mohamed Boudiaf, Didouche Mourad, Mostefa Ben Boulaïd, Larbi Ben M'hidi, Rabah Bitat, Krim Belkacem, Mohamed Khider, Ahmed Ben Bella, Hocine Aït Ahmed, Abane Ramdane, Abdelhafid Boussouf, Lakhdar Ben Tobbal, Amirouche Aït Hamouda, Ferhat Abbas, Benyoucef Ben Khedda, and Houari Boumediene.
ruling party from 1962 onward and sole legal party until 1989
following independence led successively or concurrently by Mohammed Khider, Ahmed Ben Bella, Cherif Belkacem, Kaïd Ahmed, Houari Boumediene, Mohamed Salah Yahiaoui, Chadli Bendjedid, Mohamed Cherif Messaadia, Abdelhamid Mehri

MOUVEMENT NATIONAL ALGERIEN (MNA), 1954–62
formed by Messali Hadj and composed of members of the PPA–MTLD
other leading figures: Mohamed Memchaoui, Moulay Merbah, Ahmed Mezerna, Abdallah Filali

PARTI DE LA REVOLUTION SOCIALISTE (PRS), 1962–early 1980s
founded and led by FLN founding figure Mohamed Boudiaf
initially composed of dissident members of the FLN

FRONT DES FORCES SOCIALISTES (FFS), 1963–present
founded and led by FLN founding figure Hocine Aït Ahmed
initially composed of dissident members of the FLN
supported almost exclusively by Kabyle Berbers

ORGANISATION DE LA RESISTANCE POPULAIRE (ORP), 1965–67
formed by Mohammed Harbi, Hocine Zahouane, and other leftists in the FLN opposed to the 1965 coup d'état

PARTI DE L'AVANT-GARDE SOCIALISTE (PAGS), 1966–present
name change of the PCA
leading figures: Bachir Hadj Ali, Sadek Hadjeres, Abdelhamid Benzine, El Hachemi Cherif

ORGANISATION CLANDESTINE DE LA REVOLUTION ALGERIENNE (OCRA), 1966–68
formed in exile by dissident figures of the FLN
led by Mohamed Lebjaoui and Mohand Aït El Hocine

MOUVEMENT DEMOCRATIQUE POUR LE RENOUVEAU ALGERIEN (MDRA), 1967–present
founded in exile by FLN founding figure Krim Belkacem
composed of dissident members of the FLN
led by Slimane Amirat after Krim's death

RASSEMBLEMENT UNITAIRE DES REVOLUTIONNAIRES (RUR), 1967–74
formed in exile by dissident FLN figure Bachir Boumaza

RASSEMBLEMENT NATIONAL POUR LA DEMOCRATIE ET LA REVOLUTION (RNDR), 1977–78
formed in exile by dissident FLN figures Kaïd Ahmed, Ahmed Mahsas, and Tahar Zbiri

PARTI SOCIALISTE DES TRAVAILLEURS (PST), early 1980s–present
Trotskyist party with origins in mid-1970s
led by Salah Chawki

ORGANISATION SOCIALISTE DES TRAVAILLEURS (OST), early 1980s–90
Trotskyist party with origins in mid-1970s, renamed in 1990 the PARTI DES TRA-VAILLEURS

MOUVEMENT ISLAMIQUE D'ALGERIE (MIA), 1982–87
Islamist guerrilla movement led by Mustapha Bouyali
most members later formed or joined the FRONT ISLAMIQUE DU SALUT

MOUVEMENT POUR LA DEMOCRATIE EN ALGERIE (MDA), 1984–present
formed in exile by FLN founding figure Ahmed Ben Bella
essentially composed of dissident members of the FLN

RASSEMBLEMENT POUR LA CULTURE ET LA DEMOCRATIE (RCD), 1989–present
formed by activists in the Berberist cultural movement of the 1980s and some dissidents of the FFS
led by Saïd Sadi
almost exclusively Kabyle Berber in composition

FRONT ISLAMIQUE DU SALUT (FIS), 1989–present
Islamist party led by Abassi Madani and Ali Ben Hadj
dominant political force from 1990

PARTI SOCIAL-DEMOCRATE (PSD), 1989–present
led by Ahmed Hamidi-Khodja

PARTI NATIONAL POUR LA SOLIDARITE ET LE DEVELOPPEMENT (PNSD), 1989–present
led by Rabah Bencharif

PARTI DU RENOUVEAU ALGERIEN (PRA), 1989–present
led by Nourredine Boukrouh

UNION DES FORCES DEMOCRATIQUES (UFD), 1989–present
led by former PPA–MTLD/FLN/RNDR figure Ahmed Mahsas

MOUVEMENT EL-OUMMA, 1990–present
moderate Islamist party founded by Benyoucef Ben Khedda

PARTI DES TRAVAILLEURS (PT), 1990–present
name change of OST
led by Louiza Hanoune

MOUVEMENT DE LA NAHDA ISLAMIQUE (MNI), 1990–present
  Islamist party led by Abdallah Djeballah

MOUVEMENT ALGERIEN POUR LA JUSTICE ET LE DEVELOPPEMENT (MAJD), 1990–present
  FLN schismatic group led by Kasdi Merbah

MOUVEMENT DE LA SOCIETE ISLAMIQUE (HAMAS), 1991–present
  Islamist party led by Mahfoud Nahnah

## ARABIAN PENINSULA STATES

WORKERS' COMMITTEE (Saudi Arabia), mid-1950s
  led to SONS OF THE ARABIAN PENINSULA (late 1950s)

DHOFAR LIBERATION FRONT (Oman), 1965
  offshoot: POPULAR FRONT FOR THE LIBERATION OF THE OCCUPIED ARAB GULF (1968)

NATIONAL DEMOCRATIC FRONT FOR THE LIBERATION OF OMAN AND THE ARAB GULF (NDFLOAG) (Oman), late 1960s
  merged with POPULAR FRONT FOR THE LIBERATION OF THE OCCUPIED ARAB GULF to form POPULAR FRONT FOR THE LIBERATION OF OMAN AND THE ARAB GULF (PFLOAG) (1971)
    offshoot: POPULAR FRONT FOR THE LIBERATION OF OMAN (1974)

POPULAR DEMOCRATIC PARTY (Saudi Arabia), 1970
  formed by merger of MOVEMENT OF ARAB NATIONALISTS with BA'TH.

## EGYPT

FREE NATIONALIST PARTY, 1907
  name change to PARTY OF FREE EGYPTIANS, 1908
WAFD, 1919
  split to form LIBERAL CONSTITUTIONAL PARTY, 1922
  split to form SA'DISTS, 1938
  split to form WAFDIST BLOC
SOCIALIST PARTY OF ALEXANDRIA WORKERS, 1920
  led to EGYPTIAN SOCIALIST PARTY, 1921
    name change to EGYPTIAN COMMUNIST PARTY, 1922
    split to form UNION OF PEACE PARTISANS, 1934
    split to form PEOPLE'S LIBERATION GROUP, 1939
    split to form DEMOCRATIC UNION, 1939
      split to form ISKRA, 1942
      split to form EGYPTIAN MOVEMENT FOR NATIONAL LIBERATION, 1943
      merger of ISKRA and EMNL with PEOPLE'S LIBERATION GROUP to form HADETU
        split to form REVOLUTIONARY BLOC, 1948
        split to form COMMUNIST PARTY OF EGYPT, 1948
    split to form POPULAR VANGUARD FOR LIBERATION, 1946
    overall merger to form EGYPTIAN COMMUNIST PARTY, 1957

UNIONIST PARTY, 1925
    merger with PEOPLE'S PARTY, 1936

MUSLIM BROTHERHOOD, 1927
    split to form ISLAMIC ASSOCIATIONS, 1970s and 1980s

YOUNG EGYPT, 1933
    renamed NATIONALIST ISLAMIC PARTY, 1940
    renamed SOCIALIST PARTY OF EGYPT, late 1940s

SOCIAL PEASANT PARTY, 1938
    name change to SOCIALIST PEASANT PARTY, 1945

LIBERATION RALLY, 1953
    replaced by NATIONAL UNION, 1957
    replaced by ARAB SOCIALIST UNION, 1962
        split to form: NATIONAL DEMOCRATIC PARTY, NATIONAL PROGRES-
        SIVIST UNIONIST FORUM, and SOCIALIST LABOR PARTY, 1978

SOCIALIST LABOR PARTY, 1978
    allied with MUSLIM BROTHERHOOD and SOCIALIST LIBERAL PARTY, 1987

## IRAN

SOCIAL DEMOCRATIC PARTY, 1904–10
    merged into DEMOCRAT PARTY I, 1909–21
    DEMOCRAT PARTY OF AZERBAIJAN I split away, 1917–20
        DEMOCRAT PARTY OF AZERBAIJAN II formed by former members of DEM-
        OCRAT PARTY OF AZERBAIJAN I and COMMUNIST PARTY OF IRAN,
        1945–60
            joined TUDEH in 1960

MODERATE PARTY, 1910–16
    some conservative members formed REFORMERS' PARTY, 1921?–1929?

JUSTICE PARTY I, 1917–20
    name change to COMMUNIST PARTY OF IRAN, 1920–37

REVIVAL PARTY, 1921–27
    succeeded by NEW IRAN PARTY I, 1927–31
    succeeded by PROGRESSIVE PARTY, 1931–32

COMMUNIST PARTY II (TUDEH), 1941–
    split to form short-lived COMMUNIST PARTY I, 1947
    joined by DEMOCRAT PARTY OF AZERBAIJAN II, 1960
    some members left to join KURDISH DEMOCRATIC PARTY, 1964
    split to form MARXIST-LENINIST STORM ORGANIZATION (TUFAN), 1965–
    77
    split to form REVOLUTIONARY ORGANIZATION OF THE COMMUNIST
    PARTY ABROAD, 1966
        name change to TOILERS' PARTY, 1979
    joined by faction of DEVOTEES OF THE MASSES, 1971?
    COMMITTEE FOR THE RESURRECTION OF KURDISTAN (KOMALEH),
    1942–
    name change to KURDISH DEMOCRATIC PARTY, 1945

temporary alliance with DEMOCRAT PARTY OF AZERBAIJAN, 1940s
alliance with MOJAHEDIN, 1980s
original name revived in the 1970s by Maoist group

COMRADES' PARTY, 1942–44
split to form SOCIALIST PARTY II, 1944–

FATHERLAND PARTY, 1943–44
name change to NATIONAL WILL PARTY, 1944

NATIONAL UNION PARTY, 1943–44
name change to PEOPLE'S PARTY, 1944–47

FREEDOM PARTY, 1944–46
merged with DEMOCRAT PARTY II, 1946–49

NATIONAL PARTY, 1943–53
fusion of PAYKAR, PATRIOTS' PARTY, ISTIQLAL, and AZADI KHVAKHAN
member of NATIONAL FRONT

NATIONAL FRONT I, 1949–53
consisted of: IRAN PARTY, NATIONAL PARTY, TOILERS' PARTY OF THE
IRANIAN NATION, and the THIRD FORCE

NATIONAL FRONT II, 1965
consisted of: IRAN PARTY, LIBERATION MOVEMENT OF IRAN, NATIONAL
PARTY, SOCIETY OF IRANIAN SOCIALISTS

NATIONAL FRONT III, 1977–79
consisted of: NATIONAL PARTY, SOCIETY OF IRANIAN SOCIALISTS

TOILERS' PARTY OF THE IRANIAN NATION, 1951–53
expulsion of individual leader led to creation of THIRD FORCE, 1953; name change
to SOCIETY OF IRANIAN SOCIALISTS, 1953

LIBERATION MOVEMENT OF IRAN, 1960
split to form: PEOPLE'S MOJAHEDIN ORGANIZATION OF IRAN, 1965
1975, split to form: PMOI, then name change to MUSLIM MOJAHEDIN; and PMOI,
then name change to MARXIST-LENINIST BRANCH OF THE PMOI, 1978;
then split to form: PAYKAR, 1979

NATIONALISTS' PARTY, 1957–63
succeeded by: NEW IRAN PARTY II, 1963–75
succeeded by: RESURGENCE PARTY, 1975–78

MUSLIM PEOPLE'S REPUBLICAN PARTY, 1979–80
allied with RADICAL MOVEMENT PARTY, 1979–80

COUNCIL OF NATIONAL RESISTANCE, 1981
formed outside Iran by former President Bani Sadr and PMOI leader Mas'ud Rajavi
and supported by the PMOI and the KURDISH DEMOCRATIC PARTY, among
other groups, to oppose the Ayatollah Ruhollah Khomeini and the ISLAMIC RE-
PUBLICAN PARTY.

## IRAQ

AHALI GROUP (dates not available)
    developed into NATIONAL DEMOCRATIC PARTY, 1946–61

NATIONAL BROTHERHOOD PARTY, 1931–35
    formed by merger of NATIONALIST PARTY with PEOPLE'S PARTY
    split to form NATIONAL UNITY PARTY, 1934–35

COMMUNIST PARTY OF IRAQ, 1935–79
    Auxiliary (and possibly front): NATIONAL LIBERATION PARTY, 1940s
    split to form ICP CENTRAL COMMAND, 1967–69

ARAB SOCIALIST RESURRECTION (BA'TH) PARTY, 1943–present
    joined NATIONAL UNION FRONT, 1957, a secret organization
      of opposition parties, including Communists
    formed NATIONAL PROGRESSIVE FRONT, 1968

KURDISH DEMOCRATIC PARTY, 1946–present
    split with defection of Talabani, 1964, with subsequent
    reunification and additional splits

NATIONAL SOCIALIST PARTY, 1951
    merged with REFORM PARTY

NATIONAL PROGRESSIVE FRONT, 1968?–
    formed by Ba'th government in order to co-opt opposition
    joined by ICP, 1972–75, KURDISH DEMOCRATIC PARTY, PROGRESSIVE
    KURDISH MOVEMENT

## ISRAEL

MIZRAHI, 1902
    offshoot: HAMIZRAHI WORKER, 1922
    merger of MIZRAHI and HAMIZRAHI WORKER to form NATIONAL RELIG-
    IOUS PARTY (MAFDAL), 1956
      offshoots: TAMI, 1981 (joined LIKUD in 1988), MORASHA, 1984, MEIMAD,
      1988

ZIONIST LABOR, 1905
    joined UNITY OF LABOR, 1919

YOUNG WORKER, 1905
    merged with AHDUT HA'AVODA to form MAPAI, 1930
      split to form AHDUT HA'AVODA MOVEMENT, 1944
      split to form ISRAEL WORKERS LIST (RAFI), 1965
        rejoined LABOR PARTY, 1968
        split to form STATE LIST, 1969
          joined LIKUD, 1973
          joined FOR THE PEOPLE, 1977
          joined TELEM, 1981
          formed COURAGE MOVEMENT, 1984
          rejoined LIKUD, 1988

merged with RAFI and AHDUT HA'AVODA-ZIONIST LABOR to form LA-
BOR PARTY, 1968
formed electoral bloc with UNITED WORKERS PARTY (MAPAM) to form
LABOR ALIGNMENT, 1969
renamed LABOR, 1992

ASSOCIATION OF ISRAEL (Agudat Israel), 1912
formed WORKERS OF THE ASSOCIATION OF ISRAEL, 1922
offshoot: SHAS, 1984
split to form FLAG OF THE TORA, 1988

REVISIONIST PARTY, 1925
succeeded by FREEDOM PARTY (HERUT), 1948
joined with LIBERAL PARTY to form GAHAL BLOC, 1965
joined with FREE CENTER, STATE LIST, AND LABOR MOVEMENT FOR
GREATER ISRAEL to form LIKUD, 1973
STATE LIST, LABOR MOVEMENT FOR GREATER ISRAEL, and INDE-
PENDENT CENTER form FOR THE PEOPLE within LIKUD, 1976
split to form REVIVAL PARTY (HATEHIYA), 1980
offshoot: TOGETHERNESS PARTY (YAHAD), 1984
joined LABOR, 1988

WORKERS PARTY (Hashomer Hatzair), 1946
merged with UNITY OF LABOR MOVEMENT–ZIONIST WORKERS to form
UNITED WORKERS PARTY (MAPAM), 1948
split to re-form UNITY OF LABOR MOVEMENT, 1954
joined electoral bloc with MAPAI to form LABOR ALIGNMENT, 1969
splinter (*Techelet Adom*) joined with remnant of Israel Communist Party to form
MOKED, 1973
left LABOR ALIGNMENT, 1984
joined electoral bloc with CIVIL RIGHTS MOVEMENT and SHINUI to form
MERETZ, 1992

COMMUNIST PARTY OF ISRAEL, 1948
originated in HEBREW SOCIALIST WORKERS' PARTY, 1919
succeeded by PALESTINE COMMUNIST PARTY, 1921 (See also Palestinian
Genealogy of Parties)
split to form NEW COMMUNIST LIST, 1965
formed electoral bloc: DEMOCRATIC FRONT FOR PEACE AND
EQUALITY, 1977
remaining faction joined with TECHELET ADOM, splinter from UNITED
WORKERS PARTY, to form electoral bloc: MOKED, 1973
merged with THIS WORLD PARTY and BLACK PANTHERS to form
SHELI PEACE CAMP, 1977

DEMOCRATIC MOVEMENT FOR CHANGE, 1977
succeeded by SHINUI (one of its factions), 1981

## JORDAN

ISTIQLAL (in Jordan), 1921
offshoot: JORDAN'S LIBERALS PARTY, ca. 1922

ARAB COVENANT PARTY, 1921

UMM AL-QURA PARTY, 1922

JORDANIAN PEOPLE'S PARTY I, 1927
  merged with EXECUTIVE COMMITTEE OF THE NATIONAL CONGRESS PARTY

NATIONAL CONGRESS, 1928
  split to form: EXECUTIVE COMMITTEE OF THE NATIONAL CONGRESS PARTY, 1929
    split to form: MODERATE LIBERAL PARTY, 1930
    succeeded by: JORDANIAN NATIONAL PARTY II, 1930s
    offshoot: EXECUTIVE COMMITTEE OF THE JORDANIAN CONGRESS PARTY, 1944

JORDANIAN WORKERS' PARTY, 1931

JORDANIAN NATIONAL PARTY (I)

JORDANIAN SOLIDARITY PARTY, 1933

EXECUTIVE COMMITTEE OF THE GENERAL CONGRESS OF THE JORDANIAN PEOPLE, 1933

JORDANIAN BROTHERHOOD PARTY, 1937

ARAB UNION ASSOCIATION, 1942 (in Egypt)
  formed Jordanian branch: ARAB UNION PARTY, 1940s

SYRIAN SOCIAL NATIONAL PARTY

JORDANIAN ARAB PARTY, 1946

JORDANIAN LIBERAL YOUTH ASSOCIATION, 1946

MUSLIM BROTHERHOOD ASSOCIATION (in Palestine), 1946
  split to form: LIBERATION PARTY, 1952
  formed: ISLAMIC ACTION FRONT PARTY, 1992

ARAB REVIVAL PARTY, 1947

JORDANIAN PEOPLE'S PARTY (II), 1947

ARAB SOCIALIST RESURRECTION (BA'TH) PARTY (in Jordan), 1951
  formed: NATIONAL FRONT PARTY
  split to form ARAB SOCIALIST RESURRECTION (BA'TH) PARTY—SYRIAN WING (name change: PROGRESSIVE ARAB BA'TH PARTY, 1993) and ARAB SOCIALIST RESURRECTION (BA'TH) PARTY—IRAQI WING (name change: JORDANIAN SOCIALIST ARAB BA'TH PARTY, 1993)
  offshoot: UNIONIST DEMOCRATIC BLOC, 1983
  formed: DEMOCRATIC ARAB UNIONIST PARTY—PROMISE
  offshoot: ARAB SOCIALIST RESURRECTION (BA'TH) PARTY—UNIFIED ORGANIZATION, 1989
  offshoot: JORDANIAN ARAB DEMOCRATIC PARTY, 1993

PALESTINE COMMUNIST PARTY (see also Palestinian genealogy)
  split to form: NATIONAL LIBERATION LEAGUE, 1943
  reorganized in Jordan, West Bank as JORDANIAN COMMUNIST PARTY, 1951
    formed: NATIONAL FRONT PARTY

split to form: PALESTINE COMMUNIST ORGANIZATION, 1970s; later became PALESTINE COMMUNIST PARTY (see Palestinian genealogy)

split to form: JORDANIAN COMMUNIST PARTY—REVOLUTIONARY PATH, 1989

offshoot: JORDANIAN PROGRESSIVE PARTY, 1990 (name change: FREEDOM PARTY, 1993)

split to form: JORDANIAN SOCIALIST DEMOCRATIC PARTY, 1993

NATIONAL UNION PARTY, 1952

PARTY OF THE NATION, 1954

NATIONAL SOCIALIST PARTY, 1954
formed: NATIONAL FRONT PARTY

NATIONAL FRONT PARTY, 1950s
formed by ARAB SOCIALIST RESURRECTION (BA'TH) PARTY, JORDANIAN COMMUNIST PARTY, NATIONAL SOCIALIST PARTY, MOVEMENT OF ARAB NATIONALISTS

ARAB SOCIALIST WORKERS PARTY
formed Jordanian branch: JORDANIAN REVOLUTIONARY PEOPLE'S PARTY, 1970s

PALESTINIAN COMMUNIST WORKERS PARTY (see Palestinian genealogy)
split to form: COMMUNIST WORKERS PARTY IN JORDAN, 1970s
formed: JORDANIAN DEMOCRATIC PROGRESSIVE PARTY

MOVEMENT OF ARAB NATIONALISTS, 1953 (in Jordan)
formed: NATIONAL FRONT PARTY

CONSTITUTIONAL ARAB PARTY, 1956

POPULAR FRONT FOR THE LIBERATION OF PALESTINE (see Palestinian genealogy)
formed Jordanian branch: JORDANIAN DEMOCRATIC POPULAR UNITY PARTY, 1990

DEMOCRATIC FRONT FOR THE LIBERATION OF PALESTINE (see Palestinian genealogy)
formed Jordanian branch: DEMOCRATIC FRONT ORGANIZATION IN JORDAN, 1974
formed: JORDANIAN DEMOCRATIC PEOPLE'S PARTY, 1989
split to form: JORDANIAN DEMOCRATIC PARTY, 1990
formed: JORDANIAN DEMOCRATIC PROGRESSIVE PARTY

CONSTITUTIONAL ARAB FRONT, 1975

JORDANIAN PLEDGE PARTY, 1990

DEMOCRATIC ISLAMIC ARAB MOVEMENT—THE CALL, 1990

JORDANIAN DEMOCRATIC PROGRESSIVE PARTY, 1992
formed by COMMUNIST WORKERS PARTY IN JORDAN, JORDANIAN DEMOCRATIC PARTY

JORDANIAN NATIONAL ALLIANCE PARTY, 1992

POPULAR UNITY PARTY–THE UNIONISTS, 1992

FUTURE PARTY, 1992

JUSTICE AND PROGRESS PARTY, 1993

REAWAKENING PARTY, 1993

JORDANIAN ARAB MASSES PARTY, 1993

HOMELAND PARTY, 1993

DEMOCRATIC ARAB UNIONIST PARTY–PROMISE, 1993
formed by UNIONIST DEMOCRATIC BLOC (see above)

## LEBANON

LEBANESE PEOPLE'S PARTY, 1924
split to form SOCIALIST REVOLUTION PARTY
split to form ILA AL-'AMAM (FORWARD), 1964
merged with UNION OF LEBANESE COMMUNISTS

ARAB SOCIALIST RESURRECTION (BA'TH) PARTY
split to form GROUPING OF POPULAR COMMITTEES AND LEAGUES, 1967
split to form ORGANIZATION OF SOCIALIST LEBANON
merged with ORGANIZATION OF LEBANESE SOCIALISTS to form COM-
MUNIST ACTION ORGANIZATION (see also MAN below)

MOVEMENT OF INDEPENDENT NASSERITES, 1958
split to form NATIONAL GROUPING, 1982
name change to MOVEMENT OF UNIONIST NASSERITES

FRONT OF NATIONAL AND PROGRESSIVE PARTIES, BODIES, AND PERSON-
ALITIES, 1964
reorganized and renamed GROUPING OF THE NATIONAL AND PROGRESSIVE
PARTIES, 1969
renamed LEBANESE NATIONAL MOVEMENT, 1976
composed of
PROGRESSIVE SOCIALIST PARTY
COMMUNIST PARTY OF LEBANON
COMMUNIST ACTION ORGANIZATION
SYRIAN SOCIAL NATIONAL PARTY
LEBANESE MOVEMENT IN SUPPORT OF THE REVOLUTION
POPULAR NASSERITE ORGANIZATION
ARAB SOCIALIST RESURRECTION (BA'TH) PARTY
AL-MURABITUN
LEFTIST KURDISH PARTY
NASSERITE FORCES
AL-'AFWAJ AL-'ARABIYYA
DEMOCRATIC CHRISTIANS
SOCIALIST ARAB ACTION PARTY

UNION OF THE FORCES OF THE WORKING PEOPLE, 1969
split to form NASSERITE FORCES, 1974
split to form REVOLUTIONARY NASSERITE ORGANIZATION, 1977

MOVEMENT OF ARAB NATIONALISTS
split to form ORGANIZATION OF LEBANESE SOCIALISTS

merged with ORGANIZATION OF SOCIALIST LEBANESE to form COM-
MUNIST ACTION ORGANIZATION, 1969 (see also BA'TH above)

LEBANESE KURDISH PARTY, 1975
coalition with KURDISH DEMOCRATIC PARTY to form BROAD KURDISH NA-
TIONAL FRONT, 1976
split to form LEFTIST KURDISH PARTY
split to form LEBANESE KURDISH PARTY (II), 1977

ARAB SOCIALIST UNION, 1975
split to form ARAB SOCIALIST UNION (THE NASSERITE ORGANIZATION),
1976

AMAL MOVEMENT
split to form ISLAMIC AMAL MOVEMENT, 1982
split to form YOUTHS OF 'ALI

## LIBYA

UNITED NATIONAL FRONT, 1946
split to form FREE NATIONALIST BLOC, 1946 and INDEPENDENCE PARTY,
1948
FREE NATIONALIST BLOC split to form LABOR PARTY, 1947
UNITED NATIONAL FRONT merged with NATIONALIST PARTY to form TRI-
POLITANIAN NATIONAL CONGRESS

NATIONALIST PARTY
split to form LIBERAL PARTY, 1948
NP merged with UNF to form TRIPOLITANIAN NATIONAL CONGRESS

NATIONAL CONGRESS, 1948
developed into NATIONAL CONGRESS PARTY

TRIPOLITANIAN NATIONAL CONGRESS, 1949
formed by merger of UNITED NATIONAL FRONT and NATIONALIST PARTY

MUSLIM BROTHERHOOD, 1950s
split into three factions; basic faction affiliated with anti-Qadhafi NATIONAL
FRONT FOR THE SALVATION OF LIBYA, 1981, in which it was joined by
leftists and pan-Arabists

LIBYAN NATIONAL DEMOCRATIC RALLY, 1982
formed by merger of LIBYAN NATIONAL DEMOCRATIC MOVEMENT with LIB-
YAN NATIONAL GROUPING

## MOROCCO

MOROCCAN ACTION COMMITTEE, 1934
developed into NATIONAL PARTY FOR THE REALIZATION OF THE REFORM
PLAN, 1937, and ultimately ISTIQLAL PARTY, 1943
split to form PEOPLE'S ACTION PARTY [also known as POPULAR MOVEMENT
(I)] 1937, reorganized as DEMOCRATIC PARTY OF INDEPENDENCE, 1946

PARTY OF NATIONAL REFORM (ISLAH PARTY), 1936–56
  split to form PARTY OF MOROCCAN UNITY, 1937, based in pre-independence Spanish Morocco
  in alliance with ISTIQLAL PARTY from 1947 to independence in 1956

PEOPLE'S ACTION PARTY [also known as POPULAR MOVEMENT (I)] 1937, reorganized as DEMOCRATIC PARTY OF INDEPENDENCE, 1946

ISTIQLAL PARTY, 1943–present
  split to form NATIONAL UNION OF POPULAR FORCES (UNFP), 1959, which split to form MARCH 23 MOVEMENT, 1970 and SOCIALIST UNION OF POPULAR FORCES (USFP), 1975. MARCH 23 MOVEMENT members joined USFP or ORGANIZATION OF DEMOCRATIC AND POPULAR ACTION (OADP); further split to form PARTY OF THE DEMOCRATIC SOCIALIST AVANT-GARDE, 1991

MOROCCAN COMMUNIST PARTY, 1943
  reorganized and renamed PARTY OF LIBERATION AND SOCIALISM, 1968
  renamed PARTY OF PROGRESS AND SOCIALISM (PPS), 1974
  split to form FORWARD, 1970; most members later joined USFP, PPS, and OADP

DEMOCRATIC PARTY OF INDEPENDENCE, 1946
  succeeded by DEMOCRATIC CONSTITUTIONAL PARTY, 1959; split with some members joining UNFP

POPULAR MOVEMENT (MP), 1957
  (Moroccan Action Committee and People's Action Party)
  joined FRONT FOR THE DEFENSE OF CONSTITUTIONAL INSTITUTIONS (FDIC), 1963
  split to form DEMOCRATIC AND CONSTITUTIONAL POPULAR MOVEMENT, 1967

DEMOCRATIC CONSTITUTIONAL PARTY, 1959 (see DEMOCRATIC PARTY OF INDEPENDENCE)
  joined FDIC

FRONT FOR THE DEFENSE OF CONSTITUTIONAL INSTITUTIONS (FDIC), 1963
  formed by the DEMOCRATIC CONSTITUTIONAL PARTY, POPULAR MOVEMENT, and independents to support policies of the king

ISLAMIC YOUTH, 1969
  spun off faction called the MUJAHIDIN MOVEMENT

NATIONAL FRONT I, 1970
  formed by ISTIQLAL PARTY and UNFP

NATIONAL FRONT II, 1990
  formed by ISTIQLAL, USFP, UNFP, and OADP

NATIONAL FRONT III, 1992
  reformation of NF II with addition of PPS; renamed DEMOCRATIC BLOC

FORWARD, 1970
  split from PARTY OF LIBERATION AND SOCIALISM; most of its members later joined USFP or PPS

NATIONAL RALLY OF INDEPENDENTS (RNI), 1978
  promonarchy coalition
  split to form NATIONAL DEMOCRATIC PARTY, 1981
    spin-off: NATIONAL UNION OF DEMOCRATIC STUDENTS, 1983
    further split to form CONSTITUTIONAL UNION, 1983

## PALESTINIANS

ASSOCIATION OF BROTHERHOOD AND PURITY, 1918
  armed wing of the ARAB CLUB and the LITERARY SOCIETY

YOUTH (*Al-Fatat*), 1919
  formed PARTY OF ARAB INDEPENDENCE, 1918
  offshoot: ARAB CLUB, 1919

PALESTINE COMMUNIST PARTY, 1919
  offshoot: NATIONAL LIBERATION LEAGUE, 1943
    reorganized and renamed: JORDANIAN COMMUNIST PARTY (JCP) in Jordan,
      1951, and ISRAELI COMMUNIST PARTY (ICP) in Israel, 1948
      JCP offshoot: PALESTINIAN COMMUNIST ORGANIZATION, 1975,
        which formed PALESTINE COMMUNIST PARTY, 1982; name change to
        PALESTINIAN PEOPLE'S PARTY
        offshoot: PALESTINIAN REVOLUTIONARY COMMUNIST PARTY
      ICP offshoot: NEW COMMUNIST LIST (Rakah), 1965
        formed DEMOCRATIC FRONT FOR PEACE AND EQUALITY, 1977
        (see Genealogy of Israeli Parties)

PALESTINIAN ARAB NATIONAL PARTY, 1923
  succeeded by NATIONAL DEFENSE PARTY, 1934

MUSLIM BROTHERHOOD, 1946 in Palestine
  offshoot: PARTY OF LIBERATION, 1952
  offshoot (?): ISLAMIC JIHAD, 1970s
  organized armed wing: HAMAS, 1988

FATAH (Palestinian National Liberation Movement), 1950s
  offshoot: FATAH–REVOLUTIONARY COUNCIL, 1970s
  offshoot: FATAH–UPRISING, 1982

AL ARD, 1959
  organized as ARAB SOCIALIST LIST, 1965

AL-SAI'QA, 1966
  branch of Syrian BA'TH PARTY

POPULAR FRONT FOR THE LIBERATION OF PALESTINE, 1967
  split to form DEMOCRATIC FRONT FOR THE LIBERATION OF PALESTINE,
    1968
    name change to DEMOCRATIC FRONT FOR THE LIBERATION OF PAL-
      ESTINE
      split into Hawatmeh and 'Abd Rabbuh factions, 1991
  split to form POPULAR FRONT FOR THE LIBERATION OF PALESTINE–GEN-
    ERAL COMMAND (PFLP–GC), 1968

split to form PFLP-GC B; name change to ORGANIZATION OF ARAB PAL-
ESTINE, 1968
  split to form PALESTINE LIBERATION FRONT, 1977
    split into pro-'Arafat, pro-Syrian, and pro-Iraqi factions, 1983
  split to form POPULAR REVOLUTIONARY FRONT FOR THE LIBERATION OF
  PALESTINE, 1972
  succeeded by PFLP–EXTERNAL OPERATIONS, 1970s

ARAB LIBERATION FRONT, 1969
  branch of Iraqi BA'TH PARTY

ABNA AL-BALAD (Sons of the Country), 1970s
  split to form AL ANSAR II, 1980s

**Committees, Umbrella Organizations, and Fronts**

ARAB FRONT, 1958
  split to form AL-ARD

PALESTINE LIBERATION ORGANIZATION, 1964
  legislative arm: PALESTINE NATIONAL COUNCIL
  armed wing: PALESTINE LIBERATION ARMY
    commando forces: POPULAR LIBERATION FORCES

NATIONAL ALLIANCE, 1984
  succeeded by PALESTINIAN NATIONAL SALVATION FRONT, 1985

NATIONAL DEMOCRATIC AND ISLAMIC FRONT, 1993
  formed by PFLP, DFLP, PFLP–GC, PALESTINIAN POPULAR STRUGGLE
  FRONT, PALESTINE LIBERATION FRONT, FATAH-UPRISING, PALES-
  TINIAN REVOLUTIONARY COMMUNIST PARTY, AL-SA'IQA, HAMAS,
  and ISLAMIC JIHAD (The "Damascus Ten").

DFLP
  split to form PALESTINIAN DEMOCRATIC UNION, early 1990s

**SUDAN**

SUDANESE UNION SOCIETY, 1920
  formed the WHITE FLAG LEAGUE, 1923

ASHIQQA, 1924
  became UNITY OF THE NILE VALLEY PARTY, 1944
  merged into NATIONAL UNIONIST PARTY, 1952

LIBERAL PARTY, 1945
  split to form LIBERAL SECESSIONISTS and LIBERAL UNIONISTS, 1946; former
  merged with UMMA, most of latter joined the COMMUNIST PARTY

UMMA, 1945
  formed from moderate wing of the GRADUATE CONGRESS
  merged with NATIONALIST PARTY, 1946
  coalition government with PEOPLE'S DEMOCRATIC PARTY, 1956

split into traditional faction and modernist faction, 1965
coalition with NATIONAL UNIONIST PARTY, 1966–67
coalition with DEMOCRATIC UNIONIST PARTY, 1986–89

COMMUNIST PARTY
formed SUDANESE MOVEMENT FOR NATIONAL LIBERATION, 1945
split to form SUDANESE DEMOCRATIC ORGANIZATION, 1952
formed ANTI-IMPERIALIST FRONT, 1953, to contest election
part of NATIONAL FRONT with NATIONAL UNIONIST PARTY, 1958
part of NATIONAL FRONT, 1964–65
outlawed, 1965
former members formed SOCIALIST PARTY, 1967
suppressed and dismantled, 1971

NATIONAL UNIONIST PARTY, 1952
formed by merger of UNIONIST PARTY with UNITY OF THE NILE VALLEY
PARTY and other small unionist parties
split to form INDEPENDENT REPUBLICAN PARTY, 1955
merger with Khatmi MPs to form PEOPLE'S DEMOCRATIC PARTY, 1956
in coalition with UMMA, 1966–67

SOUTHERN PARTY, 1953
renamed LIBERAL PARTY, 1964

BEJA CONGRESS, 1954
in failed bloc with NUBA MOUNTAINS FEDERATION

MUSLIM BROTHERHOOD, 1954
formed ISLAMIC CHARTER FRONT, 1964
formed NATIONAL ISLAMIC FRONT, 1986

NUBA MOUNTAINS FEDERATION, 1954
in bloc with SUDAN AFRICAN NATIONAL WING and SOUTHERN FRONT,
1968

PEOPLE'S DEMOCRATIC PARTY, 1956
merged with NATIONAL UNIONIST PARTY to form DEMOCRATIC UNIONIST
PARTY, 1967

SUDAN AFRICAN CLOSED DISTRICTS NATIONAL UNION, 1962
renamed SUDAN AFRICAN NATIONAL UNION, 1963
formed ANYA NYAI as military arm
split to form AZANIA LIBERATION FRONT (ALF), 1965
split to form SUDAN AFRICAN LIBERATION FRONT (SALF), 1968
merger of ALF and SALF to form SOUTHERN SUDANESE LIBERATION MOVE-
MENT, 1969
formed ANYA NYA II as military arm, late 1970s
merged into SUDAN PEOPLE'S LIBERATION ARMY, 1983
split into tribal factions, 1991

DEMOCRATIC UNIONIST PARTY, 1967
formed by merger of PEOPLE'S DEMOCRATIC PARTY and NATIONAL UNION-
IST PARTY
in coalition with UMMA, 1986–89

## SYRIA

OTTOMAN PARTY OF ADMINISTRATIVE DECENTRALIZATION, 1912
  offshoot: PARTY OF SYRIAN UNITY, 1918

YOUNG ARAB SOCIETY, 1912
  formed front organization: PARTY OF ARAB INDEPENDENCE, 1918

NATIONAL PARTY, 1919
  resurrected in 1947 (see NATIONAL BLOC)
  coalition with PEOPLE'S PARTY, 1954

IRON HAND SOCIETY, 1922
  Reorganized as PEOPLE'S PARTY, 1925

SYRIAN COMMUNIST PARTY (clandestine), 1924
  emerged as COMMUNIST PARTY OF SYRIA AND LEBANON, 1925
  separation of SYRIAN COMMUNIST PARTY, 1947
    joined NATIONAL PROGRESSIVE FRONT, 1972
    splinter groups, e.g., BASE ORGANIZATION, 1980, UNION FOR COMMU-
      NIST STRUGGLE

PEOPLE'S PARTY, 1925
  formed by leader of IRON HAND SOCIETY
  resurrected in 1949

NATIONAL BLOC, 1927
  formed by leaders of PEOPLE'S PARTY after suppression by the French mandatory
    authorities
  split to form PARTY OF NATIONAL UNITY, 1935
  superseded by NATIONAL PARTY, 1947

SYRIAN NATIONAL PARTY, 1934
  renamed SYRIAN SOCIAL NATIONAL PARTY, 1936

ARAB SOCIALIST RESURRECTION (BA'TH) PARTY, early 1940s
  formed by ARAB RESURRECTION
  merged with ARAB SOCIALIST PARTY, 1953
  offshoot: SOCIALIST UNIONISTS' MOVEMENT, 1961
  formed NATIONAL PROGRESSIVE FRONT, 1972

MUSLIM BROTHERHOOD, 1946
  formed ISLAMIC SOCIALIST FRONT, 1949
  split to form FIGHTING VANGUARD, 1968
  merged to form ISLAMIC FRONT IN SYRIA, 1980
  exiled leadership formed NATIONAL ALLIANCE FOR THE LIBERATION OF
    SYRIA, 1982 (see also ARAB SOCIALIST PARTY)

ARAB SOCIALIST PARTY, 1950
  merged with ARAB RESURRECTION (BA'TH) PARTY, 1953, to form ARAB SO-
    CIALIST RESURRECTION (BA'TH) PARTY
  succeeded by ARAB SOCIALIST MOVEMENT
    joined NATIONAL PROGRESSIVE FRONT, 1972

leaders joined NATIONAL ALLIANCE FOR THE LIBERATION OF SYRIA, 1982, along with exiled Islamists, Nasserists, and dissident Ba'this.

ARAB SOCIALIST UNION, 1961
split from ARAB SOCIALIST RESURRECTION (BA'TH) PARTY
joined NATIONAL PROGRESSIVE FRONT

FIGHTING VANGUARD, 1968
formed by secret cells of militant members of the MUSLIM BROTHERHOOD

NATIONAL PROGRESSIVE FRONT, 1972
formed by ARAB SOCIALIST RESURRECTION (BA'TH) PARTY to harness SYR-
IAN COMMUNIST PARTY, ARAB SOCIALIST UNION, SOCIALIST
UNIONISTS' MOVEMENT, and ARAB SOCIALIST MOVEMENT; Islamic
party added in 1990

## TUNISIA

EVOLUTIONIST PARTY OF YOUNG TUNISIANS, 1908
formed by Association des Anciens du Sadiki, 1905, and ASSOCIATION OF THE
ZAYTUNA MOSQUE STUDENTS, 1907

LIBERAL TUNISIAN CONSTITUTIONAL PARTY (DUSTUR), 1920
split to form NEO-DUSTUR PARTY, 1934
name change to DUSTURIAN SOCIALIST PARTY, 1964
split to form MOVEMENT OF SOCIALIST DEMOCRATS—SOCIALIST DEM-
OCRATIC PARTY, 1978

QURANIC PRESERVATION SOCIETY, 1970
offshoot: MOVEMENT OF ISLAMIC RENEWAL, 1978
split to form ISLAMIC TENDENCY MOVEMENT, 1979

MOVEMENT FOR POPULAR UNITY, 1973
offshoot: PARTY OF POPULAR UNITY, 1980; legalized 1983

## TURKEY

SOCIETY FOR THE DEFENSE OF THE RIGHTS OF ANATOLIA AND RUMELIA,
1919
name change to REPUBLICAN PEOPLE'S PARTY (RPP), 1923
split to form FREE PARTY, 1930, an unsuccessful attempt to establish a competitive
party under limited conditions
split to form DEMOCRAT PARTY, 1946
split to form NATION PARTY I, 1948
joined by PARTY OF GENUINE DEMOCRATS, 1949
reorganized as REPUBLICAN NATION PARTY, 1954
merged with PEASANTS' PARTY OF TURKEY to form REPUBLICAN
PEASANTS' NATION PARTY, 1958
split to form NATION PARTY II, 1962
reorganized and renamed NATIONALIST ACTION PARTY, 1969
reorganized as CONSERVATIVE PARTY, 1983
name change to NATIONALIST WORK PARTY, 1983
electoral alliance with PROSPERITY PARTY, 1991

name change to NATIONALIST ACTION PARTY (II), 1993
split to form GREAT UNITY PARTY, 1993
split to form PEASANTS' PARTY, 1952, a merger with LIBERAL PEASANTS' PARTY, formed in 1950
merged with PARTY FOR LAND, REAL ESTATE, AND FREE ENTERPRISE, 1950
split to form FREEDOM PARTY, 1955
reorganized as JUSTICE PARTY, 1961
split to form DEMOCRATIC PARTY, 1970
reorganized as GREAT TURKEY PARTY, 1983
reorganized as TRUE PATH PARTY, 1983
split to form RELIANCE PARTY (RP), 1967
name change to NATIONAL RELIANCE PARTY (NRP), 1971
dissidents joined with dissident RPP members to form REPUBLICAN PARTY, 1972
merger of NRP and RP to form REPUBLICAN RELIANCE PARTY, 1973

COMMUNIST PARTY OF TURKEY, 1920
name change to UNITED COMMUNIST PARTY OF TURKEY, 1990

SOCIALIST PARTY OF TURKEY, 1946
reorganized as SOCIALIST PARTY I, 1960

TURKISH CONSERVATIVE PARTY, 1947
name change to ISLAMIC DEMOCRATIC PARTY, 1951

SOCIALIST PARTY I, 1960
merged with WORKERS' PARTY OF TURKEY, 1962
some leaders helped establish SOCIALIST WORKERS' PARTY OF TURKEY II, 1974

PARTY FOR NATIONAL ORDER, 1970
reorganized as NATIONAL SALVATION PARTY, 1972
reorganized as PROSPERITY PARTY, 1983
electoral alliance with NATIONALIST WORK PARTY, 1991

POPULIST PARTY, 1983
merged with SOCIAL DEMOCRATIC PARTY, 1983, to form SOCIAL DEMOCRATIC POPULIST PARTY, 1985
split to form PEOPLE'S LABOR PARTY, 1990
split to form REPUBLICAN PEOPLE'S PARTY (II), 1991

NATIONALIST DEMOCRACY PARTY, 1983
merged with TRUE PATH PARTY

MOTHERLAND PARTY, 1983
split to form NEW PARTY, 1993

# INDEX

In this Index, foreign letters are alphabetized as follows:

The Arabic letter *ayin* (represented by the single right -facing apostrophe ) is treated as a silent letter which assumes the sound of the vowel which follows it. Names beginning with this letter will therefore be found under the letter which follows the *ayin* (e.g., 'Abboud is listed under the letter A).

Turkish letters are alphabetized as in the Turkish language; thus, names beginning with the letter Ç (e.g., Çiller) will be found in a separate listing following the items which begin with the letter C. Similarly, ö follows o; ü follows u.

Arabic names beginning with the definite article *al-* are alphabetized under the first letter of the family name of the individual; e.g., al-Sadat, Anwar will be found under the letter S.

Abane, Ramdane, 12, 14, 31–32, 48

Abassi, Madani, 23, 42

Abbas, Ferhat, 4, 8–9, 12, 16, 30, 33, 64, 65–66

'Abboud, Ibrahim, regime of, 481–82, 495

'Abd al-Illah, Crown Prince and Regent of Iraq, 176, 178, 180, 181, 503, 519–20

'Abd al-Rahman, Shaykh 'Umar, 112

'Abd Rabbuh, Yasir, 438–40, 465

Abdessalem, Belaid, 37

'Abduh, Muhammad, 115

'Abdullah, Amir (King of Jordan), 259–60, 262, 263, 270, 273, 279, 285, 290, 294

*Abna al-Balad* (Israel, Palestinians), 431, 433

Abu 'Ammar. *See* Arafat, Yasir; *Fatah*; Palestine Liberation Organization

Abu Dhabi, 84–85

Abu Ghanima, Subhi, 262, 273, 280, 284, 285, 287

Abu Iyad. *See Fatah*; Palestine Liberation Organization

Abu Jihad. *See Fatah*; Palestine Liberation Organization

Abu Lutuf. *See* al-Qaddumi, Faruq; *Fatah*; Palestine Liberation Organization

Abu Musa, 443

Abu Musa Group. *See Fatah*, Uprising

Abu Nidal, 442

Abu Nidal Group. *See Fatah*, Revolutionary Council

Abu Sa'id. *See Fatah*; Palestine Liberation Organization

Abu Yusuf. *See Fatah*; Palestine Liberation Organization

Abu-l-'Abbas, Muhammad, 458

Action Organization for the Liberation of Palestine (AOLP), 433–34

*Adalet Partisi. See* Justice Party

Aden Association (Yemen), 618, 626

Aden Trades Union Congress (ATUC) (Yemen), 619, 633

Adeni Club (Yemen), 617

Adjerid, Abderrahmane, 60
*Afaq Tunisiya. See* Tunisian Perspectives
al-Afghani, Jamal al-Din, 115
Aflaq, Michel. *See* Arab Socialist
  Resurrection (*Ba'th*) Party
*Agudat Yisrael. See* Association of Israel
Ahali Group (Iraq), 177, 180, 190, 195–96
*al-'Ahd. See* Arab Covenant Party; The
  Covenant; Society of the Covenant
*Ahdut Ha'avoda. See* Unity of Labor;
  Unity of Labor Movement
Aherdane, Mahjoubi, 385, 411, 418
Aït Ahmed, Hocine, 9, 13, 16, 22, 31–32,
  33, 38–40, 62
Aït Larbi, Mokrane, 63
'Alawite dynasty. *See* Hassan II; Morocco;
  Muhammad V
'Alawite sect, 306–7, 312, 365
Algeria: Charte d'Alger (1964), 17, 34;
  Charte Nationale (1976), 18, 19, 35,
  36, 65; constitution (1989), 20; coup
  d'etat (1965), 34; Soummam congress
  of FLN (1956), 13, 32
Algerian Human Rights League. *See* Ligue
  Algérienne des Droits de l'Homme
Algerian Movement for Justice and
  Development. *See* Mouvement
  Algérien pour la Justice et le
  Developpement
Algerian National Movement. *See*
  Mouvement National Algérien
Algerian Peoples Party, Movement for the
  Triumph of Democratic Liberties. *See*
  Parti du Peuple Algérien, Mouvement
  pour la Triomphe des Libertés
  Démocratiques
Algerian Popular Union. *See* Union
  Populaire Algérienne
Algerian Renewal Party. *See* Parti du
  Renouveau Algérien
Alliance and Progress Party (Iran), 146
ALN. *See* Armée de Libération Nationale
*Amal* Movement (Lebanon), 305–6, 319,
  336–41, 342, 349, 351, 357, 364. *See
  also* Islamic *Amal* Movement;
  Movement of the Disinherited; Youths
  of 'Ali
Amirat, Slimane, 46

Amis du Manifeste et de la Liberté
  (AML) (Algeria), 9, 30, 64
AML. *See* Amis du Manifeste et de la
  Liberté
ANAP. *See* Motherland Party
Anatolian Party (Turkey), 555. *See also*
  Great Anatolia Party
ANP. *See* Armée Nationale Populaire
*Al-Ansar. See* Communist Movement,
  Palestine
*Ansar* sect (Sudan), 477, 478, 481, 483,
  484, 488, 498. *See also* Mahdist
  Movement
Anti-Imperialist Front (Sudan), 489, 491
*Anya Nya* (Sudan), 481, 482, 486, 490,
  497. *See also* Sudan People's Liberation
  Army
AOLP. *See* Action Organization for the
  Liberation of Palestine
AP. *See* Justice Party
APC. *See* Assemblées Populaires
  Communales
APN. *See* Assemblée Populaire Nationale
APW. *See* Assemblées Populaires de
  Wilaya
Arab Club (Palestine; Syria), 434, 436,
  501
Arab Covenant Party (Jordan), 269, 270.
  *See also* Society of the Covenant
Arab Democratic Front for Peace (Israel),
  248
Arab Democratic Nasserist Party (Egypt),
  103–4
Arab Democratic Party (Lebanon), 306–
  7, 365
Arab Executive (Palestine), 425, 434–35,
  456, 465, 473
Arab Front. *See* Al-Ard
Arab Fury Generation, 82
Arab Higher Committee (Palestine), 425,
  428, 435, 456
Arab Independence Party. *See* Istiqlal
Arab Liberation Front (Palestinians), 435,
  472
Arab Liberation Movement (Syria), 505,
  514
Arab Liberation Party. *See* Party of Arab
  Liberation

Arab Literary Club (Yemen), 617
Arab National Union. *See* Jordan
  National Union
Arab Nationalist Movement (Jordan),
  295
Arab Nationalists Movement. *See*
  Movement of Arab Nationalists
Arab People's Party (Jordan), 295
Arab Popular Liberation Movement
  (Jordan), 295
Arab Popular Movement (Jordan), 295
Arab Reform Club (Yemen), 617
Arab Renaissance Society (Syria), 501,
  514
Arab Revival Party (Jordan), 270, 294,
  295
Arab Revolutionary Brigades (UAE), 85,
  86
Arab Socialist Ba'th Party (Yemen), 626,
  632
Arab Socialist Movement. *See* Arab
  Socialist Party
Arab Socialist Party (Syria), 500, 505,
  506, 511, 514–15, 516, 523, 524. *See
  also* Arab Socialist Ba'th Party
Arab Socialist Resurrection (Ba'th) Party:
  Aflaq, Michel, 190–91, 508, 509, 515–
  16, 518; Bitar, Salah al-Din, 190–91,
  509–10, 515–16; in Jordan (*see* Arab
  Socialist Resurrection [Ba'th] Party,
  Unified Organization; Jordanian Arab
  Democratic Party; Jordanian Socialist
  Arab Resurrection [Ba'th] Party;
  Progressive Arab Resurrection [Ba'th]
  Party; Unionist Democratic Bloc); in
  Lebanon, 307, 318, 329, 330, 364; in
  Libya, 372, 375 (*See also* Arab
  Liberation Front); National (Pan-Arab)
  Command, 190, 191, 510; Regional
  (Iraqi) Command, 182–89, 190–91,
  192, 194, 195; Sixth National (Pan-
  Arab) Congress, 509–10, 518, 527; in
  Syria (*see* Ba'th Party); in Tunisia (*see*
  Ba'th Movement); in Yemen (*see*
  Popular Vanguard Party)
Arab Socialist Resurrection (Ba'th) Party,
  unified organization (Jordan), 264,
  270–71, 280, 293, 295, 428, 435. *See*

*also* National Front Party
Arab Socialist Union (ASU) (Egypt), 93,
  97–99, 104–5, 108, 117, 118, 120, 124
Arab Socialist Union (Lebanon), 307–8
Arab Socialist Union (Libya), 371, 372
Arab Socialist Union (Syria), 510, 515,
  523–24
Arab Socialist Union (The Nasserite
  Organization) (Lebanon), 308, 330
Arab Socialist Workers Party (Jordanian
  branch), 286. *See also* Jordanian
  Revolutionary People's Party
Arab Union Party (Jordan), 271
Arab Unity Party (Jordan), 295
Arab Vanguard Movement (Jordan), 295
Arafat, Yasir, 426, 438, 439–40, 441, 442,
  443, 452, 454, 457, 459, 461, 462, 464,
  465–66, 470, 471
ARAMCO (Arabian-American Oil
  Company), 81
Al-Ard (Palestinian), 431, 436, 471
'Arif, 'Abd al-Rahman (Iraq), 184–85,
  191, 193
'Arif, 'Abd al-Salam (Iraq), 182, 183, 184,
  190–91, 195
Armée de Libération Nationale (ALN) of
  Algerian FLN, 12, 33
Armée Nationale Populaire (ANP)
  (Algeria), 33
Armenian Secret Army for the Liberation
  of Armenia (ASALA), 308
Armenians, 148, 308, 310, 314, 319, 358,
  503
Arsalan family. *See* Yazbaki family
  confederation
Arsuzi, Zaki, 515–16
Artisans' Society (Iraq), 176–77
al-Asad, Hafiz, 510, 511–12, 515, 517,
  518, 520, 522, 523–24, 527
ASALA. *See* Armenian Secret Army for
  the Liberation of Armenia
Ashiqqa (Sudan), 479, 490, 494. *See also*
  National Unionist Party
al-'Asifa. *See* Fatah; Palestine Liberation
  Organization
Assemblée Populaire Nationale (APN)
  (Algeria), 20, 26, 27
Assemblées Populaires Communales

(APC) (Algeria), 23, 24, 25, 35, 41–43
Assemblées Populaires de Wilaya (APW) (Algeria), 23, 24, 25, 35
*Association des anciens du Sadiki. See* Association of the Alumni of Sadiki
Association for National Reform (Libya). *See* Tripoli Republic
Association of Brotherhood and Purity (Palestine), 436
Association of Israel (*Agudat Yisrael*), 206, 208, 210, 216, 233, 236, 242, 252, 254
Association of the Alumni of Sadiki (Tunisia), 530, 538–39
Association of the Muslim Brotherhood. *See* Muslim Brotherhood
Association of the Zaytuna Mosque Students (Tunisia), 530, 531, 533, 539
ASU. *See* Arab Socialist Union
Atatürk, Mustafa Kemal (Pasha), 549, 556, 566, 587, 591
ATUC. *See* Aden Trades Union Congress
Awakening Party (Iraq), 176, 191
'Awn, Gen. Michel, 317, 325, 327, 329, 335, 346, 358, 359
Aybar, Mehmet Ali, 599, 607
Azania Liberation Front. *See* Sudan African National Union
Azerbaijan. *See* Democrat Party of Azerbaijan
al-Azhari, Isma'il, 479, 480–81, 483, 484, 490, 492, 494, 495


Baghdad Pact, 180, 181, 183
Bahrain, 70–73: Bahrain National Congress (1923), 70, 86; Committee of National Unity, 71; constitution (1973), 71; elections (1973), 71; Iran, relations with, 72–73; *Majlis al-Watani* (*see* Bahrain, National Assembly); National Assembly, 71–72; Sulman Shaykh 'Isa bin, 71
Bakdash, Khalid, 310–11, 503, 525–27
Bani Sadr, Abu al-Hasan, 138–39, 163, 167
al-Banna, Hasan, 115
al-Banna, Sabri Khaled. *See* Abu Nidal
al-Banna, Sayf al-Islam Hasan, 117

Banner of the Torah. *See* Flag of the Torah
Banner Party (Turkey), 555, 589
al-Baruni, Sulayman, 369, 370
al-Barzani, Mustafa, 183, 186, 194–95, 322. *See also* Kurdish Democratic Party
al-Bashir, 'Umar Hasan, 487–88, 489, 493, 497
*Ba'th* movement. *See* Arab Socialist Resurrection (*Ba'th*) Party
*Ba'th* Movement (Tunisia), 539, 547
*Ba'th* Party (Syria), 500, 504, 505–13, 514–18, 519, 520, 521–22, 523–24, 525, 526, 527; Military Committee, 509; Regional (Syrian) Command, 509, 510, 512, 513, 527. *See also* Arab Socialist Resurrection (*Ba'th*) Party
Bayar, Celal, 558–59, 560, 561, 562
Bazargan, Mehdi, 156, 161
Begin, Menachem, 214, 215, 222–23, 227, 228, 236, 236–37, 245, 250, 251, 254
Beja Congress (Sudan), 483, 488, 490
Belafrej, Ahmed, 382, 403, 404
Ben 'Ali, Zine al-'Abidin, 537, 541, 542, 545
Ben Barka, Mehdi, 385, 404, 412–13
Ben Bella, Ahmed, 9, 13, 16–17, 31, 32, 33, 34, 38, 48–50, 53, 57
Ben Hadj, Ali, 41, 42, 43
Ben Khedda, Benyoucef, 15, 32, 47, 58
Ben M'hidi, Larbi, 13, 31, 32
Ben Salah, Ahmad, 535–36, 542, 543
Ben Youssef, Salah, 534–35, 543, 547
Benazzouz, Zebda, 42
Bencharif, Rabah, 59–60
Bendjedid, Chadli, 18, 35–37, 54
Ben-Gurion, David, 213, 217–21, 241, 242, 243, 251, 255
Berbers, 38–40, 46, 62–64, 381–83, 411, 415, 418; Berber crisis (1949), 10; Berber spring (1980), 19, 39; Berberists, 10, 19, 21; Mouvement Culturel Berbère (MCB), 21, 39, 62
Berri, Nabih. *See* Birri, Nabih
Birri, Nabih, 319, 324, 338, 340, 349, 357
Bitar, Salah al-Din. *See* Arab Socialist Resurrection (*Ba'th*) Party

Black June Organization. *See Fatah*, Revolutionary Council

Black Panthers (Israel), 233–34, 235, 251

Black September, 442, 460. *See also Fatah*; Palestine Liberation Organization

Blessed Socialist Party (Egypt), 105

Block of the Faithful (*Gush Emunim*) (Israel), 234, 250

Blue Shirts (Egypt), 130

Blum-Violette bill (1937), 7–8, 52

Boran, Behice, 607, 608

Bouabid, Abderrahim, 419–20

Boudiaf, Mohamed, 11, 13, 16, 27, 31, 34, 37, 50–51

Boukrouh, Nourredine, 58–59

Boumediene, Houari, 14 passim, 32, 34–35, 49

Bourguiba, Habib, 532–37, 541, 542, 543, 544, 546

Bouteflika, Abdelaziz, 18, 35

Bouyali, Mustapha, 47

Brigades of Al-Sadr (Lebanon), 308

Broad Kurdish National Front. *See* Lebanese Kurdish Party

Brotherhood. *See* Saudi Arabia, Wahhabis

Brotherhood Party of Turkey, 555

The Call, 75–76, 83, 86. *See also Al Da'wa*; Democratic Islamic Arab Movement

CAM. *See* Moroccan Action Committee

CCE. *See* Comité de Coordination et d'Exécution

CDT. *See* Morocco, Democratic Labor Confederation

CGT. *See* Confédération Générale des Travailleurs

Charity Association. *See* Reform Association

Charte Nationale. *See* Algeria

Charter of National Action (Egypt), 104. *See also* Arab Socialist Union

CHP. *See* Republican People's Party

Civic Block (Israel), 214, 237. *See also* General Zionists

Civil Rights Movement (*Ratz*) (Israel), 209, 234, 245, 251

Clandestine Organization of the Algerian Revolution. *See* Organisation Clandestine de la Révolution Algérienne

CNDR. *See* Comité National pour la Defense de la Révolution

CNRA. *See* Conseil de la Révolution Algérienne

COM. *See* Comité d'Organisation Militaire

Comité de Coordination et d'Exécution (CCE), 13, 32

Comité des 22, 11

Comité d'Organisation Militaire (COM) (Algeria), 32

Comité National pour la Défense de la Révolution (CNDR), 50–51

Comité Révolutionaire pour l'Unité at l'Action (CRUA) (Algeria), 11

Committee for the Defense of Arab Lands (Palestinians), 436–37

Committee for the Liberation of the Occupied South. *See* Organization for the Liberation of the Occupied South

Committee for the Resurrection of Kurdistan (*Komaleh*), 159

Committee for the Unification of the Hadhramawt (Yemen), 617, 634

Communist Movement

—Algeria: Groupe Communiste Révolutionnaire (*see* Parti Socialiste des Travailleurs); Parti Communiste Algérien, 5–6, 12, 16, 17, 34, 50, 51–55; Parti Communiste Français, 5–6, 51–52, 56; Parti de l'Avant-Garde Socialiste, 17, 51–55

—Egypt: Egyptian Communist Party, 106–9

—Iran: Communist Party (*Tudeh* Party), 135, 137, 138, 139, 140, 145, 146–48, 149, 150–51, 152 3, 159, 162, 170, 171, 172; Communist Party of Iran, 146, 148, 159; Devotees of the Masses, 137, 152–53; Marxist-Leninist Branch of the People's *Mojahedin*, 166; Marxist-Leninist Storm Organization, 162; *Paykar* Organization, 164, 166, 171; Revolutionary Organization of the Communist Party Abroad, 170, 172;

Toilers' Party, 172 (*see also* Toilers' Party of the Iranian Nation)
—Iraq: Communist Party of Iraq (ICP), 176, 179, 180, 181, 182–84, 185–86, 190, 191–92, 193, 194, 196; National Liberation Party, 196
—Israel: Communist Party of Israel, 215, 234, 234–35, 246, 247, 253, 436, 437; Democratic Front for Peace and Equality, 231, 233–34, 235, 247, 248, 440, 455; New Communist List, 205, 234, 247, 430–32, 437, 440, 455; Palestine Communist Party (PCP), 248
—Jordan: Communist Workers Party in Jordan, 271, 283, 284 (*see also* Jordanian Democratic Progressive Party); Jordanian Communist Party, 274, 281–82, 286–87, 292 (*see also* Freedom Party; Jordanian Socialist Democratic Party; National Front Party); Jordanian Communist Party, revolutionary path, 282; Jordanian Communist Party, temporary command, 296; Palestine Communist Party, 296
—Lebanon: Communist Action Organization, 308–9, 329, 339, 359; Communist Party of Lebanon, 308–13, 329; Revolutionary Communist Bloc, 358; Socialist Arab Action Party, 359; Socialist Revolution Party, 311; Syrian Communist Party, 310; Toilers' League, 363; Union of Lebanese Communists, 311
—Libya: Libyan Communist Party, 374
—Morocco: Moroccan Communist Party, 384, 408; Party of Liberation and Socialism, 400, 408, 416; Party of Progress and Socialism (PPS), 389, 394, 399, 400, 408, 410, 415, 416–17
—Palestine, Palestinians: Al-Ansar, 434 (*see also* Abna al -Balad; Palestine Liberation Organization); Communist Party of Israel (see Communist Movement, Israel); Jordanian Communist Party, 428, 449, 456; National Liberation League, 281, 437, 449, 456; New Communist List (*see* Communist Movement, Israel);

Palestine Communist Party (PCP), 428, 434, 437, 438, 449, 456–57; Palestinian Communist Organization, 456–57; Palestinian Communist Workers Party, 465; Palestinian People's Party, 474; Palestinian Revolutionary Communist Party, 454, 467
—Sudan: Communist Party of Sudan, 482–85, 488, 490–91, 494; Sudanese Democratic Organization, 497
—Syria: Communist Party of Syria and Lebanon, 503; Spartacus, 503; Syrian Communist Party, 503, 506, 511, 513, 517, 521, 523–24, 525–27
—Tunisia: The Torch, 546; Tunisian Communist Party (PCT), 535, 536, 546; Tunisian Communist Workers' Party, 546; Tunisian Marxist-Leninist Group, 547
—Turkey: Communist Party of Turkey (CPT), 556–57, 605; Fatherland Party, 565–66; Revolutionary Workers'-Peasants' Party of Turkey, 596, 609; Socialist Party I, 598; Socialist Party of Turkey, 599–600; Socialist Revolution Party, 600; Socialist Workers' and Peasants' Party of Turkey, 601; Socialist Workers' Party of Turkey II, 601–2; Turkish People's Liberation Party, 603–4; United Communist Party of Turkey, 556, 605; Workers' Peasants' Party of Turkey, 609
—Yemen Arab Republic: People's Democratic Union, 621, 633, 633–34, 636 (*see also* Unified Political Organization of the National Front)
Communist Party of Iraq. *See* Communist Movement, Iraq
Communist Party of Israel. *See* Communist Movement: Israel, Palestine
Communist Party of Jordan. *See* Communist Movement, Jordan
Communist Party of Sudan. *See* Communist Movement, Sudan
Communist Party of Syria. *See* Communist Movement, Syria

Communist Party of Tunisia. *See* Communist Movement, Tunisia

Comrades' Party (Iran), 148, 171

Confédération Générale des Travailleurs (CGT), 6, 52

Confrontation Front (Lebanon). *See* Arab Democratic Party

Congrès Musulman Algérien, 7–8, 52

Conseil de la Révolution (1965), 34

Conseil de la Révolution Algérienne (CNRA), 13, 17, 32, 33

Conservative Party (Turkey), 557, 582

Constitution Party (Turkey), 557

Constitutional Arab Front (Jordan), 271

Constitutional Arab Party (Jordan), 272

Constitutional Bloc (Lebanon), 313–14, 343

Constitutional Liberal Party (Yemen), 626

Constitutional Party (Egypt), 106

Constitutional Reform Party (Egypt), 106

Constitutional Union (UC) (Morocco), 391, 394–95, 398–99, 409, 410, 411, 419

Constitutional Union Party (Iraq), 180–81, 192

Consultative Council, in Oman, 78. *See also Majlis al-Shura*

Cooperative Socialist Party (Syria), 504, 506, 518

Corrective Popular Nasserite Organization (Yemen), 626

Courage Movement (Israel), 235

Course, or Path (Lebanon), 314

The Covenant (Iraq), 175, 176, 192

CP. *See* Communist Movement, Sudan

CPT. *See* Communist Movement, Turkey

CRUA. *See* Comité Révolutionaire pour l'Unité at l'Action

Curiel, Henri, 107–8

Çakmak, Fevzi, 576–77

Çiller, Tansu, 603

Damascus Ten. *See* National Democratic and Islamic Front

Darawshe, 'Abd al-Wahhab, 235, 438

Dashnak Party, 148, 314

*al-Da'wa. See* The Call; Islamic Call

Dayan, Moshe, 219, 221–25, 226, 241, 242, 243, 251, 251–52. *See also Rafi*; State List; *Telem*

DCP. *See* Democratic Constitutional Party

DCPM. *See* Democratic and Constitutional Popular Movement

Debaghine, Lamine, 57–58

Debbih, Abdallah Demene, 54

Demirel, Süleyman, 562, 570–72, 574, 575, 603

Democracy Party (DEP) (Turkey), 558, 586. *See also* People's Labor Party

Democrat Party (DP) (Turkey), 550, 558–61, 562, 567, 567–68, 570, 576, 577, 582, 583, 585, 590, 592

Democrat Party (Iran), 135, 140–41, 149–50, 154, 162, 170

Democrat Party of Azerbaijan (Iran), 149, 150–51, 160

Democratic Alliance (Palestinians), 437–38, 453, 457, 464, 466

Democratic and Constitutional Popular Movement (DCPM) (Morocco), 399, 418

Democratic Arab Party (Israel), 209, 231, 235, 431, 438

Democratic Arab Party (Jordan), 295

Democratic Arab Unionist Party, Promise (Jordan), 272, 295. *See also* Unionist Democratic Bloc

Democratic Bloc (Kuwait), 75, 76, 86

Democratic Bloc (Morocco), 394, 395, 397, 399, 409, 410

Democratic Center Party (Turkey), 561

Democratic Constitutional Party (DCP) (Morocco), 387, 400, 401

Democratic Constitutional Rally (RCD) (Tunisia), 537, 539

Democratic Federation of Workers (Morocco), 406

Democratic Forces Union. *See* Union des forces Démocratiques

Democratic Front for Peace and Equality (Israel, Palestinians), 231, 235, 247, 431, 440

Democratic Front for the Liberation of Palestine (DFLP), 272, 282, 283, 427,

438, 438–40, 453, 463, 464, 465, 469, 472, 474. *See also* Jordanian Democratic Party; Jordanian Democratic People's Party
Democratic Front Organization in Jordan (MAJD), 272, 282, 283
Democratic Islamic Movement (Jordan), 272–73
Democratic Justice and Unity Party (Jordan), 295
Democratic Left Party (Turkey), 561
Democratic Movement for Algerian Renewal. *See* Mouvement Démocratique pour le Renouveau Algérien
Democratic Movement for Change (DMC) (Israel), 204, 209, 225–26, 227, 235, 236, 240, 251. *See also* Shinui
Democratic Movement for National Liberation (Egypt), 97
Democratic Party (Turkey), 562–64, 571
Democratic Party of Independence (DPI) (Morocco), 399, 400, 417
Democratic Socialist Party (Lebanon), 314–15
Democratic Union. *See* Communist Movement, Egypt
Democratic Union of the Algerian Manifesto. *See* Union Démocratique du Manifeste Algérien
Democratic Union Party (Turkey), 564
Democratic Unionist Party (Egypt), 106
Democratic Unionist Party (Sudan), 483, 491, 494, 495, 498. *See also* National Unionist Party; People's Democratic Party
Democratic United Corrective Front (Yemen). *See* Corrective Popular Nasserite Organization
Democratic Work Committees (Jordan), 295
Democratic Workers' Party (Turkey), 564
Development of Turkey Party, 564
Devotees of Islam (Iran), 135–36, 138, 151–52
Devotees of the Masses. *See* Communist Movement, Iran

DFLP. *See* Democratic Front for the Liberation of Palestine
Dhofar, 70, 78, 79, 87, 89, 90
Dhofar Liberation Front, 78, 87
Djeballah, Abdallah, 44–45
DMC. *See* Democratic Movement for Change
*Doğru Yol Partisi. See* True Path Party
DPI. *See* Democratic Party of Independence
Druzes. *See* Lebanon
*al-Du'a. See* Democratic Islamic Movement
Dubai, 84–85; National Front, 89
DUP. *See* Democratic Unionist Party
Dustur Party. *See* Democratic Constitutional Rally; Dusturian Socialist Party; Neo-Dustur Party; Tunisian Liberal Constitutional Party
Dusturian Socialist Party (PSD), 535, 544, 546, 547. *See also* Democratic Constitutional Rally; Neo-Dustur Party; Tunisian Liberal Constitutional Party
Duty for the Fatherland Party (Turkey), 565
DYP. *See* True Path Party

Eagles of *al-Biqa'*, 315
Ecevit, Bülent, 561, 571, 590, 592–94, 595
ECGCJP. *See* Executive Committee of the General Congress of the Jordanian People
ECNC. *See* Executive Committee of the National Congress Party
Egypt: constitution (1923), 93, 96, 113, 121–22; constitution (1930), 113; Copts, 109, 112, 117, 118, 129, 130; elections, 96, 99, 100, 101, 105, 106, 110, 113, 114, 116, 118, 121, 121–22, 122, 123, 124, 125, 127, 128, 129, 130; electoral laws, 100; Free Officers, 93, 97, 108, 114, 115–16, 128, 131; Gulf War (1991), 116–17, 118, 124, 129; Israel, relations with, 98, 99, 100, 103, 109, 116, 118, 119, 123, 124, 129; opposition parties, 99–100, 101–2, 105, 111–12, 116, 118, 123–24, 124–25,

127–30, 131–32; parties law, 94, 99, 105, 108; partisanship, attitudes toward, 94–95, 104; party system, 101–2; relations with Arab Gulf States, 89; United States, relations with, 98, 109, 116–17, 118 9, 124

Egyptian Democratic Party, 109

Egyptian Democratic People's Party, 109

Egyptian Movement for National Liberation. See Communist Movement, Egypt; Communist Movement, Sudan

Egyptian Party, 109

Egyptian Socialist Party. See Communist Movement, Egypt

Egyptian-Tripolitanian Union Party (Libya), 372

Eisenhower Doctrine. See Jordan: United States, relations with

Elections: in Algeria, 10, 16, 23–27, 36–37, 39, 52; in Egypt, 96, 99, 100, 101, 105, 106, 110, 113, 114, 116, 118, 121, 121–22, 122, 123, 124, 125, 127, 128, 129, 130; in Israel, 214, 216, 220, 221, 222, 224, 225–31, 257–58, 438, 440; in Jordan, 259, 260, 261, 263, 264, 265, 266–67, 268–69, 271, 272, 273–74, 275, 278, 280, 281, 282, 283, 284, 286, 287, 290, 291, 292, 293–94; in Kuwait, 75, 77; in Morocco, 387, 388, 390, 391, 392, 393, 396, 398, 400, 401, 406, 409, 410, 411, 413, 414, 418, 419–420; in Sudan, 480, 481, 483, 484, 485, 486–87, 488, 489, 490, 491, 495, 496, 498; in Syria, 500, 501, 502, 504, 505, 506, 507, 508, 513, 514, 515, 516, 517, 518, 522, 523, 524, 526, 527, 528; in Tunisia, 534–35, 537, 539, 543, 544, 545, 546, 547; in Turkey, 552, 558–59, 560, 561, 562, 562–63, 564, 565, 567, 570–71, 575, 576, 577, 578, 580–81, 581, 582, 583, 586, 587, 588, 589, 590, 592–93, 595, 597–98, 600, 603, 604, 606, 607; in Yemen, 623–25, 631, 638

Eminent Duty Party (Turkey), 565

Emir Khaled, 4–5, 56

ENA. See Etoile Nord-Africaine

Equality Party (Turkey), 565

Erbakan, Necmettin, 568, 578, 579, 584, 588

Ergenekon Peasants' and Workers' Party (Turkey), 565

Eshkol, Levi, 220–22, 241, 243, 244, 250, 255

Etat-Major Général (EMG), 14–16, 17, 33. See also Armée de Libération Nationale; Boumediene

Etoile Nord-Africaine (ENA), 6–7, 56

Evolutionist Party of Young Tunisians, 530–31, 539, 547. See also Association of the Zaytuna Mosque Students

Executive Committee of the General Congress of the Jordanian People (ECGCJP), 262, 274

Executive Committee of the Jordanian Congress Party, 273

Executive Committee of the National Congress Party (ECNC) (Jordan), 261, 273, 273–74, 280–81, 285, 288, 291. See also Jordanian National Party II; Moderate Liberal Party; National Congress

Fada'iyan-e Islam. See Devotees of Islam

Fada'iyan-e Khalq. See Communist Movement, Iran

Fadllalah, Shaykh Muhammad Husayn, 348–49. See also Party of God

The Family of Brotherhood. See Fadllalah, Shaykh Muhammad Husayn

Farid, Muhammad, 120–21

Farmers' and Villagers' Party (Turkey), 565

Farmers' Party (Palestine), 440

Al-Fassi, 'Allal, 382, 384, 403, 404, 405

Fatah (Palestinian), 426, 427, 441–42, 443, 454, 459, 464, 474

Fatah, Intifada. See Fatah, Uprising

Fatah Revolutionary Committee, 442

Fatah, Revolutionary Council (Palestinian), 442, 461

Fatah, Uprising (Palestinian), 443, 453, 454

Fatamid Party (Iraq), 192

al-Fatat. See Young Arab Society

Fatherland Party (Iran). *See* National Will
  Party
Fatherland Party. *See* Communist
  Movement, Turkey
Faysal bin Husayn, Emir (Iraq), 175–77,
  278–79, 434, 501–2, 514, 523
Faysal II, King (Iraq), 176, 180, 181
Faysal-Weizmann Agreement (1919), 434
FDIC. *See* Front for the Defense of
  Constitutional Institutions
Fédération des Elus Indigènes Algériens, 4
FFS. *See* Front des Forces Socialistes
FIDA. *See* Palestinian Democratic Union,
  *Al-Fidaiyya*, 443
Fighters' List (Israel), 236
Fighting Vanguard, 511, 518–19, 522
First Brigade (Yemen), 616
FIS. *See* Front Islamique du Salut
Flag of the Torah (Israel), 206, 236
FLN. *See* Front de Libération Nationale
FLOSY. *See* Front for the Liberation of
  South Yemen
Follow Up Committee on the General
  Concerns of the Arabs of Israel, 443–44
For the Fatherland Only Party (Turkey),
  566
For the People (Israel), 236, 240, 242,
  251
Forces of Marada (Lebanon), 315–16, 323
Forces of Nasser. *See* Lebanese National
  Movement
*Forqan* (Iran), 153–54
Forward (Lebanon), 311
Forward (Morocco), 400, 414
FP. *See* Free Party
Franjiyyah, Sulayman, 315–16, 326, 334,
  354
Franjiyyah, Toni, 316, 323
Free Center (Israel), 236, 240, 245
Free Democratic Party (Turkey), 566
Free Nationalist Bloc (Libya), 372, 374
Free Nationalist Party (Egypt), 109–10
Free Party (Turkey), 566–67
Free Unionist Officers Movement (Libya),
  372
Free Yemeni Movement. *See* Free Yemeni
  Party
Free Yemeni Party (FYP), 613, 614, 616,
  626, 627, 628. *See also* Grand Yemeni
  Association
Freedom Movement of Iran. *See*
  Liberation Movement of Iran
Freedom Party (Iran), 154
Freedom Party (*Herut*) (Israel), 199, 209,
  215, 219–23, 236, 236–37, 237, 238,
  244–45, 249, 250, 254. *See also* Begin,
  Menachem; Gahal; *Irgun Zvai Leumi*;
  *Likud*
Freedom Party (Jordan), 274
Freedom Party (Turkey), 559, 567, 583
Friends of the Manifest and Liberty
  (Algeria). *See* Amis du Manifeste et de
  la Liberté
Front Algérien pour la Défense et le
  Respect de la Liberté, 53
Front de Libération Nationale (FLN)
  (Algeria), 6, 10–27, 31–37, 43–44, 46,
  47–48, 54–55; army, relations with
  (1989–1992), 36–37; crisis, summer of
  1962, 33; Tripoli congress and program
  (1962), 33–34
Front des Forces Socialistes (FFS)
  (Algeria), 16, 22, 27, 38–40, 51, 62–64
Front for the Defense of Constitutional
  Institutions (FDIC) (Morocco), 387,
  400–401, 405, 418, 419
Front for the Liberation of Occupied
  South Yemen (FLOSY), 620, 627
Front Islamique du Salut (FIS) (Algeria),
  22–27, 40–43, 44–45, 47, 49; Jaza'ra
  and Salafiyya factions, 42–43
Front of Freedom and Man. *See* Lebanese
  Front
Front of the Guardians of the Cedar. *See*
  Guardians of the Cedar
Front of National and Progressive Parties,
  Personalities, and Bodies in Lebanon.
  *See* Grouping of National and
  Progressive Parties
Front of Palestinian Forces Rejecting
  Surrenderist Solutions. *See* Rejection
  Front
Future Party (Jordan), 275
FYM. *See* Free Yemeni Party
FYP. *See* Constitutional Liberal Party;

Free Yemeni Party; Grand Yemeni Association

Gahal (Israel), 199, 201, 219, 220, 221, 222, 223, 224, 236–37, 237, 238, 244, 244–45, 249. See also Begin, Menachem; Freedom Party; Likud
Garang, John, 486, 490, 497
Gathering of United Yemenis, 624–25, 627–28
General Union of Moroccan Workers, 406
General Zionists, 199, 201, 214, 215, 220, 236, 237–38, 244, 247, 248, 250, 253, 255. See also Gahal; Liberal Party; Likud
Ghazi, King (Iraq), 176, 177, 178
Ghozali, Sid Ahmed, 22, 37
Gouvernment Provisoire de la République Algérienne (GPRA), 14–16, 32 3
GPRA. See Gouvernment Provisoire de la République Algérienne
Graduates Club. See Sudan
Grand Yemeni Association (GYA), 613–14, 627, 628. See also Free Yemeni Party
Great Anatolia Party (Turkey), 555, 567. See also Anatolian Party
Great Change Party (Turkey), 567–68
Great Homeland Party (Turkey), 568
Great Power Party (Turkey), 568
Great Turkey Party, 568, 602–3. See also Justice Party; True Path Party
Great Unity Party (Turkey), 568. See also Nationalist Action Party
Greater Israel Movement, 238, 242. See also Israel, Greater Israel concept
Greater Syria concept, 259, 260, 261, 270, 271, 279, 289, 294, 360 passim, 424, 434, 502, 503, 524
Green Party (Egypt), 110
Green Shirts. See Young Egypt
Greens Party (Turkey), 568
Grouping of Popular Committees and Leagues (Lebanon), 316
Grouping of the National and Progressive Parties (Lebanon), 329, 354
Guardians of the Cedar (Lebanon), 316–17, 323, 325

Guardians of the City (Israel), 238
Guechi, Saïd, 42
Guédira, Ahmed Reda, 387, 400–401, 419
Guiding Party (Turkey), 568
Gulf War (1991), 80, 82–83, 441, 444–45
Gush Emunim. See Block of the Faithful
Gürsel, Cemal, 582–83
GYA. See Grand Yemeni Association

Habash, George, 289, 308, 359, 438, 451, 468–69
al-Habashi Group (Lebanon), 317
Hachani, Abdelkader, 42, 43
HADASH. See Communist Movement, Israel
Haddad, Wadi, 289, 468, 470
HADETU. See Communist Movement, Egypt
HAMAS (Algeria), See Mouvement de la Societé Islamique
HAMAS (Palestinians), 249, 444–45, 452, 454, 462
Hamidi-Khodja, Ahmed, 60
Hamizrahi (Israel), 210–11, 214, 214–16, 220, 239, 246, 252
Hamizrahi Worker (Israel), 208, 239, 252
Hamrouche, Mouloud, 22, 23, 27, 37
HAMTU. See Communist Movement, Egypt
Hanoune, Louiza, 55
Haolam Hazeh. See This World Party
Hapoel Hamizrahi. See Hamizrahi Worker
HASHD. See Jordanian Democratic People's Party
Hashemite monarchy. See Husayn bin Talal
Hashomer Hatsair. See Workers' Party (Israel)
Hassan II, Crown Prince and King of Morocco, 380, 382, 386–97, 398–99, 399, 400, 400–401, 402, 403–6, 407, 408, 411, 412–14, 415–16, 418, 419–21
Hatehiya. See Revival Party
Haute Comité d'Etat, 27, 37
Hawatmeh, Nayif, 272, 438–40, 469
Hawrani, Akram, 503–4, 504–5, 508, 511,

514–15, 516–17, 528. *See also* Arab
Socialist Party; *Ba'th* Party
Haykal, Muhammad Husayn, 113
Helpers Party (*Hizb al-Najjada*)
(Lebanon), 318
Heritage Movement (Israel), 236, 240,
242
Heritage Revival Society (Kuwait), 75, 87
*Herut* Party (Israel). *See* Freedom Party
*Hezbollah* (Iran), 162
Higher Committee for National Guidance
(Palestinians), 446
Higher Executive Committee (HEC)
(Bahrain; Kuwait), 71, 74
Hijazi Liberation Party (Saudi Arabia),
80, 87
*Histadrut* (General Federation of Labor).
*See* Israel
*Hizb al-Maliki* (Syria), 503, 519–20
*Hizb al-Nahda. See* Islamic Tendency
Movement
*Hizb al-Najjada. See* Helpers Party
*Hizb al-Umma* (Syria), 503, 520
*Hizbullah*, 82, 87, 94. *See also* Party of
God
*Hojjatiyeh* Organization (Iran), 156
Homeland Party (Israel), 206, 209, 231,
240, 252
Homeland Party (Jordan), 278
Hubayqa, Elie, 324, 326, 357–58
al-Hudaybi, Hasan, 115
al-Hudaybi, Mamun, 117
Hunchak Party, 319
Husayn bin 'Ali, Sharif of Mecca, 270,
295
Husayn, bin Talal (King of Jordan), 263–
65, 266, 268, 280, 290, 292–93
al-Husayni family, 425, 427, 434, 435,
450, 453, 454, 456, 465, 467
al-Husayni, Hajj Amin, 178, 288, 425,
428, 435, 456, 473
al-Husayni, Husayn, 315, 338

IAO. *See* Islamic Action Organization
ICP. *See* Communist Movement, Iraq
Iddi, Emile, 300, 330, 343. *See also*
National Bloc (Lebanon)
Iddi, Pierre, 343

Iddi, Raymond, 335, 343–45
Idris, Sayyid, 370–71, 375, 376, 378
IFLB. *See* Islamic Front for the Liberation
of Bahrain
*al-Ikhwan. See* Brotherhood
*al-Ikhwan al-Muslimum. See* Muslim
Brotherhood
*Ila al-'Amam. See* Forward (Lebanon)
*Ilal Amam. See* Forward (Morocco)
Imam of Yemen. *See* Yemen Arab
Republic
Independence Party (Iraq), 180–81, 182,
193
Independence Party (Jordan). *See* Istiqlal
Independence Party (Libya), 373
Independent Center (Israel), 236, 240,
242, 251
Independent Liberal Party (Israel), 201,
220, 240–41, 244, 249, 255. *See also*
Liberal Party; Progressive Party
Independent Republican Party (Sudan),
480–81, 492. *See also* People's
Democratic Party
Independent Turkish Socialist Party, 569
Inönü, Erdal, 597
Inönü, Ismet (Pasha), 549, 570, 591, 592,
593, 594
*Intifada. See* Israel; Palestine
Iran: Bazaaris (urban merchants), 141,
162, 164; constitution (1906, 1979),
134, 138, 141–42, 143; Constitutional
Revolution (1905–1909), 134, 140,
148, 149, 150, 156, 162, 169, 170, 171;
Council of Experts, 138, 167; Council
of National Resistance, 160, 166, 167,
168; Devotees of the Masses (*see*
Communist Movement, Iran);
Disinherited Foundation, 139;
elections, 138, 143, 144, 165, 166–67,
169; electoral system, 141–44; Friday
Mosque prayer leader network, 139,
157; Iraq, relations with, 139, 152, 147,
158, 160, 167–68; Islamic Republic,
138–40, 143–45, 153–54, 157–58, 163,
166–68; *Majles* (parliament), 134–35,
142, 143, 144–45; Martyrs Foundation,
139; Marxism, 146–47, 149, 159, 162,
166, 171–72; National Democratic

Front, 135, 163; National Front, 135, 138, 141, 143, 147, 156, 161, 163, 164, 171–72; National Resistance Movement, 161; party system, 140–41; *Pasdaran* (religious militia), 139, 160; Reconstruction Crusade, 139; Revolution, 137–40, 143, 147, 157–58, 163, 166–67; Revolutionary Council, 139, 161–62, 167; Society of Militant Clergymen, 139, 144, 157; Soviet Union, relations with, 135, 139, 147, 148, 151, 158, 159, 160, 164, 168; United States, relations with, 136, 143, 151, 156, 159, 164, 165, 168; *Velayat-e faqih* (supreme authority of the Ayatollah), 138, 143, 156, 157, 163; White Revolution, 143

Iran Party, 135, 156–57, 161, 163

*Iran Novin* Party. *See* New Iran Party

Iraq: Army, in politics, 175, 176, 177–78, 179, 182–85, 192, 195; Assyrian crisis (1933), 177; constitution, 185; Egypt, relations with, 181–82, 183, 184–85, 190, 195; elections, 174–75, 177, 178, 180, 181, 188, 189; Free Officers, 182; Germany, relations with, 178–79; "Golden Square" colonels, 178; Great Britain, relations with, 175–80; Iran, relations with, 180, 183, 186, 187, 188–89, 193, 194; Italy, relations with, 178–79; al-Kaylani, Rashid 'Ali, 177, 178–79, 180, 182, 184, 193, 195; Kurds, Kurdish Democratic Party, 183; Kuwait, relations with, 183, 184, 189; Nasser, Gamal Abdel, relations with, 181–82, 183, 184–85, 190, 195; Parliament, 175, 176, 180, 181, 182; political parties, party system, 176–77, 180, 182, 183, 188; Shi'ites, 176, 177, 179, 182, 184, 185–86, 187, 190, 191, 191–92, 192, 193, 194, 195; Soviet Union, relations with, 184, 186, 187, 192, 194; United States, relations with, 187, 189

Iron Hand Society (Syria), 502, 520, 524. *See also* People's Party

IRP. *See* Islamic Republican Party

Iskra. *See* Communist Movement, Egypt

*Islah* (Morocco), 384, 401–2, 416

Islamic Action Front (Jordan), 269, 278–79

Islamic Action Organization (IAO) (Bahrain), 72, 87

Islamic *Amal* Movement (Lebanon), 319–20, 349

Islamic Arab Rejuvenation Party (Jordan), 295

Islamic Association (Yemen), 617, 629

Islamic Associations (Egypt), 111–12

Islamic Call (Bahrain), 72

Islamic Call (Iraq), 186, 193

Islamic Charter Front (ICF) (Sudan), 482–83, 487, 488, 493. *See also* Muslim Brotherhood

Islamic Community (Lebanon), 320

Islamic Constitutional Movement (Kuwait), 77

Islamic Democratic Party (Turkey), 569–70. *See also* Party for Land, Real Estate and Free Enterprise; Turkish Conservative Party

Islamic Front for the Liberation of Bahrain (IFLB), 72–73

Islamic Front in Syria, 512, 519, 520, 522. *See also* National Alliance for the Liberation of Syria

Islamic Grouping. *See* Islamic Meeting

Islamic *Jihad* (Kuwait), 75–76

Islamic *Jihad* (Libya), 373–74

Islamic *Jihad* (Palestinian), 249, 446–47, 454, 462

Islamic Liberation Party (Libya), 374

Islamic Liberation Party (Tunisia), 541

Islamic Meeting, 320

Islamic Movement in Lebanon, 320

Islamic Movement of Algeria. *See* Mouvement Islamique d'Algérie

Islamic Party (Iraq), 183, 194

Islamic Popular Alliance (Kuwait), 77

Islamic Republic. *See* Iran

Islamic Republican Party (Iran), 138–39, 140–41, 144–45, 156, 157–58, 163, 167

Islamic Resistance Movement. *See* HAMAS

Islamic Revival Movement (Algeria). *See* Mouvement de la *Nahda* Islamique

Islamic Revolutionary Organization of the Arabian Peninsula (Saudi Arabia), 81, 87
Islamic Salvation Front (Algeria). See Front Islamique du Salut
Islamic Society Movement. See Mouvement de la Societé Islamique
Islamic Tendency Movement (MTI) (Tunisia), 537, 541
Islamic Truth Party (Jordan), 296
Islamic Unification Front (Lebanon), 320–21
Islamic Youth (Morocco), 402, 407, 409
Islamism, 267, 269, 272–73, 278–79, 288, 290, 321–22, 359, 373–74, 402, 407, 409, 429, 431–32, 444, 444–45, 452, 467–68, 480, 482, 484, 486, 487, 488–89, 493, 503, 505, 506, 509, 511, 512, 518–19, 520, 521 3, 527, 528, 536–37, 541, 542, 544, 550, 559, 568, 578, 579, 584, 585, 588, 590, 603, 617, 629, 636 7, 637–38
Israel: Altalena Affair, 218–19, 236; Arabs (Israeli Arabs), 235, 246 (see also Darawshe, 'Abd al-Wahhab; Democratic Arab Party; Democratic Front for Peace and Equality; Progressive List for Peace); Arlozoroff affair, 214; coalition politics, 199–202, 207, 216, 219, 220, 221–22, 225–26, 228–30, 231; Council of the Sages of the Torah, 233, 242, 254; Egypt, relations with, 221–22, 227, 228; Elections, 214, 216, 220, 221, 222, 224, 225–31; electoral reform, 202–3, 241; electoral system, 199–203, 228–29; ethnic divisions (Ashkenazi/Sephardi), 208, 226–27, 227–28, 230, 231, 233–34, 247, 250, 250–51, 251; Germany, relations with, 218, 236; Greater Israel concept, 213, 223, 227, 236, 238, 242, 245, 250, 251, 252, 253 (see also Greater Israel Movement; Labor movement for Greater Israel); Histadrut (General Federation of Labor), 198, 204, 208–9, 212–14, 215, 217, 218, 233, 234, 236, 236–37, 239, 242, 242–44, 244, 247, 248, 249, 253, 254, 255;

Immigrants, 216, 217, 219, 226–27, 234, 247; Intifada (Palestinian uprising), 205–6, 247; Irgun Zvai Leumi, 213, 214, 215, 218–19, 222, 228, 236, 249–50 (see also Begin, Menachem; Jabotinsky, Vladimir; Revisionist Movement); Kibbutz (collective settlement) movement, 213, 215, 218, 239, 243, 252–53, 254, 255; Knesset (parliament), 200–203; Knesset Yisrael (political organization of the Jewish community in Palestine under the Mandate), 199, 212, 215; Lavon Affair, 220, 226, 241, 242, 243; Lebanon War (1982–1985), 228, 229–30, 248; New Zionist Federation, 214, 249 (see also Revisionist Movement); occupied territories, as political issue, 205–7, 223, 227, 234, 241, 244, 245, 247, 250, 251–52, 253; Palestine Liberation Organization (PLO), 206, 228, 245, 247; Palestinians, relations with, 218, 230, 231, 234, 240, 245, 247, 248, 250, 251–52; Partition of Mandate Palestine, as an issue, 206, 213, 215, 217, 218, 234, 243; party system, 198–205, 209–31; peace with the Arabs, as an issue, 223, 227, 228, 244, 248, 250, 253, 254; PLO-Israel agreement for Gaza-Jericho autonomy (September 13, 1993), 206–7; recognition of PLO as legitimate, 463; religion as an issue, 204, 207–8, 210, 218, 228, 230, 234, 238, 239, 245, 247; religious parties, 204, 206, 207, 207–8, 208, 213–16, 218, 220, 225–26, 227, 228, 230–31, 234, 238, 239, 240, 245, 246–47, 250–51, 252; Revisionist Movement, 199, 213–14, 236–37; Sinai Campaign (1956), 218; Six Day War (1967), 221–22, 223, 227, 229, 234, 239, 242; War of Independence (1948–1949), 217; Yom Kippur War (1973), 222, 223–24, 251
Israel Workers List (Rafi), 199, 221–23, 225, 226, 241, 242, 243–44, 251, 253. See also Ben-Gurion, David; Dayan, Moshe; State List

*Istiqlal* (Jordan; Palestine; Syria), 261, 273, 278–79, 287, 468
*Istiqlal* (Morocco), 383–97, 399, 400, 401–2, 402–7, 408, 410, 411–13, 415, 416, 417, 418, 419–21

Jabotinsky, Vladimir (Zeev), 214, 249–50. *See also* Revisionist Movement
Jacquot-Descombes, Paul, 107
Jaja, Samir, 324, 325, 327, 358
*al-Jamahiriya. See* Libya, Mass Republic
Jamayyil, Amin, 324, 326, 335, 339
Jamayyil, Bashir, 315, 319, 323–25, 326, 334–35, 346, 349
Jamayyil, Pierre, 323, 326, 330–33
Jamayyil family, 335
*Jam'iyat al-'Ulama* (Algeria), 5, 7
*Jangali* movement (Iran), 134, 148, 149, 158
JCP. *See* Communist Movement, Jordan
JDP. *See* Jordanian Democratic Party
JDPP. *See* Jordanian Democratic Progressive Party
JDPUP. *See* Jordanian Democratic Popular Unity Party
Jewish Defense League (*Kach*) (Israel), 228, 241
Jeune Algérien movement, 3–5
Jibril, Ahmad, 469, 470–71
JIHA. *See* Guardians of the Cedar
*Jihad* Organization (Egypt), 112
JNP. *See* Jordanian National Party
Jordan: Baghdad Pact (1955), 264–65; constitution, national charter, 260, 261, 262, 263, 266, 368, 271, 272, 284, 292; elections, 259, 260, 261, 263, 264, 265, 266–67, 268–69, 271, 272, 273–74, 275, 278, 280, 281, 282, 283, 284, 286, 287, 290, 291, 292, 293–94; Great Britain, relations with, 259–63, 264 5, 270, 274, 279, 389, 291; Greater Syria, 259, 260, 261, 270, 271, 279, 289, 294; Husayn, King (*See* Husayn bin Talal); Iraq, relations with, 286, 290, 292; Israel, relations with, 262, 265, 266, 281, 289; national pact, 261, 273, 280, 291; Palestinians, relations with, 262, 265–66, 268, 269, 271, 272, 274, 282,

283–84, 284, 285, 287, 288, 289; political liberalization, 260, 267–69, 282, 284, 288; Syria, relations with, 262, 273, 279, 294; United States, relations with, 264–65; West Bank, 262–63, 265–66, 280, 281, 283, 288, 289, 292, 295, 446
Jordan National Union, 264, 280
Jordanian Arab Democratic Party, 280
Jordanian Arab Masses Party, 280
Jordanian Arab Party, 280
Jordanian Brotherhood Party, 281
Jordanian Democratic Party (JDP), 282 3, 283. *See also* Democratic Front for the Liberation of Palestine; Jordanian Democratic People's Party; Jordanian Democratic Progressive Party
Jordanian Democratic People's Party (*HASHD*), 272, 282–83, 439
Jordanian Democratic Popular Unity Party, 283–84. *See also* Popular Front for the Liberation of Palestine
Jordanian Democratic Progressive Party (JDPP), 271, 283, 284
Jordanian Democrats Movement, 296
Jordanian al-Khadir Party, 296
Jordanian Liberal Youth Association, 261, 284
Jordanian National Alliance Party, 284
Jordanian National Party, 262, 285
Jordanian National Party, *Urdunn*, 296
Jordanian People's Party, 260, 285
Jordanian Pledge Party, 286
Jordanian Progressive Party. *See* Freedom Party
Jordanian Revolutionary People's Party, 271, 284, 286. *See also* Popular Front for the Liberation of Palestine
Jordanian Socialist Arab Resurrection (*Ba'th*) Party, 286. *See also* Arab Socialist Resurrection (*Ba'th*) Party
Jordanian Socialist Democratic Party (JSDP), 282, 286–87
Jordanian Solidarity Party, 287
Jordanian Workers' Party, 287
Jordan's Liberals Party, 287
JP. *See* Justice Party

JSDP. *See* Jordanian Socialist Democratic Party

Jumblat, Kamal, 300, 309, 329, 352–55, 362, 364. *See also* Lebanon, Druzes

Jumblat, Walid, 303, 355–57, 364. *See also* Lebanon, Druzes

*Jundullah. See* Soldiers of God

Jungle Party (Iran), 158

Justice and Charity Movement (Morocco), 407

Justice and Progress Party (Jordan), 287–88

Justice Bloc (Jordan), 296

Justice Party (Iran), 159

Justice Party (JP) (Turkey), 550, 560, 562, 568, 570–72, 579, 580, 581, 583, 586, 592, 595, 603–3, 606. *See also* Democrat Party; Great Turkey Party; True Path Party

Justice Party (Tunisia), 542

Justice Party of Free Turkey, 572


*Kach. See* Jewish Defense League

Kahane, Meir. *See* Jewish Defense League

Kaïd, Ahmed, 34–35, 54, 61

Kamil, Mustafa, 120, 125

Kasdi, Merbah, 22, 43–44

Kashani, Ayatollah Abu al-Qasem, 136, 152, 172

Kassem, Abdel Karim. *See* Qasim, Brigadier 'Abd al-Karim

KDL. *See* Kuwait, Kuwaiti Democratic League

KDP. *See* Kurdish Democratic Party

al-Khalidi family, 472

Al Khalifa, 70, 72, 89. *See also* Bahrain

Khatib, Abdelkrim, 385, 399, 418

*Khatmiyya* sect (Sudan), 478–79, 480–81, 481–82, 488, 490, 491, 492, 494, 495, 498

Khider, Mohammed, 13, 16, 31, 32, 33, 34, 57

Khomeini, Ayatollah Ruhollah, 136, 138–40, 152, 157–58, 160, 161 2, 167

al-Khuri, Bisharah, 300, 313, 343, 353

Kishk, Jalal, 112

*Komaleh. See* Committee for the Resurrection of Kurdistan

Krim Belkacem, 13, 16, 31–32, 46

Kuchik Khan. *See Jangali* Movement

Kurdish Democratic Party, 140–41, 145, 160, 183, 194–95, 196

Kurdish Democratic Party (*Al-Parti*), 321–22, 328, 348

Kurdish Democratic Party (*Al Parti*), Provisional Leadership, 322

Kurdish Republic of Mahabad, 159, 160, 194

Kurdish Revolutionary Party (Iraq), 195

Kurdish Workers' Party (PKK), 558, 573

Kurds, 159–60, 164, 183–85, 186–87, 192, 194–95, 196, 322, 328, 348, 558, 573, 586, 587, 596, 600, 601, 607

Kuwait, 74–77, 86, 87, 88, 89, 91, 92; al-Ahmad, Shaykh Jabir, 73, 75, 141; Constituent Assembly, 74; Iran, relations with, 86; Iraq, relations with, 76–77, 183, 184, 189; al-Khatib, Ahmad, 74; National Advisory Assembly, 73–77; al-Salim, Shaykh Abdullah, 74; al-Shabiba, 73, 91

Kuwait Democratic Youth, 74, 88

Kuwaiti Democratic League, 74, 88


*La'am* (Israel). *See* For the People

Labor Alignment. *See* Labor Party of Israel

Labor Association of Israel, 236, 238, 240, 242, 252

Labor Movement for Greater Israel, 223, 236, 238, 242, 245, 250, 251. *See also* For the People; *Likud*; Revival Party

Labor New Immigration (Israel), 242

Labor Party (Libya), 374

Labor Party (Turkey), 573

Labor Party (Yemen). *See* National Democratic Front

Labor Party of Israel, 198–99, 199–200, 201–3, 206, 207, 208, 212, 213, 216–31, 234, 235, 240, 240–41, 241, 241–42, 242–44, 245–46, 246, 246–47, 248, 249, 250, 251, 253, 253–54, 254, 255

Labor Party of Turkey. *See* Workers' Party of Turkey

The Land. *See Al-Ard*

LCP. *See* Communist Movement, Lebanon

League of the Sons of Yemen, 615, 624, 630. *See also* South Arabian League

League of Yemenis. *See* League of the Sons of Yemen

Lebanese Forces (LF), 315–16, 322–25, 328, 334, 348, 356

Lebanese Front, 315, 323, 325–27, 328, 344, 346, 359

Lebanese Kurdish Party I, II (*Riz Kari*), 327–28, 328

Lebanese Monastic Order, 328–29

Lebanese Movement in Support of the Revolution. *See* Lebanese National Movement

Lebanese National Movement, 307, 322, 329–30, 337, 354, 355

Lebanese People's Party, 309

Lebanese Phalanges Party, 330–36, 347

Lebanese Youths, 336. *See also* National Bloc

Lebanon: Al-Taif Accords (1990), 299, 300–301, 321, 323, 357; constitution, 298, 299–300; Druzes, 298, 300, 303, 352–57, 362, 364; elections, 301–3, 307, 312, 315, 330–33, 334, 335, 347, 352, 353; France, relations with, 298, 300, 330, 343; Greater Lebanon, 298; Iran, relations with, 308, 320, 321, 338, 340, 348–51; Iraq, relations with, 307, 322, 345, 355; Israel, relations with, 305–6, 315, 316, 322–24, 334, 339, 340, 342, 344, 346, 348, 349, 350, 351, 352, 356, 362; Libya, relations with, 308, 337, 338, 341, 343, 362; Maronites, 398, 300, 303, 306, 312, 314, 315, 316, 322–27, 328–29, 333–35, 343–47, 364–65; National Pact, 300, 306, 325, 328, 330, 332, 354; Palestinians, relations with, 305–6, 307, 309, 310–11, 315, 316, 322, 333–34, 336–38, 340, 341–42, 344, 345, 347–48, 352, 354–55, 359, 361, 362, 363; party system, 297–304; Salvation Committee, 319, 349; Saudi Arabia, relations with, 320, 342, 364; Sectarianism, 298, 303, 312–13, 342,

362, 364–66; Shi'ites, 303, 305–6, 312–13, 314–15, 320, 336–41, 348–52, 360, 362, 365; Syria, relations with, 299, 300, 302, 303, 306–7, 314–15, 315, 316, 317, 323–25, 327, 330, 335, 337, 339–40, 342, 344, 346, 349, 352, 354, 355–57, 358, 360–64; Tripartite Agreement of December 1985, 298, 324, 357, 358; Tripartite Alliance (1968), 334, 344, 345; *Zu'ama* (political bosses), 297, 300, 303, 343–44, 353

Leftist Kurdish Party, 330. *See also* Organization of Leftist Kurdish *Parti*

LF. *See* Lebanese Forces

Liberal Constitutional Party (Syria), 502–3, 521

Liberal Constitutionalist Party (Egypt), 94, 96, 113–14, 122, 127

Liberal Democratic Party (Turkey), 573

Liberal Independents. *See* Front for the Defense of Constitutional Institutions

Liberal Labor Movement (Israel), 244

Liberal Nation Party (Turkey), 573

Liberal Party (Iraq), 180, 195

Liberal Party (Israel), 199, 201, 204, 209, 217, 220–21, 237–38, 240, 244, 245, 247, 248–49. *See also Gahal*; General Zionists; *Likud*; Progressive Party

Liberal Party (Palestine), 450

Liberal Party (Sudan), 480, 481, 493, 495, 495–96

Liberal Peasants' Party (Turkey), 574, 584, 486. *See also* Party for Land, Real Estate, and Free Enterprise; Peasants' Party of Turkey

Liberation Front Party (Yemen), 630

Liberation Movement of Iran, 137, 140, 141, 161–62, 165

Liberation Party (Jordan), 288

Liberation Party, "*al-Mu'tazala*" faction (Jordan), 296

Liberation Party of the Peninsula (Saudi Arabia), 81, 88

Liberation Rally (Egypt), 93, 97, 114–15, 119

Libya: Great Britain, relations with, 369, 370–71, 378; Italy, relations with, 369–

70, 378, 378–79; Mass Republic, 371, 378; *Sanusiya* movement, 369–71; Tripoli Republic, 370

Libya National Army. *See* National Front for the Salvation of Libya

Libyan Communist Party. *See* Communist Movement, Libya

Libyan Constitutional Union, 375

Libyan Liberation Committee, 375

Libyan Liberation Organization, 375

Libyan National Democratic Movement, 375

Libyan National Democratic Rally, 375

Libyan National Movement, 375

Libyan National Rally, 375

Life Devoted to Struggle (Yemen), 616

Ligue Algérienne des Droits de l'Homme (1985), 62

*Likud,* The National Camp (Israel), 199, 201–2, 204, 206–7, 207, 208–9, 223, 224, 225–31, 235, 236, 237, 238, 240, 241, 242, 244, 244–45, 247, 251, 253. *See also* Free Center; Freedom Party; Labor Movement for Greater Israel; Liberal Party; State List

Literary Post (Yemen), 614, 616

Literary Society (Palestine), 436, 450

LMI. *See* Liberation Movement of Iran

LNM *See* Lebanese National Movement

*Mafdal. See* National Religious Party

Mahabad. *See* Kurdish Republic of Mahabad

al-Mahdi family (Sudan): al-Mahdi, Sayyid 'Abd al-Rahman, 478, 479, 481, 490, 498; al-Mahdi, Sadiq, 483, 484, 485–87, 498

Mahdist Movement, 477–78, 498

Mahmud, Muhammad, 113–14

Mahsas, Ahmed, 62, 65

MAJD. *See* Democratic Front Organization in Jordan; Mouvement Algérien pour la Justice et le Developpement

*Majlis al-Shura:* Algeria, FIS, 41, 42; Qatar, 79–80; Saudi Arabia, 83–84. *See also* Consultative Council

*Maki. See* Communist Movement, Israel

Manifeste du Peuple Algérien (1943), 8–9, 30, 64

*Mapai. See* Labor Party of Israel

*Mapam. See* United Workers Party

March 23 Movement (Morocco), 408, 414

Maronites. *See* Lebanon

Martyr 'Izz al-Din al-Qassam Brigades. *See* Hamas

Marxist-Leninist Storm Organization. *See* Communist Movement, Iran

MB. *See* Muslim Brotherhood

MDA. *See* Mouvement pour la Démocratie en Algérie

MDRA. *See* Mouvement Démocratique pour le Renouveau Algérien

MDS. *See* Movement of Socialist Democrats

Mehri, Abdelhamid, 18, 36–37

*Meimad* (Israel), 245

Meir, Golda, 222, 223, 243–44, 244

Memchaoui, Mohamed, 58

Menderes, Adnan, 559, 560, 567, 567–68

*Meretz* Bloc (Israel), 204, 206, 207, 208, 231, 234, 245, 251, 252, 253. *See also* Civil Rights Movement; *Shinui*; United Workers Party

Messaadia, Mohamed Cherif, 18, 35, 36, 54

Messali Hadj, 6, 8, 9, 11–12, 56–58, 65. *See also* Mouvement Nationale Algérien

MIA. *See* Mouvement Islamique d'Algérie

Mihhu, Jamil, 321–22, 328, 348

Mihhu, Muhammad, 322

Minorities Lists (Israel), 246. *See also* Labor Party of Israel

al-Mirghani, Sayyid 'Ali, and family (Sudan), 478–79, 487, 490, 492, 498. *See also Khatmiyya* sect

MNA. *See* Mouvement Nationale Algérien

MNI. *See* Mouvement de la *Nahda* Islamique

Moderate Liberal Party (Jordan), 274, 288

Moderate Liberal Party (Turkey), 574

Moderate Party (Iran), 134, 162–63, 169

*Mojahedin-e Islam. See* Warriors of Islam

*Mojahedin-e Khalq. See* People's *Mojahedin* Organization of Iran

*Moked* Movement (Israel), 234, 246, 251. *See also* Communist Movement, Israel; *Sheli* Peace Camp

*Morasha. See* Heritage Movement

Moroccan Action Committee (CAM), 383, 384, 403, 408, 410, 417

Moroccan Communist Party. *See* Communist Movement, Morocco

Moroccan Labor Union (UMT), 412–13

Moroccan National Front, 408–9

Moroccan Popular Movement. *See* Popular Movement

Morocco: 'Alawite dynasty, 382; constitution, 386–87, 388–89, 394, 399, 404–5, 412, 413; Democratic Labor Confederation (CDT), 420–21; elections, 387, 388, 390, 391, 392, 393, 394–96, 398, 400, 401, 406, 409, 410, 411, 413, 414, 418, 419–20; France, relations with, 380, 381, 382–83, 400, 403–4, 408, 413, 416, 417; Iran, relations with, 409; Monarchy, 403, 404, 405, 407; Parliament, 387, 388, 390–91, 392, 394, 395, 397, 398, 399, 400, 405, 406–7, 410, 411, 412, 418, 419, 420-n21; Spain, relations with, 382–83, 384, 401–2, 411, 416; Western Sahara territories, 381, 389–91, 392, 393, 400, 405–6, 408, 411, 413–14, 414, 416–17, 420

Mosaddeq, Muhammad, 135, 136, 141, 142–43, 147, 156, 161, 163, 164, 165, 172

Motherland Party (MP), 552, 561, 574–75, 582, 603

Mouvement Algérien pour la Justice et le Developpement (MAJD), 43–44

Mouvement de la *Nahda* Islamique (MNI), 44–45

Mouvement de la Societé Islamique (HAMAS), 45–46

Mouvement de la Triomphe des Libertés Démocratique (MTLD). *See* Parti du Peuple Algérien

Mouvement Démocratique pour le Renouveau Algérien (MDRA), 46

Mouvement El-Oumma, 46–47

Mouvement Islamique d'Algérie (MIA), 47

Mouvement Nationale Algérien (MNA), 11–12, 47–48. *See also* Messali Hadj

Mouvement pour la Démocratie en Algérie (MDA), 48–50

Movement for Democracy in Algeria. *See* Mouvement pour la Démocratie en Algérie

Movement for Popular Unity (MUP) (Tunisia), 536, 542, 543. *See also* Party of Popular Unity

Movement for the Triumph of Democracy in Algeria. *See* Parti du Peuple Algérien, Mouvement pour la Triomphe des Libertés Démocratiques

Movement of Arab Lebanon. *See* Islamic Unification Front

Movement of Arab Nationalists (MAN), 88, 90, 195, 268, 288–89, 291, 308–9, 359, 375–76, 428, 439, 450–51, 468, 619, 620, 631. *See also* National Front Party (Jordan); Pan-Arabism

Movement of Independent Nasserites, "*Al-Murabitun*" (Lebanon), 329, 341–42

Movement of Islamic Renewal (Tunisia), 541, 542–43

Movement of Lebanese Nationalism. *See* Guardians of the Cedar

Movement of Socialist Democrats (MDS). *See* Social Democratic Party

Movement of the Disinherited (Lebanon), 336–41. *See also* Amal

Movement of the Pioneers of Reform (Lebanon), 342

Movement of Unionist Nasserites (Lebanon), 342. *See also* Movement of Independent Nasserites

MP. *See* Popular Movement

MPRP. *See* Muslim People's Republican Party

MTI. *See* Islamic Tendency Movement

MTLD. *See* Mouvement de la Triomphe des Libertés Démocratique

Mubarak, Husni, regime of, 93, 100–102, 111–12, 116, 117–18, 118–19, 123, 129

Mufti of Jerusalem. *See* al-Husayni, Hajj Amin

Muhammad V (Sultan and King of Morocco), 383, 384–86, 394, 400, 402, 403–4, 412, 418

Muhi al-Din, Khalid, 108, 118–19

*Mujahidin* Movement (Morocco), 409. *See also* Islamic Youth

*Mujahidin-i Islam. See* Warriors of Islam

MUP. *See* Movement for Popular Unity

"*Al-Murabitun.*" *See* Movement of Independent Nasserites

Muragha, Sa'id Musa. *See* Abu Musa

Al-Musawi, 'Abbas, 352

Al-Musawi, Husayn, 319–20, 349

Al-Musawi, Shaykh Sadiq, 320

Muslim Brotherhood, 45, 74, 75, 89, 94, 96, 97, 99, 100, 102, 111, 115–17, 123–24, 126, 129–30, 265, 266, 267, 269, 278–79, 288, 289–90, 320–21, 376, 377, 428, 444, 447, 451–52, 468, 480, 482, 484, 486, 488–89, 493, 505, 506, 509, 511, 512, 518, 520, 521–23, 527, 528. *See also Hamas*; Islamic Action Front; Islamic Associations; Islamic Charter Front; Liberation Party; National Islamic Front

Muslim *Mojahedin* (Iran), 166. *See also* People's *Mojahedin*

Muslim People's Republican Party (MPRP) (Iran), 138, 163, 169

Muslim Union (Syria), 500–501, 523

Muslim-Christian Association (Palestine), 452

*al-Mu'tadilin* (The Upright) (Syria), 502, 523

al-Nabulsi, Sulayman, 264–65, 280, 292–93, 294

Nagib, General Muhammad, 97, 114

*Al-Nahda. See* Islamic Tendency Movement

al-Nahhas, Mustafa, 121, 128–29, 130, 131

Nahnah, Mahfoud, 45–46

*Al-Najjada. See* Helpers Party

NAP. *See* Nationalist Action Party

al-Nashashibi family, 425, 435, 450, 453, 465, 467, 473. *See also* al-Husayni family

Nasser, Gamal Abdal, 92, 97, 114, 116, 181–82, 183, 184–85, 190, 195. *See also various Arab countries*

Nasserism, Nasserists, 97–98, 99, 100, 103–4, 104–5, 109, 118, 307–8, 311, 318, 329, 341–42, 342, 343, 347, 352, 354, 359, 363–64, 426, 429, 436, 437, 438, 450, 455, 509, 515, 618, 620, 626, 631

Nasserite Democratic Party (Yemen), 631

Nasserite Forces (Lebanon), 343. *See also* Union of the Forces of the Working People

Nasserite Front. *See* National Front for the Liberation of South Yemen

Nasserite Organization. *See* Union of the Forces of the Working People

Nasserite Organization of Yemen. *See* Corrective Popular Nasserite Organization

Nasserite Unionists in Jordan, 296

Nation Party I, II, III (Turkey), 559, 566, 576–78, 585, 589, 590, 605. *See also* Reformist Democracy Party; Republican Nation Party; Republican Peasants' Nation Party

National Accord (Morocco), 395, 409

National Action Front Party (Jordan), 286. *See also* Arab Socialist Resurrection Party, Unified Organization; Jordanian Revolutionary People's Party

National Alliance (Palestinians), 438, 443, 452–53, 466. *See also* Palestinian National Salvation Front

National Alliance for the Liberation of Syria, 512, 515, 519, 522. *See also* Islamic Front in Syria

National Assembly: Bahrain, 71–72, 90, 91; Kuwait, 74–76, 86, 89; Syria, 500

National Assembly of Independents. *See* National Rally of Independents

National Association (Libya), 376. *See also* 'Umar al-Mukhtar Group

National Bloc (Kuwait), 73

National Bloc (Lebanon), 326, 330, 334, 336, 343–45, 352, 364
National Bloc (Palestine), 453
National Bloc (Syria), 502–4, 516, 521, 523, 524. *See also* Party of National Unity
National Bloc Party (Jordan), 296
National Brotherhood Party (Iraq), 176, 177, 190, 195, 196
National Center Group (Kuwait), 75, 89
National Committee for the Defense of the Revolution. *See* Comité National pour la Defense de la Révolution
National Committee of Heads of Arab Local Councils (Palestinians), 453
National Confederation of the *Istiqlal. See* National Union of Popular Forces
National Conference of Popular Forces (Egypt), 104
National Congress (NC) (Jordan), 261, 273, 281, 291
National Congress (Libya), 371, 376
National Congress Party (Libya), 376–77
National Defense Party (Palestine), 425, 453–54, 472
National Democratic Front. *See* Iran
National Democratic Front (NDF) (Yemen), 632, 633, 638
National Democratic and Islamic Front (Damascus Ten) (Palestinians), 428, 440, 443, 445, 447, 454, 458, 463, 466, 467, 470, 471, 473
National Democratic Front for the Liberation of Oman and the Arab Gulf (NDFLOAG), 78, 89
National Democratic Party (NDP) (Egypt), 93, 101, 102, 117–18
National Democratic Party (NDP) (Iraq), 180, 181, 182, 195–96
National Democratic Party (PND) (Morocco), 391, 409–10, 411
National Development Party (Turkey), 578
National Front. *See* Iran
National Front (Libya), 377
National Front (Morocco), 384, 388, 392, 399, 406, 410, 413, 414. *See also* Democratic Bloc; *Istiqlal;* National

Union of Popular Forces; Organization of Democratic and Popular Action; Party of Progress and Socialism; Socialist Union of Popular Forces
National Front (UAE), 84, 89
National Front (NF) (Yemen), 620, 621, 632, 636, 638. *See also* National Front for the Liberation of South Yemen; Yemeni Socialist Party
National Front for the Liberation of South Yemen (NLF), 619–21, 627, 632, 638. *See also* National Front; Yemeni Socialist Party
National Front for the Salvation of Libya (NFSL), 376, 377
National Front Party (Jordan), 263, 281, 289, 291–92
National Grouping (Lebanon), 342
National Guidance Committee (NGC) (Palestine), 429, 454–55, 464
National Islamic Front (NIF) (Sudan), 487, 493. *See also* Islamic Charter Front; Muslim Brotherhood
National Liberal Party (Lebanon), 303, 323, 326, 334, 345–47
National Liberation Front (Algeria). *See* Front de Libération Nationale
National Liberation Front (NLFB) (Bahrain), 71, 72, 89
National Liberation Front (Saudi Arabia), 81, 89
National Liberation Front (Yemen). *See* National Front for the Liberation of South Yemen
National Liberation League. *See* Communist Movement: Israel, Jordan, Palestine
National Liberation Party (Iraq). *See* Communist Movement, Iraq
National Pact. *See* Jordan; Lebanon; Turkey; Yemen
National Party (Iran), 156, 161, 163, 164, 166
National Party (Palestine), 425. *See also* Palestinian Arab National Party
National Party (Syria), 502, 504, 506, 508, 523, 527. *See also* National Bloc
National Party for Solidarity and

Development. *See* Parti National pour la Solidarité et le Developpement

National Party for the Realization of the Reform Plan (Morocco), 383, 403, 408, 410, 417

National Party of Union and Solidarity (Morocco), 410

National Popular Movement (Morocco), 395, 409, 411, 418

National Progressive Front (Syria), 512, 513, 515, 517, 523–24, 525, 527

National Progressive Front for the Liberation of Tunisia, 543

National Progressive Unionist Forum (NPUF) (Egypt), 99, 108–9, 118–19

National Rally for Democracy and Revolution. *See* Rassemblement pour la Démocratie at la Révolution

National Rally of Independents (RNI) (Morocco), 390–91, 394, 398, 409, 411, 419

National Reform Movement (Jordan), 296

National Reliance Party. *See* Reliance Party

National Religious Party (NRP) (Israel), 201, 204, 206, 207–8, 220, 225, 228, 229, 230, 231, 234, 239, 240, 242, 246–47, 251. *See also* Hamizrahi Hamizrahi Worker; *Tami*

National Salvation Party (NSP) (Turkey), 578–80, 581, 583, 584, 588, 593, 595

National Socialist Party (Iraq), 196

National Socialist Party (Jordan), 264, 292. *See also* National Front Party

National Socialist Workers' Party of Iran, 164

National Struggle Front. *See* Jumblat, Kamal; Progressive Socialist Party

National Syrian Party. *See* Syrian Social National Party

National Tunisian Democratic Front, 543

National Union (Egypt), 93, 97, 98, 104, 119–20

National Union (Jordan), 296

National Union (Syria), 507, 508, 514, 524, 526

National Union Front (Iraq), 190, 196

National Union of Democratic Students (Morocco), 410

National Union of Moroccan Students, 412–13

National Union of Popular Forces (UNFP) (Morocco), 385, 404, 406, 408, 411–14, 414, 415, 419

National Union Party (Iran), 164, 168

National Union Party (Iraq), 180, 196

National Union Party (Jordan), 293

National Unionist Party (Sudan), 480–81, 482, 491, 492, 494, 495, 498, 499. *See also* Democratic Unionist Party

National Unity Front (Qatar), 79, 90

National Unity Party (Iraq), 196

National Will Party (Iran), 140, 164

National Women's Party of Turkey, 580

National Yemeni Congregation. *See* People's General Congress

Nationalist Action Party (Turkey), 557, 580–81, 582, 591. *See also* Conservative Party; Nationalist Work Party; Republican Peasants' Nation Party

Nationalist Democracy Party (Turkey), 581–82

Nationalist Islamic Party. *See* Young Egypt

Nationalist Movement Party. *See* Nationalist Action Party

Nationalist Party (Egypt), 94, 95, 106, 120–21

Nationalist Party (Iraq), 176–77, 195, 196

Nationalist Party (Libya), 371, 374, 377, 378

Nationalist Party (Sudan), 494. *See also* Umma Party

Nationalist Party (Yemen), 617, 634

Nationalist Work Party (NWP) (Turkey), 557, 582, 588. *See also* Conservative Party; Nationalist Action Party

Nationalists of Iran Party, 164

Nationalists' Party (Iran), 136, 140, 165, 168–69

Nazareth Democratic Front (Israel; Palestinians), 455

NC. *See* National Congress

NDF. *See* National Democratic Front

NDFLOAG. *See* National Democratic

Front for the Liberation of Oman and the Arab Gulf

NDP. *See* National Democratic Party

Neo-Dustur Party (Tunisia), 532–35. *See also* Democratic Constitutional Rally; Dusturian Socialist Party; Tunisian Liberal Constitutional Party

*Neturei Karta* (Israel). *See* Guardians of the City

New Communist List. *See* Communist Movement: Israel, Palestine

New Democratic Party (Turkey), 582

New Immigration (Israel), 215, 247

New Iran Party, 136, 140, 165, 169

New Liberal Party (Israel), 247

New Order Party (Turkey), 582

New Party (Turkey), 582

New Peasants' Party (Turkey), 582

New Turkey Party (NTP), 582–83

New Wafd Party (Egypt), 99, 129–30. *See also* Wafd

NF. *See* National Front for the Liberation of South Yemen

NFSL. *See* National Front for the Salvation of Libya

NGC. *See* National Guidance Committee

Nimeiri, Ja'far, 484–86, 491, 496, 497

NIP. *See* New Iran Party

NLF. *See* National Front for the Liberation of South Yemen

NLFB. *See* National Liberation Front (Bahrain)

Nobles' Party (Egypt), 121

NOP. *See* Party for National Order

North African Star. *See* Etoile Nord-Africaine

North Yemen. *See* Yemen Arab Republic

Northern Liberation Grouping, 327

NPUF. *See* National Progressive Unionist Forum

NRP. *See* National Religious Party

NSP. *See* National Salvation Party; National Socialist Party

NTP. *See* New Turkey Party

Nuba Mountain Federation (Sudan), 483, 490, 494

NUC. *See* Turkey, National Unity Committee

NUP. *See* National Unionist Party

al-Nuqrashi, Mahmud Fahmi, 115, 122–23

Nuri al-Sa'id (Iraq), 176–82, 192, 196, 197

NWP. *See* Nationalist Work Party

OADP. *See* Organization for Democratic and Popular Action

OAP. *See* Organization of Arab Palestine

OCRA. *See* Organisation Clandestine de la Révolution Algérienne

October 24 Movement (Lebanon), 347

OLOS. *See* Organization for the Liberation of the Occupied South

Oman, 77–78, 87, 89, 90–91; Imamate, Ibadi, 77

Oman Revolutionary Movement, 90

One Arab Movement (Jordan), 296

Organisation Clandestine de la Révolution Algérienne (OCRA), 50

Organisation de la Résistance Populaire (ORP), 34, 50

Organisation Socialiste des Travailleurs (OST). *See* Parti des Travailleurs

Organisation Spéciale (OS), 9–11, 33

The Organization (Lebanon), 347–48

Organization for the Liberation of the Occupied South (OLOS) (Yemen), 619, 620, 627, 633. *See also* Front for the Liberation of South Yemen

Organization of Arab Palestine (OAP), 456

Organization of Democratic and Popular Action (Morocco), 391, 408, 414, 415–16

Organization of Leftist Kurdish Party (Lebanon), 348

Organization of Revolutionary Brigades, 76

Organization of Revolutionary Socialist Action (Lebanon), 348

Organization of Socialist Lebanon. *See* Communist Movement, Lebanon

Organization of Yemeni Resisters. *See* National Democratic Front

ORM. *See* Oman Revolutionary Movement

ORP. *See* Organisation de la Résistance Populaire
OST. *See* Parti des Travailleurs
Ottoman Party of Administrative Decentralization (Syria), 501, 524. *See also* Party of Syrian Unity
al-Ouazzani, Muhammad, 384, 399–400, 404, 417
Oujda Clan. *See* Boumediene
Our Party (Turkey), 583
Özal, Turgut, 574–75, 582, 603

PA. *See* Party of Action
PAGS. *See* Communist Movement, Algeria
Palestine, Palestinians: "All Palestine Government," 428; Damascus Ten (*see* National Democratic and Islamic Front); Egypt, relations with, 428, 429, 451, 457, 460, 461; *Fatah* civil war (Lebanon, 1983), 461; Gaza, 428–29; Great Britain, relations with, 422, 424, 425, 452, 473; Gulf War, and, 429, 441, 444–45, 462, 474; *Intifada* (uprising), 429, 440, 443, 444–45, 447, 452, 462, 474–75 (*see also* Unified National Command of the Uprising); Iran, relations with, 454; Iraq, relations with, 435, 442, 460; Israel, Palestinians in, 430–32, 436, 436–37, 443–44, 453, 471–72; Israel, peace with, 427–28, 430, 439, 440, 442, 454, 458, 462, 465, 470, Camp David, 455; Israel, relations with, 426, 430, 459, 462–63, 466, 469, 471, Oslo secret talks (1993), 463, two-state solution, 460; Jordan, relations with, 439, 441, 446, 449, 451, 459–61, 462, 465, 468, 469; Lebanon, involvement in, 441, 443, 452, 457, 458, 459, 460–61, 462, 471, 473; Libya, relations with, 442; Palestine Central Council, 430, 463, 464; Palestine National Council (PNC), 443, 444, 458, 461, 462, 464, 471, 473; Palestinian National Authority, 430, 464, 474; Palestinian state, declaration of (1988), 461; Resolutions 242 and 338 of UN Security Council, 461, 463; Syria, relations with, 438, 442, 452, 454, 457, 458, 466, 471, 472–73; United States, relations with, 439, 458, 461; West Bank, 423, 426, 428–30, 445, 446, 448–49, 451, 454, 456, 461, 464, 468, 473; Zionism, conflict with, 422–23, 424, 425, 434, 435, 450, 453, 454–55, 464, 467, 468, 473
Palestine Arab Party, 425, 456, 472, 473
Palestine Communist Party (PCP). *See* Communist Movement: Israel, Jordan, Palestine
Palestine Democratic Union, 440
Palestine Liberation Army, 429, 457–458, 463
Palestine Liberation Front, 438, 454, 458, 464, 471. *See also* Popular Front for the Liberation of Palestine
Palestine Liberation Organization (PLO), 427–30, 433, 435, 437–38, 438–39, 441–42, 443, 444–45, 450, 451, 452, 454, 455, 456, 457, 458, 458–64, 465–66, 468, 474
Palestine National Front, 429, 438, 452, 456, 464
Palestinian Arab National Party, 453, 465. *See also* National Defense Party
Palestinian Communist Organization. *See* Communist Movement, Palestine
Palestinian Communist Workers Party. *See* Communist Movement, Palestine
Palestinian Democratic Union, 440, 465
Palestinian National Liberation Movement. *See* Fatah
Palestinian National Salvation Front (PNSF), 443, 452, 454, 461, 465–66, 469, 471, 473
Palestinian People's Party. *See* Communist Movement, Palestine
Palestinian Popular Struggle Front (PPSF), 452, 454, 466
Palestinian Revolutionary Communist Party. *See* Communist Movement, Palestine
Palestinian Society, 467
Pan-Arabism, 88, 90, 178–79, 180, 182–83, 184–85, 190, 193, 195, 268, 271, 284, 288–89, 292, 295, 359, 426, 428,

436, 450, 631. *See also* Arab Socialist Resurrection (*Ba'th*) Party; Movement of Arab Nationalists; National Front Party (Jordan); National Socialist Party (Jordan); Unionist Democratic Bloc

Pan-Iranist Party, 165

*Al-Parti. See* Kurdish Democratic Party, *Al-Parti*

Parti Communiste Algérien (PCA). *See* Communist Movement, Algeria

Parti Communiste Français (PCF). *See* Communist Movement, Algeria

Parti de la Révolution Socialiste, Comité National pour la Defense de la Révolution (PRS-CNDR), 50–51

Parti de l'Avant-Garde Socialiste (PAGS). *See* Communist Movement, Algeria

Parti des Travailleurs (PT), 55

Parti du Peuple Algérien, Mouvement pour la Triomphe des Libertés Démocratiques (PPA-MTLD), 6, 9–12, 55–58, 64–65

Parti du Renouveau Algérien (PRA), 58–59

Parti National pour la Solidarite et le Developpement (PNSD), 59–60

Parti Populaire Syrienne. *See* Syrian Social National Party

Parti Social-Démocrate (PSD), 60–61

Parti Socialiste des Travailleurs (PST), 61

The Partisans. *See* Communist Movement, Palestine

Party for Civilization, Cherishing Animals, Economy, and Agriculture (Turkey), 584

Party for Land, Real Estate, and Free Enterprise (Turkey), 569, 574, 584. *See also* Islamic Democratic Party; Liberal Peasants' Party

Party for National Order (Turkey), 578, 584–85. *See also* National Salvation Party; Prosperity Party

Party for the Defense of Islam (Turkey), 585

Party of Action (Morocco), 389, 415

Party of Advance and Preservation (Turkey), 585

Party of Arab Independence, 501, 503, 524, 529. *See also Istiqlal* (Jordan; Palestine; Syria); Young Arab Society

Party of Arab Liberation (Lebanon), 348

Party of Democrats (Turkey), 585

Party of Genuine Democrats (Turkey), 585. *See also* Nation Party I

Party of God (*Hizbullah*) (Lebanon), 320, 340, 348–52, 362

Party of Idealists (Turkey), 585

Party of Kemalist Youth (Turkey), 585

Party of Liberation (Palestinians), 467–68

Party of Liberation and Socialism. *See* Communist Movement, Morocco

Party of Moroccan Unity, 416

Party of National Reform. *See Islah*

Party of National Unity (Syria), 502, 524. *See also* National Bloc

Party of Popular Unity (Tunisia), 543. *See also* Movement for Popular Unity

Party of Progress and Socialism. *See* Communist Movement, Morocco

Party of Syrian Unity, 501, 524. *See also* Ottoman Party of Administrative Decentralization

Party of the Democratic Socialist Avant-Garde (Morocco), 415–16

Party of the Lebanese People, 503

Party of the Nation (Jordan), 293, 296

Patriotic Free Party (Turkey), 585

Patriotic Front. *See* National Front for the Liberation of South Yemen

Patriotic Union of Kurdistan (PUK) (Iraq), 196

Patriots' Party (Iran), 166

*Paykar* Organization. *See* Communist Movement, Iran

PCA. *See* Communist Movement, Algeria

PCF. *See* Parti Communiste Français

PCP. *See* Communist Movement, Palestine

PCT. *See* Communist Movement, Tunisia

PDI. *See* Democratic Party of Independence

PDP. *See* People's Democratic Party

PDRY. *See* Yemen Arab Republic, People's Democratic Republic of Yemen

PDS. *See* Socialist Democratic Party

Peace Now (Israel), 248
Peasants' Party of Turkey, 574, 585–86, 590. See also Liberal Peasants' Party; Republican Peasants' Nation Party
People's Action Party (Morocco), 408, 417
People's Bloc (Bahrain), 71, 72, 90
People's Club (Yemen), 617, 634
People's Democratic Party (PDP) (Sudan), 481, 491, 492, 494, 495, 498. See also Democratic Unionist Party
People's Democratic Union. See Communist Movement, Yemen
People's General Congress (PGC) (Yemen), 623–24, 632, 633
People's Labor Party (Turkey), 558, 586. See also Democracy Party
People's Liberation Group (Egypt). See Communist Movement, Egypt
People's Mojahedin Organization of Iran, 137, 141, 158, 166, 166–68
People's Party (Egypt), 93, 96, 113-n14, 121–22, 127
People's Party (Iran), 136, 140, 164, 168–69
People's Party (Iraq), 176, 180, 195, 196
People's Party (Syria), 502, 504, 505, 505–7, 508, 517, 520, 522, 523, 524–25, 528. See also Iron Hand Society
People's Party (Turkey), 586. See also Republican People's Party
People's Progressive Party (Sudan), 495
People's Republican Party (Turkey), 586
People's Socialist Party (PSP) (Yemen), 619, 633
Peres, Shimon, 201, 219, 221, 222, 225, 231, 241, 242, 243, 244. See also Labor Party; Rafi
PFLOAG. See Popular Front for the Liberation of Oman and the Arab Gulf; Popular Front for the Liberation of the Occupied Arab Gulf
PFLP. See Popular Front for the Liberation of Palestine
PFLP, GC. See Popular Front for the Liberation of Palestine, General Command
PGC. See People's General Congress

Phalanges Libanaises. See Lebanese Phalanges Party
Pink Panthers militia (Lebanon). See Arab Democratic Party
PKK. See Kurdish Workers' Party
PLA. See Palestine Liberation Army
PLF. See Palestine Liberation Front
PLO. See Palestine Liberation Organization
PMOI. See People's Mojahedin Organization of Iran
PND. See National Democratic Party
PNF. See Palestine National Front
PNO. See Party for National Order
PNSD. See Parti National pour la Solidarite et le Developpement PNSF. See Palestinian National Salvation Front
Poalei Agudat Yisrael. See Labor Association of Israel
Political Council of the National Liberal Party Convening in Saudico (Lebanon), 346
Popular Democratic Front for the Liberation of Palestine. See Democratic Front for the Liberation of Palestine
Popular Democratic Nationalists (Jordan), 296
Popular Democratic Party (Saudi Arabia), 81, 90
Popular Front (1974) (Bahrain), 72
Popular Front for the Liberation of Oman, 78, 90
Popular Front for the Liberation of Oman and the Arab Gulf (PFLOAG), 70, 71, 72, 78, 90
Popular Front for the Liberation of Palestine (PFLP), 283–84, 289, 359, 427, 438, 453, 454, 459, 463, 464, 466, 468–70, 472, 474. See also Jordanian Democratic Popular Unity Party; Socialist Arab Action Party
Popular Front for the Liberation of Palestine, External Operations, 470
Popular Front for the Liberation of Palestine, General Command (PFLP-GC), 348, 438, 443, 453, 454, 456, 458, 469, 470, 470–71, 472. See also Organization of Arab Palestine

Popular Front for the Liberation of the Occupied Arab Gulf (PFLOAG), 78, 90–91

Popular Front Organization in Jordan, 267, 284. See also Jordanian Democratic Popular Unity Party

Popular Liberation Forces (Palestinians), 457. See also Palestine Liberation Army

Popular Movement (Jordan), 296

Popular Movement (Morocco), 384, 385, 389, 401, 411, 415, 417, 417–18

Popular Nasserite Organization (Lebanon), 329–30, 352

Popular Resistance Organization. See Organisation de la Resistance Populaire

Popular Revolutionary Front for the Liberation of Palestine, 469, 470. See also Popular Front for the Liberation of Palestine; Popular Front for the Liberation of Palestine, External Operations

Popular Struggle. See Palestinian Popular Struggle Front

Popular Unionist Party (Egypt). See People's Party; Unionist Party

Popular Unity Party, The Unionists (Jordan), 293

Popular Vanguard for Liberation (TASHT) (Egypt). See Communist Movement, Egypt

Popular Vanguard Party (Yemen), 621, 633–34, 636. See also Unified Political Organization of the National Front (UPONF)

Populist Party (PP) (Turkey), 586, 586–87, 598. See also Social Democratic Populist Party

PPA. See Parti du Peuple Algérien, Mouvement pour la Triomphe des Libertés Démocratiques

PPS. See Communist Movement, Morocco

PPSF. See Palestinian Popular Struggle Front

PRA. See Parti du Renouveau Algérien

PRCP. See Palestinian Revolutionary Communist Party

Progressive Arab Resurrection (Ba'th) Party (Jordan), 293–94. See also Arab Socialist Resurrection (Ba'th) Party

Progressive Ideals Party of Turkey, 587

Progressive Kurdish Movement (Iraq), 197

Progressive Liberal Party, 418

Progressive List for Peace (Israel, Palestinians), 209, 248, 431, 471–72

Progressive National Movement (Jordan), 296

Progressive Party (Iran), 165, 169

Progressive Party (Iraq), 176, 197

Progressive Party (Israel), 201, 215, 220, 237, 240, 244, 247, 248–49, 255. See also General Zionists; Independent Liberal Party; Liberal Party; New Immigration; Zionist Worker

Progressive Republican Party (Turkey), 587

Progressive Socialist Party (Lebanon), 303, 329, 339, 342, 352–57

Progressive Vanguards (Lebanon), 357

Promise. See Democratic Arab Unionist Party, Promise

The Promise Movement (Jordan), 296

Promise Party (Lebanon), 357–58

Prosperity Party (Turkey), 568, 582, 588

PRS. See Parti de la Révolution Socialiste, Comité National pour la Defense de la Révolution

PSD. See Dusturian Socialist Party; Parti Social-Démocrate

PSP. See People's Socialist Party; Progressive Socialist Party; Social Progress Party

PST. See Parti Socialiste des Travailleurs

PT. See Parti des Travailleurs

PUK. See Patriotic Union of Kurdistan

The Pulpit. See Union of Popular Forces

PUP. See Party of Popular Unity

Purification and Preservation Party (Turkey), 588

al-Qaddumi, Faruq, 442

al-Qadhafi, Muammar, 372, 373, 374, 375, 376, 377, 378

Qahtan Society (Syria), 501, 525

Qasim, Brigadier 'Abd al-Karim, 181–84, 190, 192, 194, 195–96

Qatar, 79–80, 90
Qawqa, Shaykh Khalil. See Hamas
Qulaylat, Ibrahim, 341 42
Quranic Preservation Society (Tunisia), 541, 542, 544
Qutb, Sayyid, 111, 116
al-Quywwatli, Shukri, 503–4, 506, 507, 516, 517, 523, 525, 526

Rabin, Yitzhak, 206, 224–25, 244
Radical Freedom Party (Turkey), 588
Radical Party (Turkey), 588
Rafi. See Israel Workers List
Rafsanjani, 'Ali Akbar Hashemi, 157, 158
Rajavi, Mas'ud, 139, 167–68
Rakah. See Communist Movement, Israel
Rally of the United Maghrib (Tunisia), 544
Ramgavar Party, 358
Rantisi, 'Abd al-'Aziz. See Hamas
Rashid 'Ali. See al-Kaylani
Rassemblement National pour la Démocratie et la Révolution (RNDR), 61–62
Rassemblement pour la Culture et al Démocratie (RCD), 39
Rassemblement Unitaire des Révolutionaires (RUR), 64
Rastakhiz Party. See Resurgence Party
Ratz. See Civil Rights Movement
RCC. See Sudan, Revolutionary Command Council
RCD. See Democratic Constitutional Rally (Tunisia); Rassemblement pour la Culture et al Démocratie
Reawakening Party (Jordan), 294
Rebirth Party I, II (Turkey), 588
Red Hand Society (Syria), 502, 525
Reform Association (Yemen), 614, 616, 617, 634
Reform Club (Yemen), 616, 617
Reform Party (Iraq), 181, 197
Reform Party (Palestine), 472
Reform Party (Syria), 502, 525
Reform Party (Turkey), 588
Reformers' Party (Iran), 135, 169
Reformist Democracy Party (Turkey),

555, 589. See also Banner Party; Nation Party III
Reformist Party (Tunisia), 531, 533
Rejection Front (Palestinian), 460, 466, 469, 472
Reliance Party (RP) (Turkey), 589, 590, 592. See also Republican Reliance Party
Religious Bloc (1973) (Bahrain), 71, 72, 91
Religious Strugglers. See Islamic Community
Religious Worker (Israel), 249
Renaissance Party (Tunisia), 537. See also Islamic Tendency Movement
Representatives of the People (Bahrain), 71, 91
Republican Democratic Youth Party (Turkey), 589
Republican Nation Party (Turkey), 577, 586, 589–90. See also Nation Party I; Republican Peasants' Nation Party
Republican Party (Egypt), 122
Republican Party (Turkey), 589, 590, 593, 595. See also Republican Reliance Party
Republican Party (Yemen), 624, 634
Republican Peasants' Nation Party (RPNP) (Turkey), 577, 580, 586, 590–91. See also Nation Party II; Nationalist Action Party; Peasants' Party of Turkey; Republican Nation Party
Republican People's Party (RPP) (Turkey), 549–50, 558, 561, 562, 566, 567, 577, 578, 580, 583, 587, 589, 590, 591–95, 598
Republican Professional Reform Party (Turkey), 595
Republican Reliance Party (RRP) (Turkey), 589, 595–96. See also Reliance Party; Republican Party
Resurgence Party (Iran), 136–37, 139, 140, 165, 169
Revisionist Movement (Israel), 199, 213–14, 236, 236–37, 249–50. See also Irgun Zvai Leumi; Jabotinsky, Vladimir
Revival Party (Iran), 135, 165, 169, 169–70
Revival Party (Israel), 207, 209, 228, 231, 238, 242, 250. See also Block of the

Faithful; Labor Movement for Greater
Israel
Revival Party (Turkey), 596
Revolutionary Bloc (Egypt). *See*
Communist Movement, Egypt
Revolutionary Committees (Libya), 378
Revolutionary Democratic Party of
Yemen. *See* National Democratic Front
Revolutionary March Committees
(Jordan), 296
Revolutionary Marxists in Jordan, New
Leftist Formation, 296
Revolutionary Nasserite Organization
(Lebanon), 359
Revolutionary Organization in the
Occupied South Yemen. *See* National
Front for the Liberation of South
Yemen
Revolutionary Organization of the
Communist Party Abroad. *See*
Communist Movement, Iran
Revolutionary Pioneers. *See* National
Front for the Liberation of South
Yemen
Revolutionary Workers'-Peasants' Party of
Turkey. *See* Communist Movement,
Turkey
*Riz Kari*. *See* Lebanese Kurdish Party
RMU. *See* Rally of the United Maghrib
RNDR. *See* Rassemblement National pour
la Démocratie et la Révolution
RNI. *See* National Rally of Independents
RP. *See* Reliance Party
RPNP. *See* Republican Peasants' Nation
Party
RPP. *See* Republican People's Party
RRP. *See* Republican Reliance Party
RSP. *See* Socialist Rally of Progressive
Unity
RUR. *See* Rassemblement Unitaire des
Révolutionaires

Sa'adah, 'Abdallah, 362
Sa'adah, Antun, 360–62, 503, 505, 527–28
Sa'adah, George, 327, 335–36
Al Sabah Emirs of Kuwait, 73–77

SACDNU. *See* Sudan African Closed
Districts National Union
al-Sadat, Anwar, 93, 98–99, 103, 105,
116, 117, 118, 128
al-Sadawi, Bahir, 371, 373, 375, 376–77,
378
Sadi, Saïd, 39, 62–64
Sa'dist Organization (Egypt), 96, 114,
115, 122–23
Saddam Husayn (Iraq), 182, 185, 186–89,
190, 191, 194, 441
Al-Sadr, Musa (Imam), 305–6, 308, 319,
336–38, 340, 348
Sahnouni, El Hachemi, 42
Sahwa (Egypt), 112. *See also* Islamic
Associations
al-Sa'id, Nuri. *See* Nuri al-Sa'id
*al-Sa'iqa*, 453, 454, 472–73
SAL. *See* South Arabian League
Salama, Hafiz, 112
Salvation Movement (Jordan), 296
Salvation Party (Turkey), 597
SANU. *See* Sudan African National
Union
Sarraj, 'Abd al-Hamid, 506–7
Saudi Arabia, 70, 80–84, 86, 87, 88, 89,
90, 91, 92; 'Abd al -'Aziz, King Sa'ud
bin, 81; Grand Mosque incident, 81–
82; *al -Ikhwan* (The Brotherhood), 82;
Iran, relations with, 82, 86, 87, 88;
Wahhabis, 80, 86; Workers'
Committee, 81
al-Sayyid, Ahmad Lutfi, 95, 125–26
SDPP. *See* Social Democratic Populist
Party
Secret Labor Union (Bahrain), 71, 91
Secret Organization of Free Officers and
Soldiers. *See* National Front for the
Liberation of South Yemen
Secret Organization of Freeman of
Occupied South Yemen. *See* National
Front for the Liberation of South
Yemen
Sephardi Association (Israel), 250
Sephardi Association of the Observers of
the Torah. *See Shas*
September Democratic Organization
(Yemen), 635

Serenity Party (Turkey), 597
Service to the Nation Party (Turkey), 597
Sha'b. See Marxist People's Party
al-Shabiba. See Kuwait
Shach, Rabbi Eliezer, 236, 240, 250
Shafi'is. See Yemen Arab Republic
Shah Muhammad Reza (1941–1979),
    135–37, 143, 165, 168–69
Shah Reza Khan (1925–1941), 135, 169,
    169–70
Shahbandar, 'Abd al-Rahman, 502, 520,
    524
Shamir, Yitzhak, 200, 201, 228, 230, 237,
    245
Sham'un, Dani, 246. See also National
    Liberal Party
Sham'un, Duri, 346. See also National
    Liberal Party
Sham'un, Kamil, 325–26, 345–47, 355,
    361. See also National Liberal Party
Shari'atmadari, Ayatollah Muhammad
    Kazem, 138, 141, 163, 169
Sharon, Ariel, 223, 225
Shas (Israel), 206, 207, 208, 209, 230–31,
    240, 250–51
Sheli Peace Camp (Israel), 246, 251, 252
Shihab, Fu'ad, 314, 353, 361
Shi'ites. See Iraq; Lebanon; Turkey
Shinui, Center Party (Israel), 204, 209,
    230, 234, 235, 240, 245, 251
Shishakli, Adib, 505, 514, 526, 528
SHP. See Social Democratic Populist
    Party
Shuqayri, Ahmad, 459. See also Palestine
    Liberation Organization
Shukri, Ibrahim, 123–24, 131
Sidqi, Isma'il, 121–22, 127
SLP. See Socialist Labor Party
Social Center Party (Morocco), 419
Social Cultural Society (Kuwait), 75, 91
Social Democrat Party (Iran), 134, 170
Social Democratic Party (Algeria). See
    Parti Social-Démocrate
Social Democratic Party (Morocco), 388,
    419
Social Democratic Party (Turkey), 587,
    597
Social Democratic Populist Party (SDPP)
    (Turkey), 586, 587, 597–98, 603. See
    also Populist Party
Social Justice Party (Turkey), 598
Social Peasant Party (Egypt). See Socialist
    Peasant Party
Social Progress Party (PSP) (Tunisia),
    537, 545
Social Reform Society (Kuwait), 72, 91
Socialist Arab Action Party (Lebanon),
    330, 359
Socialist Christian Democratic Party, The
    Action Party (Lebanon), 359
Socialist Democratic Party (PDS)
    (Tunisia), 536, 544–45
Socialist Federation of Tunisia, 531
Socialist Labor Party (Egypt), 97, 99, 101,
    103, 112, 116, 118, 123 4, 131
Socialist Liberal Party (Egypt), 105, 116,
    123, 124–25
Socialist Party (Iran), 135, 148, 170–71
Socialist Party I, II, III (Turkey), 597,
    598–99, 600. See also Socialist Party of
    Turkey; Workers' Party of Turkey;
    Workers'-Peasants' Party of Turkey
Socialist Party of Egypt. See Young Egypt
Socialist Party of Turkey I, 598, 599–600.
    See also Socialist Party I; Workers' Party
    of Turkey
Socialist Party of Turkey II, 600
Socialist Peasant Party (Egypt), 125
Socialist Power Party (Turkey), 600. See
    also Socialist Party; Socialist Party of
    Turkey II
Socialist Rally of Progressive Unity
    (RSP), 537, 545
Socialist Republican Party (Sudan), 495
Socialist Revolution Party (Turkey). See
    Communist Movement, Turkey
Socialist Revolution Party, National
    Committee for the Defense of the
    Revolution. See Parti de la Révolution
    Socialiste, Comité National pour la
    Defense de la Révolution
Socialist Union of Popular Forces (USFP)
    (Morocco), 389–91, 406, 408, 413–14,
    415, 419–21
Socialist Unionists' Movement (Syria),
    511, 523, 525

Socialist Unity Party (Turkey), 600–601
Socialist Vanguard Party. *See* Parti de L'Avant-Garde Socialiste
Socialist Workers' and Peasants' Party of Turkey, 601
Socialist Workers' Party (Algeria). *See* Parti Socialiste des Travailleurs
Socialist Workers' Party (Iran), 171
Socialist Workers' Party of Turkey I, 601
Socialist Workers' Party of Turkey II. *See* Communist Movement, Turkey; Workers' Party of Turkey
Socialist Workers' Party of Turkey III, 602
Society for Social Reform (Bahrain), 72, 91
Society for the Defense of the Rights of Anatolia and Rumelia. *See* Republican People's Party
Society for the Liberation of the Holy Soil, 81, 91
Society of Free Youth (Bahrain), 71, 91
Society of Independent Egypt, 113
Society of Iranian Socialists, 161, 171. *See also* Third Force
Society of Palestinian Youth, 467, 473
Society of the Covenant (Syria), 501, 525
Soldiers of God (Lebanon), 359
SOMKA. *See* National Socialist Workers' Party of Iran
SONATRACH, 37
Sons of the Arabian Peninsula, 81, 91
Sons of the Country. *See* Abna al-Balad
South Arabian League (SAL) (Yemen), 617, 618–19, 620, 630, 633, 635. *See also* League of the Sons of Yemen
South Yemen. *See* Yemen Arab Republic
Southern Front (Sudan), 483–84, 494, 495
Southern Liberal Party (Sudan), 495. *See also* Southern Party
Southern Party (Sudan), 481, 495–96. *See also* Southern Liberal Party
Southern Sudan Political Association, 496
Southern Sudanese Liberation Movement (SSLM), 485, 496. *See also* Sudan African National Union

SPLA. *See* Sudan People's Liberation Army
SSLM. *See* Southern Sudanese Liberation Movement
SSNP. *See* Syrian Social National Party
SSU. *See* Sudan Socialist Union
State List (Israel), 223, 226, 235, 236, 242, 245, 251
Stern Group (Gang) (Israel), 236
The Storm. *See* Fatah; Palestine Liberation Organization
Sudan: civil war in, 481, 482, 483–87; constitution, 485, 486, 487, 494, 498; Egypt, relations with, 476–80, 490, 493, 494, 495, 498, 499; elections, 480, 481, 483, 484, 485, 486–87, 488, 489, 490, 491, 495, 496, 498; Graduates Club, 478, 479, 491, 498; Great Britain, relations with, 478, 480, 495, 498; military in politics, 481, 484, 486, 487, 497; political system, 478–89; Professionals Front, 482–83, 495; Revolutionary Command Council (RCC), 484; Supreme Council of the Armed Forces (SCAF), 481–82
Sudan African Closed Districts National Union (SACDNU), 482, 496. *See also* Sudan African National Union
Sudan African Congress, 496
Sudan African National Union (SANU), 482, 483–84, 490, 494, 496
Sudan African People's Congress, 497
Sudan People's Federal Party, 497
Sudan People's Liberation Army (SPLA), 486, 491, 497
Sudan People's Liberation Movement. *See* Sudan People's Liberation Army
Sudan Socialist Union (SSU), 485, 485–86
Sudan Unity Party, 497
Sudanese Democratic Organization. *See* Communist Movement, Sudan
Sudanese Movement for National Liberation (SMNL), 480, 490. *See also* Communist Movement, Sudan; Sudanese Democratic Organization
Sudanese Union Society (SUS), 478, 498, 499

Suicidal Forces of Husayn (Lebanon), 360
Supporters of the Call (*Ansar al-Da'wa*) (Bahrain), 72, 92
Supreme Muslim Council (Palestine), 425, 473–74
SUS. *See* Sudanese Union Society
Syria: Arab revolt against Ottoman Empire (1916), 501; constitution, 505, 507, 511–12, 524, 528; Egypt, relations with, 506 , 515, 517, 521, 522, 526, 527; elections, 500, 501, 502, 504, 505, 506, 507, 508, 513, 514, 515, 516, 517, 518, 522, 523, 524, 526, 527, 528; France, mandate, 502–3, 520, 523, 527, 528; France, relations with, 502, 508, 516, 524, 525, 526; Hama uprising (1982), 512, 519, 522; Iraq, relations with, 504, 506, 522, 524, 528; Israel, relations with, 504, 511, 518, 527; Monarchism, 503, 509–10; Nasser, 506–7, 517, 522; National Assembly, 500, 502, 503, 504, 506, 508, 514, 515, 516, 518, 523, 524, 525, 526, 528; National Council for Command of the Revolution, 509; party system, 500; People's Assembly, 511–12, 513, 515, 524, 527; United Arab Republic, 507, 517; United States, relations with, 506–7, 526
Syrian Communist Party. *See* Communist Movement, Syria
Syrian Social National Party (SSNP), 294, 324, 329, 360–63, 503, 505, 506, 526, 527–28
Syrian Union Party, 502, 528

Talabani, Jalal (Iraq; Kurds), 186, 194–95, 196
Taleqani, Ayatollah Mahmut, 160, 161–62
*Tami*, Movement for the Tradition of the People of Israel, 228, 230, 247, 251
TASHT (Egypt). *See* Communist Movement, Egypt
TCP. *See* Communist Movement, Turkey
*Tehiya. See* Revival Party
*Telem*, Movement for Renewal of Statehood (Israel), 235, 251–52

Al-Thani. *See* Qatar
Third Force (Iran), 163, 171. *See also* Society of Iranian Socialists
This World Party (Israel), 251, 252
Thorez, Maurice, 52
Those Rescued From Hell (Egypt). *See* Islamic Associations
Those Who Sacrifice Themselves. *See al-Fidaiyya*
Tigers. *See* National Liberal Party
TIP. *See* Workers' Party of Turkey
Togetherness Party. *See Yahad*
Toilers' League. *See* Communist Movement, Lebanon
Toilers' Party. *See* Communist Movement, Iran
Toilers' Party of the Iranian Nation, 163, 172
Torres, Abdel Khalek, 401–2. *See also Islah* Party
The Tribal Organization. *See* National Front for the Liberation of South Yemen
Tripolitanian National Congress (Libya), 371, 376, 378
True Path Party (Turkey), 568, 575, 598, 602–3
The Truth Party (Yemen), 624, 636. *See also* Union of Popular Forces
*Tsomet*, Movement for Zionist Renewal, 206, 207, 209, 231, 250, 252
*Tudeh* Party. *See* Communist Movement, Iran
*Tufan. See* Communist Movement, Iran
*Tunis al-Fatat. See* Young Tunisians
Tunisia: Arab world, relations with, 533, 539, 547; Bardo Treaty, 534–35; elections, 534–35, 537, 539, 543, 544, 545, 546, 547; France, relations with, 530–35, 546, 547; one-party system, 535, 536; political liberalization, 536–37, 544
Tunisian Communist Party (PCT). *See* Communist Movement, Tunisia
Tunisian Liberal Constitutional Party (*Dustur*), 531–32, 546, 546–547. *See also* Democratic Constitutional Rally;

Dusturian Socialist Party; Neo-Dustur Party
Tunisian National Progressive Front, 547
Tunisian National Resistance, 547
Tunisian Nationalist Movement, 547
Tunisian Perspectives, 547
Tunisian Socialist Study and Action Group, 547
Tunisian Worker, 547
al-Turabi, Hasan, 486, 487, 493
Türkes, Alparslan, 557, 580, 582, 590
Turkey: Alevis, 594, 606; constitution, 556, 591; elections, 552, 558–59, 560, 561, 562, 562–63, 564, 565, 567, 570–71, 575, 576, 577, 578, 580–81, 581, 582, 583, 586, 587, 588, 589, 590, 592–93, 595, 597–98, 600, 603, 604, 606, 607; electoral system, 550–51, 580, 592; Kemalism, reform program, 549, 591, 593; military in politics, 549, 550–52, 556, 557, 560, 568, 570, 571, 572, 574, 580, 581, 582–83, 587, 589, 590, 592–93, 597, 599, 603, 604; National Unity Committee (NUC), 580, 582–83; party structure, 551; party system, competitive, 549–51, 566, 578, 591–92; political violence, 551, 552, 566, 571, 573, 604; secularism and anti-secularism, 549, 550, 555, 559, 561, 568, 573, 574, 577, 578, 579, 581, 584, 585, 587, 588, 589, 590, 591, 593, 600, 602, 603, 607
Turkish Conservative Party, 569, 603. See also Islamic Democratic Party
Turkish People's Liberation Party, 603–4
Turkish Social Democratic Party, 604
26 January Collective (Tunisia), 547

UAE. See United Arab Emirates
UAR. See United Arab Republic
UC. See Constitutional Union
UDMA. See Union Démocratique du Manifeste Algérien
UDU. See Union for Democratic Unity
UFD. See Union des Forces Démocratiques
UGEMA. See Union Générale des Etudiants Musulmans Algériens

UGTA. See Union Générale des Travailleurs Algériens
UGTM. See General Union of Moroccan Workers
'Umar al-Mukhtar Group/Society (Libya), 370, 378, 379
Umm al-Qura Party (Party of Mecca) (Jordan), 295
Al-Umma Movement (Algeria). See Mouvement el-Oumma
Umma Party (Egypt), 94, 95, 120, 125–26
Umma Party (Sudan), 480, 481, 482, 483–84, 485, 486–87, 488, 491, 492, 493, 494, 495, 498
UMT. See Moroccan Labor Union
UNCU. See Unified National Command of the Uprising
UNED. See National Union of Democratic Students
UNEM. See National Union of Moroccan Students
Unified National Command of the Uprising (UNCU) (Palestinians), 249, 442, 444, 447, 463, 474–75
Unified Political Organization of the National Front (UPONF) (Yemen), 621, 634, 636. See also National Front; People's Democratic Union; Popular Vanguard Party; Yemeni Socialist Party
Union Club (Kuwait), 74, 92
Union Démocratique du Manifeste Algérien (UDMA) (Algeria), 9, 16, 52–53, 64–65
Union des Forces Démocratiques (UFD) (Algeria), 65
Union for Democratic Unity (Tunisia), 537, 547
Union Générale des Etudiants Musulmans Algériens (UGEMA), 12, 33
Union Générale des Travailleurs Algériens (UGTA), 17, 18, 34, 35, 54
Union Générale Tunisienne du Travail (UGTT), 535, 539, 542
Union of Bahraini Students, 72
Union of Peace Partisans (Egypt). See Communist Movement, Egypt
Union of People's Forces. See Union of Popular Forces

Union of Popular Forces (Yemen), 636–37. *See also* Truth Party

Union of Popular Yemeni Forces, 637

Union of the Forces of the Working People (The Nasserite Organization) (Lebanon), 343, 363–64

Union of the People of the Arabian Peninsula, 81, 92

Union of Tunisian People's Forces, 548

Union Populaire Algérienne (UPA), 65, 66

Unionist Democratic Bloc (Jordan), 272, 295

Unionist Democratic Jordanian Party, 296

Unionist Party (Egypt), 93, 96, 113–14, 122, 126–27

Unionist Party (Sudan), 480, 498. *See also* National Unionist Party

Unionist Rally for Democracy (Tunisia), 548

Unionist Socialist Movement (Jordan), 296

Unionist Socialist Movement in Jordan, New Leftist Formation, 296

Unitarian Yemeni Congregation. *See* Gathering of United Yemenis

Unitary Rally of Revolutionaires. *See* Rassemblement Unitaires des Révolutionnaires

United Arab Emirates, 84–85

United Arab Republic, 104, 120, 507, 515, 517, 522, 524, 525, 526. *See also* Egypt; Syria

United Communist Party of Turkey. *See* Communist Movement, Turkey

United Democratic Corrective Front. *See* Corrective Popular Nasserite Organization

United Front (Sudan), 482

United Front of Progressive Parties (Iran), 171

United Nasserist People's Organization (Yemen), 637

United National Front (Libya), 371, 372, 373, 378, 378–79

United National Front (Yemen), 619, 637. *See also* South Arabian League

United Political Organization, National Front. *See* Unified Political Organization of the National Front

United Popular Front (Iraq), 197

United Religious Front (Israel), 252

United Workers Party (*Mapam*) (Israel), 199, 201, 213, 215, 217, 218, 219, 229, 230, 234, 241–42, 244, 245, 246, 251, 252–53, 253, 254

Unity of Labor (Israel), 199, 201, 211, 213, 217, 221, 222, 225, 241, 242, 253, 255

Unity of Labor Movement (Israel), 253–54

Unity of Labor, Zionist Labor (Israel), 254

Unity of the Nile Valley Party (Sudan), 480, 490, 499

Unity Party (UP), Unity Party of Turkey, 571, 605–6

UNPF. *See* National Union of Popular Forces

UP. *See* Unity Party, Unity Party of Turkey

UPA. *See* Union Populaire Algérienne

UPONF. *See* Unified Political Organization of the National Front

USFP. *See* Socialist Union of Popular Forces

Vanguards of the Popular Liberation War, Forces of the Lightning Bolt. *See* al-Sa'iqa

Virtue Party (Turkey), 606

Wafd (Egypt), 94, 95–96, 97, 99, 101, 109, 113–14, 116, 121, 121–22, 122, 123, 124, 126, 126–27, 127–30, 131. *See also* New Wafd Party

Wafdist Bloc (Egypt), 96, 130. *See also* New Wafd Party

Wahhabis. *See* Saudi Arabia

Warriors of Islam (Iran), 135–36, 172

Warriors of the Islamic Revolution (Iran), 158. *See also* Islamic Republican Party

White Flag League (Sudan), 478, 498, 499

White Revolution. *See* Iran

Workers' and Farmers' Party of the Turkish Republic, 606, 606–607

Workers' and Farmers' Party of Turkey, 606
Workers' Committee. *See* Saudi Arabia
Workers' Party (Algeria). *See* Parti des Travailleurs
Workers' Party (Jordan), 296
Workers' Party (Turkey), 607
Workers' Party, *Hashomer Hatsair* (Israel), 213, 215, 253, 254
Workers' Party of Turkey I (WPT), 593, 598, 599, 600, 601, 602, 605, 607–8
Workers' Party of Turkey II, 608–9
Workers'-Peasants' Party of Turkey. *See* Communist Movement, Turkey; Revolutionary Workers'-Peasants' Party of Turkey
WPT. *See* Workers' Party of Turkey I

Yafa'i Reform Front. *See* National Front for the Liberation of South Yemen
Yafa'i Reform Movement. *See* National Front for the Liberation of South Yemen.
*Yahad* (Israel), 234, 254
Yahiaoui, Mohamed Salah, 18, 35, 54
Yasin, Shaykh Ahmad. *See Hamas*
Yazbaki Family Confederation, 355, 362, 364
Yazbaki Liberation Front (Lebanon), 364
YCR. *See* Yemeni Congregation for Reform
Yemen Arab Republic: civil war, 616, 621; constitution, 621–22, 623; Corrective Movement (1969), 620, 632; Egypt (Nasser), relations with, 615, 616, 618, 620, 626, 627, 631, 633, 637; elections, 623–25, 631, 638; Great Britain, relations with, 612, 613, 616, 617–18, 619, 620, 627, 629, 630, 633, 637; Imam Ahmad, 614–16; Imam Muhammad al-Badr, 615 6; Imam Yahya, 611, 612, 614, 616, 627; Iraq, relations with, 612, 626, 632; National Pact, 623; North Yemen, 611–16, 617, 620, 621, 624, 632, 633; party system, 623–24; People's Democratic Republic of Yemen (South Yemen), 617–21, 624, 627, 630, 631, 632, 638; Political Parties Law, 622–23; Saudi Arabia,

relations with, 616; Shafi'is, 612, 613, 615, 616, 627; Signatory Parties of the Declaration, 624; Zaydis, 611, 613, 615, 616, 627, 636, 638
Yemeni Congregation for Reform, 623–24, 637–38
Yemeni Free Forum Party. *See* Union of Popular Forces
Yemeni Labor Party. *See* National Democratic Front
Yemeni Nationalist Gathering Party, 638
Yemeni People's League Party, 638
Yemeni Socialist Party (YSP), 621, 623, 624, 636, 638. *See also* National Democratic Front; National Front; Unified Political Organization of the National Front
Yemeni Union, 615, 617
Yemeni Unity, 616
Yemenite Association (Israel), 254
Yılmaz, Mesut, 575
YMMA. *See* Young Men's Muslim Association
Young Arab Society, 278, 434, 501, 524, 528–529. *See also* Arab Club
Young Egypt, 96, 97, 123 4, 125, 130–32
Young Men's Muslim Association (Palestine), 475
Young Tunisians. *See* Evolutionist Party of Young Tunisians
Young Worker (Israel), 211, 254, 254–55
Youssoufi, Abderrahman, 420
Youth Congress (Palestine), 475
Youth League (Libya), 379
Youth of Fulayhi (Yemen), 616
Youth Organization of the Mahra District (Yemen). *See* National Liberation Front
Youth Who Enjoin Good and Forbid Evil (Yemen), 616
Youths of 'Ali (Lebanon), 364
YSP. *See* Yemeni Socialist Party

Zaghlul, Sa'd, 95, 121, 122, 126, 127 8
Za'im, Husni, 504–5
Zaydis. *See* Yemen Arab Republic
Zionist Labor, 211, 255
Zionist Labor, Left, 253, 254, 255
Zionist Worker, 215, 237, 255

# ABOUT THE EDITOR AND CONTRIBUTORS

FRANK TACHAU is Professor of Political Science at the University of Illinois at Chicago. He has been Visiting Professor at the University of Chicago, and at Bilkent University and Middle East Technical University in Ankara, Turkey. In 1993 he was Lady Davis Visiting Professor of Political Science and Senior Research Fellow at the Leonard Davis Institute for International Relations at the Hebrew University of Jerusalem. He has published a number of books and articles on Turkey and the Middle East, including *Turkey: The Politics of Authority, Democracy and Development*.

AS'AD ABUKHALIL is a member of the Department of Politics at California State University, Stanislaus. He has been Scholar-in-Residence at the Middle East Institute in Washington, D.C., and has taught at Georgetown University, George Washington University, Tufts University, and Randolph-Macon College. He is the author of numerous articles on various aspects of Middle East politics.

SHAHROUGH AKHAVI is Professor of Government and International Studies at the University of South Carolina. He is Editor of the Middle East series of the State University of New York Press; Book Review Editor of the *Journal of Iranian Studies*; and Section Editor of the *Encyclopedia of the Modern Islamic World*. He has published widely on Egyptian and Iranian politics.

ABLA AMAWI is a senior political researcher at the Centre d'Etudes et de Recherches sur le Moyen-Orient Contemporain (CERMOC) in Amman, Jordan. Her research interests include the state, civil society, democratization, and Islam and politics.

NATHAN J. BROWN is Associate Professor of Political Science and International Affairs, Associate Dean of the Elliott School of International Affairs, and Director of the Middle East Studies Program, all at George Washington University, Washington, D.C. He is the author of *Peasant Politics in Modern Egypt*, as well as of articles on Egyptian and Arab politics. In 1987 he received the Malcolm Kerr Memorial Prize of the Middle East Studies Association of North America for best dissertation in the Social Sciences.

MARIUS K. DEEB is a member of the Department of Political Science at George Washington University, Washington, D.C. He is the author of several books, including *Party Politics in Egypt: The Wafd and its Rivals, 1919–1939*, and *The Lebanese Civil War*, as well as coauthor of *Libya Since the Revolution*.

MARY-JANE DEEB is with the School of International Service of the American University, Washington, D.C. She is author of *Libya's Foreign Policy in North Africa*, and co-author of *Libya Since the Revolution*. She is Book Review Editor of the *International Journal of Middle East Studies* and a member of the Executive Board of the American-Tunisian Association.

MICHAEL R. FISCHBACH is Assistant Professor of History at Randolph-Macon College in Ashland, Virginia. He is the author of several journal articles and book chapters on land tenure in Jordan. He is also a contributor to the *Encyclopedia of the Modern Middle East*.

ARUN KAPIL is conducting research that deals with political liberalization and democracy in Algeria under former President Chadli Bendjedid. He spent 1989–90 in Algeria on a Fulbright grant. He has published articles in *Annuaire de l'Afrique du Nord*, *Maghreb-Machrek*, *Les Cahiers de l'Orient*, and *Middle East Report*.

ROBERT S. KRAMER is Assistant Professor of History at St. Norbert College in Wisconsin. In 1986–87 he was a Fulbright Fellow and Research Associate of the Institute of African and Asian Studies at Khartoum University. He is preparing a history of Omdurman during the Mahdist period. His publications and research interests concern Islam and social change in sub-Saharan Africa.

JACOB M. LANDAU is Gersten Professor of Political Science at the Hebrew University of Jerusalem. He has published extensively on the history and politics of the modern Middle East. His recent books include *Radical Politics in Modern Turkey*, *The Politics of Pan-Islam*, *The Arab Minority in Israel*, and *Jews, Arabs, Turks*.

FRED H. LAWSON is Professor of Political Science at Mills College in Oakland, California. He has conducted research on politics in several Arab countries, and is the author of *Bahrain: The Modernization of Autocracy*. He spent the 1992–93 academic year in Syria.

DAVID M. MEDNICOFF was a visiting faculty member in the Department of Political Science at Emory University, Atlanta, in 1993–94. He has done extensive research on politics in Morocco, and spent the academic year 1992–93 undertaking field research there.

TIMOTHY J. PIRO specializes on the political economy of the Arab world. He has worked in Egypt and Jordan.

REEVA SIMON is Assistant Director of the Middle East Institute of Columbia University in New York. She is the author of *Iraq Between the Two World Wars* and *The Middle East in Crime Fiction*. She is coeditor of *The Origins of Arab Nationalism* and the forthcoming *Encyclopedia of the Modern Middle East*.

MANFRED W. WENNER is Professor of Political Science at Northern Illinois University. He was Visiting Professor at Arizona State University in 1992–93. He is the author of a number of articles and books on comparative politics, most dealing with Yemen and the Middle East. He is past President of the American Institute of Yemeni Studies.

NATHAN YANAI is Professor of Israeli Studies at Haifa University in Israel. His publications include *Party Leadership in Israel: Maintenance and Change*, and an earlier study of the Mapai Party and the Lavon Affair.

ISBN 0-313-26649-2

90000>

HARDCOVER BAR CODE